(Continued from front flap)

The *WBC* is being produced with a view to
the needs of the average Christian minister,
Sunday school officer and teacher, Bible class
leader, college Bible teacher and student, and
all other alert students of the Bible who seek
help in understanding the spiritual message of
the Word of God as recorded in the Bible.

Old Testament

Volume I. GENESIS through ESTHER
Genesis and Exodus — Rev. Lee Haines, editor, Wesleyan
Methodist Sunday School Literature
Leviticus — Dr. Armor D. Peisker, editor, **Pilgrim Holiness
Advocate**
Numbers and Deuteronomy — Dr. Howard Hanke, Asbury
College
Joshua through Esther — Dr. Charles Wilson, Houghton
College
Volume II. JOB through SONG OF SOLOMON
Job — Dr. Milo A. Rediger, Dean and Vice President, Taylor
University
Psalms, 1-72 — Dr. W. Ralph Thompson, Spring Arbor College
Psalms, 73-150 — Dr. George Herbert Livingston, Asbury
Theological Seminary
Proverbs — Professor George Kufeldt, School of Theology,
Anderson College and Theological Seminary
Ecclesiastes and Song of Solomon — Professor Dennis Kin-
law, Asbury Theological Seminary
Volume III. ISAIAH through MALACHI
Isaiah and The Minor Prophets — Dr. Claude A. Ries,
Houghton College
Jeremiah, Ezekiel, and Daniel — Dr. Bert H. Hall, Chairman,
Division of Philosophy and Religion, Houghton College

New Testament

Volume V. ROMANS through PHILEMON
Romans and Galatians — Dr. Wilber T. Dayton, Professor of
New Testament and Greek, Asbury Theological Seminary
I Corinthians and Ephesians — Charles W. Carter
II Corinthians — Dr. Clarence H. Zahniser, Professor of Reli-
gion, Houghton College
Philippians and Colossians — Dr. George A. Turner, English
Bible Professor, Asbury Theological Seminary
I and II Thessalonians — W. O. Klopfenstein, Professor of
Bible, Fort Wayne Bible College
I and II Timothy and Titus — Dr. Roy S. Nicholson, Chairman,
Division of Religion, Central Wesleyan College
Philemon — Dr. George Failing, editor, **The Wesleyan Meth-
odist**
Volume VI. HEBREWS through REVELATION
Hebrews — Professor Charles W. Carter
James and Jude — Dr. Duane Thompson, Professor of Philos-
ophy and Religion, Marion College
I and II Peter — Dr. Charles S. Ball, Pastor of Newberg
Friends Church, Newberg, Oregon
I, II, III John — Dr. Leo G. Cox, Chairman, Division of Reli-
gion, Marion College
Revelation — Dr. Harvey J. S. Blaney

THE WESLEYAN BIBLE COMMENTARY
Matthew - Mark - Luke - John - Acts

The Wesleyan Bible Commentary

Editorial Board

Chairman and General Editor

CHARLES W. CARTER, M.A., Th. M.
Professor of Philosophy and Religion
Taylor University

New Testament Editor

RALPH EARLE, M.A., Th. D.
Professor of New Testament
Nazarene Seminary

Old Testament Editor

W. RALPH THOMPSON, M.A., Th.D.
Professor of Philosophy and Religion
Spring Arbor College

Associate Editor

LEE HAINES, B.D.
Office Editor
Wesleyan Methodist Sunday School Literature

Advisory Board

The Six Volumes

Wesleyan Bible Commentary

Volume Four

MATTHEW - MARK - LUKE - JOHN - ACTS

by

RALPH EARLE
Professor of New Testament
Nazarene Seminary

HARVEY J. S. BLANEY
Professor of Religion and Chairman of the Graduate Division of Theological Studies
Eastern Nazarene College

CHARLES W. CARTER
Professor of Philosophy and Religion
Taylor University

BAKER BOOK HOUSE

Grand Rapids, Michigan

The Wesleyan Bible Commentary
General Introduction

The Wesleyan Bible Commentary is a six-volume set covering the entire Bible. It consists of three volumes on the New Testament and three volumes on the Old Testament. In consideration of the important contemporary revival of interest in and emphasis upon John Wesley, the renowned English preacher and scholar of the eighteenth century, and the Father of Methodism in all of its multifold branches, a group of scholars in the Wesleyan tradition responded to what they believed to be the movings of God's Spirit in the religious climate of today to produce a set of commentaries within the Wesleyan theological frame of reference. The design of the WBC is evangelical, expositional practical, homiletical, and devotional. It is cast in the framework of contemporary evangelical Wesleyan Bible scholarship. Herein lies the justification for the title of the work: *Wesleyan Bible Commentary.*

The staff of contributors to the WBC includes approximately twenty Bible scholars from throughout the nation. They have been selected from nine different denominations, which include the Church of God (with headquarters in Anderson, Indiana), Church of the Nazarene, Evangelical United Brethren, Free Methodist, Friends, Methodists, Missionary Church Association, Pilgrim Holiness, and Wesleyan Methodist. The commentary is interdenominational in representation, nonsectarian, and non-polemical.

The aim of the WBC is to maintain both the spiritual insight and sound biblical scholarship of John Wesley and Adam Clarke, but to express these characteristics in the context of contemporary thought and life. While the WBC contributors aim to maintain the faith of the Fathers of Methodism, they have not neglected the use of the latest and best information and tools available to present-day Bible scholarship. Again, while the WBC is evangelical in the sense of expounding God's provisions for man's personal regeneration and sanctification, it does not overlook the social implications and provisions of the gospel of Jesus Christ.

The WBC aims at a high level of sound biblical scholarship, with a purpose that is practical rather than technical. It is produced with a view to the needs of the average Christian minister, Sunday school officer and teacher, Bible class leader, college Bible teacher and student, and all other alert students of the Bible who seek help in understanding the spiritual message of the Word of God as recorded in the Bible.

While the Editorial Board assumes responsibility for the general purpose and production of the WBC, the views expressed in the commentary are those of the individual contributors. The Editorial Board has aimed at a reasonable degree of uniformity in the format and general design of the commentary, but its purpose and desire have been that each contributor should realize the freedom necessary to discover the truth for himself and express his own personal insights into the unsearchable riches of God's Word. Although both the Editorial Board and the contributors represent the evangelical Wesleyan position, they lay no claim to a monopoly upon the truth of God as revealed in the Bible. They have aimed to make use of the best insights into God's revealed truth that are available in the scholarship of all communions of the Christian faith. The American Standard Version is the basic Bible text used by the contributors, and it is the text printed in the commentary. Free and large use, however, has been made of many other versions of the Bible, as also occasional individual translations by the respective contributors.

General guidance in the development and execution of the WBC has been afforded the Editorial Board by the wise counsel of a carefully selected Advisory Board consisting of eminent leaders in the field of evangelical Christianity today. This Board includes Drs. Paul S. Rees, Vice President of World Vision; Leslie R. Marston, Bishop of the Free Methodist Church; Hugh H. Benner, General Superintendent of the Church of the Nazarene; Roy S. Nicholson, formerly General President of the Wesleylan Methodist Church of America; Paul F. Elliott, President of Owosso College; Everett L. Cattell, President of Malone College; George E. Failing, Editor of the *Wesleyan Methodist*; and Paul P. Petticord, President of Western Theological Seminary.

It is the earnest desire and sincere prayer of those responsible for the production of this commentary that it will make a significant and lasting contribution to the contemporary revival of interest in vital Christian faith and practice throughout the world.

THE EDITORIAL BOARD

CHAS W. CARTER
Chairman and General Editor

RALPH EARLE
New Testament Editor

W. RALPH THOMPSON
Old Testament Editor

LEE HAINES
Associate Editor

Contents

The Gospel According to St. Matthew

by Ralph Earle

Editor's Preface to Matthew — Mark — Luke

THE AUTHOR OF THE EXPOSITION OF MATTHEW, MARK AND LUKE in the *Wesleyan Bible Commentary* is Dr. Ralph Earle, Professor of New Testament at the Nazarene Theological Seminary in Kansas City, Missouri. Professor Earle holds the following degrees: A.B., Eastern Nazarene College; M.A., Boston University; B.D. and Th.D., Gordon Divinity School. He has also done post-doctoral studies at Harvard and Edinburgh Universities.

Dr. Earle is an ordained minister in the Church of the Nazarene, and pastored churches in his denomination for a period of twelve years. He was Instructor and Professor of Biblical Literature at Eastern Nazarene College from 1933-1945. In 1945 he became Professor of New Testament at the Nazarene Theological Seminary. Dr. Earle has traveled widely, preaching in conventions, camps and churches throughout the United States, Canada, and the British Isles. His name has appeared frequently on the list of professors at the widely known Winona Lake School of Theology (now Fuller Summer Seminary).

Dr. Earle is a member and past President of the Evangelical Theological Society, and he holds membership in the American Academy of Religion, the American Schools of Oriental Research, and the Society of Biblical Literature and Exegesis. He has made three trips to the Holy Land and the Middle East. He is the author of more than a dozen books, including the *Story of the New Testament, Know Your New Testament, The Quest of the Spirit, Twice to the Holy Land, Meet the Minor Prophets, Meet the Major Prophets, Meet the Early Church, Search the Scriptures: Revelation, Search the Scriptures: Galatians,* and *Search the Scriptures: Thessalonians* (all published by Beacon Hill Press). Dr. Earle's other publications consist of *The Gospel According to Mark* (Zondervan), *The Gospel of Mark* (Baker Book House), *Aldersgate Biblical Series: Matthew* (Light and Life Press), and he is coauthor with Professor Charles W. Carter of the *Evangelical Commentary*: "The Acts of the Apostles" (Zondervan). Dr. Earle is a frequent contributor to religious periodicals of his own church and other churches, and he has contributed articles to several scholarly reference works in recent years. Few evangelical scholars today have been such prolific writers as Dr. Ralph Earle.

Out of the richness of his background of scholarship, traveling, preaching, teaching and writing on biblical themes the author of the *Wesleyan Bible Commentary*: "Matthew, Mark, and Luke" has poured his very mind and soul into the exposition of these books. The reader will find in this work that scholarship that will stimulate his mind and command his respect, and spiritual insights and revelations of divine truth that will bless and enrich his spiritual life and ministry. Here will be found a rich blend of the intellectual and the spiritual that will satisfy the quest of the mind and edify the soul in the truth of God in Christ.

CHAS. W. CARTER
Chairman and General Editor
Wesleyan Bible Commentary

Outline
The King and His Kingdom

Introduction

I. POSITION

A. IN THE NEW TESTAMENT

It is no accident that the Gospel of Matthew comes first, for it forms the natural link between the Old Testament and the New. Its very opening words — "The book of the generation of Jesus Christ, the son of David, the son of Abraham" — tie it in with the older Scriptures. Abraham was the father of the Hebrew nation, and David the founder of its permanent dynasty. The Messiah was to be "the son of David," a phrase found seven times in this Gospel.

The Gospels are logically placed first in the New Testament, for Christianity is based on the life, death, and resurrection of Jesus Christ. Without these there would have been no church, and the rest of the New Testament would never have been written.

B. IN THE CHURCH

The famous French critic Renan called the Gospel of Matthew the most important book ever written. It is the most frequently quoted Gospel in the early church, from the second century on. Today the form found in the Gospel of Matthew is most often adopted for the sayings of Jesus, as, for instance, the Lord's Prayer.

II. AUTHORSHIP

The earliest extant testimony on this point comes from Papias, about A.D. 140. He says, as quoted by Eusebius: "Matthew composed his history [logia, 'sayings'] in the Hebrew dialect, and every one translated it as he was able."[1] Irenaeus, about A.D. 185, writes: "Matthew, indeed, produced his gospel written among the Hebrews in their own dialect whilst Peter and Paul proclaimed the gospel and founded the church at Rome."[2] Pantaenus (ca. 195) was reported to have found in India "the gospel of Matthew

in Hebrew."[3] Origen (ca. A.D. 220) wrote: "The first is according to Matthew, the same that was once a publican, but afterwards an apostle of Jesus Christ, who having published it for the Jewish converts, wrote it in the Hebrew."[4]

The strong tradition of the early church, then, is that Matthew wrote a gospel for the Jews in "Hebrew" (probably Aramaic). But almost all scholars are agreed that the Gospel of Matthew, as we have it, is not a translation from the Aramaic, but was written originally in Greek. The best conclusion seems to be that Matthew rewrote his Aramaic Gospel in Greek for a wider audience. We have a striking parallel in the case of Josephus, who in the same century wrote his first draft of the *War* in either Hebrew or Aramaic for the Jews and then furnished a Greek version of it for his Roman readers. Foakes-Jackson makes this logical deduction: "May it not be permissible to enquire whether some books of the New Testament have been subjected to similar literary revision, and, though Hebraic in origin, have been Graecised almost beyond recognition?"[5] The seven books of the *War* are written in excellent Greek. But Josephus states that he used the assistance of others at Rome in order to make his Greek version suitable for cultured readers.[6] May not Matthew have done the same with his original Aramaic Gospel, and thus the smooth, non-translation Greek be accounted for?

Many scholars today deny the Matthean authorship of the First Gospel. They would assign it to a later unknown individual, or even to a group of men.[7] But it is significant that recently a leading liberal New Testament scholar, Edgar J. Goodspeed, has come out firmly in favor of the view that the First Gospel was written by the Apostle Matthew.[8]

It should be recognized, of course, that all four Gospels are anonymous. They

---

1 Eusebius, *Ecclesiastical History*, trans. C. F. Cruse, p. 127 (III. 39).   2 *Ibid.*, p. 187 (V. 8).
3 *Ibid.*, p. 190 (V. 10).   4 *Ibid.*, p. 245 (VI. 25).
5 F. J. Foakes-Jackson, *Josephus and the Jews* (R. Smith, 1930), p. xiv.
6 *Ibid.*, p. xiii.   7 Krister Stendahl, *The School of St. Matthew, passim*.
8 Edgar J. Goodspeed, *Matthew, Apostle and Evangelist*, pp. 77-98.

do not have the authors' names attached, as do most of the epistles in the New Testament. Hence the question of the authorship of Matthew is not involved in one's belief in the inspiration or authority of the canonical Scriptures. But the earliest Christians certainly knew who wrote these books, and it seems reasonable to hold that this information could and would have been transmitted correctly. Holdsworth has expressed it this way:

> From the time when the Gospels began to circulate or to be appealed to, it was the common tradition of the Christian Church that they were written by those whose names they bear. . . . This tradition rested upon no claim made within the books themselves, and the only possible explanation of it is that the tradition rested upon facts so clearly within the cognizance of the Christian Church that denial of the received authorship was held to be impossible.[9]

We first read of Matthew in connection with his call to follow Jesus (Matt. 9:9-19; Mark 2:14-22; Luke 5:27-39). He made a great feast for his old friends in order that they might meet his new Master. Then he left all to follow Christ.

In Mark and Luke he is called "Levi." This was a common Jewish name. But in his own Gospel he calls himself "Matthew." This name, meaning "gift of God," was probably given him as a disciple of Jesus — just as the Master conferred on Simon the new name "Cephas."

Matthew is never mentioned again in the New Testament, except in the lists of apostles chosen by Christ (Matt. 10:3; Mark 3:18; Luke 6:15; Acts 1:13). It is interesting to note that only in his own Gospel is he designated as "Matthew the publican" (10:3). A despised and hated tax collector, he had yet been called by the Master and actually chosen as one of His apostles. The little phrase underscores the big miracle.

III. PLACE AND TIME OF WRITING

This Gospel is traditionally held to have been written in Palestine. More recently Streeter has argued for Antioch in

Syria as the place of origin,[10] and it could probably be said that a majority of scholars today hold this position. Either view is acceptable.

The date is a greater matter of dispute. The older view placed the writing of Matthew at about A.D. 60. At present most scholars would date it about twenty years later. Streeter favors A.D. 85.[11] While conservatives very naturally prefer the earlier datings, the matter of time is not as important as it is sometimes assumed to be. It should be recognized, however, that the late date is usually — though not always — associated with the denial of Matthean authorship.

IV. SOURCES

Most scholars today hold that Matthew (as well as Luke) used the Gospel of Mark as a main source for the historical narrative in his Gospel, and a collection of "Sayings of Jesus" (Q, or the Logia) for the teaching sections. Mark seems to have more of a freshness and vividness of detail than Matthew has in recording the same incidents. The latter summarizes more. The priority of Mark strikes the careful reader. Over 90% of the material in Mark is reproduced in Matthew in language largely identical. There thus seems to be a literary interdependence.

To account for the material peculiar to Matthew — that is, not found in Mark or the supposed Q — Streeter has postulated another document, called M.[12] But if one accepts the traditional view that the Gospel was written by the Apostle Matthew, there is no need to suppose that he needed any such documentary source. The Logia, if there was such a document, was probably composed of the sayings of Jesus that Matthew himself had taken down.[13] B. C. Butler rejects the whole idea of Q and argues that Matthew was the first Gospel to be written.[14]

V. CHARACTER

A. WRITTEN FOR THE JEWS

The most obvious characteristic of the Gospel of Matthew is that it was written

[9] W. W. Holdsworth, Gospel Origins, p. 23.
[10] B. H. Streeter, The Four Gospels, pp. 500-507. [11] Ibid., pp. 523-24.
[12] Ibid., p. 150. See also G. D. Kilpatrick, The Origins of the Gospel According to St. Matthew (Oxford: Clarendon Press, 1946), p. 9. [13] See Goodspeed, op. cit., pp. 111-17.
[14] The Originality of St. Matthew (Cambridge: University Press, 1951), passim.

for the Jewish people. It begins with a Jewish genealogy, which describes Jesus as "the son of David, the son of Abraham" (1:1). It gives more attention to the fulfillment of Old Testament prophecies than do the other Gospels. A key phrase is, "that it might be fulfilled." This, or its equivalent, occurs thirteen times in Matthew (never in Mark or Luke, and only six times in John). Hayes remarks: "The first Gospel is almost a manual of Messianic prophecy."[15] He further states: "Altogether nineteen Old Testament books . . . are used by Matthew . . . . [It] is a New Testament book, but is built upon Old Testament foundations."[16] There are some sixty citations of Old Testament prophecy as fulfilled in Jesus.

It may be noted that Matthew does not explain Jewish customs, as Mark does, or give geographical data. This supports the view that this Gospel was written for the Jews.

Another typical Jewish emphasis is the repetition of the words "righteous" and "righteousness." They are found more often in Matthew than in the other three Gospels combined. This was a primary emphasis of Judaism.

One of the outstanding key phrases of the book is "the kingdom of heaven." It occurs thirty-three times in this Gospel, and nowhere else in the New Testament. Of the fifteen parables of Jesus in Matthew, twelve begin with the words: "The kingdom of heaven is like unto . . . ." The term "kingdom" is found fifty-two times in this Gospel. Mat-

thew's book is pre-eminently the Gospel of the Kingdom, presenting Jesus as the King and Messiah.

B. SYSTEMATIC ARRANGEMENT

Matthew was a tax collector. As such he had to keep books. It is not surprising, therefore, that his Gospel is marked by systematic arrangement more than any of the other three. In fact, this quality rivals the Jewishness of the Gospel for first place as the outstanding characteristic of Matthew.

Actually the one characteristic is closely allied to the other. The Jews had a literary habit of dividing their writings into five parts. The Torah — what we call the Pentateuch — is composed of five books. The Jews divided the Psalms into five books. They had five "Rolls" — Song of Songs, Ruth, Lamentations, and Esther. Later there were five books of *Sayings of the Jewish Fathers.*

So it is not surprising that Matthew has five collections of the sayings of Jesus. In fact, aside from the Infancy Narrative at the beginning and the Passion Story at the end, the Gospel is built largely around five great discourses: (1) Sermon on the Mount (chaps. 5-7); (2) Charge to the Twelve (chap. 10); (3) Seven Parables of the Kingdom (chap. 13); (4) Sayings on Repentance and Forgiveness (chap. 18); (5) Olivet Discourse (chaps. 24-25). Each one ends with the formula: "And it came to pass when Jesus had ended." One might add also ten miracles in chapters 8-9.

[15] D. A. Hayes, *The Synoptic Gospels and Acts,* p. 44. [16] *Ibid.,* p. 50.

The King and His Kingdom

I. THE PRESENTATION OF THE KING (Matt. 1:1-4:11)

A. HIS ANCESTRY (1:1-17)

1. His Titles (1:1)

1 The book of the generation of Jesus Christ, the son of David, the son of Abraham.

The Gospel According to Matthew begins with a genealogical table, showing the legal descent of Jesus from Abraham and David, through Joseph.[1] **As son of Abraham** Jesus was a true Jew. As **son of David** he was heir to the throne of David and to the promises made to Israel's greatest king.

Christ means "the Anointed One." The Hebrew equivalent is Messiah. Jesus was the Messiah of Israel, the fulfillment of the messianic promises of the Old Testament. Thus it is altogether fitting that the Gospel of Matthew should stand first in the New Testament. This verse forms the connecting link between the two parts of the Bible. It ties the New Covenant in Christ to the ancient covenants which God made with Abraham and David.

As noted in the Introduction, Matthew's Gospel was written to Jews. Hence it had to begin with a genealogy. For the first question a Jew would ask about Jesus' claim to be the Messiah would be this: Was He the son of Abraham and the son of David? If not, His messianic claims would be immediately invalidated.

2. The Pre-kingdom Period (1:2-6)

2 Abraham begat Isaac; and Isaac begat Jacob; and Jacob begat Judah and his brethren; 3 and Judah begat Perez and Zerah of Tamar; and Perez begat Hezron; and Hezron begat Ram; 4 and Ram begat Amminadab; and Amminadab begat Nahshon; and Nahshon begat Salmon; 5 and Salmon begat Boaz of Rahab; and Boaz begat Obed of Ruth; and Obed begat Jesse; 6 and Jesse begat David the king.

And David begat Solomon of her *that had been the wife* of Uriah;

One of the most striking features of this genealogy of Jesus is that it contains the names of four women. This is surprising, for women usually were not recognized by the Jews when thinking of their ancestors. There must have been a reason for this strange phenomenon. What was it?

The rather obvious answer reveals the marvelous grace of God. Two of these women were Israelites, but both are portrayed in the Old Testament as immoral. **Tamar** (v. 3) was guilty of incest (Gen. 38:13-18). **Bathsheba**, the wife of Uriah (v. 6), was involved in adultery (II Sam. 11:2-5). The other two women were foreigners. **Rahab** (v. 5) was a Canaanite. Though described as a harlot, she was saved in the destruction of Jericho because she protected the spies sent by Joshua (Josh. 6:25; Heb. 11:31). **Ruth** (v. 5) was a Moabitess, and thus under God's curse because the women of Moab had enticed the Israelites to idolatry and immorality (Num. 25:1-2). A Moabite was forbidden to enter into the assembly of the Lord (Deut. 23:3).

Now the answer becomes clear. It is God's grace triumphing over man's sin. Though the Jews utterly rejected such an idea, the gospel declared that through divine grace both sinners and foreigners could be brought into the kingdom of God. Salvation was to be offered to men of every class, every color, every creed. The gospel of Jesus Christ is a message of hope to the lowest sinner and the most remote heathen. That is the glory of the Good News.

David is identified as **the king**. A list of Judah's kings follows. But David was pre-eminently "the king" of Israel. It was to him that the promise was made that his throne should be established forever

---

[1] The Rabbis had this rule: "The descent on the father's side only shall be called a descent; the descent by the mother is not called any descent." (Samuel J. Andrews, *Life of Our Lord*, p. 61).

(II Sam. 7:16; Psa. 89:35-37). This promise was fulfilled in Jesus the Messiah, the son of David.

3. The Kingdom Period (1:7-11)

7 and Solomon begat Rehoboam; and Rehoboam begat Abijah; and Abijah begat Asa; 8 and Asa begat Jehoshaphat; and Jehoshaphat begat Joram; and Joram begat Uzziah; 9 and Uzziah begat Jotham; and Jotham begat Ahaz; and Ahaz begat Hezekiah; 10 and Hezekiah begat Manasseh; and Manasseh begat Amon; and Amon begat Josiah; 11 and Josiah begat Jechoniah and his brethren, at the time of the carrying away to Babylon.

This section consists of a list of the kings of Judah, after the kingdom was divided following Solomon's death. But there are some omissions. After **Joram** (v. 8) three names are omitted (Ahaziah, Joash, Amaziah); after **Josiah** (v. 11) Jehoiakim is left out. This is apparently because Matthew is following a pattern of three times fourteen (cf. v. 17).

4. The Post-Kingdom Period (1:12-16)

12 And after the carrying away to Babylon, Jechoniah begat Shealtiel; and Shealtiel begat Zerubbabel; 13 and Zerubbabel begat Abiud; and Abiud begat Eliakim; and Eliakim begat Azor; 14 and Azor begat Sadoc; and Sadoc begat Achim; and Achim begat Eliud; 15 and Eliud begat Eleazar; and Eleazar begat Matthan; and Matthan begat Jacob; 16 and Jacob begat Joseph the husband of Mary, of whom was born Jesus, who is called Christ.

These are names less familiar to us because they belong largely to the period between the Old and New Testaments. They are, however, good Hebrew names, such as we find elsewhere.

Special attention should be given to the verse 16. The very careful, exact wording remarkably protects the truth of the Virgin Birth, which is recounted later. The radical change from "begat . . . begat" is most significant. Joseph did not beget Jesus. Rather Joseph is identified as **the husband of Mary, of whom was born Jesus, who is called Christ.** Here it is indicated implicitly that Joseph was not the actual father of Jesus. But Jesus was the real son of Mary.

5. Summary (1:17)

17 So all the generations from Abraham unto David are fourteen generations; and from David unto the carrying away to Babylon fourteen generations; and from the carrying away to Babylon unto the Christ fourteen generations.

One of the main features of Matthew's Gospel is systematic arrangement. That is strikingly illustrated in the very first chapter. The author arranges the ancestors of Jesus, from Abraham on, into three groups of fourteen each. As we have already noted, he omits several names in order to do this. **Fourteen** was significant as being the numerical value of the Hebrew letters in the name David. Jesus is thus portrayed as the Son of David in this royal genealogy.

B. HIS BIRTH (1:18-25)

18 Now the birth of Jesus Christ was on this wise: When his mother Mary had been betrothed to Joseph, before they came together she was found with child of the Holy Spirit. 19 And Joseph her husband, being a righteous man, and not willing to make her a public example, was minded to put her away privily. 20 But when he thought on these things, behold, an angel of the Lord appeared unto him in a dream, saying, Joseph, thou son of David, fear not to take unto thee Mary thy wife: for that which is conceived in her is of the Holy Spirit. 21 And she shall bring forth a son; and thou shalt call his name JESUS; for it is he that shall save his people from their sins. 22 Now all this is come to pass, that it might be fulfilled which was spoken by the Lord through the prophet, saying,
23 Behold, the virgin shall be with child, and shall bring forth a son,
And they shall call his name Immanuel;
which is, being interpreted, God with us. 24 And Joseph arose from his sleep, and did as the angel of the Lord commanded him, and took unto him his wife; 25 and knew her not till she had brought forth a son: and he called his name JESUS.

It is typical of Matthew's business-like approach — based on his experience as a tax collector who kept records and made reports — to write: **Now the birth of Jesus Christ was on this wise.** That is a matter-of-fact way of saying: Now I am going to tell you the story of Jesus' birth.

Betrothed (v. 18) means something more binding than the modern "engaged." Among the Jews it required a formal divorce to break a betrothal. That is why Joseph is called "her husband" (v. 19) and Mary "thy wife" (v. 20) and "his wife" (v. 24). The account indicates very clearly that they had not been living together as husband and wife. It is stated explicitly that the announcement to Joseph of Jesus' coming birth was made **before they came together** (v. 18). Again, we are told that Joseph, in obedience to the angel, **took unto him his wife** (v. 24). So the terms "husband" and "wife" should not be interpreted with modern literalness.

The expression **she was found with child** (v. 18) suggests the surprise with which Joseph made the discovery. It is evident that Mary had not disclosed to him the announcement of the angel to her (Luke 1:26-38). One can well understand the delicacy of the situation and her reticence at this point. But it was a very jarring experience to Joseph.

To him there could naturally be only one explanation: his fiancée had been untrue to him. To a religious Jew the course was clear: he must divorce his betrothed. But Joseph was also a kindly man and deeply devoted to Mary. He would not expose her to public shame (v. 19). Rather he would divorce her secretly, which could be done with a minimum of two legal witnesses present.

The child was **of the Holy Spirit** (v. 18). Thus does Matthew very briefly lend support to the more complete statement found in Luke's Gospel. There we find that the angel informed Mary that the Holy Spirit would come upon her and the power of the Highest would overshadow her, so that her child would in a unique sense be the Son of God (Luke 1:35).

Just as an angel had made the announcement to Mary, so now an angel **appeared unto** Joseph **in a dream** (v. 20). The angel addressed Joseph as son of David. This was the basis on which that title could be given to Jesus. As Joseph's adopted son He was also the **son of David.** Thus His legal descent from David came through Joseph. The angel assured Joseph that he need not divorce Mary.

He could take her as his wife; **for that which is conceived in her is of the Holy Spirit.** Thus Joseph received the same announcement which had been made to Mary earlier. It was entirely necessary that he, as well as she, should have this divine disclosure.

The child was to be named **Jesus** (v. 21). This is the Greek equivalent of the Hebrew "Joshua." It means "Jehovah saves." Jesus would **save his people from their sins.** Only here in the New Testament is the meaning of this name given.

The language of the first part of this verse is reminiscent of Genesis 17:19. There God told Abraham that Sarah would bear a son, who would be named Isaac. The birth of Isaac to Sarah in her old age was a miracle. But how much greater was the miracle of the Virgin Birth. Miracles are simply God at work in history.

In verse 22 we find the first of many statements in Matthew that the events connected with Jesus were a fulfillment of Old Testament prophecy. All this came to pass **that it might be fulfilled which was spoken by the Lord through the prophet.** It was God speaking, but He spoke through His prophet (cf. Heb. 1:1-2). Thus does the New Testament declare the divine inspiration of the Old. This introductory formula for quoting the Old Testament occurs a dozen times in this Gospel, more frequently than in any other book of the New Testament.

Verse 23 is a quotation of Isaiah 7:14 in the Septuagint (Greek translation of the Old Testament, made about 200 years before Christ). There Isaiah told King Ahaz that God would give him a sign. A young woman — that is the meaning of the Hebrew word *almah* — would conceive and bear a son. Before the child came to the age of accountability the two enemy kings of Israel and Syria would be cut off (Isa. 7:16), so that Judah would be saved. All this happened in the time of Ahaz, as a sign to him. But now the prediction is caught up in its larger meaning as a messianic prophecy of Jesus' Virgin Birth. This is what is called the *telescopic* feature of prophecy. Most Old Testament passages had a nearer, partial fulfillment in the period of the prophet. But they also looked ahead to their final and complete fulfillment in Christ and His kingdom. A recognition of this principle is absolutely essential to understanding the relation of the Old and New Testaments.

In this prophecy occurs a third title for the Coming One. In the first verse He is designated as "the son of David," the Messiah who would rule on the throne of David and fulfill God's gracious promises to that good king. In verse 21 He is named "Jesus," the Savior of His people. Now He is called **Immanuel,** which means **God with us.**

What a gracious name for the Son of God who became Son of Man. Jesus is God brought near. He came to earth to reveal the heavenly Father, whose love desires to save every human being. He dwelt among men that they might see God (John 14:9). But He has also promised: "Lo, I am with you always" (Matt. 28:20).

When Joseph wakened the next morning he **did as the angel of the Lord commanded him** (v. 24). His obedience fulfilled the divine plan and purpose. God's will was carried out through man's co-operation. How many times do men attempt to frustrate God's purposes by their refusal to obey? Jesus said to Jerusalem, "How often would I have gathered thy children together . . . and ye would not" (Luke 13:34). The greatest tragedy of human life is divine blessings missed because of disobedience.

Joseph **took unto him his wife;** that is, he took Mary into his home. Thus he publicly accepted her as his wife. In doing so he also accepted the reproach and slander that would be cast in his face as one who had sexual relations with his fiancée before marriage. Both Joseph and Mary had to pay a costly price — sacrificing their reputation — in order to be God's servants in carrying out His will.

The statement that he **knew her not till she had brought forth a son** (v. 25) implies that after the birth of Jesus, Mary and Joseph did have complete marital relations. This is probably confirmed by the words of the people of Nazareth: "Is not his mother called Mary? and his brethren, James, and Joseph, and Simon, and Judas?" (13:55). The most natural interpretation is that these brothers of Jesus were sons of Mary. This idea is also suggested in the statement that "she

brought forth her firstborn son" (Luke 2:7). There is no support in Scripture for the doctrine of the Perpetual Virginity of Mary. We do not need to exalt Mary in order to worship Christ. In fact, the true human nature and the humble birth and childhood of Jesus are strongly emphasized in the New Testament. When we minimize His humanity in order to magnify His deity we are not being true to the Scriptures. Jesus was truly God and truly man. Though no finite mind can ever explain this mystery, faith accepts it as true. We do not understand the relationship, but we must believe the fact on the authority of God's word. When we do accept it, we find it filled with wonderful comfort and strength. As God He is able to save us from sin and make us more than conquerors. As man He is able to sympathize with our human weakness and help us (Heb. 2:17-18).

C. HIS VISITORS (2:1-12)

2 Now when Jesus was born in Bethlehem of Judaea in the days of Herod the king, behold, Wisemen from the east came to Jerusalem, saying, 2 Where is he that is born King of the Jews? for we saw his star in the east, and are come to worship him. 3 And when Herod the king heard it, he was troubled, and all Jerusalem with him. 4 And gathering together all the chief priests and scribes of the people, he inquired of them where the Christ should be born. 5 And they said unto him, In Bethlehem of Judaea: for thus it is written through the prophet,

6 And thou Bethlehem, land of Judah,
Art in no wise least among the princes of Judah:
For out of thee shall come forth a governor,
Who shall be shepherd of my people Israel.

7 Then Herod privily called the Wisemen, and learned of them exactly what time the star appeared. 8 And he sent them to Bethlehem, and said, Go and search out exactly concerning the young child; and when ye have found *him*, bring me word, that I also may come and worship him. 9 And they, having heard the king, went their way; and lo, the star, which they saw in the east, went before them, till it came and stood over where the young child was. 10 And when they saw the star, they rejoiced with exceeding

great joy. 11 And they came into the house and saw the young child with Mary his mother; and they fell down and worshipped him; and opening their treasures they offered unto him gifts, gold and frankincense and myrrh. 12 And being warned *of God* in a dream that they should not return to Herod, they departed into their own country another way.

Jesus was born in **Bethlehem of Judaea** (v. 1). This was the city of David, a fitting place for the birth of the Son of David (1:1). It was in Judea, the southern part of Palestine. Thus Jesus was born among the Jews, who subsequently ignored Him and finally rejected Him.

It happened in the days of **Herod the king.** This ruler was placed on the throne by a Roman emperor. He was an Idumean (Edomite) whose father had become a dominant political figure in troubled Palestine. Herod the Great ruled from 40 B.C. to 4 B.C.

The **Wise-men** were magi (Greek *magoi*). The same word occurs in Acts 13:8, where it is translated "sorcerer." But these visitors to the Christ-child were not crafty "magicians" (from the Greek *magos*). Unlike many of their profession they were good and wise. So although the Greek word does not mean "wise-men," they may properly be referred to as such.

These Magi came **from the east.** We cannot be sure of precisely what this phrase signifies. Some would refer it to Arabia, just east of Palestine, but it is more likely that the general region of Mesopotamia is meant. Probably the Magi were Persian astrologers, who had been studying the stars. Modern astronomers have calculated that there were rare conjunctions of planets, and comets, between 12 B.C. and 6 B.C. This may very well explain the excitement that caused these astrologers to make the long trek to Palestine, following the direction of a new star which had appeared.

The idea that there were three wise men has no support except in legend. It was probably deduced from the fact that three different kinds of gifts are mentioned (v. 11). Neither is there any indication that they were kings, as they are commonly portrayed today. It is true that they brought royal gifts to the

One who was to become King of kings, but if they were astrologers they probably would not also be kings.

Looking for a king, they naturally came to the capital city, **Jerusalem.** But the King they sought was born in a manger, not a palace. He was not to be a political potentate but a spiritual Savior.

Just as naturally the Magi enquired at the capital: **Where is he that is born King of the Jews** (v. 2)? They expected to find the whole city alive with excitement about the birth of a prince in the royal palace. Instead their announcement was news. No one understood what they were talking about.

When **Herod the king** heard about it, **he was troubled** (v. 3). One thing no Roman ruler could permit was a rival. Herod the Great was especially allergic to any news that threatened his throne. Because one of his sons seemed too eager, with his mother's help, to succeed his father, the jealous, wily old king instructed some of his servants at the winter palace in Jericho to teach the lad to swim under water. The idea, of course, was to see how long they could hold him under. When the distressed, enraged mother accused the king of contriving her son's death, Herod put on an elaborate state funeral to prove the sincerity of his devotion and the depth of his sorrow. But it was a veneer so thin that it was transparent. Later on he stated in his will that two of his other sons were to inherit his kingdom, but when rumors reached him that they were conspiring against him he had them put to death likewise. No wonder a Roman ruler said that it was safer to be one of Herod's pigs than one of his sons.

Not only was the king upset, but **all Jerusalem with him.** The people were afraid of violent Roman retribution if any revolutionist appeared in their midst.

It is interesting to note that Herod equated the Magi's "King of the Jews" with **the Christ** (v. 4). Though not a Jew himself, he had lived his life among the people of promise, and so was somewhat familiar with the Scriptures. So he gathered **the chief priests and scribes** — perhaps called for a special meeting of the Sanhedrin — and asked them **where the Christ should be born.** He was acquainted with the fact that the Jews were awaiting the coming of their Messiah. If this promised Deliverer had already arrived, he wanted to know where.

He did not have to wait for any search to be made in the ancient Scriptures. The answer was on the tip of every scribal Jewish tongue — **in Bethlehem of Judaea** (v. 5). It was in this ancient city of David that the Messiah was to be born.

To back up their assertion the scribes quoted Micah 5:2. This prophet of the eighth century before Christ not only looked back to the birth of David at Bethlehem. Putting the telescope of prophecy to his Spirit-anointed eyes, he looked down across the centuries and heralded the fact that from the same town would come a **governor,** who would be the **shepherd of my people Israel.** David was shepherd boy and shepherd king. His greater Son would one day declare: "I am the good shepherd: the good shepherd layeth down his life for the sheep" (John 10:11). The Shepherd of Israel was to be its Savior. Before He governed He must give His life. There was far more implied in this picture of a shepherd than the ancient prophet surmised or the contemporary scribes realized.

Herod **privily** (v. 7) — i. e., privately, secretly — summoned the wise men to the palace. Carefully he ascertained from them **exactly what time the star appeared.** Herod was as efficient as he was cunning and crafty. His notable success politically was due in part to the fact that he was a master of details. He wanted to know all the facts. Then he acted on this knowledge.

He was also the master of secret diplomacy, which usually consists largely of deceit. He sent the Magi on to Bethlehem with instructions to **search out exactly concerning the young child** (v. 8). When they had found him they were to inform the king where he was, **that I also may come and worship him.** Herod's design, however, was not to adore but to destroy.

Naturally the wise-men assumed the sincerity of the king, so they set forth again, following divine leading and royal command. When they left the city they once more saw **the star** (v. 9) and **rejoiced** greatly (v. 10). Its presence gave

them added assurance that their journey would not be in vain, but that their search would be crowned with success.

We are told that the star went before them **till it came and stood over where the young child was** (v. 9). Since Bethlehem lies only six miles south of Jerusalem, a star could only indicate general direction. Nor could it pinpoint the house where the infant Jesus was. The star had led the wise-men westward from eastern lands. When they arrived at the borders of Palestine they headed straight for the capital city, assuming that the king would be born there. At Jerusalem they were directed by the scribes and Herod to go to Bethlehem. Perhaps further inquiry there, or a sense of direct divine guidance, led them to the house where Jesus lived.

They came into the house and saw the young child (v. 11). Modern Christmas scenes often picture three wise men kneeling before the baby Jesus in a manger. But here we are told that they found **the young child** in a **house.** Luke tells us that the night Jesus was born shepherds found the babe in a manger. But the scene here is something different. Herod had inquired of the Magi "exactly what time the star appeared" (v. 7). On the basis of the information he received he ordered all the male children in Bethlehem under two years of age to be slain (v. 16). Had Jesus just been born, a six months' limit would certainly have been sufficient. The implication of the statements here is that Jesus was at least several months — perhaps a year old when the wise-men visited him. It should be recognized, too, that the long journey would take considerable time.

All this affects the dating of His birth. When the first calculation was made there was an error of at least four years. For it was discovered long ago that Herod the Great died in 4 B.C. For this reason Archbishop Ussher of Ireland — a contemporary of John Wesley — fixed the date of Jesus' birth at 4 B.C. It is Ussher's chronology that we find in most of our English Bibles. But the facts we have just noted would suggest that Jesus was born in 5 or 6 B.C. Most scholars today favor the dates of 5 B.C. for His birth and A.D. 30 for His death.[2]

---

[2] See, for instance, Andrews, *op. cit.,* pp. 51-52. However, Ethelbert Stauffer (*Jesus and His Story,* pp. 7-8) argues for 7 B.C. and A.D. 32.

Gold and frankincense and myrrh (v. 11) were costly gifts, worthy of a king. In fact, they suggest a coronation. Isaiah had predicted that Gentile kings would bring to restored Israel gifts of "gold and incense" (Isa. 60:6). There is perhaps here a hint of a partial fulfilment when these royal gifts are brought to the Restorer of Israel.

The wise-men were warned of God in a dream that they should not return to Herod (v. 12), so they departed into their own country another way. Probably they went a few miles to the northeast, then turned down the Jericho Road, crossed the Jordan, and went up the east side of the river. Thus they avoided Jerusalem and central Palestine.

The visit of the wise-men gives us in miniature the paradox of Jesus' ministry. The Jewish rulers did not care to go the short distance to Bethlehem to seek the Messiah. The earthly king of the Jews sought to kill the One who was "born King of the Jews." At the same time Gentiles sought the Savior and worshiped Him. It is a commentary on John 1:11 — "He came unto his own [things], and they that were his own received him not." His own nation rejected Him, and the Gentile church took its place as God's people.

D. HIS FLIGHT (2:13-15)

13 Now when they were departed, behold, an angel of the Lord appeareth to Joseph in a dream, saying, Arise and take the young child and his mother, and flee into Egypt, and be thou there until I tell thee: for Herod will seek the young child to destroy him. 14 And he arose and took the young child and his mother by night, and departed into Egypt; 15 and was there until the death of Herod: that it might be fulfilled which was spoken by the Lord through the prophet, saying, Out of Egypt did I call my son.

Again we find an angel appearing in a dream. This time the message to Joseph was: Arise and take the young child and his mother, and flee into Egypt (v. 13). The reason for the command was that Herod would seek to kill the supposed young rival for his throne. Jesus was Divine Love incarnate. But He was to

be pursued by human hate which would finally nail Him to a cruel, shameful cross. But all the time the heavenly Father was watching. Not until His time had come could He be killed. First He must fulfill all righteousness (3:15) in a sinless life on earth and then He must die as a sacrifice for our sins. God's eternal purpose would be carried out in spite of the efforts of wicked men. All this gives us courage and faith for the future. God's redemptive plan, which includes salvation here and hereafter for all who believe in Jesus Christ, will not fail. The outcome of the conflict between good and evil is already settled in the sovereign purpose of an infinite God.

Joseph was prompt to obey. He arose from his sleep — his dream evidently wakened him — and, taking Jesus and Mary by night, he departed into Egypt (v. 14). He wisely took no chances, but fled under cover of darkness. Southward he went, putting as much distance as quickly as possible between his family and the murderous tyrant at Jerusalem. It was a long trek of some two hundred miles to Egypt and the journey would take several weary weeks. Probably the traditional picture of Joseph walking beside the donkey which carried Mary and Jesus is correct. It appears that Joseph, though of royal blood, was a poor peasant who could very likely afford only one donkey.

How long the family stayed in Egypt we are not told. All that is stated is that it was there until the death of Herod (v. 15). As already noted, this was 4 B.C.

At a later period the Jews circulated the slander that Jesus' supposed miracle-working power was due to His having learned magic in Egypt. This is perhaps an indirect testimony to the fact that he had been there.

Out of Egypt did I call my son is quoted from the Hebrew of Hosea 11:1. What the prophet had in mind was unquestionably the Exodus. He says it was "when Israel was a child." But Matthew picks this up and applies it to Jesus, in whom was embodied the true Israel. In fulfilling this role He too would come out of Egypt. For the Exodus was a type of salvation from the slavery of sin.

E. HIS ATTEMPTED ASSASSINATION (2:16-18)

16 Then Herod, when he saw that he was mocked of the Wise-men, was exceeding wroth, and sent forth, and slew all the male children that were in Bethlehem, and in all the borders thereof, from two years old and under, according to the time which he had exactly learned of the Wise-men. 17 Then was fulfilled that which was spoken through Jeremiah the prophet, saying,

18 A voice was heard in Ramah,
Weeping and great mourning,
Rachel weeping for her children;
And she would not be comforted, because they are not.

Herod was past master in the art of deceiving others. But he did not take graciously the opposite turn of events. When he saw that he had been **mocked** (v. 16) — better "deceived" — he was **exceeding wroth,** or furiously angry. This was nothing unusual for Herod; in fact, it happened very often. Since he could not identify the Christ child, he would take no chances, so he ordered the wholesale massacre of all the **male children that were in Bethlehem** and its suburbs, **from two years old and under.** As already noted, this implies that Jesus was at least several months old. It is clear that Herod understood that Jesus had been born at the time the wise men first saw the star.

Matthew interprets this incident as a fulfillment of **that which was spoken through Jeremiah the prophet** (v. 17). Over and again the New Testament declares that events in the life of Christ fulfilled the prophecies of the Old Testament. This principle of "promise-fulfillment" is the key to understanding the unity of the Bible. Redemption is a mixture of prophecy and history, both divinely planned.

The quotation in verse 18 is taken from Jeremiah 31:15. **Ramah** was about six miles north of Jerusalem. It was on the road the Babylonians would follow when taking the Jews into captivity in 586 B.C. Clearly Jeremiah had in mind this sad event when he portrayed Rachel, the mother of Judah, weeping inconsolably because her descendants were being taken away. But, true to the telescopic principle of prophecy, Matthew applies this prophecy to the slaughter of the babes of Bethlehem by another cruel Gentile ruler. Rachel was buried near Bethlehem (Gen. 35:19; 48:7), and her tomb is still pointed out beside the road.

The slaughter of the innocents is not recorded in secular history. But it fits the known character of Herod so perfectly that no reasonable objection can be raised against its authenticity. A man who would murder his own sons and kill his favorite wife — apparently the only person he ever really loved — in a fit of jealous rage, could be counted on to have no inhibitions about the massacre of numbers of innocent children. Herod was like the Pharaoh of the Oppression and a type of the dragon of Revelation (Rev. 12:1-5).

F. HIS RETURN (2:19-23)

19 But when Herod was dead, behold, an angel of the Lord appeareth in a dream to Joseph in Egypt, saying, 20 Arise and take the young child and his mother, and go into the land of Israel: for they are dead that sought the young child's life. 21 And he arose and took the young child and his mother, and came into the land of Israel. 22 But when he heard that Archelaus was reigning over Judaea in the room of his father Herod, he was afraid to go thither; and being warned of God in a dream, he withdrew into the parts of Galilee, 23 and came and dwelt in a city called Nazareth; that it might be fulfilled which was spoken through the prophets that he should be called a Nazarene.

When Herod was dead, again the Lord spoke to Joseph **in a dream** (v. 19). Even **in Egypt** he was close to God. It is not *where* we live but *how* we live that counts. Among a people of heathen religion and pagan morals, Joseph still kept in touch with heaven. To choose selfishly, for material advantage, to live in such godless surroundings has often proved spiritually fatal, but in the center of God's will men are safe anywhere.

Again (cf. v. 13) Joseph was commanded: **Arise and take the young child and his mother** (v. 20). But this time his destination was different: **go into the land of Israel.** This must have been welcome news to the exiles far from home and loved ones.

And again (cf. v. 14) Joseph obeyed promptly. Waking from his dream, **he** arose and took the young child and his mother (v. 21). Anyone who has headed home after a long journey knows that the way back seems only half as long. With what happy hearts the little family must have come into the land of Israel.

Somewhere in the southern part of Palestine Joseph heard disturbing news. Archelaus (v. 22) had succeeded his father Herod as ruler of Judaea. Josephus the Jewish historian tells us that Archelaus was a very brutal, cruel despot, like his father. Apparently Joseph was aware of the man's character and was afraid to go thither. Again God intervened in a dream, and so Joseph withdrew into the parts of Galilee, in northern Palestine. This region was ruled by another son of Herod the Great, Antipas (the "Herod" of Jesus' public ministry), who was not as cruel as his brother. So the family settled safely in his territory.

The phrase in a dream occurs no less than five times in the first two chapters of Matthew (1:20; 2:12, 13, 19, 22). It was one of the ways by which God spoke to His people before the coming of the Holy Spirit at Pentecost. Since then it has played a minor role.

Traveling past Judea and Samaria, Joseph finally settled in Nazareth (v. 23). This town was about eighty miles north of Jerusalem. Luke informs us that the home town of Mary and Joseph was Nazareth (Luke 1:26; 2:4). Matthew omits this. But there is no contradiction in the accounts. That Nazareth was the village of Jesus' childhood and youth is clear from both.

The cited prophecy that He should be called a Nazarene is one of the most difficult in the New Testament to explain. The Old Testament reference is not at all clear; here it simply says: through the prophets. It is sometimes equated with "Nazarite," as in Judges 13:5. Others relate it to the Hebrew root *nazir* or *netzer*, translated "shoot" or "branch" in Isaiah 4:2, 11:1; Jeremiah 23:5, 33:15; Zechariah 3:8, 6:12. This is one of the still unsolved problems of Biblical study.

It should be observed that the infancy narratives in these first two chapters of Matthew are clearly focussed on the experience of Joseph. It is *his* genealogy in chapter one, and the announcement of Jesus' birth is made to him. In chapter two he is the one who is commanded to take the mother and child to Egypt, to return them to Palestine, and to settle them in Galilee. In Luke's Gospel the infancy narratives are centered chiefly on Mary.

G. HIS HERALD (3:1-12)

1 And in those days cometh John the Baptist, preaching in the wilderness of Judaea, saying, 2 Repent ye; for the kingdom of heaven is at hand. 3 For this is he that was spoken of through Isaiah the prophet, saying,

The voice of one crying in the wilderness,

Make ye ready the way of the Lord, Make his paths straight.

4 Now John himself had his raiment of camel's hair, and a leathern girdle about his loins; and his food was locusts and wild honey. 5 Then went out unto him Jerusalem, and all Judaea, and all the region around about the Jordan; 6 and they were baptized of him in the river Jordan, confessing their sins. 7 But when he saw many of the Pharisees and Sadducees coming to his baptism, he said unto them, Ye offspring of vipers, who warned you to flee from the wrath to come? 8 Bring forth therefore fruit worthy of repentance: 9 and think not to say within yourselves, We have Abraham to our father: for I say unto you, that God is able of these stones to raise up children unto Abraham. 10 And even now the axe lieth at the root of the trees: every tree therefore that bringeth not forth good fruit is hewn down, and cast into the fire. 11 I indeed baptize you in water unto repentance: but he that cometh after me is mightier than I, whose shoes I am not worthy to bear: he shall baptize you in the Holy Spirit and *in* fire: 12 whose fan is in his hand, and he will thoroughly cleanse his threshing-floor; and he will gather his wheat into the garner, but the chaff he will burn up with unquenchable fire.

Luke's Gospel (1:5-25, 39-80) tells us the miraculous details connected with the birth of John the Baptist. But Matthew introduces us immediately to his ministry.

John came preaching. The Greek word is *kerysso*, from *keryx*, a herald. It was used for the herald of a military commander who gave an important announcement, or for the herald of a king who made a proclamation. John was God's herald, proclaiming an important message. A herald does not voice his own words; he speaks for another. That is what true preaching is — not arguing, debating, discussing, or airing one's own opinions, but **proclaiming** God's message.

John was preaching **in the wilderness** of Judaea. This was the rough, rugged, largely uninhabited area between the Dead Sea and the high mountain plateau on which Jerusalem and Bethlehem were located. It consisted of hills and rocks, cliffs and canyons — a desolate wasteland.[3] Perhaps it was a symbol of the spiritual condition of the nation. In such surroundings and under such circumstances a rugged preacher of righteousness was needed. John fitted the part, and his environment suited his message.

John the Baptist's message was **Repent ye; for the kingdom of heaven is at hand** (v. 2). The keynote of all pioneer preaching is **repent**. Unfortunately, most people have superficial ideas as to what repentance is. They think it means being sorry. But that is not repentance. Someone has said it means being sorry enough to quit. That comes a little nearer the truth, but is still inadequate. The Bible declares that "godly sorrow worketh repentance unto salvation" (II Cor. 7:10). Obviously, then, sorrow is not repentance; it is what produces repentance. The Greek word for **repent** means "change one's mind." Repentance is a change of attitude. It is not an emotional feeling but a moral purpose. It is a determined decision that one is done with sin, that he has renounced the world, the flesh, and the devil.

John the Baptist told the people of his day to repent, **for the kingdom of heaven is at hand.** The King had come; the kingdom was near. But instead of repenting, Israel rejected her King, and the kingdom virtually became the Church.

The phrase **the kingdom of heaven** is found only in Matthew, where it occurs thirty-three times. It is literally "the kingdom of the heavens." Matthew was writing for the Jews, who preferred to use euphemistic substitutes for "God," such

as "Heaven" or "the Blessed One." Mark and Luke have "the kingdom of God," which Matthew has only four times.

Again Matthew quotes from the Old Testament, this time from **Isaiah the prophet** (v. 3). Isaiah was the greatest of the writing prophets, as well as the most evangelical; that is, he saw most clearly the coming of Christ and His gospel.

The quotation is from Isaiah 40:3. The prophet had primarily in mind the preparation of the return of the Jewish captives from Babylonia. But the prophetic telescope pointed on down the centuries to the coming of the Messiah. How were the people to prepare the way of His coming? By repentance. That is what is meant by **make his paths straight.** Repentance involves making straight what is crooked in one's life.

John's food and clothing are described in the fourth verse. He was dressed in **raiment of camel's hair, and a leathern girdle about his loins.** The former was a coarse, rough sackcloth that would irritate the skin. It was commonly worn by ascetics of ancient times. A leather belt held the loosely flowing garment around his waist. He ate **locusts and wild honey.** "Meat" (KJV) is an obsolete term for **food.** It does not mean animal flesh. Probably **locusts** means large insects, such as were commonly eaten by the people of Palestine. The **honey** was likely bees' honey, which would be found in the crevasses of rocks. This rugged food and clothing clearly points to Elijah, who ate and dressed in similar fashion (II Kings 1:8). John the Baptist was the Elijah of the New Testament (Matt. 17:10-13).

In spite of his rough appearance and rugged preaching — or perhaps because of it — John was a popular preacher. There went out to hear him **Jerusalem, and all Judea, and all the region round about the Jordan** (v. 5). Obviously this does not mean that everybody came to him, but that vast crowds came from these places. **Jerusalem** was at an elevation of

---

[3] It was in the same wilderness that the Qumran community was located. John the Baptist may have had some connection with this group, or with the Essenes. Millar Burrows discusses at length the possible identification of the community of Qumran with the Essenes described by Philo and Josephus (*The Dead Sea Scrolls*, pp. 279-298). His conclusion is that it is safer to call the Qumran sectarians "covenanters" rather than Essenes (p. 298). But he does point out a number of parallels between John's ministry and the beliefs and practices of the Qumran covenanters, especially in his baptism of repentance and his messianic expectations (p. 328-329). F. F. Bruce is also doubtful about identifying the Qumran community with the Essenes (*Second Thoughts on the Dead Sea Scrolls*, p. 121). But Matthew Black says the identification is "one of the best established positions about the scrolls so far reached" (*The Scrolls and Christian Origins*, p. 4).

2,500 feet, while the Jordan River was about 1,300 feet below sea level. So these people from the central highlands of Judaea had to descend some four thousand feet and then face the rugged climb back up the rough mountain road. But still they came in multitudes.

These crowds were being **baptized** by John in the Jordan River, as they were **confessing out** their sins (v. 6). That is the force of the Greek, which expresses continuous action. John refused to baptize anyone who did not confess.

The **Pharisees** (v. 7) were the Separatist party in Judaism. They were connected mainly with the synagogues in the various cities and towns, where they taught the Law to the people. The **Sadducees** were the priests, who functioned in connection with the temple at Jerusalem. They tended to be wealthy and worldly, whereas the Pharisees were strict legalists in religion. Many of both parties were insincere, greedy, selfish impostors.

When John saw representatives of these two groups coming to his baptism he greeted them as **offspring of vipers**. These are harsh words. But John saw through the thin veneer of their casual curiosity, and he discerned a deep-seated spirit of deception underneath. The Pharisees and Sadducees were like snakes hiding in the grass, waiting to bite the people rather than to help them. And like vipers fleeing before a roaring brush fire, they sought to **flee from the wrath to come**. But they were unwilling to repent and confess their sins — they probably claimed they had no sins to confess. Perhaps they would have submitted to baptism as a further security against the day of wrath, but John refused to baptize them unless they fulfilled the prerequisites of repentance and confession.

The baptizing prophet urged them to produce **fruit worthy of repentance** (v. 8). The Pharisees prided themselves on their good works. But their superficial morality was no evidence of genuine repentance.

John also warned them against trusting in the fact that they were descended from **Abraham** (v. 9). God was able by a miracle to **raise up children unto Abraham**. That is exactly what He is doing in this age. All who believe in Jesus

Christ become the spiritual children of Abraham (Rom. 4:11, 16).

What did John mean by saying that **the axe lieth at the root of the trees** (v. 10)? He referred to the fact that the coming of the Messiah meant not only hope to those who accepted Him, but also judgment to those who rejected. These latter would be **hewn down, and cast into the fire**. This figure was later used by Jesus in the Parable of the Fig Tree (Luke 13:6-9). The same words we find here were later uttered by Jesus in the Sermon on the Mount (7:19). The fig tree of the parable symbolized the nation of Israel, **every tree** the individual. This is a serious warning that if one fails to produce the good fruit of Christian character, he will ultimately be cut down and cast into the fire. There is here at least an implicit reference to the final doom of the wicked in the lake of fire (Rev. 20:15).

Verse 11 is one of the most significant ones thus far in the Gospel. John declared that while he baptized **in water**, the Coming One would baptize **in the Holy Spirit**. **In** could just as well be translated "with."

The implication of John's statement is too often ignored. There is nothing distinctively Christian about water baptism. The Jews baptized Gentile proselytes as a sign of washing away their ceremonial uncleanness. Other religions have practised water baptism. The only uniquely Christian baptism is the baptism with the Holy Spirit. A truly Christian church will give more emphasis to this than to water baptism, important though the latter may be.

What is the significance of the added words, **and in fire** (found in Luke, but not in Mark)? On the basis of the following verse these are often taken as referring to the Last Judgment. But it is difficult to see how that interpretation fits this verse. Matthew is contrasting the baptism in water with the baptism of of the Spirit. It seems best to take **and in fire** as indicating that the coming of the Holy Spirit will be a fiery, cleansing baptism of the human heart. Cleansing is an important part of salvation from sin (cf. I John 1:7, 9). Much is made in both the Old Testament and the New of the fact that God will purify His people. This purification is not done in the external rite of water baptism, but in the internal experience of the baptism with the Spirit, who fills the heart when He cleanses it (cf. Acts 15:8-9).

Verse 12 gives a picture of the Final Judgment. Different figures — which symbolize the same thing — are used in the Parable of the Tares (13:24-30) and the Parable of the Drag Net (13:47-50). Here Christ is pictured as cleansing **his threshingfloor,** a smooth area of hard earth or rock outside each village, preferably located on a high spot so as to catch the wind. Freshly harvested grain is spread out on this "floor" to a depth of about a foot and a half. Then a yoke of oxen (sometimes a horse today) pull a threshing sled over the grain. This sledge is about four feet long and two and a half feet wide, with sharp teeth of stone or metal fastened to its bottom side. These tear the grain to pieces, while the oxen tread out the kernels. The threshing sleds are often ridden by women and girls. Then a man takes a winnowing fork — here called **fan** — and throws the grain high in the air. The kernels fall to the ground, while the lighter chaff blows away in the breeze. This method is still carried on in essentially the same way as it has been done for thousands of years.

John the Baptist here states of Christ that **the chaff he will burn with unquenchable fire.** In the Greek **unquenchable** is *asbestos,* which gives us our English word. There is an intimation here of what is stated in Revelation: "And if any was not found written in the book of life, he was cast into the lake of fire" (Rev. 20:15). This is the final act of divine judgment.

John's preaching, then, can be summed up in two major emphases: *repentance* and *judgment.* The first was the only way to prepare for the second. The certainty of God's judgment demands that we repent.

H. HIS PUBLIC INAUGURATION
(3:13-17)

13 Then cometh Jesus from Galilee to the Jordan unto John, to be baptized of him. 14 But John would have hindered him, saying, I have need to be baptized of thee, and comest thou to me? 15 But Jesus answering said unto him, Suffer it now: for thus it becometh us to fulfil

all righteousness. Then he suffereth him. 16 And Jesus, when he was baptized, went up straightway from the water: and lo, the heavens were opened unto him, and he saw the Spirit of God descending as a dove, and coming upon him; 17 and lo, a voice out of the heavens, saying, This is my beloved Son, in whom I am well pleased.

All this time Jesus had been living in His home town of Nazareth. But now He comes **from Galilee to the Jordan unto John, to be baptized of him** (v. 13). Just where John was baptizing we do not know. It is generally thought to have been on the east bank of the Jordan River. But whether it was in the south, near Jericho, or farther north, near Scythopolis (ancient Beth-Shean) cannot be determined.

John would have hindered him (v. 14). "Forbade" (KJV) is incorrect. The imperfect tense suggests "tried to forbid." That he did not succeed in doing so is clearly stated. John's protest was that he needed to be baptized by Jesus, not the reverse. His attitude is thoroughly understandable. At last he was confronted by a candidate who had no need for repentance, for confession, or cleansing. Jesus is described as one "who did no sin" (I Pet. 2:22).

Why, then, was Jesus baptized? The answer is given in His reply to John: **thus it becometh us to fulfill all righteousness** (v. 15). **Righteousness** means "religious duty." The Incarnation was more than a coming in physical flesh. It was an actual entrance into the human race. In so doing Jesus identified Himself with all humanity. Though He never sinned, He united Himself in a real way with sinful men. He did not place Himself upon a pedestal, but plunged into the arena of moral conflict. He became one with us in our lowly estate. The climax of Christ's identification with sinful humanity came when He hung on the Cross in man's place, condemned as a criminal. That is the mystery of divine redemption. Only Eternal Love incarnate could have done it.

All this explains why Jesus was baptized. He would go all the way as the Representative of man in his sin and deep need. He stood there that day, not by Himself or with John only, but with the crowd. Here was the Incarnation in action, divine Love revealed.

Jesus did not have to tarry in the Jordan to confess His sins, as others did. Instead He **went up straightway from the water** (v. 16). Then there took place a most remarkable scene. The heavens opened and the Spirit of God descended upon Him as a dove. The record says **he saw** this. Mark's account declares the same (Mark 1:10). This might seem to suggest a vision seen only by Jesus. But Luke says, "The Holy Spirit descended in a bodily form, as a dove, upon him" (Luke 3:22). Furthermore, John's Gospel clearly states that this descent of the Spirit as a dove was seen by John the Baptist and was a sign to him that the recipient was the Messiah (John 1:32-34). In none of the accounts is it explicitly stated that the dove-like form was seen by the crowd.

Then a voice came from heaven: **This is my beloved Son, in whom I am well pleased** (v. 17). Thus did the Father express His approval of Jesus' submitting to baptism. In this first public act of His mission to men, Christ had the approbation of the One who sent Him. He was following the path of perfect obedience marked out for Him in His redemptive ministry.

One Biblical meaning of **beloved** is "only." Christ is *the* Son, the unique Son of God. This the Father declared at the beginning of Jesus' public career.

The baptismal scene gives us the first clear revelation of the Trinity to be found in the Bible. Intimations occur in the Old Testament, but at no place do we find the three Persons distinctly indicated. Here, however, we see Christ coming out of the water, the Holy Spirit descending upon Him, and the Father's voice calling from heaven, "This is my beloved Son." The picture is at last complete.

Whereas Matthew has **This is my beloved Son,** Mark (1:11) and Luke (3:22) have "Thou art my beloved Son." Thus Matthew makes it a *public* proclamation rather than a message addressed to Jesus. So Matthew and Luke (see above) seem to indicate clearly that this was not just a psychological spiritual event experienced by Jesus alone.

It seems clear that Christ was empowered by the Spirit to preach and also to perform miracles. Luke says that after

His baptism and temptation "Jesus returned in the power of the Spirit into Galilee" (Luke 4:14). Furthermore, Jesus Himself said to the Pharisees: "If I by the Spirit of God cast out demons, then is the kingdom of God come upon you" (Matt. 12:28). It was the Father's will that Jesus should operate in the power of the Spirit.

Was this the beginning of Jesus' clear messianic consciousness? We must avoid both extremes in this matter. Apocryphal gospels which circulated in the early church depicted Christ as a tiny infant in the cradle speaking profoundly as the Son of God, and as a baby and a young boy performing spectacular miracles. But this would make of Him a psychological monstrosity. At the other extreme are those who say that Jesus was not aware of His messianic mission until the confession at Caesarea Philippi. These extremists say that, beginning to wonder who He was, He asked His disciples. When Peter said, "Thou art the Christ," Jesus cried, "You are right; I believe I am!" That settled His lingering doubts.

Somewhere in between these extremes lies the truth. Some place the awareness of messiahship at His baptism, when the voice declared He was the Son of God. But it seems that another possible time and place would be when Jesus was twelve years old in the temple. This is the age at which boys are apt to think seriously about the meaning of life and about what they should do. Psychologically this is a sane place to put the clear understanding of His divine mission.

I. HIS PRIVATE INVITATION (4:1-11)

1 Then was Jesus led up of the Spirit into the wilderness to be tempted of the devil. 2 And when he had fasted forty days and forty nights, he afterward hungered. 3 And the tempter came and said unto him, If thou art the Son of God, command that these stones become bread. 4 But he answered and said, It is written, Man shall not live by bread alone, but by every word that proceedeth out of the mouth of God. 5 Then the devil taketh him into the holy city; and he set him on the pinnacle of the temple, 6 and saith unto him, If thou art the Son of God, cast thyself down: for it is written,

He shall give his angels charge concerning thee:

and,

> On their hands they shall bear thee up,
> Lest haply thou dash thy foot against a stone.

7 Jesus said unto him, Again it is written, Thou shalt not make trial of the Lord thy God. 8 Again, the devil taketh him unto an exceeding high mountain, and showeth him all the kingdoms of the world, and the glory of them; 9 and he said unto him, All these things will I give thee, if thou wilt fall down and worship me. 10 Then saith Jesus unto him, Get thee hence, Satan: for it is written, Thou shalt worship the Lord thy God, and him only shalt thou serve, 11 Then the devil leaveth him; and behold, angels came and ministered unto him.

The Baptism was followed immediately by the Temptation. Jesus must have not only His public inauguration but also His private initiation into the ministry.

Martin Luther was once asked, "What is the most important preparation a man needs for the ministry?" He replied, "Temptation." "What is the second most important?" Again he answered, "Temptation." When asked for the third he gave the same reply: "Temptation." We might list other factors as being more absolutely essential, but no one well acquainted with the demands and problems of the Christian ministry could doubt that testing is a very necessary preparation. A piece of steel must be carefully tested before it can serve as the mainspring of a watch. So a man must be thoroughly tested in the crucible of temptation before he is fitted to be a good minister of Jesus Christ. Only tempered steel can stand the strain.

So it was with Jesus. He was to experience all the temptations common to humanity (Heb. 4:15). He was to be confronted with opposition from His enemies and misunderstanding from His friends. Before entering the public arena of His ministry He must be tested in private.

Jesus was **led up** (v. 1) **into the wilderness.** The baptism took place in the Jordan River. This, as noted, was about 1300 feet below sea level. Now He was **led up** into the precipitous heights that rose sharply between the Jordan valley and Jerusalem.

Jesus was led into the wilderness **of**

the Spirit — more accurately, "by the Spirit." We are apt to think that the Lord always leads in the green pastures and beside the still waters (Psa. 23:2). But sometimes the Holy Spirit brings the consecrated, obedient child of God through dark tunnels, over rugged mountains, through roaring storms, over raging seas, through deep waters, over thin ice, through thick forests, over desert plains.

Jesus was **tempted of [by] the devil.** Many sophisticated scholars, and their readers, scoff at the idea of a personal devil. But the horrible sadism of Nazism and Communism in our generation well illustrates the Biblical truth that Satan is real and that he is hard at work in the world of men. There is perhaps less talk today about the "natural goodness" of man and more about a personal evil force operating in history.

Jesus fasted for **forty days and forty nights** (v. 2). This is the proverbial number for a period of probation. Moses was on Mount Sinai "forty days and forty nights" (Ex. 24:18) receiving the Law. He, too, fasted during this entire period (Ex. 34:28; Deut. 9:9). Great leaders pay a great price. Both Moses and Jesus were probably sustained by divinely given strength. Elijah, likewise, was made strong to travel "forty days and forty nights" to Mount Sinai (Horeb, I Kings 19:8). The children of Israel wandered for forty years in the wilderness before entering the Promised Land (Num. 14:33).

It may surprise some to read that **he afterward hungered.** But those who have fasted for long periods of time say that after the first few days they no longer feel hungry. This is especially true if they are intensely absorbed in some consuming interest. It appears that Jesus had little or no sense of hunger for most of this period. But at the end He felt extremely hungry again, doubtless with gnawing pangs.

It was while He was in this condition — weak and hungry — that **the tempter came** (v. 3). Taking advantage of Jesus' weakened state Satan closed in on Him for hand to hand combat, determined to destroy Him in disobedience.

The first word the devil said was **If.** One of Satan's most formidable methods is that of injecting doubt. It was thus that he approached Eve in the Garden of

Eden: "Yea, hath God said?" (Gen. 3:1).

The Father's voice from heaven had just proclaimed, "This is my beloved Son." Now the devil comes and says, **If thou art the Son of God.** This can be taken two ways. It can be thought of as simply raising doubt: Do you really think you are the Son of God? If so, why not test the matter to find out? Or it may mean: Since you are the Son of God, **command that these stones become bread.** Use your sonship to serve yourself. It is foolish for you, a son of God, to go hungry! If you are God, act like Him: show your creative power!

Jesus refused to be swept off His feet by the tempter. He answered with the Word of God. **It is written** (v. 4) is in the perfect tense in Greek. The full literal meaning is: "It has been written, and still stands written." That is, the Greek perfect indicates completed action, as does the English tense. But it especially emphasizes the continuing state resulting from the completed action. So the best simple translation is either that of our standard English versions, "It is written," or perhaps still better, "It stands written." The force of this should not be missed. It underscores the fact that God's Word is unchangeable. It implies what is stated explicitly by the Psalmist: "For ever, O Lord, thy word is settled in heaven" (Psa. 119:89).

In connection with this emphasis it is interesting that all three times Jesus quoted from Deuteronomy. The divine origin and authority of this book especially have been attacked by some critics, but it is obvious that Jesus accepted it as the Word of God.

The Scripture Jesus quoted gives us a clue to His attitude. **Man shall not live by bread alone, but by every word that proceedeth out of the mouth of God** (Deut. 8:3). It was Jesus Himself who said on another occasion: "My meat is to do the will of him that sent me, and to accomplish his work" (John 4:34). He was ruled, not by His material desires but by the will of His Father. God's Word governed His every act. He lived by the Word of God. And thus He left us an example, that we should follow His steps (I Pet. 2:21).

The contrast between this and the temptation of Adam and Eve in the garden is very striking. They were in the midst of a luxurious paradise; Jesus was in a bleak, barren wilderness. They had everything to eat; He had nothing. They had the companionship of each other; He was alone. The first Adam ate the forbidden fruit; the last Adam refused Satan's suggestion that He make bread to eat. With everything in his favor the first Adam failed and brought suffering to the whole human race. With seemingly everything against Him the last Adam triumphed and brought salvation to all mankind. Never was battle fought with greater issues at stake. Never was a more important victory won.

The second temptation was of a different type. The devil took Jesus to **the holy city** (v. 5). This designation for Jerusalem is found in the New Testament only in Matthew and Revelation. In the Old Testament it occurs in Nehemiah 11:1, 18; Isaiah 52:1; Daniel 9:24. Satan set Him on **the pinnacle of the temple.** The word for **pinnacle** literally means "wing." Probably a high "wing" of some temple building is meant, so that He would be seen by the throngs in the temple courts. Perhaps it was the dome of the sanctuary itself, which towered to a height of some 150 feet.

Again the devil cried, **If thou art the Son of God** (v. 6). The challenge this time was: **cast thyself down.** Then, appearing as an angel of light (II Cor. 11:14), Satan very piously proceeded to quote Scripture (Psa. 91:11-12). He tried to deceive Jesus into thinking He could do as He pleased and still trust God to take care of Him.

What was Jesus' answer to Satan's second suggestion? **Again it is written** (v. 7). He used one weapon — the Word of God. Once more He quoted from Deuteronomy: **Thou shalt not make trial of the Lord thy God** (Deut. 6:16). To have presumed on divine protection when He was guided by human self-interest would have been to tempt His Father. Jesus refused to do it.

There seem to have been two aspects to this temptation. The first may have been: You say that you trust God; now prove it. This is a very subtle type of thing. At first sight it would seem that to obey Satan would, in this instance, glorify God. But only those who obey the heavenly Father can claim His protection.

The second aspect was: Throw yourself down, land safely, and the people will acclaim you as Messiah. It is known that the Jews of that day expected that when the Messiah came He would make a spectacular appearance at the temple.

The third temptation presents a different setting: **the devil taketh him unto an exceeding high mountain** (v. 8). That these words should be taken figuratively, not literally, is rather obvious. For there is no mountain peak on earth from which **all the kingdoms of the world** can be seen. In spirit, or imagination, Jesus was taken to the pinnacle of the temple and to the high mountain.

This time Satan's proposal was: **All these things will I give thee, if thou wilt fall down and worship me** (v. 9). What the devil was offering was political power. But that was not what Jesus wanted. He desired to rule the hearts of men by His love. His was to be a spiritual kingdom, "not of this world" (John 18:36). To have worshiped Satan would have been to destroy the true kingdom of God.

Jesus had had enough. Sternly He commanded, **Get thee hence, Satan** (v. 10). As a parting shot He once more quoted the Scriptures: **Thou shalt worship the Lord thy God, and him only shalt thou serve** (Deut. 6:13). God's law was His will. He refused to worship or serve any one but the one true God.

The devil obeyed His command and **leaveth him** (v. 11). Satan's place was taken by **angels** who **came and ministered unto him**. This probably included the provision of physical food, as an angel once fed Elijah (I Kings 19:5-7). It certainly meant also spiritual comfort and strength.

It seems best to assume that there was no physical form visible to the eyes of Jesus, but rather that the temptations came as suggestions to His mind. For that is the way the most crucial enticements come to God's people today. Jesus' temptations have more meaning and value for us if they were in the form of mental suggestions. This seems to be Satan's favorite method of attack.

It might be noted that Luke gives the same three temptations, but in a different order from that in Matthew; the second and third are transposed. Matthew's order seems preferable, as it suggests a greater climactic effect. The advice to leap from the pinnacle of the temple sounds like an anticlimax after the offer of the kingdoms of the world. Then, too, it is at the close of Matthew's third temptation that Satan is commanded to leave. Luke doubtless had some reason for his order, but just what it was is not known.

The story of Jesus' temptation is filled with many lessons for His followers. We can note only a few of them.

(1) Jesus met every temptation with only one weapon; and that weapon is at our disposal. Paul urged the Christians of his day to take "the sword of the Spirit, which is the word of God" (Eph. 6:17). With this sword Christ defeated the devil every time.

(2) The devil often attacks Christians when they feel most weak and weary. It is then that one needs to be on special alert and rely most on divine help.

(3) Doubt is often the wedge by which Satan would pry open an entrance into the heart. If he can get one to doubt, he has won the first round. Paul wrote: "Withal taking up the shield of faith, wherewith ye shall be able to quench all the fiery darts of the evil one" (Eph. 6:16). Often "fiery darts" take the form of fiery doubts. These must be met by firm faith in God and in His Word.

(4) Man is a spiritual as well as physical being. Therefore he cannot live by bread alone, "but by every word that proceedeth out of the mouth of God."

(5) A thing may be legitimate in itself, but if it is not the will of God it must be rejected. Of itself there was nothing wrong in Jesus' turning stones into bread. But there were spiritual principles of obedience involved in this instance, and Jesus stuck by those principles.

(6) The devil has lured many people into the trap of the spectacular. Doing something spectacular draws attention to oneself, not to Christ. Jesus refused to leap from a pinnacle of the temple in order to get the crowd on His side.

(7) One should not tempt God by exposing himself to needless danger and trusting the Lord to take care of him.

(8) The end does not justify the means. To worship Satan was obviously wrong. But if it would gain for Christ the kingdoms of the world, would it not certainly be justified? Jesus answered an emphatic "No!" God will not, for example, be pleased with gifts of money

earned by compromise with evil. The devil has deceived more than one person at this point.

(9) There comes a time when one should refuse to listen longer to the voice of the tempter. Jesus said, "Get thee hence, Satan."

(10) One must refuse to worship anything or anyone other than God Himself. The early Christians had to face the crucial choice: Christ or Caesar. Some tried to compromise and save their lives by worshiping the emperor while still professing allegiance to God. But the issue is still the same as with the three Hebrew children who went to the fiery furnace rather than compromise by bowing down to the golden image. Too often today gold itself is the image to which men bow in abject servitude.

The temptation of Jesus was no play-acting on the stage. Some have put the whole emphasis on His deity until the temptation has become unreal — just something displayed for effect. But that attitude actually denies the historicity of the Gospels.

The author of Hebrews has underscored the reality of the temptation. He says that Jesus "suffered being tempted" (Heb. 2:18). That is, His temptations were as real to Him as ours are to us. There is no profit in debating the question as to whether He could have failed and what the results would have been. The truth is that in the consciousness of Christ, *He was really tempted.* Otherwise the whole thing would have been an empty farce, and the author of Hebrews could not honestly have said that He was *in all points* tempted as we are (Heb. 4:15). That means they were real temptations to Him.

II. THE POWER AND PROGRAM OF THE KING (Matt. 4:12-25:46)

A. HIS HEADQUARTERS (4:12-17)

12 Now when he heard that John was delivered up, he withdrew into Galilee; 13 and leaving Nazareth, he came and dwelt in Capernaum, which is by the sea, in the borders of Zebulun and Naphtali: 14 that it might be fulfilled which was spoken through Isaiah the prophet, saying:
15 The land of Zebulun and the land of Naphtali,
Toward the sea, beyond the Jordan,

Galilee of the Gentiles,
16 The people that sat in darkness Saw a great light,
And to them that sat in the region and shadow of death,
To them did light spring up.
17 From that time began Jesus to preach, and to say, Repent ye; for the kingdom of heaven is at hand.

When Jesus heard that **John was delivered up, he withdrew into Galilee** (v. 12). Thus in the first two Gospels the arrest and imprisonment of John the Baptist — **delivered up** can mean either "arrested" or "imprisoned" — mark the beginning of Jesus' public ministry (cf. Mark 1:14). Luke, just before his description of the Baptism and Temptation, inserts the mention of the imprisonment of John by Herod Antipas. But that insertion serves to round off his account of John's ministry and does not conflict chronologically with the statement here. John's Gospel describes an earlier Judean ministry (John 1:35—3:36); but obviously that is no contradiction of Matthew's account. We do not have in any or all of the Gospels together a full record of Jesus' ministry. Each writer selected certain parts to relate.

Leaving Nazareth (v. 13), His home town, Jesus chose **Capernaum** as the headquarters for His great Galilean ministry, which was to cover perhaps a year and a half. **Nazareth** was a tiny, obscure village, not even mentioned in the Old Testament or in Josephus. It lay nestled in the hills north of the Plain of Esdraelon, tucked away out of sight and off the main thoroughfares. On the other hand, **Capernaum** (modern Tell Hum, on the northwest shore of the Lake of Galilee) was an important city on the busy highway leading from Egypt and the south to Damascus and the north. It was a far more fitting place for Jesus to make contact with the multitudes.

The sea does not mean the Mediterranean but what Luke more accurately calls the Lake of Galilee. It was only about twelve miles long and six miles wide — just a broad spot on the Jordan River as it flowed southward. But to those who lived on its shores and fished in its waters it was "the sea."

Galilee was composed largely of the old tribal territories of **Zebulun and Naphtali**. The latter bordered on the lake, while the former lay farther west. **Borders,** as usually in the New Testament, means "district" or "region."

Once more (v. 14) the reader finds the familiar formula, **that it might be fulfilled which was spoken** (cf. 1:22; 2:15, 23). This time it was through **Isaiah the prophet.** As already noted, he was the one who foretold most fully the work of the coming Messiah. The quotation in verse 15 is from Isaiah 9:1-2. Altogether, Matthew quotes Isaiah no less than fifteen times.

Toward the sea (v. 15) is literally "the way of the sea." This refers to the main highway which led from the Mediterranean past the Lake of Galilee to Damascus. **Beyond the Jordan** would probably mean east of the Jordan River. Perhaps the reference is to Perea (ancient Gilead), which was joined with Galilee under the rule of Herod Antipas. These were the two main territories of Jesus' public ministry as described in the Synoptic Gospels.

Galilee of the Gentiles was so called because it had a larger Gentile population than did Judea in the south. This was due to the fact that it bordered on the nations to the north and had been, together with Gilead east of the Jordan, the first part of Israel to be conquered and taken into captivity (II Kings 15: 29). The strict Jews of Judea always looked down on the inhabitants of Galilee as less pure.

The people that sat in darkness (v. 16) is a reference to the fact that the Galileans were more subject to pagan influences than the Judeans. But it was precisely because they needed Him most that Jesus went to them first. In Him they **saw a great light.** Jesus, the Light of the world (John 8:12), had appeared to those who sat in the darkness of sin and partial heathenism, and thus in the **shadow of death.** The Messiah was foretold by the ancient prophet as "a light of the Gentiles" (Isa. 42:6). The phrase **light spring up** finds its most eloquent commentary in Isaiah 60:1-5.

Preach (v. 17) is the same verb that is used of John the Baptist's ministry (3:1). It means "herald, proclaim." Jesus adopted exactly the same text as John had used: **Repent ye; for the kingdom of heaven is at hand** (cf. 3:2). **Is at hand** does not mean "has come" but "has drawn near"

(perfect tense). In the person and preaching of Christ the kingdom of God had come near to men.

B. HIS FIRST FOLLOWERS (4:18-22)

18 And walking by the sea of Galilee, he saw two brethren, Simon who is called Peter, and Andrew his brother, casting a net into the sea; for they were fishers. 19 And he saith unto them, Come ye after me, and I will make you fishers of men. 20 And they straightway left the nets, and followed him. 21 And going on from thence he saw two other brethren, James the *son* of Zebedee, and John his brother, in the boat with Zebedee their father mending their nets; and he called them. 22 And they straightway left the boat and their father, and followed him.

It was now time for Jesus to choose helpers, those who would be His associates and assistants. **Walking by the sea of Galilee** (v. 18), he found the first four. **Simon** — a very common Jewish name in that day — had already been given by Jesus the new name **Peter,** a stone (John 1:42). **Andrew** played a minor role in the circle of the twelve, but will always be remembered for bringing his brother Peter to the Master (John 1:41).

Near the shore of the lake these two brothers were wading in the shallow water, **casting a net.** This was a casting-net with weights on the bottom. Its users would throw it into the lake in the hope that its mesh would enclose a school of fish. South of Capernaum there are warm springs where the fish tend to congregate.

These men were **fishers,** or fishermen. Probably Jesus chose fishermen for their qualities of patience and persistence, of hardihood and fortitude, of purpose and determination — characteristics which would equip them for their apostolic mission.

The Master's call was clear and unequivocal: **Come ye after me, and I will make you fishers of men** (v. 19). What a contrast — from gathering fish out of the lake to gather sinners out of the sea of humanity, that they might be saved in the kingdom.

The call was peremptory; the response was prompt. **Straightway,** immediately, they **left the nets, and followed him** (v. 20). There was no debating or discussing — just a decision. But it was immediate and irrevocable. They forsook their business and followed Jesus.

So also did **James** and **John** (v. 21). These two sons of **Zebedee** were partners of Peter and Andrew (Luke 5:7-10). They had pulled their fishing boat up to the shore and were sitting in it, mending their nets in preparation for the next fishing trip.

But when Jesus called, they **straightway left the boat and their father, and followed him** (v. 22). This required both courage and consecration.

These four fishermen were not only the first but also the foremost of the disciples. Three of them became the inner trio — Peter, James and John. Peter and John are associated prominently in the early part of Acts (e.g., 3:1; 8:14). Peter was the main spokesman of the apostles both in the Gospels and in the opening chapters of Acts. He it was who preached the great sermon on the day of Pentecost. James must have been a zealous worker, for he was the first of the apostles to become a martyr (Acts 12:2). Andrew played an important role at the feeding of the five thousand (John 6:8-9), though he later fades out of the foreground.

It may seem surprising that these four men answered Jesus' call so quickly and completely. But this was not their first contact with Christ. Their earlier call to fellowship with the Master is described in John 1:35-42. But this new call was to active service. There is no contradiction between the accounts.

C. HIS POPULARITY (4:23-25)

23 And Jesus went about in all Galilee, teaching in their synagogues, and preaching the gospel of the kingdom, and healing all manner of disease and all manner of sickness among the people. 24 And the report of him went forth into all Syria: and they brought unto him all that were sick, holden with divers diseases and torments, possessed with demons, and epileptic, and palsied; and he healed them. 25 And there followed him great multitudes from Galilee and Decapolis and Jerusalem and Judaea and *from* beyond the Jordan.

Verse 23 gives a summary statement of a circuit Jesus made of the towns and villages of **all Galilee**. Almost exactly the same words are found in a later, similar summary (9:35). Obviously the Gospels give us only a few high spots in the very busy ministry of the Master.

There were three distinct aspects of this early Galilean ministry: **teaching, preaching,** and **healing.** He taught in **their synagogues.** These were located in every town and were the local centers of worship, education, and judicial procedure. The three functions of the synagogues made them something different from churches today. In His ministry Jesus had the tremendous advantage, as did Paul later, of an open door, in the form of a synagogue, in each community. Here any visiting rabbi would have the privilege of speaking to the people assembled for the services (cf. Acts 13:15). The rabbis were laymen, not ordained clergymen (like the priests at the temple).

In addition to His teaching, Jesus was **preaching the gospel of the kingdom.** This was the good news that the kingdom of God belonged to all who would accept it (cf. v. 17). The word **kingdom** means primarily not a *realm,* but a *reign.* It is God's sovereign rule. When one accepts God's will as his will, he is in the kingdom, and the kingdom is in him. To accept Christ as king is to receive the kingdom.

Thirdly, Jesus was **healing all manner of disease and all manner of sickness among the people.** His power was not limited to curing functional disorders, which may respond to mental suggestion and emotional pressure — as is the case with many "healers" today. He healed organic diseases as well.

This created a great deal of excitement. **The report of him went forth into all Syria** (v. 24). Strictly speaking, Syria was a non-Jewish territory north of Palestine — similar to the modern country of Syria — though in its larger sense it took in Palestine and Phoenicia (modern Lebanon). That His fame should travel so far shows the magnitude of Jesus' miracles.

Three special classes of ill people are mentioned: demoniacs, epileptics, and paralytics. Demon possession is mentioned frequently in the Gospel accounts. It apparently was rather common in those days. Today it is popular to say that this was just an ancient, unscientific explanation for insanity, as well as for some extreme physical ailments. But the Gospels state categorically that Jesus cast out demons. In pagan lands today, well-educated missionaries whose honesty and judgment cannot be questioned affirm that they have come in contact with some cases of genuine demon possession and have witnessed a few miraculous deliverances. Those who live in the seclusion of a highly sophisticated and civilized country should be cautious about denying this intelligent testimony.

The word **epileptic** is literally "moonstruck." This word reflects the ancient superstition that insanity was caused by a stroke from the moon. The word "lunatic" comes from the Latin word for moon and is based on the same concept. For that reason some would translate the term **epileptic** as "lunatics."

This was the period of Jesus' greatest popularity: **there followed him great multitudes** (v. 25). The places from which they came provide some idea of the outreach of His ministry. People who came were not only from **Galilee**, in the northern part of Palestine proper, but also from **Decapolis**. This Greek word means "ten cities." The name was applied to a group of ten cities — or approximately that number — located east of the Jordan River and the Lake of Galilee (except Scythopolis), and also to the region where most of these were situated. It was strongly Gentile territory.

Jerusalem and **Judaea** were in the southern part of Palestine, between the Jordan Valley and the Mediterranean Sea. It was about a hundred miles from Jerusalem to Capernaum. **Beyond the Jordan**, as already noted, means Perea (literally, "across"). This territory on the east side of the Jordan, though not adjoining Galilee at any point, was also ruled by Antipas. It was likewise rather strongly Gentile.

This paragraph (vv. 23-25) forms the immediate setting for the Sermon on the Mount. Though the compassion of Christ moved Him to heal the multitudes that flocked to Him, He realized that their greatest need was for teaching. Their spiritual illness far outweighed their physical ailments. Jesus knew what they needed most and gave it to them.

D. HIS KINGDOM (5:1-7:29)

1. Children of the Kingdom (5:1-20)

a. Their Rights (5:1-12)

1 And seeing the multitudes, he went up into the mountain: and when he had sat down, his disciples came unto him: 2 and he opened his mouth and taught them, saying,

3 Blessed are the poor in spirit: for theirs is the kingdom of heaven.

4 Blessed are they that mourn: for they shall be comforted.

5 Blessed are the meek: for they shall inherit the earth.

6 Blessed are they that hunger and thirst after righteousness: for they shall be filled.

7 Blessed are the merciful: for they shall obtain mercy.

8 Blessed are the pure in heart: for they shall see God.

9 Blessed are the peacemakers: for they shall be called sons of God.

10 Blessed are they that have been persecuted for righteousness' sake: for theirs is the kingdom of heaven. 11 Blessed are ye when *men* shall reproach you, and persecute you, and say all manner of evil against you falsely, for my sake. 12 Rejoice, and be exceeding glad: for great is your reward in heaven: for so persecuted they the prophets that were before you.

Chapters 5, 6, and 7 comprise what is commonly called the Sermon on the Mount. Its keynote is *true righteousness* (5:20). It has sometimes been referred to as the Constitution of the Kingdom of Heaven. The Beatitudes (5:3-12) would then be the Preamble to the Constitution. From the British point of view it might be designated the Magna Carta of the Kingdom.

The first two verses of chapter 5 give us the setting of the sermon. Jesus went up a hill, with His disciples following. But the crowds also heard Him (7:28). Jesus **sat down**, as all Jewish rabbis did while teaching.

As Moses declared the Old Law at Mount Sinai, so Jesus set forth the New Law on a mountain. The traditional Mount of Beatitudes is a long slope at the northwest corner of the Lake of Galilee.

Some have dismissed the Sermon on the Mount as a hopeless ideal. Others have sought to relegate it to a future Millennium. But it really is the Christian's "working philosophy of life," as Jones rightly points out.[4]

The Beatitudes have been called "a sort of title-page to the teachings of Jesus."[5] They set forth the true nature of the subjects of the Kingdom. These subjects are the **poor in spirit,** the **pure in heart,** the **peacemakers,** the **persecuted,** those who **mourn,** the **meek,** the **merciful,** the ones who **hunger and thirst after righteousness.**

It is obvious that these virtues are far different from those usually stressed by the world. In the Roman Empire *virtus* meant "manliness." But too often it was military valor rather than moral courage which was emphasized. Jesus exalted a new type of ethic. He proclaimed a startlingly different set of values. He put the highest premium on the things of the spirit.

This King confronted His world with a new concept of life. Not the powerful, but the **poor in spirit,** were to be the subjects of His kingdom (cf. Isa. 11:4; 57:15). Luke (6:20) has "ye poor." But poverty is no guarantee of piety. What Jesus meant was the **poor in spirit;** that is, those who are conscious of their spiritual need. Jesus had been brought up among the humble poor of Israel, who devoutly desired the kingdom of God (cf. Luke 2:25).

Not the merrymakers, but those that **mourn,** will find true happiness. The Old Testament predicted that God's people would be **comforted** by the coming of the Messiah (Isa. 61:1-3). The compassionate Christ came to comfort sorrowing, suffering humanity.

Not the mighty, but the **meek,** will **inherit the earth** (cf. Psa. 37:11). Not the greedy, but the godly will gain the inheritance. Paul gives vivid expression to this paradox of the Christian life in II Corinthians 6:6-10. **Meek** does not mean weak or timid, but humble and trustful. It means accepting God's will rather than asserting one's rights.

Not the ones who are hungry for riches, but those that **hunger and thirst after righteousness,** will be **filled;** that is, satisfied. Righteousness means "a life fully conformed to the will of God in thought, word, worship, and act."[6]

Not the merciless, but the **merciful,** will **obtain mercy.** The Stoics considered mercy to be a vice, not a virtue.[7] Also the Jews taught that those who suffered were only getting their just deserts (cf. John 9:2). Ward comments: "Jesus had to be explicit about this requirement, for the current doctrine of suffering as reward of sin tended to stifle sympathy as does the Hindu doctrine of karma."[8]

Not the proud in spirit, but the **pure in heart,** will **see God** — here and hereafter. Sin is like dust in the eyes: it beclouds one's vision of the Eternal. Salvation includes the cleansing of the heart from all sin (I John 1:7). Purity of intention is essential if one would **see God;** that is, truly worship in His presence and enjoy His fellowship.

Not the pugnacious, but the **peacemakers,** will be called **sons of God.** In Oriental thought **sons of** means "having the nature of." Those who seek to avert quarrels, to harmonize differences, to strengthen friendship, to avoid petty bickering, to create a pleasant atmosphere, to work for a sympathetic understanding between loved ones, friends, neighbors, social classes, industrial groups, and nations — these display the divine nature of love and so will be **called sons of God** by those who observe them. One of the most important places to be a peacemaker is in the home. This is where the largest number of crises develop.

Not the persecutors, but the **persecuted,** will have membership in the Kingdom. In the first century it was the leaders of the Jewish religion who persecuted Jesus and His disciples. In the Middle Ages pompous ecclesiastics persecuted humble followers of the lowly Nazarene. Later on those who protested against this stooped to the disgraceful business of persecuting their fellow Protestants. Beyond all this there is persecution by the world in the form of ridicule and social pressure. But the one who is persecuted **for righteousness' sake** is assured of a place in the Kingdom. Because of this he should **rejoice** (cf. Acts 5:41).

Christianity has sometimes been accused of promising "pie in the sky when

[4] E. Stanley Jones, *The Christ of the Mount,* p. 11.
[5] Harvie Branscomb, *The Teachings of Jesus,* p. 173.
[6] Floyd V. Filson, *A Commentary on the Gospel According to St. Matthew,* p. 77.
[7] Epictetus, *Dissertations,* II. 24. 43.
[8] A. Marcus Ward, *The Gospel According to St. Matthew,* pp. 28-29.

you die" — **great is your reward in heaven.** Two replies may be made to this accusation. The first is that the hope of future reward is a perfectly justifiable incentive for righteous living.[9] The other is that the kingdom of God is not only a pleasant prospect but a present possession. To know Christ is to enjoy the Kingdom here and now.

b. Their Responsibilities (5:13-16)

13 Ye are the salt of the earth: but if the salt have lost its savor, wherewith shall it be salted? it is thenceforth good for nothing, but to be cast out and trodden under foot of men. 14 Ye are the light of the world. A city set on a hill cannot be hid. 15 Neither do *men* light a lamp, and put it under the bushel, but on the stand; and it shineth unto all that are in the house. 16 Even so let your light shine before men; that they may see your good works, and glorify your Father who is in heaven.

As citizens of the heavenly commonwealth, Christians have heavy responsibilities. First, they are to be **the salt of the earth.** Salt does two things: it *flavors* and *preserves.* Life without Christ is flat, insipid, tasteless. His followers are to add tone to life and zest to living, just as salt adds flavor to food. But Christianity must also be the preservative of human society. When Jesus spoke these words modern refrigeration was unknown. One of the most common ways to preserve food — such as fish shipped from the Lake of Galilee down to Jerusalem — was to salt it heavily. What would the world be today without the Church of Jesus Christ?

Secondly, Jesus said: **Ye are the light of the world.** This should be set alongside another statement of His: "I am the light of the world." The Son of God is the Sun of righteousness (Mal. 4:2). The Church is the moon which is to reflect the light of this Sun into the face of a darkened world.

A city set on a hill is a common sight in the mountainous Holy Land. Just so, Christians are on display and must give care to their influence on others.

A lamp was a very important item in a windowless Palestinian house. Burning olive oil, the tiny clay lamp (not "candle," KJV) was not to be put under a **bushel** — actually a meal tub holding about a peck. Rather, it was to be put on a **stand,** or lampstand, which was often a niche in the wall. Here it would give light to **all that are in the house.** This would imply a one-room house, such as that lived in by most of the poor people of that day.

What is the Christian's light? It is here described as his **good works.** These are even more effective witnesses than one's verbal testimony.

c. Their Righteousness (5:17-20)

17 Think not that I came to destroy the law or the prophets: I came not to destroy, but to fulfil. 18 For verily I say unto you, Till heaven and earth pass away, one jot or one tittle shall in no wise pass away from the law, till all things be accomplished. 19 Whosoever therefore shall break one of these least commandments, and shall teach men so, shall be called least in the kingdom of heaven: but whosoever shall do and teach them, he shall be called great in the kingdom of heaven. 20 For I say unto you, that except your righteousness shall exceed *the righteousness* of the scribes and Pharisees, ye shall in no wise enter into the kingdom of heaven.

A most significant statement is found in verse 17. Jesus declared that He had not come to **destroy the law or the prophets,** but rather to **fulfil.** Thus Christ Himself explained His relationship to the Old Testament. The Hebrew Scriptures were not set aside with the coming of Christianity. Rather, they were to be given a higher interpretation, which is exactly what is found in verses 21-48. Only by their fulfillment in Christ can the Old Testament writings be understood correctly. Without Him they are incomplete and incomprehensible.

Jesus further declared that not the least item of the Law would pass away until all was fulfilled.[10] This does not bind Christians to a literal adherence to the many minute regulations of the Old Testament. Since Christ fulfilled it all in His perfect

---

[9] Ward (*ibid.*, p. 30) wisely remarks: "The Christian can talk about rewards so long as he remembers that they are not deserved or acquired by him, and avoids making them a matter of exact book-keeping."

[10] **Jot** represents the smallest letter of the alphabet (*yodh* in Hebrew, *iota* in Greek). **Tittle** stands for the "horn" on a Hebrew letter which distinguishes it from similar letters.

life of absolute obedience to the will of God, men meet its demands when they by faith unite themselves with Him. To be dominated by the Spirit of Christ is to fulfill God's requirements.

Verse 20 has often been chosen as the key verse of the Sermon on the Mount. Jesus demanded of His followers a higher righteousness than that of the *scribes and Pharisees,* whose righteousness was outward, formal, ceremonial, legalistic. Christian righteousness is essentially inward, spiritual, moral, generated by love.

The point that Jesus was emphasizing was that the demands of grace are actually higher than those of the Law. But they are of a different nature. Instead of paying meticulous attention to multitudinous details, Christians are to do "one thing" (Phil. 3:13) — seek to please God continually. Filson observes: "The gospel brings mercy, comfort, and divine help, but it does not cancel the demand of God for faithful and complete obedience to his will."[11] Only "reaching the spiritual meaning of the law"[12] will permit one to **enter into the kingdom of heaven.** That is because the Kingdom is a spiritual reign, not a legal or political realm. Ward comments: "The disciple does not think in terms of rules and right but of love."[13] For the Jew **righteousness** was a slavish adherence to the letter of the Law. For the Christian it is a right attitude of the heart in desiring to do the whole will of God.

2. Characteristics of the Kingdom (5: 21-48)

In this section "Jesus takes six concrete examples from the old Law in order to illustrate the new righteousness."[14] This righteousness involves every aspect of one's daily life.

Each one of these six discussions is introduced by **Ye have heard that it was said to them of old time** (vv. 21, 33), **Ye have heard that it was said** (vv. 27, 38, 43), or simply **It was said** (v. 31). With this formula reference is made to some commandment in the Mosaic law (or, in the case of the last clause of v. 43, in the tradition of the elders).

All six times Jesus adds: **but I say unto you** (vv. 22, 28, 32, 34, 39, 44). This is even stronger in the Greek than in the English — *ego de lego hymin.* The *ego* is expressed in Greek only for added emphasis, as the **I** is included in the verb *lego,* **I say.** Furthermore, it is placed first in the clause, the most emphatic position in a Greek sentence. Either Jesus was a blatant egotist, or He was what He claimed to be — the eternal Son of God, who had the right to speak with absolute divine authority. Blair maintains that this emphasis on Christ's authority is the main characteristic of the Gospel of Matthew.[15]

a. Peaceableness (5:21-26)

21 Ye have heard that it was said to them of old time, Thou shalt not kill; and whosoever shall kill shall be in danger of the judgment: 22 but I say unto you, that every one who is angry with his brother shall be in danger of the judgment; and whosoever shall say to his brother, Raca, shall be in danger of the council; and whosoever shall say, Thou fool, shall be in danger of the hell of fire. 23 If therefore thou art offering thy gift at the altar, and there rememberest that thy brother hath aught against thee, 24 leave there thy gift before the altar, and go thy way, first be reconciled to thy brother, and then come and offer thy gift. 25 Agree with thine adversary quickly, while thou art with him in the way; lest haply the adversary deliver thee to the judge, and the judge deliver thee to the officer, and thou be cast into prison. 26 Verily I say unto thee, Thou shalt by no means come out thence, till thou have paid the last farthing.

The sixth of the Ten Commandments is: **Thou shalt not kill** (Ex. 20:13; Deut. 5:17). Jesus did not abrogate this command. Rather, He extended it to cover anger, contempt, and hatred. There seems to be an ascending scale in verse 22: (1) **angry** — "Feeling of anger without words"; (2) **Raca** — "Anger venting itself in words"; (3) **Thou fool** — "Insulting anger."[16] The precise distinction between the terms **raca** and **fool** is not known. It is thought that the first may come from a root meaning to "spit."[17]

---

[11] *Op. cit.*, p. 84.   [12] A. Carr, *The Gospel According to St. Matthew*, p. 110.   [13] *Op. cit.*, p. 33.
[14] *Ibid.*, p. 34.   [15] Edwin P. Blair, *Jesus in the Gospel of Matthew*, pp. 44ff.
[16] Carr, *op. cit.*, p. 120.   [17] *Ibid.*

Both words express contempt and condemnation.

More clear is the ascending scale of consequences. **Judgment** probably refers to the local court. **Council** is *synedrion,* the Great Sanhedrin at Jerusalem, the highest Jewish court of justice. **Hell** is *Gehenna,* the place of final torment. **Be in danger of** is a legal term meaning "is liable to." That is, the one guilty of these things is subject to the courts of justice or punishment named here.

This warning is followed by a twofold admonition to make reconciliation. If one comes to the sanctuary and remembers that he has injured his brother in any way, he must first be reconciled before his worship will be acceptable. Again, if one is being hauled before the judge, he should settle quickly out of court. Otherwise he will be **cast into prison** and kept there until he has paid the last **farthing;** or as we would say, "the last penny." Imprisonment for debt was a common practice until fairly recent times.

The point that Jesus was making is that everyone should hasten to be reconciled to God, whom all men have offended. Thus this passage has a strong evangelistic slant.

b. Purity (5:27-30)

27 Ye have heard that it was said, Thou shalt not commit adultery: 28 but I say unto you, that every one that looketh on a woman to lust after her hath committed adultery with her already in his heart. 29 And if thy right eye causeth thee to stumble, pluck it out, and cast it from thee: for it is profitable for thee that one of thy members should perish, and not thy whole body be cast into hell. 30 And if thy right hand causeth thee to stumble, cut it off, and cast it from thee: for it is profitable for thee that one of thy members should perish, and not thy whole body go into hell.

The seventh commandment says: **Thou shalt not commit adultery** (Ex. 20:14; Deut. 5:18). Jesus extended this to cover the lustful look. It is not the act but the desire that constitutes sin. This is the basic difference between the Old Law and the New. The former deals primarily with actions, the latter with attitudes; the former with deeds, the latter with desires; the former with means, the latter with motives; the former with the hand, the latter with the heart.

It is sometimes assumed that because Christians are not under law but under grace they are thereby not subject to such rigid requirements as were the Old Testament saints. But the interpretation that Jesus gives here indicates clearly that His demands go deeper and higher and further than those of the Mosaic law. Since desire is parent to the deed, it is the former that should be given prior attention.

The **eye** is the gateway to the mind, and the **hand** represents the instrument for doing evil. **Hell** is not *Hades,* the place of departed spirits, but *Gehenna,* the place of torment. Jesus declared that it was better to lose one's right **eye** or right **hand** than to be lost forever in **hell.** He was speaking figuratively, of course, when He talked of plucking out an eye or cutting off a hand. A significant application would be that of cutting off a close friendship that was leading to sin, or a loved vocation which was proving to be a source of temptation.

c. Harmony (5:31-32)

31 It was said also, Whosoever shall put away his wife, let him give her a writing of divorcement: 32 but I say unto you, that every one that putteth away his wife, saving for the cause of fornication, maketh her an adulteress: and whosoever shall marry her when she is put away committeth adultery.

Divorce is one of the oldest and most persistent problems in human society. The Mosaic law permitted divorce, but required a certificate to be given, thus putting a restriction on easy divorce (Deut. 24:13). But Jesus went on record as forbidding divorce except in the case of **fornication.** This last term is not used in its present narrow technical sense but includes adultery, which is meant here. The Christian standard is that of love and harmony in the home.

d. Honesty (5:33-37)

33 Again, ye have heard that it was said to them of old time, Thou shalt not forswear thyself, but shalt perform unto

the Lord thine oaths: 34 but I say unto you, Swear not at all; neither by the heaven, for it is the throne of God; 35 nor by the earth, for it is the footstool of his feet; nor by Jerusalem, for it is the city of the great King. 36 Neither shalt thou swear by thy head, for thou canst not make one hair white or black. 37 But let your speech be, Yea, yea, Nay, nay: and whatsoever is more than these is of the evil *one.*

The Law commanded, **Thou shalt not forswear thyself** (Lev. 19:12; Num. 30:2; Deut. 23:21), that is, "swear falsely" (RSV) or "commit perjury." It was held that if one took an oath in God's name, it was binding. So recourse was had to substitutes, such as **heaven, earth, Jerusalem,** or one's **head.** But Jesus exposed the hypocrisy of this practice. He insisted that one should say quite simply and honestly "Yes" or "No." Filson rightly observes: "The trouble with oaths is that they introduce a double standard of truth and honesty."[18]

e. Kindness (5:38-42)

38 Ye have heard that it was said, An eye for an eye, and a tooth for a tooth: 39 but I say unto you, Resist not him that is evil: but whosoever smiteth thee on thy right cheek, turn to him the other also. 40 And if any man would go to law with thee, and take away thy coat, let him have thy cloak also. 41 And whosoever shall compel thee to go one mile, go with him two. 42 Give to him that asketh thee, and from him that would borrow of thee turn not thou away.

The law of retaliation (*lex talionis*), expressed as **An eye for an eye, and a tooth for a tooth,** is the most primitive form of justice. It is stated three times in the Old Testament (Ex. 21:24; Lev. 24:20; Deut. 19:21). The intention was to deter men from seeking excessive revenge.

But Jesus enjoined the higher law of non-retaliation. The Christian is not to strike back. Rather he is to take wrong, if need be. People have been won to Christ through the practice of this principle.

Jesus gave five illustrations: (1) insult, (2) lawsuit, (3) forced service, (4) demands for gifts, (5) demands for loans.

It is obvious that a literalistic, unthinking application of these principles could do more harm than good. The higher law of unselfish love should govern conduct at these points, as at all others, but to give money to a begging drunkard — or even to a selfish child — may result in worse damage to him and to his family. Nevertheless, the general principle here enunciated by Jesus holds good.

f. Love (5:43-48)

43 Ye have heard that it was said, Thou shalt love thy neighbor, and hate thine enemy: 44 but I say unto you, Love your enemies, and pray for them that persecute you; 45 that ye may be sons of your Father who is in heaven: for he maketh his sun to rise on the evil and the good, and sendeth rain on the just and the unjust. 46 For if ye love them that love you, what reward have ye? do not even the publicans the same? 47 And if ye salute your brethren only, what do ye more *than others?* do not even the Gentiles the same? 48 Ye therefore shall be perfect, as your heavenly Father is perfect.

Thou shalt love thy neighbor was a familiar command in the Old Testament (Lev. 19:18), though **neighbor** was usually interpreted as meaning a fellow Jew. But nowhere in the ancient Scriptures were the Israelites commanded to **hate thine enemy.** The idea might be derived, however, from such passages as Deuteronomy 7:2, 23:36, 25:17-19, Psalm 137:7-9 and elsewhere in the so-called Imprecatory Psalms, where the reference is to national, not personal, enemies.

But Jesus was utterly opposed to this attitude. His command was: **Love your enemies** and **pray** for your persecutors. This is grace, not law. Thereby Christians show themselves to be **sons of your Father;** that is, they manifest the nature of God. To love those who love us is natural, but to love the ones who hate us is supernatural.

This chapter closes with a "counsel of perfection" — **Ye therefore shall be perfect, as your heavenly Father is perfect** (v. 48). This is both a command and a promise. It has been called "the impossible possibility." Taken in an absolute sense it is of course only a counsel of despair: no man can be fully like God. But this verse, like all other passages,

---

[18] *Op. cit.,* p. 88.

must be interpreted in the light of its context. James Daane has offered this very helpful explanation:

> And when God's children love their enemies, pray for those who persecute them, and bless those that curse them, then they, too, possess and reveal in their conduct that perfection of God which is His grace toward evil and unjust men. Then they are perfect as their Father in heaven is perfect. Then they have that righteousness without which they would not enter the kingdom of heaven.[19]

3. Character Qualities of the Kingdom (6:1-34)

a. Sincerity (6:1-18)

(Introduction, v. 1)

Take heed that ye do not your righteousness before men, to be seen of them: else ye have no reward of your Father who is in heaven.

In the King James Version this verse seems to be a part of the discussion of almsgiving. But the best Greek text has "righteousness" instead of "alms." So the first verse should be taken as a general introduction to this section. The Master warned His disciples not to put their piety on parade. **Righteousness** (*dikaiosyne*) means religious acts. The point is that they were not to practice their religion before men **to be seen of them.** It is the motive of wanting the praise of men that Christ was warning against.[20]

After this brief introductory statement Jesus discussed three religious acts: almsgiving, prayer, and fasting. They were the ones which were emphasized most by the Jews of the day, and almsgiving ranked first in value.

(1) Almsgiving (6:2-4)

2 When therefore thou doest alms, sound not a trumpet before thee, as the hypocrites do in the synagogues and in the streets, that they may have glory of men. Verily I say unto you, They have received their reward. 3 But when thou doest alms, let not thy left hand know what thy right hand doeth: 4 that thine alms may be in secret: and thy Father who seeth in secret shall recompense thee.

Jesus admonished His followers not to

trumpet their works of charity. One test of a man's consecration is whether he is willing to do something for God, regardless of who gets the credit.

They have received their reward is a better translation than "They have their reward" (KJV). The papyri have shown that the verb here, *apecho*, is the regular form used in receipts of that day. What Jesus is saying is this: If people do their religious acts to gain the praise of men, they have been given a receipt, "Paid in full," and they thereby have no claim on a reward in the next life. One must decide whether he puts higher value on an earthly or a heavenly reward.

Let not thy left hand know what thy right hand doeth has sometimes been misused as an excuse for refusing to make a pledge in public. The criterion in all such cases is: What is best for the kingdom of God?

(2) Prayer (6:5-15)

5 And when ye pray, ye shall not be as the hypocrites: for they love to stand and pray in the synagogues and in the corners of the streets, that they may be seen of men. Verily I say unto you, They have received their reward. 6 But thou, when thou prayest, enter into thine inner chamber, and having shut thy door, pray to thy Father who is in secret, and thy Father who seeth in secret shall recompense thee. 7 And in praying use not vain repetitions, as the Gentiles do: for they think that they shall be heard for their much speaking. 8 Be not therefore like unto them: for your Father knoweth what things ye have need of, before ye ask him. 9 After this manner therefore pray ye: Our Father who art in heaven, Hallowed be thy name. 10 Thy kingdom come. Thy will be done, as in heaven, so on earth. 11 Give us this day our daily bread. 12 And forgive us our debts, as we also have forgiven our debtors. 13 And bring us not into temptation, but deliver us from the evil *one.* 14 For if ye forgive men their trespasses, your heavenly Father will also forgive you. 15 But if ye forgive not men their trespasses, neither will your Father forgive your trespasses.

The admonition to pray **in secret** has been used as an argument against pray-

---

[19] James Daane, "The Perfection of God," *The Reformed Journal*, VIII (Dec., 1958), 6. See also Martin Lloyd-Jones, *Studies in the Sermon on the Mount*, I, 319.

[20] "Not the open benevolence of the Christian who lets his light shine that men may glorify God, but the ostentation of him whose *object* is the praise and glory coming from man" (Henry Alford, *New Testament for English Readers*, I, 37).

ing in public. But Jesus prayed publicly (John 11:41-42). The thing He was condemning throughout this section was making a display of one's piety in order to win the praise of man.

Vain repetitions are to be avoided, such as using names of deity over and over in a short prayer. This is neither respectful nor reverent. God hears the sincere petition without repetitiousness.

Simplicity is what Jesus urged in praying. As an example He gave what is known as the Lord's Prayer (vv. 9-13). It is a model of simplicity and unselfish consecration.

The Prayer may be divided into three sections. *First* is the address: **Our Father who art in heaven.** The first part of this suggests familiarity; the second demands reverence. Ward comments, "True prayer begins with adoration."[21]

The *second* section consists of three petitions. The first petition is not one for personal needs, but rather an act of worship — **Hallowed be thy name.** Literally this is "let thy name be sanctified." The Jews put much emphasis on "the sanctification of the Name."[22] The second petition, **Thy kingdom come,** enjoins us to be more concerned about the prosperity of the Kingdom than about our personal interests. Filson defines the Kingdom as meaning "the full and effective reign of God."[23] The third petition is: **Thy will be done, as in heaven, so in earth.** This is very comprehensive in its scope. It takes in all relationships of life — domestic, community, national, international; economic, religious, social — as well as one's own thoughts, words, and deeds. There is no greater prayer that anyone can pray. Jesus Himself set the example in Gethsemane (26:42).

The *third* section likewise includes three petitions. But these, unlike the previous three, are concerned with personal needs. The first is: **Give us this day our daily bread.** While the prayer for material needs to be supplied is not to come first, it has its place — even in this brief model prayer. God is interested in our physical as well as spiritual welfare. The second petition, **forgive us our debts,** has attached to it the very significant condition: **as we also have for-**

given our debtors. For the professing Christian with an unforgiving spirit this is a dangerous prayer to repeat. **Debts** means sins (cf. Luke 11:4). Man owes God complete obedience. But everyone has failed to obey and so is hopelessly in debt. The third petition is: **bring us not into temptation, but deliver us from the evil one.** The last phrase (as in 5:37) may be translated either this way or "from evil" (KJV). **Temptation** may mean "testing." The Greek fails to distinguish between these two ideas which are somewhat distinct in English. **Bring us not into** means "keep us from." While all righteous men must experience testing and endure temptation, one needs to beware of over-confidence in his own ability to overcome.

The closing doxology (KJV) is not found in the earliest Greek manuscripts and so is omitted in the Revised versions. It is a liturgical ending, added to make the Lord's Prayer more suitable for use in public worship. For that purpose it may properly be included still. It seems evident that Jesus was giving the disciples a model for private rather than public prayer. That will explain His omission of any doxology at the end.

Verses 14 and 15 are a further elaboration of the condition stated in verse 12. The importance of a forgiving spirit is underscored by the considerable attention Jesus gave to it (cf. 18:21-35; Mark 11:25).

(3) Fasting (6:16-18)

16 Moreover when ye fast, be not, as the hypocrites, of a sad countenance: for they disfigure their faces, that they may be seen of men to fast. Verily I say unto you, They have received their reward. 17 But thou, when thou fastest, anoint thy head, and wash thy face; 18 that thou be not seen of men to fast, but of thy Father who is in secret: and thy Father, who seeth in secret, shall recompense thee.

Orientals are particularly prone to emphasize fasting as a religious exercise. Jesus warned that it must not be engaged in for the sake of impressing others with one's piety. **A sad countenance** could be a hypocritical mask. It is proper to wash

21 *Op. cit.*, p. 42.
22 Cf. Isa. 29:23; Ezek. 36:23. See also A. M. Hunter, *A Pattern for Life*, p. 65.
23 *Op. cit.*, p. 95. Cf. J. W. Bowman and R. W. Tapp, *The Gospel from the Mount*, pp. 124-125.

one's face, comb the hair, and appear cheerful, not gloomy.

b. Singleness (6:19-24)

Jesus stressed great principles of godly living, rather than minute regulations such as the Pharisees emphasized. Sincerity and singleness of purpose are absolutely essential for the one who would please God.

(1) Of Investment (6:19-21)

19 Lay not up for yourselves treasures upon the earth, where moth and rust consume, and where thieves break through and steal: 20 but lay up for yourselves treasures in heaven, where neither moth nor rust doth consume, and where thieves do not break through nor steal: 21 for where thy treasure is, there will thy heart be also.

A contrast is drawn between earthly and heavenly **treasures.** An important part of an ancient Oriental's treasure was his luxurious clothing. This could be consumed by **moth and rust.** The latter term is literally "eating" and so might refer to worms that eat clothes. **Break through** is literally "dig through." Palestinian homes were made of stone and mortar, or with mud bricks, so that thieves commonly dug through the outer walls. Jesus reminded His disciples of a place, **heaven,** where alone their securities were safe. But the important principle He enunciated here is that one's hoarding will hold his heart (v. 21). To **lay up** treasures here is to be earth-bound. Jesus sounded a salutary warning against the danger of losing one's soul as well as his wealth through being tied to earthly treasure.

(2) Of Intention (6:22-23)

22 The lamp of the body is the eye: if therefore thine eye be single, thy whole body shall be full of light. 23 But if thine eye be evil, thy whole body shall be full of darkness. If therefore the light that is in thee be darkness, how great is the darkness!

Great religious writers have always recognized the supreme importance of purity of intention. To illustrate this, Jesus used the figure of **the eye** as **the lamp of the body.** A diseased (**evil**) eye

means a darkened body. A sound (**single**) eye lets in the light.

The connection with the preceding paragraph is suggested in Proverbs 28:22 — "He that hasteth to be rich hath an evil eye." Filson expresses it in slightly different fashion: "If man divides his interest and tries to focus on both God and possessions, he has no clear vision, and will live without clear orientation or direction."[24] A **single** eye is essential to spiritual vision. Basically it means the same as a pure heart (5:28).

(3) Of Inner Loyalty (6:24)

24 No man can serve two masters: for either he will hate the one, and love the other; or else he will hold to one, and despise the other. Ye cannot serve God and mammon.

This verse sums up the emphasis of the previous two paragraphs. Undivided loyalty is essential to spiritual health. The Psalmist prayed, "Unite my heart to fear thy name" (Psa. 86:11).

Jesus did not say that a man *should* not, but that he **cannot** serve two masters. **Mammon** is an Aramaic term for money or wealth. It comes from a root meaning to "trust." Here the real danger lies: When people put their trust in material things they lose their faith in God. Discipleship demands complete loyalty. Those who begin by trying to serve **God** and **mammon** end by serving mammon alone.

c. Simplicity (6:25-35)

Matthew 6 emphasizes the three great virtues of simplicity, sincerity, and singleness of heart. All three are contrasted with hypocrisy in relation to religious duties (vv. 1-18) and material possessions (vv. 19-24). Out of this grows a warning against being unduly concerned with physcial needs. Simplicity of trust in a heavenly Father is enjoined upon Christ's disciples.

(1) Faith for Food (6:25-27)

25 Therefore I say unto you, Be not anxious for your life, what ye shall eat, or what ye shall drink; nor yet for your body, what ye shall put on. Is not the life more than the food, and the body than the raiment? 26 Behold the birds of

[24] *Ibid.,* p. 100.

the heaven, that they sow not, neither do they reap, nor gather into barns; and your heavenly Father feedeth them. Are not ye of much more value than they? 27 And which of you by being anxious can add one cubit unto the measure of his life?

Be not anxious is far more accurate than "take no thought" (KJV). The latter rendering has unfortunately led to rejection of responsibility to care for the future of one's family. Jesus was not forbidding proper attention to economic security or the purchase of life insurance, but only that anxiety that amounts to denial of one's faith in God. One cannot worry and trust at the same time.

Intense anxiety about **food, drink, and clothing** are not common in modern civilized society. But with ancient Orientals this anxiety was an ever-present problem. Jesus reminded His disciples of God's care of the **birds**. He then warned that worry cannot prolong one's **measure of his life**. It is not clear whether this or "stature" (KJV) is the better translation. The Greek word has both meanings. The Revised rendering, however, fits the context better. For worry actually shortens one's life, instead of lengthening it.

(2) Faith for Clothing (6:28-30)

28 And why are ye anxious concerning raiment? Consider the lilies of the field, how they grow; they toil not, neither do they spin: 29 yet I say unto you, that even Solomon in all his glory was not arrayed like one of these. 30 But if God doth so clothe the grass of the field, which to-day is, and to-morrow is cast into the oven, *shall he* not much more *clothe* you, O ye of little faith?

Jesus' favorite illustrations were from nature. This time it was **the lilies of the field**. They neither **toil** nor **spin**. Yet God arrays them in a beauty which even Solomon could not match in his expensive robes. If the heavenly Father shows such concern for perishing **grass**, how much more will He care for His own children?

(3) Faith for All Necessities (6:31-34)

31 Be not therefore anxious, saying, What shall we eat? or, What shall we drink? or, Wherewithal shall we be clothed? 32 For after all these things do the Gentiles seek; for your heavenly Father knoweth that ye have need of all these things. 33 But seek ye first his kingdom and his righteousness; and all these things shall be added unto you. 34 Be not therefore anxious for the morrow: for the morrow will be anxious for itself. Sufficient unto the day is the evil thereof.

The closing verses summarize these truths. The warning against being **anxious** occurs in verses 25, 28, 31 and 34. It is climaxed by the general admonition not to worry about the unknown future (v. 34).

In the midst of this discussion comes one of the great commands and promises of the New Testament: **But seek ye first his kingdom, and his righteousness; and all these things shall be added unto you.** This is the primary responsibility of every disciple of Christ, and it is his assurance that all needs will be supplied. To seek the Kingdom is to order one's own life according to the divine will and work for the extension of God's reign or rule in the hearts of others.

4 Judgment in the Kingdom (7:1-29)

a. Judgment of Others (7:1-5)

1 Judge not, that ye be not judged. 2 For with what judgment ye judge, ye shall be judged: and with what measure ye mete, it shall be measured unto you. 3 And why beholdest thou the mote that is in thy brother's eye, but considerest not the beam that is in thine own eye? 4 Or how wilt thou say to thy brother, Let me cast out the mote out of thine eye; and lo, the beam is in thine own eye? 5 Thou hypocrite, cast out first the beam out of thine own eye; and then shalt thou see clearly to cast out the mote out of thy brother's eye.

Jesus put His finger on one of the most common faults of humanity when He said: **Judge not, that ye be not judged.** Ward renders this, "Stop passing judgment on men that you be not judged by God," and adds: "The opening words indicated that the whole chapter should be read in the context of the final Judgment."[25]

The disciple of Christ must live constantly in the light of the Judgment

---

[25] *Op. cit.*, p. 49. Filson agrees with this rendering. He writes: "You will be sternly judged by God if you are severe in judging others" (*op. cit.*, p. 104).

Day, when he will have to give an account for the deeds done in the body (II Cor. 5:10). So he should be charitable toward others and strict with himself, knowing that God alone is the rightful Judge of all.

The second verse states a general principle of life: You get what you give. If one judges others severely, he will himself be judged severely.

Verses 3-5 present a vivid illustration of the unreasonableness of judging others. **Mote** means "splinter" or "speck." One sees a little splinter of wood or speck of dust — some trifling fault — in his brother's eye, when he has a saw log — a harsh, critical spirit — in his own. This is a typical Oriental hyperbole.

b. Judgment of Oneself (7:6)

6 Give not that which is holy unto the dogs, neither cast your pearls before the swine, lest haply they trample them under their feet, and turn and rend you.

The traditional interpretation of this seemingly isolated verse is that one should use discrimination in presenting sacred truths to wicked' men. But E. Stanley Jones points out the fact that this idea fits neither the context nor the mind and spirit of Christ. He offers this alternative interpretation: "We are not to take the holy thing of personality that is being perfected and give it to the dogs of desire, nor take the pearl of our spiritual life and cast it before the swine of our lower appetites, lest they trample that holy thing in the mire, and turn and rend the most precious thing we have, namely, our spiritual life."[26]

c. Judgment of One's Status (7:7-12)

7 Ask, and it shall be given you; seek, and ye shall find; knock, and it shall be opened unto you: 8 for every one that asketh receiveth; and he that seeketh findeth; and to him that knocketh it shall be opened. 9 Or what man is there of you, who, if his son shall ask him for a loaf, will give him a stone; 10 or if he shall ask for a fish, will give him a serpent? 11 If ye then, being evil, know how to give good gifts unto your children, how much more shall your Father who is in heaven give good things to them that ask him? 12 All things therefore whatsoever ye would that men should do unto you,

even so do ye also unto them: for this is the law and the prophets.

The basis of assurance of answered prayer is one's relationship to God as His child. If human (relatively **evil**) parents give **good gifts** to their children, how much more will the heavenly Father give **good things** (Luke 11:13 has "the Holy Spirit") to those **that ask him.** Here is the incentive to prayer: An all-loving Father delights to hear His children's requests and to give them **good things;** that is, what is really good for them. As will any wise parent, God will sometimes say "No" to misguided petitions for things that would not be best for one's spiritual welfare.

Ask — seek — knock — these are three levels of prayer. If asking does not bring results, one should **seek** over a period of time, persistently praying and waiting on God to know His will. If seeking does not succeed, then one should desperately **knock.** This suggests earnest, intense, urgent prayer, that will not be satisfied until some kind of an answer comes. Always the disciple must follow his Master in saying: "Nevertheless not as I will, but as thou wilt" (26:39).

The last verse of this paragraph (v. 12) expresses the so-called Golden Rule. This had previously been stated in negative form — "What you hate, do not do to any one"[27] — but so far as is known never before in positive form. The latter demands far more than refraining from *hurting* others. It requires *helping* those who are in need. Yet the Golden Rule is not the heart of Christianity, as some have claimed. Jesus said the Rule was **the law and the prophets;** that is, it summarized the Old Testament requirements for social relationships. But it is also binding on Christians.

d. Judgment of Ways (7:13-14)

13 Enter ye in by the narrow gate: for wide is the gate, and broad is the way, that leadeth to destruction, and many are they that enter in thereby. 14 For narrow is the gate, and straitened the way, that leadeth unto life, and few are they that find it.

The theme of the two ways was a familiar one to readers of the Old

---

[26] *Op. cit.,* p. 250.   [27] *Tobit* 4:15.

Testament (Psa. 1; Jer. 1:8). Jesus intensified and enriched this theme, emphasizing the entrance to each of these ways. **Narrow** is the correct meaning of "strait" (KJV). **Straitened** is in the Greek a strong term meaning literally "compressed" or "confined." **Many** are going the broad way that leads to **destruction** (perishing), but only a **few** actually **find** the way that leads to **life.** It is a very sobering statement.

e. Judgment of Fruits (7:15-20)

15 Beware of false prophets, who come to you in sheep's clothing, but inwardly are ravening wolves. 16 By their fruits ye shall know them. Do *men* gather grapes of thorns, or figs of thistles? 17 Even so evey good tree bringeth forth good fruit; but the corrupt tree bringeth forth evil fruit. 18 A good tree cannot bring forth evil fruit, neither can a corrupt tree bring forth good fruit. 19 Every tree that bringeth not forth good fruit is hewn down, and cast into the fire. 29 Therefore by their fruits ye shall know them.

As in the Old Testament period there were false prophets, so there are in the New. Coming in **sheep's clothing,** they are actually **ravening** [ravenous] **wolves,** bent on devouring the flock.

Jesus said, **By their fruits ye shall know them,** (vv. 16, 20). At first sight this may seem to conflict with the first verse of this chapter. But there He is talking about a harsh, critical spirit. Here He is stating the simple principle that one cannot avoid recognizing people's true character by the **fruit** in their outward lives.

Once more Ward points out the relation to judgment. He says: "The disciple's life is set in the perspective of the final Judgment which will reveal the manner in which Jesus' words have been put into practice."[28]

f. Judgment of Professors (7:21-23)

21 Not every one that saith unto me, Lord, Lord, shall enter into the kingdom of heaven; but he that doeth the will of my Father who is in heaven. 22 Many will say to me in that day, Lord, Lord, did we not prophesy by thy name, and by thy name cast out demons, and by thy name do many mighty works? 23 And then will I profess unto them, I never

knew you: depart from me, ye that work iniquity.

Not profession but possession is what makes one a true disciple of Christ. It is not calling Him **Lord,** but doing the **will** of the Father. That is the one requirement for membership in the **kingdom of heaven.** For the Kingdom is the reign or rule of God. It is not an outward organization but a living organism. It is composed of those who have submitted their hearts to the will of God and who seek to work out the divine will in their daily lives.

Ability to **prophesy, to cast out demons,** to do **many mighty works** (miracles) is no proof that one is a true follower of Christ. The only valid test is: Does one do the will of God?

g. Judgment of Listeners (7:24-27)

24 Every one therefore that heareth these words of mine, and doeth them, shall be likened unto a wise man, who built his house upon the rock: 25 and the rain descended, and the floods came, and the winds blew, and beat upon that house; and it fell not: for it was founded upon the rock. 26 And every one that heareth these words of mine, and doeth them not, shall be likened unto a foolish man, who built his house upon the sand: 27 and the rain descended, and the floods came, and the winds blew, and smote upon that house; and it fell: and great was the fall thereof.

Jesus closed His sermon with a warning that there were two types of listeners in His congregation. The one who not only **heareth** but **doeth** His words will be like a **wise man, who built his house** [his life] **upon the rocks,** so that it withstood the storms. The one who **heareth** His words but **doeth them not** will be like a **foolish man, who built his house upon the sand,** so that it fell before the **floods.**

The point seems clear. If one would build strong Christian character that will stand the stress and strain of life, he must order his ways according to God's Word. Thus he shows himself a true member of the Kingdom.

Filson offers an alternative suggestion as to the interpretation of **floods.** He writes: "Probably he means not recurrent

---

[28] *Op. cit.,* p. 52.

crises or trials in life, but as in vv. 21-23 the final crisis at the last day."[29] The Judgment will be the supreme test of character.

h. Judgment of Jesus as Teacher (7:28-29)

28 And it came to pass, when Jesus had finished these words, the multitudes were astonished at his teaching: 29 for he taught them as *one* having authority, and not as their scribes.

The people were astonished at Christ's teaching. They were accustomed to hearing the scribes quote other authorities — the rabbis of the past. But Jesus spoke with His own authority. The difference was startling. The crowds recognized that they were not listening to human opinions but to divine truth. Here was something that gripped their hearts and held them.

Jesus is not only Teacher but Judge. Commenting on the phrase, "Lord, Lord," (v. 21), Filson says: "The assumption of Jesus here and elsewhere is that he will speak the decisive word at the final judgment; this indicates clearly that he did not think of himself or want others to think of him merely as a good man."[30]

The Sermon on the Mount is the first of five great discourses in Matthew around which the Gospel is largely built. Each one ends with a formula similar to that found in verse 28 (cf. 11:1; 13:53; 19:1; 26:1).

E. HIS POWER (8:1-9:38)

Chapters eight and nine contain no less than ten miracles performed by Jesus. They were "the credentials of the King."[31] All were done in answer to human need, showing the compassion of the King. All were done in response to the divine will, showing the power of the King. Nine were miracles of healing. The other was a nature miracle — the stilling of the storm.

The grouping of these miracles illustrates one of the main characteristics of Matthew — systematic arrangement. The first group of three — healing a leper, a paralytic, and Peter's mother-in-law — is followed by the demand that disciples leave all to follow Him (vv. 18-22). The second group — the stilling of the storm, and the healing of two demoniacs and another paralytic — is followed by the call of Matthew (v. 9). The third group — the healing of the hemorrhaging woman and the dead daughter (treated together), of the two blind men, and of the dumb demoniac — ends with a teaching, preaching, healing tour of Galilee. Thus Jesus displayed His authority over men, as well as over disease, demons, and death.

Lenski maintains that Matthew relates these miracles in the order of their occurrence.[32] But a comparison with Mark 1:21-45 (cf. vv. 29, 32, 35) suggests that Mark gives the correct chronological order, whereas Matthew groups them together in one place for topical rather than chronological reasons.

It is appropriate that these two chapters should come immediately after the three containing the Sermon on the Mount. The new Moses, like the old, was not only a law-giver, but also a miracle-worker. The one who declared, "But I say unto you!" must give adequate evidence of His divine authority. These were Jesus' credentials to a doubting nation.

1. Over Leprosy (8:1-4)

1 And when he was come down from the mountain, great multitudes followed him. 2 And behold, there came to him a leper and worshipped him, saying, Lord, if thou wilt, thou canst make me clean. 3 And he stretched forth his hand, and touched him, saying, I will; be thou made clean. And straightway his leprosy was cleansed. 4 And Jesus saith unto him, See thou tell no man; but go, show thyself to the priest, and offer the gift that Moses commanded, for a testimony unto them.

As in the case of Moses, Jesus came down from the mountain to find **great** multitudes awaiting Him. But there was one in the crowd who had a special need. This **leper** approached Jesus and

[29] *Op. cit.*, p. 108.   [30] *Ibid.*, p. 107.
[31] Charles R. Erdman, *The Gospel of Matthew*, p. 64.
[32] R. C. H. Lenski, *The Interpretation of St. Matthew's Gospel*, p. 316.

fell on his knees before Him. He was sure of Jesus' power to heal him, but not quite certain of His willingness. But the Master **touched** him, and the **leprosy was cleansed.** In the Old Testament the leper was considered unclean. His healing is therefore spoken of as a "cleansing" (Lev. 14:2). The fact that Jesus **touched** the leper would render Him unclean in the eyes of the Jews. But such was His holy power and His divine compassion that He cleansed the uncleanness of the poor outcast.

Jesus cautioned the man not to publicize the miracle, but to report to the priest and **offer the gift that Moses commanded.** The instructions for this are given very fully in Leviticus 14:1-32. **For a testimony unto them** evidently means to the priests, not the people, since Jesus had said, "Tell no man."

2. Over Paralysis (8:5-13)

5 And when he was entered into Capernaum, there came unto him a centurion, beseeching him, 6 and saying, Lord, my servant lieth in the house sick of the palsy, grievously tormented. 7 And he saith unto him, I will come and heal him. 8 And the centurion answered and said, Lord, I am not worthy that thou shouldest come under my roof; but only say the word, and my servant shall be healed. 9 For I also am a man under authority, having under myself soldiers: and I say to this one, Go, and he goeth; and to another, Come, and he cometh; and to my servant, Do this, and he doeth it. 10 And when Jesus heard it, he marvelled, and said to them that followed, Verily I say unto you, I have not found so great faith, no, not in Israel. 11 And I say unto you, that many shall come from the east and the west and shall sit down with Abraham, and Isaac, and Jacob, in the kingdom of heaven: 12 but the sons of the kingdom shall be cast forth into the outer darkness: there shall be the weeping and the gnashing of teeth. 13 And Jesus said unto the centurion, Go thy way; as thou hast believed, so be it done unto thee. And the servant was healed in that hour.

The Mount of the Beatitudes is near Capernaum, the town which Jesus had chosen as His headquarters (4:13). When He entered that city a **centurion** — officer over one hundred men — came to Him with the request that He heal his servant of a very painful paralysis. The Greek word *pais* (servant) may also mean "son." But Luke uses the term *doulos* (Luke 7:10), which means "slave."

Jesus offered to go to the centurion's home. But the latter protested that he was not worthy to have the Master come. All that was necessary was a **word.** Jesus spoke this word, and the servant was healed **in that hour.** Christ expressed His astonishment at the faith of this foreigner. The unbelief of His own people was a sad contrast (v. 10). At the messianic banquet, He prophesied, many Gentiles would be present (v. 11), while the **sons of the kingdom** — the Jews of Jesus' day who rejected Him — would be cast forth **into the outer darkness: There shall be the weeping and the gnashing of teeth** (v. 12). This is one of several passages in which Christ sounds a stern warning against the horrors of hell.

Both the leper and the centurion (a Gentile) were considered outcasts by the Jews. But Jesus responded to their call for help.

3. Over Fever (8:14-17)

14 And when Jesus was come into Peter's house, he saw his wife's mother lying sick of a fever. 15 And he touched her hand, and the fever left her; and she arose, and ministered unto him. 16 And when even was come, they brought unto him many possessed with demons: and he cast out the spirits with a word, and healed all that were sick: 17 that it might be fulfilled which was spoken through Isaiah the prophet, saying, Himself took our infirmities, and bare our diseases.

It appears that Jesus made **Peter's house** His home at Capernaum. Here one day He found Peter's mother-in-law **sick of a fever.** He **touched her hand,** and she was immediately well. This miracle contrasts with the healing of the centurion's servant, which came simply by a word spoken at a distance, or the healing of the man born blind, when Jesus used clay made of soil and spittle (John 9:6). Jesus was not bound by certain methods. In every case it was the power of His command which brought the results.

That same evening, when the sabbath ended (cf. Mark 1:21), the people of Capernaum flocked to Jesus, bringing their sick friends and relatives. Especially prominent were those **possessed with demons,** a common affliction in those days. With His word of command the Master **cast out the** evil **spirits** and **healed all that were sick.** Thus He fulfilled Isaiah's prophecy (Isa. 53:4). **Took** and **bare** may be rendered "took and bore away."[33] Isaiah 53 deals primarily with the sufferings of Christ. Here Matthew applies the passage to Jesus' removal of **infirmities** and **diseases.** Physical healing is not involved in the atonement in the same sense as salvation is, but all blessings come to Christians now by way of the Cross.

4. Over Disciples (8:18-22)

18 Now when Jesus saw great multitudes about him, he gave commandment to depart unto the other side. 19 And there came a scribe, and said unto him, Teacher, I will follow thee withersoever thou goest. 20 And Jesus saith unto him, The foxes have holes, and the birds of the heaven *have* nests; but the Son of man hath not where to lay his head. 21 And another of the disciples said unto him, Lord, suffer me first to go and bury my father. 22 But Jesus saith unto him, Follow me; and leave the dead to bury their own dead.

Constantly thronged by the crowds, Jesus finally gave orders to go to the **other side,** the east side of the Lake of Galilee. This shore was not so heavily inhabited as were the west and north shores.

As He was leaving, an impetuous scribe volunteered to follow Him. Jesus warned him that **the Son of man** had no home.

The expression **the Son of man** (v. 20) is found here for the first time in Matthew. It is used in the Gospels only by Jesus and always as a designation of Himself (31 times in Matthew, 14 in Mark, 25 in Luke, and 13 in John). Outside the Gospels it occurs in the New Testament only in Acts 7:56 (without the article in Heb. 2:6; Rev. 1:13; 14:14).

In the Psalms "Son of man" is equivalent to "man" (e.g., Psa. 8:4). In Ezekiel it refers to the prophet (e.g., Ezek. 2:1). But the most significant Old Testament occurrence of this term is to be found in Daniel 7:13, where it is said that the Son of man will come "with the clouds of heaven." This apocalyptic meaning is heightened in the apocryphal Book of Enoch, where it is used to designate a pre-existent, personal Messiah. By using the term, Jesus made the claim to be this Messiah.

Another disciple wanted to follow Jesus, but he would have to wait, he said, until his father and mother died — which might entail a delay of several years. Jesus told him to let the spiritually **dead** bury their physical **dead.** The disciple's duty was: **Follow me.** Thus Jesus asserted His authority over not only men's bodies but their minds and lives as well.

5. Over Storms (8:23-27)

23 And when he was entered into a boat, his disciples followed him. 24 And behold, there arose a great tempest in the sea, insomuch that the boat was covered with the waves: but he was asleep. 25 And they came to him, and awoke him, saying, Save, Lord; we perish. 26 And he saith unto them, Why are ye fearful, O ye of little faith? Then he arose, and rebuked the winds and the sea; and there was a great calm. 27 And the men marvelled, saying, What manner of man is this, that even the winds and the sea obey him?

As they were crossing the lake a great **tempest** arose. The Greek word is *seismos,* the usual meaning of which is "earthquake." It underscores the violence of the storm, which shook the ship. But still Jesus kept on sleeping (imperfect tense).

Finally the disciples could stand it no longer. They wakened Jesus and called on Him to save them. After reproving them for being **fearful** (literally, cowardly) He **rebuked** the storm, as if it were a person. The result was **a great calm.** Not only did the winds cease to blow, but the waves ceased to roll. It is no wonder that the men **marvelled.** They had never witnessed anything like this before.

Some scholars seek to explain this miracle on purely psychological grounds. Jesus calmed the minds of the men, not the waves of the sea. But why not both?

[33] A. B. Bruce, "The Synoptic Gospels," *The Expositor's Greek Testament,* I, 141.

One who has had the tempest within his soul quieted by the Savior's voice has no difficulty in believing that the Creator could exercise authority over His creation.

6. Over Demons (8:28-34)

28 And when he was come to the other side into the country of the Gadarenes, there met him two possessed with demons, coming forth out of the tombs, exceeding fierce, so that no man could pass by that way. 29 And behold, they cried out, saying, What have we to do with thee, thou Son of God? art thou come hither to torment us before the time? 30 Now there was afar off from them a herd of many swine feeding. 31 And the demons besought him, saying, If thou cast us out, send us away into the herd of swine. 32 And he said unto them, Go. And they came out, and went into the swine: and behold, the whole herd rushed down the steep into the sea and perished in the waters. 33 And they that fed them fled, and went away into the city, and told everything, and what was befallen to them that were possessed with demons. 34 And behold, all the city came out to meet Jesus: and when they saw him, they besought *him* that he would depart from their borders.

The **country of the Gadarenes** was east of the Lake of Galilee and named after the nearest large city, Gadara, which was six miles to the southeast. The King James Version has "Gergesenes." Probably Gergasa was the modern Khersa, the ruins of which are on the eastern shore. Some Greek manuscripts have "Gerasenes." Gerasa lay thirty miles southeast of the lake.

Matthew mentions **two** demoniacs, whereas Mark and Luke tell of only one. Evidently Mark and Luke mention only the prominent one of the two. These demoniacs were so **fierce** that travelers avoided the area.

When the demons saw Jesus they noisily acclaimed Him as **Son of God.** They recognized Him as their Judge, who would finally consign them to torment. When given permission to enter a herd of hogs grazing nearby, they caused the whole herd to commit mass suicide. The swineherds rushed into the city to report the disaster. **All the city** turned out to see what had happened. Jesus was asked to leave. The people did not wish to lose any more of their pigs.

It has often been said that these people had no right to keep hogs, since the eating of these animals was forbidden as unclean in the law of Moses. But the owners were probably Gentiles, not Jews. The fact that Jesus permitted a herd of hogs to be destroyed in order to save two men should not give rise to quibbling criticism. The deliverance of the demoniacs was related to the destruction of the pigs. The fate of the latter highlighted for the healed men the desperateness of their previous condition and the miracle of their deliverance.

What are the lessons of this incident? (1) There is the fact of the existence of demons. This has already been discussed in the comments on 4:24. (2) Jesus has power over the spirit world. The demons could not defy His command, **Go** (v. 32). (3) "Both insanity and demon-possession are symbols of the more terrible tyranny of sin."[34] (4) Sin, like these demons, seeks the destruction of its victims. (5) Men are usually more concerned about their own material property than the welfare of souls. The Gadarenes did not want Jesus around if He was going to interfere with their business. (6) Jesus leaves when asked to, but those who reject Him sustain the greater loss.

7. Over Paralysis (9:1-8)

1 And he entered into a boat, and crossed over, and came into his own city. 2 And behold, they brought to him a man sick of the palsy, lying on a bed: and Jesus seeing their faith said unto the sick of the palsy, Son, be of good cheer; thy sins are forgiven. 3 And behold, certain of the scribes said within themselves, This man blasphemeth. 4 And Jesus knowing their thoughts said, Wherefore think ye evil in your hearts? 5 For which is easier, to say, Thy sins are forgiven; or to say, Arise, and walk? 6 But that ye may know that the Son of man hath authority on earth to forgive sins (then saith he to the sick of the palsy), Arise, and take up thy bed, and go unto thy house. 7 And he arose, and departed to his house. 8 But when the multitudes saw it, they were afraid, and glorified God, who had given such authority unto men.

[34] Erdman, *op. cit.,* p. 70.

Jesus got into a boat and **crossed over** to the northwest side of the lake and returned to **his own city,** Capernaum. Here they brought to Him **a man sick of the palsy** — all one word in the Greek *paralyticon.* When Jesus saw their **faith** — probably the faith of both the paralytic and those who brought him — He said to the man, **Thy sins are forgiven.** The paralysis may have been induced, at least in part, by a severe guilt complex. It was commonly held by the Jews that sickness was caused by sin in one's life (John 9:2). In any case, Jesus recognized the man's greater spiritual need and met that first.

Some scribes sitting there muttered to themselves, **This man blasphemeth.** Only God, they thought, could forgive sins (Isa. 43:25). But Jesus read their **thoughts** and challenged them with a question. The answer is not so obvious as might at first appear. Actually it was easier to say, **Thy sins are forgiven,** because no one could prove or disprove the results. But to say **Arise, and walk** would put Jesus "on the spot." Nevertheless, He proceeded to say it. The physical miracle was outward proof of the inner miracle. The effect on the people was that they were **afraid;** that is, in awe, and they glorified God for this display of divine power.

A careful comparison of Matthew's account with the parallel accounts in Mark 2:3-12 and Luke 5:18-26 will show how many details of the incident are omitted here. Mark's record, especially, is far more vivid. One of the characteristics of Matthew is his brevity of description. He devotes more words to the teachings of Jesus than does Mark, but fewer to the details of the narrative.

8. Over Matthew (9:9)

9 And as Jesus passed by from thence, he saw a man, called Matthew, sitting at the place of toll: and he saith unto him, Follow me. And he arose, and followed him.

The call of Matthew — named Levi in Mark 2:14 and Luke 5:27 — is recorded very briefly in all three Synoptics. He was sitting at the **place of toll** (KJV, "receipt of custom"). The exact meaning of the Greek word is not certain. Perhaps "tax office" (RSV) is most satisfactory. This much we know: it was a place connected with tax, toll, or custom.

Jesus' command, **Follow me,** was met with instant obedience. It has already been noted that John's Gospel indicates a previous contact with the earliest disciples before their call to active service. Probably the same was true in the case of Matthew. He had doubtless been observing Jesus and listening to His teaching for some time before this day of decision.

In some ways Matthew's response called for greater consecration than that of the four fishermen. They could return to their fishing at any time, but not he to the job he forsook.

9. Over Sin (9:10-13)

10 And it came to pass, as he sat at meat in the house, behold, many publicans and sinners came and sat down with Jesus and his disciples. 11 And when the Pharisees saw it, they said unto his disciples, Why eateth your Teacher with the publicans and sinners? 12 But when he heard it, he said, They that are whole have no need of a physician, but they that are sick. 13 But go ye and learn what *this* meaneth, I desire mercy, and not sacrifice: for I came not to call the righteous, but sinners.

Levi, or Matthew, made a great feast for Jesus at his spacious home (Luke 5:29). To this banquet he invited many of his friends and colleagues. They are called **publicans and sinners.** "Publicans" is more correctly rendered "tax collectors" or "tax gatherers." "Sinners" refers to those who were careless about ceremonial requirements and so were labeled as "sinners" by the strict religious leaders. The tax collectors necessarily had too much contact with the "unclean" Gentiles.

The **Pharisees** were the Separatists of Jesus' day, priding themselves on their ceremonial purity. So they found fault, asking the disciples why their **Teacher** ate with such defiling people. By way of answer Jesus indicated that He came as the great Physician to heal those who were sick in sin. He was not able to help those who considered themselves to be **righteous.** Only **sinners** can be saved.

Thus Jesus set the example for His followers. The unsaved cannot be reached by those who hold themselves aloof with a "holier than thou" attitude. Christians must be willing to associate with all men in order to win them to Christ.

10. Over Fasting (9:14-17)

14 Then come to him the disciples of John, saying, Why do we and the Pharisees fast oft, but thy disciples fast not? 15 And Jesus said unto them, Can the sons of the bridechamber mourn, as long as the bridegroom is with them? but the days will come, when the bridegroom shall be taken away from them, and then will they fast. 16 And no man putteth a piece of undressed cloth upon an old garment; for that which should fill it up taketh from the garment, and a worse rent is made. 17 Neither do *men* put new wine into old wine-skins: else the skins burst, and the wine is spilled, and the skins perish: but they put new wine into fresh wine-skins, and both are preserved.

This time it was the disciples of John who took a critical attitude. They and the Pharisees were observing a fast, while Jesus' disciples were eating.

In defense of His disciples Jesus used three parabolic figures. The first was that of sons of the bridechamber, or "friends of the bridegroom" (RSV). It would not be fitting for them to fast at the time of the wedding. In the same way Christ's presence precluded fasting or mourning.

The second comparison was with a patch of unshrunk cloth. If sewed on an old garment it would shrink and tear the garment, leaving it in worse condition than before.

The third figure was that of new wine put into old wineskins. When the wine ferments the already stretched and brittle wineskins burst and the wine is lost. New wine must be put into fresh wineskins. The clean skins will not cause fermentation so rapidly and they can stretch without breaking.

The application is rather obvious. The new wine of Christianity must not be poured into the old wineskins of Judaism. It must have fresh concepts to convey new truths, a fresh language to communicate spiritual ideals. The church must take the place of the synagogue, the gospel the place of the law. The Book of Acts demonstrates the fact that Christianity could not be contained in Judaism. Ward comments: "Jesus comes with effervescence of new wine bursting the constraints of tradition."[35] The Epistle to the Galatians underscores Paul's emphasis on the same truth.

II Over Hemorrhaging (9:20-22)

20 And behold a woman, who had an issue of blood twelve years, came behind him, and touched the border of his garment: 21 for she said within herself, If I do but touch his garment, I shall be made whole. 22 But Jesus turning and seeing her said, Daughter, be of good cheer; thy faith hath made thee whole. And the woman was made whole from that hour.

The healing of the woman with an issue of blood is sandwiched into the account of the raising of Jairus' daughter. This is true in all three Synoptic Gospels (cf. Mark 5:22-43; Luke 8:41-56). Again a comparison will show that Matthew's record of this double incident is both shorter and less vivid than the other two.

The woman had been afflicted for twelve years, so that her case was considered hopeless. When she heard how Jesus had healed others, her hope sprang up anew. Timidly she came behind Him, in order not to be noticed, and quickly touched the border of his garment. This was the tassel of His robe (cf. Num. 15:38), a reminder of God's presence. She had faith that if she could do this she would be made whole. The Greek word is most commonly used in the Epistles for being "saved." But in the Gospels it is employed for physical healing.

It was not touching the tassel of Jesus' robe that healed the woman, but her faith. It may have been tinged a bit with superstition, but it was genuine faith. The Master graciously accommodated Himself to her understanding and rewarded her confidence in Him. She was instantly and permanently healed of her affliction.

12. Over Death (9:18-19, 23-26)

18 While he spake these things unto them, behold, there came a ruler, and worshipped him, saying, My daughter is even now dead: but come and lay thy

35 *Op. cit.*, p. 63.

hand upon her, and she shall live. 19 And
Jesus arose, and followed him, and *so did*
his disciples.

23 And when Jesus came into the ruler's
house, and saw the flute-players, and the
crowd making a tumult, 24 he said, Give
place: for the damsel is not dead, but
sleepeth. And they laughed him to scorn.
25 But when the crowd was put forth,
he entered in, and took her by the hand;
and the damsel arose. 26 And the fame
hereof went forth into all that land.

While Jesus was teaching, He was approached by a **ruler,** an official in the
local synagogue. The distracted father
reported that his daughter was dead.
But he, like the woman, had great faith.
He believed that if Jesus would lay His
hand upon her, she would live. The
Master and His disciples accompanied
the father toward his home.

After the healing of the hemorrhaging
woman on the way, they proceeded to
the ruler's house. There they found that
the ceremonial mourning was already
under way. Hired **flute-players** were
sounding out their funeral dirges. The
crowd was **making a tumult.** This Oriental custom, that of making as much noise
as possible at such a time, seems strange
indeed to Occidental minds. The body
was normally buried the very day the
person died, so no time was lost in
getting the mourning into full swing.

Into this scene of confusion and death
walked the Creator of life. Calmly He
asserted that the **damsel** was **not dead,**
but sleeping. Mourning turned to mocking as they **laughed him to scorn.** Such
an atmosphere is a serious hindrance to
belief, so Jesus asked the crowd to leave.
Then He quietly entered the room and
took the hand of the girl. Immediately
the father's faith was rewarded; his restored child rose from the bed.

Both these closely connected incidents
emphasize the importance of faith in
Christ. The woman herself believed for
her healing, but the dead daughter had
to depend on her father's faith. This suggests two types of sinners. The one
comes to Christ with deep repentance
and eager faith. The other seems helpless to make a move and is saved as a
result of the earnest prayers of someone
else. In both cases today, however,
sinners must have personal faith in the
Savior.

13. Over Blindness (9:27-31)

27 And as Jesus passed by from thence,
two blind men followed him, crying out,
and saying, Have mercy on us, thou son
of David. 28 And when he was come
into the house, the blind men came to
him: and Jesus saith unto them, Believe
ye that I am able to do this? They say
unto him, Yea, Lord. 29 Then touched
he their eyes, saying, According to your
faith be it done unto you. 30 And their
eyes were opened. And Jesus strictly
charged them, saying, See that no man
know it. 31 But they went forth, and
spread abroad his fame in all that land.

Matthew is fond of pairs. So here he
mentions **two blind men.** They cry for
Jesus to **have mercy** on them, calling
Him **son of David.** This was a messianic
title and reflects the popular hopes of
many Jews in Jesus' day. The report
of raising the dead girl had circulated
widely (v. 26). This doubtless gave added
incentive to the faith of the blind men.
When Jesus asked them if they believed
He could heal them, they replied, **Yea,
Lord.** Their persistent faith, shown when
they followed Him into the house, was
fully rewarded. The Master **touched their
eyes.** Unable to see, they needed His
comforting, reassuring touch.

**According to your faith be it done
unto you** still stands as a constant challenge to every follower of Christ.

Jesus **strictly charged** the healed men
not to report the miracle. The verb is
a very strong one in the Greek, indicating extreme emotion. It emphasizes
the fact that Jesus was very desirous
that nothing should be done to hinder
His preaching ministry. But the men
disobeyed His stern command.

14. Over Dumbness (9:32-34)

32 And as they went forth, behold, there
was brought to him a dumb man possessed with a demon. 33 And when the
demon was cast out, the dumb man spake:
and the multitudes marvelled, saying, It
was never so seen in Israel. 34 But the
Pharisees said, By the prince of the demons casteth he out demons.

As **they** — Jesus and His disciples —
went out of the house a dumb demoniac
was brought to Him. Whereas the healing of the two blind men had taken
place in the seclusion of the home, this
miracle was witnessed by the **multitudes,**

who **marvelled**. It was impossible for Jesus to keep secret His miracle-working. The reaction of the crowd was enthusiastic: never had they seen such miracles before.

The Pharisees, however, had an explanation ready: Jesus was casting out demons by the power of the prince of demons. Jesus gave no reply to this absurd, slanderous charge at this time, but later He answered the illogic and folly of their position (12:24-32).

15. Over Disease (9:35-38)

35 And Jesus went about all the cities and the villages, teaching in their synagogues, and preaching the gospel of the kingdom, and healing all manner of disease and all manner of sickness. 36 But when he saw the multitudes, he was moved with compassion for them, because they were distressed and scattered, as sheep not having a shepherd. 37 Then saith he unto his disciples, The harvest indeed is plenteous, but the laborers are few. 38 Pray ye therefore the Lord of the harvest, that he send forth laborers into his harvest.

Another summary of Jesus' Galilean ministry is given in verse 35. It is almost identical with that in 4:23. In both places there is emphasized the threefold aspect of Christ's ministry: **teaching, preaching, healing.** The last was not limited to easy cases of functional disorders. Jesus healed all kinds of **disease** and **sickness.** The two words mean much the same, with the latter stressing the idea of weakness.

The sight of so much need moved the Master to deep **compassion.** This was more than human pity. The word literally means a "suffering with." To Him the **multitudes** were as **sheep** without a shepherd, harrassed and fearful. **Distressed** and **scattered** are both perfect passive participles. The former means "worn out" and the latter "prostrate," or "thrown to the ground." Both express a continual state of distraction and dejection.

Then the figure changes. In the multitudes Jesus sees a **harvest** that is ripe and **plenteous,** ready to be reaped. Unfortunately, **the laborers** are few. The Master urges His disciples to pray that God, the Lord of the harvest, will send laborers out into the ripened fields. **Send**

forth is literally "cast out." It suggests the strong compulsion of the missionary call, based on the great need.

F. HIS MESSENGERS (10:1-42)

1. Their Number (10:1)

1 And he called unto him his twelve disciples, and gave them authority over unclean spirits, to cast them out, and to heal all manner of disease and all manner of sickness.

The reason for having **twelve disciples** was probably that there were twelve tribes of Israel. So the New Israel would be represented by the twelve apostles. This does not mean, of course, that each of the disciples was from a different tribe, but simply that the speciality of the number twelve was retained.

To these chosen followers Jesus gave **authority** to cast out unclean spirits and heal all kinds of illness. Thus His ministry would be multiplied through them.

2. Their Names (10:2-4)

2 Now the names of the twelve apostles are these: The first, Simon, who is called Peter, and Andrew his brother; James the *son* of Zebedee, and John his brother; 3 Philip, and Bartholomew; Thomas, and Matthew the publican; James the *son* of Alphaeus, and Thaddaeus; 4 Simon the Cananaean, and Judas Iscariot, who also betrayed him.

The word **apostles** means "ones sent on a mission." Lists of the **twelve** occur in each of the three Synoptic Gospels (cf. Mark 3:16-19; Luke 6:14-16) and in Acts 1:13. In every case the name **Peter** comes first. His given name was **Simon,** a very common Jewish name at that time. But Jesus called him *Petros,* "a rock."

The four fishermen are always at the top of the list, as having been called first. That **Simon** and **James** were frequently used names is shown by the fact that among the twelve apostles there were two men named Simon and two named James. Only in this Gospel list is Matthew identified as **the publican.** This reflects the humility of the writer. Though a despised tax collector, he had been chosen by Jesus as one of His apostles.

The second **Simon** is identified as **the Cananaean.** This is more correct than "Canaanite" (KJV). Luke explains the meaning of this by calling him "the Zealot" (Luke 6:15; Acts 1:13). This could mean simply that he was a very zealous individual, but it may be that he belonged to the party that later was to be known prominently as "the Zealots." They were ardent nationalists who desired to break the yoke of Rome.

Judas is always named last (except in Acts, after his death), and always he carries the shameful epithet, **who also betrayed him.** The word **Iscariot** probably means "man of Kerioth," a village in Judah. If so, Judas was the only non-Galilean among the apostles.

3. Their Mission (10:5-15)

5 These twelve Jesus sent forth, and charged them, saying, Go not into *any* way of the Gentiles, and enter not into any city of the Samaritans: 6 but go rather to the lost sheep of the house of Israel. 7 And as ye go, preach, saying, The kingdom of heaven is at hand. 8 Heal the sick, raise the dead, cleanse the lepers, cast out demons: freely ye received, freely give. 9 Get you no gold, nor silver, nor brass in your purses; 10 no wallet for *your* journey, neither two coats, nor shoes, nor staff: for the laborer is worthy of his food. 11 And into whatsoever city or village ye shall enter, search out who in it is worthy; and there abide till ye go forth. 12 And as ye enter into the house, salute it. 13 And if the house be worthy, let your peace come upon it: but if it be not worthy, let your peace return to you. 14 And whosoever shall not receive you, nor hear your words, as ye go forth out of that house or that city, shake off the dust of your feet. 15 Verily I say unto you, It shall be more tolerable for the land of Sodom and Gomorrah in the day of judgment, than for that city.

The twelve were sent out with the charge that they were not to visit the **Gentiles** or **Samaritans.** Jesus was still offering Himself as the Messiah to the Jews. Only after they finally and officially rejected Him was the door opened to the Gentiles. That the policy enunciated here was not intended to be a permanent one is shown conclusively by Acts 1:8. But on this brief, quick tour they were to go only to **the lost sheep of the house of Israel.**

They were to preach the same message that John and Jesus had declared: **The kingdom of heaven is at hand.** The King was already present. His power would be shown through them in healing the sick, raising the dead, cleansing lepers, and casting out demons. These were manifestations of the kingdom, evidences that it was already present. All the people had to do was to receive it into their hearts by submitting to God's reign in their lives.

The warning against taking along money and extra clothes can be understood only in the context of the situation. This was to be a hurried trip. The climate was warm. And since it was the custom in those days to offer hospitality to strangers, food and shelter would be no problem.

This was not a synagogue ministry. The apostles were to be guests in a worthy private home in each community and apparently were to make that the main scene of their labors. Whenever they were rejected, they were to **shake off the dust** of their feet as a sign that the rejecting home or city was, because of its own act, rejected by God. Pharisees were in the habit of wiping off their feet the "unclean" dust of foreign countries. This act of the disciples would suggest the uncleanness of any Jews who rejected God's messengers.

Then Jesus sounded the solemn warning that it would be more **tolerable** for **Sodom and Gomorrah** in the judgment day than for the city that refused the Kingdom. Several times in the New Testament the destruction of Sodom is cited as an example of divine judgment on sin (cf. 11:23, 24; Luke 10:12; 17:29; Rom. 9:29; II Pet. 2:6; Jude 7). The destruction of Jerusalem by the Romans in A.D. 70 was a horrible fulfillment of this statement of Jesus.

4. Their Courage (10:16-23)

16 Behold, I send you forth as sheep in the midst of wolves: be ye therefore wise as serpents, and harmless as doves. 17 But beware of men: for they will deliver you up to councils, and in their synagogues they will scourge you; 18 yea and before governors and kings shall ye be brought for my sake, for a testimony to them and to the Gentiles. 19 But when they deliver you up, be not anxious how or what ye shall speak: for it shall be given you in that hour what ye shall speak. 20 For it is not ye that speak, but the Spirit of your Father that speaketh in you. 21 And brother shall deliver up

brother to death, and the father his child: and children shall rise up against parents, and cause them to be put to death. 22 And ye shall be hated of all men for my name's sake: but he that endureth to the end, the same shall be saved. 23 But when they persecute you in this city, flee into the next: for verily I say unto you, Ye shall not have gone through the cities of Israel, till the Son of man be come.

The figure of sheep and wolves was to become a very familiar one to the disciples. The Jewish leaders proved to be rapacious wolves in their treatment of Christ and His followers. This rapacity is especially evident in the Book of Acts.

Because of the danger, the apostles were to be wise as serpents and at the same time harmless as doves. The first adjective means "prudent," possessing practical wisdom. The second means "pure" (unmixed), "simple," or "sincere." No amount of wisdom will make up for lack of sincerity, but the combination of both virtues is a strong asset.

The Master warned His men that they would be turned over to councils — plural of sanhedrin — and scourged in synagogues. Besides the Great Sanhedrin at Jerusalem each town and village had its own local sanhedrin, or court of justice. These were connected with the synagogues, where punishment was administered. The disciples would even be brought before governors (e.g., Felix and Festus) and kings (e.g., Agrippa). But the Spirit of God would stand by them (v. 20).

Christ is inevitably a divider of men, for everyone must take sides either for or against Him. The result is that sometimes a believer's worst enemy is his own brother. Jesus further warned His disciples that they would be hated of all men. But the one who endureth to the end will be saved (v. 22). There are three tenses in one's salvation. The born-again believer *has been* saved in conversion, *is being* saved as he daily believes and obeys, and *will be* ultimately saved if he endures to the end. While Jesus applied this particularly to the persecuted, the principle is applicable to all believers.

The disciples were urged to keep moving, for they would not reach all the cities of Israel till the Son of man be come. What does this last clause mean?

It may have reference to the time leading up to the destruction of Jerusalem in A.D. 70, and yet it may apply to the continuing missionary work that will last until Christ returns.[36] A third interpretation applies it to the manifestation of Christ in the coming of His kingdom in the hearts of men.[37] In any case, the urgency of the hour is emphasized.

5. Their Comfort (10:24-33)

24 A disciple is not above his teacher, nor a servant. above his lord. 25 It is enough for the disciple that he be as his teacher, and the servant as his lord. If they have called the master of the house Beelzebub, how much more them of his household! 26 Fear them not therefore: for there is nothing covered that shall not be revealed; and hid, that shall not be known. 27 What I tell you in the darkness, speak ye in the light; and what ye hear in the ear, proclaim upon the house-tops. 28 and be not afraid of them that kill the body, but are not able to kill the soul: but rather fear him who is able to destroy both soul and body in hell. 29 Are not two sparrows sold for a penny? and not one of them shall fall on on the ground without your Father: 30 but the very hairs of your head are all numbered. 31 Fear not therefore: ye are of more value than many sparrows. 32 Every one therefore who shall confess me before men, him will I also confess before my Father who is in heaven. 33 But whosoever shall deny me before men, him will I also deny before my Father who is in heaven.

If the Master must suffer, it is not to be expected that His servants will escape persecution. The Pharisees called Him Beelzebub, or prince of demons (best Greek text, *Beelzebul;* meaning uncertain); they will malign His followers worse.

The second clause of verse 28 has caused considerable discussion. Who is it that can destroy both soul and body in hell? Carr says it means either God or Satan, "into whose power the wicked surrender themselves."[38] A. B. Bruce notes that most commentators say that it means "God," but he takes issue with them. He thinks the passage means: "Fear not the persecutor, but the tempter, not the man who kills you for your fidelity, but the man who wants to buy you off, and the devil whose agent he is."[39] But it seems

---

[36] Carr, *op. cit.,* p. 166.   [37] Filson, *op. cit.,* p. 132.   [38] *Op. cit.,* p. 167.   [39] EGT, I, 166.

best to take the traditional interpretation. Allen explains it this way: "Fear
the wrath of God against unfaithfulness
to Him, for He can destroy both soul and
body together in Gehenna."[40]

Having given this warning, Jesus proceeded to comfort His disciples. **Two
sparrows** — food for the poorest people
— were sold for a **penny**. This last word
is not to be confused with the usual
word for penny in the Gospels, which is
denarius, worth about twenty cents. This
one is the *assarion,* a small copper coin
about equal in value to an American cent.
In spite of its cheap price, the heavenly
Father notes the fall of each sparrow.
Furthermore, the **hairs** of every head are
numbered. This suggests God's providential care over the least details in the lives
of His children.

The paragraph closes with a promise
and a warning. Those who confess Christ
will find Him standing by them in the
heavenly realm, but those who deny Him
will be rejected by Him.

6. Their Consecration (10:34-39)

34 Think not that I came to send
peace on the earth: I came not to send
peace, but a sword. 35 For I came to set
a man at variance against his father, and
the daughter against her mother, and the
daughter in law against her mother in
law: 36 and a man's foes *shall be* they of
his own household. 37 He that loveth
father or mother more than me is not
worthy of me; and he that loveth son
or daughter more than me is not worthy
of me. 38 And he that doth not take
his cross and follow after me, is not
worthy of me. 39 He that findeth his life
shall lose it; and he that loseth his life
for my sake shall find it.

Christ is often portrayed as "the gentle
Jesus, meek and mild," and the angels
announced Him as bringing peace on
earth (Luke 2:14). Yet here Christ declares that He did not come to bring
peace on the earth, but rather **a sword.**
How can these two statements be reconciled?

The context of the whole passage
points the way to the correct answer.
Jesus did not come to cause division.
But His coming demands a decision. No

man can remain indifferent or neutral in
His presence. Since some refuse to follow Him, inevitable divisions in families
result.

The main emphasis here is that Christ
requires the absolute loyalty of His followers. He must have the disciple's first
love (v. 37). No one can follow Him
unless he is willing to take up the cross
of complete submission to His will (v.
38).

Verse 39 contains one of the most frequently repeated sayings of Jesus (Mark
8:35; Luke 9:34; 17:33; John 12:25). Carr
gives its meaning clearly as follows: "He
that findeth the life of external comfort
and pleasure, shall lose the eternal life
of spiritual joy; and conversely, he who
loseth his earthly life for my sake shall
find the truer and more blessed life in
heaven."[41]

7. Their Care (10:40-42)

40 He that receiveth you receiveth me,
and he that receiveth me receiveth him
that sent me. 41 He that receiveth a
prophet in the name of a prophet shall
receive a prophet's reward: and he that
receiveth a righteous man in the name
of a righteous man shall receive a righteous man's reward. 42 And whosoever
shall give to drink unto one of these
little ones a cup of cold water only, in the
name of a disciple, verily I say unto you
he shall in no wise lose his reward.

The close relation of Christ and His
church is already anticipated in verse 40.
Later Jesus said to Saul, "Why persecutest thou me?" (Acts 9:4). The Head
was feeling the hurt inflicted on the body.
This is both a consoling and a sobering
thought.

In the name of is a Hebraism meaning
"for the sake of." He who **receiveth,** or
welcomes, a **prophet** or a **righteous man**
will receive the reward due to these. The
idea of oneness with Christ and with
His followers continues to be stressed.

What is the meaning of **little ones**
(v. 42)? Some take it as referring to the
less prominent disciples. Others think that
Jesus may have indicated children standing nearby. Still others refer it to new
converts, those who were less instructed
than the apostles. In any case, the
thought is that of showing kindness to

[40] W. C. Allen, *A Critical and Exegetical Commentary on the Gospel According to St. Matthew,* p. 109.
[41] *Op. cit.,* p. 168.

those who may be novices in spiritual education. This kindness is the Spirit of Christ.

G. HIS MESSENGER (11:1-30)

1. Jesus in Galilee (11:1)

1 And it came to pass when Jesus had finished commanding his twelve disciples, he departed thence to teach and preach in their cities.

When Jesus had given instructions to the Twelve and sent them on their mission, He himself undertook a preaching-teaching tour of Galilee. His purpose was to evangelize as many **cities** as possible. Galilee was very heavily populated at this time.

2. Jesus and John (11:2-19)

a. Victim (11:2-6)

2 Now when John heard in the prison the works of the Christ, he sent by his disciples 3 and said unto him, Art thou he that cometh, or look we for another? 4 And Jesus answered and said unto them, Go and tell John the things which ye hear and see: 5 the blind receive their sight, and the lame walk, the lepers are cleansed, and the deaf hear, and the dead are raised up, and the poor have good tidings preached to them. 6 And blessed is he, whosoever shall find no occasion of stumbling in me.

John was in prison. Jesus was preaching, teaching, healing. Finally the lonely Baptist — accustomed to the wide open wilderness, but now confined in a cramped cell — could scarcely endure his imprisonment any longer. He had introduced Jesus as the Messiah. Doubtless he expected Him quickly to vanquish the enemy (the Romans) and set up His own kingdom, ruling the world in righteousness. But nothing like this was happening.

Faith tested, patience exhausted, John sent his disciples to Jesus to ask if He were truly **he that cometh.** This was "a classic expression, somewhat veiled, to designate the Messiah."[42]

Jesus' answer to John's question was simply His own words and works. They would speak for themselves. His healing miracles fulfilled Isaiah's prediction of the Messiah's coming (Isa. 35:5-6). The crowning phase of His ministry was preaching the gospel to the poor (cf. Isa. 61:1). John evidently expected the Messiah to be a military conqueror, a political ruler. But Jesus fulfilled the true Messianic role of ministering divine love to suffering humanity.

To John the idea of a Suffering Servant was an **occasion of stumbling** (v. 6). The cross of Christ is still a stumblingblock (I Cor. 1:23).

b. Vindication (11:7-11)

7 And as these went their way, Jesus began to say unto the multitudes concerning John, What went ye out into the wilderness to behold? a reed shaken with the wind? 8 But what went ye out to see? a man clothed in soft *raiment?* Behold, they that wear soft *raiment* are in kings' houses. 9 But wherefore went ye out? to see a prophet? Yea, I say unto you, and much more than a prophet. 10 This is he of whom it is written,

Behold, I send my messenger before thy face,

Who shall prepare thy way before thee.

11 Verily I say unto you, Among them that are born of women there hath not arisen a greater than John the Baptist: yet he that is but little in the kingdom of heaven is greater than he.

Having gently reproved John for his lack of faith, Jesus vindicated him before the people. He asked them what they went out to see. Why had they made the arduous journey to the wilderness of Judea? Was it to see **a reed shaken with the wind** — a vacillating coward? No, John's courage was the cause of his imprisonment. Was it **a man clothed in soft raiment** ("dressed in silks and satins" —NEB)? No, John was dressed for the wilderness (3:4), not the king's court. Was it **a prophet?** Ah, yes, and **much more than a prophet** (v. 9). John the Baptist was the Lord's **messenger** foretold in Malachi 3:1.

Then Jesus paid John the highest tribute possible. He declared that among all men there had never been a greater than the Baptist. Yet the least person in the kingdom of heaven is **greater than he** (v. 11). In what way? Because he has the greater privilege of living in the

[42] Suzanne de Dietrich, "The Gospel According to Matthew," *Layman's Bible Commentary,* Vol. 16, p. 69.

light of the Cross. In a very real sense John belonged to the old dispensation, though he was the herald of the new.

c. Violence (11:12-15)

12 And from the days of John the Baptist until now the kingdom of heaven suffereth violence, and men of violence take it by force. 13 For all the prophets and the law prophesied until John. 14 And if ye are willing to receive *it*, this is Elijah, that is to come. 15 He that hath ears to hear, let him hear.

The meaning of verse 12 is not immediately clear, nor is its relation to verse 13. Luke (16:16) has a similar statement, paralleling these two verses. The thought seems to be: ". . . only the man who is desperately in earnest, only the man in whom the violence of devotion matches and defeats the violence of persecution will in the end enter into it."[43]

Jesus then declared that John the Baptist fulfilled the predicted role of Elijah (Mal. 4:5) He was the forerunner of the Messiah.

d. Vilification (11:16-19)

16 But whereunto shall I liken this generation? It is like unto children sitting in the marketplaces, who call unto their fellows 17 and say, We piped unto you, and ye did not dance; we wailed, and ye did not mourn. 18 For John came neither eating nor drinking, and they say, He hath a demon. 19 The Son of man came eating and drinking, and they say, Behold, a gluttonous man and a winebibber, a friend of publicans and sinners! And wisdom is justified by her works.

Jesus compared His generation to spoiled children, who are never satisfied. Green puts it well: "The picture of the children playing alternately at weddings and funerals . . . suggests a change in the temper of the people who now react neither to John nor Jesus but are indifferent to both."[44]

People are always quick to condemn someone they do not understand. John's asceticism seemed so strange to his contemporaries that they said he had a demon. His unsociable nature, they thought, proved that there was something drastically wrong with him.

Jesus' social behavior was quite different from that of John: He came **eating and drinking** (v. 19). He joined the people at their meals and made himself friendly with all levels of society. This displeased the Jewish leaders, who thought He should keep Himself aloof, should lead a separated, not sociable, life. The primary meaning of "Pharisees" was "separated ones." But this connoted mainly ceremonial separation; that is, avoiding contact with all "unclean" objects, including **publicans and sinners**. So the Pharisees castigated Jesus as **a gluttonous man and a winebibber**. They despised Him.

It may be that **wisdom** should be capitalized here; that is, personified and so meaning God (cf. Phillips). This is suggested in Proverbs 8. The oldest Greek manuscript of the New Testament extant today, Codex Vaticanus (4th cent.), has **works** in place of "children" (KJV). Adam Clarke, after considering different interpretations, settles on this: "It is likely, however, that by *children* our Lord simply means the *fruits* or *effects* of wisdom, according to the Hebrew idiom, which denominates the fruits or effects of a thing, its children."[45] In any case, **wisdom is justified**, or "approved," by its consequences, the most significant of which is the conduct of its followers.

3. Judgment on Cities (11:20-24)

20 Then began he to upbraid the cities wherein most of his mighty works were done, because they repented not. 21 Woe unto thee, Chorazin! woe unto thee, Bethsaida! for if the mighty works had been done in Tyre and Sidon which were done in you, they would have repented long ago in sackcloth and ashes. 22 But I say unto you, it shall be more tolerable for Tyre and Sidon in the day of judgment, than for you. 23 And thou, Capernaum, shalt thou be exalted unto heaven? thou shalt go down unto Hades: for if the mighty works had been done in Sodom which were done in thee, it would have remained until this day. 24 But I say unto you that it shall be more tolerable for the land of Sodom in the day of judgment, than for thee.

[43] William Barclay, *The Gospel of Matthew*, II, 9.
[44] F. W. Green, *The Gospel According to Saint Matthew*, "The Clarendon Bible," p. 176.
[45] Adam Clarke, *The New Testament of Our Lord and Saviour Jesus Christ*, I, 130.

Jesus began to **upbraid** — "reproach" or "rebuke" — the cities where most of His miracles (**mighty works,** literally "powers") had been done. They should have **repented** — had a change of heart and mind — at this display of divine power. Instead their souls were hardened in sin. It is obvious that the inhabitants of these places were free to repent, or Jesus could not have reproached them.

The force of **Woe unto thee** (v. 21) has been debated. Adam Clarke writes: "It would be better to translate the word *ouai soi, alas for thee,* than *wo to thee.* The former is an exclamation of pity; the latter a denunciation of wrath."[46] Modern translators largely concur in this. But in any event Jesus' statement was a declaration of divine judgment on these unrepentant cities.

The exact location of **Chorazin** is unknown, but it clearly was near the northwest corner of the Lake of Galilee. Its very disappearance is a testimony to Christ's judgment on it. The same can be said for **Bethsaida,** which was located on the east bank of the Jordan River where it flows into the Lake. **Tyre and Sidon,** about twenty miles apart, were far north on the coast of the Mediterranean, in ancient Phoenicia, the modern country of Lebanon. Both are small towns today, though the old site of Tyre is largely in ruins. It is said that, in the time of Christ, Tyre equaled Jerusalem in population. Jesus said these cities **would have repented** if they had seen the miracles He performed in Palestine. **Sackcloth** was a very coarse material, irritating to the skin. It was worn as a sign of fasting or of mourning. Extreme grief was shown by sprinkling **ashes** on the head. The significance of the combination is shown in Jeremiah 6:26 — "Gird thee with sackcloth, and wallow thyself in ashes: make thee mourning, as for an only son, most bitter lamentation." Jesus used the expression to mean an evidence of genuine grief and sorrow, which the heathen cities would have shown but Irsael did not.

Verse 22 suggests that the crime for which men will be most severely condemned at the Judgment is impenitence. Those who have been ignorant of the ways of God will fare far better than the ones who have had the evidence presented but have rejected it.

Capernaum (v. 23) was located near the northwest corner of the Lake of Galilee. There are still some impressive ruins to be seen there, but no town remains. This verifies the Master's prophetic declaration that it would be cast down to **Hades** — the place of death, and so, of utter destruction.

"Which art exalted unto heaven" (KJV) is better translated **shalt thou be exalted to heaven?** The former translation would be a description of the heavenly privilege Capernaum had enjoyed as the headquarters of Jesus' Galilean ministry. The town had experienced His presence and power. The latter translation would suggest a proud, arrogant attitude on the part of Capernaum, exalting itself to heaven. Many modern translators prefer the form of a question, which is more striking.

Sodom was in ancient times a synonym for sin. Yet Jesus asserted that if Sodom had enjoyed Capernaum's privileges it would not have been destroyed. The principle is clearly enunciated here that responsibility is measured by privilege, and judgment by one's light (v. 24).

4. Joy in Simplicity (11:25-27)

25 At that season Jesus answered and said, I thank thee, O Father, Lord of heaven and earth, that thou didst hide these things from the wise and understanding, and didst reveal them unto babes: 26 yea, Father, for so it was well-pleasing in thy sight. 27 All things have been delivered unto me of my Father: and no one knoweth the Son, save the Father; neither doth any know the Father, save the Son, and he to whomsoever the Son willeth to reveal *him.*

Only a few of Jesus' prayers are recorded in the Gospels, though frequent reference is made to His praying. Here is one of the rare gems (vv. 25-26).

Thank is the same verb which is translated "confess" in connection with people confessing their sins when John baptized them (3:6; Mark 1:5). It literally means "speak the same thing out of." Here it may mean "fully agree with." Jesus was

[46] *Ibid.*

in full agreement with His Father's policy.

These things probably refers to the nature of the Kingdom, as described in the Sermon on the Mount. This Kingdom was to be a spiritual *reign* of God in the hearts of individuals, not a political *realm* as the Jewish religious leaders expected.

God had chosen to **hide** this mystery, because they would not receive it, from **the wise and understanding** — the scribes and Pharisees, who prided themselves on their wisdom, but who actually showed supreme folly in rejecting Jesus as Messiah. Instead He revealed it to **babes** — "To the poor, the ignorant, and the obscure; the teachable, the simple, the humble."[47]

Jesus acquiesced fully in the will of His Father (v. 26). This is the only truly Christian attitude one can take today.

The first statement of verse 27 is echoed throughout the New Testament. For the carrying out of the plan of redemption, the Father has given **all things** to the Son (cf. 28:18; John 3:35; 13:3; 17:2; I Cor. 15:27). This verse is paralleled almost verbatim in Luke 10:22.

The declaration that no one **knoweth** the Son except the Father must of course be taken in the absolute sense. For salvation consists in *knowing* Jesus Christ (John 17:3). But no one except God can understand the Incarnation nor the full nature of the Son of God. Also no one can know the **Father** but the **Son** Himself and those to whom He **willeth to reveal Him** — not simple future, "will reveal" (KJV). No man knows God except through the revelation in Jesus Christ. In a very real sense Jesus is *God revealed* (John 1:18). The combination of divine sovereignty and human freedom is brought out clearly by a comparison of this verse with John 7:17 — "If any man is willing to do His will, he shall know" (literal translation).

5. Joy in Humility (11:28-30)

28 Come unto me, all ye that labor and are heavy laden, and I will give you rest. 29 Take my yoke upon you, and learn of me; for I am meek and lowly in heart: and ye shall find rest unto your souls. 30 For my yoke is easy, and my burden is light.

This is one of the most beautiful passages in the entire Bible. And admittedly it is one of many where it would be difficult to improve on the beauty of the King James Version. Every Christian would do well to memorize it in that form.

It begins with the gracious invitation: **Come unto me.** This is an expression of the Divine Nature — pure, unselfish, redemptive Love.

The phrase, **all ye that labor and are heavy laden** has at least three applications. It referred first of all to the Jews, whose yoke of the Law (supplemented by "the tradition of the elders," Mark 7:3), constituted a burden too heavy to bear (23:4; Acts 15:10). In the second place, it has reference to all sinners, who are carrying on their backs a crushing load of guilt (cf. *Pilgrim's Progress*). But th[is] invitation should also be accepted [by] Christians who feel weighed down [by] the cares of life and perplexing [prob]lems too difficult for human solu[tion]. Jesus Christ is the great Burden-be[arer].

I will give you rest is literall[y "I] will rest you." It is His presence [that] gives rest to the weary soul. That [is] why He said, "Come unto me."

The **yoke** (v. 29) symbolizes submission to someone's authority. To take Christ's yoke is to acknowledge fully His lordship in one's life. It was also used in the sense of discipleship, of accepting the teachings of a certain person. This thought is borne out by the clause following: **and learn of me.** To take Jesus' yoke means to accept His way of life.

What aspect of that is emphasized here? **I am meek and lowly in heart.** Those who are humble **find rest.** Pride breeds restlessness, but humility brings restfulness. **Meek** may be translated "gentle." The gentleness of Jesus is the answer to the violent strife of a wicked world.

One thinks of yokes as hard and burdens as heavy. But the loving Master said: **My yoke is easy, and my burden is light** (v. 30). To one who loves Christ, doing His will is easy. Someone has well said, "Love makes all burdens light."

[47] Albert Barnes, *Notes on the New Testament: Matthew and Mark*, ed. Robert Frew, p. 123.

H. HIS CRITICS (12:1-50)

1. The Cause (12:1-21)

a. Harvesting on the Sabbath (12:1-8)

1 At that season Jesus went on the sabbath day through the grainfields; and his disciples were hungry and began to pluck ears and to eat. 2 But the Pharisees, when they saw it, said unto him, Behold, thy disciples do that which it is not lawful to do upon the sabbath. 3 But he said unto them, Have ye not read what David did, when he was hungry, and they that were with him; 4 how he entered into the house of God, and ate the showbread, which it was not lawful for him to eat, neither for them that were with him, but only for the priests? 5 Or have ye not read in the law, that on the sabbath day the priests in the temple profane the sabbath, and are guiltless? 6 But I say unto you, that one greater than the temple is here. 7 But if ye had known what this meaneth, I desire mercy, and not sacrifice, ye would not have condemned the guiltless. 8 For the Son of man is lord of the sabbath.

In the Synoptic Gospels we find Jesus in frequent conflict with the Pharisees. One of the main causes of these clashes was the question of sabbath desecration. Perhaps the most important single distinguishing feature of Judaism in the time of Christ was its supreme emphasis on the observance of the sabbath. In the Talmud no less than twenty-four chapters were devoted to the subject. This and circumcision were the two principle things that set the Jews apart from the Gentiles.

Grainfields is more accurate for American readers than "corn" (KJV). However, in the British Isles wheat is still called "corn" (cf. NEB). The grain here was either wheat or barley, probably the former. So **ears** ("ears of corn," KJV) should be "heads."

Working on the sabbath day was a major crime according to Judaism. In the eyes of the Pharisees the disciples of Jesus were guilty on three specific counts: (1) they were plucking the heads of wheat, which was *harvesting;* (2) they were rubbing off the husks in their hands, which was *threshing;* (3) they were blowing the chaff away from the kernels, which was *winnowing.* This is a good example of the picayunish way the legalistic Pharisees applied the Mosaic prohibition against working on the sabbath (Ex. 20:10).

Jesus defended His followers against the Pharisaic condemnation (v. 2). He cited the example of David, the revered king of the Old Testament, who ate the showbread, which only the priests were permitted to eat (vv. 3-4). This does not necessarily mean that Christ defended David's action. But why, He asked, did they condone David and condemn the disciples for something far less important?

The Master used a second illustration. The priests in the temple **profane the sabbath** by their slaying and offering of sacrifices, yet are **guiltless** (v. 5). The trouble with the Pharisees was their failure to recognize that something **greater than the temple** was on hand (v. 6). Jesus was the actual representation of God, whereas the temple was only a **symbol** of the divine presence.

Then Jesus laid His finger on the real sore spot. The Pharisees were long on **sacrifice** (offering of animals) but short on **mercy.** They needed less legalism and more love. Christ quoted Hosea 6:6 to show God's preference for the latter.

The Master concluded with a general statement which has sweeping implications. If the **son of man is lord of the sabbath** (v. 8), the only duty of the Christian is to do on the Lord's Day what he honestly believes would be pleasing to his Lord.

b. Healing on the Sabbath (12:9-14)

9 And he departed thence, and went into their synagogue: 10 and behold, a man having a withered hand. And they asked him, saying, Is it lawful to heal on the sabbath day? that they might accuse him. 11 And he said unto them, What man shall there be of you, that shall have one sheep, and if this fall into a pit on the sabbath day, will he not lay hold on it, and lift it out? 12 How much then is a man of more value than a sheep! Wherefore it is lawful to do good on the sabbath day. 13 Then saith he to the man, Stretch forth thy hand. And he stretched it forth; and it was restored whole, as the other. 14 But the Pharisees went out, and took counsel against him, how they might destroy him.

The second cause of conflict was Jesus' habit of healing on the sabbath day. This is noted in all four Gospels. The specific instance here was the case of **a man having a withered hand** (v. 10) — literally, "all dried up." This incident happened in **their synagogue** (v. 9), probably at Capernaum (cf. Mark 2:1; 3:1). There were Pharisees present who were spying on Jesus, to see whether He would heal the man on the sabbath (Mark 3:2). They asked Him a loaded question: **Is it lawful to heal on the sabbath day?** They were not seeking for information, but for an opportunity to **accuse him** (v. 10).

In reply Christ asked if they would not on the sabbath pull out a sheep that had fallen into a pit (v. 11). How much more valuable was **a man** than **a sheep** (v. 12). Then the Master stated His single regulation for sabbath observance: **Wherefore it is lawful to do good on the sabbath day.** This was His answer to their question. He proceeded to apply this principle by ordering the man to stretch out his withered hand (v. 13). The latter might have said, "I can't." Instead he exerted his *will* to obey, and found that Christ furnished the *power* to carry out His command. This obedience is the secret of victory in every phase of life.

The Pharisees left the synagogue and **took counsel,** or "held a council" (KJV), against Jesus, determined to **destroy him** (v. 14). It was all right for them to plot against His life on the sabbath, but not for Him to heal a helpless victim! The only ones who fail to see the inconsistency of legalism are the legalists themselves.

c. Helping the Sick (12:15-21)

15 And Jesus perceiving *it* withdrew from thence: and many followed him; and he healed them all, 16 and charged them that they should not make him known: 17 that it might be fulfilled which was spoken through Isaiah the prophet, saying,
18 Behold, my servant whom I have chosen;
My beloved in whom my soul is well pleased:
I will put my Spirit upon him,
And he shall declare judgment to the Gentiles.
19 He shall not strive, nor cry aloud;
Neither shall any one hear his voice in the streets.
20 A bruised reed shall he not break,
And smoking flax shall he not quench,
Till he send forth judgment unto victory.
21 And in his name shall the Gentiles hope.

Jesus did not stay around to be arrested. Instead He withdrew to the seashore (Mark 3:7), where He would be safer. There great crowds gathered to Him, and He **healed them all.** He forbade them to publicize His miracles (v. 16), for He did not want false messianic hopes raised, that might result in a political uprising.

As is his frequent custom, Matthew quotes an Old Testament passage (Isa. 42:1-4). He is especially fond of quoting Isaiah (cf. 1:23; 3:3; 4:14; 13:14; 15:7). The passage here is taken from the first of the so-called Servant Songs.

The second poetic line of verse 18 was echoed at the baptism of Jesus (3:17). It was there also that the **Spirit** came upon Him (3:16), in order that He might **declare judgment to the Gentiles**; that is, provide salvation for all men, not simply for the Jews.

The gentleness of Jesus' ministry is here described (v. 19). He did not come to lead a political revolution, but to initiate a spiritual reformation. He did not come to **break** the **bruised reed** of Roman power, nor to **quench** the **smoking flax** (v. 20) of flickering authority. The second figure used here is much more clearly indicated in the Old Testament translation — "a dimly burning wick" (Isa. 42:3). When the oil is low a wick burns dimly and threatens to flicker out.

Just what application Jesus had in mind is not certain. In addition to that given above there are at least two others. He may have referred to the flickering light in Judaism and the bruised reed of religious authority, due to the fact that too often the people had lost confidence in their leaders. Another interpretation is that Jesus did not wish to snuff out the weakened spiritual life of the least child of the Kingdom. That is, He seeks to conserve, rather than destroy. It is very likely that all three of these applications are valid and should be given consideration.

2. The Criticism (12:22-30)

22 Then was brought unto him one possessed with a demon, blind and dumb: and he healed him, insomuch that the dumb man spake and saw. 23 And all the multitudes were amazed, and said, Can this be the son of David? 24 But when the Pharisees heard it, they said, This man doth not cast out demons, but by Beelzebub the prince of the demons. 25 And knowing their thoughts he said unto them, Every kingdom divided against itself is brought to desolation; and every city or house divided against itself shall not stand: 26 and if Satan casteth out Satan, he is divided against himself; how then shall his kingdom stand? 27 And if I by Beelzebub cast out demons, by whom do your sons cast them out? therefore shall they be your judges. 28 But if I by the Spirit of God cast out demons, then is the kingdom of God come upon you. 29 Or how can one enter into the house of the strong *man*, and spoil his goods, except he first bind the strong *man*? and then he will spoil his house. 30 He that is not with me is against me; and he that gathereth not with me scattereth.

Since Jesus was healing all kinds of illness, the people brought to him an impossible case — a blind, dumb demoniac. But the Master was equal to the situation: He made the man see and speak.

It was obvious that this spectacular healing was a display of supernatural power. Two explanations were offered. The **multitudes** (v. 23) thought the miracle-worker must be **the son of David;** that is, the Messiah. On the other hand, **the Pharisees** (v. 24) declared that Jesus received His power to cast out demons from **Beelzebub** (Greek, *Beelzebul*) , **the prince of the demons.**

Immediately Christ pointed out how utterly illogical was their reasoning. A divided kingdom or house cannot stand; surely Satan would not be casting out Satan (vv. 25-26) . Then He asked a pointed question: if He was casting out demons by Beelzebub, by what power were their **sons** doing it (v. 27)? Their success in exorcising demons — a familiar practice in that day — would condemn the critics. If, on the other hand, Jesus was doing it **by the Spirit of God,** this was proof that the kingdom of God was in

their midst (v. 28). The Master then made the application. He had entered the domain of the **strong man** (Satan), conquered him, and was now able to **spoil his goods** by delivering men from his demonic power (v. 29).

On the surface, the statement, **He that is not with me is against me** (v. 30), seems to be in contradiction with Luke 9:50 — "he that is not against us is for us." But Jesus had two very different things in mind. In the saying reported by Matthew He declared that whoever was not inwardly loyal to Him was actually against Him. But in an entirely different context He asserted that a man who did not openly oppose Him must be treated as on His side. In Luke He is talking against a narrow sectarian attitude. In Matthew He is warning against a divided loyalty.

3. The Curse (12:31-32)

31 Therefore I say unto you, Every sin and blasphemy shall be forgiven unto men; but the blasphemy against the Spirit shall not be forgiven. 32 And whosoever shall speak a word against the Son of man, it shall be forgiven him; but whosoever shall speak against the Holy Spirit, it shall not be forgiven him, neither in this world, nor in that which is to come.

A great deal has been said and written about the so-called Unpardonable Sin. Jesus defines it here in its simplest terms as **blasphemy against the Spirit.** The context, especially as stated in Mark 3:30, indicates the true nature of it: "The *unpardonable sin,* as some term it, is neither less nor more than *ascribing the miracles Christ wrought, by the power of God, to the spirit of the devil.*"[48] On verse 32 Barnes comments: "He that speaks against me as a man of Nazareth — that speaks contemptuously of my humble birth, etc., may be pardoned; but he that reproaches my divine nature, charging me with being in league with Satan, and blaspheming the power of God manifestly displayed *by me,* can never obtain forgiveness."[49] The modern counterpart would seem to be deliberately, obstinately, and wilfully attributing to wrong sources the manifest working of the Holy Spirit. It is generally accepted today that anyone

---

[48] Adam Clarke, *op. cit.,* p. 138.   [49] *Op. cit.,* p. 132.

who is concerned lest he may have committed the unpardonable sin, and who sincerely desires forgiveness, gives evidence thereby that he is not guilty of this horrible curse.

4. The Contrast (12:33-37)

33 Either make the tree good, and its fruit good; or make the tree corrupt, and its fruit corrupt: for the tree is known by its fruit. 34 Ye offspring of vipers, how can ye, being evil, speak good things? for out of the abundance of the heart the mouth speaketh. 35 The good man out of his good treasure bringeth forth good things: and the evil man out of his evil treasure bringeth forth evil things. 36 And I say unto you, that every idle word that men shall speak, they shall give account thereof in the day of judgment. 37 For by thy words thou shalt be justified, and by thy words thou shalt be condemned.

The Master drew a contrast between good and evil trees, and also between good and evil men. It is the *fruit* that shows, in each case, the nature of the tree or of the man.

Jesus called the Pharisees **offspring of vipers** (v. 34). John the Baptist, the stern, ascetic prophet of the wilderness, had earlier described them thus (3:7). The language seems strange on the lips of the loving Christ. What must be recognized was that this was no mere exhibition of peevish anger, but simply a declaration of the true nature of the Pharisees. They were **corrupt** trees (v. 33), whose fruit was corrupting the nation. Since they were **evil** they could not say **good things,** for the mouth speaks from the overflow of the heart. The **good man** from the **good treasure** in his heart brings forth **good things,** while the converse is true of the **evil man** (v. 35).

The warning in verse 36 is startling, to say the least. If the adjective **idle** were to be taken in its common, literal sense today, most good people would be under condemnation. But the context clearly indicates that **idle** here means not just careless or thoughtless, but false, injurious, malicious, wicked — the kind of words the Pharisees were saying. Since one's speech is the expression of his heart, everyone will be **justified** or **condemned** by his **words** (v. 37).

5. The Craving (12:38-42)

38 Then certain of the scribes and Pharisees answered him, saying, Teacher, we would see a sign from thee. 39 But he answered and said unto them, An evil and adulterous generation seeketh after a sign; and there shall no sign be given to it but the sign of Jonah the prophet: 40 for as Jonah was three days and three nights in the belly of the whale; so shall the Son of man be three days and three nights in the heart of the earth. 41 The men of Nineveh shall stand up in the judgment with this generation, and shall condemn it: for they repented at the preaching of Jonah; and behold, a greater than Jonah is here. 42 The queen of the south shall rise up in the judgment with this generation, and shall condemn it: for she came from the ends of the earth to hear the wisdom of Solomon; and behold, a greater than Solomon is here.

One of the evidences of lack of true spirituality is the craving for external signs. It is really an indication of a materialistic attitude toward spiritual things.

Some of the **scribes and Pharisees** sought such a **sign** from the **teacher.** Jesus rebuked them as an **evil and adulterous generation,** or race. Christ was Himself the supreme Sign. But they had rejected Him and also His miracles, which were signs of His divine power. What they wanted was some spectacular sign from heaven, that would satisfy their carnal curiosity. But Jesus never wrought miracles to fulfill this craving.

One sign would be given to that wicked, rebellious nation. The resurrection of Jesus is the crowning proof of His deity (Rom. 1:4). Jonah's experience in the stomach of the "seamonster" (margin) was a type of the death, burial, and resurrection of Christ.

The statement that the Son of man would be **three days and three nights** in the heart of the earth (v. 40) has raised some questions about the time of the crucifixion. If this took place on Friday, how can one possibly find three days and nights before Sunday. It should be noted that the most frequently suggested alternative, Wednesday, is equally unsatisfactory, unless one places the resurrection on Saturday afternoon. Thursday seems best to fit the description, but very few hold to this day. It should be recognized, of course, that the Jews counted parts of days as a whole day. We have portions of Friday, Saturday and Sunday without difficulty. The problem lies in explaining the *three nights*. Over against this we have the statement that Christ would rise "the third day" (16:21), which fits neither Wednesday nor Thursday. The overwhelming early-church tradition that Jesus was crucified on Friday cannot easily be set aside. It seems best to take the expression **three days and three nights** in a general sense, in keeping with those times, and not to insist on the scientific exactness which is demanded today.

Verses 41-42 are very similar in emphasis to 11:20-24. There Jesus used the examples of Tyre, Sidon, and Sodom. Here He refers to **the men of Nineveh** and **the queen of the south** (the Queen of Sheba, I Kings 10:1). The former **repented at the preaching of Jonah** and the latter **came from the ends of the earth to hear the wisdom of Solomon.** But a greater than Jonah or Solomon was present, yet the Jews refused to repent or to listen to His wisdom. This was the crowning condemnation of the Jews of Jesus' day — rejection of the Son of God as their Messiah.

6. The Consequences (12:43-45)

43 But the unclean spirit, when he is gone out of the man, passeth through waterless places, seeking rest, and findeth it not. 44 Then he saith, I will return into my house whence I came out; and when he is come, he findeth it empty, swept, and garnished. 45 Then goeth he, and taketh with himself seven other spirits more evil than himself, and they enter in and dwell there: and the last state of that man becometh worse than the first. Even so shall it be also unto this evil generation.

To illustrate the sad situation, Christ told the story of a man, from whom an **unclean spirit** had been cast out. The demon is pictured as passing through **waterless places** (barren deserts), **seeking rest.** Not finding any place to settle down it returns to the man, finds his heart like an **empty** house, and moves back in, accompanied by seven other demons more evil than itself. The result is that the last state of the man is worse than his first.

Thus it was with **this evil generation** (v. 45). It had experienced Christ's presence and power, casting out many demons. But when the Jews rejected Jesus, they found themselves in a worse state than ever before. Wicked demons drove them on to their doom, in the destruction of Jerusalem in A.D. 70.

The warning for individuals is that reformation is not enough. One must not only cast off bad habits, but allow his heart to be filled with Jesus Christ and his life with worthwhile activity. Otherwise he will find himself a victim to worse habits than before. No heart can long stay **empty.** One's only safety lies in keeping both heart and life filled with the good, that there may be no room for the bad.

7. The Clan (12:46-50)

46 While he was yet speaking to the multitudes, behold, his mother and his brethren stood without, seeking to speak to him. 47 And one said unto him, Behold, thy mother and thy brethren stand without, seeking to speak to thee. 48 But he answered and said unto him that told him, Who is my mother? and who are my brethren? 49 And he stretched forth his hand towards his disciples, and said, Behold, my mother and my brethren! 50 For whosoever shall do the will of my Father who is in heaven, he is my brother, and sister, and mother.

Jesus' **mother** and **brethren** (probably sons of Joseph and Mary) wanted to speak to Him, but apparently the crowd made it difficult. So someone told the Master of their desire.

Christ's reply was startling. He asked who His mother and brethren were (v. 48). Pointing to His disciples He said: **Behold, my mother and my brethren** (v. 49). Then He defined His family as consisting of all those who do the will of His Father (v. 50). The point He was making was that spiritual relationships are the highest and holiest in life. He did not repudiate His earthly family, but He added the new concept of a heavenly family.

I. HIS PARABLES (13:1-52)

The thirteenth chapter of Matthew contains seven parables of the Kingdom. This is in line with Matthew's custom of collecting items together by topics. It also highlights his central emphasis on the kingdom of heaven. Each of these parables portrays the Kingdom in one of its aspects. There are three pairs of parables: the Tares and the Dragnet, the Mustard Seed and the Leaven, the Hidden Treasure and the Pearl of Great Price. Each of these begins with the formula: "The kingdom of heaven is like." But the first parable, that of the Sower, has no such introductory phrase. It is clear, however, that it is a true parable of the Kingdom.

1. The Sower (13:1-23)

a. Declaration (13:1-9)

1 On that day went Jesus out of the house, and sat by the sea side. 2 And there were gathered unto him great multitudes, so that he entered into a boat, and sat; and all the multitudes stood on the beach. 3 And he spake to them many things in parables, saying, Behold, the sower went forth to sow; 4 and as he sowed, some *seeds* fell by the way side, and the birds came and devoured them: 5 and others fell upon the rocky places, where they had not much earth: and straightway they sprang up, because they had no deepness of earth: 6 and when the sun was risen, they were scorched; and because they had no root, they withered away. 7 And others fell upon the thorns; and the thorns grew up and choked them: 8 and others fell upon the good ground, and yielded fruit, some a hundredfold, some sixty, some thirty. 9 He that hath ears, let him hear.

Capernaum was located on the shore of the Lake of Galilee. **The house** was probably Peter's home in that city, where Jesus usually stayed. Now the Master left the town and went out beside the **sea** (i.e., the lake). When **great multitudes** thronged Him, He got into a **boat** —probably Peter's fishing boat — and pushed out a little from land to escape the crowd. He **sat**, as did all Jewish rabbis when teaching, while the crowd **stood on the beach.** The sloping shore formed a natural amphitheater, so that the thousands of people could hear Him.

For the first time in Matthew we read of Jesus teaching in **parables.** The Greek word *parabole* literally means something "laid beside," and so "a comparison." It is used specifically to mean "the pictures and narratives drawn from nature and human life which are characteristic of the synoptic teaching of our Lord."[50] It may be defined as follows: "A parable is a short discourse that makes a comparison; it expresses a (single) complete thought."[51] C. H. Dodd says: "At its simplest the parable is a metaphor or simile drawn from nature or common life, arresting the hearer by its vividness or strangeness, and leaving the mind in sufficient doubt about its precise application to tease it into active thought."[52]

Jesus did not originate the parabolic method of teaching. There are parables in the Old Testament, and the rabbis added to the list. But Christ surpassed them all. Buttrick writes: "Jesus is Master of parable because He is Master of Life."[53]

It is usually stressed that each parable was intended to illustrate just one point, and that the student of the Gospels should avoid seeking a spiritual meaning in every part of a parable. This emphasis is sometimes questioned today. In any case it is obvious that the Parable of the Sower is of an allegorical nature, for Jesus Himself gives the allegorical interpretation of it (vv. 18-23). But this, together with the Parable of Tares, seems to be an exception to the rule.

According to Trench's list of thirty, only three parables are common to each of the Synoptics. The Parable of the Sower is one of them (cf. Mark 4:1-12; Luke 8:4-10). It is generally held by scholars that there are no parables in the Gospel of John. If one takes the word "parable" in its simplest sense, Matthew includes fifteen, Mark four, and Luke nineteen.

Perhaps as Jesus sat in the boat a man strode across a nearby field, scattering seed with wide sweeps of his hand. Beckoning toward him, the Master cried: **Behold, the sower went forth to sow.** The audience may have turned to see the familiar sight.

This story could more accurately be called the Parable of the Soils, for its

[50] G. Abbott-Smith, *A Manual Greek Lexicon of the New Testament*, p. 338.
[51] W. F. Arndt and F. W. Gingrich, *A Greek-English Lexicon of the New Testament and Other Early Christian Literature*, p. 617.
[52] C. H. Dodd, *The Parables of the Kingdom*, p. 16.
[53] George A. Buttrick, *The Parables of Jesus*, p. xiii.

emphasis is on four different types of soil: the beaten path, the shallow soil on rock, the thorn-infested patch, and the good ground. The seed **by the way side** was quickly devoured by birds. That which fell on **rocky places** (i.e., thin soil on solid rock) sprang up quickly because of the heated, moist earth. But the sun's rays soon dried out the dirt, and the rootless plants withered away. In the third case **thorns grew up and choked** the wheat or barley before it could reach maturity. But some fell upon **good ground.** This brought forth a rich yield of grain.

b. Defense (13:10-17)

10 And the disciples came, and said unto him, Why speakest thou unto them in parables? 11 And he answered and said unto them, Unto you it is given to know the mysteries of the kingdom of heaven, but to them it is not given. 12 For whosoever hath, to him shall be given, and he shall have abundance: but whosoever hath not, from him shall be taken away even that which he hath. 13 Therefore speak I to them in parables; because seeing they see not, and hearing they hear not, neither do they understand. 14 And unto them is fulfilled the prophecy of Isaiah, which saith,
By hearing ye shall hear, and shall in no wise understand;
And seeing ye shall see, and shall in no wise perceive:
15 For this people's heart is waxed gross, And their ears are dull of hearing, And their eyes they have closed; Lest haply they should perceive with their eyes, And hear with their ears, And understand with their heart, And should turn again, And I should heal them.
16 But blessed are your eyes, for they see; and your ears, for they hear. 17 For verily I say unto you, that many prophets and righteous men desired to see the things which ye see, and saw them not; and to hear the things which ye hear, and heard them not.

The disciples wondered why their Master had adopted the parabolic method of teaching. So they came and asked Him the reason.

His reply was that to them, but not to the multitudes, it was given to know the mysteries of the Kingdom. The Greek word *mysterion* is found in the Gospels only here and in the parallel passages in Mark (4:11) and Luke (8:10). Omitted in Acts, it occurs twenty times in Paul's epistles and four times in Revelation. The greatest mystery is that God has chosen to save in Christ both Jews and Gentiles. The **mysteries of the kingdom of heaven** are the truths connected with the divine rule in human hearts — the spiritual nature of the Kingdom in this age.

The twelfth verse states a general principle of life. Its truth is illustrated in connection with the Parable of the Talents (25:29). Meyer expresses well its meaning here: "With the knowledge you have already acquired, you are ever penetrating more deeply and fully into the things of God's kingdom; the multitude, on the other hand, would lose altogether the little capacity it has for understanding divine truth, unless I were to assist its weak powers of apprehension by parabolic illustrations."[54]

In the thirteenth verse Jesus states more specifically why He spoke in parables. It was because those who listened to Him did not understand His teachings. So He sought to make the truth more plain by illustrating it, comparing the unknown with the known. Again Isaiah is quoted as describing this type of hearer (Isa. 6:9-10).

c. Delineation (13:18-23)

18 Hear then ye the parable of the sower. 19 When any one heareth the word of the kingdom, and understandeth it not, *then* cometh the evil *one,* and snatcheth away that which hath been sown in his heart. This is he that was sown by the way side. 20 And he that was sown upon the rocky places, this is he that heareth the word, and straightway with joy receiveth it; 21 yet hath he not root in himself, but endureth for a while; and when tribulation or persecution ariseth because of the word, straightway he stumbleth. 22 And he that was sown among the thorns, this is he that heareth the word; and the care of the world, and the deceitfulness of riches, choke the word, and he becometh unfruitful. 23 And he that was sown upon the good ground, this is he that heareth the word, and understandeth it; who verily beareth fruit, and bringeth forth,

---

[54] H. A. W. Meyer, *Critical and Exegetical Hand-book to the Gospel of Matthew*, p. 254.

some a hundredfold, some sixty, some thirty.

After the brief discussion of the reason for speaking in parables, the Master proceeded to interpret the Parable of the Sower. He first described the *Stolid Heart*, symbolized by the soil trodden hard by the traffic of life. Then He indicated the *Shallow Heart*, the thin life typified by the top soil on a ledge of rock. It does not take much heat of **tribulation or persecution** for such to wither away. The third picture is that of the *Strangled Heart*. The **thorns** which **choke the word** are **the care of the world** and **the deceitfulness of riches**. Herein lies the gravest danger for every Christian. The fourth is the *Steady Heart*, the **good ground** that brings forth a harvest.

It is to be noted that not only are there four different kinds of soil, but three degrees of fruit-bearing. One should seek not only to have a good heart, but one that bears abundant fruit in Christian life and service.

2. The Tares (13:24-30, 34-43)

a. Declaration (13:24-30)

24 Another parable set he before them, saying, The kingdom of heaven is likened unto a man that sowed good seed in his field: 25 but while men slept, his enemy came and sowed tares also among the wheat, and went away. 26 But when the blade sprang up and brought forth fruit, then appeared the tares also. 27 And the servants of the householder came and said unto him, Sir, didst thou not sow good seed in thy field? whence then hath it tares? 28 And he said unto them, An enemy hath done this. And the servants say unto him, Wilt thou then that we go and gather them up? 29 But he saith, Nay; lest haply while ye gather up the tares, ye root up the wheat with them. 30 Let both grow together until the harvest: and in the time of the harvest I will say to the reapers, Gather up first the tares, and bind them in bundles to burn them; but gather the wheat into my barn.

The Parable of the Tares is related to that of the Sower not because of teaching the same or a similar lesson, but because both have to do with sowing.

In the Parable of the Sower the truth is emphasized that the results of sowing depend to a considerable extent on the soil upon which the seed falls. Jesus was warning His hearers against having hard, shallow, or cluttered hearts, which would hinder the seed of the Word from growing.

In the Parable of the Tares the Master warns the people that bad seed, as well as good, will be sown. They must give heed as to what they receive.

The word **tares** refers to a bearded "darnel" (NEB) that looks almost exactly like wheat and cannot be distinguished from it until it ripens. The task of sorting out the tares from the wheat is a very tedious one, done by women and children. But it is important to do this. "If tares are ground into meal they spoil the flour, and often cause dizziness and nausea when eaten."[55]

The servants reported to their master the presence of the darnel among the wheat and asked if they should weed it out. But the **householder** instructed them to let both grow together until harvest. A. M. Hunter suggests the point as this: "The parable sounds like Jesus' reply to a critic — probably a Pharisee (the very name meant 'separatist') — who had objected: "If the Kingdom of God is really here, why has there not been a separating of sinners from saints in Israel?"[56]

At **the time of harvest** the reapers would **gather up first the tares** and bundle them to use as fuel — a very scarce item in Palestine. Jeremias suggests how this may have been done: "By the gathering out of the darnel we are not to understand that it was rooted up immediately before the reaping of the grain, but that, as the reaper cut the grain with his sickle, he let the darnel fall, so that it was not gathered into the sheaves."[57]

b. Delineation (13:36-43)

36 Then he left the multitudes, and went into the house: and his disciples came unto him, saying, Explain unto us the parable of the tares of the field. 37 And he answered and said, He that soweth the good seed is the Son of man;

[55] Madeleine S. Miller and J. Lane Miller, *Harper's Bible Dictionary*, p. 727.
[56] A. M. Hunter, *Interpreting the Parables of Jesus*, p. 46.
[57] Joachim Jeremias, *The Parables of Jesus*, trans. S. H. Hooke, p. 156.

38 and the field is the world; and the good seed, these are the sons of the kingdom; and the tares are the sons of the evil *one;* 39 and the enemy that sowed them is the devil: and the harvest is the end of the world; and the reapers are angels. 40 As therefore the tares are gathered up and burned with fire; so shall it be in the end of the world. 41 The Son of man shall send forth his angels, and they shall gather out of his kingdom all things that cause stumbling, and them that do iniquity, 42 and shall cast them into the furnace of fire: there shall be the weeping and the gnashing of teeth. 43 Then shall the righteous shine forth as the sun in the kingdom of their their Father. He that hath ears, let him hear.

After some intervening parables given to the crowds, Jesus entered **the house** — probably Peter's in Capernaum. There the disciples requested an explanation of the Parable of the Tares. Again the Master gave an allegorical interpretation, as in the case of the Parable of the Sower. The sower is identified as **the Son of man,** the field as **the world,** the good seed as **the sons of the kingdom** — rather than the Word of God, as in the previous parable — the tares as **the sons of the evil one,** the enemy as **the devil,** the harvest as **the end of the world,** and the reapers as **angels.** Jesus indicated that at the end of the age the angels would gather out of the Kingdom the wicked people and cast them into the **furnace of fire,** where there will be **the weeping and the gnashing of teeth** (v. 42). The latter phrase is used five times by Matthew (see 8:12; 22:13; 24:51; 25: 30) and once by Luke (13:28). In several of these other passages it is connected with "outer darkness." The reference here is clearly to Gehenna (Greek for "hell").

This parable teaches two things: (1) it is not our task to separate saints from sinners; (2) there will be a final and eternal separation at the end of this period of probation.

3. The Mustard Seed (13:31-32)

31 Another parable set he before them, saying, The kingdom of heaven is like unto a grain of mustard seed, which a man took, and sowed in his field: 32

which indeed is less than all seeds; but when it is grown, it is greater than the herbs, and becometh a tree, so that the birds of the heaven come and lodge in the branches thereof.

Botanically speaking, the mustard seed is not **less than all seeds.** But Jesus' statement was a practical one based on the fact that in that day it was thought of as the smallest seed. Plummer comments: " 'Small as a mustard seed' was a Jewish proverb to indicate a very minute particle."[58]

But this tiny seed **becometh a tree.** Dr. Thomson tells of seeing a mustard tree more than twelve feet high near the Jordan River.[59]

This parable, like that of the Sower, is found in all three Synoptic Gospels (cf. Mark 4:30-32; Luke 13:18-19). It was clearly considered important.

4. The Leaven (13:33)

33 Another parable spake he unto them; The kingdom of heaven is like unto leaven, which a woman took, and hid in three measures of meal, till it was all leavened.

This parable is also recorded by Luke (13:20-21), but not by Mark. It is obviously a doublet with the previous parable. So the interpretation of the two can be treated together.

Leaven, of course, is yeast. **Three measures** (about a bushel) may be suggested by Genesis 18:6. There is probably no significance in the number three. Just as the mustard seed was sown in the ground, so the leaven was mixed in the meal. Both had to go out of sight in order to grow. These parables illustrate Jesus' statement that the kingdom of God "cometh not with observation" (Luke 17:20); that is, not with outward show. Its real work is done in the hearts of human beings.

The vast majority of commentators from earliest times have interpreted these two parables as relating to the growth of the church. The former describes its outward growth (like a tree), while the latter depicts its inward growth. The church would flourish throughout the earth, in spite of its very small begin-

---

58 Alfred Plummer, *An Exegetical Commentary on the Gospel According to Matthew,* p. 194.
59 William H. Thomson, *The Land and the Book,* II, 163.

nings. At the same time its unseen influence would "leaven" human society.

In the last century a very different interpretation has been suggested. It presupposes the idea that leaven is *always* a symbol of evil. Therefore it is intended here to indicate the insidious influence of heretical teaching and worldly outlook in the church, by which it lost its pristine purity. The rapid growth of the mustard plant symbolizes the great outward expansion of the Roman Catholic Church as a world organization. The **birds** in the **branches** are the godless men who took office in the various branches of the church. Thus both parables teach the growth of evil in the outward church.

It seems wisest to follow the judgment of the best commentators of the centuries and interpret these parables as referring to the rapid spread of Christianity throughout the world and to the leavening influence of the gospel of Jesus Christ. It appears more likely that this was what the Master had in mind.

5. The Hidden Treasure (13:44)

44 The kingdom of heaven is like unto a treasure hidden in the field; which a man found, and hid; and in his joy he goeth and selleth all that he hath, and buyeth that field.

Jesus told of a man discovering a hidden treasure in a field. So valuable was it that he sold all his possessions to purchase the property in order to get this treasure.

6. The Pearl of Great Price (13:45-46)

45 Again, the kingdom of heaven is like unto a man that is a merchant seeking goodly pearls: 46 and having found one pearl of great price, he went and sold all that he had, and bought it.

This pair of parables is found only in Matthew. Rather obviously both teach the same lesson.

Two applications have been given: (1) that Christ gave His all to purchase the church; (2) that a man should be willing to give his all in order to gain salvation. The second is more likely what Jesus had in mind. For He says that the kingdom of heaven is like the hidden treasure and the precious pearl. The lesson, then, is that salvation is worth one's complete consecration.

There is one slight difference in the two parables. In the first the man stumbles accidentally on a hidden treasure; in the second the merchant is seeking valuable pearls and finally finds one. This suggests two types of converts. One is confronted suddenly with the gospel and receives it joyfully. The other searches long for a religion that will satisfy and at last discovers the truth in Jesus Christ.

7. The Dragnet (13:47-50)

47 Again, the kingdom of heaven is like unto a net, that was cast into the sea, and gathered of every kind: 48 which, when it was filled, they drew up on the beach; and they sat down, and gathered the good into vessels, but the bad they cast away. 49 So shall it be in the end of the world: the angels shall come forth, and sever the wicked from among the righteous, 50 and shall cast them into the furnace of fire: there shall be the weeping and the gnashing of teeth.

This parable forms a doublet with the Parable of the Tares. Both are found only in Matthew. Both teach the same lesson: a final day of judgment is coming, when the evil will be separated from the good. The **bad** will be **cast away**. The **good** will be **gathered** safely. Again it is the **angels** who do the work of separation at the end of the age. As in the previous parable (v. 42), the wicked are cast into the **furnace of fire** and there is **weeping and gnashing of teeth** (v. 50).

These are solemn parables of warning about the seriousness of divine judgment. Jesus was concerned with the attitude of many of His hearers who would be lost.

The distinctive emphasis of this parable is on the large seine that is dragged through the water, enclosing a multitude of fish, both good and bad. So the Gospel-net catches both good and bad. But the separation of these is to be left for the final judgment day.

Trench gives the main lesson of this parable as follows: "That we be not content with being included within the Gospel-net, since 'they are not all Israel who are of Israel'; . . . since despite of all the confusions of the visible Church, 'the Lord knoweth them that are His,' and will one day bring these confusions to an end, separating the precious from the vile."[60]

8. The Householder (13:51-52)

51 Have ye understood all these things? They say unto him, Yea. 52 And he said unto them, Therefore every scribe who hath been made a disciple to the kingdom of heaven is like unto a man that is a householder, who bringeth forth out of his treasure things new and old.

This is often listed as one of the parables of Jesus, though it is not, strictly speaking, a full-fledged parable. However it is a comparison — between a scribe of the kingdom of heaven and a householder, who brings out of his treasure **things new and old.** Perhaps Jesus was seeking to emphasize the fact that His teaching was rooted in the Old Testament and yet contained a new interpretation. Good preaching combines the old and the new.

J. HIS PROVISION (14:1—15:39)

1. Fearless John (14:1-12)

1 At that season Herod the tetrarch heard the report concerning Jesus, 2 and said unto his servants, This is John the Baptist; he is risen from the dead; and therefore do these powers work in him. 3 For Herod had laid hold on John, and bound him, and put him in prison for the sake of Herodias, his brother Philip's wife. 4 For John said unto him, It is not lawful for thee to have her. 5 And when he would have put him to death, he feared the multitude, because they counted him as a prophet. 6 But when Herod's birthday came, the daughter of Herodias danced in the midst, and pleased Herod. 7 Whereupon he promised with an oath to give her whatsoever she should ask. 8 And she, being put forward by her mother, saith, Give me here on a platter the head of John the Baptist. 9 And the king was grieved; but for the sake of his oaths, and of them that sat at meat with him, he commanded it to be given; 10 and he sent and beheaded John in the prison. 11 And his head was brought on a platter, and given to the damsel: and she brought it to her mother. 12 And his disciples came, and took up the corpse, and buried him; and they went and told Jesus.

Tetrarch literally means "ruler of a fourth part" and was used in Greek and then Roman circles for one who governed a tetrarchy. But it finally came to be used loosely for the ruler of a small territory. **Herod the tetrarch** was governor of Galilee and Perea. He was one of three sons of Herod the Great who were given parts of their father's former domain (Luke 3:1). His name was Antipas, so that he is properly referred to as Herod Antipas.

When this guilty governor heard of the miracles that Jesus was performing in his territory, his conscience plagued him with superstitious fear. He thought that John the Baptist had risen from the dead.

At this point the story of John's death is told. It is a gory tale of drunken debauch and dancing daughter, with a determined demon working behind the scenes.

On a visit to Rome, Herod Antipas had stayed in the home of his brother Philip. He repaid the hospitality of his host by stealing his wife, Herodias. When Herod returned to Galilee with his ill-gotten gain, having renounced his own wife, John the Baptist denounced his deed (v. 4). For this John was put in prison.

Herod would liked to have executed John but was afraid to do so, because the crowds considered John a prophet. However, Herodias was watching for an opportunity. She took advantage of Herod's birthday party and had her daughter go in and dance before the assembled guests. Herod was delighted and promised to give the girl whatever she desired. At her mother's instigation — **being put forward** (v. 8) is literally "having been incited or instructed" — she asked for the Baptist's head on a **platter.** "Charger" (KJV) is older English for "a large plate or flat dish for carrying a large joint of meat; a platter."[61]

Herod is called **the king.** Actually he did not hold this title but was popularly called that by his people. The king **was grieved** (v. 9). This does not seem to agree with what is said in the fifth verse about his desire to kill John. But the account in Mark (6:14-29) indicates that Herod was torn between two forces — fear of his wife and fear of John. It was

---

[60] R.C. Trench, *Notes on the Parables of Our Lord,* p. 118.
[61] *Oxford English Dictionary,* II, 287.

Herodias' purpose to place him in such a position that he had to carry out her desire. In this she succeeded completely. John was *beheaded* — Josephus says at the fortress of Machaerus, east of the Dead Sea.[62]

The disciples of John picked up the headless corpse and gave it a decent burial. Then **they went and told Jesus.** Their own leader was gone. How many of them transferred their loyalty to Christ — to whom John had pointed them — is not told.

The lesson of the incident is clear. Herod could stop the tongue of the preacher but he could not still the voice of conscience within. The ghost of John the Baptist rose to haunt his guilty soul.

2. Five Thousand Fed (14:13-21)

13 Now when Jesus heard *it*, he withdrew from thence in a boat, to a desert place apart: and when the multitudes heard *thereof*, they followed him on foot from the cities. 14 And he came forth, and saw a great multitude, and he had compassion on them and healed their sick.

15 And when even was come, the disciples came to him, saying, The place is desert, and the time is already past; send the multitudes away, that they may go into the villages, and buy themselves food. 16 But Jesus said unto them, They have no need to go away; give ye them to eat. 17 And they say unto him, We have here but five loaves, and two fishes. 18 And he said, Bring them hither to me. 19 And he commanded the multitudes to sit down on the grass; and he took the five loaves, and the two fishes, and looking up to heaven, he blessed, and brake and gave the loaves to the disciples, and the disciples to the multitudes. 20 And they all ate, and were filled; and they took up that which remained over of the broken pieces, twelve baskets full. 21 And they that did eat were about five thousand men, besides women and children.

When Jesus heard what had happened He **withdrew.** Micklem says: "Previous action by Herod had prompted an earlier retirement, 4:12, and there was danger now that having swept from his path one popular teacher he might proceed to seize Jesus also (cf. Acts 12:3)."[63]

Desert place means a deserted place, not necessarily a sandy waste. Taking a **boat,** Christ crossed the Lake of Galilee to the eastern shore, where few people lived. There He could expect a quiet time with His disciples. They had probably been seriously disconcerted by the news of John's death. They needed both encouragement and instruction.

The anticipated vacation failed to materialize. Instead the crowds followed **on foot** (or, "by land") circling the north end of the lake. They were ready to greet Jesus on His arrival (v. 14).

One might expect the Master to have resented their presence. Instead He had compassion on them and healed those who were ill.

As evening drew on the disciples became concerned. Who was going to feed this crowd? It would be best to send them, before it got dark, to the nearby villages for food. But the reply of the Master was: **Give ye them to eat** (v.16). This seemed utterly absurd. They had only **five loaves, and two fishes** (v. 17). The loaves were about the size of a flat biscuit or small pancake. The fish were probably sardines. Yet with this lunch for one person (John 6:9) the disciples did actually feed five thousand men, **besides women and children** (v. 23).

How did they do it? Simply by cooperating with Christ. He blessed and broke the loaves, while the disciples served the crowd. To facilitate the serving Jesus commanded the people to **sit** — the Greek says "recline" — **on the grass.** At the close of the meal the disciples filled their twelve lunch **baskets** with the broken fragments that were left over. Thus they had their own food for the next day.

This incident furnishes both challenge and encouragement to the Christian worker. One must give Christ all His resources. But when he does so he finds that the Master multiplies what seems nothing into an abundant supply.

3. Fear and Faith (14:22-27)

22 And straightway he constrained the disciples to enter into the boat, and to go before him unto the other side, till he should send the multitudes away. 23 And after he had sent the multitudes away, he went up into the mountain apart to pray: and when even was come, he was there alone. 24 But the boat was now

---

[62] *Ant.* XVIII, 5, 2.　　[63] Philip A. Micklem, *St. Matthew.* "Westminster Commentaries," p. 152.

in the midst of the sea, distressed by the waves; for the wind was contrary. 25 And in the fourth watch of the night he came unto them, walking upon the sea. 26 And when the disciples saw him walking on the sea, they were troubled, saying, It is a ghost; and they cried out for fear. 27 But straightway Jesus spake unto them, saying, Be of good cheer; it is I; be not afraid.

The reason why Jesus **constrained** or "compelled" His disciples to embark in a boat and head for the opposite shore while He dismissed the crowd is suggested in John's Gospel (6:15). There it is indicated that the people wanted to make Him king. It was necessary to get the disciples out of this atmosphere of political revolution. Jesus Himself went up alone to a quiet hillside, and there He spent the night in prayer. It was one of the crises of His life, and He needed fellowship with the Father.

The expression **when even was come** (v. 23) seems to conflict with the same phrase in verse 15. But evidently the earlier use refers to what has sometimes been called the "first evening," from about three o'clock in the afternoon until sunset. The "second evening" (v. 23) means from sunset on. The literal meaning of the word for **even** is "late." Arndt and Gingrich observe: "The context often makes it easier to decide just what time is meant, whether before or after sundown."[64]

The Lake of Galilee is about six or seven miles across, near its northern end. The boat was **in the midst of the sea** (v. 24). Some ancient manuscripts read: "held away many *stadia* from the land." John says that they had rowed about twenty-five or thirty *stadia*, or "furlongs" (John 6:19). That would be about three or four miles. Presumably they had been rowing for about nine hours. Matthew says they were **distressed** by the heavy waves. The word literally means "tortured" or "tormented." The reason they had gone such a short distance was that **the wind was contrary.** That is, it was blowing fiercely from the north or west and hindered their progress seriously.

In the fourth watch of the night (3:00-6:00 A.M.) Jesus approached, walking on the sea. Not unnaturally, when the disciples saw Him they were **troubled** (v. 26). A better translation would be "terrified." Calling it a **ghost** (Greek, *phantasma*), they **cried out.** Perhaps "screamed" or "shrieked" would describe the case more adequately. Like most ancients — and many moderns — these Galileans had a superstitious horror of ghosts. All this was added to the terror of the storm.

Immediately Jesus called to them: "Have courage; it is I; stop being afraid" (v. 27). That is what the Greek literally says. It was in similar fashion that Jesus several times allayed the fears of His disciples.

4. Faith and Fear (14:28-33)

28 And Peter answered him and said, Lord, if it be thou, bid me come unto thee upon the waters. 29 And he said, Come. And Peter went down from the boat, and walked upon the waters to come to Jesus. 30 But when he saw the wind, he was afraid; and beginning to sink, he cried out, saying, Lord, save me. 31 And immediately Jesus stretched forth his hand, and took hold of him, and saith unto him, O thou of little faith, wherefore didst thou doubt? 32 And when they were gone up into the boat, the wind ceased. 33 And they that were in the boat worshipped him, saying, Of a truth thou art the Son of God.

This incident is recorded only in Matthew, who seems to show a special interest in Peter. He calls him the "first" of the apostles (10:2) and mentions him frequently.

If it be thou (v. 28) does not express doubt. It quite evidently means "since it is you." Peter's request to walk on the water is characteristic of his impetuous, impulsive nature. It seems to reflect a mixture of faith and presumption. Philip Schaff, in an appended note in Lange's *Commentary*, remarks: "Peter's fault lay in the words: 'Bid *me*,' which betray an ambitious and overconfident desire to outdo and outdare the other disciples, and may be regarded as a prelude of the boastful: 'Although *all* shall be offended at Thee, yet will not *I*.' "[65]

To come to Jesus (v. 29) is in the

---

[64] *Op. cit.*, p. 606.　　　[65] J. P. Lange, *Commentary on the Holy Scriptures: Matthew,* p. 272.

two oldest Greek manuscripts "and [or, then] came to Jesus." This fits well with the indication that when he started to sink he was within arm's length of the Master (v. 31). Peter started out in faith, failed through fear, but turned once more to Jesus for help.

Some have questioned the credibility of such a miracle as a man walking on water. Plummer has answered the objection thus: "What is told us in these four verses (28-31) is so in harmony with Peter's character, is such an anticipation of his conduct of a year later, and is so beautiful in itself as an illustration of Christ's way of dealing with His apostles, that we may safely regard it as beyond the power of any early Christian to invent."[66]

The lesson of this incident is well expressed in these words:

> In which plight of Peter, as in a sacred drama, we see graphically represented the spiritual experience of many of Christ's disciples when they are in 'deep waters.' As long as they look steadfastly to Jesus, their heart is strong and their footsteps are firm. But the moment that they look away, and occupy themselves with their difficulties, as viewed apart from their Strength, they tremble and begin to sink. Their sinking recalls to their mind the presence of the very present One; and hence the piercing cry, Lord, save me! The Lord hearkens, and hears, and delivers.[67]

5. Furnishing Health (14:34-36)

34 And when they had crossed over, they came to the land, unto Gennesaret. 35 And when the men of that place knew him, they sent into all that region round about, and brought unto him all that were sick; 36 and they besought him that they might only touch the border of his garment: and as many as touched were made whole.

Gennesaret is the name of a plain some three miles long and a mile and a half wide, located near the northern end of the western shore of the Lake of Galilee. It had the reputation of being one of the most fertile spots in Palestine.

Here Jesus was again surrounded by crowds of people who sought to take advantage of His healing power. They begged to be allowed to touch only the border of his garment (v. 36). This could be translated "tassel of His robe." The Israelites were supposed to wear a tassel on the four corners of their outer garments.

Matthew states that all those who touched were made whole. This is a strong compound, suggesting that they were fully cured.

6. Fussing Pharisees (15:1-20)

1 Then there come to Jesus from Jerusalem Pharisees and scribes, saying, 2 Why do thy disciples transgress the tradition of the elders? for they wash not their hands when they eat bread. 3 And he answered and said unto them, Why do ye also transgress the commandment of God because of your tradition? 4 For God said, Honor thy father and thy mother: and, He that speaketh evil of father or mother, let him die the death. 5 But ye say, Whosoever shall say to his father or his mother, That wherewith thou mightest have been profited by me is given to God; 6 he shall not honor his father. And ye have made void the word of God because of your tradition. 7 Ye hypocrites, well did Isaiah prophesy of you, saying,
8 This people honoreth me with their lips;
   But their heart is far from me.
9 But in vain do they worship me,
   Teaching as their doctrines the precepts of men.
10 And he called to him the multitude, and said unto them, Hear, and understand: 11 Not that which entereth into the mouth defileth the man; but that which proceedeth out of the mouth, this defileth the man. 12 Then came the disciples, and said unto him, Knowest thou that the Pharisees were offended, when they heard this saying? 13 But he answered and said, Every plant which my heavenly Father planted not, shall be rooted up. 14 Let them alone: they are blind guides. And if the blind guide the blind, both shall fall into a pit. 15 And Peter answered and said unto him, Declare unto us the parable. 16 And he said, Are ye also even yet without understanding? 17 Perceive ye not, that whatsoever goeth into the mouth passeth into the belly, and is cast out into the draught? 18 But the things which proceed out of the mouth come forth out of the heart; and they defile the man. 19 For out of the heart come forth evil thoughts, murders, adulteries, fornications,

[66] Alfred Plummer, op. cit., p. 209.
[67] James Morison, A Practical Commentary on the Gospel According to St. Matthew, pp. 255-56.

thefts, false witness, railings: 20 these are the things which defile the man; but to eat with unwashen hands defileth not the man.

The fact that **Pharisees and scribes** would come all the way from Jerusalem (about a hundred miles) to see Jesus shows that He was attracting national attention. While the Sadducees had charge of the temple worship, the **Pharisees** considered themselves to be particularly the custodians of the Law. The **scribes** not only copied the Scriptures, but also were the teachers of the Law. They decided it was time to scrutinize this new prophet of Galilee.

The tradition of the elders (v. 2) consisted of interpretations and applications of the law of Moses which had been made by various rabbis. They sought to "build a fence around the Law," as they expressed it, by making hundreds of minute rules and regulations as to how the Law was to be carried out. This tradition circulated in oral form in Jesus' day but was later reduced to writing.

The particular complaint the Pharisees had at this time was that the disciples did not **wash** their hands before eating. The question was not one of sanitation, but rather of religious ceremony. The disciples doubtless washed the dirt off their hands before they ate, but they did not go through the elaborate ceremonial ablutions demanded by the scribes.

In reply Jesus charged them with transgressing **the commandment of God** by observing their tradition (v. 3). In other words, they had, probably unconsciously, given a higher authority to their man-made rules and regulations than to the divinely revealed Scriptures — a tendency that still appears in many ecclesiastical circles.

Jesus proceeded to document His indictment by giving a specific example. **Honor thy father and thy mother** (v. 4) is the fifth of the Ten Commandments — the very heart of the law of Moses. But the rabbis had made a rule that a son could tell his parents that the money he should be using to care for their needs had been **given to God** (v. 5). Thus they **made void** ("revoked," "invalidated"; literally, "made without authority") the word of God for the sake of their own **tradition** (v. 6).

On the basis of this, Jesus called them hypocrites (v. 7). He quoted Isaiah 29: 13 to show that while they rendered God lip-service, their hearts were far from Him. Instead of proclaiming the Word of God they were teaching **the precepts of men** (v. 9).

Jesus then called the people together and enunciated the real difference between "clean" and "unclean" — a distinction that was given central emphasis by the scribes. He declared that it was not what went into a man's mouth — "unclean" foods — that defiled him, but what came out of his mouth (v. 11).

The disciples were worried. They reported to their Master that the Pharisees were **offended** (*eskandalisthesan,* "scandalized") at His statement (v. 12). Christ's answer implied that the scribes were not **planted** by His Father, and so would be **rooted up** (v. 13). That is, they and their work would not endure. They were **blind guides,** who were leading the people blindly. Both would fall **into a pit** (v. 14); or, as we would say, "into the ditch."

The disciples themselves did not understand Jesus' interpretation of cleanness and uncleanness. So Peter, their main spokesman, asked the Master for an explanation of this **parable** (v. 15); that is, this "comparison" or "similitude." Jesus reproved them for not seeing the obvious (v. 16). The difficulty was that they failed to distinguish between the material and the spiritual. What a man eats affects him physically (v. 17), but not spiritually. It is what comes from his **heart** that defiles him. Thinking unclean thoughts and saying unclean words **defile** (literally "make common"; that is, "make ceremonially unclean," or "profane") a man (vv. 18-19). To eat with hands that were not ceremonially cleansed does not defile (v. 20).

7. Faith of a Foreigner (15:21-28)

21 And Jesus went out thence, and withdrew into the parts of Tyre and Sidon. 22 And behold, a Canaanitish woman came out from those borders, and cried, saying, Have mercy on me, O Lord, thou son of David; my daughter is grievously vexed with a demon. 23 But he answered her not a word. And his disci-

ples came and besought him, saying, Send
her away; for she crieth after us. 24 But
he answered and said, I was not sent but
unto the lost sheep of the house of Israel.
25 But she came and worshipped him,
saying, Lord, help me. 26 And he answered and said, It is not meet to take
the children's bread and cast it to the
dogs. 27 But she said, Yea, Lord: for even
the dogs eat of the crumbs which fall
from their masters' table. 28 Then Jesus
answered and said unto her, O woman,
great is thy faith: be it done unto thee
even as thou wilt. And her daughter was
healed from that hour.

This is Jesus' second withdrawal from
Galilee (cf. 14:13). This time He and
His disciples went forth north to the
parts (not "coasts," KJV) of Tyre and
Sidon — ancient Phoenicia, modern
Lebanon. He was eager to get away
from the thronging crowds and carping
Pharisees. From now on He would spend
an increasing proportion of His time
preparing His disciples to take over when
He must leave. So He sought a quiet
region where He was little known.

But even here His miracle-working
fame had preceded Him. There came
to Him a Canaanitish woman (v. 22).
Meyer observes: "Several tribes of the
Canaanites, who were the original inhabitants of Palestine, went and settled
in the north, and founded what was
subsequently known as the Phoenician
nation."[68] The statement that she came
out from these borders (literally "boundaries"; not "coasts," KJV) would seem
to imply that Jesus had come merely to
the edge of the territory of Phoenicia.

This Gentile woman greeted Him as
Lord, thou son of David. This seems
a bit surprising. Williams comments:
"Living among a mixed population of
Jews and Gentiles, she had heard this
title applied to Jesus; she knew something of the hopes of the Hebrew nation,
that they were expecting a Messiah, son
of the great King David, who should
preach to the poor and heal the sick, as
she heard that Jesus had done."[69] She
clearly had faith that Christ could cast
the demon out of her daughter.

The Master met her request with
silence (v. 23). The disciples, irked at

her crying after them, begged Jesus to
send her away. His answer was that He
was sent to minister to Jews, not Gentiles.
Obviously this referred only to His
earthly ministry.

The persistent woman pressed her case.
Drawing near, she worshipped him [that
is, "fell on her face before Him"], saying,
Lord, help me. The last verb means
literally "to run at the cry of one who
calls for aid."

Christ's answer (v. 26) seems very
strange. But the woman's reply (v. 27)
showed that she took it in the spirit in
which it was intended. The Jews considered all the Gentiles to be dogs. But
Jesus used a word which means "little
dogs" or "puppies" — not the despised
scavenger mongrels of an Oriental village but the pet dogs in the house.
Weatherhead makes the further suggestion that Jesus used this language as a
reproof of His disciples' attitude in
resenting this foreign woman, and that
He may even have spoken with a meaningful twinkle in His eye.[70] In any case
the Master praised her faith and honored
it by granting her request (v. 28).

8. Faith for Healing (15:29-31)

29 And Jesus departed thence, and
came nigh unto the sea of Galilee; and
he went up into the mountain, and sat
there. 30 And there came unto him great
multitudes, having with them the lame,
blind, dumb, maimed, and many others,
and they cast them down at his feet; and
he healed them: 31 insomuch that the
multitude wondered, when they saw the
dumb speaking, the maimed whole, and
the lame walking, and the blind seeing:
and they glorified the God of Israel.

Jesus now returned to the general
area of the sea of Galilee. But Mark
(7:31) indicates that He went to the
east side of the lake, to the Decapolis.
So He was still avoiding the territory
of Herod Antipas.

The Master had two favorite places of
teaching — by the seashore and on a
mountain. This time it was the latter,
though it probably overlooked the lake.
Here great multitudes (v. 30) once more
brought the sick for Him to heal. Some-

[68] Op. cit., p. 284.
[69] A. L. Williams, "St. Matthew" (Exposition), Pulpit Commentary, ed. H. D. M. Spence and J. S.
Exell, XV, II, 99.   [70] Leslie D. Weatherhead, It Happened in Palestine, pp. 198-202.

thing of the prevalence of illness is emphasized in the enumeration here — **lame, blind, dumb, maimed** — as well as the ability of Christ to heal every case. The effect was that people **glorified the God of Israel.**

9. Four Thousand Fed (15:32-39)

32 And Jesus called unto him his disciples, and said, I have compassion on the multitude, because they continue with me now three days and have nothing to eat: and I would not send them away fasting, lest haply they faint on the way. 33 And the disciples say unto him, Whence should we have so many loaves in a desert place as to fill so great a multitude? 34 And Jesus said unto them, How many loaves have ye? And they said, Seven, and a few small fishes. 35 And he commanded the multitude to sit down on the ground; 36 and he took the seven loaves and the fishes; and he gave thanks and brake, and gave to the disciples, and the disciples to the multitudes. 37 And they all ate, and were filled: and they took up that which remained over of the broken pieces, seven baskets full. 38 And they that did eat were four thousand men, besides women and children. 39 And he sent away the multitudes, and entered into the boat, and came into the borders of Magadan.

Probably many of the people who flocked to Jesus had come from some distance. They had stayed with Him for **three days** and now had nothing left to eat. Characteristically Christ was moved with compassion toward them.

This time there were seven loaves and a few small fish on hand, all that was left in the supply of food the disciples had brought. Again Christ commanded the people to **sit down** (v. 35). A different verb is used from that in 14:18. There it literally meant to "lie back," here to "fall back." Both words are correctly translated "recline." In connection with the feeding of the five thousand He "blessed" the bread (14:19). Here he **gave thanks.** Both terms are used today for "saying grace" (a third expression) before meals. Then He broke the loaves and the disciples served the crowd of **four thousand men, besides women and children** (v. 38). As in the case of the previous feeding, there were some of the latter along, but they were probably a relatively small group.

Just as the number of loaves differed from the number on hand at the previous feeding, so did the number of baskets. This time there were **seven baskets full** (v. 37). And a different word for "basket" is used. In the earlier account the term referred to the lunch baskets of the twelve apostles. Here the word may be translated "hamper" — an item sometimes used as a receptacle for wheat. So it is possible that the seven hampers may have held more than the twelve lunch baskets.

When Jesus had dismissed the crowd, He again embarked and crossed over to the **borders** (boundaries) of **Magadan.** Magdala (KJV) is an obvious scribal "correction." Since the location of Magadan is completely unknown, and apparently was so in the Middle Ages, some copyist changed it to the well-known Magdala. But the earliest Greek manuscripts have Magadan.

K. HIS TEACHINGS (16:1—20:34)

1. Messiahship and Majesty (16:1 — 17:27)

a. Perverted Desire (16:1-4)

1 And the Pharisees and Sadducees came, and trying him asked him to show them a sign from heaven. 2 But he answered and said unto them, When it is evening, ye say, *It will* be fair weather: for the heaven is red. 3 And in the morning, *It will be* foul weather to-day: for the heaven is red and lowering. Ye know how to discern the face of the heaven; but ye cannot *discern* the signs of the times. 4 An evil and adulterous generation seeketh after a sign; and there shall no sign be given unto it, but the sign of Jonah. And he left them, and departed.

This time it was the **Pharisees and Sadducees** who came to Jesus. The former are named one hundred times in the New Testament, the latter only fourteen times — seven of these times in Matthew (once each in Mark and Luke, and five times in Acts). While they had to work together in the Great Sanhedrin at Jerusalem, there was normally considerable friction between the two groups. But both united in **trying him.** The verb *peirazo* may also be translated "test" (RSV) or "tempting" (KJV). In this context the last seems to fit best.

They asked Him to show them a **sign**

from heaven. Robinson comments: "The *Sign from heaven* seems to be a general reference to the expectations of popular eschatology, based on Joel iii. 3, and Jesus is being challenged to prove himself to be the Messiah."[71]

Earlier some scribes and Pharisees had asked for a sign (12:38). There He had offered only the sign of the prophet Jonah. The saying in verse 4 here is almost identical with that in 12:39, following which it is explained more percisely in 12:40. No such explanation is given here.[72]

b. Perverse Doctrine (16:5-12)

5 And the disciples came to the other side and forgot to take bread. 6 And Jesus said unto them, Take heed and beware of the leaven of the Pharisees and Sadducees. 7 And they reasoned among themselves, saying, We took no bread. 8 And Jesus perceiving it said, O ye of little faith, why reason ye among yourselves, because ye have no bread? 9 Do ye not yet perceive, neither remember the five loaves of the five thousand, and how many baskets ye took up? 10 Neither the seven loaves of the four thousand, and how many baskets ye took up? 11 How is it that ye do not perceive that I spake not to you concerning bread? But beware of the leaven of the Pharisees and Sadducees. 12 Then understood they that he bade them not beware of the leaven of bread, but of the teaching of the Pharisees and Sadducees.

Once more Jesus and His disciples went to the **other side** — probably the east or northeast. The ones responsible for providing food had forgotten to take along some loaves of bread. So when Jesus bade them beware of the **leaven of the Pharisees and Sadducees** (v. 6) they thought He was referring to this lack. Always their thinking tended to be materialistic, and for this the master reproved them. He reminded them of His power to provide loaves for the five thousand and four thousand and of the surplus they had garnered.

It has sometimes been contended that the stories of the two miraculous feedings are variant accounts of the same incident. But the careful distinctions maintained

refute this theory. In all six references to the feeding of the five thousand (Matt. 14:20; 16:9; Mark 6:43; 8:19; Luke 9:17; John 6:13) the word *kophinos* is used for "baskets." In all four references to the feeding of the four thousand (Matt. 15:37; 16:10; Mark 8:8, 20) the word *spyris* is used. Such careful and complete consistency cannot be explained except on the basis of accurate accounts of two different miracles.

One of the characteristics of Matthew is that of giving added explanations of the meaning of what Jesus said (cf. 17:13). So here he indicates that **leaven** meant **teaching** (v. 12). "Doctrine" (KJV) carries a theological connotation that is too strong for both the Greek word (*didache*) and the context.

c. Peter's Confession (16:13-20)

13 Now when Jesus came into the parts of Caesarea Philippi, he asked his disciples, saying, Who do men say that the Son of man is? 14 And they said, Some *say* John the Baptist; some, Elijah; and others, Jeremiah, or one of the prophets. 15 He saith unto them, But who say ye that I am? 16 And Simon Peter answered and said, Thou art the Christ, the Son of the living God. 17 And Jesus answered and said unto him, Blessed art thou, Simon Bar-Jonah: for flesh and blood hath not revealed it unto thee, but my Father who is in heaven. 18 And I also say unto thee, that thou art Peter, and upon this rock I will build my church; and the gates of Hades shall not prevail against it. 19 I will give unto thee the keys of the kingdom of heaven: and whatsoever thou shalt bind on earth shall be bound in heaven; and whatsoever thou shalt loose on earth shall be loosed in heaven. 20 Then charged he the disciples that they should tell no man that he was the Christ.

This paragraph describes a fourth withdrawal of Jesus, to get away from the crowds and instruct His disciples (cf. 14:13; 15:21, 29). This time He went far north again, to the region around **Caesarea Philippi**. It was so named to distinguish it from the Caesarea on the coast of the Mediterranean, which Herod the Great built as his capital city and

---

[71] Theodore H. Robinson, *The Gospel of Matthew*, "The Moffatt New Testament Commentary", p. 138.

[72] The reply of Jesus in verses 2 and 3 is omitted in the two oldest Greek manuscripts (Vaticanus and Sinaiticus), as well as the Old Syriac version and Origen. It is placed in brackets in the Nestle text, but retained in RSV.

named in honor of Caesar Augustus. This one was built by Herod's son, Philip, and named for Tiberius Caesar.

It was located at the foot of Mount Hermon, which is snow-capped the year around (9,166 ft.). Near the city was the main source of the Jordan River, where it leaps forth from a cleft in the rock. Here had been carried on the worship of the Roman god Pan ("All"), so that the town had been called Paneas (modern Banias). It was about twenty-five miles north of Bethsaida Julias, which was on the northeastern shore of the Lake of Galilee. Here at the worship of the ancient All-god, Jesus called forth a confession of His messiahship.

He began by asking how people identified **the Son of man.** This was the name by which Jesus most frequently (over 80 times in the Gospels) referred to Himself. In reply the disciples mentioned John the Baptist, Elijah, and Jeremiah. Then came the crucial question: "But *you,* who do you say me to be?" (v. 15, literal translation). Peter, the spokesman for the apostles, rose fully to the occasion. With firm faith he declared: **Thou art the Christ** [the "Messiah"], **the Son of the living God** (v. 16). The first concept was primarily Jewish, the second Greek. Both combined to express correctly who Jesus was.

Peter was **blessed** because he had learned this truth not from men but by a direct revelation from God. One does not believe in the deity of Jesus by any theological argument or ecclesiastical dogma but only because of a divine revelation, an inner certification by the Spirit.

Verse 18 is a much controverted passage. It has been asserted that the church of Jesus Christ is built upon Peter as its foundation. However, Paul stated: "For other foundation can no man lay than that which is laid, which is Jesus Christ" (I Cor. 3:11).

The Greek for **Peter** is *petros,* which means "stone." The word for **rock** is *petra,* "a mass of live rock as distinct from *petros,* a detached stone or boulder."[73] It is often contended that Jesus spoke in Aramaic, where only one word, *Kepha,* could be used. But the possibility that Jesus may have spoken in Greek on this occasion cannot be ruled out entirely.

On the other side of the picture should be noted the words of Paul in Ephesians 2:20 — "Being built upon the foundation of the apostles and prophets, Christ Jesus himself being the chief corner stone." Bengel cites another passage also in support of Peter as the rock. He writes: "The Church of Christ is certainly (Rev. 21:14) built on the apostles, inasmuch as they were the first believers, and the rest have been added through their labours; in which matter a certain especial prerogative was conspicuous in the case of Peter, without damage to the equality of apostolic authority; for he first converted many Jews (Acts 2), he first admitted the Gentiles to the Gospel (Acts 10)."[74] But Bengel also goes on to say: "He does not say, *on this rock* I WILL FOUND; for Peter, nevertheless is not the foundation."[75]

Many Protestant scholars feel constrained to favor the interpretation of W. C. Allen: "Upon this rock of revealed truth I will build my Church . . . it shall be the central doctrine of the Church's teaching."[76]

The expression **the gates of Hades** is paralleled in Isaiah 38:10 — "the gates of Sheol." *Sheol* is the Hebrew equivalent of the Greek *Hades.* Both mean the place of death, or of departed spirits. They should not be rendered "hell" (KJV), which is the proper translation of *Gehenna* — place of torment or everlasting burning.

Gates is in the Scriptures a symbol of power. The power of Hades will not **prevail against,** or "win a victory over,"[77] the Church of Jesus Christ.

Verse 19 is also the despair of many interpreters. In what sense did Peter receive **the keys of the kingdom of heaven?** It seems best to explain this language in the light of the Book of Acts. At Pentecost Peter used the keys to unlock the door of the kingdom of heaven to Jews and proselytes, and three thousand entered that day. A little later he used the same keys to unlock the door of the kingdom to the Gentiles in the house of Cornelius, and thus began the mission

---

[73] Abbott-Smith, *op. cit.,* p. 359.
[74] John Albert Bengel, *Gnomon of the New Testament,* rev. and ed. A. R. Faussett, 5 vols., I, 323.
[75] *Ibid.,* p. 324.   [76] *Op. cit.,* p. 176.   [77] Arndt and Gingrich, *op. cit.,* p. 425.

to the nations. Robertson well remarks: "Every preacher uses the keys of the kingdom when he proclaims the terms of salvation in Christ."[78]

Jesus went on to say that whatever Peter would **bind** on earth would be bound in heaven and whatever he would **loose** on earth would be loosed in heaven. The background of these terms is well known: "In rabbinical language to **bind** and to **loose** is to declare certain actions forbidden or permitted."[79]

To say that this delegated to Peter the authority to settle the destinies of individuals is manifestly absurd. A little later Jesus made this same statement to all the apostles (18:18). But it was first given to Peter. Alford makes this application: "Of the *binding,* the case of Ananias and Sapphira may serve as an eminent example: of the *loosing* . . . the lame man at the beautiful gate of the Temple."[80] In a similar vein Wesley writes: "Under the terms of *binding* and *loosing* are contained all those acts of discipline which Peter and his brethren performed as apostles; and undoubtedly, what they thus performed on earth, God confirmed in heaven."[81]

The paragraph concludes with Jesus' command to His disciples to tell no one that He was the Christ; that is, the Messiah. The reason for this is obvious. In view of the popular conception of political messiah, to publicize Jesus' messiahship would have been to risk precipitating a revolution against Rome. This Christ sought to avoid.

d. Passion Foretold (16:21-28)

21 From that time began Jesus to show unto his disciples, that he must go unto Jerusalem, and suffer many things of the elders and chief priests and scribes, and be killed, and the third day be raised up. 22 And Peter took him, and began to rebuke him, saying, Be it far from thee, Lord: this shall never be unto thee. 23 But he turned, and said unto Peter, Get thee behind me, Satan: thou art a stumbling-block unto me: for thou mindest not the things of God, but the things of men. 24 Then said Jesus unto his disciples, If any man would come after me, let him deny himself, and take

up his cross, and follow me. 25 For whosoever would save his life shall lose it: and whosoever shall lose his life for my sake shall find it. 26 For what shall a man be profited, if he shall gain the whole world, and forfeit his life? or what shall a man give in exchange for his life? 27 For the Son of man shall come in the glory of his father with his angels; and then shall he render unto every man according to his deeds. 28 Verily I say unto you, There are some of them that stand here, who shall in no wise taste of death, till they see the Son of man coming in his kingdom.

It was altogether fitting that the first prediction of the passion should come immediately after Jesus' messiahship had been acknowledged. The confession at Caesarea Philippi was the central event in Christ's ministry. That is suggested by the language of verse 21. **From that time** Jesus began to show His disciples what was the real goal of His mission. The heart of His earthly ministry, as well as its climax, would be His death on the Cross. But that would be followed by His resurrection. The story of the passion was the central theme of Jesus' private ministry to His disciples, and this theme would be His major interest from now on.

The prediction here (v. 21) is remarkably specific. He was going up to Jerusalem, where He would **suffer many things** at the hands of the **elders and chief priests and scribes** — the three groups that comprised the Great Sanhedrin — would **be killed,** and on the third day be **raised up.** This prediction summarizes the Passion.

Peter in his excitement appears to have taken hold of Jesus. He began to **rebuke,** or "censure," his Master. **Be it far from thee** is *hileos soi,* "May God be merciful to Thee." He continued: "This shall by no means be to Thee" (literal translation).

Jesus **turned** — probably facing Peter — and said: **Get thee behind me, Satan** (v. 23). These are the same words that He spoke to the devil at the close of His temptation in the wilderness (4:10). Was Peter actually Satan? Certainly not. But Jesus saw in his words the same tempta-

[78] A. T. Robertson, *Word Pictures in the New Testament,* I, 135.
[79] Sherman Johnson, "The Gospel According to St. Matthew" (Exegesis), *The Interpreter's Bible,* ed. G. A. Buttrick, *et al.,* VII, 453.
[80] Henry Alford, *The Greek Testament,* rev. E. F. Harrison, I, 174.
[81] John Wesley, *Explanatory Notes upon the New Testament,* p. 82.

tion which the devil had presented to Him at the beginning of His career. It was the suggestion that He take the easy way, avoiding the path of suffering. Christ could not entertain these thoughts for a single moment. So He rebuked Peter — really Peter's words — in the sharpest manner.

The word **stumbling-block** is *skandalon* (scandal), which means the "bait-stick" or "trigger of a trap or snare," and also "the trap itself." Peter was unconsciously setting a snare for His Master's feet, and Christ refused to be trapped.

Verse 24 contains one of the most important sayings of Jesus (cf. 10:38; Mark 8:34; Luke 9:23; 14:27). The Master must face the Cross, and so must His disciples.

Three things Christ demanded of the one who would take His way. First, he must **deny himself.** The first step toward God involves self-denial, the renouncing of self. Everyone who enters the kingdom of God must come in through the Door of Humiliation. He must humble himself and confess his sins.

The second thing demanded is that he must **take up his cross.** This speaks of death to self, of being crucified with Christ (Rom. 6:6; Gal. 2:20), of full surrender of one's own will to the will of God. Dietrich Bonhoeffer, who was hanged at 39 years of age in a Nazi concentration camp (April 9, 1945), has written these cogent words: "Just as Christ is Christ only in virtue of his suffering and rejection, so the disciple is a disciple only in so far as he shares his Lord's suffering and rejection and crucifixion. Discipleship means adherence to the person of Jesus, and therefore submission to the law of Christ which is the law of the cross."[82]

It is striking that the first two verbs, **deny** and **take** up are in the aorist tense. They suggest the crises of conversion and consecration. But the third, **follow me,** is in the present tense (continuous action), suggesting a lifelong task of following Christ.

The saying in verse 25 is also given prominence in the Gospels (10:39; Mark 8:35; Luke 9:24; 17:33; John 12:25). To hold on to one's life for temporal advantage is to lose it eternally. On the other hand, to lose it in loving service

for God and others is to find it in a larger life both here and hereafter.

Verse 26 (cf. Mark 8:36-37) asks an unanswerable question: What does a man gain if he should get the whole world but **forfeit his life** ("lose his own soul," KJV)? The noun here is *psyche.* In the King James Version it is translated "life" in verse 25, but "soul" in verse 26. The Revised Versions more consistently translate it the same way in both verses. Actually *psyche* is about as ambiguous in Greek as "soul" is in English. We speak of a ship going down and so many "souls" being lost; that is, so many lives. In religious circles we use "soul," with quite a different connotation, to mean that in man which is immortal. It is of interest to note that in the King James Version *psyche* is translated "soul" 58 times, "life" 40 times, "mind" 3 times, and "heart" once. The exact meaning in any given passage must be determined by the context (cf. Acts 27:37). Here it seems to refer to "life" in its largest meaning, as related to both time and eternity.

The statement in verse 28 is often taken as a prediction of the Transfiguration, which immediately follows it in Mark (9:1) and Luke (9:27). But the possibility of some of the disciples dying within a week's time seems very remote. It seems best to refer **coming in his kingdom** to the coming of the spiritual kingdom at Pentecost and during the apostolic age.

e. Preview of Glory (17:1-8)

1 And after six days Jesus taketh with him Peter, and James, and John his brother, and bringeth them up into a high mountain apart: 2 and he was transfigured before them; and his face did shine as the sun, and his garments became white as the light. 3 And behold, there appeared unto them Moses and Elijah talking with him. 4 And Peter answered, and said unto Jesus, Lord, it is good for us to be here: if thou wilt, I will make here three tabernacles; one for thee, and one for Moses, and one for Elijah. 5 While he was yet speaking, behold, a bright cloud overshadowed them: and behold, a voice out of the cloud, saying, This is my beloved Son, in whom I am well pleased; hear ye him. 6 And when the disciples heard it, they

---

[82] Dietrich Bonhoeffer, *The Cost of Discipleship,* p. 77.

fell on their face, and were sore afraid. 7 And Jesus came and touched them and said, Arise, and be not afraid. 8 And lifting up their eyes, they saw no one, save Jesus only.

After six days — a week after the previous incident — Jesus took along with Him Peter, James, and John, and gave them the priceless privilege of viewing His transfiguration. On two other occasions He chose to have with Him the same inner circle of three disciples — at the raising of Jairus' daughter (Mark 5:37) and in the Garden of Gethsemane (26:37).

Jesus led them up privately to a **high mountain.** This has traditionally been identified as Mount Tabor, at the eastern end of the Plain of Esdraelon. But this is a rather low, rounding hill, only about one thousand feet high, and it apparently had a fortress on it at this time. So it does not seem to have been a fitting place for the Transfiguration. Therefore many scholars today think that this event took place on one of the spurs of lonely, lofty Mount Hermon, at the head of the Jordan Valley.

Jesus was **transfigured** before them (v. 2). The Greek word occurs only four times in the New Testament. It is used in the parallel passage in Mark 9:2. It also occurs in Romans 12:2, where it is rendered "transformed." Finally it is found in II Corinthians 3:18, where it is translated "changed." The verb is *metamorphoo,* from which comes "metamorphosis" — a change from one state to another. So it suggests a "spiritual metamorphosis," or "the transfigured life."

The transfiguration is described vividly: **his face did shine as the sun, and his garments became white as the light.** While Christ was in close fellowship with His Father, His divine nature radiated an incandescent glow, which penetrated through the veil of His flesh, and the three disciples caught a glimpse of His eternal glory. It was a high moment in their experience and one to which Peter referred at the close of his life (II Pet. 1:16-18).

Two heavenly visitants appeared — **Moses and Elijah** (v. 3). Peter was overwhelmed at finding himself in such august company and wanted to make the situation permanent. He offered to build three booths of boughs — **tabernacles** (v. 4) — one each for Jesus, Moses, and Elijah. One is reminded of the recurring phrase in some books on Oriental philosophy — "Confucius, the Buddha, and the Christ." But the eternal Son of God is not to be placed on the same level with mere men. **A bright cloud,** reminder of the Shekinah of the Old Testament, **overshadowed them** (v. 5), and a voice from above rebuked Peter's careless speech with these words: **This is my beloved Son . . . hear ye him** (not Peter). **Beloved** may also be translated "only" (cf. 3:17). Jesus is the Son of God in an utterly unique sense.

Peter's attitude is easily understood. People want to stay on the mount of vision, to enjoy the almost ecstatic state of glorious fellowship in the place of prayer. But at the foot of the mountain was a man in desperate need with a demonized son. And still today the multitudes wait at the foot of the mountain for the ministry of those who have glimpsed God's glory in the face of Jesus Christ.

When the experience was over, **they saw no one, save Jesus only** (v. 8). This was the permanent deposit, the real value of the vision. The test of any supposed ecstatic experience is whether it leaves one with inflated spiritual pride and fanatical dogmatism, or with a true humility based on a continuing consciousness of Christ's presence.

f. Prophet Identified (17:9-13)

9 And as they were coming down from the mountain, Jesus commanded them, saying, Tell the vision to no man, until the Son of man be risen from the dead. 10 And his disciples asked him, saying, Why then say the scribes that Elijah must first come? 11 And he answered and said, Elijah indeed cometh, and shall restore all things: 12 but I say unto you, that Elijah is come already, and they knew him not, but did unto him whatsoever they would. Even so shall the Son of man also suffer of them. 13 Then understood the disciples that he spake unto them of John the Baptist.

On the way down the mountain Jesus charged His three disciples not to tell anyone about the Transfiguration **until the Son of man be risen from the dead.** Only then could the vision be properly understood (Rom. 1:4).

The disciples had a perplexing question, acutely activated by the sight of the ancient prophet on the mount. Why did the scribes say that Elijah must precede the Messiah? If Jesus was the Messiah, why had not Elijah appeared prior to His ministry and not momentarily on the mountain?

In reply Jesus declared that Elijah would come and **restore all things** (v. 11); that is, initiate a new order which would finally result in the restoration of all things through Christ (Col. 1:16; Eph. 1:9-11). Indeed he had already come, but had been unrecognized and ill-treated (v. 12). Matthew adds the typical explanation that the disciples then understood that the reference was to John the Baptist (v. 13).

g. Powerless Disciples (17:14-21)

14 And when they were come to the multitude, there came to him a man, kneeling to him, and saying, 15 Lord, have mercy on my son: for he is epileptic, and suffereth grievously; for oft-times he falleth into the fire, and oft-times into the water. 16 And I brought him to thy disciples, and they could not cure him. 17 And Jesus answered and said, O faithless and perverse generation, how long shall I be with you? how long shall I bear with you? bring him hither to me. 18 And Jesus rebuked him; and the demon went out of him: and the boy was cured from that hour.

19 Then came the disciples to Jesus apart, and said, Why could not we cast it out? 20 And he saith unto them, Because of your little faith: for verily I say unto you, If ye have faith as a grain of mustard seed, ye shall say unto this mountain, Remove hence to yonder place; and it shall remove; and nothing shall be impossible unto you.

At the foot of the mountain they found the crowd still waiting for them. A distraught father at once knelt before Jesus and besought Him to heal his **epileptic** son. The Greek word literally means "moonstruck" (cf. KJV "lunatick," from Latin *luna,* the moon). It was commonly held in ancient times that insanity was due to the influence of the moon.

The description of the epileptic seizures (v. 15) is typical of this malady.

The father had brought his boy to the disciples, but found them powerless to help (v. 16). Jesus expressed His great disappointment at their failure (v. 17). He had previously commissioned and empowered them to cast out demons (10:8). But now they were ineffective. The Master Himself had to perform the cure (v. 18).

Naturally the disciples wondered why they had lost their power, and questioned Jesus (v. 19). In reply He said: **Because of your little faith** (v. 20). If they had pure faith, even as a tiny mustard seed (cf. 13:32), nothing would be **impossible** to them. The disciples had failed to realize that spiritual power comes only through a life of prayer.[83]

h. Passion Foretold Again (17:22-23)

22 And while they abode in Galilee, Jesus said unto them, The Son of man shall be delivered up into the hands of men; 23 and they shall kill him, and the third day he shall be raised up. And they were exceeding sorry.

This second prediction of the Passion mentions Christ's arrest (v. 22) and once more His death and resurrection (v. 23). This time the reaction of the disciples is noted. Their hearts were filled with sorrow.

i. Paying the Temple Tax (17:24-27)

24 And when they were come to Capernaum, they that received the half-shekel came to Peter, and said, Doth not your teacher pay the half-shekel? 25 He saith, Yea. And when he came into the house, Jesus spake first to him, saying, What thinkest thou, Simon? the kings of the earth, from whom do they receive toll or tribute? from their sons, or from strangers? 26 And when he said, From strangers, Jesus said unto him, Therefore the sons are free. 27 But, lest we cause them to stumble, go thou to the sea, and cast a hook, and take up the fish that first cometh up; and when thou hast opened his mouth, thou shalt find a shekel: that take, and give unto them for me and thee.

On Jesus' return to Capernaum, the collectors of the annual tax for the up-

---

[83] Verse 21 is omitted in the Revised Versions because it is absent in the earliest Greek manuscripts. In Mark 9:29 the statement about prayer is genuine, but the reference to fasting is not in the oldest manuscripts.

keep of the temple at Jerusalem approached Peter and asked: **Doth not your teacher pay the half-shekel?** The Greek word for this coin is *didrachma*. It was worth about thirty-two cents. This tax was to be paid by every male Jew over twenty years of age (Ex. 30:11-16). About a month before the Passover the temple tax was collected in the outlying territories.

Peter's answer, **yea** (v. 25), shows that Jesus was in the habit of doing His duty as a Jew. However, He asked Peter whether kings usually received **toll** (taxes on goods) or **tribute** (taxes on persons) — indirect and direct taxation — from sons or **strangers;** that is, those outside the royal family. When Peter indicated the latter, Jesus said: **Therefore the sons are free** (v. 26). He, as Son of God, should be exempt from this obligation.

Nevertheless, Jesus would pay the tax (v. 27). The lesson He apparently sought to teach in this incident was that Christians should go "the second mile" in doing what is expected of them, even though they may feel that they deserve exemption. Specifically, Christ's followers are to pay their taxes (cf. 22:21).

Peter was instructed to go to the **sea** (Lake of Galilee, on which Capernaum was located), cast a line, and catch a fish. In its mouth he would find a **shekel** (Greek, *stater*), which would pay the required half-shekel for both of them. Presumably the other disciples were to find some way of paying their taxes also.

This miracle has often been criticized as being preposterous. The fact that it is not stated that Peter actually caught a fish and found a coin in its mouth is sometimes cited as favoring the idea that Jesus was speaking figuratively: Catch a fish, sell it, and use the money to pay our tax. While this may not be impossible, the most natural interpretation is to take the account as describing what actually did take place. The important thing is the lesson Jesus was teaching.

2. Offences and Forgiveness (18:1-35)

a. Little Children (18:1-10)

1 In that hour came the disciples unto Jesus, saying, Who then is greatest in the kingdom of heaven? 2 And he called to him a little child, and set him in the midst of them, 3 and said, Verily I say unto you, Except ye turn, and become as little children, ye shall in no wise enter into the kingdom of heaven. 4 Whosoever therefore shall humble himself as this little child, the same is the greatest in the kingdom of heaven. 5 And whoso shall receive one such little child in my name receiveth me: 6 but whoso shall cause one of these little ones that believe on me to stumble, it is profitable for him that a great millstone should be hanged about his neck, and *that* he should be sunk in the depth of the sea. 7 Woe unto the world because of occasions of stumbling! for it must needs be that the occasions come; but woe to that man through whom the occasion cometh! 8 And if thy hand or thy foot causeth thee to stumble, cut it off, and cast it from thee: it is good for thee to enter into life maimed or halt, rather than having two hands or two feet to be cast into the eternal fire. 9 And if thine eye causeth thee to stumble, pluck it out, and cast it from thee: it is good for thee to enter into life with one eye, rather than having two eyes to be cast into the hell of fire. 10 See that ye despise not one of these little ones: for I say unto you, that in heaven their angels do always behold the face of my Father who is in heaven.

The question of the disciples (v. 1) betrays a carnal attitude of selfish ambition and self-seeking. In reply Jesus called a **little child** for an object lesson (v. 2). Pointing to it, He said that unless the disciples would **turn** (turn themselves about, or "change") and **become as little children** they could never enter the kingdom of heaven (v. 3). Then He gave a direct answer to their question: The one who would **humble himself as this little child** would be greatest in the kingdom of heaven (v. 4). Humility is the main mark of true greatness. An attitude of complete dependence on God, of trust in Him rather than oneself, is central to Christianity.

Jesus' love for children is shown in His statement that anyone who would **receive** (welcome) a little child was in reality welcoming Him (v. 5). On the other hand, if one should cause a young convert to **stumble** (Greek *skandalizo*) it would be better for him if **a great millstone** — literally "a millstone of a donkey"; that is, a large stone turned by a donkey, in contrast with the small millstones turned by women — were fastened to his neck and he were consigned to the sea (v. 6). This underscores the seriousness that Christ attached to wrongly influencing children or new Christians.

Jesus then warned against **occasions of stumbling** ("offences," KJV). The Greek word *skandalon,* as already noted (see on 16:23) is exceedingly difficult to translate. Lenski writes: "The figure is that of an animal caught by touching the bait affixed to the crooked stick in a dead-fall trap."[84] He also says that the terms *skandalon* and *skandalizo* "go beyond the idea of stumbling (from which one may rise) and always denote spiritual destruction."[85] In this passage Lenski translates the verb "entrap" and the noun "entrapment."

Jesus warned that such "entrapments" would come, but woe to the one through whom they came (v. 27). So serious is the matter that if one's hand or foot "entraps" him he had better cut it off and cast it away than lose his soul (v. 8). Even if his most precious physical organ, the eye, should become the occasion of tempting him to sin, he should **pluck it out** and throw it away (v. 9). Any alternative is better than being cast into **eternal fire** (v. 8) or **hell** (*Gehenna,* v. 9).

The application of these verses is clear. *Anything* that is a source of mortal temptation should be eliminated.

These little ones (v. 10) may refer to little children (vv. 3-5) or young converts (v. 6) — probably both. **Their angels** suggests the familiar figure of guardian angels watching over little children.

b. Lost Sheep (18:11-14)[86]

12 How think ye? if any man have a hundred sheep, and one of them be gone astray, doth he not leave the ninety and nine, and go unto the mountains, and seek that which goeth astray? 13 And if so be that he find it, verily I say unto you, he rejoiceth over it more than over the ninety and nine which have not gone astray. 14 Even so it is not the will of your Father who is in heaven, that one of these little ones should perish.

The Parable of the Lost Sheep (vv. 12-14) is also found in Luke 15:4-7, in a variant form. It is a beautiful picture of a shepherd's sacrificial, searching love for even one lost sheep. It could as well be called the Parable of the Seeking Shepherd.

The Oriental shepherd knew all his sheep and knew them by name. To lose one was almost like losing his own child. The picture of the shepherd going to the mountains, where the sheep had grazed during the day, to seek the lost one is a parable of Jesus' search for the lost sheep of the human race on the mountains of His earthly ministry — Temptation, Transfiguration, Gethsemane, Calvary.

God does not design or desire that any child should be lost (v. 14). Peter describes Him as "not wishing that any should perish, but that all should come to repentance" (II Pet. 3:9).

c. Local Church (18:15-20)

15 And if thy brother sin against thee, go, show him his fault between thee and him alone: if he hear thee, thou hast gained thy brother. 16 But if he hear *thee* not, take with thee one or two more, that at the mouth of two witnesses or three every word may be established. 17 And if he refuse to hear them, tell it unto the church, and if he refuse to hear the church also, let him be unto thee as the Gentile and the publican. 18 Verily I say unto you, What things soever ye shall bind on earth shall be bound in heaven; and what things soever ye shall loose on earth shall be loosed in heaven. 19 Again I say unto you, that if two of you shall agree on earth as touching anything that they shall ask, it shall be done for them of my Father who is in heaven. 20 For where two or three are gathered together in my name, there am I in the midst of them.

This section anticipates the time when there would be local congregations of believers. It gives essential teaching on how "offences" in the church should be taken care of.

The instructions are plain and precise. **If thy brother sin against thee**[87] [not you against him], **go, show him his fault between thee and him alone**. It almost goes without saying that if this

---

[84] *Op. cit.,* p. 686.   [85] *Ibid.*
[86] Verse 11 is omitted in the Revised Versions because it is absent in the earliest Greek manuscripts.
[87] The two oldest Greek manuscripts have simply: "If thy brother should sin."

first rule were obeyed the vast majority of "church fusses" would never come about. If the offender refuses to listen, the offended party should take one or two witnesses along for another private conference, so that they can verify what is actually said. If he refuses to listen to this "committee," then — but not before then — the matter should be taken to the church. If he will not pay any attention to the peaceful efforts of the congregation he is to be treated as an outsider — the Gentile and the publican (v. 17). He will be a sinner in need of salvation, having taken himself out of the fellowship of the believers. He will still be the object of the Christians' prayers and evangelistic efforts.

The word church occurs only three times in the Gospels,[88] all in Matthew (twice here in v. 17 and once in 16:18). In the earlier instance it refers to the general Church of Jesus Christ, which He declared He would build. Here it indicates a local congregation.

The Greek word is *ekklesia*, which literally means a congregation of "called out ones." It was used for an assembly of free, voting citizens in a Greek city-state. But the most significant background for its meaning in the New Testament is its use in the Septuagint (Greek translation of O.T.) for the "congregation" of Israel. The Septuagint was the Bible of the apostolic church. So here it refers to the congregation of God's people.

In verse 18 Jesus repeats what He had said to Peter (16:19), but applies it to the whole group of twelve apostles. They are at the moment the *ecclesia*, the nucleus of the church that was to be after Pentecost. So in their hands lies the primitive discipline, just discussed (v. 17). The binding and loosing evidently refer to discipline and judgment in the early church.

Verse 19 appears to be a projection of this thought. A compact between two earnest, sincere individuals praying in the will of God in a sense binds God to answer their request. This paradox is holy ground and requires a delicate balance of thought between divine sovereignty and human freedom. But the statement here is clear and emphatic.

The paragraph closes with a beautiful promise that where **two or three** are congregated in Christ's name, He will be present (v. 20). This can be true only because He is infinite and omnipresent.

d. Law of Forgiveness (18:21-35)

21 Then came Peter and said to him, Lord, how oft shall my brother sin against me, and I forgive him? until seven times? 22 Jesus saith unto him, I say not unto thee, Until seven times; but, Until seventy times seven. 23 Therefore is the kingdom of heaven likened unto a certain king, who would make a reckoning with his servants. 24 And when he had begun to reckon, one was brought unto him, that owed him ten thousand talents. 25 But forasmuch as he had not *wherewith* to pay, his lord commanded him to be sold, and his wife, and children, and all that he had, and payment to be made. 26 The servant therefore fell down, and worshipped him, saying, Lord, have patience with me, and I will pay thee all. 27 And the lord of that servant, being moved with compassion, released him, and forgave him the debt. 28 But that servant went out, and found one of his fellow-servants, who owed him a hundred shillings: and he laid hold on him, and took *him* by the throat, saying, Pay what thou owest. 29 So his fellow-servant fell down and besought him, saying, Have patience with me, and I will pay thee. 30 And he would not: but went and cast him into prison, till he should pay that which was due. 31 So when his fellow-servants saw what was done, they were exceeding sorry, and came and told unto their lord all that was done. 32 Then his lord called him unto him, and saith to him, Thou wicked servant, I forgave thee all that debt, because thou besoughtest me: 33 shouldest not thou also have had mercy on thy fellow-servant, even as I had mercy on thee? 34 And his lord was wroth, and delivered him to the tormentors, till he should pay all that was due. 35 So shall also my heavenly Father do unto you, if ye forgive not everyone his brother from your hearts.

The implication of verse 15 is that one should forgive an offending brother, if he repents. Peter wanted to know how often he had to forgive such a person: **Until seven times?** Jesus' an-

---

[88] Twenty-one times in Acts, 62 times in Paul's Epistles, twice in Hebrews, 4 times in the General Epistles, and 20 times in Revelation.

swer was astounding: **Until seventy times seven** (v. 22). The Greek word is used in the Septuagint at Genesis 4:24 for "seventy-seven" ("seventy *and* seven" rather than "seventy *times* seven"). But it seems best to follow the English versions here. What Jesus was saying was that one should forgive an *infinite* number of times. He who counts the times knows nothing of the true spirit of forgiveness.

To illustrate this law of forgiveness Jesus told the striking Parable of the Unmerciful Servant (vv. 23-35, only in Matt.). He purposely used hyperbole to make the truth startling so that it would stick. He told of a servant who owed his king **ten thousand talents.** Since a talent was worth about a thousand dollars, this debt would amount to ten million dollars — a preposterous sum and one that the slave could never repay. The king commanded the servant to be sold, with his family and possessions, and the debt paid. When the slave begged for mercy, the king forgave him and canceled the debt.

That servant found a fellow servant who owed him **a hundred shillings** (v. 28). The Greek *denarius* was worth about twenty cents. So this would be twenty dollars — a mere trifle in comparison with the ten million. Yet when this fellow servant begged for patience, the wicked, cruel servant (cf. v. 28b) threw him into prison till he should pay the debt. The sequel (vv. 31-34) is only what would be expected.

The lesson of this parable is too obvious to call for much comment. Every believer has been forgiven a mammoth debt of sin which he could never repay. Yet some professing Christians refuse to forgive a fellow Christian for some petty, imagined wrong — a passing remark or an impatient word, sometimes even something said in fun. Grudges are harbored for years. It should be said once and for all than an unforgiving spirit is utterly unchristian.

Jesus Himeslf applied the parable. He said that a similar fate — eternal punishment — would be meted out to all who did not forgive their brothers **from your hearts** (v. 35). There is no place here for the oft-expressed attitude of forgiving but not forgetting. One does not really forgive until he also forgets.

3. Divorce and Discipleship (19:1-30)
a. Divorce (19:1-12)

1 And it came to pass when Jesus had finished these words, he departed from Galilee, and came into the borders of Judaea beyond the Jordan; 2 and great multitudes followed him; and he healed them there.

3 And there came unto him Pharisees, trying him, and saying, Is it lawful *for a man* to put away his wife for every cause? 4 And he answered and said, Have ye not read, that he who made *them* from the beginning made them male and female, 5 and said, For this cause shall a man leave his father and mother, and shall cleave to his wife; and the two shall become one flesh? 6 So that they are no more two, but one flesh. What therefore God hath joined together, let not man put asunder. 7 They say unto him, Why then did Moses command to give a bill of divorcement, and to put *her* away? 8 He saith unto them, Moses for your hardness of heart suffered you to put away your wives: but from the beginning it hath not been so. 9 And I say unto you, Whosoever shall put away his wife, except for fornication, and shall marry another, committeth adultery: and he that marrieth her when she is put away committeth adultery. 10 The disciples say unto him, If the case of the man is so with his wife, it is not expedient to marry. 11 But he said unto them, Not all men can receive this saying, but they to whom it is given. 12 For there are eunuchs, that were so born from their mother's womb: and there are eunuchs, that were made eunuchs by men: and there are eunuchs, that made themselves eunuchs for the kingdom of heaven's sake. He that is able to receive it, let him receive it.

Jesus **departed from Galilee,** probably for the last time, and began His final journey to Jerusalem. But first He came into the borders of **Judaea beyond the Jordan.** This area was known as Perea, on the east side of the Jordan River. Pilgrims from Galilee preferred to come down the east side of the Jordan, to avoid going through "unclean" and unfriendly Samaria. Here in Perea Jesus carried on a healing ministry (v. 2).

Once more the Pharisees came to test Him. This time the subject was divorce — already discussed by Christ in the Sermon on the Mount (5:31-32). They asked if it was lawful for a man to divorce his wife **for every cause** (v. 3).

Jesus began His answer by calling attention to the original plan of God in creation — one man and one woman. He quoted Genesis 2:24. A man should **leave** his parents and **cleave** to his wife (v. 5). These are strong verbs in the Greek. Literally they mean "leave behind" and "be glued to." One of the causes of domestic difficulty is that some husbands — and wives — do not really *leave* their parents. One is tempted to pray: "God give us more glue in the modern marriage."

The last clause of verse 5 and the first sentence of verse 6 indicate that there is to be a physical, as well as spiritual, union. That is what makes marriage sacred, something different from any other contract or association in life. It is for this reason that true marriage is unbreakable.

The Pharisees enquired why it was, then, that Moses commanded to give a divorce certificate and put one's wife away (v. 7; cf. Deut. 24:1-4). Jesus answered that this was a concession to the hardness of their hearts, but not God's first plan and purpose.

It should be recognized that Moses was not hereby encouraging divorce. The opposite was the case: he was putting restrictions on it to prevent easy divorce. The Moslem today needs only to say to his wife three times, "I divorce thee," and it is legally done. Moses insisted that a man must seek out a scribe and have legal papers drawn up. This would tend to discourage divorce.

The Pharisees had asked: **for any cause?** Jesus said: "No, only for **fornication**" (v. 9). To get a divorce for any other reason and then remarry is to commit **adultery.** He who marries a person not Scripturally divorced also is guilty of adultery.

The question of the Pharisees (v. 3) reflects the contemporary dispute between the two schools of Hillel and Shammai. It revolved around the interpretation of a clause in Deuteronomy 24:1 — "if she find no favor in his eyes." Shammai held that this referred to uncleanness or fornication. Hillel was much more liberal. He would allow a man to divorce his wife if she did anything he disliked; for instance, if she burned his food

when cooking it. Jesus revolted against all such chicanery. He placed Himself squarely on the side of Shammai in this debate.

The disciples remarked that if matters were going to be as strict as this it was better not to marry (v. 10). They still showed themselves to be children of their times and badly in need of the Spirit of Christ.

Jesus picked up their callous, crude remark and lifted the idea to a higher level. For some, celibacy was the better way, but only for those who could **receive** this state properly (v. 11). He then went on (v. 12) to indicate three classes of **eunuchs** (the word comes directly from the Greek). First there were those born with a defect. The second group was composed of those **made eunuchs** by men. Originally a eunuch was "keeper of the bed-chamber in any Oriental harem . . . , a jealous office, which could be entrusted only to such as were . . . emasculated."[89] In the third place, some had made themselves eunuchs for the sake of the kingdom. They were eunuchs ethically rather than physically. Only some were able to **receive it;** that is, adopt the celibate life for higher purposes of undistracted service (cf. I Cor. 7:32-25).

b. Displaced Persons (19:13-15)

13 Then were there brought unto him little children, that he should lay his hands on them, and pray: and the disciples rebuked them. 14 But Jesus said, Suffer the little children, and forbid them not, to come unto me: for to such belongeth the kingdom of heaven. 15 And he laid his hands on them, and departed thence.

The relation of this to what precedes may not at once be apparent. But children of divorced parents are among the most pathetic D.P.'s of any generation. Whether or not Matthew so intended it, the beautiful picture of Jesus blessing the little children is certainly appropriate at this point. The disciples **rebuked** the parents who brought their infants. Jesus in turn rebuked the disciples for their callousness. **Suffer** (v. 14) should be "let" or "permit." **To such belongeth the kingdom of heaven** and "of such is the kingdom of heaven" (KJV) are equally

89 EGT, I, 247.

accurate translations of the Greek, though the latter is more literal. Actually the Kingdom both belongs to and is composed of such ones. Often the Greek is ambiguous and allows for more than one interpretation.

c. Discipleship (19:16-26)

16 And behold, one came to him and said, Teacher, what good thing shall I do, that I may have eternal life? 17 And he said unto him, Why askest thou me concerning that which is good? One there is who is good: but if thou wouldest enter into life, keep the commandments. 18 He saith unto him, Which? And Jesus said, Thou shalt not kill, Thou shalt not commit adultery, Thou shalt not steal, Thou shalt not bear false witness, 19 Honor thy father and thy mother; and, Thou shalt love thy neighbor as thyself. 20 The young man saith unto him, All these things have I observed: what lack I yet? 21 Jesus said unto him, If thou wouldest be perfect, go sell that which thou hast, and give to the poor, and thou shalt have treasure in heaven: and come follow me. 22 But when the young man heard the saying, he went away sorrowful; for he was one that had great possessions.

23 And Jesus said unto his disciples, Verily I say unto you, It is hard for a rich man to enter into the kingdom of heaven. 24 And again I say unto you, It is easier for a camel to go through a needle's eye, than for a rich man to enter into the kingdom of God. 25 And when the disciples heard it, they were astonished exceedingly, saying, Who then can be saved? 26 And Jesus looking upon *them* said to them, With men this is impossible; but with God all things are possible.

The story of the Rich Young Ruler is found also in Mark (10:17-30) and Luke (18:18-30). Matthew indicates that he was **young** (v. 20) and had **great possessions** (v. 22). **Luke** calls him a "ruler" and says he was "very rich" (Luke 18:18, 23). Hence the title.

The young man came with a question: **Teacher, what good thing shall I do, that I may have eternal life?** Mark and Luke have the "good" before "teacher" (cf. KJV here) and give Jesus' reply as, "Why callest thou me good?" The oldest Greek manuscripts support the Revised rendering here in Matthew. Why did the ruler ask **concerning that which**

is good? Only God is good in the absolute sense.

The wording in Matthew is more difficult to interpret than that in Mark and and Luke. But one must begin with the young man's question. He thought he could obtain eternal life by *doing* some **good thing**. This was the way of legalism. Perhaps he thought that Jesus had discovered some spiritual secret that he had missed.

Jesus' reply amounts to this: "Why do you ask me about the good? You need to turn to God and to His Word. There you will find the answer, the way of God's will for men." The answer to the man's question had already been revealed in the Scriptures.

When Jesus mentioned keeping the **commandments** (v. 17), the ruler asked, **Which?** (v. 18). In reply Christ enumerated the sixth, seventh, eighth, ninth, and fifth of the Ten Commandments, adding the great commandment, **Thou shalt love thy neighbor as thyself** (v. 19). This one summed up the last six Commandments, which relate to man's duties to his fellow men. It was probably assumed that this man had kept the first four (duties to God), though his subsequent action showed that he had broken the first. He really had another god before Jehovah. It was Mammon.

The reply of the young man is striking. After asserting that he had kept all these commandments, he asked: **what lack I yet?** (v. 20). This showed some nobility and certainly great earnestness.

Jesus met the challenge with a crucial demand. If the ruler wanted to be **perfect** — *teleios*: complete, having reached the goal (*telos*) — he must sell all his possessions and give the proceeds to the poor, thus laying up treasures in heaven. Then, and then only, he would be ready to follow Jesus.

The young man failed the test. His love of money proved to be the strongest force in his life. He went away **sorrowful** (v. 22); or, as the Greek says, "sorrowing." Disobedience always depresses.

By his disobedience the man showed his disbelief in Jesus. Dietrich Bonhoeffer has well said: "Only he who believes is obedient, and only he who is obedient believes"; and again, "For faith is only real when there is obedience, never without it, and faith only becomes faith in the act of obedience."[90]

Jesus then made what were to His disciples two very startling statements: **It is hard for a rich man to enter the kingdom of heaven** (v. 23) and **It is easier for a camel to go through a needle's eye, than for a rich man to enter into the kingdom of God** (v. 24). Some have tried to reduce the **camel** to a "rope" (similar root in Aramaic), while others have tried to increase the **needle's eye** to a small postern gate in the wall of Jerusalem. Both efforts are ill-advised, and rejected by reputable scholars. This is a striking hyperbole and Jesus intended it as such. It was similar to His speaking of swallowing a camel (23:24).

The disciples were **astonished exceedingly** (v. 25). The Jews looked upon material prosperity as a sign of divine favor. What could Jesus mean? The Master, **looking upon them** with tender compassion and concern, explained that while this (salvation of the rich) was impossible with men, yet **with God all things are possible** (v. 26).

d. Dedication (19:27-30)

27 Then answered Peter and said unto him, Lo, we have left all, and followed thee; what then shall we have? 28 And Jesus said unto them, Verily I say unto you, that ye who have followed me, in the regeneration when the Son of man shall sit on the throne of his glory, ye also shall sit upon twelve thrones, judging the twelve tribes of Israel. 29 And every one that hath left houses, or brethren, or sisters, or father, or mother, or children, or lands, for my name's sake, shall receive a hundredfold, and shall inherit eternal life. 30 But many shall be last *that are* first; and first *that are* last.

Peter had been thinking of the rich young ruler who refused to part with his possessions. Now the spokesman of the disciples volunteered the reminder that he and his fellow disciples had **left all** to follow Christ. What were they going to get out of it? (v. 27). It was a mercenary question, but Jesus gave a kind reply. First, they would be richly rewarded in the next life (v. 28). **Regeneration** means the "renewal" of all things at the end of this age. When that came,

His disciples who had shared the privations of His earthly ministry would likewise share in the glories of His kingdom. How literally the **twelve thrones** and **twelve tribes** are to be taken is a matter for each person to settle in his own mind. Probably the language is figurative.

In the second place, Jesus asserted that there was a reward even in this life. Those who had left property and loved ones would receive a **hundredfold** here, plus **eternal life** (v. 29). Franzmann correctly oberves: "The homeless and landless shall find home and land enough in the generous fellowship of the church — an indication that Jesus makes no blanket rule of poverty for all disciples."[91]

The last statement of the chapter is found again in 20:16, as well as Mark 10:31 and Luke 13:30. Evidently it was uttered more than once by Jesus. It may have two applications here. The rich young ruler seemed **first,** but he turned out to be **last,** while the opposite was true of the disciples. But Jesus' statement may also have been a rebuke to Peter's self-complacency and a call for humility.

4. Service and Self-seeking (20:1-34)

a. Parable of Laborers in the Vineyard (20:1-16)

1 For the kingdom of heaven is like unto a man that was a householder, who went out early in the morning to hire laborers into his vineyard. 2 And when he had agreed with the laborers for a shilling a day, he sent them into his vineyard. 3 And he went out about the third hour, and saw others standing in the market-place idle; 4 and to them he said, Go ye also into the vineyard, and whatsoever is right I will give you. And they went their way. 5 Again he went out about the sixth and the ninth hour, and did likewise. 6 And about the eleventh *hour* he went out, and found others standing; and he saith unto them, Why stand ye here all the day idle? 7 They say unto him, Because no man hath hired us. He saith unto them, Go ye also into the vineyard. 8 And when even was come, the lord of the vineyard saith unto his steward, Call the laborers, and pay them their hire beginning with the last unto the first. 9 And when

---

[90] *Op. cit.,* p. 54.
[91] Martin H. Franzmann, *Follow Me: Discipleship According to Saint Matthew,* p. 176.

they came that *were hired* about the eleventh hour, they received every man a shilling. 10 And when the first came, they supposed that they would receive more; and they likewise received every man a shilling. 11 And when they received it, they murmured against the householder, 12 saying, These last have spent *but* one hour, and thou hast made them equal unto us, who have borne the burden of the day and the scorching heat. 13 But he answered and said to one of them, Friend, I do thee no wrong: didst not thou agree with me for a shilling? 14 Take up that which is thine, and go thy way; it is my will to give unto this last, even as unto thee. 15 Is it not lawful for me to do what I will with mine own? or is thine eye evil, because I am good? 16 So the last shall be first, and the first last.

This parable, found only in Matthew, was apparently given in further answer to Peter's question, "What are we going to get out of this?" (19:27). Specifically, it was an expansion of the proverb with which the previous chapter closes. Those who came last were the first to receive their wages. It is significant that this saying (19:30; 20:16) immediately precedes and follows the parable, which, coming between, explains and illustrates its meaning. As a wise preacher, Jesus illustrated His text and then repeated it at the close.

Trench has well expressed the purpose of the parable. He writes: "The question itself, 'What shall we have?' was not a right one; it put their relation to their Lord on a wrong footing; there was a tendency in it to bring their obedience to a calculation of so much work, so much reward. There lurked, too, a certain self-complacency in this speech. That spirit of self-exalting comparison of ourselves with others. . . ."[92]

The word for **householder** is a combination of *oikos*, house, and *despotes*, master. So it means literally "the master of a house." This man went out **early in the morning**, probably about sunrise, to hire workers for his vineyard. He agreed with them on a daily wage of a **shilling** — Greek *denarius*, worth about twenty cents. About **the third hour** (9:00 A.M.) he found others standing idle in the **marketplace** (Agora), and hired them.

At the **sixth** (noon) and the **ninth hour** (3:00 P.M.) he did likewise. Finally he went out about the **eleventh hour** (5:00 P.M.) and found more men standing in the Agora. When asked why they were not working, they gave the simple answer that no one had hired them. So the house-master put them to work also.

At the end of the day the owner instructed his **steward** (v. 8) — *epitropos*, administrator — to pay the men their wages, **beginning from the last unto the first** (cf. 19:30; 20:16). Those hired at the eleventh hour each received a denarius. When those who had worked all day were given the same wage, they complained (v. 12). But the owner justified his action as being fair to all (vv. 13-15). The point is that those who had worked only one hour needed the denarius to supply food for their families just as much as those who had labored all day. The implication is that they would have worked the full day had they had the opportunity. As Buttrick points out, "Divine judgment . . . is according not alone to the measure of work done but also *according to the measure of opportunity.*"[93]

One error that must be avoided in interpreting this parable is the idea that the equality of wages suggests eternal life. Salvation is not *earned*. It is received alone by faith in Jesus Christ. This parable deals only with the matter of rewards and suggests that the amount will depend more on motive than activity.

b. Passion Foretold Once Again (20: 17-19)

17 And as Jesus was going up to Jerusalem, he took the twelve disciples apart, and on the way he said unto them, 18 Behold, we go up to Jerusalem; and the Son of man shall be delivered unto the chief priests and scribes; and they shall condemn him to death, 19 and shall deliver him unto the Gentiles to mock, and to scourge, and to crucify: and the third day he shall be raised up.

For the third time Jesus predicted His coming Passion (cf. 16:21; 17:22-23). It was on their way up to Jerusalem for the last passover of His ministry. He took the twelve aside and talked to them privately. The nearer the end, the more

---

[92] *Op. cit.*, p. 138.   [93] George A. Buttrick, *op. cit.*, p. 164.

important became His instruction to the disciples.

This prediction is more full and specific than the two previous ones. First He will be **delivered** (KJV, "betrayed"; cf. 10:4) to the Sanhedrin, which would **condemn him to death.** Then He would be turned over to the Gentiles. They would **mock, scourge,** and **crucify** Him. On the third day He would rise. The important new item here is the indication that His death would be by Roman crucifixion, not Jewish stoning.

c. Place-seeking Disciples (20:20-28)

20 Then came to him the mother of the sons of Zebedee with her sons, worshipping *him,* and asking a certain thing of him. 21 And he said unto her, What wouldest thou? She saith unto him, Command that these my two sons may sit, one on thy right hand, and one on thy left hand, in thy kingdom. 22 But Jesus answered and said, Ye know not what ye ask. Are ye able to drink the cup that I am about to drink? They say unto him, We are able. 23 He saith unto them, My cup indeed ye shall drink: but to sit on my right hand, and on *my* left hand, is not mine to give; but *it is for them* for whom it hath been prepared of my Father. 24 And when the ten heard it, they were moved with indignation concerning the two brethren. 25 But Jesus called them unto him, and said, Ye know that the rulers of the Gentiles lord it over them, and their great ones exercise authority over them. 26 Not so shall it be among you: but whosoever would become great among you shall be your minister; 27 and whosoever would be first among you shall be your servant; 28 even as the Son of man came not to be ministered unto, but to minister, and to give his life a ransom for many.

Mark (10:35) tells of James and John, rather than their mother, making the request. But there is no contradiction here. Matthew says she came **with her sons.** The request was the desire of all three — perhaps initiated by the mother, ambitious for her sons — and presented jointly to Jesus.

The request was that James and John might have the seats of highest honor on either side of Christ in His kingdom. It is evidence that the recent confession

of Him as Messiah (16:13-20) had whetted their anticipation that He was about to set up His earthly kingdom at Jerusalem. They wanted to get in their bids for first place promptly.

Jesus must have been deeply grieved by this spirit of self-seeking. He was thinking of a cross, they of crowns. His mind was filled with sacrifice, theirs with selfishness. Their request was especially inappropriate at this time, coming right after the prediction of His Passion.

But the Master dealt patiently with His men. He asked if they were able to drink His **cup** — symbol of sorrow and suffering (cf. Psa. 75:8). They replied, **We are able.** Jesus indicated that they would, in a measure, share His sufferings, but that He did not have authority to assign them seats (v. 23).

When the other ten apostles heard about this, they were **moved with indignation.** The sad thing is that possibly some of them regretted they had not thought to ask first. More probably they covered themselves with a cloak of smug self-complacency because they had not stooped to ask for themselves. In any event the whole incident reflects badly on the spiritual condition of all.

The Master called the whole group together and took advantage of the occasion to give a much needed lesson in humility. Rulers of the Gentile nations **lord it over them** (v. 25), but Christ's disciples were to be different. Whoever would be great must be their **minister** (*diakonos,* "servant"). Whoever would be first must be **servant** (*doulos,* "slave"). Christ was their example. He came **not to be ministered unto, but to minister** —better, "not to be served, but to serve" (*diakoneo*).

The use of **ransom** here (v. 28) is exceedingly significant. The Greek word is *lytron,* from *lyo,* "loose." So the essential idea is that of a release; then, that by which the release is obtained. Deissmann shows that *lytron* was used for the redemption money paid for freeing slaves.[94] The word occurs only here and in the parallel passage in Mark (10:45).

The preposition **for** is *anti.* It carried at the time the idea of substitution. In their *Vocabulary of the Greek Testament*

---

[94] Adolf Deissmann, *Light from the Ancient East,* pp. 327-28.

Illustrated from the Papyri and Other Non-literary Sources J. H. Moulton and George Milligan say: "By far the commonest meaning of *anti* is the simple 'instead of.' "[95] This strongly supports the doctrine of Christ's substitutionary atonement for the sins of **many**.

d. Pleading Rewarded (20:29-34)

29 And as they went out from Jericho, a great multitude followed him. 30 And behold, two blind men sitting by the way side, when they heard that Jesus was passing by, cried out, saying, Lord, have mercy on us, thou son of David. 31 And the multitude rebuked them, that they should hold their peace: but they cried out the more, saying, Lord, have mercy on us, thou son of David. 32 And Jesus stood still, and called them, and said, What will ye that I should do unto you? 33 They say unto him, Lord, that our eyes may be opened. 34 And Jesus, being moved with compassion, touched their eyes; and straightway they received their sight, and followed him.

Jericho was located near the Jordan River, some fifteen miles from Jerusalem. It was the last city through which Jesus would pass.

Matthew mentions **two blind men**; Mark (10:46) and Luke (18:35) only one. Mark names the more vocal and probably better known one, Bartimaeus. It is very possible that Bartimaeus was an active Christian when Mark wrote, and had often told this incident, whereas the other man had dropped out of sight. But Matthew, the bookkeeper, was mathematically inclined. He noted carefully that there were two blind men who were healed. The same characteristic appears in 8:28 and 9:27.

The blind men called: **Lord, have mercy on us, thou son of David.** This is almost exactly the same as the cry of the Syro-Phoenician woman (15:22). They were appealing to the Messiah to help them.

When the multitude with Jesus tried to quiet the two men, they cried the louder (v. 31). The Master heard their cry and called them to Him. When asked what they wanted, they requested that their eyes be opened. Jesus, **moved with compassion** — the aorist tense is better translated "*gripped* with compassion" —

touched their eyes, as He usually did with those who could not see Him, to help their faith. When they **straightway** received their sight, they **followed him** — became His disciples.

L. HIS LAST WEEK (21:1—25:26)

1. Presenting Himself to the Nation (21:1-27)

a. Coming into Jerusalem (21:1-11)

1 And when they drew nigh unto Jerusalem, and came unto Bethphage, unto the mount of Olives, then Jesus sent two disciples, 2 saying unto them, Go into the village that is over against you, and straightway ye shall find an ass tied, and a colt with her: loose *them,* and bring *them* unto me. 3 And if any one say aught unto you, ye shall say, The Lord hath need of them; and straightway he will send them. 4 Now this is come to pass, that it might be fulfilled which was spoken through the prophet, saying,
5 Tell ye the daughter of Zion,
Behold, thy King cometh unto thee,
Meek, and riding upon an ass,
And upon a colt the foal of an ass.
6 And the disciples went, and did even as Jesus appointed them, 7 and brought the ass, and colt, and put on them their garments; and he sat thereon. 8 And the most part of the multitude spread their garments in the way; and others cut branches from the trees, and spread them in the way. 9 And the multitudes that went before him, and that followed, cried, saying, Hosanna to the son of David. Blessed is he that cometh in the name of the Lord; Hosanna in the highest. 10 And when he was come into Jerusalem, all the city was stirred, saying, Who is this? 11 And the multitudes said, This is the prophet, Jesus, from Nazareth of Galilee.

The so-called Triumphal Entry, occurring on Sunday of Passion Week, is recorded in all four Gospels, though somewhat more briefly in John's Gospel. The importance of it cannot be missed. Jesus was presenting Himself to the nation as its Messiah. The Jews were given their last opportunity to accept Him. Instead they rejected Him and condemned Him to die.

In the interval between the last verse of the previous chapter and the first verse of this one, Jesus and His disciples, accompanied by a large group of Galilean

[95] P. 46.

pilgrims on their way to the Passover, had walked up the steep, winding road from Jericho to Jerusalem. John's Gospel intimates that they reached Bethany, two miles east of Jerusalem, on Friday afternoon (John 12:1). Here they rested over the Sabbath (sunset Friday to sunset Saturday). On Sunday Jesus went on into Jerusalem.

When they reached the village of **Bethphage** (pronounced beth-fa-jee, "house of figs"), on the slopes of the **mount of Olives,** Jesus commissioned two of His disciples to secure a colt on which He might ride into the city. If anyone should ask why they were untying the donkey and its colt, they were to answer, **The Lord hath need of them,** and permission would be granted. Matthew explains that all this was to be in fulfillment of the prophecy of Zechariah 9:9 (quoted also by John). The implication is clear: Jesus was presenting Himself officially as the Messiah, fulfilling the Messianic role described by Zechariah. Not with lordly pomp, like a Roman conqueror on a charger, but **meek** and lowly, riding on a donkey. He was coming as the Prince of Peace (Isa. 9:6). But Jerusalem later rejected Him as such, and soon horrible war and destruction overtook it.

The disciples brought **the ass, and the colt** (v. 7). The other Gospels mention only the colt. Matthew shows here again his fondness for doubles, or pairs — a feature occurring throughout the Gospel. He also says they put their **garments** on **them** and that Jesus sat "on them" (literal Greek). Some have gone so far as to claim that Matthew pictures Jesus as riding two animals at once. The most plausible interpretation is to take the last "them" as referring to the garments placed on the colt.[96]

Jesus was given a royal welcome by the crowds. They even spread their outer **garments** on the road as a "red carpet" for the king to ride on. Others, less zealous, **cut branches** from trees along the way and spread them on the path (v. 8). Some ran on ahead of Him, and some followed behind, but all cried **Hosanna** (literally "Save, we pray," but perhaps here like "God save the King!") **to the son of David** (i.e., the Messiah).

This and the words that follow are quoted from Psalm 118:25-26. Mark gives them a strong messianic connotation by adding a reference to "the kingdom" (Mark 11:10). Luke also identifies **he that cometh** (a messianic term) as "the King" (Luke 19:38). This was indeed a triumphal procession, at least in its beginnings.

Only Matthew relates that when Jesus reached Jerusalem, **all the city was stirred** (v.10). People cried, **Who is this?** This all-important question was answered by a simple statement of fact, with no interpretation: **This is the prophet, Jesus, from Nazareth of Galilee** (v. 11). Evidently people were afraid to say, "This is the Messiah."

The crowds that gave Jesus such an enthusiastic reception on Palm Sunday were composed mainly of Galilean pilgrims on their way to the Passover. They had earlier wanted to proclaim Him as king (John 6:15). Now they were virtually doing this. But the religious leaders at Jerusalem scornfully rejected Him. By so doing, they sealed the doom of the city.

b. Cleansing the Temple (21:12-17)

12 And Jesus entered into the temple of God, and cast out all them that sold and bought in the temple, and overthrew the tables of the money-changers, and the seats of them that sold the doves; 13 and he saith unto them, It is written, My house shall be called a house of prayer: but ye make it a den of robbers. 14 And the blind and the lame came to him in the temple; and he healed them. 15 But when the chief priests and the scribes saw the wonderful things that he did, and the children that were crying in the temple and saying, Hosanna to the son of David; they were moved with indignation, 16 and said unto him, Hearest thou what these are saying? And Jesus saith unto them, Yea: did ye never read, Out of the mouth of babes and sucklings thou hast perfected praise? 17 And he left them, and went forth out of the city to Bethany, and lodged there.

Mark indicates that Jesus surveyed the temple on Sunday afternoon and then returned to Bethany for the night. It was on Monday that He cleansed the temple (Mark 11:11, 12, 15). In keep-

---

[96] See Kenneth S. Wuest, *The New Testament: An Expanded Translation, in loco.*

ing with his usual custom, Matthew "telescopes" the Triumphal Entry and the Cleansing of the Temple into one narrative, as if they happened the same day. Since this habit of his is clear, there should be no difficulty about it.

The Cleansing of the Temple, a second messianic act, is described in all four Gospels, though John places it at the beginning of Jesus' ministry (John 2:13-17). It could be that John put it at that point for dramatic effect, or there could have been two cleansings. The possibility of the latter should not be dismissed too lightly. Conditions in the temple could certainly have reverted to the same sad state within three years' time.

Jesus drove out those who were buying and selling in the **temple** — the Greek word is *hieron*, "temple area," not the building — and turned over the **tables of the money-changers** and the **seats** of those selling **doves**. This market was located in the spacious Court of the Gentiles, on the eastern edge of the temple area (about 25 acres). The reason for it was obvious. Jews were required to offer for sacrifice animals that were "without blemish" (Ex. 12:5; 29:1, plus 16 times in Lev. and seven in Num.). One could never be positive that the officiating priest would approve his sheep or ox, *unless* it was bought in the temple market — which was run by the family of the high priest.[97] **Doves** were used for some offerings, especially by the poor people (Lev. 12:8).

The **money-changers** were there because the temple tax (cf. 17:24) had to be paid each year with the Phoenician silver half-shekel (worth about one-third of a dollar). But the people in daily transactions used the Roman *denarius* or Greek *drachma*, each worth about twenty cents. It is claimed that the priests collected about fifteen per cent for making the exchange — a very lucrative business.

As Jesus cleared the temple area of its dirty, noisy, smelly market, He quoted Isaiah 56:7 and Jeremiah 7:11. God's house was intended to be a house of prayer. But they had made it a **den of robbers** (v. 13). The word for den literally means "cave" or "cavern." In that day robbers in Palestine commonly lived

in caves. There is a technical difference between **robbers** and "thieves" (KJV), in English as well as Greek. A robber is one who takes by force. A first century rabbi charged that the servants of the high priest beat the people with sticks.

The **chief priests and scribes** — Sadducees and Pharisees — were disturbed to hear the children crying **Hosanna** in the temple (v. 15). When they complained to Jesus, He replied by quoting Psalms 8:2. Leaving these disgruntled religious leaders, who were jealous of His popularity, He went out to **Bethany** to spend the night (v. 17).

c. Cursing the Fig Tree (21:18-22)

18 Now in the morning as he returned to the city, he hungered. 19 And seeing a fig tree by the way side, he came to it, and found nothing thereon, but leaves only; and he saith unto it, Let there be no fruit from thee henceforward for ever. And immediately the fig tree withered away. 20 And when the disciples saw it, they marvelled, saying, How did the fig tree immediately wither away? 21 And Jesus answered and said unto them, Verily I say unto you, If ye have faith, and doubt not, ye shall not only do what is done to the fig tree, but even if ye shall say unto this mountain, Be thou taken up and cast into the sea, it shall be done. 22 And all things, whatsoever ye shall ask in prayer, believing, ye shall receive.

This incident is recorded by both Matthew and Mark — though, as already noted, the latter places the Cleansing of the Temple after it. Instead of this event Luke includes, at an earlier point (13:6-9), the Parable of the Fig Tree. They teach much the same lesson but should not be confused.

It was Monday morning. Jesus was returning from the suburb, Bethany, into the city. Being hungry, He stopped to eat some figs from a tree beside the road. But when He came to it, He found only leaves. He pronounced a curse on it, and **immediately** it **withered away** (v. 19) — whereas Mark (11:20) indicates that it was on Tuesday morning that the disciples noted the withering. This is another example of Matthew's custom of "telescoping" a series of in-

97 Alfred Edersheim, *Life and Times of Jesus the Messiah*, I, 369-373.

cidents into one story, without punctilious regard for the passage of time. Probably **immediately** should be interpreted as "very quickly," which would harmonize with Mark's statement that the effect was visible the next day.

Jesus used this incident to teach a lesson on faith (v. 21). Whatever one asks **in prayer, believing,** he will receive (v. 22).

But this parabolic act also carried a warning to the Jewish nation. It had the **leaves** of a profession of piety, but no fruit of genuine righteousness. For this reason it was to be cursed and would soon **wither away.** This could be applied to Israel's loss of position as the special "people of God" or to the destruction of Jerusalem in A.D. 70. In either case, the prophesied event happened very quickly.

d. Challenged by Chief Priests (21: 23-27)

23 And when he was come into the temple, the chief priests and the elders of the people came unto him as he was teaching, and said, By what authority doest thou these things? and who gave thee this authority? 24 And Jesus answered and said unto them, I also will ask you one question, which if ye tell me, I likewise will tell you by what authority I do these things. 25 The baptism of John, whence was it? from heaven or from men? And they reasoned with themselves, saying, if we shall say, From heaven; he will say unto us, Why then did ye not believe him? 26 But if we shall say, From men; we fear the multitude; for all hold John as a prophet. 27 And they answered Jesus, and said, We know not. He also said unto them, Neither tell I you by what authority I do these things.

When he reached the city and arrived in the temple — which was just inside the east wall, near the gate where He entered — He was confronted by the **chief priests and the elders of the people** (members of the Sanhedrin).

This chapter (cf. v. 15) is the first place in the Synoptic Gospels where we find the Sadducees in opposition to Jesus. Heretofore it had been the scribes and Pharisees. The reason for the change is that, by His cleansing of the temple, Jesus

had threatened both the authority and income of the chief priests. Naturally, they were infuriated. From this time forward it was they who led the attack on Jesus and finally compassed His death (cf. 27:1, 12; Mark 14:55; 15:10). It is for this reason that E. F. Scott calls the Cleansing of the Temple *the* crisis of Jesus' life which precipitated His death.[98]

The question of the chief priests was a definite challenge: **By what authority doest thou these things?** — that is, cleansing the temple and performing miracles (**wonderful things,** v. 15). **What** is literally "what kind." Tied in with the following question, it seems to indicate the question: "Are you doing these things by divine or human authority?" Of course it may mean simply: "What temple official gave you permission to carry on here?"

Jesus countered by asking a very pertinent question: Was John's baptism of divine or of human origin? (v. 25). The chief priests dared not say **From heaven** or Jesus would ask why they did not believe John. On the other hand, if they said **From men** they would get in trouble with the people. So they answered, **We know not** (v. 27), which was a deliberate and dishonest evasion. The reasoning of these religious leaders, concerned only with expediency and not with ethics, is a sad commentary on the Judaism of Jesus' day.

Christ's refusal to answer their question, since they would not answer His, was perfectly fair. The whole point was that the correct answer to both questions was the same.

2. Preaching in Parables (21:28-22:14)

a. The Two Sons (21:28-32)

28 But what think ye? A man had two sons; and he came to the first, and said, Son, go work today in the vineyard. 29 And he answered and said, I will not: but afterward he repented himself, and went. 30 And he came to the second, and said likewise. And he answered and said, I go, sir: and went not. 31 Which of the two did the will of his father? They say, The first. Jesus saith unto them, Verily I say unto you, that the publicans and the harlots go into the kingdom of God before you. 32 For

---

[98] *The Crisis in the Life of Jesus: The Cleansing of the Temple and Its Significance, passim.*

John came unto you in the way of righteousness, and ye believed him not; but the publicans and the harlots believed him: and ye, when ye saw it, did not even repent yourselves afterward, that ye might believe him.

This parable is found only in Matthew. A man had two **sons** (literally, children). When he asked the first to work in his vineyard, he refused, but later **repented** (felt regret) and went to work. The other promised to go, but failed to do so. Which one carried out the will of his father? The leaders answered correctly, **The first** (v. 31).

Jesus then made the application. **The publicans and the harlots,** who at first rebelled, would go into the Kingdom before the chief priests. This indicates that Jesus placed the latter outside the Kingdom, not only because they refused to repent at the preaching of John the Baptist (v. 32), but also because they continued in their impenitence.

b. The Wicked Husbandmen (21:33-46)

33 Hear another parable: There was a man that was a householder, who planted a vineyard, and set a hedge about it, and digged a winepress in it, and built a tower, and let it out to husbandmen, and went into another country. 34 And when the season of the fruits drew near, he sent his servants to the husbandmen, to receive his fruits. 35 And the husbandmen took his servants, and beat one, and killed another, and stoned another. 36 Again, he sent other servants more than the first: and they did unto them in like manner. 37 But afterward he sent unto them his son, saying, They will reverence my son. 38 But the husbandmen, when they saw the son, said among themselves, This is the heir; come, let us kill him, and take his inheritance. 39 And they took him, and cast him forth out of the vineyard, and killed him. 40 When therefore the lord of the vineyard shall come, what will he do unto those husbandmen? 41 They say unto him, He will miserably destroy those miserable men, and will let out the vineyard unto other husbandmen, who shall render him the fruits in their seasons. 42 Jesus saith unto them, Did ye never read in the scriptures,
The stone which the builders rejected,
The same was made the head of the corner;
This was from the Lord,

And it is marvellous in our eyes? 43 Therefore say I unto you, The kingdom of God shall be taken away from you, and shall be given to a nation bringing forth fruits thereof. 44 And he that falleth on this stone shall be broken to pieces: but on whomsoever it shall fall, it will scatter him as dust. 45 And when the chief priests and the Pharisees heard his parables, they perceived that he spake of them. 46 And when they sought to lay hold on him, they feared the multitudes, because they took him for a prophet.

This is the third and last parable (cf. 13:3-9, 31-32) which is found in all three Synoptic Gospels (adopting Trench's list of 30). It is closely associated with the one immediately preceding it.

A **householder** (*oikodespotes*) planted a vineyard, built a **hedge** (probably of stone) around it, dug a **winepress** (lined with stone or mortar), and built a **tower** — a wooden booth covered with branches and serving as a watch tower. Rabbinical rules required that this should be fifteen feet high and six feet square. He leased it to husbandmen ("vinedressers") and went abroad.

As the **season of the fruits** approached (v. 34) — September to December, on the fifth year after planting (Lev. 19:23-25) — the owner sent servants to get his share of the crop. The tenants mistreated these slaves, beating one, killing another, and stoning a third (v. 35). He sent more slaves and they were treated in similar fashion (v. 36). Finally he sent his son. But the tenants conspired against him and killed him (vv. 38-39). The inevitable result was that the vinedressers would themselves be destroyed, and the vineyard leased to others (v. 41).

Jesus then quoted Psalm 118:22-23. **Rejected** means "cast aside after careful examination." **Head of the corner** signifies either the cornerstone of a building or the keystone of an arch.

Christ concluded with a definite, twofold application. In line with His parable, He declared that **the kingdom of God** would be taken away from the Jewish leaders and given to another nation that would return the fruits of righteousness. Thus He announced the founding of the Gentile church. Applying the quotation from the Psalms, He said that whoever fell on this **stone**

(Christ Himself) would be broken (cf. Isa. 8:14-15), and whoever it fell upon would be ground to dust (cf. Dan. 2:34, 44-45). These are strong warnings of the judgment that awaits those who reject Jesus Christ.

It is not surprising that when the chief priests and Pharisees heard these two parables **they perceived that he spake of them** (v. 45). The point was altogether obvious. But instead of repenting, they sought to arrest Jesus. Only fear of the crowds, who held Him a prophet of God, kept them from carrying out their desires.

c. The Marriage Feast (22:1-14)

1 And Jesus answered and spake again in parables unto them, saying, 2 The kingdom of heaven is likened unto a certain king, who made a marriage feast for his son, 3 and sent forth his servants to call them that were bidden to the marriage feast: and they would not come. 4 Again he sent forth other servants, saying, Tell them that are bidden, Behold, I have made ready my dinner; my oxen and my fatlings are killed, and all things are ready: come to the marriage feast. 5 But they made light of it, and went their ways, one to his own farm, another to his merchandise; 6 and the rest laid hold on his servants, and treated them shamefully, and killed them. 7 But the king was wroth; and he sent his armies, and destroyed those murderers, and burned their city. 8 Then saith he to his servants, The wedding is ready, but they that were bidden were not worthy. 9 Go ye therefore unto the partings of the highways, and as many as ye shall find, bid to the marriage feast. 10 And those servants went out into the highways, and gathered together all as many as they found, both bad and good: and the wedding was filled with guests: 11 But when the king came in to behold the guests, he saw there a man who had not on a wedding-garment: 12 and he saith unto him, Friend, how camest thou in hither not having a wedding-garment? And he was speechless. 13 Then the king said to the servants, Bind him hand and foot, and cast him out into the outer darkness; there shall be the weeping and the gnashing of teeth. 14 For many are called, but few chosen.

The Parable of the Marriage Feast is found only in Matthew, though it is similar in many respects to the Parable of the Great Supper, found only in Luke (14:16-24). But the differences stand out. Here it is a **king** who makes a **marriage feast for his son;** there it is a "man" who made "a great supper." Here the invited guests not only refuse to come (v. 3) but they make light of the invitation (v. 5) and finally they mistreat and kill the servants. There they make excuses. In this parable the king sends his armies and destroys the murderers. In the other parable the man is angry and declares that none of the invited guests shall eat his supper. The closest similarity lies in the urgent instructions to the servants to go out into the highways and bring in everybody they can get.

The lesson is clear. The Jews were the invited guests. Because they refused to come to the messianic banquet, the Gentiles and despised sinners would be welcomed into the kingdom of God. This parable, like the previous two, is one of warning of judgment.

Matthew adds one interesting item: the man without the wedding garment (vv. 11-13). The point of this seems to be a warning against assuming that all Gentiles and sinners will be saved. Only those who have on the garments of Christ's righteousness may partake of the marriage supper of the Lamb (Rev. 19: 9).

The saying with which this paragraph closes fits the parable very appropriately, but the theological implication conveyed thereby should not be missed. The ones who were not **chosen** suffered loss not because they were not **called** but because they did not choose to accept the call.

3. Probed by Enemies (22:15-45)

a. Tribute to Caesar (22:15-22)

15 Then went the Pharisees, and took counsel how they might ensnare him in *his* talk. 16 And they send to him their disciples, with the Herodians, saying, Teacher, we know that thou art true and teachest the way of God in truth and carest not for any one: for thou regardest not the person of men. 17 Tell us therefore, What thinkest thou? Is it lawful to give tribute unto Caesar, or not? 18 But Jesus perceived their wickedness, and said, Why make ye trial of me ye hypocrites? 19 Show me the tribute money. And they brought unto him a denarius. 20 And he saith unto them

Whose is the image and superscription?
21 They say unto him, Caesar's. Then
saith he unto them, Render therefore
unto Caesar the things that are Caesar's;
and unto God the things that are God's.
22 And when they heard it, they marvelled, and left him, and went away.

This incident is recorded in all three
Synoptic Gospels. The **Pharisees** wanted
to **ensnare** — a rare hunting term, used
only here in the New Testament and
nowhere in classical Greek — Jesus **in
his talk**. This is literally "in a word" or
"in a statement." Arndt and Gingrich
render the clause: "in order that they
might entrap him with something that he
said."[99] In other words, they hoped to
trick Jesus into saying something that
would get Him into trouble.

To this end they took along some
Herodians. Josephus does not mention
this group, but the name indicates that
they were supporters of the Roman regime in Palestine. Since the Pharisees
were ardent nationalists, they naturally
hated the Herodians. But in common
opposition to Jesus, the Pharisees were
willing to associate with their political
enemies just as they had earlier united
with their religious rivals, the Sadducees,
in seeking to trap Jesus (21:45-46).

The combined group approached Christ
with fawning flattery. The language of
verse 16 was intended to throw Him off
His guard and get Him to make some
strong statement carelessly. Deferentially
they asked for His opinion (v. 17), then
sprang their trap: Was it **lawful** (permitted, proper) **to give tribute** (pay taxes)
to Caesar — the Roman emperor. Schürer
indicates that in provinces people had to
pay both poll taxes and property taxes.[100]

The questioners assumed that they had
Jesus trapped. Whichever way He answered He would be caught on one of
the two horns of a dilemma. If He said,
"No," the Herodians would immediately
report Him to the Romans as one who
was guilty of sedition against the government. (Now it becomes evident why the
Pharisees wanted Herodians along.) If
He said, "Yes," the Pharisees would cry
to the people: "See, he is not loyal to

our nation." There was no escape for
Jesus — so they thought.

But after reproving them for their
hypocritical wickedness (v. 18), Christ
made one simple request: **Show me the
tribute money** — "the coin for paying
the tax."[101] They brought Him a **denarius**, the most common coin in Palestine in
that day. Turning it over in His hand
He asked: **Whose is this image and
superscription?**[102] When they answered,
Caesar's, Jesus made one of the most
important statements He ever uttered
(v. 21). **Render** is literally "give back."
They asked if they should **give** taxes to
Caesar (v. 17). Jesus virtually said: "No,
you cannot *give* Caesar what already belongs to him, but you must *pay* your
taxes." This principle is repeated by Paul
(Rom. 13:6).

Then Christ added a most significant
second command: **and unto God the
things that are God's**. One cannot *give*
his tithe; he *pays* his tithe, for it belongs
to God. The human soul also bears the
imprint of God's image — though marred
by the Fall — and so should be given back
to its Maker. In the ultimate sense, all
belongs to God — health and strength,
time and talents.

b. Ties in the Resurrection (22:23-33)

23 On that day there came to him
Sadducees, they that say that there is
no resurrection: and they asked him, 24
saying, Teacher, Moses said, If a man
die, having no children, his brother shall
marry his wife, and raise up seed unto
his brother. 25 Now there were with
us seven brethren: and the first married
and deceased, and having no seed left
his wife unto his brother; 26 in like
maner the second also, and the third, unto the seventh. 27 And after them all,
the woman died. 28 In the resurrection therefore whose wife shall she
be of the seven? For they all had her.
29 But Jesus answered and said unto
them, Ye do err, not knowing the scriptures, nor the power of God. 30 For in
the resurrection they neither marry, nor
are given in marriage, but are as angels in
heaven. 31 But as touching the resurrection of the dead, have ye not read that

[99] *Op. cit.*, p. 607.
[100] Emil Schürer, *A History of the Jewish People in the Time of Jesus Christ*, I, I, 109.
[101] Arndt and Gingrich, *op. cit.*, p. 543.
[102] Exact reproductions of both sides of this denarius, bearing the picture of the reigning Emperor Tiberius (A.D. 14-37), may be seen in most large Bible dictionaries.

which was spoken unto you by God, saying, 32 I am the God of Abraham, and the God of Isaac, and the God of Jacob? God is not *the God* of the dead, but of the living. 33 And when the multitudes heard it, they were astonished at his teaching.

The very same day the **Sadducees** came with their question. Their main contention with the Pharisees was about the **resurrection.** They used an argument with which they may have many times discomfited their opponents. It was the highly hypothetical case of a woman who lost her husband and was left childless. According to the law of levirate marriage (Deut. 25:5), the deceased husband's brother should marry the widow. The first child of this union would carry the first husband's name, so that the line would not end.

The Sadducees posed the theoretically possible but practically impossible situation of a woman outliving seven husbands, all of whom died childless. In the resurrection whose wife would she be? (v. 27).

In reply Jesus charged the Sadducees with erring because they did not know the Scriptures nor the power of God (v. 29). This is the root difficulty of all who err in doctrine. He went on to say that there is no marriage in the next life. Then He used the Scripture (Ex. 3:6) to support belief in the resurrection (vv. 31-32).

c. Two Greatest Commandments (22: 34-40)

34 But the Pharisees, when they heard that he had put the Sadducees to silence, gathered themselves together. 35 And one of them, a lawyer, asked him a question, trying him: 36 Teacher, which is the great commandment in the law? 37 And he said unto him, Thou shalt love the Lord thy God with all thy heart, and with all thy soul, and with all thy mind. 38 This is the great and first commandment. 39 And a second like *unto it* is this, Thou shalt love thy neighbor as thyself. 40 On these two commandments the whole law hangeth, and the prophets.

The **Pharisees** had been worsted once. But when they heard that Jesus had silenced the Sadducees, they decided to try again. One of their number, a **lawyer**

— teacher of the Mosaic law, not lawyer in the modern sense — came, asking: "What kind of commandment is greatest in the Law?" (literal translation). This was a matter of constant dispute among the rabbis.

For an answer Jesus referred the lawyer to a sweeping command in Deuteronomy 6:5. One must love the Lord with all his **heart** and **soul** and **mind** (v. 37); that is, with his whole being. Christ labeled this **the great and first commandment** (v. 38). Then, for good measure (cf. 5:41), He added a second: **Thou shalt love thy neighbor as thyself** (v. 39). These two summarize the **law** and the **prophets;** that is, the Old Testament. The first defines one's basic duty to God (first four of the Ten Commandments). The second summarizes one's duties to his fellow men (the remaining six). It was as if He had said: "Here are the two tablets of the Law. All else is commentary."

One might note that all three questioners address Jesus as **Teacher** (vv. 16, 24, 36). This is the correct term, rather than "Master," with which the King James Version translates seven different Greek words in the New Testament.

d. Turning the Tables (22:41-46)

41 Now while the Pharisees were gathered together, Jesus asked them a question, 42 saying, What think ye of the Christ? whose son is he? They say unto him, *The son* of David. 43 He saith unto them, How then doth David in the Spirit call him Lord, saying,
44 The Lord said unto my Lord,
   Sit thou on my right hand,
   Till I put thine enemies underneath thy feet?
45 If David then calleth him Lord, how is he his son? 46 And no one was able to answer him a word, neither durst any man from that day forth ask him any more questions.

While Jesus had the Pharisees before Him, He propounded a question to them. He first asked whose son the Messiah was. They reflected the common belief of the day in their answer: **The son of David** (v. 42). This messianic concept was based on such Scriptures as Isaiah 9:2-7; 11:1-9; Jeremiah 23:5-6; 33:14-18; Ezekiel 34:23-24; 37:24; Psalm 89:20-37.

Now came the real question: **How then doth David in the Spirit call him Lord?** To support this Jesus quoted the first verse of Psalm 110 — the outstanding messianic Psalm, quoted five other times in the New Testament (Acts 2:34; Heb. 1:13; 5:6; 7:17, 21). **The Lord said unto my Lord** is "Jehovah (or Yahweh) said to my Adonai." In the King James Version of the Old Testament LORD usually translates the Hebrew *Yahweh* and Lord the Hebrew *Adonai*. But in the Greek one word, *kyrios*, has to do for both.

The phrase **in the Spirit** (v. 43) is of great significance. It attributes divine inspiration to David in writing this Psalm. These are not simply the words of a man, but of a man inspired by the Holy Spirit. This is one of several passages in the New Testament which assert the inspiration of the Old.

The question of verse 45 found no answer in the minds of these Jewish teachers of the Scripture because of their rigid, monolithic monotheism — similar to that of Moslems today. It still is the greatest single stumbling-block in the way of Jews accepting Christ as a divine Savior.

But for Christians the answer is clear. The solution lies in the fact of the Incarnation. The eternal Son of God, David's Lord, became David's son at Bethlehem.

Jesus had silenced all His opponents, answering their three questions to the astonishment of the crowds (vv. 22, 23), and then asked them a question they could not answer. From that day the questioning ceased (v. 46). The Pharisees and Sadducees were not ready to risk another public debate.

4. Pronouncing Woes on Pharisees (23:1-39)

a. Sitting on Moses' Seat (23:1-12)

1 Then spake Jesus to the multitudes and to his disciples, 2 saying, The scribes and the Pharisees sit on Moses' seat: 3 all things therefore whatsoever they bid you, *these* do and observe: but do not ye after their works; for they say, and do not. 4 Yea, they bind heavy burdens and grievous to be borne, and lay them on men's shoulders; but they themselves will not move them with their finger.

5 But all their works they do to be seen of men: for they make broad their phylacteries, and enlarge the borders *of their garments*, 6 and love the chief place at feasts, and the chief seats in the synagogues, 7 and the salutations in the market-places, and to be called of men, Rabbi. 8 But be not ye called Rabbi: for one is your teacher, and all ye are brethren. 9 And call no man your father on the earth: for one is your Father, *even* he who is in heaven. 10 Neither be ye called masters: for one is your master, *even* the Christ. 11 But he that is greatest among you shall be your servant. 12 And whosoever shall exalt himself shall be humbled; and whosoever shall humble himself shall be exalted.

Seat is *kathedra*. The phrase *ex cathedra* means literally "from the seat"; that is, by official authority. Jesus said that **the scribes and the Pharisees** spoke *ex cathedra*, because they sat on Moses' seat; that is, they were the authorized teachers of the Law. Therefore **all things** that they enjoined were to be observed (v. 3). Taken in an absolute sense, this seems to conflict with Christ's earlier strictures of the Pharisees for substituting their own "tradition of the elders" for the Word of God (15:1-6). Evidently the thought here is: "Do all things that they teach, in so far as this is in harmony with the spirit of the Mosaic law."[103] **For they say, and do not** does not mean that the Pharisees neglected to practice their religion. Actually they were over-scrupulous in their observance of its many requirements, but they missed the central things in the Law, such as justice, mercy, and faith (v. 23).

The **heavy burdens** (v. 4) were the minute, multitudinous rules and regulations with which the scribes had saddled the religion of Israel. There were so many detailed items that the common people could not observe them all. Religion, instead of being a joy and inspiration, had become an unbearable burden. Yet the scribes refused to lighten this load (v. 4b) by simplifying the system.

Jesus made a serious charge against the Pharisees: their practice of religion was in order **to be seen of men** (v. 5). They made broad their **phylacteries**. These were tiny boxes made from the skin of

103 Allen, *op. cit.*, p. 244.

ceremonially clean animals and worn on the forehead and left arm. The head phylactery had four compartments, each with a passage from the Old Testament (Ex. 13:1-10; 11-16; Deut. 6:4-9; 11:13-21). The arm phylactery contained all four passages in one compartment. The custom of wearing these arose from a very literal interpretation of Deuteronomy 6:8; 11:18. The Pharisees often made these phylacteries **broad** to prove their great piety. For them religion was something external, to be put on parade. They also enlarged the **borders** of their outer garments; that is, wore long tassels on the corners of their robes. These were supposed to be the mark of a pious Jew.

The Pharisees also sought the chief places at feasts and in the synagogues. They failed to realize that love of prominence is one of the surest denials of genuine piety. They loved to be called **Rabbi.** Jesus warned His disciples against such a haughty attitude (vv. 8-10). These instructions should be taken as warning against a spirit of ostentation and pride, rather than specific rules about the use of technical titles.

The principle that Jesus sought to enforce is declared in verse 11 (cf. 20:26). Humility and service are the true marks of piety. Verse 12 expresses the life principle that "the way up is down."

b. Seven Woes (23:13-36)

(1) Closing the Kingdom (23:13)

13 But woe unto you, scribes and Pharisees, hypocrites! because ye shut the kingdom of heaven against men: for ye enter not in yourselves, neither suffer ye them that are entering in to enter.

Jesus pronounced seven woes on the Pharisees. The King James Version has eight, but verse 14 is omitted in the earliest Greek manuscripts.

Woe unto you may be translated "Alas for you!" (cf. 11:21). The note of judgment here is better expressed by the former. On the other hand, the latter reflects more clearly the compassion of Christ. Perhaps both expressions should be retained.

Six of the woes (exception, v. 16) are addressed specifically to **scribes and Pharisees, hypocrites.** The first accuses them of closing the Kingdom **against men.** The Greek says "before men"; that is, in their

faces as they seek to enter. By their legalistic interpretation of the Old Testament, the scribes closed the door of faith in the faces of those they taught.

(2) Compassing the Earth (23:15)

15 Woe unto you, scribes and Pharisees, hypocrites! for ye compass sea and land to make one proselyte; and when he is become so, ye make him twofold more a son of hell than yourselves.

A **proselyte** (literally, "one who has come over") was a convert from paganism to Judaism. The proselyting zeal of the Jews at this time is amply corroborated by Philo and other writers. They compassed **sea and land** — we would say, "land and sea" — in the effort to make **one proselyte.** This suggests the difficulty of getting Gentiles to be circumcised and observe all the many requirements of the Jewish law, even though numbers of them were ready to turn from idolatry and polytheism to the worship of the true God.

(3) Confusing the Sacred (23:16-22)

16 Woe unto you, ye blind guides, that say, Whosoever shall swear by the temple, it is nothing; but whosoever shall swear by the gold of the temple, he is a debtor. 17 Ye fools and blind: for which is greater, the gold, or the temple that hath sanctified the gold? 18 And, Whosoever shall swear by the altar, it is nothing; but whosoever shall swear by the gift that is upon it, he is a debtor. 19 Ye blind: for which is greater, the gift, or the altar that sanctifieth the gift? 20 He therefore that sweareth by the altar, sweareth by it, and by all things thereon. 21 And he that sweareth by the temple, sweareth by it, and by him that dwelleth therein. 22 And he that sweareth by the heaven, sweareth by the throne of God, and by him that sitteth thereon.

The pathetic casuistry of scribes is illustrated by this passage. If one swore by the **temple** — naos, "sanctuary," not hieron, "temple area" (21:12) — one's oath was not valid, but if by the gold on the sanctuary, it was binding. To refute this, Jesus asked the obvious question concerning which was greater, the gold or the sanctuary that **sanctifieth** (makes sacred) the gold. Again, one who swore by the **altar** — the "brazen" altar on which animal sacrifices were offered — was not bound, while one who swore by the gift on it was. But it is the altar that **sanctifieth the gift.** Oaths by the **altar** (v. 20), the **temple** (v. 21), or **heaven** (v. 22) were all binding.

(4) Confounding Values (23:23-24)

23 Woe unto you, scribes and Pharisees, hypocrites! for you tithe mint and anise and cummin, and have left undone the weightier matters of the law, justice, and mercy, and faith: but these ye ought to have done, and not to have left the other undone. 24 Ye blind guides, that strain out the gnat, and swallow the camel!

The Pharisees were very scrupulous in paying their tithes. They even counted the seeds, and took out one in ten. They tithed **mint** — literally, sweet-smelling — and **anise** — possibly dill, or another plant with seeds similar to caraway seeds — and **cummin** — the seeds of which were used as spice for bread and meat, and also for medicinal purposes. These were three common garden herbs, all used in cooking. But the scribes neglected the **weightier** (more important, or possibly "harder" to fulfill) **matters of the law, justice, and mercy, and faith** (or fidelity). **These** (the latter) they should have practiced and not **left the other** (the former) unpracticed.

Strain out the gnat (v. 24) is the correct translation. The verb means "filter out," especially out of wine. The picture is that of a strict Pharisee straining his drinking water through a cloth — to make sure he did not swallow the smallest "unclean animal," the gnat — and meanwhile gulping down a whole camel. Obviously Jesus had a sense of humor and intended this as a ridiculous hyperbole for dramatic effect. Every hearer could see the vivid picture and remember it.

"Strain at" (KJV) is definitely misleading for the reader today. The first English version, Wycliffe's, had "clensenge" (cleansing). Tyndale, the first to translate from the original Greek, "strayne out." The King James Version is the *only* English translation that has "strain at" — which suggests a man trying

to catch a gnat. Goodspeed maintains that this is a "sheer misprint," which should have been corrected long ago, as hundreds of other misprints in the 1611 edition were corrected.[104] It may possibly be that the King James translators were following a usage that had gained some currency,[105] but if so, they were certainly unwise in their choice.

(5) Cleansing the Outside (23:25-26)

25 Woe unto you, scribes and Pharisees, hypocrites! for ye cleanse the outside of the cup and of the platter, but within they are full from extortion and excess. 26 Thou blind Pharisee, cleanse first the inside of the cup and of the platter, that the outside thereof may become clean also.

This paragraph sums up the essential difference between the Judaism of that day and the religion of Jesus. The former gave primary importance to the **outside** (v. 25), the latter to the **inside** (v. 26). The former was concerned with ceremonial cleansings, the latter with a clean heart.

"Full of" (KJV) is correctly translated **full from** (v. 25). The preposition suggests that the contents of the dishes were obtained by **extortion** — the Greek word means "plundering," or "robbery" — and **excess,** or "lack of self-control." In other words, the cups and plates of the hypocrites were filled with the fruits of dishonesty and self-indulgence. To **cleanse** the **inside** means to get rid of unrighteous practices. Jesus' admonition reduces to this: Religion is righteousness, not ritual (cf. Amos and Micah).

(6) Corrupting the Inside (23:27-28)

27 Woe unto you, scribes and Pharisees, hypocrites! for ye are like unto whited sepulchres, which outwardly appear beautiful, but inwardly are full of dead men's bones, and of all uncleanness. 28 Even so ye also outwardly appear righteous unto men, but inwardly ye are full of hypocrisy and iniquity.

A month before the Passover, all the tombs were supposed to be whitewashed, so that no one would accidentally come

---

[104] Edgar J. Goodspeed, *Problems of New Testament Translation*, pp. 38-39.
[105] *Oxford English Dictionary*, X, 1067.

in contact with one, and thus be rendered ceremonially unclean and barred from eating the Passover (Num. 19:16). Since this was the Passover season, Jesus compared the scribes to the freshly whitewashed graves (**whited sepulchres**) — good appearance outwardly, but full of corruption inwardly. Their besetting sins were **hypocrisy and iniquity** (v. 28). The latter is literally "lawlessness." This term is particularly striking in view of the fact that these very Pharisees claimed that they, and they alone, really kept the Law. But they were the actual lawbreakers (cf. v. 23).

(7) Continuing the Persecution (23:29-36)

29 Woe unto you, scribes and Pharisees, hypocrites! for ye build the sepulchres of the prophets, and garnish the tombs of the righteous, 30 and say, If we had been in the days of our fathers, we should not have been partakers with them in the blood of the prophets. 31 Wherefore ye witness to yourselves, that ye are sons of them that slew the prophets. 32 Fill ye up then the measure of your fathers. 33 Ye serpents, ye offspring of vipers, how shall ye escape the judgment of hell? 34 Therefore, behold, I send unto you prophets, and wise men, and scribes: some of them shall ye kill and crucify; and some of them shall ye scourge in your synagogues, and persecute from city to city: 35 that upon you may come all the righteous blood shed on the earth, from the blood of Abel the righteous unto the blood of Zachariah son of Barachiah, whom ye slew between the sanctuary and the altar. 36 Verily I say unto you, All these things shall come upon this generation.

It is the tendency of almost every religious group to worship its past. Just so in Jesus' day did the Jews **build** and **garnish** (decorate) the tombs of their martyred prophets and **righteous** men. They declared if they had lived in the days of their forefathers they would not have killed the prophets (v. 30). But by their actions they showed that they were sons of their fathers, for they rejected John the Baptist and sought to kill Jesus. Grimly Christ bade them fill up the measure of sin (v. 32). The language of verse 34 is explained only in the light of their murderous hatred of Jesus, whose death they would soon bring about.

Not content with that ultimate crime, they would **persecute** and even **kill** the Christian messengers (v. 34). Therefore upon them would come **all the righteous blood** that had been shed from the beginning of history, from that of **Abel** to that of **Zachariah son of Barachiah** (v. 35). The last phrase is difficult, since the Zechariah slain between the **sanctuary** and the **altar** (of sacrifice) is declared to be the son of Jehoiada (II Chron. 24:20-22). The son of Berechiah was the prophet (Zech. 1:1). The phrase is omitted in the original text of Sinaiticus, and may be the mistaken insertion of a copyist — though its presence in the rest of the ancient manuscripts does pose a problem which at present seems insoluble.

The prediction of verse 36 was horribly fulfilled in A.D. 70, the year with which **this generation** ended. Jerusalem was taken, its temple destroyed, and its inhabitants killed or sent into slavery.

c. Sorrowing over Jerusalem (23:37-39)

37 O Jerusalem, Jerusalem, that killeth the prophets, and stoneth them that are sent unto her! how often would I have gathered thy children together, even as a hen gathereth her chickens under her wings, and ye would not! 38 Behold, your house is left unto you desolate. 39 For I say unto you, Ye shall not see me henceforth, till ye shall say, Blessed is he that cometh in the name of the Lord.

This is one of the most plaintive cries of the compassionate Christ. It was His parting word to "the city of the great king" (5:35), which had nevertheless just rejected its King (chap. 21). Instead of being sheltered (v. 37) it would be forsaken (v. 38). Never would it see Him again until it welcomed Him as Messiah (v. 39). **And ye would not** (v. 37) are among the saddest words ever written.

5. Preparing His Disciples (24:1-25:46)

a. Three Predictions (24:1-51)
(Opening Occasion, (24:1-2)

1 And Jesus went out from the temple, and was going on his way; and his disciples came to him to show him the buildings of the temple. 2 But he answered and said unto them, See ye not all these things? verily I say unto you,

There shall not be left here one stone upon another, that shall not be thrown down.

As Jesus was leaving the **temple** (*hieron*, temple area), His disciples pointed out the wonder of its magnificent buildings, built by Herod the Great. It is claimed that the Sanctuary was about one hundred fifty feet in height and one of the most beautiful sacred edifices in the world of that day. It was constructed of white marble, its roof gilded with gold.[106] But Jesus predicted that not one stone would be left upon another (v. 2). That this was fulfilled very literally in A.D. 70 is verified by the Jewish historian, Josephus.[107]

(1) The End of the Age (24:3-14)

3 And as he sat on the mount of Olives, the disciples came unto him privately, saying, Tell us, when shall these things be? and what *shall be* the sign of thy coming, and of the end of the world? 4 And Jesus answered and said unto them, Take heed that no man lead you astray. 5 For many shall come in my name, saying, I am the Christ; and shall lead many astray. 6 And ye shall hear of wars and rumors of wars; see that ye be not troubled: for *these things* must needs come to pass; but the end is not yet. 7 For nation shall rise against nation, and kingdom against kingdom; and there shall be famines and earthquakes in divers places. 8 But all these things are the beginning of travail. 9 Then shall they deliver you up unto tribulation, and shall kill you: and ye shall be hated of all the nations for my name's sake. 10 And then shall many stumble, and shall deliver up one another, and shall hate one another. 11 And many false prophets shall arise, and shall lead many astray. 12 And because iniquity shall be multiplied, the love of the many shall wax cold. 13 But he that endureth to the end, the same shall be saved. 14 And this gospel of the kingdom shall be preached in the whole world for a testimony unto all the nations; and then shall the end come.

As Jesus was sitting on the Mount of Olives, facing the temple 200 feet below, His disciples came to Him **privately** and asked Him three questions: (1) **when shall these things be?** (2) **what shall be**

the **sign of thy coming?** (3) **and of the end of the world** (better, "age") ? In answer to these questions Christ gave what is called the Olivet Discourse, the only long one found in all three Synoptic Gospels (cf. Mark 13, Luke 21).

If the three questions had been answered in order, the exposition of this chapter would be great simplified. What one finds here is much overlapping, with apparently double application of some passages.

This paragraph seems to relate primarily to the signs of the end of the age. First Jesus warned against false messiahs (v. 5), of whom Bar Cochba (A.D. 135) is the outstanding example. Then he predicted **wars and rumors of wars** (v. 6), which have happened in every century since, as have **famines and earthquakes** (v. 7). These are the beginning of **travail** (v. 8). The word means "birth-pangs." The rabbis had a phrase, "birth-pangs of the Messiah," which fits well here. These sufferings would precede the birth of the Messianic Age.

Jesus went on to predict tribulation and death (v. 9), defection and betrayal (v. 10), false prophets and apostasy (v. 11), iniquity and loss of love (v. 12). Then comes the promise of verse 13 — salvation is the reward of endurance — and the prophecy of verse 14. The Gospel shall be **preached** ("heralded, proclaimed") in the whole **world** ("inhabited earth") to **all the nations;** then the end will come. Has this sign been fulfilled yet? The answer depends on the interpretation of **nations.** The word is *ethnos*, which in the King James Version is translated "Gentiles" 93 times and "nation" 64 times (plus "heathen," 5; "people," 2). How far is the division into ethnic groups to be carried? All *tribes* have not heard the gospel, but some would claim that all **nations** have. If this sign is not actually fulfilled, one could say that it is approximately so.

(2) The Destruction of Jerusalem (25:15-28)

15 When therefore ye see the abomination of desolation, which was spoken of through Daniel the prophet, standing in the holy place (let him that readeth

---

[106] Shailer Matthews, *New Testament Times in Palestine*, p. 205.   [107] *War*, VII. I. I.

understand), 16 then let them that are in Judaea flee unto the mountains: 17 let him that is on the housetop not go down to take out the things that are in his house: 18 and let him that is in the field not return back to take his cloak. 19 But woe unto them that are with child and to them that give suck in those days! 20 And pray ye that your flight be not in the winter, neither on a sabbath: 21 for then shall be great tribulation, such as hath not been from the beginning of the world until now, no, nor ever shall be. 22 And except those days had been shortened, no flesh would have been saved: but for the elect's sake those shall be shortened. 23 Then if any man shall say unto you, Lo, here is the Christ, or, Here; believe *it* not. 24 For there shall arise false Christs, and false prophets, and shall show great signs and wonders; so as to lead astray, if possible, even the elect. 25 Behold, I have told you beforehand. 26 If therefore they shall say unto you, Behold, he is in the wilderness; go not forth: Behold, he is in the inner chambers; believe *it* not. 27 For as the lightning cometh forth from the east, and is seen even unto the west; so shall be the coming of the Son of man. 28 Wheresoever the carcase is, there will the eagles be gathered together.

Does the language of this prophecy refer to the destruction of Jerusalem in A.D. 70 or to the coming of Christ? This question could be debated endlessly. The only satisfactory answer seems to be: "Both."

The cryptic phrase, **abomination of desolation** (v. 15) is the key to this paragraph. The latter word means "devastation, destruction, desolation." The first word signifies "detestable thing"; literally, "anything that must not be brought before God because it arouses his wrath."[108] The phrase may be translated, *"the detestable thing causing the desolation* of the holy place."[109]

This **abomination of desolation** was spoken of through Daniel (9:27; 11:31; 12:11). The expression is found also in the apocryphal I Maccabees (1:54), where it refers to the pagan altar of Zeus set up in the temple at Jerusalem by Antiochus Epiphanes (168 B.C.) Apparently this is the primary reference in Daniel's prophecy written beforehand.

In the New Testament the phrase occurs elsewhere only in the parallel passage in Mark (13:14). Luke (21:20) has "when ye see Jerusalem compassed with armies, then know that her desolation is nigh" — followed by the admonition to flee to the mountains, as in Matthew and Mark. "Compassed with armies" is the way Luke interpreted the Jewish phrase **abomination of desolation** for his Gentile readers. "Her desolation is nigh" seems to be a clear reference to the destruction of Jerusalem in A.D. 70. It would seem, therefore, that the phrase in Matthew and Mark must be taken as referring primarily to this event. But it may also point forward to the Antichrist and to the setting up of his image (Rev. 13:14).

The holy place can be taken three ways: (1) Palestine; (2) Jerusalem; (3) the temple. For Luke the reference is to the pagan armies of Rome surrounding the Holy City. All three accounts seem clearly to describe an invasion by an enemy. **Let him that readeth understand** is obviously an insertion by the Evangelist (found also in Mark), since Jesus was speaking, not writing. Luke omits this clause and substitutes, instead of the enigmatic phrase found in Matthew and Mark, a simple, understandable explanation.

The command for those in Judea to **flee unto the mountains** (v. 16) was literally carried out during the siege of Jerusalem in A.D. 70. Eusebius relates it thus: "The whole body, however, of the church at Jerusalem, having been commanded by a divine revelation, given to men of approved piety there before the war, removed from the city, and dwelt at a certain town beyond the Jordan, called Pella."[110] Two occasions may have given opportunity for this flight. A first siege by the Roman governor of Syria was routed by the Jews. Later while Vespasian was attacking Jerusaiem the Emperor at Rome died and Vespasian was called to succeed him, leaving his son Titus in charge of the army in Palestine. The change of generals may have given the Christians a chance to flee.

The urgency of the flight is highlighted in verses 17-19. In verse 20 Matthew adds for his Jewish readers, **neither on a sab-**

---

[108] Arndt and Gingrich, *op. cit.*, p. 137.   [109] *Ibid.*
[110] Eusebius, *Ecclesiastical History*, trans. C. F. Cruse, III, 5.

bath — appropriately missing in Mark, who wrote for the Romans.

Verse 21 is commonly taken as referring to the so-called Great Tribulation at the end of this age. Doubtless it does have reference to that; but can the strong language here also be applied to the destruction of Jerusalem in A.D. 70? Josephus gives some support when he says: "It appears to me that the misfortunes of all men, from the beginning of the world, if they be compared to these of the Jews, are not so considerable as they were."[111] Admittedly, however, the statement, "No, nor ever shall be," in its fullest sense would have to apply to the end of this age.

Verse 22 perhaps has reference to the brevity of the Roman siege of A.D. 70. It lasted only about four and a half months.

Again reference is made to false messiahs (vv. 23-25; cf. v. 5). Reports that Christ has returned and is to be found in the *wilderness* or *inner chambers* are not to be believed (v. 26). His coming will not be secret, but seen by all (v. 27).

Verse 28 is an enigmatic statement. **Eagles** evidently means "vultures." But to what does this saying refer?

Chrysostom, Jerome, and other church Fathers interpret the verse as applying to the Second Coming. The **eagles** are the saints who will be gathered to the **carcase,** Christ. Erasmus, Calvin, Zwingli, Beza, and others of the Reformation period repeat this view. The Puritans carried the matter still further, portraying the eagles to be saints feeding on the sacrificed body of Christ.[112] Filson returns to the early Fathers, when he writes: "Jesus seems to mean that wherever the disciples are, the returning Christ will appear."[113]

Bengel furnishes a more historical interpretation. He writes: "The *carcase,* therefore, must be carnal Judaism, upon which, as upon a carcase left to them, the eagles will pounce greedily and in great numbers," and adds, "These eagles are partly the false Christs and false prophets, partly the Roman forces."[114] A. B. Bruce agrees with this,[115] as do John Wesley and Adam Clarke. Allen refers the saying to the Second Coming. He says: "Just as when life has abandoned a body, and it becomes a corpse, the vultures immediately swoop down upon it; so when the world has become rotten with evil, the Son of man and His angels will come to execute the divine judgment."[116] The best interpretation is probably that which gives the double reference, as follows: "When Jerusalem is ready for destruction, the Roman armies will gather and destroy it; when the world lies awaiting the final appearance of Christ to judgment, he will come."[117]

(3) The Coming of the Son of Man (24:29-44)

29 But immediately after the tribulation of those days the sun shall be darkened, and the moon shall not give her light, and the stars shall fall from heaven, and the powers of the heavens shall be shaken: 30 and then shall appear the sign of the Son of man in heaven: and then shall all the tribes of the earth mourn, and they shall see the Son of man coming on the clouds of heaven with power and great glory. 31 And he shall send forth his angels with a great sound of a trumpet, and they shall gather together his elect from the four winds, from one end of heaven to the other.

32 Now from the fig tree learn her parable: when her branch is now become tender, and putteth forth its leaves, ye know that the summer is nigh; 33 even so ye also, when ye see all these things, know ye that he is nigh, *even* at the doors. 34 Verily I say unto you, This generation shall not pass away, till all these things be accomplished. 35 Heaven and earth shall pass away, but my words shall not pass away. 36 But of that day and hour knoweth no one, not even the angels of heaven, neither the Son, but the Father only. 37 And as *were* the days of Noah, so shall be the coming of the Son of man. 38 For as in those days which were before the flood they were eating and drinking, marrying and giving in marriage, until the day that Noah entered into the ark, 39 and they knew not until the flood came, and took them all away; so shall be the coming of the Son of man. 40 Then shall two men be in the field; one is taken, and one is left: 41 two women *shall be* grinding

111 *War*, Preface, 4.
112 See John Trapp, *Commentary on the New Testament*, p. 249.   113 *Op. cit.*, p. 256.
114 *Op. cit.*, I, 426.   115 *Op. cit.*, pp. 257-58.   116 *Op. cit.*, pp. 257-58.
117 John A. Broadus, *Commentary on the Gospel of Matthew*, "American Commentary," p. 489.

at the mill; one is taken, and one is left. 42 Watch therefore: for ye know not on what day your Lord cometh. 43 But know this, that if the master of the house had known in what watch the thief was coming, he would have watched, and would not have suffered his house to be broken through. 44 Therefore be ye also ready; for in an hour that ye think not the Son of man cometh.

The language of verse 29 is a reflection of the apocalyptic imagery of the Old Testament (cf. Isa. 13:10; 34:4; Ezek. 32:7-8; Joel 2:31; 3:15). "Such signs are symbolical of any great manifestation of Jehovah's power."[118]

The first part of verse 30 is found only in Matthew. It would be useless to speculate as to what **the sign of the Son of man** is, unless it be the lightning-like flash at His coming (v. 27). Matthew is the only one who tells of the disciples asking about "the sign of thy coming" (v. 3); so he alone gives the answer. The statement that the people of the earth will **mourn** (cf. Zech. 12:12) underscores the fact that Christ will be coming in judgment. **Coming on the clouds** is reminiscent of Daniel 7:13. Before the doom strikes, the **elect** (His chosen ones) will be gathered from all directions (**four winds**) and the remotest part of the earth (**from one end of heaven to the other**, meaning the rim of the sky).

Jesus sought to prepare for His coming by giving the **parable** of the **fig tree** (v. 32). When its leaves appear, that is a sign that summer is coming soon. So, **when ye see all these things** — presumably what had been described so far in this chapter — **then know that he** (probably better than KJV "it," though the Greek can mean either) is right **at the doors** (v. 33).

The statement in verse 34 is another difficult one. On the surface it seems to say that Christ would return during that very generation. Two expressions need analysis: **generation** and **all these things.** Does the second refer to the destruction of Jerusalem in A.D. 70 or to the Second Coming? The former is implied in vv. 2-3; the latter is involved definitely at many points in the chapter. How then can one explain Jesus' statement? The destruction of Jerusalem did

take place in that generation but not Christ's return.

The word for **generation** is *genea.* Its first meaning is "family, descent," and so "race." It may mean "nation," or even "age" (period of time). But its primary meaning, especially in the Gospels, is this: "basically, the sum total of those born at the same time, expanded to include all those living at a given time *generation, contemporaries.*"[119]

If **generation** is to be taken in this strict sense, then **all these things** must be limited to the events culminating in A.D. 70. Chrysostom and Origen interpreted it as the generation of believers. Jerome thought it meant either the race of men or Jewish race. While these interpretations should not be ruled out arbitrarily, it seems safer to recall that the occasion of the Olivet Discourse was Jesus' prediction of the destruction of the temple, and to take **all these things** (cf. vv. 2-3) as referring primarily to that event. The majority of the best scholars today insist that **generation** be taken in its strictest sense.

Heaven and earth (everything material) will pass away, but **my words** will stand forever (v. 35). Jesus exhibited a strong consciousness of full divine authority. His words were God's Word.

All setting of dates for the Second Coming is forbidden by Christ's statement in verse 36. **Day and hour** means appointed time, and does not, as some have claimed, leave one free to predict the year. The phrase **neither the Son** (found only in Mark in KJV) is supported here by the earliest manuscripts.

Jesus used **the days of Noah** (v. 37) as a parallel for the time preceding His coming. There is nothing wrong with the four things mentioned in verse 38. The people's sin consisted in their living their lives without any reference to God. The primary emphasis here seems to be on the fact that life went on as usual, until suddenly *catastrophe* (Greek word for "overthrow," II Pet. 2:6) struck in devastating judgment. The word for **flood** (v. 39) is *kataklysmos* ("cataclysm"). The phrase, **the coming of the Son of man,** occurs here for the third and last time in the chapter (cf. vv. 27, 37).

---

[118] Allen, *op. cit.,* p. 258. [119] Arndt and Gingrich, *op. cit.,* p. 153.

The return of Christ will be a time of sad separation (vv. 40-41). The **mill** was the small hand mill, which women used each morning to grind the wheat or barley for the day. One can still occasionally see in Palestine two women sitting on the ground, both grasping the same handle on the upper millstone — about the same in diameter as a dinner plate — as they turn it rapidly about. Two people in close daily fellowship will suddenly find themselves parted forever. It is a solemn warning.

The keyword of the Olivet Discourse is **watch** (v. 42; 25:13). There is much here that one cannot explain; but this admonition is clear and forceful. This was the purpose for which Jesus gave the discourse. The verb is in the present imperative: "Keep on watching continually." Literally it means "be awake," and figuratively "be on the alert" or "be vigilant." It may well be translated, "Keep wide awake!" The reason for this warning is that we do not know when Christ will come. If the owner had known when the burglar was coming to break into his home, he would have **watched** ("kept awake" — same verb with literal meaning) and not allowed his house to be **broken through** (literally, "dug through"). Walls made of sun-dried brick or flimsy stone were rather easy to dig through.

This section closes with another admonition and warning: **Be ye also ready** (prepared), because the Son of man will come **in an hour that ye think not** (v. 44). The unexpectedness of His coming will catch many asleep or off guard.

(Closing Warning, 24:45-51)

45 Who then is the faithful and wise servant, whom his lord hath set over his household, to give them their food in due season? 46 Blessed is that servant, whom his lord when he cometh shall find so doing. 47 Verily I say unto you, that he will set him over all that he hath. 48 But if that evil servant shall say in his heart, My lord tarrieth; 49 and shall begin to beat his fellow-servants, and shall eat and drink with the drunken; 50 the lord of the servant shall come in a day when he expecteth not, and in an hour when he knoweth not, 51 and shall cut him asunder, and appoint his portion

with the hypocrites: there shall be the weeping and the gnashing of teeth.

Jesus used the illustration of a master going away and leaving a **servant** ("slave") in charge of his **household** (his "household slaves"; Greek word only here in N.T.). If that servant is **faithful** in discharging his responsibilities and **wise** ("prudent," knowing that there will be a reckoning time when his master returns), he will be **blessed** (i.e., "rewarded"). But the **evil servant** who assumes the master will delay his coming, and carouses with drunkards, will be severely punished. A very strong term is used, **cut him asunder** (v. 51), which is what the verb literally signifies ("cut in two"). Perhaps it means here to "cut" with a whip.

The expression **the weeping and the gnashing of teeth** is found seven times in the New Testament (Matt. 8:12; 13: 42, 50; 22:13; 24:51; 25:30; Luke 13:28). It is a vivid warning of the horrors of hell.

b. Three Parables (25:1-46)

(1) The Ten Virgins (25:1-13)

1 Then shall the kingdom of heaven be likened unto ten virgins, who took their lamps, and went forth to meet the bridegroom. 2 And five of them were foolish, and five were wise. 3 For the foolish, when they took their lamps, took no oil with them: 4 but the wise took oil in their vessels with their lamps. 5 Now while the bridgroom tarried, they all slumbered and slept. 6 But at midnight there is a cry, Behold, the bridegroom! Come ye forth to meet him. 7 Then all those virgins arose, and trimmed their lamps. 8 And the foolish said unto the wise, Give us of your oil; for our lamps are going out. 9 But the wise answered, saying Peradventure there will not be enough for us and you: go ye rather to them that sell, and buy for yourselves. 10 And while they went away to buy, the bridegroom came; and they that were ready went in with him to the marriage feast: and the door was shut. 11 Afterward came also the other virgins, saying, Lord, Lord, open to us. 12 But he answered and said, Verily I say unto you, I know you not. 13 Watch therefore, for ye know not the day nor the hour.

All the material in chapter 25 is found only in Matthew. It is his addition to the Olivet Discourse. That it was a part of that discourse is suggested by the recurring refrain in verse 13 (cf. 24:42).

Appropriate to Matthew's Gospel, the Parable of the Ten Virgins begins: **Then shall the kingdom of heaven be likened unto.** The **ten virgins** took **lamps** (Greek, *lampadas*) and went out to meet the bridegroom, who would come with his male attendants to the bride's house. The five **foolish** (Greek, *morai,* from which comes "moron") maidens did not take an extra supply of oil, but the five **wise** ("thoughtful, prudent") ones did.

The bridegroom probably had to wash and dress, as well as eat, after finishing work. His companions may have been slow in assembling at his house for the procession to the bride's home. After waiting for some hours, the virgins all became drowsy. They **slumbered** ("nodded, dozed, fell asleep") and **slept** ("kept on sleeping"). [120]

At midnight, when least expected, there came a cry: **Behold, the bridegroom!** The ten virgins quickly rose and trimmed the wicks of their tiny clay lamps, which burned olive oil. The foolish asked for oil; for their lamps were **going out** (not "gone out," KJV) — a warning against the danger of letting one's spiritual experience get low. But the wise knew they could not spare any of their own supply. So the foolish had to go in search of oil.

Meanwhile the bridegroom came (v. 10). Those that were **ready** (same word as in 24:44) went in with him to the **marriage feast,** which usually lasted from one to three weeks, **and the door was shut.** This is the language of settled destiny. The foolish virgins returned and cried for the door to be opened — but their cries were in vain. The bridegroom disowned those who were outside in the dark.

The main lesson is given by Jesus: **Watch, therefore, for ye know not the day nor the hour** (v. 13). This vivid parable is a warning that there is such a thing as being too late, that once the door of eternal destiny is closed it cannot be reopened. The story is an admonition to be filled with the Spirit (typified by the oil) and always ready for Christ's return.

120 The first verb is aorist, the second imperfect.

(2) The Talents (25:14-30)

14 For *it is* as *when* a man, going into another country, called his own servants, and delivered unto them his goods. 15 And unto one he gave five talents, to another two, to another one; to each according to his several ability; and he went on his journey. 16 Straightway he that received the five talents went and traded with them, and made other five talents. 17 In like manner he also that *received* the two gained other two. 18 But he that received the one went away and digged in the earth, and hid his lord's money. 19 Now after a long time the lord of those servants cometh, and maketh a reckoning with them. 20 And he that received the five talents came and brought other five talents, saying, Lord, thou deliveredst unto me five talents: lo, I have gained other five talents. 21 His lord said unto him, Well done, good and faithful servant: thou hast been faithful over a few things, I will set thee over many things; enter thou into the joy of thy lord. 22 And he also that *received* the two talents came and said, Lord, thou deliveredst unto me two talents: lo, I have gained other two talents. 23 His lord said unto him, Well done, good and faithful servant: thou hast been faithful over a few things, I will set thee over many things; enter thou into the joy of thy lord. 24 And he also that had received the one talent came and said, Lord, I knew thee that thou art a hard man, reaping where thou didst not sow, and gathering where thou didst not scatter; 25 and I was afraid, and went away and hid thy talent in the earth: lo, thou hast thine own. 56 But his lord answered and said unto him, Thou wicked and slothful servant, thou knewest that I reap where I sowed not, and gather where I did not scatter; 27 thou oughtest therefore to have put my money to the bankers, and at my coming I should have received back mine own with interest. 28 Take ye away therefore the talent from him, and give it unto him that hath the ten talents. 29 For unto every one that hath shall be given, and he shall have abundance: but from him that hath not, even that which he hath shall be taken away. 30 And cast ye out the unprofitable servant into the outer darkness: there shall be the weeping and the gnashing of teeth.

The Parable of the Ten Virgins teaches the necessity of keeping one's inward Christian experience up-to-date, with full spiritual glow fed by the oil of the Spirit. The Parable of the Talents emphasizes the need of being active in service for the Lord. These two — the subjective and the objective, the inner and the outer, the passive and the active — are both equally important as essential parts of one's preparation for the coming of Christ.

The Parable of the Talents is somewhat parallel to the Parable of the Pounds (Luke 19:11-28). In both cases, money is given to servants, the reports of three are recorded, the first two are commended, and the third is condemned for hoarding his money rather than using it. On the other hand, the differences are numerous. Here one servant is given **five talents,** another **two,** and another **one** — to each according to his several ability (v. 15). In Luke, ten servants each receive a pound. In Matthew, the first servant doubles his five talents, and the second doubles his two talents. In Luke, the first reports that his pound has gained ten pounds, the second that his has gained five pounds. The commendation is exactly the same for the two in Matthew, who did equally well. In Luke, the first is put over ten cities, the second over five cities. The two parables were intended to enforce much the same lesson — faithfulness in service.

Talents refers to amounts of money. Each talent was worth about a thousand dollars. Today the term "talents" is used to mean gifts or abilities — a fact which gives added though originally unintended significance to the story.

The one who doubled his two talents was given exactly the same commendation as the one who had doubled his five talents, for they both had worked equally hard. The master said: **Well done, good and faithful servant** (vv. 21, 23). He did not reward them for their cleverness or skill. Only two things were demanded of them: that they be good and faithful — something that everyone can be, however limited his background or native ability.

The parable sounds a warning that it is often the one-talent man who refuses to do anything in the work of the Kingdom, excusing himself by saying that he cannot do much. But the spirit and attitude of the man with the one talent should put such on their guard. The

servant who did nothing blamed his master for his own failure (v. 24-25). He failed to realize that it was only the master's ownership of property which gave him the opportunity for successful service. It was true that the owner had the servants do the work, but he was the one who clothed and fed and cared for them.

Because of his selfish, sinful attitude the master addressed him as **wicked and slothful servant** (v. 26). The second adjective literally means "shrinking, hesitating, timid." These attitudes can frustrate effective Christian service (cf. Rom. 2:11).

Perhaps the last part of verse 26 should be a question rather than an assertion — the Greek bearing both translations equally well. "So you knew . . . ?" Then double reason why you should have given my money to the **bankers** ("money-changers"), so that I would have my capital **with interest** (v. 27).

Verse 29 states a truism of life. The one who uses his talents gains more; the one who fails to use what he has soon loses it. The really valuable things in life can only be retained as they are employed and exercised. The one who fails to use his talents will gain only eternal loss (v. 30).

3. The Sheep and the Goats (25:31-46)

31 But when the Son of man shall come in his glory, and all the angels with him, then shall he sit on the throne of his glory: 32 and before him shall be gathered all the nations: and he shall separate them one from another, as the shepherd separateth the sheep from the goats; 33 and he shall set the sheep on his right hand, but the goats on the left. 34 Then shall the King say unto them on his right hand, Come, ye blessed of my Father, inherit the kingdom prepared for you from the foundation of the world: 35 for I was hungry, and ye gave me to eat; I was thirsty, and ye gave me drink; I was a stranger, and ye took me in; 36 naked, and ye clothed me; I was sick, and ye visited me; I was in prison, and ye came unto me. 37 Then shall the righteous answer him, saying, Lord, when saw we thee hungry, and fed thee? or athirst, and gave thee drink? 38 And when saw we thee a stranger, and took thee in? or naked, and clothed thee? 39 And when saw we thee sick, or in prison, and came unto thee? 40 And the King shall an-

swer and say unto them, Verily I say unto you, Inasmuch as ye did it unto one of these my brethren, *even* these least, ye did it unto me. 41 Then shall he say also unto them on the left hand, Depart from me, ye cursed, into the eternal fire which is prepared for the devil and his angels: 42 for I was hungry, and ye did not give me to eat; I was thirsty, and ye gave me no drink; 43 I was a stranger, and ye took me not in; naked, and ye clothed me not; sick, and in prison, and ye visited me not. 44 Then shall they also answer, saying, Lord, when saw we thee hungry, or athirst, or a stranger, or naked, or sick, or in prison, and did not minister unto thee? 45 Then shall he answer them, saying, Verily I say unto you, Inasmuch as ye did it not unto one of these least, ye did it not unto me. 46 And these shall go away into eternal punishment; but the righteous into eternal life.

The question is often raised as to whether this is actually a parable. Filson reflects the attitude of many when he says: "Vss. 31-46 give not a parable but a description of the last judgment."[121] But they are included in many lists of parables of Jesus.[122] The value of the passage is not affected by this question.

Christ pictured Himself seated on the **throne of his glory,** after His coming. All the **nations** will be gathered before Him, and He will separate **them** — not nations (neuter), but people, individuals (masculine pronoun). It is manifestly unreasonable to think of Christ consigning nations as such to **eternal punishment** or **eternal life** (v. 46). It is clear that **all the nations** (v. 32) means "all the people of the world."

Sheep are proverbially good creatures, and **goats** bad. The **right hand** is the place of honor, **the left** that of dishonor (v. 33). Judgment is on the basis of the way individuals have acted toward the needy about them (vv. 34-36). The **righteous** are surprised to learn that they have merited commendation (v. 37-39) — a forceful example of the humility of true piety. They learn that what they have done to the sick and suffering, the lonely and the needy, they have in reality done to Christ Himself (v. 40).

In contrast, those **on the left hand** are not commended but condemned. Instead of **Come, ye blessed** (v. 34), it is **Depart from me, ye cursed** (v. 41). Instead of **the kingdom prepared for you from the foundation of the world** (v. 34), it is **the eternal fire which is prepared for the devil and his angels** (v. 41). This is because they have failed to minister to those in need (vv. 42-45). Not the least contrast is the final fate of both groups — **eternal punishment** for the one, **eternal life** for the other (v. 46). If the second is eternal, so is the first.

This passage stands as a strong indictment of the church for its lack of social conscience. Had the church carried out fully the teachings of Jesus as set forth here, there would have been no place for the rise of the so-called social gospel.

John Wesley is one of the finest examples of an evangelical Christian who practiced what Jesus preached. He devoted a good deal of his time to ministering to the poor and imprisoned, at the same time winning thousands of converts to Christ.

III. PASSION OF THE KING (Matt. 26: 1-28:20)

A. His Betrayal and Arrest (26:1-56)

1. Betrayal (26:1-29)

a. Conspiracy (26:1-5)

1 And it came to pass, when Jesus had finished all these words, he said unto his disciples, 2 Ye know that after two days the passover cometh, and the Son of man is delivered up to be crucified. 3 Then were gathered together the chief priests, and the elders of the people, unto the court of the high priest, who was called Caiaphas; 4 and they took counsel together that they might take Jesus by subtlety, and kill him. 5 But they said, Not during the feast, lest a tumult arise among the people.

It appears that the Olivet Discourse was given on Tuesday afternoon of Passion Week. For here Jesus says, **after two days the passover cometh,** and He is pictured as eating the passover meal with the Twelve on Thursday evening, the night before His crucifixion (vv. 17, 20). This suggests that the Master and His disciples spent Wednesday in se-

[121] *Op. cit.*, p. 266.   [122] E.g., Adam Fahling and A. T. Robertson, but not Trench.

clusion, while He instructed them privately.

The chief priests, and the elders of the people is an expression for the Great Sanhedrin at Jerusalem, the supreme court of the Jewish nation. This convened in **the court of the high priest,** which was located either in the western part of the city or just northwest of the temple area. **Caiaphas** was **high priest** about A.D. 18-36.

The Jewish leaders conspired to take Jesus **by subtlety** — literally, "by deceit"; the word originally meant a "bait" or "snare." They wanted to catch Him craftily and **kill him.** But they wished to avoid doing it during the Passover, lest there be a **tumult** ("uproar").

b. Complaint (26:6-13)

6 Now when Jesus was in Bethany, in the house of Simon the leper, 7 there came unto him a woman having an alabaster cruse of exceeding precious ointment, and she poured it upon his head, as he sat at meat. 8 But when the disciples saw it, they had indignation, saying, To what purpose is this waste? 9 For this *ointment* might have been sold for much, and given to the poor. 10 But Jesus perceiving it said unto them, Why trouble ye the woman? for she hath wrought a good work upon me. 11 For ye have the poor always with you; but me ye have not always. 12 For in that she poured this ointment upon my body, she did it to prepare me for burial. 13 Verily I say unto you, Wheresoever this gospel shall be preached in the whole world, that also which this woman hath done shall be spoken of for a memorial of her.

This anointing of Jesus at Bethany is also recorded by Mark (14:3-9) and John (12:2-8). It is not to be confused with the one in Luke 7:36-50. That was by a sinful woman in Galilee, this by Mary of Bethany (John 12:3) in Judea. It is evidently just a coincidence that in both cases the name of the host was Simon — a very common name in that day (at least ten are mentioned in the N.T.). This **Simon the leper** was probably a well-known person who had been cured by Jesus.

Alabaster cruse is simply *alabastron* in

Greek. It was probably a flask, "a vessel with rather a long neck which was broken off when the contents were used."[123] **Exceeding precious** is *barytimos* (literally, "heavy in value"). **Sat at meat** is better translated "reclined at the table."

When the woman broke the neck of the flask and poured the precious perfume on Jesus' head, the disciples complained at **this waste.** They were still shackled with a materialistic point of view, unable to appreciate the higher values of love and devotion.

Jesus rebuked them for their attitude. **Good** (v. 10) may also be translated "beautiful." In His eyes, illuminated by love, what the woman did was a beautiful deed. After He was gone, the poor would **always** remain to be cared for. But Mary had caught something of the significance of this critical moment. She anointed His body, consciously or unconsciously, in preparation for His burial (v. 12). It is significant that among the Marys who bought spices after Jesus' death to anoint His corpse (Mark 16:1), Mary of Bethany was missing. While sitting at His feet (Luke 10:39), had she understood, as no one else did, what was going to happen to Him?

The promise of verse 13 has been fulfilled beyond anything that Mary could possibly have imagined: uncounted millions of people have read this story in the Gospels and honored the memory of this woman who loved the Master with deep devotion.

c. Compact (26:14-16)

14 Then one of the twelve, who was called Judas Iscariot, went unto the chief priests, 15 and he said, What are ye willing to give me, and I will deliver him unto you? And they weighed unto him thirty pieces of silver. 16 And from that time he sought opportunity to deliver him *unto them.*

What a vivid contrast is the act of Judas with that of Mary. John (12:6) tells us that Judas was the dishonest treasurer of the Twelve, and especially resented the "waste." Filled with greed, he bargained with the **chief priests** to betray Jesus for **thirty pieces of silver** — about twenty or twenty-five dollars.

[123] Arndt and Gingrich, *op. cit.,* p. 33.

d. Cooperation (26:17-19)

17 Now on the *first day* of unleavened bread the disciples came to Jesus, saying, Where wilt thou that we make ready for thee to eat the passover? 18 And he said, Go into the city to such a man, and say unto him, The Teacher saith, My time is at hand; I keep the passover at thy house with my disciples. 19 And the disciples did as Jesus appointed them; and they made ready the passover.

The first day of unleavened bread would be the day the passover lamb was slain. Strictly speaking, this was called the Passover, followed by seven days of the Feast of Unleavened Bread (Lev. 23: 5-6). But Josephus indicates that by this time the latter name was applied to the whole period. He writes: "We celebrate for eight days the feast called that of unleavened bread."[124]

Jesus had been in the habit of eating the Passover with His disciples. The regulation was that the lamb was to be eaten by each family, or by two families if one was too small to eat it (Ex. 12:3-4). This was now specified as not less than ten or more than twenty persons. So Jesus and the Twelve would make just the right-sized group. Furthermore, the Passover was to be eaten between sunset and midnight. The lamb was slain at about three o'clock in the afternoon and eaten that evening. Also it was required that the Passover be celebrated in or near Jerusalem (Deut. 16:7). The feast commemorated the fact that the first-born male child among the Israelites was saved by the sprinkling of blood the night the Egyptian first-born were slain (Ex. 12: 12-14).

The **disciples** were to go **into the city** (Jerusalem) and find **such a man.** The latter ambiguous expression is explained by Mark (14:13) and Luke (22:10) as "a man bearing a pitcher of water." Mark also indicates that only two disciples were sent on this errand, and Luke (22:8) identifies them as Peter and John. They were to inform the man that **the Teacher** was going to eat the Passover with His disciples at his house. It is probable that Jesus had previously made arrangements with this individual.[125] The disciples went into Jerusalem and **made ready the passover.**

e. Confusion (26:20-25)

20 Now when even was come, he was sitting at meat with the twelve disciples; 21 and as they were eating, he said, Verily I say unto you, that one of you shall betray me. 22 And they were exceeding sorrowful, and began to say unto him every one, Is it I, Lord? 23 And he answered and said, He that dipped his hand with me in the dish, the same shall betray me. 24 The Son of man goeth, even as it is written of him: but woe unto that man through whom the Son of man is betrayed! good were it for that man if he had not been born. 25 And Judas, who betrayed him, answered and said, Is it I, Rabbi? He saith unto him, Thou hast said.

Sitting at meat should be "reclining at the table." In the larger homes — and this would be one — the Jews followed the Roman custom of reclining on couches around the table, leaning with their left elbow on a cushion, and eating with the right hand. In fact the typical table with a head table and two wings was called *triclinium* (literally, "three-couch").

At this last supper of Jesus with His disciples He threw them into confusion by announcing that one of the Twelve was going to betray Him. Filled with sorrow, they began asking, **Is it I?** This showed a wholesome humility and distrust of themselves. Jesus answered that it was one who **dipped his hand with me in the dish** (v. 23). Probably several were eating out of the same common dish — the people used no silverware in those days. John makes it more specific by saying that Jesus identified the betrayer by offering him a "sop" (John 13:26). Surprisingly, Judas himself finally asked — probably as a cover-up — **Is it I, Rabbi?** (v. 25). Both here and in verse 22 the Greek form of the question indicates that a negative answer was expected: "It is not I, is it?" It is to be noted that while the other disciples addressed Jesus as **Lord** (v. 22) Judas called Him **Rabbi.**

f. Comfort (26:26-29)

26 And as they were eating, Jesus took bread, and blessed, and brake it; and he gave to the disciples, and said, Take, eat; this is my body. 27 And he took a cup, and gave thanks, and gave to them,

---

[124] *Ant.* II. 15. 1.   [125] See further discussion on Mark 14:13.

saying, Drink ye all of it; 28 for this is my blood of the covenant, which is poured out for many unto remission of sins. 29 But I say unto you, I shall not drink henceforth of this fruit of the vine, until that day when I drink it new with you in my Father's kingdom.

Apparently Judas left the room at this point (cf. John 13:30). Then Jesus instituted the Lord's Supper. He **blessed** a tiny, biscuit-sized loaf of **bread**, broke it into fragments, and gave each disciple a piece. Among Orientals this was a solemn sign of close fellowship and faithful friendship. It was a comforting assurance to the disciples that their Master was still one with them. His announcement that one of them would betray Him had not made them enemies.

But this act signified far more. Jesus declared: **This is my body**. It is quite obvious that the meaning is: "This *symbolizes* my body," or "This *represents* my body." Actually His physical body was still intact.

Then Jesus took **a cup** (v. 27), gave thanks, and offered it to them. **Drink ye all of it** misrepresents the Greek, which clearly says, "All of you drink from it." It was not that they were to drink all the contents of the cup. Rather the one cup was passed around the circle and each disciple was to take a sip from it. Since this saying is repeated thousands of times in communion services it is unfortunate that it was not translated correctly.

Jesus explained . that the cup represented or symbolized **my blood of the covenant** that He was soon to shed for the **remission of sins** (v. 28). It was common in those days to seal a solemn covenant with the blood of the one making it. The reference here is probably to Exodus 24:8 (cf. also Heb. 9:22) . **Remission** means "forgiveness" and "release."

The Master declared that this would be the last time He would drink the cup with His disciples until the Kingdom came. Thus He pointed them forward to the new day of His return.

2. Arrest (26:30-56)

a. Boasting of Peter (26:30-35)

30 And when they had sung a hymn, they went out into the mount of Olives.

31 Then saith Jesus unto them, All ye shall be offended in me this night: for it is written, I will smite the shepherd, and the sheep of the flock shall be scattered abroad. 32 But after I am raised up, I will go before you into Galilee. 33 But Peter answered and said unto him, If all shall be offended in thee, I will never be offended. 34 Jesus said unto him, Verily I say unto thee, that this night, before the cock crow, thou shalt deny me thrice. 35 Peter saith unto him, Even if I must die with thee, *yet* will I not deny thee. Likewise also said all the disciples.

The **hymn** they sang after the passover meal was the latter part of the Great Hallel (Psalms 115-118). Jesus and the eleven disciples then left the city, crossed the Kidron valley, and started up the western slope of the **mount of Olives**.

Offended is the verb *skandalizo* (v. 31) . Probably the best translation here is "stumble." The disciples would stumble over the fact that Jesus did not set up the expected messianic kingdom in Jerusalem, but rather allowed Himself to be taken and killed. He quoted Zechariah 13:7 as a prophecy that His disciples would be **scattered** when their Shepherd was smitten. That is what happened immediately, but they came together again. Jesus also promised to meet them in Galilee (v. 32). That was a call to them to reassemble.

With his usual impetuosity Peter declared that though all others should be "caused to stumble" (**offended**), he would never. Jesus warned Simon that he would deny Him three times that very night. Peter and all the disciples declared they would die first. They did not know their own weakness.

b. Bitter Grief of Jesus (26:36-46)

36 Then cometh Jesus with them unto a place called Gethsemane, and saith unto his disciples, Sit ye here, while I go yonder and pray. 37 And he took with him Peter and the two sons of Zebedee, and began to be sorrowful and sore troubled. 38 Then saith he unto them, My soul is exceeding sorrowful, even unto death: abide ye here, and watch with me. 39 And he went forward a little, and fell on his face, and prayed, saying, My Father, if it be possible, let this cup pass away from me: nevertheless, not as I will, but as thou wilt. 40 And he cometh

unto the disciples, and findeth them sleeping, and saith unto Peter, What, could ye not watch with me one hour? 41 Watch and pray, that ye enter not into temptation: the spirit indeed is willing, but the flesh is weak. 42 Again a second time he went away, and prayed, saying, My Father, if this cannot pass away, except I drink it, thy will be done. 43 And he came again and found them sleeping, for their eyes were heavy. 44 And he left them again, and went away, and prayed a third time, saying again the same words. 45 Then cometh he to the disciples, and saith unto them, Sleep on now, and take your rest: behold, the hour is at hand, and the Son of man is betrayed into the hands of sinners. 26 Arise, let us be going: behold, he is at hand that betrayeth me.

The story of Jesus praying in the Garden is told in all three Synoptic Gospels. **Gethsemane** (used only here and Mark 14:32) means "oil-press"; that is, a press for squeezing oil out of olives. There are still many olive trees on the slopes of the Mount of Olives.

Jesus left eight of the disciples at the entrance of the grove, taking with Him Peter, James, and John. These two details are recorded only in Matthew and Mark. The Master then shared with the inner circle the sorrow that weighed Him down, even to the point of death (v. 38). Asking them to **watch** with Him, He went forward a little — Luke (22:41) says "about a stone's cast" — **and fell on his face** — "fell on the ground" (Mark); "kneeled down" (Luke) — **and prayed** (all three). One can almost see Christ, staggering under the load of a world's sin, stumble and finally fall. The deep, dark horror of the Cross was already filling His consciousness.

The prayer is given in very similar form in all three Synoptics (cf. Mark 14:36; Luke 22:42). Jesus would like to have been spared this cup. But He submitted: **Not as I will, but as thou wilt.** This is the greatest prayer anyone can pray. It is the heart of Christian consecration.

Returning to the three disciples, the Master found them sleeping (v. 40). Gently He reproved boasting Peter: Could he not watch **one hour?** Then He gave the combined command and warning: **Watch and pray, that ye enter not into temptation** (v. 41; same in Mark

14:38). **Flesh** evidently means the physical body. The disciples were weary with the busy emergencies of Passion Week.

A second time Jesus went away and prayed the same prayer (cf. Mark 14:39 — "the same words"); with emphasis on the second half (v. 42). Once more He found the disciples asleep. **Their eyes were heavy** (v. 43) suggests that they fought to keep awake, but in vain. A third time He prayed (only in Matt.), **saying again the same words** (v. 44).

Verses 45 and 46 (cf. Mark 14:41-42) do not fit together, but clash (in KJV and ASV). The conflict is resolved in the obviously correct translation of the opening words of Jesus (v. 45): "Are you still sleeping and taking your rest?" (RSV). It was no time to sleep, for already the enemy was approaching.

c. Betrayal by Judas (26:47-56)

47 And while he yet spake, lo, Judas, one of the twelve, came, and with him a great multitude with swords and staves, from the chief priests and elders of the people. 48 Now he that betrayed him gave them a sign, saying, Whomsoever I shall kiss, that is he: take him. 49 And straightway he came to Jesus, and said, Hail, Rabbi; and kissed him. 50 And Jesus said unto him, Friend, *do* that for which thou art come. Then they came and laid hands on Jesus, and took him. 51 And behold, one of them that were with Jesus stretched out his hand, and drew his sword, and smote the servant of the high priest, and struck off his ear. 52 Then saith Jesus unto him, Put up again thy sword into its place: for all they that take the sword shall perish with the sword. 53 Or thinkest thou that I cannot beseech my Father, and he shall even now send me more than twelve legions of angels? 54 How then should the scriptures be fulfilled, that thus it must be? 55 In that hour said Jesus to the multitudes, Are ye come out as against a robber with swords and staves to seize me? I sat daily in the temple teaching, and ye took me not. 56 But all this is come to pass, that the scriptures of the prophets might be fulfilled. Then all the disciples left him, and fled.

While Jesus was still rousing His sleepy disciples, Judas appeared at the head of a procession from the Sanhedrin. It was composed of a **multitude** — Stauffer thinks it was a small army of a thousand soldiers,"[126] prepared to "cordon off the Mount of Olives, and to search with lanterns and torches every hiding-place."[127]   But this overlooks the statement that Judas "knew the place" (John 18:2). There may have been scores in the motley band, but probably not hundreds.

Judas had given a sign: he would identify Jesus with a kiss (v. 48). The greeting seemed especially inappropriate: *chaire* (Hail), literally "rejoice," or "be glad" — "I am glad to see you," a common term of greeting at that time. Then he kissed Jesus. The word is a compound, perhaps suggesting "kissed him much" (ASVm.). Jesus responded: Friend (literally "comrade" or "companion"), do that for which thou art come. The issue had already been settled by Christ in the Garden.

When the soldiers or officers seized Jesus, one of His disciples — John (18: 10) identifies him as Peter — drew his sword and swung it at the head of a slave of the high priest, who was assisting in the arrest. The servant evidently "ducked" and lost only his ear (v. 51). Christ commanded Simon to sheathe his sword again, and stated the oft-proved principle: all they that take the sword shall perish with the sword (v. 52). He reminded the desperate disciple that He could have called for twelve legions of angels (a Roman legion normally numbered about 6,000). But the Scriptures must be fulfilled (v. 54).

Turning to the mob surrounding Him, Jesus chided them for seizing Him in this way with swords and staves, as if He were a robber (v. 55). They had seen Him teaching daily in the temple; why had they not arrested Him then? But the Scriptures had to be fulfilled (v. 56), especially Isaiah 53. Since there was apparently nothing they could do and their own lives were in danger, all the disciples forsook Jesus and fled.

B. HIS TRIALS AND EXECUTION (26:57-27:66)

1. Jewish Trial (26:57-27:10)

a. Jesus Defamed (26:57-68)

57 And they that had taken Jesus led him away to *the house of* Caiaphas the high priest, where the scribes and the elders were gathered together. 58 But Peter followed him afar off, unto the court of the high priest, and entered in, and sat with the officers, to see the end. 59 Now the chief priests and the whole council sought false witness against Jesus, that they might put him to death; 60 and they found it not, though many false witnesses came. But afterward came two, 61 and said, This man said, I am able to destroy the temple of God, and to build it in three days. 62 And the high priest stood up, and said unto him, Answerest thou nothing? what is it which these witness against thee? 63 But Jesus held his peace. And the high priest said unto him, I adjure thee by the living God, that thou tell us whether thou art the Christ, the Son of God. 64 Jesus saith unto him, Thou hast said: nevertheless I say unto you, Henceforth ye shall see the Son of man sitting at the right hand of Power, and coming on the clouds of heaven. 65 Then the high priest rent his garments, saying, He hath spoken blasphemy: what further need have we of witnesses? behold, now ye have heard the blasphemy: 66 what think ye? They answered and said, He is worthy of death. 67 Then did they spit in his face and buffet him: and some smote him with the palms of their hands, 68 saying, Prophesy unto us, thou Christ: who is he that struck thee?

Jesus was led to the home of Caiaphas the high priest.   John (18:12-13) mentions a preliminary, informal hearing before Annas, father-in-law of Caiaphas. The high priest presided over the Sanhedrin — the scribes and the elders (cf. Mark 14:53, "the chief priests and the elders and the scribes") — as it tried Jesus.   Evidently a meeting of this august body had been called hastily.   Were Nicodemus and Joseph of Arimathea intentionally not notified?

Peter followed him afar off — a dangerous procedure, which got him into trouble.   But he deserves a degree of commendation for following at all.   He entered the large, open court, or "courtyard," around which the high priest's palace was built.   Sitting down with the officers — "attendants," probably members of the temple guard — he waited to see the end (v. 58). He was overcome with pessimistic despair.

The Sanhedrin sought false witness against Jesus — a sad commentary on the ecclesiastical leaders — in order to **put him to death.** This aim was the object of the whole procedure. But they had difficulty getting what they wanted. Finally two witnesses agreed in declaring that Jesus had said: **I am able to** (Mark 14:58 — "I will") **destroy the temple of God,** and build it again in three days. This was a distorted report of the saying found in John 2:19 — "Destroy this temple, and in three days I will raise it up." Of course, Jesus was referring to His body. Perhaps these witnesses had heard of Jesus' prediction that the temple of Jerusalem would be destroyed (24:2). If so, they presented a garbled combination that was a clear falsehood.

The most sensitive point with the Jews was their sacred temple. This testimony roused the group to action. The high priest curtly asked Jesus why He did not respond (v. 62). Getting no reply, he put Jesus under oath to state whether or not He was the Messiah (**the Christ**), **the Son of God.** Jesus answered, **Thou hast said** (v. 64). Some have interpreted this as meaning, "That is what you say." But that (the statement that Jesus was the Son of God) is precisely *not* what the high priest affirmed. Evidently the words mean, "You said it" (cf. Mark 14:62 — "I am").

Then Jesus applied to Himself the language of Daniel 7:13 and Psalm 110:1. This was all the high priest wanted. He **rent his garments** — a sign of extreme grief and shocked surprise. The high priest was forbidden to do this in a case of personal sorrow (Lev. 10:6; 21:10), but this was an official act. He now declared Jesus' guilt: **He hath spoken blasphemy** (v. 65), in claiming to be the fulfillment of these prophecies in Daniel and the Psalms. No further witnesses were needed — an evident relief to Jesus' prosecutors.

When the presiding high priest asked, **What think ye?** (v. 66), the answer was a foregone conclusion: **He is worthy of death.** Thus the Sanhedrin condemned Jesus to die for blasphemy.

The ensuing actions were utterly unsuited to a supreme court of justice, and especially one that was also a religious body. The chief priests and elders of the people stooped so low as to **spit in his face** (v. 67). They blindfolded Him

(cf. Mark 14:65) and slapped His face, then mockingly told Him to prove He was the Messiah by identifying the one who struck Him (v. 68).

b. Jesus Denied (26:69-75)

69 Now Peter was sitting without in the court: and a maid came unto him, saying, Thou also wast with Jesus the Galilaean. 70 But he denied before them all, saying, I know not what thou sayest. 71 And when he was gone out into the porch, another *maid* saw him, and saith unto them that were there, This man also was with Jesus of Nazareth. 72 And again he denied with an oath, I know not the man. 73 And after a little while they that stood by came and said to Peter, Of a truth thou also art *one* of them; for thy speech maketh thee known. 74 Then began he to curse and to swear, I know not the man. And straightway the cock crew. 75 And Peter remembered the word which Jesus had said, Before the cock crow, thou shalt deny me thrice. And he went out, and wept bitterly.

Peter was sitting in the open courtyard, warming himself at the fire (cf. Mark 14:67). A servant **maid** charged him with being associated with the man on trial. Emphatically Peter denied the charge (v. 70). To escape further detection, he went out to the **porch** — more correctly, the "vestibule" between the courtyard and the outer door opening onto the street. But here **another maid** spied him and made the same charge (v. 71). Again he denied, this time **with an oath** (v. 72), making himself guilty of perjury. A little later **they that stood by** affirmed that he certainly was **one of them; for thy speech maketh thee known** (v. 73) — "bewrayeth" (KJV) should be "betrayeth." What they were saying was: "Your accent gives you away." Just as there are differences of speech in various parts of most countries today, so it was in ancient Palestine (cf. Judges 12:5-6).

In answer to this third accusation Peter began **to curse and to swear, I know not the man** (v. 74). This sounds as if he resorted to profanity to prove that he was no follower of Jesus. But what is meant is that he placed himself under solemn oath and bound himself by a curse if he were not telling the truth.

Just then **the cock crew.** Peter recalled his Master's prediction (cf. v. 34). He went out and **wept bitterly** (v. 75). It was Peter's most bitter hour.

One who uses a harmony of the Gospels will note some variation in the accounts of the three denials. The simplest solution is that there was considerable confusion in the courtyard and that Peter was accused by several individuals. All four Gospels agree that he definitely denied his Master three times.

c. Jesus Doomed (27:1-2)

1 Now, when morning was come, all the chief priests and the elders of the people took counsel against Jesus to put him to death: 2 and they bound him, and led him away, and delivered him up to Pilate the governor.

The Jewish trial at night was illegal. To make the matter official, the Sanhedrin (cf. Mark 15:1 — "the whole council") met at dawn and passed the death sentence on Jesus. However, at this time the Jewish Sanhedrin was not allowed the authority for capital punishment. Except in the case of a Gentile who entered the sacred precincts of the temple, only the Roman governor could have a man put to death. So the Sanhedrin had to turn the prisoner over to Pilate (v. 2).

d. Judas Disillusioned (27:3-10)

3 Then Judas, who betrayed him, when he saw that he was condemned, repented himself, and brought back the thirty pieces of silver to the chief priests and elders, 4 saying, I have sinned in that I have betrayed innocent blood. But they said, What is that to us? see thou *to it.* 5 And he cast down the pieces of silver into the sanctuary and departed; and he went away and hanged himself. 6 And the chief priests took the pieces of silver, and said, It is not lawful to put them into the treasury, since it is the price of blood. 7 And they took counsel, and bought with them the potter's field, to bury strangers in. 8 Wherefore the field was called, The field of blood, unto this day. 9 Then was fulfilled that which was spoken through Jeremiah the prophet, saying, And they took the thirty pieces of silver, the price of him that was priced, whom *certain* of the children of Israel did price; 10 and they gave them for the potter's field, as the Lord appointed me.

The story is told only by Matthew. The callousness of the Jewish religious leaders stands in painful contrast to the compassion of Christ. Having returned the money, Judas went and **hanged himself** (v. 5). This seems to be contradicted by the account in Acts 1:18. But the ruggedness of the terrain around Jerusalem makes it altogether possible that the hanging took place overlooking a precipice, where the breaking of either the rope or the limb of a tree could cause his body to be battered on the rocks below.[128] There is also a seeming disparity between verse 8 and Acts 1:19, as to the reason why the place was called **The field of blood.** But there is no reason why both explanations should not have been current in that day and both correct.[129]

In keeping with his usual custom, Matthew quotes an Old Testament prophecy to show that it was fulfilled in Christ (v. 9). But there is a real problem here. The nearest passage to this in the Old Testament is Zechariah 11:13. How did the name of **Jeremiah** come in? The first suggestion would be a copyist's error. But **Jeremiah** is found in practically all the Greek manuscripts and early versions. Morison does indeed suggest — after listing a dozen possible solutions — that this is a sort of typographical error made by the first scribe who copied the author's original manuscript.[130] This is not at all impossible. In the *Pulpit Commentary* Williams has a good treatment of the problem. He favors the idea that Matthew had in mind reminiscenses of certain passages in Zechariah, but concludes: "Too much has been made of what, after all, may be simply an *erratum* perpetuated from an ancient copy."[131]

2. Roman Trial (27:11-32)

a. Mistried by Pilate (27:11-26)

11 Now Jesus stood before the governor: and the governor asked him, saying, Art thou the King of the Jews? And Jesus said unto him, Thou sayest. 12 And when he was accused by the chief priests and elders, he answered nothing. 13 Then saith Pilate unto him, Hearest thou not how many things they witness against thee? 14 And he gave him no answer,

---

128 See Charles W. Carter and Ralph Earle, *The Acts of the Apostles,* "The Evangelical Commentary," p. 20.   129 *Ibid.,* p. 21.   130 *Op. cit.,* p. 573.   131 *Op. cit.,* p. 583.

not even to one word: insomuch that the governor marvelled greatly. 15 Now at the feast the governor was wont to release unto the multitude one prisoner, whom they would. 16 And they had then a notable prisoner, called Barabbas. 17 When therefore they were gathered together, Pilate said unto them, Whom will ye that I release unto you? Barabbas, or Jesus who is called Christ? 18 For he knew that for envy they had delivered him up. 19 And while he was sitting on the judgment-seat, his wife sent unto him, saying, Have thou nothing to do with that righteous man; for I have suffered many things this day in a dream because of him. 20 Now the chief priests and the elders persuaded the multitudes that they should ask for Barabbas, and destroy Jesus. 21 But the governor answered and said unto them, Which of the two will ye that I release unto you? And they said, Barabbas. 22 Pilate saith unto them, What then shall I do unto Jesus who is called Christ? They all say, Let him be crucified. 23 And he said, Why, what evil hath he done? But they cried out exceedingly, saying, Let him be crucified. 24 So when Pilate saw that he prevailed nothing, but rather that a tumult was arising, he took water, and washed his hands before the multitude, saying, I am innocent of the blood of this righteous man; see ye *to it*. 25 And all the people answered and said, His blood *be* on us, and on our children. 26 Then released he unto them Barabbas; but Jesus he scourged and delivered to be crucified.

Pilate is here called the **governor**. The Greek term is *hegemon,* which was popularized in Sholem Asch's book, *The Nazarene*. It occurs in verses 2, 11 (twice,) 14, 15, 21, 27, as well as 28:14. The correct Latin title for Pilate was "procurator."

The first question that Pilate asked Jesus was, **Art thou the King of the Jews?** (so in all three Synoptics). This is probably due to the opening accusation of the Jewish leaders that Jesus claimed to be a king (Luke 23:2). Christ's answer was brief: **Thou sayest**. Filson gives the best interpretation of this ambiguous answer: "I could truthfully use the title, but you give it a meaning I cannot accept, so I cannot give you a clear Yes."[132] In other words, Pilate had in mind a political kingdom, Jesus a spiritual one.

When accused by the **chief priests and elders** — mainly Sadducees, who now led in the prosecution — Jesus kept silent. This puzzled Pilate, who was accustomed to vehement defense by prisoners. He asked Christ why He did not answer, but Christ made no reply (v. 14). There was no use in Jesus' trying to defend Himself against the **many things** (v. 13) with which the chief priests falsely accused Him. So He maintained a dignified and discreet silence. The governor **marvelled greatly** at His perfect poise.

The custom of releasing a prisoner at the feast time in Judea is not mentioned outside the Gospels. But it is in line with the sometimes generous policies of Roman rule. **Barabbas** is an Aramaic term (*Bar-abba*), meaning "son of the father." The Jews would be conscious of the play on words, since this was exactly what Jesus claimed to be. Pilate asked them whether he should release Barabbas or the Messiah (v. 17). This question was obviously an attempt on his part to set Jesus free without further trial. He was keen enough to see that the real trouble was the **envy** (v. 18) of the Jewish leaders.

The incident recorded in verse 19 is only recorded in Matthew's Gospel. Pilate's wife sent word to him that she had been distressed in a dream about Jesus. The governor had left early for the **judgment-seat** (cf. John 18:28), and evidently his wife had wakened later from her horrible **dream.** She wanted this **righteous man** released. Whether or not she had had any contact with Christ's disciples is a matter of sheer speculation. Early tradition pictures her as becoming a Christian.

While Pilate's attention was diverted by this perplexing message from his wife, the **chief priests** were busy persuading the gathered crowd to ask for the release of Barabbas and the death of Jesus (v. 20). When the governor repeated his question, the people answered, **Barabbas** (v. 21). Distracted, Pilate asked, **What then shall I do with Jesus who is called Christ?** — a question that today confronts every man. The reply was, **Let him be crucified** (v. 22). Again Pilate demurred, wanting to know what **evil** Jesus had done. This shows his pitifully

[132] *Op. cit.,* p. 289.

weak character. Stirred to frenzy by their religious leaders, the people **cried out exceedingly** with the same slogan (v. 23). Filled with cowardly fear in the face of an unruly mob, Pilate gave in. He had allowed himself to be maneuvered into a corner by the scheming Sadducees, and he saw no escape. He lacked the moral courage to do what he knew was right and also what was his responsibility as governor.

Pilate's washing his hands before the crowd (v. 24) is recorded only by Matthew. It did not cleanse his conscience, nor did it remove his guilt. His desire to placate the Jews by letting them have their way did him no good. Six years later he was summoned to Rome by the emperor to answer charges of misrule. Banished to Gaul, he is said to have committed suicide.

The governor released Barabbas and **scourged** Jesus. The Roman scourge was a short whip made of strips of leather, with sharp pieces of metal or bone fastened to the ends. The victim's back was lacerated to shreds; some men even died under the lash. There is no excuse for Pilate's adding this cruel torture, unless it was an absolute requirement before crucifixion.

b. Mocked by Soldiers (27:27-32)

27 Then the soldiers of the governor took Jesus into the Praetorium, and gathered unto him the whole band. 28 And they stripped him, and put on him a scarlet robe. 29 And they platted a crown of thorns and put it upon his head, and a reed in his right hand; and they kneeled down before him, and mocked him, saying, Hail, King of the Jews! 30 And they spat upon him, and took the reed and smote him on the head. 31 And when they had mocked him, they took off from him the robe, and put on him his garments, and led him away to crucify him.

32 And as they came out, they found a man of Cyrene, Simon by name: him they compelled to go *with them,* that he might bear his cross.

When Jesus was turned over to the soldiers they took Him into the **Praetorium.** The location of this place is much debated. The two alternatives are

Herod's palace — in the southwestern part of Jerusalem, near the present Jaffa Gate — or the Tower of Antonia at the northwest corner of the temple area. Josephus seems to suggest the former,[133] as does Philo[134] — both being Jewish writers of the first century. The regular residence of the Roman governor of Judea was in Caesarea. Schürer writes: "On special occasions, especially during the chief Jewish feasts, when, on account of the crowds of people that streamed into Jerusalem, particularly careful oversight was necessary, the procurator went up to Jerusalem and resided then in what had been the palace of Herod."[135] Sanday also argues for this as the location of the **praetorium,**[136] as does Dalman[137] — two of the best authorities on New Testament topography.

But Herod Antipas was in Jerusalem at this time (Luke 23:7). Some scholars feel that he was staying in the palace built by his father, Herod the Great. The question cannot be settled.

Christ had evidently been scourged publicly, before the crowds that demanded His crucifixion. Was this done to show that Pilate was carrying out their wishes with a vengeance? Or, possibly, may he yet have had a faint hope that they might be moved to desire mercy? There is no way of knowing. In any event, the soldiers now led Jesus inside the courtyard (cf. Mark 15:16), where they called together the whole **band,** or "cohort" — the tenth part of a Roman legion, and so about six hundred men. Perhaps two hundred or so would be on duty at this time.

First the soldiers **stripped him** (that is, took off His outer garment) and placed on Him the **scarlet robe** (v. 28) of a Roman legionnaire. Then they braided a **crown of thorns** and put it on His head, and a **reed** (mock sceptre) in His hand. Having arrayed Him like a king, they **kneeled down** in front of Him and **mocked** Him, hailing Him jeeringly as **King of the Jews.** It was as callous and cruel a performance as one can imagine. To add to the insult, they **spat** on Him, and grabbing the mock sceptre, hit Him with it on the head, doubtless driving the thorns into His brow.

[133] *War,* II. 14. 8.   [134] *Legat. ad Cajum.* 38.   [135] *Op. cit.,* I, i, 48.
[136] William Sanday, *Sacred Sites of the Gospels,* pp. 52-55.
[137] Gustaf Dalman, *Sacred Sites and Ways,* trans. Paul Levertoff, pp. 335-342.

When they were surfeited with mocking Him, they took off the scarlet robe, put on His own outer garment, and led Him out to crucifixion. On the way they pressed into service a certain **Simon** from **Cyrene** — an African, but not necessarily a Negro — and compelled him to carry the heavy wooden cross. It was the custom for a condemned criminal to bear his own cross — or at least the crossbeam — to the place of execution. Jesus started out bearing His (John 19:17), but apparently He was so weakened by the agonies of Gethsemane and the terrible scourging that He staggered under the load and had to be relieved.

3. Execution (27:33-66)

a. Placed on Cross (27:33-44)

33 And when they were come unto a place called Golgotha, that is to say, The place of a skull, 34 they gave him wine to drink mingled with gall: and when he had tasted it, he would not drink. 35 And when they had crucified him, they parted his garments among them, casting lots; 36 and they sat and watched him there. 37 And they set up over his head his accusation written, THIS IS JESUS THE KING OF THE JEWS. 38 Then are there crucified with him two robbers, one on the right hand and one on the left. 39 And they that passed by railed on him, wagging their heads, 40 and saying, Thou that destroyest the temple, and buildest it in three days, save thyself: if thou art the Son of God, come down from the cross. 41 In like manner also the chief priests mocking *him*, with the scribes and elders, said, 42 He saved others; himself he cannot save. He is the King of Israel; let him now come down from the cross, and we will believe on him. 43 He trusteth on God; let him deliver him now, if he desireth him: for he said, I am the Son of God. 44 And the robbers also that were crucified with him cast upon him the same reproach.

Golgotha is a modified transliteration of the Aramaic word for **skull.** The Greek for the latter is *kranion* ("cranium"). The reference is probably to a skull-shaped hill.[138] But precisely where it was located is not certain. Many Protestants favor Gordon's Calvary, a skull-shaped rock north of the city wall near the Jericho Road, between Herod's Gate

[138] Filson, *op. cit.,* p. 295.

and the Damascus Gate. Hebrews 13:12 suggests that the crucifixion took place outside the city. The traditional site in the present Church of the Holy Sepulcher is inside the walls, but may have been outside the north wall of that time. Archaeology has not yet furnished a final answer to this question.

The soldiers offered Jesus **wine . . . mingled with gall** (v. 34). This was intended as a narcotic to deaden the pain of hanging on the cross. Tradition says that the women of Jerusalem furnished this mercifully for crucified criminals. When Jesus had **tasted** it and recognized what it was, He refused to drink it. He wanted to be fully conscious during these hours of suffering for sin.

The soldiers stripped Him for crucifixion and divided His few **garments** among them (v. 35). These probably consisted of sandals, an under garment (short and sleeveless), a long white robe, a girdle, and the turban (headdress). John 19:23-24 explains more clearly the reference to **casting lots,** and the matter will be discussed there. John's account also indicates that there were four soldiers who **sat and watched** Him.

The wording of the inscription over His head differs somewhat in the four Gospels. John (19:20) says it was written in Hebrew (Aramaic), Latin, and Greek. So the form may have varied. Mark (15:26) gives the shortest form: "The King of the Jews," which is incorporated in all four forms. Putting them all together we have: "This is Jesus of Nazareth, the King of the Jews."

Two **robbers** (not "thieves") were crucified with Jesus, one on each side. People passing by **railed on him,** and mockingly shook their heads at Him (v. 39). Taunting Him with His supposed claim that He could rebuild the temple in three days, they said, **Save thyself.** If He was the Son of God, why did He not prove it by coming down from the cross (v. 40)? What they could not perceive was that He proved Himself the Son of God by *staying* on the cross. Divine love, not spectacular power, is the greatest demonstration of deity. **He saved others; himself he cannot save** (v. 42), said the members of the Sanhedrin (v. 41). They spoke better than they knew. He could not save Himself from the Cross and still save others.

The scathing sting of the words in verse 43 also goes beyond the intellect and intention of these Jewish leaders. Since He claimed to be the Son of God, let God deliver Him if He wishes to have Him. The awful fact was that the Father had to turn His back on His beloved Son and forsake Him when He took man's place as a condemned sinner. This was the heart of the meaning of the Cross, but the religious leaders missed it entirely. To them Jesus was a blasphemous impostor, who deserved to die.

The statement of verse 44 seems out of harmony with Luke 23:40. But it may well be that at first both suffering robbers bitterly reproached the man on the middle cross, but that finally one of them was so impressed with Jesus' attitude toward those who mocked Him that he turned to Him in repentance and faith.

b. Praying in Despair (27:45-56)

45 Now from the sixth hour there was darkness over all the land until the ninth hour. And about the ninth hour Jesus cried with a loud voice, saying, Eli, Eli, lama sabachthani? that is, My God, my God, why hast thou forsaken me? 47 And some of them that stood there, when they heard it, said, This man calleth Elijah. 48 And straightway one of them ran, and took a sponge, and filled it with vinegar, and put it on a reed, and gave him to drink. 49 And the rest said, Let be; let us see whether Elijah cometh to save him. 50 And Jesus cried again with a loud voice, and yielded up his spirit. 51 And behold, the veil of the temple was rent in two from the top to the bottom; and the earth did quake; and the rocks were rent; 52 and the tombs were opened; and many bodies of the saints that had fallen asleep were raised; 53 and coming forth out of the tombs after his resurrection they entered into the holy city and appeared unto many. 54 Now the centurion, and they that were with him watching Jesus, when they saw the earthquake, and the things that were done, feared exceedingly, saying, Truly this was the Son of God. 55 And many women were there beholding from afar, who had followed Jesus from Galilee, ministering unto him: 56 among whom was Mary Magdalene, and Mary the mother of James and Joses, and the mother of the sons of Zebedee.

This is the Holy of Holies of the Gospels and should be entered only in a reverent spirit. This was the most important moment in human history. The salvation of mankind depended on it.

From the **sixth hour** (noon) until the **ninth hour** (3:00 P.M.) there was darkness over all the **land**. The Greek word is *ge* (pronounced gay), which means "earth," but in the varying senses of "soil," or "land," or "ground," or "globe." An interesting inconsistency of translation is found in the King James Version, which has "whole land" here, but "whole earth" in the parallel passage in Luke 23:44. Probably the former translation, "land," found in all three Synoptics in the Revised versions, is correct. The darkness covered the land of Judea, or possibly Palestine (cf. 2:6, 20). This could not have been caused by an ordinary eclipse of the sun, for the moon is always full at the Passover season. (Each month in the Jewish calendar began with the new moon, and since the Passover was on the fifteenth it was always at full moon.) Probably a heavy, black cloud shut off the sun's light. Storm clouds were thought of as signs of divine judgment.

At the **ninth hour** — the time for the offering of the evening sacrifice — Jesus cried out in Hebrew (quoting Ps. 22:1): **My God, my God, why hast thou forsaken me?** (v. 46). This was the price He had to pay for man's salvation. The Incarnate Son of God took the torturous trail of a lost soul, walking out into the labyrinthine depths of outer darkness. Hebrews 2:9 says that He tasted death for every man. For a few moments He experienced in His consciousness the unspeakable horrors of eternal doom. The darkness that covered the land was but a symbol of the deeper spiritual darkness that shrouded His soul. His cry of dereliction reveals the measure of His sacrifice. On the cross He paid the penalty for sin, which is separation from God.

When they heard Him cry **Eli**, some thought He was calling for **Elijah** (v. 47). One bystander soaked a sponge in **vinegar** — the sour wine commonly drunk by laborers (Ruth 2:14) and soldiers — put it on **reed** (John 19:29 says "hyssop"), and offered it to Jesus. Again Christ cried out — it is not said what He uttered — **and yielded up his spirit**. His death was voluntary (John 10:18). He gave Himself as a sacrifice for men's sins.

At the moment of His death the **veil** — the inner veil shutting off the Holy of Holies in the sanctuary — was torn in two, from top to bottom. The writer of Hebrews (9:1-14; 10:19-22) gives the significance of this. It symbolized the fact that through the rent veil of Christ's flesh the way was now opened for every believer to come into the holy presence of God. It may also have prefigured the destruction of the temple in A.D. 70. God no longer dwells in a temple made with hands, but in the sanctuary of human hearts (I Cor. 3:16; 6:19).

The incident recorded in verses 51b-53 — the earthquake, opening of tombs, and resurrection of many saints — is found only in Matthew. The **bodies of the saints** were **raised** (v. 52). After **his resurrection** (that is, Christ's) they came out of their tombs and entered **the holy city** (cf. 4:5). What finally happened to these resurrected saints we are not told. Instead of laboring with the problems involved, it seems best to appreciate the spiritual symbolism suggested. Morison puts it this way: "In the Death of Christ is the true victory over death, and the true entrance into life. His death was the death of death, and the genesis of life everlasting."[139]

The **centurion** (officer in charge of a hundred men; what we would call "captain") and those with him were filled with fear, and said: **Truly this was the Son of God** (v. 54). There has been considerable comment about the change to "a son of God" (RSV). The simple fact is that the definite article is not used here, and the Greek language has no indefinite article. The safest translation is "God's Son" (Berkeley Version). But should "son" be capitalized or not?

A significant item, often forgotten, is that Luke reports the centurion as saying: "Certainly this was a righteous man" (Luke 23:47). That is the way he interpreted it for his Greek readers. (Or, did the centurion say both?) Does "son of God" then mean a godly person, "a righteous man"? Would the pagan cen-

turion have had the religious background for understanding "the Son of God"?

Many feel that the centurion was the firstfruits of Christ's victory on the Cross. The difficulty of interpreting this passage is shown by W. C. Allen's treatment of it. He prints the translation, "a Son of God," but comments: "The centurion, who may well have known that Jesus was popularly understood to claim to be the Son of God, expresses his conviction that the circumstance of His death pointed to the reality of the claim."[140]

E. C. Colwell has made a careful study of the use and non-use of the article in the New Testament. He concludes that ". . . definite predicate nouns which precede the verb usually lack the article."[141] This means that the phrase here should be translated "the Son of God." C. F. D. Moule agrees with Colwell.[142] It is to be noted that exactly the same phrase occurs in 14:33, where the Revised Standard Version gives the obviously correct translation: "Truly you are the Son of God." That may be the best rendering here.

Many women from Galilee watched the crucifixion. Three are named (v. 56). **Mary Magdalene** was one of the most loyal followers of Christ. Another **Mary** is identified as **the mother of James** ("the less," Mark 15:40) **and Joses.** The third woman was **the mother of the sons of Zebedee,** perhaps named "Salome" (cf. Mark 15:40).

c. Placed in Tomb (27:57-61)

57 And when even was come, there came a rich man from Arimathaea, named Joseph, who also himself was Jesus' disciple: 58 this man went to pilate, and asked for the body of Jesus. Then Pilate commanded it to be given up. 59 And Joseph took the body, and wrapped it in a clean linen cloth, 60 and laid it in his own new tomb, which he had hewn out in the rock: and he rolled a great stone to the door of the tomb, and departed. 61 And Mary Magdalene was there, and the other Mary, sitting over against the sepulchre.

When even was come — evidently between three o'clock and sunset — Joseph of Arimathea, a secret disciple of Jesus

[139] *Op. cit.,* p. 601.   [140] *Op. cit.,* p. 297.   [141] *Journal of Biblical Literature,* LII (1933), 20.
[142] *An Idiom Book of New Testament Greek,* p. 116.

(John 19:38), asked Pilate for the corpse. When it was given him he wrapped it in a **clean linen cloth** and laid it in a **new tomb**, which was cut in the face of a cliff. His actions showed the love and reverence he had for Christ. Rolling **a great stone** across the entrance to the tomb, he **departed,** for the sabbath began at sunset, and all labor must cease. Two women watched his work — **Mary Magdalene** (i.e., from the city of Magdala) and **the other Mary.** The latter is apparently the woman mentioned in verse 56.

d. Placed Under Guard (27:62-66)

62 Now on the morrow, which is *the day* after the Preparation, the chief priests and the Pharisees were gathered together unto Pilate, 63 saying, Sir, we remember that that deceiver said while he was yet alive, After three days I will rise again. 64 Command therefore that the sepulchre be made sure until the third day, lest haply his disciples come and steal him away, and say unto the people, He is risen from the dead: and the last error will be worse than the first. 65 Pilate said unto them, Ye have a guard: go, make it as sure as ye can. 66 So they went, and made the sepulchre sure, sealing the stone, the guard being with them.

This story is told only by Matthew. It describes what took place on Saturday. The Preparation is a technical term for Friday, the day before the Sabbath (Saturday). **The chief priests** (Sadducees) and the **Pharisees** came to Pilate. They remembered that **that deceiver** (impostor) had predicted He would rise after three days. So they wanted His tomb guarded with special care, lest His disciples steal His body and report it as a miraculous resurrection. In that case the last **error** — "imposture," same root as **deceiver** (v. 62) — would be worse than the first (i.e., His claim to be the Messiah). The connection of the same Greek roots should be shown by translating either "deceiver . . . deception," or "impostor . . . imposture." **Ye have a guard** may be rendered, "Take a guard." They evidently took four Roman soldiers, sealed the sepulcher, and left the soldiers to guard it.

This passage throws some light on the much debated question concerning how long Jesus was in the tomb. "Three days and three nights" (12:40) sounds like seventy-two hours, which would obviously rule out a Friday crucifixion. It is claimed that **after three days** (v. 63) also does. But the Jewish leaders asked that a guard be set **until the third day** (v. 64). Assuming that this means beginning with Friday, the third day would be Sunday. The expression "on the third day" is used seven times for the resurrection of Christ (Matt. 16:21; 17:23; 20:19; Luke 24:7, 21, 46; I Cor. 15:4). It seems clear that the Gospel writers used "after three days" (twice) and "on the third day" as equivalent. Since the latter occurs far more often and is more specific, it appears reasonable to take it as definitive, and thus to hold that Jesus died on Friday afternoon and rose Sunday morning.

C. HIS RESURRECTION (28:1-20)

1. Revelation to Women (28:1-10)

1 Now late on the sabbath day, as it began to dawn toward the first *day* of the week, came Mary Magdalene and the other Mary to see the sepulchre. 2 And behold, there was a great earthquake; for an angel of the Lord descended from heaven, and came and rolled away the stone, and sat upon it. 3 His appearance was as lightning, and his raiment white as snow: 4 and for fear of him the watchers did quake, and became as dead men. 5 And the angel answered and said unto the women, Fear not ye; for I know ye seek Jesus, who hath been crucified. 6 He is not here; for he is risen, even as he said. Come, see the place where the Lord lay. 7 And go quickly, and tell his disciples, He is risen from the dead; and lo, he goeth before you into Galilee; there shall ye see him: lo, I have told you. 8 And they departed quickly from the tomb with fear and great joy, and ran to bring his disciples word. 9 And behold, Jesus met them, saying, All hail. And they came and took hold of his feet, and worshipped him. 10 Then saith Jesus unto them, Fear not: go tell my brethren that they depart into Galilee, and there shall they see me.

Late on the sabbath day is better rendered "after the sabbath" (cf. Mark 16:1), for the sabbath ended at sunset on Saturday, and this was Sunday morning. The two Marys (cf. 15:56, 61) came **to see the sepulchre.** Matthew (alone again) mentions a second **earthquake** and at the same time an **angel** descending from heaven and rolling the stone back from the door. His appearance struck the guards with terror (vv. 2-3).

The **angel** (v. 5) is described as "a young man" (Mark 16:5). Interestingly it is Luke, rather than Matthew, who speaks this time of "two men" (Luke 24: 4). The women were greeted with the typical words, **Fear not ye** (cf. v. 10), and informed that Jesus had risen. They were invited to look into the empty tomb and then tell His disciples He had risen and would meet them in Galilee (v. 7). The two women **ran** to share the good news with the sad-hearted disciples. On the way **Jesus met them** (v. 9). He confirmed the announcement of the angels that He would meet His followers in Galilee (v. 10). The beautiful name **brethren** would comfort their hearts. He was still one with them.

This meeting of the disciples with their Master in Galilee is described in verses 16-20. But Mark, Luke, and John all tell of appearances of Jesus on the very day of the resurrection in or near Jerusalem. It seems evident that the earliest appearances took place in Judea, followed by two in Galilee (vv. 16-20 and 21), and finally by the concluding ones — on the Mount of Olives and at His ascension.

2. Report of Guard (28:11-15)

11 Now while they were going, behold, some of the guard came into the city, and told unto the chief priests all the things that were come to pass. 12 And when they were assembled with the elders, and had taken counsel, they gave much money unto the soldiers, 13 saying, Say ye, His disciples came by night, and stole him away while we slept. 14 And if this come to the governor's ears, we will persuade him, and rid you of care. 15 So they took the money, and did as they were taught: and this saying was spread abroad among the Jews, *and continueth* until this day.

As Matthew is the only Gospel-writer who records the posting of the guards at the tomb (27:62-66), so he is the only one who gives the sequel. While the women who had seen Jesus were hurrying to tell the disciples, **some of the guard** went into the **city** (Jerusalem) and told

the **chief priests** what had happened. The latter called a meeting of the Sanhedrin and decided to bribe the soldiers to say that the disciples stole Jesus' body at night while the guards slept. Since death was the penalty for a sentry caught sleeping on duty, the Jewish leaders promised to protect the soldiers (v. 14). The spread of this false report among the Jews **until this day** — the time when the Evangelist wrote — is his obvious reason for recording the incident here. He wished to set the record straight.

3. Rendezvous in Galilee (28:16-20)

16 But the eleven disciples went into Galilee, unto the mountain where Jesus had appointed them. 17 And when they saw him they worshipped *him;* but some doubted. 18 And Jesus came to them and spake unto them, saying, All authority hath been given unto me in heaven and on earth. 19 Go ye therefore, and make disciples of all the nations, baptizing them into the name of the Father and of the Son and of the Holy Spirit: 20 teaching them to observe all things whatsoever I commanded you: and lo,· I am with you always, even unto the end of the world.

The **eleven disciples** — Judas was now gone — went to a mountain in Galilee **where Jesus had appointed them.** This suggests that the Master had made definite arrangements with His disciples before His crucifixion (cf. 26:32). Even when they saw Jesus and **worshipped him** (cf. v. 9), yet **some doubted.** The latter reference cannot be connected with Thomas (John 20:24-25), since the disciples could hardly have made the round trip to Galilee (at least 150 miles) between the first and second Sunday nights. The various accounts suggest that Jesus' appearance was in some way different after His resurrection, for in several cases people fail to recognize Him at first (cf. John 20:15; Luke 24:16, 37). The exact nature of Christ's resurrection body is a matter of sheer speculation.

On this mountain in Galilee the Master gave the Great Commission to His disciples. **All authority** (*exousia*) was given to Him **in heaven and on earth** (v. 18). Morison comments: *"All authority in heaven:* So that He can make use of all the resources of heaven. *All authority upon earth:* So that He can turn every institution and power and person on earth to account."[143]

On the basis of this authority came the command, Go. They were to make disciples of all nations. The verb is from the noun *mathetes* "disciple" (literally, a learner). Tasker comments: "A disciple is not one who has already learned, but one who is always learning. The 'school-days' of a Christian are never over."[144]

Baptizing them into the name seems awkward. Since in Hellenistic Greek *eis* (into) is already beginning to encroach on the functions of *en* (in) — and has completely replaced the latter in Modern Greek — it is doubtful that the translation into should be insisted upon (cf. KJV, Moffatt, Goodspeed, RSV, NEB). This does not mean that Jesus' main emphasis was on a rigid baptismal formula. Baptizing and indoctrinating are closely allied, as the next verse indicates. But a Christian is one who has accepted the Trinity and sworn allegiance to Father, Son, and Holy Spirit.

Teaching is an important part of evangelism. Making new converts is not enough. They must be taught how to live the Christ life.

With the Go (v. 19) comes the Lo (v. 20). Always is literally "all the days." This is something more than mere chronology. It means that whatever kind of days may be the lot of the Christian, Christ is there — a most comforting assurance. And this is promised unto the end of the world (better, "age"). The Gospel of Matthew thus ends with a command and a promise conditioned on obedience to the commission.

Since this book is called a "Gospel" (*evangel*) it is altogether fitting that the closing emphasis should be on the evangelization of all men everywhere. McNeile comments on the last clause thus: "A world-wide mission, imperative because of Christ's limitless *exousia*, is also possible because of His perpetual presence."[145]

---

[143] *Op. cit.*, p. 623.
[144] R. V. G. Tasker, *The Gospel According to St. Matthew,* "The Tyndale New Testament Commentaries," p. 277.
[145] A. H. McNeile, *The Gospel According to St. Matthew,* p. 437.

Bibliography

Commentaries Used

Alford, Henry. *The Greek Testament*, E. F. Harrison. Vol. I. Chicago: Moody Press, 1958.

————. *New Testament for English Readers.* Chicago: Moody Press, n.d.

Allen, W. C. *A Critical and Exegetical Commentary on the Gospel According to St. Matthew.* "The International Critical Commentary." (3rd ed.) Edinburgh: T. & T. Clark, 1912.

Barclay, William. *The Gospel of Matthew.* (2nd ed.) 2 vols. Philadelphia: Westminster Press, 1958.

Barnes, Albert. *Notes on the New Testament: Matthew and Mark,* ed. Robert Frew. Grand Rapids: Baker Book House, 1949.

Bengel, John Albert. *Gnomon of the New Testament.* (4th ed.) Edinburgh: T. & T. Clark, 1860. Vol. I.

Broadus, John A. *Commentary on the Gospel of Matthew.* "An American Commentary on the New Testament." Philadelphia: American Baptist Publication Society, 1886.

Bruce, A. B. "The Synoptic Gospels." *The Expositor's Greek Testament.* Vol. I. Grand Rapids: Wm. B. Eerdmans Publishing Co., n.d.

Carr, A. *The Gospel According to St. Matthew.* "Cambridge Greek Testament." Cambridge: University Press, 1886.

Clarke, Adam. *The New Testament of Our Lord and Saviour Jesus Christ.* Vol. I. New York: Methodist Book Concern, n.d.

Dietrick, Suzanne de. "The Gospel According to Matthew." *The Layman's Bible Commentary,* ed. B. H. Kelly, *et al.* Vol. 16. Richmond, Va.: John Knox Press, 1961.

Erdman, Charles R. *The Gospel of Matthew.* Philadelphia: Westminster Press, 1920.

Filson, Floyd V. *A Commentary on the Gospel According to St. Matthew.* "Harper's New Testament Commentaries." New York: Harper & Brothers, 1960.

Green, F. W. *The Gospel According to Saint Matthew.* "The Clarendon Bible." (2nd ed.) Oxford: Clarendon Press, 1945.

Johnson, Sherman. "The Gospel According to St. Matthew" (Exegesis). *The Interpreter's Bible,* ed. G. A. Buttrick, *et al.* Vol. VII. New York: Abingdon-Cokesbury Press, 1951.

Lange, John Peter. *Commentary on the Holy Scriptures: Matthew.* Trans. and ed.

Philip Schaff. Grand Rapids: Zondervan Publishing House, n.d.

Lenski, R. C. H. *The Interpretation of St. Matthew's Gospel.* Columbus, O.: Wartburg press, 1943.

McNeile, A. H. *The Gospel According to St. Matthew.* London: Macmillan & Co., 1915.

Meyer, H. A. W. *Critical and Exegetical Hand-book to the Gospel of Matthew.* New York: Funk & Wagnalls, 1884.

Micklem, Philip A. *St. Matthew.* "Westminster Commentaries." London: Methuen & Co., 1917.

Morison, James. *A Practical Commentary on the Gospel According to St. Matthew,* London: Hodder & Stoughton, 1899.

Plummer, Alfred. *An Exegetical Commentary on the Gospel According to St. Matthew.* London: Elliot Stock, 1909.

Robinson, Theodore H. *The Gospel of Matthew.* "Moffatt's New Testament Commentary." New York: Harper & Brothers, 1927.

Tasker, R. V. G. *The Gospel According to St. Matthew.* "The Tyndale New Testament Commentaries." Grand Rapids: Wm. B. Eerdmans Publishing Co., 1961.

Trapp, John. *Commentary on the New Testament.* Grand Rapids: Zondervan Publishing House, 1958.

Ward, A. Marcus. *The Gospel According to St. Matthew.* "Epworth Preacher's Commentaries." London: Epworth Press, 1961.

Wesley, John. *Explanatory Notes on the New Testament.* London: Epworth Press, 1941.

Williams, A. L. "St. Matthew" (Exposition). *Pulpit Commentary.* Vol. XV. Grand Rapids: Wm. B. Eerdmans Publishing Co., 1950.

Other Works Cited

Abbott-Smith, G. *A Manual Lexicon of the New Testament.* (2nd ed.) Edinburgh: T. & T. Clark, 1923.

Andrews, Samuel J. *The Life of Our Lord.* Grand Rapids: Zondervan Publishing House, 1954.

Arndt, W. F., and Gingrich, F. W. *A Greek-English Lexicon of the New Testament and Other Early Christian Literature.* Chicago: University of Chicago Press, 1957.

Black, Matthew. *The Scrolls and Christian*

Origins. New York: Charles Scribner's Sons, 1961.

Blair, Edward P. *Jesus in the Gospel of Matthew.* New York: Abingdon Press, 1960.

Bonhoeffer, Dietrich. *The Cost of Discipleship.* (2nd ed.) New York: Macmillan Co., 1959.

Bowman, J. W. and Tapp, R. W. *The Gospel from the Mount.* Philadelphia: Westminster Press, 1957.

Branscomb, Harvie. *The Teaching of Jesus.* New York: Abingdon Cokesbury Press, 1931.

Bruce, F. F. *Second Thoughts on the Dead Sea Scrolls.* Grand Rapids: Wm. B. Eerdmans Publishing Co., 1956.

Burrows, Millar. *The Dead Sea Scrolls.* New York: Viking Press, 1955.

Buttrick, George A. *The Parables of Jesus.* New York: Harper & Brothers, 1928.

Carter, Charles W., and Earle, Ralph. *The Acts of the Apostles.* "Evangelical Commentary." Grand Rapids: Zondervan Publishing House, 1959.

Daane, James. "The Perfection of God," *The Reformed Journal* (Grand Rapids), VIII (December, 1958), 6ff.

Dalman, Gustaf. *Sacred Sites and Ways.* Trans. Paul Levertoff. London: Society for Promoting Christian Knowledge, 1935.

Deissmann, Adolf. *Light from the Ancient East,* trans. L. R. M. Strachan. (Rev. ed.) New York: George H. Doran Co., 1927.

Dodd, C. H. *The Parables of the Kingdom.* (Rev. ed.) London: Nisbet & Co., 1936.

Edersheim, Alfred. *The Life and Times of Jesus the Messiah:* (8th ed.) 2 vols. New York: Longmans, Green & Co., 1903.

Epictetus. *Dissertations. Encyclopaedia Britannica,* Chicago; 1952.

Eusebius. *Ecclesiastical History.* Trans. C. F. Cruse. Grand Rapids: Baker Book House, 1955.

Foakes-Jackson, F. J. *Josephus and the Jews.* New York: Richard R. Smith, 1930.

Franzmann, Martin H. *Follow Me: Discipleship According to Saint Matthew.* St. Louis, Mo.: Concordia Publishing House, 1961.

Goodspeed, Edgar J. *Matthew, Apostle and Evangelist.* Philadelphia: John C. Winston Co., 1959.

Hayes, D. A. *The Synoptic Gospels and Acts.* New York: Methodist Book Concern, 1919.

Holdsworth, W. W. *Gospel Origins.* New York: Charles Scribner's Sons, 1913.

Hunter, A. M. *Interpreting the Parables of Jesus.* Naperville, Ill.: SCM Book Club, 1960.

―――. *A Pattern for Life.* Philadelphia: Westminster Press, 1953.

Jeremias, Joachim. *The Parables of Jesus.* Trans. S. H. Hooke. New York: Charles Scribner's Sons, 1955.

Jones, E. Stanley. *The Christ of the Mount.* New York: Abingdon Press, 1931.

Josephus, Flavius. *Works.* Trans. William Whiston. Philadelphia: Henry T. Coates, n.d.

Lloyd-Jones, D. Martyn. *Studies in the Sermon on the Mount.* 2 vols. Grand Rapids: Wm. B. Eerdmans Publishing Co., 1959-60.

Matthews, Shailer. *New Testament Times in Palestine.* (Rev. ed.) New York: Macmillan Co., 1933.

Miller, Madeleine S., and Miller, J. Lane. *Harper's Bible Dictionary.* New York: Harper & Brothers, 1952.

Moule, C. F. D. *An Idiom Book of New Testament Greek.* Cambridge: University Press, 1953.

Moulton, J. H., and Milligan, George. *The Vocabulary of the Greek Testament.* Grand Rapids: Wm. B. Eerdmans Publishing Co., 1949.

Oxford English Dictionary, ed. J. A. H. Murray, et al. 13 vols. Oxford: Clarendon Press, 1933.

Robertson, A. T. *Word Pictures in the New Testament.* Vol. I. New York: Richard R. Smith, 1930.

Sanday, William. *Sacred Sites of the Gospels.* Oxford: Clarendon Press, 1903.

Schürer, Emil. *A History of the Jewish People in the Time of Jesus Christ.* Division I (2 vols.). Division II (3 vols.) Edinburgh: T. & T. Clark, 1885.

Scott, E. F. *The Crisis in the Life of Jesus: The Cleansing of the Temple and Its Significance.* New York: Charles Scribner's Sons, 1952.

Stauffer, Ethelbert. *Jesus and His Story.* Trans. Richard and Clara Winston. New York: Alfred A. Knopf, 1960.

Stendahl, Krister. *The School of Matthew.* Uppsala, 1954.

―――. (ed.). *The Scrolls and the New Testament.* New York: Harper & Brothers, 1957.

Streeter, B. H. *The Four Gospels.* (Rev. ed.) London: Macmillan and Co., 1930.

Thomson, William H. *The Land and the Book.* 3 vols. New York: Harper & Brothers, 1882.

Trench, R. C. *Notes on the Parables of Our Lord.* Philadelphia: William Sychelmoore, 1878.

Weatherhead, Leslie D. *It Happened in Palestine.* New York: Abingdon Press, 1936.

Wuest, Kenneth S. *The New Testament: An Expanded Translation.* Grand Rapids: Wm. B. Eerdmans Publishing Co., 1961.

The Gospel According to St. Mark
by Ralph Earle

Outline
The Servant and His Service

III. THE SERVANT'S SACRIFICE (14:1-16:20)

A. Foes and Friends (14:1-31)
1. Conspiracy and Comfort (14:1-11)
a. Council to Kill (14:1-2)
b. Comfort of Consecration (14:3-9)
c. Conspiracy for Capture (14:10-11)
2. Passover and Prediction (14:12-31)
a. Preparation for Passover (14:12-16)
b. Passover with Disciples (14:17-21)
c. Presentation of Eucharist (14:22-25)
d. Prediction about Peter (14:26-31)
B. Gethsemane and Golgotha (14:32-15:57)
1. Agony and Arrest (14:32-52)
a. Bitterness of Cup (14:32-42)
b. Betrayal by Companion (14:43-50)
c. Befriending by Youth (14:51-52)
2. Trial and Denial (14:53-72)
a. Trial by Sanhedrin (14:53-65)
b. Denial by Peter (14:66-72)
3. Pilate and People (15:1-21)
a. Problem of Pilate (15:1-5)
b. Plea of People (15:6-15)
c. Persecution in Praetorium (15:16-21)
4. Execution and Entombment (15:22-47)
a. Railing and Robbers (15:22-32)
b. Darkness and Death (15:33-41)
c. Kindness and Courtesy (15:42-47)
C. Resurrection and Reappearance (16:1-20)
1. Resurrection (16:1-8)
2. Reappearances (16:9-20)
a. To Mary Magdalene (16:9-11)
b. To Two Disciples (16:12-13)
c. To the Eleven (16:14-18)
3. Reinstatement (16:19-20)

Introduction

I. AUTHORSHIP

The testimony of the early church is unanimous in asserting that the Second Gospel was written by John Mark. This view is seldom questioned today.

Papias (A.D. 140) is the first witness. Eusebius quotes him as affirming: "John the presbyter also said this, Mark being the interpreter of Peter, whatsoever he recorded he wrote with great accuracy, but not however, in the order in which it was spoken or done by our Lord, for he neither heard nor followed our Lord, but as before said, he was in company with Peter, who gave him such instruction as was necessary, but not to give a history of our Lord's discourses."[1]

Justin Martyr (A.D. 150) refers to this Gospel as "Peter's Memoirs." Irenaeus (A.D. 185) says that after the "departure" (death?) of Peter and Paul, who had been preaching in Rome, "Mark, the disciple and interpreter of Peter, also transmitted to us in writing what had been preached by Peter."[2]

Clement of Alexandria (A.D. 195), as quoted by Eusebius, speaks more explicitly. He says: "When Peter had proclaimed the word publicly at Rome . . .; as there was a great number present, they requested Mark, who had followed him from afar, and remembered well what he had said, to reduce these things to writings, and that after composing the gospel he gave it to those who requested it of him."[3] Clement adds: "Which, when Peter understood, he directly neither hindered nor encouraged it."[4]

Other quotations could be given. But these will serve to show the twofold testimony of the early church that in this Gospel Mark has given the preaching of Peter. The only thing that is uncertain is whether the Gospel was written before or after Peter's death.

The author's full name was John Mark. John was a common Jewish name. Marcus was his Roman name. He would be called by the former when among Jews, but by the latter in the Gentile world.

The first mention of Mark is in the Book of Acts. While Peter was in prison, a prayer meeting was held on his behalf in the home of "Mary the mother of John, whose surname was Mark" (Acts 12:12). It is possible that this was the location of the Last Supper and Pentecost.

Mark accompanied Paul and Barnabas from Jerusalem to Antioch (Acts 12:25) and then became their attendant on the first missionary journey (Acts 13:5). But at Perga in Pamphylia he left them and returned home to Jerusalem. For this reason Paul refused to take him along on the second journey (Acts 15:36-41). Mark went with Barnabas to Cyprus, while Paul chose a new associate Silas. It looked as though Mark was through, as far as Paul was concerned.

Such was not the case. The young man finally made good. Paul twice mentions Mark as being with him in Rome (Col. 4:10; Philemon 24). He is identified as the "cousin of Barnabas" (Col. 4:10). In the great apostle's last letter he writes: "take Mark, and bring him with thee; for he is useful to me for ministering" (II Tim. 4:11). He could not have paid any higher compliment to the former "quitter" than to request his presence in those last days on earth.

II. DATE

Most American and British scholars today date Mark at A.D. 65-70, or at least between 60 and 70. Some place it a decade or two later. The traditional conservative dating is in the 50's. This dating was even defended by the noted German liberal scholar Harnack.[5]

The reasoning behind this is that Acts was written about A.D. 62, at the end of Paul's two years of inprisonment at Rome, that Matthew and Luke was written somewhat earlier (ca. A.D. 60), and

---

[1] Eusebius, *Ecclesiastical History*, p. 127 (III, 39).
[2] *Ibid.*, p. 188 (V, 8). [3] *Ibid.*, p. 234 (VI, 14). [4] *Loc. cit.*
[5] Adolph Harnack, *The Date of the Acts and the Synoptic Gospels*, trans. J. A. Wilkinson, pp. 126-133.

that the latter two used Mark as a source. This reasoning would place the composition of Mark's Gospel back in the 50's.

As is the case with many other historical questions, we cannot reach a dogmatic conclusion. The best we can say is that Mark was almost certainly written between 50 and 70.

III. PLACE

On this point there is little question. The early church affirmed that the Gospel was written in Rome. Internal evidence tends to corroborate this.

IV. CHARACTER

The personality of Peter is reflected clearly in the main characteristics of this Gospel. His active, impulsive disposition is prominent here, as it was in his preaching. Mark caught the spirit, as well as the voice, of the apostle.

The first characteristic is *rapidity of action.* The narrative moves along swiftly, with often many incidents in each chapter. The frequent occurrence of "and" is noticeable. The Greek word translated "straightway" (ASV) is found over forty times. This book is pre-eminently the Gospel of action. Only one long discourse of Jesus is found here, the Olivet Discourse (chap. 13). Mark gives more of Jesus' works and fewer of His words than do the other three Gospels. He records eighteen of the Master's miracles, as compared with twenty each in the much longer books of Matthew and Luke. But he includes only four parables, as compared with fifteen in Matthew and nineteen in Luke.[6]

This emphasis on action fits in well with the tradition that Mark's Gospel was written in Rome. The Romans emphasized activity rather than speech. Incidentally, it is noticeable that this Gospel has ten Latin words, some of which are not found elsewhere in the New Testament. It also furnishes explanations of Jewish words and customs. This shows that it was written for Gentile readers.

A second distinctive characteristic is *vividness of detail.* Though Mark's Gospel is the shortest, it often gives vivid details that make the action more pictorial. This can easily be seen in any harmony of the Gospels. Mark gives more attention than the other Evangelists to the looks and gestures of Jesus.

A third prominent characteristic is *picturesqueness of description.* In connection with the feeding of the five thousand, Mark is the only one who says that the people sat down in "ranks" (literally, "flower beds") on the "green grass." The picture impressed Peter, who described it in his preaching, and Mark has preserved it for all time. One can almost see the hundreds of people attired in bright Oriental garments of red and yellow, looking like flower beds on the green hillside.

The Roman character of the Gospel confronts the reader at the very beginning. There is no genealogy here, as in Matthew and Luke. The Romans were not so much concerned about where a man came from as what he could do. They cared more about power than pedigree. So Mark presented Jesus to them as the great *Conqueror,* who conquered demons, disease, and death. He also portrayed Him as the *Servant of the Lord.* Servants do not parade pedigrees. They offer service instead. That is what Jesus did.

The most striking thing about the beginning of Mark is that it has no infancy narratives. With only a brief introduction — consisting of an account of the ministry of John the Baptist, and the baptism and temptation of Jesus — the Gospel narrative plunges immediately into the public ministry of the Master. The short 13 verses here are in startling contrast to the 76 verses in Matthew and 183 in Luke before we reach this point. Mark presents Jesus as the Wonder Worker.

D. A. Hayes has called this "The Gospel of the Strenuous Life." He says: "Mark alone has recorded the fact that twice in his ministry neither Jesus nor those who were working with him had even time to eat."[7]

---

[6] This assumes a total of thirty, as listed in R. C. Trench, *Notes on the Parables of Our Lord.* Some scholars list many more.

[7] D. A. Hayes, *The Synoptic Gospels and the Book of Acts,* p. 129.

The Servant and His Service

I. THE SERVANT'S SETTING (1:1-13)

A. IN ETERNITY (1:1)

1 The beginning of the gospel of Jesus Christ, the Son of God.

In the case of several of the Old Testament prophets the first verse is the heading of the book. This kind of opening is found, for example, in Isaiah, Jeremiah, and most of the Minor Prophets. Many of the early church fathers held that this is the function of the first verse of Mark. John Wesley and Adam Clarke agreed, as do the majority of recent writers. This seems preferable to the view of some that this verse is simply the heading for John the Baptist's ministry. **The beginning of the gospel** is to be found in the life, death and resurrection of Jesus Christ.

Gospel means "good news." It is the glad tidings *about* Jesus Christ and the salvation He has provided (cf. 10:45). "Evangel" comes directly from the Greek word for gospel.

Son of God is missing in a few of the early manuscripts and so is omitted in some modern translations. But it is retained in the standard versions (ASV, RSV, NEB). It is fully in keeping with Mark's emphasis on the deity of Jesus. The Savior is the eternal Son of God.

B. IN TIME (1:2-13)

1. His Introduction (1:2-8)

2 Even as it is written in Isaiah the prophet,
Behold, I send my messenger before thy face,
Who shall prepare thy way;
3 The voice of one crying in the wilderness,
Make ye ready the way of the Lord,
Make his paths straight;
4 John came, who baptized in the wilderness and preached the baptism of repentance unto remission of sins. 5 And there went out unto him all the country of Judaea, and all they of Jerusalem; and they were baptized of him in the river Jordan, confessing their sins. 6 And John was clothed with camel's hair, and *had* a leathern girdle about his loins, and did eat locusts and wild honey. 7 And he preached, saying, There cometh after me he that is mightier than I, the latchet of whose shoes I am not worthy to stoop down and unloose. 8 I baptized you in water; but he shall baptize you in the Holy Spirit.

John the Baptist was the forerunner of Jesus. He appeared on the scene to prepare the way for the coming of Christ. His function was to introduce to the Jews their Messiah.

For the full implication of the phrase **it is written** see the comment on Matthew 4:4. **Isaiah the prophet** is the correct reading here rather than "the prophets" (KJV). It is easy to understand why some copyist would change to the latter, since the first part of the quotation (v. 2) is from Malachi 3:1. Only in verse 3 does Mark quote from Isaiah (40:3). It would appear that he had mainly in mind the words from Isaiah and then inserted the ones from Malachi as "an afterthought."[1] Matthew (3:3) and Luke (3:4) have only the quotation from Isaiah.

It is a striking phenomenon that the last book of the Old Testament, Malachi, ties in so closely with the New Testament. It contained two specific predictions of the forerunner who would prepare the way for the Messiah (Mal. 3:1; 4:5).

The imagery of verse 3 alludes to the ancient custom of provinces preparing the way for the coming of a conqueror by making straight roads to facilitate his travel. **Crying** is literally "calling out." It suggests the eagerness and earnestness with which John proclaimed the coming of the Messiah.

John the Baptist **came,** or "appeared," **in the wilderness** (v. 4). This was the wilderness of Judea (cf. Matt. 3:1), a

---

[1] Alexander Maclaren, *Expositions of Holy Scripture*, VIII, 15.

very desolate region north and west of the Dead Sea. John **baptized** in the lower Jordan valley.

For the meaning of **preached** see on Matthew 3:1. John's message was a baptism of repentance unto remission of sins; that is, a baptism which was the outward sign of an inward repenting of one's sins, leading to forgiveness. The Greek word *aphesis,* **remission,** means literally *"dismissal, release"* but metaphorically in the New Testament *"pardon, remission* of penalty."[2] In the King James Version it is translated "forgiveness" six out of the seventeen times it occurs. For the meaning of **repentance** see on Matthew 3:2.

John's popularity is indicated in verse 4. **Judaea** took in the southern part of Palestine, reaching from the Jordan valley to the Mediterranean Sea. Since **Jerusalem** is at an elevation of 2,500 feet, and the Jordan River twenty miles away is nearly 1,300 feet below sea level, the "Jerusalemites" (literal Greek) had to descend some four thousand feet to hear John preach. But they were willing to put up with the rugged road and the strenuous effort of the return trip in order to see what was going on. The imperfect tense, "were going out," suggests a steady stream of travelers up and down the Jericho Road.

Were baptized is literally "were being baptized." But this was taking place as the people "were confessing out" (*exomologoumenoi*) their sins. The implication is clear that John baptized only those who repented and confessed their sins. Baptism was an outward sign of these inner attitudes, not a substitute for them.

The food and clothing of this rugged prophet of the wilderness are graphically described in verse 6 (see on Matt. 3:4). These fitted his virile, austere style of preaching.

John **preached** ("heralded, proclaimed") that a **mightier** One was coming after him (v. 7). He was only the introducer, unfit even to **stoop down** and untie the thongs of Jesus' sandals (**shoes**). The humble spirit shown here is in startling juxtaposition with the prophet's rugged

preaching. For the significance of verse 8 see on Matthew 3:11.

2. His Installation (1:9-11)

9 And it came to pass in those days, that Jesus came from Nazareth of Galilee, and was baptized of John in the Jordan. 10 And straightway coming up out of the water, he saw the heavens rent asunder, and the Spirit as a dove descending upon him: 11 and a voice came out of the heavens, Thou art my beloved Son, in thee I am well pleased.

The baptism of Jesus by John is described in all three Synoptic Gospels, most fully by Matthew (see on Matt. 3:13-17). Mark's fondness for strong, vivid words — reflecting Peter's preaching — is illustrated here, as in many other places. Matthew and Luke say the heavens were "opened." But Mark says **rent asunder** (*schizomenous*).[3]

The slight differences of wording in parallel accounts in the Synoptic Gospels with often no divergence of meaning is also illustrated here. Mark has **the Spirit** (v. 10), whereas Matthew has "the Spirit of God" and Luke "the Holy Spirit." These are equivalent expressions.

3. His Initiation (1:12-13)

12 And straightway the Spirit driveth him forth into the wilderness. 13 And he was in the wilderness forty days tempted of Satan; and he was with the wild beasts; and the angels ministered unto him.

The Temptation is described at greater length by Matthew and Luke, both of whom indicate three climactic assaults by Satan (see on Matt. 4:1-11; Luke 4:1-13). But while Mark's account is much briefer, he has here, as usual, one or two distinctive items not included in the other Gospels. He says that the Holy Spirit **driveth him forth** (*ekballei*) into the wilderness, a much stronger term than the other two have. Taylor says it "appears to indicate strong, if not violent, propulsion."[4] Mark alone mentions the **wild beasts** as being with Jesus (v. 13), rending the night air with their weird howls. The first of these two items illustrates Mark's characteristic picturesque-

2 Abbott-Smith, *op. cit.,* p. 70.
3 KJV has "opened" in all three places, ignoring the change in Greek.
4 Vincent Taylor, *The Gospel According to St. Mark,* p. 163.

ness of description; the second exemplifies his vividness of detail.

In referring to the tempter, Matthew and Luke use the term "the devil" — *diabolos*, "slanderer," or "false accuser" — which Mark never uses. Instead he has **Satan**, which means "adversary" — a Hebrew word transliterated into Greek and then into English. In the New Testament *diabolos* occurs 38 times, *Satanas* 36 times.

II. THE SERVANT'S SERVICE (1:14-13:37)

1. Beginning of Ministry (1:14-15)

14 Now after John was delivered up, Jesus came into Galilee, preaching the gospel of God, 15 and saying, The time is fulfilled, and the kingdom of God is at hand: repent ye, and believe in the gospel.

The great Galilean ministry of Jesus began with the imprisonment of John the Baptist. **Delivered up** can be translated either "put in prison" (KJV) or "arrested." Most recent translations[5] prefer the latter.

When John was taken from the scene, Jesus took his place as the prominent prophetic figure. He began **preaching** (proclaiming) **the gospel of God.** This phrase is found several times in Paul's Epistles. It signifies the good news which comes from God.

The specific emphasis here was: "The time has been fulfilled and the kingdom of God has come near" (perfect tenses). **Time** is *kairos*, which means *"the right, proper, favorable time . . . . definite fixed time . . . .* one of the chief eschatological terms . . . *the time of crisis, the last times."*[6] This was the "opportune moment" for the Jewish nation to accept the *kingdom of God* in the person of the Messiah. But the moment (His ministry) passed, the nation that rejected God's reign was punished severely by Rome.

Matthew and Mark both indicate that Jesus echoed John in preaching, **repent ye.** But the latter adds: **and believe in the gospel.** This was the new, distinctive, Christian note. Repentance and faith are the two prerequisites to salvation.[7]

2. Call of Fishermen (1:16-20)

16 And passing along by the sea of Galilee, he saw Simon and Andrew the brother of Simon casting a net in the sea; for they were fishers. 17 And Jesus said unto them, Come ye after me, and I will make you to become fishers of men. 18 And straightway they left the nets, and followed him. 19 And going on a little further, he saw James the *son* of Zebedee, and John his brother, who also were in the boat mending the nets. 20 And straightway he called them: and they left their father Zebedee in the boat with the hired servants, and went after him.

The accounts of this incident in Matthew and Mark are almost exactly the same (see on Matt. 4:18-22). The one distinctive item in Mark is the mention of Zebedee's **hired servants.** James and John did not leave their father desolate when they forsook the fishing business to follow Jesus.

3. Day in Capernaum (1:21-34)

a. Healing a Demoniac (1:21-28)

21 And they go into Capernaum; and straightway on the sabbath day he entered into the synagogue and taught. 22 And they were astonished at his teaching: for he taught them as having authority, and not as the scribes. 23 And straightway there was in their synagogue a man with an unclean spirit; and he cried out, 24 saying, What have we to do with thee, Jesus thou Nazarene? art thou come to destroy us? I know thee who thou art, the Holy One of God. 25 And Jesus rebuked him, saying, Hold thy peace, and come out of him. 26 And the unclean spirit, tearing him and crying with a loud voice, came out of him. 27 And they were all amazed, insomuch that they questioned among themselves, saying, What is this? a new teaching! with authority he commandeth even the unclean spirits, and they obey him. 28 And the report of him went out straightway everywhere into all the region of Galilee round about.

For the significance of **Capernaum** see on Matthew 4:13. The particular incident described here is omitted by Matthew, but closely paralleled in Luke 4:31-37. It is the first miracle of Jesus recorded by Mark and Luke.

---

[5] E.g., Moffatt, Williams, Goodspeed, RSV, NEB.
[6] Arndt and Gingrich, *op. cit.*, pp. 395-96.
[7] For the meaning of "kingdom of God" see on Matt. 4:23 and the Special Note in Ralph Earle, *The Gospel According to Mark*, p. 33; also George Ladd, "The Kingdom of God — Reign or Realm?" *JBL*, LXXXI (1962), 230-38.

This was a busy day in Jesus' life, doubtless typical of many such during His public ministry. Since it was the **sabbath day** — Saturday, the Jewish sabbath — He went to the **synagogue**. This word means literally "a gathering together." As in the case of "church," it was used first for the congregation and then for the building. The latter is the meaning here.

In the synagogue He **taught**. The imperfect tense means "began to teach." It was the custom of local synagogues to invite traveling rabbis to speak in the services (cf. Acts 13:15).

The worshipers in the synagogue were **astonished at his teaching**. The scribes were in the habit of quoting the opinions of earlier rabbis. But Jesus spoke with direct divine **authority** that amazed His hearers.

At the service was a man **with an unclean spirit** — literally, "in an unclean spirit," or under its power. **He cried out;** probably "screamed" or "yelled" would describe it correctly.[8] **What have we to do with thee** is literally, "What to us and to thee?" That is, "What is there between us?" Moffatt renders it: "What business have you with us?" That probably expresses the meaning well.

The demoniac identified Jesus as the **Holy One of God**. Though some have denied that this was a designation for the Messiah, Vincent Taylor correctly observes that while it "is not a known Messianic title," yet it is probably used here "with Messianic significance."[9]

The Master silenced the demon and commanded it to come out of the man. **Hold thy peace** (v. 25) is literally, "Be muzzled!" Jesus did not want testimony from such a quarter. It is also likely that He was banning any public proclamation of His messiahship, lest there should be a political revolution against Rome.

The sadistic cruelty of the unclean spirit is revealed in verse 26. **Tearing him** is better rendered "having convulsed him." Luke (4:35) says that the demon did not permanently injure him.

Again the people were amazed at the Master. First their astonishment had been caused by His authority in teaching (v. 22). Now they marveled at His

authority in casting out demons. This was something **new**. It is not surprising that the **report** of what happened at this synagogue service spread **straightway** throughout all Galilee (v. 28). It was exciting news.

b. Healing in Peter's House (1:29-31)

29 And straightway, when they were come out of the synagogue, they came into the house of Simon and Andrew, with James and John. 30 Now Simon's wife's mother lay sick of a fever; and straightway they tell him of her: 31 and he came and took her by the hand, and raised her up; and the fever left her, and she ministered unto them.

This incident is recorded in all three Synoptic Gospels (see on Matt. 8:14-15). Mark alone mentions that the four fishermen disciples accompanied Jesus home from the synagogue. It was the custom at that time not to eat before attending service on the sabbath day. The five men arrived hungry, expecting a good meal to be awaiting them. Instead they found Peter's mother-in-law in bed with a raging fever. But, as always, the Master was in control of the situation. Soon the sick lady was well and serving the meal.

c. Healing at Sunset (1:32-34)

32 And at even, when the sun did set, they brought unto him all that were sick, and them that were possessed with demons. 33 And all the city was gathered together at the door. 34 And he healed many that were sick with divers diseases, and cast out many demons; and he suffered not the demons to speak, because they knew him.

The Jewish sabbath lasted from sunset Friday night until sunset Saturday. So **when the sun did set** the crowds, excited by the news of the two miracles Jesus had performed that day, came hurrying to Peter's house. Now that the sabbath was over they could carry their **sick** and those **possessed with demons**. To Matthew's and Luke's accounts Mark adds typically: **And all the city was gathered together at the door** (v. 33). At least so it seemed to Peter, and Mark captured his vivid description of that sunset heal-

[8] Cf. NEB, "shrieked." [9] Op. cit., p. 174.

ing service. Again the Master muzzled the demons[10] who sought to testify to His deity (cf. Luke 4:41).

4. Tour of Galilee (1:35-45)

a. Praying at Sunrise (1:35-39)

35 And in the morning, a great while before day, he rose up and went out, and departed into a desert place, and there prayed. 36 And Simon and they that were with him followed after him; 37 and they found him, and say unto him, All are seeking thee. 38 And he saith unto them, Let us go elsewhere into the next towns, that I may preach there also; for to this end came I forth. 39 And he went into their synagogues throughout Galilee, preaching and casting out demons.

Matthew does not record this incident, though Luke (4:42-44) does. The sunset healing service was followed by a sunrise prayer meeting. But for the latter there were no jostling, noisy throngs — just the Master alone in fellowship with His Father. He needed strength and guidance for the new day.

The two opening clauses of verse 35 are very strong in the Greek: "And very early in the morning, while it was still night." Jesus left the disciples asleep, and sought the solitude of a **desert place**; that is, a lonely spot outside of town.

Finally Peter wakened. Missing the Master, he and his fellow disciples "hunted Him down" (*katedioxen*). When they finally discovered Him, they reported that all Capernaum was looking for Him (v. 37). Doubtless there were many people who failed to make it to the healing service the night before.

But in the time of prayer Jesus had received His orders for the day. He must not return to Capernaum at this time, but proceed to **the next towns.** There He must **preach**, for people needed spiritual salvation more than physical healing. Then He added: **To this end came I forth.** This could refer to His leaving Capernaum early that morning. But it probably has reference to His coming forth from heaven.[11] His mission to earth was to save mankind.

Verse 39 consists of a summary state-

ment of a synagogue ministry throughout Galilee. Along with His preaching He cast out demons.

b. Cleansing a Leper (1:40-45)

40 And there cometh to him a leper, beseeching him, and kneeling down to him, and saying unto him, If thou wilt, thou canst make me clean. 41 And being moved with compassion, he stretched forth his hand, and touched him, and saith unto him, I will; be thou made clean. 42 And straightway the leprosy departed from him, and he was made clean. 43 And he strictly charged him, and straightway sent him out, 44 and saith unto him, See thou say nothing to any man: but go show thyself to the priest, and offer for thy cleansing the things which Moses commanded, for a testimony unto them. 45 But he went out, and began to publish it much, and to spread abroad the matter, insomuch that Jesus could no more openly enter into a city, but was without in desert places: and they came to him from every quarter.

This miraculous cure is recorded in three Synoptics (see Matt. 8:1-4). **Moved with compassion** (only in Mark) is the aorist passive participle and is better translated "being gripped with compassion." The use of the aorist tense suggests Jesus' sudden and immediate reaction when faced with human need.

Mark (with Luke) says that **straightway,** or immediately, the leper was cleansed (v. 42). In verse 43 he alone uses a strong word for **strictly charged.** Originally the Greek verb meant to snort like a horse. It indicated the deep feeling with which Jesus commanded the leper to tell no one except the priest about his healing. Christ knew that the unfriendly priests would not report the matter. He was seeking to avoid undue publicity, because the vast throngs, wanting to be healed or to witness miracles, were hindering Him from carrying out His most important mission — preaching the gospel.

But it was all to no avail. Mark (alone) adds that the healed man went out and published abroad the matter (v. 45). The result was that Jesus had to avoid the cities and hide away in solitary places. Yet the people sought Him

---

[10] "Devils" (KJV, NEB) is incorrect. The Greek carefully distinguishes between *diabolos* (always singular) and *daimonion*. There is only one "devil," but there are many "demons."

[11] So Klostermann, Lagrange, Plummer, Swete.

out and kept coming (imperfect tense) to Him from everywhere.

5. Back in Capernaum (2:1-17)

a. Healing a Paralytic (2:1-12)

1 And when he entered again into Capernaum after some days, it was noised that he was in the house. 2 And many were gathered together, so that there was no longer room *for them,* no, not even about the door: and he spake the word unto them. 3 And they come, bringing unto him a man sick of the palsy, borne of four. 4 And when they could not come nigh unto him for the crowd, they uncovered the roof where he was: and when they had broken it up, they let down the bed whereon the sick of the palsy lay. 5 And Jesus seeing their faith saith unto the sick of the palsy, Son, thy sins are forgiven. 6 But there were certain of the scribes sitting there, and reasoning in their hearts, 7 Why doth this man thus speak? he blasphemeth: who can forgive sins but one, *even* God? 8 And straightway Jesus, preceiving in his spirit that they so reasoned within themselves, saith unto them, Why reason ye these things in your hearts? 9 Which is easier, to say to the sick of the palsy, Thy sins are forgiven; or to say, Arise, and take up thy bed, and walk? 10 But that ye may know that the Son of man hath authority on earth to forgive sins (he saith unto the sick of the palsy), 11 I say unto thee, Arise, take up thy bed, and go unto thy house. 12 And he arose, and straightway took up the bed, and went forth before them all; insomuch that they were all amazed, and glorified God, saying, We never saw it on this fashion.

As usual Mark's account is more vivid than that in Matthew (see on Matt. 9:1-8) or Luke (5:17-26). He alone definitely names **Capernaum.** The people of this city (Matt. — "his own city") had eagerly awaited His return since that wonderful Saturday of healing (1:21-34). Now **it was noised that he was in the house.** A better translation would be: "It was heard, 'He is at home.' "

The people's hope that He would continue His healing ministry was not disappointed. While He was teaching the **many** who flocked to hear Him, a paralytic was brought. The Master stopped

His message long enough to perform the miracle.

Verse 2 is found only in Mark. He tells us such a great crowd gathered that there was no longer any room, even by the door. **He spake the word unto them** — imperfect tense, kept on speaking. The reference to **the word** here is intriguing. What does it mean in this early context? Alexander gives a minimum meaning when he defines it as: "What he had to say of himself and of his kingdom."[12] Johnson simply says, "the Good News."[13] Plummer comments that the use of the same phrase again in 4:33 "shows that the first Christians use *ho logos* as a technical term for 'the good tidings.' "[14]

Mark alone tells us that there were four men who brought the paralytic to Jesus. Each one grasped a corner of the quilt on which he lay and the four carried the helpless man to the Master. **A man sick of the palsy** is all one word in the Greek — *paralyticon* (paralytic) .

Mark's language in verse 4 is especially graphic. When the paralytic's four friends found that the way to Jesus was blocked by the crowd that was packed closely around Him, they did not despair. Instead they carried the cripple up the outside stairway which led to the flat roof of the one-story home. There they uncovered the roof — the Greek says "unroofed the roof" — over the place where Jesus was. That is, they scraped away the dirt which had been packed hard to shed rain. This would be a laborious task, but these men were determined to get the paralytic to Christ. Mark adds another vivid touch: **when they had broken it up;** literally, "dug it out." Luke (5:19) says, "through the tiles." They had to dig down through the slabs and branches that had been laid over the crossbeams to hold the dirt of this typical Palestinian roof. It is likely that the graphic language here reflects Peter's telling of the incident. After all, it was his house, and he had to repair the roof!

Then they let down the **bed** on which the paralytic lay. Three different words are used by three Synoptic writers. Matthew (9:2) — as also Luke (5:18) — has *kline,* something upon which a person rests. In his parallel statement Luke

12 J. A. Alexander, *Commentary on the Gospel of Mark,* p. 34.
13 Sherman Johnson, *A Commentary on the Gospel According to St. Mark,* p. 55.
14 Alfred Plummer, *The Gospel According to St. Mark,* p. 81.

(5:19) uses *klinidion,* a diminutive form. But Mark has *krabbatos* — a translation of the Latin *grabatus,* a camp cot. It signifies a rude pallet, like a heavy blanket or padded quilt. This is one of Mark's numerous Latinisms not found in Matthew or Luke. These words are appropriate in a book written in Rome for Romans.

One can imagine the astonishment of the people as they saw the pallet descending through the hole in the roof. Doubtless hands below reached up to finish the task when the men above had lowered the paralytic as far as they could.

The first thing Jesus did was not to heal the man's paralysis but to forgive his sins. **Thy sins are forgiven** is what the Greek says, not "thy sins be forgiven thee" (KJV) — which suggests a wish. Many Greek manuscripts have the perfect tense — "have been forgiven." The Son of God graciously exercised His authority to forgive sins (see further on Matt. 9:3-6).

b. Calling Levi (2:13-14)

13 And he went forth again by the sea side; and all the multitude resorted unto him, and he taught them. 14 And as he passed by, he saw Levi the *son* of Alphaeus setting at the place of toll, and he saith unto him, Follow me. And he arose and followed him.

Levi is better known as Matthew, the author of the First Gospel (cf. Matt. 9:9). His is the only disciple's call besides that of the four fishermen (1:16-20) that is recorded in the Synoptic Gospels.

For the meaning of **place of toll** see on Matthew 9:9. Mark alone notes that this incident took place **by the sea side.** This may suggest that Levi's tax office was located by the fishing pier, in order to collect duty on the catches of fish.

c. Eating with Sinners (2:15-17)

15 And it came to pass, that he was sitting at meat in his house, and many publicans and sinners sat down with Jesus and his disciples: for there were many, and they followed him. 16 And the scribes of the Pharisees, when they saw that he was eating with the sinners and publicans, said unto his disciples, *How is it* that he eateth and drinketh

with publicans and sinners? 17 And when Jesus heard it, he saith unto them, They that are whole have no need of a physician, but they that are sick: I came not to call the righteous, but sinners.

Matthew showed the normal reaction in wanting to share his new-found Friend with his colleagues and acquaintances. Wisely he invited them to a great feast at his house, where they might meet Jesus. Mark alone notes that many of these **followed him** (v. 15). Christ had an especially strong appeal to the **sinners,** as He still does today. For the meaning of this term see on Matthew 9:10-13. On the term **followed** Swete has this observation: "*Akolouthein* in the Gospels usually implies moral attraction."[15] There was a power the Master possessed which almost compelled people to follow Him.

6. Conflict with Pharisees (2:18-3:6)

a. Question of Fasting (2:18-22)

18 And John's disciples and the Pharisees were fasting: and they come and say unto him, Why do John's disciples and the disciples of the Pharisees fast, but thy disciples fast not? 19 And Jesus said unto them, Can the sons of the bride-chamber fast, while the bridegroom is with them? as long as they have the bridegroom with them, they cannot fast. 20 But the days will come, when the bridegroom shall be taken away from them, and then will they fast in that day. 21 No man soweth a piece of undressed cloth on an old garment: else that which should fill it up taketh from it, the new from the old, and a worse rent is made. 22 And no man putteth new wine into old wine-skins; else the wine will burst the skins, and the wine perisheth, and the skins: but *they put* new wine into fresh wine-skins.

With his typical attention to details, Mark *alone* gives the setting for this incident. He says that **John's disciples and the Pharisees were fasting** — not "used to fast" (KJV). The occasion for this controversy was a fast day scheduled by the Jews and observed meticulously by the Pharisees and the disciples of John the Baptist. But Jesus' disciples were eating. The question in the latter part of verse 18 is literally: "Why are your disciples not fasting?" Mark thus

15 H. B. Swete, *The Gospel According to St. Mark,* p. 39.

points up the drama of the situation: Jesus' disciples were less "religious" than those of John and the Pharisees. The problem was that the critics were measuring religion by outward, ceremonial acts rather than inward attitudes.

Christ's answer to this criticism is given similarly in all three Synoptics (see on Matt. 9:14-17). Fasting should be a voluntary choice, not a legal duty. Legalism is the bane of religion.

b. Question of Sabbath Observance (2:23-3:6)

(1) Working on Sabbath (2:23-28)

23 And it came to pass, that he was going on the sabbath day through the grainfields; and his disciples began, as they went, to pluck the ears. 24 And the Pharisees said unto him, Behold, why do they on the sabbath day that which is not lawful? 25 And he said unto them, Did ye never read what David did, when he had need, and was hungry, he, and they that were with him? 26 How he entered into the house of God when Abiathar was high priest, and ate the showbread, which it is not lawful to eat save for the priests, and gave also to them that were with him? 27 And he said unto them, The sabbath was made for man, and not man for the sabbath: 28 so that the Son of man is lord even of the sabbath.

For discussion of this incident (found in all three Synoptics) see on Matthew 12:1-8. The last clause of verse 23 is literally, "His disciples began to make a way, plucking the heads of grain." Mark and Luke give only one of the two illustrations that Jesus used in answering the criticisms of the Pharisees — that of David and his associates eating the showbread.

But in this connection there appears a difficult problem. It says here that David did this when Abiathar was high priest (v. 26). But I Samuel 21 declares that it was Ahimelech, Abiathar's father, who was high priest at that time. Morison gives ten solutions to the problem that have been proposed by different writers. He prefers the tenth, which is a sound solution. It is this: "The phrase refers to the lifetime of the highpriest,

not to the time of his pontificate."[16] That is, this incident took place during the days of Abiathar, who became the famous high priest of that period.

Mark alone gives Jesus' important observation: **The sabbath was made for man, and not man for the sabbath** (v. 27). It has been proved over and over that man needs one day a week for his spiritual, mental, and physical well-being. Bishop Ryle wrote: "National prosperity and personal growth in grace are intimately bound up in the maintenance of a holy Sabbath."[17]

(2) Healing on Sabbath (3:1-6)

1 And he entered again into the synagogue; and there was a man there who had his hand withered. 2 And they watched him, whether he would heal him on the sabbath day; that they might accuse him. 3 And he saith unto the man that had his hand withered, Stand forth. 4 And he saith unto them, Is it lawful on the sabbath day to do good, or to do harm? to save a life, or to kill? But they held their peace. 5 And when he had looked round about on them with anger, being grieved at the hardening of their heart, he saith unto the man, Stretch forth thy hand. And he stretched it forth; and his hand was restored. 6 And the Pharisees went out, and straightway with the Herodians took counsel against him, how they might destroy him.

This incident is also recorded in all three Synoptic Gospels (see on Matt. 12: 9-14). It is the last in a series of five conflicts that Jesus had with the fault-finding Pharisees (2:1—3:6): (1) healing the paralytic; (2) eating with sinners; (3) fasting; (4) harvesting on the Sabbath; (5) healing on the Sabbath.

Watched (v. 2) is a strong word in the Greek. It means "watch closely, observe narrowly."[18] Arndt and Gingrich note that from its context it can take on the meaning, "watch maliciously, lie in wait for."[19] The expression could be translated, "They were spying on Him" (imperfect tense). The wicked purpose of trapping Jesus shows clearly in the narrative. Healing on the Sabbath was traditionally allowed only when it was necessary to save a life.[20] This did not seem to be the case with this man. But

16 James Morison, *A Practical Commentary on the Gospel According to St. Mark*, p. 62.
17 J. C. Ryle, *Expository Thoughts on the Gospels: Mark*, p. 42.
18 Abbott Smith, *op. cit.*, p. 343.   19 *Op. cit.*, p. 628.   20 Edersheim, *op. cit.*, II, 59-61.

Jesus held that it was proper to do good, not harm (v. 4).

Mark's attention to the looks and gestures of Jesus appears again in verse 5. Mark records that Christ looked around at the Pharisees **with anger, being grieved at the hardening of their heart.** To some it may seem shocking that Jesus was angry. But a lack of righteous indignation betrays an absence of moral sensitivity, and the combination here is most significant — anger mingled with grief. Furthermore, **looked around** is in the aorist tense, while **being grieved** is present (continuous action). Swete points out the implication: "The look was momentary, the sorrow habitual."[21] Mark alone notes that the Pharisees took counsel **with the Herodians to destroy Jesus** (v. 6). These sworn enemies could unite in their common enmity to Christ (see on Matt. 22:16).

7. Popularity with People (3:7-35)

a. Healing the Many (3:7-12)

7 And Jesus with his disciples withdrew to the sea: and a great multitude from Galilee followed; and from Judaea, 8 and from Jerusalem, and from Idumaea, and beyond the Jordan, and about Tyre and Sidon, a great multitude, hearing what great things he did, came unto him. 29 And he spake to his disciples, that a little boat should wait on him, because of the crowd, lest they should throng him: 10 for he had healed many insomuch that as many as had plagues pressed upon him that they might touch him. 11 And the unclean spirits, whensoever they beheld him, fell down before him, and cried, saying, Thou art the Son of God. 12 And he charged them much that they should not make him known.

The statement in verse 7 is similar to that already noted in Matthew 4:25. **Idumea** (v. 8) is named only here in the New Testament. It was the territory in the southern part of Judea where the Edomites settled during the Babylonian captivity of the Jews. **Beyond the Jordan** refers to Perea, east of the Jordan River. **Tyre and Sidon** were cities of ancient Phoenicia (modern Lebanon) on the coast of the Mediterranean north of Palestine. It is noticeable that Samaria, though closer, is not

mentioned (cf. John 4:9). The Samaritans would not be welcomed by the Jews.

Another graphic touch by Mark is given in verse 9. So crowded was Jesus that He had to ask for a small boat in which He could push off from shore, lest the crowd crush Him. **Pressed upon him** (v. 10) is literally "were falling upon Him." Hundreds of sick people were anxious to reach and **touch him.** His physical safety was actually endangered by the pushing crowd.

Again we find the **unclean spirits** proclaiming Him as Son of God and Jesus silencing them (vv. 11-12). **Charged them much** is literally "kept charging them many times." He did not want the witness of demons to His deity.

b. Appointing the Twelve (3:13-19a)

13 And he goeth up into the mountain, and calleth unto him whom he himself would; and they went unto him. 14 And he appointed twelve, that they might be with him, and that he might send them forth to preach, 15 and to have authority to cast out demons: 16 and Simon he surnamed Peter; 17 and James the *son* of Zebedee, and John the brother of James; and them he surnamed Boanerges, which is, Sons of thunder: 18 and Andrew, and Philip, and Bartholomew, and Matthew, and Thomas, and James the *son* of Alphaeus and Thaddaeus, and Simon, the Cananaean, 19 and Judas Iscariot, who also betrayed him.

The power of Jesus' personality is strikingly illustrated in verse 13. Whomever He wished He called, and they came. From among His followers He appointed **twelve** (see on Matt. 10:1).

A twofold purpose was involved in this choice: (1) **that they might be with him;** (2) **that he might send them forth to preach** (v. 14). This suggests the significant truth that a call to preach implies a call to prepare. Furthermore, one must know Jesus before he can share Him. Williams observes: "Fellowship with Him must precede preaching about Him."[22]

The list given here is essentially the same as that found in Matthew (see on Matt. 10:2-4), as well as those in Luke and Acts, with some variation in the order and form of the names.[23] The dis-

---

[21] *Op. cit.,* p. 50.
[22] George Williams, *The Student's Commentary on the Holy Scriptures,* p. 734.
[23] See Earle, *op. cit.,* pp. 53-55; also Carter and Earle, *op. cit.,* pp. 14-15.

tinctive item here is the designation of James and John as **Sons of thunder** (v. 17). **Boanerges** is a difficult term to explain. Cranfield says, "The word is doubtless a corrupt transliteration of an Aramaic or Hebrew phrase," and adds: "Though this word is not used in the sense of thunder in Hebrew or Aramaic texts, the related Arabic word is used for thunder."[24]

c. Disputing with Scribes (3:19b-30)

And he cometh into a house. 20 And the multitude cometh together again, so that they could not so much as eat bread. 21 And when his friends heard it, they went out to lay hold on him: for they said, He is beside himself. 22 And the scribes that came down from Jerusalem said, He hath Beelzebub, and, By the prince of the demons casteth he out the demons. 23 And he called them unto him, and said unto them in parables, How can Satan cast out Satan? 24 And if a kingdom be divided against itself, that kingdom cannot stand. 25 And if a house be divided against itself, that house will not be able to stand. 26 And if Satan hath risen up against himself, and is divided, he cannot stand, but hath an end. 27 But no one can enter into the house of the strong *man,* and spoil his goods, except he first bind the strong *man*; and then he will spoil his house. 28 Verily I say unto you, All their sins shall be forgiven unto the sons of men, and their blasphemies wherewith soever they shall blaspheme: 29 but whosoever shall blaspheme against the Holy Spirit hath never forgiveness, but is guilty of an eternal sin: 30 because they said, He hath an unclean spirit.

The last part of verse 19 belongs with this paragraph, rather than with the previous one, for it gives the setting for the new incident. **And he cometh into a house** is better translated: "And He comes home." This would mean back once more to Capernaum.

Again a great crowd gathered, as always happened when Jesus came home. This time He was kept so busy ministering to the multitudes that He and His disciples could not find time to eat. **Eat bread** is literally "eat a loaf" (or biscuit). Furthermore, **eat** is the aorist infinitive. The modern equivalent would be: "They didn't even have a chance to grab a bite to eat."

His friends (v. 21) may be translated "his family." The latter is the more common meaning in the papyri for the Greek phrase which is literally "those from beside him." The context also suggests that it was His family (cf. v. 31). **Went out** probably means "came out from Nazareth."

He is beside himself is literally, "He is standing out of himself." It suggests, "He is out of his mind." Even Jesus' friends thought He had gone crazy over religion. Zeal for God's kingdom is something the world cannot understand.

His opponents had another explanation (v. 22). **Scribes** had even come from **Jerusalem,** about a hundred miles away. It would take most of the week between sabbaths to walk it, especially if they crossed to the east side of the Jordan to avoid going through "unclean," unfriendly Samaria. **Down** seems odd, since they went north. But every devout Jew went "up" to Jerusalem and "down" whenever he left the Holy City.

These **scribes** — teachers of the Law — said that Jesus had **Beelzebub** (Greek, "Beelzebul"). This was a name given to **the prince of the demons.** That Christ cast out demons not even His enemies dared deny. Branscomb has well said: "That Jesus did cure cases of possession is one of the best supported facts of the history."[25] The Talmud accuses Him of practicing magic,[26] an accusation similar to that hurled by the scribes.

But when the scribes declared that it was by the prince of demons that Jesus cast out demons, He showed the folly of their charge. He first asked (only in Mark): **How can Satan cast out Satan?** (v. 23). Then he stated the obvious truth (also recorded in Matt. and Luke) that a **kingdom** or **house** which is divided against itself cannot stand (vv. 24-25). If Satan is fighting against himself, he **hath an end** (v. 26). But Jesus had entered into the house of the **strong man,** Satan, and was spoiling his goods (v. 27) by casting demons out of human beings.

The word **parables** (v. 23) here indicates short parabolic statements. Three of these are given (vv. 24, 25, 27). A

[24] C. E. B. Cranfield, *The Gospel According to Saint Mark,* p. 131.
[25] Harvie Branscomb, *The Gospel of Mark,* p. 31.   [26] *Ibid.,* p. 69.

parable, in its simplest, most uncomplicated form, is a terse metaphorical statement, and that is what these are.

For an interpretation of the so-called
"unpardonable sin" (vv. 28-30) see on
Matthew 12:31-32. **Guilty of an eternal
sin** (v. 29) is really stronger than "in
danger of eternal damnation" (KJV).
One meaning of the word for **guilty** is
"held in the grip of." To be found
eternally as a slave to sin, with no
escape from the sense of guilt — that is
hell at its worst.

Mark alone adds the explanation in
verse 30. This was a solemn warning
to the scribes of the seriousness of their
sin.

d. Identifying His Family (3:31-35)

31 And there come his mother and his
brethren; and, standing without, they
sent unto him, calling him. 32 And a
multitude was sitting about him; and
they say unto him, Behold, thy mother
and brethren without seek for thee. 33
And he answereth them, and saith, Who
is my mother and my brethren? 34 And
looking round on them that sat around
about him, he saith, Behold, my mother
and my brethren! 35 For whosoever shall
do the will of God, the same is my
brother, and sister, and mother.

This incident is recorded in all three
Synoptics (see on Matt. 12:46-50). Mark
has just one distinctive detail (v. 34a).
It underscores again Mark's attention to
the looks of Jesus. Literally it reads,
"when he had looked around at those
sitting around him in a circle."

8. Teaching in Parables (4:1-34)

a. Parable of Sower (4:1-9)

1 And again he began to teach by the
sea side. And there is gathered unto him
a very great multitude, so that he entered
into a boat, and sat in the sea; and all
the multitude were by the sea on the
land. 2 And he taught them many things
in parables, and said unto them in his
teaching, 3 Hearken: Behold, the sower
went forth to sow: 4 and it came to pass,
as he sowed, some *seed* fell by the way
side, and the birds came and devoured it.
5 And other fell on the rocky *ground*,
where it had not much earth; and
straightway it sprang up, because it had
no deepness of earth: 6 and when the sun
was risen, it was scorched; and because
it had no root, it withered away. 7 And

other fell among the thorns, and the
thorns grew up, and choked it, and it
yielded no fruit. 8 And others fell into
the good ground, and yielded fruit, growing up and increasing; and brought forth,
thirtyfold, and sixtyfold, and a hundredfold. 9 And he said, Who hath ears to
hear, let him hear.

For this parable, found in all three
Synoptic Gospels, see on Matthew 13:1-9.
Sat in the sea is obviously "sat in a boat
on the sea." For the meaning of the
word **parables** (v. 2) see especially on Matthew 13:3. The three records of this
parable are almost exactly the same.
Mark alone adds at the end of verse 7:
and it yielded no fruit.

b. Explanation of Parable (4:10-20)

10 And when he was alone, they that
were about him with the twelve asked
of him the parables. 11 And he said unto
them, Unto you is given the mystery of
the kingdom of God: but unto them that
are without, all things are done in parables: 12 that seeing they may see, and
not perceive; and hearing they may hear,
and not understand; lest haply they
should turn again, and it should be forgiven them. 13 And he saith unto them,
Know ye not this parable? and how shall
ye know all the parables? 14 The sower
soweth the word. 15 And these are they
by the way side, where the word is sown;
and when they have heard, straightway
cometh Satan, and taketh away the word
which hath been sown in them. 16 And
these in like manner are they that are
sown upon the rocky *places,* who, when
they have heard the word, straightway
receive it with joy; 17 and they have
no root in themselves, but endure for a
while; then, when tribulation or persecution ariseth because of the word, straightway they stumble. 18 And others are
they that are sown among the thorns;
these are they that have heard the word,
19 and the cares of the world, and the
deceitfulness of riches, and the lusts
of other things entering in, choke the
word, and it becometh unfruitful. 20
And those are they that were sown upon
the good ground; such as hear the word,
and accept it, and bear fruit, thirtyfold,
and sixtyfold, and a hundredfold.

Before explaining the Parable of the
Sower Jesus set forth His reason for
speaking in parables (see on Matt. 13:10-
17). The wording in Mark (v. 12) and
Luke (8:10) poses a problem. Why should
Christ use parables **that** (literally, "in

order that") people should **not understand?** This seems utterly unreasonable and unlike Him. But Maclear suggests that this speaking in parables was *"Penal,* as testing the disposition of those who listened to them; withdrawing the light from such as loved darkness and were wilfully blind, and protecting the truth from the mockery of the scoffer."[27] That is, those who were willing to understand would do so, while those who were unwilling would miss the truth entirely. It underscores again the fact that unbelief — and in some cases ignorance — is more a moral than a mental difficulty.

Another interesting example of difference in wording without any variance in meaning is found here. Mark (v. 15) uses the name **Satan,** whereas Matthew has "the evil one" and Luke "the devil."

The explanation of the **thorns** as given in Mark is especially striking. Jesus names three things in verse 19 (Matt. has only the first two). **The cares of the world** is literally "the anxieties of the age." This is one of the most serious dangers confronting the child of God. Too many become obsessed with anxiety about material matters and lose their spiritual glow. **The deceitfulness of riches** is a very significant phrase. Possessions promise peace, but usually give the opposite. Many a man has been deceived by the love of money into doing things he never dreamed he would do. **The lusts of other things** is literally "the desires concerning the remaining things." This includes everything else that might strangle the spiritual life of the believer. Wrong desire is the root of all man's troubles.

c. Lamp on Lampstand (4:21-25)

21 And he said unto them, Is the lamp brought to be put under the bushel, or under the bed, and not to be put on the stand? 22 For there is nothing hid, save that it should be manifested; neither was *anything* made secret, but that it should come to light. 23 If any man hath ears to hear, let him hear. 24 And he said unto them, Take heed what ye hear: with what measure ye mete it shall be measured unto you; and more shall be given unto you. 25 For he that hath, to him shall be given: and he that hath not,

from him shall be taken away even that which he hath.

In Jesus' day a small clay **lamp,** with a tiny wick in olive oil, was the main means of lighting the often windowless Palestinian home. It would be placed on a **stand,** or a niche in the wall, not under a **bushel** — really a peck "measure" — or **bed.** The latter is not a "thick mat" or "pallet" (cf. 2:4), which would lie flat on the floor. Another word is used which means "couch," something on which one can recline. The point Christ was making was similar to that in Matthew 5:15-16. The disciples were to let the light of the gospel shine out.

Verse 22 states a general principle. Only valuable things are hidden, and he who hides them does so with the intent of some day revealing them.

The context suggests the meaning of verse 24 as being that the measure of one's listening will be the measure of his learning. The one who receives retains; but the one who neglects loses what little he already has (v. 25).

d. Seed Growing Secretly (4:26-29)

26 And he said, So is the kingdom of God, as if a man should cast seed upon the earth; 27 and should sleep and rise night and day, and the seed should spring up and grow, he knoweth not how. 28 The earth beareth fruit of herself; first the blade, then the ear, then the full grain in the ear. 29 But when the fruit is ripe, straightway he putteth forth the sickle, because the harvest is come.

This is the only parable found in Mark alone. It fits into the context of the Parable of the Sower. It stresses the fact that even on good ground "the production of fruit is a gradual process demanding time."[28]

Cast is aorist, whereas **sleep** and **rise** are in the present tense. "The sowing is once for all; the sleeping and rising are a daily habit."[29]

Of herself is *automate,* "automatically." The word is used elsewhere in the New Testament only in Acts 12:10, to describe the gate opening of its own accord. **Blade** is literally "grass," referring to the shoot. **Ear** should be "head," because the grain was wheat or barley.

[27] G. F. Maclear, *Gospel According to St. Mark,* p. 56.
[28] Bruce, *op. cit.,* p. 168.   [29] Earle, *op. cit.,* p. 66.

The emphasis of this parable is on "the need of patience on the part of the Christian worker."[30] One must give time for the seed he has sown to issue in conversion and Christian living in the case of the hearer.

e. Mustard Seed (4:30-32)

30 And he said, How shall we liken the kingdom of God, or in what parable shall we set it forth? 31 It is like a grain of mustard seed, which, when it is sown upon the earth, though it be less than all the seeds that are upon the earth, 32 yet when it is sown, groweth up, and becometh greater than all the herbs, and putteth out great branches; so that the birds of the heaven can lodge under the shadow thereof.

For this parable, which is found in all three Synoptic Gospels, see on Matthew 13:31-32.

f. Many Parables (4:33-34)

33 And with many such parables spake he the word unto them, as they were able to hear it; 34 and without a parable spake he not unto them: but privately to his own disciples he expounded all things.

This brief paragraph is closely paralleled in Matthew 13:34-35. Mark adds in verse 33: as they were able to hear it; and in verse 34: but privately to his own disciples he expounded all things.

B. IN SURROUNDING AREAS (4:35—9:50)

1. First Retreat and Return (4:35-6:29)

a. Storm on the Lake (4:35-41)

35 And on that day, when even was come, he saith unto them, Let us go over unto the other side. 36 And leaving the multitude, they take him with them, even as he was, in the boat. And other boats were with him. 37 And there ariseth a great storm of wind, and the waves beat into the boat, insomuch that the boat was now filling. 28 And he himself was in the stern, asleep on the cushion: and they awake him, and say unto him, Teacher, carest thou not that we perish? 39 And he awoke, and rebuked the wind, and said unto the sea, Peace, be still. And the wind ceased, and there was a great

calm. 40 And he said unto them, Why are ye fearful? have ye not yet faith? 41 And they feared exceedingly, and said one to another, Who then is this, that even the wind and the sea obey him?

Mark adds a few details to Matthew's description of this incident (see on Matt. 8:23-27). He says that due to the **storm of wind** (same in Luke 8:23), the boat **was now filling** (v. 37). Obviously the statement that it was "full" (KJV) is incorrect, for in that case it would already have sunk. The Greek clearly says, "was being filled."

All three accounts state that Jesus was asleep. Mark alone notes the place: **in the stern . . . on the cushion.** Probably this was the leather pad on the steersman's seat. Mark also gives the words Jesus uttered in the teeth of the raging storm. Facing the winds and the waves, He sternly demanded: **Peace, be still** (v. 39). The latter is literally, "Be muzzled." Lenski brings out the double meaning of the perfect tense by translating it: "Put the muzzle on and keep it on!"[31] The elements immediately obeyed the voice of their Creator.

Typically, Mark uses stronger language than the others to describe the reactions of the disciples. He says that they **feared exceedingly** — literally, "feared a great fear." This was not because of the storm but because of the miraculous display of divine power they had witnessed.

This and other "nature miracles" in the Gospels are rejected by many scholars today. But Rawlinson has an excellent answer for that attitude. He writes: "The broad truth of the Christian doctrine of the Incarnation once assumed, no wise person will proceed rashly to draw the limits between what is and what is not possible."[32]

b. Demoniac of Gerasa (5:1-20)

1 And they came to the other side of the sea, into the country of the Gerasenes. 2 And when he was come out of the boat, straightway there met him out of the tombs a man with an unclean spirit, 3 who had his dwelling in the tombs: and no man could any more bind him, no, not with a chain; 4 because that he had been often bound with fetters and chains,

[30] Loc. cit.   [31] R. C. H. Lenski, The Interpretation of St. Mark's Gospel, p. 201.
[32] A. E. J. Rawlinson, St. Mark, p. 60.

and the chains had been rent asunder by him, and the fetters broken in pieces: and no man had strength to tame him. 5 And always, night and day, in the tombs and in the mountains, he was crying out, and cutting himself with stones. 6 And when he saw Jesus from afar, he ran and worshipped him; 7 and crying out with a loud voice, he saith, What have I to do with thee, Jesus, thou Son of the Most High God? I adjure thee by God, torment me not. 8 For he said unto him, Come forth, thou unclean spirit, out of the man. 9 And he asked him, What is thy name? And he saith unto him, My name is Legion; for we are many. 10 And he besought him much that he would not send them away out of the country. 11 Now there was there on the mountain side a great herd of swine feeding. 12 And they besought him, saying, Send us into the swine, that we may enter into them. 13 And he gave them leave. And the unclean spirits came out, and entered into the swine: and the herd rushed down the steep into the sea, *in number* about two thousand; and they were drowned in the sea. 14 And they that fed them fled, and told it in the city, and in the country. And they came to see what it was that had come to pass. 15 And they come to Jesus, and behold him that was possessed with demons sitting, clothed and in his right mind, *even* him that had the legion: and they were afraid. 16 And they that saw it declared unto them how it befell him that was possessed with demons, and concerning the swine. 17 And they began to beseech him to depart from their borders. 18 And as he was entering into the boat, he that had been possessed with demons besought him that he might be with him. 19 And he suffered him not, but saith unto him, Go to thy house unto thy friends, and tell them how great things the Lord hath done for thee, and *how* he had mercy on thee. 20 And he went his way, and began to publish in Decapolis how great things Jesus had done for him: and all men marvelled.

For the lessons here taught and also the location of this incident — the country of the Gadarenes, **Gerasenes,** or Gergesenes — see on Matthew 8:28-34. In the case of each of the Synoptic Gospels, all three words are found in different Greek manuscripts. But they all indicate a region on the east side of the Lake of Galilee. As one stands today on the western shore near Tiberias he can see almost opposite him the one hill that

comes close enough to the beach to fulfill the happening described here — the swine rushing down the slope into the water.

As usual, Mark adds vivid touches to the account. He alone says: **And no man could any more bind him, no, not with a chain** (v. 3). While Luke (8:29) mentions the **fetters and chains,** Mark adds: **And no man had strength to tame him.** (v. 4). Also, verse 5 is peculiar to this Gospel. These three verses suggest a threefold portrait of sin. It is suicide (v. 3a), insanity (vv. 3b, 4), and self-destruction (v. 5). Only Christ can deliver those enslaved by sin.

The last clause of verse 16 is significantly added by Mark: **and concerning the swine.** The people were more concerned about their hogs than human beings. They wanted no more of this Man whose miracles interfered with their business. So they asked Him to leave, and He left.

Mark and Luke record how the cured demoniac begged Jesus to let him go with Him (v. 18). The Master enjoined him instead to return home and tell his friends and relatives what the Lord had done for him. This the man did with great enthusiasm and thus made it possible for Jesus to receive a better welcome when He later revisited this area (7:31). For the meaning and location of **Decapolis** see on Matthew 4:25. These are the only three places in the New Testament where this word occurs.

c. Plea of Jairus (5:21-24)

21 And when Jesus had crossed over again in the boat unto the other side, a great multitude was gathered unto him; and he was by the sea. 22 And there cometh one of the rulers of the synagogue, Jairus by name; and seeing him, he falleth at his feet, and beseecheth him much, saying, My little daughter is at the point of death: *I pray thee,* that thou come and lay thy hands on her, that she may be made whole, and live. 24 And he went with him; and a great multitude followed him, and they thronged him.

Jesus and His disciples crossed over again to the **other side,** which means the west side of the Lake of Galilee, or perhaps the northwest corner near Capernaum. This area is where He had His busiest ministry. As usual, a great **multitude** quickly **gathered,** thronging to the beach (**by the sea**) to see and hear Him.

One of the **rulers of the synagogue** — whose duty it was to have charge of the services, indicating the ones to read the Scriptures and say the prayers — pushed his way through the crowd until he reached Jesus. So crushed with concern was he that he **falleth at his feet** — in spite of the fact that he was one of the leaders in the community. With extreme earnestness — **beseecheth him much** — he begged the Master to come at once. His **little daughter** — Mark is fond of diminutives — was **at the point of death** (literally, "at her last gasp"). Jesus immediately went with Jairus. Matthew (9:18) says that the father reported the girl was "even now dead." But he omits the report of the daughter's death received on the way to Jairus' house found in Mark (v. 38) and Luke (8:49). So it seems best to treat this seeming contradiction as an example of Matthew's habit of telescoping details: "Matthew combines these two phrases into one."[33]

d. Woman with Hemorrhage (5:25-34)

25 And a woman, who had an issue of blood twelve years, 26 and had suffered many things of many physicians, and had spent all that she had, and was nothing bettered, but rather grew worse, 27 having heard the things concerning Jesus, came in the crowd behind, and touched his garment. 28 For she said, If I touch but his garments, I shall be made whole. 29 And straightway the fountain of her blood was dried up; and she felt in her body that she was healed of her plague. 30 And straightway Jesus, perceiving in himself that the power *proceeding* from him had gone forth, turned him about in the crowd, and said, Who touched my garments? 31 And his disciples said unto him, Thou seest the multitude thronging thee, and sayest thou, Who touched me? 32 And he looked round about to see her that had done this thing. 33 But the woman fearing and trembling, knowing what had been done to her, came and fell down before him, and told him all the truth. 34 And he said unto her, Daughter, thy

faith hath made thee whole; go in peace, and be whole of thy plague.

For general treatment of this incident see on Matthew 9:20-22. Mark's account is much more vivid with details. His unique statement in verse 26 that she had **suffered many things of many physicians** is well explicated by Adam Clarke, who describes the many foolish concoctions that were prescribed for this ailment, as well as arduous ordeals recommended by the rabbis.[34] Speaking as a layman, Mark observes that the unfortunate woman **was nothing bettered, but rather grew worse.** But Luke, writing as a physician, says that "she could not be healed of any," though he agrees with Mark that she had "spent all her living upon physicians" (Luke 8:43).

When the woman had touched Jesus, she felt in her body that **she was healed of her plague** (v. 29, only in Mark). The Master recognized that **power** (*dynamis*) had gone from Him to produce the healing (v. 30). So He turned and asked who **touched** Him. To the disciples this question seemed absurd, since Jesus was jammed in by the jostling crowd. But He knew that someone had touched Him by faith and received healing power from Him. Too many today brush against Jesus, as it were, in church services and elsewhere, but do not touch Him by faith and thus do not gain spiritual help from His presence.

The Master (v. 32) "kept on looking around" (imperfect tense) — typical of Mark's attention to the looks of Jesus. Finally the woman, **fearing and trembling** — according to the Mosaic law (Lev. 15:19) she was unclean and had rendered Jesus unclean by touching Him — fell down before Him and **told him all the truth.**

It may seem strange that Christ should force this timid, trembling woman out into the open. But He did it for her good. He knew that testifying publicly would bring spiritual blessing. She gained a double dividend when He added: "**Go in peace** (v. 34). She was to be permanently **whole** of her **plague.** What comfort those words must have brought to her heart.

---

[33] Basil F. C. Atkinson, "The Gospel According to Matthew," *The New Bible Commentary*, ed. F. Davidson, 2nd ed., p. 785.   [34] *Op. cit.*, I, 304, 305.

e. Daughter of Jairus (5:35-43)

35 While he yet spake, they come from the ruler of the synagogue's *house,* saying, Thy daughter is dead: why troublest thou the Teacher any further? 36 But Jesus, not heeding the word spoken, saith unto the ruler of the synagogue, Fear not, only believe. 37 And he suffered no man to follow with him, save Peter, and James, and John the brother of James. 38 And they come to the house of the ruler of the synagogue; and he beholdeth a tumult, and *many* weeping and wailing greatly. 39 And when he was entered in, he saith unto them, Why make ye a tumult, and weep? the child is not dead, but sleepeth. 40 And they laughed him to scorn. But he, having put them all forth, taketh the father of the child and her mother and them that were with him, and goeth in where the child was. 41 And taking the child by the hand, he saith unto her, Talitha cumi; which is, being interpreted, Damsel, I say unto thee, Arise. 42 And straightway the damsel rose up, and walked; for she was twelve years old. And they were amazed straightway with a great amazement. 43 And he charged them much that no man should know this: and he commanded that *something* should be given her to eat.

While Jesus was talking with the woman, a messenger arrived from the house of Jairus to inform him that his daughter had just died. There was no need to trouble the Teacher any further. Very likely there was thinly veiled cynicism in these words. If Jesus had cared about the need of the dying girl He would have hurried to her side and healed her, instead of standing around in the street talking to some woman! One can easily imagine how the faith of the anxious father must already have been tested severely by Christ's delaying action.

But Jesus ignored the probably reproachful words of the messenger. It seems that **not heeding** (v. 36) is better than "heard" (KJV). The Greek verb used here regularly means "ignore" in the Septuagint. The only other passage in the New Testament where it occurs is Matthew 18:17 (twice), and there it clearly means "refuse to hear." Gould prefers "overheard" here.[35] Swift

makes the wise observation: "Perhaps both meanings are implicit here. Jesus overheard the message and deliberately set it aside in giving a word of assurance to Jairus."[36]

At any rate Christ turned to the grief-stricken father and said: "Stop being afraid; just keep on believing" (literal translation). What a challenge to Jairus' faith! Though the child was dead, the Master was still equal to the emergency.

Jesus permitted only **Peter, and James and John** (v. 37) to accompany Him to the house of mourning. This is the first of three occasions upon which the Master took the inner trio with Him. The other two were the Transfiguration and the prayer in Gethsemane.

Mark paints a vivid picture of the scene that followed in the girl's bedroom. With just the parents and the three disciples present He took the child by the hand and said **Talitha cumi.** It has been suggested that these Aramaic words may well have been the very ones the mother habitually used to waken her daughter. This time they roused her from the sleep of death. The Master's word was with power. The twelve-year-old daughter was restored to her parents. They were **amazed straightway with a great amazement** (v. 42). The Greek says they stood out of themselves with great "ecstasy."

Jesus again commanded that no publicity should be given to the miracle. He was already too much beset by crowds wanting to be healed in body, when He needed to minister to the souls of men.

Then follows a beautiful touch of loving thoughtfulness. Christ commanded something to be given the girl to eat. The implication of this is well expressed by Swete, when he writes: "Life restored by miracle must be supported by ordinary means; the miracle has no place where human care or labour will suffice."[37]

f. Rejection at Nazareth (6:1-6)

1 And he went out from thence; and he cometh into his own country; and his disciples followed him. 2 And when the sabbath was come, he began to teach in the synagogue: and many hearing him

[35] Ezra P. Gould, *A Critical and Exegetical Commentary on the Gospel According to St. Mark,* p. 100.
[36] C. E. Graham Swift, "The Gospel According to Mark," *The New Bible Commentary,* ed. F. Davidson, p. 1.   [37] *Op. cit.,* p. 104.

were astonished, saying, Whence hath this man these things? and, What is the wisdom that is given unto this man, and *what mean* such mighty works wrought by his hands? 3 Is not this the carpenter, the son of Mary, and brother of James, and Joses, and Judas, and Simon? and are not his sisters here with us? And they were offended in him. 4 And Jesus said unto them, A prophet is not without honor, save in his own country, and among his own kin, and in his own house. 5 And he could there do no mighty work, save that he laid his hands upon a few sick folk, and healed them. 6 And he marvelled because of their unbelief.
And he went round about the villages teaching.

Jesus **went out from thence** — that is, from Capernaum, where He made His headquarters during His Galilean ministry — and came into **his own country;** that is, His home town, Nazareth.

When the **sabbath** came, He attended the service in the synagogue. There He taught the people who had gathered for worship. They were **astonished** (the imperfect tense suggests a growing astonishment) and wondered where He got His wisdom and His miracle-working power. To them He was simply a "home town boy," the former village **carpenter** (Matt. 13:55 — "carpenter's son"). They were well acquainted with His mother, as also His brothers and sisters. Four of His brothers are named here. It has been generally held that **James** and **Judas** were the writers, respectively, of the Epistles of James and Jude. **Joses** is short for Joseph, and so was named after his father. **Simon** was one of the most common Jewish names of that day. Nearly a dozen Simons are mentioned in the New Testament. We do not know how many **sisters** Jesus had. In keeping with the customs of the times, their names are not given. They were all probably children of both Joseph and Mary — not "cousins," as is sometimes held.

Because they knew Jesus and His family, the people of Nazareth **were offended in him.** The verb is *skandalizo* ("scandalize"). The evident meaning is that they "stumbled" over the fact that He was such a familiar figure to them. They could not believe that He was the miracle-working Messiah. Jesus quoted

to them a well-known proverb (v. 4), which is applicable in every age.

The result of their attitude was that He could do there **no mighty work** (*dynamis,* power) — which Mark immediately modifies by saying that He did lay His hands on **a few sick folk** and healed them. This is in full agreement with Matthew's statement that He did "not many mighty works there" (Matt. 13:58).

Mark adds that Jesus **marvelled** at their unbelief (v. 6). In only one other place is it said that Christ marveled, and then it was at the faith of a Gentile, a Roman centurion (Matt. 8:10; Luke 7:9). What a sad contrast! Even today new converts often have a more simple and complete faith in Christ than do older church members.

The last part of verse 6 contains one of several such summary statements. **Round about** is literally "in a circle" (Greek, *cyclo*). Jesus' main concern was teaching the people.

g. Sending of the Twelve (6:7-13)

7 And he calleth unto him the twelve, and began to send them forth by two and two; and he gave them authority over the unclean spirits; 8 and he charged them that they should take nothing for *their* journey, save a staff only; no bread, no wallet, no money in their purse; 9 but *to go* shod with sandals: and, *said he,* put not on two coats. 10 And he said unto them, Wheresoever ye enter into a house, there abide till ye depart thence. 11 And whatsoever place shall not receive you, and they hear you not, as ye go forth thence, shake off the dust that is under your feet for a testimony unto them. 12 And they went out, and preached that *men* should repent. 13 And they cast out many demons, and anointed with oil many that were sick, and healed them.

For the significance of the number **twelve** see on Matthew 10:1. Mark alone adds the statement that Jesus sent forth His apostles **by two and two.** Traveling in pairs was a common custom in ancient times (cf. Luke 7:19; Acts 13:1-3), and still has great value today. If one gets discouraged or falls ill, the other is there to give needed help. Also they can agree together in prayer (cf. Matt. 18: 19). Two are stronger than one.

Send . . . forth is literally "send on a

mission." The twelve "apostles" (same Greek root as **send forth**) were to be Christ's missionaries to the lost sheep of Israel (Matt. 10:5-6). They were to make a missionary tour of Galilee, since it was impossible for Jesus Himself to cover all the many hundreds of villages in this area.

Matthew gives the list of twelve apostles at this point (Matt. 10:2-4). But Mark has given it earlier (3:13-19).

The instructions for the journey (vv. 8-11) seem rather startling. They were not to take any food or extra clothing (for the reasons for this see on Matt. 10:9-10). They were allowed one **staff**, or walking stick. The seeming prohibition against even this in Matthew 10:10 and Luke 9:3 means that if they did not already have one, they were not to get one (Matt. 10:9).

Wallet does not mean billfold, as it usually does today. A better translation would be "bag." It probably refers to a leather pouch for carrying food.[38] **Money** is the same word in Greek as in the parallel passage in Matthew (10:9), where it is translated "brass." It refers to copper coins, the cheapest money then, as now. **Purse** is "belt," the place where money was carried in those days. Plummer indicates the climactic effect of these three prohibitions, thus: "no food, no wallet for carrying food that might be given, no money for buying food."[39]

They were to wear **sandals**, not even taking an extra pair of "shoes" (Matt. 10:10). Moreover they were not to have two **coats** (so all three Gospels). The word does not mean what we understand by a "coat," but rather refers to the under garment, or tunic. The nearest equivalent today would be "shirt."

They were to stay in only one house in each community, lest they be accused of carrying gossip from one home to another. For the meaning of **shake off the dust** (v. 11) see on Matthew 10:14. The act would indicate that the offending city "is reckoned as heathen."[40] Paul and Barnabas did this very thing at Pisidian Antioch (Acts 13:51).

The twelve apostles had a threefold mission (vv. 12-13). (1) They **preached that men should repent**, as John and Jesus had done before them; (2) **they cast out many demons**, using the authority Jesus had given them (v. 7); (3) they **anointed with oil many that were sick, and healed them.** The only other place in the New Testament where this method is mentioned is James 5:14. The anointing with olive-oil was probably intended as a symbol of God's outpoured grace.

h. Death of John (6:14-29)

14 And king Herod heard *thereof;* for his name had become known: and he said, John the Baptizer is risen from the dead, and therefore do these powers work in him. 15 But others said, It is Elijah. And others said, *It is* a prophet, *even* as one of the prophets. 16 But Herod, when he heard *thereof,* said, John, whom I beheaded, he is risen. 17 For Herod himself had sent forth and laid hold upon John, and bound him in prison for the sake of Herodias, his brother Philip's wife; for he had married her. 18 For John said unto Herod, It is not lawful for thee to have thy brother's wife. 18 And Herodias set herself against him, and desired to kill him; and she could not; 20 for Herod feared John, knowing that he was a righteous and holy man, and kept him safe. And when he heard him, he was much perplexed; and he heard him gladly. 21 And when a convenient day was come, that Herod on his birthday made a supper to his lords, and the high captains, and the chief men of Galilee; 22 and when the daughter of Herodias herself came in and danced, she pleased Herod and them that sat at meat with him; and the king said unto the damsel, Ask of me whatsoever thou wilt, and I will give it thee. 23 And he sware unto her, Whatsoever thou shalt ask of me, I will give it thee, unto the half of my kingdom. 24 And she went out, and said unto her mother, What shall I ask? And she said, The head of John the Baptizer. 25 And she came in straightway with haste unto the king, and asked, saying, I will that thou forthwith give me on a platter the head of John the Baptist. 26 And the king was exceeding sorry; but for the sake of his oaths, and of them that sat at meat, he would not reject her. 27 And straight-

---

[38] Deissmann (*op. cit.,* pp. 108-110) thinks the reference is to a bag used by beggars for collecting food.   [39] *Op. cit.,* p. 160.

[40] T. W. Manson, "The Gospel According to St. Mark," *The Mission and Message of Jesus,* by H. D. A. Major, T. W. Manson, & C. J. Wright, p. 368.

way the king sent forth a soldier of his guard, and commanded to bring his head: and he went and beheaded him in the prison, 28 and brought his head on a platter, and gave it to the damsel; and the damsel gave it to her mother. 29 And when his disciples heard *thereof*, they came and took up his corpse, and laid it in a tomb.

As usual, Mark's account is much more vivid than that in Matthew (see on Matt. 14:1-12) or Luke (3:19-20; 9:7-9). The story told here is filled with drama and pathos.

King Herod is correctly called "the tetrarch" by Matthew and Luke (see on Matt. 14:1). Mark uses the popular title that was commonly employed in Galilee. Also it was the habit in Rome to refer to Eastern rulers by this title, and Mark was writing for Romans.

When Herod heard of Jesus' miracles, his conscience plagued him. This must be **John the Baptizer**. Others identified Christ as **Elijah** or **one of the prophets** (v. 15). But Herod was sure it was **John, whom I beheaded** (v. 16).

Then follows the story of John's arrest and imprisonment, which had taken place some time before (cf. 1:14). This was due to John's reproof of Herod because he had **married** his brother's wife.

The primary source of this evil was Herodias. **Set herself against him** (v. 19) is literally "had it in for him." That exactly expresses her attitude. She wished **to kill him,** but **could not.** Why not? Mark alone gives the answer. It was because **Herod feared John** and **kept him safe** (v. 20) — apparently from the murderous designs of Herodias. Matthew (14:5) says that Herod "feared the multitude." There is no contradiction here, as is sometimes claimed. Herod was primarily a politician, and also a man of weak character and vacillating actions, as was Ahab in the Old Testament. Herodias was like Jezebel — utterly without conscience in her cruel conniving and devilish determination. Both women succeeded in carrying out their planned murder of a righteous man.

Was much perplexed is almost exactly the same in the Greek as "did many things" (KJV). But the former has the support of the oldest manuscripts.

Scheming, wily Herodias waited for a **convenient day** (v. 21). Herod's birthday proved to be just that. When he made a great feast for the civil magistrates, military officers, and leading men of his country, Herodias plotted the climactic act. In order to bring about the death of the prophet whom she hated she was willing to degrade her own daughter, assigning her the disgraceful role of dancing before the assembled crowd. Her sensual movements roused the drunken king to the place where he promised her anything she wished (v. 22), even to **half of my kingdom** (v. 23). There was only one thing Herodias wanted — John the Baptist's head. At the evil queen's behest, the daughter asked for this bloody trophy, and received it. Thus died the chosen forerunner of the Messiah.

2. Second Retreat and Return (6:30-7:23)

a. Feeding of Five Thousand (6:30-44)

30 And the apostles gathered themselves together unto Jesus; and they told him all things, whatsoever they had done, and whatsoever they had taught. 31 And he saith unto them, Come ye yourselves apart into a desert place, and rest a while. For there were many coming and going, and they had no leisure so much as to eat. 32 And they went away in the boat to a desert place apart. 33 And *the people* saw them going, and many knew *them*, and they ran together there on foot from all the cities, and outwent them. 34 And he came forth and saw a great multitude, and he had compassion on them, because they were as sheep not having a shepherd: and he began to teach them many things. 35 And when the day was now far spent, his disciples came unto him, and said, The place is desert, and the day is now far spent; 36 send them away, that they may go into the country and villages round about, and buy themselves somewhat to eat. 37 But he answered and said unto them, Give ye them to eat. And they say unto him, Shall we go and buy two hundred shillings' worth of bread, and give them to eat? 38 And he saith unto them, How many loaves have ye? *go and see.* And when they knew, they say, Five, and two fishes. 39 And he commanded them that all should sit down by companies upon the green grass. 40 And they sat down in ranks, by hundreds, and

by fifties. 41 And he took the five loaves and two fishes, and looking up to heaven, he blessed, and brake the loaves; and he gave to the disciples to set before them; and the two fishes divided he among them all. 42 And they all ate, and were filled. 43 And they took up broken pieces, twelve basketfuls, and also of the fishes. 44 And they that ate the loaves were five thousand men.

Mark and Luke place this incident immediately after the return of the twelve apostles from their preaching mission (v. 30). The Master realized that His men needed rest and relaxation before joining Him again in ministering to the multitudes, so He graciously invited them — just the twelve — to come apart with Him to a quiet place. **Desert place** does not mean a sandy waste, but a lonely spot where they could escape the thronging crowds. So constant was the pressure of milling multitudes that Jesus and His disciples did not even have leisure to eat (v. 31).

So they took a **boat** — probably Peter's fishing craft — to the east side of the lake, where only a few people lived. But some saw them leaving and **knew them** — better, "recognized them"; that is, "saw what was happening" (cf. Matt. 14:13; Luke 9:11). So they ran around the north end of the Lake of Galilee **on foot** (or, "by land"). They perhaps traveled about eight miles while the boat traversed some four or five miles — a commentary on the slowness of sailing in those days — and arrived first on the eastern shore.

So Jesus' vacation plans were suddenly shattered. Arriving at their destination the thirteen men found **a great multitude** (v. 34). How did the Master react? He **had compassion**: the aorist tense suggests that He "was gripped with compassion." That was always His immediate reaction to human need. And so He **began to teach them**. That was their greatest necessity. Matthew (14:14) says He "healed their sick." Luke combines the two in his statement that Jesus "spake to them of the kingdom of God, and them that had need of healing he cured" (Luke 9:11). This is a good example of the essential agreement in thought, together with some differences in form, that one finds in the three Gospel records of the same incident.

Actually the feeding of the five thousand is the only miracle of Jesus which is recorded in all four Gospels. John's account (6:1-13) is fuller.

As evening drew on, the disciples became concerned about where the vast crowd was going to get its supper. Orientals feel a deep sense of obligation to feed their guests when mealtime arrives. So the Twelve suggested that the Master had better send the multitudes away to the surrounding farms and villages in order that they might buy something to eat.

To say the least, Jesus' answer was startling: **Give ye them to eat** (v. 37). The Greek is even stronger: "you yourselves give them to eat" (same in all three Synoptics). The command seemed utterly unreasonable. But the important point is that the disciples actually did exactly the impossible thing Jesus told them to do: they fed the whole crowd. He furnished the miracle; they furnished the hands; and the deed was done. Christ's disciples still have only one responsibility — obedience. It is His responsibility to provide the enabling power, as He did back there.

The reaction of the Twelve to the command was perfectly natural. Were they to go and buy **two hundred shillings' worth of bread** — 200 denarii, worth about forty dollars? Since a denarius was a day's wage (Matt. 20:2), this would represent a laborer's income for seven months.

Ignoring their incredulous question, Jesus asked how many **loaves** (the size of a small pancake) they had. They investigated and reported that there were only **five** on hand, plus **two fishes** (v. 38). The latter were probably the size of sardines (John uses a word meaning "small fish"). The whole was enough to feed one person, but Jesus fed five thousand.

The Master commanded that all the men should be made to **sit down** (Greek "recline") on the **green grass** (v. 39). Only Mark mentions the latter but it fits perfectly with John's statement that the passover was "at hand" (John 6:4), for the grass is usually green in Palestine only in March, April and May. They were to recline **by companies,** so that they might be conveniently fed in an orderly fashion.

They reclined in **ranks** (v. 40). This is one of Mark's picturesque words. Literally it means "garden beds." When Peter saw the crowd grouped by hundreds, and by fifties — which would facilitate the count — the people in their bright Oriental garments of red and yellow looked to him like flower beds against the green grass.

b. Walking on the Water (6:45-52)

45 And straightway he constrained his disciples to enter into the boat, and to go before *him* unto the other side to Bethsaida, while he himself sendeth the multitude away. 46 And after he had taken leave of them, he departed into the mountain to pray. 47 And when even was come, the boat was in the midst of the sea, and he alone on the land. 48 And seeing them distressed in rowing, for the wind was contrary unto them, about the fourth watch of the night he cometh unto them, walking on the sea; and he would have passed by them: 49 but they, when they saw him walking on the sea, supposed that it was a ghost, and cried out; 50 for they all saw him, and were troubled. But he straightway spake with them, and saith unto them, Be of good cheer: it is I; be not afraid. 51 And he went up unto them into the boat; and the wind ceased: and they were sore amazed in themselves; 52 for they understood not concerning the loaves, but their heart was hardened.

When the meal was ended and the twelve disciples had filled their lunch baskets with the fragments left over, Jesus constrained (or, compelled) them to embark in their boat and go ahead of Him unto the other side to Bethsaida. This statement seems strange, since apparently they were on the east side of the lake and the only Bethsaida that we know (Bethsaida Julia) was on the east bank of the Jordan River at the point where it enters the Lake of Galilee. Furthermore, Luke 9:10 says that the feeding of the five thousand took place near this city. How are these statements to be harmonized?

It has been suggested that the disciples headed northward across the small bay just south of Bethsaida, expecting to take Jesus on board at that city, but were instead driven by north winds out into the center of the lake. Some scholars think it likely that there was a fishing village named Bethsaida on the western shore near Capernaum. Either one of

these solutions is acceptable, but which is preferable it is difficult to say. John (6:17) says that the disciples "were going over the sea unto Capernaum." This was apparently their final destination that night.

The story of Jesus' walking on the water is recorded also by Matthew (see on Matt. 14:22-27) and John, but not Luke. A contrary wind was making it difficult for the disciples out on the lake. Distressed (v. 48) is a better translation than "toiling" (KJV). The Greek word (used also by Matthew) means "tortured" or "tormented."

Mark alone says that Jesus would have passed by them. This probably does not mean that that was His full intention, but only that it seemed thus to the disciples. When they cried out with fear, troubled or "disturbed" by what they saw, He comforted them by His words and His presence. When He boarded the boat, the wind ceased. The verb literally means "grow weary." Like a restless child who has stormily refused to be quiet, the wind finally sank into a restful slumber.

c. Healing in Gennesaret (6:53-56)

53 And when they had crossed over, they came to the land unto Gennesaret, and moored to the shore. 54 And when they were come out of the boat, straightway *the people* knew him, 55 and ran round about that whole region, and began to carry about on their beds those that were sick, where they heard he was. 56 And wheresoever he entered, into villages, or into cities, or into the country, they laid the sick in the marketplaces, and besought him that they might touch if it were but the border of his garment: and as many as touched him were made whole.

This incident is given only here and in Matthew (see on Matt. 14:34-36). As is usually the case in narrative sections, Mark's account is fuller and more graphic. He relates that as soon as they had anchored on the western shore of the lake, straightway (immediately) the people ran round about (Greek compound verb found only here in the New Testament) and began to carry about (another compound with *peri*) on their beds ("pallets," or thickly padded quilts) the sick where they heard he was. These added items in Mark paint a vivid picture. One can see stretcher cases being rushed to Jesus from every direction. It was a typical scene in His busy ministry.

Verse 56 may be thought of as a general description of what took place throughout the Master's great Galilean ministry, and not here alone. The three kinds of human habitation of that day are mentioned. People lived in **villages** (unwalled towns) or cities (usually with walls) or the **country** (plural, "country places"). In the singular this word means "a field." But in the plural it refers to all the area outside the cities and villages.

They laid the sick in the **marketplaces.** The Agora, like the Plaza of Latin America towns, was the central meeting place of the community for buying and selling, as well as for social fellowship. Here the crowds flocked around Jesus.

d. Conflict over Cleansing (7:1-23)

1 And there are gathered together unto him the Pharisees, and certain of the scribes, who had come from Jerusalem, 2 and had seen that some of his disciples ate their bread with defiled, that is, unwashen, hands. 3 (For the Pharisees, and all the Jews, except they wash their hands diligently, eat not, holding the tradition of the elders; 4 and *when they come* from the marketplace, except they bathe themselves, they eat not; and many other things there are, which they have received to hold, washings of cups, and pots, and brasen vessels.) 5 And the Pharisees and the scribes ask him, Why walk not thy disciples according to the tradition of the elders, but eat their bread with defiled hands? 6 And he said unto them, Well did Isaiah prophesy of you hypocrites, as it is written,
This people honoreth me with their lips,
But their heart is far from me.
7 But in vain do they worship me,
Teaching *as their* doctrines the precepts of men.
8 Ye leave the commandment of God, and hold fast the tradition of men. 9 And he said unto them, Full well do ye reject the commandment of God, that ye may keep your tradition. 10 For Moses said, Honor thy father and thy mother; and, He that speaketh evil of father or mother, let him die the death: 11 but ye say, If a man shall say to his father or his mother, That wherewith thou mightest have been profited by me is Corban, that is to say, Given *to God;*
12 ye no longer suffer him to do aught for his father or his mother; 13 making void the word of God by your tradition, which ye have delivered: and many such like things ye do. 14 And he called to him the multitude again, and said unto them, Hear me all of you, and understand: 15 there is nothing from without the man, that going into him can defile him; but the things which proceed out of the man are those that defile the man. 17 And when he was entered into the house from the multitude, his disciples asked him the parable. 18 And he saith unto them, Are ye so without understanding also? Perceive ye not, that whatsoever from without goeth into the man, *it* cannot defile him; 19 because it goeth not into his heart, but into his belly, and goeth out into the draught? *This he said,* making all meats clean. 20 And he said, That which proceedeth out of the man, that defileth the man. 21 For from within, out of the heart of men, evil thoughts proceed, fornications, thefts, murders, adulteries, 22 covetings, wickednesses, deceit, lasciviousness, an evil eye, railing, pride, foolishness: 23 all these evil things proceed from within, and defile the man.

Matthew and Mark both give a record of this controversy of the Pharisees with Jesus over the matter of ceremonial cleansings (see on Matt. 15:1-20). As the number of verses indicates, the two accounts are similar in length. The small difference is due to Mark's furnishing (in parentheses) for his Gentile readers an explanation of the Jewish custom of washing the hands ceremonially before eating (vv. 3-4).

As usual Mark, and he alone, graphically portrays the setting of the incident. Both he and Matthew state that scribes and Pharisees had come the long distance from Jerusalem to see what was going on in Galilee. But only Mark says that, when they **had seen** the disciples eating, they found fault. In other words, they had come with the specific purpose of trying to find some infraction of the Pharisaic regulations on the part of Jesus or His disciples, and they succeeded. With hawklike eyes they watched, and then pounced on their victims.

What they saw was that the Master's disciples ate their food with **defiled, that is, unwashen, hands.** The Greek word for **defiled** is literally "common." With the Pharisees this meant "unclean" or "unhallowed." That which was not sacred was "common." A thing was rendered sacred by being ceremonially cleansed. **Unwashen** does not mean that the disciples had not washed their hands at all before eating. It merely indicates that they had not gone through the elaborate procedure which was prescribed by the Pharisaic code.[41]

Then Mark explains for his Roman readers what this Jewish custom was. **All the Jews** — this does not mean every individual Jew, but refers to the general practice — and especially **the Pharisees**, the strict observers and teachers of the Law, did not eat unless they washed their hands **diligently**. This is *pygme* in the Greek. In the King James Version it is translated "oft." Literally it means "with the fist." But just what this signifies is a matter of dispute. Some very good scholars interpret it "to the wrist." Others say, "up to the elbow." The two best authorities (Swete and Taylor) would take the word literally, "with the fist," perhaps meaning that they washed one hand with the closed fingers of the other. The translation **diligently** probably conveys the correct idea. The Revised Standard Version leaves the word untranslated, because of the uncertainty of its meaning, as does also the New English Bible (1961).

When the strict Jews returned from the marketplace the first thing they did was to **bathe** themselves. The oldest Greek manuscripts have a word which means "sprinkle," which would be a sort of ceremonial cleansing. Later manuscripts have "baptize." The meaning is apparently much the same. It was a religious act, done for sacredness rather than sanitation.

For his Roman readers Mark adds that there are **many other things** which the Jews observed. He spells out **the washings of cups, and pots, and brazen vessels**.[42] The word **washings** is in the Greek *baptismous*, "baptisms." The term is used for ritual cleansings. **Pots** is perhaps better rendered "pitchers." It refers to a container holding about a pint. The **brazen vessels** were probably caldrons used for cooking. The fact that the Jews gave great attention to the matter of ceremonial washing of dishes is abundantly corroborated by the Mishna, thirty chapters of which are devoted to this subject.

The scribes and Pharisees asked Jesus why His disciples were not walking according to **the tradition of the elders**. See this phrase explained in the notes on Matthew 15:2. The word **walk** is used here alone in the Synoptic Gospels in the Hebrew sense of "live," though this usage is very common in Paul's Epistles.

In answer Jesus quoted Isaiah 29:13. The prophet's description of the people in the eighth century B.C. applied equally well to those in the first century A.D. In both cases they were honoring God with their lips, while their hearts were not submissive to His will. In this they were **hypocrites** (v. 6). The word occurs only this once in Mark's Gospel, though it is found fourteen times in Matthew and three times in Luke. It is an exact transliteration of the Greek word which was used for actors on the stage. In those days when there were no modern electronic amplification systems the actors found it difficult to carry their voices throughout an amphitheater seating 25,-000 people. So they wore large masks in which were hidden small megaphones. Thus a hypocrite is one who wears a false face, who appears to be what he is not.

Jesus accused the scribes of teaching the **precepts of men** (v. 7). They forsook the divine Law and held fast the **tradition of men** (v. 8). He was evidently speaking ironically when He said: **Full well do ye reject** ("set aside") **the commandment of God, that ye may keep your tradition.** This is still done by those who forget the greatest command of all, to love one another, while they harshly criticize those who fail to keep their man-made traditions.

To illustrate His point, Christ gave an example from their own practice. He first quoted the fifth commandment. The way this quotation is introduced is most striking. **Moses said** is in Matthew, "God said." Thus the divine authority

---

[41] The last clause of verse 2 in the King James Version, "they found fault," is not in the oldest manuscripts. It was added to complete the sentence, which is grammatically incomplete in the Greek.
[42] The addition of "tables" (literally "couches") in KJV is not in the oldest manuscripts. It does not fit well into the context.

and inspiration of the Mosaic code is forcibly emphasized. The Law came from God through Moses.

To the fifth of the Ten Commandments (Ex. 20:12) Jesus added a quotation from Exodus 21:17. **Die the death** is a Hebraism. Literally it means "let him come to an end by death." The Old Testament passage gives the correct idea in English — "surely die."

In contrast to what God said through Moses, the rabbis said that a man might withhold from his aged father or mother the financial support they sorely needed. This was done by the fiction of **Corban**. Mark explains for his Roman readers that this Hebrew word means a gift which has been consecrated to God. The cognate term *corbanas* is used in Matthew 27:6 for the temple "treasury." But there seems to be good evidence that the use of **Corban** does not mean necessarily that the money was actually given to the temple. No less an authority than the great Jewish scholar, Montefiore, writes: "'Corban' does not mean that the property was dedicated to the use of the Temple. The word is used here as a mere oath."[43]

So all a man had to do was to say "Corban!" and the rabbis no longer permitted him to do anything for his needy parents, because of his oath. No wonder Jesus charged the scribes with **making void the word of God by your tradition** (v. 13). The primary law of God is love, and everything that is contrary to true love is a denial of divine authority.

Mark adds the general condemnation: **and many such like things ye do.** It is difficult to understand the cruel attitude of the Jewish rabbis who condoned such a custom. When religion ceases to be human, it is no longer divine.

Then Jesus returned to the original question of the Pharisees, which involved the true nature of uncleanness. In order to make sure that no one missed the point, He called the crowd together again and urged the people to **hear** and **understand** (v. 14). Then He made a startling statement: Not what goes into a man defiles him, but what comes out (v. 15).[44]

When Christ had dismissed the crowd and gone indoors, **his disciples** — Mat-

thew says "Peter" — asked Him to explain **the parable** (v. 17). We generally think of a parable (literally, "something laid alongside" for purposes of comparison) as a story. But the term is sometimes applied, as here, to a short parabolic saying.

The question in the first part of verse 18 may literally be translated: "Thus even you are without understanding?" It was bad enough to have the crowds misunderstanding Him. But that not even His disciples, after all this time with Him, could grasp what He was saying was indeed disappointing.

It is difficult for a Christian today to realize how utterly revolutionary Jesus' teaching sounded to those who first heard it. They had been taught from childhood that eating unclean meat (such as pork) defiled a person. This was part of the Mosaic law (cf. Lev. 11). But the Pharisees had magnified it all out of proportion and made it a major emphasis. Jesus clearly declared that religion is a spiritual, not a material, affair. It is not the stomach, but the heart, which counts. The Master's primary emphasis was on inner attitudes, not outward things.

The last clause of verse 19 is interpreted in the Revised Versions differently from the way it is rendered in the King James Version. The reason for the change is that the participle *katharizon* ("cleansing") is masculine in the best Greek text, not neuter, and so refers to Christ. Mark, following Peter (cf. Acts 10:15), makes this comment concerning what Jesus meant: Christ's teaching at this point abolished for all His followers the Judaistic distinction between clean and unclean meats. The Book of Acts shows that the first generation of Jewish Christians had difficulty in absorbing this truth.

Jesus declared that it was what flowed out of the heart of man which defiled him. **Evil thoughts** (or "designs") is probably a general term introducing the list of sins. Twelve specific items are mentioned, six in the plural and six in the singular. The enumeration is similar to that of "the works of the flesh" (Gal. 5:19-21). Paul has several such

[43] C. G. Montefiore, *The Synoptic Gospels*, I, 164.
[44] Verse 16 is omitted in the two oldest extant Greek manuscripts. The words are genuine in 4:23.

lists in his epistles, but this is the longest in the Gospels.

The sins listed here are the things that are really unclean in God's sight. One should note the unsavory company in which the so-called sins of the spirit — conveting, deceit, envy (an evil eye), pride, and foolishness — are found. In the X-ray gaze of a holy God these are just as sinful as fornication, theft, murder, and adultery. All of these are sins against love.

3. Third Retreat and Return (7:24-8:13)

a. Woman of Phoenicia (7:24-30)

24 And from thence he arose, and went away into the borders of Tyre and Sidon. And he entered into a house, and would have no man know it; and he could not be hid. 25 But straightway a woman, whose little daughter had an unclean spirit, having heard of him, came and fell down at his feet. 26 Now the woman was a Greek, a Syrophoenician by race. And she besought him that he would cast forth the demon out of her daughter. 27 And he said unto her, Let the children first be filled: for it is not meet to take the children's bread and cast it to the dogs. 28 But she answered and saith unto him, Yea, Lord; even the dogs under the table eat of the children's crumbs. 29 And he said unto her, For this saying go thy way; the demon is gone out of thy daughter. 30 And she went away unto her house, and found the child laid upon the bed, and the demon gone out.

Leaving Capernaum, Jesus withdrew some 40 or 50 miles northward to the borders (literally "boundaries") of Tyre and Sidon. These were the two main cities of ancient Phoenicia and were noted for their seafaring sailors. This area lay north of Palestine on the coast of the Mediterranean.

In this foreign, Gentile territory the Master sought seclusion with His disciples, that He might give them the private instruction they needed. But he could not be hid, even in a house. His reputation had outrun Him. This little detail is added by Mark.

Among those who searched Him out was a Greek-speaking Syrophoenician woman. Phoenicia was part of the general area of Syria. Mark, writing in Rome, uses this compound to distinguish her from the Libyo-Phoenicians of North Africa.

This interesting incident is recorded also by Matthew (see on Matt. 15:21-28). The two accounts are very similar in thought, though considerably different in wording. Mark identifies the "little dogs" (both Gospels) as being under the table (v. 28) — a typical picturesque detail. He also reports Jesus as saying to the distressed mother: the demon has gone out of thy daughter (v. 29). Then he concludes with the graphic touch that when the mother returned home, in obedient faith, she found the child laid upon the bed, and the demon gone out. Thus he confirms Jesus' promise to the woman.

This is the only case which Mark records of the Master's healing someone at a distance. Matthew adds that of the centurion's servant (Matt. 8:5-13). Both times it was a Gentile who displayed such amazing faith. Even today new converts often exhibit greater faith than seasoned Christians.

b. Deaf Mute of Decapolis (7:31-37)

31 And again he went out from the borders of Tyre, and came through Sidon unto the sea of Galilee, through the midst of the borders of Decapolis. 32 And they bring unto him one that was deaf, and had an impediment in his speech; and they beseech him to lay his hand upon him. 33 And he took him aside from the multitude privately, and put his fingers into his ears, and he spat, and touched his tongue; 34 and looking up to heaven he sighed, and saith unto him, Ephphatha, that is, Be opened. 35 And his ears were opened, and the bond of his tongue was loosed, and he spake plain. 36 And he charged them that they should tell no man: but the more he charged them, so much the more a great deal they published it. 37 And they were beyond measure astonished, saying, He hath done all things well; he maketh even the deaf to hear, and the dumb to speak.

Leaving the borders of Tyre, Jesus returned southward to the Lake of Galilee. The statement that He went through Sidon is surprising, for this city is north of Tyre. It implies that Jesus took a swing some twenty miles northward before turning east and south.

Christ did not return to Galilee, however, but went into **Decapolis** on the east side of the Lake of Galilee. There were probably two reasons why He avoided Galilee. Its ruler, Herod Antipas, had killed John the Baptist and now threatened the life of Jesus (Luke 13:31). In the second place, the opposition of the Pharisees had grown sharper. Since the Decapolis ("Ten Cities," see on Matt. 4:25) was mainly Gentile territory, Christ would be relatively free there from interference by the Pharisees. Added to these two reasons was the fact that He was seeking to avoid the large crowds that always flocked around Him in Galilee. He wanted at this stage to be alone with His disciples to instruct them.

The healing of the deaf mute in the Decapolis is recorded only by Mark. Matthew mentions many healings at this point.

The word for **deaf** can mean either deaf or dumb. But Mark employs it only in the former sense. **Had an impediment in his speech** is all one word in the Greek — *mogilalos* (literally, "speaking with difficulty"). It is probable that this man was not completely dumb. For when he was healed, Mark says, he spoke **plain** (v. 35).

Typically, Mark describes how Jesus took the man away from the crowd **privately** (v. 33). Not able to hear, the patient needed quiet, careful attention, and the Great Physician gave it to him. To bolster the man's faith and also to indicate that He planned to heal his tongue and ears, Jesus placed His fingers into the poor fellow's ears, and touched his tongue. This showed how gracious and thoughtful Jesus was in dealing with men.[45]

Ephphatha is an Aramaic word. The Greek word used to translate it means "open completely." **Ears** (v. 35) is literally "hearings." The Master Physician did a thorough job of healing.

It is not to be wondered that the crowd was **beyond measure** (literally, "above exceedingly") **astonished.** Their testimony to Jesus was very appropriate —

He hath done all things well.

c. Feeding of Four Thousand (8:1-10)

1 In those days, when there was again a great multitude, and they had nothing to eat, he called unto him his disciples, and saith unto them, 2 I have compassion on the multitude, because they continue with me now three days, and have nothing to eat: 3 and if I send them away fasting to their home, they will faint on the way; and some of them are come from far. 4 And his disciples answered him, Whence shall one be able to fill these men with bread here in a desert place? 5 And he asked them, How many loaves have ye? And they said, Seven. 6 And he commandeth the multitude to sit down on the ground: and he took the seven loaves, and having given thanks, he brake, and gave to his disciples, to set before them; and they set them before the multitude. 7 And they had a few small fishes; and having blessed them, he commanded to set these also before them. 8 And they ate, and were filled: and they took up, of broken pieces that remained over, seven baskets. 9 And they were about four thousand: and he sent them away. 10 And straightway he entered into the boat with his disciples, and came into the parts of Dalmanutha.

Whereas the Feeding of the Five Thousand is recorded in all four Gospels, the Feeding of the Four Thousand is related only by Matthew and Mark. In this case the Markan and Matthean accounts are almost exactly the same (see Matt. 15:32-39). Mark adds one little detail in verse 3, when he says that many of the people had **come from far,** and so would faint by the way if they had to return home for food. Characteristically Mark uses the more vivid historical present tense in verse 6, where Matthew has the aorist participle.

At the close of the incident he says that Jesus crossed the lake to **Dalmanutha.** Matthew has "Magadan." Neither location is known today. But presumably both terms refer to the heavily populated Plain of Gennesaret (cf. Mark 6:53), which was on the west side of the lake.

Critics have often questioned how the disciples could have asked what is recorded in verse 4, after they had witnessed the miracle of feeding five thousand people with five loaves and two fish.

---

[45] Adam Clarke thinks the man himself touched his own tongue and ears, to show his need. But most commentators favor the interpretation given above.

But it is recorded in Mark 6:52 that they did not understand the meaning of the earlier incident. A long time had elapsed between the two events, and it is characteristic human nature to forget God's blessings in the past. Moreover, the question of the disciples can be interpreted as expressing a hint of anticipation, rather than complete incredulity. When Jesus posed the problem of what to do with a famished multitude (vv. 1-3), the apostles answered that, while they were unable to do anything about it, perhaps Jesus would do something. Allen writes: "The words mean just what they put into them, and that may well have been a note of expectation, 'Whence . . . unless you provide?' "[46]

d. Request for Sign (8:11-13)

11 And the Pharisees came forth, and began to question with him, seeking of him a sign from heaven, trying him. 12 And he sighed deeply in his spirit, and saith, Why doth this generation seek a sign? verily I say unto you, There shall no sign be given unto this generation. 13 And he left them, and again entering into *the boat* departed to the other side.

The rabbis said that when the Messiah came He would show a light from heaven as proof that He really was the Messiah. Apparently that was what the Pharisees were demanding here.

This will explain the seeming discrepancy between this account and Matthew's. The latter says that no sign would be given but that of Jonah (Matt. 16:4). Mark declares that **no sign** would be given to that generation. What he evidently means is that there would be no sign of the kind the Pharisees were seeking.

Actually, the many miracles which Jesus had already performed were adequate testimony to His deity. But the scribes demanded some spectacular sign to show that His work was supernatural.

Too often that attitude prevails today. People are not satisfied with the glowing evidence of transformed lives and redeemed personalities. The craving for the sensational is not a sign of godliness, but rather of a carnal heart. Just

as Jesus had refused Satan's suggestion that He leap from the pinnacle of the Temple (Matt. 4:6), so now He rejected the temptation to do something spectacular. It is only a fickle crowd which is won by the sensational. People who are sensible and spiritual desire what is sane and significant, not a circus stunt.

The Master's reaction to the Pharisees' demand is graphically expressed by Mark in the word *anastenaxas*, translated **sighed deeply.** It is a strong compound term, found only here in the New Testament. It shows how deeply disturbed He was by the selfish, superficial, unreasonable attitude displayed by the religious leaders of His nation. So "having embarked" (literal Greek), He "went away" **to the other side** — probably the eastern shore of the Lake of Galilee.

4. Fourth Retreat and Return (8:14-9:50)

a. Leaven of Pharisees (8:14-21)

14 And they forgot to take bread; and they had not in the boat with them more than one loaf. 15 And he charged them, saying, Take heed, beware of the leaven of the Pharisees and the leaven of Herod. 16 And they reasoned one with another, saying, We have no bread. 17 And Jesus perceiving it saith unto them, Why reason ye, because ye have no bread? do ye not yet perceive, neither understand? have ye your heart hardened? 18 Having eyes, see ye not? and having ears, hear ye not? and do ye not remember? 19 When I brake the five loaves among the five thousand, how many baskets full of broken pieces took ye up? They say unto him, Twelve. 20 And when the seven among the four thousand, how many basketfuls of broken pieces took ye up? And they say unto him, Seven. 21 And he said unto them, Do ye not yet understand?

On their way across the lake Jesus solemnly admonished His disciples to beware of the leaven of the **Pharisees** and **Herod.** Matthew in his parallel account says "the leaven of the Pharisees and Sadducees" (Matt. 16:6). This phrase might be explained as legalism and ceremonialism. The **leaven of Herod** would probably signify worldly politics — something that should have no place what-

[46] W. C. Allen, *The Gospel According to Saint Mark*, p. 113.

ever in the Christian church. Luke (12:1) identifies "the leaven of the Pharisees" as "hypocrisy." Legalists are always inconsistent, if not insincere. They make a fetish out of some minor item, while transgressing the major emphasis of the law, which is love.

The materialistically-minded disciples thought that their Master was reproving them for having neglected to take along some loaves as they went to the sparsely inhabited east side of the lake. Their misunderstanding may have been due in part to the rabbinical custom of referring to ordinary bread as "leaven," to distinguish it from unleavened bread.

For a discussion of the significance of the different Greek words for **basket** see the notes on Matthew 16:5-12. How pathetic is Jesus' closing question in verse 21!

b. Blind Man of Bethsaida (8:22-26)

22 And they come unto Bethsaida. And they bring to him a blind man, and beseech him to touch him. 23 And he took hold of the blind man by the hand, and brought him out of the village; and when he had spit on his eyes, and laid his hands upon him, he asked him, Seest thou ought? 24 And he looked up, and said, I see men; for I behold *them* as trees, walking. 25 Then again he laid his hands upon his eyes; and he looked stedfastly, and was restored, and saw all things clearly. 26 And he sent him away to his home, saying, Do not even enter into the village.

Bethsaida Julias was located on the east bank of the Jordan River, near where it flows into the north end of the Lake of Galilee. Formerly a village, it had been rebuilt and enlarged by Philip the tetrarch (son of Herod the Great) as his capital of Gaulonitis. He called it Julias in honor of Julia, the daughter of Emperor Augustus.

The miracle recorded here is found only in Mark's Gospel. The account evidences Mark's love for vivid details, based probably on the keen observations of Peter. We are told that Jesus took the blind man by the hand and led him outside the village. Here we see the tender thoughtfulness of the Great Physician. The blind man would be distracted by the clamor of crowds all around him. So Jesus took him to a quiet spot, where He could have the man's full attention. Probably He wanted this to be a spiritual experience for the afflicted fellow, as well as a physical healing. Then, too, He wished to avoid undue publicity.

This incident and the healing of the deaf mute of Decapolis (7:31-37) are the only two miracles that are recorded by Mark alone. They have much in common. In fact, the language of verse 23 is very similar to that in 7:33. In both cases Jesus took the man aside from the crowd. Both times He put His hand on the afflicted parts of the body and used spittle. This was evidently to bolster the faith of these needy men. Spittle was sometimes thought to possess medicinal qualities, and Christ may have used it as a symbol of His healing power.

The healing of the blind man of Bethsaida is unique among the miracles performed by Jesus in being the only one that took place in two stages. After the first touch Christ asked the man if he saw anything. His reply was literally: "I behold the men, for as trees I see them walking." In other words, he saw what looked like trees. But they were moving; so they must be men. His vision was still very vague.

After the second touch the man **looked stedfastly**. The Greek verb is a compound, *diablepo*. Literally, he "saw through"; that is, he "saw clearly." He was **restored** to seeing and saw all things **clearly**. The Greek word means "at a distance clearly." His sight was perfect — and continued that way, as the imperfect tense implies.

Why did this miracle take place progressively, rather than instantly? The suggestion that the first touch healed the man's physical organs, while the second gave him mental apperception, does not seem to fit. His sight was **restored**, indicating that he had had previous experience of interpreting objects. It is more likely that Jesus accommodated "the pace of His power to the slowness of the man's faith."[47]

Christ charged the healed man not to enter the village. At this stage in His ministry, perhaps, the Master was more concerned about teaching than healing

---

[47] Maclaren, *op. cit.*, p. 326.

and did not wish to be hindered by thronging multitudes bringing the sick.

c. Pronouncement of Peter (8:27-30)

27 And Jesus went forth, and his disciples, into the villages of Caesarea Philippi: and on the way he asked his disciples, saying unto them, Who do men say that I am? 28 And they told him, saying, John the Baptist; and others, Elijah; but others, One of the prophets. 29 And he asked them, But who say ye that I am? Peter answereth and saith unto him, Thou art the Christ. 30 And he charged them that they should tell no man of him.

Peter's confession at Caesarea Philippi is recorded in all three Synoptic Gospels (cf. Matt. 16:13-20; Luke 9:18-21). In this case Matthew's account is by far the fullest (see the notes there). Mark has only two, very minor, unique details. He says that Jesus and the disciples went forth into the **villages** of Caesarea Philippi — i.e., the suburbs — whereas Matthew uses the word "parts." Mark also indicates that it was while they were **on the way** that the questioning took place. He gives a shorter form of the confession: **Thou art the Christ;** i.e., the Messiah.

Jesus **charged** the disciples not to publicize His messiahship. The verb, used in all three accounts of this incident, is a strong compound, occurring twenty-nine times in the New Testament. All but five of these times it is translated "rebuke" in the King James Version (cf. vv. 32, 32). It is used of Christ's rebuking demons and nature. Here it should be rendered "charged strictly." Jesus did not want a public proclamation of His messiahship that might precipitate a revolution against Roman rule. Political conditions in Palestine were tense in the first century, and it would not have taken much of a spark to ignite the inflammable tinder of nationalism. This was exactly what Jesus sought to avoid.

The significance of this incident is well expressed by Stamm: "The journey of Jesus and His disciples to Caesarea Philippi is the midpoint of Mark's Gospel as well as the turning point of Jesus' minis-

try . . . . Now a new theme is introduced: The Son of man must suffer and die."[48]

d. Prediction of Passion (8:31-9:1)

31 And he began to teach them, that the Son of man must suffer many things, and be rejected by the elders, and the chief priests, and the scribes, and be killed, and after three days rise again. 32 And he spake the saying openly. And Peter took him, and began to rebuke him. 33 But he turning about, and seeing his disciples, rebuked Peter, and saith, Get thee behind me, Satan; for thou mindest not the things of God, but the things of men. 34 And he called unto him the multitude with his disciples, and said unto them, If any man would come after me, let him deny himself, and take up his cross, and follow me. 35 For whosoever would save his life shall lose it; and whosoever shall lose his life for my sake and the gospel's shall save it. 36 For what doth it profit a man, to gain the whole world, and forfeit his life? 37 For what should a man give in exchange for his life? 38 For whosoever shall be ashamed of me and of my words in this adulterous and sinful generation, the Son of man also shall be ashamed of him, when he cometh in the glory of his Father with the holy angels. 1 And he said unto them, Verily I say unto you, There are some here of them that stand *by*, who shall in no wise taste of death, till they see the kingdom of God come with power.

The word *began* (v. 31) is significant. It marks a new departure in Jesus' ministry. Hitherto the Master had been dealing mainly with the multitudes — healing, teaching, preaching. From now on He would spend most of His time instructing His disciples, preparing them for the time when He must leave them and they would have to carry on the work of the Kingdom.

A main topic in this private teaching was His coming death and resurrection. In common with all Jews, the apostles expected a Messiah who would come in glory to reign over an earthly kingdom. It was necessary that the Master should correct this misconception in the minds of His disciples. They must be taught that the **Son of man** (the Messiah) would suffer and die, but after three days rise

[48] Raymond T. Stamm, "The Gospel According to Mark," *New Testament Commentary*, ed. Herbert C. Allenman, p. 265.

again. For the details of the prediction, see the notes on Matthew 16:21-28.

This was the first of three predictions of the Passion (see 9:31; 10:32-34). All three Synoptics emphasize this phase of Jesus' private ministry to His disciples. Mark adds one observation here: **And he spake this saying openly** (or, "plainly"). As a result Peter **took him.** The aorist middle participle literally means "having taken him to himself." It seems to mean that the apostle sought to take the Master to one side, to reprove Him for speaking thus. But when Peter began to **rebuke** Him, Jesus **rebuked** the disciple in turn. **Turning about** probably means that Christ turned so as to face both Peter and the disciples.

Jesus declared that some of His hearers would not die until they had seen the kingdom of God coming **with power.** This last phrase is found only in Mark.

By a strange inconsistency this verse is placed at the beginning of chapter nine in Mark, as if it referred to the Transfiguration (see on Matt. 16:28), whereas in Matthew it goes with the previous chapter. The latter is the correct division. Mark 9:1 belongs with chapter eight.

On the meaning of this verse Alexander has a very helpful comment. He writes:

> The solutions of this question which have been proposed are objectionable, chiefly because too exclusive and restrictive of the promise to a single point of time, whereas it really has reference to a gradual or progressive change, the institution of Christ's kingdom in the hearts of men and in society at large, of which protracted process the two salient points are the effusion of the Spirit on the day of Pentecost, and the destruction of Jerusalem more than a quarter of a century later, between which points, as those of its inception and its consummation, lies the lingering death of the Mosaic dispensation, and the gradual erection of Messiah's kingdom.[49]

The kingdom of God came **with power** on the day of Pentecost and during the Apostolic Age. That seems to be what Jesus was predicting here.

e. Transfiguration of Jesus (9:2-8)

2 And after six days Jesus taketh with him Peter and James, and John, and bringeth them up into a high mountain apart by themselves; and he was transfigured before them; 3 and his garments became glistering, exceeding white, so as no fuller on earth can whiten them. 4 And there appeared unto them Elijah with Moses: and they were talking with Jesus. 5 And Peter answereth and saith to Jesus, Rabbi, it is good for us to be here: and let us make three tabernacles; one for thee, and one for Moses, and one for Elijah. 6 For he knew not what to answer; for they became sore afraid. 7 And there came a cloud overshadowing them: and there came a voice out of the cloud, This is my beloved Son: hear ye him. 8 And suddenly looking round about, they saw no one any more, save Jesus only with themselves.

This was one of the high moments in the earthly ministry of the Son of God. Perhaps its purpose was at least partly to confirm Peter in the truth of his recent declaration of the deity of Jesus (8:29). Now he and the other two of the inner circle were privileged to glimpse the glory of God in the face of Jesus Christ.

Mark's account is closely parallel to Matthew's (see on Matt. 17:1-13). The latter alone says of Jesus that "his face did shine as the sun." Mark adds to the description of the glistening white garments: "so as no fuller on earth can whiten them" (v. 3). Significantly he says of Peter: "For he knew not what to answer" (v. 6 cf. Luke 9:33). He did not know what to say; so he said something. That was Peter!

f. Identification of Elijah (9:9-13)

9 And as they were coming down from the mountain, he charged them that they should tell no man what things they had seen, save when the Son of man should have risen again from the dead. 10 And they kept the saying, questioning among themselves what the rising again from the dead should mean. 11 And they asked him, saying, How is it that the scribes say that Elijah must first come? 12 And he said unto them, Elijah indeed cometh first, and restoreth all things: and how is it written of the Son of man, that he should suffer many things and be set at nought? 13 But I say unto you, that Elijah is come, and they have also done

[49] *Op. cit.*, p. 230.

unto him whatsoever they would, even as it is written of him.

On the way down the mountain Christ told the three disciples not to tell anybody about His transfiguration until after He had risen again from the dead. Mark alone adds that they were "questioning among themselves what the rising again from the dead should mean" (v. 10). Though the Resurrection had been included in the first prediction of the Passion (8:31), the disciples had not understood what Jesus meant, nor did they now grasp the truth.

Matthew and Mark both record the question of the disciples as to the prophecy that Elijah would precede the Messiah. Jesus answered that Elijah had already come to restore all things (see on Matt. 17:11). Matthew alone adds the explanation that Jesus was referring to John the Baptist. This emphasis on the fulfillment of prophecy is one of the characteristics of that Gospel.

g. Healing of Epileptic (9:14-29)

14 And when they came to the disciples, they saw a great multitude about them, and scribes questioning with them. 15 And straightway all the multitude, when they saw him, were greatly amazed, and running to him saluted him. 16 And he asked them, What question ye with them? 17 And one of the multitude answered him, Teacher, I brought unto thee my son, who hath a dumb spirit; 18 and wheresoever it taketh him, it dasheth him down: and he foameth, and grindeth his teeth, and pineth away: and I spake to thy disciples that they should cast it out; and they were not able. 19 And he answereth them and saith, O faithless generation, how long shall I be with you? how long shall I bear with you? bring him unto me. 20 And they brought him unto him: and when he saw him straightway the spirit tare him grievously; and he fell on the ground, and wallowed foaming. 21 And he asked his father, How long time is it since this hath come unto him? And he said, From a child. 22 And oft-times it hath cast him both into the fire and into the waters, to destroy him: but if thou canst do anything, have compassion on us, and help us. 23 And Jesus said unto him, If thou canst! All things are possible to him that believeth. 24 Straightway the father of the child cried out, and said, I believe; help thou mine unbelief.

25 And when Jesus saw that a multitude came running together, he rebuked the unclean spirit, saying unto him, Thou dumb and deaf spirit, I command thee, come out of him, and enter no more into him. 26 And having cried out, and torn him much, he came out: and *the boy* became as one dead; insomuch that the more part said, He is dead. 27 But Jesus took him by the hand, and raised him up; and he arose. 28 And when he was come into the house, his disciples asked him privately, *How is it* that we could not cast it out? 29 And he said unto them, This kind can come out by nothing, save prayer.

Most of the incidents in this section of the Gospel are recorded in all three Synoptics. We noted that Matthew has the longest account of Peter's confession at Caesarea Philippi. He and Mark devote about equal space to the events occurring between that occasion and this. But here Mark resumes his usual pattern of giving more vivid details in his narrative than do the others.

Verse 15 is peculiar to this Gospel. It would seem that the crowd was excited by the appearance of Jesus' face. Perhaps the afterglow of His transfiguration still lingered there. We have a parallel in the case of Moses. When he came down from Mount Sinai, after spending forty days in close fellowship with God, his face shone so brightly that the people were afraid to come near him (Ex. 34:30). The strong compound Greek verb translated **greatly amazed** suggests something similar in Jesus' case.

Matthew alone identifies the boy as an epileptic (see on Matt. 17:15). But Mark (v. 18) and Luke (9:39) describe the epileptic seizures in similar terms. They also agree in stating that when Jesus asked for the boy to be brought to Him, the demon viciously took out his last spite on the poor victim (v. 20; Luke 9:42). Mark adds that the lad **fell on the ground, and wallowed foaming.** The description is clearly that of epilepsy, apparently induced in his case by demon-possession.

Mark alone tells how the father in desperation cried out: **if thou canst do anything, have compassion on us, and help us** (v. 22). The American Standard Version points out the force of Jesus' reply: **If thou canst!** (v. 23). The Greek literally says: "The 'if thou canst.'"

That is, the Master picked up the very words the man had used and threw them back to him. He seems to imply: What do you mean by saying, "If thou canst"? The uncertainty is not on my part, but yours. **All things are possible to him that believeth.** I am able and willing, but you must have faith.

Humbly and sincerely, the man met Jesus' challenge. He cried out: **I believe; help thou mine unbelief** (v. 24). He was exercising what William James called "the will to believe." He realized that he had to have divine assistance in order to believe, that naturally his heart inclined toward unbelief. The Greek word for **help** literally means "run at the cry for help." The man recognized his immediate need. And his request was granted.

Mark alone tells of the crowd **running together** and gives the words of Jesus to the unclean spirit: **Thou dumb and deaf spirit, I command thee, come out of him, and enter no more into him** (v. 25). The last clause must have been a very comforting assurance to the distracted father. To know that there would never be a recurrence of the affliction was a wonderful consolation.

With malicious hatred the demon screamed in anger, and having **torn him much** — better, "convulsed him greatly" — came out, leaving the victim apparently dead (v. 26). But Jesus raised him up and restored him to his father.

When the disciples privately inquired as to why they could not cast out the demon, Jesus informed them that spiritual power comes only through **prayer** (v. 29). The added phrase, "and fasting" (KJV), is not found in the two earliest Greek manuscripts (4th cent.).

h. Prediction of Passion (9:30-32)

30 And they went forth from thence, and passed through Galilee; and he would not that any man should know it. 31 For he taught his disciples, and said unto them, The Son of man is delivered up into the hands of men, and they shall kill him; and when he is killed, after three days he shall rise again. 32 But they understood not the saying, and were afraid to ask him.

This second prediction of Christ's passion occurred as He and His disciples returned southward through Galilee from their journey north to Caesarea Philippi. Because of the inevitable crowds that always thronged around Him in Galilee, Jesus sought to keep His movements secret (v. 30). The reason for this is given in verse 31: **For he taught** (literally, "was teaching") **his disciples.** The most important ministry of the Master was now to His apostles, whom He had chosen to carry on after His death. He did not want the curious crowds to interfere with this.

The second prediction was very similar to the first (cf. 8:31). **Is delivered** (literally, "is being delivered") emphasizes the imminence and certainty of his coming betrayal, death, and resurrection. But even yet the disciples **understood not** the meaning of what their Master was saying (v. 32).

i. Back in Capernaum (9:33-37)

33 And they came to Capernaum: and when he was in the house he asked them, What were ye reasoning on the way? 34 But they held their peace: for they had disputed one with another on the way, who *was* the greatest. 35 And he sat down, and called the twelve; and he saith unto them, If any man would be first, he shall be last of all, and servant of all. 36 And he took a little child, and set him in the midst of them: and taking him in his arms, he said unto them, 37 Whosoever shall receive one of such little children in my name, receiveth me: and whosoever receiveth me, receiveth not me, but him that sent me.

One of the main, most frequently recurring emphases in Jesus' teaching was on the supreme importance of humility. He came back to this again and again (cf. 10:15, 43-44; Matt. 10:40; 18:1-5; 20:26-27; Luke 9:46-48; 10:16; 18:17; 22:26). There is no such thing as Christlikeness without deep, sincere humility.

When Jesus got back to His headquarters city of Capernaum, He asked His disciples an embarrassing question: **What were ye reasoning on the way?** They were so ashamed of themselves that **they held their peace.** For they had been arguing as to who was greatest — Matthew says, "greatest in the kingdom of heaven" (Matt. 18:1).

The proud selfishness and self-seeking of these disciples, after many months with the Master, is disconcerting. They had learned so little from His example! Yet the same attitude shows up too often in church circles today. The Christian should seek spiritual power rather than ecclesiastical position. He should be more concerned with service than status.

All three Synoptics tell how Jesus used a little child as an example of humility. Characteristically Mark adds, **and taking him in his arms** (v. 36). The tender love of the Master made an impression on burly Peter.

In my name (v. 37) is used in the Jewish Talmud as meaning "on my account, for my sake." That is the sense here. **Receive** means "welcome." It suggests treating with kindness, not turning coldly away.

j. Rebuke of Sectarianism (9:38-50)

38 John said unto him, Teacher, we saw one casting out demons in thy name; and we forbade him, because he followed not us. 39 But Jesus said, Forbid him not: for there is no man who shall do a mighty work in my name, and be able quickly to speak evil of me. 40 For he that is not against us is for us. 41 For whosoever shall give you a cup of water to drink, because ye are Christ's, verily I say unto you, he shall in no wise lose his reward. 42 And whosoever shall cause one of these little ones that believe on me to stumble, it were better for him if a great millstone were hanged about his neck, and he were cast into the sea. 43 And if thy hand cause thee to stumble, cut it off: it is good for thee to enter into life maimed, rather than having thy two hands to go into hell, into the unquenchable fire. 45 And if thy foot cause thee to stumble, cut it off: it is good for thee to enter into life halt, rather than having thy two feet to be cast into hell. 47 And if thine eye cause thee to stumble, cast it out: it is good for thee to enter into the kingdom of God with one eye, rather than having two eyes to be cast into hell; 48 where their worm dieth not, and the fire is not quenched. 49 For every one shall be salted with fire. 50 Salt is good: but if the salt have lost its saltness, wherewith will ye season it? Have salt in yourselves, and be at peace one with another.

This incident (recorded also in Luke 9:49-50) reveals a narrow, sectarian attitude on the part of the apostle John. Perhaps the mention of "in my name" reminded him of an incident that had just taken place. Having observed a man casting out demons **in thy name,** he **forbade him.** The imperfect tense is more accurately translated, "tried to restrain him." The reason was that **he followed not us.** Note that he does not say, "He was not following thee." The modern parallel would be that of opposing someone who labored in Christ's name, just because he did not belong to our sect or denomination. Sectarianism is a denial of New Testament Christianity. John Wesley put it this way: "to confine religion to them that follow us is a narrowness of spirit which we should avoid and abhor."[50]

Jesus' reply was literally: "Stop trying to restrain him." Then Mark alone adds the Master's sane observation that no one who was working miracles in His name would quickly speak evil of Him (v. 39).

On the surface verse 40, **For he that is not against us is for us,** seems like a contradiction of "he that is not with me is against me" (Matt. 12:30; Luke 11:23). But the first has to do largely with outward conduct, while the second relates to inner attitude. Plummer notes that the former is to be used in "judging other people," the latter in "judging ourselves." He adds: "If we are not sure that others are against Christ, we must treat them as being for Him; if we are not sure that we are on His side, we have reason to fear that **we are against Him.**"[51]

Verse 41 continues the teaching of Jesus regarding children which had been interrupted by John. **Because ye are** is literally "in name that ye are." Even the act of giving a cup of water to a humble follower of Jesus will not go unrewarded. Instead of rebuking those who do not follow us we should treat them with kindness.

The Master then issued some very solemn warnings against causing **one of these little ones that believe on me** — even the weakest convert to Christ — **to stumble.** For the meaning of **stumble** and **great millstone** see the notes on Matthew 18:6 9.

---

[50] *Explanatory Notes Upon the New Testament*, p. 170.   [51] *Op. cit.*, p. 225.

Hell (v. 43) is not here Hades, the place of departed spirits, but *Gehenna,* the place of torment. It is described as the **unquenchable** (Greek, *asbestos*) **fire.** The name *Gehenna* referred originally to the Valley of Hinnom, just south of the walls of Jerusalem. Here the Israelites in the time of Manasseh had offered their children to the heathen idol, Moloch (Jer. 7:31). Later Josiah desecrated the place (II Kings 23:10), and it became the city dump, where the garbage and refuse were taken. Its continually burning fires became a fit symbol of hell. Jesus took over the Jewish usage of this term.

Bickersteth has a good application of the warnings given in verses 43, 45, and 47. He says: "If your relative or your friend, who is useful or dear to you as your hand, your foot, or your eye, is drawing you into sin, cut him off from you, lest he draw you into hell."[52]

It will be noted that verses 44 and 46 are omitted in the Revised Versions. That is because they are not found in the earliest Greek manuscripts (Aleph BCL). But they are identical with verse 48, which is genuine.

In the Valley of Hinnom worms and fire destroyed the refuse. In Jesus' use of these two symbols, the **worm** could be thought of as the gnawings of a guilty conscience, and **fire** as the unquenchable memories of one's past life, with its lost opportunities to be saved from sin and its penalty.

This is a terrible description of eternal torment. It should be noted that these strongest warnings against the horrors of hell fell from the lips of the supposedly "meek and mild Jesus." The "gentle Galilean" could and did speak out with unforgettable sternness about the eternal consequences of sin. One had better lose everything in this life than lose his soul forever in hell.

Verse 49 — the second clause is omitted in the oldest manuscripts — has proved a very difficult one for scholars to explain. The best interpretation, connecting it with **fire** in verse 48, seems to be this:

'I say "fire" advisedly, for it is with fire that every man shall be purified' (literally, salted) : i.e., everyone must pass

through a 'cleansing fire'; what this 'fire' is may be seen from the Baptist's saying about Christ (Matt. 3:11), that He 'shall baptize with the Holy Spirit and with fire': it is the Spirit which shall purify away all dross, i.e., all that makes a man unfit for the 'sacrifice' of himself to the service of Christ.[53]

The first part of verse 50 is paralleled closely in Luke 14:34 and Matthew 5:13 (see the notes there). Jesus was warning the disciples that by their selfishness and self-seeking they were in danger of becoming savorless salt. The combination of **salt** and **peace** in the last part of the verse (found only in Mark) may be due to the Oriental custom of using salt as the symbol of friendship. The disciples needed the purifying salt of Christ's Spirit, that they might be at peace with each other.

C. IN PEREA (10:1-52)

1. Teaching in Perea (10:1)

1 And he arose from thence, and cometh into the borders of Judaea and beyond the Jordan: and multitudes come together unto him again; and, as he was wont, he taught them again.

Here begins a new stage in Jesus' ministry. Making His final departure from Galilee, the center of most of His public life, He **cometh** — Mark's favorite historical present — to **the borders of Judaea and beyond the Jordan.** The expression **beyond the Jordan** clearly refers to Perea, ruled by Herod Antipas. It seems strange that **Judaea** should be mentioned first, since the Galilean Jews normally journeyed to Jerusalem (in Judea) by way of Perea. The simplest explanation is that this is a general statement of the fact that the closing months of Christ's ministry were spent in Perea and Judea.

Once more Jesus was beset by crowds. It appears that He reverted to His earlier **custom** and **taught them again** in parables. This seems to be supported by the fact that Luke places many of the parables in this later period of Jesus' ministry.

---

[52] E. Bickersteth, "St. Mark" (Exposition), *The Pulpit Commentary,* eds. H. D. M. Spence and Joseph S. Excell, II, 8.

[53] A. F. Hort, *Gospel According to St. Mark,* the Greek text edited with introduction and notes, p. 132.

2. Question of Divorce (10:2-12)

2 And there came unto him Pharisees, and asked him, Is it lawful for a man to put away *his* wife? trying him. 3 And he answered and said unto them, What did Moses command you? 4 And they said, Moses suffered to write a bill of divorcement, and to put her away. 5 But Jesus said unto them, For your hardness of heart he wrote you this commandment. 6 But from the beginning of the creation, Male and female made he them. 7 For this cause shall a man leave his father and mother, and shall cleave to his wife; 8 and the two shall become one flesh: so that they are no more two, but one flesh. 9 What therefore God hath joined together, let not man put asunder. 10 And in the house the disciples asked him again of this matter. 11 And he saith unto them, Whosoever shall put away his wife, and marry another, committeth adultery against her: 12 and if she herself shall put away her husband, and marry another, she committeth adultery.

Divorce was another important question that Jesus dealt with more than once (cf. Matt. 5:31, 32; Luke 16:18). Matthew's account of this incident is somewhat fuller than Mark's (see notes on Matt. 19:3-12). Matthew discusses the case of eunuchs, not touched on by Mark.

A typical example of slight, but insignificant differences in the Synoptic Gospels is found here. Mark says that Jesus asked the Pharisees: **What did Moses command you?** (v. 3). Matthew says that the Pharisees asked: "Why then did Moses command . . . ?" (Matt. 19:7). But the second question may have followed close on the heels of the first, so that the accounts are not contradictory. In any case, the meaning is essentially the same.

The main difference in the two records is that Matthew adds to the original question of the Pharisees the phrase "for every cause" (cf. v. 2 and Matt. 19:3), and then has Jesus add to His answer "except for fornication" (cf. v. 11 and Matt. 19:9). Matthew was writing to Jews, who would be interested in Jesus' reactions to the differing views of the two rabbis, Hillel and Shammai (see notes on Matt. 19:3). The Romans, to whom Mark was writing, would not know about this.

Typically, Mark adds one definite detail. He says that Jesus' statement about divorce and remarriage was given to the disciples **in the house,** where they asked Him (privately?) for more information on the subject (v. 10). But Matthew finally brings in the disciples separate from the Pharisees (Matt. 19:10).

That Christ felt very strongly about divorce is obvious. In a day of very careless thought and action on the subject, Christians are wise to examine afresh their Lord's clear teachings on the subject and conform to them. This is one of many instances in which the standards of the church must be different from the standards of the world.

3. Reception of Children (10:13-16)

13 And they were bringing unto him little children, that he should touch them: and the disciples rebuked them. 14 But when Jesus saw it, he was moved with indignation, and said unto them, Suffer the little children to come unto me; forbid them not: for to such belongeth the kingdom of God. 15 Verily I say unto you, Whosoever shall not receive the kingdom of God as a little child, he shall in no wise enter therein. 16 And he took them in his arms, and blessed them, laying his hands upon them.

For the relation of this paragraph to the preceding one, see the notes on Matthew 19:13-15. All three Synoptics give this incident in almost exactly the same words (cf. Luke 18:15-17). Typically, Matthew has "kingdom of heaven" where Mark and Luke have "kingdom of God." Typically also, Mark adds one vivid detail: **And he took them in his arms** (v. 16). Where Mark and Luke tell of the children brought to Jesus that He might **touch** them (v. 13; Luke 18:15), Matthew says "that he should lay his hands on them and pray" (Matt. 19:13). This reflects the Jewish custom of blessing, which would not be familiar to the Gentile readers of Mark and Luke.

4. Way of Eternal Life (10:17-22)

17 And as he was going forth into the way, there ran one to him, and kneeled to him, and asked him, Good Teacher, what shall I do that I may inherit eternal life? 18 And Jesus said unto him, Why callest thou me good? none is good save one, *even* God. 19 Thou knowest the commandments, Do not kill, Do not

commit adultery, Do not steal, Do not bear false witness, Do not defraud, Honor thy father and mother. 20 And he said unto him, Teacher, all these things have I observed from my youth. 21 And Jesus looking upon him loved him, and said unto him, One thing thou lackest: go, sell whatsoever thou hast, and give to the poor, and thou shalt have treasure in heaven: and come, follow me. 22 But his countenance fell at the saying, and he went away sorrowful: for he was one that had great possessions.

This story of the Rich Young Ruler is also recorded fully in all three Synoptics (cf. Luke 18:18-30 and the notes on Matt. 19:16-26). It is an excellent illustration of the call to Christian discipleship, which this young man heard but rejected.

Characteristically, Mark gives a number of graphic details. He says that there **ran one to him and kneeled to him** (v. 17). This shows the eagerness of the man's search. What a contrast between the quick approach and the sad, slow departure (v. 22)!

Mark also adds that Jesus **looking upon him loved him** (v. 21). Here was a model young man. From his youth he had kept all the Mosaic law, at least as far as his outward conduct was concerned. He was eager and earnest about his religious life. It is not surprising that Jesus stood for a moment, looking on the man with fond affection. Here indeed was a beautiful stone to fit into the building of the new church.

Yet the Master dealt faithfully with this seeker after the higher life. He said to him; **One thing thou lackest** — so Mark and Luke (18:22), in place of Matthew's "If thou wouldest be perfect." It was only one thing, but it was actually everything. He lacked what Jesus defined as the central core of the Law — loving God with all the heart and one's neighbor as himself (12:29-31). This was the one thing wrong with the church at Ephesus, but it demanded repentance and doing the first works (Rev. 2:2-5).

So Jesus asked the young man to sell all he had and give the proceeds to the poor. It is perfectly obvious that this is not a universal requirement for all of Christ's followers. But in this case it was necessary, for the young ruler's wealth

was his idol. Until he surrendered this he could not be saved. Anything that takes the place of God in our lives must go.

Graphically Mark gives the man's reaction: **his countenance fell** (v. 22). The Greek word used here is found elsewhere in the New Testament only in Matthew 16:3, where it is said that the sky is "lowering." It means "gloomy." Disobedience always brings gloom and sadness.

5. Warning Against Riches (10:23-31)

23 And Jesus looked round about, and saith unto his disciples, How hardly shall they that have riches enter into the kingdom of God! 24 And the disciples were amazed at his words. But Jesus answereth again, and saith unto them, Children, how hard is it for them that trust in riches to enter into the kingdom of God! 25 It is easier for a camel to go through a needle's eye, than for a rich man to enter into the kingdom of God. 26 And they were astonished exceedingly, saying unto him, Then who can be saved? 27 Jesus looking upon them saith, With men it is impossible, but not with God: for all things are possible with God. 28 Peter began to say unto him, Lo, we have left all, and have followed thee. 29 Jesus said, Verily I say unto you, There is no man that hath left house, or brethren, or sisters, or mother, or father, or children, or lands, for my sake, and for the gospel's sake, 30 but he shall receive a hundredfold now in this time, houses, and brethren, and sisters, and mothers, and children, and lands, with persecutions; and in the world to come eternal life. 31 But many *that are* first shall be last; and the last first.

Once more Mark notes the looks of Jesus. He alone says that the Master **looked round about** (v. 23). He was about to make an important observation, and He wanted the full attention of His disciples. Then He declared that it is hard for rich people to enter the Kingdom, because too often their wealth blocks the way. They are not willing to push it to one side and let God have first place in their lives.

Mark alone records the amazement of the disciples and Jesus' reply to it (v. 24). Their surprise was due to the fact that many Old Testament passages seem to imply that material prosperity is a sign of divine favor. But Christ was fully aware of the mastery that money often gets over men. So He reiterated His former statement in still stronger terms. According to the oldest extant Greek text, He declared literally: "How hard it is to enter the kingdom of God!"[54] It is not an easy thing to be a follower of Christ. There is nothing in the world more demanding than Christian discipleship — and nothing more rewarding and satisfying.

Another example of the slight difference in wording with no essential difference in meaning is found in a comparison of verse 29 with Matthew 19:29 and Luke 18:29. Mark has **for my sake, and for the gospel's sake.** Matthew reads, "for my name's sake." Luke has, "for the kingdom of God's sake." All mean the same thing.

6. Prediction of Passion (10:32-34)

32 And they were on the way, going up to Jerusalem; and Jesus was going before them: and they were amazed; and they that followed were afraid. And he took again the twelve, and began to tell them the things that were to happen unto him, 33 *saying*, Behold, we go up to Jerusalem; and the Son of man shall be delivered unto the chief priests and the scribes; and they shall condemn him to death, and shall deliver him unto the Gentiles: 34 and they shall mock him, and shall spit upon him, and shall scourge him, and shall kill him; and after three days he shall rise again.

One of the typical vivid details found only in Mark occurs in verse 32. As Christ and His disciples were on their last journey to Jerusalem, Jesus **was going before them: and they were amazed; and they that followed were afraid.** Apparently the set, stern look of determination on the Master's face astonished the apostles. He had told them He was going to Jerusalem to die. Why then did He press on toward the end? There was an ominous sense of destiny here.

Many scholars feel that the followers mentioned in the last clause quoted above were Galilean pilgrims, a separate group from the disciples. These were filled with fear. They could not understand

what was going on, but they felt a strange sense of threatening calamity.

This third and final prediction of the Passion is more full and specific than the previous ones (see notes on Matt. 20:17-19). This is true in all three Synoptic Gospels (cf. Luke 18:31-34). The end was approaching fast.

7. Politics of Disciples (10:35-45)

35 And there come near unto him James and John, the sons of Zebedee, saying unto him, Teacher, we would that thou shouldest do for us whatsoever we shall ask of thee. 36 And he said unto them, What would ye that I should do for you? 37 And they said unto him, Grant unto us that we may sit, one on thy right hand, and one on *thy* left hand, in thy glory. 38 But Jesus said unto them, Ye know not what ye ask. Are ye able to drink the cup that I drink? or to be baptized with the baptism that I am baptized with? 39 And they said unto him, We are able. And Jesus said unto them, The cup that I drink ye shall drink; and with the baptism that I am baptized withal shall ye be baptized: 40 but to sit on my right hand or on *my* left hand is not mine to give; but *it is for them* for whom it hath been prepared. 41 And when the ten heard it, they began to be moved with indignation concerning James and John. 42 And Jesus called them to him, and saith unto them, Ye know that they who are accounted to rule over the Gentiles lord it over them; and their great ones exercise authority over them. 43 But it is not so among you: but whosoever would become great among you shall be your minister; 44 and whosoever would be first among you, shall be servant of all. 45 For the Son of man also came not to be ministered unto, but to minister, and to give his life a ransom for many.

The ambitious, self-seeking spirit of James and John looks especially black and ugly, as it is seen against the backdrop of Jesus' determined progress toward a cross, where He would give Himself as a sacrifice for man's sin (see notes on Matt. 20:20-28). The sinfulness of selfishness shows up here in all its stark reality.

Matthew depicts Jesus asking the disciples if they are able to drink the cup

---

[54] The added phrase "for them that trust in riches" is not found in Vaticanus and Sinaiticus.

that He is about to drink. Mark adds: **or to be baptized with the baptism that I am baptized with?** Jews would understand quickly the significance of **cup** (cf. Ps. 75:8). The well-known incident of Socrates drinking the cup of poison hemlock would add poignancy to the figure. Its connotation was only too familiar.

Baptism would suggest being drowned with sorrow (cf. Isa. 43:2). On the relation of the two terms Alford says, speaking first of the cup: "*It* here seems to signify more the *inner* and spiritual bitterness, resembling the agony of the Lord Himself, — and the *baptism*, which is an important addition in Mark, more the *outer* accession of persecution and trial."[55]

When the disciples — certainly without recognizing fully the implications — said, **We are able,** the Master assured them that they would share His **cup** and **baptism** (v. 39). James was the first martyr among the apostles; he was put to death by Herod Agrippa I in A.D. 44 (Acts 12:2). John suffered banishment on the Isle of Patmos (Rev. 1:9), and probably experienced other persecutions. To follow Christ means that we must suffer with Him before we can reign with Him. This was the lesson the disciples needed to learn. For the Christian, as for his Lord, the cross must precede the crown.

Verse 45 (found also in Matt. 20:28; see notes there) is perhaps the most important theological passage in the Synoptic Gospels. It states clearly and categorically the doctrine of the vicarious atonement of Christ for human sin. It is being increasingly realized that Mark's main purpose for writing his Gospel was theological, rather than biographical or historical. He presents Jesus as Son of God and Savior.

8. Healing of Bartimaeus (10:46-52)

46 And they come to Jericho: and as he went out from Jericho, with his disciples and a great multitude, the son of Timaeus, Bartimaeus, a blind beggar, was sitting by the way side. 47 And when he heard that it was Jesus the Nazarene, he began to cry out, and say, Jesus, thou son of David, have mercy on me. 48 And many rebuked him, that he

should hold his peace: but he cried out the more a great deal, Thou son of David, have mercy on me. 49 And Jesus stood still, and said, Call ye him. And they call the blind man, saying unto him, Be of good cheer, rise, he calleth thee. 50 And he, casting away his garment, sprang up, and came to Jesus. 51 And Jesus answered him, and said, What wilt thou that I should do unto thee? And the blind man said unto him, Rabboni, that I may receive my sight. 52 And Jesus said unto him, Go thy way; thy faith hath made thee whole. And straightway he received his sight, and followed him in the way.

This incident is recorded in all three Synoptic Gospels (cf. Luke 18:35-43 and the notes on Matt. 20:29-34). Mark alone gives the man's name, **Bartimaeus.** This is Aramaic for **son of Timaeus.** He was a **blind beggar.**

As usual, Mark gives one or two vivid touches not found in the other accounts. He alone tells of the people calling the blind man, in response to Jesus' command, with the words: **Be of good cheer: rise, he calleth thee** (v. 49). What welcome words those must have been in the blind man's ears!

Then, typically, Mark says: **And he, casting away his garment, sprang up, and came to Jesus.** Peter was an embodiment of quick, impulsive action, and he appreciated it in others. The blind man threw aside his cloak, so as not to be hindered in his movements, and **sprang up.** This might better be rendered "leaped up." The strong Greek verb is found only here in the New Testament. The three aorists — **casting, sprang, came,** — all add to the description of the man's eager haste in reaching Christ.

The blind man addressed Jesus as **Rabboni,** a word that occurs only here and in John 20:16. It is a strengthened form of the common term "rabbi." They both mean "my master." The stronger title was a sign of higher honor.

In answer to the man's plea, Jesus said to him: **Go thy way** (v. 53), and assured him that his faith had made him whole. Instantly receiving his sight, the man began following the Master and kept on following Him (imperfect tense).

---

[55] Henry Alford, *The Greek Testament,* I, 204.

D. IN JUDEA (11:1-13:37)

1. Coming to Jerusalem (11:1-24)

a. Acclaim of Crowd (11:1-10)

1 And when they draw nigh unto Jerusalem, unto Bethphage and Bethany, at the mount of Olives, he sendeth two of his disciples, 2 and saith unto them, Go your way into the village that is over against you: and straightway as ye enter into it, ye shall find a colt tied, whereon no man ever yet sat; loose him, and bring him. 3 And if any one say unto you, Why do ye this? say ye, The Lord hath need of him; and straightway he will send him back hither. 4 And they went away, and found a colt tied at the door without in the open street; and they loose him. 5 And certain of them that stood there said unto them, What do ye, loosing the colt? 6 And they said unto them even as Jesus had said: and they let him go. 7 And they bring the colt unto Jesus, and cast on him their garments; and he sat upon him. 8 And many spread their garments upon the way; and others branches, which they had cut from the fields. 9 And they that went before, and they that followed, cried, Hosanna; Blessed *is* he that cometh in the name of the Lord: 10 Blessed *is* the kingdom that cometh, *the kingdom* of our father David: Hosanna in the highest.

When we come to the last week of our Lord's ministry we find the account more full and detailed. It is interesting to note that John's Gospel is, in its treatment of this week, in close correlation with the Synoptics. Previous to this John has not had much in common with them except the story of the feeding of the five thousand. Now John's account dovetails in with the earlier Gospels at several points.

The so-called Triumphal Entry is recorded in all four Gospels (see Luke 19:29-44; John 12:12-19; and the notes on Matt. 21:1-11). As usual, Mark makes the narrative somewhat more vivid with his use of the historical present — **draw nigh** and **sendeth** (v. 1), **loose** (v. 4), **bring** (v. 7).

Mark and Luke both mention **Bethphage** and **Bethany**. Since Matthew mentions only the former, it would seem that this was the village where the colt was found.

Bethany was located on the southeastern slopes of the Mount of Olives, about two miles out from Jerusalem on the road to Jericho. It is represented today by El-Azariyeh, "Village of Lazarus," where his supposed tomb is shown to tourists.

The location of **Bethphage** is a much more difficult problem. It is not mentioned in the Old Testament and only in this connection in the New. The Talmud says it was very near Jerusalem, and suggests that for purposes of eating the Passover it was treated as a sacred area adjacent to the city.[56] This proximity would be necessary, since Jerusalem inside the walls would not furnish adequate space for the multitudes of Passover pilgrims. Andrews suggests: "Bethphage was the name given to a district extending a Sabbath day's journey east of the city up the slopes of Olivet, and regarded as holy."[57]

The Greek text of verse 3 indicates that Jesus promised to return the colt to its owners. Literally it reads thus: "And if anyone should say to you, 'Why are you doing this?', say, 'The Lord has need of it, and immediately He sends it again hither.'" This assurance would allay any fears the disciples had about failing to obtain the animal.

Mark goes on to say that the two disciples — were these Peter and John (cf. Luke 22:8)? — **found a colt tied at the door without in the open street** (v. 4). This is a typical vivid detail given only in this Gospel. One can still see donkeys tied outside doorways in the narrow cobblestone streets of Jerusalem. "A place where two ways met" (KJV) is an attempt to translate the Greek word *amphodon* (only here in N.T.), which literally means "a road around." But at this time it was used simply to mean "street."

The disciples placed their outer garments on the colt, to form a saddle. Many of the jubilant Galilean pilgrims even cast their robes on the path as a carpet for Jesus to ride on. Others cut from the fields **branches** — not the same Greek word for "branches" in Matthew 21:8, but literally "litters of leaves." They were giving a royal welcome to their "King," as Luke 19:38 indicates. Mark

---

[56] Gustaf Dalman, *Sacred Sites and Ways*, trans. Paul P. Levertoff, pp. 252-254.
[57] Samuel Andrews, *The Life of Our Lord*, p. 432.

reports their cry thus: **Blessed is the kingdom that cometh, the kingdom of our father David.** All this shows that the Galileans were ready to accept Jesus as their Messiah, even though the Jerusalem Jews rejected Him.

b. Coming to Temple (11:11)

11 And he entered into Jerusalem, into the temple; and when he had looked round about upon all things, it being now eventide, he went out unto Bethany with the twelve.

Mark alone adds that when Jesus had entered the temple and **looked round about** — a very typical Markan expression — since it was **eventide** (late in the afternoon), He went out to Bethany with the twelve (v. 11). It would seem that during the Passover week they lodged in some home there, perhaps that of Mary, Martha, and Lazarus.

c. Cursing of Fig Tree (11:12-14)

12 And on the morrow, when they were come out from Bethany, he hungered. 13 And seeing a fig tree afar off having leaves, he came, if haply he might find anything thereon: and when he came to it, he found nothing but leaves; for it was not the season of figs. 14 And he answered and said unto it, No man eat fruit from thee henceforward forever. And his disciples heard it.

This incident (see the notes on Matt. 21:28-29) occurred on Monday morning, as Jesus and His disciples were returning to Jerusalem from Bethany. He was hungry — had they left before breakfast? At any rate, when He saw at a distance a fig tree with leaves on it, He came to it, thinking He might find some fruit on it.

A. M. Hunter calls this "one of the most perplexing stories in the Gospels."[58] Several problems present themselves. Why should Jesus destroy the helpless fig tree? But God commanded Jeremiah to break a potter's vessel as a symbolic warning to the people of Judah (Jer. 19). Why then should not Christ destroy a fig tree to teach a solemn lesson to the Jewish nation in His day? Matthew tells us that the fig tree was "by the way

side" (Matt. 21:19). So there was no destruction of private property. Nor was it a case of vindictive vengeance because of His disappointment at not finding fruit. Rather it was an enacted parable, signifying that the Holy City would be destroyed (A.D. 70) for rejecting its King, and the nation would wither away. Trench answers well the objections raised, when he says: "His miracles of mercy were numberless, and on men; His miracle of judgment was but one, and on a tree."[59]

Another problem is the question of why Jesus would expect to find ripe figs in early April. Mark indeed observes that **it was not the season of figs** (v. 13). There seems to be general agreement among the best authorities that green figs do appear in early spring, before the leaves come out, but that ripe, edible figs are not available till June.[60]

Why, then, would Jesus be looking for figs to eat? It should be noted that expression **if haply** (v. 13) is in the Greek "if therefore." That is, since the tree had leaves, He expected it to have at least some kind of fruit on it. He punished it for making a false profession. It had no fruit at all.

It should be remembered that the Master and His disciples had just come from sub-tropical Jericho (700 feet below sea level), where they doubtless ate ripe figs. Here in Jerusalem (2500 feet above sea level), He saw a fig tree with leaves. When He found no fruit on it, He pronounced its doom as a dramatic parable on the sinfulness of hypocrisy. The Jews displayed the leaves of religious profession, but they lacked the fruit of sincere piety.

d. Cleansing of Temple (11:15-19)

15 And they come to Jerusalem: and he entered into the temple, and began to cast out them that sold and them that bought in the temple, and overthrew the tables of the money-changers, and the seats of them that sold the doves; 16 and he would not suffer that any man should carry a vessel through the temple. 17 And he taught, and said unto them, Is it not written, My house shall be called a house of prayer for all the nations? but ye have made it a den of robbers. 18 And the

[58] A. M. Hunter, *The Gospel According to St. Mark*, p. 110.
[59] R. C. Trench, *Notes on the Miracles of Our Lord*, p. 345.
[60] See, e.g., J. C. Trevor, "Fig Tree, Fig," *The Interpreter's Dictionary of the Bible*, ed. George A. Buttrick *et al.*, II, 267.

chief priests and the scribes heard it, and sought how they might destroy him: for they feared him, for all the multitude was astonished at his teaching.

19 And every evening he went forth out of the city.

For the differences in the accounts in John and Matthew, see the notes on Matthew 21:12-17. Luke, who omits the cursing of the Fig Tree, records this incident right after the Triumphal Entry (Luke 19:45-48). Mark alone notes that it was on Monday, after the Cursing of the Fig Tree.

Mark's account of the actual cleansing (v. 15) is almost exactly the same as Matthew's (21:12). Verse 16 is an addition in Mark. The Temple Area, located in the eastern part of the city, covered some twenty-five or thirty acres. People going from the southwestern part of Jerusalem to the northeastern found it convenient to take a short cut through the court of the Gentiles in the Temple. Thus they lost the sense of its holiness as the house of God. Jesus forbade such careless traffic through the sacred precincts. The same warning needs to be sounded today against desecrating the sanctuary of the church. It should be used as a place of worship, not of secular business.

In the quotation from Isaiah 56:7, Matthew and Luke omit the last phrase, **for all the nations,** which Mark includes (v. 17) for his Roman readers. Why Luke, who also wrote for Gentiles, omits this is not clear. Evidently it was the divine intention in Old Testament times that Israel should lead the other nations in the worship of the true God.

Enraged by what Jesus had done, the **chief priests** and **scribes** (Sadducees and Pharisees) wanted to destroy Him. But **they feared him** (v. 18), because of His tremendous influence on the crowds.

The literal translation of verse 19 is: "And when evening came, he was going forth outside the city." The Revised rendering **every evening** takes the imperfect tense here as indicating customary action. It can be taken either way. Apparently it was Jesus' policy to keep out of Jerusalem at night (until Thursday evening). This may have been partly to avoid the danger of assassination in the dark, narrow streets of the city.

e. Character of Faith (11:20-25)

20 And as they passed by in the morning, they saw the fig tree withered away from the roots. 21 And Peter calling to remembrance saith unto him, Rabbi, behold, the fig tree which thou cursedst is withered away. 22 And Jesus answering saith unto them, Have faith in God. 23 Verily I say unto you, Whosoever shall say unto this mountain, Be thou taken up and cast into the sea; and shall not doubt in his heart, but shall believe that what he saith cometh to pass; he shall have it. 24 Therefore I say unto you, All things whatsoever ye pray and ask for, believe that ye receive them, and ye shall have them. 25 And whensoever ye stand praying, forgive, if ye have aught against any one; that your Father also who is in heaven may forgive you your trespasses.

The Cursing of the Fig Tree was intended to teach two lessons. The first, already noted, was the tragic consequences of hypocrisy. The second was a lesson on faith. When on Tuesday morning on their way into the city, the disciples noticed that the fig tree had withered from its roots, **Peter** (so Mark notes) expressed their astonishment. Jesus' answer was **Have faith in God** (v. 22). Then He went on to declare that if one should command a **mountain** to be cast into the sea, and did not **doubt in his heart,** but believed it would happen, it would take place. Obviously the Master was not talking about some physical mountain. Rather, He was referring to mountainous obstacles and difficulties in the work of the Kingdom. These can be removed by the power of prayer and faith. But faith and doubt do not mix.

The challenge of verse 24 is tremendous. Literally it reads: "On account of this I say to you, all things as many as you are praying and asking for, keep on believing that you received, and they shall be to you." **Believe** is the present imperative of continuous action. We are to have a stedfast faith that holds on to God's promises and refuses to doubt. "Received" is the aorist tense (past action), which means we believe that in God's purpose our prayer is already answered and the fulfillment of our request is now on the way.

But there is an important condition attached to praying in faith: we must have a forgiving spirit. If we refuse to forgive those who have wronged us, our heavenly Father will not forgive our trespasses. This is implicit in verse 25. The twenty-sixth verse, which contains an explicit negative statement, is not found here in the oldest manuscripts, but it is genuine in Matthew 6:15. That Jesus attached great importance to the need for a forgiving spirit is found in His repeated teaching on the subject (cf. Matt. 6:12, 14; 18:35; Luke 11:4).

The word **trespasses** occurs only here in Mark's Gospel. The Greek word means literally "a falling beside," and so suggests a false step or blunder. It finally took on ethical connotations and became one of the important words for "sin" in the New Testament.

2. Challenge to Jesus (11:27-12:37)

a. Question of Authority (11:27-33)

27 And they come again to Jerusalem: and as he was walking in the temple, there come to him the chief priests, and the scribes, and the elders; 28 and they said unto him, By what authority doest thou these things? or who gave thee this authority to do these things? 29 And Jesus said unto them, I will ask of you one question, and answer me, and I will tell you by what authority I do these things. 30 The baptism of John, was it from heaven, or from men? answer me. 31 And they reasoned with themselves, saying, If we shall say, From heaven; he will say, Why then did ye not believe him? 32 But should we say, From men — they feared the people: for all verily held John to be a prophet. 33 And they answered Jesus and say, We know not. And Jesus saith unto them, Neither tell I you by what authority I do these things.

This incident occurs in almost identical language in all three Synoptic Gospels (see Luke 20:1-8 and the notes on Matt. 21:23-27). In verse 30 Mark adds: **answer me.** Doubtless Jesus was distressed with the obdurate, obstinate attitude of the Jewish religious leaders in refusing to acknowledge the obvious. Their answer betrays a tragic lack of concern for truth.

Twice in verse 33 Mark uses the historical present where Matthew has a past tense. When the men refused to answer His question directly, Jesus declined to answer theirs.

The **chief priests,** the **scribes,** and the **elders** (v. 27) were the three groups that composed the Great Sanhedrin at Jerusalem. So it was the "Supreme Court" of the Jewish nation which challenged Jesus' authority to cleanse the Temple.

b. Question of Stewardship (12:1-12)

1 And he began to speak unto them in parables. A man planted a vineyard, and set a hedge about it, and digged a pit for the winepress, and built a tower, and let it out to husbandmen, and went into another country. 2 And at the season he sent to the husbandmen a servant, that he might receive from the husbandmen of the fruits of the vineyard. 3 And they took him, and beat him, and sent him away empty. 4 And again he sent unto them another servant; and him they wounded in the head, and handled shamefully. 5 And he sent another; and him they killed: and many others; beating some, and killing some. 6 He had yet one, a beloved son: he sent him last unto them, saying, They will reverence my son. 7 But those husbandmen said among themselves, This is the heir; come, let us kill him, and the inheritance shall be ours. 8 And they took him, and killed him, and cast him forth out of the vineyard. 9 What therefore will the lord of the vineyard do? he will come and destroy the husbandmen, and will give the vineyard unto others. 10 Have ye not read even this scripture:

The stone which the builders rejected,
The same was made the head of the corner;

11 This was from the Lord,
And it is marvellous in our eyes?
12 And they sought to lay hold on him; and they feared the multitude; for they perceived that he spake the parable against them: and they left him, and went away.

The Parable of the Wicked Husbandmen is one of the very few found in all three Synoptic Gospels (see Luke 20:9-19 and the notes on Matt. 21:33-46). It conveyed essentially the same warning as the incident of the withered fig tree: the Jewish nation was to be destroyed.

Instead of "winepress" (Matt.), Mark has a **pit for the winepress.** This is all one word in the Greek and found only here in the New Testament. It was the trough under the winepress, into which the grape juice could flow. Sometimes the winepress was cut out of solid rock. A typical one may be seen today near the Garden Tomb.

As usual, Matthew telescopes the narrative a bit by twice mentioning "servants" sent by the householder. Mark and Luke indicate three different servants sent in succession, and what happened to each. The first was beaten and sent away empty (v. 3). The second was **wounded in the head, and handled shamefully** (v. 4). Finally the climax was reached when the wicked tenants **killed** the third slave (v. 5). Mark adds, **and many others,** which agrees with Matthew's phrase "more than the first" (Matt. 21:36).

All three accounts record the final sending of the son. Mark and Luke have **beloved son** (v. 6), which properly means "only son."

What would the **lord of the vineyard** do? There was only one logical conclusion: the wicked tenants must be destroyed. Typical of the slight differences in the Synoptic accounts is the fact that here Matthew says "they" (the crowd, or the disciples) answered the question, whereas Mark (v. 9) and Luke have Jesus answering His own questions. But may there not have been a general response simultaneously with His reply?

The quotation from Psalm 118:22-23 is given in all three Synoptics, which shows its great importance. The expression **head of the corner** is somewhat ambiguous. It may mean a corner stone, or a cornice at the top of the wall, or even the keystone of the arched doorway. In any case, Christ is the Stone which the builders (the Jewish leaders) had rejected, but which God had chosen. In Isaiah 28:16 (quoted in I Pet. 2:6), the Messiah is referred to as the "precious corner stone."

The meaning of this parable is rather obvious. The slaves sent by the owner of the vineyard represent the prophets of the Old Testament, many of whom were shamefully handled, and some killed. The "beloved son" is God's own Son, who was killed by the Jews, represented here by the tenants. Matthew gives the implication of the parable in these words: "The kingdom of heaven shall be taken away from you, and shall be given to a nation bringing forth the fruits thereof" (Matt. 21:43). The Jewish nation was to be replaced by the Gentile church as God's own people.

All three accounts indicate that the leaders of the Jews recognized that the parable was directed against them. Infuriated, they wanted to arrest Him, thus fulfilling their role in the parable. But fear of the crowd prevented their doing it at this time.

c. Question of Taxes (12:13-17)

13 And they send unto him certain of the Pharisees and of the Herodians, that they might catch him in talk. 14 And when they were come, they say unto him, Teacher, we know that thou art true, and carest not for any one; for thou regardest not the person of men, but of a truth teachest the way of God: Is it lawful to give tribute unto Caesar, or not? 15 Shall we give, or shall we not give? But he, knowing their hypocrisy, said unto them, Why make ye trial of me? bring me a denarius, that I may see it. 16 And they brought it. And he saith unto them, Whose is this image and superscription? And they said unto him, Caesar's. 17 And Jesus said unto them, Render unto Caesar the things that are Caesar's, and unto God the things that are God's. And they marvelled greatly at him.

It was perhaps Tuesday afternoon or possibly Wednesday. The three Synoptic Gospels agree closely here in giving three questions asked of Jesus, His replies, and then a final question which He asked of His opponents and which silenced them permanently.

The first question was about paying taxes to Caesar (see Luke 20:20-26 and the notes on Matt. 22:15-22). The Pharisees and Herodians tried to **catch** Him in a statement. The Greek word (found only here in the N.T.) meant "to *catch* or *take* by hunting or fishing."[61] They thought that Jesus would be fairly easy prey, but in that they were mistaken.

In spite of their semblance of sincerity, Christ saw through their **hypocrisy** (v. 15). Matthew says "wickedness," and Luke "craftiness." They were wearing a religious mask to cover their wicked malice toward Him.

Instead of answering their question directly — which would have got Him into trouble — Jesus asked for a *denarius* (worth about twenty cents). This coin was particularly hated by the Jews, be-

61 Abbott-Smith, *op. cit.*, p. 7.

cause it carried on it the image of the emperor. They resented the necessity of handling it.

Christ's teaching on the payment of taxes is clear. **Render** is literally "give back." Taxes are a debt that every citizen owes to his government for protection and other services rendered. In effect, Jesus said to the Jews: "If this coin has Caesar's picture on it, then it must belong to him. So give it back to him." Paul (Rom. 13:7) and Peter (I Pet. 2:13-14) echo Jesus' teaching here.

As often, Mark here uses a vivid term to express the reaction of the crowd. He says that they **marvelled greatly** — one word in the Greek, a strong compound verb found only here in the New Testament. Bickersteth well says: "He vaulted over the trap they set for him, leaving them entangled in it."[62]

This section ties in logically with the previous one, on stewardship. For Jesus declared that we must "give back" to God what belongs to Him, and this includes all that we are and have. Christian stewardship demands the consecration of our all to Christ.

d. Question of Resurrection (12:18-27)

18 And there come unto him Sadducees, who say that there is no resurrection; and they asked him, saying, 19 Teacher, Moses wrote unto us, If a man's brother die, and leave a wife behind him, and leave no child, that his brother should take his wife, and raise up seed unto his brother. 20 There were seven brethren: and the first took a wife, and dying left no seed; 21 and the second took her, and died, leaving no seed behind him; and the third likewise: 22 and the seven left no seed. Last of all the woman also died. 23 In the resurrection whose wife shall she be of them? for the seven had her to wife. 24 Jesus said unto them, Is it not for this cause that ye err, that ye know not the scriptures, nor the power of God? 25 For when they shall rise from the dead, they neither marry, nor are given in marriage; but are as angels in heaven. 26 But as touching the dead, that they are raised; have ye not read in the book of Moses, in *the place concerning* the Bush, how God spake unto him, saying, I *am* the God of Abraham, and the God of Isaac, and the God

of Jacob? 27 He is not the God of the dead, but of the living: ye do greatly err.

The second question was about the resurrection (see Luke 20:27-38 and the notes on Matt. 22:23-33). Matthew indicates that it was asked on the same day as the previous one.

Having seen their rivals, the Pharisees, silenced, the Sadducees decided they would try to entangle Jesus before the people, and embarrass and discredit Him, by their favorite question about the resurrection. Perhaps they had "stumped" the Pharisees with it more than once. This simple Galilean with no formal theological training would be an easy victim. So they posed their hypothetical, really ridiculous, case of a woman whose seven successive husbands all died and left her childless. They were worried about whose wife she would be in the resurrection!

Jesus' first words in reply were a rebuke to their sophistry. He said they erred because they knew neither the Scriptures nor the power of God. As priests, the Sadducees should have known both. Only a good knowledge of the Word of God, plus a personal experience of the power of God, can save one from error today.

Christ declared that earthly marriages do not carry over into the heavenly realm. The redeemed will be **as angels in heaven** (v. 25). This agrees with Paul's teaching on the resurrection in I Corinthians 15, where he says (v. 44): "It is sown a natural body, it is raised a spiritual body." It does seem reasonable, however, to hold that we shall know our loved ones in heaven. But relationships there will far transcend those that we experience here.

The Sadducees had quoted Moses (v. 19). Now Jesus meets them on their own ground by quoting another text from Moses (Ex. 3:6). It was in the passage called **the Bush** (v. 26); that is, the one that told about the burning bush where Moses received his call and commission. The point Jesus made was that **I am the God of Abraham** shows that the venerable patriarch is still a *living* person (v. 27). Then, for good measure, He added: **ye do greatly err** (only in Mark). The trouble with the Sadducees was

---

[62] *Pulpit Commentary: Mark*, II, 155.

that they had for their religion a dead, cold, formal ritualism. They had no sense of a living Presence with them. But to one who has experienced "the power of His resurrection" (Phil. 3:10) there is no doubt about the reality of the resurrection.

e. Question of Priority (12:28-34)

28 And one of the scribes came, and heard them questioning together, and knowing that he had answered them well, asked him, What commandment is the first of all? 29 Jesus answered, The first is, Hear, O Israel; The Lord our God, the Lord is one: 30 and thou shalt love the Lord thy God with all thy heart, and with all thy soul, and with all thy mind, and with all thy strength. 31 The second is this, Thou shalt love thy neighbor as thyself. There is none other commandment greater than these. 32 And the scribe said unto him, Of a truth, Teacher, thou hast well said that he is one; and there is none other but he: 33 and to love him with all the heart, and with all the understanding, and with all the strength, and to love his neighbor as himself, is much more than all whole burnt-offerings and sacrifices. 34 And when Jesus saw that he answered discreetly, he said unto him, Thou art not far from the kingdom of God. And no man after that durst ask him any question.

The third question related to what commandment (literally, "what kind of commandment") was the first of all (see Luke 20:39-40 and the notes on Matt. 22:34-40). Was the main emphasis of true religion ceremonial or moral? Is ritual or righteousness more important? This may have been some of the background for this question, over which the rabbis often argued.

Mark says that one of the scribes (a Pharisee) heard the dialogue between the Sadducees and Jesus, and knowing that he had answered well, proceeded to pose the new question. On the surface this may seem to disagree with the picture presented in Matthew 22:35, where we read of a lawyer "tempting" Him (KJV). "Trying" (ASV) is less difficult. But here the scribe seems almost friendly. Probably even individual Pharisees felt mixed reactions to this Galilean Prophet.

For the beginning of Jesus' reply Mark alone gives the first part of the Shema — the great declaration of the unity of God (v. 29). This was repeated by every faithful Pharisee twice a day. It is taken from Deuteronomy 6:4-5. The first commandment, said Christ, is to love God with all the **heart, soul, mind** and **strength**. The Hebrew text has heart, soul, and might. The Septuagint (Greek) of Deuteronomy says "understanding, soul, and might." Jesus combined all four different terms (so Mark and Luke). The implication is clear: we are to love God with all there is of us.

Unsolicited, the Master voiced a second command: to love one's neighbor as oneself (Lev. 19:18). Then He added (only Mark): **There is none other commandment greater than these** (v. 31).

The reply of the scribe (vv. 32-33) is found only in Mark. This teacher of the Law felt a high appreciation for the keen spiritual discernment shown by the master Teacher. He showed his own true insight by declaring that love of God and one's neighbor was worth more than all ceremony and ritual. No wonder Jesus said: **Thou art not far from the kingdom of God** (v. 34). But there is no evidence that the man entered the Kingdom.

f. Question in Reply (12:35-37)

35 And Jesus answered and said, as he taught in the temple, How say the scribes that the Christ is the son of David? 36 David himself said in the Holy Spirit,

The Lord said unto my Lord,
Sit thou on my right hand,
Till I make thine enemies the footstool of thy feet.

37 David himself calleth him Lord; and whence is he his son? And the common people heard him gladly.

After Christ had silenced His opponents (v. 34) and successfully answered the three questions posed by the Pharisees, the Sadducees, and a certain scribe, He proceeded to ask one Himself (see Luke 20:41-44 and the notes on Matt. 22:41-46). Mark alone indicates that it was **as He taught in the temple** (v. 35). This means the open courts of the Temple Area.

The scribes taught that the Messiah (**Christ**) would be **the son of David**. This was the heart of the messianic hope of that day — a regal, ruling Messiah. Yet David calls Him Lord. How can these two concepts be reconciled? The Incarnation is the answer.

It seems apparent that Jesus posed this question in order to correct the popular misconceptions concerning the Messiah. He was seeking to pave the way for the people to accept Him as the true Messiah, sent by God. As usual, **the common people heard him gladly** (only in Mark).

3. Condemnation and Commendation (12:38-44)

a. Condemnation of Scribes (12:38-40)

38 And in his teaching he said, Beware of the scribes, who desire to walk in long robes, and *to have* salutations in the marketplaces, 39 and chief seats in the synagogues, and chief places at feasts: 40 they that devour widows' houses, and for a pretence make long prayers; these shall receive greater condemnation.

This section is given almost identically in Luke 20:45-47 and much more fully in Matthew 23:1-12 (see notes there). The Master warned His men to beware of the scribes who set a sad example of pride and love of place.

The **long robes** were supposed to indicate wealth or nobility. The **chief seats** refer to a bench before the ark in front of the synagogue, facing the audience. The **chief places** were the couches for reclining at the head table. **Feasts** can be translated "banquets" (Moffatt).

Along with all this religious pretense and outward show, the scribes — at least some of them — were robbers at heart. One can hardly conceive greater hypocrisy than that of dishonest cruelty to poor, helpless widows — cruelty covered up by making long prayers in public. The scribes took advantage of the fact that people had to employ them for drawing up legal papers. There is evidence that some of them practised sheer dishonesty, while others heartlessly foreclosed mortgages, leaving widows homeless and penniless. It must be remembered that in those days a widow ordinarily could not find employment, as she might today.

Condemnation (v. 40) is better than "damnation" (KJV). The Greek word simply means "judgment." This will be eternal in the case of the unrepentant sinner.

b. Commendation of Widow (12:41-44)

41 And he sat down over against the treasury, and beheld how the multitude cast money into the treasury: and many that were rich cast in much. 42 And there came a poor widow, and she cast in two mites, which make a farthing. 43 And he called unto him his disciples, and said unto them, Verily I say unto you, This poor widow cast in more than all they that are casting into the treasury: 44 for they all did cast in of their superfluity; but she of her want did cast in all that she had, *even* all her living.

The story of the widow's mite is given by Mark and Luke (21:1-4). Jesus sat down opposite **the treasury**. This was located in the Court of the Women. Coming into the Temple Area, one would enter first the Court of the Gentiles, the most extensive part, where Jesus taught vast crowds. A marble wall punctuated with nine gateways separated this from the Court of the Women, which no Gentile was permitted to enter. In 1871 there was discovered the Greek sign which guarded this point. It read:

No foreigner may enter within the balustrade and enclosure around the Sanctuary. Whoever is caught will render himself liable to the death penalty which will inevitably follow.[63]

Inside the Court of the the Women was the Court of the Israelites, which only male Jews could enter. Inside this was the Court of the Priest, with its altar of sacrifice and the Sanctuary.

It is said that the Court of the Women could hold 15,000 people. Here Jesus sat down and observed the different people depositing their offerings in the thirteen large, trumpet-shaped receptacles that were placed there. The rich cast in coins by the handful, but in a careless gesture of unconcern.

But the Master was particularly interested in a certain poor widow. She had only two **mites** — lepta, the smallest copper coins then in use, worth only about a quarter of a cent each. So the **two mites** equalled about half an American

---

[63] Jack Finegan, *Light from the Ancient Past*, p. 246.

penny. But this represented all her **living** (v. 44), or "livelihood."

Jesus said that she cast in more than all the rest (v. 43). This was true both in the proportion and in the spirit of her giving. She gave her all, and so exceeded everybody else. Giving is not measured by the amount given, but by what is left over. It is the spirit of devotion and sacrifice which pleases God, and only He can judge fully as to that. It is the gift of love which brings joy to the heart of the heavenly Father. Cold, careless giving is never rewarded, no matter how much the amount of the gift.

4. Concerning the Future (13:1-37)

a. Prediction of Destruction (13:1-2)

1 And as he went forth out of the temple, one of his disciples saith unto him, Teacher, behold, what manner of stones and what manner of buildings! 2 And Jesus said unto him, Seest thou these great buildings? there shall not be left here one stone upon another, which shall not be thrown down.

The Olivet Discourse — so called because uttered on the Mount of Olives — is found in all three Synoptic Gospels (see Luke 21:5-36 and the notes on Matt. 24). Mark 13 is often referred to as "The Little Apocalypse." The word "apocalypse" is the Greek for "revelation." Literally it means "uncovering." Truth that was hidden now becomes uncovered.

It is a striking fact that the only long discourse found in Mark, and so the only one in all three Synoptics, is eschatological; that is, it deals with "last things." Eschatology played an important role in the teaching of Jesus — though not the dominant one, as some have claimed. It is altogether fitting that this new emphasis should come just before the Crucifixion, for that event was fraught with great eschatological significance. The "last days" had already begun.

As Jesus was leaving the Temple, one of His disciples exclaimed about the beautiful **stones** and **buildings** — as usual, Mark is more specific than Matthew. Josephus mentions the magnitude of the stones. He says: "Now the temple was

built of stones that were white and strong, and each of their length was twenty-five cubits, their height was eight, and their breadth about twelve."[64] Figuring at eighteen inches to the cubit, this would indicate stones thirty-seven feet long, twelve feet high, and eighteen feet thick. Some of these stones of Herod's temple can still be seen at the old Wailing Wall, which formed part of the west wall of the Temple Area.

Then Jesus made a shocking prediction. He said that the beautiful, magnificent buildings of the Temple would all be **thrown down,** until one stone would not be left on another. How literally this was fulfilled in A.D. 70 is indicated by this statement of the first-century Jewish historian, Josephus: "It was so thoroughly laid even with the ground by those that dug it up to the foundation, that there was left nothing to make those that came thither believe it had ever been inhabited."[65]

b. Plea of Disciples (13:3-8)

3 And as he sat on the mount of Olives over against the temple, Peter and James and John and Andrew asked him privately, 4 Tell us, when shall these things be? and what *shall be* the sign when these things are all about to be accomplished? 5 And Jesus began to say unto them, Take heed that no man lead you astray. 6 Many shall come in my name, saying, I am *he;* and shall lead many astray. 7 And when ye shall hear of wars and rumors of wars, be not troubled: *these things* must needs come to pass; but the end is not yet. 8 For nation shall rise against nation, and kingdom against kingdom; there shall be earthquakes in divers places; there shall be famines: these things are the beginning of travail.

Again Mark is more specific than Matthew. The latter says "the disciples" (24:3). Mark names the four fishermen whom Jesus had first called. The Master was sitting on the Mount of Olives, **over against the temple.** The Temple Area lies about two hundred feet below the top of the hill, and about half a mile away. The best view of the city of Jerusalem is from the summit of the Mount of Olives.

Shocked deeply by their Master's pre-

---

[64] *Ant.* XV. 2. 3.   [65] *War,* VII. 1. I.

diction of the destruction of the sacred temple — symbol of God's presence in the midst of His people — the four disciples asked when this would happen, and what sign would precede it. In reply, Jesus warned them against being led astray by deceivers. He said that many false Messiahs would appear. Furthermore, there would be wars, earthquakes, and famines. There is evidence for a number of these in the period between A.D. 30 and A.D. 70.

c. Persecution of Disciples (13:9-13)

9 But take ye heed to yourselves: for they shall deliver you up to councils; and in synagogues shall ye be beaten; and before governors and kings shall ye stand for my sake, for a testimony unto them. 10 And the gospel must first be preached unto all the nations. 11 And when they lead you *to judgment*, and deliver you up, be not anxious beforehand what ye shall speak: but whatsoever shall be given you in that hour, that speak ye; for it is not ye that speak, but the Holy Spirit. 12 And brother shall deliver up brother to death, and the father his child; and children shall rise up against parents, and cause them to be put to death. 13 And ye shall be hated of all men for my name's sake: but he that endureth to the end, the same shall be saved.

Again Jesus says, **Take heed** (v. 9; cf. v. 5). In perilous times one must watch carefully. Literally the verb means, "See!" or "Look!" Maintaining a constant alert is the price of safety.

Once more Mark is more detailed than Matthew. He records Christ's warning that His followers will be delivered up (or, betrayed) to **councils** (sanhedrins), and beaten in the **synagogues** (which also served as local courts), and brought before **governors** and **kings.** The former two refer to Jewish persecution, the latter two to Gentile. Paul stood before the governors Felix and Festus, as well as King Agrippa. **For a testimony unto them** suggests that these persecutions would actually give opportunity for a witness to Christ (cf. Luke 21:13). Verse 14 is paralleled by Matthew 24:14 (see the notes there).

When betrayed and brought before rulers, the disciples were not to be anxious as to what they should say. The Holy Spirit would guide them when the time came. (This has nothing to say about preparation for preaching.) Matthew's parallel to verses 9, 11, and 12 is found in Matthew 10:17-21 (see notes there).

The first statement of verse 13 is a startling one. Why should all men hate Jesus' followers? The answer is that Christ's way cuts right straight across the world's way, and this causes inevitable conflict. Those who are not willing to surrender their wills and take the Christian path in life resent the presence of disciples of the Master. They show their resentment in hatred and some form of persecution.

Only those will be saved who endure **to the end** (v. 13). F. C. Grant says that the phrase means "to the last degree, to the final pitch of endurance."[66] Perhaps a simpler view would be to take it as meaning to the end of life.

d. Prediction of Desolation (13:14-23)

14 But when ye see the abomination of desolation standing where he ought not (let him that readeth understand) , then let them that are in Judaea flee unto the mountains: 15 and let him that is on the housetop not go down, nor enter in, to take anything out of his house: 16 and let him that is in the field not return back to take his cloak. 17 But woe unto them that are with child and to them that give suck in those days! 18 And pray ye that it be not in the winter. 19 For those days shall be tribulation, such as there hath not been the like from the beginning of the creation which God created until now, and never shall be. 20 And except the Lord had shortened the days, no flesh would have been saved; but for the elect's sake, whom he chose, he shortened the days. 21 And then if any man shall say unto you, Lo, here is the Christ; or, Lo, there; believe *it* not: 22 for there shall arise false Christs and false prophets, and shall show signs and wonders, that they may lead astray, if possible, the elect. 23 But take ye heed: behold, I have told you all things beforehand.

The phrase **abomination of desolation** is taken from Daniel, as Matthew indicates (see the notes on Matt. 24:15-38). "Spoken of by Daniel the prophet"

66 "Mark" (Exegesis), *The Interpreter's Bible*, ed.   George Buttrick *et al.*, Vol. 7, p. 860.

(KJV) is not in the oldest Greek manuscripts of Mark.

The primary application of this passage seems to be to the destruction of Jerusalem in A.D. 70. The **abomination of desolation** is thought by some to refer to the horrible desecration that took place during the Roman siege, when an army of Zealots massacred their fellow Jews in the Temple Area. Josephus gives a vivid description of this and relates that there was an ancient oracle to the effect that when the Jews themselves would "pollute the temple of God," the city would be captured and the sanctuary burned.[67]

When the Christians saw this sign take place, they were to flee to the mountains (see on Matt. 24:16). There was to be no tarrying, for the opportunity for flight would be brief. If a person was on the flat roof of the house he was to hurry down the outside stairway, and not go inside to take anything with him. If he was working in the field, he was not to return home for his outer cloak. The urgency of the situation could not have been expressed more graphically. It was flee immediately, or risk death.

It would be very hard on expectant and nursing mothers (v. 17), for they would have to seek safety beyond the Jordan. It would be especially difficult in winter (v. 18), when the nights are cold, and the rainy season is on. Also the Jordan River would be swollen with the winter rains and might well be impassable. Thus the fugitives would be trapped.

The word **tribulation** (v. 19) comes from the Latin *tribulum*, which was a flail for threshing grain. The Greek word here is *thlipsis,* which comes from the verb *thlibo,* "press." It was used for pressing grapes in a winepress. The two ideas give a graphic illustration of what tribulation really is. It is a beating, battering impact made by the circumstances of life; it is also the "squeeze" that one sometimes feels in a situation that seems to imprison its victim.

Again comes the admonition, **take ye heed** (v. 23). Times of temptation and tribulation call for special watchfulness, lest the believer be tripped or trapped. The primary purpose of the Olivet Dis-

course was to forewarn the disciples of what would happen in their generation.

e. Prediction of Darkness (13:24-27)

24 But in those days, after that tribulation, the sun shall be darkened, and the moon shall not give her light, 25 and the stars shall be falling from heaven, and the powers that are in the heavens shall be shaken. 26 And then shall they see the Son of man coming in clouds with great power and glory. 27 And then shall he send forth the angels, and shall gather together his elect from the four winds, from the uttermost part of the earth to the uttermost part of heaven.

Matthew and Mark are closely parallel in this section (see notes on Matt. 24:29-31). It would seem that the previous paragraph (vv. 14-23) refers especially to the destruction of Jerusalem in A.D. 70. But this one (and to the end of the chapter) appears to deal with the signs of the Second Coming. Whether the language here is literal or symbolical has been much debated. It is of course well known that the apocalyptic vocabulary is usually figurative and marked by poetic fancy. The primary reference here is probably to political and social upheavals. But the amazing developments of this atomic age, with its exploration of space, should caution one against saying what cannot happen. Perhaps the terminology here is more literal than any previous generation could have guessed. Just how much of physical "cataclysm" and "catastrophe" — both good Greek words — may precede the return of Christ, no one on earth knows.

Concerning His **coming in clouds** (v. 26), Morison offers this good comment: "The clouds, which will be rolling over the troubled sky, and which are the fitting symbols at once of the impending crisis and of the impenetrable mystery that surrounds the throne of Him who rules over it, will be, as it were, the sublime drapery of His presence, illumined 'with the brightness of His coming' (II Thess. 2:8)."[68]

The idea of the **elect** (v. 27) comes from the Old Testament (cf. Isa. 11:11; 27:12). The **four winds** (cf. Zech. 2:6) means the four points of the compass. The phrasing of the last part of the verse is unique.

[67] *War*, IV. 6. 3.   [68] *Op. cit.*, p. 369.

It apparently means "from horizon to horizon," that is, from all parts of the earth.

f. Parable of the Fig Tree (13:28-32)

28 Now from the fig tree learn her parable: when her branch is now become tender, and putteth forth its leaves, ye know that the summer is nigh; 29 even so ye also, when ye see these things coming to pass, know ye that he is nigh, *even* at the doors. 30 Verily I say unto you, This generation shall not pass away, until all these things be accomplished. 31 Heaven and earth shall pass away: but my words shall not pass away. 32 But of that day or that hour knoweth no one, not even the angels in heaven, neither the Son, but the Father.

The words of this parable are given in almost identical language in Matthew and Mark (see notes on Matt. 24:32-44), and rather similarly in Luke (21:29-33). The main point is clear enough. But verse 30 poses a problem. In addition to the solutions mentioned in the notes on Matthew 24:34, one more might be cited. Some have suggested the idea that the generation living when these signs begin to be fulfilled will see the culmination of them. That is, the final "wind-up" of this age will all take place within one generation. In view of the incredible acceleration of events in the last two decades, this interpretation may have some validity.

h. Plea for Watchfulness (13:33-37)

33 Take ye heed, watch and pray: for ye know not when the time is. 34 *It is* as *when* a man, sojourning in another country, having left his house, and given authority to his servants, to each one his work, commanded also the porter to watch. 35 Watch therefore: for ye know not when the lord of the house cometh, whether at even, or at midnight, or at cockcrowing, or in the morning; 36 lest coming suddenly he find you sleeping. 37 And what I say unto you I say unto all, Watch.

For the fourth time in this chapter (cf. vv. 5, 9, 23) we find the warning admonition: **Take ye heed** (v. 33). This time there is added: **watch and pray.** Why? **For ye know not when the time is.** Since the hour of Christ's return is un-certain, believers must be watching and ready at every moment.

Verse 34 gives just a hint of Matthew's Parable of the Talents (Matt. 25:14-30) and Luke's Parable of the Pounds (Luke 19:11-28). It emphasizes the necessity for faithfulness and watchfulness.

Mark's account of the Olivet Discourse closes with an emphatic repetition of the key word of this message — **watch.** Verse 35 begins with it, and it is the last word of verse 37 and of this discourse. It literally means "Keep awake!" No one can interpret fully the signs of the times. Those who try the hardest often fail the most miserably. But everyone can and must keep watching.

The four-time notices in the latter part of verse 35 refer to the four watches of the night, adopted by the Jews from the Romans. These closed at 9:00 P.M., midnight, 3:00 A.M., and 6:00 A.M. So **even, midnight, cockcrowing,** and **morning** were appropriate names.

In the hectic, uncertain days of the mid-twentieth century, the words of the Olivet Discourse take on added significance. No longer can one say that everything is going to continue just as it always has. Discoveries and inventions follow on each other's heels with dizzying rapidity. One never knows what to expect when unfolding the morning newspaper. "In days like these" the most needful thing is to watch and pray, always being ready for the return of our Lord.

III. THE SERVANT'S SACRIFICE (14:1-16:20)

A. FOES AND FRIENDS (14:1-31)

1. Conspiracy and Comfort (14:1-11)

a. Counsel to Kill (14:1-2)

1 Now after two days was *the feast of the passover* and the unleavened bread: and the chief priests and the scribes sought how they might take him with subtlety, and kill him: 2 for they said, Not during the feast, lest haply there shall be a tumult of the people.

Matthew (26:1-5) and Mark both have this time reference — two days before the Passover. Presumably this would be Tuesday evening or Wednesday afternoon. In Jewish usage **after two days** could mean "on the next day."

The great annual festival is here called

the passover and the unleavened bread. Strictly speaking, the Passover was one day, followed by seven days of Unleavened Bread (Lev. 23:5, 6). But at this time the whole period of eight days was often referred to by either name.

Here we have the definite conspiracy of the **chief priests and the scribes** (the Sadducees and the Pharisees) to arrest Jesus and put Him to death. They were afraid to attempt it during the feast, knowing that the thousands of Galilean pilgrims were on His side and would cause an uproar. But in divine Providence the arrest did take place apparently during the feast time.

b. Comfort of Consecration (14:3-9)

3 And while he was in Bethany in the house of Simon the leper, as he sat at meat, there came a woman having an alabaster cruse of ointment of pure nard very costly; *and* she brake the cruse, and poured it over his head. 4 But there were some that had indignation among themselves, *saying,* To what purpose hath this waste of the ointment been made? 5 For this ointment might have been sold for above three hundred shillings, and given to the poor. And they murmured against her. 6 But Jesus said, Let her alone; why trouble ye her? she hath wrought a good work on me. 7 For ye have the poor always with you, and whensoever ye will ye can do them good: but me ye have not always. 8 She hath done what she could; she hath anointed my body beforehand for the burying. 9 And verily I say unto you, Wheresoever the gospel shall be preached throughout the whole world, that also which this woman hath done shall be spoken of for a memorial of her.

The anointing of Jesus at Bethany is recorded also by Matthew (see notes on Matt. 26:6-13). It is evidently the same incident as that described in John 12:2-8, but definitely not the same as that in Luke 7:36-50.

John says that the anointing took place "six days before the passover." On the surface this conflicts with the time notice here and in Matthew. The consensus of scholars is that the statement in John is more definite and determinative, and that the anointing actually took place on Friday or Saturday evening before the Triumphal Entry. It would seem that Matthew and Mark bring in the incident rather parenthetically in connection with the conspiracy against Jesus' life. The difference in attitudes of His foes and friends presents a striking contrast. It perhaps should be recognized that some good scholars prefer the Markan chronology at this point. We cannot be dogmatically certain as to the day of the anointing.

Pure nard is probably more accurate than "spikenard" (KJV). The Greek adjective appears to mean "genuine." In other words this was high quality, **very costly,** perfume that Mary poured on Jesus' head.

Mark's statement that she **broke the cruse** (Greek, *alabastron*) indicates the utter abandon of her consecration. She did not pour out a few drops of perfume. Rather, in an act of spontaneous love and uncalculating devotion, she broke the narrow neck of the alabaster flask and poured all its contents on the Master's head. It is one of the most beautiful examples of love and consecration to be found in the Scriptures.

Both Mark and John note that the value of the perfume was about three hundred denarii. It will be remembered that a denarius was worth about twenty cents in American money, but that it also represented a day's wage. So this amount would be nearly a year's earnings. Mary may well have saved the amount over a period of many years. But now she gave it all, gladly and spontaneously.

Mark adds that some **murmured** against her (v. 5). The verb could be translated "growled," or "were angry." It literally means "snorted." These complainers resented what they considered a sheer waste of something valuable.

Jesus' reply was, **Let her alone** (v. 6). He fully defended her action. The last part of the verse is best rendered: "She has done a beautiful thing to me" (RSV).

The idea of true consecration is forcefully expressed in another addition by Mark: **She hath done what she could.** That is the most — and least — that God expects of anyone.

The last part of verse 8 reads literally: "She anticipated to anoint my body for the preparation for burial." Mary of Bethany seems to be the only follower of Jesus who caught the significance of His teaching about His coming death and resurrection. Often love understands better than reason.

c. Conspiracy for Capture (14:10-11)

10 And Judas Iscariot, he that was one of the twelve, went away unto the chief priests, that he might deliver him unto them. 11 And they, when they heard it, were glad, and promised to give him money. And he sought how he might conveniently deliver him *unto them.*

For this brief description of the arrangement Judas Iscariot made with the chief priests to betray Jesus to them, see the notes on Matthew 26:14-16. The contrast between Mary of Bethany and Judas Iscariot is sharp and shattering.

Why did Judas betray his Master? It may have been a mixture of motives. He is thought to have been the only Judean among the apostles, and he may have despised the Galileans. But why then did He join the group? Some have suggested that Judas was trying to force Jesus' hand. He would put Him in a situation where He would have to declare and demonstrate His messiahship. Thus Judas was seeking to precipitate the setting up of the messianic kingdom. But probably the main motive was love of money — his besetting sin.

2. Passover and Prediction (14:12-31)

a. Preparation for Passover (14:12-16)

12 And on the first day of unleavened bread, when they sacrificed the passover, his disciples say unto him, Where wilt thou that we go and make ready that thou mayest eat the passover? 13 And he sendeth two of his disciples, and saith unto them, Go into the city, and there shall meet you a man bearing a pitcher of water: follow him; 14 and wheresoever he shall enter in, say to the master of the house, The Teacher saith, Where is my guest-chamber, where I shall eat the passover with my disciples? 15 And he will himself show you a large upper room furnished *and* ready: and there make ready for us. 16 And the disciples went forth, and came into the city, and found as he had said unto them: and they made ready the passover.

For the regulations on the Passover see the notes on Matthew 26:17-19 (cf. Luke 22:7-38). To make the time specific, Mark adds:**when they sacrificed the pass-over.** This would be the afternoon of the fourteenth day of the month Nisan. That evening, which would be the fifteenth — the Jewish day began at sunset — the Passover lamb was to be eaten.

Jesus sent **two of his disciples.** Luke (22:8) identifies then as Peter and John. They were instructed that they would meet a man **bearing a pitcher of water** — a very unsual sight. Men carried water in large goatskins, but not in jars on their heads. Only women did the latter. So it would be easy to spot their man.

Why did Jesus give these cryptic instructions? Why did He not simply indicate the house where they would eat the Passover together?

The answer might be that He did not want Judas to know where it was, lest he should go and make arrangements to have the Jewish rulers seize Him there. Christ wanted an uninterrupted evening with His disciples at what He knew would be His last supper with them.

When the two disciples reached the house they were to quote their Teacher as asking, **Where is my guest-chamber?** This implies that Jesus had already made arrangements with the owner for the use of the place that evening. **Guest-chamber** is the same Greek word which is translated "inn" at Luke 2:7. It was a **large upper room,** where a group could assemble. It is possible that Pentecost occurred in this very same place.

The room would be **furnished and ready;** literally, "spread, prepared." There would be carpets on the floor, and cushions on the couches on which the guests would recline as they ate. The disciples were to **make ready for us.** That is, they were to get the food for the evening meal and prepare it for serving.

The three Synoptic Gospels all give the impression very definitely that this was the Passover meal. But a real problem arises when we read in John 18:28 that the Jews would not enter Pilate's Praetorium the next morning "that they might not be defiled, but might eat the passover." How could this be if they had already eaten the Passover meal the night before? John seems to suggest that Jesus died at the very time that the Passover lamb was being slain. This presents a very attractive symbolism, but how can it be harmonized with the Synoptics?

Branscomb thinks the Last Supper was not a Passover meal. He stresses the fact that no mention is made of the lamb, the bitter herbs, or the unleavened bread.[69] Plummer suggests that Jesus knew He could not celebrate the Passover at the regular time, and so He ate it with His disciples a day early.[70] Vincent Taylor writes: "Probably most British scholars are justified in holding that the Last Supper and the Crucifixion preceded the Passover."[71] A. M. Hunter agrees that modern scholars, with very few exceptions, prefer the Johannine chronology, rather than the Synoptic, at this point.

On the other hand, Samuel Andrews uses about thirty pages in the effort to prove that the Last Supper was really a Passover meal. He harmonizes the Johannine and Synoptic statements by asserting that John uses the term "passover" in the larger sense, as including the seven days of Unleavened Bread.[72] The Jewish leaders did not wish to be defiled and thus prevented from continuing to participate in the feast. The great German scholar, Joachim Jeremias, insists that the Last Supper was indeed the Passover.[73]

Two new solutions have recently been suggested. In an article entitled, "Are Both the Synoptics and John Correct about the Date of Jesus' Death?," Massey H. Shepherd writes: "In that particular year the Jews in Palestine observed Passover on Saturday; those in Dispersion observed it on Friday."[74] Mark followed the Dispersion calendar, while John adopted the Palestinian. So both are right.

The other is by David Noel Freedman, in an article, "When Did Christ Die?" He claims that the Dead Sea Scrolls indicate that many pious Jews held to the older solar calendar in which every year began on the same day, so that 14th Nisan — the day the Passover lamb was to be slain — always came on Tuesday. Freedman thinks that Jesus ate the Passover with His disciples on Tuesday night, whereas the chief priests and rulers of the Jews ate it on Friday night. He believes that this gives more time for the Jewish and Roman trials of Jesus.[75]

We cannot know whether any of the above theories is correct. But at least they show that there are ways of harmonizing the accounts and thus solving the most difficult problem in the chronology of the Gospels.

b. Passover with Disciples (14:17-21)

17 And when it was evening he cometh with the twelve. 18 And as they sat and were eating, Jesus said, Verily I say unto you, One of you shall betray me, *even* he that eateth with me. 19 They began to be sorrowful, and to say unto him one by one, Is it I? 20 And he said unto them, *It is* one of the twelve, he that dippeth with me in the dish. 21 For the Son of man goeth, even as it is written of him: but woe unto that man through whom the Son of man is betrayed! good were it for that man if he had not been born.

For the explanation of several terms used here, see the notes on the parallel account in Matthew 26:20-25. The order in Luke is somewhat different (cf. Luke 22:14-23).

To the announcement that one of the Twelve would betray his Master, Mark alone adds: **even he that eateth with me** (v. 18). This made Judas' crime all the more heinous. F. C. Grant comments: "To betray a companion after eating with him was, and still is among the Arabs, the grossest conceivable perfidy."[76]

Solemnly Jesus asserted that it would have been better for the betrayer if he had never been born (v. 21). This statement underscores the serious responsibility that every human being carries for the decisions he makes. Judas was free to choose, and his decision determined his destiny.

c. Presentation of Eucharist (14:22-25)

22 And as they were eating, he took bread, and when he had blessed, he brake it, and gave to them, and said, Take ye: this is my body. 23 And he took a cup, and when he had given thanks, he gave to them: and they all drank of it. 24 And he said unto them, This is my blood of

[69] *Op. cit.*, pp. 249-255.   [70] *Op. cit.*, p. 310.   [71] *Op. cit.*, p. 607.   [72] *Op. cit.*, pp. 452-481.
[73] *The Eucharistic Words of Jesus*, pp. 14-37.   [74] *Journal of Biblical Literature*, LXXX (1961), 125.
[75] *Perspective*, III (1962), 52-57.   [76] *Op. cit.*, VII, 875.

the covenant, which is poured out for many. 25 Verily I say unto you, I shall no more drink of the fruit of the vine, until that day when I drink it new in the kingdom of God.

The Last Supper became the Lord's Supper. Mark's account is almost exactly the same as Matthew's (see notes on Matt. 26:26-29). There is only one small addition here: **and they all drank of it** (v. 23). Probably Judas Iscariot had already left the room, but the remaining eleven apostles all partook of the sacrament.

In verse 24 the King James Version reads, "This is my blood of the new testament." The word "new" is omitted in the Revised Version because it is missing in the earliest and best Greek manuscripts. Also "testament" is better translated *covenant*. The Greek word has both meanings. But since "covenant" is a prominent Old Testament term, and since the Jews made covenants rather than testaments (wills), it is very clear that **covenant** is the correct translation.

The Last Supper was in many ways a sad and solemn occasion. But it ended with a note of hope. Some day the kingdom of God would come, and Jesus would be with them again in joyous fellowship. This promise had a partial fulfillment at Pentecost, but also points forward to the Second Coming.

d. Prediction about Peter (14:26-31)

26 And when they had sung a hymn, they went out unto the mount of Olives.

27 And Jesus saith unto them, All ye shall be offended: for it is written, I will smite the shepherd, and the sheep shall be scattered abroad. 28 Howbeit, after I am raised up, I will go before you into Galilee. 29 But Peter said unto him, Although all shall be offended, yet will not I. 30 And Jesus saith unto him, Verily I say unto thee, that thou to-day, *even* this night, before the cock crow twice, shalt deny me thrice. 31 But he spake exceeding vehemently, If I must die with thee, I will not deny thee. And in like manner also said they all.

For explanation of the **hymn** and other items here see the notes on Matthew 26: 30-35. Characteristically Mark uses the historical present **saith** (v. 30) where Matthew and Luke have "said." He adds the specific prediction that before the cock

crew **twice,** Peter would deny Him thrice. This suggests that even after the warning of the first cockcrowing Peter would continue to deny his Lord. The Greek word for **deny** is a strong compound, meaning "deny utterly." Mark says that the denial would take place not only **this night** (so also Matthew) but **today.** Since the Jewish day began at sunset, it was already Friday. The emphatic **thou** is in answer to Peter's emphatic **I** (v. 29).

A good example of Mark's attention to vivid details is found in his (alone) description of Peter's strong feelings: **But he spake exceeding vehemently** (v. 31). Poor Peter was impetuous and impulsive, but at this stage he was not steady and established. **I will not** is a double negative in Greek (also in Matthew). The full force of the assertion is: "I will by no means deny you," or "I will never deny you." And Peter meant it. But he did not know how weak he was without the power of the Holy Spirit in his heart. After Pentecost Peter would witness to Christ, not deny Him (Acts 1:8).

B. GETHSEMANE AND GOLGOTHA (14:32-15:47)

1. Agony and Arrest (14:32-52)

a. Bitterness of Cup (14:32-42)

32 And they come unto a place which was named Gethsemane: and he saith unto his disciples, Sit ye here, while I pray. 33 And he taketh with him Peter and James and John, and began to be greatly amazed, and sore troubled. 34 And he saith unto them, My soul is exceeding sorrowful even unto death: abide ye here, and watch. 35 And he went forward a little, and fell on the ground, and prayed that, if it were possible, the hour might pass away from him. 36 And he said, Abba, Father, all things are possible unto thee; remove this cup from me: howbeit not what I will, but what thou wilt. 37 And he cometh, and findeth them sleeping, and saith unto Peter, Simon, sleepest thou? couldest thou not watch one hour? 38 Watch and pray, that ye enter not into temptation: the spirit indeed is willing, but the flesh is weak. 39 And again he went away, and prayed, saying the same words. 40 And again he came, and found them sleeping, for their eyes were very heavy; and they knew not what to answer him. 41 And he cometh the

third time, and saith unto them, Sleep on now, and take your rest: it is enough; the hour is come; behold, the Son of man is betrayed into the hands of sinners. 42 Arise, let us be going: behold, he that betrayeth me is at hand.

Again Matthew and Mark are closely parallel (see notes on Matt. 26:36-46). For greater vividness Mark uses the historical present, **taketh** (v. 33). In place of Matthew's "sorrowful," he has **greatly amazed** — a strong compound that only he uses. It can be translated "terrified." As the time drew near, the horrors of the Crucifixion struck Jesus with blinding force. His sorrow over a world's sins was crushing, almost killing, Him.

As in other places, Mark adds a vivid touch. Whereas Matthew says that Jesus "fell" (aorist), Mark says that He "was falling" (imperfect tense). Staggering under an insufferable burden, He was stumbling and falling on the ground.

The word **Abba** — found only here (v. 36), Romans 8:15, and Galatians 4:6 — is Aramaic for "father." In moments of high emotional tension Jesus naturally spoke in the common language of the home. Both Greek and Aramaic were spoken in Palestine at that time. The **cup** was perhaps most specifically the separation from His Father's face that must take place when Jesus accepted the penalty for the sins of all mankind.

The reproof of Peter is more full and vivid in Mark. Where Matthew reports the Master as saying, "What, could ye not watch with me one hour," Mark has: **Simon, sleepest thou? Couldest thou not watch one hour?** (v. 37). Peter would remember well the shame he felt when Jesus wakened them and not only reproved all three for sleeping, but chided him personally.

Some think that Jesus spoke ironically when He said: **Sleep on now, and take your rest** (v. 41). But Redlich has well observed: "The hour was too solemn for Jesus to be guilty of speaking in irony, and the only way in which verses 41 and 42 give a clear meaning is by translating the opening words of our Lord in verse 41 as a question."[77] The Greek can be translated either way with equal accuracy. **It is enough** (only in Mark) is one word in Greek. It probably means, "You

have slept long enough now." **The hour is come** was a significant declaration. It was the hour of His betrayal and crucifixion when it seemed that man's hate and sin had conquered. But it was also the hour of the world's redemption.

In the shadows of the trees it might have been expected that Jesus would have sought to elude those who came to seize Him. But the hour had come for His surrender to them. **Let us go** (v. 42) does not mean "Let us flee," but "Let us go to meet them." After His agonizing hour of prayer in Gethsemane, the Master was calm and ready to face His foes and the Cross that lay beyond.

b. Betrayal by Companion (14:43-50)

43 And straightway, while he yet spake, cometh Judas, one of the twelve, and with him a multitude with swords and staves, from the chief priests and the scribes and the elders. 44 Now he that betrayed him had given them a token, saying, Whomsoever I shall kiss, that is he; take him, and lead him away safely. 45 And when he was come, straightway he came to him, and saith, Rabbi; and kissed him. 46 And they laid hands on him, and took him. 47 But a certain one of them that stood by drew his sword, and smote the servant of the high priest, and struck off his ear. 48 And Jesus answered and said unto them, Are ye come out, as against a robber, with swords and staves to seize me? 49 I was daily with you in the temple teaching, and ye took me not: but *this is done* that the scriptures might be fulfilled. 50 And they all left him, and fled.

The betrayal and arrest in the garden are given in considerable detail by all four Gospels (see the notes on Matt. 26:47-56; cf. Luke 22:47-53 and John 18:2-12). All three Synoptics say it was **while he yet spake** that the mob appeared. Christ had finished His praying just in time. Also all three Synoptics note that the leader of the group was Judas, **one of the twelve.** This underscores again the enormity of his crime.

The crowd sent by the Sanhedrin — **the chief priests and the scribes and the elders** — was armed with swords and clubs. Apparently they expected some resistance on the part of the disciples.

But the accounts suggest that the only one they intended to arrest was Jesus.

Judas had given the mob a **token** (v. 44). The compound (found only here) suggests a sign agreed upon beforehand. The horrible depravity of his heart is shown by the fact that he chose to betray his Master with a kiss. He warned the soldiers to seize Jesus **and lead him away safely.** This little addition (given only by Mark) indicates Judas' concern that the plot should not fail. Many times the Jewish rulers had sought to arrest Jesus, but always they had failed. Now was the time to succeed. This hardly comports with the idea that Judas expected his Master once more to elude His enemies.

Rabbi means "my master." This simply indicates that Judas was a disciple ("learner") of Jesus. The term "was the usual form of address with which the learned were greeted."[78] But on the lips of the betrayer it was sheer hypocrisy.

c. Befriending by Youth (14:51-52)

51 And a certain young man followed with him, having a linen cloth cast about him, over *his* naked *body*: and they lay hold on him; 52 but he left the linen cloth, and fled naked.

Why is this little incident inserted here by Mark alone. The only obvious answer is that John Mark was himself the young man involved. As it were, he initials his description of the scene, thus saying, "I was there."

The reconstruction is not difficult to make, especially if we assume that the Last Supper took place in the home of John Mark's mother, which was an early meeting place of the Christians in Jerusalem (Acts 12:12). When Judas left the upper room, between the Last Supper and the Lord's Supper to complete the plans for seizing Jesus, he would naturally expect to return there for the actual arrest. But by the time the mob had been gathered together, Christ had left, with His disciples, for the Mount of Olives.

When the crowd arrived at the house of the Last Supper, probably the place was dark. Young John Mark, awakened by the noise, would look out to see what was going on. When he saw the swords and clubs, visible in the light of the torches the men carried, he would know that all this did not bode well for the Master.

As the crowd headed off down the street, going to the place where Judas knew Jesus often went (cf. John 18:2), John Mark may have had a sudden impulse to try to warn Christ of the impending danger. Grabbing a **linen cloth** for an improvised night robe, he hastened out into the dark streets. But by the time he arrived at the garden, the crowd was already arresting Jesus. In the confusion that followed, one of the soldiers tried to seize him. Slipping out of the linen cloth, he fled back home to bed — but probably not to sleep.

2. Trial and Denial (14:53-65)

a. Trial by Sanhedrin (14:53-65)

53 And they led Jesus away to the high priest: and there come together with him all the chief priests and the elders and the scribes. 54 And Peter had followed him afar off, even within, into the court of the high priest; and he was sitting with the officers, and warming himself in the light *of the fire.* 55 Now the chief priests and the whole council sought witness against Jesus to put him to death; and found it not. 56 For many bare false witness against him, and their witness agreed not together. 57 And there stood up certain, and bare false witness against him, saying, 58 We heard him say, I will destroy this temple that is made with hands, and in three days I will build another made without hands. 59 And not even so did their witness agree together. 60 And the high priest stood up in the midst, and asked Jesus, saying, Answerest thou nothing? what is it which these witness against thee? 61 But he held his peace, and answered nothing. Again the high priest asked him, and saith unto him, Art thou the Christ, the Son of the Blessed? 62 And Jesus said, I am: and ye shall see the Son of man sitting at the right hand of Power, and coming with the clouds of heaven. 63 And the high priest rent his clothes, and saith, What further need have we of witnesses? 64 Ye have heard the blasphemy: what think ye? And they all condemned him to be worthy of death. 65 And some began to spit on him, and to cover his face, and to buffet him, and to say unto him, Pro-

---

[78] Gustaf Dalman, *The Words of Jesus,* trans. D. M. Kay, p. 331.

phesy: and the officers received him with blows of their hands.

Matthew's and Mark's accounts are very closely parallel at this point (see the notes on Matt. 26:57-68 and compare Luke 22:54, 63-71). John records a preliminary hearing before Annas, ex-high priest and father-in-law of the high priest then in office. But he agrees with the Synoptics in saying that Jesus was then sent to the **high priest,** whom Matthew and John identify as Caiaphas.

Thereupon there took place a meeting of the Sanhedrin, here mentioned by its three constituent elements (v. 53; cf. v. 43). Meanwhile below in the open courtyard Peter sat **warming himself in the light of the fire.** This little addition by Mark reflects the fact that the nights are chilly in Jerusalem, which is at an elevation of about 2500 feet.

The false witness recorded in verse 58 is somewhat more explicit than that in Matthew (26:16). Mark adds: **And not even so did their witness agree together** (v. 59). In spite of dishonest efforts at collusion, the whole attempt failed.

When the high priest put Jesus under oath, He gave a simple, but very specific affirmative answer — **I am** (v. 62). This is as definite a declaration of deity as anyone could desire.

The action of the members of the Sanhedrin at this time is utterly without defense or excuse. They displayed a spiteful hatred that is difficult to understand.

b. Denial by Peter (14:66-72)

66 And as Peter was beneath in the court, there cometh one of the maids of the high priest; 67 and seeing Peter warming himself, she looked upon him, and saith, Thou also wast with the Nazarene, *even* Jesus. 68 But he denied, saying, I neither know, nor understand what thou sayest: and he went out into the porch; and the cock crew. 69 And the maid saw him, and began again to say to them that stood by, This is *one* of them. 70 But he again denied it. And after a little while again they that stood by said to Peter, Of a truth thou art *one* of them; for thou art a Galilaean. 71 But he began to curse, and to swear, I know not this man of whom ye speak. 72 And straightway the second time the cock crew. And Peter called to mind the word, how that Jesus said unto him, Before the cock crow

twice, thou shalt deny me thrice. And when he thought thereon, he wept.

The four Gospels differ considerably in their accounts of Peter's denials. But it appears that he was challenged a number of times by different individuals and groups. That there were three specific denials all the accounts agree.

There are several distinctive items in Mark. He identifies the first accuser as **one of the maids of the high priest** (v. 66), and intimates that she recognized him by the light of the fire. Mark uses a different Greek word for porch from that found in Matthew (26:71). The one here literally means "forecourt." The reference seems to be to the "vestibule" between the inner court and the outer door. Here, away from the light of the fire, Peter hoped to escape detection. But it was of no avail. The same maid, or another one (cf. Matt. 26:71; Luke 22: 58), declared that he was **one of them.** Instead of being thankful for the special privilege he enjoyed, Peter denied it all.

Consistent with his report of Jesus' prediction (v. 30), Mark here relates a second cockcrowing (v. 72). At last Peter came to his senses. Fleeing the place of compromise, he went out to weep bitter tears of repentance.

3. Pilate and People (15:1-21)

a. Problem of Pilate (15:1-5)

1 And straightway in the morning the chief priests with the elders and scribes, and the whole council, held a consultation, and bound Jesus, and carried him away, and delivered him up to Pilate. 2 And Pilate asked him, Art thou the King of the Jews? And he answering saith unto him, Thou sayest. 3 And the chief priests accused him of many things. 4 And Pilate again asked him, saying, Answerest thou nothing? behold how many things they accuse thee of. 5 But Jesus no more answered anything; insomuch that Pilate marvelled.

The Jewish trial of Jesus at night was illegal (see the notes on Matt. 27:1-2). So now the whole **council** (Sanhedrin) met at daybreak to make its earlier sentence of death (14:64) official. It is interesting to note that more frequently than the other Gospel writers Mark names the three constituent groups in the Great Sanhedrin at Jerusalem (cf. 14:53 and parallel in Matt. 26:57). The phrasing here, however, is a bit unusual — **the chief priests with the elders and scribes.** This underscores the fact that whereas earlier it was the scribes (Pharisees) who opposed Jesus and hounded His steps, now it was the chief priests (Sadducees) who headed the opposition. Apparently this was the result of His cleansing the Temple, when He threatened both the power and pocketbooks of the priestly hierarchy. In the early chapters of Acts it is noticeable that the Sadducees are the main persecutors of the Christian disciples.

Bound Jesus means "put Jesus in chains" (NEB). It is shocking to think of the compassionate Christ, whose loving hands had healed the sick, been laid in blessing on the heads of little children, and broken the biscuits to feed the multitudes, being handcuffed and led through the streets of His own Holy City in chains. This was one of those dramatic ironies of history. His body was bound that men's souls might be set free.

The Sanhedrin, having condemned Jesus to death, delivered Him up to the governor, who alone had the power of execution. Pilate was procurator of Judea for ten years (A.D. 26-36). His regular place of residence was down on the coast of the Mediterranean, at Caesarea. But the Passover tended to excite the nationalistic feelings of the Jews, often leading to riots. So the governor found it safer to be on hand in Jerusalem at the feast times.

Josephus indicates that Pilate was hated by the Jews because of his greed, stubbornness, and cruelty.[79] He was finally recalled by the emperor and banished into exile.

When confronted by Christ, Pilate asked contemptuously, *"You,* are you the King of the Jews?"* As far as outward appearance was concerned, Jesus did not look much like a king.

Christ's answer is rather enigmatic. **Thou sayest** is a literal translation of the Greek. But what does it mean? Is it equivalent to the slang expression, "You said it!" — a strong affirmation? Or does it mean, "That's what you say." It would seem that Jesus purposely gave an ambiguous answer (cf. NEB — "The words are yours") because Pilate would mis-

understand a categorical "Yes." His ideas of kingship would be very different from those of Jesus (see notes on Matt. 27:11).

Mark records that the chief priests accused Christ of **many things.** They were vicious and violent in their opposition. On one thing they were determined — that Pilate should not release Jesus, but put Him to death.

The Master's perfect poise in the face of false accusations has left an example for His followers. The governor was amazed. He had never had before him a prisoner like this one. In the light of these facts Pilate is utterly without excuse for condemning the Sinless One to die.

b. Plea of People (15:6-15)

6 Now at the feast he used to release unto them one prisoner, whom they asked of him. 7 And there was one called Barabbas, *lying* bound with them that had made insurrection, men who in the insurrection had committed murder. 8 And the multitude went up and began to ask him *to do* as he was wont to do unto them. 9 And Pilate answered them, saying, Will ye that I release unto you the King of the Jews? 10 For he perceived that for envy the chief priests had delivered him up. 11 But the chief priests stirred up the multitude, that he should rather release Barabbas unto them. 12 And Pilate again answered and said unto them, What then shall I do unto him whom ye call the King of the Jews? 13 And they cried out again, Crucify him. 14 And Pilate said unto them, Why, what evil hath he done? But they cried out exceedingly, Crucify him. 15 And Pilate, wishing to content the multitude, released unto them Barabbas, and delivered Jesus, when he had scourged him, to be crucified.

The custom of releasing a prisoner at the feast time is referred to only in the Gospels (see notes on Matt. 27: 11-26). **Barabbas** is described more fully by Mark, perhaps because this Gospel was written in Rome, where the legal aspects involved would be of particular interest. Here it is stated that Barabbas was **bound with them that had made insurrection, men who in the insurrection had committed murder** (v. 7). Luke (23:19) also mentions the insurrection and the murder. Gould points out the significance

---

[79] *Ant.* XVIII. 3. I; *War* ii. 9. 2-4.

of this, when he writes: "He was just what the Jews accused Jesus of being, a man who had raised a revolt against the Roman power."[80]

When the crowd began to demand the release of a prisoner, Pilate seized at the opportunity to get rid of his difficulty. He was convinced of Jesus' innocence, yet the chief priests were demanding that He be put to death. Here perhaps was a way out of the dilemma.

So the governor asked, **Will ye that I release unto you the King of the Jews?** An affirmative answer would have been an easy solution to the problem. Jesus was obviously innocent. Barabbas was just as clearly guilty. Why not release the good man, and execute the criminal?

The sad truth is that Pilate cared more about the attitude of the crowd than the character of Christ. He was more concerned with his own political fortunes than he was with seeing that this prisoner received justice. He was actuated by selfish motives. As often happens in such cases, his personal welfare finally suffered loss, for he was banished from his position.

It was not difficult for Pilate to see that it was **for envy** (NEB — "out of spite") that the **chief priests** had delivered up Jesus to him. They were still smarting under the blow He had inflicted on them when He cleansed the Temple. For that He would never be forgiven. They must get rid of Him.

So they **stirred up the multitude** (v. 11). Kagawa gives a graphic portrayal of what might well have taken place. He pictures the servants of Annas moving through the crowd, handing out coins, and whispering to the people to demand Jesus' death.[81] The Greek verb translated **stirred up** comes from *seismos,* "an earthquake." The chief priest caused earthquake disturbances in the crowd, until Pilate felt helpless to cope with the situation. Again he asked, probably sarcastically, what he should do with the one **whom ye call the King of the Jews.** If only the populace would accept their King, as they had done the previous Sunday in the Triumphal Entry, the governor would be freed from further responsibility in the case.

But Pilate's hopes were dashed to the ground, as the crowd yelled, "Crucify him!" Again the governor pleaded: "**Why, what evil hath he done? (v. 14).** This question, given in all three Synoptic Gospels, shows the weak, vacillating character of the governor.

Once more the governor was frustrated. The clamor was becoming an uproar, as thousands shouted, **crucify him.** Finally Pilate literally "caved in" under the pressure of the crowd. **Wishing to content** (better, "satisfy") the multitude, he **released unto them Barabbas.** The Jewish rulers preferred having a murderer loose in their midst than having Jesus going about healing the sick, raising the dead, and preaching good tidings to the poor. This is another dramatic example of the awful insanity of sin. Peter pointed up the contrast when he said later to this same crowd: "Whom ye delivered up, and denied before the face of Pilate when he had determined to release him. But ye denied the Holy and Righteous One, and asked for a murderer to be granted unto you, and killed the Prince of life" (Acts 3:13-15). Every sinner is hugging a murderer to his bosom and rejecting the Source of eternal life. This is the folly of sin.

Before sending Jesus to the place of execution, Pilate had Him **scourged.** This was a gesture of utter cruelty. It has been suggested that this was a legal requirement before crucifixion, but the matter is not certain. Others think that the governor may have been appealing to the sympathies of the people, hoping that they might yet ask for Jesus' release. In any case it was a horrible act (see notes on Matt. 27:36).

c. Persecution in Praetorium (15:16-21)

16 And the soldiers led him away within the court, which is the Praetorium; and they call together the whole band. 17 And they clothe him with purple, and platting a crown of thorns, they put it on him; 18 and they began to salute him, Hail, King of the Jews! 19 And they smote his head with a reed, and spat upon him, and bowing their knees worshipped him. 20 And when they had mocked him, they took off from him the purple, and put on him his garments. And they lead him out to crucify him.

---

[80] *Op. cit.,* p. 285.   [81] Toyohiko Kagawa, *Behold the Man,* p. 302.

21 And they compel one passing by, Simon of Cyrene, coming from the country, the father of Alexander and Rufus, to go *with them*, that he might bear his cross.

Luke, who alone tells that Pilate sent Jesus to Herod and that the latter's soldiers mocked the Galilean prophet (Luke 23:4-12), omits the account here of the mockery of the governor's soldiers. But Matthew again closely parallels Mark at this point (see notes on Matt. 27: 27-23).

It would seem that the scourging was done outside before the crowd, for it is stated that the soldiers led Jesus within the court. In the King James Version the Greek word is translated "palace" in 14:54, 66 and "hall" here. But it means "courtyard," and should be so rendered in every case. J. H. Moulton and George Milligan affirm: "So far as we have observed, there is nothing in the *Koine* to support the contention that in the N.T. *aule* ever means the house itself."[82]

For the location of the **Praetorium**, as well as the meaning of **band**, see the notes on Matthew 27:27. Instead of **purple** (v. 17), Matthew has "a scarlet robe." The two words are used together to describe the clothing of the Scarlet Woman in Revelation 17:4, and they also occur in conjunction in a Tebtunis papyrus of the third century.[83] Apparently they refer to the same thing. Souter holds that the Greek word for **purple** signifies here "a red-coloured cloak" worn by a common soldier.[84]

Then they braided a **crown** of thorns. The Greek word was used for the laurel wreath that the emperor wore in token of a military victory. **Spat** (v. 19) is the imperfect tense — "were spitting" repeatedly. The Greek word suggests the very sound of spitting. Mark adds: **and bowing their knees worshipped him.** This was the crowning act of insult.

Simon of Cyrene is further identified in Mark (alone) as the father of **Alexander and Rufus.** Some scholars feel that the latter is the same Rufus who is mentioned in Romans 16:13. If so, these two men were probably two well-known members of the church at Rome. It was natural that Mark, writing in Rome, should call attention to this interesting family connection. Since there was a large Jewish colony at Cyrene, in North Africa, it is likely that Simon (the most common Jewish name of that day)[85] was a Jew (not a Negro) who had come to Jerusalem for the Passover. **Coming from the country** suggests that Simon was just coming in through a northern gate of the city as the soldiers were leading Jesus out.

4. Execution and Entombment (15:22-47)

a. Railing and Robbers (15:22-32)

22 And they bring him unto the place Golgotha, which is, being interpreted, The place of a skull. 23 And they offered him wine mingled with myrrh: but he received it not. 24 And they crucify him, and part his garments among them, casting lots upon them, what each should take. 25 And it was the third hour, and they crucified him. 26 And the superscription of his accusation was written over, THE KING OF THE JEWS. 27 And with him they crucify two robbers; one on his right hand, and one on his left. 29 And they that passed by railed on him, wagging their heads, and saying, Ha! thou that destroyest the temple, and buildest it in three days, 30 save thyself, and come down from the cross. 31 In like manner also the chief priests mocking *him* among themselves with the scribes said, He saved others; himself he cannot save. 32 Let the Christ, the king of Israel, now come down from the cross, that we may see and believe. And they that were crucified with him reproached him.

Once more Matthew and Mark are closely parallel, while Luke (23:33-43) varies the order somewhat (see the notes on Matt. 27:33-44). Apparently just before Jesus was placed on the cross He was offered a drink of sour wine, mixed with myrrh. Matthew calls this concoction "gall," which is here probably used as the equivalent of myrrh.[86] The wine was drugged to deaden the pain of crucifixion. But Jesus refused to take any sedative.

Mark alone says that Christ was cru-

[82] *Vocabulary of the Greek Testament*, p. 92.   [83] *Ibid.*, p. 352.
[84] Alexander Souter, *A Pocket Lexicon to the Greek New Testament*, p. 211.
[85] Joseph A. Fitzmeyer, "The Name Simon," *Harvard Theological Review*, LVI (Jan., 1963), 4.
[86] Abbott-Smith, *op. cit.*, p. 482.

cified at **the third hour** (v. 25). According to the Jewish reckoning this would be nine o'clock in the morning. This seems to clash with the statement, in John 19:14, that Pilate sat down on the judgment seat "about the sixth hour." But by Roman computation this would be six o'clock in the morning. So there is no contradiction here, except for those who deny that John followed the Roman method of reckoning the day as beginning at midnight. There is no denying a problem here, but the above solution seems reasonable.

It was customary to put a title over the cross, indicating the crime for which the victim was being executed. But the only sin of which Jesus was guilty was that of being THE KING OF THE JEWS. Barabbas, the murderer, belonged on the middle cross between the **two robbers.**

It is of interest to note that there are five historic presents in verses 21 through 27 — compel (v. 21), **bring** (v. 22), **crucify** and **part** (v. 24), **crucify** (v. 27). This feature — probably an echo of Peter's frequent use of the present tense in recounting these incidents — adds vividness to the narrative. Though frowned upon by many rhetoricians, then and now, it is sometimes forceful.

Verse 28 (KJV) is not in the oldest Greek manuscripts, and so is rightly omitted in the Revised Versions. It was probably copied by some scribe from Luke 22:37.

The scene of mockery (vv. 29-32) calls to mind the language of Isaiah 53 and Psalm 22 (especially verses 7 and 8). It must have been particularly painful to Jesus to be jeered by the rulers of His own nation. One could find some partial excuse for the hardened Roman soldiers. But who can condone the attitudes and actions of these religious leaders?

b. Darkness and Death (15:33-41)

33 And when the sixth hour was come, there was darkness over the whole land until the ninth hour. 34 And at the ninth hour Jesus cried with a loud voice, Eloi, Eloi, lama sabachthani? which is, being interpreted, My God, my God, why hast thou forsaken me? 35 And some of them

that stood by, when they heard it, said, Behold, he calleth Elijah. 36 And one ran, and filling a sponge full of vinegar, put it on a reed, and gave him to drink, saying, Let be; let us see whether Elijah cometh to take him down. 37 And Jesus uttered a loud voice, and gave up the ghost. 38 And the veil of the temple was rent in two from the top to the bottom. 39 And when the centurion, who stood by over against him, saw that he so gave up the ghost, he said, Truly this man was the Son of God. 40 And there were also women beholding from afar: among whom *were* both Mary Magdalene, and Mary the mother of James the less and of Joses, and Salome; 41 who, when he was in Galilee, followed him, and ministered unto him; and many other women that came up with him unto Jerusalem.

Again Matthew follows Mark very closely (see notes on Matt. 27:45-56). All three Synoptics mention the darkness over the land from noon until three o'clock in the afternoon (cf. Luke 23:44). Mark and Matthew give the so-called "cry of dereliction" (v. 34). The form **Eloi** is Aramaic, "Eli" (Matt. 27:46) Hebrew. Both mean **My God.** The cry is quoted from Psalm 22:1. Lenski has stated well its significance: "All that we can say is that only thus, by Jesus' being actually forsaken, could the full price of our redemption be paid."[87]

Adam Clarke seems to miss the point when he interprets the cry as meaning, "To what sort of persons hast thou left me?"[88] John Wesley, however, speaks of Jesus "lamenting His Father's withdrawing the tokens of His love, and treating Him as an enemy, while He bare our sins."[89] That seems to be the true sense. It was necessary that Jesus experience the awful separation from God's presence which is the penalty for sin. That does not mean that His divine nature left Him. But in His human consciousness He felt utterly lost. James Morison, another Wesleyan writer, has expressed it thus: "He had been *forsaken* or *left* by the Father; not, of course, physically or metaphysically, but politically, or governmentally."[90]

Behold, he calleth Elijah (v. 35) was probably said in cruel mockery. Many

[87] *Op. cit.,* p. 718.   [88] *The New Testament of Our Lord and Saviour Jesus Christ,* I, 277.
[89] *Op. cit.,* p. 192.   [90] *Op. cit.,* p. 435.

of the bystanders doubtless considered Jesus to be a deluded fanatic. However, one person, apparently moved by pity, offered the Sufferer some sour wine to assuage His thirst.

Saying (v. 36) is singular in the Greek. This raises a bit of a problem, since Matthew reads: "The rest said" — followed by essentially the same quotation. The simplest solution would be that the bystanders said to the one who was filling the sponge, "Let him alone"; that is, do not give Him a drink (Matt.). But the man replied to his objectors, "Let me alone" (Mark), and went right ahead with his act of mercy. Gould offers a good explanatory paraphrase for the last part of the verse: "Let me give him this, and so prolong his life, and then we shall get an opportunity to see whether Elijah comes to help him or not."[91]

Gave up the ghost was an unfortunate translation when the King James Version was made (1611) and is inexcusable in the American Standard Version (1901). The Greek says very simply and clearly, "expired." The verb literally means, "breathe out." That is, He stopped breathing. Matthew (27:50) emphasizes the voluntariness of His death — "yielded up his spirit."

For a careful discussion of the phrase **the Son of God** (v. 39) see the notes on Matthew 27:54. It might be added that every reference to a Roman **centurion** — Mark alone uses the Latin term, writing in Rome — in the New Testament shows him in a good light (e.g., Acts 10:1-2; 27:43; Matt. 8:5-13). As a class they seem to have been men of high character and ability. They show up better than the governors above them or the common soldiers beneath them.

After naming apparently the same three women (v. 40) as in Matthew (27: 56), Mark adds: **and many other women that came up with him unto Jerusalem.** These were Jesus' most devoted, loyal followers. They doubtless took good care of His material needs, besides listening lovingly to His teaching. In the face of opposition from enemies, and dull misunderstanding from friends, they must have been a great comfort to Him.

It should be noted that women were the last at the cross and the first at the

91 *Op. cit.*, p. 295.

tomb. Their devotion often puts men to shame.

c. Kindness and Courtesy (15:42-47)

42 And when even was now come, because it was the Preparation, that is the day before the sabbath, 43 there came Joseph of Arimathaea, a councillor of honorable estate, who also himself was looking for the kingdom of God; and he boldly went in unto Pilate, and asked for the body of Jesus. 44 And Pilate marvelled if he were already dead: and calling unto him the centurion, he asked him whether he had been any while dead. 45 And when he learned it of the centurion, he granted the corpse to Joseph. 46 And he bought a linen cloth, and taking him down, wound him in the linen cloth, and laid him in a tomb which had been hewn out of a rock; and he rolled a stone against the door of the tomb. 47 And Mary Magdalene and Mary the *mother* of Joses beheld where he was laid.

Even here evidently means late afternoon, what is sometimes called "the first evening" (3:00 P.M. to sunset). The second evening would be about 6:00-9:00 P.M.

Preparation means Friday, as indicated here. The Jewish **sabbath** was from sunset Friday evening to sunset Saturday evening. The Greek word for preparation is still used for Friday in the Greek Orthodox Church.

Joseph of Arimathea (a town between Jerusalem and the coast) is identified by Mark as **a councillor of honorable estate;** that is, a wealthy member of the Sanhedrin.

Mark adds to Matthew's account (see notes on Matt. 27:57-61) the statement that Pilate was surprised to hear that Jesus had died so quickly, and sent a centurion to check the report (vv. 44, 45). Ordinarily crucified criminals hung for days on the cross before they finally expired.

C. RESURRECTION AND REAPPEARANCE (16:1-20)

1. Resurrection (16:1-8)

1 And when the sabbath was past, Mary Magdalene, and Mary the *mother* of James, and Salome, bought spices, that they might come and anoint him. 2 And

very early on the first day of the week, they come to the tomb when the sun was risen. 3 And they were saying among themselves, Who shall roll us away the stone from the door of the tomb? 4 and looking up, they see that the stone is rolled back: for it was exceeding great. 5 And entering into the tomb, they saw a young man sitting on the right side, arrayed in a white robe; and they were amazed. 6 And he saith unto them, Be not amazed: ye seek Jesus, the Nazarene, who hath been crucified: he is risen; he is not here: behold, the place where they laid him! 7 But go, tell his disciples and Peter, He goeth before you into Galilee: there shall ye see him, as he said unto you. 8 And they went out, and fled from the tomb; for trembling and astonishment had come upon them: and they said nothing to any one; for they were afraid.

The three women of verse one are the same as those in 15:40. Mark says that **when the Sabbath was past** — that is, after sunset Saturday evening — they bought spices. Luke (23:56) declares that the women "prepared spices and ointments" on Friday evening, before the sabbath began at sunset. The probability is that they began their purchases on Friday, but had to stop at sunset, and finished getting the fragrant perfume (Greek, *aroma*) on Saturday night.

Mark states that the women came to the tomb at sunrise. Probably they left Bethany, two miles away, while it was still dark, but arrived as the sun was rising.

As the women approached the sepulcher they were wondering who would roll back the heavy stone that blocked the entrance. But soon they discovered that the stone had already been rolled away from the door of the tomb. It was **exceeding great;** that is, very heavy.

The details differ in the three Synoptic accounts, but the essential features are the same. Mark says that a **young man** was sitting inside the tomb (v. 5). Matthew (28:5) identifies him as an "angel." Luke says the women found "two men." Obviously there is no contradiction here. Swete makes the sage comment: "The very diversity of the accounts strengthens the probability that the story rests upon a basis of truth; the impres-

sions of the witnesses differed, but they were agreed upon the main facts."[92]

Mark makes a significant addition in verse 7 — **and Peter.** This was probably an intimation that his three denials had been forgiven. He needed special comfort and encouragement at this time.

With **trembling and astonishment the women** fled from the empty sepulcher. The statement that **they said nothing to any one** does not contradict Matthew's affirmation that they "ran to bring his disciples word." It simply means that they talked with no one on the way.

2. Reappearances (16:9-20)

a. To Mary Magdalene (16:9-11)

9 Now when he was risen early on the first day of the week, he appeared first to Mary Magdalene, from whom he had cast out seven demons. 10 She went and told them that had been with him, as they mourned and wept. 11 And they, when they heard that he was alive, and had been seen of her, disbelieved.

In the two oldest Greek manuscripts of the New Testament the Gospel of Mark ends with verse 8. A few manuscripts have another (shorter, and very different) ending. The question of the genuineness of these last twelve verses has not been finally and fully settled, but their authenticity is definitely open to question. They give a brief summary of several post-resurrection appearances of Jesus. That to Mary Magdalene (v. 9) is described very dramatically in John 20:1-18.

b. To Two Disciples (16:12-13)

12 And after these things he was manifested in another form unto two of them, as they walked, on their way into the country. 13 And they went away and told it unto the rest; neither believed they them.

The appearance of Christ to two men (v. 12) as they were walking out into the country (to Emmaus) is narrated beautifully in Luke 24:13-35.

c. To the Eleven (16:14-18)

14 And afterward he was manifested unto the eleven themselves as they sat at meat; and he upbraided them with

92 *Op. cit.*, p. 374.

their unbelief and hardness of heart, because they believed not them that had seen him after he was risen. 15 And he said unto them, Go ye into all the world, and preach the gospel to the whole creation. 16 He that believeth and is baptized shall be saved; but he that disbelieveth shall be condemned. 17 And these signs shall accompany them that believe: in my name shall they cast out demons; they shall speak with new tongues; 18 they shall take up serpents, and if they drink any deadly thing, it shall in no wise hurt them; they shall lay hands on the sick, and they shall recover.

The visit with the eleven (Judas Iscariot having taken his own life) as they were eating (v. 14) is probably the same as that described in Luke 24:36-43 and John 20:19-25. John's statement that Thomas was not with the other disciples on that first Sunday night (the day of the Resurrection) is not contradicted by the use of the eleven in Mark. The latter employs the expression as a general designation for the group after Judas Iscariot's default.

The Great Commission is given more briefly in Mark (v. 15) than in Matthew (28:19-20), but the main thrust is the same. There is a strong emphasis on baptism (v. 16), but it does not say that those who are not baptized will be lost.

The passage on the signs (vv. 17-18) is strikingly different from what is found in this section of the other Gospels. Five signs are specified: (1) casting out demons in His name; (2) speaking with tongues; (3) taking up serpents; (4) drinking deadly poison without being harmed; (5) laying hands on the sick and healing them. The disciples had already cast out demons (Luke 10:17). At Pentecost they spoke in tongues (Acts 2:4). Paul accidentally took up a deadly serpent, but was not hurt (Acts 28:3-6). James 5:14-15 indicates that healing was practiced in the early church.

3. Reinstatement (16:19-20)

19 So then the Lord Jesus, after he had spoken unto them, was received up into heaven, and sat down at the right hand of God. 20 And they went forth, and preached everywhere, The Lord working with them, and confirming the word by the signs that followed. Amen.

Christ, who had come to earth to be the Savior of mankind, was now reinstated in His eternal glory. The Ascension, mentioned briefly here, is described more fully in Luke 24:50-53 and Acts 1:9-12. The glorified Jesus sat down at the right hand of God as the rightful Heir of the Kingdom. In obedience to their Master's command the disciples went forth to preach in the power of the Spirit. The story of their mission is told in the Book of Acts.

Bibliography

Commentaries

Alexander, J. A. *Commentary on the Gospel of Mark.* Grand Rapids: Zondervan Publishing House, n.d.

Alford, Henry. *The Greek Testament.* Revised by Everett F. Harrison. Vol. I. Chicago: Moody Press, 1958.

Allen, W. C. *The Gospel According to St. Mark.* "Oxford Church Biblical Commentary." New York: Macmillan Co., 1915.

Bickersteth, E. *St. Mark* (Exposition). "The Pulpit Commentary." Edited by H. D. M. Spence and Joseph S. Excell. Vol. II. Grand Rapids: Wm. B. Eerdmans Publishing Co., 1950.

Branscomb, Harvie. *The Gospel of Mark.* "The Moffatt New Testament Commentary." New York: Harper & Brothers, 1937.

Clarke, Adam. *The New Testament of Our Lord and Savior Jesus Christ.* Vol. I. New York: Methodist Book Concern, n. d.

Cranfield, C. E. B. *The Gospel According to Saint Mark.* "Cambridge Greek Testament Commentary." Cambridge: University Press, 1959.

Earle, Ralph. *The Gospel According to Mark.* "The Evangelical Bible Commentary." Grand Rapids: Zondervan Publishing House, 1957.

Gould, Ezra P. *A Critical and Exegetical Commentary on the Gospel According to St. Mark.* "The International Critical Commentary." New York: Charles Scribner's Sons, 1896.

Grant, F. C. *The Gospel According to St. Mark* (Exegesis). "The Interpreter's Bible." Edited by George A. Buttrick *et al.* Vol. VII. New York: Abingdon-Cokesbury Press, 1951.

Hort, A. F. *Gospel According to St. Mark.* The Greek text edited with introduction and notes. Cambridge: University Press, 1902.

Hunter, A. M. *The Gospel According to St. Mark.* "Torch Bible Commentaries." Edited by John Marsh *et al.* London: SCM Press, 1948.

Johnson, Sherman. *A Commentary on the Gospel According to St. Mark.* "Harpers New Testament Commentaries." New York: Harper & Brothers, 1960.

Lenski, R. C. H. *The Interpretation of St. Mark's Gospel.* Columbus, Ohio: Wartburg Press, 1951.

Maclaren, Alexander. *Expositions of Holy Scripture.* Grand Rapids: Wm B. Eerdmans Publishing Co., 1944.

Maclear, G. F. *Gospel According to St. Mark.* "Cambridge Greek Testament." Cambridge: University Press, n.d.

Manson, T. W. "The Gospel According to St. Mark." *The Mission and Message of Jesus,* by H. D. A. Major, T. W. Manson, and C. J. Wright. New York: E. P. Dutton & Co., 1938.

Montefiore, C. G. *The Synoptic Gospels.* Vol. I. London: Macmillan & Co., 1909.

Morison, James. *A Practical Commentary on the Gospel According to St. Mark.* 6th ed. London: Hodder and Stoughton, 1889.

Plummer, Alfred. *The Gospel According to St. Mark.* "Cambridge Greek Testament." New series. Cambridge: University Press, 1914.

Rawlinson, A. E. J. *St. Mark.* "Westminster Commentaries." London: Methuen & Co., 1925.

Redlich, Basil. *St. Mark's Gospel.* London: Gerald Duckworth & Co., 1948.

Ryle, J. C. *Expository Thoughts on the Gospels: Mark.* Grand Rapids: Zondervan Publishing House, n.d.

Stamm, Raymond T. *The Gospel According to Mark.* "New Testament Commentary." Edited by Herbert C. Alleman. Rev. ed. Philadelphia: Muhlenberg Press, 1944.

Swete, H. B. *The Gospel According to St. Mark.* London: Macmillan & Co., 1898.

Swift, C. E. G. "The Gospel According to Mark." *The New Bible Commentary.* Edited by F. Davidson. 2nd ed. Grand Rapids: Wm. B. Eerdmans Publishing Co., 1954.

Taylor, Vincent. *The Gospel According to St. Mark.* London: Macmillan & Co., 1952.

Wesley, John. *Explanatory Notes Upon the New Testament.* London: Epworth Press, 1941 (reprint).

Williams, George. *The Student's Commentary on the Holy Scriptures.* Grand Rapids: Kregel Publications, 1949.

Other Works Cited

Abbott-Smith, G. *A Manual Greek Lexicon of the New Testament.* Edinburgh: T. & T. Clark, 1937.

Andrews, Samuel. *The Life of Our Lord.* Grand Rapids: Zondervan Publishing House, 1954 (reprint).

Arndt, W. F. and Gingrich, F. W. *A Greek-English Lexicon of the New Testament and Other Early Christian Literature.* Chicago: The University of Chicago Press, 1957.

Atkinson, Basil F. C. *The Gospel According to Matthew.* "The New Bible Commentary." Edited by F. Davidson. 2nd ed. Grand Rapids: Wm. B. Eerdmans Publishing Co., 1954.

Carter, Charles W. and Earle, Ralph. *The Acts of the Apostles.* Grand Rapids: Zondervan Publishing House, 1959.

Dalman, Gustaf. *Sacred Sites and Ways.* Translated by Paul P. Levertoff. London: Society for Promoting Christian Knowledge, 1935.

————. *The Words of Jesus.* Translated by D. M. Kay. Edinburgh: T. & T. Clark, 1909.

Deissmann, Adolf. *Light from the Ancient East.* Translated by L.R.M. Strachan. New York: George H. Doran Co., n.d.

Edersheim, Alfred. *The Life and Times of Jesus the Messiah.* 2 vols. New York: Longmans, Green, and Co., 1896.

Finegan, Jack. *Light from the Ancient Past.* Princeton: University Press, 1946.

Harnack, Adolph. *The Date of the Acts and the Synoptic Gospels.* Translated by J. A. Wilkinson. London: Williams & Norgate, 1911.

Hayes, D. A. *The Synoptic Gospels and the Book of Acts.* New York: Methodist Book Concern, 1919.

Jeremias, Joachim. *The Eucharistic Words of Jesus.* Translated by Arnold Ehrhardt. New York: Macmillan Co., 1955.

Kagawa, Toyohiko. *Behold the Man.* New York: Harper & Brothers, 1941.

Moulton, J. H. and Milligan, George. *Vocabulary of the Greek Testament.* Grand Rapids: Wm. B. Eerdmans Publishing Co., 1949.

Souter, Alexander. *A Pocket Lexicon to the Greek New Testament.* Oxford: Clarendon Press, 1916.

Trench, R. C. *Notes on the Miracles of Our Lord.* Philadelphia: Wm. Sychelmoore, n.d.

————. *Notes on the Parables of Our Lord.* Philadelphia: Wm. Sychelmoore, 1878.

Articles

Fitzmeyer, Joseph A. "The Name Simon," *Harvard Theological Review,* LVI (January, 1963).

Freedman, David Noel. "When Did Christ Die?" *Perspective,* III (1962).

Ladd, George E. "The Kingdom of God — Reign or Realm?" *Journal of Biblical Literature,* LXXXI (1962).

Shepherd, Massey H. "Are Both the Synoptics and John Correct About the Date of Jesus' Death?" *Journal of Biblical Literature,* LXXX (1961).

Trevor, J. C. "Fig Tree, Fig." *The Interpreter's Dictionary of the Bible.* Edited by George A. Buttrick *et al.* Vol. II. New York: Abingdon Press, 1962.

The Gospel According to St. Luke
by Ralph Earle

Outline
The Master and His Message

Introduction

I. AUTHORSHIP

A. EXTERNAL EVIDENCE

Papias, the earliest extant witness to Matthew and Mark, is silent about Luke. So our earliest evidence comes from Justin Martyr (ca. A.D. 150). Plummer writes: "That Justin Martyr used the Third Gospel (or an authority which was practically identical with it) cannot be doubted."[1] He also says: "That his pupil Tatian possessed this Gospel is proved by the Diatessaron."[2] In this same period (middle of the second century) Marcion adopted Luke as the only Gospel, editing out the passages with which he disagreed.

When we come to the latter part of the second century the evidence is very full and definite. "Irenaeus, who represents the traditions of Asia Minor and Rome and Gaul in the second half of the second century, quotes it many times and quotes from nearly every chapter."[3] Irenaeus wrote: "And Luke the companion of Paul, committed to writing the gospel preached by him, i.e., Paul."[4] This suggests a strong Pauline influence on Luke which is borne out in a study of the Gospel, as the commentary will show. While the connection between Paul and the Gospel of Luke may not be as close as that between Peter and the Gospel of Mark, yet it is definitely noticeable.

Clement of Alexandria "quotes the Gospel very frequently" and "definitely assigns it to Luke."[5] Tertullian, speaking for the church of North Africa, "not only quotes the Gospel frequently in his other works, but in his treatise against Marcion he works through the Gospel from chapter 4 to the end, often calling it Luke's."[6] The Muratorian Fragment assigns it to Luke. Wikenhauser correctly states: "From the second half of the second century at latest the unanimous tradition of the early Church attributes the third Gospel to Luke the physician who accompanied St. Paul on his journeys."[7]

The foremost Biblical scholar of the early church was Origen. Writing near the beginning of the third century, he says: "And the third, according to Luke, the gospel commended by Paul, which was written for the converts from the Gentiles."[8] So Origen corroborates the earlier tradition that Luke's Gospel was influenced by Paul and adds the statement that it was written for Gentile converts. The contents of the Gospel support both these ideas.

The external evidence for the Lukan authorship of the Third Gospel is early and strong. It is particularly significant that the name of such an obscure character should be attached to this the longest book in the New Testament. Yet that is the unanimous witness of the early church.

B. INTERNAL EVIDENCE

Luke is mentioned by name only three times in the New Testament. In Philemon 24 Paul lists him among "my fellow-workers." In Colossians 4:14 he calls him "the beloved physician," and in II Tim. 4:11 he writes: "Only Luke is with me." These references tell us that Luke was a physician and that he was a companion of Paul.

That the Gospel of Luke and the Book of Acts were written by the same author is so abundantly evident that very few scholars have ever questioned the fact. The close similarity of style and vocabulary is overwhelmingly convincing to any open mind. Both books are addressed to Theophilus, mentioned nowhere else in the New Testament. It is generally recognized that any arguments for the authorship of Acts may be taken as evidence also for the authorship of the Third Gospel.

---

[1] Alfred Plummer, *A Critical and Exegetical Commentary on the Gospel According to St. Luke*, p. xv. [2] *Ibid.* [3] *Ibid.*, p. xvi.
[4] Eusebius Pamphilus, *Ecclesiastical History*, trans. C. F. Cruse, p. 188 (V. 8).
[5] Plummer, *op. cit.*, p. xvi. [6] *Ibid.*
[7] Alfred Wikenhauser, *New Testament Introduction*, trans. Joseph Cunningham, p. 206.
[8] Eusebius, *op cit.*, pp. 245, 246 (VI. 25).

Granted this premise, the "we-passages" in Acts take on great importance. These so-called "we-sections" are Acts 16:10-18; 20:5-21:17; 27:1-28:16. They indicate that the author of Acts joined the Pauline party on the second missionary journey at Troas, accompanied Paul to Philippi, and apparently stayed there for several years (perhaps as pastor of the new church). When Paul arrived at Philippi on his third journey, the author rejoined the party, and continued with it until the arrival at Jerusalem. There the "we" is dropped. What was the writer doing during the two years that Paul was a prisoner at Caesarea? The most logical answer is that he was gathering materials for his Gospel. Especially important would be his interview with Mary, the aged mother of Jesus. This seems to be the most logical source for his infancy narratives in the first two chapters of the Gospels. When Paul left Caesarea for Rome, the "we" is resumed, showing that the author was with him on that fateful voyage. He evidently stayed rather close to the apostle for the rest of his days.

The suggestion has been made that the "we-passages" may be excerpts from someone else's diary which the author has incorporated in Acts. But Major makes this observation: ". . . a very precise examination of the style and language of these 'We' sections proves, it may be said almost beyond doubt, that the author of the 'We' sections is also the author of the Third Gospel and the Acts."[9]

The capstone of the argument is this. Of the men mentioned prominently by Paul in his Epistles as companions of his, only two are not named in Acts — Luke and Titus. Of these two, "Titus is excluded because he was at the Apostolic Council with Paul (Gal. 2:13), and Acts 15 is not a 'We passage.' "[10] That leaves only Luke as the logical candidate for author. The early church unites with one voice in declaring that he was.

There is a subsidiary argument which might be mentioned. In 1882 Hobart published a book in which he assembled an immense amount of material from the Greek medical writers to show that the author of Luke and Acts was a physician.[11] Unfortunately, he overstated the case. Many of the so-called technical medical terms which he cited have been shown by Professor Cadbury to have been commonly used by non-medical writers of that period.[12] It is rather commonly assumed today that Cadbury has completely exploded Hobart's theory, though it was accepted as basically valid by Harnack, Plummer, Ramsay, and Zahn. For instance, the last of these scholars says: "W. K. Hobart has proved to the satisfaction of anyone open to conviction, that the author of the Lucan work was familiar with the technical language of Greek medicine, and hence was a *Greek physician.*"[13]

It is time that the pendulum swung back to a sensible center, a mediating view between that of Hobart and Cadbury. Such is the position of a number of recent scholars. For instance, Wikenhauser says: "So we cannot regard the linguistic argument by itself as proof that only a physician could have composed the two books. Nevertheless the tradition . . . may still be sustained, for the author displays familiarity with medical terminology."[14] Major concurs. He writes: "Nevertheless, there are passages in the Lukan writings, which although they cannot be said to prove, yet do support the hypothesis, that the author was a physician."[15] Even Creed says of Cadbury's work: "But he has not demolished the relevance of *some* of the evidence which has been collected, and in a few cases he has unduly depreciated the force of the medical parallels."[16] In other words, there is a residuum of evidence that the author of this Gospel shows a medical interest. Some examples will be pointed out in the course of the commentary.

II. DATE

The traditional date for Luke's Gospel is in the early 60's. The argument for

[9] H. D. A. Major, "Incidents in the Life of Jesus," *The Mission and Message of Jesus*, by H. D. A. Major, T. W. Manson, and C. J. Wright, pp. 251, 252.
[10] Wikenhauser, *op. cit.*, p. 208.
[11] William K. Hobart, *The Medical Language of St. Luke, passim*.
[12] Henry J. Cadbury, *The Making of Luke-Acts*, pp. 118-120.
[13] Theodor Zahn, *Introduction to the New Testament*, trans. J. M. Trout, *et al.*, p. 146.
[14] *Op. cit.*, p. 209. [15] *Op. cit.*, p. 253.
[16] J. M. Creed, *The Gospel According to St. Luke*, p. xix.

this dating is that, since Acts ends with Paul's two-year imprisonment in Rome (A.D. 59-61), that book must have been written soon after. But clearly the Gospel of Luke was written before Acts (cf. Acts 1:1). Therefore, Luke must have been written soon after A.D. 60.

Today most scholars prefer a later date. For instance, Wikenhauser, a Catholic scholar, says: "So probably the Gospel of St. Luke was not written until after 70 A.D. However, there is no reason for placing it later than about 80 A.D."[17] Zahn, a conservative Protestant, writes: "It may be assumed with practical certainly that Luke wrote his work about year 75."[18] Plummer suggests: "The intermediate date of A.D. 75-80 has very much more to recommend it."[19] And Taylor concludes: ". . . on the whole there is most to be said for the period A.D. 80-5."[20] Streeter favors "about A.D. 80."[21]

Many, if not most, conservative Protestants will nevertheless prefer to hold to a date soon after A.D. 60.

III. PLACE OF WRITING

There is some tradition from the early church that Luke wrote his Gospel in Achaia (Greece). While nothing can be known certainly, this is as good a guess as any.

IV. CHARACTER

Of the three Synoptic Gospels, Luke's is the most unique. It has been called "The most beautiful book ever written." We can do no more than list briefly some of its main characteristics. It is the Gospel of:

(1) *The Poor.* Often Luke speaks out against riches, as in the Parable of the Rich Fool and in the story of the Rich Man and Lazarus.

(2) *The Sinner.* There is a great deal of emphasis in this Gospel on lostness (cf. 19:10, the key verse of the book). In chapter 15 there are the three parables of the Lost Sheep, the Lost Coin, and the Lost Son. The conversion of Zac-

chaeus, the despised tax collector, is related only here.

(3) *The Samaritan.* Only Luke gives the Parable of the Good Samaritan and the story of the Samaritan leper who returned to thank Jesus.

(4) *Women.* There is first Anna, the prophetess, in the Temple. Then we find the widow of Nain, the many women who followed Jesus from Galilee, Mary and Martha, the woman who lost her coin, and the parable of the importunate widow and the unjust judge.

(5) *Children.* Especially is this shown in the fact that Luke alone tells us anything about the childhood of Jesus.

(6) *Prayer.* This is shown in two ways. In the first place, Luke tells about Jesus praying in six instances where the other Gospels do not. These instances will be found in the course of the commentary. In the second place, Luke gives us more than do Matthew and Mark of the teaching of Jesus on prayer. Here alone do we find the parables of the Importunate Friend at Midnight, the Pharisee and the Publican, and the Importunate Widow. Thus Jesus taught prayer by example and precept.

(7) *Joy.* This shows up strongly in the great hymns of praise in the first two chapters of the Gospel. Hayes writes: "This Gospel begins with songs and ends with songs, and there is singing and rejoicing all the way along."[22]

(8) *The Holy Spirit.* This is not only the keynote of the Book of Acts. It shows up much more prominently in Luke's Gospel than in the other two Synoptics.

(9) *The Home.* It is in this Gospel alone that we have a fascinating little glimpse of the domestic life of Mary and Martha, as well as a touch of Jesus' childhood in a home.

Luke shows a greater appreciation of the psychology of human nature than the other Evangelists. He is describing Jesus as the Son of man and the human touch predominates throughout the Gospel.

---

[17] *Op. cit.,* p. 221. [18] *Op. cit.,* III, 159. [19] *Op. cit.,* p. xxxi.
[20] Vincent Taylor, *The Gospels,* p. 73. [21] B. H. Streeter, *The Four Gospels,* p. 529.
[22] D. A. Hayes, *The Synoptic Gospels and the Books of Acts,* p. 262.

The Master and His Message

I. THE COMING OF THE SON OF MAN (1, 2)

A. LUKE'S PREFACE (1:1-4)

1 Forasmuch as many have taken in hand to draw up a narrative concerning those matters which have been fulfilled among us, 2 even as they delivered them unto us, who from the beginning were eyewitnesses and ministers of the word, 3 it seemed good to me also, having traced the course of all things accurately from the first, to write unto thee in order, most excellent Theophilus; 4 that thou mightest know the certainty concerning the things wherein thou wast instructed.

It was the custom of Luke's day to begin a work with a formal literary preface, dedicating the book to the writer's patron, and stating the reasons for writing and the method followed. Josephus, the Jewish historian of the first century, has an impressive Preface to his *Antiquities of the Jews*. The opening words are strikingly similar to those found here at the beginning of Luke's Preface. Josephus says: "Those who undertake to write histories, do not, I perceive, take that trouble on one and the same account, but for many reasons, and those such as are very different one from another."[1]

Luke's Preface is written in the best classical Greek of any part of the New Testament. This implies that he was a highly-educated, well-read scholar. But after the formal Preface he chooses to write in the common literary style of the people.

The very opening word in Greek is striking. Plummer describes it as "a stately compound, suitable for a solemn opening."[2]

Luke indicates that **many** lives of Christ had been written. What happened to them we do not know. Plummer suggests: "Probably all the documents here alluded to were driven out of existence by the manifest superiority of the four Canonical Gospels."[3]

Have been fulfilled is better than "most surely believed" (KJV). While the latter is the correct meaning of the phrase when it is applied to persons (cf. Rom. 4:21), in connection with things it means "fulfilled" or "accomplished." The perfect tense indicates a permanent state resulting from a completed action. "The expression also points to the fact that in Jesus the divine promises of the Old Dispensation have been fulfilled and that a new era has been inaugurated."[4]

Luke seems clearly to indicate that he was not one of the disciples who followed Jesus during the Master's earthly ministry. He says that the facts that had been accomplished were **delivered** — the Greek word suggests the handing down of tradition — by those **who from the beginning were eyewitnesses and ministers of the word** (v. 2). Farrar observes: "The words imply that the attempted Gospels to which St. Luke alludes were *secondhand* — that they were *rearrangements of a tradition* received from the apostles and original disciples."[5]

The author of this Gospel gave careful attention to his preparation for writing. He describes it thus: **having traced the course of all things accurately from the first.** This is preferable to "having had a perfect understanding of all things from the very first" (KJV). The verb means "follow along closely beside." On the basis of this thorough investigation Luke purposes to write **in order.** This does not necessarily indicate chronological order, though it probably implies it. Primarily it means an orderly arrangement of the materials that perhaps others had presented in somewhat disorderly fashion.

[1] Flavius Josephus, *Works*, trans. William Whiston, p. 29.
[2] Alfred Plummer, *A Critical and Exegetical Commentary on the Gospel According to St. Luke*, p. 2.
[3] *Ibid.*   [4] Norval Geldenhuys, *Commentary on the Gospel of Luke*, p. 56.
[5] F. W. Farrar, *The Gospel According to St. Luke*, p. 84.

The statement of the second verse outlines four points in Luke's purpose: (1) He is going back to the beginning — **from the first.** It is significant that this Gospel is the only one that takes the reader back to the announcement and birth of John the Baptist. Also it gives more fully than do the others the narrative of Jesus' birth and the attendant circumstances. Furthermore it is the only one that tells us anything of His childhood. As a historian, Luke was interested in how things began.

(2) He has made a thorough investigation. He has traced the course of **all things.** He has done his spade work as every careful historian must — collecting, evaluating, discarding, retaining, arranging. Now he is ready to write.

(3) He has carried on his research **accurately.** One of the great contributions that Sir William Ramsay made was to show that Luke never makes a mistake in his references to the secular governments and rulers connected with his narrative. He could not have worked his way through the complicated, changing picture of Palestinian politics if he had not done accurate research.

(4) He is determined to give an *orderly account* of what took place. He was evidently dissatisfied with **many** narratives he found. They were either inaccurate, incomplete, or disorderly.

The Preface is addressed to **most excellent Theophilus.** The name means "friend of God." The adjective **most excellent** is used in Acts (23:26; 24:3; 26:25) for governors of Judea. It implies that Theophilus was a high-ranking nobleman. *The Recognitions of Clement* (10:71) say that Theophilus was a citizen of Antioch who had opened his large home for Christian services. This fits in well with the early church tradition that Luke was from Antioch. It is possible that Theophilus was a wealthy patron who paid for the publication of this Gospel. It was the custom in those days to dedicate a literary work to such a patron.

Luke wants Theophilus to **know the certainty** of what he has been taught. This idea of certifying the truth of the Christian gospel — based on the life, death and resurrection of Jesus Christ — is the primary purpose of this Gospel. **Thou wast instructed** is a translation

of the Greek word from which comes "catechize." It refers to oral instructions. Theophilus had been catechized in the Christian faith. Whether this means that he was merely a catechumen, or had become a full church member, is not clear. But he was evidently a convert.

B. THE ANNOUNCEMENT OF JOHN THE BAPTIST'S BIRTH (1:5-25)

1. Zechariah and Elisabeth (1:5-7)

5 There was in the days of Herod, king of Judaea, a certain priest named Zacharias, of the course of Abijah: and he had a wife of the daughters of Aaron, and her name was Elisabeth. 6 And they were both righteous before God, walking in all the commandments and ordinances of the Lord blameless. 7 And they had no child, because that Elisabeth was barren, and they both were *now* well stricken in years.

After the Preface, which precedes the Gospel proper, Luke begins like the good historian he was, with the historical setting. His story begins **in the days of Herod,** king of Judaea. This is Herod the Great who was appointed as King of the Jews by Antony in 40 B.C. at Rome. He landed in Palestine the next year. But two years passed before he put down his opponents and began his actual rule in 37 B.C. He reigned until 4 B.C. Fortunately Josephus, in his *Antiquities of the Jews* (Books 15-17), has given us a full account of the colorful career of Herod the Great, together with his ten wives and fifteen children. The whole story is written up in a fascinating way by Stewart Perowne.[6]

There was **a certain priest named Zacharias.** (It is better to use the Old Testament form, Zechariah). He was of **the course of Abijah,** the eighth of the twenty-four classes into which the priests were divided. Each course served for a week at a time in the Temple at Jerusalem.

This priest had followed the highest custom by marrying one of **the daughters of Aaron,** who thus herself belonged to a priestly family. In fact, she was named after Aaron's wife (Exod. 6:23). Her name was Elisabeth, which means "God is an oath"; that is, the faithful, covenant-keeping God. His name means "Jehovah

[6] *The Life and Times of Herod the Great* (New York: Abingdon Press, 1956).

is strength." They were both righteous before God, walking in all the commandments and ordinances of the Lord blameless (v. 6). This is about as high a compliment as could be paid to saints under the Old Testament regime. On the distinction between commandments and ordinances Farrar says, " 'Commandments' mean the moral precepts . . . . 'Ordinances' had come to be technically used of the *ceremonial* Law."[7]

The devout piety of this couple was difficult to reconcile with the fact that they had no child (v. 7). In Psalm 128: 1-4 it is stated that the man who fears the Lord and walks in His ways will be blessed with children. Then too, a childless woman was robbed of any chance of being the mother of the Messiah. Childlessness was considered a real calamity in any Jewish house. The case of this couple now seemed hopeless, for they were well stricken in years; or, as the Greek says, "advanced in their days."

2. The Announcement to Zechariah (1:8-23)

> 8 Now it came to pass, while he executed the priest's office before God in the order of his course, 9 according to the custom of the priest's office, his lot was to enter into the temple of the Lord and burn incense. 10 And the whole multitude of the people were praying without at the hour of incense. 11 And there appeared unto him an angel of the Lord standing on the right side of the altar of incense. 12 And Zacharias was troubled when he saw *him,* and fear fell upon him. 13 But the angel said unto him, Fear not, Zacharias: because thy supplication is heard, and thy wife Elisabeth shall bear thee a son, and thou shalt call his name John. 14 And thou shalt have joy and gladness; and many shall rejoice at his birth. 15 For he shall be great in the sight of the Lord, and he shall drink no wine nor strong drink; and he shall be filled with the Holy Spirit, even from his mother's womb. 16 And many of the children of Israel shall he turn unto the Lord their God. 17 And he shall go before his face in the spirit and power of Elijah, to turn the hearts of the fathers to the children, and the disobedient *to walk* in the wisdom of the just; to make ready for the Lord a people prepared *for him.* 18

> And Zacharias said unto the angel, Whereby shall I know this? for I am an old man, and my wife well stricken in years. 19 And the angel answering said unto him, I am Gabriel, that stand in the presence of God; and I was sent to speak unto thee, and to bring thee these good tidings. 20 And behold, thou shalt be silent and not able to speak, until the day that these things shall come to pass, because thou believedst not my words, which shall be fulfilled in their season. 21 And the people were waiting for Zacharias, and they marvelled while he tarried in the temple. 22 And when he came out, he could not speak unto them: and they perceived that he had seen a vision in the temple: and he continued making signs unto them, and remained dumb. 23 And it came to pass, when the days of his ministration were fulfilled, he departed unto his house.

One day when Zechariah's course was on duty, the lot fell to him to enter into the temple — *naos,* the Sanctuary, not *hieron,* the Temple Area — and burn incense (v. 9). The Mosiac law commanded that fresh incense should be burned on the altar of incense each morning and evening (Exod. 30:7, 8), "that offered in the morning being *previous* to the offering of the burnt-offering, and that in the evening . . . coming *after* it, so that the daily burnt-offering was, as it were, girt round with the offering of incense."[8]

This was the most momentous day in Zechariah's life. Early that morning lots had been drawn to see which priest would have the privilege of offering incense this particular day. This great honor could come only once in a lifetime, as it is claimed that there were twenty thousand priests at that time. So Zechariah was without question in an exalted frame of mind as he went into the Sanctuary. He was entering the Holy Place, furnished only with the gold-covered table of the Bread of the Presence, the seven-branched lampstand, and the altar of incense right before the inner veil that closed off the Holy of Holies. To a pious priest like Zechariah this would be the most sacred moment he had ever experienced.

Meanwhile, the whole multitude of the people was praying outside (v. 10). "The

---

[7] *Op. cit.,* p. 88.
[8] Emil Schürer, A *History of the Jewish People in the Time of Jesus Christ,* II, I, 289, 290.

number of people in attendance is perhaps an indication that the evening offering is here thought of."[9] It may have been a sabbath or feast day.

The setting was a perfect one for a vision. And it came. Suddenly Zechariah saw **an angel of the Lord standing on the right side of the altar of incense** (v. 11). Luke gives more attention than the other Evangelists to the ministry of angels (cf. 1:26; 2:9, 13:21; 12:8; 15:10; 16:22; 22:43; 24:4,23).

The effect of such supernatural visions was almost invariably that of **fear** (v. 12) as the Old Testament instances show. But the first words of the heavenly visitant were usually, as here, **fear not** (v. 13) — literally, "stop being afraid." Bengel comments: "This is the first address from heaven in the opening dawn of the New Testament which is most charmingly described by Luke."[10]

Zechariah was assured that his prayer had been heard. **Supplication** means "petition" or entreaty. Thayer says that the Greek word "gives prominence to the expression of need."[11] Some think that, while God's presence pervaded the sanctuary, Zechariah had presented his petition once more that he and his wife might have a child. Now the promise was given: **thy wife Elisabeth shall bear thee a son, and thou shalt call his name John** — which means "God is gracious." His birth would bring **joy and gladness** to Zechariah and rejoicing to many (v. 14). The Greek words for **joy** and **gladness** Bruce explains as signifying: "a joy, and exaltation; joy in higher, highest degree; joy over a son late born, and such a son as he will turn out to be."[12]

In view of the whole context here it may be best to reject the idea that Zechariah was praying for a son. Donald Miller suggests that the priest must already have given up all hope, as is evidenced by his unbelief (v. 18). What he was really praying for was the redemption of Israel. Thus verse 13 says two distinct things. "First, your prayer for the redemption of Israel is heard. Second, as an instrument of preparing the way for this redemption, you will have a son."[13]

The prophetic description of John is comprehensive and striking. He would be **great in the sight of the Lord** (v. 15) and would not drink wine or **strong drink** — the term was applied to any intoxicating drinks not made from grape juice. Instead he would be **filled with the Holy Spirit** from birth. This same contrast between being drunk and being filled with the Spirit is found in Ephesians 5:18. It is often assumed that John was a Nazarite. But since nothing is said about letting his hair grow, we cannot be certain about this.

John's future ministry is also described graphically. It was predicted that he would turn to the Lord **many of the children of Israel** (v. 16). He would appear **in the spirit and power of Elijah** (v. 17) "to make ready for the Lord, a people well prepared." This was an indication that he would be the forerunner of the Messiah. The reference is to Malachi 4:5 (cf. Matt. 11:14).

In spite of his prayer, Zechariah was not prepared for the promise. He could not believe it possible that the answer to his petition should come. He asked, **Whereby shall I know this?** (v. 18). He thought he was too old, and his wife also. He should have remembered that Isaac was born to Abraham and Sarah when they were extremely old.

In reply the angel identified himself as **Gabriel, that stand in the presence of God** (v. 19). He is mentioned by name again in verse 26, and nowhere else in the Bible except Daniel 8:16; 9:21. The only other archangel named in the Scriptures is Michael (Dan. 10:21). "Gabriel is the angel of mercy, Michael the angel of judgment."[14]

It was **good tidings** that the angel brought to Zechariah. But since he disbelieved, he was to suffer the loss of his speech until the promise was fulfilled in the birth of his son (v. 20). He had asked for a sign (v. 18) and he got one.

Outside, the people were still waiting

[9] J. M. Creed, *The Gospel According to St. Luke*, p. 10.
[10] John Albert Bengel, *Gnomon of the New Testament*, trans. A. R. Fausset, II, 12.
[11] J. H. Thayer, *A Greek-English Lexicon of the New Testament*, p. 126.
[12] A. B. Bruce, "The Synoptic Gospels." *The Expositor's Greek Testament*, ed. W. Robertson Nicoll, I, 462.
[13] Donald G. Miller, "The Gospel According to Luke," *The Layman's Bible Commentary*, ed. Balmer H. Kelly, p. 26.   [14] Plummer, *op. cit.*, p. 16.

for Zechariah to come out (v. 21). Ordinarily it took only a short time for the priest to offer the incense. Then he was supposed to appear on the steps of the Sanctuary and bless the people.

When Zechariah finally did appear, he was unable to pronounce the benediction (v. 22). The people somehow recognized that he had seen a vision in the Temple. Perhaps his face still carried a reflection of the encounter. **He continued making signs unto them.** He "had to keep motioning for some time before the people understood that they were this time to go home without the usual benediction."[15]

When Zechariah had fulfilled **the days of ministration** (v. 23) — the evening of one sabbath to the morning of the next — he went home. But he carried his dumbness with him.

3. Elisabeth's Conception (1:24, 25)

24 And after these days Elisabeth his wife conceived; and she hid herself five months, saying, 25 Thus hath the Lord done unto me in the days wherein he looked upon *me,* to take away my reproach among men.

The Greek word for **conceived** is used only by Luke in the New Testament in this sense (1:24, 31, 36; 2:21). This is one of the many little items that add up to considerable evidence of Luke's medical interest (see Introduction). Hobart makes the statement: "The number of words referring to pregnancy, barrenness, etc., used by St. Luke, is almost as large as that used by Hippocrates."[16]

Elisabeth **hid herself five months.** The implication (cf. v. 26) seems to be that it was the first five months, though Lenski disagrees. He says: "For the last five months she kept herself in the customary retirement."[17] As to her motive for doing so Farrar writes: "It may have been devotional; or precautionary; or she may merely have wished out of deep modesty to avoid as long as possible the idle comments and surmises of her neighbors."[18] Elisabeth's use of the term **reproach** reveals the reaction of those days to women who had no children. This tended to be considered as evidence of a lack of divine favor.

C. THE ANNOUNCEMENT OF JESUS' BIRTH (1:26-56)

1. The Annunciation (1:26-38)

26 Now in the sixth month the angel Gabriel was sent from God unto a city of Galilee, named Nazareth, 27 to a virgin betrothed to a man whose name was Joseph, of the house of David; and the virgin's name was Mary. 28 And he came in unto her, and said, Hail, thou that art highly favored, the Lord *is* with thee. 29 But she was greatly troubled at the saying, and cast in her mind what manner of salutation this might be. 30 And the angel said unto her, Fear not, Mary: for thou hast found favor with God. 31 And behold, thou shalt conceive in thy womb, and bring forth a son, and shalt call his name JESUS. 32 He shall be great, and shall be called the Son of the Most High: and the Lord God shall give unto him the throne of his father David: 33 and he shall reign over the house of Jacob for ever; and of his kingdom there shall be no end. 34 And Mary said unto the angel, How shall this be, seeing I know not a man? 35 And the angel answered and said unto her, The Holy Spirit shall come upon thee, and the power of the Most High shall overshadow thee: wherefore also the holy thing which is begotten shall be called the Son of God. 36 And behold, Elisabeth thy kinswoman, she also hath conceived a son in her old age; and this is the sixth month with her that was called barren. 37 For no word from God shall be void of power. 38 And Mary said, Behold, the handmaid of the Lord; be it unto me according to thy word. And the angel departed from her.

Gabriel, the same angel that had foretold to Zechariah the birth of John the Baptist, now announced to Mary the birth of Jesus. This announcement took place **in the sixth month** after Zechariah's vision. This is the only passage which indicates that John was six months older than Jesus.

Mary was living in **a city of Galilee, named Nazareth.** This expression is found only in Luke and fits in with the fact that he was writing to Gentiles unfamiliar with Palestine.

The angel Gabriel was sent from God **to a virgin betrothed to a man whose**

---

[15] R. C. H. Lenski, *The Interpretation of St. Luke's Gospel,* p. 57.
[16] William K. Hobart, *The Medical Language of St. Luke,* p. 91.
[17] *Op. cit.,* p. 58. [18] *Op. cit.,* p. 94.

name was **Joseph** (v. 27). "The interval between betrothal and marriage was
commonly a year, during which the bride
lived with her friends. But her property
was vested in her future husband, and
unfaithfulness on her part was punished,
like adultery, with death."[19]

Joseph was **of the house of David.** Since
Jesus was the legal, though not actual,
son of Joseph, this made Him the "son
of David" — a title which is given Him
a number of times in the Gospels. It
is also probable that He was a blood descendant of David through Mary His
mother (see notes on 3:23). This idea
is stated definitely here in the Sinaitic
Syriac manuscript: "because both of them
were of the house of David."

The angel suddenly appeared to Mary,
as he had done to Zechariah, and greeted
her with the words: **Hail, thou that art
highly favored, the Lord is with thee**[20]
(v. 28). The Roman Catholic hymn, *Ave
Maria* ("Hail, Mary"), dating in its present form from the sixteenth century, is
based on this verse. **Thou that art highly
favored** is all one word in the Greek.
It is translated in the Vulgate *gratia
plena,* "full of grace." This became the
basis of the idea that Mary could bestow grace on those who supplicated her.
But Bengel, an older contemporary of
John Wesley, had a good answer: "She
is so called, not as the mother of grace,
but as the daughter of grace."[21] She
was the recipient, not bestower, of divine
grace.

Quite naturally, Mary was **troubled** —
"greatly troubled," a stronger word than
in verse 12 — and **cast in her mind** ("considered" or "reasoned") **what manner of
salutation this might be;** that is, "what
it might signify."

She did not have long to wait. The
angel cushioned the coming shock with
the same comforting words he had used
with Zechariah (v. 13: **Fear not;** literally,
"stop being afraid"). Then came the
shattering announcement — to a pure
virgin — of verse 31. The son to be
born to her would be **great** (cf. v. 15),

and shall be called ("shall be") **the Son
of the Most High** (v. 32) — an appellation
often used as synonym for God, frequently in the Old Testament (cf. II Sam.
7:12; Isa. 11:1, 10; 16:5; Jer. 23:5; 30:9;
Ezek. 34:24; Dan. 7:14; Hos. 3:4; Micah
4:7; 5:4). This passage is especially
reminiscent of Isaiah 9:6, 7. The kingdom
of this One who will be both Son of
God and son of David will last forever
(v. 33).

The question Mary asked in reply (v.
34) was inevitable. The thing the angel
had announced was biologically impossible. But theology is above and beyond
biology.

The answer which the angel gave (v.
35) is simple, clear and beautiful. The
Holy Spirit would take the place of the
human father. The language here is
reminiscent of Genesis 1:2 — "and the
Spirit of God was brooding upon the
face of the waters" (ASV margin). It
was altogether fitting that the Holy
Spirit, who was the active Agent in the
original creation, should thus inaugu-
rate a New Creation, the Christ of God.
The virgin birth is clearly presented
here as an act of divine creation. Admittedly it is a mystery. But Bishop
Ryle has well said: "In a religion which
really comes down from heaven there
must needs be mysteries. Of such mysteries in Christianity, the incarnation
is one."[22]

The doctrine of the Virgin Birth has
come under sharp attack in this century.
Much has been made of the fact that only
two writers of the New Testament, Matthew and Luke, refer definitely to it.
But they are the only two who record
the birth of Jesus at all. The other
writers, of course, assume it. Bruce is
correct when he writes: "The more we
appreciate the uniqueness of this incarnation, the more may we recognize
how fitting — indeed, how inevitable
— it is that the means by which it was
brought about should also be unique."[23]

The theological thrust of the Virgin
Birth is well expressed by Donald Miller,

---

[19] Plummer, *op. cit.,* p. 21.
[20] The added words, "blessed art thou among women" (KJV) are not in the two oldest Greek
manuscripts of the New Testament (Vaticanus and Sinaiticus). They were probably borrowed from
verse 42.   [21] *Op. cit.,* II, 15, 16.
[22] J. C. Ryle, *Expository Thoughts on the Gospels: Luke,* p. 27.
[23] F. F. Bruce, "The Person of Christ: Incarnation and Virgin Birth," *Basic Christian Doctrines,*
ed. Carl F. H. Henry, p. 128.

as follows: "One must believe that in the Virgin Birth God entered human life redemptively, and that *he did so for me.*"[24]

The angel further announced to Mary that Elisabeth her **kinswoman** — "cousin" (KJV) is more definite than the Greek will allow — had **conceived a son in her old age** (v. 36). The reason for this disclosure was to strengthen Mary's faith. "If God worked such an astounding miracle in the case of Elisabeth, then Mary could with confidence await the fulfillment of God's promise made to her."[25]

The translation of verse 37 accords well with the Greek (better than KJV). **Word** is not *logos* but *rhema* (properly, "a spoken word").

Mary's acquiescence in the will of God for her is one of the most beautiful examples of consecration ever recorded. **Handmaid** is literally "bondmaid" or "slave." The implications of this submission are pointed out by Miller. He says: "To be God's servant, Mary had to expose herself to the misunderstanding of Joseph (Matt. 1:18-25), to the possible loss of her reputation and the curse of being considered a sinful woman, and to possible death by stoning (Deut. 22: 23-24)."[26]

2. The Magnificat (1:39-56)

39 And Mary arose in these days and went into the hill country with haste, into a city of Judah; 40 and entered into the house of Zacharias and saluted Elisabeth. 41 And it came to pass, when Elisabeth heard the salutation of Mary, the babe leaped in her womb; and Elisabeth was filled with the Holy Spirit; 42 and she lifted up her voice with a loud cry, and said, Blessed *art* thou among women, and blessed *is* the fruit of thy womb. 43 And whence is this to me, that the mother of my Lord should come unto me? 44 For behold, when the voice of thy salutation came into mine ears, the babe leaped in my womb for joy. 45 And blessed *is* she that believed; for there shall be a fulfilment of the things which have been spoken to her from the Lord. 46 And Mary said,
My soul doth magnify the Lord,
47 And my spirit hath rejoiced in God my Saviour.

48 For he hath looked upon the low estate of his handmaid:
For behold, from henceforth all generations shall call me blessed.
49 For he that is mighty hath done to me great things;
And holy is his name.
50 And his mercy is unto generations and and generations
On them that fear him.
51 He hath showed strength with his arm;
He hath scattered the proud in the imagination of their heart.
52 He hath put down princes from *their* thrones,
And hath exalted them of low degree.
53 The hungry he hath filled with good things;
And the rich he hath sent empty away.
54 He hath given help to Israel his servant,
That he might remember mercy
55 (As he spake unto our fathers)
Toward Abraham and his seed for ever.
56 And Mary abode with her about three months, and returned unto her house.

Mary went to the home of Zechariah and Elisabeth in **a city of Judah,** which was in **the hill country** (v. 39). The exact location is uncertain. Some have thought it was Hebron, twenty miles south of Jerusalem, because that was a city where many priests lived. But tradition places the birth of John the Baptist at Ain Karem, a modern village about four miles west of Jerusalem. This would have meant a journey of over eighty miles on foot.

When Mary greeted Elisabeth, the unborn babe leaped within the latter, she was filled with the Holy Spirit, and she broke forth with inspired utterance (vv. 41-45). **Blessed art thou among women** has been overworked by the Roman Catholic Church (cf. v. 28). Elisabeth addressed Mary as **the mother of my Lord** (v. 43). This is a high theological note, but gives no support to calling Mary "the Mother of God." She was the earthly mother of Jesus in His humanity, but in no sense the mother of the eternal God.

Mary is pronounced **blessed** because she believed (v. 45). This is a striking

[24] *Op. cit.,* p. 32.   [25] William F. Arndt, *The Gospel According to St. Luke,* p. 51.
[26] *Op. cit.,* p. 29.

contrast to Zechariah, who was cursed temporarily with loss of speech because of his unbelief. Thus the hint is given to us at the very beginning of the Gospel that we must read it in faith,[27] not balking at the miraculous but believing it.

The "Magnificat" is so named from the first word in the Latin version. It is a magnificent hymn-poem, covering verses 46-55. It bears striking resemblance to the Song of Hannah (I Sam. 2:1-10) and is much like the Psalms in content and spirit. In fact, it is almost a mosaic of quotations from the Old Testament. Maclaren remarks: "Birds sing at dawn and sunrise. It was fitting that the last strains of Old Testament psalmody should prelude the birth of Jesus."[28]

In a similar vein van Oosterzee writes: "The Magnificat . . . and the Benedictus of Zechariah, vss. 68-79, . . . are the Psalms of the New Testament, and worthily introduce the history of Christian hymnology. They prove the harmony of poetry and religion. They are the noblest flowers of Hebrew lyric poetry, sending their fragrance to the approaching Messiah. They are full of reminiscences of the Old Testament, entirely Hebrew in tone and language, and can be rendered almost word for word."[29]

Regarding the timing of these two hymns of praise he makes the further observation: "The angel's visit was vouchsafed to Mary later than to Zacharias, yet her song of thanksgiving is uttered long before his: faith is already singing for joy, while unbelief is compelled to be silent."[30]

Due to the limitations set by this commentary, it will be impossible to give any extended treatment to these poems. The most satisfactory way to study them is to look up all the Old Testament references given in the margin, and interpret the hymns in the light of these.

After three months, Mary left and returned to Nazareth (v. 56). Whether this was before or after the birth of John the Baptist we are not told. Consequently the commentators differ. Creed says: "Mary returns to her home before the birth of Elisabeth's child."[31] Lenski

agrees with this view and adds the following reason for Mary's return: "We judge that Mary hastens home because she wanted to avoid the people who would soon throng the house of Elisabeth."[32] Geldenhuys agrees exactly with this.

On the other hand, Farrar thinks it "probable that the Virgin Mary remained at least until the birth of the Baptist."[33] Meyer likewise says of her return: "but not until the delivery of Elisabeth."[34] And Plummer concludes: "Luke mentions her return before mentioning the birth in order to complete one narrative before beginning another,"[35] just as he does in 3:20, 21. Where the doctors disagree it seems best to withhold any personal opinion.

D. THE BIRTH OF JOHN (1:57-80)

1. The Naming of John (1:57-66)

57 Now Elisabeth's time was fulfilled that she should be delivered; and she brought forth a son. 58 And her neighbors and her kinsfolk heard that the Lord had magnified his mercy towards her; and they rejoiced with her. 59 And it came to pass on the eighth day, that they came to circumcise the child; and they would have called him Zacharias, after the name of his father. 60 And his mother answered and said, Not so; but he shall be called John. 61 And they said unto her, There is none of thy kindred that is called by this name. 62 And they made signs to his father, what he would have him called. 63 And he asked for a writing tablet, and wrote, saying, His name is John. And they marveled all. 64 And his mouth was opened immediately, and his tongue *loosed*, and he spake, blessing God. 65 And fear came on all that dwelt round about them: and all these sayings were noised abroad throughout all the hill country of Judaea. 66 And all that heard them laid them up in their heart, saying, What then shall this child be? For the hand of the Lord was with him.

When Elisabeth gave birth to a son, all her **neighbors** and **kinsfolk** rejoiced with her (vv. 57, 58). On the eighth day they all gathered for their important cere-

[27] Miller, *op. cit.*, p. 23.   [28] Alexander Maclaren, *Expositions of Holy Scripture; St. Luke*, I, 17.   [29] J. J. van Oosterzee, "Luke," *Commentary on the Holy Scriptures*, ed. John Peter Lange, trans. Philip Schaff, p. 25.   [30] *Ibid.*   [31] *Op. cit.*, p. 24.   [32] *Op. cit.*, p. 94.   [33] *Op. cit.*, p. 101.
[34] H. A. W. Meyer, *Critical and Exegetical Hand-Book to the Gospels of Mark and Luke*, trans. R. E. Wallis, rev. and ed. W. P. Dickson, Am. Edition, p. 249.   [35] *Op. cit.*, p. 34.

mony of circumcising the baby boy (v. 59). It was the custom to name the child at the time of its circumcision. Alford says: "The names of children were given at circumcision, because, at the institution of that rite, the names of Abram and Sarai were changed to Abraham and Sarah."[36]

They would have called him exactly represents the force of the imperfect tense in Greek, which is missed in the translation "they called him" (KJV). "They tried to, they wished to, they would have" — that is what the Greek says.

The neighbors and relations wanted to call him Zechariah, after his father.[37] But his mother demurred: **he shall be called John** (v. 60). When a debate arose over the matter they appealed to the father for a decision. The statement that they **made signs** implies that Zechariah was deaf as well as dumb.

When he had been given a **writing tablet** — a piece of wood with wax or sand on it — he wrote: **His name is John** (v. 63). There was no uncertainty or even futurity (cf. v. 60) about it. The name had already been fixed by the angel's message in the Temple. All the people **marvelled** at this strange coincidence. But it seems extremely likely that Zechariah had already communicated to his wife the name assigned by the Lord.

As soon as Zechariah completed his obedience to the angel's directions, the punishment for his unbelief was lifted. Immediately his **mouth was** opened, and **his tongue loosed** (vv. 64). He used his regained powers of speech **blessing God.** The miracle caused a great stir in that whole countryside (vv. 65, 66). People somehow felt that this was an unusual child.

2. The Benedictus (1:67-79)

67 And his father Zacharias was filled with the Holy Spirit, and prophesied, saying.
68 Blessed be the Lord, the God of Israel;
For he hath visited and wrought redemption for his people,
69 And hath raised up a horn of salvation for us
In the house of his servant David

70 (As he spake by the mouth of his holy prophets that have been from of old),
71 Salvation from our enemies, and from the hand of all that hate us;
72 To show mercy towards our fathers, And to remember his holy covenant;
73 The oath which he sware unto Abraham our father,
74 To grant unto us that we being delivered out of the hand of our enemies
Should serve him without fear,
75 In holiness and righteousness before him all our days.
76 Yea and thou, child, shalt be called the prophet of the Most High;
For thou shalt go before the face of the Lord to make ready his ways;
77 To give knowledge of salvation unto his people
In the remission of their sins,
78 Because of the tender mercy of our God,
Whereby the dayspring from on high shall visit us,
79 To shine upon them that sit in darkness and the shadow of death;
To guide our feet into the way of peace.

Just as Elisabeth was "filled with the Holy Spirit" (v. 41) in her prophetic utterance to Mary (vv. 42-45) so Zechariah was **filled with the Holy Spirit, and prophesied** (v. 67). The word **prophesied** fits in with the nature of the song that follows. Plummer notes: "As the *Magnificat* is modelled on the psalms, so the *Benedictus* is modelled on the prophecies. . . . And while the tone of the *Magnificat* is regal, that of the *Benedictus* is sacerdotal."[38] Farrar calls the Benedictus "the last Prophecy of the Old Dispensation, and the first of the New."[39]

The Benedictus, as was the case of the Magnificat, is named after the first word in the Latin version. Like the psalmists and prophets of old, Zechariah blesses the Lord. From the Greek word comes the English "eulogize." Arndt summarizes the main thrust of the song thus: "Its general theme is the praise of God, who through the sending of the Messiah now is providing the rescue which he had promised long ago through the prophets."[40] He divides the poem into

---

[36] Henry Alford, *The Greek Testament*, rev. E. F. Harrison, I, 451.
[37] Sons were frequently named after the father, but more frequently after the grandfather (Creed, *op. cit.*, p. 24). [38] *Op. cit.*, pp. 38, 39. [39] *Op. cit.*, pp. 103, 104. [40] *Op. cit.*, p. 66.

two parts. The first eulogizes God for providing redemption (vv. 68-75). "The second part is addressed to the infant John and prophesies the role which he is to play as the forerunner of the Messiah, giving at the same time the contents of his message (76-79)."[41]

The birth of John the Baptist and the anticipated coming of the Messiah are interpreted by Zechariah as meaning that the Lord has **visited and wrought redemption for his people** (v. 68). God was breaking into history in a new way. He has now raised up a **horn of salvation** (v. 69). The *horn* is a frequent symbolical term in the Old Testament for "strength" (e.g., I Sam. 2:10; Psa. 131:17; Ezek. 29:21).

This **horn** was to be a descendant of **David**. Since John the Baptist was from the tribe of Levi (not Judah), the reference is clearly to Christ. Geldenhuys comments: "Just as the power of an animal is, as it were, concentrated in its horn, so all the redeeming power of God that was promised to the house of David will be concentrated in the Messiah — Redeemer."[42]

All this was in fulfillment of what the Lord spoke **by the mouth of his holy prophets** from ancient times (v. 70). This takes in the entire Old Testament (cf. 24:44; Heb. 1:1). This verse is parenthetical, so that verse 71 picks up the word **salvation** from verse 69 and enlarges on it. Just as the Lord had **visited** (v. 68) His people long ago in their Egyptian bondage and delivered them, so He would again give **salvation from our enemies,** delivering from bondage to Rome.

But the Song of Zechariah seems clearly to go beyond the hope for national salvation from foreign enemies. His desire is that God's people may **serve him without fear, in holiness and righteousness before him all our days** (vv. 74, 75). This implies that holiness of heart and righteousness of life are part of what **salvation** means. Paul combines these two words in Ephesians 4:24, and I Thessalonians 2:10. They give the twofold emphasis of the Christian life — **holiness** toward God, and **righteousness** toward men.

Then Zechariah turned to his son, the boy whose birth had been a miracle.

He echoed the prophecy the angel had made (cf. vv. 16, 17) that John would prepare the way of the Lord in the hearts of the people (vv. 76, 77). The goal of **salvation** was the **remission of their sins.** The **dayspring** (v. 78) is "the dawn." This seems to be a reflection of the promise in Malachi 4:2 — "But unto you that fear my name shall the sun of righteousness arise with healing in its wings."

3. The Preparation of John (1:80)

80 And the child grew, and waxed strong in spirit, and was in the deserts till the day of his showing unto Israel.

This verse emphasizes John's physical growth and his mental and spiritual development. Since his parents were elderly when he was born, it is likely that the boy was left an orphan before he had grown completely to manhood. He lived the life of an ascetic recluse in the **desert;** that is, the wild and desolate Wilderness of Judea.

E. THE BIRTH OF JESUS (2:1-20)

1. The Birth in Bethlehem (2:1-7)

1 Now it came to pass in those days, there went out a decree from Caesar Augustus, that all the world should be enrolled. 2 This was the first enrolment made when Quirinius was governor of Syria. 3 And all went to enrol themselves, every one to his own city. 4 And Joseph also went up from Galilee, out of the city of Nazareth, into Judaea, to the city of David, which is called Bethlehem, because he was of the house and family of David; 5 to enrol himself with Mary, who was betrothed to him, being great with child. 6 And it came to pass, while they were there, the days were fulfilled that she should be delivered. 7 And she brought forth her firstborn son; and she wrapped him in swaddling clothes, and laid him in a manger, because there was no room for them in the inn.

Luke always writes as a historian. This fact is evident again (cf. 1:5) in the first verse here. He mentions both the Roman emperor and the ruling governor of Syria. He starts out with a typical historical phrase: **Now it came to pass in those days.** The Greek word for **decree** is *dogma.* It is used in Acts 16:4 for the

41 *Ibid.*   42 *Op. cit.,* p. 93.

"decrees" of the Council of Jerusalem and in Acts 17:7 for the "decrees" of Caesar.

Caesar Augustus reigned 30 B.C.-A.D. 14. Both parts of this ruler's name are titles. Caesar is from the same root as Czar and Kaiser. Augustus means "reverend," a title assumed by the Roman emperors. Caesar Augustus was one of the greatest rulers the world has ever seen, reigning as absolute monarch over the Roman Empire for forty-four years and maintaining order and peace. This helped to prepare the way for the rapid spread of Christianity.

Caesar decreed that all the world (Roman Empire) should be enrolled. This is more accurate than "taxed" (KJV). A different Greek word is used for the latter. The term used here refers only to drawing up lists with information that could be used for a later taxation.

There is no other passage in the New Testament that has been attacked so severely with regard to its historical accuracy as has Luke 2:1-4. A number of nineteenth-century critics thought that they had completely demolished its historicity and trustworthiness.

But time is always on the side of truth. Donald Miller writes: "More recent study, however, has produced evidence tending to support Luke in his historic facts."[43] This evidence has come mostly from recent archaeological discoveries, which have repeatedly confirmed Luke's exact historical accuracy in details previously disputed.

The first quarrel has been with the statement of verse 2: "This was the first enrollment made when Quirinius was governor of Syria." It is maintained that Quirinius did not become governor of Syria until A.D. 6. At that time he did institute a Roman census, which produced tumultuous opposition in Palestine. Critics claim that Luke has confused this with the one he reports at this time. But Sir William Ramsay, the greatest modern authority on the history of western Asia in the first century, wrote an entire book to prove the historicity of Luke 2:1-4. In it he shows that it was the custom in the first century to have a Roman

enrollment every fourteen years.[44] The previous census, then, would have been held about 8 B.C. But it usually took several years to complete an enrollment, so that it could have been going on in 6 or 5 B.C. In fact, a Roman census undertaken in Gaul in 27 B.C. dragged on for more than forty years because of the opposition of the Gallic tribal chiefs.[45]

But the important point made by Stauffer is that Quirinus was not only governor at a later date but also commander-in-chief for Oriental affairs from 12 B.C. So he could easily have instituted a census in the days of King Herod.[46] The oft-repeated contention that Herod's royal realm would not have been invaded for a census is completely refuted by Stauffer.[47]

Serious objection has also been made to the statement of verse 3: And all went to enroll themselves, every one to his own city. It used to be said that there was no evidence for such a custom. But Deissmann gives the text and translation of an edict written by a praefect of Egypt on papyrus and dated A.D. 104. It reads in part: "The enrollment by household being at hand, it is necessary to notify all who for any cause soever are outside their homes to return to their domestic hearths."[48] Thus, there is support for the statement that Joseph had to go from Nazareth to Bethlehem, because he was of the house and family of David (v. 4).

Moulton and Milligan have expressed graphically the change of tone in this field. They write: "The deduction so long made from Luke's shocking blunders about the census apparently survives the demonstration that the blunder lay only in our lack of information: the microbe is not yet completely expelled. Possibly the salutary process may be completed by our latest inscriptional evidence that Quirinius was a legate in Syria for census purposes in B.C. 8-6."[49]

While Joseph and Mary were in Bethlehem, she brought forth her firstborn son (v. 7). The word firstborn does not prove, but it may imply, that Mary had other children later. The dogma of the Perpetual Virginity of Mary has no Scriptural support whatever.

[43] Op. cit., p. 35.   [44] W. M. Ramsay, Was Christ Born in Bethlehem? p. 154.
[45] Ethelbert Stauffer, Jesus and His Story, trans. Richard and Clara Winston, p. 23.
[46] Ibid., p. 30.   [47] Ibid., pp. 26-29
[48] Adolf Deissmann, Light From the Ancient East, trans. L. R. M. Strachan, rev. ed., p. 271.
[49] James Hope Moulton and George Milligan, The Vocabulary of the Greek New Testament, p. 60.

It is said of Mary that she wrapped the baby in **swaddling clothes,** or swathing bands. It appears that she had no midwife to help and so had to perform this task herself. Then she **laid him in a manger.** Tradition says this was in a cave stable in the hillside. **There was no room for them in the inn.** The Greek word is used for "guest-chamber" in 22:11, and that might be its meaning here, though **inn** seems preferable. We are apt to think of this as working a special hardship on Joseph and Mary, particularly the latter. But it is possible that the animal heat in the stable made it safer for both mother and child than it would have been in the cold room in the inn.

2. The Visit of the Shepherds (2:8-20)

8. And there were shepherds in the same country abiding in the field, and keeping watch by night over their flock. 9 And an angel of the Lord stood by them, and the glory of the Lord shone round about them: and they were sore afraid. 10 And the angel said unto them, Be not afraid; for behold, I bring you good tidings of great joy which shall be to all the people: 11 for there is born to you this day in the city of David a Saviour, who is Christ the Lord. 12 And this *is* the sign unto you: Ye shall find a babe wrapped in swaddling clothes, and lying in a manger. 13 And suddenly there was with the angel a multitude of the heavenly host praising God, and saying,

14 Glory to God in the highest,
And on earth peace among men in whom he is well pleased.

15 And it came to pass, when the angels went away from them into heaven, the shepherds said one to another, Let us now go even unto Bethlehem, and see this thing that is come to pass, which the Lord hath made known unto us. 16 And they came with haste, and found both Mary and Joseph, and the babe lying in the manger. 17 And when they saw it, they made known concerning the saying which was spoken to them about this child. 18 And all that heard it wondered at the things which were spoken unto them by the shepherds. 19 But Mary kept all these sayings, pondering them in her heart. 20 And the shepherds returned, glorifying and prais-

ing God for all the things that they had heard and seen, even as it was spoken unto them.

The night Christ was born there were shepherds keeping watch over their flock in the field (v. 8). This statement has caused some to say that Jesus could not have been born on December 25, because it would be too cold to spend the night in the open field. October has been suggested as an alternative. But after a careful investigation of relevant data Andrews comes to this conclusion: "There seems, then, so far as climate is concerned, no good ground to affirm that shepherds could not have been pasturing their flocks in the field during the month of December."[50] Edersheim agrees with this and adds the suggestion that these flocks may have been "destined for Temple-sacrifice."[51] Barclay picks up this idea and applies it thus: "It is a lovely thought that the shepherds who looked after the Temple lambs were the first to see the Lamb of God who takes away the sin of the world."[52]

Suddenly an angel appeared to them. We have already seen how Luke mentions angels more frequently than the other Gospel writers. **The glory of the Lord shone round about them** (v. 9), like the shekinah ("glory," or apprehensible presence) of the Old Testament. The natural reaction of the shepherds was one of fear at this manifestation of the supernatural, fear such as is often seen in the Old Testament. They were **sore afraid** (literally, "feared a great fear"). The first words of the angel were the same — except for the change from singular to plural — as to Zechariah (1:13) and to Mary (1:30): **Be not afraid** (literally, "stop being afraid").

Having quieted the shepherds' fears, the angel made the greatest announcement ever heard on earth. It was **good tidings** (or "good news") **of great joy which shall be to all people** (v. 10). **I bring . . . . good tidings** is all one word in Greek, **euangelizomai** ("evangelize").

The good news is found in verse 11: **For there is born to you this day in the city of David a Saviour, who is Christ**

50 Samuel J. Andrews, *The Life of Our Lord,* p. 16.
51 Alfred Edersheim, *The Life and Times of Jesus the Messiah,* I, 186.
52 William Barclay, *The Gospel of Luke,* p. 17.

the Lord. No newspaper ever carried headlines more significant than this. No more important event was ever heralded. It was particularly fitting that this announcement should be made by an angel. He came as God's "messenger" (literal meaning of "angel"), to deliver the greatest divine message man had ever heard.

Note the three titles given the newborn babe. The first is **Saviour.** That is why he was called Jesus, which means "Saviour" (Matt. 1:21). Appropriately this is the primary designation. For the main purpose of Jesus' appearance on earth was the salvation of mankind. The Greek word for **Saviour** means "deliverer" or "preserver." The one believing in Jesus is delivered from sin and preserved from evil.

The second title is **Christ.** The Greek *Christos* is equivalent to the Hebrew "Messiah." Both mean the "anointed one." Jesus came as the Messiah predicted and promised in the Old Testament. He was the fulfillment of the Messianic hopes of the centuries. Tragically, the Jewish nation rejected Him as its Messiah.

The third title is **the Lord.** This One who came as the Messiah of Israel and "the Saviour of the world" (I John 4:14) is the Lord of all. That He is the Lord of history is shown by the fact that almost all civilized nations date their events Before Christ (B.C.) or In The Year of Our Lord (A.D.). Millions of times a day around the world silent tribute is paid to the Lordship of Jesus Christ. Every time a date is affixed to a letter, bill, check, receipt, or legal document fresh acknowledgment is made of the fact that the birth of Christ is the watershed of human history.

Yet how is this "Lord of all" identified? **Ye shall find a babe wrapped in swaddling clothes and lying in a manger.** What a paradox! The *Eternal One* caught in a moment of time. *Omnipresence* corralled in a cave manger. *Omnipotence* cradled in a helpless infant who could not even raise His head from the straw. *Omniscience* confined in a baby who could not say a word. The *Christ* who created the heavens and the earth

cradled in a manger in a cave stable. What condescending love! And what divine wisdom! For when God would draw near to cold, cruel, sinful, suffering humanity, He placed a baby in a manger at Bethlehem. The quickest way to the human heart is by way of an innocent little child. In infinite wisdom God planned it thus. And so today the story most loved the world around is the one found in Luke 2:1-20.

Another significance of this humble birth is pointed out by Erdman, who says: "A redeemer who was cradled in a manger has known what it is to endure poverty and suffering and neglect, and now he can sympathize with the lowly and distressed, even as he is abundantly able to save."[53]

Suddenly the single messenger was joined by **a multitude of the heavenly host** (v. 13), who were singing the **Gloria in Excelsis** (v. 14). To God on high be glory, and to men on earth peace.

The translation of the latter part of verse 14 has been a matter of considerable comment. The King James Version has "on earth peace, good will toward men." But in the oldest Greek manuscripts the word for "good will" is in the genitive case — "of good will." But scholars are agreed that "peace to men of good will" is not the proper Biblical concept. The American Standard Version probably represents the true idea correctly: **peace among men in whom he is well pleased.** The Latin Vulgate "is often rendered 'men of good-will,' i.e., good men of a right spirit and intention. The Hebraistic Greek would rather mean 'men in whom God is well pleased.' "[54] Plummer renders it "men whom the Divine favour has blessed."[55]

The shepherds hurried into Bethlehem and found Joseph and Mary, with the baby lying in a manger. Their report caused considerable excitement in that area. **But Mary kept all these sayings, pondering them in her heart.** "There seems to be a clear hint here that Mary is, as we should naturally expect, the ultimate source of our information about the birth of Christ and what preceded it."[56]

[53]Charles R. Erdman, *The Gospel of Luke*, p. 33.
[55] *Op. cit.*, p. 58.
[56] H. Balmforth, *The Gospel According to St. Luke*, p. 128.
[54] Lonsdale Ragg, *St. Luke*, p. 32.

A. THE CIRCUMCISION AND PRESENTATION (2:21-39)

1. The Circumcision (2:21)

21 And when eight days were fulfilled for circumcising him, his name was called JESUS, which was so called by the angel before he was conceived in the womb.

The law of Moses stipulated that after the birth of a male child the mother was considered ceremonially unclean for seven days. On the eighth day the boy was to be circumcised. For thirty-three days more the mother was not to come into the sanctuary or touch any sacred thing, until "the days of her purifying" were fulfilled (Lev. 12:1-4). Circumcision, however, antedated Moses. The custom was enjoined upon Abraham as the sign or symbol of God's covenant with him, and it was to be performed on the eighth day (Gen. 17:9-12).

The significance of this rite and of the one that follows is thus stated by Spence: "These ancient rites — circumcision and purification — enjoined in the Mosaic Law were intended as perpetual witnesses to the deadly taint of imperfection and sin inherited by every child of man."[57]

Of course Jesus did not need this for Himself. But this was a part of His fulfilling all righteousness for us. Sadler says: "Thus His circumcision was the first stage in that outward life of submission to the will of His Father by which He redeemed us."[58]

At the time of his circumcision the child was given his name (cf. 1:59). In this case it was JESUS, which means "Jehovah is salvation," or "Jehovah saves" (Matt. 1:21). "The name was fairly common in the first century; Josephus mentions nineteen persons called Jesus."[59]

Luke is careful to call attention to the fact that this name was assigned to Christ by the angel before His birth. In His case, it carried special prophetic significance. He was to be the Savior of mankind.

"Jesus" is the most common designation for the Son of God. The name occurs nearly a thousand times in the New Testament, whereas "Christ" is found less than six hundred times. "Jesus" carries a twofold emphasis on both the humanity and the saviorhood of Christ. It has always held high place in the devotional literature of the church and in its hymnology. Bernard of Clairvaux wrote:

Jesus, the very thought of Thee
  With sweetness fills my breast;
But sweeter far Thy face to see,
  And in Thy presence rest.

No voice can sing, no heart can frame,
  Nor can the memory find
A sweeter sound than Thy blest name,
  O Saviour of Mankind.

2. The Presentation in the Temple (2:22-24)

22 And when the days of their purification according to the law of Moses were fulfilled, they brought him up to Jerusalem, to present him to the Lord 23 (as it is written in the law of the Lord, Every male that openeth the womb shall be called holy to the Lord), 24 and to offer a sacrifice according to that which is said in the law of the Lord, A pair of turtledoves, or two young pigeons.

Actually two Mosaic rites are combined in this paragraph: the purification of the mother and the presentation of the child. Their purification is what the Greek text says. "Her purification" (KJV) is a late reading introduced because the Levitical law speaks only of the purification of the mother. It has practically no support in the Greek.[60] There has been some difference of opinion concerning what their purification means. Godet interprets thus: "This pronoun refers primarily to Mary, then to Joseph, who is, as it were, involved in her uncleanness, and obliged to go up with her."[61]

[57] H. D. M. Spence, "St. Luke" (Exposition), *The Pulpit Commentary*, ed. H. D. M. Spence and Joseph S. Exell, p. 39.   [58] M. F. Sadler, *The Gospel According to St. Luke*, p. 53.
[59] F. C. Grant, "Jesus Christ," *The Interpreter's Dictionary of the Bible*, ed. George A. Buttrick, II, 869.
[60] Plummer writes: "No uncial and perhaps only one cursive (76) supports the reading *autes* (her), which spread from the Complutensian Polyglott Bible (1514) to a number of editions. It is a remarkable instance of a reading which had almost no authority becoming widely adopted" (*op. cit.*, p. 63).   [61] F. L. Godet, *Commentary on the Gospel of St. Luke*, p. 136.

These days of purification would be forty in number (Lev. 12:2, 4). **According to the law of Moses** reminds us of the fact that Jesus was "born of a woman, born under the law" (Gal. 4:4), and that He kept the Law completely. This was a part of His fulfilling all righteousness in order that He might be the perfect Sacrifice for sin.

Joseph and Mary **brought him up to Jerusalem.** Bethlehem was about six miles south of Jerusalem and on higher ground. But one always went "up" to the Holy City. Luke shows a greater interest in Jerusalem than do the other Synoptists. "Altogether it is mentioned no less than 96 times in Luke-Acts."[62]

The last of the ten plagues in Egypt was the death of the firstborn son in every home which did not have the blood sprinkled on the doorposts. So when the Israelites left Egypt, the Lord said to Moses: "Sanctify unto me all the first-born, whatsoever openeth the womb . . . . is mine" (Exod. 13:2). Verse 23 is a free quotation of this passage.

The tribe of Levi was taken in place of the first-born sons of Israel to minister to the Lord. The surplus number of the first-born was taken care of by assessing a poll tax of five shekels (Num. 3: 44-51). Finally this rule was extended to all the first-born (Num. 18:15, 16). Presumably Jesus paid this fee at this time, though it is not mentioned.

What is stated is that they offered the prescribed sacrifice for Mary's purification — **A pair of turtledoves, or two young pigeons** (v. 24). Brown gives the following summary of the situation:

> The proper sacrifice was a lamb for a burnt offering, and a turtle-dove or a young pigeon for a sin offering. But if a lamb could not be afforded, the mother was to bring two turtle-doves or two young pigeons; and if even this was beyond the family means, then a portion of fine flour, but without usual fragrant accompaniments of oil and frankincense, because it represented a sin offering (Lev. 12:6-8; v. 7-11). From this we gather that our Lord's parents were in poor circumstances (2 Cor. 8, 9), and yet

not in abject poverty; as they brought neither the lamb, nor availed themselves of the provision for the poorest, but presented the intermediate offering.[63]

3. The Adoration of Simeon (2:25-35)

25 And behold, there was a man in Jerusalem, whose name was Simeon; and this man was righteous and devout, looking for the consolation of Israel: and the Holy Spirit was upon him. 26 And it had been revealed unto him by the Holy Spirit, that he should not see death, before he had seen the Lord's Christ. 27 And he came in the Spirit into the temple: and when the parents brought in the child Jesus, that they might do concerning him after the custom of the law, 28 then he received him into his arms, and blessed God, and said,
29 Now lettest thou thy servant depart, Lord,
  According to thy word, in peace;
30 For mine eyes have seen thy salvation,
31 Which thou hast prepared before the face of all peoples;
32 A light for revelation to the Gentiles, And the glory of thy people Israel.
33 And his father and his mother were marvelling at the things which were spoken concerning him; 34 and Simeon blessed them, and said unto Mary his mother, Behold, this *child* is set for the falling and the rising of many in Israel; and for a sign which is spoken against; 35 yea and a sword shall pierce through thine own soul; that thoughts out of many hearts may be revealed.

From the reading of the Gospels one may sometimes get the impression that all the Jews were dead spiritually. But here is a notable exception. Simeon was **righteous and devout.** The former may refer more particularly to his outward life, the latter to his inner attitude of reverence for God. He was looking for **the consolation of Israel.** In general, this phrase means the fulfillment of the Messianic hope. More specifically, "the Consoler" was "recognized as one of the names of the Messiah."[64]

The Holy Spirit was **upon** Simeon. By special revelation he had been shown that he would live to see the Messiah (v. 26). He was a representative of what

[62] W. R. F. Browning, *The Gospel According to St. Luke*, p. 51.
[63] David Brown, "Matthew — John," *A Commentary Critical, Experimental and Practical on the Old and New Testaments*, by Robert Jamieson, A. R. Fausset, and David Brown, V. 229.
[64] Farrar, *op. cit.*, p. 117.

was best in Israelite religion at that time. Leany suggests also that "Symeon by his age and piety is the very personification of ancient Israel, the servant of God."[65]

The song of Simeon (vv. 29-32) is called the *Nunc Dimittis* — again after the first words in Latin. It is the last of five songs that occur in the first two chapters of this Gospel. Their presence shows that Luke was by nature a poet.

Simeon addresses God as **Lord** (v. 29). This is not the common word for Lord, *kyrios,* but the rare word *despotes,* which has been taken over into English. This is the only place where it occurs in the Gospels. Thayer says that it "denoted absolute ownership and uncontrolled power."[66] The word for **servant** means "slave." It was because Simeon was the submissive slave of his Master that he was given the great privilege of holding in his arms the infant Jesus and of being the first to welcome Him as the Messiah. Had the whole Jewish nation adopted Simeon's attitude, how different would have been its subsequent history.

This song echoes the sentiments of Mary's *Magnificat* and Zechariah's *Benedictus.* Simeon acclaims the coming of the Messiah as meaning **salvation** (v. 30). But he prophesies that it will be for **all peoples** (v. 31). Specifically it will be (v. 32):

A light for revelation to the Gentiles,
And the glory of thy people Israel.

The **Gentiles** were always thought of as dwelling in darkness (cf. Isa. 9:1, 2; Matt. 4:15, 16). The coming of Christ caused a great **light** — "the Light of the world" (John 8:12) — to shine on them. But the Messiah would also be **the glory of thy people Israel.** The shekinah of His presence would once more be manifested to them as it was to the ancient Israelites when they came out of Egypt. Israel's only hope of salvation — both individual and national — lay in accepting Jesus as Messiah and Master. This it refused to do.

The idea of salvation for all who will accept Christ is more prominent in Luke than in the other Gospels (see Introduction). Manson says of Simeon's song: "The utterance harmonizes with Luke's own conception of the Christian religion as bringing to the Greeks for the first time the 'sure word' of truth for which they were waiting (i.4) while at the same time it provides the final verification of Israel's ancient faith."[67]

The expression **his father** (v. 33) seems a bit surprising in view of Luke's clear statement of the Virgin Birth. But Joseph was Jesus' legal, though not actual, father. The parents **were marvelling** at the things that were being said about their Son.

Prophetically Simeon declared that Jesus **is set** (literally, "lies") **for the falling and the rising of many in Israel** (v. 34). "The metaphor is taken from a stone which may become either a 'stone of stumbling' and 'a rock of offence' (Is. 8:14; Rom. 9:32, 33; I Cor. 1:23), or 'a precious corner-stone' (I Pet. 2:7, 8; Acts 4:11; I Cor. 3:11)."[68] To put it in slightly different form, Christ is for all men either a stumbling-stone, over whom they will fall in judgment, or a stepping-stone into the presence of God.

But He will also be **for a sign which is spoken against.** This same compound verb is found in Acts 28:22. The Jews at Rome said to Paul: "For as concerning this sect, it is known to us that everywhere it is spoken against."

Mary had already paid a high price for the privilege of being the mother of the Messiah. Doubtless she suffered much reproach and slander for what many would consider her illegitimate child. But the worst was yet to come. A sharp **sword** would pierce her soul (v. 35). This took place at the Crucifixion, and to a lesser extent at other times. The result of Christ's coming would be that **thoughts out of many hearts may be revealed;** "that is, upon this occasion, men will **show themselves,** will discover, and so distinguish, themselves."[69] Bond puts it more briefly: "Christ's sufferings are the touchstone of men's sentiments."[70]

---

[65] A. R. C. Leany, *A Commentary on the Gospel According to St. Luke,* p. 99.
[66] *Op. cit.,* p. 130.   [67] William Manson, *The Gospel of Luke,* p. 21.   [68] Farrar, *op. cit.,* p. 118.
[69] Matthew Henry, *Commentary on the Whole Bible,* V, 605.
[70] John Bond, *The Gospel According to St. Luke,* p. 89.

4. The Adoration of Anna (2:36-39)

36 And there was one Anna, a prophetess, the daughter of Phanuel, of the tribe of Asher (she was of a great age, having lived with a husband seven years from her virginity, 37 and she had been a widow even unto fourscore and four years), who departed not from the temple, worshipping with fastings and supplications night and day. 38 And coming up at that very hour she gave thanks unto God, and spake of him to all them that were looking for the redemption of Jerusalem. 39 And when they had accomplished all things that were according to the law of the Lord, they returned into Galilee, to their own city Nazareth.

Anna — same as Hannah (I Sam. 1:20), meaning "grace" or "compassion" — was a **prophetess,** like Miriam, Deborah, and Huldah in the Old Testament. Her father's name was **Phanuel,** which means "the face of God." It is the same word as Peniel (Gen. 32:30). The importance of having godly parents and a good home is reflected here. There would be more Annas if there were more Phanuels.

This woman was married for **seven years** (v. 36). She had now reached the age of 84 (v. 37). This fact is brought out more clearly in **even unto** (*heos*, best Greek text) than in the "about" (*hos*) of the King James Version. The latter might suggest that she had been a widow for 84 years.

The statement that Anna **departed not from the temple** may mean that as a prophetess she lived there, or simply that she was always present at the morning and evening hours of prayer. She was **worshipping** (or, "serving") with **fastings and supplications night and day.** This is echoed in the words of Paul: "Now she that is a widow indeed, and desolate, hath her hope set on God, and continueth in supplications and prayers night and day" (I Tim. 5:5).

Coming up (literally, "standing by" or "being present"), Anna **gave thanks**[71] **unto God** for the coming of the Messiah. She talked about Him **to all them that were looking for the redemption of Jerusalem** (v. 38). There were in Jerusalem faithful souls who were waiting for the

Messiah. And they knew each other in a fellowship of obedient expectancy.

Mary and Joseph were careful to carry out all the requirements of the Law (v. 39). This reflected their own piety. It was also a necessary part of Jesus' fulfilling all righteousness. When they had completed all their obligations at the Temple in Jerusalem, they **returned into Galilee, to their own city Nazareth** — a journey of eighty miles.

B. THE CHILDHOOD AND YOUTH OF JESUS (2:40-52)

1. Early Growth (2:40)

40 And the child grew, and waxed strong, filled with wisdom: and the grace of God was upon him.

The humanity of Jesus is emphasized here. He grew — the same word is used for John the Baptist (1:80) — **and waxed strong.**[72] **Filled with wisdom** is literally "becoming filled with wisdom," Jesus had a steady physical and mental development. Also He grew spiritually — **the grace of God was upon him.**

2. Visit to the Temple (2:41-51)

41 And his parents went every year to Jerusalem at the feast of the passover. 42 And when he was twelve years old, they went up after the custom of the feast; 43 and when they had fulfilled the days, as they were returning, the boy Jesus tarried behind in Jerusalem; and his parents knew it not; 44 but supposing him to be in the company, they went a day's journey; and they sought for him among their kinsfolk and acquaintance: 45 and when they found him not, they returned to Jerusalem, seeking for him. 46 And it came to pass, after three days they found him in the temple, sitting in the midst of the teachers, both hearing them, and asking them questions: 47 and all that heard him were amazed at his understanding and his answers. 48 And when they saw him, they were astonished; and his mother said unto him, Son, why hast thou thus dealt with us? behold, thy father and I sought thee sorrowing. 49 And he said unto them, How is it that ye sought me? knew ye not that I must be in my Father's house? 50 And they understood not the saying which he spake

---

[71] The Greek verb, found only here in the New Testament, suggests "gave thanks in turn"; that is, responsively to Simeon.

[72] "In spirit" (KJV), genuine in 1:80, is not found here is the oldest Greek manuscripts.

unto them. 51 And he went down with them, and came to Nazareth; and he was subject unto them: and his mother kept all *these* sayings in her heart.

Every adult male Jew was required to attend **the feast of the passover** each year. It was held in March or April, as Easter is celebrated today, because the Jewish months always began at the time of a new moon. Women were not obliged to go to the three great annual feasts (Deut. 16:16). But both of the **parents** of Jesus, being unusually pious, **went every year.** When Jesus was **twelve years old,** He accompained them to Jerusalem for the Passover. Every Jewish boy at the age of thirteen is supposed to go through a solemn ceremony by which he becomes *Bar Mitzvah* (Aramaic for "Son of the Law"; the Hebrew is *Ben Torah*). But there is some evidence that in the time of Christ it might have been held when a boy was either twelve or thirteen. So this may have been Jesus' *Bar Mitzvah.* Schürer allows for this when he says that the ceremony was held when the boy reached puberty, which would normally be at either twelve or thirteen years of age.[73] Later the age was fixed definitely at thirteen.

If Jesus did have *Bar Mitzvah* at this time it would form a perfect setting for the incident described here. For at that ceremony a Jewish boy became a member of the congregation of Israel. He could worship with the men in the synagogue, instead of having to be with his mother in the secluded, curtained space assigned to the women. He was no longer called "little" but "grown up." The modern counterpart is what is known as Confirmation in some churches.

When they had **fulfilled the days** — the seven days of the Feast of Unleavened Bread — they started back home. Since there was a large group of people from Nazareth traveling together Mary and Joseph did not know that Jesus had stayed behind in Jerusalem. They supposed that He was in **the company** — the caravan from their home town. It was not until they stopped for the night that they discovered His absence. As it was not safe to travel in the dark, they had to wait until the morning to start back to Jerusalem. It must have been an anxious night for His mother.

After three days (v. 46) — one day traveling toward home, a second day returning to Jerusalem, and part of a third day looking for Him — they found Him in the Temple. He was sitting in the midst of the teachers, listening to them and also asking them questions. People were **amazed** at His understanding (v. 47). But why should His parents have been **astonished** to find Him in the Temple?

Reproachfully His mother said to Him: **Son, why hast thou thus dealt with us?** (v. 48). The word **Son** should be "child." The Greek word is from the verb meaning "to bear a child." Morgan draws a modern parallel. He says: "It is a word that has exactly the value of the Scotch word 'bairn.' When a Scotchwoman talks of her bairn, she means the child she has borne."[74]

Mary went on to say: **thy father and I have sought thee sorrowing.** But Jesus reminded her that God was His real Father. He said: **Knew ye not that I must be in my Father's house?** The Greek literally reads: "in the things of my Father," but the papyri point to the Revised rendering (rather than KJV) as the correct reading.[75]

His parents did not understand what He meant (v. 50). But the young lad went home with them to Nazareth, and **was subject unto** them (v. 51). Mary treasured in her heart the memory of what had happened.

3. Further Development (2:52)

52 And Jesus advanced in wisdom and stature, and in favor with God and men.

This verse indicates that Jesus had a normal development mentally, physically, spiritually and socially. He was human as well as divine.

The word which is translated **stature** means "a stage of growth whether measured by age or stature."[76] In John 9:21, 23 it clearly means "age." The parents of the man who had been born blind said: "He is of age; ask him." The same is true of Hebrews 11:11. Sarah conceived "when she was past age." But in

---

[73] *Op. cit.,* II, ii, 50-52. [74] G. Campbell Morgan, *The Gospel According to Luke,* p. 45.
[75] James Hope Moulton, *A Grammar of New Testament Greek,* Vol. I., "Prolegomena," p. 103.
[76] G. Abbott-Smith, *A Manual Greek Lexicon of the New Testament,* p. 199.

Luke 19:3 it just as obviously means "stature." Zacchaeus could not see Jesus in the crowd "because he was little of stature." Since "the prevailing usage in the Septuagint and the papyri" is in favor of "age,"[77] some translators prefer that here. Goodspeed has: "As Jesus grew older he gained in wisdom and won the approval of God and men" (cf. NEB — "As Jesus grew up he advanced in wisdom and in favour with God and men"). The latter translation may be purposely somewhat ambiguous. But it seems rather preferable in this passage to use "stature" (so RSV).

A comparison of the infancy narratives in Matthew and Luke shows that they have an entirely different set of incidents, aside from the statement of Jesus' birth. Luke records the announcement of the birth of John the Baptist, the announcement (to Mary) of the birth of Jesus, Mary's visit to Elisabeth, the birth of John the Baptist, the birth of Jesus, the visit of the shepherds, Jesus' circumcision and presentation to the Lord, and His visit to Jerusalem at the age of twelve. Matthew has the annunciation to Joseph, the visit of the wise men, the flight into Egypt and the return to Nazareth (see notes on Matt. 2:19-23).

II. THE PERIOD OF PREPARATION (3:1-4:1)

A. THE MINISTRY OF JOHN THE BAPTIST (3:1-20)

1. A Baptism of Repentance (3:1-6)

1 Now in the fifteenth year of the reign of Tiberius Caesar, Pontius Pilate being governor of Judaea, and Herod being tetrarch of Galilee, and his brother Philip tetrarch of the region of Ituraea and Trachonitis, and Lysanias tetrarch of Abilene, 2 in the highpriesthood of Annas and Caiaphas, the word of God came unto John the son of Zacharias in the wilderness. 3 And he came into all the region round about the Jordan, preaching the baptism of repentance unto remission of sins; 4 as it is written in the book of the words of Isaiah the prophet,
The voice of one crying in the wilderness,
Make ye ready the way of the Lord,
Make his paths straight.
5 Every valley shall be filled,

And every mountain and hill shall be brought low;
And the crooked shall become straight,
And the rough ways smooth;
6 And all flesh shall see the salvation of God.

Luke's role as a historian appears in sharp focus in the first two verses of this chapter. There is nothing like it in the other Gospels. No less than five rulers plus two high priests are mentioned, and then the Forerunner of the Messiah. Thus the stage is set for the beginning of Christ's ministry. Ewald says that Luke is "the first writer who frames the Gospel History into the great history of the world."[78]

Tiberius Caesar was the second emperor of the Roman Empire (A.D. 14-37). He was the adopted stepson of Augustus, the first emperor (30 B.C.-A.D. 14), who ruled when Christ was born. At first a wise and beneficent ruler, he had by this time become cruel and tyrannical. Luke states that John the Baptist began his ministry in the **fifteenth year** of Tiberius' reign. The problem is raised here as to whether this means the fifteenth year of his sole rulership, which began in A.D. 14 — thus making John the Baptist's ministry begin in A.D. 29 — or whether the time is to be reckoned from Tiberius' association with Augustus as ruler of the empire, in A.D. 11 or 12. The latter would place the beginning of John's ministry in A.D. 26, which seems to fit better into the chronology of Christ's life.[79]

Pontius Pilate was **governor** — his official Latin title was Procurator — of Judea (A.D. 26-36). So he was the new ruler of the central and southern parts of Palestine (Samaria, Judea, Idumea) when Jesus began His public ministry. He was cruel and yet weak, as the Gospels show. The first inscription bearing his name was found on June 15, 1961, at Caesarea. It was discovered by an Italian archaeologist among the ruins of the ancient capitol of Roman rule in Palestine.[80]

Herod was **tetrarch of Galilee,** and also of Perea, east of Jordan (4 B.C.-A.D. 39). This was Herod Antipas, son of Herod the Great and his Samaritan wife, Malthace. **Tetrarch** literally means "ruler

77 *Ibid.*   78 Quoted by Farrar, *op. cit.*, p. 126.   79 Andrews, *op. cit.*, pp. 21-29.
80 *Israel Digest*, July 7, 1961.

of a fourth part." "But by this time it was used in a less specific sense. As a title it is lower than 'king,' and implies limitation and dependency."[81] It was used as a "general term for a subordinate native ruler."[82] On the death of Herod the Great (4 B.C.) his kingdom was partitioned between one ethnarch (Archelaus, who received Judea but was deposed for misrule in A.D. 6) and two tetrarchs (Antipas and Philip).

Antipas' **brother Philip** was the son of Herod the Great and Cleopatra. Considered the best of the Herods, he ruled from 4 B.C. until his death in A.D. 33 or 34. His territory included **Ituraea** and **Trachonitis,** which are northeast of Galilee.

Lysanias was **tetrarch of Abilene.** Very little is known about this man from ancient sources, and Luke has often been charged with historical inaccuracy in this reference. But Creed cites an inscription which mentions a tetrarch named Lysanias in the time of Tiberius, and concludes: "It is therefore reasonable to suppose that Luke's statement that a Lysanias ruled over Abilene at the time of the ministry of John the Baptist is true."[83] Abilene was far to the north, near Damascus.

The reference to the **highpriesthood of Annas and Caiaphas** seems very odd. There was supposed to be only one high priest at a time, and the office was for life. But the Roman rulers at this period were appointing and dismissing high priests according to their own whims. In the seventy-five years between the birth of Jesus (5 B.C.) and the destruction of the Temple in A.D. 70 (and so the end of a functioning priesthood) there were no less than twenty-five men who held this office — an average of one every three years. **Annas** was high priest A.D. 6-15. But he continued to exercise a dominant influence over the office, which was held by five of his sons, as well as his son-in-law, **Caiaphas,** who acted as high priest A.D. 18-36.

In the period thus designated in a sixfold way, **the word of God came unto John** (cf. I Sam. 15:10; II Sam. 7:4; I Kings 17:2; Jer. 2:1). Donald Miller says: "The belief was widespread . . . that when the Messianic Age came, prophecy

would reappear (Joel 2:28; Mal. 3:1; 4:5)."[84] He was **in the wilderness** when God spoke to him. This was probably the Wilderness of Judea. From there John emerged into **the region round about the Jordan.** Here he was **preaching the baptism of repentance unto remission of sins** (v. 3). For the meanings of these terms see the comments on Matthew 3:1, 2 and Mark 1:4.

For an identification of John's mission, Luke quotes Isaiah 40:3-5. (Matthew and Mark quote only the third verse.) This passage suggests God's fourfold formula for a revival: (1) filling in the valleys; (2) cutting down the mountains; (3) straightening out the curves; (4) smoothing out the bumps. When this is done, **all flesh shall see the salvation of God** (v. 6). When the church takes the divine prescription, sinners will be saved.

2. The Fruits of Repentance (3:7-14)

7 He said therefore to the multitudes that went out to be baptized of him, Ye offspring of vipers, who warned you to flee from the wrath to come? 8 Bring forth therefore fruits worthy of repentance, and begin not to say within yourselves, We have Abraham to our father: for I say unto you, that God is able of these stones to raise up children unto Abraham. 9 And even now the axe also lieth at the root of the trees: every tree therefore that bringeth not forth good fruit is hewn down, and cast into the fire. 10 And the multitudes asked him, saying, What then must we do? 11 And he answered and said unto them, He that hath two coats, let him impart to him that hath none; and he that hath food, let him do likewise. 12 And there came also publicans to be baptized, and they said unto him, Teacher, what must we do? 13 And he said unto them, Extort no more than that which is appointed you. 14 And soldiers also asked him, saying, And we, what must we do? And he said unto them, Extort from no man by violence, neither accuse any one wrongfully; and be content with your wages.

Verses 7-9 are closely parallel to Matthew 3:7-10 (see the comments there). Luke alone goes on to give John's specific instructions to three groups: (1) **the multitudes** (vv. 10, 11); (2) **the**

[81] S. Sandmel, "Tetrarch," *The Interpreter's Dictionary of the Bible* (hereafter cited as IDB), ed. George A. Buttrick, IV, 579. [82] Creed, *op. cit.,* p. 49. [83] *Ibid.,* p. 309. [84] *Op. cit.,* p. 43.

publicans (vv. 12, 13); (3) the soldiers (v. 14).

When the multitudes asked, What then must we do (v. 10), John the Baptist told them to share their clothing and food with those who lacked. This is simply practicing the Golden Rule (Matt. 7:12). Coats is literally "shirts" (Moffatt); that is, the undergarments worn next to the skin.

The publicans came with the same question on their lips. These were the "tax collectors" of that day. To them John said, Extort no more than that which is appointed unto you (v. 13). The Roman government farmed out the collection of taxes to certain individuals called *publicani*. These, in turn, employed local individuals to do the actual collecting of the taxes in small areas. The latter were "tax collectors," not publicans, and are the ones mentioned here and elsewhere in the Gospels. Since each tax collector was responsible for turning in a certain amount to his superior, it was common practice to extort — better, "exact" (KJV); extort is too strong for the Greek — as much as possible from the people. The collector would then pocket the difference.

Lastly came soldiers (v. 14) — literally, "ones serving as soldiers" — with the same question. Extort . . . by violence is a strong verb (found only here in NT), very different from "extort" in the previous verse. It literally means to shake as with an earthquake. Some soldiers would force men, through threats of violence, to give them what they demanded. John the Baptist warned against this violation of human rights. Accuse wrongfully — rather "accuse falsely" (KJV) — is a rare word, in the Greek (*sykophanteo*) found only here and in 19:8 (of Zacchaeus). It is compounded of two roots, the first meaning "fig" and the second "bring to light." Thayer gives this as one explanation for the origin of the term: "At Athens those were called *sykophantai* whose business it was to inform against any one whom they might detect exporting figs out of Attica; and as sometimes they seem to have extorted money from those loath to be exposed, the name *sykophantes* from the time of Aristophanes down was a general term of op-

probrium to designate a *malignant informer*."[85] This gives the modern term "*sycophant*." Furthermore, the soldiers were to be content with their wages. Since soldiers have always been poorly paid, this was a necessary admonition.

3. The Baptism with the Holy Spirit (3:15-17)

15 And as the people were in expectation, and all men reasoned in their hearts concerning John, whether haply he were the Christ; 16 John answered, saying unto them all, I indeed baptize you with water; but there cometh he that is mightier than I, the latchet of whose shoes I am not worthy to unloose: he shall baptize you in the Holy Spirit and *in* fire: 17 whose fan is in his hand, thoroughly to cleanse his threshing-floor, and to gather the wheat into his garner; but the chaff he will burn up with unquenchable fire.

Verse 15 is only in Luke. It indicates the reason why John made the statements found in the following verses. The Christ means "the Messiah." People were wondering if perhaps John the Baptist might be the promised Messiah.

Verses 16 and 17 are closely paralleled in Matthew 3:11, 12. For their interpretation see the discussion there. We add only one comment here: "The 'fire' connected with the baptism of the Holy Spirit likely refers to the purifying of the Spirit's work."[86]

4. The Imprisonment of John (3:18-20)

18 With many other exhortations therefore preached he good tidings unto the people; 19 but Herod the tetrarch, being reproved by him for Herodias his brother's wife, and for all the evil things which Herod had done, 20 added this also to them all, that he shut up John in prison.

This incident actually took place at a later time (cf. Matt. 14:3, 4; Mark 6:17, 18, and the comments there). Luke places it here in order to finish his discussion of John the Baptist. To John's reproving Herod for his illegal marriage to his brother's wife, Luke alone adds: and for all the evil things which Herod had done (v. 19). John was a stern Puritan and was appalled at the luxury and licentiousness of Herod's living.

B. THE BAPTISM OF JESUS (3:21, 22)

21 Now it came to pass, when all the people were baptized, that, Jesus also having been baptized, and praying, the heaven was opened, 22 and the Holy Spirit descended in a bodily form, as a dove, upon him, and a voice came out of heaven, Thou art my beloved Son; in thee I am well pleased.

For discussion of this incident and its significance, see the comments on Matthew 3:13-17. Luke has two additional details not found in the other two Synoptics. He notes that Jesus was **praying.** This is the first of six times that Luke mentions the prayer life of Jesus where the other Gospels do not mention it at all (see Introduction). The other detail is that the Holy Spirit descended **in a bodily form** upon Jesus. This is more definite than the other two accounts and emphasizes that the coming was visible to human eyes. **As a dove** (in all three Synoptics) could be taken metaphorically.

On the meaning of the Baptism, Miller has this to say: "He was baptized for the sins of others. Isaiah 53 makes this clear. . . . He took upon himself all the sins which all the people brought to the Jordan."[87]

C. THE GENEALOGY OF JESUS (3:23-38)

23 And Jesus himself, when he began *to teach,* was about thirty years of age, being the son (as was supposed) of Joseph, the *son* of Heli, 24 the *son* of Matthat, the *son* of Levi, the *son* of Melchi, the *son* of Jannai, the *son* of Joseph, 25 the *son* of Mattathias the *son* of Amos, the the *son* of Nahum, the *son* of Esli, the *son* of Naggai, 26 the *son* of Maath, the *son* of Mattathias the *son* of Semein, the *son* of Josech, the *son* of Joda, 27 the *son* of Joanan, the *son* of Rhesa, the *son* of Zerubbabel, the *son* of Shealtiel, the *son* of Neri, 28 the *son* of Melchi, the *son* of Addi, the *son* of Cosam, the *son* of Elmadam, the *son* of Er, 29 the *son* of Jesus, the *son* of Eliezer, the *son* of Jorim, the *son* of Matthat, the *son* of Levi, the *son* of Symeon, the *son* of Judas, the *son* of Joseph, the *son* of Jonam, the *son* of Eliakim, 31 the *son* of Melea, the *son* of Menna, the *son* of Mattatha, the *son* of Nathan, the *son* of David, 32 the *son* of Jesse, the *son* of Obed, the *son* of

Boaz, the *son* of Salmon, the *son* of Nahshon, 33 the *son* of Amminadab, the *son* of Arni, the *son* of Hezron, the *son* of Perez, the *son* of Judah, 34 the *son* of Jacob, the *son* of Isaac, the *son* of Abraham, the *son* of Terah, the *son* of Nahor, 35 the *son* of Serug, the *son* of Reu, the *son* of Peleg, the *son* of Eber, the *son* of Shelah, 36 the *son* of Cainan, the *son* of Arphaxad, the *son* of Shem, the *son* of Noah, the *son* of Lamech, 37 the *son* of Methuselah, the *son* of Enoch, the *son* of Jared, the *son* of Mahalaleel, the *son* of Cainan, 38 the *son* of Enos, the *son* of Seth, the *son* of Adam, the *son* of God.

There are several differences between this genealogy and the one found in Matthew 1:2-17. The most obvious one is that while Matthew begins with Abraham and follows the chosen line down to Christ, Luke begins with Jesus and goes backward to **Adam, the Son of God** (v. 38). Thus Luke, in keeping with his purpose in writing for Gentile readers, gives a complete genealogy rather than just a Jewish one.

Another striking difference is the fact that the names between David and Christ are not the same. Various theories have been proposed to account for this. One that has the support of many of the best scholars is that "Matthew gives Joseph's legal descent as successor to the throne of David," while Luke "gives Joseph's real parentage."[88] Robertson, however, thinks that the "most plausible solution yet suggested makes Matthew give the real descent of Joseph, and Luke the real descent of Mary."[89] This is in keeping with the fact that the infancy narratives in Matthew are focused on the experience of Joseph and those in Luke center on Mary. The best explanation and defense of this view is that presented by Godet. He would translate the last part of verse 23: "being a son — as was thought, of Joseph — of Heli."[90] So it is the genealogy of Heli, the father of Mary, which is followed.

In keeping with Luke's historical interest is his statement — found only here — that Jesus was **about thirty years of age, when He began to teach** (v. 23). This was the usual time for men to begin public life.

87 *Ibid.,* p. 47.
88 A. T. Robertson, *A Harmony of Gospels for Students of the Life of Christ,* p. 260.
89 *Ibid.,* p. 261.   90 *Op. cit.,* p. 201.

D. THE TEMPTATION OF JESUS (4:1-13)

1 And Jesus, full of the Holy Spirit, returned from the Jordan, and was led in the Spirit in the wilderness 2 during forty days, being tempted of the devil. And he did eat nothing in those days: and when they were completed, he hungered. 3 And the devil said unto him, if thou art the Son of God, command this stone that it become bread. 4 And Jesus answered unto him, It is written, Man shall not live by bread alone. 5 And he led him up, and showed him all the kingdoms of the world in a moment of time. 6 And the devil said unto him, To thee will I give all this authority, and the glory of them: for it hath been delivered unto me; and to whomsoever I will I give it. 7 If thou therefore wilt worship before me, it shall all be thine. 8 And Jesus answered and said unto him, it is written, Thou shalt worship the Lord thy God, and him only shalt thou serve. 9 And he led him to Jerusalem, and set him on the pinnacle of the temple, and said unto him, If thou art the Son of God, cast thyself down from hence: 10 for it is written,

He shall give his angels charge concerning thee, to guard thee:

11 and,

On their hands they shall bear thee up,

Lest haply thou dash thy foot against a stone.

12 And Jesus answering said unto him, It is said, Thou shalt not make trial of the Lord thy God.

13 And when the devil had completed every temptation, he departed from him for a season.

For an extended discussion of this crisis in Christ's life, see the notes on Matthew 4:1-11. We shall note here mainly the distinctive items in Luke.

In the first verse Luke alone has the expression **full of the Holy Spirit**. This is the key phrase of the Book of Acts, which was also written by Luke. His interest in the Holy Spirit is very marked. The Spirit is mentioned more times in this Gospel than in any of the others, and over fifty times in Acts — many times more than in any other book of the New Testament.

Luke reports that when Satan was offering Jesus the authority of the kingdoms of the world if He would worship him, the devil said: **for it hath been delivered unto me; and to whomsoever I will I give it.** The striking fact is that Christ did not deny the devil's claim. Three times in the Gospel of John we find Jesus referring to Satan as "the prince of this world" (John 12:31; 14:30; 16:11).

The significance of this second temptation is thus expressed by Burton: "The objective point at which the tempter aimed was, as in the first temptation, to shift Jesus from the Divine purpose, to detach His will from the Father's will, and to induce Him to set up a sort of independence."[91]

Luke concludes the story of the Temptation by saying that **when the devil had completed every temptation** — which suggests that the three recorded were only the climactic ones of a long series — he left Jesus **for a season** (v. 13). The last words are ominous, suggesting that he would be back.

III. THE GALILEAN MINISTRY (4:14-9:50)

A. BEGINNING OF PUBLIC MINISTRY (4:14-30)

1. Return to Galilee (4:14, 15)

14 And Jesus returned in the power of the Spirit into Galilee: and a fame went out concerning him through all the region round about. 15 And he taught in their synagogues, being glorified of all.

All three Synoptic Gospels note the fact that Jesus moved northward to Galilee (cf. Matt. 4:12; Mark 1:14). But Luke alone says that He returned to His home territory **in the power of the Spirit.** This is a typical Lukan emphasis (cf. Acts 1:8). The Holy Spirit came down upon Jesus at His baptism, then led Him out into a desolate wilderness for a period of severe testing. As a result of those two experiences He was now ready to begin His ministry. Thus Luke has twice (cf. 4:1) pointed out the importance of the Holy Spirit in the life of Christ. If He needed to be consciously filled and empowered with the Spirit, how much more do we.

Because of His power, His ministry created a sensation. His fame spread throughout all that region (cf. Matt. 4:

91 Henry Burton, *The Gospel According to St. Luke*, pp. 119, 120.

24; Mark 1:28). A Spirit-filled ministry is always effective.

In all the towns that Jesus visited He found an open door for teaching in the synagogues. This was a situation perhaps unparalleled by any in the world today. As a visiting rabbi, He would be invited to speak (cf. Acts 13:15). This gave Him an opportunity to speak the Good News.

Not much is known about the origin of the synagogue. But the consensus today is that this institution had its beginning during the period of Babylonian captivity, when the Jews had no temple in which to worship. Following the Jews' return to Judea it became firmly established under the influence of the scribes. Though leading scholars disagree in details, "they all set the beginning of the synagogue in the Babylonian exile but its consolidation in Palestine as a result of Ezra's work."[92]

Luke says that Jesus was **glorified** by all. This is also a favorite Lukan term. "Glory" and "glorify" are found more frequently in this Gospel than in the other two Synoptics, though not as many times as in John's Gospel. "Glory" and "power" were prominent in Luke's thinking.

Plumptre's comment on this closing phrase of verse 15 is worth quoting. He writes: "The dawn of the day of work was bright. Wonder, admiration, glory, waited on the New Prophet. Soon, however, when His preaching involved a demand on men's faith and obedience beyond what they had expected, it roused opposition, and the narrative that follows is the first stage of that antagonism."[93]

2. Rejection at Nazareth (4:16-30)

16 And he came to Nazareth, where he had been brought up: and he entered, as his custom was, into the synagogue on the sabbath day, and stood up to read. 17 And there was delivered unto him the book of the prophet Isaiah. And he opened the book, and found the place where it was written,
18 The Spirit of the Lord is upon me, Because he anointed me to preach good tidings to the poor:

He hath sent me to proclaim release to the captives,
And recovering of sight to the blind, to set at liberty them that are bruised,
19 To proclaim the acceptable year of the Lord.
20 And he closed the book, and gave it back to the attendant, and sat down: and the eyes of all in the synagogue were fastened on him. 21 And he began to say unto them, Today hath this scripture been fulfilled in your ears. 22 And all bare him witness, and wondered at the words of grace which proceeded out of his mouth: and they said, Is not this Joseph's son? 23 And he said unto them, Doubtless ye will say unto me this parable, Physician, heal thyself: whatsoever we have heard done at Capernaum, do also here in thine own country. 24 And he said, Verily I say unto you, No prophet is acceptable in his own country. 25 But of a truth I say unto you, There were many widows in Israel in the days of Elijah, when the heaven was shut up three years and six months, when there came a great famine over all the land; 26 and unto none of them was Elijah sent, but only to Zarephath, in the land of Sidon, unto a woman that was a widow. 27 And there were many lepers in Israel in the time of Elisha the prophet; and none of them was cleansed, but only Naaman the Syrian. 28 And they were all filled with wrath in the synagogue, as they heard these things; 29 and they rose up, and cast him forth out of the city, and led him unto the brow of the hill whereon their city was built, that they might throw him down headlong. 30 But he passing through the midst of them went his way.

Matthew (13:53-58) and Mark (6:1-6) both record a visit of Jesus to His home town of Nazareth, but they place it at a later point in the chronology. As Gilmour notes, putting it here makes it "a dramatic frontispiece to Jesus' public ministry."[94]

There has been considerable dispute as to whether this is the same visit as that related by Matthew and Mark. The best scholars are divided on this point. For instance, Alford, A. B. Bruce, Farrar, and Geldenhuys favor one visit, as does Creed. Alford cites several arguments in support of this position. Farrar says

---

[92] I. Sonne, "Synagogue," *Interpreter's Dictionary of the Bible*, IV, 479.
[93] E. H. Plumptre, "The Gospel According to St. Luke," *Commentary on the Whole Bible*, ed. C. J. Ellicott, VI, 264.
[94] S. MacLean Gilmour, "The Gospel According to St. Luke" (Exegesis), *The Interpreter's Bible*, VIII, p. 89.

more simply: "This is probably the visit related in unchronological order in Matt. 13:53-58; Mark 6:1-6, since after so violent and decisive a rejection as St. Luke describes, it is unlikely that He should have preached at Nazareth again."[95]

But we have already noted that Luke describes the imprisonment of John the Baptist at an earlier point than it actually took place (see 3:18-20). So why may he not have done the same thing here? This is the view of Geldenhuys, who thinks that Luke wanted to describe the nature of Jesus' ministry and show His interest in the salvation of the Gentiles.[96]

On the other hand, the idea of two visits is favored by Andrews, Ellicott, Godet, Meyer, and others. Andrews says: "The points of difference are more numerous, and more plainly marked."[97] Both he and Godet[98] present these differences in detail.

In the face of such general disagreement it is difficult to make a decision. And if we settle for one visit, as probably most Biblical scholars do today, we are still left with the question of whose chronology is preferable, that of Matthew and Mark, or that of Luke. The language of verse 23 implies a period of miracle-working at Capernaum. But that could perhaps be equated with the statement in verse 14.

As his custom was (v. 16) points to a lifelong habit of attending the synagogue on the sabbath day. In this respect Jesus set an example for our going to church every Lord's Day, the Christian sabbath.

It was apparently the custom that one who wished to read the Scripture lesson **stood up to read** (v. 16). The attendant handed to Jesus **the book** — that is, a "scroll" of **the prophet Isaiah** (v. 17). This would have been after the repeating of the Shema (Deut. 6:4-9; 11:13-21; Num. 15:37-41), a prayer, and the reading of the prescribed lesson from the Law (the Pentateuch). The readings from both the Law and the Prophets were in Hebrew, with an Aramaic paraphrase (Targum) added so that the listeners would understand. "The Law was read through over a period of three years — one year in Babylonia — but the reader

chose his own selection from the Prophets."[99]

The lesson Jesus selected was from Isaiah 61:1, 2. **The Spirit of the Lord is upon me, Because he anointed me** refers to the recent Baptism, when the Holy Spirit descended on Christ. **To preach good tidings to the poor** is a strong emphasis in Luke. He has more to say for the poor than do other Evangelists (see Introduction). The poor people were willing to hear and heed the message, while too often the learned and wealthy spurned it. As climactic proof of His messiahship, Jesus told the disciples of John the Baptist to report to him "the poor have good tidings preached to them" — literally, "poor people are being evangelized." It is the same verb here — "to evangelize poor people." This is the glory of the gospel, that it is Good News for all who will accept. It is a striking fact that while the verb *euangelizo* is found only once in Matthew and not at all in Mark or John, it occurs ten times in Luke and fifteen times in Acts (written by Luke) — twenty-five out of a total of fifty-five times in the New Testament. It is definitely a Lukan emphasis.

The words "to heal the broken-hearted" (KJV) are omitted in the Revised Versions because they are not found in most of the very earliest Greek manuscripts. But they are in the passage in Isaiah, which Jesus was reading. Godet, the great French commentator, thinks "they form the almost indispensable basis of the word of Jesus, ver. 23."[100] So he would retain them, holding that their omission in some manuscripts is due to carelessness in copying a long series of infinitives. But Plummer asserts: "The evidence against the clause . . . is decisive." At any rate the words are in the Old Testament, and we cannot give any explanation as to why they may have been omitted here.

He hath sent me is in the perfect tense in Greek, as in English, whereas *he anointed* (above) is aorist. Plummer points out the significance of this: "He anointed Me (once for all); He hath sent Me (and I am here)."[101] The Greek perfect emphasizes not only a completed act, but even more forcibly a continuing state. The verb **sent** is not the more general

[95] *Op. cit.*, pp. 148, 149.　　[96] *Op. cit.*, p. 166.
[99] Gilmour, *op. cit.*, p. 90.　　[100] *Op. cit.*, p. 234.
[97] *Op. cit.*, p. 219.　　[98] *Op. cit.*, 1, 240, 241.
[101] *Op. cit.*, p. 121.

term *pempo* but the stronger one *apostello*, which "adds the idea of a delegated authority making the person sent to be the envoy or representative of the sender."[102] It means "sent on a mission."

The first thing (as recorded here) for which Jesus was sent was to **proclaim release to the captives.** The Greek word for **proclaim** is the same as that used for the preaching of John the Baptist (3: 3). The word for **release** is translated both "forgiveness" and "remission" in regard to sins. **Captives** is literally "prisoners of war." This has led most commentators to assume that the primary application of the passage in Isaiah was to the return of the Jewish exiles from Babylonian captivity. Jesus now applied it to His mission of proclaiming release from the captivity of sin.

The second purpose of His coming was to proclaim **recovering of sight to the blind.** It is evident that Jesus intended these words to be taken figuratively rather than literally, for the whole context suggests this. Nevertheless Christ did restore sight to many eyes that were blinded physically. This He did for two reasons: (1) out of compassion for afflicted people, and (2) as an illustration of His greater mission in giving sight to men's eyes that were blinded spiritually.

The third, **To set at liberty them that are bruised** "is imported (by Luke probably) from Isa. 58:6, the aim being to make the text in all respects a programme for the ministry of Jesus."[103] But it does not seem impossible to suppose that Jesus may have inserted this item from an earlier chapter to fill out the description of the nature of His mission. **Bruised** is a strong perfect passive participle. Plummer observes that it "is here applied to those who are shattered in fortune and broken in spirit."[104]

Jesus closed His reading with the climactic expression, **To proclaim the acceptable year of the Lord.** This leads Godet to interpret the entire passage in terms of the Hebrew year of jubilee (Lev. 25). He says: "On the first day of the year of jubilee, the priests went all through the land, announcing with sound of trumpets the blessings brought by the opening year."[105] The words **to proclaim release** fit perfectly the idea of the year of jubilee (which came every fifty years). For at that time all Hebrew slaves were set free. The Greek for **release** is *aphesin.* Godet notes: "This word *aphesin* is found at almost every verse, in the Septuagint, in the statute enjoining this feast."[106]

Very wisely Plummer makes the double application of this Scripture that Jesus read. He says: "It is obvious that both figures, the return from exile and the release at the jubilee, admirably express Christ's work of redemption."[107]

When Jesus had finished reading, He **closed the book** — rather, He "rolled up the scroll" — **and gave it back to the attendant** (v. 20). This was the *hazzan,* who acted as assistant to the *archisynagogos,* or "ruler of the synagogue" (cf. 13:14). "He assigned the functions during the worship, handed the Torah and the prophetic scroll to the reader. . ., and received them after the reading."[108]

Then Jesus **sat down.** It was the custom among the Jews to stand to read the Scriptures (cf. v. 16), out of reverence for them, and then to sit while explaining them and teaching the people. As usual, Christ conformed to such established customs.

Jesus now had the attention of everyone — **the eyes of all in the synagogue were fastened on him.** "Their intense interest was caused by His reputation as a teacher and as a worker of miracles, as well as by His having been brought up amongst them; perhaps also by His look and manner of reading."[109]

Then He began **to speak** (v. 21). This word "points to the solemnity of the moment when His words broke the silence of universal expectations."[110] His first pronouncement was: **Today hath this scripture been fulfilled in your ears;** that is, "this preaching to which you are now listening is itself the realization of this prophecy."[111]

It has often been pointed out that Jesus stopped His reading of the lesson from the Prophets right in the middle of a sentence. But had He read the next clause of Isaiah 61:2, "and the day of vengeance of our God," He could not have said that it was now fulfilled. Christ

---

[102] *Ibid.*   [103] A. B. Bruce, *op. cit.,* p. 490.   [104] *Op. cit.,* p. 122.   [105] *Op. cit.,* p. 234.
[106] *Ibid.,* p. 106.   [107] *Op. cit.,* p. 121.   [108] Sonne, IDB, IV, 489.
[109] Plummer, *op. cit.,* p. 123.   [110] *Ibid.*   [111] Godet, *op. cit.,* p. 235.

came the first time in mercy to bring salvation. He will come the second time in judgment, to set up His kingdom of righteousness and peace.

The effect on the audience was impressive: **all bare him witness, and wondered** — or, "were witnessing and wondering" — **at the words of grace which proceeded out of his mouth** (v. 22).

The word **grace** (*charis*) is not found in Matthew or Mark. It is characteristic of Luke's emphasis on God's grace shown in the salvation of all who will believe, whether Jew or Gentile, that he uses the term eight times in his Gospel and sixteen times in Acts. (It is found four times in John.) It is one of the great words in Paul's vocabulary, occurring over a hundred times. Plummer gives such an excellent summary of the changing meanings of this term, that we quote it at length:

> The very first meaning of *charis* . . . is "comeliness, winsomeness" (Hom. *Od.* 8.175; Eccles. 10:12; Ps. 44:3 . . .; Col. 4:6): and in all these passages it is the winsomeness of *language* that is specially signified. From this objective attractiveness it easily passes to subjective "favor, kindness, goodwill", especially from a superior to an inferior (Acts 2:47 . . .); and hence in particular, of finding "favour" with God (1:30; Acts 7:46 . . .). From the sense of God's favour generally (2:40, 52; John 1:14, 16) we come to the special theological sense of "God's favour to sinners, the free gift of His grace" (Acts 14:3, 20, 24, 32; and frequently in the Pauline Epistles).[112]

But surprise was mixed with incredulity. The hearers began asking, **Is not this Joseph's son?** This suggests that the people of Nazareth considered Joseph to be the actual father, rather than foster-father, of Jesus. Apparently Joseph was a very ordinary man, whose son could not be expected to have such a spectacular career as this Prophet. Or the question may simply indicate that the people considered the passage in Isaiah to be Messianic, and could not see how a child of Nazareth could fill that role.

In answer Jesus suggested that His fellow townspeople would probably like to quote to Him the familar **parable** ("proverb") **Physician, heal thyself** (v. 23). This is similar to the modern saying,

"Charity begins at home." The application is made here: the miracles which they heard He was performing at **Capernaum** should be done also in Nazareth. This remark is often taken as indicating a later date for this visit to Nazareth, in keeping with the Markan and Matthean chronology, when His fame as miracle-worker would have gained proportions. But probably a sufficient answer to this argument is found in verse 14: "A fame went out concerning him through all the region round about."

Jesus went on to balance this with another proverb: **No prophet is acceptable in his own country** (v. 24). To illustrate this He cited the case of Elijah who was hated in his own country but was cared for by a widow **of Zarephath** (a city between Tyre and Sidon). Also there were **many lepers in Israel** in Elisha's day. Yet none of them was cleansed. Instead **Naaman the Syrian,** a general in the army of Israel's enemy, was healed.

This was more than the hearers in the synagogue could take. They rushed Jesus out of the city and tried to throw Him over **the brow of the hill** — a rocky cliff. But Jesus **passing through the midst of them went his way** (v. 30). Whether this involved the use of "His divine power," as Geldenhuys[113] thinks, we have no way of being certain.

B. MINISTRY AT CAPERNAUM (4:31-43)

1. Deliverance of Demoniac (4:31-37)

31 And he came down to Capernaum, a city of Galilee. And he was teaching them on the sabbath day: 32 and they were astonished at his teaching; for his word was with authority. 33 And in the synagogue there was a man, that had a spirit of an unclean demon; and he cried out with a loud voice, 34 Ah! what have we to do with thee, Jesus thou Nazarene? art thou come to destroy us? I know thee who thou art, the Holy One of God. 35 And Jesus rebuked him, saying, Hold thy peace, and come out of him. And when the demon had thrown him down in the midst, he came out of him, having done him no hurt. 36 And amazement came upon all, and they spake together, one with another, saying, What is this word? for with authority and power he commandeth the unclean spirits, and they

---

[112] *Op. cit.*, pp. 124, 125.   [113] *Op. cit.*, p. 169.

come out. 37 And there went forth a rumor concerning him into every place of the region round about.

This incident is recorded also by Mark, but not by Matthew. The accounts agree closely (see comments on Mark 1:21-28). We note here only the distinctive items given by Luke. Since he was writing for people living outside Palestine, he adds the identification of **Capernaum** as **a city of Galilee** (v. 31). He uses the term **demon** twice (vv. 33, 35), while Mark simply says "unclean spirit." Being a physician, Luke adds the observation concerning the condition of the delivered demoniac that the demon came out, **having done him no hurt** (v. 35). This is one of the many little items in this Gospel which suggests that it was written by a physician (see Introduction).

2. Healing of Peter's Mother-in-Law (4:38, 39)

38 And he rose up from the synagogue, and entered into the house of Simon. And Simon's wife's mother was holden with a great fever; and they besought him for her. 39 And he stood over her, and rebuked the fever; and it left her: and immediately she rose up and ministered unto them.

This miracle is recorded in all three Synoptics (see the comments on Matt. 8:14-17; Mark 1:29-31). Luke again shows a physician's interest in his description of the woman's affliction. He says she was **held with a great fever** (v. 38). This expression was commonly used by such physicians as Galen. Also Luke describes the healing with the distinctive statement that Jesus **rebuked the fever** (v. 39). Hobart notes that this language "would more naturally come from a medical writer than another."[114]

3. Sunset Healing Service (4:40, 41)

40 And when the sun was setting, all they that had any sick with divers diseases brought them unto him; and he laid his hands on every one of them, and healed them. 41 And demons also came out from many, crying out, and saying, Thou art the Son of God. And rebuking them, he suffered them not to speak, because they knew that he was the Christ.

This is also found in all three Synoptic

Gospels (see comments on Matt. 8:16-17; Mark 1:32-34). Luke is a bit more definite in specifying that the demons knew Jesus to be **the Christ** (v. 41); that is, the Messiah.

4. Sunrise Prayer Time (4:42, 43)

42 And when it was day, he came out and went into a desert place: and the multitudes sought after him, and came unto him, and would have stayed him, that he should not go from them. 43 But he said unto them, I must preach the good tidings of the kingdom of God to the other cities also: for therefore was I sent.

This description of Jesus praying in the early morning is found in Mark, but not Matthew (see comments on Mark 1:35-38). One minor difference in the accounts is that Mark says that "Simon and they that were with him" sought Jesus, while Luke simply says **the multitudes.** Whereas Mark reports Jesus as saying that He must "preach" (*kerusso*, "herald") in other towns, Luke has his favorite verb *evangelize* — **preach the good tidings.** In other words, He wanted to evangelize other cities besides Capernaum.

C. PREACHING AND HEALING (4:44—5:16)

1. Tour of Preaching (4:44)

44 And he was preaching in the synagogues of Galilee.

This brief summary statement is paralleled in Mark 1:39. It indicates that Jesus made a preaching tour of the synagogues of **Galilee.** It will be noted that some modern versions (e.g., RSV, NEB) have "Judea." That is because Judea is the reading in the two oldest Greek manuscripts (Vaticanus and Sinaiticus), as well as some others. If "Judea" is the original reading here, the word must be taken in its wider connotation as referring to all of Palestine, the country of the Jews. Plummer says: "Luke often uses *Ioudaia* in this sense . . . . Classic writers use the term in much the same manner."[115]

2. Call of Four Fishermen (5:1-11)

1 Now it came to pass, while the multitude pressed upon him and heard the

word of God, that he was standing by the lake of Gennesaret; 2 and he saw two boats standing by the lake: but the fishermen had gone out of them, and were washing their nets. 3 And he entered into one of the boats, which was Simon's, and asked him to put out a little from the land. And he sat down and taught the multitudes out of the boat. 4 And when he had left speaking, he said unto Simon, Put out into the deep, and let down your nets for a draught. 5 And Simon answered and said, Master, we toiled all night, and took nothing: but at thy word I will let down the nets. 6 And when they had done this, they inclosed a great multitude of fishes; and their nets were breaking; 7 and they beckoned unto their partners in the other boat, that they should come and help them. And they came, and filled both the boats, so that they began to sink. 8 But Simon Peter, when he saw it, fell down at Jesus' knees, saying, Depart from me; for I am a sinful man, O Lord. 9 For he was amazed, and all that were with him, at the draught of the fishes which they had taken; 10 and so were also James and John, sons of Zebedee, who were partners with Simon. And Jesus said unto Simon, Fear not; from henceforth thou shalt catch men. 11 And when they had brought their boats to land, they left all, and followed him.

Matthew and Mark record the call of two pairs of brothers — Peter and Andrew, James and John. Here the entire conversation is with Peter. James and John are mentioned, but not Andrew.

It is inevitable that the question should rise as to whether or not this is the same incident as that described in Matthew and Mark. Godet contends that it is. He says: "The call related here by Luke is certainly the same as that which is related, in a more abridged form, by Matthew (4:18-22) and Mark 1:16-20)."[116] On the other hand, Geldenhuys writes: "This story is by no means the same as that in Matthew 4:18-22 and Mark 1: 16-21."[117] Plummer is more nearly correct when he says that "the identity of this incident with that narrated by Matthew and Mark can neither be affirmed nor denied with certainty."[118] Luke's account is much more full than the others'. He alone records the miraculous draught of fish, which was Jesus'

generous payment for the use of Peter's fishing boat as a pulpit.

The **multitude** was (literally) "lying upon Him" to hear **the word of God.** Concerning the last phrase Lowther Clarke says: "This technical term, used of the Apostolic preaching, is found in Luke only of the Gospels, cp. Acts 4:31, 6:2, etc."[119]

The Gospels of Matthew and Mark refer repeatedly to "the sea of Galilee" and always call it "the sea." But Luke never does. Matthew and Peter (whose preaching is reflected in Mark's Gospel) both lived on the lake. To them it was "the sea." But Luke had sailed the Mediterranean many times, so he correctly called this small body of water, about thirteen miles long and seven miles wide, **the Lake of Gennesaret.** Only here is this name found in the New Testament. The Greek word for **lake** occurs only in Luke (5 times) and in Revelation (5 times, always of the lake of fire). The name **Gennesaret** is also used for a small plain on the northwestern shore of the lake (Matt. 14:34; Mark 6:53).

Two boats were standing near the shore, while the fishermen washed their nets after a night of fishing. Jesus got into one of them, which belonged to Simon Peter, and asked him to pull away from the beach a bit. Sitting in the boat the Master was then able to address the crowd that thronged the shore.

When He had finished His message to the people, Jesus bade Simon push out into the deep water and let down his net. Peter protested that they had **toiled** all night and taken nothing. But he addressed Jesus as *epistata* (**Master**), a term found only in Luke (7 times). It means "commander." Plummer says: "Here it is used of one who has a right to give orders."[120] So Peter said: **at thy word I will let down the nets** (v.5).

Immediately the nets enclosed a great school of fish, for which the Lake of Galilee is famous. So many were there that their nets **were breaking** (v. 6) — perhaps better "on the point of breaking." Obviously "their nets brake" (KJV) is not accurate, because in that event they would have lost their fish.

116 *Op. cit.,* p. 255.   117 *Op. cit.,* p. 181.   119 *Op. cit.,* p. 142.
119 W. K. Lowther Clarke, *Concise Bible Commentary,* p. 753.   120 *Op. cit.,* p. 143.

Unable to handle the situation, **they** (Peter and Andrew?) **beckoned** — today one would say "waved" — to **their partners** to come and help them. These **partners** are identified as James and John (v. 10). It appears that they had stayed on shore while Peter's boat put out into the deep water — the lake is about 150 feet deep — and were too far away to call by voice. The partners came and both boats were filled with fish, almost to the sinking point.

The effect on impulsive Peter was typical. He fell at Jesus' feet, crying out: **Depart from me; for I am a sinful man, O Lord** (v. 8). A display of divine power always tends to bring conviction on sinners and a deeper sense of humility to saints.

The Master's reply to Peter was: **Fear not; from henceforth thou shalt catch men** (v. 10). The Greek says, "catch alive." As Geldenhuys points out, these words show that this event is intended to be understood "symbolically in connection with evangelism." He adds: "In spite of all failures in the past, the church of Christ must again and again renew its energetic attempts under His guidance to gather in souls for His kingdom, and must do this not merely in the 'shallow waters' but in the 'deep water' — not only in the vicinity of settled ecclesiastical life, but also among the great masses of people where the need is so great."[121] Gore writes: "Few narratives are so full of encouragement to workers in the cause of the Kingdom, liable as they are to a sense of hopelessness due to failure in their efforts."[122]

When the boats loaded with fish reached shore, the four fishermen **left all** to follow Jesus. Probably they made provision for their families out of the proceeds from the sale of the large catch of fish.

3. Healing of a Leper (5:12-16)

12 And it came to pass, while he was in one of the cities, behold, a man full of leprosy: and when he saw Jesus, he fell on his face, and besought him, saying, Lord, if thou wilt, thou canst make me clean. 13 And he stretched forth his hand, and touched him, saying, I will;

be thou made clean. And straightway the leprosy departed from him. 14 And he charged him to tell no man: but go thy way, and show thyself to the priest, and offer for thy cleansing, according as Moses commanded, for a testimony unto them. 15 But so much the more went abroad the report concerning him: and great multitudes came together to hear, and to be healed of their infirmities. 16 But he withdrew himself in the deserts, and prayed.

This is another incident recorded in all three Synoptic Gospels (see the notes on Matthew 8:1-3; Mark 1:40-45). Here again we see the hand of the physician, Luke, who describes the man as **full of leprosy.** Creed comments: *"Pleres* ["full"] is frequently used in Greek medical writers of disease."[123]

The pleading leper doubted Jesus' willingness, but not His power. The Master settled the matter by saying, **I will.** Immediately the leprosy left the man. Jesus charged him to report to the priest and make the required offering for his cleansing, as a **testimony** to **them** — probably the priests. But such a miracle was bound to attract attention. Soon the report of it **went abroad** (v. 15). Great crowds gathered to hear Jesus and to be healed by Him. Once more He withdrew Himself **in the deserts** (uninhabited areas), **and prayed.** This is the second time that Luke alone records Jesus' praying (cf. 3:21). In every great crisis the Master spent time in prayer. Before it was at the Baptism; now it was prior to selecting His twelve apostles.

D. CONTROVERSIES WITH THE PHARISEES (5:17-16:11)

1. Forgiving Sins (5:17-26)

17 And it came to pass on one of those days, that he was teaching; and there were Pharisees and doctors of the law sitting by, who were come out of every village of Galilee and Judaea and Jerusalem: and the power of the Lord was with him to heal. 18 And behold, men bring on a bed a man that was palsied: and they sought to bring him in, and to lay him before him. 19 And not finding by what *way* they might bring him in because of the multitude, they went up to the housetop, and let him down through the tiles

---

[121] *Op. cit.*, p. 183.
[122] Charles Gore, "The Gospel According to St. Luke," *A New Commentary on Holy Scripture,* ed. Charles Gore, H. L. Goudge, and Alfred Guillanme, III, 217. [123] *Op. cit.*, p. 76.

with his couch into the midst before Jesus. 20 And seeing their faith, he said, Man, thy sins are forgiven thee. 21 And the scribes and the Pharisees began to reason, saying, Who is this that speaketh blasphemies? Who can forgive sins, but God alone? 22 But Jesus perceiving their reasonings, answered and said unto them, Why reason ye in your hearts? 23 Which is easier, to say, Thy sins are forgiven thee; or to say, Arise and walk? 24 But that ye may know that the Son of man hath authority on earth to forgive sins (he said unto him that was palsied), I say unto thee, Arise, and take up thy couch, and go unto thy house. 25 And immediately he rose up before them, and took up that whereon he lay, and departed to his house, glorifying God. 26 And amazement took hold on all, and they glorified God; and they were filled with fear, saying, We have seen strange things to-day.

This is the first of four controversies — recorded in all three Synoptics — that Jesus had with the Pharisees. The first concerned Christ's authority to forgive sins — only God could do this. The second had to do with His eating with "sinners"; that is, those who were ceremonially defiled because of not observing all the religious regulations. The third was related to the question of fasting, which had received great emphasis among the Pharisees. The fourth dealt with what was one of the most prominent features of Judaism — the observance of the sabbath day. In all four areas Jesus came into sharp conflict with the Pharisees and their legalistic religion.

The question of the right to forgive sins arose in connection with the healing of the paralytic (see comments on Matthew 9:1-8; Mark 2:1-12). Luke is the only one who specifically mentions the Pharisees, and he refers to them twice (vv. 17, 21). However, Matthew and Mark mention the scribes, who were Pharisees. Luke adds the designation doctors of the law (v. 17). This is one word in the Greek, a compound which occurs elsewhere in the New Testament only in Acts 5:34 and I Timothy 1:7. It means teachers of the Jewish law and is equivalent to "scribes." Luke says that these had come out of every village of Galilee and Judaea and Jerusalem (100

miles away). This shows how far Jesus' fame had reached. The leaders of the Pharisees were investigating what He was doing and saying.

They did not have long to wait. Luke says that the power of the Lord was with him to heal — the first phrase is typically Lukan. Soon a difficult case presented itself. A paralytic was brought to Jesus (v. 18). Matthew and Mark use the Greek word *paralytikos*. But Luke says that was palsied; that is, paralyzed. He alone uses the verb (here, v. 24, and twice in Acts). Again Hobart comments: "St. Luke's use is in strict agreement with that of the medical writers."[124]

The description of breaking up the roof of Peter's house in order to lower the paralytic in front of Jesus is told most graphically, as usual, by Mark. But Luke alone mentions the tiles that covered the roof (v. 19). He also uses a different word for couch, found only here and in verse 24. It is a diminutive of the word for bed (v. 18 and Matthew 9:2). Hobart remarks: "The variety of words employed by St. Luke for the beds of the sick is remarkable. He uses four, two of which are common to him with the other Evangelists . . . and two peculiar to himself."[125]

The addition that the healed man was glorifying God (v. 25) is typically Lukan, although all three Synoptics say that the onlookers glorified God (v. 26).

2. Eating with Sinners (5:27-32)

a. Call of Levi (5:27-28)

27 And after these things he went forth, and beheld a publican, named Levi, sitting at the place of toll, and said unto him, Follow me. 28 And he forsook all, and rose up and followed him.

For discussion of this incident see the notes on Matthew 9:9 and Mark 2:13-14. Luke alone notes here that Levi was a publican; that is, a tax collector.

b. Feast at Levi's House (5:29-32)

29 And Levi made him a great feast in his house: and there was a great multitude of publicans and of others that were sitting at meat with them. 30 And the Pharisees and their scribes murmured

---

[124] *Op. cit.*, p. 6. The only non-Lukan use of the verb is in Heb. 12:12, in a quotation from the Septuagint.   [125] *Ibid.*, p. 116.

against his disciples, saying, Why do ye eat and drink with the publicans and sinners? 31 And Jesus answering said unto them, They that are in health have no need of a physician; but they that are sick. 32 I am not come to call the righteous but sinners to repentance.

See comments on Matthew 9:9-13 and Mark 2:15-17. Luke is the only one who states specifically that Levi made him a great feast in his house. It is evident that he had become well-to-do, if not wealthy, as a tax collector. However, there is no implication here, as in the case of Zacchaeus (19:8), that he had been dishonest in accumulating money.

Again Luke's medical interest appears. Whereas Matthew and Mark say, "They that are whole," Luke says, They that are in health (v. 31). This is the participle of a verb (from which we get "hygiene") which occurs only in Luke's Gospel (3 times), in the Pastoral Epistles (8 times) — did Luke write these for Paul? — and once in III John 2. In the Pastorals the verb is used in a metaphorical sense ("sound doctrine," "sound speech"). Hobart writes: "St. Luke is the only New Testament writer who uses *hygiainein* in this, its primary sense, 'to be in sound health', which the exception of St. John 3 Ep. 2. For this meaning it is the regular word in the medical writers."[126]

3. Fasting (5:33-39)

33 And they said unto him, The disciples of John fast often, and make supplications; likewise also the *disciples* of the Pharisees; but thine eat and drink. 34 And Jesus said unto them, Can ye make the sons of the bride-chamber fast, while the bridegroom is with them? 35 But the days will come; and when the bridegroom shall be taken away from them, then will they fast in those days. 36 And he spake also a parable unto them: No man rendeth a piece from a new garment and putteth it upon an old garment; else he will rend the new, and also the piece from the new will not agree with the old. 37 And no man putteth new wine into old wineskins; else the new wine will burst the skins, and itself will be spilled, and the skins will perish. 38 But new wine must be put into fresh wine-skins. 39 And no man having drunk old *wine* desireth new; for he saith, The old is good.

For discussion of this paragraph see the comments on Matthew 9:14-17 and Mark 2:18-22. There is very little distinctive material in Luke. However, in verse 33 he adds: but thine eat and drink. It is obvious from this and the previous incident that Jesus was no extreme ascetic. Those who wish to emphasize strict asceticism as an essential element in the Christian life can find no support for this in the life of Christ.

Fasting is an important phase of true piety, when it is used as an aid to more intensive, uninterrupted praying. It is most effective when a person becomes so burdened in prayer that he does not care to eat. Engaged in as a legalistic duty it can do more harm than good. Tittle cites an example which observation shows is not an isolated case. He writes: "A certain clergyman made it a point of honor to fast on holy days. On those days, according to members of his church staff, he was especially morose, irritable, and dictatorial!"[127] The test of any religious practice is: does it make us more Christlike? If not, it is hurting rather than helping the Kingdom.

Luke alone labels as a parable the sayings of Jesus about putting a new patch on an old garment and pouring new wine into old wineskins. (vv. 36-38).

Barclay makes an interesting application of the latter figure: " 'Don't,' says Jesus, 'let your mind become like an old wineskin' . . . . The whole passage is Jesus' condemnation of the shut mind and his plea that men should not reject new ideas."[128]

Luke adds verse 39: And no man having drunk old wine desireth new; for he saith, The old is good. The purpose of this verse is thus stated by Farrar: "The spirit for which our Lord here (as it were) offers an apology is the deep-rooted human tendency to prefer old habits to new lights, and stereotyped formulae to fresh truths."[129]

Geldenhuys makes another helpful application of the saying about wineskins. He writes: "Just as the new forms of religion brought by Jesus could not tolerate any compromise with the old forms, so it is also with the new life which every regenerated person finds in Christ"; and adds: "There must be no mixing

126 *Ibid.*, p. 10.   127 Ernest F. Tittle, *The Gospel According to Luke*, p. 55.
128 *Op. cit.*, p. 65.   129 *Op. cit.*, p. 174.

with the former kind of life to which a man was accustomed before his conversion."[130] Not only is Christianity a new religion, but the Christian life is a new life. Older Christians need to recapture the freshness of new converts.

In a special note Geldenhuys gives a good brief summary of the subject of "Fasting." He calls attention to the fact that the Old Testament law prescribes only one fast, that of the Day of Atonement (Lev. 16:29). Fasting was, however, used as a sign of mourning (II Sam. 1:12). "During the Babylonian exile, as a result of the lack of the sacrificial services, the opinion arose more and more that fasting was a meritorious work that would be rewarded by God."[131] This idea was opposed by the prophets (e.g., Zech. 7:5ff.). But the situation reached its legalistic worst among the Pharisees. Geldenhuys says: "Jesus' attitude towards fasting briefly amounts to this, that He rejects it as a religiously meritorious ceremony bearing a compulsory, ceremonial character; but He practiced it Himself at times and permits it as a voluntary form of spiritual discipline."[132]

That states the case very clearly. Fasting should always be purely voluntary and not considered either a legal requirement or an evidence of piety.

4. Observing the Sabbath (6:1-11)

a. Working on the Sabbath (6:1-5)

1 Now it came to pass on a sabbath, that he was going through the grainfields; and his disciples plucked the ears, and did eat, rubbing them in their hands. 2 But certain of the Pharisees said, Why do ye that which it is not lawful to do on the sabbath day? 3 And Jesus answering them said, Have ye not read even this, what David did, when he was hungry, he, and they that were with him; 4 how he entered into the house of God, and took and ate the showbread, and gave also to them that were with him; which it is not lawful to eat save for the priests alone? 5 And he said unto them, The Son of man is lord of the sabbath.

The three accounts of this incident are closely parallel (see notes on Matthew 12:1-8 and Mark 2:23-28). Attention will be given here mainly to the distinctive features in Luke.

A sabbath is in the King James Version "the second sabbath after the first." The latter — literally, "a second-first sabbath" — is the reading in a considerable number of manuscripts dated as far back as the fifth century. The Greek compound meaning "second-first" has no precedent. Plummer says: "In the whole of Greek literature, classical, Jewish, or Christian, no such word is found independently of this text."[133] So he considers it spurious.

On the other hand, Gilmour echoes the opinions of both Scrivener and Tischendorf (great textual critics) when he says of this additional reading: "Its very difficulty is an argument in its favor."[134] He adds: "A reckoning in terms of post-Passover sabbaths is given in Lev. 23:15-16, and perhaps Luke had in mind the second sabbath in such a series."[135]

Jesus was walking **through the grainfields** on the sabbath day when the disciples began to pluck the heads of grain. Luke adds: **rubbing them in their hands.** This would perhaps indicate that the grain was wheat, rather than barley. The verb **rubbing** is found only here in the New Testament. Plummer says that it "seems to occur elsewhere only in the medical writer Nicander."[136] This may be another hint of Luke's medical background.

In the minds of the legalistic Pharisees plucking the heads of grain was harvesting, rubbing them out in the hand was threshing, and blowing the husks away was winnowing. Gilmour writes: "The Old Testament prohibition of sabbath labor had been supplemented in rabbinical tradition by a list of thirty-nine 'major occupations' that were proscribed, among them harvesting and threshing."[137]

b. Healing on the Sabbath (6:6-11)

6 And it came to pass on another sabbath, that he entered into the synagogue and taught: and there was a man there, and his right hand was withered. 7 And the scribes and the Pharisees watched him, whether he would heal on the sabbath; that they might find how to accuse him. 8 But he knew their thoughts; and he said to the man that had his hand withered, Rise up, and stand forth in the midst. And he arose and stood forth. 9 And Jesus said unto them, I ask you, Is it lawful on the sabbath to do good,

---

[130] *Op. cit.*, p. 197.   [131] *Op. cit.*, p. 198.   [132] *Ibid.*   [133] *Op. cit.*, p. 166.
[134] *Op. cit.*, p. 10.   [135] *Ibid.*   [136] *Op. cit.*, p. 167.   [137] *Op. cit.*, p. 111.

or to do harm? to save a life, or to destroy it? 10 And he looked round on them all, and said unto him, Stretch forth thy hand. And he did *so*: and his hand was restored. 11 But they were filled with madness; and communed one with another what they might do to Jesus.

For full discussion of this incident see the notes on Matthew 12:9-14 and Mark 3:1-6. The accounts are similar.

Luke indicates that it was **another sabbath** when Jesus attended the synagogue; he adds: **and taught.** All three Synoptists tell about the man with a withered hand, but only Luke specifies that it was his **right hand.** Hobart says: "The medical writers invariably state whether it is the right or left member that is affected."[138]

The "they" of Matthew 12:10 and Mark 3:2 are identified by Luke as **the scribes and the Pharisees** (v. 7). Mark and Luke say they **watched him** — better, "were watching Him." Plummer notes: "The verb signifies 'watch narrowly,' especially with sinister intent, perhaps from looking sideways out of the corner of one's eyes."[139]

The scribes and Pharisees were trying to find some occasion for accusing Jesus. Luke adds: **But he knew their thoughts** — the Greek word means "reasoning" or "inward questioning." So He answered their unspoken thought by the command (most specific in Luke) to the afflicted man to **Rise up, and stand forth in the midst** (v. 8). Jesus was going to do everything right out in the open, where everyone could see. If these enemies wanted to watch Him, He would help them out! He was not ashamed of what He was doing, and so had nothing to hide. Then He posed the question, with a pointed **I ask you** (only in Luke). The interrogation was twofold, and answers itself. Godet says: "The skilfulness of the question proposed by the Lord [v. 9] consists in its representing good *omitted* as evil *committed*," and adds: "This question is one of those marks of genius, or rather one of those inspirations of the heart, which enhance our knowledge of Jesus."[140]

Then Christ healed the man. The effect on the Pharisees was powerful (v. 11). They were **filled with madness** (only

in Luke). The last word is literally "senselessness." Here it means "foolish rage." Plummer defines it as "the phrensy or loss of reason which is caused by extreme excitement."[141] The main concern of the scribes was **what they might do to Jesus.** Mark and Matthew put it more strongly here: His opponents "took counsel against him, how they might destroy him." Already the Master's days were numbered.

The Pharisees were meticulous not only in their minute regulations against working on the sabbath, but also in the rules concerning healing on that day. Schürer says: "Medical assistance was only allowed on the assumption that life was in danger."[142]

Obviously this was not the case with the man who had a withered hand. Specifically the rabbinical ruling was: "A fracture (of a limb) may not be attended to. If any one has sprained his hand or foot, he may not pour cold water on it."[143] Edersheim says that the Law "prohibited the application or use on the Sabbath of any remedies that would bring improvement or cure to the sick."[144]

The attitude of Christ was exactly the opposite of this. Manson writes (particularly with regard to verse 9): "Jesus will recognize no alternative to the doing of good except the doing of evil. The refusal to save life is tantamount to the taking of it."[145]

E. SERMON ON THE MOUNT (6:12-49)

1. Choosing the Twelve (6:12-16)

12 And it came to pass in these days, that he went out into the mountain to pray; and he continued all night in prayer to God. 13 And when it was day, he called his disciples; and he chose from them twelve, whom he also named apostles: 14 Simon, whom he also named Peter, and Andrew his brother, and James and John, and Philip and Bartholomew, 15 and Matthew and Thomas, and James *the son* of Alphaeus, and Simon who was called the Zealot, 16 and Judas *the son* of James, and Judas Iscariot, who became a traitor;

While Matthew gives a list of the twelve apostles (Matthew 10:2-4), it is Mark and Luke who relate their appoint-

---

[138] *Op. cit.*, p. 7.   [139] *Op. cit.*, p. 169.   [140] *Op. cit.*, p. 292.   [141] *Op. cit.*, p. 170.
[142] *Op. cit.*, II, ii, 287.   [143] *Ibid.*   [144] *Op. cit.*, II, 787.   [145] *Op. cit.*, p. 60.

ment by Christ (see notes on Mark 3:13-19).

For the third time (cf. 3:21; 5:16), Luke mentions that Jesus prayed. This time He went up on a mountain and **continued all night in prayer to God.** The selection of His associates was one of the critical decisions of His life and He wanted clear and definite guidance from His Father.

In the morning He called together His disciples and **chose from them twelve, whom also he named apostles** (v. 13). The name, as often noted, means "ones sent on a mission" (or with a commission). The main point of interest here is the substitution of **Judas the son** (or, brother) **of James** in place of "Thaddaeus" of the other two lists. Luke does the same thing in his list of the Eleven in Acts 1:13.

2. Setting of the Sermon (6:17-19)

17 and he came down with them, and stood on a level place, and a great multitude of his disciples, and a great number of the people from all Judaea and Jerusalem, and the sea coast of Tyre and Sidon, who came to hear him, and to be healed of their diseases; 18 and they that were troubled with unclean spirits were healed. 19 And all the multitude sought to touch him; for power came forth from him, and healed *them* all.

The question of the relation of the rest of this chapter to the Sermon on the Mount in Matthew will continue to be debated until the end of time. Plummer seems to prefer the theory of two different sermons, but confesses that "a multitude of commentators adopt the view that the main portions of the reports given by Matthew and Luke represent one and the same discourse."[146] Godet favors one sermon.[147]

Geldenhuys goes a step further. He heads this section (6:17-49), "The Sermon on the Mount," and remarks: "If we assume, together with a majority of expositors, that verses 17-49 reproduce the same sermon (though greatly abbreviated) as Matthew 5, 6, 7 . . . ."[148]

It has often been claimed that the Sermon on the Mount in Matthew was delivered to the disciples only (cf. Matthew 5:1), but Matthew 7:28 indicates that a

large crowd heard Him. Both discourses end with the same striking illustration of the two houses, one founded on a rock and the other built on the sand. And both, while not at all identical, contain similar sayings.

The main argument for two discourses is that Matthew says Jesus "went up into the mountain" (Matthew 5:1), whereas Luke says **He came down with them, and stood on a level place** (v. 17). It has often been suggested that this could have been a plateau part way up the hill. Plummer prefers level ground at the foot. He says: "Hither it would be more likely that multitudes would come and bring their sick, than to a plateau high up the mountain."[149] But Robertson sees no great difficulty here. His explanation is that Jesus first went up onto the mountain to pray (v. 12), then came down to a lower, level place to heal the sick (v. 17), then went up a little higher on the hill where He could see and teach the multitudes.[150]

A striking phrase occurs here — **a great multitude of his disciples** (v. 17). This indicates that large numbers of people at this time were followers of Jesus. With them were **a great number of people,** not only **all Judaea and Jerusalem,** but also from **the sea coast of Tyre and Sidon,** far to the north. **Power came forth from him, and healed them all** is a typical Lukan expression.

3. The Beatitudes (6:20-23)

20 And he lifted up his eyes on his disciples, and said, Blessed *are* ye poor: for yours is the kingdom of God. 21 Blessed *are* ye that hunger now: for ye shall be filled. Blessed *are* ye that weep now: for ye shall laugh. 22 Blessed are ye, when men shall hate you, and when they shall separate you *from their company,* and reproach you, and cast out your name as evil, for the Son of man's sake. 23 Rejoice in that day, and leap *for joy*: for behold, your reward is great in heaven; for in the same manner did their fathers unto the prophets.

In this section Jesus is addressing mainly **his disciples** (v. 20), as in Matthew's account of the Sermon on the Mount (Matthew 5:1). Whereas in Matthew the

[146] *Op. cit.,* p. 177.   [147] *Op. cit.,* pp. 307-311.   [148] *Op. cit.,* p 209.
[149] *Op. cit.,* p. 175.
[150] A. T. Robertson, *A Harmony of the Gospels for Students of the Life of Christ,* p. 274.

sermon begins with eight (or nine) Beatitudes, Luke records four Beatitudes and four Woes. Another difference is that Matthew gives a spiritual cast to the description of the blessed, while Luke seems to be speaking in economic terms. This will appear in connection with the discussion of each Beatitude. A third difference is that the Beatitudes in Matthew are in the third person, while here they are in the second person.

In the first Beatitude Jesus says, **Blessed are ye poor.** This is not a blanket blessing on poverty as such. For observation shows that poverty does not guarantee piety. But, as Plummer paraphrases it, "to *you,* My disciples, poverty is a blessing, because it preserves you in your dependence on God, and helps you to be truly His subjects."[151] Some of these disciples had become poor by leaving all to follow Jesus.

Manson has a helpful comment at this point: "The meaning of the word 'poor' is given by such passages as Ps. 69:29-36. In the Judaism of the last two centuries B.C. the term was practically a synonym for *Hasid,* i.e., 'saintly' or 'pious,' in the best sense."[152]

But there is a rich reward for them: **yours is the kingdom of God.** It is not only the future kingdom, but God's presence with you now.

The second Beatitude is: **Blessed are ye that hunger now.** Paul mentions the fact that he had often been without food — "in hunger and thirst, in fastings often" (II Cor. 11:27). In the early days of the church, many Jewish Christians suffered through economic boycott by their fellow Jews. And in the Orient, then as now, being poor meant actually going without food — not a lack of money in the bank and two cars in the garage! **Ye shall be filled.** This is the same verb as in Matthew 5:6. Originally used for animals being filled with fodder, in the New Testament it primarily signifies filled with abundance — physically or spiritually.

The third Beatitude is: **Blessed are ye that weep now** (cf. Matt. — "Blessed are they that mourn"). Whereas the term in Matthew speaks more of inward sorrow, the Greek word for **weep** suggests the outward manifestation of this in loud weeping. Again, Matthew says, "they shall be comforted" (inwardly). Here it is, **ye shall laugh,** implying outward mirth.

In the case of each of these first three Beatitudes Matthew gives a spiritual connotation to the condition described: it is the "poor in spirit," those that "hunger and thirst after righteousness," those that "mourn." Plummer points out the significance of the terms Luke uses: "*Actually* poverty, sorrow and hunger are declared to be blessed (as being opportunities for the exercise of internal virtues); and this doctrine is emphasized by the corresponding Woes pronounced upon wealth, jollity, and fullness of bread (as being sources of temptation)."[153]

The fourth Beatitude is more like the the corresponding one in Matthew, both in form and in extent (cf. Matt. 5:10-12). These early disciples were soon to undergo severe persecution by their fellow Jews. The Master was seeking to prepare them for it. Men would **hate them** and **separate** them. The latter would occur religiously (excommunicated from the synagogue), socially (treated as outcasts), and economically (boycotted in business). Converts on the mission field have often suffered a similar fate, involving sometimes exclusion from the use of the village well — the only source of water. One has to become acquainted with the foreign missionary work of the church in order to understand and appreciate many of the references in the New Testament. In the sheltered life of lands favorable to evangelical Christianity some of these things seem remote and irrelevant. But these passages speak in a particularly meaningful way to Christian converts in Asia or Africa today. As in Matthew, those persecuted **for the Son of man's sake** are to **rejoice,** because their reward in heaven will be **great.**

4. The Woes (6:24-26)

24 But woe unto you that are rich! for ye have received your consolation. 25 Woe unto you, ye that are full now! for ye shall hunger. Woe *unto you,* ye that laugh now! for ye shall mourn and weep. 26 Woe *unto you,* when all men shall

---

[151] *Op. cit.,* p. 180.
[152] T. W. Manson, "The Sayings of Jesus," *The Mission and Message of Jesus,* by H. D. A. Major, T. W. Manson, and C. J. Wright, p. 339.   [153] *Ibid.,* p. 179.

speak well of you! for in the same manner did their fathers to the false prophets.

Luke gives four Woes, corresponding to the four Beatitudes just noted. While the poor are blessed, Jesus says: **Woe unto you that are rich!** Christ Himself suffered opposition from the wealthy Jews of His day. The Epistle of James indicates that these same people were persecuting the early Christians (James 5:16). The same condemnation of the rich is found in the Minor Prophets (e.g., Amos 6:1-6). It is also one of the distinctive features of Luke's Gospel. He is the only one who records Jesus' parables of the Rich Fool, and the Rich Man and Lazarus. This is the Gospel of the Poor, and that fact is reflected clearly here.

Concerning the word **Woe** Geldenhuys says: "In the mouth of Jesus it expresses lament, not denunciation: 'alas for you!' "[154]

To the rich, Jesus said: **ye have received your consolation.** For the significance of **received** see the notes on Matthew 6:2. Plummer comments here: " 'Ye have to the full'; so that there is nothing more left to have. The poor consolation derived from the riches in which they trusted is all that they get; they have no treasure in heaven."[155]

The second Woe is: **Woe unto you, ye that are full now!** (v. 25). He refers to those who are satiated with the abundance of material goods, such as the rich man at whose gate Lazarus was laid and the rich fool who was burdened with excessive surplus. He says that such **shall hunger.** This has several applications. Some wealthy men have suddenly lost their fortunes, and in some cases have become extremely poor. Others have lost their health, so that they could not eat and enjoy food. And all who have been selfish and God-forgetting have finally found themselves destitute spiritually.

The third Woe is: **Woe unto you, ye that laugh now!** This is not to be construed as a general condemnation of laughter. When a person thinks that in order to be pious he must never laugh, he is probably heading for a mental institution. Laughter is one of the most therapeutic blessings in life, especially the ability to laugh at one's own mistakes and blunders. What Jesus is talking about here is the gay mirth of those who mock what is highest and most sacred in life. There is coming a time when those who gaily forget God and their own spiritual and social responsibilities will **mourn and weep.** It was Jesus who said, "There shall be weeping and gnashing of teeth" (13:28; Matt. 8:12; 13:42, 50; 22:13; 24:51; 25:30).

The fourth Woe is: **Woe unto you, when all men shall speak well of you!** (v. 26). The Bible is its own best commentary here. James writes, "Know ye not that the friendship of the world is enmity with God?" (James 4:4). Jesus said: "If ye were of the world, the world would love its own" (John 15:19). The politician whose only concern is to please everybody for the sake of winning votes is the classical example of what Christ is talking about here. Those who want the world's applause pay too high a price for it. The **false prophets** played this role, and so do false men today.

5. Love and Mercy (6:27-38)

27 But I say unto you that hear, Love your enemies, do good to them that hate you, 28 bless them that curse you, pray for them that despitefully use you. 29 To him that smiteth thee on the *one* cheek offer also the other; and from him that taketh away thy cloak withhold not thy coat also. 30 Give to every one that asketh thee; and of him that taketh away thy goods ask them not again. 31 And as ye would that men should do to you, do ye also to them likewise. 32 And if ye love them that love you, what thank have ye? for even sinners love those that love them. 33 And if ye do good to them that do good to you, what thank have ye? for even sinners do the same. 34 And if ye lend to them of whom ye hope to receive, what thank have ye? even sinners lend to sinners, to receive again as much. 35 But love your enemies, and do *them* good, and lend, never despairing; and your reward shall be great, and ye shall be sons of the Most High: for he is kind toward the unthankful and evil. 36 Be ye merciful, even as your Father is merciful. 37 And judge not, and ye shall not be judged: and condemn not, and ye shall not be condemned: release, and ye shall be released: 38 give, and it shall be given unto you; good measure, pressed down, shaken together, running over, shall they

---

[154] *Op. cit.,* p. 216.   [155] *Ibid.,* p. 182.

give into your bosom. For with what measure ye mete it shall be measured to you again.

Verse 27 is parallel to Matthew 5:44 — "Love your enemies, and pray for them that persecute you." The second clause is elaborated by Luke in verse 38. **Curse you and despitefully use you** describes the treatment that Christians received from their persecutors. To love one's enemies requires the grace of God in one's heart. This is not natural; it is supernatural. Christ demands more, but "He giveth more grace." Geldenhuys writes: "Never before or after Jesus did anyone lay down such high standards of how one should live in thought and action towards God and one's fellow-men. His law is nothing less than absolute perfection in love."[156]

Verses 28-36 run fairly parallel to Matthew 5:39-48 (see notes there). On verse 29 Plummer has this significant comment: "A violent blow with the fist seems to be meant rather than a contemptuous slap, for *siagon* (cheek) means 'jaw-bone'. . . . In what follows also it is an act of violence that is meant; for in that case the upper and more valuable garment (*himation*) would be taken first. In Matthew 5:40 the spoiler adopts a legal method of spoliaton (*krithenai*) and takes the under and less indispensable garment (*chitona*) first."[157]

The policy of giving to everyone who asks is one that must be practiced with some measure of good judgment (as we noted in the comments on Matthew 5: 42), lest one do more harm than good. Plummer has a very penetrating observation at this point: "Love knows no limits but those which love itself imposes. When love resists or refuses, it is because compliance would be a violation of love, not because it would involve loss or suffering."[158]

Verse 31 gives Luke's form of the Golden Rule (cf. Matthew 7:12). It is generally agreed by scholars that Jesus was the first one ever to state this in positive form. Creed calls attention to numerous examples of earlier negative statements. For instance, the great Rabbi Hillel said: "That which thou hatest, do

not to thy fellow; this is the whole Law and all the rest is commentary."[159] The Stoics, Confucius, and Buddhism all give it in negative form. Tsze-kung said: "What you do not want done to yourself, do not do to others."[160]

Verse 35 repeats the command to love your enemies. The phrase, **never despairing**, has presented considerable difficulty. In the King James Version it is rendered, "hoping for nothing again." Creed defends that translation here. He says: "The context imperatively demands the meaning 'without hoping to receive anything back.' "[161] Though admitting that the verb "consistently means elsewhere 'to despair,' or 'to despair of,' " he concludes: "But this interpretation cannot be reconciled with the context."[162]

Plummer disagrees. He writes, "The usual meaning of *apelpizo*, 'I give up in despair,' makes excellent sense; either 'despairing of nothing,' or 'despairing of no one.' "[163] Meyer also favors "never despairing," but refers it to "the everlasting recompense."[164]

The majority of commentators, however, stand with the King James Version rendering, "hoping for nothing again." This is the view of Bruce,[165] Godet,[166] and Geldenhuys.[167]

Luke is the only New Testament writer who uses **the Most High** as a proper name for God (Luke 1:32, 35, 76; 6:35; Acts 7:48). Manson writes: "It was a term admirably fitted to form a bridge between Judaism and the higher Greek religion, between the one Lord of Jewish monotheism and the First Principle of Greek thought."[168]

Be ye merciful, even as your Father is merciful (v. 36), seems to be Luke's parallel to Matthew's, "Ye therefore shall be perfect, as your heavenly Father is perfect" (Matt. 5:48). On Luke's use of **merciful** instead of "perfect" Bruce says: "a legitimate substitution, as the perfection inculcated referred to loving enemies."[169]

The warning against judging others (v. 37) is a parallel to Matthew 7:1, 2. **Release** means "forgive." Verse 38, found only in Luke, is a beautiful promise of abundant reward for a generous spirit.

[156] *Op. cit.*, p. 215.   [157] *Op. cit.*, p. 185.   [158] *Ibid.*   [159] Creed, *op. cit.*, p. 94.
[160] *Ibid.*   [161] *Ibid.*, p. 95.   [162] *Ibid.*   [163] *Op. cit.*, p. 163.
[164] *Op. cit.*, pp. 337, 338.   [165] EGT,I,507.   [166] *Op. cit.*, p. 326.   [167] *Op. cit.*, p. 217.
[168] T. W. Manson, *op. cit.*, p. 347.   [169] EGT, I, 507.

T. W. Manson says that they (shall give) is "probably — as in the Rabbinic literature — a way of referring to God."[170] On the meaning of **bosom** Barnes says: "The word *bosom* here has reference to a custom among Oriental nations of making the bosom or front part of their garments **large**, so that articles could be carried in them, answering the purpose of our pockets."[171]

6. Judging and Fruit-bearing (6:39-45)

39 And he spake also a parable unto them, Can the blind guide the blind? shall they not both fall into a pit? 40 The disciple is not above his teacher: but every one when he is perfected shall be as his teacher. 41 And why beholdest thou the mote that is in thy brother's eye, but considerest not the beam that is in thine own eye? 42 Or how canst thou say to thy brother, Brother, let me cast out the mote that is in thine eye, when thou thyself beholdest not the beam that is in thine own eye? Thou hypocrite, cast out first the beam out of thine own eye, and then shalt thou see clearly to cast out the mote that is in thy brother's eye. 43 For there is no good tree that bringeth forth corrupt fruit; nor again a corrupt tree that bringeth forth, good fruit. 44 For each tree is known by its own fruit. For of thorns men do not gather figs, nor of a bramble bush gather they grapes. 45 The good man out of the good treasure of his heart bringeth forth that which is good; and the evil *man* out of the evil *treasure* bringeth forth that which is evil: for out of the abundance of the heart his mouth speaketh.

Again Jesus spake a **parable** (v. 39) — here a brief parabolic saying, found also in Matthew 15:14. Verse 40 is paralleled in Matt. 10:24, 25 (cf. John 13:16; 15:20). Lampe points out its relation to the preceding verse: "In Luke it means that to avoid becoming a blind guide one must exercise self-criticism."[172] Verses 41-42 are parallel to Matthew 7:3-5 (see notes there). Verses 43-44 correspond to Matthew 7:16-20 (see comments there). Verse 45 is parallel to Matthew 12:34-35. A man's speech, flowing out of what is in his heart (v. 45) is

compared to the good and bad fruit produced by good and bad trees.

7. Two Houses (6:46-49)

46 And why call ye me, Lord, Lord, and do not the things which I say? 47 Every one that cometh unto me, and heareth my words, and doeth them, I will show you to whom he is like: 48 he is like a man building a house, who digged and went deep, and laid a foundation upon the rock: and when a flood arose, the stream brake against that house, and could not shake it: because it had been well builded. 49 But he that heareth, and doeth not, is like a man that built a house upon the earth without a foundation; against which the stream brake, and straightway it fell in; and the ruin of that house was great.

Verse 46 is parallel to Matthew 7:21. Verses 47-49 close this "sermon" with the same illustration as that at the close of the Sermon on the Mount in Matthew (see notes on Matt. 7:24-27). The difference in the two houses was not in the superstructure, but in the foundation. The only sure, stable foundation is obedience to the word of God. **Went deep** (v. 48) has obvious devotional and homiletical overtones.

F. HEALING MINISTRY (7:1-17)

1. Healing of Centurion's Slave (7:1-10)

1 After he had ended all his sayings in the ears of the people, he entered into Capernaum. 2 And a certain centurion's servant, who was dear unto him, was sick and at the point of death. 3 And when he heard concerning Jesus, he sent unto him elders of the Jews, asking him that he would come and save his servant. 4 And they, when they came to Jesus, besought him earnestly, saying, He is worthy that thou shouldest do this for him; 5 for he loveth our nation, and himself built us our synagogue. 6 And Jesus went with them. And when he was now not far from the house, the centurion sent friends to him, saying unto him, Lord, trouble not thyself; for I am not worthy that thou shouldest come under my roof: 7 wherefore neither thought I myself worthy to come unto thee: but say the word, and my servant shall be healed. 8 For I also am a man set under authority, having under myself soldiers: and I say

---

[170] *Op. cit.,* p. 348.

[171] Albert Barnes, *Notes on the New Testament: Luke and John,* ed. Robert Frew, p. 47.

[172] G. W. H. Lampe, "Luke," *Peake's Commentary on the Bible,* ed. Matthew Black and H. H. Rowley, p. 831.

to this one, Go, and he goeth; and to another, Come, and he cometh; and to my servant, Do this and he doeth it. 9 And when Jesus heard these things, he marvelled at him, and turned and said unto the multitude that followed him, I say unto you, I have not found so great faith, no, not in Israel. 10 And they that were sent, returning to the house, found the servant whole.

This miracle is recorded also in Matthew 8:5-13 (see the notes there). Both Gospels indicate that it took place in **Capernaum,** on the northwestern shore of the Lake of Galilee, where Jesus evidently made His headquarters in Peter's house.

The Greek word for **centurion** (v. 2) is a compound meaning "ruler of a hundred." The centurion was an officer in charge of a Roman "century," composed of one hundred infantrymen.

The word **servant** is *doulos;* literally, "slave" (v. 2). Matthew uses a different term, *pais,* which may mean either "child" or "servant." Strangely, in this passage Luke does not state the nature of the illness, while Matthew does. But Luke describes the slave as **dear** — honored, valued, precious — to his master, and also as **at the point of death** — literally, "about to come to an end."

When the centurion heard about Jesus, and the healing miracles He was performing, he sent to Him **elders of the Jews** — leaders of the local synagogue — asking Him to come and **save** his slave. This verb is *sozo,* which is used frequently in the Gospels for physical healing and in the Epistles for spiritual salvation; that is, healing of the soul. It basically means "*to save* from peril, injury or suffering."[173]

The elders came to Jesus, earnestly pleading the case of the centurion. They said: **He is worthy that thou shouldest do this for him; for he loveth our nation, and himself built us our synagogue** (v. 4). It is an interesting fact that centurions are always spoken of in a favorable way in the New Testament. All one has to do to verify that fact is to check the passages listed under "centurion" in a concordance.

Jesus went with them (v. 6); literally, "was going," or "started to go" with them. But before He reached the man's house

He was met by another delegation, this time of the centurion's **friends.** It is obvious that this Roman soldier was highly thought of in the Jewish community. The friends brought the message that the centurion did not consider himself worthy of having the Master come into his home; **wherefore neither thought I myself worthy to come unto thee** (v. 7).

When we compare this with Matthew's account, we immediately run into a difficulty. Matthew says that the centurion came to Jesus, beseeching Him (Matt. 8:5). When the Master said, "I will come and heal him," the centurion answered, "Lord, I am not worthy that thou shouldest come under my roof" (Matt. 8:8). How can these two accounts be reconciled?

The answer in this case is rather simple. Matthew has a regular habit of "telescoping" narratives, leaving out the details of the procedure. There are so many examples of this (see, for instance, the notes on Matthew 21:1-22) that this feature cannot be questioned. So here Matthew simply says that the centurion **came, beseeching,** and **answered,** while Luke spells out the details, showing that the centurion did all this through his friends. This is perfectly proper and understandable.

The centurion's reasoning was logical. He knew what it was to exercise authority over his soldiers and slaves (v. 8). He believed that Jesus had complete authority over disease. So all that was necessary was: **say the word, and my servant shall be healed** (v. 7).

The Greek word for **servant** is different from that used previously. In verse 2 it was *doulos,* "slave." But here it is *pais,* which can mean either "child" or "servant." Here it is used in the way that a servant in a British household would be called "boy."

Jesus **marvelled** at the centurion's strong, intelligent faith. He said: **I have not found so great faith, no, not in Israel** (v. 9). Only one other time is it recorded that Jesus marvelled, and that was at the unbelief of His own townspeople (Mark 6:6).

When the ones who had been sent by the centurion returned to the house, they

173 G. Abbott-Smith, *A Manual Greek Lexicon of the New Testament,* p. 436.

found the slave **whole**. This is the participle of *hygiainio* (see notes on 5:31).

2. Raising of Widow's Son (7:11-17)

11 And it came to pass soon afterwards, that he went to a city called Nain; and his disciples went with him, and a great multitude. 12 Now when he drew near to the gate of the city, behold, there was carried out one that was dead, the only son of his mother, and she was a widow: and much people of the city was with her. 13 And when the Lord saw her, he had compassion on her, and said unto her, Weep not. 14 And he came nigh and touched the bier: and the bearers stood still. And he said, Young man, I say unto thee, Arise. 15 And he that was dead sat up, and began to speak. And he gave him to his mother. 16 And fear took hold on all: and they glorified God, saying, A great prophet is arisen among us: and, God hath visited his people. 17 And this report went forth concerning him in the whole of Judaea, and all the region round about.

This incident is recorded only by Luke. It is a typical picture of Christ's compassion, such as Luke loves to paint.

In the Gospels there are three cases of Jesus raising someone from the dead. In climactic order they would be: (1) Jairus' daughter, who had just died; (2) the widow's son at Nain, who had been dead for a few hours and was on the way to the cemetery; (3) Lazarus, who had been in the grave for four days. These, in a sense, prefigured Christ's own resurrection.

Nain is now an Arab village called Nein. It is on the lower slope of a knoll called "Little Hermon," located between Mount Gilboa and Mount Tabor in the Plain of Esdraelon (which forms a natural boundary between Galilee and Samaria). It is five or six miles southeast of Nazareth and about twenty-five miles (a day's journey) from Capernaum, where the previous incident occurred. While this place today is only a small village of about two hundred inhabitants, the ruins of ancient Nain show that it was once a large town.

When Jesus drew near **the gate of the city** — which shows that it was a walled city — He passed the cemetery. (Tombs can still be found on the hillside at this point.) As He approached, a funeral procession came out through the gate.

The dead person was **the only son of his mother, and she was a widow** (v. 12). That she was a **widow** was quickly evident from the fact that no husband walked by her side. That the deceased was her **only son** was revealed by the absence of young men accompanying her in her mourning. She was a lonely soul.

It is difficult for people in modern western civilization to appreciate the full measure of the woman's sorrow, and the reasons for it. In the first place, the woman had lost her husband. In the Orient this is a much greater tragedy than in the Occident. The situation here was not as bad as that in recent India, where a young widow was often blamed for the death of her husband. But a widow's state in Israel was anything but a happy one.

When the father in a home died, the oldest son succeeded him as head of the house. This widow had only one son. He was her only support — both socially and economically. All her affection and attention were showered on him. He was her only source of income.

When he died, it seemed as if all the lights went out. Not only was she left to live alone, but she was bereft of all financial support. In those days a widow did not find a job in office, store, or factory. She faced not only loneliness but even the threat of starvation, except as her neighbors might come to her rescue. This was no ordinary funeral; it was a black, bleak one.

Jesus took in this whole picture at a glance. **When the Lord** — Luke's favorite designation of Christ — **saw her, he had compassion on her** (v. 13) — better, "was gripped with compassion" (aorist tense). That was His immediate reaction to human need. He bore the sorrows of humanity not only on the cross in those last awful hours, but also on His heart during the days of His earthly ministry.

First Jesus addressed Himself to the mourning mother: **Weep not**; literally, "Do not go on weeping." Then He came near and touched **the bier** (v. 14). This was not a closed casket, but, as was customary among the Jews, an open one — perhaps only a board on which the body was carried. Due to the lack of modern embalming techniques, and also to the hot weather in Palestine, it was required by law that the corpse be buried the same day the person died. So the deceased had been dead only a few hours.

Then Jesus addressed the corpse: **Young man, I say unto thee, Arise.** To everyone's astonishment, the dead man **sat up** (v. 15). The verb occurs only here and in Acts 9:40, where Dorcas sat up when restored to life. Hobart writes: "In this intransitive sense its use seems, with a few exceptions, to be almost altogether confined to the medical writers, who employ it to describe patients sitting up in bed."[174]

The fact that the young man **began to speak** was full proof that he was now alive. It would be interesting to know what his first words were when restored to life. Jesus gave the young man **to his mother.** He did not ask this man to follow Him, because his mother needed him. God does not unreasonably ignore human responsibility when He calls one to full-time service.

Once more we have the twofold reaction of the crowd: first, **fear;** then **they glorified God** (v. 16) — a typical Lukan expression (cf. 5:25, 26). The people said: **God hath visited his people.** Plummer observes, "The verb was specially used of the 'visits' of a physician," and adds this comment: "After the weary centuries during which no Prophet had appeared, it was indeed a proof of Jehovah's visiting His people that one who excelled the greatest Prophets was among them."[175]

This **report** (*logos,* "word") went out into all Judaea. Gilmour says: "Judea, as in 1:5; 4:44; and 6:17, is the whole of Palestine."[176] **All the region round about** would take in Syria and Phoenicia.

G. JESUS AND JOHN THE BAPTIST (7:18-35)

1. The Concern of John (7:18-23)

18 And the disciples of John told him of all these things. 19 And John calling unto him two of his disciples sent them to the Lord, saying, Art thou he that cometh, or look we for another? 20 And when the men were come unto him, they said, John the Baptist hath sent us unto thee, saying, Art thou he that cometh, or look we for another? 21 In that hour he cured many of diseases and plagues and evil spirits; and on many that were

blind he bestowed sight. 22 And he answered and said unto them, Go and tell John the things which ye have seen and heard; the blind receive their sight, the lame walk, the lepers are cleansed, and the deaf hear, the dead are raised up, the poor have good tidings preached to them. 23 And blessed is he, whosoever shall find no occasion of stumbling in me.

This section is found only here and in Matthew 11:2-19 (see notes there for further discussion).

The **disciples of John** — who evidently were still loyal to him, though following Jesus while John was in prison — reported to their master **all these things.** This report refers primarily to the two healing incidents just noted.

John called two of his disciples and sent them to **the Lord** (Luke's favorite designation again). They were to ask: **Art thou he that cometh, or look we for another?** (v. 19). The last word is *heteros,* "another of a different kind."

He that cometh is a phrase with a long history. Mowinckel made it the title of his monumental work on the Messiah concept in the Old Testament and later Judaism.[177] It would be impossible to summarize in a brief compass his more than five hundred pages of closely written material. Suffice to say that the hopes of the centuries focused on "the Coming One" — first conceived of as a political figure and finally also as a supernatural Son of man.

Luke's account is fuller than that of Matthew. Verses 20 and 21 are found only here. Verse 21 forms a logical prelude to verse 22 which is found almost verbatim in Matthew 11:4, 5.

Verse 22 reveals the value that Jesus put on evangelism. After enumerating the various types of miracles He was performing — healing the blind, lame, lepers, deaf, and raising the dead — He climaxed it all with what was most important of all: **the poor have good tidings preached to them** (literally, "are being evangelized"). This was a greater miracle than all the rest. Here was His true Messianic mission (cf. 4:18). This was the greatest evidence that He was the Messiah.

Then Jesus sounded a note which was perhaps a bit of warning to John: **And**

---

[174] *Op. cit.,* p. 11.   [175] *Op. cit.,* p. 200.   [176] *Op. cit.,* p. 133.
[177] Sigmund Mowinckel, *He That Cometh,* trans. G. W. Anderson.

blessed is he, whosoever shall find no occasion of stumbling in me (v. 23). The verb is *skandalizo* ("scandalize"), found commonly in Matthew and Mark, but seldom in Luke (only here and 17:2). Its meaning has already been discussed in the notes on Matthew 16:23; 18:6-9. Plummer says: "The verb combines the notions of 'trip up' and 'entrap,' and in the New Testament is always used in the figurative sense of 'causing to sin.' "[178]

There have been several suggestions as to why John asked this question. Chrysostom thought that the question was asked for the sake of John's disciples, and not for his own sake. This idea was adopted by Luther and Calvin, as well as others later. Some have suggested that John's own faith was failing. Plummer prefers a third view: that it was his patience, not his faith, that was failing. He was anxious for the Kingdom to be set up and for the Jews to be delivered from Roman bondage.[179] It must be confessed that the form of John's question seems to favor the second view, that his faith was failing. But we should like to prefer the third.

2. The Commendation of John (7:24-35)

24 And when the messengers of John were departed, he began to say unto the multitudes concerning John, What went ye out into the wilderness to behold? a reed shaken with the wind? 25 But what went ye out to see? a man clothed in soft raiment? Behold, they that are gorgeously apparelled, and live delicately, are in kings' courts. 26 But what went ye out to see? a prophet? Yea, I say unto you, and much more than a prophet. 27 This is he of whom it is written,
Behold, I send my messenger before thy face,
Who shall prepare thy way before thee.
28 I say unto you, Among them that are born of women there is none greater than John: yet he that is but little in the kingdom of God is greater than he. 29 And all the people when they heard, and the publicans, justified God, being baptized with the baptism of John. 30 But the Pharisees and the lawyers rejected for themselves the counsel of God, being not baptized of him. 31 Whereunto then shall I liken the men of this generation, and to what are they like? 32 They are

like unto children that sit in the market-place, and call one to another; who say, We piped unto you, and ye did not dance; we wailed, and ye did not weep. 33 For John the Baptist is come eating no bread nor drinking wine; and ye say, He hath a demon. 34 The Son of man is come eating and drinking; and ye say, Behold, a gluttonous man, and a wine-bibber, a friend of publicans and sinners! 35 And wisdom is justified of all her children.

It would seem that Jesus had gently reproved John for having asked the question he did. But immediately he proceeded to commend the Baptist before the crowd. He intimated that John was no **reed shaken with the wind** (v. 24), nor **a man clothed in soft raiment** (v. 25). Was he a prophet? **Yea . . . much more than a prophet** (v. 26). He was God's **messenger,** predicted in Malachi 3:1 (v. 27). Jesus climaxed His commendation by asserting that among all men who had been born, **there is none greater than John** (v. 28). This is a surprising statement. Of John's piety and dedication there can be no doubt. But was he a greater character than some of the leading Old Testament saints? Plummer writes: "John's superiority lay, not in his personal character, but in his office and mission: the glory of being the immediate forerunner of the Messiah was unique."[180]

The second part of the verse seems almost more surprising than the first: **yet he that is but little in the kingdom of heaven is greater than he.** To say that the expression **but little** (literally, "lesser") refers to Christ, as being younger than John and baptized by him, seems very questionable. Probably the correct meaning is expressed by Godet when he says: "The weakest disciple has a more spiritual intuition of divine things than the forerunner. He enjoys in Jesus the dignity of a son, while John is only a servant."[181] In a similar vein Farrar writes: "The simple meaning of these words seems to be that in blessings and privileges, in knowledge, in revealed hope, in conscious admission into fellowship with God, the humblest child of the new kingdom is superior to the greatest prophet of the old."[182]

Verses 29 and 30 are not paralleled at this point in Matthew but are somewhat

[178] *Op. cit.*, p. 203. [179] *Ibid.*, p. 202. [180] *Ibid.*, p. 205. [181] *Op. cit.*, p. 351.
[182] *Op. cit.*, p. 202.

similar to Matthew 21:31, 32. There has been considerable discussion as to whether these words are a part of Jesus' discourse, or whether they are a historical observation by the writer of the Gospel. If the former, it means **all the people when they heard** the preaching of John the Baptist. This is the view of Geldenhuys. He says: "These words form part of what Jesus said on this occasion. Then we have a connected address of our Lord running from verse 24b to verse 35."[183] Plummer agrees: "A comment inserted in the middle of Christ's words, and with no indication that it is a comment, is without a parallel and improbable."[184]

The common people and the publicans, as the result of hearing the preaching of John, **justified God, being baptized.** That is, they "admitted the righteousness of God (in making these claims upon them and granting them these opportunities) *by* being baptized. Their accepting baptism was an acknowledgement of His justice."[185]

On the other hand, **the Pharisees and the lawyers rejected for themselves the counsel of God,** refusing to be baptized — better, "They frustrated the counsel of God *concerning* themselves."[186] God's counsel, or purpose, was their salvation. By their rejection of John the Baptist's preaching of repentance they nullified God's purpose to save them.

The word **lawyers** is almost a Lukan term. He uses it six times. Elsewhere in the New Testament it occurs only three times (Matt. 22:35; Titus 3:9, 13). The term does not refer to lawyers in the modern sense, but to teachers of the Mosaic law. Luke often uses the word in place of "scribes," evidently fearing that his Gentile readers might not know the main function of the scribes, which was to teach the Law.

The **then** (or, "therefore") of verse 31 ties in with the interpretation just given for verses 29 and 30. The Pharisees and lawyers were like children who stand sullenly on the side lines and refuse to play wedding (Jesus' offer of the gospel) or funeral (John's rugged repentance-preaching). The application is made very clearly here. John the Baptist was an ascetic; so the Pharisees said he was demon-possessed. Jesus was sociable and loved to eat with people; so He was, His enemies said, **a gluttonous man, and a winebibber, a friend of publicans and sinners** (v. 34). It is impossible to please antagonistic critics. Jesus is saying: "John failed through his austerity; I shall fail through my gentleness; neither under one form nor another will you obey God. Nevertheless there are those whose conduct by condemning you justifies God."[187]

H. JESUS AND PENITENT WOMAN (7: 36-50)

36 And one of the Pharisees desired him that he would eat with him. And he entered into the Pharisee's house, and sat down to meat. 37 And behold a woman who was in the city, a sinner; and when she knew that he was sitting at meat in the Pharisee's house, she brought an alabaster cruse of ointment, 38 and standing behind at his feet, weeping, she began to wet his feet with her tears, and wiped them with the hair of her head, and kissed his feet, and anointed them with the ointment. 39 Now when the Pharisee that had bidden him saw it, he spake within himself, saying, This man, if he were a prophet, would have perceived who and what manner of woman this is that toucheth him, that she is a sinner. 40 And Jesus answering said unto him, Simon, I have somewhat to say unto thee. And he saith, Teacher, say on. 41 A certain lender had two debtors: the one owed five hundred shillings, and the other fifty. 42 When they had not *wherewith* to pay, he forgave them both. Which of them therefore will love him most? 43 Simon answered and said, He, I suppose, to whom he forgave the most. And he said unto him, Thou hast rightly judged. 44 And turning to the woman, he said unto Simon, Seest thou this woman? I entered into thy house, thou gavest me no water for my feet: but she hath wetted my feet with her tears, and wiped them with her hair. 45 Thou gavest me no kiss: but she, since the time I came in, hath not ceased to kiss my feet. 46 My head with oil thou didst not anoint: but she hath anointed my feet with ointment. 47 Wherefore I say unto thee, Her sins, which are many, are forgiven; for she loved much: but to whom little is forgiven, *the same* loveth little. 48 And he said unto her, Thy sins are forgiven. 49 And they that sat at meat with him began to say within themselves, Who is this that even forgiveth sins? 50

183 *Op. cit.,* p. 230. 184 *Op. cit.,* p. 205. 185 *Ibid.,* p. 206. 186 *Ibid.*
187 Godet, *op. cit.,* p. 357.

And he said unto the woman, Thy faith hath saved thee; go in peace.

What motive the Pharisee had in inviting Jesus to dinner we do not know. From the rude, discourteous way he treated his Guest, it would seem that he was not kindly disposed toward Christ. **Sat down to meat** should be "reclined at the table." In the better homes of those days it was the custom to recline on couches around the table while eating, with the bare feet at the outer edge of the couch.

During the meal a woman who was a **sinner** (street-walker) **in the city** (v. 37) entered the dining room. To some this might seem strange, but in that warm climate it was customary to have the eating area open to the outside for better ventilation.

The woman brought **an alabaster cruse of ointment.** Weeping with penitence and loving gratitude, she washed His feet with her tears, and wiped them with her own hair, kissing[188] His feet, and anointing them with ointment. Perhaps the very perfume which she had formerly used in plying her trade, she now poured out in pure love, as she stood at His feet and kept on **weeping** (present participle of continuous action).

It was a scene to make angels weep with joy (cf. 15:10), but the Pharisee met it with cold, cruel criticism. He reasoned to himself that if Jesus were a prophet, **He** would know that it was a **sinner** who was touching Him (v. 39). In his own thinking he called Jesus **this man.** The Greek has simply "this one." The expression in the Gospels is often used as an epithet of contempt on the part of Jesus' enemies — "this fellow."

The self-righteous host was particularly disgusted that this woman **toucheth him.** According to the rabbis no good man would ever in public talk to a woman — not even his own wife, mother, or sister — or let a woman get within six feet of him. Jesus was violating both rules. By letting this woman touch His feet, He rendered Himself ceremonially unclean. So thought the Pharisee. But instead

Jesus made the sinful woman clean. The touch of divine power brings purity.

Soon Jesus was **answering** Simon's thoughts. As Augustine well expressed it, "He heard the Pharisee thinking."[189] To be sure that His host got the point, Jesus put the truth in the form of a parable — the Parable of the Two Debtors (vv. 41-42). A certain **lender** ("money-lender") had two debtors. One owed him 500 denarii, or about a hundred dollars, and the other 50 denarii, or about ten dollars.[190]

When they were unable to pay, the money-lender freely **forgave** them both. The verb is built on the root *charis*, meaning "grace." Plummer well observes: "In *echarisato*, 'he made them a present' of what they owed him, we trace the Pauline doctrine of free grace and salvation for all."[191]

Then Jesus posed the question: **"Which of them therefore will love him most?"** (v. 42). Simon replied: **He, I suppose,[192] to whom he forgave the most** (v. 43). Jesus assured him that he had answered correctly, and then made the application. First, He asked His host to look at the woman whom he had been treating with scornful contempt. When Christ entered the Pharisee's house, He was offered no water for His feet. This was a real insult to a guest. In those days men wore open sandals and no socks. On the hot dusty roads the traveler's feet would become grimy with dirt and perspiration. The first thing any thoughtful host did was to have a servant wash the guest's feet, or at least to offer him water for the purpose (cf. Gen. 18:3; 19:2). But Simon showed his real attitude toward Jesus by omitting this common courtesy. The woman had made up for this lack by washing His feet with her tears. It was also customary for the host to greet each guest — only men ate together at these dinners — with a kiss. Simon could not bring himself to kiss One whom he apparently despised in his heart. But the grateful, penitent woman **since the time I came in, hath not ceased to kiss my feet** (v. 45). A third custom was the additional courtesy of pouring a little

---

[188] The Greek compound in the imperfect tense suggests: "She continued to kiss tenderly."
[189] Quoted by Farrar, *op. cit.*, p. 207.
[190] The Roman denarius was worth about twenty cents, but represented a fair day's wage (cf. Matt. 20:2).   [191] *Op. cit.*, p. 212.
[192] The Greek verb is used only by Luke in the New Testament. Farrar comments: "The word has a shade of supercilious irony" (*op. cit.*, p. 208).

oil on a favored guest's head. Simon deliberately omitted this also, but the woman had anointed Jesus' feet with perfume, which would be more costly than the olive oil customarily used.

Then the Master made His conclusion. The many sins of the woman **are forgiven** — the Greek says, "have been forgiven" — **for she loved much** (v. 47). This last statement has caused a great deal of debate. It seems to say that the woman was forgiven because she loved much — which is what the Roman Catholic commentators hold. Plummer points out the fallacy of this view: "It is quite at variance (a) with the parable which precedes; (b) with the second half of the verse . . .; (c) with the ver. 50, which states that it was *faith*, not love, which had been the means of salvation; a doctrine which runs through the whole of the New Testament."[193]

Adam Clarke thinks that *hoti*, for, is here equivalent to *dioti*, "wherefore."[194] Perhaps a simpler solution is the one proposed by Godet. He illustrates it thus: "We may say, It is light, for the sun is risen; but we may also say, The sun is risen, for (I say this because) it is light."[195] That is, "for" may be used to introduce the result as well as the cause. So here. Because the woman loves much you can readily discern that her sins have been forgiven her.

Then Jesus turned to the woman and said, **Thy sins are forgiven** (v. 48) — rather, "have been forgiven." Apparently Christ ignored the criticisms of the other guests[196] — **Who is this that even forgiveth sins?** (v. 49) — for He added a closing benediction to the woman: **Thy faith hath saved thee; go in peace** (v. 50). This answered the question of the critics; it was her faith that saved. **Go in peace** is a beautiful Hebrew blessing.

I. TEACHER AND WONDER-WORKER (8:1-56)

1. The Ministering Women (8:1-3)

1 And it came to pass soon afterwards, that he went about through cities and villages, preaching and bringing the good tidings of the kingdom of God, and with him the twelve, 2 and certain women who had been healed of evil spirits and infirmities: Mary that was called Magdalene, from whom seven demons had gone out, 3 and Joanna the wife of Chuzas Herod's steward, and Susanna, and many others, who ministered unto them of their substance.

Among other characteristics which it possesses, Luke's is the Gospel of Women (see Introduction). This is one of the several brief paragraphs in the book which support that statement. It is not paralleled in the other Gospels.

Farrar notes that the opening expression of this chapter "marks a new phase, a new departure, in Christ's mode of action. Hitherto He had made Capernaum His head-quarters . . . . at this period . . . He began a wider range of wandering and of missions."[197]

Jesus made another tour of Galilee's **cities and villages** — the Greek suggests, "city by city and village by village" — **preaching** (proclaiming, heralding) **and bringing the good tidings of** — one word in the Greek "evangelizing" — the kingdom of God. The good news was that the kingdom of God was now offered to all who would enter it.

Not only did Jesus have with Him **the twelve,** but also **certain women.** Farrar comments that Luke "is fond of dwelling on the graciousness and tenderness of Jesus even to a class so much despised and neglected as Eastern women."[198]

Three women are named here. The first is **Mary that was called Magdalene;** that is, "of Magdala," a city on the western shore of the Lake of Galilee. Magdala is the Aramaic-Greek form of Migdol, meaning "watch-tower." Mary is probably designated thus (as usually in the Gospels) to distinguish her from Mary of Bethany and other Marys of the New Testament. We would agree with Plummer when he says: "The *hamartolos* (sinner, 7:37) and Mary Magdalene and Mary of Bethany are three distinct persons."[199] Jesus had cast **seven demons** out of Mary Magdalene, and she was everlastingly grateful to Him.

The second woman was **Joanna, the wife of Chuzas, Herod's steward.** She is mentioned elsewhere only in 24:10, where

193 *Op. cit.,* p. 213.
194 Adam Clarke, *The New Testament of Our Lord and Saviour Jesus Christ,* I, 415.
195 *Op. cit.,* p. 361.   196 **Within themselves** may be translated "among themselves."
197 *Op. cit.,* p. 211.   198 *Ibid.*   199 *Op. cit.,* p. 216.

she is also associated with Mary Magdalene. Her husband's position would make her a woman of means, so that she was able to help generously in ministering to Jesus' needs. The Greek word for steward here is not the common one, *oikonomos*, which literally means "house-manager," but *epitropos*, which "conveys the impression of a higher rank than 'steward.' "[200]

The third woman was **Susanna,** which means "Lily." Nothing more is known about her. She and the other women **ministered unto them**[201] **of their substance.** These women kept Jesus and His disciples supplied with necessary food and clothing.

Women have always played an important part in the work of the Kingdom. Too often their contribution has been unnoticed and their praises unsung. It is to Luke's everlasting credit that he bore witness to the charity of these good women.

2. The Parable of the Sower (8:4-15)

a. Declaration of the Parable (8:4-8)

4 And when a great multitude came together, and they of every city resorted unto him, he spake by a parable: 5 The sower went forth to sow his seed: and as he sowed, some fell by the way side; and it was trodden under foot, and the birds of the heaven devoured it. 6 And other fell on the rock; and as soon as it grew, it withered away, because it had no moisture. 7 And other fell amidst the thorns; and the thorns grew with it, and choked it. 8 And other fell into the good ground, and grew, and brought forth fruit a hundredfold. As he said these things, he cried, He that hath ears to hear, let him hear.

Once more Luke emphasizes the vastness of the crowds that thronged Jesus — **when a great multitude came together, and they of every city resorted unto him.** The power of His preaching, the uniqueness of His teaching, and the wonder of His miracles drew in the people from every side.

To this crowd Jesus gave the Parable of the Sower. Its purpose was to warn the people that a responsibility was involved in listening to His teaching. The

Master suggested that there were four characteristic types of soil represented in the hearts of the hearers. So this is sometimes called the Parable of the Soils. It is one of the three parables which are recorded in all three Synoptic Gospels[202] (see the notes on Matt. 13:1-23 and Mark 4:1-20).

Up to this point Luke has given only a few brief parables. But now the parabolic method becomes dominant in the teaching of Jesus. Plummer suggests the reason why. Speaking of parables, he says: "They have the double property of revealing and concealing. They open the truth, and impress it upon the minds of those who are ready to receive it: but they do not instruct, though they may impress, the careless (v. 10)."[203] More specifically, he adds: "As the hostility to His teaching increased, Jesus would be likely to make more use of parables, which would benefit disciples without giving opportunity to His enemies."[204]

As to the exact meaning of the word **parable,** Farrar says: "A parable is a pictorial or narrative exhibition of some spiritual or moral truth, by means of actual and not fanciful elements of comparison."[205] In not being fanciful it differs from a fable.

The distinctive items in Luke's account of the Parable of the Sower are few. In connection with the seed that **fell by the wayside,** he adds: **and it was trodden under foot** (v. 5). This is perhaps implied in the other accounts, but not explicitly stated. Again he notes regarding the seed which fell **on the rock** that it withered away **because it had no moisture** (v. 6), while Matthew and Mark say, "Because it (they) had no root."

Thorns are particularly prevalent in the Plain of Gennesaret, near where Jesus was giving this parable, and seed sown among them would be **choked** (v. 7).

In connection with the seed sown on good ground Luke does not mention the thirtyfold and the sixtyfold, but only the **hundredfold** (v. 8). This generous yield seems to have been fairly common on the Plain of Gennesaret, which was renowned for its fruitfulness. "With a rich, loamy, well-watered soil, today as

---

[200] *Ibid.*   [201] So the best Greek text, rather than "him" (KJV).
[202] The other two are the Parables of the Mustard Seed (13:18-19) and the Wicked Husbandmen (20:9-16).   [203] *Op. cit.,* p. 217.   [204] *Ibid.*   [205] *Op. cit.,* p. 213.

in the Bible times, it is extraordinarily fertile; the only easily tillable land bordering the Sea of Galilee."[206]

In the latter part of verse 8, Luke uses a stronger word than Mark. He says that Jesus cried. Plummer comments: "The introductory *ephonei*, 'He cried aloud,' indicates a raising of the voice, and gives a solemnity to this concluding charge."[207] All three Synoptics give the admonition: He that hath ears to hear, let him hear. The meaning is: "This teaching is worthy the deepest attention of those who have the moral and spiritual capacity to understand it."[208]

b. Explanation of the Parable (8:9-15)

9 And his disciples asked him what this parable might be. 10 And he said, Unto you it is given to know the mysteries of the kingdom of God: but to the rest in parables; that seeing they may not see, and hearing they may not understand. 11 Now the parable is this: The seed is the word of God. 12 And those by the way side are they that have heard; then cometh the devil, and taketh away the word from their heart, that they may not believe and be saved. 13 And those on the rock *are* they who, when they have heard, receive the word with joy; and these have no root, who for a while believe, and in time of temptation fall away. 14 And that which fell among the thorns, these are they that have heard, and as they go on their way they are choked with cares and riches and pleasures of *this* life, and bring no fruit to perfection. 15 And that in the good ground, these are such as in an honest and good heart, having heard the word, hold it fast, and bring forth fruit with patience.

A typical example of difference in wording without any distinction in meaning in parallel passages in the Synoptic Gospels is found at v. 12. Luke says the devil, while Matthew has "the evil one" and Mark has "Satan." They all refer, of course, to the same person. All three Synoptists use the name "Satan," but Mark never uses "the devil." In this same verse (12) Luke alone adds: that they may not believe and be saved.

This is in line with Luke's stronger emphasis on salvation. It reflects the Pauline influence on his thinking. Similarly, in verse 13, Luke has who for a while believe, whereas Matthew and Mark have "but endure for a while." Here again is Paul's doctrine of salvation through faith.

In the same verse (13) there are two other items of interest. The first is Luke's substitution of in time of temptation for Matthew's and Mark's "when tribulation or persecution ariseth because of the word." The difference is significant. Matthew and Mark use the form which fitted into the prevailing Jewish persecution of Christians in their day. Luke has a broader concept in mind, writing for Gentiles everywhere and Christians of all time. In time of temptation has a more universal application than the two specific situations suggested in the other accounts.

The second item is the last word of verse 13. Matthew and Mark have "stumble (th) ." This is the oft-occurring verb *skandalizo* (see on Matt. 18:6) . How does Luke interpret the meaning of this difficult word[209] for his Gentile readers? He says, fall away. Cremer says it means "to dissolve the union formed with God by faith and obedience."[210] Perhaps Luke's interpretation here should be considered in our understanding of the meaning of *skandalizo* elsewhere in the New Testament.

In the explanation of the seed sown among thorns, the three Synoptics have somewhat different wording, while at the same time they give essentially the same thought. Luke mentions three items, as does Mark (Matt. only two) . Luke has as they go on their way they are choked with cares and riches and pleasures of this life (v. 14). The first two items, cares and riches, are paralleled in both Matthew and Mark. The third, pleasures of this life, is Luke's version of "the lusts of other things" (Mark). Both emphasize the fact that a life of self-indulgent pleasure (satisfying only one's own desires) is destructive of spiritual life.

In the explanation of the seed sown in

[206] Merrill C. Tenney (ed.), *The Pictorial Bible Dictionary*, p. 307.
[207] *Op. cit.*, p. 219. [208] Farrar, *op. cit.*, p. 215.
[209] He uses it only two times in his Gospel, whereas it is found fourteen times in Matthew and eight in Mark.
[210] Hermann Cremer, *Biblico-theological Lexicon of New Testament Greek*, trans. William Urwick, p. 308.

good soil Luke alone has: **these are such as in an honest[211] and good heart** (v. 15). This is the meaning of **good ground**. He also says that having heard the Word, **they hold it fast** (Mark: "accept it"; Matt.: "understand it"). To the statement that they bring forth fruit he adds: **with patience** (better, "steadfastness"). This relates to **hold it fast**. Endurance is the price of final salvation. Jesus said: "He that endureth to the end, the same shall be saved" (Matt. 10:22).

3. The Lighted Lamp (8:16-18)

16 And no man, when he hath lighted a lamp, covereth it with a vessel, or putteth it under a bed; but putteth it on a stand, that they that enter in may see the light. 17 For nothing is hid, that shall not be made manifest; nor *anything* secret, that shall not be known and come to light. 18 Take heed therefore how ye hear: for whosoever hath, to him shall be given; and whosoever hath not, from him shall be taken away even that which he thinketh he hath.

In this brief paragraph (see notes on Mark 4:21-25) Jesus seems to be explaining the reason for His use of parables. The truth is not to be hidden, like a **lamp** covered with a **vessel** — Mark has "bushel" (or "peck measure"). Rather it is to be put on a **stand** (or "niche in the wall"), **that they that enter in may see the light** in a windowless Palestinian home of that day.

But if anything is **hid**, it is in order that it may be **made manifest** (v. 17); or **secret** — be **known and come to light**. If the truth of Jesus' teaching seemed to be hidden in parables, it was for the purpose of finally making it known to those who would listen with open hearts to receive it.

Jesus further admonished: **Take heed therefore how ye hear** (v. 18). Mark has "what ye hear." Both are important. Here the emphasis is on the fact that we must listen with open, receptive hearts.

The last part of verse 18 expresses the important principle that only those who take in truth can receive more, for the new can be understood only in relation to the old. The one who **hath not** —

who has carelessly failed to learn — will lose **even that which he thinketh he hath.** The only way to retain knowledge is to keep adding to it.

4. The Family of God (8:19-21)

19 And there came to him his mother and brethren, and they could not come at him for the crowd. 20 And it was told him, Thy mother and thy brethren stand without, desiring to see thee. 21 But he answered and said unto them, My mother and my brethren are these that hear the word of God, and do it.

For the meaning of this interesting incident see the notes on Matthew 12:46-50 and Mark 3:31-35. Luke's account is by far the briefest of the three. The only distinctive item which he adds is the statement that Jesus' mother and brethren **are these that hear the word of God, and do it** (v. 21). This ties in closely with what precedes in Luke. Matthew and Mark both place this incident before the Parable of the Sower, and so do not have this reference to hearing the Word.

5. The Stilling of the Storm (8:22-25)

22 Now it came to pass on one of those days, that he entered into a boat, himself and his disciples; and he said unto them, Let us go over unto the other side of the lake; and they launched forth. 23 But as they sailed he fell asleep: and there came down a storm of wind on the lake; and they were filling *with water,* and were in jeopardy. 24 And they came to him, and awoke him, saying, Master, master, we perish. And he awoke, and rebuked the wind and the raging of the water: and they ceased, and there was a calm. 25 And he said unto them, Where is your faith? And being afraid they marvelled, saying one to another, Who then is this, that he commandeth even the winds and the water, and they obey him?

The miracle is related in all three Synoptic Gospels (see the notes on Matt. 8:23-27; Mark 4:35-41). Luke again uses **lake** (vv. 22, 23) where the others have "sea" (see on 5:1, 2). In keeping with this, he shows his background of having sailed the Mediterranean. He alone has **launched forth** (v. 22). In the Greek this

---

[211] This is not the usual meaning of *kalos*, which is here associated with *agathos* (good). The distinction usually made is that *kalos* basically describes aesthetic goodness — it may be translated "beautiful" — and *agathos* ethical goodness. A. B. Bruce (EGT,1, 520) translates the phrase here: "in a noble and generous heart."

is a nautical term used by Homer, Herodotus, and Thucydides. It means "put to sea." In the New Testament it is used by Luke (here and 13 times in Acts).

Verse 23 reflects a further use of nautical terms. The Greek word for **sailed** is found only here and in Acts (4 times). (Incidentally, the Greek verb for **fell asleep** occurs only here.) For **filling** Luke uses a different word — found only here, 9:51, and Acts 2:1 — from that in Mark.

The breaking of the storm is thus described by Plummer: "There came down a violent squall of wind, from the heights which surround the lake. These are furrowed with ravines like funnels, down which winds rush with great velocity."[212] The writer of this commentary well remembers being caught in such a sudden storm on the Lake of Galilee in the summer of 1953. The gigantic waves that broke furiously over the bow seemed determined to sink the boat. Luke adds the comment that Jesus and His companions **were in jeopardy**.

Terrified, the disciples woke Him, crying, **Master, master.** The Greek is *epistata*, found only in Luke (see note on 5:5 for its meaning). The term is particularly appropriate here, for it was used to mean a pilot of a ship.[213] The verb **commandeth** (v. 25) fits well with the idea of a "commander" of the boat.

The spiritual application of this incident is obvious. The Christian is safe as long as he has Jesus on board his bark. No matter how furiously the storms of life may beat on men's souls, they need not fear if He is with them.

6. The Gerasene Demoniac (8:26-39)

26 And they arrived at the country of the Gerasenes, which is over against Galilee. 27 And when he was come forth upon the land, there met him a certain man out of the city, who had demons; and for a long time he had worn no clothes, and abode not in *any* house, but in the tombs. 28 And when he saw Jesus, he cried out, and fell down before him, and with a loud voice said, What have I to do with thee, Jesus, thou Son of the Most High God? I beseech thee, torment me not. 29 For he was commanding

the unclean spirit to come out from the man. For oftentimes it had seized him: and he was kept under guard, and bound with chains and fetters; and breaking the bands asunder, he was driven of the demon into the deserts. 30 And Jesus asked him, What is thy name? And he said, Legion; for many demons were entered into him. 31 And they entreated him that he would not command them to depart into the abyss. 32 Now there was there a herd of many swine feeding on the mountain: and they entreated him that he would give them leave to enter into them. And he gave them leave. 33 And the demons came out from the man, and entered into the swine: and the herd rushed down the steep into the lake, and were drowned. 34 And when they that fed them saw what had come to pass, they fled, and told it in the city and in the country. 35 And they went out to see what had come to pass; and they came to Jesus, and found the man, from whom the demons were gone out, sitting, clothed and in his right mind, at the feet of Jesus: and they were afraid. 36 And they that saw it told them how he that was possessed with demons was made whole. 37 And all the people of the country of the Gerasenes round about asked him to depart from them, for they were holden with great fear: and he entered into a boat, and returned. 38 But the man from whom the demons were gone out prayed him that he might be with him: but he sent him away, saying, 39 Return to thy house, and declare how great things God hath done for thee. And he went his way, publishing throughout the whole city how great things Jesus had done for him.

This miracle also is recorded in all three of the Synoptics (see the commentary on Matt. 8:28-34; Mark 5:1-20). It doubtless made a great impression on all who saw it or heard about it.

The best Greek text has **Gerasenes** (v. 26), rather than "Gadarenes" (KJV). For a discussion of the variant readings see the notes on Matt. 8:28 and Mark 5:1.

The Greek word for **arrived** is found only here in the New Testament. It means "sail to land" or "put in." This is another one of Luke's nautical terms which reflect his wide travels.

Instead of **out of the city** (v. 27), Matthew and Mark have "out of the tombs." But there is no contradiction here. As

---

[212] *Op. cit.*, p. 226.
[213] H. G. Liddell and Robert Scott, *A Greek-English Lexicon*, rev. H. S. Jones, I, 659.

Plummer says, "The man belonged to the city, but he came out of the tombs to meet Jesus."[214] In the description of the demoniac, Luke adds the item: **and for a long time he had worn no clothes.** This shows what a desperate maniac the poor wretch was.

Fell down before him (v. 28) is Luke's correct interpretation of Mark's "worshipped him." Obviously there was no heart worship here, just a posture of the body.

The use of the expression **the Most High God** may suggest that the demoniac was not a Jew. For this divine title was apparently a favorite with Gentiles. It was used by Melchizedek (Gen. 14:20, 22), Balaam (Num. 24:16), the king of Babylon (Isa. 14:4), and frequently in the proclamations of the Babylonian kings (Dan. 3:26, 4:24, 32; 5:18, 21; 7:18, 22, 25, 27); also by the heathen girl at Philippi (Acts 16:17).

In the further description of the demoniac Luke adds that the man was **kept under guard** and that he was **driven of the demon into the deserts** (v. 29); — "regarded as a peculiar haunt of Azazel and other demons."[215]

Jesus asked **the unclean spirit** (v. 29): **What is thy name?** (v. 30). Creed comments: "The knowledge of the demon's name would, according to ancient belief, give the exorcist an advantage over the demon."[216]

The demons begged not to be sent **into the abyss** (v. 31).[217] Elsewhere the word (*abyssos*) is found only in Romans 10:7 and seven times in Revelation ("the bottomless pit"). When Jesus gave them permission, the demons entered a herd of hogs nearby, which stampeded into the lake and perished.

The moral question of Jesus' destruction of private property has created much discussion. Plummer suggests some possible solutions. One is: "Like earthquakes, shipwrecks, pestilences, and the like, the destruction of the swine is part of the mystery of evil, and insoluble."[218] Another, perhaps more helpful, is this: "A visible effect of the departure of the demons was necessary to convince the demoniacs and their neighbors of the completeness of the cure. Brutes and

private property may be sacrificed, when the sanity and lives of persons are concerned."[219]

7. Two Intertwined Miracles (8:40-56)

a. The Plea of Jairus (8:40-42)

40 And as Jesus returned, the multitude welcomed him; for they were all waiting for him. 41 And behold, there came a man named Jairus, and he was a ruler of the synagogue: and he fell down at Jesus' feet, and besought him to come into his house; 42 for he had an only daughter, about twelve years of age, and she was dying. But as he went the multitudes thronged him.

These two miracles, the healing of the hemorrhaging woman and the raising of Jairus' daughter, are described together in all three Synoptic Gospels (see notes on Matt. 9:18-26; Mark 5:21-43). We shall discuss here only the points peculiar to Luke.

Jesus had been on the east side of the Lake of Galilee, in the country known as Decapolis (see on Mark 5:20). Now He returned to the western shore, which was more heavily populated and so the main center of His Galilean ministry. He found a **multitude** ready to welcome Him, **for they were all waiting for him** (v. 40). This indicates well the eagerness of the common people to enjoy His teaching and healing ministry.

Luke notes that the dying daughter of Jairus was **about twelve years of age** (v. 42). Mark has this item at the close of his account. But it is natural that a physician should record the girl's age immediately.

b. Healing of the Woman with Hemorrhage (8:43-48)

43 And a woman having an issue of blood twelve years, who had spent all her living upon physicians, and could not be healed of any, 44 came behind him, and touched the border of his garment: and immediately the issue of her blood stanched. 45 And Jesus said, Who is it that touched me? And when all denied, Peter said, and they that were with him, Master, the multitudes press thee and crush *thee.* 46 But Jesus said, Some one did touch me; for I perceived that power had gone forth from me. 47 And when

[214] *Op. cit.*, p. 229.
[215] Farrar, *op. cit.*, p. 222. Cf. Matt. 12:43.　　[216] *Op. cit.*, p. 121.
[217] Mark has simply "out of the country."　　[218] *Op. cit.*, p. 228.　　[219] *Ibid.*

the woman saw that she was not hid, she came trembling, and falling down before him declared in the presence of all the people for what cause she touched him, and how she was healed immediately. 48 And he said unto her, Daughter, thy faith hath made thee whole; go in peace.

In the description of the woman Mark presents the typical view of a layman. He says that she "had suffered many things of many physicians and had spent all that she had, and was nothing bettered, but rather grew worse" (Mark 5: 26). This does not reflect very well on the doctors! Luke, being a physician, seeks to protect his profession. He admits that she **had spent all her living upon physicians,** but adds, **and could not be healed of any** (v. 43). That is, medically speaking, hers was an incurable case.

The woman's confession is given more fully by Luke than by Mark (not at all by Matthew). Luke says that she **declared in the presence of all the people for what cause she touched him, and how she was healed immediately** (v. 47). A physician would be interested in exactly this sort of testimony.

c. Raising of Jairus' Daughter (8:49-56)

49 While he yet spake, there cometh one from the ruler of the synagogue's *house,* saying, Thy daughter is dead; trouble not the Teacher. 50 But Jesus hearing it, answered him, Fear not: only believe, and she shall be made whole. 51 And when he came to the house, he suffered not any man to enter in with him, save Peter, and John, and James, and the father of the maiden and her mother. 52 And all were weeping, and bewailing her: but he said, Weep not; for she is not dead, but sleepeth. 53 And they laughed him to scorn, knowing that she was dead. 54 But he, taking her by the hand, called, saying, Maiden, arise. 55 And her spirit returned, and she rose up immediately: and he commanded that *something* be given her to eat. 56 And her parents were amazed: but he charged them to tell no man what had been done.

All three Gospels say that when Jesus bade the mourners be quiet, because the girl was only sleeping, **they laughed him to scorn.** Only Luke adds, **knowing that she was dead** (v. 53). He was naturally interested in the matter of whether the girl actually had died before Jesus raised her.

Luke alone records the nature of her restoration: **her spirit returned** (v. 55). Again, Mark puts at the very last the command of Jesus that the girl should be given something to eat, relating first the amazement created by the miracle. But Luke, being a physician, puts the command first (v. 55), and then the reaction of the parents (v. 56). The important thing was to see that the body restored to life should have nourishment to keep it alive.

J. CLOSE OF GALILEAN MINISTRY (9: 1-50)

1. Mission of the Twelve (9:1-6)

1 And he called the twelve together, and gave them power and authority over all demons, and to cure diseases. 2 And he sent them forth to preach the kingdom of God, and to heal the sick. 3 And he said unto them, Take nothing for your journey, neither staff, nor wallet, nor bread, nor money; neither have two coats. 4 And into whatsoever house ye enter, there abide, and thence depart. 5 And as many as receive you not, when ye depart from that city, shake off the dust from your feet, for a testimony against them. 6 And they departed, and went throughout the villages, preaching the gospel, and healing everywhere.

This event is described in the three Synoptic Gospels (see notes on Matt. 10:1-15; Mark 6:7-13). Jesus summoned **the twelve,** gave them **power** (*dynamis*) and **authority** (*exousia*) over all **demons** and **to cure diseases.** Thus equipped spiritually, they set out on their mission. As far as their physical equipment was concerned, they were to travel light. They were to take with them no food or money and no extra clothing. It is interesting to note that while we find "brass" in Matthew and **money** in Mark and Luke (v. 3), the Greek has "brass" in Matthew and Mark, and "silver" in Luke.

The twofold mission of the twelve apostles was to **preach the kingdom of God, and to heal the sick** (v. 2). They carried out their commission, **preaching the gospel** — evidently equated with the Kingdom — **and healing** everywhere. Thus they were spreading their Master's ministry farther than He could go in person.

2. Herod's Uneasy Conscience (9:7-9)

7 Now Herod the tetrarch heard of all that was done: and he was much perplexed because that it was said by some, that John was risen from the dead; 8 and by some, that Elijah had appeared; and by others, that one of the old prophets was risen again. 9 And Herod said, John I beheaded: but who is this, about whom I hear such things? And he sought to see him.

When **Herod the tetrarch** — same in Matthew 14:1; "king Herod" in Mark 6: 14 (see notes on Luke 3:1) — heard of the miracles Jesus was performing, **he was much perplexed** (cf. Mark 6:20). Some were saying that John the Baptist had risen from the dead, others that Elijah had come or one of the prophets had risen. Herod knew he had beheaded John; but who was this? He wished to see Jesus. But the Master did not reciprocate his desire.

3. Feeding of the Five Thousand (9: 10-17)

10 And the apostles, when they were returned, declared unto him what things they had done. And he took them, and withdrew apart to a city called Bethsaida. 11 But the multitudes perceiving it followed him: and he welcomed them, and spake to them of the kingdom of God, and them that had need of healing he cured. 12 And the day began to wear away; and the twelve came, and said unto him, Send the multitude away, that they may go into the villages and country round about, and lodge, and get provisions: for we are here in a desert place. 13 But he said unto them, Give ye them to eat. And they said, We have no more than five loaves and two fishes; except we should go and buy food for all this people. 14 For they were about five thousand men. And he said unto his disciples, Make them sit down in companies, about fifty each. 15 And they did so, and made them all sit down. 16 And he took the five loaves and the two fishes, and looking up to heaven, he blessed them, and brake; and gave to the disciples to set before the multitude. 17 And they ate, and were all filled: and there was taken up that which remained over to them of broken pieces, twelve baskets.

This is the only miracle of Jesus which is recorded in all four Gospels (cf. Matt.

14:13-23; Mark 6:3; John 6:1-13). In Mark and Luke the incident is preceded by the return of the Twelve from their tour of preaching. The Master knew that His men needed a vacation, and He wished to give them private instruction. So He withdrew with them to **a city called Bethsaida.** This was presumably Bethsaida Julias, which was located on the east bank of the Jordan River near where it empties into the north part of the Lake of Galilee. Apparently they went to a quiet spot south of Bethsaida.

The vacation never materialized. The people, seeing which way the boat was heading, **followed him** (v. 11). Mark tells vividly how the people ran around the northern end of the Lake and reached Jesus' destination before He did (Mark 6:23). John tells us it was just before the Passover (John 6:4). Perhaps the pilgrims were already beginning to gather, to go to the feast at Jerusaelm one hundred miles away — a week's journey each way.

When Jesus saw the large and eager crowd of people awaiting Him, He did not resent their presence. Instead He **welcomed** them. He preached to them about **the kingdom of God** and healed the needy ones. Then He fed the whole multitude of five thousand men with a young lad's lunch of **five loaves and two fishes** (v. 13; cf. John 6:9). The account in Luke is definitely shorter and less vivid than that in Mark.

In verse 16 **brake** is in the aorist tense, suggesting a simple act, while **gave** is in the imperfect tense of continuous action.

With regard to the **twelve baskets** (v. 17) which were filled with the broken bread that was left over, Farrar writes that they were probably wicker baskets. "Every Jew carried such a basket about with him to avoid the chance of his food contracting any Levitical pollution in heathen places."[220]

4. At Caesarea Philippi (9:18-27)

a. Peter's Confession (9:18-20)

18 And it came to pass, as he was praying apart, the disciples were with him: and he asked them, saying, Who do the multitudes say that I am? 19 And they answering said, John the Baptist; but others *say*, Elijah; and others, that one

[220] Farrar, *op. cit., pp.* 233, 234.

of the old prophets is risen again. 20 And he said unto them, But who say ye that I am? And Peter answering said, The Christ of God.

Matthew (16:13-20) and Mark (8:27-30) — see notes there — both indicate that Peter's confession was made near Caesarea Philippi. Luke alone says that Jesus was **praying** just before this (v. 18). This is the fourth time that Luke has mentioned the prayer life of Jesus where the other Gospels do not (cf. 3:21; 5:16; 6:12).

This was a climactic incident in the life of Christ. Farrar says: "This event may well be regarded as the **culminating point** in His ministry. He had now won **the deliberate faith and conviction** of those who had lived in close intercourse with Him."[221]

b. Prediction of Passion (9:21-27)

21 But he charged them, and commanded *them* to tell this to no man; 22 saying, The Son of man must suffer many things, and be rejected of the elders and chief priests and scribes, and be killed, and the third day be raised up. 23 And he said unto all, If any man would come after me, let him deny himself, and take up his cross daily, and follow me. 24 For whosoever would save his life shall lose it; but whosoever shall lose his life for my sake, the same shall save it. 25 For what is a man profited, if he gain the whole world, and lose or forfeit his own self? 26 For whosoever shall be ashamed of me and of my words, of him shall the Son of man be ashamed, when he cometh in his own glory, and *the glory* of the Father, and of the holy angels. 27 But I tell you of a truth, There are some of them that stand here, who shall in no wise taste of death, till they see the kingdom of God.

The first prediction of the Passion is somewhat similar in all three Synoptics (see the notes on Matt. 16:21-28; Mark 8:31). All mention that the elders, the chief priests, and the scribes — the constituent parts of the Great Sanhedrin at Jerusalem — would reject Christ, that He would be killed and rise the third day. It is difficult to see how the disciples could have failed to understand what He was saying. But they did fail.

Luke omits the protest of Peter, given

in Mark and Matthew. But he does join them in giving the great challenge to consecration found in verses 23-25. He adds one significant word in verse 23: the follower of Christ is to take up his cross **daily**. There must be not only a crisis of complete consecration, but also a daily submission to God's will.

For the meaning of verse 27, see the comments on Matthew 16:28 and Mark 9:1. It does not seem best to take this verse as a prediction of the Transfiguration.

5. The Transfiguration (9:28-36)

28 And it came to pass about eight days after these sayings, that he took with him Peter and John and James, and went up into the mountain to pray. 29 And as he was praying, the fashion of his countenance was altered, and his raiment *became* white *and* dazzling. 30 And behold, there talked with him two men, who were Moses and Elijah: 31 who appeared in glory, and spake of his decease which he was about to accomplish at Jerusalem. 32 Now Peter and they that were with him were heavy with sleep: but when they were fully awake, they saw his glory, and the two men that stood with him. 33 And it came to pass as they were parting from him, Peter said unto Jesus, Master, it is good for us to be here: and let us make three tabernacles; one for thee, and one for Moses, and one for Elijah: not knowing what he said. 34 And while he said these things, there came a cloud, and overshadowed them: and they feared as they entered into the cloud. 35 And a voice came out of the cloud, saying, This is my Son, my chosen: hear ye him. 36 And when the voice came, Jesus was found alone. And they held their peace, and told no man in those days any of the things which they had seen.

This was one of the great crises in the life of Christ. Appropriately it is recorded in all three Synoptic Gospels (see the notes on Matt. 17:1-8; Mark 9:2-8).

Luke says it was **about eight days after these sayings.** Matthew and Mark say "after six days." Both expressions mean "a week later."

Once more, for the fifth time, Luke mentions Jesus as praying (cf. v. 18). He does not use the word "transfigured" (Matt. 17:2; Mark 9:2), but instead describes the changed appearance of Christ — **As he was praying, the fashion of his countenance was altered** (v. 29).

Luke's most important contribution to this incident is found in verses 31 and 32. He says that Moses and Elijah appeared in glory and **spake of his decease which he was about to accomplish at Jerusalem.** The word **decease** is *exodos* in the Greek, an "exodus" or "going out." Bengel writes: "The subject was a great one: the term describing it a very weighty one, wherein are contained the Passion, Cross, Death, Resurrection, and Ascension of Christ."[222]

In spite of the momentousness of the occasion, **Peter and they that were with him were heavy with sleep** (v. 32) The next clause is uncertain as to translation and interpretation. It reads here, **but when they were fully awake,** which implies that they had been sleeping, or at least dozing. The margin gives: "having remained awake."

Arndt and Gingrich allow both of these meanings, without choosing between them.[223] Abbott-Smith cites both meanings, but prefers "to be fully awake."[224] On the other hand, Thayer prefers "to remain awake."[225]

Alford says, "Not 'when they were awake', as E.V. — but *having kept awake* through the whole," and adds: "It seems to be expressly used here to shew that it was *not merely a vision,* seen in sleep."[226] A. B. Bruce interprets it: "Having thoroughly wakened up, so as to be able to see distinctly what passed (here only in N.T.)."[227] He also says: "They fell asleep while their Master prayed, as at Gethsemane."[228] Godet agrees: "They were asleep during the prayer of Jesus . . . . This verb denotes their return to self-consciousness through (*dia*) a momentary state of drowsiness."[229] Farrar translates the clause: "suddenly starting into full wakefulness."[230] Creed also agrees that they had been asleep.[231]

Meyer says that they "were weighed down with sleep (drowsy); as they nevertheless remained awake, were not actually asleep, they saw."[232] He adds that the verb "is not to be explained as it usually is, as 'after they became awake,' but as

when, however, they had thoroughly awakened."[233]

Perhaps this explanation by Meyer is as near as we can come to the correct meaning. Plummer leaves the matter uncertain.

6. Healing of Epileptic Boy (9:37-43a)

37 And it came to pass, on the next day, when they were come down from the mountain, a great multitude met him. 38 And behold, a man from the multitude cried, saying, Teacher, I beseech thee to look upon my son; for he is mine only child: 39 and behold, a spirit taketh him, and he suddenly crieth out; and it teareth him that he foameth, and it hardly departeth from him, bruising him sorely. 40 And I besought thy disciples to cast it out; and they could not. 41 And Jesus answered and said, O faithless and perverse generation, how long shall I be with you, and bear with you? bring hither thy son. 42 And as he was yet a coming, the demon dashed him down, and tare *him* grievously. But Jesus rebuked the unclean spirit, and healed the boy, and gave him back to his father. 43 And they were all astonished at the majesty of God.

Luke says that it was **on the next day** that Jesus and His three disciples came down from the Mount. This implies that the vision took place at night. It also helps to explain why the disciples were drowsy.

For the meaning of this incident, see the notes on Matt. 17:14-20 and Mark 9:14-29. Luke's account is much briefer and less vivid than Mark's. Both Mark and Luke say that the demon convulsed the boy — **tare him grievously** (v. 42).

Luke concludes the narrative by saying that Jesus **healed the boy,** and **gave him back to his father** (v. 42), and then registers the reaction of crowd: **And they were all astonished at the majesty of God** (v. 43). The last expression is typically Lukan.

7. Second Prediction of the Passion (9:43b-45)

But while all were marvelling at all the things which he did, he said unto his disciples, 44 Let these words sink into your ears: for the Son of man shall be de-

---

[222] *Op. cit.,* II, 83.
[223] W. F. Arndt. and F. W. Gingrich, *A Greek-English Lexicon of the New Testament,* p. 181.
[224] *Op. cit.,* p. 106.   [225] *Op. cit.,* p. 135.   [226] *Op. cit.,* I, 530.   [227] ECT, I, 532.   [228] *Ibid.*
[229] *Op. cit.,* p. 423.   [230] *Op. cit.,* p. 238.   [231] *Op. cit.,* p. 134.
[232] *Op. cit.,* p. 369.   [233] *Ibid.*

livered up into the hands of men. 45
But they understood not this saying, and
it was concealed from them, that they
should not perceive it; and they were
afraid to ask him about this saying.

Luke's account of this is much less
detailed than those in Matt. 17:22-23
and Mark 9:30-32 (see the notes there).
But he agrees with Mark in underscoring
the fact that the disciples did not understand the warning of their Master's coming death.

8. Dispute over Position (9:46-48)

46 And there arose a reasoning among
them, which of them was the greatest.
47 But when Jesus saw the reasoning of
their heart, he took a little child, and
set him by his side, 48 and said unto
them, Whosoever shall receive this little
child in my name receiveth me: and whosoever shall receive me receiveth him
that sent me: for he that is least among
you all, the same is great.

Again Luke is the briefest (see comments on Matthew 18:1-5, Mark 9:33-37).
The disciples were quarreling about who
would be greatest. Luke reports: **when
Jesus saw the reasoning of their heart**
(v. 47), he gave them an illustrated sermon, using a child as an example. At
the conclusion, Jesus says: **for he that is
least among you all, the same is great** (v.
48).

9. Rebuke of Sectarianism (9:49-50)

49 And John answered and said, Master,
we saw one casting out demons in thy
name; and we forbade him, because he
followeth not with us. 50 But Jesus
said unto him, Forbid *him* not: for he
that is not against you is for you.

This little incident is recorded also
by Mark (see notes on Mark 9:38-41).
Luke again uses his unique word for
Master, *epistata*, whereas Mark typically
says "Teacher." Jesus rebuked the narrow, sectarian spirit which John showed.
He concluded: **he that is not against you
is for you** (Mark says "us"). Christians
should not take an antagonistic attitude
toward people because they belong to a
different denomination, but should welcome all true believers as brothers and
sisters in the Lord.

234 *Op. cit.*, p. 260.

IV. THE PEREAN MINISTRY (9:51 – 19:28)

Luke begins at this point to tell of
a new stage in the ministry of Jesus.
During the days of His great Galilean
ministry the Master went up to Jerusalem for the annual feasts. Some of these
visits are described in John's Gospel. But
now He is leaving Galilee for the last
time. This long block of Luke, which
has traditionally been labeled "the Perean
Ministry," covers that final journey to
Jerusalem. It consists of alternating accounts of the teachings and miracles of
the Master.

Perhaps the term "Perean" should be
explained. A look at a map of Palestine
in the time of Christ will show that
Perea lay east of the Jordan River, across
from Judea and Samaria. The word
Perea simply means "across." The modern
equivalent is Transjordan.

Concerning this section of Luke's Gospel, Plummer observes: "Although this
period is only one-third as long as the
preceding one, it is described with much
greater minuteness, and the narrative is
nearly one-third longer." He adds about
Luke: "From 11:51 to 18:14 he is almost alone, and he gives us information
which we obtain from no other
source."234

A. THE DEPARTURE FROM GALILEE (9:51-62)

1. An Unfriendly Samaritan Village (9:51-56)

51 And it came to pass, when the days
were well-nigh come that he should be
received up, he stedfastly set his face to
go to Jerusalem, 52 and sent messengers
before his face: and they went, and entered into a village of the Samaritans,
to make ready for him. 53 And they did
not receive him, because his face was
as though he were going to Jerusalem.
54 And when his disciples James and
John saw *this*, they said, Lord, wilt thou
that we bid fire to come from heaven,
and consume them? 55 But he turned,
and rebuked them. 56 And they went to
another village.

When the days were well-nigh come
is literally, "When the days were being
fulfilled." The Greek verb occurs elsewhere in the New Testament only in

8:23 and Acts 2:1. The latter is an exact parallel in usage to this passage. Christ was going to die at the Passover season, which was drawing near. The allotted days for His public ministry "were being fulfilled." There were only a few left. **Received up** refers to His ascension, preceded by His death and resurrection. **He steadfastly set his face to go to Jerusalem.** This meaningful statement highlights His determination to carry out to completion His mission on earth, though in the days ahead it would involve indescribable agony and suffering. He was going to Jerusalem to die, and He knew it.

When He left Galilee with His disciples, He **sent messengers before his face** (v. 52) to arrange for overnight lodging for the group. This is the first time that we read of His doing this. But the time was getting short, and also they were entering unfriendly territory, where they could not be sure of receiving hospitality.

The **messengers** (Greek, *angelous,* from which comes "angels") entered a Samaritan village to make arrangements for the night. But because it was obvious that Jesus was headed for Jerusalem, His request for lodging was refused (v. 53).

There is a long history back of this reaction of the Samaritans. These people were descendants of a mixed race of Jews and Gentiles. Shalmanezer, king of Assyria, conquered Samaria (the capital of the northern Kingdom of Israel) in 722 B.C. He thereupon proceeded to deport the Israelites and to bring in people from Mesopotamia and the East to populate the district (II Kings 17). The result was a half-breed race with half-breed religion — a syncretism of Jehovah-worship mingled with idolatry.

When the Babylonian exiles from the southern Kingdom of Judah returned to Jerusalem to rebuild its walls and Temple, the Samaritans opposed them and sought to hinder their efforts (Ezra 4; Nehemiah 2:4). When Nehemiah refused to permit these half-heathens to participate in the building at Jerusalem, they eventually erected their own temple on Mount Gerizim. It was destroyed by the Jewish ruler, John Hyrcanus, in 129 or 128 B.C. He forced the Samaritans to be subservient to the Jews. In 63 B.C.

Pompey freed them from the Jewish yoke. In Jesus' day they were united with Judea and Idumea under the Roman governor Pilate. But they were despised by the Jews, and they retaliated with hatred and spite.

When **James and John,** the two "sons of thunder" (Mark 3:17) saw the reaction of the Samaritan village to their Master's request, they wanted lightning to strike the place. They were ready to pray for the fire to fall! But Jesus restrained them. In fact, **he . . . rebuked them.**[235] Jesus practiced what He preached (non-retaliation) by going to another village (v. 56). Whether this was another Samaritan town, or not, is not stated. Apparently Jesus wanted to take the shortest route from Galilee to Judea, through Samaria. It rather looks as though He changed His plans and crossed the Jordan to go down the east side. This route was preferred by many of the Galilean pilgrims, to avoid going through the hostile — and "unclean" — territory of Samaria.

2. Tests of Discipleship (9:56-62)

57 And as they went on the way, a certain man said unto him, I will follow thee whithersoever thou goest. 58 And Jesus said unto him, The foxes have holes, and the birds of the heaven *have* nests; but the Son of man hath not where to lay his head. 59 And he said unto another, Follow me. But he said, Lord, suffer me first to go and bury my father. 60 But he said unto him, Leave the dead to bury their own dead; but go thou and publish abroad the kingdom of God. 61 And another also said, I will follow thee, Lord; but first suffer me to bid farewell to them that are at my house. 62 But Jesus said unto him, No man, having put his hand to the plow, and looking back, is fit for the kingdom of God.

While the previous incident is recorded only by Luke, this has a parallel in Matthew 8:19-22 (see notes there). However, Matthew tells of only two individuals in conversation with Christ, whereas Luke has three.

The first was **a certain man** who impetuously declared: **I will follow thee whithersoever thou goest** (v. 57). Plummer remarks: "His peril lies in relying on his feelings at a moment of enthusiasm."[236]

---

[235] The rest of verse 55, as also the last clause of verse 54 (KJV), is not in the oldest Greek manuscripts and so is omitted in the Revised Versions. [236] *Op. cit.,* p. 265.

It is not enough to have enthusiasm; it takes endurance to succeed.

Jesus was glad to receive new disciples. But they must realize that there was a price to pay. Christian discipleship is costly — the most costly thing in the world. This man was doubtless accustomed to a comfortable home. Jesus warned him that **the Son of man hath not where to lay his head** (v. 58). He had been expelled from Nazareth. He had left the shelter of Peter's home in Capernaum. The Samaritans had refused Him lodging. He was headed for a hostile Jerusalem. All that Jesus could promise a would-be disciple was the fellowship of His sufferings, as far as this life was concerned.

To another the Master said, **Follow me** (v. 59). But the man begged permission first to bury his father. The language of verse 60 seems harsh on the surface, but the need was for someone to go *now* and **publish abroad the kingdom of God.**

A third aspirant to discipleship offered to follow Jesus. But he wanted first to go back and **bid farewell** to those at his house (v. 61). Was that not a reasonable request? The trouble was that this bidding farewell in typical Oriental style would have taken days, perhaps weeks, and possibly months. But the time was short. Anybody that wanted to join Christ's forces must do so at once, for the end of His earthly warfare was near.

Then Jesus uttered a warning for all people and for all time. Said He: **No man, having put his hand to the plow, and looking back, is fit for the kingdom of God** (v. 62). Bishop Ryle rightly observes: "We learn from this saying that it is impossible to serve Christ with a divided heart. If we are looking back to any thing in the world we are not fit to be disciples."[237]

B. THE MISSION OF SEVENTY (10:1-24)

1. Sending of the Seventy (10:1-16)

1 Now after these things the Lord appointed seventy others, and sent them two and two before his face into every city and place, whither he himself was about to come. 2 And he said unto them, The harvest indeed is plenteous, but the laborers are few: pray ye therefore the Lord of the harvest, that he send forth laborers into his harvest. 3 Go your ways; behold, I send you forth as lambs in the midst of wolves. 4 Carry no purse, no wallet, no shoes; and salute no man on the way. 5 And into whatsoever house ye shall enter, first say, Peace *be* to this house. 6 And if a son of peace be there, your peace shall rest upon him: but if not, it shall turn to you again. 7 And in that same house remain, eating and drinking such things as they give: for the laborer is worthy of his hire. Go not from house to house. 8 And into whatsoever city ye enter, and they receive you, eat such things as are set before you: 9 and heal the sick that are therein, and say unto them, The kingdom of God is come nigh unto you. 10 But into whatsoever city ye shall enter, and they receive you not, go out into the streets thereof and say, 11 Even the dust from your city, that cleaveth to our feet, we wipe off against you: nevertheless know this, that the kingdom of God is come nigh. 12 I say unto you, It shall be more tolerable in that day for Sodom, than for that city. 13 Woe unto thee, Chorazin! woe unto thee, Bethsaida! for if the mighty works had been done in Tyre and Sidon, which were done in you, they would have repented long ago, sitting in sackcloth and ashes. 14 But it shall be more tolerable for Tyre and Sidon in the judgment, than for you. 15 And thou, Capernaum, shalt thou be exalted unto heaven? thou shalt be brought down unto Hades. 16 He that heareth you heareth me; and he that rejecteth you rejecteth me; and he that rejecteth me rejecteth him that sent me.

The mission of the Twelve is recorded in three Synoptics, the sending of the Seventy only in Luke. This is in keeping with the point of view of this Evangelist. Plummer puts it this way: "This incident would have special interest for the writer of the Universal Gospel, who sympathetically records both the sending of the Twelve to the tribes of Israel (11:1-6), and the sending of the Seventy to the nations of the earth."[238] In Perea, where these servants of Christ were sent, the population was more Gentile than in Judea. Yet it was predominantly Jewish. While nothing is said about the Gentiles in the instructions to the Seventy, neither is there any prohibition against preaching to them, as there was in the case of the Twelve (Matt. 10:5-6).

[237] *Op. cit.,* p. 341.   [238] *Op. cit.,* p. 270.

The question has often been raised as to why Jesus sent seventy. There are several parallels. The most obvious one, perhaps, is that of the seventy elders of ancient Israel (Num. 11:16-25). Another is the Sanhedrin, with its seventy members. But the most significant one is the traditional view that there were seventy nations on the earth (cf. Gen. 10). This fits the picture best.

The designation of Jesus as **the Lord** (v. 1) is found sixteen times in Luke, and only once each in Matthew (21:3) and Mark (11:3) — and these are parallel passages, making one usage. The Greek word for **appointed** is found only here and in Acts 1:24 (Lukan). Here it means "to consecrate, set apart,"[239] or "appoint, commission."[240] **Others** points back to the sending of the twelve (9:1-6). **Seventy** is "seventy-two" in a number of older manuscripts (including Vaticanus). But the balance of evidence seems to favor the reading here (adopted by KJV and RSV). Some modern translations have "seventy-two" (e.g., NEB, Goodspeed).

The Seventy were sent in pairs, as the Twelve had been. This was primarily for the sake of companionship, but also that they might bear joint witness. They were sent as advance agents to every town to prepare the way for His coming.

The saying in verse 2 is found verbatim in Matthew 9:37-38, where it occurs before the sending of the Twelve. Both these missionary groups were fulfillments of this prayer. Also, the warning that they would be as **lambs in the midst of wolves** occurs in connection with the earlier mission (Matt. 10:16).

The instructions about traveling light (v. 4) are similar to what are recorded in all three Synoptics as directions for the Twelve. Here it is simply: **Carry no purse** — no wallet ("bag"), **no shoes** (better, "sandals"); **and salute no man on the way** (Luke only). This last sounds strange on the lips of Christ, as if He were advocating discourtesy. But it must be remembered that salutations take longer in eastern lands, and even in Latin America, than they do in the United States. The custom was for each person, on meeting, to inquire about the health of the other, and then the health of the father, mother, grandfather, etc., etc. All this was very time-consuming. These

men must go forth with haste and urgency.

Son of peace (v. 6) is a typical Hebraism for "peaceful person." Where such a person received them into his house, they were to remain, eating what was provided for them, **for the laborer is worthy of his hire** (v. 7). Jesus Himself enunciated this principle, and it is echoed by Paul (I Tim. 5:18). The specific warning is given: **Go not from house to house.** Trouble can be created by Christian workers carrying gossip from home to home, or seeming to show partiality. The advice, **eat such things as are set before you** (v. 8) is also important. These messengers were to **heal the sick** and proclaim the nearness of the Kingdom (v. 9). Wherever they were rejected, the missionaries were to wipe the dust of the place off their sandals as a symbolic warning (vv. 10, 11).

Then Jesus pronounced woes on the main cities of His earthly ministry — **Chorazin, Bethsaida,** and **Capernaum** (see notes on Matt. 11:21-24). Note the form of a question in the first part of verse 15. This is much more effective than the declarative form (KJV). The Greek will support either form equally well. Verse 16 is paralleled in Matt. 10:40. Jesus identified Himself with His representatives, even as they needed to identify themselves with Him.

2. Return of the Seventy (10:17-20)

17 And the seventy returned with joy, saying, Lord, even the demons are subject unto us in thy name. 18 And he said unto them, I beheld Satan fallen as lightning from heaven. 19 Behold, I have given you authority to tread upon serpents and scorpions, and over all the power of the enemy: and nothing shall in any wise hurt you. 20 Nevertheless in this rejoice not, that the spirits are subject unto you; but rejoice that your names are written in heaven.

The seventy missionaries had a very successful tour. They came back rejoicing and reporting that even the demons were subject to them in Christ's name.

The answer of Jesus was: **I beheld Satan fallen as lightning from heaven** (v. 18). The connection with the previous verse is pointed out by Plummer: "In the defeat of the demons He saw the

239 Abbott-Smith, op. cit., p. 29.   240 Arndt and Gingrich, op. cit., p. 53.

downfall of their chief."[241] Some have related this statement to the fall of Lucifer and the Angels (Jude). But probably a better view is to recognize that "it refers to the success of the disciples regarded as a symbol and earnest of the complete overthrow of Satan."[242]

Verse 19 indicates that Christ gives to those commissioned by Himself all the power and protection they need to carry out their assignments. Whatever hostile forces they meet, physical or spiritual, they can overcome.

But there was something greater in importance and wonder than casting out demons; that is, **that your names are written in heaven** (v. 20). This is the highest honor and greatest glory that can come to anyone.

3. Rejoicing of Jesus (10:21-24)

21 In that same hour he rejoiced in the Holy Spirit, and said, I thank thee, O Father, Lord of heaven and earth, that thou didst hide these things from the wise and understanding, and didst reveal them unto babes: yea, Father; for so it was well-pleasing in thy sight. 22 All things have been delivered unto me of my Father: and no one knoweth who the Son is, save the Father; and who the Father is, save the Son, and to whomsoever the Son willeth to reveal *him*. 23 And turning to the disciples, he said privately, Blessed *are* the eyes which see the things that ye see: 24 for I say unto you, that many prophets and kings desired to see the things which ye see, and saw them not; and to hear the things which ye hear, and heard them not.

Rejoiced in the Holy Spirit is obviously stronger than "rejoiced in spirit" (KJV). The former has much firmer support in the earliest manuscripts. The verb translated **rejoiced** is a strong one, meaning "exult" or "rejoice greatly." This was a rare moment of self-revelation, when the disciples were given the privilege of seeing the Man of Sorrows overflowing with joy.

The thanksgiving to the Father (vv. 21-22) is closely parallel to Matthew 11: 25-27 (see notes there). Verses 23 and 24 are paralleled in Matthew 13:16, 17. **Many prophets and kings** had longed to see the coming of the Messiah. But

this high privilege belonged to the disciples. No wonder Jesus said: **Blessed are the eyes which see the things that ye see.**

C. EARLY INCIDENTS (10:25-42)

1. A Lawyer's Question (10:25-29)

25 And behold, a certain lawyer stood up and made trial of him, saying, Teacher, what shall I do to inherit eternal life? 26 And he said unto him, What is written in the law? how readest thou? 27 And he answering said, Thou shalt love the Lord thy God with all thy heart, and with all thy soul, and with all thy strength, and with all thy mind; and thy neighbor as thyself. 28 And he said unto him, Thou hast answered right: this do, and thou shalt live. 29 But he, desiring to justify himself, said unto Jesus, And who is my neighbor?

A **lawyer** — teacher of the Mosaic Law — **stood up** — which may suggest that they were in a synagogue — **and made trial of him** — or "tempted him" (KJV), or "testing him." It is not indicated in the context that his motive was a sinister one. The question, **Teacher, what shall I do to inherit eternal life,** reminds one of the query of the rich young ruler (18: 18). It has been suggested that this lawyer represents "the wise and understanding" (v. 21), from whom divine truth was hidden, while the disciples are the "babes" to whom it was revealed. As in the case of the rich young ruler, Jesus answered by turning the man's attention to the Law: **how readest thou?** He replied by summing up all the Law in two great commandments (cf. Matt. 22:37-40; Mark 12:29-31).

Jesus told him that if he obeyed this, he would **live** (v. 28). No one can love the Lord with all the heart and be spiritually dead. The lawyer, **desiring to justify himself,** asked: **And who is my neighbor?** (v. 29). In reply Jesus told the man a striking story.

2. The Parable of the Good Samaritan (10:30-37)

30 Jesus made answer and said, A certain man was going down from Jerusalem to Jericho; and he fell among robbers, who both stripped him and beat him, and departed, leaving him half dead. 31 And by chance a certain priest was going down

[241] *Op. cit.,* p. 278.   [242] *Ibid.*

that way: and when he saw him, he passed by on the other side. 32 And in like manner a Levite also, when he came to the place, and saw him, passed by on the other side. 33 But a certain Samaritan, as he journeyed, came where he was: and when he saw him, he was moved with compassion, 34 and came to him, and bound up his wounds, pouring on *them* oil and wine; and he set him on his own beast, and brought him to an inn, and took care of him. 35 And on the morrow he took out two shillings, and gave them to the host, and said, Take care of him; and whatsoever thou spendest more, I, when I come back again, will repay thee. 36 Which of these three, thinkest thou, proved neighbor unto him that fell among the robbers? 37 And he said, He that showed mercy on him. And Jesus said unto him, Go, and do thou likewise.

The Master of parables told of a man **going down from Jerusalem to Jericho** who **fell among robbers**. These **stripped** and **beat** him, and **departed, leaving him half dead** (v. 30). The Jericho Road is a lonely way which winds around the hills and descends steeply through a desolate wilderness. It provided an excellent set-up for robbers to ambush unsuspecting travellers. Even in modern times there have been many robbers on this road.

While the man lay there half dead, a **priest** chanced to come down that way. A large number of priests lived in Jericho. Evidently this man had been ministering in the Temple and was now on his way home. He reached the place where the victim lay, but **when he saw him, he passed by on the other side** (v. 31). He may have soliloquized something like this: "The man looks as if he might be dead. If I go near him, I'll be defiled, and that will be very inconvenient. Anyhow, I can recognize his face now, and I remember offering a sacrifice for him on the altar. So I have done my duty by him and have no further responsibility."

Then a **Levite also, when he came to the place, and saw him, passed by on the other side** (v. 32). Perhaps he said to himself: "Poor fellow. It looks as if he's done for. I guess he's beyond hope. So there's nothing I can do about it."

But then came a Samaritan — one who was despised by the Jews as being a "dirty dog." He saw the victim — probably a

Jew — lying there helpless. Immediately **he was moved with compassion** — the same phrase which is often used of Christ's reaction to human need. He went to the man, knelt beside him, **bound up his wounds, pouring on them oil and wine.** The wine would act as an antiseptic, and the olive oil as a balm. Then he put the weakened victim on his own donkey and brought him safely to an inn. There he **took care of him** — put him up for the night and made him as comfortable as possible. In the morning he gave the innkeeper two shillings (two days' wages), with instructions to take care of the man. He even promised to pay any further expenses involved, when he returned.

Then Jesus asked the question: Who acted as neighbor to the man in need? There was only one possible answer, and the man gave it. Said the Master to him: **Go, and do thou likewise** (v. 37).

The lawyer had asked, "Who is my neighbor?" Jesus turned it around and asked, "To whom can you be a neighbor?" Or, if we wish to answer the lawyer's question directly, we could say: "Your neighbor is anyone who needs you." Geographical proximity is not the basic factor, but the need of help.

Three different philosophies of life are represented in this story Jesus told. The robbers said, "What's yours is ours and we'll take it." The priest and the Levite muttered, "What's ours is our own and we'll keep it." But the good Samaritan said, "What's mine is yours and we'll share it." These three philosophies can be put even more briefly. That of the robbers was, "Beat him up!" That of the priest and Levite was, "Pass him up!" That of the Samaritan was, "Pick him up!"

It is a disturbing experience to ask oneself the question: "Which of these three philosophies do I practice in my daily life?" Of course any Christian would renounce the first right away and plead, "Not guilty." But what about the choice of the other two. Too often the church has followed the way of the ecclesiastical figures in this story. If people want to come to church services, believers usually do their best to preach to them, teach them, and show them the way of salvation. But what about the man beside the road, beaten and robbed by life? Do

Christians pick him up, or do they pass him by? That is a very disconcerting question. But this parable belongs to believers today just as much as to the people of the first century.

3. Mary and Martha (10:38-42)

38 Now as they went on their way, he entered into a certain village: and a certain woman named Martha received him into her house. 39 And she had a sister called Mary, who also sat at the Lord's feet, and heard his word. 40 But Martha was cumbered about much serving; and she came up to him, and said, Lord, dost thou not care that my sister did leave me to serve alone? bid her therefore that she help me. 41 But the Lord answered and said unto her, Martha, Martha, thou art anxious and troubled about many things: 42 but one thing is needful: for Mary hath chosen the good part, which shall not be taken away from her.

These two sisters are such vivid examples of two personality types that it is impossible to forget them or their names. Mary was by nature an introvert, Martha an extrovert. Mary was a meditative mystic. Martha was a practical provider, hustling and bustling about, hurried and flurried and worried. These two saw things through different eyes.

The **certain village** was Bethany, called "the village of Mary and her sister Martha" (John 11:1). It was two miles southeast of Jerusalem, on the opposite side of the Mount of Olives.

Martha received him into her house. This suggests that Martha was the older sister and perhaps owned the home. She may have been married; probably Mary was not. Mary **sat at the Lord's feet, and heard his word** (v. 39). **But Martha was cumbered about much serving** (v. 40). These two brief statements pinpoint the differences in personality. Mary was quiet and receptive. Martha was busy and outgoing. While Mary was more keenly aware of the supreme value of feasting spiritually at the Master's feet, she may have been somewhat remiss in her duty of helping her sister. To put it in modern terms, perhaps she should have been paying some attention to helping out in the kitchen, as well as listening to Jesus as intently as she could.

At any rate, Martha became more and more disconcerted. Instead of scolding her sister she scolded Jesus! "Why don't you tell my sister to help me?" Martha was probably too disgusted with her sister to speak to her. But in her hasty anger or impatience she said something of which she must have been heartily ashamed afterward.

Jesus' reply was twofold. To Martha He said: **Thou art anxious and troubled** (v. 41). Plummer makes this comment: "The verb is a strong one, 'thou art anxious,' and implies division and distraction of mind (*merizo*), which believers ought to avoid." The second part he would translate, "And art in a tumult, bustle." He concludes: "In any case, *merimnas* refers to the mental distraction and the second verb to the external agitation."[243]

Martha was anxious and troubled **about many things.** She was distracted by the multiplicity of her activities. Quietly Jesus told her: **But one thing is needful: for Mary hath chosen the good part which shall not be taken away from her** (v. 42). In sitting at Jesus' feet and feasting on the spiritual truth He gave, Mary had chosen what was eternal and could not be taken away from her.

The best Greek text of the first clause of this verse reads literally: "but of few things is there need, or one." Apparently Jesus is saying to Martha: "We need only a simple meal — just a few things, or even one dish. I would prefer that you come and enjoy spiritual fellowship. That is the most important thing, because it is eternal." Perhaps sometimes the Master today wants us and our worship more than our busy, bustling service.

D. VARIOUS TEACHINGS (11:1-54)

1. Concerning Prayer (1:1-13)

a. The Lord's Prayer (11:1-4)

1 And it came to pass, as he was praying in a certain place, that when he ceased, one of his disciples said unto him, Lord, teach us to pray, even as John also taught his disciples. 2 And he said unto them, When ye pray, say, Father, Hallowed be thy name. Thy kingdom come. 3 Give us day by day our daily bread. 4 And forgive us our sins; for we ourselves also forgive every one that is indebted to us. And bring us not into temptation.

---

[243] *Op. cit.*, p. 291.

For the sixth and last time (cf. 9:29), Luke mentions Jesus as praying, where the other Evangelists do not. This time it was before giving the so-called Lord's Prayer.

As Jesus was praying one day it made a strong impression on those who heard. One of His disciples requested that He teach them to pray, even as John the Baptist had taught his followers. Literally he said: "Lord, teach us to be praying." He did not say, "Teach us *how* to pray," though that may be implied. One can only learn to pray by praying. Reading good books on prayer will help. But just as one could read a book on how to drive a car and yet be unable to drive, so one might study a dozen books on prayer and not know how to pray. In this area, as in all others, only practice makes perfect.

In response to the disciple's plea, the Master of prayer suggested a pattern for praying. It is extremely brief, consisting only of five petitions. At the same time it is amazingly comprehensive, covering all the essential needs of an individual.

A comparison of the King James Version and American Standard Version of verses 2-4 will quickly reveal that the latter form is considerably shorter. Specifically, there are three clauses in the former that are missing in the latter, besides the word "Our" with **Father.** These clauses are "which art in heaven," "Thy will be done, as in heaven, so in earth," and "deliver us from evil." The evidence of the manuscripts seems clearly against the genuineness of these petitions.

But there is another factor which is significant. "The express testimony of Origen [early 3rd century] that in the texts of Luke known to him the clauses were wanting would in itself be almost conclusive; and about the second and third omitted clauses we have the express testimony of Augustine also."[244] It seems very probable that these clauses were added from Matthew's version of the Lord's Prayer by copyists who were familiar with the liturgical use of the longer form in the churches. For the meaning of the various parts of the Lord's Prayer see the comments on Matthew 6:9-13. We note only a few additional thoughts here.

On the clause, **Hallowed be thy name** — literally, "let thy name be sanctified" — Creed calls attention to the use in the Mishna of the expression "the sanctification of the name." This is the heading for what is called the "third benediction," which reads: "Thou art holy and thy name is holy, and holy beings praise thee daily."[245]

The Greek word translated **daily** is *epiousion.* Its meaning is uncertain. Creed notes that there has been found just one occurrence of it in secular Greek.[246] Arndt and Gingrich call attention to several interpretations which have been offered: (1) "necessary for existence"; (2) "for today"; (3) "for the following day."[247] Probably **daily** is as good a rendering as anyone can give.

Give is in the present imperative, followed by **day by day;** that is, "Continue to give us day by day." In Matthew the verb is in the aorist and is followed by "this day"; that is, "give us right now for today." The two ideas supplement each other. Both petitions are proper for the Christian to pray. Geldenhuys adds the observation: " 'Bread' here stands for everything that man really needs for his earthly existence."[248]

For Matthew's "forgive us our debts" Luke has **forgive us our sins** (*hamartias*). Yet the second clause has, **every one that is indebted to us,** which is parallel to Matthew's "our debtors." Perhaps Luke felt that "debts" would be less clear to his Gentile readers than the more familiar term **sins.**

The last petition is, **bring us not into temptation.** On this, Creed says: "To be interpreted generally of a situation which involved especially grave temptation to sin."[249] He quotes this Jewish prayer: "Bring me not into the power of sin, nor into the power of guilt, nor into the power of temptation." Both wisdom and humility teach us that we ought to pray thus.

b. Parable of the Importunate Friend (11:5-13)

5 And he said unto them, Which of you shall have a friend, and shall go unto him at midnight, and say to him, Friend, lend me three loaves; 6 for a friend of mine is come to me from a journey, and

---

244 *Ibid.,* p. 204. 245 Creed, *op. cit.,* p. 157.
248 *Op. cit.,* p. 320. 249 *Op. cit.,* p. 157. 246 *Op. cit.,* p. 157. 247 *Op. cit.,* p. 297.

I have nothing to set before him; 7 and he from within shall answer and say, Trouble me not: the door is now shut, and my children are with me in bed; I cannot rise and give thee? 8 I say unto you, Though he will not rise and give him because he is his friend, yet because of his importunity he will arise and give him as many as he needeth. 9 And I say unto you, Ask, and it shall be given you; seek, and ye shall find; knock, and it shall be opened unto you. 10 For everyone that asketh receiveth; and he that seeketh findeth; and to him that knocketh it shall be opened. 11 And of which of you that is a father shall his son ask a loaf, and he give him a stone? or a fish, and he for a fish give him a serpent? 12 Or if he shall ask an egg, will he give him a scorpion? 13 If ye then, being evil, know how to give good gifts unto your children, how much more shall *your* heavenly Father give the Holy Spirit to them that ask him?

This is one of the many parables found only in Luke. It is also one of the three parables on prayer. The other two are in 18:1-14.

The story is vivid and appealing. A man goes to a **friend** at **midnight,** saying, **Friend lend me three loaves.** The Greek word for **lend** is not the common one, meaning "to lend on interest," as a business transaction, but one found only here in the New Testament and meaning "grant the use of, as a friendly act."[250] **Three loaves** could well represent the man's feeling that he should have one loaf (the size of a small pancake) for his guest, one for himself as he courteously ate with him, and an extra one for the guest if he wanted it. The guest's arrival at **midnight** may reflect the Eastern custom of traveling at night to avoid the heat of the day.

The friend to whom the request was made replies that his door is **shut** (i.e., "locked") and his children with him in bed. In a poorer home this might be literally true. A quilt-like pad would be placed on the dirt floor, the whole family would lie down on it, and a big blanket would be pulled over them all. If the man got up he would disturb the entire family.

Jesus concluded the story by saying that although friendship alone would not cause the man to rise and open the door, yet he would do it because of his friend's **importunity.** The Greek word means "shamelessness." It was that which the unprepared host showed in coming at such an unseasonable hour and in continuing to beg until he received the bread. Abraham's prayer is a good example of persistent prayer (Gen. 18:23-33). Isaiah wrote: "Ye that are Jehovah's remembrancers, take ye no rest and give him no rest, till he establish, and till he make Jerusalem a praise in the earth" (Isa. 62:6).

The lesson of this parable is obvious — the need of persistence in prayer. Farrar comments: "Although idle repetitions in prayer are forbidden, persistency and importunity in prayer — wrestling with God, and not letting Him go until He has blessed us — are here distinctly taught."[251]

Then Jesus proceeded to make the application:

Ask, and it shall be given you;
Seek, and ye shall find;
Knock, and it shall be opened unto you.

The three words seem to suggest degrees of intensity in prayer. If one should **ask,** and seemingly not receive an answer, he should become more earnest and **seek.** If the answer still does not appear; then in desperation he should **knock** until he gets results. This is earnest, definite, desperate praying, and every Christian should face the challenge of it.

Verses 9-13 are closely paralleled in Matthew 7:7-11 (see notes there). Jesus promises that all those who ask will receive, those who seek will find; and those who knock will discover doors opened.

To the two figures that Matthew uses of a father's giving — a **loaf** instead of a **stone** and a **fish** instead of a **serpent** — Luke adds a third: an **egg** instead of a **scorpion.** Then he points up his argument. If human parents, being relatively **evil** (in comparison with God), love to give good gifts to their children, **how much more shall your heavenly Father give the Holy Spirit to them that ask him.** In Matthew the Father gives "good things," whereas Luke's version says, **give**

250 Thayer, op. cit., p. 125.
251 Op. cit., p. 261.

the Holy Spirit. This is in keeping with Luke's interest in the Holy Spirit.

2. Concerning Casting Out Demons (11: 14-26)

14 And he was casting out a demon *that was* dumb. And it came to pass, when the demon was gone out, the dumb man speak; and the multitudes marvelled. 15 But some of them said, By Beelzebub the prince of the demons casteth he out demons. 16 And others, trying *him*, sought of him a sign from heaven. 17 But he, knowing their thoughts, said unto them, Every kingdom divided against itself is brought to desolation; and a house *divided* against a house falleth. 18 And if Satan also is divided against himself, how shall his kingdom stand? because ye say that I cast out demons by Beelzebub. 19 And if I by Beelzebub cast out demons, by whom do your sons cast them out? therefore shall they be your judges. 20 But if I by the finger of God cast out demons, then is the kingdom of God come upon you. 21 When the strong *man* fully armed guardeth his own court, his goods are in peace: 22 but when a stronger than he shall come upon him, and overcome him, he taketh from him his whole armor wherein he trusted, and divideth his spoils. 23 He that is not with me is against me; and he that gathered not with me scattereth. 24 The unclean spirit when he is gone out of the man, passeth through waterless places, seeking rest, and finding none, he saith, I will turn back unto my house whence I came out. 25 And when he is come, he findeth it swept and garnished. 26 Then goeth he, and taketh *to him* seven other spirits more evil than himself; and they enter in and dwell there: and the last state of that man becometh worse than the first.

The paragraph opens with the incident of Jesus **casting out a demon that was dumb** (v. 14). This verse is paralleled in Matthew 9:32-33. Apparently the case was considered hopeless, **for the multitudes marvelled** at Christ's power to cure.

Some, however, said that it was by **the prince of the demons** that He was casting out demons (v. 15). These **some** are identified by Matthew (9:34) as "the Pharisees," and by Mark (3:22), as "the scribes that came down from Jerusalem."

The latter were the most vicious in their treatment of Christ.

Beelzebub (v. 15) is a spelling which has no support in the Greek, but comes from the Latin Vulgate. The two oldest Greek manuscripts (Vaticanus and Sinaiticus, 4th cent.) call the demon "Beezebul." But a third-century papyrus (45) and the manuscripts from the fifth century onward refer to him as "Beelzebul." So it would be a choice between these two, with the familiar "Beelzebub" ruled out.

As to the meaning of this term, Plummer writes: "*Beelzeboul* may mean either, 'Lord of the dwelling,' i.e., of the heavenly habitation, or, 'Lord of dung,' i.e., of idolatrous abomination. 'Lord of idols,' 'Prince of false gods,' comes close to 'Prince of the demons.' "[252]

Others, trying him, sought of him a sign from heaven (v. 16). Matthew 12: 38 attributes this request to "certain of the scribes and Pharisees." **Trying him** may be translated "testing him," or "tempting him." All three shades of meaning are found in the one Greek word. One can only choose on the basis of the context, which is not always determinative. Any one of the three would seem to fit here.

One would think that casting out the demon would be a sufficient sign. But the Jews expected that when the Messiah came He would give some spectacular **sign from heaven** to prove that He was the Messiah. The Pharisees were now demanding this sort of demonstration from Jesus. But He refused to acquiesce.

Knowing their thoughts — the motives and reasonings that lay behind their words — Christ pointed out the folly of their accusation that He was casting out demons by Beelzebul. For a **kingdom** or **house** which is **divided against itself** cannot stand, but will fall. In the same way, if **Satan** is **divided against himself**, his **kingdom** will fall (v. 18). Then Jesus made a brilliant thrust: **if I by Beelzebub cast out demons, by whom do your sons cast them out?** (v. 19). The Jews of that day practiced exorcism (casting out demons). While only one case of demon-possession is related in the Old Testament, that of Saul (I Sam. 16:14-16; 18:10; 19:9), exorcism shows up in the apocryphal literature written in the intertestamental period (e.g., Tobit 6:7, 16-17; 8:3). But the most definite testimony to the contemporary practice of exorcism is found in Josephus, the great Jewish historian of the first century. He says of Solomon:

God also enabled him to learn that skill which expels demons . . . . He composed such incantations also by which distempers are alleviated. And he left behind him the manner of using exorcisms, by which they drive away demons, so that they never return; and this method of cure is of great force unto this day; for I have seen a certain man of my own country, whose name was Eleazar, releasing people that were demoniacal in the presence of Vespasian. . . .The manner of the cure was this: He put a ring that had a root of one of those sorts mentioned by Solomon to the nostrils of the demoniac, after which he drew out the demon, through his nostrils; and when the man fell down immediately, he adjured him to return into him no more, making still mention of Solomon, and reciting the incarnations which he composed. And when Eleazar would persuade and demonstrate to the spectators that he had such, he set a little way off a cup or basin full of water, and commanded the demon, as he went out of the man, to overturn it, and thereby to let the spectators know that he had left the man.[253]

Does this last sentence suggest a reason why Jesus may have permitted the legion of demons in the Gadarene demoniac to go into the herd of swine? (8:33). Was it to give proof to both the demoniac and the onlookers that the demons had really left?

A contemporary of Josephus, Rabbi Johanan ben Zakkai, prescribed this technique for casting out demons: "Take roots of herbs, burn them under him (the possessed person), and surround him with water, whereupon the spirit will flee."[254]

Obviously, this is magic. Josephus is probably mistaken in attributing exorcism to Solomon. But his witness to the practice among the Jews of Jesus' day cannot be questioned.

There is a reference to professional Jewish exorcists at Ephesus in Acts 19:13-14. They tried to expel demons by saying, "I adjure you by Jesus whom Paul

preacheth" (cf. also Mark 9:38).

How did Jesus cast out demons? His explanation was: **by the finger of God** (v. 20). This is a typical Hebraistic expression to designate "the power of God." The meaning is made specific in Matthew's parallel passage. He says, "by the Spirit of God" (Matt. 12:28). This was proof that **the kingdom of God has come upon you.**

Christ then used another parabolic figure. While a **strong man fully armed guardeth his own court,** his possessions are safe (v. 21). But if a **stronger than he** confronts and overcomes him, the man loses both his armor and his goods (v. 22). The meaning is clear. **The strong man is Satan.** The **stronger than he** is Christ, who is in the process of defeating and despoiling the devil.

For the meaning of verse 23 see the notes on the exact parallel in Matthew 12:30. In the contest between Christ and Satan no one can be neutral. Those who are not gathering souls into the Kingdom are scattering them abroad to be captured and destroyed by the devil.

The meaningful material in verses 24-26 is paralleled almost verbatim in Matthew 12:43-45 (see notes there). Geldenhuys gives the following excellent application: "Even purely psychological considerations render it imperative that, when a person has passed through a crisis which has contributed to his renunciation of former sins and evil practices in his life, he must immediately in place thereof let his life be filled with what is beautiful and noble, otherwise the old sins and evils will return in renewed violence. . . . There cannot be a vacuum in man's soul."[255]

3. Concerning True Blessedness (11:27-28)

27 And it came to pass, as he said these things, a certain woman out of the multitude lifted up her voice, and said unto him, Blessed is the womb that bare thee, and the breasts which thou didst suck. 28 But he said, Yea rather, blessed are they that hear the word of God, and keep it.

This little item is found only in Luke. It forever condemns raising Mary, the mother of Jesus, to a special place of reverence. Christ said that those who hear the word of God and keep it (v. 28) are the ones who are truly blessed (the same word as in the Beatitudes).

4. Concerning Signs (11:29-32)

29 And when the multitudes were gathering together unto him, he began to say, This generation is an evil generation: it seeketh after a sign; and there shall no sign be given to it but the sign of Jonah. 30 For even as Jonah became a sign unto the Ninevites, so shall also the Son of man be to this generation. 31 The queen of the south shall rise up in the judgment with the men of this generation, and shall condemn them: for she came from the ends of the earth to hear the wisdom of Solomon; and behold, a greater than Solomon is here. 32 The men of Nineveh shall stand up in the judgment with this generation, and shall condemn it: for they repented at the preaching of Jonah; and behold, a greater than Jonah is here.

For the meaning of this paragraph see the comments on Matthew 12:39-42. Luke omits Matthew's reference to the "three days and three nights" that Jonah was in the whale and Jesus would be in the grave. The queen of the south (v. 31) is called in the Old Testament "the queen of Sheba." She apparently lived in the southern part of Arabia.[256] The identification of Sheba with Ethiopia (Abyssinia), which Josephus makes, is probably wrong, though the Sabeans did found colonies in Ethiopia.

5. Concerning Single Intention (11:33-36)

33 No man, when he hath lighted a lamp, putteth it in a cellar, neither under the bushel, but on the stand, that they which enter in may see the light. 34 The lamp of thy body is thine eye: when thine eye is single, thy whole body also is full of light; but when it is evil, thy body also is full of darkness. 35 Look therefore whether the light that is in thee be not darkness. 36 If therefore thy whole body be full of light, having no part dark, it shall be wholly full of light, as when the lamp with its bright shining doth give thee light.

Verse 33 is paralleled in Matthew 5:15 and verses 34-35 in Matthew 6:22-23 (see

notes on those passages). Besides duplicating Matthew's reference to putting the lamp under the bushel, Luke adds in a cellar. The Greek reads "into a crypt" (*krypte,* only here in N.T.) ; that is "a hidden place" (from *krypto,* "I hide").

The connection with the context is this: Jesus was not refusing to show the Jews a sign because He wanted to hide the light of divine truth. But the trouble was with them. Their eye was evil (v. 34), because they refused the revelation of God which Christ was giving. The meaning of eye is thus explained by Farrar: "The eye . . . . is the 'inward eye' of conscience; the 'illuminated eye of the heart,' Eph. 1:17, 18."[257] Single means "free from distortion, normal, sound"; evil means "diseased." Plummer adds this observation: "Faith, when diseased, becomes the darkness of superstition; just as the eye, when diseased, distorts and obscures."[258]

Farrar gives this literal translation of verse 36: "If then thy body be wholly illumined . . . it shall be illumined wholly as when the lamp with its bright shining illumines thee."[259] When one's heart is fully opened to receive the sunlight of God's truth, there is no part dark, but all is bright.

6. Conflict with the Pharisees (11:37-54)

a. A Critical Host (11:37-41)

37 Now as he spake, a Pharisee asketh him to dine with him: and he went in, and sat down to meat. 38 And when the Pharisee saw it, he marvelled that he had not first bathed himself before dinner. 39 And the Lord said unto him, Now ye the Pharisees cleanse the outside of the cup and of the platter; but your inward part is full of extortion and wickedness. 40 Ye foolish ones, did not he that made the outside make the inside also? 41 But give for alms those things which are within; and behold, all things are clean unto you.

This brief incident is found only in Luke. A Pharisee asked Jesus to dine with him. The Greek verb occurs elsewhere in the New Testament only in John 21:12, 15, where the meaning clearly is 'have breakfast." So the reference here is not to a dinner, but to a light

[256] See D. Harvey, "Sheba, Queen of," IDB,IV,311.   [257] *Op. cit.,* p. 267.
[258] *Op. cit.,* p. 308.   [259] *Op. cit.,* p. 267.

meal earlier in the day, perhaps what is now popularly known as "brunch" — breakfast and lunch combined. **Sat down to meat** should be translated "reclined at the table."

The host **marvelled** that his guest had not first **bathed himself** before breakfast. The verb is *baptizo,* but probably refers here to simply washing the hands. But the Pharisees, in their "tradition of the elders," had built up an elaborate system of ablutions accompanied by long prayers. With the incisive scissors of common sense and good religion Jesus cut through all this "red tape" and got down to the business of eating. That He did offer thanks for the food is shown by His customary doing of this on other occasions. Here He deliberately vaulted the unnecessary fence which the Pharisees had put around the Law. The Pharisees were primarily interested in protecting the Law, Jesus in promoting piety in the human heart.

Again Luke uses the expression **the Lord** (v. 39). For Jesus is speaking with divine authority in setting aside this man-made system of rules and regulations that had actually become a hindrance rather than a help to true religion. The Pharisees were interested in cleansing the outside, Jesus the inside.

Verse 39 is closely parallel to Matthew 23:25. But Matthew 23:26 reads (in part): "Cleanse first the inside of the cup and of the platter, that the outside thereof may become clean also," while Luke has: **But give for alms those things which are within; and behold, all things are clean unto you** (v. 41). What does this mean?

It has been pointed out that in the Aramaic *dakki* means "cleanse" and *zakki* means "give alms." It is suggested that "Luke has followed a mistaken, or else a literal, translation from the Aramaic."[260]

Torrey translates this verse: "Nay, make right what is within, and you will have all clean."[261] He suggests that Luke had before him a corrupted Aramaic text.[262]

Accepting the Greek text here as the true reading, Plummer gives this interpretation, among others: " 'The contents of your cup and platter give ye in alms, and, lo, all things are clean to you,' i.e., benevolence is a better way of keeping meals free from defilement than scrupulous cleansing of vessels."[263] Perhaps it is the part of humility and wisdom to say that we cannot be certain about the meaning of this obscure passage.

b. Denunciation of Pharisees (11:42-44)

42 But woe unto you Pharisees! for ye tithe mint and rue and every herb, and pass over justice and the love of God: but these ought ye to have done, and not to leave the other undone. 43 Woe unto you Pharisees! for ye love the chief seats in the synagogues, and the salutations in the marketplaces. 44 Woe unto you! for ye are as the tombs which appear not, and the men that walk over *them* know it not.

Verse 42 is parallel to Matthew 23:23, verse 43 to Matthew 23:6-7, and verse 44 to Matthew 23:27. The Pharisees are depicted here as proud, self-seeking, and like defiling tombs that men unconsciously come into contact with. It is a sad picture of the religious leaders of God's chosen people. It constitutes a warning to Christians today not to become Pharisaical.

c. Denunciation of Lawyers (11:45-52)

45 And one of the lawyers answering saith unto him, Teacher, in saying this thou reproachest us also. 46 And he said, Woe unto you lawyers also! for ye load men with burdens grievous to be borne, and ye yourselves touch not the burdens with one of your fingers. 47 Woe unto you! for ye build the tombs of the prophets, and your fathers killed them. 48 So ye are witnesses and consent unto the works of your fathers: for they killed them, and ye build *their tombs.* 49 Therefore also said the wisdom of God, I will send unto them prophets and apostles; and *some* of them they shall kill and persecute; 50 that the blood of all the prophets, which was shed from the foundation of the world, may be required of this generation; 51 from the blood of Abel unto the blood of Zachariah, who perished between the altar and the sanctuary: yea, I say unto you, it shall be required of this gen-

[260] C. J. Mullo-Weir, "Old Testament Languages — Hebrew and Aramaic," *A Companion to the Bible,* ed. T. W. Manson, p. 24.   [261] C. C. Torrey, *The Four Gospels,* p. 146.   [262] *Ibid.,* p. 310.
[263] *Op. cit.,* p. 311.

eration. 52 Woe unto you lawyers! for ye took away the key of knowledge: ye entered not in yourselves, and them that were entering in ye hindered.

One of the lawyers — teachers of the Mosaic law — got himself into trouble by complaining that in talking thus about the Pharisees Jesus was reproaching them also. This became the occasion for the Master's pronouncement of three solemn woes on the lawyers.

The first *Woe* was that they loaded men with **burdens grievous to be borne** (v. 46), but would not lift a finger to help carry them (cf. Matt. 23:4). Plummer comments: "The reference is to the intolerably burdensome interpretations by which the scribes augmented the written Law. They made it far more severe than it was intended to be, explaining every doubtful point in favor of rigorous ritualism."[264]

The second *Woe* (v. 47) was that they built **the tombs of the prophets** which their fathers had killed (cf. Matthew 23:29-31). By rejecting John and crucifying Jesus (Acts 7:51-52) they did actually **consent** to what their fathers did (v. 48). These Pharisees were denying the Christ whom the prophets foretold.

Verses 49-51 are parallel to Matthew 23:34-36 (see the notes there). The one distinctive note in Luke is: **Therefore also said the wisdom of God** (v. 49). What follows is not a direct quotation of any Old Testament passage. The meaning probably is, "God in His wisdom said."[265] Then comes a composite of Old Testament ideas.

The third *Woe* (v. 52) scored the lawyers for taking away the key of knowledge. They not only refused to enter the kingdom themselves but were hindering others from doing so. The **key of knowledge** is the revelation of the knowledge of salvation.

d. Enmity of Scribes (11:53-54)

53 And when he was come out from thence, the scribes and the Pharisees began to press upon *him* vehemently, and to provoke him to speak of many things; 54 laying wait for him, to catch something out of his mouth.

These two verses, together with verse 52, are found only in Luke. In this paragraph we see the animosity of the Pharisees at its unreasonable worst. As Jesus left the house, **the scribes and the Pharisees** began to harass Him, trying to provoke Him to say something for which they could get Him into trouble. They were lying in wait for Him, **to catch something out of his mouth.** Their malicious motives and diabolical attitudes bespoke the denatured religion they represented — a legalistic distortion of the true revelation from God.

The verb **catch** means literally "to hunt." These religious leaders who were supposed to be leading men to God, to bring them into the way of His salvation, were instead hunting the Savior, trying to trap Him in His talk. They were more interested in saving their system than they were in saving souls.

E. VARIOUS WARNINGS (12:1-59)

1. Against Hypocrisy (12:1-12)

1 In the mean time, when the many thousands of the multitude were gathered together, insomuch that they trod one upon another, he began to say unto his disciples first of all, Beware ye of the leaven of the Pharisees, which is hypocrisy. 2 But there is nothing covered up, that shall not be revealed; and hid, that shall not be known. 3 Wherefore whatsoever ye have said in the darkness shall be heard in the light; and what ye have spoken in the ear in the inner chambers shall be proclaimed upon the housetops. 4 And I say unto you my friends, Be not afraid of them that kill the body, and after that have no more that they can do. 5 But I will warn you whom ye shall fear: Fear him, who after he hath killed hath power to cast into hell; yea, I say unto you, Fear him. 6 Are not five sparrows sold for two pence? and not one of them is forgotten in the sight of God. 7 But the very hairs of your head are all numbered. Fear not: ye are of more value than many sparrows. 8 And I say unto you, Every one who shall confess me before men, him shall the Son of man also confess before the angels of God; 9 but he that denieth me in the presence of men shall be denied in the presence of the angels of God. 10 And every one who shall speak a word against the Son of man, it shall be forgiven him: but unto him that blasphemeth against the Holy Spirit it shall not be forgiven. 11 And when they bring

---

[264] *Op. cit.,* p. 312.   [265] *Ibid.*

you before the synagogues, and the rulers, and the authorities, be not anxious how or what ye shall answer, or what ye shall say: 12 for the Holy Spirit shall teach you in that very hour what ye ought to say.

Great crowds had gathered to see and hear Jesus. **Many thousands** is in the Greek *myriadon* ("myriads"); literally, "the tens of thousands." Plummer suggests a possible reason for this: "The commotion inside and outside the Pharisee's house had attracted an immense crowd which was divided in its sympathy, some siding with the Pharisees, others disposed to support Christ." He adds: "His addressing His words to His disciples rather than to the multitude indicates that the latter were in the main not friendly."[266]

A. B. Bruce agrees that it was probably the Pharisees' assaults on Jesus that drew **the multitude**. Concerning *myriadon* he says: "a hyperbolical expression for an 'innumerable multitude,' pointing, if the words are to be taken in earnest, to the largest crowd mentioned anywhere in the Gospels."[267]

The meaning of **first** (v. 1) has been debated. Does it mean that this was the first topic that Jesus discussed, or that He addressed Himself first to the disciples and then to the crowd? The Greek could mean either. And both could be true.

The first warning was: **Beware ye of the leaven of the Pharisees, which is hypocrisy.** The last clause is found only in Luke (cf. Matt. 16:6; Mark 8:15). **Hypocrisy** means literally the wearing of a mask, such as was done by the actors of that day. The Pharisees were wearing the mask of false piety, while their hearts were filled with envy, jealousy, and hate.

Verses 2-9 are parallel to Matthew 10:26-33 (see notes there). **Covered up** and **revealed** is literally "veiled over" and "unveiled." Farrar suggests that the meaning of this verse is: "You will be made *responsible* for any part of my teaching which you conceal."[268]

In the darkness (v. 3) means "in obscurity." **In the inner chambers** is literally "in the storehouses." It suggests secret or inner rooms. Since thieves could dig through the outer walls of a house the treasure was kept in a secret place. But everything hidden will finally come to light. Hypocrisy is foolish, for it will finally be unmasked. In an Oriental city it was customary to make proclamations **upon the housetops.**

Persecutions are coming. The Master warns His disciples not to be afraid of those who kill the body, but can do no more (v. 4). Rather they are to fear the one who has **power** — "authority" — **to cast into hell** (*Gehenna*) (v. 5). Who is the one who has this power? Plummer says, "There is little doubt that this refers to God and not to the devil," and adds: "we are not in Scripture told to fear Satan, but to resist him . . . . although the evil one tries to bring us to Gehenna, it is not he who has authority to send us thither."[269]

A typical minor difference in wording in parallel accounts with no distinction in meaning occurs in connection with verse 6. Matthew says: "two sparrows sold for a penny" (*assarion*, worth about one cent). Luke has: **five sparrows sold for two pence** (getting one sparrow free). But in spite of the trivial commercial value of these small birds **not one of them is forgotten in the sight of God.** Such infinite Divine Providence is utterly beyond our comprehension. Then Jesus made the application: **the very hairs of your head are all numbered** — again we stagger at the infinity of it — **ye are of more value than many sparrows** (v. 7).

To deny Christ here is to have Him deny us there. To deny Christ now is to have Him deny us then.

What is the sin that **shall not be forgiven?** There have been many attempts to define the so-called Unpardonable Sin. Plummer puts it well when he writes: "Constant and consummate opposition to the influence of the Holy Spirit, because of a deliberate preference of darkness to light, renders repentance, and therefore forgiveness, morally impossible."[270] This blasphemy against the Holy Spirit is usually identified with the sin unto death of I John 5:16. It is also described in Matthew 12:31-32 and Mark 3:29-30.

Then Jesus gave His disciples a warning that they would be persecuted by the Jews (**synagogues**) and by the Gentiles

---

[266] *Ibid.,* p. 317.   [267] EGT, I, 555.   [268] *Op. cit.,* p. 273.
[269] *Op. cit.,* p. 319.   For the meaning of Gehenna see the notes on Mark 9:43.
[270] *Ibid.,* p. 321.

(rulers and authorities). But they need not fear, for the **Holy Spirit** will teach them what to say (12).

2. Against Covetousness (12:13-21)

a. Plea for Help (12:13-15)

13 And one out of the multitude said unto him, Teacher, bid my brother divide the inheritance with me. 14 But he said unto him, Man, who made me a judge or a divider over you? 15 And he said unto them, Take heed, and keep yourselves from all covetousness: for a man's life consisteth not in the abundance of the things which he possesseth.

A man in the crowd asked Jesus to order his brother to divide the family inheritance with him. Christ's reply was: **Who made me a judge or a divider over you?** Then the Master took advantage of the situation to deliver a strong warning against **covetousness.** He also enunciated a great general principle: **a man's life consisteth not in the abundance of things which he possesseth.** Material possessions do not mean abundant life.

b. Parable of the Rich Fool (12:16-21)

16 And he spake a parable unto them, saying, The ground of a certain rich man brought forth plentifully: 17 and he reasoned within himself, saying, What shall I do, because I have not where to bestow my fruits? 18 And he said, This will I do: I will pull down my barns, and build greater; and there will I bestow all my grain and my goods. 19 And I will say to my soul, thou hast much goods laid up for many years; take thine ease, eat, drink, be merry. 20 But God said unto him, Thou foolish one, this night is thy soul required of thee; and the things which thou hast prepared, whose shall they be? 21 So is he that layeth up treasure for himself, and is not rich toward God.

Jesus told the story of a man who was embarrassed with abundance. His greatest concern was the problem of what to do with his surplus. He finally decided to tear down his barns and build bigger ones. Then he would take his ease. **But God** saw things differently. His verdict was, **Thou foolish one.** The man was foolish because he forgot God, forgot his own spiritual condition, and forgot the needy ones around him. Why

did he not distribute his surplus to the poor people, instead of storing it up, possibly to rot? Also the man was foolish because he thought more of his body than his soul, more of time than eternity, more of himself than others.

This is one of the considerable number of parables found only in Luke. It is a part of his condemnation of the selfish rich who have no concern for the needy poor.

3. Against Anxiety (12:22-34)

22 And he said unto his disciples, Therefore I say unto you, Be not anxious for *your* life, what ye shall eat; nor yet for your body, what ye shall put on. 23 For the life is more than the food, and the body than the raiment. 24 Consider the ravens, that they sow not, neither reap; which have no store-chamber nor barn; and God feedeth them: of how much more value are ye than the birds! 25 And which of you by being anxious can add a cubit unto the measure of his life? 26 If then ye are not able to do even that which is least, why are ye anxious concerning the rest? 27 Consider the lilies, how they grow: they toil not, neither do they spin; yet I say unto you, Even Solomon in all his glory was not arrayed like one of these. 28 But if God doth so clothe the grass in the field, which to-day is, and to-morrow is cast into the oven; how much more *shall he clothe* you, O ye of little faith? 29 And seek not ye what ye shall eat, and what ye shall drink, neither be ye of doubtful mind. 30 For all these things do the nations of the world seek after: but your Father knoweth that ye have need of these things. 31 Yet seek ye his kingdom, and these things shall be added unto you. 32 Fear not, little flock; for it is your Father's good pleasure to give you the kingdom. 33 Sell that which ye have, and give alms; make for yourselves purses which wax not old, a treasure in the heavens that faileth not, where no thief draweth near, neither moth destroyeth. 34 For where your treasure is, there will your heart be also.

Verses 22-31 are closely parallel to Matthew 6:25-33 (see notes there). Jesus warns His hearers: **Be not anxious** — much more accurate than "Take no thought" (KJV) — about food or clothing. Life consists of more than these material things, as is illustrated vividly in the Parable of the Rich Fool.

Verse 25 asks a striking question. **Which of you by being anxious can add a cubit unto the measure of his life?** The last five words replace "his stature" (KJV). Which is correct? The Greek word *helikia* can mean either length of body or length of life (see notes on 2:52). Which it means here is uncertain. The Berkeley Version reads, "Who of you can add a foot to his height by worrying?" But it adds the footnote: "'one moment to his span of life' is an equally true translation." The difficulty of deciding between the two is highlighted by the fact that whereas the Revised Standard Version has "his span of life," the New English Bible has "his height." In either case **cubit** must be taken somewhat figuratively.

Neither be ye of doubtful mind (v. 29) is a clause which Matthew does not include. **Be ye of doubtful mind** is one word in the Greek, a verb which is found only here in the New Testament. It comes from an adjective meaning: "(a) in mid air; (b) buoyed up; (c) in suspense."[271] So the verb in the passive (as here) means either, "to be elated, puffed up," or "to be anxious, in suspense."[272]

Thayer says of its meaning (in the active): "by a metaphor taken from ships that are tossed about on the deep by winds and waves, *to cause one to waver or fluctuate in mind . . . ; to agitate or harass with cares.*" For this passage he suggests "and waver not between hope and fear."[273] Arndt and Gingrich say that the adjective from which the verb comes means: "hovering between hope and fear, restless, anxious."[274]

Alexander Maclaren heads his exposition of this clause with the title, "Stillness in Storm." He points out the relation of this passage to the total context of the chapter in these words: "The rich fool stretching himself out to rest on the pile of his possessions, and the poor fool tossing about on the billows of unquiet thought, are at bottom under the influence of the same folly"[275] — that of depending on themselves rather than trusting God.

One of the many beautiful passages which occur only in Luke is verse 32:

Fear not, little flock; for it is your Father's good pleasure to give you the kingdom. Christ's own were once, like all others, sheep who had gone astray (Isa. 53:6). But Jesus has become their Good Shepherd, who gave His life for the sheep and now leads and feeds them (John 10). They seem to be a **little flock,** in comparison with earth's millions outside the fold. But some day they will be "a great multitude, which no man could number" (Rev. 7:9). Though they are not exempt from the calamities of life, they have a Father in heaven to care for them. Simeon asks: "Why should they be afraid of *want* who have God for their Father, and a kingdom for their inheritance?"[276]

Verses 33-34 are parallel to Matthew 6:19-21 (see notes there). Luke adds: **Sell that which ye have, and give alms** (v. 33). Plummer observes: "As in 5:29, 30, we have a rule given, not that it may be kept literally, but that it may illustrate a principle." He adds that almsgiving is not only for the benefit of the needy recipient, but "also for the good of the giver, that his heart may be freed from covetousness."[277] This is one of the reasons why giving is an essential means of grace. The soul of the Christian who gives generously is abundantly blessed by God.

4. Concerning the Second Coming (12:35-59)

a. Need for Watchfulness (12:35-40)

35 Let your loins be girded about, and your lamps burning; 36 and be ye yourselves like unto men looking for their lord, when he shall return from the marriage feast; that, when he cometh and knocketh, they may straightway open unto him. 37 Blessed are those servants, whom the lord when he cometh shall find watching: verily I say unto you, that he shall gird himself, and make them sit down to meat, and shall come and serve them. 38 And if he shall come in the second watch, and if in the third, and find *them* so, blessed are those *servants.* 39 But know this, that if the master of the house had known in what hour the thief was coming, he would have watched, and not have left his house to be broken through. 40 Be ye also ready: for in an hour that ye think not the Son of man cometh.

---

[271] Abbott-Smith, *op. cit.,* p. 288.   [272] *Ibid.*   [273] *Op. cit.,* p. 407.   [274] *Op. cit.,* p. 515.
[275] *Op. cit.,* p. 353.   [276] Charles Simeon, *Expository Outlines on the Whole Bible,* XII, 480.
[277] *Op. cit.,* p. 329.

Verses 35-38 are found only in Luke. The twofold admonition of verse 35 is striking: **Let your loins be girded about, and your lamps burning.** Both figures of speech were familiar to Christ's hearers. When one wished to go to work or go on a journey he would "gird" himself, pulling on his flowing robe and then tying the sash to hold it all together. So, said Jesus, we need to prepare for His coming again by girding ourselves with prayer. We must also keep our **lamps burning.** This is the Parable of the Ten Virgins (Matt. 25:1-13) in a nutshell.

Jesus said that the attitude of the Christian is to be like that of servants who are expecting momentarily the return of their master. They must be ready to open to him the moment he knocks at the street door. The servants whom the master finds watching will be **blessed.** He will serve them. The **second watch** (9:00 P.M. to midnight) and the **third** (12:00-3.00 A.M.) are the times when it is hardest to keep fully awake and alert.

Verses 39-40 are parallel to Matthew 24:43-44 (see notes there). The emphasis here is on the unexpectedness of the time of the Second Coming. If a man had known what hour of the night the burglar would break in, he would be watching for him. So we are to be always on the alert, for Christ will come **in an hour that ye think not** (v. 40).

b. Need for Faithfulness (12:41-48)

41 And Peter said, Lord, speakest thou this parable unto us, or even unto all? 42 And the Lord said, Who then is the faithful and wise steward, whom his lord shall set over his household, to give them their portion of food in due season? 43 Blessed is that servant, whom his lord when he cometh shall find so doing. 44 Of a truth I say unto you, that he will set him over all that he hath. 45 But if that servant shall say in his heart, My lord delayeth his coming; and shall begin to beat the menservants and the maidservants, and to eat and drink, and to be drunken; 46 the lord of that servant shall come in a day when he expecteth not, and in an hour when he knoweth not, and shall cut him asunder, and appoint his portion with the unfaithful. 47 And that servant, who knew his lord's will, and made not ready, nor did according

to his will, shall be beaten with many *stripes;* 48 but he that knew not, and did things worthy of stripes, shall be beaten with few *stripes.* And to whomsoever much is given, of him shall much be required: and to whom they commit much, of him will they ask the more.

Peter wanted to know whether **this parable** of the watching servants was only for the disciples, or for all the crowd. In reply Jesus gave another "parable," that of the faithful steward (vv. 42-46). This is paralleled in Matthew 24:45-51 (see notes there).

Verses 47-48 are found only in Luke and constitute a significant passage. It seems to be clearly indicated here that there will be degrees of punishment in the next life — which justice would seem to demand. The basic distinction will be the light that one has. The criterion of judgment will be the reaction of each person to what he knows is **his lord's will.** Those with much light have greater demands placed upon them — both by life and by the Lord Himself.

c. Divided Loyalties (12:49-53)

49 I came to cast fire upon the earth; and what do I desire, if it is already kindled? 50 But I have a baptism to be baptized with; and how am I straitened till it be accomplished! 51 Think ye that I am come to give peace in the earth? I tell you, Nay; but rather division: 52 for there shall be from henceforth five in one house divided, three against two, and two against three. 53 They shall be divided, father against son, and son against father; mother against daughter, and daughter against her mother; mother in law against her daughter in law, and daughter in law against her mother in law.

What did Christ mean when He said that He came **to cast fire upon the earth?** It seems to refer to strife and division (cf. v. 51). This perhaps harks back to the beginning of this chapter, a situation rising out of the opposition of the Pharisees to Christ. On the meaning of **fire** here, A. B. Bruce says: "the fire of a new faith, or religion, a burning enthusiasm in believers, creating fierce antagonism in unbelievers: deplorable but inevitable."[278]

---

[278] EGT, I, 562.

The second part of verse 49 might be translated: "How earnestly I wish that it were already kindled." Creed says: "Christ wishes that the fire were already kindled, because it must needs be so before the kingdom of God can come."[279]

Plummer prefers the meaning, "What more have I to desire, if it be already kindled!" He writes: "Christ came to set the world on fire, and the conflagration had already begun."[280]

But there is perhaps another meaning of fire to be added to this. John the Baptist had said of the coming Messiah, "he shall baptize you in the Holy Spirit and in fire," and "the chaff he will burn up with unquenchable fire" (3:16, 17). Farrar offers this suggestion: "The metaphor is probably to be taken in all its meanings: fire as a spiritual baptism; the refining fire to purge gold from dross, and burn up the chaff of all evil in every imperfect character; and the fire of retributive justice."[281] Christ longed for the beginning of the purifying work of the Holy Spirit in the hearts of believers, which would come after the Crucifixion and the outpouring of the Spirit at Pentecost.

How is verse 50 related to verse 49? Plummer makes this suggestion about the metaphors of fire and water: "The one sets forth the results of His coming as it affects the world, the other as it affects Himself. The world is lit up with flames, and Christ is bathed in blood."[282]

The last part of verse 50 gives us a glimpse of the burden that already lay heavily on Christ's heart. He was straitened — "oppressed, afflicted" — until His Passion should be completed. "The prospect of His sufferings was a perpetual Gethsemane."[283]

Verses 51-53 are parallel to Matthew 10:34-36 (see notes there). Luke is more specific in spelling out the division often occasioned in a home where some choose to follow Christ and others refuse to do so. He illustrates by citing the example of a family of five that will be divided, **three against two** (v. 52). But then it appears as though he goes on to name six. A little thought, however, will show that the **mother** and **mother-in-law** (v. 53) are the same person. It was the custom of a man to take his bride to his father's

home, so this son's mother would at the same time be his wife's mother-in-law.

d. Signs of the Time (12:54-59)

54 And he said to the multitudes also, When ye see a cloud rising in the west, straightway ye say, There cometh a shower; and so it cometh to pass. 55 And when *ye see* a south wind blowing, ye say, There will be a scorching heat; and it cometh to pass. 56 Ye hypocrites, ye know how to interpret the face of the earth and the heaven; but how is it that ye know not how to interpret this time? 57 And why even of yourselves judge ye not what is right? 58 For as thou art going with thine adversary before the magistrate, on the way give diligence to be quit of him; lest haply he drag thee unto the judge, and the judge shall deliver thee to the officer, and the officer shall cast thee into prison. 59 I say unto thee, Thou shalt by no means come out thence, till thou have paid the very last mite.

Verses 54-56 are somewhat parallel to Matthew 16:2-3, though the weather signs cited are different. In Matthew Christ notes that red sky at night is a sign of good weather, whereas a red and dismal ("lowering") sky in the morning is a bad sign. Along the Atlantic coast, where the writer of this commentary was brought up, the old saying was:

> Red sky at night,
> Sailor's delight;
> Red sky in the morning,
> Sailor's take warning.

But here it is **a cloud rising in the west** (over the Mediterranean) that signifies a **shower** coming, and **a south wind** (from the desert) that meant **scorching heat.** Palestine lies between the desert and the sea.

Jesus challenged His hearers. If they could interpret **the face of the earth and the heaven** (the sky), why could they not **interpret this time?** (v. 56). The use of **hypocrites** here is thus explained by Farrar: "Their insincerity consisted in the fact that though the signs of the Kingdom were equally plain they *would* not see them, and pretended not to see them."[284] The miracles He performed were Messianic signs (cf. Isa. 35:4-6), as also the preaching of John the Baptist.

[279] *Op. cit.,* p. 178.   [280] *Op. cit.,* p. 334.   [281] *Op. cit.,* p. 281.   [282] *Ibid.*
[283] *Ibid.*   [284] *Op. cit.,* p. 282.

Why could they not themselves **judge** what was right (v. 57), without His having to point out these obvious facts to them?

Verses 58-59 are parallel to Matthew 5:25-26 (see notes there). At the beginning of verse 58 the King James Version translators left out the **For**, perhaps because they could not see any connection between what follows and what precedes. But A. B. Bruce has pointed out that link, in these words: "It is implied that if they had the necessary moral discernment they would see that a judgment day was at hand, and understand that the duty of the hour was to come to terms with their adversary by a timely repentance."[285]

To be quit of is a legal term in the Greek, and here means to be freed from any further legal involvement with one's **adversary**. **Drag** (literally, "drag away") is a strong term, found only here in the New Testament. **Officer** is *practor*. In Athens it was used for "one who exacts payments, a collector."[286] The word is found only here in the New Testament (different from "officer" in Matthew 5: 25), but is frequent in the papyri of that period. Deissmann thinks that here it means simply "officer of the court."[287] Arndt and Gingrich say that in this passage it signifies: "A court functionary who is under the judge's orders, something like a *bailiff* or *constable*, who is in charge of the debtor's prison."[288] **Mite** (v. 59) was the smallest coin in use, worth about one-eighth of a cent. The Greek word literally means "peeled, thin, small."

Jesus was warning His hearers to get things straightened out with the great Judge of all, before it was too late. Godet observes: "In the application, God is at once adversary, judge, and officer: the first by His holiness, the second by His justice, the third by His power."[289]

But the literal application to one's relationship with his fellow men should not be forgotten or neglected in giving attention to the ultimate reference to the divine-human encounter. For our standing with God involves our standing with men. The Jewish Talmud has a wise saying on this point: "The offences between man and God the Day of Atonement doth atone for. The offences between man and his neighbour the Day of Atonement atoneth for, only when he hath agreed with his neighbor."[290] We cannot maintain peace with God unless we continually pursue peace with all men (Heb. 12:14).

F. MIRACLES AND PARABLES (13:1-17: 10)

1. Repent or Perish (13:1-5)

1 Now there were some present at that very season who told him of the Galilaeans, whose blood Pilate had mingled with their sacrifices. 2 And he answered and said unto them, Think ye that these Galilaeans were sinners above all the Galilaeans, because they have suffered these things? 3 I tell you, Nay: but, except ye repent, ye shall all in like manner perish. 4 Or those eighteen, upon whom the tower in Siloam fell, and killed them, think ye that they were offenders above all the men that dwell in Jerusalem? 5 I tell you, Nay: but, except ye repent, ye shall all likewise perish.

This paragraph is found only in Luke. It consists of references to two incidents which took place in or near Jerusalem and the application Jesus made.

There were some present — or, "there came some" — who told Jesus of a recent tragedy. Evidently Pilate had become displeased with a group of Galileans and had them killed right in the Temple, so that their blood was mingled with that of their sacrifices. While no record of this has been found elsewhere, it is in keeping with what is known of the cruel character of Pilate and the revolutionary fanaticism of the Galileans. Josephus records many horrible massacres that took place in this period.[291] So it is not surprising that this one, in which perhaps only a few were killed, did not receive much attention. It is possible that it was this incident which caused Herod Antipas, ruler of Galilee, to be at enmity with Pilate (23:12). He may have been angered at Pilate's treatment of his Galilean subjects.

[285] EGT, I, 563.   [286] Abbott-Smith, *op. cit.*, p. 376.
[287] Adolf Deissmann, *Bible Studies*, trans. Alexander Grieve, p. 154.   [288] *Op. cit.*, p. 704.
[289] *Op. cit.*, II, 116.   [290] Quoted in Plummer, *op. cit.*, p. 337.
[291] *Ant.* XVII. 9.3; XV. 5:3; *War*, II. 9.4.

Jesus seized upon this opportunity to enforce an important truth. Doubtless some of the Jerusalem Jews may have concluded that these Galileans were hypocritical, wicked men. But Jesus said their tragic fate did not prove that they were worse sinners than those who survived. This is a warning to all who would interpret calamities as evidence of wickedness. This is not a situation for condemnation but one for compassion. So Christ warned His hearers: **except ye repent, ye shall all in like manner perish** (v. 3). Then he cited the eighteen upon whom **the tower of Siloam** (southern part of Jerusalem) fell. This incident, also, is not reported elsewhere. But this is not at all surprising. Building was not then done as carefully as it is done today. It was not an uncommon thing for walls to fall. But the men who died were not necessarily worse than the rest of the people in Jerusalem. Again Jesus declared, **except ye repent, ye shall all likewise perish** (v. 5) The master's warning to His hearers was: repent or perish!

2. Parable of the Barren Fig Tree (13: 6-9)

6 And he spake this parable; A certain man had a fig tree planted in his vineyard; and he came seeking fruit thereon, and found none. 7 And he said unto the vinedresser, Behold, these three years I come seeking fruit on this fig tree, and find none: cut it down; why doth it also cumber the ground? 8 And he answering saith unto him, Lord, let it alone this year also, till I shall dig about it, and dung it: 9 and if it bear fruit thenceforth, *well;* but if not, thou shalt cut it down.

The lesson of this parable is fairly obvious. The **fig tree** is the Jewish nation, which had failed to bring forth fruit for **three years.** This may refer to the failure of the Jewish leaders to respond to Jesus during the three years of His ministry. But this point should not be overemphasized. Since the nation was given forty more years of probation, the **three years** may refer to Israel's past. The owner bade the vinedresser cut the tree down. The vinedresser pleaded for one more year for the tree, to give it another chance. Presumably, his plea was granted, but we are not told the outcome of the story.

The application clearly is that if the nation of Israel did not show signs of repentance and exhibit the fruits of pious living, it would have to be cut down. This actually happened to the nation in A.D. 70, when Jerusalem was destroyed.

This parable in Luke takes the place of the incident of Jesus' cursing of the barren fig tree, recorded in Matthew (21:18-19), and Mark (11:12-14). The main lesson of both is the same; namely, that if Israel fails to bear fruit, she must be destroyed.

But one should not miss the application of this parable to the individual. For it is part of the warning to repent, and is the natural consequent of the passage immediately preceding it. The person who does not repent will perish, just as surely as will the impenitent nation.

3. Healing of the Infirm Woman (13: 10-17)

10 And he was teaching in one of the synagogues on the sabbath day. 11 And behold, a woman that had a spirit of infirmity eighteen years; and she was bowed together, and could in no wise lift herself up. 12 And when Jesus saw her, he called her, and said to her, Woman, thou art loosed from thine infirmity. 13 And he laid his hands upon her: and immediately she was made straight, and glorified God. 14 And the ruler of the synagogue, being moved with indignation because Jesus had healed on the sabbath, answered and said to the multitude, There are six days in which men ought to work: in them therefore come and be healed, and not on the day of the sabbath. 15 But the Lord answered him, and said, Ye hypocrites, doth not each one of you on the sabbath loose his ox or his ass from the stall, and lead him away to watering? 16 And ought not this woman, being a daughter of Abraham, whom Satan had bound, lo, *these* eighteen years, to have been loosed from this bond on the day of the sabbath? 17 And as he said these things, all his adversaries were put to shame: and all the multitude rejoiced for all the glorious things that were done by him.

This miracle is recorded only by Luke. It took place **on the sabbath day,** and that was what caused the conflict.

True to his medical profession, Luke records the fact that the woman had been afflicted for eighteen years. By this time she would have given up all hope of any help. She was bowed over and unable to straighten up.

When Jesus saw her, He was moved to do something about her case. Summoning her, He pronounced her cured. When He laid His hands on her, she **immediately** straightened up, and **glorified God** — a typically Lukan expression.

The ruler of the synagogue was indignant because Jesus had healed someone on the sabbath day. He told the people to come during the week to be healed, and not on the sabbath.

This piece of senseless legalism stirred the Master. Boldly He called the Pharisees **hypocrites.** They customarily lead their animals to water on the sabbath day (v. 15). How much more should this afflicted woman be freed on the sabbath — this one **whom Satan hath bound** (v. 16). To Jesus, sin and Satan were the ultimate causes of sickness.

All of Jesus' adversaries were shamed and silenced by what He said. But the multitude **rejoiced** at what had happened.

4. Two Parables of the Kingdom (13:18-21)

a. Parable of the Mustard Seed (13:18-19)

18 He said therefore, Unto what is the kingdom of God like? and whereunto shall I liken it? 19 It is like unto a grain of mustard seed, which a man took, and cast into his own garden; and it grew, and became a tree; and the birds of the heaven lodged in the branches thereof.

For the meaning of this parable see the notes on Matthew 13:31-32. The rapid visible growth of the kingdom of God seems to be the main point.

b. Parable of the Leaven (13:20-21)

20 And again he said, Whereunto shall I liken the kingdom of God? 21 It is like unto leaven, which a woman took and hid in three measures of meal, till it was all leavened.

For the meaning of this parable see the comments on Matthew 13:33. These twin parables teach much the same lesson, except that the former emphasizes the outward growth of the Kingdom, and the latter its inward growth and influence.

5. Teachings on the Way to Jerusalem (13:22-35)

a. The Narrow Door (13:22-30)

22 And he went on his way through cities and villages, teaching, and journeying on unto Jerusalem. 23 And one said unto him, Lord, are they few that are saved? And he said unto them, 24 Strive to enter in by the narrow door: for many, I say unto you, shall seek to enter in, and shall not be able. 25 When once the master of the house is risen up, and hath shut to the door, and ye begin to stand without, and to knock at the door, saying, Lord, open to us; and he shall answer and say to you, I know you not whence ye are; 26 then shall ye begin to say, We did eat and drink in thy presence, and thou didst teach in our streets; 27 and he shall say, I tell you, I know not whence ye are; depart from me, all ye workers of iniquity. 28 There shall be the weeping and the gnashing of teeth, when ye shall see Abraham, and Isaac, and Jacob, and all the prophets, in the kingdom of God, and yourselves cast forth without. 29 And they shall come from the east and west, and from the north and south, and shall sit down in the kingdom of God. 30 And behold, there are last who shall be first, and there are first who shall be last.

Verse 22 consists of a summary statement of Jesus' last journey to Jerusalem. He was going **through cities and villages,** teaching the people as He journeyed toward the Holy City.

Someone asked Him a pertinent question. Jesus had been emphasizing the certainty of judgment and the necessity of repentance, and the inquirer asked: **Lord, are they few that are saved?** (v. 23).

In answer Jesus urged: **Strive to enter in by the narrow door** (v. 24) — for many would try to and **not be able.** This is a brief statement of what is found in Matthew 7:13-14. The implication here — not as explicit as in Matthew — is an affirmative answer to the question. Oddly, Matthew seems to answer the question in Luke. He quotes Jesus as saying: "and few are they that find it" (Matt. 7:14). It has always been true, and still is, that the genuine Christians are in the minority. But this fact is neither surprising nor confusing, for Christ predicted it.

The verb **strive** is *agonizo* ("agonize"). It was used first for striving in an athletic contest, then in the sense of "fight" or "struggle." Arndt and Gingrich suggest for this passage: "Strain every nerve to enter."[292]

Jesus indicated that there would come a time when the period of probation would be over. Then the door would be **shut** (v. 25), and those outside (the Kingdom) would knock desperately, but in vain.

The language of the last part of verse 25 is similar to what is found in the Parable of the Ten Virgins (cf. Matthew 25:11-12). In both cases the sadly solemn words are uttered: **I know you not**. Those on the outside would plead that they knew Him: He had taught in their very streets! But the master would insist that He did not know them. As in Matthew, the horror of hell is described here as **weeping** and **gnashing of teeth** (v. 28). Luke adds **when ye shall see Abraham, and Isaac, and Jacob, and all the prophets in the kingdom. . . , and yourselves cast forth without.**

Verse 29 is parallel to Matthew 8:11, and verse 30 to Matthew 19:30. People will come from all directions to **sit down in the kingdom of God**. The **last** are rather obviously the Gentiles, the **first** the Jews. But in the church of Jesus Christ the Gentiles have become the dominant force.

b. Lament over Jerusalem (13:31-35)

31 In that very hour there came certain Pharisees, saying to him, Get thee out, and go hence: for Herod would fain kill thee. 32 And he said unto them, Go and say to that fox, Behold, I cast out demons and perform cures to-day and to-morrow, and the third *day* I am perfected. 33 Nevertheless I must go on my way to-day and to-morrow and the *day* following: for it cannot be that a prophet perish out of Jerusalem. 34 O Jerusalem, Jerusalem, that killeth the prophets, and stoneth them that are sent unto her! how often would I have gathered thy children together, even as a hen *gathereth* her own brood under her wings, and ye would not! 35 Behold, your house is left unto you *desolate*: and I say unto you, Ye shall not see me, until

ye shall say, Blessed *is* he that cometh in the name of the Lord.

Certain Pharisees warned Jesus that He had better leave Herod Antipas' territory, before Herod managed to kill Him. Jesus' reply was fearless and forceful. He called Herod Antipas **that fox** (v. 32) — a reference to the crafty, wily character of this ruler. Christ further enjoined them to tell Herod that He was going to **cast out demons and perform cures today and tomorrow** — that is, for a short time longer — and on **the third day** He would be **perfected**; that is, His earthly ministry would be "completed" (literal meaning of **perfected**). But He must hurry on to Jerusalem, the city where they kill prophets. Probably the references here to days are not to be taken literally as meaning 24-hour days, but rather figuratively — a short period of time. Plummer writes: "The three days have been interpreted to mean (1) three actual days, (2) the three years of the ministry, (3) a long time, (4) a short time, (5) a definite time." He prefers the last, and says: "The course of the Messiah is determined, and will not be abbreviated or changed because of the threats of a Herod."[293] Olshausen likewise interprets the phrase as indicating a definite time. He specifies it thus: "The expression today, to-morrow, and the day after, is therefore a symbolic description of the whole public ministry of Jesus, which is in point of time exactly measured off, and which no earthly power can shorten."[294]

The actual lament (vv. 34-35) is almost a word-for-word parallel to Matthew 23:37-39.

It is a sad thing that Jerusalem should have to be identified with the epithet, **that killeth the prophets**. In spite of the city's wickedness, divine compassionate love is described under the tender figure of a mother hen gathering her brood of chicks **under her wings**, to warm and protect them. Yet God's people refused — **and ye would not** (v. 34). Jesus warns Jerusalem that it would not see Him again (after His Ascension) until its inhabitants should say: **Blessed is he that cometh in the name of the Lord** (v. 35).

[292] *Op. cit.*, p. 15. [293] *Op. cit.*, pp. 349, 350.
[294] Hermann Olshausen, *Biblical Commentary on the New Testament*, trans. A. C. Kendrick, II, 41.

6. In the House of a Chief Pharisee (14:1-24)

a. Healing of Man with Dropsy (14:1-6)

1 And it came to pass, when he went into the house of one of the rulers of the Pharisees on a sabbath to eat bread, that they were watching him. 2 And behold, there was before him a certain man that had the dropsy. 3 And Jesus answering spake unto the lawyers and Pharisees, saying, Is it lawful to heal on the sabbath, or not? 4 But they held their peace. And he took him, and healed him, and let him go. 5 And he said unto them, Which of you shall have an ass or an ox fallen into a well, and will not straightway draw him up on a sabbath day? 6 And they could not answer again unto these things.

For a third time (cf. 7:36; 11:37) Luke (alone) mentions Jesus' eating in the home of a Pharisee. In view of the Pharisaic opposition to Him, this seems a bit surprising. Christ's acceptance of the invitation shows His generous, forgiving spirit. He was glad to go anywhere that He might be of help. It is a suggestion to Christians today that one should not shun social opportunities for ministering to those who would not otherwise be reached and brought into the Kingdom.

This feast was **on a sabbath.** Farrar comments: "Sabbath entertainments of a luxurious and joyous character were the rule among the Jews, and were even regarded as a religious duty. . . .all the food was however cooked on the previous day."[295] The meal followed the morning service at the synagogue, and so was eaten about noon.

As Jesus waited, **they were watching him.** This verb is used four times in the Gospels and always of the Pharisees seeking to entrap Christ (cf. 6:7; 20:20; Mark 3:2). It means "to watch closely, observe narrowly."[296] The compound verb properly signifies "to stand beside and watch." The context of these passages shows that in the Gospels it indicates "to watch insidiously"[297]; that is, with evil intent. Geldenhuys comments: "From the context it appears as if the Pharisees, who were now watching Jesus continually

with growing hate, intentionally arranged matters in such a way that the dropsical man was in the dining-room so that they might see whether he would again contravene the sabbath laws."[298]

Apparently these teachers of the Law had not taken to heart one passage in their Scriptures: "The wicked watcheth the righteous, and seeketh to slay him" (Psa. 37:32). These self-righteous religious leaders were playing the part of the wicked. **And behold, there was before him** — apparently placed so that Jesus could not fail to see the man's pitiful condition — **a certain man that had the dropsy** (v. 2). **That had the dropsy** is in the Greek all one word (hydropikos) found only here in the New Testament. It comes from the word for "water," which indicates the nature of the disease — "a disproportionate effusion of watery fluid into the tissues or cavities of the body."[299] The Greek word here was a term which was "widely used by medical practitioners from Hippocrates onward."[300] This is another of many evidences that the writer of this Gospel may well have been a physician.

Jesus, **answering** the unspoken thoughts of His enemies, said to the **lawyers and Pharisees** — the **lawyers** were all **Pharisees** — **Is it lawful to heal on the sabbath, or not?** (v. 3) Thus the Master placed His opponents in an inescapable dilemma. If they said "No" the people would be offended. If they said "Yes" they could never again object to His healing on the sabbath day. So **they held their peace** (v. 4). "It was the silence of the splenetic pride and obstinacy which while *secretly* convinced determined to remain unconvinced. But such silence was His complete public justification."[301] For by saying nothing they tacitly gave permission for Jesus to perform the miracles, according to the rule, "Silence gives consent."

So Christ healed the man and released him. Then He turned to the sullen Pharisees and asked which of them would have **an ass or an ox** — the best Greek reading seems to be "a son or (even) an ox" — that would fall into a **well** (or "pit") and they would not **straightway** pull it out (cf. Matthew 12:11). Why

295 Op. cit., p. 293.   296 Abbott-Smith, op. cit., p. 343.   297 Thayer, op. cit., p. 486. 298 Op. cit., p. 386. For the Jewish regulations about healing on the sabbath, see the comments on 6:6-11.   299 R. K. Harrison, "Dropsy," IDB, I, 872.   300 Ibid.   301 Farrar, op. cit., p. 294.

then should not Christ be compassionate toward this afflicted man and heal him on the sabbath day? In the face of such logic it is not surprising that **they could not answer again unto those things** (v. 6).

b. Parable of Ambitious Guests (14: 7-11)

7 And he spake a parable unto those that were bidden, when he marked how they chose out the chief seats; saying unto them, 8 When thou art bidden of any man to a marriage feast, sit not down in the chief seat; lest haply a more honorable man than thou be bidden of him, 9 and he that bade thee and him shall come and say to thee, Give this man place; and then thou shalt begin with shame to take the lowest place. 10 But when thou art bidden, go and sit down in the lowest place; that when he that hath bidden thee cometh, he may say to thee, Friend, go up higher: then shalt thou have glory in the presence of all that sit at meat with thee. 11 For everyone that exalteth himself shall be humbled; and he that humbleth himself shall be exalted.

The word **parable** suggests that a spiritual "comparison" is intended. "Through the medium of a counsel of prudence relating to ordinary social life He communicates a lesson of true wisdom concerning the higher sphere of religion."[302]

Jesus noted that the guests who were invited to the feast at the Pharisee's house were choosing the **chief seats** — literally, "first couches." Apparently the healing miracle took place before the guests moved to the tables. Now they were selecting their couches, on which they would recline while eating.

Christ then admonished them that when they were invited to **a marriage feast** — "here representing all great social functions at which ambition for distinction is called into play"[303] — they were not to recline on the "first couch." For **a more honorable man** might have been invited, and the host would then ask the self-ambitious guest to give up his place. The result would be embarrassment before the whole crowd, as the first guest had to move down to the **lowest place** (literally, "last place"). Thus Jesus showed pointedly the folly

of pride. Humility is not only a divine grace, but it accords with common sense. Pride always makes men look foolish.

The Master went on to suggest that if the invited guest would take **the lowest place**, the probabilities were that when the host came he would say, **Friend, go up higher** (better, "come up higher"). Thus the guest would receive **glory** ("honor") from all who were reclining at the table (v. 10).

Then Jesus enunciated the great principle of life (cf. Matt. 23:12). He showed that "the way up is down," that "Pride goeth before destruction and a haughty spirit before a fall" (Prov. 16:18). Alexander Pope's familiar lines fit well here:

He that is down need fear no fall,
    He that is low no pride.
He that is humble ever shall
    Have God to be his guide.

c. Entertaining the Poor (14:12-14)

12 And he said to him also that had bidden him, When thou makest a dinner or a supper, call not thy friends, nor thy brethren, nor thy kinsmen, nor rich neighbors; lest haply they also bid thee again, and a recompense be made thee. 13 But when thou makest a feast, bid the poor, the maimed, the lame, the blind: 14 and thou shalt be blessed; because they have not *wherewith* to recompense thee: for thou shalt be recompensed in the resurrection of the just.

Christ also had a word for His host, as well as for the guests. He admonished him that when he made **a dinner or a supper** — "a dinner or a banquet" (RSV) — he should not **call** (present imperative, "habitually call") his **friends . . . brethren . . . kinsmen, nor rich neighbors.** Jesus did not mean that one should never entertain his relatives, but that he should also show hospitality to the needy. The **poor** would not have the money, nor **the maimed, the lame, the blind** (v. 13) the physical ability, to furnish entertainment. He who entertained them would be **blessed** — same word as in the Beatitudes — and **recompensed** ("paid back") in the **resurrection of the just** (or, "righteous"). The last phrase may reflect the idea of two resurrections (cf. I Cor. 15:23; I Thess.

302 A. B. Bruce, *The Parabolic Teaching of Christ*, p. 310.   303 EGT, I, 572.

4:16; Rev. 20:5, 6). Or it may simply refer to the character of those who entertain the poor.

Books have been written containing the "table talk" of Martin Luther and more recently of Karl Barth. The last two paragraphs, with the one that follows, might be called "the table talk of Jesus."

d. Parable of the Great Supper (14: 15-24)

15 And when one of them that sat at meat with him heard these things, he said unto him, Blessed is he that shall eat bread in the kingdom of God. 16 But he said unto him, A certain man made a great supper; and he bade many: 17 and he sent forth his servant at supper time to say to them that were bidden, Come; for *all* things are now ready. 18 And they all with one *consent* began to make excuse. The first said unto him, I have bought a field, and I must needs go out and see it; I pray thee have me excused. 19 And another said, I have bought five yoke of oxen, and I go to prove them; I pray thee have me excused. 20 And another said, I have married a wife, and therefore I cannot come. 21 And the servant came, and told his lord these things. Then the master of the house being angry said to his servant, Go out quickly into the streets and lanes of the city, and bring in hither the poor and maimed and blind and lame. 22 And the servant said, Lord, what thou didst command is done, and yet there is room. 23 And the lord said unto the servant, Go out in the highways and hedges, and constrain *them* to come in, that my house may be filled. 24 For I say unto you, that none of these men that were bidden shall taste of my supper.

For the main differences between this and the Parable of the Wedding Feast see the notes on Matthew 22:1-10. If one wishes a more detailed list it will be found in Trench.[304] There is little question but that these are two distinct parables: the differences far outweigh the similarities. Plummer writes:

The parable in Matthew is a comment on an attempt to arrest Christ (xxi.46), and tells of rebels put to death for insulting and killing their sovereign's messengers; this is a comment on a pious remark, perhaps ignorantly or hypo-critically made, and tells of discourteous persons who, through indifference, lose the good things to which they were invited. It is much less severe in tone than the other; and even in those parts which are common to the two has very little similarity of wording."[305]

The occasion of the parable is given in this case, which is unusual. One of the guests reclining at the table with Jesus said: **Blessed is he that shall eat bread in the kingdom of God** (v. 15). This reflects the Jewish belief that the Messianic age would begin with a great banquet. Blessed were those who would be privileged to participate in that feast.

In reply Jesus indicated that there would be many invited to the Messianic banquet who would fail to be there, because they considered other things more important. Not all who are called by Christ accept.

The parable tells of a man who made a great **supper** — "feast" or "banquet" (same word as "supper" in v. 12). He bade **many**. This suggests the free grace of God which is bountifully offered to all. However, the context shows that the primary application is to the Jews. They were the first guests invited to the feast of the kingdom of God, through the preaching of both John the Baptist and Jesus.

At supper time (literally, "at the hour of the feast") the man sent **his servant** (Greek, "slave") to tell the invited guests that the banquet was **now ready** (v. 17). The custom of sending a second invitation still prevails in some places, and is considered an important part of good etiquette. "To refuse the second summons would be an insult, which is equivalent among the Arab tribes to a declaration of war."[306]

But they all — general designation for the invited guests — **began to make excuse** (v. 18). The **first** had bought a field and must see it. Then **another** had bought five yoke of oxen and needed to prove them. Still **another** had just married and said, **I cannot come** (v. 20). Trench suggests that the first represents those who are elated with their acquired possessions, the second those who feel the care of this life, the third those who want to enjoy the pleasures of this world

304 R. C. Trench, *Notes on the Parables of Our Lord*, pp. 171, 172.
305 *Op. cit.*, p. 305.   306 Quoted by Plummer, *op. cit.*, p. 360.

rather than follow Christ.[307] The last is related to Paul's admonition in I Cor. 7:29-31, and all the excuses find an adequate answer in verse 26, which follows this parable.

When the slave told his master what the invited guests had said, the master was very angry. He told his slave to go out into the streets and lanes of the city, and bring in the poor and maimed and blind and lame (v. 21; cf. v. 13). The slave soon reported that he had fulfilled this command, and yet there is room (v. 22). Then the master ordered his slave to go outside the city to the highways and hedges and constrain them to come in, for his house must be filled (v. 23). This typifies God's bountiful love in desiring all men to be saved. But those who were invited and refused to come would lose their opportunity of enjoying the feast.

It seems logical to say that the invited guests who rejected the summons represent the leaders of the Jewish nation — or most of the Jews — who refused to accept Christ's invitation into the Kingdom. The poor and afflicted who were brought in from the streets and lanes of the city typify the poorer Jews, "the common people" who heard Jesus gladly, the publicans and harlots (Matthew 31:31). Those who were brought in from outside the city represent the Gentiles who were called and accepted the gospel invitation.

The central significance of this parable is pointed out clearly by T. W. Manson. He says:

> Jesus does not here teach either a mechanically operating predestination, which determines from all eternity who shall or shall not be brought into the Kingdom. Neither does He proclaim that man's entry into the Kingdom is purely his own affair. The two essential points in His teaching are that no man can enter the Kingdom without an invitation of God, and that no man can remain outside it but by his own deliberate choice.[308]

7. Counting the Cost (14:25-35)

25 Now there went with him great multitudes: and he turned, and said unto them, 26 If any man cometh unto me, and hateth not his own father, and mother, and wife, and children, and brethren, and sisters, yea, and his own life also, he cannot be my disciple. 27

---

[307] Op. cit., p. 280.   [308] Op. cit., p. 422.

Whosoever doth not bear his own cross, and come after me, cannot be my disciple. 28 For which of you, desiring to build a tower, doth not first sit down and count the cost, whether he have *wherewith* to complete it? 29 Lest haply, when he hath laid a foundation, and is not able to finish, all that behold begin to mock him, 30 saying, This man began to build, and was not able to finish. 31 Or what king, as he goeth to encounter another king in war, will not sit down first and take counsel whether he is able with ten thousand to meet him that cometh against him with twenty thousand? 32 Or else, while the other is yet a great way off, he sendeth an ambassage, and asketh conditions of peace. 33 So therefore whosoever he be of you that renounceth not all that he hath, he cannot be my disciple. 34 Salt therefore is good: but if even the salt have lost its savor, wherewith shall it be seasoned? 35 It is fit neither for the land nor for the dunghill: *men* cast it out. He that hath ears to hear, let him hear.

Apparently the conversation at the table ended. Jesus is now once more thronged by great multitudes. To them He turned and spoke. Alluding to the Parable of the Great Supper, He indicated that if anyone loves anyone or anything more than he loves Him, he cannot be His disciple (v. 26). It is obvious that hateth here means "loves less." Jesus, who is Love Incarnate, is not the author of hate. What He is talking about is a conflict of loyalties. Our first commitment must always be to Christ, never to anyone else. We cannot permit anyone, no matter how near and dear, to come between us and Him.

Verse 27 goes a step further. To be a disciple of Christ means that one must bear his own cross (cf. Matthew 10:38). This means complete and continuous submission to the will of God. The Cross means death to self, in order that one may be fully alive to Christ.

Having pointed out in strong, graphic, almost shocking terms the real cost of discipleship, Jesus proceeded to give two brief illustrations of the necessity of counting the cost before one begins to be a disciple. The first is that of a man who wants to build a tower (vv. 28-30). Unless he sits down first and counts the cost, and makes sure that he has enough money to finish, he may be left with a tower half-built that will be a laughing-stock for those who mock his failure. The second is that of a king going to war against another king (vv. 31, 32). Unless he is assured of being able to defeat his enemy he had better not launch the attack. Instead he would be wise to sue for peace.

Then Jesus made the application: **So therefore whosoever he be of you that renounceth not all that he hath, he cannot be my disciple** (v. 33). Complete self-renunciation is the cost of discipleship. Renouncing all one's possessions will do no good unless one renounces self (cf. v. 26). The giving up of this thing or that thing in our lives may be a token sign of our consecration. But it must go deeper than that. It must be an inward surrender of our will to His will, of our way to His way, of our desires — little and big — to His supreme desire. It is saying: "Not my will, but thine, be done."

At first sight verses 34 and 35 seem to stand alone, isolated from their context. But a little thought will show their connection. The Master is still dealing with the spirit of sacrifice that His disciples must have (cf. Matt. 5:13; Mark 9:49, 50).

Godet calls attention to the two functions of salt — flavoring and preserving. Then he says: "In this twofold relation, it is the emblem of the sharp and austere savour of holiness, of the action of the gospel on the natural life, the insipidity and frivolity of which are corrected by the Divine Spirit."[309]

The relationship of these sayings on salt to what precedes is indicated by Plummer's comment on verse 35. He says: "Savourless salt is not even of this much use: and disciples without the spirit of self-devotion are like it."[310]

The closing verses of this chapter contain a sharp warning against the danger of backsliding and apostasy (cf. Heb. 6: 4-12; 10:26-39). The importance of this truth is emphasized by Jesus' repetition of the proverbial expression: **He that hath ears to hear, let him hear** (cf. Matt. 11:15; 13:9, 43; Mark 4:9, 23; 7:16; Luke 8:8; Rev. 2:7, 11, 17, 29; 2:6, 13, 22; 13: 9).

Lang links together the three closing

"pictures" of discipleship: (1) building a tower; (2) fighting a battle; (3) acting as salt. He says: "The first is costly, the second is arduous, the third is perilous."[311] In connection with the first, he notes that the Lord in giving this stern teaching to the multitudes, "sifted and sorted them, as once He had done with Gideon's great army."[312] The work of God is arduous toil, and one must be willing to pay this price.

But it is also a warfare. No soldier on duty can be entangled with the things of this life (II Tim. 2:4). That was the fatal fault of those who asked to be excused from the feast. Discipleship involves the costly sacrifice of being a soldier.

In the third place, it is like salt. "This is another picture of battle, for salt does its work by *antagonizing* what is around it. It is unlike and contrary to corruption." Lang continues: "This demands that the disciple must be unlike the man of the world in all moral and religious respects."[313]

The three "inexorable conditions of this high calling" are summarized by Lang. He says, in part:

> 1. First, that the Lord shall have such undisputed hold on the affections and will that even the dearest, the plainly God-created relationships shall recede. . . .
> 2. The second condition is that the disciple must "bear his own cross" and take the road in life that Christ took here. The former condition is death to *all other persons* in comparison with Christ; this condition means death to *myself* as an object of service. Not that I trim my life of this or that indulgence, but that I put *self itself* on the cross and deny it any attention or provision. This theme is taken up in Rom. 6:6ff., Gal. 2:19, 20.
> 3. The third condition of discipleship has relation to *possessions.* He cannot be a follower of Jesus who regards Himself as the *owner* of *anything* . . . cannot be such until he renounces all that he has to the sovereign disposition of the Lord.[314]

8. Three Parables on Lostness (15:1-32)

a. Introduction (15:1, 2)

1 Now all the publicans and sinners were drawing near unto him to hear him.

309 *Op. cit.,* II. 142.　310 *Op. cit.,* p. 366.
311 G. H. Lang, *The Parabolic Teaching of Scripture,* p. 241.　312 *Ibid.,* p. 242.
313 *Ibid.,* p. 243.　314 *Ibid.,* pp. 243, 244.

2 And both the Pharisees and the scribes murmured, saying, This man receiveth sinners, and eateth with them.

The opening statement of this chapter is very significant. In the Parable of the Last Supper, Christ had intimated that the Jewish leaders had rejected His call, and now the "street" people were being invited to enter the Kingdom. Apparently they joyfully responded, for we read: **Now all the publicans and sinners were drawing near unto him to hear him.** It is not surprising to learn next that **the Pharisees and the scribes** were complaining and criticizing. Their objection was: **This man receiveth sinners.** This criticism of the Pharisees points up sharply the main difference between Judaism and Christianity. The Judaism of Jesus' day was more concerned about avoiding all association with sinners, for fear of being defiled, than it was about saving them. But the glory of Christianity is that it receives sinners and by the grace of God turns them into saints. A religion which is concerned only with keeping the status quo is already dead, even if not yet buried.

Godet has well observed: "What drew those sinners to Jesus was their finding in Him not that righteousness, full of pride and contempt, with which the Pharisees assailed them, but a holiness which was associated with tenderest love."[315]

Murmured is a strong compound, found only here and 19:7 (murmuring against Jesus going with Zacchaeus, "a sinner"). Literally it is, "they were murmuring among themselves." **Receiveth** is also a compound, meaning "to receive to oneself, receive favorably, admit, accept."[316] The climax of His crimes was that **He eateth with them.** This no self-respecting rabbi would do. Farrar says: "He associated with sinners that He might save them. . . .It is this yearning of redemptive love which finds its richest illustration in these three parables."[317]

Bengel classifies the three parables as follows: "The lost sheep, the lost drachma (piece of money), and the lost son, express respectively the stupid (senseless) sinner, the sinner altogether ignorant of himself, and the knowing and willful (voluntary) sinner."[318]

The first two are joined closely together by "or" (v. 8). They form a pair and teach the same lesson, as is suggested by "or". But the third is separated from the other two by "and he said" (v. 11), which suggests something new.

The Parable of the Lost Sheep is found also in Matthew 18:12-14 (see notes there). The other two occur only in Luke. All three are based on the Lukan theme of lostness. The first two are vivid illustrations of the key verse of this Gospel: "For the Son of man came to seek and to save that which was lost" (19:10).

The relation of the three to the Trinity has also been suggested. The Parable of the Lost Sheep portrays the *Son* as the Seeking Shepherd. The Parable of the Lost Coin represents the work of the *Holy Spirit,* diligently searching out every lost sinner. The Parable of the Lost Son shows the *Father* waiting for the penitent sinner to come home.

b. The Lost Sheep (15:3-7)

3 And he spake unto them this parable, saying, 4 What man of you, having a hundred sheep, and having lost one of them, doth not leave the ninety and nine in the wilderness, and go after that which is lost, until he find it? 5 And when he hath found it, he layeth it on his shoulders, rejoicing. 6 And when he cometh home, he calleth together his friends and his neighbors, saying unto them, Rejoice wth me, for I have found my sheep which was lost. 7 I say unto you, that even so there shall be joy in heaven over one sinner that repenteth, *more* than over ninety and nine righteous persons, who need no repentance.

Jesus' claim to be the Good Shepherd is developed at length in John 10:1-18. It is one of the main motifs in the art of the ancient Catacombs. No picture is better loved today than the Good Shepherd. "No simile has taken more hold upon the mind of Christendom."[319]

Of verse 4 Trench says: "There is a peculiar fitness in this image as addressed to the spiritual rulers of the Jewish people. They too were shepherds."[320] They had been charged with the care of God's sheep, but had failed their trust (Ezek. 34; Zech. 11:16). Now they find

315 *Op. cit.,* p. 143.   316 Abbott-Smith, *op. cit.,* p. 384.   317 *Op. cit.,* p. 302.
318 *Op. cit.,* II, 136.   319 Plummer, *op. cit.,* p. 368.   320 *Op. cit.,* p. 288.

fault with the Good Shepherd[321] who comes to seek and save the lost whom they had neglected.

Jesus portrays the picture of a shepherd who has a **hundred sheep, but one is lost.** He leaves the **ninety and nine in the wilderness.** The idea of **wilderness** might be misleading. Trench observes that the term signifies "No sandy or rocky desert, the haunt of wild beasts or of wandering robber hordes; rather, wide, extended, grassy plains. . . , called 'desert' because without habitations of men."[322] The ninety-nine were left here in the care of under-shepherds, while the shepherd himself went in search of the one lost sheep.

The climax of this verse is reached in the last clause — **until he find it.** "This is the point of the first two parables — the particular love of God for each individual soul."[323]

On the identification of the main items in verse 4 Godet suggests this: "The *hundred sheep* represent the totality of the theocratic people; the *lost sheep*, that portion of the people which has broken with legal ordinances, and so lives under the impulses of its own passions; the *ninety and nine,* the majority which has remained outwardly faithful to the law."[324]

In the context of the opening verses of this chapter it is evident that Christ is defending Himself against the criticism of the Pharisees: that He "receiveth sinners" (v. 2). All three parables portray Divine Love as seeking and accepting the lost. To the Pharisees **that which is lost** (v. 4) would be specifically "the publicans and sinners" (v. 1).

Layeth it on his shoulders (v. 5) is a particularly tender touch, found only in Luke. The lost sheep would be worn out with its wandering, perhaps, unable to walk the long trail home. Paul said: "For while we were yet weak, in due season Christ died for the ungodly" (Rom. 5:6).

In contrast to the sour, critical attitude of the Pharisees toward the "sinners" who came to Jesus is the rejoicing of the shepherd and his neighbors over the finding of his lost sheep (v. 6). This

is humanity's "finest hour." Christ declared that likewise there was joy in heaven — in the heart of God and among the holy angels — **over one sinner that repenteth.**

The additional words — **more than over ninety and nine righteous persons, who need no repentance** (v. 7) — seem strange. Do not all men need to repent? Farrar suggests the answer: "There is a shade of irony both in the words *'just'* [KJV for "righteous"] and *'repentance.'* Neither word can be understood in its full and true sense; but only in the inadequate senses which the Pharisees attached to them."[325] The Parable of the Pharisee and the Publican was spoken to those who "trusted in themselves that they were righteous" (18:9). This was the great crime and tragedy of the Pharisees, that they depended on their self-righteousness and rejected the righteousness which Christ preached, and died to provide.

c. The Lost Coin (15:8-10)

8 Or what woman having ten pieces of silver, if she lose one piece, doth not light a lamp, and sweep the house, and seek diligently until she find it? 9 And when she hath found it, she calleth together her friends and neighbors, saying, Rejoice with me, for I have found the piece which I had lost. 10 Even so, I say unto you, there is joy in the presence of the angels of God over one sinner that repenteth.

This brief but vivid story is attached closely to the preceding parable by the word **or,** as already noted. It portrays the same truth in another figure. Godet comments: "The idea common to both is the solicitude of God for sinners; the difference is, that in the first instance this solicitude arises from the compassion with which their *misery* inspires Him, in the second from the *value* which He attaches to their persons."[326]

The **pieces of silver** were drachmas. The drachma (named only here in the New Testament) was the basic Greek silver coin and was approximately equal in value to the Roman denarius (mentioned often in the Gospels). Each was

---

[321] The thought of God as Shepherd appears prominently in the Psalms and the Prophets (e.g., Ps. 23; 80:1; Isa. 40:11; Jer. 31:10; Ezek. 34:12; 37:24; Zech. 8:7).
[322] *Op. cit.,* p. 289.   [323] Plummer, *op. cit.,* p. 368.   [324] *Op. cit.,* pp. 144, 145.
[325] *Op. cit.,* p. 303.   [326] *Op. cit.,* p. 144.

worth somewhere between fifteen and twenty cents, but represented a day's wage (Matthew 20:2). So the woman's loss of her "shilling" or "quarter" would be like our loss of a twenty-dollar bill.

The distracted woman will do three things: **light a lamp** — not a "candle" (KJV), but a small clay oil-burning lamp — **sweep the house** — probably a dirt floor — and **seek diligently until she find it.** The picture is that of the Holy Spirit, through the Spirit-filled Church, lighting the lamp of God's Word (Psa. 119:103, 130), sweeping even the corners, seeking diligently to find every lost individual.

Trench makes a significant observation at this point: "In the preceding parable the shepherd went to look for his strayed sheep *in the wilderness;* but *in the house* this piece of money is lost, and in the house therefore it is sought and found."[327] This reminds us of the fact that our children may be lost right in our homes — still participating in family worship, perhaps, but without Christ in their hearts. Also, people may be lost right in our churches — attending Sunday School and regular services, but unsaved. The challenge to every Christian is to be concerned about such persons and to seek definitely the salvation of their souls.

As did the shepherd of the previous parable, the woman, when she finds the lost coin, calls together her **friends** and **neighbors.** But, as might be expected, the words here are in the feminine gender in the Greek, not masculine as in the Parable of the Lost Sheep. A. B. Bruce points out a possible implication of this: "The finding would appeal specially to feminine sympathies if the lost drachma was not part of a hoard to meet some debt, but belonged to a string of coins worn as an ornament round the head, then as now, by married women in the East."[328]

Again it is declared that there is **joy in the presence of the angels of God over one sinner that repenteth** (v. 10). This joy is reflected in the hearts of the saints on earth when a sinner is converted. One of the greatest thrills that can come to any human individual is to have a burden for a lost soul and then see that individual surrender to Christ. And what rejoicing it causes in a church when a sinner is saved.

d. The Lost Son (15:11-32)

11 And he said, A certain man had two sons: 12 and the younger of them said to his father, Father, give me the portion of *thy* substance that falleth to me. And he divided unto them his living. 13 And not many days after, the younger son gathered all together and took his journey into a far country; and there he wasted his substance with riotous living. 14 And when he had spent all, there arose a mighty famine in that country; and he began to be in want. 15 And he went and joined himself to one of the citizens of that country; and he sent him into his fields to feed swine. 16 And he would fain have filled his belly with the husks that the swine did eat: and no man gave unto him. 17 But when he came to himself he said, How many hired servants of my father's have bread enough and to spare, and I perish here with hunger! 18 I will arise and go to my father, and will say unto him, Father, I have sinned against heaven, and in thy sight: 19 I am no more worthy to be called thy son: make me as one of thy hired servants. 20 And he arose, and came to his father. But while he was yet afar off, his father saw him, and was moved with compassion, and ran, and fell on his neck, and kissed him. 21 And the son said unto him, Father, I have sinned against heaven, and in thy sight: I am no more worthy to be called thy son. 22 But the father said to his servants, Bring forth quickly the best robe, and put it on him; and put a ring on his hand, and shoes on his feet: 23 and bring the fatted calf, *and* kill it, and let us eat, and make merry: 24 for this my son was dead, and is alive again; he was lost, and is found. And they began to be merry. 25 Now his elder son was in the field: and as he came and drew nigh to the house, he heard music and dancing. 26 And he called to him one of the servants, and inquired what these things might be. 27 And he said unto him, Thy brother is come; and thy father hath killed the fatted calf, because he hath received him safe and sound. 28 But he was angry, and would not go in: and his father came out, and entreated him. 29 But he answered and said to his father, Lo, these many years do I serve thee, and I never transgressed a commandment of thine; and *yet* thou never gavest me a kid, that I might make merry with my friends: 30 but when this thy son came, who hath devoured thy living with harlots, thou killedst for him the fatted calf. 31 And he said unto him,

---

[327] *Op. cit.,* p. 296. [328] EGT, I, 579.

Son, thou art ever with me, and all that is mine is thine. 32 But it was meet to make merry and be glad: for this thy brother was dead, and is alive *again;* and *was* lost, and is found.

This is sometimes called the Parable of the Two Sons. For while verses 11-24 describe the younger of the two, verses 25-32 deal with the older brother. Also the opening words are: **A certain man had two sons.** The parable seems to have a twofold purpose: (1) to show that God's love stands ready to restore the lowest sinner who will repent and return to Father's house; (2) to picture the Pharisees in their harsh lack of love for repentant sinners. A. B. Bruce points out the relationship of this parable to the previous two in this way: "These two parables showed the Pharisees how they ought to have acted towards Jesus as the friend of the publicans and sinners. The third parable assails them in another way, not by showing them how they ought to have acted, but by showing them how they did act."[329] As Lang says, "Here the scribes and Pharisees are made to see themselves."[330]

Probably more sermons have been preached on this parable than on any other in the Bible. The figure of the Prodigal Son has universal appeal. In all lands and in all ages there have been prodigal sons. A Greek papyrus letter from the second century A.D. has striking parallels to this parable. In this letter, a young man says that he prays daily for his mother's health. But he is ashamed to come home, "because I walk about in rags. . . .I beseech thee, mother, be reconciled to me. Furthermore I know what I have brought upon myself. I have been chastened . . . . I know that I have sinned."[331] The letter abounds in significant words found in the Greek New Testament.

The first part of the parable (vv. 11-24 lends itself to a simple outline: (1) the Possessor (vv. 11, 12); (2) the Prodigal (v. 13); (3) the Pauper (vv. 14-16); (4) the Penitent (vv. 17-19); (5) the Pardoned (vv. 20-24).

The story begins with the **younger** son asking for his portion of the family estate (v.12). In response the father divided

unto them — both sons — **his living.** The older son would get two-thirds and the younger son one-third (Deut. 21:17). The expression **the portion . . . . that falleth to me** is "a technical formula . . . . in the Papyri" for a son receiving his share of "the paternal inheritance."[332] Creed notes further: "Besides testamentary disposition of property, later Jewish law recognized disposition by gift in the man's life-time."[333] But the author of the apocryphal Ecclesiasticus (33:19-23, Goodspeed) warns against doing this. He says: "To a son or a wife, to a brother or a friend, Do not give power over yourself as long as you live, and, do not give your money to someone else. . . . When the days of your life reach their end, at the time of your death distribute your property."

Soon after the distribution was made, the younger son **gathered all together,** went into a **far country** — to get away from his father's authority — and there **wasted his substance with riotous living** (v. 13) — literally, "living prodigally." Abbott-Smith says that the Greek word (only here in the New Testament) indicates "wastefully," but "not necessarily dissolute."[334] On the other hand, Arndt and Gingrich give "dissolutely, loosely."[335] It is evident that the exact meaning cannot be known with certainty. Probably Manson gives the best conclusion when he says: "The Greek adverb translated 'with riotous living' may mean that he spent his money 'extravagantly,' or that he spent it on dissolute pleasures, or both."[336] However, common sense suggests that a young man far away from home and wasting his family inheritance would not be apt to live a circumspect life.

One day the prodigal found himself with an empty purse — and an empty soul. A famine in that land compelled him to **feed swine** (v. 15) for a living. So hungry was he that he envied the hogs their diet of **husks** (v. 16) — that is, "pods of the carob tree."

In Jewish thinking, this young prodigal had "hit bottom." The Talmud has this saying: "Cursed is the man who rears swine, and cursed is the man who teaches his son Greek philosophy."[337] Another

---

[329] *Parabolic Teaching,* p. 263.   [330] *Op. cit.,* p. 251.   [331] Deissmann, LAE, p. 188.
[332] Deissmann, *Bible Studies,* p. 230.   [333] *Op. cit.,* p. 198.   [334] *Op. cit.,* p. 66.
[335] *Op. cit.,* p. 119.   [336] T. W. Manson, *op. cit.,* p. 579.   [337] *Ibid.,* p. 580.

rabbinical saying is this: "When the Israelites are reduced to eating carobpods, then they repent"; and still another: "When a son (abroad) goes barefoot (through poverty), then he remembers the comfort of his father's house."[338] So it was with the prodigal.

He came to himself (v. 17), is the literal Greek, and also good Latin and English idiom, meaning "came to his senses." He had been acting insanely; but sin is insanity.

Contrasting his destitute condition with the plenty which his father's servants enjoyed, the Prodigal Son decided that he would go home. He planned carefully the speech of penitence that he would make (vv. 18, 19). **Against heaven** means "against God," the Jews preferring to avoid using the sacred name. **In thy sight** means "against thee."

But good resolutions will never save anyone. Too many stop at that point. But this young man **arose** and **came to his father** (v. 20). Both verbs — the first is a participle — are in the aorist tense. There was no delay, no "dawdling." Immediately, with decision and determination, he headed back home.

The welcome he received far exceeded his fondest hopes. While he was still coming — just as God meets the repentant sinner more than half way — the father ran to meet him and gave him the kiss of forgiveness. The son tried to make his speech (v. 21). But the father stopped him.[339] He commanded his servants: **Bring forth quickly the best robe, and put it on him.** This is literally, "the first robe"; that is, the one of highest quality. Concerning **quickly** (not in KJV), A. B. Bruce writes: "*Tachu,* quick! a most probable reading (Aleph BL), and a most natural exclamation; obliterate the traces of the wretched past as soon as possible; off with these rags!"[340]

Besides the best robe, the servants were to put **a ring on his hand.** This was the sign and symbol of the fact that he was once more in the family. But it indicated more than that. Probably this was the father's official signet ring, with which he stamped the soft sealing wax on letters and goods he sent. Giving the son the ring may have meant that he was thereby authorized to do business again in his father's name. If so, nothing could show more dramatically the fact that the son was now fully a member of the family. Here is a picture of the complete, unlimited forgiveness which God gives to every penitent sinner.

But one thing more was necessary — **shoes on his feet.** The young man was not to sit around the house, where no shoes were worn, but to go to work. One of the surest ways to save new converts from backsliding is to set them to work doing something useful. Work is one of God's best gifts to man. Without it, almost all men would be ruined. Work has high therapeutic value — physically, mentally, morally, emotionally, and spiritually.

Having clothed his son properly, the father now ordered the servants to prepare the best feast possible. They were to kill the **fatted calf** (v. 23); that is, the one that had been fed in the stall (cf. Amos 6:4; Mal. 4:2), and reserved for just such an occasion as this. What greater event to celebrate than the fact that his son who was dead, is **alive again,** who was lost, is **found.**

In the midst of all the merriment, the older son came in from the field. As he approached the house he heard **music and dancing** (v. 25) — in those days the men and women danced separately. Calling one of the servants, he inquired what was going on. When told, **he was angry** (v. 28), and refused to join the celebration. His father went out to him, and **entreated him.**[341] Angry and sullen, the older son gave vent to his feelings in a very unlovely and unloving tirade. He showed that he was far from being a true son of his generous-hearted father.

It is noticeable that the older brother said **this thy son** (v. 30) — "this son of yours," said comtemptuously. He put the very worst construction possible on the younger son's actions while away from home.

But the father reversed the situation. He said, **Son** — not the word for "son" in the previous verse, but literally,

---

[338] *Ibid.*
[339] The last clause of verse 19 is found at this point in some of the oldest manuscripts, and may be genuine.   [340] EGT, I, 582.
[341] Literally, "was entreating him." The Greek suggests that the older brother interrupted his father. He had built up so much pressure inside that he exploded.

"child," an endearing term — **thou art ever with me** — all the family privileges have been yours all the time — **and all that is mine is thine** — your inheritance is safe. Furthermore, you could have had a feast with your friends at any time. But it is obvious that the elder brother was not the kind who could have enjoyed such festivities. He is a type of those in church circles who live outwardly above reproach, who are faithful in doing their duty, but who endure their religion instead of enjoying it. Their harsh, unloving legalism makes them, as well as those around them, unhappy. The older son, too, was lost — at home.

9. Stewardship (16:1-31)

a. Parable of the Unjust Steward (16:1-13)

1 And he said also unto the disciples, There was a certain rich man, who had a steward; and the same was accused unto him that he was wasting his goods. 2 And he called him, and said unto him, What is this that I hear of thee? render the account of thy stewardship; for thou canst be no longer steward. 3 And the steward said within himself, What shall I do, seeing that my lord taketh away the stewardship from me? I have not strength to dig; to beg I am ashamed. 4 I am resolved what to do, that, when I am put out of the stewardship, they may receive me into their houses. 5 And calling to him each one of his lord's debtors, he said to the first, How much owest thou unto my lord? 6 And he said, A hundred measures of oil. And he said unto him, Take thy bond, and sit down quickly and write fifty. 7 Then said he to another, And how much owest thou? And he said, A hundred measures of wheat. He saith unto him, Take thy bond, and write fourscore. 8 And his lord commended the unrighteous steward because he had done wisely: for the sons of this world are for their own generation wiser than the sons of the light. 9 And I say unto you, Make to yourselves friends by means of the mammon of unrighteousness; that, when it shall fail, they may receive you into the eternal tabernacles. 10 He that is faithful in a very little is faithful also in much: and he that is unrighteous in a very little is unrighteous also in much. 11 If therefore ye have not been faithful in the unrighteous mammon, who will commit to your trust the true *riches?* 12 And if ye have not been faithful in that which is another's, who will give you that which is your own? 13 No servant can serve two masters: for either he will hate the one, and love the other; or else he will hold to one, and despise the other. Ye cannot serve God and mammon.

This is one of the many parables found only in Luke. Like the several that precede it, it is anti-Pharisaic in emphasis. Thus it forms a part of the inevitable conflict between divine love and human legalism. Of the stories in this chapter Plummer says: "These two parables, like the previous three, are directed against special faults of the Pharisees. The former three combated their hard exclusiveness, self-righteousness, and contempt for others. These two combat their self-indulgence."[342]

The interpretation of this parable is admittedly difficult. Farrar writes: "No parable has been more diversely and multitudinously explained than this." But he goes on to say: "We *cannot* be wrong if we seize as the *main* lesson of the parable, the one which Christ Himself attached to it (8-12), namely, the use of earthly gifts of wealth and opportunity for heavenly and not for earthly aims."[343] In other words, just as the unjust steward made use of present opportunities to provide for the future, so the follower of Christ should use the material things of this life in helping to provide for the next life. One cannot purchase salvation with money. But what one does with his money will have much to do with the ultimate salvation of his soul. Trench puts the matter very briefly: "I am persuaded that we have here simply a parable of Christian prudence, — Christ exhorting us to use the world and the world's good, so to speak, *against* the world, and *for* God."[344]

The **steward** was a sort of business manager for his master. The word literally means "house-manager." In those days stewards carried great responsibility and were held in high esteem.

This steward was accused to his master that he was **wasting** — same word as in 15:13 — **his goods.** So the master summoned and ordered him to give an ac-

[342] *Op. cit.*, p. 380.   [343] *Op. cit.*, p. 312.   [344] *Op. cit.*, p. 324.

counting of his stewardship, at the same time dismissing him from his position (v. 2).

The steward had to do some quick thinking. He was too weak to dig, too proud to beg (v. 3). Suddenly he had a "bright idea" — a plan by which he would make his master's many debtors obligated to him so that they would receive him into their houses (v. 4).

Summoning those who were in debt to his master, he asked each one how much he owed. Then he proceeded to discount a percentage from each bill — fifty per cent from one, twenty per cent from another, and so on probably clear down the line of all those who owed his master anything. It has been suggested that the reduced bills may have represented the correct amount, that the steward may have been "padding" them for his own profit. This kind of dishonesty was very common. If this was the case here, the master still received what was due him, but the debtors were now also in debt to show gratitude to the steward. A hundred measures [baths] of oil (v. 6), would amount to about 868 gallons. This seems like a large quantity of olive oil. But great amounts of it were consumed in those days when it was used with food, as a balm, and for fuel in clay lamps. A hundred measures [cors] of wheat (v. 7) would be about 1,086 bushels. Again the amount seems large. But wheat was the main staple of diet in that time.

Bond (vv. 6, 7) is better rendered "bill" (KJV, RSV). The Greek word is gramma, which first referred to letters of the alphabet (cf. "grammar") and then to written documents. Often, as here, the plural word is used for a single piece of writing. For this passage Arndt and Gingrich suggest "a promissory note."[345]

On the matter of changing the amounts on these notes or bills, Farrar makes this accurate observation: "Since Hebrew numerals were letters, and since Hebrew letters differed but slightly from each other, a very trivial forgery would represent a large difference."[346] This custom of using letters of the alphabet to represent numbers was followed in Hebrew, Greek, and Latin. The Arabs made a great contribution to mathematics by giving us separate symbols, the so-called Arabic numerals — which are much easier to read than the Roman (Latin) numerals in common use a few generations ago.

His lord commended the unrighteous steward (v. 8). This is clearer than "the lord" (KJV), which could be taken as meaning Christ. "The master" (RSV) is still better. It is true that A. B. Bruce does prefer identifying this lord with Jesus.[347] But in this he stands against the vast majority of commentators. The more general view is expressed by Farrar, when he writes: "The Lord is of course only the landlord of the parable."[348] Wisely "does not mean 'wisely' (a word which is used in a higher sense), but prudently."[349] On this most commentators agree. This was Wycliffe's translation and should have been followed.

The sons of this world (Greek, "age") means those who live for this world, who belong to this age, who do not live for eternity. Sons of light refers to those who have been enlightened by the Spirit of God, and who are walking in the light of His Word. What Jesus is saying is that worldly people are more farsighted and often more earnest in carrying on secular business than are the saints in doing the work of the Kingdom. This, of course, is not always true, but sometimes it is. Are we as eager, enthusiastic, and persistent in seeking to win people to Christ as successful salesmen are in closing deals? That is what Jesus was talking about, and it is an embarrassing question for most Christians.

Trench gives a good paraphrase for the last part of verse 8: "The children of this world are wiser in their generation (in worldly matters) than the children of light, in their, that is, in heavenly matters; the children of light being thus rebuked that they give not half the pains to win heaven which the children of this world do to win earth."[350]

After giving the parable (vv. 1-8), Jesus proceeded to make the application (vv. 9-13). Verse 9 seems on a first reading to be rather obscure. The expression mammon of unrighteousness perhaps suggests two things: (1) that wealth is often

---

[345] Op. cit., p. 164.   [346] Op. cit., p. 313.
[349] Ibid.   [350] Op. cit., p. 335.

[347] EGT, I, 585.   [348] Op. cit., p. 313.

accumulated by unjust means: (2) that its use is too often an abuse. On the meaning of Jesus' exhortation here Farrar comments: "We turn mammon into a friend, and make ourselves friends by its means, when we use riches not as our own to squander, but as God's to employ in deeds of usefulness and mercy."[351]

When it shall fail can be interpreted either of two ways: (1) when money fails you; (2) when you shall die. But actually these two become one in large measure. For it is at death that money fails for everyone, though it may fail earlier for some.

Who is meant by **they?** Geldenhuys suggests that the word designates those who have been benefited by our means. He asks the pertinent question: "Do we use our worldly possessions in such a manner that there will be persons in Eternity who will be glad to receive us?"[352] But he also states in an exegetical note, "The indefinite 'they' in this context is really a substitute for 'God,'" and quotes support for this from Strack-Billerbeck.[353]

Jesus continued to make the application. **Very little** and **much** (v. 10) seem to be explained as meaning **unrighteous mammon** and **true riches** (v. 11). The **very little** relates to this life, the **much** to the next. The same truth seems to be put in slightly different form in verse 12. **Another's** means God's, for everything we have here on earth belongs to Him, not to us. In a sense we shall enjoy in eternity what is our **own.**

The principle enunciated in verse 13 is paralleled in Matthew 6:24. It stresses the crucial truth that ultimately one can have only one master. Everyone has to choose between God and mammon. No one can serve both, though many try. One of the greatest curses of popular Christianity is that of divided loyalty.

b. Lovers of Money (16:14-17)

14 And the Pharisees, who were lovers of money, heard all these things; and they scoffed at him. 15 And he said unto them, Ye are they that justify yourselves in the sight of men; but God knoweth your hearts: for that which is exalted among men is an abomination in the sight of God. 16 The law and the proph-

ets *were* until John: from that time the gospel of the kingdom of God is preached, and every man entereth violently into it. 17 But it is easier for heaven and earth to pass away, than for one tittle of the law to fall.

While it appears that the Pharisees did not usually live in ostentatious wealth, as did the worldly, politically-minded Sadducees, yet here they are described as **lovers of money.** The meaning seems to be that they were covetous. Plummer says: "The covetousness of the Pharisees is independently attested, and they regarded their wealth as a special blessing for their carefulness in observing the Law."[354] When they heard Jesus talking about the right use of money, **they scoffed at him.** The Greek is literally, "they were turning up their noses at Him."

Jesus accused them of self-righteousness, of justifying themselves before men (v. 15). But God read their hearts. **That which is exalted among men is an abomination in the sight of God.**

The supreme example of this is the Pharisee who went up to the Temple to pray (18:9-14). He showed a conceited self-righteousness that although it may have been **exalted among men** was an **abomination in the sight of God.** Selecting a prominent place, where many could see and hear him, he sought to **justify** himself **in the sight of men** by reciting his virtues for all to hear, and telling God how much better he was than other men. This is religious pride at its worst, and this is the sort of thing that Jesus was attacking here.

Verse 16 is parallel to Matthew 11:13, 12 (see notes there). The statement that **the law and the prophets were until John** is a clear indication on the part of Jesus that the old dispensation had come to a close, and a new one was now beginning. **From that time** — the time of John the Baptist — **the gospel of the kingdom of God** (cf. Matt. 4:23; Mark 1:14) **is preached** — *evangelizetai*, "proclaimed as glad tidings" — **and every man entereth violently into it** — "is making *forcible* entrance into it." Farrar says: "The allusion is to the eagerness with which the message of the kingdom was

---

351 *Op. cit.*, p. 314.   352 *Op. cit.*, p. 417.   353 *Ibid.*, p. 419.   354 *Op. cit.*, pp. 387, 388.

accepted by the publicans and the people generally."[355]

On the surface there might seem to be no connection between verses 16 and 17. But Meyer suggests that "the announcement of the kingdom, and the general endeavor after the kingdom which had begun from the time of John, might easily throw upon Jesus the suspicion of putting back the old principle, that of law, into the shade."[356] But no, not one thing of the Law would fail.

Verse 17 is parallel to Matthew 5:18 (see notes there). The **tittle** (literally, "horn") refers to the tiny projection which distinguishes similar Hebrew letters of the alphabet. Some of these are so small that one has to look carefully to decide which letter is intended. The rabbis declared that if one of these little horns was changed on a letter in the Law, the world would be destroyed.[357] This reflects the undue veneration the Jews gave to the exact letter of the Law, while they missed its spirit. But we may be thankful for the extreme care in copying the Old Testament Scriptures which resulted from this attitude.

Jesus declared that not the least item in the Law would **fall**; that is, fail of fulfillment (cf. Matt. 5:18 — "till all these things be accomplished"). The Christian does not have to keep all the ceremonial requirements of the Mosaic law because they have been fulfilled in Christ and His atoning death. By accepting Him and living in Him we fulfill the real purpose of the Law.

c. Divorce (16:18)

18 Every one that putteth away his wife, and marrieth another, committeth adultery: and he that marrieth one that is put away from a husband committeth adultery.

This seems to have no connection with what precedes or follows, but rather to stand as an isolated saying. But Plummer suggests a solution: "Perhaps this introduces an example of the durability of the moral law in spite of human evasions. Adultery remains adultery even when it has been legalized, and legalized by men who jealously guarded every fraction of the letter, while they flagrantly

violated the spirit of the Law."[358] The crowning example was Rabbi Hillel's interpretation of Deuteronomy 24:1, permitting a man to divorce his wife if she did a bad job of cooking his dinner.

The question of divorce was an important topic in the teaching of Jesus. He touched on it a number of times (cf. Matt. 5:32; 19:9 Mark 10:11 — and the notes on those passages).

d. The Rich Man and Lazarus (16: 19-31)

19 Now there was a certain rich man, and he was clothed in purple and fine linen, faring sumptuously every day: 20 and a certain beggar named Lazarus was laid at his gate, full of sores, 21 and desiring to be fed with the *crumbs* that fell from the rich man's table; yea, even the dogs came and licked his sores. 22 And it came to pass, that the beggar died, and that he was carried away by the angels into Abraham's bosom: and the rich man also died, and was buried. 23 And in Hades he lifted up his eyes, being in torments, and seeth Abraham afar off, and Lazarus in his bosom. 24 And he cried and said, Father Abraham, have mercy on me, and send Lazarus, that he may dip the tip of his finger in water, and cool my tongue; for I am in anguish in this flame. 25 But Abraham said, Son, remember that thou in thy lifetime receivedst thy good things, and Lazarus in like manner evil things: but now here he is comforted, and thou art in anguish. 26 And besides all this, between us and you there is a great gulf fixed, that they that would pass from hence to you may not be able, and that none may cross over from thence to us. 27 And he said, I pray thee therefore, father, that thou wouldest send him to my father's house; 28 for I have five brethren; that he may testify unto them, lest they also come into this place of torment. 29 But Abraham saith, They have Moses and the prophets; let them hear them. 30 And he said, Nay, father Abraham: but if one go to them from the dead, they will repent. 31 And he said unto him, If they hear not Moses and the prophets, neither will they be persuaded, if one rise from the dead.

It is sometimes debated as to whether this story is a parable or not. Some object that to treat it as such would weaken

---

[355] *Op. cit.* p. 316.   [356] *Op. cit.*, p. 473.   [357] Edersheim, *op. cit.*, I, 538.
[358] *Op. cit.*, p. 389.

its doctrinal force. But that is illogical thinking. A parable has to be true to life, or it is a fable, not a parable. This one begins with the same introductory phrase as the Parable of the Unjust Steward — there was a certain rich man (cf. v. 1). Almost all commentators, both conservative and liberal, label this a parable. Geldenhuys writes: "Although Luke does not expressly state that this is a parable and although the Saviour has given the beggar a name, it is by no means necessary to assume that we have here the story of something that really happened and not a parable."[359]

In this story Jesus picks up again His emphasis on the right use of money. He had dealt with this in the Parable of the Unjust Steward and its application (vv. 1-13). The Pharisees are labeled "lovers of money" (v. 14). Now the Master gives the vivid illustration of a man who misused his money for self-indulgence.

The rich man is described as clothed in purple and fine linen, faring sumptuously every day (v. 19). This man is often referred to as Dives, which is simply the Latin for "a rich man." The Greek word for purple was used first for the *murex*, or purple fish, and then for the dye made from the fish. It was very expensive, because so scarce. Lydia is called "a seller of purple" (Acts 16: 14), and she was evidently a prosperous business woman, for she kept the whole missionary party at her house. The Greek word for fine linen was first used for Egyptian flax and then for the expensive linen made from it. This refers to the under garment, while purple indicated the outer robe.

Faring sumptuously every day is literally, "making merry every day, splendidly." For this man life was one long, gay party. What a contrast to his life after death!

At the gate (high, ornamented portico) of the rich man's mansion there had been laid (pluperfect passive) a beggar named Lazarus. Perhaps his name is given because it means "God has helped." He was full of sores, (an expression only here in New Testament). It was "the regular medical term for 'to be ulcerated.'"[360]

The beggar was desiring to be fed with the leftovers from the rich man's table (v. 21). How well his desire was met we are not told. The only ones who took pity on him were the dogs, who licked his sores, perhaps out of pity.

Finally, the beggar died (v. 22). Nothing is said about a funeral or burial. But he had angels for pallbearers. They carried him into Abraham's bosom. Plummer says: "Lazarus in Sheol reposes with his head on Abraham's breast, as a child in his father's lap, and shares his happiness." He adds: "The expression is not common in Jewish writings; but Abraham is sometimes represented as welcoming the penitent into paradise."[361]

Finally the time came when the rich man also died — as all men must — and was buried. With what pomp and ceremony this was done can well be imagined. But no mention is made of angels.

The rich man found himself in Hades — the equivalent of the Hebrew *Sheol*. Arndt and Gingrich say of Hades: "(originally proper noun, name of god of the underworld), *the underworld* as the place of the dead."[362] That it does not always mean a place of torment seems indicated in Acts 2:27, 31 and I Cor. 15:55, where it is translated "grave" (KJV). But Laird Harris makes this observation: "The New Testament sometimes has the Old Jewish usage of Hades for Sheol, 'the grave,' but sometimes as in Luke 16:23 and probably in Matthew 11:23 and Luke 10:15 it shows an advanced terminology referring to the place of punishment of the wicked dead."[363]

At any rate, the rich man was in Hades and he was in torments. Seeing Abraham afar off and Lazarus in his bosom, he cried for help. Even a drop of cold water on his tongue would ease the awful agony and anguish.

In reply Abraham reminded the rich man that in his lifetime he enjoyed good things, while Lazarus endured evil things (v. 25). Now their positions were reversed. The next life will right the wrongs of this life. In the end justice will triumph. That is the consolation that all the afflicted and oppressed people of God have in this world.

[359] *Op. cit.*, p. 428.   [360] Hobart, *op. cit.*, p. 31.   [361] *Op. cit.*, p. 393.   [362] *Op. cit.*, p. 16.
[363] R. Laird Harris, "The Meaning of the Word Sheol as Shown by Parallels in Poetic Texts," *Bulletin of the Evangelical Theological Society*, IV (1961), 129.

But there was a **great gulf** fixed between Paradise and Torment, so that Lazarus could not minister to the suffering man's needs (v. 26). Despairing of any help for himself, the man asked that Lazarus be sent to warn his five brothers, so that they would not **come into this place of torment** (v. 28). When Abraham answered that they had **Moses and the prophets** — the Scriptures, which would give them sufficient warnings, if they would **hear them** (v. 29) — the rich man argued that if one went **from the dead, they will repent** (v. 30). Then Abraham made the significant statement: **If they hear not Moses and the prophets, neither will they be persuaded, if one rise from the dead** (v. 31). This truth is strikingly confirmed and illlustrated by the case of a Lazarus who did rise from the dead. What was the attitude of the Jewish leaders toward him? "But the chief priests took counsel that they might put Lazarus also to death; because that by reason of him many of the Jews went away, and believed on Jesus" (John 11:10, 11). This is ample evidence that if people will not listen to the Word of God, the written Scriptures, they would not be convinced by any miracle. Unbelief is primarily a moral rather than mental matter. In most cases people do not believe because they *will* not believe.

10. Forgiveness and Faith (17:1-10)

a. Forgiveness (17:1-4)

1 And he said unto his disciples, It is impossible but that occasions of stumbling should come; but woe unto him, through whom they come! 2 It were well for him if a millstone were hanged about his neck, and he were thrown into the sea, rather than that he should cause one of these little ones to stumble. 3 Take heed to yourselves: if thy brother sin, rebuke him; and if he repent, forgive him. 4 And if he sin against thee seven times in the day, and seven times turn again to thee, saying, I repent; thou shalt forgive him.

Parallels to this paragraph are found in Matthew 18:7, 6, 15, 21, 22 and Mark 9:42. Jesus is warning against two things: (1) causing others to stumble; (2) having an unforgiving spirit.

The Master declared that **occasions of stumbling** will inevitably come (v. 1), but that it was better to be drowned in the sea than to **cause** another to

stumble (v. 2). The noun is *skandalon*, the verb *skandalizo*. The former is found only here in Luke (though five times in Matthew); the latter occurs also in 7:23 (14 times in Matthew, 8 in Mark). For the meaning of these significant terms see the notes on Matthew 18:6. All three Synoptic Gospels give in graphic language Jesus' warning against causing **one of these little ones to stumble** (v. 2). This calls for careful, consistent Christian living. No wonder that Christ said: **Take heed to yourselves** (v. 3). This should go with the first two verses as the climax of the warning.

The language of the first part of verse 2 is very vivid. Literally it reads: "It is profitable for him if a millstone is hanging around his neck and he has been hurled into the sea (and is still lying there)." Christ could hardly have used stronger words to describe the awfulness of causing even **one** (emphatic in Greek) of **these little ones** (weak believers) to stumble. This is a warning which we cannot and must not ignore.

If one's **brother** (fellow believer) sins, one should **rebuke him** (v. 3). That this is not to be done publicly is shown by the parallel passage: "Go, show him his fault between thee and him alone" (Matthew 18:15). And that it should be done in the spirit of love and humility is indicated in Galatians 6:1 — "Brethren, even if a man be overtaken in any trespass, ye who are spiritual, restore such a one in a spirit of gentleness; looking to thyself, lest thou also be tempted."

The important second step is: **and if he repent, forgive him.** This suggests that forgiveness is based on repentance. God cannot forgive the sinner until he repents.

Even if one's brother should sin against him seven times **in the day** (only Luke), and seven times say, **I repent, he is to be forgiven** (v. 4). This is Luke's way of summarizing the conversation between Peter and Jesus in Matthew 18:21, 22. By **seven times** is meant unlimited forgiveness.

b. Faith (17:5-10)

5 And the apostles said unto the Lord, Increase our faith. 6 And the Lord said, If ye had faith as a grain of mustard seed, ye would say unto this sycamine tree, Be thou rooted up, and be thou

planted in the sea; and it would obey you. 7 But who is there of you, having a servant plowing or keeping sheep, that will say unto him, when he is come in from the field, Come straightway and sit down to meat; 8 and will not rather say unto him, Make ready wherewith I may sup, and gird thyself, and serve me, till I have eaten and drunken; and afterward thou shalt eat and drink? 9 Doth he thank the servant because he did the things that were commanded? 10 Even so ye also, when ye shall have done all the things that are commanded you, say, We are unprofitable servants; we have done that which it was our duty to do.

The foregoing command of Christ staggered the **apostles** — the word occurs only once each in Matthew (10:2) and Mark (6:30), but six times in Luke (see notes on 5:17; 7:13). **Increase our faith.** The disciples felt that they needed greater faith to appropriate more grace if they were going to meet such a demand. But **the Lord** replied that if they had faith as a tiny grain of mustard seed — — a proverbial expression for what is smallest — they could say to **this sycamine tree** (black mulberry) — evidently pointing to one nearby — **Be thou rooted up** (instantly, aorist tense), **and it would obey you.** T. W. Manson well says: "This word of Jesus does not invite Christians to become conjurers and magicians, but heroes like those whose exploits are celebrated in the eleventh chapter of Hebrews."[364]

Verses 7-10 are often called the Parable of the Unprofitable Servant. It is obvious that Jesus is not now talking primarily to His disciples (v. 1), because He says, **who is there of you** (v. 7). The disciples did not have **a servant** (literally, "a slave") **plowing or keeping sheep.**

Straightway is properly placed with **come.** The King James Version puts it with "say," and furthermore translates it "by and by." The original meaning of this phrase was "immediately," but now it means the opposite. The same thing has happened to a number of other words and phrases in the King James Version. This shows the absolute necessity for having an up-to-date translation of the Bible if we are going to know accurately what the Word of God actually says.

Sit down to meat is in the Greek "recline (to eat)."

The master does not say to his slave: "You recline at the table, and I will serve you." Rather he says: "Prepare something for my dinner, put on an apron, and serve me." Jesus is simply calling attention to the custom of the times, not endorsing the master-slave relationship. Then He makes the application: When you have done everything commanded you, say that you are **unprofitable servants** (v. 10) — meaning that you have "made no profit" for your master. "The point is that man can make no just **claim** for having done **more** than was due."[365] God is never in debt to us; we are always in debt to Him.

Plummer summarizes the "four sayings of Christ" in verses 1-10 as follows: "The Sin of Causing Others to Sin (1, 2); The Duty of Forgiveness (3, 4); The Power of Faith (5,6); and, The Insufficiency of Works (7-10)."[366] He notes also the distinction between "the severity of vv. 1 and 2, 'when thou sinnest against another,' and the tenderness of vv. 3 and 4, 'when others sin against thee.'"[367]

G. JOURNEY TO JERUSALEM (17:11-19:28)

1. Healing of Ten Lepers (17:11-19)

11 And it came to pass, as they were on their way to Jerusalem, that he was passing along the borders of Samaria and Galilee. 12 And as he entered into a certain village, there met him ten men that were lepers, who stood afar off: 13 and they lifted up their voices, saying, Jesus, Master, have mercy on us. 14 and when he saw them, he said unto them, Go and show yourselves unto the priests. And it came to pass, as they went, they were cleansed. 15 And one of them, when he saw that he was healed, turned back, with a loud voice glorifying God; 16 and he fell upon his face at his feet, giving him thanks: and he was a Samaritan. 17 And Jesus answering said, Were not the ten cleansed? but where are the nine? 18 Were there none found that returned to give glory to God, save this stranger? 19 And he said unto him, Arise, and go thy way: thy faith hath made thee whole.

This incident is found only in Luke. It happened as Jesus and His disciples were **on the way to Jerusalem** for the

[364] Op. cit., p. 433.   [365] Plummer, op. cit., p. 402.   [366] Ibid., p. 398.   [367] Ibid., p. 399.

climax and completion of the Master's ministry (cf. 9:51; 13:22).

Along the borders of Samaria and Galilee (v. 11) is much better than "through the midst of Samaria and Galilee" (KJV). The latter would suggest that they were going northward from Jerusalem through Samaria into Galilee. But this verse distinctly says that they were on the way to Jerusalem. Actually they were going "between" (*dia* in its original sense) Samaria and Galilee, heading eastward to cross the Jordan and go down the east side of the river, so as to avoid passing through the unclean, unfriendly territory of the Samaritans. This suggests a fresh beginning for the journey to Jerusalem, rather than its third stage. The chronological and geographical sequence is not maintained. Apparently Luke did not consider it important. Farrar suggests: "The most natural place chronologically for this incident would have been after ix. 57. St. Luke places it here to contrast man's thanklessness to God which is asserted by spiritual pride"[368] (cf. v. 9).

As Jesus entered a village in this area, He was met by ten lepers, **who stood afar off.** This separation was required by the Law (Lev. 13:45, 46). They called loudly to Him: **Master** [*epistata*], **have mercy on us** (v. 13). No one else could help them.

In reply Jesus said: **Go and show yourselves unto the priests** (v. 14). Only the priest could legally pronounce them clean (Lev. 13). **But while they went, they were cleansed.** Blessing came in the path of obedience, as it always does.

One of the ten, when he saw that he was healed, returned to Jesus, **with a loud voice glorifying God** (v. 15) — a typically Lukan expression. He fell on his face at Christ's feet, thanking Him; **and he was a Samaritan** (v. 16). Once more Luke places the foreigner in a good light, as he does in the Parable of the Good Samaritan. This was part of his emphasis on God's interest in the Gentiles as well as the Jews.

Jesus asked: **But where are the nine?** (v. 17). That question still stands as a constant reproach to all who fail to thank the Lord for His many blessings. Unthankfulness is one of the most prevalent and yet most inexcusable sins of humanity.

The one who returned to give thanks received a double blessing, as always happens to those who praise God for His goodness. Jesus said to him: **Thy faith hath made thee whole** (v. 19). This could be translated, "has saved you." The verb is *sozo*, which is generally used to express physical healing in the Gospels and spiritual salvation in the Epistles. It is not definitely stated that this thankful Samaritan received a spiritual blessing — healing of soul as well as body — but this may probably be inferred from Jesus' words. No one ever thanks God without receiving more for which to thank Him.

2. The Coming of the Kingdom (17: 20-37)

a. The Nature of the Kingdom (17: 20, 21)

20 And being asked by the Pharisees, when the kingdom of God cometh, he answered them and said, The kingdom of God cometh not with observation: 21 neither shall they say, Lo, here! or, There! for lo, the kingdom of God is within you.

The Pharisees asked Jesus when the Kingdom of God was coming. They were looking, as were the disciples, for an earthly, outward, visible kingdom. As is the case with all who expect that kind of a kingdom, they were interested in dates. Christ's answer was: **The kingdom of God cometh not with observation** (v. 20); "that is, in such a way that its rise can be observed."[369] The Greek word for **observation** is found only here in the New Testament. It was employed "to denote medical observation of disease."[370] The meaning of Jesus' reply is: "There will be no such signs as would enable a watcher to date the arrival. A spiritual kingdom is slow in producing conspicuous material effects; and it begins in ways that cannot be dated."[371]

The first part of verse 21 looks like a flat contradiction of verse 23. Rather obviously the meaning here is that no one can *rightly* or *reasonably* say this. Verse 23 indicates that some will say it, though not on good grounds.

[368] *Op. cit.*, p. 323. [369] Ardt and Gingrich, *op. cit.*, p. 628. [370] Hobart, *op. cit.*, p. 153.
[371] Plummer, *op. cit.*, p. 405.

In opposition to the **Lo, here!** or, **There!** Jesus asserted **lo, the kingdom of God is within you.** The last two words have been discussed endlessly. The translation here (same in KJV, Goodspeed, Weymouth, Williams) means that the Kingdom is inward and spiritual, not outward and political. But the Greek words can be translated "among you" (NEB) or "in the midst of you" (RSV; cf. Berkeley, Moffatt — "in your midst"). Geldenhuys writes: "*Entos hymon* should, according to the ordinary and natural use of *entos,* be translated by 'within you' . . . . Nevertheless there are instances in the Classics . . . . where it means 'among you.' "[372] Liddell and Scott give as the primary classical meaning of *entos,* "within, inside."[373] Phillips adopted the second, stronger word ("inside") for his translation.

Geldenhuys states his position emphatically. He says: "The contention of some critics that the Saviour by these words taught that the kingdom of God is merely an inner, spiritual condition in the human heart, must very definitely be rejected."[374] Creed agrees that while "within" is probably the "most natural interpretation of *entos* for a Greek," yet "among" is "more easily harmonized with the general usage of the Gospels than the interpretation 'within you.' "[375] He ends up by leaving the matter somewhat undecided.

So does Plummer. After noting that usage will permit either translation, "within" or "among," he says: "The latter seems to suit the context better; for the kingdom of God was not in the hearts of the Pharisees, who are the persons addressed."[376] However, after further discussion he concludes: "But this rendering of *entos* lacks confirmation in *Scripture,* and the context is not *decisive* against the other."[377] It should be noted that although Jesus was addressing the Pharisees, He could have meant "within people's hearts." It is difficult to escape the impression that He was primarily emphasizing the spiritual nature of the Kingdom.

Meyer contends that the idea of the Kingdom as an internal "ethical condition" is *"modern,* not historico-biblical."[378] Farrar disputes this statement, but still prefers "among you." He concludes: "But in either case our Lord implied that His Kingdom had *already* come while they were straining their eyes forward in curious observation."[379]

T. W. Manson admits that the proper meaning of *entos* is "within." But after discussing the possible Aramaic background he says: "The Kingdom of God is not here under discussion as a state of mind or a disposition of men. It is thought of as something which is to come." He concludes: "The whole weight of the teaching of Jesus elsewhere seems to be in favour of saying, 'Lo, the Kingdom of God is among you.' "[380]

Alford argues definitely for "among you." However, he does say: "The meaning 'among you' includes of course the deeper and personal one 'within each of you,' but the two are not convertible."[381]

It should be recognized that "within you," meaning "in your hearts," was the popular (though not universal) interpretation among the early Church Fathers, as also in the Reformation period (Erasmus, Luther, Calvin).

A slightly variant rendering has been recently suggested by Roberts. He argues from the evidence of the papyri that the Greek could mean "in your possession" — if you want it (cf. NEB margin). However, he states that "there is hardly a modern theologian" who does not favor "among."[382]

Conzelmann thinks the exact meaning of *entos* "is not as important as is often supposed. Whether we take the word to mean 'intra' or 'inter,' it does not vitally affect Luke's conception of eschatology."[383]

Perrin favors "among you." He declares that "if the word is to be translated 'within,' then we have here an understanding of Kingdom of God without further parallel in the recorded teaching of Jesus."[384]

[372] *Op. cit.,* p. 443.   [373] *Op. cit.,* p. 577.   [374] *Op. cit.,* p. 443.   [375] *Op. cit.,* p. 219.
[376] *Op. cit.,* p. 406.   [377] *Ibid.*   [378] *Op. cit.,* p. 491.   [379] *Op. cit.,* p. 325.
[380] *Op. cit.,* p. 596.   [381] *Op. cit.,* I, 610.
[382] C. H. Roberts, "The Kingdom of Heaven (Luke 17:21)," *Harvard Theological Review,* XLI (Jan., 1948), p. 1.
[383] Hans Conzelmann, *The Theology of St. Luke,* trans. Geoffrey Buswell, p. 124.
[384] Norman Perrin, *The Kingdom of God in the Teaching of Jesus,* pp. 175, 176.

Lundstrom also adopts "among you." He writes: "What is new about Jesus is that He preached the purely eschatological Kingdom which is to come in the future as being already present."[385] He goes on to say: "The present Kingdom is concentrated in Jesus, the Son of Man and Servant of the Lord, who is to give His life as a ransom for many."[386]

Since *entos* in its only other occurrence in the New Testament (Matthew 23:26) clearly means "within," it would seem that this translation should at least be given serious consideration here. On the other hand, it does not seem necessary to go to the other extreme and say with Olshausen: "The explanation of *entos hymon,* by 'among you' . . . must be utterly rejected for this reason, that the clause so understood forms no contrast to the antecedent 'lo here.' "[387] Olshausen, however, recognized that in the discourse to the disciples that follows (vv. 22-37) the Kingdom is presented as eschatological. He says: "Yet this twofold conception and portraiture of the manifested kingdom of God . . . . present it under those two aspects which mutually complete each other. The kingdom of God shows itself as purely spiritual in its origin, and also external in its perfection."[388]

To the present writer it seems the part of wisdom to allow both translations, "within you" and "among you," without presuming to think that we can be sure which Jesus primarily intended. The context suggests that He was emphasizing the fact that the Kingdom is inward and spiritual, not outward and observable with the physical eyes. At the same time the Kingdom was "among" them in His own Person, for He is the King. The promises of the coming of the Kingdom will find their final fulfillment when Christ is universally recognized as King (Rom. 14:11).

b. The Day of the Son of Man (17:22-37)

22 And he said unto the disciples, The days will come, when ye shall desire to see one of the days of the Son of man, and ye shall not see it. 23 And they shall say to you, Lo, there! Lo, here! go not away, nor follow after *them*: 24 for as the lightning, when it lighteneth out of the one part under the heaven, shineth unto the other part under heaven; so shall the Son of man be in his day. 25 But first must he suffer many things and be rejected of this generation. 26 And as it came to pass in the days of Noah, even so shall it be also in the days of the Son of man. 27 They ate, they drank, they married, they were given in marriage, until the day that Noah entered into the ark, and the flood came, and destroyed them all. 28 Likewise even as it came to pass in the days of Lot; they ate, they drank, they bought, they sold, they planted, they builded; 29 but in the day that Lot went out from Sodom it rained fire and brimstone from heaven, and destroyed them all: 30 after the same manner shall it be in the day that the Son of man is revealed. 31 In that day, he that shall be on the housetop, and his goods in the house, let him not go down to take them away: and let him that is in the field likewise not return back. 32 Remember Lot's wife. 33 Whosoever shall seek to gain his life shall lose it: but whosoever shall lose his life shall preserve it. 34 I say unto you, In that night there shall be two men on one bed; the one shall be taken, and the other shall be left. 35 There shall be two women grinding together; the one shall be taken, and the other shall be left. 37 And they answering say unto him, Where, Lord? And he said unto them, Where the body *is*, thither will the eagles also be gathered together.

Jesus declared that the time would come — after His return to heaven — when they would **desire** ("long for") one of **the days of the Son of man** (v. 22). The same expression occurs in verse 26. What does it mean? Strack and Billerbeck say: " 'The days of the Messiah' is in the Rabbinical writings the usual expression for the Messianic period."[389] Dodd connects it with the Old Testament expression: "The Day of Jehovah."[390] Leany says that for Luke it meant the Transfiguration, the revelation of the glory of the Son of man, which will reach its culmination in His "final appearance."[391]

---

[385] Gösta Lundström, *The Kingdom of God in the Teaching of Jesus,* p. 234.
[386] *Ibid.,* p. 235. [387] *Op. cit.,* II, 89. [388] *Ibid.*
[389] Hermann L. Strack and Paul Billerbeck, *Kommentar zum Neuen Testament aus Talmud und Midrasch,* II, 237. [390] C. H. Dodd, *The Parables of the Kingdom,* p. 81, n. 1.
[391] *Op. cit.,* pp. 70, 231.

The suddenness of the Second Coming is vividly portrayed in verse 24, in the figure of a flash of **lightning**. It is difficult to harmonize this with the popular theory that the Rapture will be something secret and invisible to the world, unless one applies that not to the Rapture but to what is often called the Revelation — the coming of Christ with His saints to reign on earth.

Again (v. 25) Jesus refers to His coming Passion, which He had already twice predicted (see 9:43). He goes on to compare **the days of the Son of man** to **the days of Noah** (v. 26). This is paralleled in Matthew 24:37-39 (see notes there). There was nothing wicked in the fact that the antediluvians **ate** and **drank** and **married,** and **were given in marriage** (v. 27). Their sin consisted basically in ignoring God altogether — which is the besetting sin today of millions of people in so-called Christian lands. A similar comparison is made (only in Luke) to **the days of Lot** (vv. 28-30). These are likened to **the day that the Son of man is revealed** (v. 30). This could refer in a real sense to the revelation of Christ in this age, in the Gospel and in the Church. But the final application seems to be to His coming again.

The instructions in verse 31 are similar to those in Matthew 24:17, 18 and Mark 13:15, 16. Luke adds the significant warning, **Remember Lot's wife** (v. 32). Verse 33 is parallel to Matthew 16:25; verses 34-37 to Matthew 24:40, 41; verse 37 to Matthew 24:28 (see notes on those passages).

The last part of verse 37 has one of those enigmatic statements such as are often found in apocalyptic literature — **Where the body is, thither will the eagles also be gathered together.** To what do **body** and **eagles** refer?

Since the preceding context relates to the Second Coming — "the day that the Son of man is revealed" (v. 30) — some of the Church Fathers took this as meaning that where the glorified body of Christ is, the "eagle saints" will be gathered together. But this interpretation seems to be definitely ruled out by the fact that instead of *soma* (**body**) Matthew (24:28) has *ptoma*, "carcass."

In classical Greek *soma* was used for a dead body.

One of the better treatments of this obscure saying is that by Plummer, which we therefore quote at length:

> This was perhaps a current proverb. The application is here quite general. "Where the conditions are fulfilled, then and there only will the revelation of the Son of Man take place." Or possibly, "Where the dead body of human nature, clinging to earthly things, is, there the judgments of God will come . . . ." Jesus thus sets aside all questions as to the *time* (vs. 20) or *place* (v. 37) of His return. One thing is certain; that *all* who are not ready will suffer (vv. 27, 29). Upon all who are dead to the claims of the Kingdom ruin will fall (v. 37).[392]

Geldenhuys says that in the light of the context verse 37b means: "Where the spiritually dead people are, there the judgment will be executed."[393] Brown writes: " 'As birds of prey scent out the carrion, so wherever is found a mass of incurable moral and spiritual corruption, there will be seen alighting the ministers of Divine judgment'; a proverbial saying terrifically verified at the destruction of Jerusalem, and many times since, though its most tremendous illustration will be at the world's final day."[394]

The reference seems to be to the return of Christ in judgment at the end of this age. The best commentary on this passage is Revelation 19:17, 18 — ". . . . an angel . . . . saying to all the birds that fly in mid heaven, Come and be gathered together unto the great supper of God; that ye may eat the flesh of kings, . . . and the flesh of all men." This will be the greatest destruction the world has ever seen. The means of mass annihilation now being perfected form a prelude to the final judgments of God.

3. Two Parables on Prayer (18:1-14)

a. The Unjust Judge (18:1-8)

1 And he spake a parable unto them to the end that they ought always to pray, and not to faint; 2 saying, There was in a city a judge, who feared not God, and regarded not man; 3 and there was a widow in that city; and she came oft

unto him, saying, Avenge me of mine adversary. 4 And he would not for a while: but afterward he said within himself, Though I fear not God, nor regard man; 5 Yet because this widow troubleth me, I will avenge her, lest she wear me out by her continual coming. 6 And the Lord said, Hear what the unrighteous judge saith. 7 And shall not God avenge his elect, that cry to him day and night, and *yet* he is longsuffering over them? 8 I say unto you, that he will avenge them speedily. Nevertheless, when the Son of man cometh, shall he find faith on the earth?

Luke's Gospel is the great Gospel of prayer (see Introduction). Chapter 11 contains the so-called Lord's Prayer and the Parable of the Importunate Friend at Midnight. This chapter begins with the Parable of the Unjust Judge (or the Importunate Widow) and the Parable of the Pharisee and the Publican.

The purpose of this parable is stated in the first verse — **that they ought always to pray, and not to faint.** This is tied in with what precedes. "The connexion is, that, although the time of Christ's return to deliver His people is hidden from them, yet they must not cease to pray for deliverance."[395] This same command to pray continually, following a statement that no one knows the hour of Christ's coming, is found in 21:36 and also in Mark 13:33. It is clear that unceasing prayer is the most important preparation for the Second Coming.

The word translated **ought** is *dei*, which literally means, "it is necessary," This parable teaches that persistent praying is not only a duty but a necessity. Only here and in verse 9 do we find the purpose and meaning of a parable given as a preface to it. **To faint** is literally "to lose heart." It is a favorite word with Paul.

The exhortation to pray **always** (cf. I Thess. 5:17 — "Pray without ceasing") is contrary to Jewish teaching "that God must not be wearied with incessant prayer . . . . A man ought not to pray more than three times a day. Hourly prayers are forbidden."[396]

The description of the judge — **feared not God, and regarded not man** (v.2) — shows that he was utterly unfitted to

hold this position. He was a cynic with no moral consciousness. Probably he is thought of as a Gentile Official.[397]

In the same city was a widow who **came oft** (imperfect tense, "kept coming") to the judge with the plea: **Avenge me of mine adversary** (v. 3). Arndt and Gingrich translate this: "See to it that I get justice against my opponent."[398] In the Greek there is a play on words which it is difficult to bring out in English. **Avenge** and **adversary** are developed from the same root, meaning "justice." **Adversary** properly means "an opponent in a lawsuit." It seems likely that some wealthy person was taking legal action against the poor woman, perhaps foreclosing a mortgage on her home and threatening to take it from her. Jesus accused the scribes of doing this — "they that devour widows' houses, and for a pretense make long prayers" (Mark 12: 40). So the widow kept pleading with the judge, "Vindicate my rights against my opponent." The status of a widow in the ancient Orient was a very unhappy one. Time and again the Israelites were warned against oppressing widows, but often this cruel sin was perpetrated.

At first the judge kept refusing (imperfect tense) to take care of the woman's case. But finally her persistence wore him down. Though he did not fear God, nor even have respect for man, yet he decided to take action, **lest she wear me out by her continual coming** (v. 5; literally, "coming to the end)." This translation is better than "weary me" (KJV), which is altogether too weak. The verb in Greek is a very strong one. Literally it means, "to strike under the eye, give a black eye."[399] It is found only here and in I Cor. 9:27, where Paul says, "But I beat and bruise my body" (Goodspeed). Probably the word is used metaphorically in both passages, though one is tempted to allow the possibility that the exasperated woman might literally give the judge a black eye. It is not likely, however, that this could happen.

Then Jesus made the application. If an unjust judge would finally surrender to persistent pleading, how much more would a faithful God of love **avenge his elect,** that cry continually to Him (v.7).

395 Plummer, *op. cit.*, p. 411.   396 *Ibid.*   397 *Ibid.*   398 *Op. cit.*, p. 238.
399 Abbott-Smith, *op. cit.*, p. 463.

The exact meaning of the last clause of verse 7 — **and yet he is longsuffering over them** — is disputed. Geldenhuys objects to the word **yet** in this version. It will be noticed that the term is in italics, indicating that it is not in the original. He prefers the English Revised Version (1881), which reads: "and he is longsuffering over them."[400] Plummer suggests: "while he is slow to act for them."[401] The Revised Standard Verson gives a different slant by putting this in the form of a question: "Will he delay long over them?" — implying a negative answer. This seems to fit best with what follows in verse 8.

The parable closes with a disquieting question: **Nevertheless, when the Son of man cometh, shall he find faith on the earth?** Since *pistis* (**faith**) carries the definite article, some take this as "the faith," meaning Christianity. Others refer it to personal trust. Geldenhuys says that it "clearly refers to the faith that is here being discussed — faith in Jesus as the Christ, the Messianic Son of Man, through whom God will vindicate the cause of the elect."[402]

b. The Pharisee and the Publican (18:9-14)

9 And he spake also this parable unto certain who trusted in themselves that they were righteous, and set all others at nought: 10 Two men went up into the temple to pray; the one a Pharisee, and the other a publican. 11 The Pharisee stood and prayed thus with himself, God, I thank thee, that I am not as the rest of men, extortioners, unjust, adulterers, or even as this publican. 12 I fast twice in the week; I give tithes of all that I get. 13 But the publican, standing afar off, would not lift up so much as his eyes unto heaven, but smote his breast, saying, God, be thou merciful to me a sinner. 14 I say unto you, This man went down to his house justified rather than the other: for every one that exalteth himself shall be humbled; but he that humbleth himself shall be exalted.

The purpose of this parable also is given (cf. v. 1). Jesus spoke it as a word of warning to **certain** (scribes and Pharisees) **who trusted in themselves that they** were righteous, and set all others at nought (v. 9). **Set at nought** is a strong verb, meaning "despise, disdain." It is one of numerous words used only by Luke and Paul, suggesting a definite Pauline influence on the writer of Luke and Acts.

Two men went up into the temple (v. 10), which was situated on Mount Moriah, called the "Hill of the House." They went **to pray** — probably at one of the regular hours of prayer, 9:00 A.M. or 3:00 P.M. One of the men was a **Pharisee**, the other a **publican**; that is, a "tax collector."

The Pharisee **stood and prayed** (v. 11) — literally, "having taken his stand he was praying." He chose a prominent place where everyone could see him. He was doing exactly what Jesus commanded not to be done — parading his piety (see notes on Matthew 6:1). He **prayed thus with himself, God, I thank thee.** Plummer observes: "He glances at God, but contemplates himself."[403] Edersheim comments: "Never, perhaps, were words of thanksgiving spoken in less thankfulness than these."[404]

He thanked God that he was not **as the rest of men.** This is the most obnoxious pride imaginable. And yet some professing Christians unintentionally come dangerously close to having this unchristian attitude. The Pharisee enumerated some classes of people to whom he was superior. **Extortioners** is literally "rapacious," but perhaps here means "swindlers."[405] On the phrase, **or even as this publican,** Ragg remarks: "an arrogant comparison (not uncommon among Christians) which 'fills up the cup' of his self-righteousness."[406]

Having shown how he was different from the rest of men negatively, the Pharisee proceeded to show how he was different positively. Said he, **I fast twice in the week.** This practice of the Jews is corroborated in the *Didache* (2nd century), where they are called, "hypocrites." The passage reads thus: "But let not your fastings be appointed in common with the hypocrites; for they fast on the second day of the week and on the fifth; but do ye fast during the fourth,

---

400 *Op. cit.* p. 448.   401 *Op. cit.*, p. 414.   402 *Op. cit.*, p. 449.
403 *Op. cit.*, p. 417.   404 *Op. cit.*, II, 289.   405 Arndt and Gingrich, *op. cit.*, p. 108.
406 *Op. cit.*, p. 235.

and the preparation day."[407] That is, the Jews fasted on Monday and Thursday, the Christians on Wednesday and Friday. The law of Moses prescribed only one fast — on the Day of Atonement, in September or October. This is still referred to as "the Fast" in Acts 27:9. After the Babylonian captivity the Jews added four other fasts (Zech. 8:19) to commemorate certain calamities that had befallen the nation.

The Pharisee also reminded the Lord: **I give tithes of all that I get** (not "possess," (KJV). The Mishna gives this picture of a Pharisee: "He tithes all that he eats, all that he sells, and all that he buys, and he is not a guest with an unlearned person"[408]; that is, he does not risk eating food that may not have been tithed.

Quite the opposite was the attitude of the **publican. Standing afar off** — perhaps in the outer Court of the Gentiles, rather than in the inner Court of Israel — he did not even look up. Farrar says: "The Jews usually stood with arms outspread, the palms turned upwards, as though to receive the gifts of heaven, and the eyes raised."[409] The Psalmist expresses vividly the man's feelings, when he writes: "Mine iniquities have taken such hold upon me that I am not able to look up" (Psa. 40:12).

Instead of lifting his eyes, the man **smote his breast** — a common way of expressing grief, in both Old and New Testament times (cf. 23:48; Nahum 2:7; Jer. 31:19). **Be thou merciful** is literally, "be propitiated." The Greek word occurs elsewhere in the New Testament only in Hebrews 2:17, where it is translated, "make propitiation" (for sins). The root of the word is that which is used for the mercy seat, where atonement was made annually for the sins of the people by sprinkling it with the blood of the sin offering. The publican wanted God to meet him with mercy and forgiveness.

Jesus declared that the penitent publican went home **justified** (v. 14) — literally, "having been justified." His sins were forgiven, and he was made right with God. This Pauline term occurs five times in Luke, only twice elsewhere in the Gospels (Matthew 11:9; 12:37), twice in Acts, twenty-seven times in Paul's Epistles

(fifteen in Romans and eight in Galatians), three times in James, and once in Revelation. Luke's frequent use of it again shows Pauline influence.

The twofold principle enunciated in verse 14b is one that operates in life constantly. To exalt oneself is to deny one's dependence on God. This is the essence of sin, and one who is guilty of it has already fallen. When one realizes his utter dependence on the Lord, he will inevitably feel humble, His humility will be deep and genuine, not a surface mask for a dominant pride of heart. Honest, intelligent thinking will cause one to feel sincerely humble.

4. Blessing the Children (18:15-17)

15 And they were bringing unto him also their babes, that he should touch them: but when the disciples saw it, they rebuked them. 16 But Jesus called them unto him, saying, Suffer the little children to come unto me, and forbid them not: for to such belongeth the kingdom of God. 17 Verily I say unto you, Whosoever shall not receive the kingdom of God as a little child, he shall in no wise enter therein.

This brief but beautiful incident is found in all three Synoptic Gospels (see notes on Matthew 19:13-15; Mark 10:13-16). About the only distinctive item in Luke's Gospel is his change from "little children" to **babes** — literally "infants." Geldenhuys remarks: "Possibly most of the children were about a year old."[410] Plummer notes: "On the first anniversary of their birth Jewish children were sometimes brought to the Rabbi to be blest."[411] **Touch them** is more exactly defined by Matthew — "That he should lay his hands on them, and pray" (Matt. 19:13). This was evidently the custom of the rabbis who blessed the little children.

The **disciples rebuked** those who brought the infants. They evidently felt that their Master was too busy to be bothered with such "unimportant matters." But Jesus told them to "stop forbidding" the children to come to Him, **for to such belongeth the kingdom of God** (v. 16). Plummer comments: "It is not these children, nor all children, but

---

[407] *Teaching of the Twelve Apostles,* trans. R. D. Hitchcock and Francis Brown, p. 15.
[408] Quoted in Edersheim, *op. cit.,* II, 291.   [409] *Op. cit.,* p. 332.   [410] *Op. cit.,* p. 455.
[411] *Op. cit.,* p. 421.

those who are childlike in character, especially in humility and trustfulness, who are best fitted for the Kingdom."412

5. The Rich Young Ruler (18:18-30)

18 And a certain ruler asked him, saying, Good Teacher, what shall I do to inherit eternal life? 19 And Jesus said unto him, Why callest thou me good? none is good, save one, *even* God. 20 Thou knowest the commandments, Do not commit adultery, Do not kill, Do not steal, Do not bear false witness, Honor thy father and mother. 21 And he said, All these things have I observed from my youth up. 22 And when Jesus heard it, he said unto him, One thing thou lackest yet: sell all that thou hast, and distribute unto the poor, and thou shalt have treasure in heaven: and come, follow me. 23 But when he heard these things, he became exceeding sorrowful; for he was very rich. 24 And Jesus seeing him said, How hardly shall they that have riches enter into the kingdom of God! 25 For it is easier for a camel to enter in through a needle's eye, than for a rich man to enter into the kingdom of God. 26 And they that heard it said, Then who can be saved? 27 But he said, The things which are impossible with men are possible with God. 28 And Peter said, Lo, we have left our own, and followed thee. 29 And he said unto them, Verily I say unto you, there is no man that hath left house, or wife, or brethren, or parents, or children, for the kingdom of God's sake, 30 who shall not receive manifold more in this time, and in the world to come eternal life.

This interesting incident is recorded in all three Synoptics (see notes on Matthew 19:16-30; Mark 10:17-31). **A certain ruler** came to Jesus, saying, **Good Teacher, What shall I do to inherit eternal Life?** Christ replied: **Why callest thou me good?** Was Jesus denying that He was good? Certainly not. Plummer gives the correct interpretation: "You suppose me to be a mere man, and you ought not to call any human being good. That title I cannot accept, unless I am recognized as God."413 Then Jesus went on to say: **none is good, save one, even God** (v. 19). This was emphatically the position of the Jews. Edersheim writes: ". . . in no recorded instance was a

Jewish Rabbi addressed as 'Good Master.' " He adds: "The designation of God as the only One 'good' agrees with one of the titles given Him in Jewish writings: 'The Good One of the world.' "414 In connection with the fact that Jesus immediately referred the young man to the **commandments** (v. 20), attention should be called to this statement in the Talmud: "There is nothing else that is good but the Law."415

All three Synoptics quote the same **commandments**, except that Mark adds: "Do not defraud." The ruler's reply was: **All these things have I observed from my youth up** (v. 21). Plummer remarks: "The reply exhibits great ignorance of self and duty, but is perfectly sincere."416

Thereupon Jesus informed the young man: **One thing thou lackest** (v. 22). Leany observes: "This verse is perhaps the best testimony by the synoptics to the faithfulness of Paulinism to the essential gospel."417 Luke clearly reflects Paul's teaching more than the other Gospels.

Christ asked the rich ruler to **sell** all he had and **distribute** to the poor. Ragg notes that while this is "in one sense a general counsel to all Christians," in that "material wealth is always to be at Christ's disposal," yet this had special application to the ruler. Ragg adds: "It is renunciation, not poverty as such, that discipleship demands."418

The young man failed the test. He went away **exceeding sorrowful** (strong compound in Greek), because he was **very rich** and would not surrender his possessions.

The statement that it is easier for a camel to go through a needle's eye than for a rich man to enter the Kingdom (v. 25) should be taken at face value, without reducing the **camel** to a rope, nor increasing the **needle's eye** to a postern gate in the walls of Jerusalem. The latter appears to exist only in the imagination of modern guides. Jesus used a startling hyperbole to drive the truth home more vividly and emphatically. Plummer says: "In the Talmud an elephant passing through the eye of a needle is twice used of what is impossible."419 Jesus was talking about what was impossible apart from God's

412 *Op. cit.*, p. 421.   413 *Op. cit.*, p. 422.   414 *Op. cit.*, II, 339.   415 *Ibid.*
416 *Op. cit.*, p. 423.   417 *Op. cit.*, p. 237.   418 *Op. cit.*, p. 239.   419 *Op. cit.*, p. 425.

grace, not what was only difficult. That is indicated by verse 27.

The disciples were shocked at their Master's statements about the extreme difficulty of a rich man entering the Kingdom. They had been taught all their lives that material prosperity was a sign of God's favor. Their reaction was: **"Then who can be saved?"** (v. 26).

Peter reminded his Master that he and the other disciples had left all to follow Him (v. 28). Jesus replied that all who had done so would receive abundant reward in this life, plus eternal life in the next.

6. Third Prediction of Passion (18:31-34)

31 And he took unto him the twelve, and said unto them, Behold, we go up to Jerusalem, and all the things that are written through the prophets shall be accomplished unto the Son of man. 32 For he shall be delivered up unto the Gentiles, and shall be mocked, and shamefully treated, and spit upon: 33 and they shall scourge and kill him: and the third day he shall rise again. 34 And they understood none of these things; and this saying was hid from them, and they perceived not the things that were said.

This important item is found also in Matthew (20:17-19) and Mark (10:32-34). For full discussion, see the comments there. Luke adds: **and all the things that are written through the prophets shall be accomplished** (v. 31). At the close of the incident he makes the observation: **And they understood none of these things; and this saying was hid from them, and they perceived not the things that were said** (v. 34). The disciples were still blind spiritually. To a sad degree they shared the ignorance of their day. Geldenhuys says: "No Jewish teachers or believers of those times seem to have understood the Old Testament prophecies of the Suffering Servant in a Messianic sense."[420]

7. Jesus at Jericho (18:35 — 19:28)

a. Healing of Blind Man (18:35-43)

35 And it came to pass, as he drew nigh unto Jericho, a certain blind man sat by the way side begging: 36 and hearing a multitude going by, he inquired what this meant. 37 And they told him that Jesus of Nazareth passeth by. 38 And he cried, saying, Jesus, thou son of David, have mercy on me. 39 And they that went before rebuked him, that he should hold his peace: but he cried out the more a great deal, Thou son of David, have mercy on me. 40 And Jesus stood, and commanded him to be brought unto him: and when he was come near, he asked him, 41 What wilt thou that I should do unto thee? And he said, Lord, that I may receive my sight. 42 And Jesus said unto him, Receive thy sight; thy faith hath made thee whole. 43 And immediately he received his sight, and followed him, glorifying God: and all the people, when they saw it, gave praise unto God.

This incident is recorded in the first three Gospels (see notes on Matt. 20:29-34; Mark 10:46-52). One problem of harmonization confronts the reader right at the beginning. Matthew and Mark indicate that the healing of the blind man took place as Jesus and His disciples **went out from Jericho**, while Luke says, **as he drew nigh unto Jericho**.

There are two possible solutions. The simpler one is to take **drew nigh unto** as meaning "in the vicinity of." That is, Luke is merely placing the miracle near Jericho.

The second one is based on the fact that there is more than one Jericho. Today one can visit the sites of Old Testament Jericho and New Testament Jericho, besides traveling through modern Jericho. These are a little more than a mile apart. Geldenhuys suggests as a solution "that Bartimaeus was cured of his blindness at some point after Jesus had passed through Old Jericho (the site of the Canaanite city), that He then passed through New Jericho (the recently built Herodian city), where He had His interview with Zacchaeus."[421]

Son of David (v. 38) is used as a Messianic title in the Song of Solomon (17:23), which was written about 50 B.C. Plummer says: "This shows that he recognizes Jesus as the Messiah."[422]

Two different Greek words are translated **cried** in verses 38 and 39. The first means to cry out for help. The second is used for any loud outcry showing strong emotion.

---

[420] *Op. cit.*, p. 465.   [421] *Op. cit.*, p. 467.   [422] *Op. cit.*, p. 431.

The expression **glorified God** is found three times in Matthew, once in Mark (2:12), but eight times in Luke. It fits in well with Luke's emphasis on the blessing which Christ and His gospel bring to men.

b. Conversion of Zacchaeus (19:1-10)

1 And he entered and was passing through Jericho. 2 And behold, a man called by name Zacchaeus; and he was a chief publican, and he was rich. 3 And he sought to see Jesus who he was; and could not for the crowd, because he was little of stature. 4 And he ran on before, and climbed up into a sycamore tree to see him: for he was to pass that way. 5 And when Jesus came to the place, he looked up, and said unto him, Zacchaeus, make haste, and come down; for to-day I must abide at thy house. 6 And he made haste, and came down, and received him joyfully. 7 And when they saw it, they all murmured, saying, He is gone in to lodge with a man that is a sinner. 8 And Zacchaeus stood, and said unto the Lord, Behold, Lord, the half of my goods I give to the poor; and if I have wrongfully exacted aught of any man, I restore fourfold. 9 And Jesus said unto him, To-day is salvation come to this house, forasmuch as he also is a son of Abraham. 10 For the Son of man came to seek and to save that which was lost.

This incident, found only in Luke, fits in with his emphasis on the salvation of sinners. It also forms a significant prelude to verse 10, which is the key verse of this Gospel.

Jesus was **passing through Jericho**, on His way to Jerusalem. The chief tax collector of the district was a man named Zacchaeus. Apparently he was not living up to his name ("righteous one"). He had doubtless become **rich** by taking unfair advantage of others.

Zacchaeus wanted to see Jesus, but, being **little of stature** he was unable to do so on account of the crowd. So he ran on ahead and climbed up into **a sycamore tree**; that is, a fig mulberry. Those who want to see Christ will overcome all difficulties to do so.

When Jesus arrived at the place, He called Zacchaeus to come down out of the tree, announcing that He was going home with him (v. 5). **Joyfully** the tax

collector **received** him. This is a compound verb, meaning "to receive under one's roof, receive as a guest, entertain hospitably."[423]

The crowd murmured its disapproval. How could any self-respecting rabbi **lodge with a man that is a sinner** (v. 7)? **Lodge** is a verb which means "loose thoroughly," and so "destroy" or "demolish." Only here and in 9:12 does it have the sense of loosing one's garments and resting from a journey.

Apparently Zacchaeus overheard the complaints. So he **stood** still and told Jesus in the presence of all that he was going to give half his possessions to the poor. Moreover, if he had **wrongfully exacted** — for the meaning of this verb see the notes on 3:14 — anything from anyone — the Greek indicates that he knew he had — he would **restore fourfold**. This was the penalty the Law prescribed for one who had stolen a sheep (Exod. 22:1).

That the Pharisees labeled the "publicans" as "sinners" is abundantly evident. We find these two terms frequently together not only in the Gospels, but also in the writings of the Jewish Fathers. Bamberger says: "The rabbinic sources repeatedly bracket tax collectors with robbers."[424]

The confession and promised restitution showed that Zacchaeus had received **salvation** (v. 9). He was a true **son of Abraham**: not only a Jew, but a believer. The story climaxes with the key verse of Luke's Gospel: **For the Son of man came to seek and to save that which was lost** (v. 10). Zacchaeus was a good example of a lost sheep whom the seeking Shepherd had found (cf. 15:3-7).

c. Parable of the Pounds (19:11-27)

11 And as they heard these things, he added and spake a parable, because he was nigh to Jerusalem, and because they supposed that the kingdom of God was immediately to appear. 12 He said therefore, A certain nobleman went into a far country, to receive for himself a kingdom, and to return. 13 And he called ten servants of his, and gave them ten pounds, and said unto them, Trade ye *herewith* till I come. 14 But his citizens hated him, and sent an ambassage after him, saying, We will not that this man

---

[423] Abbott-Smith, *op. cit.*, p. 460.   [424] B. J. Bamberger, "Tax Collector," IDB, IV, 522.

reign over us. 15 And it came to pass, when he was come back again, having received the kingdom, that he commanded these servants, unto whom he had given the money to be called to him, that he might know what they had gained by trading. 16 And the first came before him, saying, Lord, thy pound hath made ten pounds more. 17 And he said unto him, Well done, thou good servant: because thou wast found faithful in a very little, have thou authority over ten cities. 18 And the second came, saying, Thy pound, Lord, hath made five pounds. 19 And he said unto him also, Be thou also over five cities. 20 And another came, saying, Lord, behold, *here is* thy pound, which I kept laid up in a napkin: 21 for I feared thee, because thou art an austere man: thou takest up that which thou layedst not down, and reapest that which thou didst not sow. 22 He saith unto him, Out of thine own mouth will I judge thee, thou wicked servant. Thou knewest that I am an austere man, taking up that which I laid not down, and reaping that which I did not sow; 23 then wherefore gavest thou not my money into the bank, and I at my coming should have required it with interest? 24 And he said unto them that stood by, Take away from him the pound, and give it unto him that hath the ten pounds. 25 And they said unto him, Lord, he hath ten pounds. 26 I say unto you, that unto every one that hath shall be given; but from him that hath not, even that which he hath shall be taken away from him. 27 But these mine enemies, that would not that I should reign over them, bring hither, and slay them before me.

This story has a number of similarities to the Parable of the Talents (Matt. 25: 14-30). But the differences far outweigh the resemblances, so that we may consider them as two distinct parables. The main differences are listed as follows by Plummer:

(1) In the Talents we have a householder leaving home for a time, in the Pounds a nobleman going in quest of a crown; (2) the Talents are unequally distributed, the Pounds equally; (3) the sums entrusted differ enormously in amount; (4) in the Talents the rewards are the same, in the Pounds they differ and are proportionate to what has been gained; (5) in the Talents the unprofitable servant is severely punished, in the Pounds

he is merely deprived of his pound. Out of about 302 words in Matthew and 286 in Luke, only about 66 words are common to the two. [425]

In addition to these there are three items found in only Luke: (1) the introduction, verse 11; (2) the hatred of his citizens, verse 14; (3) the vengeance on these enemies, verse 27. So there seems little doubt about their being two separate parables.

Once more (cf. 18:1, 9) Luke gives the reason for Jesus uttering a parable.[426] In this case it was **because he was nigh to Jerusalem** — Jericho was about seventeen miles away — **and because they supposed that the kingdom of God was immediately to appear** (v. 11). This reminds one of the attitude of the disciples, expressed in Acts 1:6 — "Lord, dost thou at this time restore the kingdom to Israel?" There was obviously a strong Messianic expectation at this time, and it had been focused on Jesus. The Galilean pilgrims who accompained Him to the Passover had high hopes. This is evidenced in the Triumphal Entry (vv. 29-39).

Verses 12 and 14 seem to be a clear reference to an historical event familiar to Jesus' hearers. When Herod the Great died in 4 B.C., he left his kingdom to his son Archelaus, though his earlier will had named Antipas as successor. It was necessary for Archelaus to go to Rome to receive confirmation of his appointment. But the Jews hated him and sent an embassy of fifty to oppose him. After the Emperor Augustus had listened to both sides and weighed the various claims, he granted to Archelaus half his father's kingdom with the title of ethnarch (not king).[427] Farrar suggests: "The facts here alluded to would naturally be brought both to His mind, and to those of the Galileans, by the sight of the magnificent palace at Jericho which Archelaus had rebuilt."[428]

The nobleman called **ten** of his **servants** ("slaves") and gave them **ten pounds** (v. 13). Apparently each one received a pound (cf. vv. 16, 18). **The pound** (*mna*, or *"mina"*) was worth about sixteen to twenty dollars. The word is found seven times here, but nowhere else in the New Testament. He told them to **trade** until he returned. The verb,

[425] *Ibid.*, p. 437.   [426] **Added and spake** is a Hebraistic construction (cf. Gen. 38:5).
[427] Josephus, *Ant.* XVII. 8.1; 9.3; 11.4; *War*, II. 6.1,3.   [428] *Op. cit.*, p. 341.

found only here in the New Testament, means "'Carry on business,' especially as a banker or trader."[429] It can also mean "engage in State business."[430] From the small sums given to these slaves it is suggested that the nobleman wanted to test their faithfulness and abilities, with a view to giving them greater responsibilities (cf. vv. 17, 19). Jesus had already said: "He that is faithful in a very little is faithful also in much" (16:10).

It appears that **ten** was used as a round number in Palestine, just as we say "about a dozen." Examples of this usage are the ten virgins (Matt. 25:1), the ten plagues in Egypt, and the ten times the Israelites tempted God in the wilderness. **Having received the kingdom** (v. 15) — as Archelaus did in a modified form — the ruler commanded the servants to whom he had entrusted money to be brought in before him, so that he might know how much each had **gained** — literally, "who had gained what" — **by trading**. This is a compound of the verb found in verse 13.

The first reported that his pound had gained **ten pounds** (v. 16). As a reward he was given **authority over ten cities** (v. 17). The second related that his pound had gained **five pounds** (v. 18). He was given authority over **five cities** (v. 19).

Finally came **another** — literally, "the other." The Greek word suggests "another of a different kind" (*heteros*). He returned the master's pound which he had **kept laid up in a napkin** (v. 20). The Greek word for **napkin** is a loan-word from the Latin, found here, John 11:44; 20:7, and Acts 19:12. "The word seems to signify some kind of scarf or neck cloth used in Palestine to protect the head and back of the neck from the heat of the sun."[431]

The question has been raised as to why only three servants are mentioned as reporting. Plummer gives this explanation: "The three mentioned are samples of the whole ten. Some gained immensely, some considerably, and some not at all. The two first classes having been described, the representative of the remaining class may be spoken of as *ho heteros,* especially as he is of quite a different kind."[432]

This servant pleaded that he was afraid because he knew that his master was an **austere** man (v. 21). The Greek word *austeros* occurs only here and in the following verse. "It obviously means 'strict, exacting,' a man who expects to get blood out of a stone."[433] The last part of verse 21 may well have been a current proverb (usually recited in the third person).

The illogic of the servant's thinking was quickly exposed by his master. If he thought the nobleman was so severe, it was all the more reason why he should have worked hard to gain all he possibly could with the pound entrusted to him. Probably the last part of verse 22 should be treated as a question, with a question mark at the end of the verse: "So you knew. . .?" "Why then. . .?" (v. 23). He could at least have put the money in the **bank** so that it could draw **interest**.

The third slave is addressed as **wicked servant** (v. 22). This suggests that we may need to revise our thinking a bit concerning what constitutes wickedness in God's sight. The slave did not steal his master's money. He did not rob anyone. At least so it appears. But in reality he did steal the interest he should have gained and which rightfully belonged to his master. There are sins of omission as well as sins of commission. People will be punished not only for the bad things they did but also for the good things they failed to do. Christian stewardship is a matter of vital importance — in relation to both the success of the Kingdom and the salvation of our souls. We cannot do nothing and at the same time be good. He who fails to do good is a bad person. Then, too, the servant's attitude expressed in words showed the wickedness of his heart. To have a mean selfish attitude is to be **wicked**.

The master thereupon ordered those standing by to take the pound away from this slave and give it to the one who had ten pounds (v. 24). Then Jesus made the application (v. 26). This is almost exactly parallel to Matthew 25:29 (see notes there). It is in connection with the last servant that the two parables have the closest similarity. The meaning of verse 26 is thus summed up by Plummer: "The point is that *to neglect opportunities is to lose them;* and that *to*

---

[429] Plummer, *op. cit.,* p. 439.   [430] T. W. Manson, *op. cit.,* p. 607.   [431] *Ibid.,* p. 608.
[432] *Op. cit.,* p. 441.   [433] Moulton and Milligan, VGT, p. 93.

make the most of opportunities is to gain others.[434] He also makes this apt observation: "He alone possesses, who uses and enjoys his possessions."[435]

This parable carried a very pointed warning to the Jews. They needed to beware lest they play the role of the wicked servant, failing to use the wonderful spiritual heritage that God had given them. Worse still, they were like the rebellious citizens. Of Jesus Christ they said: "We will not have this man reign over us" (v. 14). Their fate is portrayed in verse 27. And this overtook them forty years later, in A.D. 70, when God permitted the Romans to punish His people for their sins.

But there is a personal note of warning here for all. T. W. Manson says: "Beneath the grim imagery is an equally grim fact, the fact that the coming of Jesus to the world puts every man to the test, compels every man to a decision. And that decision is no light matter. It is a matter of life and death."[436]

The main lesson of the parable for us today must not be missed. Christ is the nobleman who has gone away to receive a kingdom. He has been gone a long time. But some day He will return. The only way that we can be ready to meet Him is to be busily occupied in the work of the Kingdom, making the most of the "working capital" He has given us — which includes the power of the Holy Spirit — and seeking to multiply our own Christian experience in that of many new converts that we win to Him. In this respect the main thrust of the Parable of the Pounds is very nearly the same as that of the Parable of the Talents.

d. Leaving for Jerusalem (19:28)

28 And when he had thus spoken, he went on before, going up to Jerusalem.

Having given this important parable — the significance of which would be clearer to the disciples after the Crucifixion, the Resurrection, the Ascension, and the Pentecost — Jesus pushed on toward Jerusalem. The last climb up the rough, steep Jericho Road was but a symbol of the rugged climb to Calvary, via Gethsemane, which lay right ahead of Him.

V. JESUS IN JERUSALEM (19:29—21: 38)

A. THE TRIUMPHAL ENTRY (19:29-44)

1. Triumph (19:29-40)

29 And it came to pass, when he drew nigh unto Bethphage and Bethany, at the mount that is called Olivet, he sent two of the disciples, 30 saying, Go your way into the village over against *you;* in which as ye enter ye shall find a colt tied, whereon no man ever yet sat: loose him, and bring him. 31 And if any one ask you, Why do ye loose him? thus shall ye say, The Lord hath need of him. 32 And they that were sent went away, and found even as he had said unto them. 33 And as they were loosing the colt, the owners thereof said unto them, Why loose ye the colt? 34 And they said, The Lord hath need of him. 35 And they brought him to Jesus: and they threw their garments upon the colt, and set Jesus thereon. 36 And as he went they spread their garments in the way. 37 And as he was now drawing nigh, *even* at the descent of the mount of Olives, the whole multitude of the disciples began to rejoice and praise God with a loud voice for all the mighty works which they had seen; 38 saying, Blessed *is* the King that cometh in the name of the Lord: peace in heaven, and glory in the highest. 39 And some of the Pharisees from the multitude said unto him, Teacher, rebuke thy disciples. 40 And he answered and said, I tell you that, if these shall hold their peace, the stones will cry out.

The so-called Triumphal Entry of Jesus into Jerusalem on Sunday morning of Passion Week is described in all four Gospels, though most briefly in the Gospel of John. (See the notes on Matt. 21: 1-11; Mark 11:1-11; cf. John 12:12-19.) It was the beginning of the end.

Mark and Luke mention **Bethphage and Bethany,** Matthew only **Bethphage.** So apparently that was the village where the colt was secured. Some think that Bethphage was not a village, but a whole district which included Bethany and everything between it and Jerusalem. Godet notes that such was a view of Lightfoot and other scholars. He continues:

According to the Rabbins, Jerusalem was to the people what *the camp* had formerly been to Israel in the wilderness. As at

[434]. *Op. cit.,* p. 444.   [435] *Ibid.,* p. 443.   [436] *Op. cit.,* p. 609.

the great feasts the city could not contain all the pilgrims who came from a distance, and who should strictly have found an abode *in the camp* (the city), and there celebrated the feast, there was added . . . to Jerusalem, to make it sufficient, all this district situated on the side of the Mount of Olives, which bore the name of *Bethphage* (*place of figs*). Bethany was the beginning of this district where the pilgrims encamped.[437]

In that case, the meaning would be that as Jesus reached the district of Bethphage He sent two disciples into the village of Bethany. That would explain the problem of why Bethphage is named first. We might paraphrase the opening words here thus: "And it came to pass (*kai engeneto*, Luke's favorite way of introducing a narrative) when Jesus came near to the district of Bethphage, and specifically to the village of Bethany."

It is thought that Bethphage means "house of unripe figs" and Bethany "house of dates." These put with the Mount of Olives would indicate the three main fruits raised in that area.

The phrase, **the mount that is called Olivet,** suggests that Luke was writing to Gentiles who were unfamiliar with Palestine. This feature shows up a number of times.

The Synoptic accounts of the Triumphal Entry run rather closely parallel. We shall give attention here largely to the distinctive items in Luke.

But first it will be profitable to take notice of a phrase found in all three — **The Lord hath need of him** (v. 31). The title for Himself that Jesus uses implies that the owner of the colt was acquainted with Jesus, if not actually His disciple. However, this does not decide the question as to whether previous arrangements had been made for using the animal at this time. While this is possible, Plummer observes: "But the impression produced by the narratives is that the knowledge is supernatural, which on so momentous an occasion would be in harmony with His purpose."[438]

Luke alone notes that the two disciples who were sent to the village found **even as he had said unto them** (v. 32). But he and Mark, both writing for Gentiles, omit the quotation from Zechariah 9:9 which is found in Matthew and John.

Luke mentions **the owners** (literally, "lords" or "masters," *kyrioi*). Probably the best interpretation is that given by Plummer: "The owner of the colt and those with him."[439] Luke also notes that when the colt was brought, they **set Jesus thereon** (v. 35), treating Him as a king.

Verse 37 is peculiar to Luke's Gospel. As Christ began the descent of the western slope of the Mount of Olives toward Jerusalem, **the whole multitude of the disciples began to rejoice and praise God with a loud voice for all the mighty works which they had seen.** This is typically Lukan language. From the top of the Mount of Olives the view of Jerusalem — half a mile away and two hundred feet below — is a breath-taking sight. The whole city lies spread out before one's gaze.

Luke does not use the word "Hosanna," found in Matthew and Mark. Instead he has **glory** (v. 38), which is evidently the way he seeks to convey the meaning of the Hebrew term to his Greek readers.

Verses 39 and 40 are likewise found only in this Gospel. Some of the Pharisees told Jesus to **rebuke** His disciples. They were doubtless afraid of the Roman reaction to this loud outburst of praise. The situation was loaded with dynamite and they did not wish to see a revolution break forth. Their fear is understandable, but it was due to their rejection of Jesus as Messiah.

Christ's reply was that if the people should remain silent, the very stones would cry out. It is sad when human beings, the crown of God's creation and made in His image, refuse to praise Him. Too often it is the children and new converts who lead the way in this paean of praise.

2. Tragedy (19:41-44)

41 And when he drew nigh, he saw the city and wept over it, 42 saying, If thou hadst known in this day, even thou, the things which belong unto peace! but now they are hid from thine eyes. 43 For the days shall come upon thee, when thine enemies shall cast up a bank about

---

[437] *Op. cit.,* II, 227.   [438] *Op. cit.,* p. 446.   [439] *Op. cit.,* p. 446.

thee, and compass thee round, and keep thee in on every side, 44 and shall dash thee to the ground, and thy children within thee; and they shall not leave in thee one stone upon another; because thou knewest not the time of thy visitation.

This paragraph is found only in Luke. The so-called Triumphal Entry ended in a tragedy of tears. When Jesus drew near the city, He **wept over it**. The verb is a strong one; "it implies wailing and sobbing."[440] **If thou hadst known** (v. 42) probably means, "Oh, that thou hadst known." "The words imply that there have been various opportunities, of which this is the last."[441] **The things which belong unto peace** reminds one of the announcement of the angels to the shepherds (2:14). Christ came to earth to bring peace to the hearts of those who would receive Him. Unfortunately, His own city, the Holy City (Matt. 4:5), rejected Him. The result: **days shall come upon thee** when the city would be captured with horrible destruction and massacre. The language here was literally fulfilled in A.D. 70, in the destruction of Jerusalem by the Romans.

The word for **bank** (only here in New Testament) is literally "palisades" or "ramparts." Josephus tells how Titus, during the siege of Jerusalem, ordered his soldiers to "bring timber together, and raise banks against the city; and . . .he placed those that shot darts and the archers in the midst of the banks that were then raising."[442]

The wholesale massacre of the inhabitants and the total destruction of buildings and walls is graphically described in verse 44. The reason for all this was: **because thou knewest not the time of thy visitation.** The Greek word for **visitation** is *episkope,* from which comes "episcopal." It literally means "a visit of inspection." Thayer says that in Biblical Greek it means "that act by which God looks into and searches out the ways, deeds, character, of men, in order to adjudge them their lot accordingly, whether joyous or sad; **inspection, investigation, visitation.**"[443] He says that here it means the time "in which God showed himself gracious toward thee and offered thee **salvation** through Christ."[444]

B. JESUS IN THE TEMPLE (19:45-48)

1. Cleansing of the Temple (19:45, 46)

45 And he entered into the temple, and began to cast out them that sold, 46 saying unto them, It is written, And my house shall be a house of prayer: but ye have made it a den of robbers.

This is told more briefly than in Matthew 21:12-17 and Mark 11:15-19 (see notes there). There are no distinctive items in Luke's account.

2. Teaching in the Temple (19:47, 48)

47 And he was teaching daily in the temple. But the chief priests and the scribes and the principal men of the people sought to destroy him: 48 and they could not find what they might do; for the people all hung upon him, listening.

Luke has two additional details here. He says of Jesus that He was **teaching daily in the temple** (v. 47). This was during Passion Week. Christ was giving the people their last opportunity to hear Him and accept His salvation. In addition to **the chief priests and the scribes** (also in Mark), Luke has: **and the principal men of the people.** These all **sought** (Greek, "were seeking") to slay Him. The rulers of Israel were determined to destroy Jesus.

But they could not find a way to carry out their designs, **for all the people hung upon him, listening** (v. 48). What a tragedy that their religious leaders would not help them in accepting and understanding their Messiah, but instead turned the tide against Him. While Jesus was busy doing good, trying to help the souls and bodies of men, the members of the Great Sanhedrin were busy plotting His death. To what depths had religion sunk!

C. CONFLICT WITH THE RULERS OF THE NATION (20:1-47)

As the time for the Crucifixion drew near, the conflict between Christ and His enemies erupted with greater frequence and violence. In this section it comes into focus. From Mark's Gospel we judge that all the events related in chapters 20 and 21 took place on Tuesday

---

440 Plummer, *op. cit.,* p. 449.   441 *Ibid.,* p. 450.   442 *War,* V. 62.
443 *Op. cit.,* p. 242.   444 *Ibid.*

of Passion Week. This is sometimes called "The Day of Questions." There were six altogether: (1) the Sanhedrin questioning Jesus' authority; (2) His counter-question about John the Baptist's authority; (3) the question of the Pharisees and Herodians about paying taxes; (4) that of the Pharisees about the resurrection; (5) that of the scribe as to what was the first commandment; (6) that of Jesus about how David's Son could be David's Lord. Plummer, who calls attention to these, writes: "Of hardly any day in our Lord's life have we so full a report." He adds: "The day may be considered the last working-day of Christ's ministry, the last of his public teaching, the last of activity in the temple, the last of instruction to the people and of warning to their leaders."[445]

1. Challenge to Christ's Authority (20:1-8)

1 And it came to pass, on one of the days, as he was teaching the people in the temple, and preaching the gospel, there came upon him the chief priests and the scribes with the elders; 2 and they spake, saying unto him, Tell us: By what authority doest thou these things? or who is he that gave thee this authority? 3 And he answered and said unto them, I also will ask you a question; and tell me: 4 The baptism of John, was it from heaven, or from men? 5 And they reasoned with themselves, saying, If we shall say, From heaven; he will say, Why did ye not believe him? 6 But if we shall say, From men; all the people will stone us: for they are persuaded that John was a prophet. 7 And they answered, that they knew not whence it was. 8 And Jesus said unto them, Neither tell I you by what authority I do these things.

For detailed discussion of this incident see the notes on Matthew 21:23-27 and Mark 11:27-33. At this stage Luke follows the other two Synoptics more closely than at any other point in his Gospel.

The items peculiar to Luke's account are few and meagre. In the first verse occurs a typically Lukan expression — **preaching the gospel**. This is all one word in the Greek — *evanglizomenou*, evangelizing. Luke uses this verb ten times in the Book of Acts. Evangelism was one of the primary interests of this

Greek, who was thrilled that the gospel was offered freely to all men — the Gentiles as well as the Jews, the poor as well as the rich, the "publicans and sinners" as well as the scribes and Pharisees. At this he never ceased to marvel, and about this he wrote with enthusiasm.

In verse 6 in place of "they feared the people" (Mark 11:32), Luke has **all the people will stone us.** This shows something of the feeling of the common people toward their hypocritical leaders. The people especially resented ecclesiastical criticism of John the Baptist. For over three centuries Israel had been without a prophet. It seemed that God would never speak again. But now a true prophet had risen in the person of John. The people were ready to turn on their leaders for not accepting John. The Sanhedrists knew they dared not *deny* the Baptist's divine authority. But they would not *affirm* it. So they replied that they did not know (v. 7). Plummer remarks: "This shameful and dishonest avowal is excelled a few days later by their answer to Pilate, 'We have no king but Caesar' (Jn. xix. 15) ."[446]

There are a few other points of especial interest in this paragraph. The first verse begins with *kai egeneto,* **and it came to pass** — Luke's favorite beginning phrase. **There came upon him** is one word in Greek, *epestesan.* Luke uses this verb seven times in his Gospel and eleven times in Acts. Elsewhere in the New Testament it is used three times by Paul, and that is all. In Acts 17:5 it is translated "assault." It is obvious that these religious leaders **came upon Jesus** with no good intent.

Who is he that gave thee this authority? (v. 2) may have been intended as a deliberate insult. Jesus had neither academic diploma nor ecclesiastical ordination, and the leaders knew it well. They may have wished to discredit Him before the people. Daube says of the term **scribes** that "in the New Testament it normally denotes 'the learned theologians,' as it often does in Rabbinic sources."[447] These challenged Jesus' right to teach, as well as to cleanse the Temple. Edersheim says: "There was no principle more firmly established by universal consent than that *authorita-*

---

[445] *Op. cit.,* p. 455.   [446] *Ibid.,* p. 457.
[447] David Daube, *The New Testament and Rabbinic Judaism,* p. 210.

tive teaching required previous authorization."[448]

2. Parable of the Wicked Husbandmen (20:9-18)

9 And he began to speak unto the people this parable: A man planted a vineyard, and let it out to husbandmen, and went into another country for a long time. 10 And at the season he sent unto the husbandmen a servant, that they should give him of the fruit of the vineyard: but the husbandmen beat him, and sent him away empty. 11 And he sent yet another servant: and him also they beat, and handled him shamefully, and sent him away empty. 12 And he sent yet a third: and him also they wounded, and cast him forth. 13 And the lord of the vineyard said, What shall I do? I will send my beloved son; it may be they will reverence him. 14 But when the husbandmen saw him, they reasoned one with another, saying, This is the heir; let us kill him, that the inheritance may be ours. 15 And they cast him forth out of the vineyard, and killed him. What therefore will the lord of the vineyard do unto them? 16 He will come and destroy these husbandmen, and will give the vineyard unto others. And when they heard it, they said, God forbid. 17 But he looked upon them, and said, What then is this that is written,

The stone which the builders rejected,
The same was made the head of the corner?

18 Every one that falleth on that stone shall be broken to pieces; but on whosoever it shall fall, it will scatter him as dust.

Again the three accounts move closely together (see notes on Matt. 21:33-46; Mark 12:1-12). In fact, **let it out** (v. 9) is the same Greek verb in all three Gospels, and it occurs nowhere else in the New Testament. At the end of verse 9, Luke adds **for a long time**. He seems to have some insight — by the help of the Holy Spirit and the apostle Paul — into the fact that there would be a considerable delay in the return of Christ.

Verse 10 indicates that in the terms of this lease it was specified that the rent be paid in kind, rather than in money. While both methods were used by the Jews, the former was more common.

He sent (v. 11) is literally, "he added

to send" (a Hebraism). The owner did not punish his renters for their disgraceful treatment of the first servant, but in addition sent another. The teaching of this parable underscores heavily the long-suffering of God. The same phrase occurs in verse 12 — "he added to send a third."

Wounded is the verb *traumatizo*, found only here and in Acts 19:16. The noun *trauma*, which has been taken over into English, occurs only in the Parable of the Good Samaritan (10:34).

Luke alone pictures **the lord of the vineyard** saying, **What shall I do?** (v. 13). He was perplexed by the attitudes and actions of his tenants. He finally decided that the only solution was to send his **beloved son** (or, "only son"). A. B. Bruce comments: "In Luke the reference to the son has a theological colour."[449] **It may be** is one word, an adverb, *isos* (literally, "equally"). It means "perhaps" or "probably." It occurs only here in the New Testament and only once in the Septuagint (I Sam. 25:21), where the English versions translate it "surely." Godet favors "undoubtedly" here,[450] and that certainly fits the context well.

Amazingly, the wicked husbandmen went so far as to kill the owner's son (v. 15). Jesus outlined the severe punishment — destruction — which must follow such a crime (v. 16). The vineyard would be given to others.

The reaction of the crowd was swift and shocked. They said, **God forbid.** In the Greek it is *me genoito*; literally, "may it not be." This is the only place in the New Testament where this expression is found outside Paul's Epistles, where it occurs fourteen times (ten in Rom., three in Gal., one in I Cor.). Burton says: "The phrase *me genoito* is an Optative of Wishing which strongly deprecates something suggested by a previous question or assertion."[451]

The context clearly suggests that the phrase was a vigorous exclamation of disagreement. It is of interest to note that this is the only place in which the Revised Standard Version translates *me genoito* with "God forbid." In Romans it has "By no means!" In I Corinthians 6:15 it is "Never!" In Galatians it is twice, "Certainly not!" These variations apparently reflect the preferences of the

[448] *Op. cit.*, II, 381.   [449] EGT, I, 613.   [450] *Op. cit.*, II, 239.
[451] Ernest DeWitt Burton, *Syntax of the Moods and Tenses in New Testament Greek*, p. 79.

different translators. All represent well the strong negative wish expressed in the original.

In response to the exclamation of the crowd, Jesus **looked upon them** (v. 17); that is, fixed His gaze on them (only in Luke). Then He asked, **What then is this?** If this is not to happen as you suggest, how will the Scripture be fulfilled? Solemnly He quoted Psalm 118: 22,[452] then sounded the double warning of verse 18. This seems to be adapted from Isaiah 8:14 and Daniel 2:34, 35, 44. The last clause is correctly translated, **it will scatter him as dust** (that is, "it will be pulverized and blown away"), rather than, "it will grind him to powder" (KJV). The reference is clearly to Daniel 2:35. When the stone "cut out without hands" struck the image of metals, "Then was the iron, the clay, the brass, the silver, and the gold, broken in pieces together, and became like the chaff of the summer threshing-floors: and the wind carried it away."

This is the figure that is used here. During His earthly ministry Christ was a stumbling-stone to the Jewish leaders. They fell over Him and were **broken to pieces.** He was there for them to stumble over because they, **the builders** (v. 17), had **rejected** Him. Instead of using Him in building the spiritual Temple of God's presence in their midst, they had thrown Him aside. But in the divine plan and purpose He was made **the head of the corner.** "Not the key-stone of the arch, but a corner-stone uniting two walls; but whether a foundation-stone at the base of the corner, or a completing stone at the top of it, is uncertain."[453]

The general meaning of the parable is clear. It lends itself almost inevitably to an allegorical interpretation. The "man" who planted the vineyard is God. The "vineyard" is the nation of Israel. The "husbandmen" are the leaders of the nation. The "servants" are the Old Testament prophets whom God sent to His people. These were often persecuted by the leaders, and some were killed. Finally God sent His "beloved Son." And now they were about to kill Him, too. The message was so clear it could not be missed.

There has been some dispute as to

what is meant by the "vineyard." Plummer writes: "The vineyard is not the nation, but its spiritual privileges. The nation was not to be transferred to other rulers, but its privileges were to be transferred to other nations."[454]

Geldenhuys says: "We cannot agree with this. The vineyard was throughout the Old Testament used as a symbol of the people of Israel. So here also it will stand for the true Israel, the real people of God."[455]

In spite of the difficulties involved it seems better to adopt the latter interpretation. It seems less complicated and more Biblical.

There is one other item in the parable that calls for a word of comment. Many critics have pointed out the fact that the reasoning of the wicked husbandmen seems ridiculous. How could they hope to gain the son's inheritance by killing him. The very idea is preposterous. But Geldenhuys has a good answer for this. He writes: ". . . it is precisely Jesus' intention to call attention to the folly of the Jewish leaders' attitude towards Him by using as an example the foolish reasonings of the husbandmen."[456]

3. Question About Paying Taxes (20: 19-26)

19 And the scribes and the chief priests sought to lay hands on him in that very hour; and they feared the people: for they perceived that he spake this parable against them. 20 And they watched him, and sent forth spies, who feigned themselves to be righteous, that they might take hold of his speech, so as to deliver him up to the rule and to the authority of the governor. 21 And they asked him, saying, Teacher, we know that thou sayest and teachest rightly, and acceptest not the person of *any*, but of a truth teachest the way of God: 22 Is it lawful for us to give tribute unto Caesar, or not? 23 But he perceived their craftiness, and said unto them, 24 Show me a denarius. Whose image and superscription hath it? And they said, Caesar's. 25 And he said unto them, Then render unto Caesar the things that are Caesar's, and unto God the things that are God's. 26 And they were not able to take hold of the saying before the people. and

---

[452] "The Rabbis recognized it as Messianic" (Plummer, *op. cit.*, p. 462).   [453] *Ibid.*
[454] *Ibid.*, p. 458.   [455] *Op. cit.*, p. 500.   [456] *Ibid.*

they marvelled at his answer, and held their peace.

For extended discussion of this paragraph see the notes on Matthew 22:15-22 and Mark 12:13-17. We shall confine ourselves here largely to treating the items found only in Luke.

So enraged were the **scribes and the chief priests** (v. 19) — that is, the Pharisees and the Sadducees — that they sought to seize Christ **in that very hour** (in Luke only). Fear of the people restrained them. It would have been a very difficult thing to arrest Jesus, surrounded as He was by a great crowd of admiring Galileans, who had two days earlier acclaimed Him King (19:38).

One thing that especially angered these leaders at this time was that **they perceived that he spake this parable against them.** The main meaning of what Jesus said was so utterly obvious that probably few of the hearers failed to catch the point. Instead of discrediting Christ before the crowd, as they had set out to do with their question about authority, they had been discredited. Frustrated and furious, Jesus' enemies determined now to wreak vengeance on Him by securing His death.

Luke says **they watched him,**[457] **and sent forth spies** (literally, "men hired to lie in wait"). Mark identifies these as "certain of the Pharisees and of the Herodians" (Mark 12:13). Matthew (22:15, 16) also names the two groups, but indicates that the Pharisees took the initiative. These **spies** "played the hypocrite," as the Greek suggests; they **feigned** (*hypokrinomenuus*) **themselves to be righteous** (v. 20). They were wolves in sheep's clothing. Their main object was to **take hold of his speech.** It is interesting to note how the three Synoptists say the same thing, but in different words. Matthew and Mark both use rare terms for hunting or trapping (see notes there). Luke employs still a third term, but one that is more common. They all agree that the purpose of the Pharisees and Herodians was to catch Him in an unguarded statement which they could use as a club to knock Him down. Luke completes the disclosure of their objective; **so as to deliver him up to the rule**

and to the authority of the governor.

The hypocrisy of these spies is shown in the insincere flattery they showered on Jesus as they addressed Him (v. 21). Plummer says: "The falseness of these fulsome compliments in their mouths . . . stamps this as one of the most dastardly of the attacks on Christ."[458]

The question they asked was: **Is it lawful to give tribute unto Ceasar, or not?** (v. 22). All three Synoptists use the word **tribute** here. But Mark and Matthew use a different Greek word, from the Latin *census.* Luke's term is *phoros.* This comes from the verb *phero,* which means "bear" or "carry." So it indicates a burden to be borne — which is what all taxes are. Abbott-Smith says that *phoros* means *"tribute* paid by a subject nation."[459] It was probably a poll tax, as the word used in Matthew and Mark indicates. A "census" was taken for one purpose only — the assessing and collecting of taxes. This poll tax was particularly hated for two reasons. The first was that the coin which was used carried the image of the emperor. This seemed to the Jews to be idolatrous. The second reason was that it was a constant reminder to the Jews that they were not free, but were in subjection to Rome.

The similarity of meaning with difference of wording shows up also in verse 23. **Perceived** is a different Greek word in each case. For **craftiness** Matthew has "wickedness" and Mark "hypocrisy." These spies were characterized by all three.

In verse 25 **render unto Caesar the things that are Caesar's** was especially needed by the Pharisees, while **unto God the things that are God's** was needed by the Herodians. The latter were evidently followers and supporters of Herod Antipas. They were politicians, not religious leaders. Josephus does not even mention them. But the Pharisees were using them for a purpose — though ordinarily they would have had nothing to do with them.

And they were not able to take hold of the saying before the people (v. 26) is found only in Luke. A popular saying of that time was: "He whose coin

---

[457] "Him" is not in the original and perhaps should not be supplied in English. The verb may mean "watching for an opportunity" (aorist participle).
[458] *Op. cit.,* p. 465.   [459] *Op. cit.,* p. 473.

is current is king of the land." The Pharisees had agreed to this. Jesus reiterated this fact. "The point was this — their national acceptance of Caesar's coinage was an admission of Caesar's right. Tribute to them was no longer an offering, but a due."[460]

4. Question About the Resurrection (20:27-40)

27 And there came to him certain of the Sadducees, they that say that there is no resurrection; 28 and they asked him, saying, Teacher, Moses wrote unto us, that if a man's brother die, having a wife, and he be childless, his brother should take the wife, and raise up seed unto his brother. 29 There were therefore seven brethren: and the first took a wife, and died childless; 30 and the second: 31 and the third took her; and likewise the seven also left no children, and died. 32 Afterward the woman also died. 33 In the resurrection therefore whose wife of them shall she be? for the seven had her to wife. 34 And Jesus said unto them, The sons of this world marry, and are given in marriage: 35 but they that are accounted worthy to attain to that world, and the resurrection from the dead, neither marry, nor are given in marriage: 36 for neither can they die any more: for they are equal unto the angels; and are the sons of God, being sons of the resurrection. 37 But that the dead are raised, even Moses showed, in *the place concerning* the Bush, when he calleth the Lord the God of Abraham, and the God of Isaac, and the God of Jacob. 38 Now he is not the God of the dead, but of the living: for all live unto him. 39 And certain of the scribes answering said, Teacher, thou hast well said. 40 For they durst not any more ask him any question.

For discussion of this paragraph see the notes on Matthew 22:23-33 and Mark 12:18-27. The accounts are very similar. The **Sadducees** are mentioned only here in Luke's Gospel, though several times in Acts (also only this one place in Mark). The question they asked was not a dangerous one, as was the previous query. Evidently the intention of the Sadducees was to hold Jesus up to ridicule before the crowd because He would not be able to answer the impossible question they posed. Plummer says: "The question is a plausible appeal to

the rough common sense of the multitude, and is based upon the coarse materialistic views of the resurrection which then prevailed."[461]

The words of Jesus in verses 34-36 are mostly found only in this Gospel. The Master contrasted **the sons of this world** ("age") with those **accounted worthy to attain to that world** ("age"). Entrance into "that age" is through the **resurrection from the dead**. Since one of the main purposes of marriage is the propagation of the human race, when death is abolished there will be no need for marriage. We shall live on so much higher a plane of spiritual fellowship that probably social companionship, as we know it here, will be superseded.

These three verses (34-36) are strongly reminiscent of Paul. The opening words of verse 35 remind one of Philippians 3: 11. The closing words of verse 38 are similar to Romans 14:8. Luke shows much Pauline influence in His Gospel.

5. Jesus' Question About David's Son (20:41-44)

41 And he said unto them, How say they that the Christ is David's son? 42 For David himself saith in the book of Psalms,

The Lord said unto my Lord,
Sit thou on my right hand,
43 Till I make thine enemies the footstool of thy feet.
44 David therefore calleth him Lord, and how is he his son?

For notes on his passage see those on Matthew 22:41-46 and Mark 12:35-37. Matthew indicates that Jesus took advantage of the presence of a large number of Pharisees to ask them a question. Different groups had stood and asked questions of Him. Now it was His turn to ask them. It is not surprising that they could not answer.

The question was how the Messiah could be both David's Son and David's Lord. The answer is found in the Incarnation. Jesus was both human and divine, so that He could fill both roles.

6. Denunciation of the Scribes (20:45-47)

45 And in the hearing of all the people he said unto his disciples, 46 Beware

460 Farrar, *op. cit.*, p. 354.   461 *Op. cit.*, p. 468.

of the scribes, who desire to walk in long robes, and love salutations in the market-places, and chief seats in the synagogues, and chief places at feasts; 47 who devour widows' houses, and for a pretence make long prayers: these shall receive greater condemnation.

This brief paragraph is similar to Mark 12:38-40 (see notes there). Ostentatiousness was apparently one of the besetting sins of the Pharisees. They loved to walk around in **long robes** — one word in the Greek, *stole,* which has been taken over into English for a cape or shawl. These **long robes** had wide, conspicuous fringes of blue — to prove that the wearers were pious. The scribes literally paraded their piety.

The crowning hypocrisy of the scribes was the fact that they would **devour widows' houses,** and then for a pretence make long prayers. No wonder Jesus said: **These shall receive greater condemnation.** To cover up a wicked life with a mask of religion is a serious insult to God who knows us altogether.

This incident marks the final break between Jesus and the Pharisees. He denounced them for their hpyocrisy, and now the battle line was drawn. The only outcome must be His death.

D. THE WIDOW'S MITE (21:1-4)

1 And he looked up, and saw the rich men that were casting their gifts into the treasury. 2 And he saw a certain poor widow casting in thither two mites. 3 And he said, Of a truth I say unto you, This poor widow cast in more than they all: 4 for all these did of their superfluity cast in unto the gifts; but she of her want did cast in all the living that she had.

This significant little incident is recorded also in Mark 12:41-44 (see the comments there). Luke's briefer account has practically nothing unique in it.

Both describe a **poor widow** (v. 2). The adjective which Mark uses is a very common one in the New Testament. Literally it means "crouching, cowering," and so "beggarly" (cf. Gal. 4:9). But usually it has the broader connotation, "poor." On the other hand, the term which Luke uses is found only here in the New Tesament. It means "needy, poor."

Luke's vocabulary indicates a wider knowledge of Greek literature than that possessed by other writers of the New Testament.

The story of the widow's mite may be recorded here because of the reference to the scribes as those who "devour widows' houses" (20:47; Mark 12:40). It is significant that Mark and Luke have both passages, while Matthew has neither. Donald Miller makes another suggestion. He writes: "The connection between this incident and the condemnation of the scribes which immediately precedes it is clear. In contrast to a piety which paraded in public for self-gain, the poor widow gave all she had in love for God."[462]

Luke alone says that Jesus **looked up.** Plummer suggests: "The long discussions had wearied Him, and He had been sitting with downcast or closed eyes."[463] Farrar registers the same thought and and then adds: "But this last little incident is 'like a rose amid a field of thistles,' — an act genuinely beautiful in the desert of 'official devotion.' "[464]

The poor widow cast into one of the trumpet-mouthed receptacles in the treasury **two mites.** "The *lepton* or *prutah* was the smallest of coins, and the Rabbis did not allow any one to give less than two."[465]

Jesus' supernatural knowledge is shown in the fact that He knew this woman had **cast in all the living that she had.** Beyond this no one's giving could go. "The essence of charity is self-denial."[466]

E. THE OLIVET DISCOURSE (21:5-36)

This is called the Olivet Discourse because it was delivered on the slopes of the Mount of Olives. It is the only long discourse recorded in all three Synoptic Gospels (see notes on Matthew 24; Mark 13). John's Gospel has in place of it the Last Discourse in the upper room (John 14-16).

In this Olivet Discourse Jesus deals with two topics: (1) the destruction of Jerusalem and its Temple in A.D. 70; (2) the signs of the Second Coming and the end of the age. As noted in the commentary on Matthew, it is very difficult to separate the particular verses

---

[462] *Op. cit.,* p. 145. [463] *Op. cit.,* p. 475. [464] *Op. cit.,* p. 356.
[465] *Ibid.,* p. 359. [466] *Ibid.*

LUKE, CHAPTER 21   325

which deal with each. This is especially true of Matthew and Mark. Geldenhuys affirms: "In Luke the classification is much clearer."[467] He goes on to say: "Luke, although he does not give such a full report of the Prophetic Discourse as Matthew, was evidently the most successful in so relating it that we can see comparatively clearly which portions refer to the destruction of Jerusalem and preceding events, and which refer to the final Judgment."[468] He thinks that verses 5-24 deal mostly with the destruction of Jerusalem, verses 25-28 with the signs of the Second Coming, verses 29-33 with watching for the former, and verses 34-36 with watching for the latter.

1. Introduction (21:5-9)

5 And as some spake of the temple, how it was adorned with goodly stones and offerings, he said, 6 As for these things which ye behold, the days will come, in which there shall not be left here one stone upon another, that shall not be thrown down. 7 And they asked him, saying, Teacher, when therefore shall these things be? and what *shall be* the sign when these things are about to come to pass? 8 And he said, Take heed that ye be not led astray: for many shall come in my name, saying, I am *he*; and, The time is at hand: go ye not after them. 9 And when ye shall hear of wars and tumults, be not terrified: for these things must needs come to pass first; but the end is not immediately.

Luke is more indefinite in his notations of time and place than the other two Synoptists. From his account one would assume that this prophetic discourse was given in the Temple. But Mark indicates that the remarks about the Temple came as He was leaving the Sacred Enclosure (Matthew, after He left) and that the disciples' questions were asked and answered "as he sat on the Mount of Olives" (same in Matthew). Furthermore, Luke says some spoke about the Temple, while Matthew identifies them as "his disciples" and Mark as "one of his disciples."

For Josephus' description of the goodly stones of the Temple, see the comments on Mark 13:1. The magnificence of the

edifice was renowned in that day. Tacitus the Roman historian when writing of the events of A.D. 70, said about Jerusalem: "There stood a temple of immense wealth."[469] Many had given offerings to adorn it. Lavish votive gifts had been presented by Ptolemy Philadelphus of Egypt, by the Emperor Augustus, and others. Especially impressive was the great golden vine given by Herod the Great. Josephus writes: "And over these, but under the crown-work, was spread out a golden vine, with its branches hanging down from a great height, the largeness and fine workmanship of which was a surprising sight to the spectators."[470]

But Jesus predicted that the magnificent Temple — which Herod began building about 20 B.C., and which was not completed until about A.D. 64 — would be completely destroyed. The words here were literally fulfilled in A.D. 70.

Josephus says that Titus did not want to destroy the Temple, but that in spite of his wishes it was set afire. As Josephus expresses it, "God had, for certain, long ago doomed it to the fire."[471] Josephus also says that Titus was so amazed at the strong fortifications of the Temple that he exclaimed: "We have certainly had God for our assistant in this war, and it was no other than God who ejected the Jews out of these fortifications; for what could the hands of men or any machines do towards overthrowing these towers?"[472]

Again Luke uses an indefinite **they** (v. 7). Matthew says, "The disciples," and Mark more specifically: "Peter and James and John and Andrew." These **asked Him** ("privately," Matthew and Mark) a twofold question (threefold in Matthew). The first was, **When** will these things be? The second was, **What** will be the **sign** when these things are about to happen? **These things** (in both questions) refers naturally to what Jesus had just predicted — the destruction of the Temple. This is as far as the questions go in Mark and Luke. But Matthew changes the second question to a double one: "What shall be the sign of thy coming and of the end of the world (Greek, 'age')?" In all three Gos-

---

[467] *Op. cit.*, p. 523.   [468] *Ibid.*   [469] *Histories, The Annals and the Histories*, p. 296 (V 8).
[470] *Ant.*, XV. 11. 3.   [471] *War*, VI.4.5.
[472] *War*, VI. 9.1. For a detailed description of Herod's Temple, see A. T. Olmstead, *Jesus in the Light of History*, pp. 81-91.

pels Christ seems to answer the threefold question of Matthew.

In reply to these questions Jesus warned that false Messiahs would come (v. 8; cf. Matthew 24:5); there would be **wars** (v. 9). Luke adds: **and tumults.** The word means "disturbances, disorders."[473] For this passage Arndt and Gingrich suggest "insurrections."[474] That this prophecy was fulfilled is attested by Tacitus. Writing about the year A.D. 69, just before the destruction of Jerusalem, he says: "I am entering on the history of a period rich in disasters, frightful in its wars, torn by civil strife, and even in peace full of horrors."[475]

In spite of these signs, Jesus said: **The end is not immediately.** This seems to refer to the end of the age, rather than the destruction of Jerusalem. But Farrar observes: "The Fall of Jerusalem was the Close of that Aeon and a symbol of the Final End."[476] Here we have that blending of the Near and the Far which we find throughout the Olivet Discourse. Speaking of the Synoptic accounts of this, Plummer says: "But in all three records the outlines of the two main events, with their signs, cannot always be disentangled. Some of the utterances clearly point to the Destruction of Jerusalem; others equally clearly to the Return of the Christ. But there are some which apply to either or both; and we, who stand between the two, cannot be sure which one, if only one, is intended."[477]

2. Tribulation and Persecution (21:10-19)

10 Then said he unto them, Nation shall arise against nation, and kingdom against kingdom; 11 and there shall be great earthquakes, and in divers places famines and pestilences; and there shall be terrors and great signs from heaven. 12 But before all these things, they shall lay their hands on you, and shall persecute you, delivering you up to the synagogues and prisons, bringing you before kings and governors for my name's sake. 13 It shall turn out unto you for a testimony. 14 Settle it therefore in your hearts, not to meditate beforehand how to answer: 15 for I will give you a mouth and wisdom, which all your adversaries shall not be able to withstand

or to gainsay. 16 But ye shall be delivered up even by parents, and brethren, and kinsfolk, and friends; and *some* of you shall they cause to be put to death. 17 And ye shall be hated for all men for my name's sake. 18 And not a hair of your head shall perish. 19 In your patience ye shall win your souls.

This paragraph gives a dark picture of the days ahead which the disciples must face. The Book of Acts records the fulfillment of many of these predictions as we shall see. The first century was a turbulent time, especially the latter half. Four Roman emperors — Nero, Galba, Otho, and Vitellius — either were assassinated or committed suicide.

Then said he unto them (v. 10) is found only in Luke. Plummer calls it: "A new introduction to mark a solemn utterance."[478] Creed also says: "The formula marks a transition from the warnings of vv. 8-9 to the definitely prophetic passage which follows."[479]

The fulfillment of the prediction that **nation shall rise against nation, and kingdom against kingdom** is abundantly corroborated by Tacitus. But in addition to these political upheavals there were signs in nature. A number of **earthquakes** took place during the decade preceding the destruction of Jerusalem. In A.D. 61 there was a severe one in Phrygia (in Asia Minor), which did a great deal of damage. Another earthquake destroyed Laodicea, Hierapolis, and other cities in A.D. 67 or 68. **Famines and pestilences** is in the Greek *loimoi kai limoi* — a play on words. Josephus mentions both of these as taking place when vast crowds came to Jerusalem for the Passover, and found themselves besieged by the Roman army. He says: ". . . there came a pestilential destruction upon them, and soon afterward such a famine, as destroyed them more suddenly."[480] Acts 11:28 mentions a "great famine" that took place in the reign of Claudius (A.D. 41-54).

Then Luke (alone) adds a startling prediction: **and there shall be terrors and great signs from heaven.** Josephus mentions a comet which hung over the city for a year. He also says that after the Passover, ". . . before sunsetting, chariots and troops of soldiers in their armour

---

[473] Thayer, *op. cit.*, p. 21.   [474] *Op. cit.*, p. 29.
[476] *Op. cit.*, p. 360.   [477] *Op. cit.*, pp. 477, 478.
[480] *War*, VI.9.3.

[475] *Histories*, I, 2. (*op. cit.*, p. 189).
[478] *Ibid.*, p. 478.   [479] *Op. cit.*, p. 255.

were seen running about among the clouds, and surrounding of cities."[481] He says that at the feast of Pentecost the priests ". . . felt a quaking, and heard a great noise, and after that they heard a sound as of a great multitude, saying, 'Let us remove hence.' "[482] God had forsaken His city, and the people would do well to leave it. Tacitus also mentions these wonders.[483]

Luke (alone) goes on to say: But before all these things, they shall lay their hands on you, and shall persecute you (v. 12). Confirmation of this comes in Acts 4, 5, 6, 7, 8, 12, 13, 14, 16, 18, 21. Synagogues indicates Jewish persecution, which came first. "Bringing you before kings and governors" was fulfilled in Paul's case (Acts 24, 25, 26). But all of this would give them an opportunity to witness for Christ (v. 13).

When imprisoned and facing trial they were not to meditate beforehand how to answer (v. 14). The verb meditate beforehand is found only here in the New Testament. Arndt and Gingrich note that it was a "technical term for practising a speech."[484] Answer is the verb apologeo, which means "defend oneself" — make one's "apology" in the original sense of that term ("defense") and not in the modern sense ("I'm sorry"). So the whole phrase here could be translated "prepare one's defense."[485] The Lord promised that He Himself (the I is emphatic in the Greek) would give His persecuted disciples a mouth and wisdom which all their adversaries would not be able to withstand or gainsay (v. 15). The Greek has here a play on words — three terms beginning with anti (against). Literally it reads: "which all those lying against you shall not be able to stand against or to speak against."

A sad note is injected here. Believers would be betrayed (delivered up [v. 16] — same verb used of Judas betraying Jesus) by relatives and friends, even by parents. That sort of thing is happening in Communist countries today. For the meaning of hated of all men (v. 17), see the notes on Mark 13:13. Luke alone adds the comforting assurance: And not a hair of your head shall perish (v. 28) — God's perfect care of His children. Since Christ has already said that some

of them would be put to death (v. 16), it is obvious that this promise must be taken in a spiritual sense. Meyer interprets it: "You shall not come by the slightest harm as to the Messianic salvation."[486]

On the surface, Luke's In your patience ye shall win your souls (v. 19) seems rather different from Matthew's and Mark's "But he that endureth to the end, the same shall be saved." However, in the Greek the connection is closer than in English. For patience has the same root as "endureth." The Greek word translated patience (KJV) is more accurately rendered "endurance" (RSV). It is not a negative, passive attitude, but a positive, active one. That point is often missed in our common English version (e.g., Heb. 12:1).

Win is literally "gain." "Souls" may be translated "lives." This verse is tied in with the spiritual interpretation of the previous verse. "There the loss of eternal salvation is spoken of as death. Here the gaining of it is called winning one's life."[487]

3. Destruction of Jerusalem (21:20-24)

20 But when ye see Jerusalem compassed with armies, then know that her desolation is at hand. 21 Then let them that are in Judaea flee unto the mountains; and let them that are in the midst of her depart out; and let not them that are in the country enter therein. 22 For these are days of vengeance, that all things which are written may be fulfilled. 23 Woe unto them that are with child and to them that give suck in those days! for there shall be great distress upon the land, and wrath unto this people. 24 And they shall fall by the edge of the sword, and shall be led captive into all the nations: and Jerusalem shall be trodden down of the Gentiles, until the times of the Gentiles be fulfilled.

In Matthew and Mark the warning sign is, "When ye see the abomination of desolation standing where it ought not" (Mark 13:14). Luke has, When ye see Jerusalem compassed with armies (v. 20) The Greek says, "being surrounded." When the encircling of the city was completed, it would be too late to es

481 War, VI.5.3.   482 Ibid.   483 Histories, V.13.   484 Op. cit., p. 715.   485 Ibid.
486 Op. cit., p. 529.   487 Plummer, op. cit., p. 481.

cape. The Christians must flee when they saw the siege beginning. Luke adds: **then know that her desolation is at hand.** Here Luke brings in the word **desolation** which is found in the parallel passage in Matthew and Mark, and nowhere else in the New Testament. It means "a laying waste." Instead of the glorification of Jerusalem as the capital of the Messianic kingdom — which the disciples expected — Jesus predicted its desolation.

The first clause of verse 21 is identical in all three accounts.[488] But in the rest of the verse Luke differs from the other two (cf. Matt. 24:17; Mark 21:21). He says: **and let them that are in the midst of her** — that is, those living in Jerusalem — **depart out; and let not them that are in the country enter therein.** One of the things that added greatly to the miseries of the siege was that thousands of Jews poured into Jerusalem from the surrounding countryside, besides the multitudes of pilgrims that came to the Passover. It is no wonder that famine and pestilence soon plagued the city.

Luke alone adds: **For these are days of vengeance, that all things which are written may be fulfilled** (v. 22). The phrase **days of vengeance** in the Greek comes from the Septuagint of Hosea 9:7. It means the days of divine retribution on Jerusalem for putting to death its Messiah, the Son of God (cf. 20:16). Thus was **fulfilled** Deuteronomy 28:15-68.

Many scholars have maintained that Luke's change from "the abomination of desolation" to **Jerusalem compassed with armies** shows that he was writing after A.D. 70 and interpreting Jesus' words in the light of what happened then. But a simpler explanation is that Luke knew the apocalyptic phrase "abomination of desolation" (taken from Daniel), which Christ used in talking to a Jewish audience, would be meaningless to his Gentile readers. So he interpreted Jesus' Aramaic words into something concrete, in the light of the Master's own prediction of the destruction of Jerusalem (v. 6) — which implied a siege. Torrey goes

so far as to affirm that the Lukan form is the original one. "When you see the city in a state of siege, then get out."[489]

The first part of the verse 23 is identical in Matthew (24:19) and Mark (13:17). But in the latter part Luke differs. He says: **there shall be great distress upon the land** (Judea), **and wrath unto this people** (the Jews living there). This is probably Luke's explanation of why all this trouble was taking place. It was divine wrath upon the Jews for rejecting Jesus.

Verse 24 is found only in Luke. There was a horrible massacre of the people in Jerusalem when it was finally captured in A.D. 70. Josephus writes that "eleven hundred thousand" (1,100,000) perished during the siege, and that 97,000 were carried into captivity.[490] Tacitus says that the population of Jerusalem at this period was 600,000.[491] However, Josephus calls attention to the fact that the city was crowded with multitudes of pilgrims to the Passover. The main problem in accepting his almost fantastic figures is that it does not seem possible that so many people could get inside the walls of Jerusalem at one time. The Old City within the walls covers only about one-fourth of a square mile today. How much larger it may have been in Jesus' time is uncertain.

The times of the Gentiles refers to "the whole period during which the Gentile world-powers are in command."[492] Jerusalem has been under the domination of the Gentiles most of the time since its capture by the Babylonians in 586 B.C., after serving as the capital of the independent nation for only about four hundred years (David began to reign about 1000 B.C.).

4. Coming of the Son of Man (21:25-28)

25 And there shall be signs in sun and moon and stars; and upon the earth distress of nations, in perplexity for the roaring of the sea and the billows; 26 men fainting for fear, and for expectation of the things which are coming on the

[488] For Eusebius' account of the flight of the Christians from Jerusalem, see the notes on Matthew 24:17. This may have taken place when the army of Cestius Gallus was repulsed from the city in October of A. D. 66. Geldenhuys interprets the "abomination of desolation" as "the symbol of the pagan, hostile forces that will invade the Holy Land and threaten the city" (*op. cit.*, p. 532).
[489] C. C. Torrey, *Documents of the Primitive Church*, p. 20. For a striking quotation from an article by C. H. Dodd, see Geldenhuys, *op. cit.*, p. 533.
[490] *War.* VI. 9. 3. [491] *Histories*, V. 13. [492] Geldenhuys, *op. cit.*, p. 536.

world: for the powers of the heavens shall be shaken. 27 And then shall they see the Son of man coming in a cloud with power and great glory. 28 But when these things begin to come to pass, look up, and lift up your heads; because your redemption draweth nigh.

Matthew and Mark also mention **signs in sun and moon and stars.** But the rest of verse 25 and most of verse 26 are found only in Luke. These words form a graphic description of the **fear** which will seize men's hearts as they see the horrors of divine judgment descending on the earth and wonder what may be coming next. The Greek compound verb for **fainting** is found only here in the New Testament. It means "swooning." In other words, so shocking will be the events that men will swoon away. **World** here is the "inhabited earth" (oikoumene).

Verse 27 is paralleled in Matthew 24: 30 and Mark 13:26. But verse 28 is found only here. Warning changes to exhortation, as believers are encouraged to **look up.** When the outlook is at its blackest, the uplook is still bright with the promises of God. The darkest hour is just before the dawn. **Redemption** means "release" or "deliverance," which will come to Christians at the second advent of Christ.

5. Parable of the Fig Tree (21:29-33)

29 And he spake to them a parable: Behold the fig tree, and all the trees: 30 when they now shoot forth, ye see it and know of your own selves that the summer is now nigh. 31 Even so ye also, when ye see these things coming to pass, know ye that the kingdom of God is nigh. 32 Verily I say unto you, this generation shall not pass away, till all things be accomplished. 33 Heaven and earth shall pass away: but my words shall not pass away.

This brief parable is found in all three Synoptics in almost identical language (see notes on Matt. 24:32-36; Mark 13: 28-32). While the figure of a tree growing leaves in the spring, as a harbinger of summer, has a general application, the **fig tree** has often been taken as typifying Israel. If this is valid, it raises the question as to whether the setting up of the new nation of Israel on May 15,

1948, may not be a fulfillment of this prophecy. For almost exactly two thousand years — from 63 B.C., when Pompey took Jerusalem for the Romans, until A.D. 1948 — there had been no independent nation of Israel. Certainly this seems to be one of the signs that **the kingdom of God is nigh** (v. 31). This is Luke's substitute for Matthew's and Mark's "he is nigh" — which can as well be translated, "it is nigh." For explanation of the difficult statement in verse 32, see the notes on Matthew 24:34 and Mark 13:30.

6. Necessity of Watching (21:34-36)

34 But take heed to yourselves, lest haply your hearts be overcharged with surfeiting, and drunkenness, and cares of this life, and that day come on you suddenly as a snare: 35 for so shall it come upon all them that dwell on the face of all the earth. 36 But watch ye at every season, making supplication, that ye may prevail to escape all these things that shall come to pass, and to stand before the Son of man.

This brief paragraph does not have any close parallel in Matthew or Mark. It is a warning against careless living (vv. 34, 35) and an exhortation to watch continually (v. 36).

Overcharged is literally "burdened." Arndt and Gingrich comment: "Of hearts that become heavy, i.e., lose their sensitiveness (cf. Exod. 7:14) in drunkenness."[493] **Surfeiting** is "both *carousing, intoxication,* and its results *drunken headache, hangover,* since it means *dizziness, staggering,* when the head refuses to function."[494] The word for **drunkenness** occurs only here and twice in Paul's Epistles (Rom. 13:13; Gal. 5:21). It is a distinct shock to discover in what bad company **cares** (rather, "anxieties") **of this life** are found. Many Christians who would never dream of getting drunk will yet allow anxiety to hamper their spiritual growth (cf. 8:14) and hinder their service in the Kingdom.

The warning is that the day of Christ's return will come **suddenly as a snare,** just as a trap springs shut. So the exhortation is given to **watch . . . at every season,** keeping prayerful (**making supplication**) so that one may prevail to escape the judgments that are coming on the earth, **and to stand before the Son of man.**

F. JESUS' DAILY PROGRAM (21:37, 38)

37 And every day he was teaching in the temple; and every night he went out, and lodged in the mount that is called Olivet. 38 And all the people came early in the morning to him in the temple, to hear him.

During the closing days of His ministry Jesus spent the daytime hours **teaching in the temple** and the nights lodging on the Mount of Olives. Whether this means that He slept in the open or stayed in Bethany with friends, is not clear.

All the people **came early** (Greek verb found only here in the New Testament) to the Temple **to hear him.** The common people still clung eagerly to the words of Jesus, even though their rulers rejected Him and finally condemned Him to death.

VI. THE PASSION (22:1–23:56)

A. THE PLOT AGAINST JESUS (22:1-6)

1. Desire of the Rulers (22:1, 2)

1 Now the feast of unleavened bread drew nigh, which is called the Passover. 2 And the chief priests and the scribes sought how they might put him to death; for they feared the people.

Matthew and Mark say it was two days before the Passover. Luke simply says that **the feast of unleavened bread drew nigh, which is called the Passover.** Strictly speaking, the Passover came on the 14th Nisan, and then the Feast of Unleavened Bread was celebrated for the next seven days, the 15th to 21st Nisan (Lev. 23:5, 6; Num. 28:16, 17; II Chron. 30:15, 21; Ezra 6:19, 22). Mark's reference conforms more nearly to this: "the passover and the unleavened bread" (Mark 14:1). Josephus sometimes combines the two. For instance, he writes: "We keep a feast for eight days, which is called the feast of unleavened bread."[495] At other times he separates them. For example, he states that on the fourteenth day of the lunar month Nisan the Jews sacrifice the Passover, and then adds: "The feast of unleavened bread succeeds that of the passover, and

falls on the fifteenth day of the month, and continues seven days."[496] But the correctness of the Lukan usage is confirmed by this passage: "This happened at the time when the feast of unleavened bread was celebrated, which we call the passover."[497]

The chief priests and the scribes — Sadducees and Pharisees — **sought** — literally, "were seeking" — **how they might put him to death.** This verb is used almost exclusively by Luke. Matthew and Mark use a more common verb, translated, "kill." The rulers were determined to kill Jesus, but they wanted to find some secret way of doing it, because they were afraid of the people.

2. Covenant with Judas (22:3-6)

3 And Satan entered into Judas who was called Iscariot, being of the number of the twelve. 4 And he went away, and communed with the chief priests and captains, how he might deliver him unto them. 5 And they were glad, and covenanted to give him money. 6 And he consented, and sought opportunity to deliver him unto them in the absence of the multitude.

This nefarious compact is related in all three Synoptics (see the notes on Matthew 26:14-16; Mark 14:10, 11). Luke alone says that **Satan entered into Judas.** Some have wondered how this could be harmonized with John 13:27, which says that after Judas Iscariot had received the sop from Jesus at the Last Supper "then entered Satan into him." Godet offers a good suggestion. Speaking of Luke, he says:

He means to remark here, in a general way, the intervention of the superior agent in this extraordinary crime; while John, seeking to characterize its various *degrees,* more exactly distinguishes the time when Satan put into the heart of Judas the first thought of it (comp.xiii.2) , and the moment when he *entered into him* so as to take entire possession of his will (xiii. 27). According to the biblical view, this intervention of Satan did not at all exclude the liberty of Judas.[498]

Farrar also has a helpful treatment of this phrase, as well as the motives of Judas' betrayal. He writes:

[495] *Ant.* II. 15. 1.   [496] *Ant.* III. 10. 5.   [497] *Ant.* XIV. 2. 1.   [498] *Op. cit.,* pp. 279, 280.

No other expression seems adequately to explain his wickedness. It began in avarice, disappointment, and jealousy; and, when he had long weakened his soul by indulgence in these dark, besetting sins, the imaginary loss of the "300 pence" of which he would have had the disposal (John xii.4,5; Mark xiv.10), — the now undisguised announcement of our Lord that He should be not only rejected but *crucified* (Matthew xx.19) — the consequent shattering of all Messianic hopes — the growing sense that he was becoming distasteful to his Master and his fellows — the open rebuke which he had drawn on his own head by his hypocritic greed at Bethany (John xii.6) — the rumored hostility of all the most venerated authorities of the nation — all these formed the climax of his temptations: — and then, at last, the tempting opportunity met the susceptible disposition.[499]

All three accounts register the fact that Judas Iscariot was one of **the twelve.** This underscored the depth of his depravity. He was Christ's chosen companion and trusted helper, yet he turned against his Master and betrayed Him.

All three Gospels say that Judas' agreement was made with **the chief priests.** Because of Christ's cleansing of the Temple, the Sadducees were infuriated with Him. They were determined to get Him out of the way. Luke adds, **and captains.** Plummer defines the term thus: "They are the leaders of the corps of Levites, which kept guard in and about the temple. . . . These officers would be consulted, because they had to take part in carrying out the arrest."[500]

Judas then **sought** ("began seeking") an opportune time to **deliver him** ("betray him") to the chief priests **in the absence of the multitude** (v. 6). It seems likely that the rulers had planned to wait until after the feast before trying to arrest Jesus. But when Judas made his offer they decided they had better accept it.

B. THE LAST PASSOVER (22:7-38)

1. The Preparation of the Passover (22:7-13)

7 And the day of unleavened bread came, on which the passover must be sacrificed. 8 And he sent Peter and John, saying, Go and make ready for us the passover, that we may eat. 9 And they said unto him, Where wilt thou that we make ready? 10 And he said unto them, Behold, when ye are entered into the city, there shall meet you a man bearing a pitcher of water; follow him into the house whereinto he goeth. 11 And ye shall say unto the master of the house, The Teacher saith unto thee, Where is the guest chamber, where I shall eat the passover with my disciples? 12 And he will show you a large upper room furnished: there make ready. 13 And they went, and found as he had said unto them: and they made ready the passover.

Mark and Luke are closely parallel at this point (see notes on Mark 14: 12-16; also on Matthew 26:17-19). Luke names **Peter and John** as the two disciples who were to go into Jerusalem and prepare the passover meal.

Probably most scholars would hold that Jesus had made earlier arrangements with the owner of the house. But Plummer says: "The Evangelists seem to intimate that Christ's knowledge was supernatural rather than the result of previous arrangement."[501]

2. The Last Supper (22:14-23)

14 And when the hour was come, he sat down, and the apostles with him. 15 And he said unto them, With desire I have desired to eat this passover with you before I suffer: 16 for I say unto you, I shall not eat it, until it be fulfilled in the kingdom of God. 17 And he received a cup, and when he had given thanks, he said, Take this, and divide it among yourselves: 18 for I say unto you, I shall not drink from henceforth of the fruit of the vine, until the kingdom of God shall come. 19 And he took bread, and when he had given thanks, he brake it, and gave to them, saying, This is my body which is given for you: this do in remembrance of me. 20 And the cup in like manner after supper, saying, This cup is the new covenant in my blood, *even* that which is poured out for you. 21 But behold, the hand of him that betrayeth me is with me on the table. 22 For the Son of man indeed goeth, as it hath been determined: but woe unto that man through whom he is betrayed! 23 And they began to question among themselves, which of them it was that should do this thing.

499 *Op. cit.*, p. 367.   500 *Op. cit.*, pp. 490, 491.   501 *Op. cit.*, p. 494.

The parallelism between the three Synoptists is rather close, although Luke presents the material in a different order from the other two (see notes on Matthew 26:20-29; Mark 15:17-25).

Matthew and Mark place the prediction of the betrayal at the beginning of the meal, Luke at the end. Apparently Luke was not concerned about chronological sequence.

Sat down (v. 14) is literally "fell up." It means "reclined." Many of the Jews had copied the Roman custom of reclining on couches around the table while eating.

Verses 15 and 16 are peculiar to Luke. With infinite tenderness Jesus said to the disciples: **With desire I have desired to eat this passover with you before I suffer.** It was to be His last time of fellowship with His chosen apostles. Twenty-four hours from then He would be in the grave, His cause apparently lost. It was the last time He would eat the Passover, **until it be fulfilled in the kingdom of God.** The Passover, as a type, was to be fulfilled in a spiritual sense in the death of Christ and in the coming of the Holy Spirit at Pentecost, to make the church one in fellowship with her living Lord.

Jesus declared that He would no more drink of the fruit of the vine **until the kingdom of God shall come** (v. 18). This is often interpreted as meaning, "until the Millennium." But the kingdom of God has come in a very real way, as a result of the Crucifixion, the Resurrection, and Pentecost. So some would say that the reference is to fellowship with the risen Lord at the Lord's Supper.

The description here of the inauguration of the Lord's Supper (vv. 19, 20) is more closely akin to Paul's words in I Corinthians 11:23-25 than are the accounts in Matthew and Mark. This is what one would expect, because of the close association of Paul and Luke. In all four accounts of the institution of the Lord's Supper it is stated that the **bread** represents Christ's body and **the cup** (meaning its contents) His blood.

Some object to the use of "represents" for **is.** They take their stand on a literal interpretation of **This is my body.** But Jesus' physical body was still intact when He uttered these words. Are we to take Christ literally when He said, "I am the door" (John 10:7)? Paul uses figurative language constantly. Speaking of the rock in the wilderness from which Moses brought forth water, he says, "That rock was Christ" (I Cor. 10:4). Pertinent to the passage here is his statement, "The bread which we break, is it not the communion of the body of Christ?" (I Cor. 10:16).

The correct interpretation of **This is my body . . . . my blood** is given by Jesus Himself in John's Gospel. Discoursing on the Bread of Life, the Master said: "I am the living bread which came down out of heaven: if any man eat of this bread, he shall live for ever: yea and the bread which I will give is my flesh, for the life of the world" (John 6:51). How did the religious leaders ("the Jews") take this? In a totally materialistic way. They asked, "How can this man give us his flesh to eat?"

As if to confound them further, Jesus became more specific: "Except ye eat the flesh of the Son of man and drink his blood, ye have not life in yourselves. He that eateth my flesh and drinketh my blood hath eternal life. . . . He that eateth my flesh and drinketh my blood abideth in me" (John 6:53-56).

Even the disciples had by now become confused. They said: "This is a hard saying; who can hear it?" (John 6:60). The Master then made a profound statement regarding Biblical interpretation. He said: "It is the spirit that giveth life; the flesh profiteth nothing: the words that I have spoken unto you are spirit, and are life" (John 6:63).

This eucharistic passage in John's Gospel fixes the correct interpretation of Jesus' words at the Last Supper. They must be interpreted spiritually. The bread and wine were physical symbols of spiritual reality. Likewise **body** and **blood** were symbolical terms, representing the *nature* of Christ. We eat His body and drink His blood when we meditate on Him and His words and by faith through the Spirit absorb His nature into our nature. Just as physical mastication helps the food we eat to become a living part of our body, so spiritual meditation makes it possible for the nature of Christ to become a part of our nature. "You are what you eat" is true physically. But it is also true intellectually and spiritually.

Verse 22 pinpoints one of the great paradoxes of Scripture. Jesus said: **the Son of man indeed goeth, as it hath been determined.** But He added: **woe unto that man through whom he is betrayed.** Here is the inescapable paradox of divine sovereignty and human freedom. God had decreed that His Son should die for men's sins. But He did not make Judas betray Jesus. Judas was free to choose — else his act would have no moral meaning and no guilt could be attached to it. To say that God determines men's actions and then punishes them for those acts is to make Him the worst moral monster imaginable. We must hold to *both* divine sovereignty and human freedom if we are to be true to the Scriptures and to life.

3. Strife About Rank (22:24-30)

24 And there arose also a contention among them, which of them was accounted to be greatest. 25 And he said unto them, The kings of the Gentiles have lordship over them; and they that have authority over them are called Benefactors. 26 But ye *shall* not be *so*: but he that is the greater among you, let him become as the younger; and he that is chief, as he that doth serve. 27 For which is greater, he that sitteth at meat, or he that serveth? is not he that sitteth at meat? but I am in the midst of you as he that serveth. 28 But ye are they that have continued with me in my temptation; 29 and I appoint unto you a kingdom, even as my Father appointed unto me, 30 that ye may eat and drink at my table in my kingdom; and ye shall sit on thrones judging the twelve tribes of Israel.

Matthew (20:20-28) and Mark (10: 35-45) give earlier pictures of the quarreling of the disciples about who should be **greatest.** But Luke indicates that they carried this **contention** (strong Greek word, only here in New Testament) even to the table at the Last Supper. Their carnal propensities showed up here in a very selfish, sordid way. They badly needed the cleansing of their hearts that was to take place at Pentecost (cf. Acts 15:8, 9). Probably here they were jockeying for the best position at the table.

Jesus pointed out the difference between the political kingdoms of this world and His spiritual kingdom. He said that **the kings of the Gentiles have lordship** over their subjects. Those that have authority **are called Benefactors** (v. 25). The same form in Greek (in the present tense) may be either middle or passive. Our English translation takes it as the latter. But probably Bengel is correct when he treats it as middle voice: "call themselves," or "would have themselves called." He says: "They claim this title to themselves."[502] A famous example is the king Ptolemy Euergetes (same Greek word as here) — "Ptolemy the Benefactor." The prevalence of this desire to be called Benefactor is shown by the following statement from Deissmann: "It would not be difficult to collect from the inscriptions . . . over a hundred instances, so widespread was the custom."[503] The irony of the situation was that some who called themselves Benefactors were the worst tyrants. Such was the case with Ptolemy Euergetes, Greek king of Egypt.

Christ then said emphatically: **But ye shall not be so** (v. 26). This states a universal principle for Christian living: we are not to be like the world. Instead, if one seems to be **the greater,** said Jesus, **let him become as the younger.** In the Oriental home **the younger** was the one who did the menial tasks, acting as servant to the older ones. And **he that is chief** — literally, "the one ruling" or leading — **as he that doth serve** — literally, "as the one serving." Jesus gave a magnificent example of this when He washed the disciples' feet on this very occasion (John 13:3-10). Exactly the same phrase in the Greek occurs at the end of verse 27: **I am in the midst of you as he that serveth** — "as the one serving." This was true not only at the Last Supper but throughout His ministry.

Verses 28-30 are found only in Luke. On **they that have continued with me** Plummer comments: "The idea of *persistent loyalty* is enforced by the compound verb, by the perfect tense, and by the preposition . . . : who have perseveringly remained with Me and continue to do so."[504]

Temptations (v. 28) may be translated "trials." It refers to "the trials to which

502 *Op. cit.,* II. 197.   503 *LAE,* p. 253.   504 *Op. cit.,* p. 502.

He had been subjected during His ministry, and especially the latter portion of it. These, even to Him, were temptations to abandon His work."505

Because of the loyalty of the disciples, Jesus said to them: **I appoint unto you a kingdom** (v. 29). The absence of the definite article suggests that **kingdom** should be translated "authority." Geldenhuys506 favors Moffatt's translation of this passage: "So, even as my Father has assigned me royal power, I assign you the right of eating and drinking at my table in my Realm." The Jews conceived of the Messianic kingdom as a royal banquet, and Jesus' words seem to fit into this picture. He promised His disciples that they would **sit on thrones judging** — that is, "ruling" — **the twelve tribes of Israel** (probably meaning all the people of God). As the disciples had shared the trials of their Master, so they would share His triumph.

4. Prediction of Peter's Denial (22:31-34)

31 Simon, Simon, behold, Satan asked to have you, that he might sift you as wheat: 32 but I made supplication for thee, that thy faith fail not; and do thou, when once thou hast turned again, establish thy brethren. 33 And he said unto him, Lord, with thee I am ready to go both to prison and to death. 34 And he said, I tell thee, Peter, the cock shall not crow this day, until thou shalt thrice deny that thou knowest me.

Verse 31 is peculiar to Luke. It is a touching statement. The repetition of the name, **Simon, Simon,** shows how concerned Christ was. Of the verb **ask,** Plummer says: "The aorist of the compound verb necessarily implies *success* in the petition"507 (cf. the margin, "obtained you by asking"). **You** is plural in the Greek, indicating that Satan asked and received the privilege of testing all the apostles. One is reminded of the opening chapter of Job where Satan asks the opportunity to afflict that godly man, to test his loyalty. So it was to happen to the disciples. They were all tested and they all failed. When their Master was arrested in the Garden, "they all left him, and fled" (Mark 14:50).

Yet Peter, as the leader of the apostles

was the special object of Satan's attack. For Jesus said, **I made supplication for thee, that thy faith fail not.** The compound verb in the aorist tense suggests "fail not utterly." That prayer was answered. While Peter did deny his Lord under pressure, he did not give up his faith. Jesus admonished him that when he had **turned again,** he should **establish** his **brethren.** After Pentecost Peter became a pillar in the church.

Against Christ's insinuation that he would fall and have to turn again, Peter protested eagerly and emphatically: **Lord, with thee I am ready to go both to prison and to death** (v. 33). And of course he meant it. But he did not know his inner weakness. The form of his assertion here is not so obnoxious as in Matthew (26:33) and Mark (14:29) — "Although all shall be offended, yet will not I." But the Master solemnly announced that before morning Peter would thrice deny Him. **This day** must be understood in the light of the fact that the Jewish day began at sunset. It was in the early morning hours that the denials took place.

5. Warning of Coming Conflicts (22:35-38)

35 And he said unto them, When I sent you forth without purse, and wallet, and shoes, lacked ye anything? And they said, Nothing. 36 And he said unto them, But now, he that hath a purse, let him take it, and likewise a wallet; and he that hath none, let him sell his cloak, and buy a sword. 37 For I say unto you, that this which is written must be fulfilled in me, And he was reckoned with transgressors: for that which concerneth me hath fulfilment. 38 And they said, Lord, behold, here are two swords. And he said unto them, It is enough.

This paragraph is found only in Luke. Jesus reminded the disciples that when He sent them out to preach (9:3), He had told them to go **without purse, and wallet, and shoes.** He had given the same instructions to the Seventy (10:4). Now He asks the apostles if they had lacked anything when they went penniless and with no provisions. They answered. **Nothing.**

Now the Master reversed His orders.

505 *Ibid.* 506 *Op. cit.,* p. 565. 507 *Op. cit.,* p. 503.

The time of peace had changed to one of war. "There was no spontaneous hospitality, no peaceful acceptance, no honoured security, to be looked for now."[508]

So the disciples would need to take a **purse** for money and a **wallet** for carrying provisions. If they had no sword, they had better sell their outer garment and buy one. They might need it for self-defense. For the things predicted of Him in Isaiah 53:12 were about to take place (v. 37), and His disciples would be caught up in the conflict. But they were not to use their swords in His defense, as Peter tried to do in the Garden (John 18:10, 11), since His death was in divine order. It seems best to take Christ's words about getting a sword in a metaphorical sense. He used this startling expression to gain their attention. Farrar says: "It was to warn them of days of hatred and opposition in which *self-defense* might become a daily necessity, though not aggression."[509]

The disciples replied, **Lord, behold here are two swords** (v. 38). These men who had lived so long with Christ were still afflicted with the unfortunate diseases of literalism and materialism. But passing centuries have seen worse misuse made of these words. In his papal bull, *Unam Sanctam* (A.D. 1302), Boniface VIII used this text to support his claim that the Pope has a right to use the **two swords** of secular and spiritual authority.

Finally Jesus said, **It is enough** — "Not of course meaning that two swords were enough, but sadly declining to enter into the matter any further, and leaving them to meditate on His words."[510]

C. JESUS IN GETHSEMANE (22:39-53)

1. The Prayer (22:39-46)

39 And he came out, and went, as his custom was, unto the mount of Olives; and the disciples also followed him. 40 And when he was at the place, he said unto them, Pray that ye enter not into temptation. 41 And he was parted from them about a stone's cast; and he kneeled down and prayed, 42 saying, Father, if thou be willing, remove this cup from me: nevertheless not my will, but thine, be done. 43 And there appeared unto him an angel from heaven, strengthening

him. 44 And being in an agony he prayed more earnestly; and his sweat became as it were great drops of blood falling down upon the ground. 45 And when he rose up from his prayer, he came unto the disciples, and found them sleeping for sorrow, 46 and said unto them, Why sleep ye? rise and pray, that ye enter not into temptation.

The story of the agony in the Garden is told in all three Synoptic Gospels (see the notes on Matthew 26:36-46; Mark 14:32-42). Matthew's account is the fullest, with Mark's nearly as long. But Luke does not distinguish the three prayers of Christ, so that he has nothing parallel to the last four verses in each of the other two. John omits the agony in the Garden altogether.

Luke says that Jesus went, **as his custom was** (v. 39), to the Mount of Olives, with His disciples following Him. This is in line with the statement made earlier that each night during Passion Week Christ went out to the mount (21:37).

Matthew and Mark both relate that Jesus came to a place ("a piece of land") called Gethsemane. Luke simply says: **When he was at the place,** using the most general term (*topos*) for **place.** There He urged them to **pray that ye enter not into temptation** (v. 40).

Again, Luke does not distinguish the two groups of disciples, the smaller one inside the Garden, the larger one outside. Nor does he tell of Jesus' expression of deep sorrow as He entered the Garden. He says that Christ was **parted from them about a stone's cast,** and prayed. The prayer (v. 42) is basically the same in all three accounts. It is a very moving prayer of dedication to do His Father's will, no matter what the cost.

Verses 43 and 44 tell of an angel coming from heaven to strengthen Him as He wrestled in deep agony of soul. There has been some question about the genuineness of these two verses. They are omitted in Vaticanus (4th cent.), Alexandrinus (5th cent.), and the Washington manuscript (4th or 5th cent.), besides a number of other Greek manuscripts.

Perhaps the best judgment that we can get on the subject is that of Hort in the second volume of Westcott and Hort's Greek Testament. Hort had spent twen-

[508] Farrar, *op. cit.,* p. 373.   [509] *Op. cit.,* pp. 373, 374.   [510] *Ibid.* p. 374.

ty years of intensive research in the text of the New Testament. After showing that both internal and external evidence are against the genuineness of these two verses — that is, against the contention that they formed a part of the original Gospel of Luke — he concludes with this:

On the other hand it would be impossible to regard these verses as a product of the inventiveness of scribes. They can only be a fragment from the traditions, written or oral, which were, for a while at least, locally current beside the canonical Gospels, and which doubtless included matter of every degree of authenticity and intrinsic value. These verses and the first sentence of xxiii.34 may be safely called the most precious among the remains of this evangelic tradition which were rescued from oblivion by the scribes of the second century.[511]

When Jesus returned to His disciples (v. 45), He found them sleeping **for sorrow** (only in Luke). Their hearts were heavy and soon their eyes became heavy with sleep. The Master gently urged them to **rise and pray, that ye enter not into temptation** (v. 46). This suggests the important truth that the only reliable safeguard against being overcome by temptation is prayer.

2. The Arrest (22:47-53)

47 While he yet spake, behold, a multitude, and he that was called Judas, one of the twelve, went before them; and he drew near unto Jesus to kiss him. 48 But Jesus said unto him, Judas, betrayest thou the Son of man with a kiss? 49 And when they that were about him saw what would follow, they said, Lord, shall we smite with the sword? 50 And a certain one of them smote the servant of the high priest, and struck off his right ear. 51 But Jesus answered and said, Suffer ye *them* thus far. And he touched his ear, and healed him. 52 And Jesus said unto the chief priests, and captains of the temple, and elders, that were come against him, Are ye come out, as against a robber, with swords and staves? 53 When I was daily with you in the temple, ye stretched not forth your hands against me: but this is your hour, and the power of darkness.

Again the accounts in Matthew and Mark are longer and fuller (see the notes on Matthew 26:47-56; Mark 14:43-52).

Once more Judas is identified in all three records as **one of the twelve** (v. 47). This shocking fact could not be forgotten. The betrayal by a kiss is likewise in all three. But Luke adds the question of Jesus: **Judas, betrayest thou the Son of man with a kiss?** (v. 48).

Verse 49 is found only in Luke. Jesus had spoken about the need of having a sword (v. 36). Now it appeared that the occasion had arrived that proved the wisdom of His warning. Excitedly the disciples cried: **Lord, shall we smite with the sword?**

Without waiting for a reply, one of them swung his sword at a man who was participating in the arrest of Jesus. Fortunately this **servant of the high priest** "ducked" his head so that he only lost **his right ear** — perhaps only the lobe of the ear (Mark uses a word which literally means "little ear"). Luke alone records: **And he touched his ear, and healed him** (v. 51). He does not say that He put the ear back on, but simply that He touched the ear. This would definitely suggest that it was just the lobe that was severed.

It was altogether appropriate that this healing miracle should be recorded by the Evangelist who was also a physician.

Luke also mentions more specifically who were included in the mob that seized Christ. He names **the chief priests, and captains of the temple, and elders** (v. 52). The first and third groups were members of the Sanhedrin. The middle group comprised the Temple guard.

To the question as to why the leaders had not seized Him while teaching daily in the Temple (all three accounts) Luke adds; **but this is your hour, and the power of darkness** (v. 53). These men preferred to arrest Him in the darkness of the night because their deed was evil. This was their **hour** — the time when God permitted them to take over and do their nefarious work.

D. THE JEWISH TRIAL (22:54-71)

1. Peter's Denials (22:54-62)

54 And they seized him, and led him *away*, and brought him into the high priest's house. But Peter followed afar off. 55 And when they had kindled a fire in the midst of the court, and had

511 B. F. Westcott and F. J. Hort, *The New Testament in the Original Greek*, II, Appendix, p. 67.

sat down together, Peter sat in the midst of them. 56 And a certain maid seeing him as he sat in the light of the fire, and looking stedfastly upon him, said, This man also was with him. 57 But he denied, saying, Woman, I know him not. 58 And after a little while another saw him, and said, Thou also art one of them. But Peter said, Man, I am not. 59 And after the space of about one hour another confidently affirmed, saying, Of a truth this man also was with him; for he is a Galilaean. 60 But Peter said, Man, I know not what thou sayest. And immediately, while he yet spake, the cock crew. 61 And the Lord turned, and looked upon Peter. And Peter remembered the word of the Lord, how that he said unto him, Before the cock crow this day thou shalt deny me thrice. 62 And he went out, and wept bitterly.

The small army that arrested Jesus led to the high priest's house. Mark mentions his name, Caiaphas. All three Synoptists say that Peter followed afar off. Who has not felt the warning note in these words? All who follow Christ afar off are going to find themselves in situations where they will deny their Lord in one way or another.

Luke notes that they had kindled a fire in the midst of the court, or "courtyard" (v. 55). Jerusalem is at an elevation of about 2,500 feet, and in the early spring the nights are cold.

Unfortunately Peter sat down by the fire. That proved to be his undoing, for a maid saw his face by the light of the fire. Looking stedfastly at him, she exclaimed, This man also was with him (v. 56). Then came the first denial: Woman, I know him not (v. 57). After a while another said to Peter: Thou also art one of them (v. 58). Emphatically Peter said; Man, I am not. About one hour later (only Luke) another confidently affirmed that Peter was with Jesus, for he is a Galilean (v. 59). Again the apostle denied the charge. Just then the cock crew (v. 60). Here Luke alone adds a very dramatic touch: And the Lord turned, and looked upon Peter (v. 61). This broke Peter's heart. He went out and wept bitterly (v. 62).

2. Mockery of Jesus (22:63-65)

63 And the men that held Jesus mocked him, and beat him. 64 And they

blindfolded him, and asked him, saying, Prophesy: who is he that struck thee? 65 And many other things spake they against him, reviling him.

This is related at a slightly earlier point in Matthew and Mark, before the account of Peter's denials (see notes on Matthew 26:59-75; Mark 14:55-72). The mockery of Jesus by the Jews was absolutely inexcusable. It reveals something of the terrible depth of depravity in the human heart.

3. Condemnation by the Sanhedrin (22: 66-71)

An official meeting of the Sanhedrin was held at daybreak to make legal the illegal sentence of condemnation passed during the night (cf. Matthew 27:1; Mark 15:1). Luke's account of this session is more detailed than the other two. He says that as soon as it was day, the assembly of the elders (v. 66) — ("presbytery") — was gathered together. This consisted of both chief priests and scribes — Sadducees and Pharisees. They led Him into their council (Greek, *synedrion*, "sanhedrin"). This seems to refer to the hall where the Sanhedrin met. It seems best to take *presbyterion* and *synedrion* as both meaning the Great Sanhedrin, but *synedrion* here as referring particularly to the place of meeting (cf. twofold use of "church" and "synagogue" for the congregation and also for the building).

On the reason for the morning meeting of the Sanhedrin, Geldenhuys says: "No session of the Jewish Council was regarded as valid if it were held during the night. Although the Jewish authorities held preliminary trials of the Saviour during the night, they must nevertheless assemble after daybreak and try Him again."[512]

The Sanhedrin first challenged Jesus to declare whether He was the Messiah (v. 67). This He refused to do, because, If I tell you ye will not believe. Regardless of what He said, they would not receive Him as their Messiah. And if I ask you, ye will not answer (v. 68) seems to be Jesus' protest against the unfair trial they had been giving Him. When He declared that they would see the Son of man seated at the right hand of the power of God, they asked him point-blank: Art thou then the **Son of God?** His answer was, **Ye say that I am** (v. 70). This can be translated: "Ye say, because I am." But this is perhaps not what was intended. His answer may have purposely been ambiguous, because of their misconceptions of what was meant by Messiah (*Christ, Son of man,* and *Son of God*).

It is noticeable that there is some overlapping of the language here with that of night sessions described earlier. But this was almost inevitable. Plummer writes: "That portions of what is recorded of one examination should resemble portions of what is recorded of another is natural. . . .at this last and only valid trial everything of importance would have to be repeated."[513]

E. THE ROMAN TRIAL (23:1-25)

1. The Accusation Before Pilate (23:1-7)

1 And the whole company of them rose up, and brought him before Pilate. 2 And they began to accuse him, saying, We found this man perverting our nation, and forbidding to give tribute to Caesar, and saying that he himself is Christ a king. 3 And Pilate asked him, saying, Art thou the King of the Jews? And he answered him and said, Thou sayest. 4 And Pilate said unto the chief priests and the multitudes, I find no fault in this man. 5 But they were the more urgent, saying, He stirreth up the people, teaching throughout all Judaea, and beginning from Galilee even unto this place. 6 But when Pilate heard it, he asked whether the man were a Galilaean. 7 And when he knew that he was of Herod's jurisdiction, he sent him unto Herod, who himself also was at Jerusalem in these days.

The Sanhedrin had gone as far as it could with Jesus' case: it had condemned Him to death. Strangely enough, Luke does not state this. In fact, he gives practically nothing of the night session of the Sanhedrin, describing only Peter's denials at that time. The actual questioning of Jesus by the Sanhedrin which he relates was at the daylight official meeting of that body. This he describes in some detail (22:66-71), whereas Matthew and Mark mention it in only a sentence (Matthew 17:1, 2; Mark 14:1). Either Luke did not have information about the night trial, or else it did not fit into his purpose to tell about it.

Klausner claims that the Sanhedrin was at this time pretty much under the control of the Sadducees, that it was not until later that the Pharisees were able to introduce and enforce more equitable and mild rules for the handling of criminal cases, especially those involving capital punishment. He thinks that the regulations often cited from the Mishna came into force after the time of Christ. The harsh treatment of Jesus and His condemnation to death by the Sanhedrin, Klausner blames on the wicked high priest and his henchmen, the Sadducees.[514] This may very well be the case, as the Gospels portray the chief priests leading the opposition to Christ at this point.

From Matthew (26:65, 66) and Mark (14:64) we learn that Jesus was charged with blasphemy and condemned to be liable to death. The question as to whether or not the Sanhedrin could at this time inflict the death sentence has been much debated. Klausner says: ". . . at that time the Jews could not pass sentence of death, at least not in a case affecting a Messiah, i.e., a political question."[515]

In an article in *The Interpreter's Dictionary of the Bible*, Burkill deals with this subject at some length. He calls attention to the statement in the Talmud that "the power to pass capital sentences was taken away from the Jews forty years before the destruction of the tempel,"[516] but questions the validity of it. He concludes in favor of the idea that the Sanhedrin could "execute any Jewish citizen accused and found guilty of a capital offense against the law of his religion."[517]

Unquestionably there was one case in which the Sanhedrin could put a man to death. "An inscription discovered in 1871 by Clermont-Ganneau definitely shows that the Jewish authorities were formally entitled by the imperial government to put any Gentile to death if he ventured to pass into the sanctuary beyond the second enclosure of the temple."[518]

The most significant statement in the Bible on this point is John 18:31. When Pilate said to the Jewish rulers, "Take

---

513 *Op. cit.,* p. 518.   514 Joseph Klausner, *Jesus of Nazareth,* trans. Herbert Danby, pp. 339-344.
515 *Ibid.,* p. 345.   516 T. A. Burkill, "Sanhedrin," IDB, IV, 217.   517 *Ibid.,* p. 218.   518 *Ibid.*

him yourselves, and judge him according to your law," they replied, "It is not lawful for us to put any man to death." The next verse adds: "that the word of Jesus might be fulfilled, which he spake, signifying by what manner of death he should die" — that is, by crucifixion, which was a Roman, not Jewish method of execution. This passage might seem to settle the question conclusively. But it might be interpreted this way: Pilate, recognizing the Roman law, told the Jews to try Him by their religious law. But because of the favorable attitude of the people toward Jesus, the Jewish rulers preferred to have Pilate handle the case. So they hid behind a (supposed?) rule that they could not put a man to death. All we can say is that we do not have sufficient historical evidence for giving a final answer to this question.

Luke says that **the whole company of them** (that is, all the Sanhedrin) brought Jesus to Pilate (v. 1). Stauffer comments: "In Palestine it was the general practice in all official affairs to confront the Roman authorities with as noisy and large a delegation of dignitaries as could be mustered."[519]

As already noted, the charge on which the Sanhedrin condemned Jesus to death was the charge of blasphemy, of claiming to be the Son of God (Matthew 26: 63-66; Mark 14:61-64). But the Jewish rulers knew well that this would carry no weight whatever in a Roman court of justice. So before Pilate they brought political charges. There were three: (1) **perverting our nation**; (2) **forbidding to give tribute to Caesar**; (3) **saying that he himself is Christ a king** (v. 2). The last two could be considered treason. Two things the Roman government could not tolerate. One was failure to pay taxes to support the expensive regime of Rome. The other was political revolution. The Jewish leaders knew that Pilate would be shaken by hearing these accusations against Jesus.

The falseness of these charges is apparent. Far from **perverting our nation**, Christ had carefully indicated that He did not come to "destroy" the law of Moses but to "fulfill" it (Matthew 5:17); that is, to fill it full of spiritual meaning. His ethical teachings were in line with those of the best rabbis — so much so that some modern Jewish writers have claimed that Jesus taught nothing essentially new.

But the chief priests intended this as a serious accusation. "They imply that the perversion of the nation was seditious. The excitement caused by Christ's ministry was notorious, and it would not be easy to prove that it had no political significance."[520]

So far as the second charge was concerned — **forbidding to give tribute to Caesar** — this was nothing but a brazen lie; Christ had precisely refused to endorse this position of the Jewish zealots. He had said clearly and emphatically: "Render unto Caesar the things that are Caesar's" (20:25). Jesus taught that people should pay their taxes, and Paul reiterated this truth for the Church (Rom. 13:6).

The third charge — **saying that he himself is Christ a king** — was both true and false. Jesus did claim to be the Messiah (**Christ**), and He did not deny that He was a king (v. 3). But He was not the kind of king or Messiah that the Jews had in mind. The implication of their accusation was that He was a political king, and that, of course, was the way they wanted Pilate to take it. Viewed in this light, the third charge, like the others, was false. The Jewish leaders were dishonest in presenting their case.

Seizing on this third charge, Pilate asked Jesus, **Art thou the King of the Jews?** (v. 3). In the Greek **thou** (*su*) occurs first, in the emphatic position. This would "imply that His appearance was very much against such a claim."[521]

Christ's answer, **Thou sayest,** seems ambiguous. What do the words mean? Creed thinks "it was understood to imply assent," and adds: "But the personal pronoun. . . must be significant: 'the statement is yours,' i.e., a certain protest against the question is implied."[522]

The best explanation is furnished by Plummer. He would link this passage with John 18:33-38. He says of the answer of Jesus here: "It condenses a conversation given at greater length by Jn., without whose narrative that of the three is scarcely intelligible."[523] John tells how Jesus informed Pilate: "My kingdom is

[519] Ethelbert Stauffer, *Jesus and His Story*, trans. R. and C. Winston, p. 128.
[520] Plummer, *op. cit.*, p. 520.   [521] *Ibid.*, p. 521.   [522] *Op. cit.*, p. 279.   [523] *Op. cit.*, p. 521.

not of this world: if my kingdom were of this world, then would my servants fight, that I should not be delivered to the Jews" (John 18:36).

This satisfied the governor that Christ was not a king in the ordinary sense, but only a harmless religious fanatic. So he said to the chief priests and the multitudes — evidently a crowd had gathered by this time — I find no fault in this man (v. 4). This was not a character endorsement, for the governor was speaking as a judge in court. Morgan is right when he affirms: "It was a legal finding, in the very terminology of the law-court of the time; just as in an English court of justice, the verdict would be, 'Not guilty.' "[524] This makes all the more reprehensible Pilate's final verdict of death for a prisoner he had declared innocent.

Why this miscarriage of justice? The next words give a partial answer: He stirreth up the people (v. 5). The Jewish leaders were trying to make stick their accusation of "perverting our nation," interpreting it as being sedition. They were the more urgent in pressing their charges against Christ. They must secure His conviction at whatever cost.

When the chief priests mentioned Jesus' teaching in Galilee, Pilate seized eagerly on the possible chance of getting rid of the responsibility for making a decision that was rapidly becoming more difficult. After confirming the fact that Christ was actually a Galilean, he sent him to Herod (v. 7). This was Herod Antipas, ruler of Galilee, who happened to be in Jerusalem for the Passover.

2. Jesus Before Herod (23:8-12)

8 Now when Herod saw Jesus, he was exceeding glad: for he was of a long time desirous to see him, because he had heard concerning him; and he hoped to see some miracle done by him. 9 And he questioned him in many words; but he answered him nothing. 10 And the chief priests and the scribes stood, vehemently accusing him. 11 And Herod with his soldiers set him at nought, and mocked him, and arraying him in gorgeous apparel sent him back to Pilate. 12 And Herod and Pilate became friends with each other that very day: for before they were at enmity between themselves.

This incident is recorded only by Luke, who shows great interest in the Herodian family, both in the Gospel and in Acts. Herod Antipas was the one who had killed John the Baptist and who, when he heard of Jesus' miracles, thought that John had come to life again (Mark 6: 14). This indicated how superstitious he was. Now he was exceeding glad to meet Christ, whom he had wished for a long time to see (v. 8). Idle curiosity made him want to witness some miracle. This suggests the measure of his religious depth.

Eagerly Herod questioned Jesus with many words (v. 9). But Christ was not interested in satisfying the selfish desires of this wicked ruler. So He answered him nothing. He knew He could not help this man. Then the chief priests and the scribes let loose a torrent of abuse, vehemently accusing him (v. 10). There was no use in trying to answer their false charges; so Jesus maintained a discreet silence.

When Herod saw he was not going to get any satisfaction out of this prisoner his "baffled curiosity" took cruel revenge. Here we glimpse the heart of one of these Herods. They were noted for their harsh cruelty. So Antipas set him at nought (v. 11). The verb means "despise utterly, treat with contempt."[525] Arraying Jesus in gorgeous apparel ("brilliant clothing"), he sent him back to Pilate. So the governor was still confronted with the demand that he make a decision, as is every man who comes into contact with Christ.

That day Herod and Pilate became friends (v. 12). Probably their enmity had stemmed from a quarrel about administrative jurisdiction (cf. 13:1).

3. Pilate's Injustice (23:13-25)

13 And Pilate called together the chief priests and the rulers and the people, 14 and said unto them, Ye brought unto me this man, as one that perverteth the people: and behold, I, having examined him before you, found no fault in this man touching those things whereof ye accuse him: 15 no, nor yet Herod: for he sent him back unto us; and behold, nothing worthy of death hath been done by him. 16 I will therefore chastise him, and release him. 18 But they cried out

---

[524] G. Campbell Morgan, *The Gospel According to Luke*, p. 260.   [525] Abbott-Smith, *op. cit.*, p. 161.

all together, saying, Away with this man, and release unto us Barabbas: — 19 one who for a certain insurrection made in the city, and for murder, was cast into prison. 20 And Pilate spake unto them again, desiring to release Jesus; 21 but they shouted, saying, Crucify, crucify him. 22 And he said unto them the third time, Why, what evil hath this man done? I have found no cause of death in him: I will therefore chastise him and release him. 23 But they were urgent with loud voices, asking that he might be crucified. And their voices prevailed. 24 And Pilate gave sentence that what they asked for should be done. 25 And he released him that for insurrection and murder had been cast into prison, whom they asked for; but Jesus he delivered up to their will.

The first charge that the Jewish leaders had brought against Jesus was that He was "perverting our nation" (v. 2). That this seemed serious to Pilate is shown by the fact that he now says: **Ye brought unto me this man, as one that perverteth the people** (v. 14). But afer examining Him in their presence, he **found no fault**, or "crime," in relation to the accusation. Neither had Herod found Him guilty (v. 15). **He sent him back unto us** has better manuscript support than "I sent you to him" (KJV) and makes much better sense in the passage. Also **by him** is much more preferable than "to him" (KJV), because the latter makes no sense. The Greek (dative case without a preposition), can equally well be translated either way.

Here we see one of the features that is prominent in the book of Acts. There the frequent picture is that of Roman officials protecting Christians against Jewish persecution. So here Pilate defended Jesus. But he lacked the courage to do what he knew was right.

The governor suggested that he would **chastise** Christ and **release** Him (v. 16). The Greek word for **chastise** means literally to "train a child," then "chasten," or "chastise." It was a very mild term for Pilate to use for the cruel Roman scourging, which sometimes was fatal. But he seemed willing to do almost anything if he could only get Jesus off his hands without having to execute Him.[526]

But he was foiled in this attempt also. The people, instigated by the chief priests (Mark 15:11), all began to shout: **Away with this man, and release unto us Barabbas** (v. 18). In Aramaic (the language of Palestine in that day) **Bar** means "son" and *abba* "father." So **Barabbas** literally means "son of a father." This seems to be a striking coincidence. The people chose "son of a father" — who was guilty of **insurrection** and **murder** — and rejected the One who was truly the Son of the Father. But the majority of people today are still making the same choice — holding on to the Old Man of self, rather than accepting the New Man in Christ Jesus.

The historical significance of the decision the Jews made should not be missed. Barabbas was a representative of that very revolutionary spirit which the Sanhedrin was accusing Jesus of having. To demand the crucifixion of Christ and the release of Barabbas "was to repudiate the spirit of submission and faith which had distinguished the whole work of Jesus, and which might have saved the people. It was at the same time to let loose the spirit of revolt which was to carry them to their destruction"[527] (in A.D. 70). In this case the consequences of wrong choice show up in glaring vividness. One cannot deliberately choose the wrong without paying a tragic price for doing so.

Pilate was still **desiring to release Jesus** (v. 20). But as soon as he suggested this again to the people, **they shouted** — "kept shouting" (imperfect of strong verb used only by Luke) — **Crucify, crucify him.**

For the **third time** the governor asserted: **I have found no cause of death in him** (v. 22; cf. vv. 4, 14). **Cause** is the same in Greek as "fault" in verses 4 and 14. Since Jesus was innocent Pilate wanted to **chastise** and **release** Him, as he had suggested earlier after his second declaration that Jesus was "not guilty" (see vv. 14, 16). The reaction of the crowd, impelled by the high priests, was by now predictable: **But they were urgent** — literally, "were pressing upon" — **with loud voices, asking** that Jesus should be crucified (v. 23). The participle **asking** (*aitoumenoi*) is in the middle voice,

---

[526] Verse 17 (KJV) is missing in some of the oldest manuscripts. It seems to have been imported here from Matt. 27:15 and Mark 15:6. It does not fit here as well as it does in those Gospels.

[527] Godet, *op. cit.*, II, 324.

which is probably somewhat stronger than active.[528] In general, the middle "is used of requests in commerce and so as a rule in the New Testament. . . .In the papyri the middle preponderates in business style."[529] So the chief priests (through the crowd) were demanding a business deal with Pilate: Jesus must be crucified. The result was: **their voices prevailed.** The verb means "to overpower, prevail against."[530] Pilate was overpowered by the "bulldozing" tactics of the chief priests.

So the governor **gave sentence** — the compound verb is used only here in the New Testament — that what they demanded should be done. When he made this decision he abdicated all right to rule as Roman governor, even though he continued in office for another half dozen years. Then his cruelties caught up with him, and he was sent into exile (A.D. 36).

Verse 25 is a sad closing summary of this paragraph. Pilate deliberately released into society a man who was a murderer and insurrectionist — guilty of two of the top crimes in the Roman catalog. In doing so he disregarded all the principles of Roman justice, which underlie our jurisprudence today. At the same time he delivered to execution a man that he had three times publicly pronounced "Not guilty" and whom he knew to be innocent. Never was there a worse miscarriage of justice.

F. THE CRUCIFIXION (23:26-49)

1. Simon of Cyrene (23:26)

26 And when they led him away, they laid hold upon one Simon of Cyrene, coming from the country, and laid on him the cross, to bear it after Jesus.

Since Luke has already recorded the mocking of Jesus by Herod and his soldiers (v. 11), he omits the mockery by the soldiers of the governor (Matthew 27:27-31; Mark 15:16-20). All three Synoptists give this little item of Simon carrying Jesus' cross (cf. Matt. 27:32; Mark 15:21). Since Mark mentions Simon's two sons, who were probably well-known members of the church at Rome (cf. Rom. 16:13), it would appear that this man from North Africa became a Christian. He must have cherished greatly this unexpected contact with Christ on His way to Calvary.

2. The Weeping Women (23:27-31)

27 And there followed him a great multitude of the people, and of women who bewailed and lamented him. 28 But Jesus turning unto them said, Daughters of Jerusalem, weep not for me, but weep for yourselves, and for your children. 29 For behold, the days are coming, in which they shall say, Blessed are the barren, and the wombs that never bare, and the breasts that never gave suck. 30 Then shall they begin to say to the mountains, Fall on us; and to the hills, Cover us. 31 For if they do these things in the green tree, what shall be done in the dry?

This brief paragraph is peculiar to Luke. As has often been said, this is the Gospel of Women. Luke gives far more attention to the women who followed Jesus and ministered to Him than do the other Evangelists (see 8:1-3).

But this is a different group. They are called **Daughters of Jerusalem** (v. 28). They were evidently sympathetic women from that city.

For if they do these things in the green tree, what shall be done in the dry? (v. 31) is obviously an obscure question. What does it mean? Creed suggests: "If the innocent Jesus. . . meets such a fate, what will be the fate of the guilty Jerusalem?"[531] Similarly, Godet says: "The green wood is Jesus led to death as a rebel. . .; the dry wood is the Jewish people, who, by their spirit of revolt, will . . .bring down on themselves the sword of the Romans."[532] A. B. Bruce expresses the same idea in slightly different form: "What is happening to me now is nothing to what is going to happen to this people. The green tree represents innocence, the dry tree guilt, ripe for the fire of judgment."[533]

3. Companions in Crucifixion (23:32)

32 And there were also two others, malefactors, led with him to be put to death.

---

[528] Moulton, *Grammar*, I, 160.
[529] F. Blass and A Debrunner, *A Greek Grammar of the New Testament and Other Early Christian Literature*, trans. R. W. Funk, pp. 165, 166.   [530] *Abbott-Smith.*, p. 241.
[531] *Op. cit.*, p. 286. [532] *Op. cit.*, II, 331.   [533] EGT, I, 639.

The statement that there were two malefactors ("evil-workers") crucified with Jesus is brought in later by Matthew (27:38) and Mark (15:27). In these other two Gospels they are identified as "robbers" (not "thieves," KJV). They may have been bandits who had taken part in the same insurrection with Barabbas. If so, Barabbas belonged on the middle cross, and Christ literally died in his place.

4. Mockery of Rulers and Soldiers (23: 33-38)

33 And when they came unto the place which is called The skull, there they crucified him, and the malefactors, one on the right hand and the other on the left. 34 And Jesus said, Father, forgive them; for they know not what they do. And parting his garments among them, they cast lots. 35 And the people stood beholding. And the rulers also scoffed at him, saying, He saved others; let him save himself, if this is the Christ of God, his chosen. 36 And the soldiers also mocked him, coming to him, offering him vinegar, 37 and saying, If thou art the King of the Jews, save thyself. 38 And there was also a superscription over him, THIS IS THE KING OF THE JEWS.

This shocking scene is recorded in all three Synoptics (see the notes on Matthew 27:33-44; Mark 15:22-32). Luke has a different order of details from the other two Gospels.

The place of crucifixion is identified in Matthew, Mark and John (19:17) by its Hebrew name "Golgotha." But Luke, writing to Greeks, omits this. However, he joins the other three in using the Greek word *kranion* (cf. "cranium"), which means **skull**. It is found in these four parallel passages in the Gospels, and nowhere else in the New Testament. Strangely, the King James Version has "Calvary" (Latin, *calvarium*, "skull") here in Luke, but "skull" in the other three Gospels. It is the same Greek word in all four places.

Three of the Seven Sayings from the Cross are found in Luke's Gospel. The first is recorded in verse 34 — **Father, for-** give them; for they know not what they do.[534]

People stood around the cross, watching. Some were friends, some were enemies. **The rulers** (Jewish religious leaders) **scoffed at him** (v. 35). The literal Greek is "turned up their noses at Him." The verb is found (in N.T.) only here and in 16:14. **The soldiers** joined in mocking Him (v. 36). For the wording of the **superscription** (v. 38) see the notes on Matthew 27:37.

5. Winning a Lost Soul (23:39-43)

39 And one of the malefactors that were hanged railed on him, saying, Art not thou the Christ? save thyself and us. 40 But the other answered, and rebuking him said, Dost thou not even fear God, seeing thou art in the same condemnation? 41 And we indeed justly; for we receive the due reward of our deeds: but this man hath done nothing amiss. 42 And he said, Jesus, remember me when thou comest in thy kingdom. 43 And he said unto him, Verily I say unto thee, To-day shalt thou be with me in Paradise.

This beautiful incident, found only here, is in line with Luke's emphasis on the fact that "The Son of man came to seek and to save that which was lost" (19:10). Even on the cross, in His dying hours of agony, Jesus rescued another lost sheep and brought him safely into the fold.

Matthew (27:44) and Mark (15:32) say that the two robbers who were crucified with Christ "reproached him." But there is no contradiction between that and Luke's statement that while one robber **railed on him,** the other rebuked his fellow robber and pleaded with Jesus for mercy. Either of two explanations will take care of the problem adequately. It may be that both robbers started in abusing Jesus, and that one of them finally repented and found forgiveness. Or it may be that the difference between "reproached" (Matt., Mark) and **railed** (Luke) should be emphasized. Both, in the heat of their suffering, "reproached" Christ. But only one **railed** on Him, using insulting language.

[534] This saying of Jesus is omitted in some of the earliest manuscripts, including Sinaiticus. Once more, as in the case of 22:43, 44, we quote from Westcott and Hort (*op. cit.*, II, Appendix, p. 68): "Few verses of the Gospels bear in themselves a surer witness to the truth of what they record than this first of the Words from the Cross; but it need not therefore have belonged originally to the book in which it is now included. We cannot doubt that it comes from an extraneous source. Nevertheless, like xxii. 43f., Mt. xvi. 2f., it has exceptional claims to be permanently retained, with the necessary safeguards, in its accustomed place."

The rebuke given by the Penitent Robber was well spoken. The two robbers were justly condemned and crucified, receiving the due reward of their deeds. But Jesus had done **nothing amiss** (literally, "out of place" and so "unbecoming").

The Penitent Robber requested: **Jesus, remember me when thou comest in thy kingdom** (v. 42). We have no way of knowing exactly what background this criminal had. But presumably he was a Jew and had general familiarity with the Old Testament. Plummer says: "The robber knew that he had only a few hours to live, and therefore this prayer implies a belief in a future state in which Jesus is to receive him in His kingdom."[535]

The Savior's answer to this poor, dying sinner must have brought inestimable comfort: **To-day shalt thou be with me in Paradise** (v. 43). This is Jesus' second Word from the Cross, as recorded by Luke. "The promise implies the continuance of consciousness after death. If the dead are unconscious, the assurance to the robber that he will be with Christ after death would be empty of consolation."[536]

The word **Paradise** occurs in only two other places in the New Testament (II Cor. 12:4; Rev. 2:7). The term comes originally from the Persian and meant "a park." But it came into English from the Greek. Although it does not occur at all in the King James Version of the Old Testament, it is found about fifty times in the Septuagint (Greek O.T.) — thirteen times in the second and third chapters of Genesis alone. It is used for the "garden" of Eden. In the Apocrypha and Pseudepigrapha it refers to a place of blessedness above the earth. That is the thought related in II Corinthians: Paul was "caught up into Paradise." It appears that in the New Testament the term applies to the abode of the righteous dead.

6. Jesus' Death (23:44-49)

44 And it was now about the sixth hour, and a darkness came over the whole land until the ninth hour, 45 the sun's light failing: and the veil of the temple was rent in the midst. 46 And Jesus, crying with a loud voice, said, Father, into thy hands I commend my spirit: and having said this, he gave up the ghost. 47 And when the centurion saw what was done, he glorified God, saying, Certainly this was a righteous man. 48 And all the multitudes that came together to this sight, when they beheld the things that were done, returned smiting their breasts. 49 And all his acquaintance, and the women that followed with him from Galilee, stood afar off, seeing these things.

Luke omits the so-called Cry of Dereliction (Matthew 27:46; Mark 15:34). All three Synoptics tell of the rending of the inner veil of the Temple (cf. Matthew 27:51; Mark 15:38).

The third Word from the Cross recorded by Luke is **Father, into thy hands I commend my spirit** (v. 46). Realizing that death was near, Jesus committed His spirit into the care of His loving Father. Plummer notes: "The voluntary character of Christ's death is very clearly expressed in this last utterance."[537]

Having said this, Jesus **gave up the ghost.** It is difficult to see why this archaic expression was retained in the American Standard Version. The Greek says very clearly and simply, "He expired" (literally, "breathed out").

The centurion — thus designated in all three Synoptic Gospels, and so probably in charge of the crucifixion — when he saw what had happened, **glorified God** (v. 47). This phrase occurs eight times in Luke making it one of the key phrases of this Gospel (cf. 2:20; 5:25, 26; 7:16; 13:13; 17:15; 18:43).

In the New Testament, and outstandingly in Luke's writings, the Roman centurions are always spoken of in a favorable light. They appear to have been better than the soldiers below them or the governors above them. "The good character of the centurions in the New Testament confirms the statement of Polybius, that as a rule the best men in the army were promoted to this rank."[538]

The centurion expressed his reaction to Christ's death by saying: **Certainly this was a righteous man** (v. 47). For a careful comparison of this expression with Matthew's and Mark's "the Son of God," see the notes on Matthew 27:54.

The content of verse 48 is found only in Luke. It reveals the shocked sorrow of the **multitudes** who had gathered to witness the crucifixion. Among the on-lookers were many Galilean followers of Christ. But they apparently, with the women, stayed at a safe distance (v. 49).

G. THE BURIAL (23:50-56)

50 And behold, a man named Joseph, who was a councillor, a good and right-eous man 51 (he had not consented to their counsel and deed), *a man* of Arimathaea, a city of the Jews, who was looking for the kingdom of God: 52 this man went to Pilate, and asked for the body of Jesus. 53 And he took it down, and wrapped it in a linen cloth, and laid him in a tomb that was hewn in stone, where never man had yet lain. 54 And it was the day of the Preparation, and the sabbath drew on. 55 And the women, who had come with him out of Galilee, followed after, and beheld the tomb, and how his body was laid. 56 And they returned, and prepared spices and ointments.

Luke's account is very closely parallel to those of the other two Synoptics (see the notes on Matthew 27:57-61; Mark 15:42-47). He gives a little fuller de-scription of Joseph of Arimathea, adding that he was a good and righteous man (he had not consented to their counsel and deed) (vv. 50, 51). This shows, what we should expect of this "secret disciple," that as a member of the Sanhedrin he did not concur in voting the death sen-tence for Jesus.

The fact that the sepulcher was a "new tomb" (Matthew 27:60) is under-scored further by Luke's phrase: where never man had yet lain (v. 53).

The Greek word for Preparation is still the official designation of Friday in the Greek Orthodox Church. In fact, it is used that way in the second-century *Didache* (VIII), which speaks of fasting during the fourth day of the week (Wednesday) "and the preparation" (*paraskeue*). This ought to be sufficient evidence that the Crucifixion took place on Friday — and not on Wednesday, as some modern writers have held.

The women who had followed Jesus from Galilee, watched to see where He was buried. Then they went and pre-pared spices and ointments, with which to anoint His body, and on the sabbath they rested according to the command-ment. That is, they did what they could

before sunset and then rested during the Jewish sabbath day (sunset Friday night to sunset Saturday).

VII. THE RESURRECTION (24:1-53)

A. THE RESURRECTION DAY (24:1-43)

1. The Empty Tomb (24:1-12)

And on the sabbath they rested ac-cording to the commandment. 1 But on the first day of the week, at early dawn, they came unto the tomb, bringing the spices which they had prepared. 2 And they found the stone rolled away from the tomb. 3 And they entered in, and found not the body of the Lord. 4 And it came to pass, while they were perplexed thereabout, behold, two men stood by them in dazzling apparel: 5 and as they were affrighted and bowed down their faces to the earth, they said unto them, Why seek ye the living among the dead? 6 He is not here, but is risen: remember how he spake unto you when he was yet in Galilee, 7 saying that the Son of man must be delivered up into the hands of sinful men, and be crucified, and the third day rise again. 8 And they remem-bered his words, 9 and returned from the tomb, and told all these things to the eleven, and to all the rest. 10 Now they were Mary Magdalene, and Joanna, and Mary the *mother* of James: and the other women with them told these things unto the apostles. 11 And these words ap-peared in their sight as idle talk; and they disbelieved them. 12 But Peter arose, and ran unto the tomb; and stoop-ing and looking in, he seeth the linen cloths by themselves; and he departed to his home, wondering at that which was come to pass.

There is a great deal of variety in the Resurrection narratives of the four Gos-pels. However, in this section the three Synoptics have much in common.

All three emphasize the fact that the women came to the tomb very early on Sunday morning — Luke says at early dawn (literally, "at deep earliness"). He further says, they came. The pronoun they evidently refers to the women mentioned at the close of the previous chapter. But they are only identified there as being from Galilee. Not until we get down to the tenth verse do we find their names — "Mary Magdalene, and Joanna, and Mary the mother of

James." It is added: "and the other women with them."

The other two Synoptics have them named in the first verse. Matthew names two — "Mary Magdalene and the other Mary." Mark lists three — "Mary Magdalene and Mary the mother of James, and Salome." John gives first the story of Mary Magdalene at the sepulcher, and Jesus' appearance to her.

These women were **bringing the spices which they had prepared.** Not able to accomplish the anointing on Saturday evening after sunset, when the Sabbath thing Sunday morning. To their joyful surprise they discovered that the heavy stone at the mouth of the sepulcher had ended, they came very early, the first been rolled back. So they **entered** the empty tomb. There they did not find **the body of the Lord Jesus** (v. 3).

While they stood there, **two men** stood by them — evidently angels. Mark says "a young man"; Matthew has "the angel." The **men** asked the women, **Why seek ye the living among the dead?** Then they informed them, as is found in the three Synoptics: **He is not here, but is risen.** They reminded them of the Master's words in Galilee, when He had predicted not only His death, but also His resurrection (v. 7). This truth had not yet registered in their thinking.

Then the women remembered that Jesus had said that. Eagerly they returned from the tomb to tell **the eleven, and all the rest** (v. 9). Then come the names of the reporters. All the Gospels name Mary Magdalene as being in the first group to come to the tomb. She loved Jesus much because He had done so much for her, casting seven demons out of her.

A vivid human touch comes in here. When the women reported what they had heard and seen at the empty tomb, their words seemed to the sophisticated men as **idle talk** (v. 11). This is one word in the Greek, found only here in the New Testament. It means "silly talk, nonsense."[539] Hobart says that it ". . .is applied in medical language to the wild talk of the sick during delirium: the way St. Luke uses it here much resembles that of Hippocrates."[540] The men doubt-less thought the women were "crazy." So they **disbelieved them.**[541]

2. The Emmaus Disciples (24:13-35)

13 And behold, two of them were going that very day to a village named Emmaus, which was threescore furlongs from Jerusalem. 14 And they communed with each other of all these things which had happened. 15 And it came to pass, while they communed and questioned together, that Jesus himself drew near, and went with them. 16 But their eyes were holden that they should not know him. 117 And he said unto them, What communications are these that ye have one with another, as ye walk? And they stood still, looking sad. 18 And one of them, named Cleopas, answering said unto him, Dost thou alone sojourn in Jerusalem and not know the things which are come to pass there in these days? 19 And he said unto them, What things? And they said unto him, The things concerning Jesus the Nazarene, who was a prophet mighty in deed and word before God and all the people: 20 and how the chief priests and our rulers delivered him up to be condemned to death, and crucified him. 21 But we hoped that it was he who should redeem Israel. Yea and besides all this, it is now the third day since these things came to pass. 22 Moreover certain women of our company amazed us, having been early at the tomb; 23 and when they found not his body, they came, saying, that they had also seen a vision of angels, who said that he was alive. 24 And certain of them that were with us went to the tomb, and found it even so as the women had said: but him they saw not. 25 And he said unto them, O foolish men, and slow of heart to believe in all that the prophets have spoken! 26 Behooved it not the Christ to suffer these things, and to enter into his glory? 27 And beginning from Moses and from all the prophets, he interpreted to them in all the scriptures the things concerning himself. 28 And they drew nigh unto the village, whither they were going: and he made as though he would go further. 29 And they constrained him, saying, Abide with us; for it is toward evening, and the day is now far spent. And he went in to abide with them. 30 And it came to pass, when he had sat down with them to meat, he took the bread and blessed; and breaking it he gave to them. 31 And

---

[539] Abbott-Smith, *op. cit.*, p. 268. [540] *Op. cit.*, p. 178.
[541] Verse 12 (KJV) is missing in the Western text and so is omitted in RSV. But it has strong manuscript support and should probably be retained. It summarizes John 20:2-8.

their eyes were opened, and they knew him; and he vanished out of their sight. 32 And they said one to another, Was not our heart burning within us, while he spake to us in the way, while he opened to us the scriptures? 33 And they rose up that very hour, and returned to Jerusalem, and found the eleven gathered together, and them that were with them, 34 saying, The Lord is risen indeed, and hath appeared to Simon. 35 And they rehearsed the things *that happened* in the way, and how he was known of them in the breaking of the bread.

This incident is recorded only by Luke. On **that very day**, two disciples were going to **Emmaus**, located sixty **furlongs**, or "stadia" (about seven miles) from **Jerusalem**. As they walked along, they **communed** with each other. The verb comes from a noun meaning "crowd" or "throng." So at first it signified "to be in company with." But in the New Testament (used only by Luke) it means "converse with." They were talking about the exciting events that had just taken place in Jerusalem.

Suddenly Jesus put in His appearance and joined them in their walk. These disciples of His did not recognize Him. When He asked what they were discussing, **they stood still, looking sad** (v. 17). Their hearts were heavy with sorrow over Christ's death.

One of the disciples is named, but not the other. We do not know with certainty who **Cleopas** was. Creed thinks that he is perhaps identical with Clopas of John 19:25. Others question this. At any rate, Cleopas expressed surprise that Jesus should be ignorant of the startling things that were happening in Jerusalem. When Christ asked **What things?**, they expressed the faith they had had that Jesus was the Messiah — **he who should redeem Israel** (v. 20).

Furthermore, this was **the third day** since the Crucifixion (v. 21). To add to the confusion, **certain women of our company** reported finding the tomb empty and seeing **a vision of angels,** who said that Jesus was alive (v. 23). Verse 24 is a clear reference to the visit of Peter and John to the sepulcher on Sunday morning (John 20:2-10).

After chiding them gently for their lack of understanding and belief in the prophetic writings of the Old Testament and for their failure to apply the teaching on a suffering Messiah (v. 26), Jesus gave these men an unforgettable experience of being taken through the Old Testament in a rapid survey of its Messianic teaching (v. 27). Plummer says: "There is nothing incredible in the supposition that He quoted from one of the Prophets."[542] It is still true that if we would find the real truth of the older Scriptures, we must seek Christ there.

Finally they neared Emmaus. Jesus naturally acted as if He were going on farther. But when they **constrained him,** because evening was coming on, He consented to stay.

A familiar scene now opened their eyes. When Christ blessed and broke the tiny loaves of bread, handing some to each of them, they suddenly recognized who He was. But immediately He vanished; literally, "He became invisible." Their significant testimony was that their hearts had burned as He had opened to them the Scriptures on the way.

That very hour these Emmaus disciples **returned**, walking once more the seven miles to Jerusalem. There they found **the eleven** gathered — a general name for the group, since we know from John that Thomas was not present — **and them that were with them** (v. 33). Before the two from Emmaus could get in their report, they were told: **The Lord is risen indeed, and hath appeared to Simon** (v. 34). Then the two men related their story (v. 35). By now the Resurrection was a well-certified reality.

3. Appearance to the Disciples (24:36-43)

36 And as they spake these things, he himself stood in the midst of them, and saith unto them, Peace *be* unto you. 37 But they were terrified and affrighted, and supposed that they beheld a spirit. 38 And he said unto them, Why are ye troubled? and wherefore do questionings arise in your heart? 39 See my hands and my feet, that it is I myself: handle me, and see; for a spirit hath not flesh and bones, as ye behold me having. 40 And when he had said this, he showed them his hands and his feet. 41 And while they still disbelieved for joy, and wondered, he said unto them, Have ye here anything

---

[542] *Op. cit.*, p. 555.

to eat? 42 And they gave him a piece of broiled fish. 43 And he took it, and ate before them.

While the two Emmaus disciples were still telling the wonderful news, suddenly Jesus **stood in the midst of them** (v. 36). As always on such occasions, He calmed their fears with, **Peace be unto you.** In spite of this they were **terrified and affrighted**, supposing they were seeing a **spirit** (v. 37); that is, a ghost. But Jesus bade them look at His nail-pierced **hands** and **feet**. A ghost does not have **flesh and bones** (v. 39). While they still **disbelieved** for joy, He asked for something to eat. When they **gave** Him a piece of broiled fish, He ate it before them, apparently to prove that He was not a ghost, but that He had a real body. Plummer suggests that it was a glorified body, not needing food, but capable of receiving it.[543] That is what the account here suggests.

B. THE PROMISE OF THE HOLY SPIRIT (24:44-49)

44 And he said unto them, These are my words which I spake unto you, while I was yet with you, that all things must needs be fulfilled, which are written in the law of Moses, and the prophets, and the psalms, concerning me. 45 Then opened he their mind, that they might understand the scriptures; 46 and he said unto them, Thus it is written, that the Christ should suffer, and rise again from the dead the third day; 47 and that repentance and remission of sins should be preached in his name unto all the nations, beginning from Jerusalem. 48 Ye are witnesses of these things. 49 And behold, I send forth the promise of my Father upon you: but tarry ye in the city, until ye be clothed with power from on high.

Just when or where this brief discourse took place we cannot tell. Luke was not primarily interested in the geographical and chronological setting, but in the message that came through.

While Jesus was with them, before His death, He had frequently indicated that the Scriptures must be **fulfilled** (v. 44). In the Hebrew canon there were three main divisions — **the law, the prophets, and the psalms** (or "the Writings"). The Law

consisted of the first five books of the Old Testament. The Prophets took in Joshua, Judges, Samuel, and Kings, as well as Isaiah, Jeremiah, Ezekiel, and the twelve Minor Prophets. Everything else went into the Writings, or the Psalms. What is implied here is that every part of the Old Testament speaks of Christ in some way. The older Scriptures teach a suffering Messiah (v. 45). Jesus doubtless called their attention to the twenty-second Psalm and the fifty-third chapter of Isaiah. He further indicated that the program of evangelizing **all the nations** was in the mind of God in the previous days.

Then He promised them the Holy Spirit, whom He calls **the promise of my Father** (v. 49). Along with the promise came a command: **but tarry ye in the city until ye be clothed with power from on high.** The same command is given in Acts 1:4.

C. THE ASCENSION (24:50-53)

50 And he led them out until *they were* over against Bethany: and he lifted up his hands, and blessed them. 51 And it came to pass, while he blessed them, he parted from them, and was carried up into heaven. 52 And they worshipped him, and returned to Jerusalem with great joy: 53 and were continually in the temple, blessing God.

The Ascension is recorded only in the last chapter of Luke and the first chapter of Acts, just as the decree of Cyrus for the return of the Jews to Palestine is given at the end of II Chronicles and the beginning of Ezra. In both cases these suggest unity of authorship.

Over against Bethany can very well mean the top of the Mount of Olives, the traditional site of the Ascension. That would be the logical place to go from Jerusalem. In the familiar act of blessing, He was taken from them. After pausing for worship, the disciples returned to the city. There they were **continually in the temple, blessing God.** This probably means that they attended faithfully the hours of prayer every day. For Acts indicates that they also tarried in the upper room.

543 *Ibid.,* p. 560.

Bibliography

(All books listed are either quoted or cited in the commentary.)

I. COMMENTARIES

Alford, Henry. *The Greek Testament.* Revised by E. F. Harrison. 2 double vols. Chicago: Moody Press, 1958.

Arndt, William F. *The Gospel According to St. Luke.* "Bible Commentary." St. Louis: Concordia Publishing House, 1956.

Balmforth, H. *The Gospel According to St. Luke.* "The Clarendon Bible." Oxford: Clarendon Press, 1930.

Barclay, William. *The Gospel of Luke.* "The Daily Study Bible." 2nd ed. Philadelphia: Westminster Press, 1956.

Barnes, Albert. *Notes on the New Testament: Luke and John.* Edited by Robert Frew. Grand Rapids: Baker Book House, 1949 (reprint).

Bengel, John Albert. *Gnomon of the New Testament.* Translated by A. R. Fausset. 4th ed. 5 vols. Edinburgh: T. & T. Clark, 1860.

Brown, David. *Matthew-John.* "A Commentary Critical, Experimental and Practical on the Old and New Testaments," by Robert Jamieson, A. R. Fausset, and David Brown. Grand Rapids: Wm. B. Eerdmans Publishing Co., 1948 (reprint).

Browning, W. R. F. *The Gospel According to St. Luke.* "Torch Bible Commentaries." New York: Macmillan Co., 1960.

Bruce, A. B. *The Synoptic Gospels.* "The Expositor's Greek Testament." Edited by W. Robertson Nicoll. Grand Rapids: Wm. B. Eerdmans Publishing Co., n.d.

Burton, Henry. *The Gospel According to St. Luke.* "The Expositor's Bible." Edited by W. R. Nicoll. New York: A. C. Armstrong and Son, 1896.

Cadbury, Henry J. *The Making of Luke-Acts.* 2nd ed. London: S.P.C.K., 1958.

Clarke, Adam. *The New Testament of Our Lord and Saviour Jesus Christ.* Vol. I. New York: Methodist Book Concern, n.d.

Clarke, W. L. Lowther. *Concise Bible Commentary.* New York: Macmillan Co., 1953.

Creed, J. M. *The Gospel According to St. Luke.* London: Macmillan and Co., 1930.

Erdman, Charles R. *The Gospel of Luke.* Philadelphia: Westminster Press, 1931.

Farrar, F. W. *The Gospel According to St. Luke.* "Cambridge Greek Testament." Cambridge: University Press, 1884.

Geldenhuys, Norval. *Commentary on the Gospel of Luke.* "New International Commentary on the New Testament." Grand Rapids: Wm. B. Eerdmans Publishing Co., 1951.

Gilmour, S. MacLean. *The Gospel According to St. Luke* (Exegesis). "The Interpreter's Bible." Edited by George A. Buttrick *et al.* VIII. New York: Abingdon-Cokesbury Press, 1952.

Godet, F. L. *Commentary on the Gospel of Luke.* Grand Rapids: Zondervan Publishing House, n.d.

Gore, Charles. *The Gospel According to St. Luke.* "A New Commentary on Holy Scripture." Edited by Charles Gore, H. L. Goudge, and Alfred Guillaume. New York: Macmillan Co., 1928.

Lampe, G. W. H. *Luke.* "Peake's Commentary on the Bible." Edited by Matthew Black and H. H. Rowley. London: Thomas Nelson & Sons, 1962.

Leany, A. R. C. *A Commentary on the Gospel According to St. Luke.* "Harper's New Testament Commentaries." New York: Harper & Brothers, 1958.

Lenski, R. C. H. *The Interpretation of St. Luke's Gospel.* Columbus, O.: Wartburg Press, 1946.

Maclaren, Alexander. *Expositions of Holy Scripture.* Vol. IX. Grand Rapids: Wm. B. Eerdmans Publishing Co., 1944 (reprint).

Major, H.D.A. "Incidents in the Life of Jesus." *The Mission and Message of Jesus.* H. D. A. Major, T. W. Manson, and C. N. Wright. New York: E. P. Dutton & Co., 1938.

Manson, T. W. "The Sayings of Jesus." *The Mission and Message of Jesus.* H. D. A. Major, T. W. Manson, and C. J. Wright. New York: E. P. Dutton & Co., 1938.

Manson, William. *The Gospel of Luke.* "The Moffatt New Testament Commentary." New York: Harper and Brothers, [1930].

Meyer, H. A. W. *Critical and Exegetical Hand-book to the Gospels of Mark and Luke.* Translated by R. E. Wallis. Revised and edited by W. P. Dickson. American Edition. New York: Funk and Wagnalls, 1884.

Miller, Donald G. *The Gospel According to Luke.* "The Layman's Bible Commentary." Edited by Balmer H. Kelly. Richmond, Va.: John Knox Press, 1959.

Morgan, G. Campbell. *The Gospel According to Luke.* New York: Fleming H. Revell Co., 1931.

Olshausen, Hermann. *Biblical Commentary on the New Testament.* Translated by A. C. Kendrick. 6 vols. New York: Sheldon & Co., 1860.

Oosterzee, J. J. van. *Luke.* "Commentary on the Holy Scriptures." Edited by John Peter Lange. Translated, with additions, by Philip Schaff. Grand Rapids: Zondervan Publishing House, n.d.

Plummer, Alfred. *A Critical and Exegetical Commentary on the Gospel According to St. Luke.* "The International Critical Commentary." New York: Charles Scribner's Sons, 1896.

Plumptre, E. H. *The Gospel According to St. Luke.* "Commentary on the Whole Bible." Edited by C. J. Ellicott. Grand Rapids: Zondervan Publishing House, 1954 (reprint).

Ragg, Lonsdale. *St. Luke.* "Westminster Commentaries." London: Methuen & Co., 1922.

Ryle, J. C. *Expository Thoughts on the Gospel.* 4 vols. Grand Rapids: Zondervan Publishing House, n.d.

Sadler, M. F. *The Gospel According to St. Luke.* 2nd ed. rev. New York: James Pott & Co., 1888.

Simeon, Charles. *Expository Outlines on the Whole Bible.* Vol. XII. Grand Rapids: Zondervan Publishing House, n.d.

Spence, H. D. M. *St. Luke* (Exposition). D. M. Spence and Joseph S. Exell. Vol. "The Pulpit Commentary." Edited by H. D. M. Spence and Joseph S. Exell, Vol. XVI. Grand Rapids: Wm. B. Eerdmans Publishing Co., 1950 (reprint).

Strack, Hermann L., and Billerbeck, Paul. *Kommentar Zum Neuen Testament aus Talmud und Midrasch.* Munchen: C. H. Beck'sche Verlagsbuchhandlung, 1956. Band II.

II. OTHER BOOKS

Abbott-Smith, G. *A Manual Greek Lexicon of the New Testament.* 2nd ed. Edinburgh: T. & T. Clark, 1923.

Andrews, Samuel J. *The Life of Our Lord.* Grand Rapids: Zondervan Publishing House, 1954 (reprint of 1891 rev. ed.)

Arndt, W. F., and Gingrich, F. W. *A Greek-English Lexicon of the New Testament and Early Christian Literature.* Chicago: University of Chicago Press, 1957.

Blass, F., and Debrunner, A. *A Greek Grammar of the New Testament and Other Early Christian Literature.* Translated and revised by Robert W. Funk. Chicago Press, 1961.

Bruce, A. B. *The Parabolic Teaching of Christ.* 3rd ed. rev. New York: A. C. Armstrong & Son, 1896.

Burton, Ernest DeWitt. *Syntax of the Moods and Tenses in New Testament Greek.* 2nd ed. rev. Chicago: University Press, 1892.

Cadbury, Henry J. *The Making of Luke-Acts.* 2nd ed. London: S.P.C.K., 1958.

Conzelmann, Hans, *The Theology of St. Luke.* Translated by Geoffrey Buswell. London: Faber and Faber, 1960.

Cremer, Hermann. *Biblico-theological Lexicon of New Testament Greek.* Translated by William Urwick. Edinburgh: T. & T. Clark, 1878.

Daube, David. *The New Testament and Rabbinic Judaism.* London: Athlone Press, 1956.

Deissmann, Adolf. *Bible Studies.* Translated by Alexander Grieve. Edinburgh: T. & T. Clark, 1901.

—————. *Light From the Ancient East.* Translated by L. R. M. Strachan. Rev. ed. New York: George H. Doran Co., 1927.

Edersheim, Alfred. *The Life and Times of Jesus the Messiah.* 2 vols. 8th ed. rev. New York: Longmans, Green, and Co., 1903.

Eusebius Pamphilus. *Ecclesiastical History.* Translated by C. F. Cruse. Grand Rapids: Baker Book House, 1955.

Hayes, D. A. *The Synoptic Gospels and the Book of Acts.* New York: Methodist Book Concern, 1919.

Henry, Carl F. H. (ed.) *Basic Christian Doctrines.* New York: Holt, Rinehart and Winston, 1962.

Hobart, William K. *The Medical Language of St. Luke.* Grand Rapids: Baker Book House, 1954 (reprint of 1882 edition).

Josephus, Flavius. *Works.* Translated by William Whiston. Philadelphia: Henry T. Coates & Co., n.d.

Klausner, Joseph. *Jesus of Nazareth.* Translated from the original Hebrew by Herbert Danby. New York: Macmillan Co., 1925.

Lang, G. H. *The Parabolic Teaching of Scripture.* Grand Rapids: Wm. B. Eerdmans Publishing Co., 1955.

Liddell, H. G., and Scott, Robert. *A Greek-English Lexicon.* Revised by H. S. Jones. Oxford: Clarendon Press, 1940.

Lundström, Gösta. *The Kingdom of God in the Teaching of Jesus.* Translated by Joan Bulman. Richmond, Va.: John Knox Press, 1963.

Morgan, G. Campbell. *The Gospel According to Luke.* New York: Fleming H. Revell Co., 1931.

Moulton, James Hope. *A Grammar of New Testament Greek.* Vol. I, "Prolegomena." 3rd ed. Edinburgh: T. & T. Clark, 1908.

Moulton, James Hope, and Milligan, George. *The Vocabulary of the Greek Testament.* Grand Rapids: Wm. B. Eerdmans Publishing Co., 1949.

Olmstead, A. T. *Jesus in the Light of History.* New York: Charles Scribner's Sons, 1942.

Perowne, Stewart. *The Life and times of Herod the Great.* New York: Abingdon Press, [1956].

Perrin, Norman. *The Kingdom of God in the Teaching of Jesus.* Philadelphia: Westminster Press, 1963.

Ramsay, William M. *Was Christ Born in Bethlehem?* New York: G. P. Putnam's Sons, n.d.

Schürer, Emil. *A History of the Jewish People in the Time of Jesus Christ.* 2 vols. Edinburgh: T. & T. Clark, 1885.

Stauffer, Ethelbert. *Jesus and His Story.* Translated from the German by Richard and Clara Winston. New York: Alfred A. Knopf, 1959.

Streeter, B. H. *The Four Gospels.* 5th Impression, Revised. London: Macmillan & Co., 1936.

Tacitus, P. Cornelius. *The Annals and the Histories.* Chicago: Encyclopaedia Britannica, 1952.

Taylor, Vincent. *The Gospels.* 7th ed. London: Epworth Press, 1952.

Teaching of the Twelve Apostles. Translated by R. D. Hitchcock and Francis Brown. New York: Charles Scribner's Sons, 1884.

Tenney, Merrill C. (ed.). *The Pictorial Bible Dictionary.* Grand Rapids: Zondervan Publishing House, 1963.

Thayer, J. H. *A Greek-English Lexicon of the New Testament.* New York: American Book Co., 1889.

Tittle, Ernest F. *The Gospel According to Luke.* New York: Harper & Brothers, 1951.

Torrey, C. C. *The Four Gospels.* New York: Harper & Brothers, 1933.

Trench, R. C. *Notes on the Parables of Our Lord.* Philadelphia: William Syckelmoore, 1878.

Westcott, B. F., and Hort, F. J. *The New Testament in the Original Greek.* Vol. II., Appendix. New York: Harper & Brothers, 1882.

Wikenhauser, Alfred. *New Testament Introduction.* Translated by Joseph Cunningham. New York: Herder and Herder, 1958.

Zahn, Theodor. *Introduction to the New Testament.* Translated under direction of M. W. Jacobs. 3 vols. Grand Rapids: Kregel Publications, 1953 (reprint).

III. ARTICLES

Bamberger, B. J. "Tax Collector." *The Interpreter's Dictionary of the Bible.* Edited by George Buttrick *et al.* New York: Abingdon Press, 1962. Vol. IV. Hereafter cited as IDB.

Burkill, T. A. "Sanhedrin." IDB, Vol. IV.

Harrison, R. K. "Dropsy." IDB, I, 872.

Mendelsohn, I, "Exorcism." IDB., Vol. II.

Mullo-Weir, C. J. "Old Testament Languages — Hebrew and Aramaic." *A Companion to the Bible.* Edited by T. W. Manson. Edinburgh: T. & T. Clark, 1939.

Roberts, C. H. "The Kingdom of Heaven (Lk. XVII. 21)." *Harvard Theological Review,* XLI (Jan., 1948).

Sandmel, S. "Tetrarch." IDB, Vol. IV.

The Gospel According to St. John
by Harvey J. S. Blaney

Editor's Preface to John

THE AUTHOR OF THE EXPOSITION OF THE GOSPEL ACCORDING TO JOHN in the *Wesleyan Bible Commentary* is Dr. Harvey J. S. Blaney, Professor of Religion and Chairman of the Graduate Division of Theological Studies at Eastern Nazarene College. Professor Blaney holds the following degrees: A.B., Eastern Nazarene College; B.D., Yale University; S.T.M., Harvard University; and Th. D., Boston University. Dr. Blaney has held his present position at Eastern Nazarene College since 1945. His teaching field is in the areas of Old and New Testament studies. A recent summer was spent teaching at Pasadena College, Pasadena, California.

Dr. Blaney is an ordained minister in the Church of the Nazarene, and has pastored Baptist, Congregational, and Nazarene congregations in New Brunswick, Canada, Maine, Connecticut, and Massachusetts. He is co-author of *Exploring the New Testament,* and author of the *College Workbook* for the foregoing volume (Beacon Hill Press). He has written extensively for religious publications.

Professor Blaney is a member of the National Association of Biblical Instructions, the Society of Biblical Literature and Exegesis, and the American Schools of Oriental Research. He is a past President of Boston Biblical Club.

The author of the Commentary on John has had a long and rich ministry of preaching, in addition to his many fruitful years of work in the classroom. The richness of his scholarship and the force of his practical ministry are abundantly evident in his expositions of the Gospel According to John. Here the mind and soul of the Apostle is made to live anew under the deft pen of Professor Blaney. His pleasing style and penetrating insights into the spiritual depth of the Apostle's teachings are a continual delight to the reader. The Gospel According to John well qualifies as a true religious classic by reason of its universal appeal to human nature and its ability to satisfy the deepest needs of man's spiritual nature. Professor Blaney has admirably portrayed those qualities of this great Gospel in his expositions of John.

CHAS. W. CARTER
Chairman and General Editor
Wesleyan Bible Commentary

Outline

Introduction

I. PRESCRIPT

The Gospel of John has always been greatly loved by the Christian Church and has been used consistently as a choice portion of the Bible in introducing the Gospel of Jesus Christ to the unconverted. Isaiah's description of "The way of Holiness" as one in which "the wayfaring man, yea fools, shall not err" (Isa. 35:8), has been given fresh meaning for the Christian by John's Gospel. At the same time, it contains some of the most profound concepts and problems to be found in the study of man and the universe, in the study of the Bible, and in the understanding of Jesus Christ and His work of Redemption. It is like a clear pool of water which delights the beholder, slakes his thirst and reflects the beauties of nature to his sight. Yet, this pool has within its depths mysteries to challenge the interest and absorb the attention of the keenest students of the physical sciences. This Gospel is a mingling of simplicity and profundity, and the attempts to unravel its problems and probe its depths of truth continue unabated.

The author of this Gospel was "a mystic with the creative imagination of the artist," howbeit a mystic whose center was Christ and not Absolute Being, a mystic who was the counterpart of the Hebrew Prophet.[1] His primary goal was not to write mere history, for the very evident reason that his interest was not only in the Jesus of history but in Jesus as the *Logos* of God. To him "the earthly life of Jesus . . . appears as the dramatic interlude in the life of the Eternal Logos."[2] His interest was the Word made Flesh which had dwelt among men. This is not to say that this Gospel cannot be used in the effort to reconstruct the life of Jesus, because it tells of Him who had lived in time and made history of the profoundest sort, of Him who was before history (1:1) and who continues to exist beyond history (14:

1-3). But the author himself stood above history as he wrote, at the same time being involved in the historical process. He wrote from the point of view of his subject who transcended history, time and space. In John "Christian experience has taken up the pen to write."[3] The history of Jesus is necessary to his narrative in order to show that the whole was not just the mystical experience of the believing community, but the history is subsumed under the view of Jesus as the Eternal Son of God. "Every part of his narrative is referred to one final truth made clear by experience, that 'Jesus is the Christ, the Son of God.' "[4]

The reader must try to stand where the author stood if he would understand his message, a message deeply concerned with "the relation between what is finite and temporal and what is infinite and eternal, between 'flesh' and Spirit, and between 'flesh' and Word."[5] B. H. Streeter says that the Fourth Gospel belongs to the "Library of Devotion." It will be misunderstood unless it is approached in a spirit comparable to that in which we approach the *Confessions* of Augustine or the *Imitation* of à Kempis."[6]

II. AUTHORSHIP AND DATE

The design and scope of the present work preclude an exhaustive treatment of the problems associated with the authorship and date of John's Gospel. These problems have been treated by qualified authorities with special interest in this area, and the material is easily available in works listed in the accompanying bibliography. It will be sufficient here to sketch the broad lines of the various arguments involved, the conclusions which have been suggested, and the position which might be considered most tenable on a problem which is still awaiting further evidence for its final answer.

From the last half of the second cen-

---

[1] B. H. Streeter, *The Four Gospels*, pp. 383, 366, 368.
[2] R. H. Strachan, *The Fourth Evangelist*, p. 31.   [3] *Ibid.*, p. 22.
[4] B. F. Westcott, *The Gospel According to St. John*, p. xlii.
[5] E. C. Hoskyns, *The Fourth Gospel*, ed. F. N. Davey, p. 20.   [6] *Op. cit.*, p. 365.

tury A.D. until the eighteenth century the accepted author was the Apostle John, son of Zebedee, who wrote late in life near the close of the first century. An excellent statement of this position is given by B. F. Westcott,[7] whose essential argument is given by Alfred Plummer,[8] and George Salmon,[9] and by many conservative writers since the turn of the present century. It is safe to say that this conclusion is in general acceptance in evangelical Christianity today.

This argument in brief is that the author was a Jew, a Jew of Palestine, an eyewitness of what he described, an apostle, and thus the Apostle John. This evidence is derived from the book itself, the language and form of which show that the author was acquainted with and understood the Old Testament, the Jewish faith, and the land and customs of Palestine. He also had firsthand knowledge of many events in the life of Christ, the times in which He lived, and of His associations with the Twelve.

In addition, there is the external evidence, made up of references to the Gospel from early Christian writers. Westcott says:

> In reviewing these traces of the use of the Gospel in the first three-quarters of a century after it was written, we readily admit that they are less distinct and numerous than those might have expected who are unacquainted with the character of the literary remains of the period. But it will be observed that all the evidence points in one direction. There is not, with one questionable exception, any positive indication that doubt was anywhere thrown upon the authenticity of the Book . . . . all the new evidence which has come to light has supported this universal belief of the Christian Society, while it has seriously modified the rival theories which have been set up against it.[10]

A more penetrating analysis of this position has been given by H. S. Holland,[11] whose work, along with that of Westcott, may be considered normative for British scholars of that period. These men were set in strict opposition to the critical school, not because they were

opposed to the tools of critical investigation, with which they were fully familiar, but because they were better oriented in early Christian tradition than their opponents.[12]

The traditional view has held to a late first-century date for the writing of John's Gospel. This is based upon the tradition that John lived in Ephesus following the departure of the Apostle Paul from the city, that he remained there to old age, and that he received the apocalyptic vision on the Isle of Patmos late in life. In addition, the contents of the Gospel reveal an assumed acquaintance with the Synoptic Gospels on the part of the Christian community, and the author, dealing with beliefs and conditions in both the church and the world of a date later than that of the Synoptic writers and Paul, relies upon his own eye-witness reminiscences. A changed attitude toward the Jews is also evident.

In opposition to the traditional school was the critical school, stemming largely from Germany. The results of liberal criticism were set forth in their most extreme form by Johannas Strauss in his *Life of Christ* and by F. C. Baur, founder of the so-called Tübingen school of thought. In brief this position may be summarized as follows.

The critical view rejected the traditional position on the basis of the assumed evolution of Christian tradition Jesus was a man with a message and a following who allowed Himself to be martyred at the darkest hour of His career, in the hope of inspiring His disciples to a renewed zeal for the new movement. It proved to be a master move, and as the years passed and the church was established in His name, more marvels came to be attributed to Him. They felt Him so near that they began to believe that He had risen from the dead. Then miracles were attributed to Him, and soon they believed that in His ministry Jesus had promised all that they were experiencing. Someone took the name of John, a disciple, and used it in writing what he called an eyewit-

---

[7] *Op. cit.*　　[8] Alfred Plummer (ed.), *The Gospel According to St. John*, Introduction.
[9] George Salmon, *A Historical Introduction to the Study of Books of the New Testament*, Ch. XII.
[10] *Ibid.*, p. xxxii.　　[11] H. S. Holland, *The Fourth Gospel*, ed. W. J. Richmond, pp. 38-134.
[12] Hoskyns, *op. cit.*, p. 36. Hoskyns gives what is probably the best and most comprehensive analysis available of the entire Johannine problem.

ness account of the life and teachings of his Lord, who had been known to be divine from the beginning and had lived and died according to a prescribed plan of God.

The Gospel was condemned because the whole claim to the deity of Jesus was false. John the Apostle could not have written it — the claim of the author to being an eyewitness and the disciple whom Jesus loved was also false. The Gospel was of very late origin, perhaps as late as the second half of the second century, and the author was utterly unknown.

While this criticism came chiefly from Germany, the field was not undivided on the continent, as W. F. Howard shows.[13] Theodor Zahn and Bernhard Weiss stood for the traditional view, H. Holzmann, Paul W. Schmiedel and Adolf Jülicher for the liberal view, while Adolf von Harnack took a middle position. William Sanday, the British scholar, represented a blindness to some of the progressive movements in Europe, notably the theological emphasis which has had a profound influence upon later scholarship. B. W. Bacon, the American scholar at Yale, served as a significant mediating force.[14] Sanday, however, was rather sarcastic concerning the work of Bacon.[15]

Out of the virtual deadlock the mediating position arose, and it continues in many modifications to the present day. It is based largely upon considerations which the conservatives had neglected or ignored or which were not even available to them, but which were forced into the discussion by the results of literary criticism and archaeological findings. Even Westcott had been conscious that the external evidence was not conclusive. Doubt had been cast upon the John referred to in some of the sources as well as upon certain references to the Gospel. A second look had to be taken at the reference from Papias that John the Apostle had suffered early martyrdom with his brother James, for this tradition was admittedly very late. It was realized that the solution of the Synoptic problem was

a literary solution, some form of a source hypothesis. Thus the Gospel of John also "stood in a literary relationship."[16] The various discrepancies, both literary and chronological, between the Synoptics and the Fourth Gospel could no longer be ignored. The complete historical accuracy of both could not be acknowledged at one and the same time; in general the Synoptics were preferred above John with the exception of the Passion story. In addition, John's Gospel itself produced a real problem when it was recognized that the discourses of Jesus are in the style of the author and that they are not always distinguishable from the exhortations of the author.

The reconstructed position allows for the Gospel to be Johannine without of necessity claiming John the Apostle as actual author. The author may be another John — John the Elder or Presbyter. It is also seen that the authorship of this Gospel cannot be solved without considering all revelant materials. This position is well represented by Wm. Temple[17] who supports the apostolic authority of the Gospel, the actual writer being John the Elder, a close disciple of John the Apostle. He is little more than a recorder, while the Apostle remains the *witness* and **the disciple whom Jesus loved**. This position is taken essentially by B. W. Robinson,[18] who holds the author to be John the Presbyter, identical with the author of the Johannine Epistles. J. H. C. Macgregor suggests that the author was a younger follower of John, the beloved disciple.[19] Two writers of more recent date have argued the same case, largely from external evidence.[20]

Another argument for the newer stance is given by B. P. W. S. Hunt, who contends that the Gospel was edited by some "authoritative persons" after the death of the author, who was the Apostle John. The language, Hunt argues, could have been applicable only in Alexandria; John founded the church there, and he never was in Ephesus (the traditionally accepted evidence is very weak). He

[13] W. F. Howard, *The Fourth Gospel in Recent Criticism and Interpretation*, p. 71.
[14] Hoskyns, *op. cit.*, p. 36f.   [15] Wm. Sanday, *The Criticism of the Fourth Gospel*, p. 24.
[16] Reginald H. Fuller (ed.), *The New Testament in Current Study*, p. 102.
[17] Wm. Temple, *Reading in St. John's Gospel*, p. x.
[18] B. W. Robinson, *The Gospel of John*, Ch. 1.
[19] J. H. C. Macgregor, *The Gospel of John*, "The Moffatt New Testament Commentary," p. xiv.
[20] R. A. Edwards, *The Gospel According to St. John*, and Wm. Barclay, *The Gospel of John*, passim.

accepts the tradition, coming from Papias, that John the Apostle suffered early martyrdom (although this tradition is generally considered weak, coming from the 7th to 9th centuries). The original writing of the Gospel is placed before A.D. 70 "when the cult of Philo was at its height among the Jews of Alexander."[21]

Barrett holds essentially the same ultimate opinion on milder grounds. John the Apostle died at an unknown but relatively early date, leaving behind him a group of pupils and a body of unpublished writings. Three, or perhaps four, pupils were responsible for the Apocalypse, the Epistles and the Gospel. It was because the reference to the beloved disciple (John the Apostle) became associated with the authorship that the traditional Johannine authorship became mistakenly established.[22]

Since the discovery of the Dead Sea Scrolls in 1947 a new dimension has been added to the study of John's Gospel, a dimension which has as yet uncertain implications for its date and authorship. Traditionally it was assumed that the Christian Church developed through Judaism to Hellenism. The Hellenistic element in John's Gospel, especially in the prologue, seemed to argue for a late date. W. F. Howard, as early as 1935, recognized the strength of the Jewish element and said, ". . . we do not need to go beyond Judaism for the idea of the Logos, and . . . Hellenistic mysticism, rather than Stoicism, in its impact upon the life and thought of the Diaspora, had prepared the way for some of the notable phrases of this Gospel."[23]

Recent literature on the background of Christianity in the light of the Dead Sea Scrolls points to a possible connection between John the Baptist and the Essenes of the Qumran Community, and thus through the disciples of John between Jesus and the Qumran sect. "Such a direct connection, however, cannot be proved with certainty."[24]

Further, some relationship is also suggested between the Fourth Gospel and the Hellenists, and between the Fourth Gospel and the Qumran sect. In positing a three-way connection between the Gospel, the Hellenists, and the Qumran sect, Oscar Cullman associates the term "Hellenist" with a Jewish group similar to those at Qumran, Hellenism being about the only term applicable to those not belonging to normative Judaism.[25] If these conclusions prove to be valid, it may turn out that ". . . John has its strong affinities, not with the Greek world, or Philonic Judaism, but with Palestinian Judaism. . . . So that rather than being the most Hellenistic of the Gospels, John now proves to be in some ways the most Jewish."[26]

In an excellent review of the present status of the Johannine problem, A. M. Hunter claims that the Dead Sea Scrolls have established the essential Jewishness of the Gospel of John. Comparisons of the thought world of John have no need to go to Hellenistic Gnosticism of the second century, because the closest parallels to the antithetical expressions in the Gospel are found in the Qumran documents.[27]

The most decisive piece of evidence which has contributed to the dating of the Gospel of John was the discovery of the Robert's Fragment of the Gospel, found in Egypt in 1935 and now in the John Ryland's Library in Manchester, England. While it contains only five verses (18:31-33; 37f.) it has been dated, on paleological grounds, in the first quarter of the second century. Allowing for time for acceptance and for circulation as far as Egypt, it could not have been written much later than A.D. 90. A fragment of an apocryphal gospel in the same library, dated in the middle of the second century, which gives evidence of the author's use of the Gospel of John, provides data of the same kind. Thus the traditional date, A.D. 90-100 is again acceptable to scholars, both liberal and conservative.

No more is being attempted at this point than to indicate that the problem of the authorship of John's Gospel has not yet been solved to the complete satisfaction of scholars, and to sketch the present trend of discussions on the sub-

21 B. P. W. S. Hunt, *Some Johannine Problems*, p. 113.
22 C. K Barrett, *The Gospel According to St. John*, pp. 113-114.   23 *Op. cit.*, pp. 25-26.
24 Krister Stendahl (ed.), *The Scrolls and the New Testament*, p. 24.   25 *Ibid.*, pp. 18f.
26 Frank M. Cross, Jr., *The Ancient Library of Qumran*, pp. 215-216.
27 A. M. Hunter, "Recent Trends in Johannine Studies," *Expository Times* (March, 1960), pp. 166-167.

ject. These discussions show little resemblance in approach and method to those of either the extreme liberals or the extreme conservatives. But whatever can reveal the earliest possible associations of the Gospel materials, if not for the Gospel itself, brings it closer to apostolic authority and to the concept of eyewitness reporting.

The traditional theory of authorship is not held today on the basis of new and original research, but on the basis of the earlier work of Westcott and others. The weight of modern scholarship takes a middle-of-the-road trend toward a noncommittal or even an indifferent position. This is indicative of the fact that Biblical criticism as hitherto defined seems to have run its course in deference to the new interest in Biblical theology. Hoskyns, in the minds of some people the successor to Westcott in Johannine scholarship, does not try to identify the author. In fact, he suggests:

> The author has done his best, apparently with intention, to cover up his tracks. . . . He does not intend us to busy ourselves with him as though he were himself the goal of our inquiry. He has, in fact, so burnt himself out of his book that we cannot be certain that we have anywhere located him as a clear, intelligible figure in history. At the end of our inquiry he remains no more than a voice bearing witness to the glory of God.[28]

He further suggests that it is impossible that the answer to the problem of authorship, as well as to other problems, will ever be found as the result of the investigation of the historical and human elements in the Gospel. It will, he thinks, ever remain a restless Gospel, because the theme of the book is beyond human knowledge.

C. H. Dodd does not deny the possibility of the Gospel resting upon the personal reminiscences of a Palestinian Jew, although he does not discuss the authorship in his major work on the Gospel of John.[29]

It is now time to evaluate the present status of the Johannine problem concerning date and authorship and to state what can be safely believed to be the position of responsible scholarship today.

The approximate date of the Gospel has been established beyond a peradventure. The traditional date — A.D. 90-100 — appears secure.

Concerning the author, the Johannine authority may be held while the Johannine authorship is rejected. The Johannine authorship is held on grounds of internal evidence and rejected on external or historical grounds. The latter position is held largely by positing a separation between history and theology — the presupposition that the Gospel is theological interpretation and therefore cannot be reliable history. But Westcott in his day warned against dividing the two elements in the Gospel story and made the claim that Christian theology is history. This prophetic warning has been honored by the increasing recognition that all written history is an interpretation of the events recorded. Events must be seen in relation to contemporary events, in the light of their consequences, and with the judgment of time placed upon them, in order to be understood and evaluated in terms of the truth to which they witness as the revelation of God.[30] It can no longer be said, as it once was, that the Synoptic Gospels are factual recording of history whereas the Gospel of John is interpretive in character. The Synoptic Gospels too were written with selectivity of materials and the understanding of the life and ministry of Christ. And so John's claim to being an eyewitness account bears more weight today than ever before, since the Synoptics make no such claim, even though they have been assigned the greater historicity when comparisons have been made between the two. Differences between them, which have been a major stumbling block in Johannine scholarship, can now be brought together and reconciled. John's Gospel stands in as clear historical light as do the other Gospels.

We are thus left largely to internal evidence for the identification of the author. On this basis there has grown up a strong emotional attachment for authorship by John the Apostle, because of the references to "the beloved disciple" who "leaned on Jesus' breast," and because what we know of John from

28 Op. cit., pp. 18-20.   29 C. H. Dodd, The Interpretation of the Fourth Gospel, p. 449.
30 Hoskyns, op. cit., p. 115.

church tradition seems to fit so perfectly the mood of the Gospel. Love for the Gospel has gone hand in hand with love for the author, until we seem to know the one almost as well as the other. If this seems to be more of feeling and faith than of reason and research, who would wish to destroy its value by more argument? Does not this Gospel carry its readers at every point beyond reason to insight, beyond comprehension to appreciation? In fact it is impossible to follow this author without a measure of the same intuitive discernment which he himself demonstrates. Nothing short of this can grasp this Gospel's portrayal of Christ as the eternal, resurrected, incarnate Word of God.

The uncertainty of research scholarship in giving an answer to this question of authorship, and its present growing indifference to the details of such a discussion, plus the heartening emphasis upon the theological teachings of John's Gospel, have left the field to the only respected position which has had the positive stamp of both scholarship and tradition upon it — the claim for John the Apostle.

Lightfoot says that the "detailed discussion" since the time of Westcott "has gone to show both how difficult the problem is, and how little light those who reject the traditional authorship are able to throw upon it."[31] Alan Richardson strikes the same note when he says, "The evidence, such as it is, does not exclude the possibility that the tradition which connects the Fourth Gospel with the name of John the son of Zebedee may be right after all."[32] A. M. Hunter says that while "very few critics are now prepared to defend the *direct* apostolic authorship . . . . we must go on to say that the conservative position does not look nearly as indefensible as it did, say, twenty years ago [1930]."[33]

The present author's lifelong attachment for this position has not been shattered by the preceding research and summary. After allowing for the dearth of adequate historical proof to solve the problem, and leaving the door open for new evidence, the present commentary will proceed by placing the authorship back into the hands of John the Apostle. The terms "The Fourth Gospel" and "the author" will be omitted in favor of those titles for this Gospel which include the name John.

III. BACKGROUND OF JOHN'S GOSPEL

It has already been noted that the literature of the Dead Sea Community has had a marked effect upon the study of the Gospel of John through an increased understanding of the environment in which the early church arose. This has had some influence upon the discussions concerning date and authorship and has thrown this Gospel back into the conflicting and interacting streams of life in the first century. No longer can John be seen as a solitary witness to the Christ nor in conflict with the Synoptics. The early Church recognized no discrepancy between the Synoptics and John, and this spirit continued until the critical period of the nineteenth century. Schmiedel[34] represented the skeptical school of thought which saw irreconcilable contradictions between the Synoptics and John, and in addition he held that John was wholly unreliable historically. At about the same time Drummond criticized this approach which demanded that historical truth be only the "truth of fact." He sought for insight into "higher truth": "The facts in themselves are utterly barren. In history, as in religion, it is the spirit that quickens, and unless we can penetrate the spirit of great historical transactions, interpret the principles out of which they sprung, and throw ourselves with sympathetic imagination into the passions which animated the great human drama, we miss the only truth which is worth receiving."[35]

We would not want to discredit the value of historical facts, for John built solidly upon the fact of the incarnation, earthly life and crucifixion of Jesus, but we should see them in proper perspective in the whole narration.

The itinerary of Jesus as given by John,

[31] R. H. Lightfoot, *St. John's Gospel*, p. 7.
[32] Alan Richardson, *The Gospel According to St. John*, p. 14.
[33] A. M. Hunter, *Interpreting the New Testament*, p. 85.
[34] Paul W. Schmiedel, *The Johannine Writings*, trans. M. A. Canney, *passim*.
[35] James Drummond, *An Inquiry into the Character and Authorship of the Fourth Gospel*, p. 29.

placing the greater portion of His ministry in Judea, may be a better framework on which to reconstruct the life and ministry of Jesus than that given in Mark and the other Synoptics. The stress upon the Galilean ministry in the Synoptics may in part rise from the fact that all the disciples but Judas Iscariot were from Galilee. Even Matthew records the instructions of Jesus to the Twelve in terms of a Judean ministry: "Go not into any way of the Gentiles, and enter not into any city of the Samaritans; but go rather to the lost sheep of the house of Israel" (Matt. 6:10). A further indication of this might be seen in the statement of Jesus to the Canaanitish woman: "I was not sent but unto the lost sheep of the house of Israel" (Matt. 15:24). The Synoptic record leaves room for a Judean ministry and John's Gospel may reflect the idealistic interest of John in showing Jesus teaching and dying at the seat of the Jewish religion, as Macgregor suggests.[36]

It was on this basis of proper perspective of the whole that Moffatt claimed that the problem of the relationship between the Synoptics and John was "too delicate and complex" to be solved by stress upon the rigid factual antithesis between the two. They were being brought closer together by the recognition that the Synoptics are not "objective chronicles," and that "in Mark, especially, the presence of . . . interpretation has been proved."[37]

Other discrepancies or contrasts between the record of John and the Synoptics can be largely reconciled on the basis of the choice of materials, emphasis, and interpretation of events of the various authors. John's Gospel states that the miracles of Jesus were signs for the purpose of engendering faith in Christ on the part of the observers; in the Synoptics miracles were performed in answer to faith. In contrast to the Synoptics, John neglects some of the more human elements of the Person of Jesus, such as the temptations. This Gospel also stresses the deity of Jesus from the very beginning of His ministry, while the Synoptics portray a gradual development of this consciousness until the time of the Crucifixion. These are not so much contradictions of historical fact as differences of emphasis for a fuller understanding of Christ and His work. The outstanding example of this is found in the two accounts of the Crucifixion. All four Gospels place it on Friday, but for the Synoptics it was the 15th of Nisan, the day following the Passover, while for John it was the 14th, the day of the Passover Feast. John is probably correct.[38]

There are also many similarities between the Gospel of John and the Synoptic Gospels, but these are found in words and phrases and do not of themselves represent dependence, the one upon the other. The Gospel of John reveals an independence on the part of the Evangelist, an independence not of essential historical material, but of environment and perspective and interpretation. The lengthy discourses in John may be as true to the teachings of Jesus as the clipped, proverbial manner of expression in the Sermon on the Mount in Matthew, neither of them intending to merely repeat the bare words and expressions of our Lord. Neither meant to be a tape recorder, but rather an instrument in the hands of God, each being a voice of the church, a living interpreter of the teachings and spirit of Christ.

There is no doubt that John either was acquainted with the Synoptics or that he shared with them a common tradition, especially with Mark, as Moffatt shows.[39] Barnett and Lightfoot believe that John is dependent upon the Synoptics. That he made use of them cannot be proven, for even identity of expression and thought does not guarantee dependence. The generally accepted date of John (90-100) and the rather late dating of the Synoptics (70-90), which is commonly accepted today, emphasize the probability that the two represent basic stores of material held by the church in some ordered form which each adapted according to his own purpose under the guidance of the Holy Spirit.[40] The tendency today is to stress the independence of John.[41] The greater

[36] Op. cit., p. xiv.   [37] James Moffatt, An Introduction to the Literature of the New Testament, p. 540.
[38] Macgregor, op. cit., pp. xiii-xiv.   [39] Op. cit., pp. 226f.
[40] P. Gardner-Smith, St. John and the Synoptic Gospels, pp. 88-97.
[41] J. A. T. Robinson, Twelve New Testament Studies, passim.

maturity of thought of John's Gospel may not be indicative of later growth of thought in the church, but rather of the maturity of thought of John himself.

The two records will not fit perfectly together as a jigsaw puzzle, but they do give a wonderful picture of Him who was at one and the same time both human and divine, the Son of God as well as the Son of Man, Israel's Messiah and the hope of the Gentiles, the One who could save others but could not save Himself (Mark 15:31). John and the Synoptics may be seen as giving a stereographic portrayal of Christ and His ministry, emphasizing both contrasts and harmonies. "It should be remembered that the church has never been aware of any fundamental incompatibility between the portrait of the Lord in John's Gospel and that in the other three. This question has long ago been settled by the religious consciousness of Christendom."[42]

Concerning the dualistic thought pattern of John's Gospel, it is no longer necessary to go to the Hellenistic Gnosticism of the second century as has been argued by R. Bultmann and others. Even those who disclaim any dependence of John upon Gnosticism were free to see him attempting to refute its philosophy. Now, however, sufficient parallels to the Gospel in this respect may be found in the *Manual of Discipline* of the Qumran Sect. The dualism of John is seen to be a modified dualism — "monotheistic, ethical, and eschatological" rather than "physical or substantial (as in the Greek Gnostics)."[43] The Gospel "is not to be interpreted against the background of Gnostic presuppositions, but against that of Palestinian, Old Testament, theological thinking, and of a piety rooted and grounded in the Bible."[44]

The *Logos* concept is, in the New Testament, peculiar to John's Gospel. It has been customary to discover John's use of the term in a development from Greek Philosophy. In the sixth century B.C., Heraclitus used it to designate the rational principle of the universe. The idea is also found in Indian, Egyptian and Persian thought. Philo and the Alex-

andrian philosophers combined the term with the Old Testament wisdom or Word of God by which God created the heavens and the earth, and came up with an intermediate principle or messenger from God, at times little more than the activity of God and at others more of a personal, independent representative of God.

The Targums substituted the "Word of God" for "God in action" — such and such an event, for example, came to pass "by the Word of God." Philo was acquainted with this usage, and although he sought confirmation of his Greek concept of Logos as Reason from the Old Testament, he remained an abstract philosopher and was not able to bring the two together. John chose the more concrete term, the Word, and so the two uses of the *Logos* by Philo and John stand in contrast, the one to the other.

> Philo, following closely in the track of Greek philosophy, saw in the Logos the divine Intelligence in relation to the universe: the Evangelist, trusting firmly to the ethical basis of Judaism, sets forth the Logos mainly as the revealer of God to man, through creation, through theophanies, through prophets, through the Incarnation. . . . In short, the teaching of St. John is characteristically Hebraic and not Alexandrine.[45]

W. F. Howard confirms this conclusion with his opinion that "it is not necessary . . . to go beyond Judaism for the idea of the Logos in John."[46] This is not to say that John may not have had Greek-speaking people in mind when he wrote; rather it signifies that the background of the prologue was not necessarily that of Greek philosophy. Howard points out further that "though the writer of this Gospel wrote with simple ease in a style of the Greek *Koine* that bears many resemblances to modern vernacular Greek, there are yet many idioms which suggest that he thought in Aramaic."[47]

While the *Logos* concept is not expressed in this Gospel beyond the prologue, it has been assumed that at least the impression lingers throughout. Scott thinks that this is true to a degree, and that the author sought "to discover the presence of the Logos in the earthly life

---

[42] Lightfoot, *op. cit.*, p. 1.   [43] A. M. Hunter, *op. cit.*, p. 166.
[44] Joachim Jeremias, "The Qumran Texts and the New Testament," *The Expository Times* (Dec., 1948), p. 68.   [45] Westcott, *op. cit.*, pp. xvii-xviii. For the complete discussion see pp. xv-xviii.
[46] *Op. cit.*, pp. 25-26. For the opposite view see E. F. Scott, *The Fourth Gospel*, p. 154f.
[47] *Ibid.*, p. 26.

of Jesus." This can be seen, Scott believes, in the miracles performed by Jesus, in the attribution to Him of omniscience (2:25), supernatural powers (8:59; 9:35) and majesty of person (7:46; 12:21); in the aloofness of Jesus from the common element of the world, and in His spirit of independence and self-determination (7:30; 8:20; 10:18; 19:11), as well as His manner of speech (6:63; 6:68).[48]

It has been customary to say that Philo popularized the *Logos* concept and that John borrowed it, put a more personal meaning in it, and used it for a fitting portrayal of Jesus who was the revealed *word* or *reason* of God in human form. It is evident that John's interest was not in the philosophical principle, but in the fact that "the Word became flesh." C. H. Dodd argues that the use which John made of the *Logos* concept can only be determined by an understanding of "the purport of the gospel as a whole."[49] Floyd Filson says: "The historical redemptive role of the incarnate Son has a full-bodied vitality which the Logos concept is hardly fitted to express, and the fact that the author drops the term before the Prologue is concluded makes it clear that it is not capable of expressing adequately what he wants to say about Jesus."[50]

How much of the philosophy of his day was consciously or unconsciously embedded in the thinking of John, or how much he may have borrowed from others, far and near, may never be known with certainty. But it becomes increasingly clear that this Gospel is a thoroughly Christian treatise, having as its prime purpose the setting forth of Him who was the pre-existent Christ of God, in order that men might believe on Him and have eternal life. It is also clear that John stood mid-stream in the onflowing of the Gospel message, influenced, but not too strongly, by the currents around him. While others wrote of their faith in terms of historical events, he spoke of historical events in terms of his faith. He was a man of both faith and vision.

Lloyd C. Douglas in *The Robe*, describing the soldier who stood by as Stephen was stoned, has the soldier say,

"That man is looking at something." John was looking at something — Somebody. And every student of John's Gospel must try to see what John saw.

IV. THE BELOVED DISCIPLE

From the time of Irenaeus, who first made specific reference to the identification, until the modern period of critical Bible study, the Beloved Disciple has been identified with John the Apostle and continues to be by many scholars. In the last chapter of John's Gospel the Beloved Disciple is the eye-witness who wrote it. He chose this term for himself, probably not feeling it necessary to distinguish himself from the other man of the same name, John the Baptist; he calls the latter *John* while the Synoptics refer to him by the full title. The Synoptic Gospels say that the Twelve (Luke uses the term Apostles) met with Jesus for the Last Supper, while John says that the disciples were there, no number being specified. It must be supposed that the Beloved Disciple was among them. F. F. Bruce expresses the traditional position when he says that "we should naturally expect that the beloved disciple would be one" of the three who were repeatedly with Jesus on special occasions: Peter, James and John.[51] James was martyred before the time of the writing of this Gospel. Peter is distinguished from this disciple at the last supper (13:24), at the tomb (20:2), and at one of the resurrection appearances (21:20). John alone of all the disciples is left to lay claim to the title of The Beloved Disciple.

John's Gospel uses the word *agapan*, love, more than any of the other Gospels — 44 times as against 14 times in Luke and even fewer times in Matthew and Mark. This points also to John as being conscious of a love relationship with his Master.

A recent attempt has been made to identify the Beloved Disciple as Lazarus. Four times before the last supper Jesus is said to have a special love for him (11:3; 11:5; 11:11; 11:36). By observing a close unity between chapters twelve and thirteen, it is suggested that the one whom Jesus loved in Bethany (Laza-

---

[48] *Ibid.*, p. 163. [49] *Op. cit.*, pp. 3-4.
[50] Wm. Klassen and G. F. Snyder, *Current Issues in New Testament Interpretation*, pp. 111-112.
[51] F. F. Bruce, *The New Testament Documents*, p. 48.

rus) is the same beloved one at supper. Moreover, Lazarus, a near native of Jerusalem, fits some of the circumstances better than a Galilean fisherman. And the fact that the Beloved Disciple first perceived that Jesus was risen from the tomb, having outrun Peter in his eagerness, seems to point to Lazarus who himself had just experienced a resurrection.[52]

This suggestion could arise only in the uncommitted climate of Johannine scholarship today. It provides food for thought, but it is not conclusive even in the view of its originator. It is a by-product of his high regard for the "substantial unity" of John's Gospel.

V. LITERARY STRUCTURE

There is a dramatic quality about John's Gospel which is not found in the Synoptics — the natural use of language and style of an unconscious artist which places John in a class by himself. With a small vocabulary, he has been able to express himself clearly and impressively. The repeated use of certain favorite words, combined with a sameness of phraseology, takes the reader through an impression of monotony onward to a great sense of the effectiveness of the whole. There are several major emphases in the Gospel, each of which may be seen to rise to a dramatic climax. For instance, the Gospel may be seen as a Gospel witness to Jesus as the Christ, punctuating the expressed purpose in 20:31. First, John the Baptist is presented as a "man, sent from God" (1:6) — yet inferior to Christ, the word of God — who testified, "Behold, the Lamb of God, that taketh away the sin of the world! This is he of whom I said, After me cometh a man who is before me: for he was before me" (1:29-30).

Nathanael, a Galilean, next witnesses to Jesus, proclaiming, "Rabbi, thou art the Son of God; thou art King of Israel" (1:49). This was the result of Christ's ability to judge character upon first sight. Then a miracle — the turning of water into wine at the Cana wedding — reveals the power of Christ over nature and its laws. For John, all of the miracles were for the purpose of witnessing to Christ's deity. Next comes the Samaritan woman at Jacob's well at Sychar. After her ex-

tended conversation with Jesus, she hurried to the city with what may be called a believing rather than a doubting question on her lips: "Can this be the Christ?" (4:29). As a result, many of the Samaritans believed on Him, not only because she had spoken, but also because they had heard for themselves. There is the witness of the people who were miraculously fed with the loaves and fishes (ch. 6), the witness of those who saw Jesus walk on the water (ch. 6), also of the people whom He taught at the Feast of Tabernacles (ch. 7), and the testimony of the man born blind (ch. 9). Others could be listed, but the whole scheme of witness comes to its climax when Thomas is brought onto the imaginary stage. His testimony is more meaningful because he was a doubter, albeit an honest doubter. His testimony is that which John sought to draw from each and all who read his Gospel: "My Lord and my God" (20:28).

An equally significant emphasis of the Gospel presents Jesus as a witness to His own Messiahship. He witnesses to Nicodemus, the Jew (ch. 3), to the Samaritan woman at the well (ch. 4), to the Gentile nobleman whose son He healed (ch. 4), to the mixed multitude by various signs (chs. 5:12), to the inner circle of disciples (chs. 13-17), and, in the final climax, to the whole world for all generations to see, upon the cross.

This Gospel may also be seen as the Gospel of Life. In the prologue, the life of all creation finds its source in Christ the Word. "All things were made through him; and without him was not anything made that hath been made. In him was life" (1:3-4). Faith in Christ gives eternal life (3:36); His words are spirit and life (6:63). He is "the bread of life" (6:35; 6:51), "the resurrection, and the life" (11:25), and "the way, and the truth, and the life" (14:6). To Nicodemus Jesus said, "Ye must be born anew" (3:7); to the Samaritan woman He offered "living water" (4:10).

In chapters five and six there are two miracles — the healing of the paralytic and the feeding of the multitude — followed by discourses by Jesus on Himself as the giver and sustainer of life. Chapters seven and eight contain another discourse which is a commentary on "In

[52] Floyd Filson in Klassen and Snyder, op. cit., pp. 119-123.

him was life and the life was the light of men." He is presented as the source of truth and light, and this is illustrated (ch. 9) by the giving of physical and spiritual light to the blind man. The climax is reached with the raising of Lazarus from the dead (ch. 10).[53]

Marcus Dods has said:

> In the whole range of literature there is no composition which is a more perfect work of art, or which more rigidly excludes whatever does not subserve its main end. . . . Part hangs together with part in perfect balance. The sequence may at times be obscure, but sequence there always is. The relevancy of this or that remark may not at first sight be apparent, but irrelevancy is impossible to this writer.[54]

No other book of the New Testament has its purpose so explicitly stated as the Gospel of John. "Many other signs therefore did Jesus in the presence of the disciples, which are not written in this book: but these are written, that ye may believe that Jesus is the Christ, the Son of God; and that believing ye may have life in his name" (20:30-31). This purpose is evident throughout the Gospel as John sought not only to inform, but also to convince. By referring to certain events which he did not include in his Gospel, he acknowledged that he was selective in the use of material, choosing only those things which would best serve his purpose. The inference is that this purpose, not the relationship of his materials in any kind of time sequence, determined form and arrangement in the Gospel. In other words, John did not write what we would term a Life of Christ; when he thought that the time of an incident was important he located it for his readers. He said that the miracle at the wedding in Cana was "the beginning of signs" which Jesus did (evidently early in His ministry), while sometimes he introduced an event or series of events by the phrase "after these things" or "again." At times John placed events in either Judea or Galilee. This kind of association of events is not basic. In one instance (6:1) Jesus is back in Galilee without any reference being made to His return from Jerusalem

or to how the events of chapter six are related to those of chapter five.

We are told also that John chose those things which occurred when Jesus and His disciples were together: those events needed for his purpose. Repeatedly he told that the disciples were with Jesus — at Cana in Galilee (2:2); at Capernaum (2:12); at the baptismal services in Judea (3:22); at Jacob's well (4:1); at the feeding of the multitude (6:3); during the stormy night on the Sea of Galilee (6:16-21); at the healing of the blind man (9:2) at the raising of Lazarus from the dead (11:8); at the anointing of Jesus by Mary of Bethany (12:1-8); at the Triumphal Entry (12:16); at the time of the great discourses (13-17); and of course they were intimately aware of all that transpired at the Crucifixion and Burial. There are only a few instances where John failed to indicate the presence of the disciples with Jesus — at the feast in Jerusalem when Jesus healed the man at the pool (5); by inference, only disciples were with Jesus at the Feast of Tabernacles (7).

Perhaps this is little more than the reiteration of what is apparent but not so frequently expressed — that Jesus always had followers about Him and that the Twelve especially were close to Him. But John made a point of it: his witness to Jesus and His work has the support of the disciples who saw His wondrous works and believed in Him because of them (2:11).

The purpose of John's Gospel takes full recognition of the tension under which the ministry of Jesus was conducted. The opposition of His enemies is set off against the loyalty of His friends. His words and works demand decisions. Men were never able to be neutral toward Jesus. He set good over against evil, light against darkness, truth against falsehood, life against death. Men responded either by acceptance or rejection, belief or unbelief. "As many as received him, to them gave he the right to become children of God, even to them that believe on his name" (1:12). The disciples saw the miracles and believed (2:11) along with many others (2:23). Because of the testimony of the

[53] See Klassen and Snyder, op. cit., pp. 111-123 for a very good discussion of this topic.
[54] Marcus Dods, The Gospel of St. John, Vol. I, "The Expositor's Bible," p. ix.

woman at Jacob's well many Samaritans believed (4:39) and many more believed when they heard Jesus for themselves (4:41-42). The nobleman and his entire household believed as the result of the healing of his son (4:53). Following the discourse of Jesus on the light of the world, many believed on Him (8: 30). The blind man who was healed believed when he learned who Jesus was (9:38). Beyond Jordan many believed on Him (10:42). After the raising of Lazarus many believed on Him (11:45). Later, many Jews who saw Lazarus also believed (12:11). Following His last public discourse, many of the religious leaders believed (12:42).

Many times John said that the response was one of unbelief. When Jesus sought to identify Himself as the bread of life, whose flesh was meat and whose blood was drink, many of the disciples said, "This is more than we can stomach" (Weymouth) and turned away in disbelief (6:66). His "brethren did not believe on him" (7:5). When many of the multitude expressed belief, the Pharisees and chief priests sent officers to take Jesus (7:32). The Jews did not believe that Jesus had really healed the blind man (9:18). The raising of Lazarus caused a council to be called among the priests and Pharisees to try to prevent the people from believing on Jesus because of the miracle (11:47). Those who did not believe could not because they were blind to the truth (12:39-40). Four times the disciples did not apprehend the meaning of some words of Jesus (2:22; 8:27; 11:6; 12:16).

These are but a few of the cases where either belief or unbelief is recorded as the response to the words and work of Jesus. In this way John showed not only that he wrote his Gospel that men might believe, but also that Jesus taught and performed miracles for the same purpose. He claimed that the purpose of Christ's entire life and ministry was summed up in his own purpose for writing the Gospel.

The use of tension between opposing forces by John seems to arise out of a basic sort of dualism in his thought, corresponding somewhat to the upper and lower levels of Gnosticism. He told

of Jesus' saying to the Pharisees, "Ye are from beneath; I am from above: Ye are of the world; I am not of this world" (8:23). There is antinomy between spirit and flesh, light and darkness, life and death, goodness and evil, truth and falsehood. Out of this scheme arises a series of allegories when Jesus, seeking to portray spiritual truth in terms of the mundane world, was not understood. "Stupid" questions were asked: Nicodemus asked how a man could have a second physical birth. At first the Samaritan woman could think only of water drawn from the well. Both of these people were looking down rather than up. Jesus was speaking of a life which came from above. To them it was wholly mysterious, although Jesus chided Nicodemus for being so lacking in perception when he was supposed to be versed in the Old Testament Scriptures. The incident of the foot-washing follows this pattern — the upper spiritual world of light and faith and truth pitted against the lower world of darkness, unbelief and falsehood. But John was sure that the darkness could not overcome the light (1:5).

The frequent use of symbolism is characteristic of John's Gospel. It is commonly said that the Synoptics have parables while this Gospel contains only allegories. A. M. Hunter questions this sharp distinction, showing that some parables are allegorical in nature — the wicked vinedressers, for instance; while he refers to some Johannine sayings as parables — the woman in travail (16: 21) as an example.[55]

While recognizing the overlapping of these two literary forms, the distinction between parable and allegory comes from the manner in which they are interpreted. In the allegory the thing signifying and the thing signified are blended together, while in the parable they are kept side by side. The interpretation of the parable must be brought to it from the knowledge of the hearers, while the interpretation of the allegory is inherent.[56] In general this distinction is valid for interpreting the teachings in the Synoptics and the Gospel of John.

In some instances a parable has a parallel allegory — for instance the parable of

55 A. M. Hunter, *Interpreting the Parables*, pp. 10-11.   56 C. H. Dodd, *op. cit.*, p. 134.

the lost sheep (Matt. 18:12-14; Luke 15:4-7). The fact that in the interpretation which Jesus gave of the parable of the Sower and the Seed (Mark 4:2-20) he treated it as an allegory contributes to the breaking down of the common distinction between the two. Some readers might be concerned to ask which form Jesus Himself actually used. The answer cannot be one or the other, nor would it be entirely correct to say that He used both. Both parable and allegory rise out of the proverbial form of speaking with which Jesus and His disciples were acquainted, for the manner of teaching in that day among rabbis was to concentrate a discourse into proverbial form for use of memorization.[57]

The distinction between proverb, parable and allegory did not seem to be important to the Gospel writers, perhaps not being as evident as it is to us today. Witness the fact that most of the early church Fathers interpreted the parables as allegories. Our English translations have done much to create the distinctions. Luke 4:23 quotes a model proverb — "Physician, heal thyself" — and calls it a *parabolee*. This term is variously translated "proverb" (KJV, RSV, NEB) and "parable" (ASV). In the Synoptics the term is consistently used to describe the standard parable form. Yet neither Thayer's *Lexicon* nor that of Liddell and Scott give "parable" as the meaning of *paraboleen*.

John's Gospel does not use *parabolee*, but *paroimia*. This also has been translated in various ways: "parable" and "proverb" (KJV), "figure" (RSV), "parable" and "figure of speech" (NEB), and "parable" and "dark saying" (ASV) with "proverb" and "parable" as marginal alternatives.

The conclusion must be that the New Testament writers did not observe the fineness of meaning between parable and allegory that is placed upon them today. They were acquainted with the general comparative method of presenting truth, and the reason for the use of the two words, *parabolee* and *paroimia,* may have been little more than authors' choices, determined largely by the peculiar method by which each approached the life and ministry of Jesus.

John portrayed Jesus in bolder perspective than did the Synoptics — he said He is not only *like* something, He *is* something. He is not just *like* bread; He *is* bread, the Bread of life. He is not only *like* a good shepherd, but He *is* the Good Shepherd who lays down His life for His sheep. To illustrate the meaning of this, John omitted the Lord's Supper probably because it was foreign to his thinking to make the kind of comparison between bread and Christ's body that the Synoptics make — the bread is Christ's body. His thought was not merely of the Crucified Jesus but also of the Risen Christ, the Eternal Son of God who is both the source and the sustainer of life, "the resurrection, and the life," "the bread of life."

Another instance of this same principle at work is the account of Jesus talking with the Samaritan woman (4:7-42). One would naturally expect Him to say, "I am the water of life." But having gone beyond the concept of His being like water and of His being water, He went to the very heart of what all of His teaching was about — He openly proclaimed Himself the hoped-for Messiah. The woman had caught the lesson inherent in the comparison between the well water and the water Jesus offered her. It reminded her of the promised Messiah and the blessings of the messianic age — perhaps "with joy shall ye draw water out of the wells of salvation" (Isa. 12:3), and she suggested the relationship to Jesus. He replied, "I that speak unto you am he." Most certainly she did not understand all that this meant, but her mind had been turned from water to Christ — and this was the whole intent of Jesus as He spoke and of John as he wrote.

John thus went beyond making comparisons between Jesus and familiar things around him. With true genius and profound spiritual insight he saw Jesus at the center of life in all of its forms, present by His Spirit, present for man in all of his needs. Jesus not only shows the way — He *is* the way; He not only teaches the truth — He *is* the truth; He not only gives life — He *is* life. And the believer becomes the possessor of the attributes of Jesus by virtue of a shared

[57] A. M. Hunter, *A Pattern for Life*, p. 12.

relationship through faith. Faith in Christ brings a new life and the supply of all that life demands. Thus did John see Jesus.

No better approach has been made than that of John witnessing to the deity of Jesus — to explain the unexplainable, to describe the undescribable, in brief, to witness in the clearest fashion to Him who was God Incarnate. Donald M. Baillie says that "it is only as Christians that we can hope to understand the Incarnation. Why then should we as theologians work with any other conception of God than that which we as Christians believe to be true?"[58] And so John presented the Incarnate Christ that people might come to know God.

No sacred writer has succeeded as well as John in making clear the meaning of the Incarnation for the salvation of the world. But even he did not say the last word. He could not depict the Christ sufficiently clear for all who read. Each must pick up where John left off, and by the insight of faith complete the picture to his own salvation. The beautiful and vivid wording of John's Gospel is at best an imperfect vehicle for picturing the Christ as John saw Him. But when the words are supplemented by the faith of the beholder, Christ becomes to him a living reality.

The great work of art by Leonardo da Vinci, *The Last Supper,* has spoken so convincingly of Christ in the center of the group of disciples, symbolic of His central place in Christianity, that the Christian world has all but forgotten that the artist did not complete the portrait of the Christ. Finally, unable to portray what he himself saw and felt, he cried out, "I cannot finish the face of the Christ; no one can finish it." No man can perfectly depict Christ for another. Each man must see Him for himself. This is what John meant; he witnessed in order that men might believe and live.

IV. CONTENTS

A wide variety of outlines are found in many commentaries on John's Gospel, but all of them recognize the simple division into Introduction (1:1-2:12), Public Ministry (2:13-12:50), Private

---

[58] Donald M. Baillie, *God Was in Christ,* p. 119.

Ministry (12:1-17:26), Passion Story (18: 1-20:31), and Appendix (21:1-25). Some scholars prefer to use only the Prologue (1:1-18) for the Introduction, including 1:19-2:11 in the Public Ministry.

In lieu of a summary of the life of John the Apostle, the following imaginative poem is here appended. It catches the spirit of John's Gospel and suggests much of the tradition which grew up around the Apostle's name in the early days of the church. It has been impossible to identify the author of this poem.

A REVERIE OF JOHN
THE BELOVED

At evening time it shall be light.
I'm growing very old. This weary head
That hath so often leaned on Jesus' breast
In days long past that seem almost a dream,
Is bent and hoary with its weight of years.
These limbs that followed Him — my Master — oft,
From Galilee to Judah, that stood
Beneath the cross, and trembled with His groans,
Refuse to bear me even through the streets
To preach unto my children. E'en my lips
Refuse to form the words my heart sends forth,
Of my dear children gathered round my couch;
God lays His hand upon me — yea, His hand
And not His rod — the gentle hand that I
Felt, those three years, so often pressed in mine,
In friendship such as passeth woman's love.

I'm old; so old I cannot recollect
The faces of my friends; and I forget
The words and deeds that make up daily life,
But that dear face, and every word He spoke,
Grow more distinct as others fade away,
So that I live with Him and holy dead
More than with living.

Some seventy years ago
I was a fisher by the sacred sea.
It was at sunset. How the tranquil tide
Bathed dreamily the pebbles! How the
    light
Crept up the distant hills, and in its
    wake,
Soft purple shadows wrapped the dewy
    fields!
And then He came and called me. Then
    I gazed
For the first time on that sweet face.

    Those eyes,
From out of which, as from a window,
    shone
Divinity, looked on my inmost soul,
And lighted it forever. Then His words
Broke on the silence of my heart and
    made
The whole world musical. Incarnate Love
Took hold of me and claimed me for its
    own.
I followed in the twilight, holding fast
His mantle.

    O, what holy walks we had,
Through harvest fields, and desolate
    dreary wastes!
Wearied and wayworn. I was young and
    strong,
And so upbore Him. Lord, now I am
    weak,
And old, and feeble! Let me rest on
    Thee!
So, put Thine arm around me. Closer
    still!
How strong Thou art! The twilight
    draws apace.
Come, let us leave these noisy streets
    and take
The path to Bethany; for Mary's smile
Awaits us at the gate, and Martha's hands
Have long prepared the evening meal.
Come, James, the Master waits; and
    Peter, see,
Has gone some steps before.

    What say you, friends?
That this is Ephesus, and Christ has gone
Back to His kingdom? Ay, 'tis so, 'tis so.
I know it all; and yet, just now, I
    seemed
To stand once more upon my native hills,
And touch my Master. Oh, how oft I've
    seen
The touching of His garments bring back
    strength

To palsied limbs! I feel it has to mine.
Up! bear me once more to my church!
    Once more
There let me tell them of a Saviour's
    love;
For, by the sweetness of my Master's voice
Just now, I think He must be very near —
Coming, I trust, to break the veil, which
    time
Has worn so thin that I can see beyond,
And watch His footsteps.

    So, raise my head.
How dark it is! I cannot seem to see
The faces of my flock. Is that the sea
That murmurs so, or is it weeping? Hush,
My little children! God so loved the
    world
He gave His Son. So love ye one another.
Love God and man. Amen. Now bear
    me back.
My legacy unto an angry world is this.
I feel my work is finished. Are the streets
    so full?
What, call the folk my name? The Holy
    John. Nay, write me rather, Jesus
    Christ's beloved.
And lover of my children.

    Lay me down
Once more upon my couch, and open
    wide
The eastern window. See, there comes
    a light
Like that which broke upon my soul at
    eve,
When, in the dreary Isle of Patmos,
    Gabriel came
And touched me on the shoulder. See
    it grows
As when we mounted toward the pearly
    gates.
I know the way! I trod it once before.
And hark! It is the song the ransomed
    sang
Of glory to the Lamb! How loud it
    sounds!
And that unwritten one — methinks my
    soul
Can join it now. But who are these who
    crowd
The shining way? Say! — joy! 'tis the
    eleven,
With Peter first! How eagerly he looks!
How bright the smiles are beaming on
    James' face!
I am the last. Once more we are com-
    plete

To gather round the Pascal feast. My place
Is next my Master. O, my Lord, my Lord!
How bright Thou art! and yet the very same
I loved in Galilee! 'Tis worth the hundred years
To feel this bliss! So lift me up, dear Lord,
Unto Thy bosom. There shall I abide.

— H. J. S. B.

Commentary on John's Gospel

I. INTRODUCTION: (1:1-2:12)

A. PROLOGUE: THE WORD BECAME FLESH (1:1-18)

1 In the beginning was the Word, and the Word was with God, and the Word was God. 2 The same was in the beginning with God. 3 All things were made through him; and without him was not anything made that hath been made. 4 In him was life; and the life was the light of men. 5 And the light shineth in the darkness; and the darkness apprehended it not. 6 There came a man, sent from God, whose name was John. 7 The same came for witness, that he might bear witness of the light, that all might believe through him. 8 He was not the light, but *came* that he might bear witness of the light. 9 There was the true light, *even the light* which lighteth every man, coming into the world. 10 He was in the world, and the world was made through him, and the world knew him not. 11 He came unto his own, and they that were his own received him not. 12 But as many as received him, to them gave he the right to become children of God, *even* to them that believe on his name: 13 who were born, not of blood, nor of the will of the flesh, nor of the will of man, but of God. 14 And the Word became flesh, and dwelt among us (and we beheld his glory, glory as of the only begotten from the Father), full of grace and truth. 15 John beareth witness of him, and crieth, saying, This was he of whom I said, He that cometh after me is become before me: for he was before me. 16 For of his fulness we all received, and grace for grace. 17 For the law was given through Moses; grace and truth came through Jesus Christ. 18 No man hath seen God at any time; the only begotten Son, who is in the bosom of the Father, he hath declared *him*.

Both the Jewish and the Greek readers of John's Gospel would have been familiar with his use of the term **Word** (*Logos*) with which the Gospel is introduced. The Jews were in the habit of substituting "the Word of God" for God Himself in their concept of Wisdom, which is very close in meaning to Reason, which in turn is one of the meanings of *Logos*. The Greeks thought of *Logos* as the great ruling principle of life and the universe. When John sought for a term to convey the idea of the Eternal Christ of God, he found one close at hand. While the term is not found in the Gospel beyond the prologue (1:1-18), the meaning of *Logos* as it is used for the person of Christ is there. John descends, so to speak, to the use of Christ's given name Jesus when referring to Him, but this is apparently an accommodation to Christ's earthly existence, which is all-important, because the **Word became flesh.** At the same time, John's understanding of the Person of Jesus finds its truest expression in the words of the woman of Samaria: "Is not this the Christ?" (4:29); of Nathanael: "Rabbi, thou art the Son of God" (1:49); of Martha: "Yea, Lord: I have believed that thou art the Christ, the Son of God" (11:27); and of Thomas: "My Lord and my God" (20:28).

The *Logos* was Jesus, and Jesus was Christ the Son of God. The term Christ becomes the focus of the body of this Gospel. Christ is both Creator and Revelator.

In the beginning was the Word. Not just from the beginning, but when the beginning began to be, the Word was. He was not a product of the beginning process, neither did He begin with the beginning, but in the beginning the Word was already there. Explaining when the beginning began is tantamount to explaining how long eternity is. John's problem is more than a problem of expression; it is also one of understanding. For when he has gone back as far as the human mind will go, already the Word had existence. What power and meaning the Apostle has packed into those six short words!

We cannot proceed as though we were

ignorant of what John meant by the **Word**. By one great sweep of his pen, dipped in the purest rhetoric, he has introduced Christ as having existence further back than man can philosophize. He did not introduce Him as a new virgin-born babe, or as a man starting his ministry, as do the Synoptics, but he proclaimed Him as the Eternal One. There was no time when Christ was not. "The only perspective in which the work of Jesus, and His relation to the Father, could be truly seen and estimated was that of eternity."[1]

The Word was with God. The idea expressed here is that of the **Word** standing face to face with God. The initial idea is that of two distinct persons, while the next phrase unites them into one: **The Word was God.** Perhaps a distinction can be made for our thinking which will stop short of seeming to make God a duality, and thus maintain His essential unity. Let us think of God in His essential being and also in His creative and redemptive activity. We can only know God as He has chosen to reveal Himself. **The Word** — Jesus — is the revealer of God, which says that we do not know God except in the Incarnation. Thus it becomes possible to say that Jesus was with God, standing face to face with Him, equal to Him. The Greek *pros* does not help us much here. It means "direction towards," or "standing over against or by something." To avoid the danger of supposing two persons involved, consider both a stamp or seal and its imprint. The one is expressive and the other receptive. The seal is set over against the impression, yet it is inseparable from it. The author of the Epistle to the Hebrews expressed a similar concept in speaking of Christ as the "image" or stamp of the substance of God. While a materialist might still insist on a twoness in this description, the authors of these two New Testament books find such analogies quite sufficient to convey truth, even though they of necessity fall short of exact description. The object behind the language is Christ, God Incarnate.

And the Word was God. We cannot read this in reverse — God was the Word. "The subject must be the Word, for

John is not trying to show us who is God, but who is the Word."[2] Vincent says that if John had changed the order of the sentence, he would have destroyed the distinction just made between God as substance and God as Incarnate Word. It should be noted also that the past tense of the verb — **was** — should not be thought to convey the idea that the previous relationship between God and Jesus had come to an end with the Incarnation. John is careful to quote Jesus, "I and the Father are one." He was God and He still is God.

Verse 2 merely repeats what verse 1 has said, but with greater force — the *Logos* is eternal and is the revelation of God to man. This follows the pattern of Hebrew parallelism, and some writers think that the prologue was a hymn to the *Logos* which John adapted to his purpose, or that he himself composed it for his Gospel. The least that can be said is that it has the marks of a Hebrew poem when the passages about John the Baptist are disregarded.

All things were made through him. The entire universe is the creation of the *Logos*, Christ. He was not just the agent of God in creation, after the fashion of the Gnostic Demiurge; He was God revealing Himself as Creator. All life finds its source in Him. Life, more than any other phenomenon, has eluded the grasp of scientists. They have not been able to isolate it, neither reproduce it. Even the shocking attempt to unite living sperm and egg under glass or in a test tube and produce a living creature, if successful, would be no more than perpetuation of life under abnormal circumstances. And though nuclear science has reduced everything to energy, which goes far beyond our common concept of what is material, it still has stopped short of the life dimension of things. John says that life comes only from God as He reveals Himself in the creative process.

The Word became flesh. This concept is more profound than **the light shineth in the darkness** and **He was in the world,** both of which suggest the Incarnation. The eternal *Logos,* Christ, became flesh, took upon Himself the full form of humanity, and became man in the truest

[1] C. K. Barrett, *The Gospel According to St. John*, p. 125.
[2] Marvin R. Vincent, *Word Studies in the New Testament*, Vol. II, p. 34.

sense of the term, without ceasing to be the *Logos*. The assumption of a temporal form did not rob Him of His eternal form; the adoption of human flesh did not terminate His existence as eternal spirit. St. Paul suggests in his great *kenosis* passage (Phil. 2:5-8) that Christ laid aside, or emptied Himself of, something at the time of the Incarnation. But neither the addition (John) or subtraction (Paul) has changed His essential Godhead. Deity became "veiled in flesh," truly God and truly man. Yet it was not only that He became "a man"; He became "man," took upon Himself the flesh of mankind.

In addition to becoming flesh, The *Logos* **dwelt among us.** "Tabernacled" is a more accurate translation of the verb, and it suggests an analogy which throws some light upon the mystery of the Incarnation. The picture of the wilderness tabernacle of the Old Testament comes to mind, especially the "glory of Jehovah [which] filled the tabernacle" (Exod. 40:34). The glory, or Shekinah, represented God's presence among the people, which presence usually came to a specific place. The Ark of the Covenant represented the same Presence, as well as clouds in which God came to talk with Moses, or which led the Israelites from Egypt. John apparently had this comparison in mind when he wrote of the Word becoming flesh and dwelling with man. "What the tabernacle had been, the dwelling of God in the midst of the people, the humanity of the *Logos* now was."[3] Paul says that the light which shines within the Christian is the revelation of God — "the knowledge of the glory of God in the face of Jesus Christ" (II Cor. 4:6).

This manifestation of the glory of God was replete with both grace and truth — grace, the efforts of God on man's behalf, and truth, the understanding of what God has done in Christ. It was also one of a kind; it owed its quality to no prior pattern, for it was the fullness of God in Jesus Christ. In contrast to this gracious revelation of God was the law which came through Moses. The law, too, was from God; but its agent, Moses, was human, while the conveyor of grace and truth was the Incarnate Word. Here can be seen the contrast between the Old economy and the New.

John realized, as have others, that the fact of the Incarnation is not easily understood; but with great insight he wrote, "No man hath seen God at any time; the only begotten Son, who is in the bosom of the Father, he hath declared him" (v. 18). Light on the mystery surrounding this topic begins to break when we realize that we only know God as He has revealed Himself or, in John's thought, in the Incarnation. Donald M. Baillie has made some valuable suggestions for a better understanding of this problem. He writes,

> We are apt to start with some conception of God, picked up we know not where . . . which is different from the Christian conception; and then to attempt the impossible task of understanding how such a God could be incarnate in Jesus. If the Incarnation has supremely revealed God, shown Him to us in a new and illuminating light, put a fresh meaning into the very word that is His name, *that* is the meaning that we must use in facing the problem of the Incarnation, because that is what God really is. It is only as Christians that we can hope to understand the Incarnation. Why then should we as theologians work with any other conception of God than that which as Christians we believe to be true?[4]

The life was the light of men. Jesus is both life and light. Life and light, as we experience them, are interdependent. The life of which John spoke was eternal life, the life of God who revealed Himself to man, and was thus light to the sin-darkened world. The world is darkness; Christ is light. Life and light correspond to grace and truth (1:7): the fact of what God has done and the understanding of it. The acceptance of this life brings one into the light, the knowledge of God. It gives light to every man. Not that every man receives it or walks according to it. John made this clear by distinguishing between those who believe on Christ and those who do not believe. Belief or faith is the acceptance of what God in Christ has done.[5]

---

[3] *The Expositor's Greek Testament*, Vol. 1, p. 690.
[4] Donald M. Baillie, *God Was in Christ*, p. 119.
[5] See commentary on 8:12 for a further discussion of light.

There was a man, sent from God, whose name was John (v. 6). In this brief, poetic treatise on Christ the Word, two men are introduced in contrast to Christ. The first is John the Baptist (1:6-8, 15). Jesus *was* — John *was sent.* They in no way should be confused or thought of as equals or as leaders of rival movements. Jesus was the Christ; John was only a witness to Him. The Baptist denied all status in contrast to Christ; he claimed to be only a voice crying in the wilderness. He had no original message of his own; he spoke the words of another (Isaiah) in his witness to Christ. There was no rivalry between him and Christ. Each knew his calling and role in life, John no less than Christ. John was a voice; Jesus was the God-man. John was a witness; Jesus was the truth. This great sense of the subordination of John to Jesus made the Apostle John feel that any rehearsal of the early life and ministry of the Baptist was irrelevant to his narrative, even the baptism of Jesus by John. The Baptist himself said of Jesus, **He that cometh after me is become before me: for he was before me"** (v. 15).

Moses is also mentioned. **The Law was given through Moses; grace and truth came through Jesus Christ** (v. 17). In a sense this is a contrast between the Old and the New — between Judaism and the Gospel, and the Apostle John probably meant it to be. But it is only a partial contrast. According to common belief, Old Testament religion was a religion of law while New Testament religion is one of grace; law is void of grace, and grace abrogated the law when Christ came. Consequently the Old Testament is of little, if any, value for Christian teaching and instruction. But this is not what John had in mind. The grace of God is abundantly evident throughout Judaism, and the Gospel is the strongest possible support for the moral law of Moses. The Apostle sought only to show that the revelation through Christ was greater than that through Moses, thereby giving greater emphasis to Christ. **No man** (not even Moses) **hath seen God at any time;** but Jesus has made Him known — Jesus **the only begotten Son** or "God only begotten,"

as some manuscripts allow.[6] In deference to human limitations, Jesus revealed God as Father: "In this connection the description of the relation of the Word of God . . . is seen to be complementary to that of the relation of the Son to the Father. The one marks an absolute relation in the Godhead. The other a relation apprehended with regard to creation."[7]

This introduction of the concept of God as Father, and this relationship of God to both Father and Son — or vice versa — was the beginning of John's portrayal of God's revelation as Trinity. Father, Son, and Spirit — in the totality of their expression — constitute all we know of the nature of God.

B. TESTIMONY OF THE BAPTIST (1: 19-34)

19 And this is the witness of John, when the Jews sent unto him from Jerusalem priests and Levites to ask him, Who art thou? 20 And he confessed, and denied not; and he confessed, I am not the Christ. 21 And they asked him, What then? Art thou Elijah? And he saith, I am not. Art thou the prophet? And he answered, No. 22 They said therefore unto him, Who art thou? that we may give an answer to them that sent us. What sayest thou of thyself? 23 He said, I am the voice of one crying in the wilderness, Make straight the way of the Lord, as said Isaiah the prophet. 24 And they had been sent from the Pharisees. 25 And they asked him, and said unto him, Why then baptizest thou, if thou art not the Christ, neither Elijah, neither the prophet? 26 John answered them, saying, I baptize in water: in the midst of you standeth one whom ye know not, 27 *even* he that cometh after me, the latchet of whose shoe I am not worthy to unloose. 28 These things were done in Bethany beyond the Jordan, where John was baptizing.

29 On the morrow he seeth Jesus coming unto him, and saith, Behold, the Lamb of God, that taketh away the sin of the world! 30 This is he of whom I said, After me cometh a man who is become before me: for he was before me. 31 And I knew him not; but that he should be made manifest to Israel, for this cause came I baptizing in water. 32 And John bare witness, saying, I have beheld the Spirit descending as a dove out of heaven; and it abode upon him.

[6] Vincent, *op. cit.*, p. 59. [7] B. F. Westcott, *The Gospel According to St. John*, p. 15.

33 And I knew him not: but he that sent me to baptize in water, he said unto me, Upon whomsoever thou shalt see the Spirit descending, and abiding upon him, the same is he that baptizeth in the Holy Spirit. 34 And I have seen, and have borne witness that this is the Son of God.

The testimony of John the Baptist was given in the most forthright way before priests and Levites who were sent from Jerusalem to question him. He disclaimed being the Christ, Elijah (whose bodily return the Jews expected), and **the prophet,** probably the one mentioned in Deuteronomy 18:15. In their minds he should have claimed to be one of them in order to validate his particular brand of baptism. But rather than answering them directly, he seized the opportunity to announce the presence among them of One whose work would exceed the fullest significance of Jewish baptism. That One was as much more worthy than John himself as a man is more worthy than his shoe lace. He did not attempt further identification of Christ, apparently because doing so, to cynics and unbelievers, would have been "casting pearls before swine." At any rate, what John said was not very convincing to them because their curiosity was not aroused sufficiently to ask him any questions.

This encounter between John the Baptist and the Jews took place in Bethany beyond the Jordan. This was not the home of Mary, Martha and Lazarus, which was not far from Jerusalem. This Bethany has never been identified. The Jews, who in John's Gospel are always in opposition to Jesus, apparently returned home after the first day's encounter. No mention is made of their presence during this whole "week of witnessing"; and John the Baptist's freedom of expression concerning Christ's identity, in contrast to his previous vague allusion, seems to indicate an absence of any persons who would be unappreciative of his announcement.

On the second day Jesus appeared, and John, in true priestly fashion — for he was an hereditary priest — cried out, **Behold, the Lamb of God, that taketh away the sin of the world!** Doubtless John had baptized Jesus before this time, although John's Gospel does not say so;

John said that he recognized Jesus as the Messiah at His baptism when the Spirit descended upon Him like a dove. Moreover, one purpose of his rite of baptism was this very thing; to discover the Messiah, baptize Him, and announce Him to the world. God had revealed this to him, thus calling him to "make straight the way of the Lord." In other words, John's baptismal ceremony may have been the ritual cleansing of an eschatological group which, among others — such as the Essenes, looked for the coming of the Messiah. This expectation by many was part of the general preparation for the coming of Christ. John's spiritual perception was keener than that of the others. He alone could hear and see what God was doing. He alone recognized Jesus, who He was and what He came to do.

The day following John revealed his great discovery to two of his followers, who immediately left him and went with Jesus. Only one of them is identified — Andrew, Simon Peter's brother. They addressed Him as Rabbi (Teacher) and asked Him the question that a prospective student of that day would ask: "Where do you live?" Their understanding of who Jesus was fell far short of even the Jewish expectation of a political Messiah. John had been unable to convey all that he himself knew. A revelation such as he had received may be described, but it can never be communicated successfully to others at will. The deep things of the Spirit can be received only by hearts and minds prepared to comprehend them — prepared by the Spirit of God.

The meeting between Jesus and the two men was casual and the conversation very commonplace. "What are you looking for?" Where do you live?" "Come and see." Yet it was the beginning of a fellowship in a tightly knit little group which has been unmatched in the entire drama of human history.

The Synoptic Gospels tell much about John the Baptist, but John's Gospel catches his spirit and the central purpose of his life. He was a man called and prepared by God, a man of true humility, of great insight into the character of men and the things of the Spirit, whose genuine greatness consisted in the contribution he made to the initial work of Christ. It might be questioned why he continued to preach and baptize, in seeming opposition to Jesus, after he had introduced Him. Not all of his disciples were persuaded to follow Jesus, and a John the Baptist party continued after John had died. Why did he not cast his lot with Jesus and become one of His disciples? The answer is that he was called to be only a voice, preparing the way for Jesus in the hearts and minds of the people; this he continued to do until his arrest by Herod. He was not distressed, but rather he rejoiced, when he learned that crowds were flocking to Jesus for baptism. He refused to become embroiled with a Jew who wanted to debate the issue of his baptism versus that of Jesus. In words of today he said, "Jesus is the bridegroom; I am only the best man. His work will increase from now on; mine will decrease to eventual oblivion. For this I am happy, for God has planned it this way." While the title "Christian" was never ascribed to John, his example of humble, dedicated service might well become the pattern for the church in our day of over-ambition in the work of the Lord.

John the Baptist was a prophet in the truest sense of the word. He could feel the pulse of things around him; he had his ear tuned both to the world around him and to God; and his entire life and ministry sounded out God's message of salvation — the forgiveness of sins and the baptism by the Holy Spirit. Perhaps he recognized the fact that he had been signally endued with the Spirit all through his life, sensing a dynamic flowing through him which was not available to the average man. Be that as it may, he did envision the work of the Spirit as being applicable to all men. He had experienced the Spirit's anointing for his specialized calling; the day would come when all could be partakers of the Spirit for the task of normal living. This thought helps us to understand what Jesus meant when He said that John the Baptist was one of the greatest of men, yet less than the least of those in the kingdom of God.

More than this, John associated the work of the Spirit with that of Christ, who would baptize with the Spirit even as John himself baptized with water.

As the Spirit came upon Jesus at His baptism, even so would Christ bestow the Spirit upon His followers. John's ministry thus became a preparation for Pentecost, when the Spirit was poured out upon the people assembled in the upper room. Christ and the Spirit are spoken of as distinctly separate and different, but as we proceed through this Gospel we will find the Spirit spoken of as the Spirit of Christ. The problem of the Trinity is involved here, to which we will come in due time.

C. JESUS CHOOSES DISCIPLES (1:35-51)

35 Again on the morrow John was standing, and two of his disciples; 36 and he looked upon Jesus as he walked, and saith, Behold, the Lamb of God! 37 And the two disciples heard him speak, and they followed Jesus. 38 And Jesus turned, and beheld them following, and saith unto them, What seek ye? And they said unto him, Rabbi (which is to say, being interpreted, Teacher), where abidest thou? 39 He saith unto them, Come, and ye shall see. They came therefore and saw where he abode; and they abode with him that day: it was about the tenth hour. 40 One of the two that heard John speak, and followed him, was Andrew, Simon Peter's brother. 41 He findeth first his own brother Simon, and saith unto him, We have found the Messiah (which is, being interpreter, Christ). 42 He brought him unto Jesus. Jesus looked upon him, and said, Thou art Simon the son of John: thou shalt be called Cephas (which is by interpretation, Peter).

43 On the morrow he was minded to go forth into Galilee, and he findeth Philip: and Jesus saith unto him, Follow me. 44 Now Philip was from Bethsaida, of the city of Andrew and Peter. 45 Philip findeth Nathanael, and saith unto him, We have found him, of whom Moses in the law, and the prophets, wrote, Jesus of Nazareth, the son of Joseph. 46 And Nathanael said unto him, Can any good thing come out of Nazareth? Philip saith unto him, Come and see. 47 Jesus saw Nathanael coming to him, and saith of him, Behold, an Israelite indeed, in whom is no guile! 48 Nathanael saith unto him, Whence knowest thou me? Jesus answered and said unto him, Before Philip called thee, when thou wast under the fig tree, I saw thee. 49 Nathanael answered him,

Rabbi, thou art the Son of God; thou art King of Israel. 50 Jesus answered and said unto him, Because I said unto thee, I saw thee underneath the fig tree, believest thou? thou shalt see greater things than these. 51 And he saith unto him, Verily, verily, I say unto you, Ye shall see the heaven opened, and the angels of God ascending and descending upon the Son of man.

At this time Jesus began to recruit disciples, more especially that small band of twelve men who later were to be called apostles. We do not have the record of the call of each one, but, in the account given us by John, three elements of the call stand out. First, there is the drawing power of Christ. It was not John the Baptist's introduction as much as something in Jesus which caused Andrew to go from the one to the other. There is a magnetism about Christ and the Gospel which draws men to Him, those who are not insulated against Him by prejudice or willful sin. Second, there is the testimony of dedicated people. John the Baptist brought Andrew, who in turn brought Peter; Philip brought Nathanael. There is a naturalness, for the one who believes in Him, to testify about Jesus. In a straightforward way Andrew testified, **We have found him, of whom Moses in the law, and the prophets, wrote, Jesus of Nazareth.** In order, on the one hand, to guard against a reticence which staunches the flow of words and, on the other, an over-compulsion which claims every acquaintance as an object of solicitation, let us observe that this early witnessing or introducing of people to Christ started with close companions, even with brothers, who were apparently of similar age and cultural status. Andrew and Philip started with those who knew them and trusted them. This is more difficult than witnessing to a total stranger whom we may never see again, but it is more effective because it can be followed up by a godly life and Christlike attitudes. This suggests that witnessing for Christ is more than speech, however enthusiastic. Speech is worth little unless there are evidences of a measure of Christian character, and unless the one witnessing is a channel through which the Spirit can speak.

In the third place, there is the invitation of Christ. Prior to His appeal to Philip, **Follow me,** there is the picture of the seeking Christ who found Philip. Had Andrew and Peter told him of Christ? (They were from the same city.) Had Jesus learned of Philip and gone in search of him? It is enough for us to know that at the side of every impassioned disciple who testifies of his Lord is the Lord Himself, the seeking Savior, the Shepherd of the lost sheep. The same thing, yet thought of in different terms, is the drawing power of the Holy Spirit. Testifying or witnessing to the person and power of Christ to the unconverted is most effective when the message is an ingrained ingredient of the Christian's life, and when human efforts are fortified by the anointing of the Holy Spirit.

Not everyone responds to the call to follow Christ as readily as did Andrew and Philip. There was Nathanael who was more like Thomas in his sceptical approach to what his friends claimed to be true. Philip's answer to this attitude was equal to the occasion: "Come and find out for yourself." Nathanael came, and seeing was believing, largely because of Christ's superior knowledge and insight. Jesus could say, **Behold, an Israelite indeed, in whom is no guile!,** because **he himself knew what was in man** (2:25) and because Nathanael was an exceptional example of a chosen people, one in whom the moral law of Moses had become effective. Nathanael's reply showed a high degree of perceptivity and perhaps spiritual insight. But he still could not think in universal terms as did John the Baptist; to him the Messiah would be no more than the King of Israel. This understanding of Christ, marvelous as far as it went, was only the beginning. On the basis of his faith Jesus promised him **greater things than these. Ye shall see the heaven opened, and the angels of God ascending and descending upon the Son of man.** In referring to Himself as **Son of man,** Jesus was focusing attention upon His visible person and not upon His essential being. The purpose of this was that the disciples might not fail to observe what He, the Incarnate One, would accomplish in His human form. Their attention was "directed thither in order that they may see that which is beyond historical

observation. Jesus is the place of revelation."[8] Open heavens and descending
angels clearly have reference to Jacob's
experience at Bethel on his way to
Paddanaram (Gen. 28:10-17). According
to the Epistle to the Hebrews angels
were God's messengers of revelation in
the times of the prophets. Jesus spoke
of Himself as the ladder upon which angels of God descend and ascend. The
method of Jesus was to start with earthly
things and then turn the disciples' minds
to heavenly or spiritual things.

D. THE WEDDING AT CANA (2:1-11)

1 And the third day there was a marriage in Cana of Galilee; and the mother
of Jesus was there: 2 and Jesus also was
bidden, and his disciples, to the marriage.
3 And when the wine failed, the mother
of Jesus saith unto him, They have no
wine. 4 And Jesus saith unto her, Woman, what have I to do with thee? mine
hour is not yet come. 5 His mother saith
unto the servants, Whatsoever he saith
unto you, do it. 6 Now there were six
waterpots of stone set there after the
Jews' manner of purifying, containing two
or three firkins apiece. 7 Jesus saith unto
them, Fill the waterpots with water.
And they filled them up to the brim.
8 And he saith unto them, Draw out
now, and bear unto the ruler of the feast.
And they bare it. 9 And when the ruler
of the feast tasted the water now become
wine, and knew not whence it was (but
the servants that had drawn the water
knew), the ruler of the feast calleth the
bridegroom, 10 and saith unto him, Every
man setteth on first the good wine; and
when *men* have drunk freely, *then* that
which is worse: thou hast kept the good
wine until now. 11 This beginning of
his signs did Jesus in Cana of Galilee, and
manifested his glory; and his disciples
believed on him.

Jewish weddings were prolonged affairs,
running for a whole week and sometimes
two weeks. The bridegroom brought his
bride to his home in a procession, and
there followed games, dancing and singing, banqueting and much wine drinking.
Songs in mutual adoration were sung by
the bride and groom, symbolic rites were
performed; but there seems to have been
no formal pronouncement of the union,
as we know it today by a minister. All

of the friends and neighbors, as well as
the relatives, were invited.[9]

We do not know why Jesus, His
mother Mary, probably His brothers (v.
12), and His disciples were invited to
the wedding. His brothers would be
either sons of Joseph by a former marriage or younger sons of Joseph and
Mary. The inclusion of the disciples
(perhaps no more than the four mentioned earlier) seems to indicate that by
this time these men had become recognized as Jesus' followers and would be
expected to be with Him wherever He
went. At this wedding something took
place which was of far greater importance than the wedding itself, which is
not described (nor are its bride and
groom named). Jesus was there and, as
always, His presence made the difference.

The failure of the supply of wine,
which was an embarrassment to the host
and an insult to the guests, provided the
opportunity for Christ's first miracle,
which John interpreted as a sign in his
Gospel of witness. Significantly, Mary
was the first to notice the lack of bever-
age and the first to suggest that something should be done immediately to
remedy the situation. Her seeming casual remark, **They have no wine,** was
taken by Jesus to mean that she expected
Him to do something. How like a woman! How like a mother! Of course
that was what she meant. His answer —
Woman, what have I to do with thee? —
was not a rebuke or an expression of dis-
respect. "The address is that of courteous
respect, even of tenderness."[10]

This is one of the few glimpses which
we get of Mary the Virgin Mother in
the New Testament. She has been almost totally overshadowed by her Son,
except in the Roman Catholic Church.
F. W. Robertson has suggested that the
veneration for Mary to the point of worship came about because the Christian
virtues enumerated by Jesus — meekness,
purity, and the like — are feminine virtues, whereas the virtues of the Old
Testament were masculine: courage, wisdom, strength.[11] Be that as it may, it
serves as a reminder that the Protestant
Church should recognize Mary as the

[8] E. C. Hoskyns, *The Fourth Gospel*, p. 51.
[9] Henri Daniel-Rops, *Daily Life in the Times of Jesus*, pp. 141f.
[10] Westcott, *op. cit.*, p. 36.   [11] F. W. Robertson, *Sermons*, p. 388.

greatest example of motherhood to be found in life or literature. Let us say with all due reverence that the deity of Christ of itself does not fully explain why Jesus was the kind of man the New Testament pictures Him to be. He was also human, born a baby, reared a child, and brought to manhood by the same general processes by which all men take their places in life. He had a mother who loved and cared for Him, who taught Him and corrected Him, for it was given her of God to help shape His Life as He "advanced in wisdom and stature, and in favor with God and men" (Luke 2: 52). It has been said that when God wants to change the world He causes a baby to be born; and this has never been more true than in the case of the Babe of Bethlehem. It has been said that the hand that rocks the cradle is the hand that rules the world; this too has its application in the case of Mary. Perhaps the Christian virtues are feminine, but they are not of the weaker kind because of it, since they are the virtues which marked Mary's life and which she helped to infuse into the life of her Son. Meekness is not weakness. Love is life's strongest tie. Humility is basic to all the other virtues. If a good reason is needed for celebrating Mother's Day in our churches, and if it can be done with reverence and in full consciousness of Christ's divine nature, no better reason could be found than to give opportunity to recognize the mother of our Lord as the highest exemplar of womanhood and the best example of motherhood.

Jesus did not respond at once to Mary's suggestion that He do something about the wine shortage. Did she expect Him to perform a miracle? Jesus appears to have thought so at first, or at least His mother's remark caused Him to think of the responsibility. How else could He have done anything under the circumstances? But He hesitated. **Mine hour is not yet come.** John gives the strong impression throughout his Gospel that Jesus was living by a divine timetable. His reply to Mary was a reminder that, although the time had come for Him to reveal His power, and although she had sensed that a crucial hour had arrived, His directions on specific occasions must come from His Heavenly Father and not

from His earthly mother. How closely Mary must have watched the development of her Son, and followed Him with her prayers as He struggled with the great issues of life, as in the wilderness temptations! A mother's love had followed Him, a mother's prayers had supported Him, a mother's instinct knew what was going on, and a mother's insight began to map the career on which He was embarking. This is a beautiful thing to observe.

Jesus' reference to His hour which was to come — the proper time to start His miracles — seems to contain a hint of hesitancy on His part; a very natural approach to such a great undertaking, a beautiful expression of His humility. Jesus never was found to flaunt His powers or His views. The recognition, especially at this early date, that He possessed the power of miracle must have been overwhelming to the human. And so His mother gave Him the encouragement He needed. **Whatsoever he saith unto you, do it,** she said to the servants. Whereupon Jesus gave instructions to have the water pots filled — and the wine appeared. In this view of the occasion we not only see Jesus performing a miracle, but we also catch a glimpse of the relationship between Jesus and Mary, and therefrom we draw lessons for God's servants as mothers and as Christian workers. When we behold Christ in His humanity and see Him as One who experienced the characteristic normal reactions in life with which we struggle, even while He was the Son of God, we understand better our own calling and potential in the work of the Lord. He was divinely human. He was also humanly divine.

The amount of water which turned to wine was perhaps as much as one hundred eighty gallons. But the large amount constituted no essential part of the miracle, except to punctuate it in the eyes of those present. The real significance lies in the purpose for which it was done. Jesus was not merely helping out the host in an embarrassing situation, nor satisfying the already over-quenched thirst of the guests. The water which became wine was water normally used for ceremonial cleansing, **after the Jews' manner of purifying.** The miracle became the symbol of His work of atonement, "the outward and visible sign that the water of Judaism was being changed into the wine of Christian faith."[12] The Jews were ready enough to acclaim the new supply as the best wine of the feast, but they were less ready to accept the Gospel in place of the Law.

II PUBLIC MINISTRY (2:13-12:50)

A. CLEANSING OF THE TEMPLE (2:12-25)

12 After this he went down to Capernaum, he, and his mother, and *his* brethren, and his disciples; and there they abode not many days.
13 And the passover of the Jews was at hand, and Jesus went up to Jerusalem. 14 And he found in the temple those that sold oxen and sheep and doves, and the changers of money sitting: 15 and he made a scourge of cords, and cast all out of the temple, both the sheep and the oxen; and he poured out the changers' money, and overthrew their tables; 16 and to them that sold the doves he said, Take these things hence; make not my Father's house a house of merchandise. 17 His disciples remembered that it was written, Zeal for thy house shall eat me up. 18 The Jews therefore answered and said unto him, What sign showest thou unto us, seeing that thou doest these things? 19 Jesus answered and said unto them, Destroy this temple, and in three days I will raise it up. 20 The Jews therefore said, Forty and six years was this temple in building, and wilt thou raise it up in three days? 21 But he spake of the temple of his body. 22 When therefore he was raised from the dead, his disciples remembered that he spake this; and they believed the scripture, and the word which Jesus had said. 23 Now when he was in Jerusalem at the passover, during the feast many believed on his name, beholding his signs which he did. 24 But Jesus did not trust himself unto them, for that he knew all men, 25 and because he needed not that any one should bear witness concerning man; for he himself knew what was in man.

The suggestion of a human reaction on Jesus' part, takes on a new meaning as we next observe Him, still with His mother, going to Capernaum-on-the-Lake for a few days of relaxation, his brothers joining them (if they had not already

been with Him). Jesus had not yet left the family circle. The little company may have left Cana following the wedding and gone back home to Nazareth (Matt. 4-13), after which the entire family (Joseph probably having died) went for a last trip together, a kind of farewell gathering together on the eve of Jesus' leaving home permanently. Capernaum was about fifteen or twenty miles northeast of Nazareth on the Sea of Galilee almost due east of Cana. The company went **down** — from the highlands down to the shore of Galilee.

Following this, Jesus left His kinfolk and went with His disciples to Jerusalem to the Feast of the Passover. This was one of three great Jewish festivals. The Feast of the Passover, or of Unleavened Bread, which commemorated the deliverance of Israel from Egyptian bondage, was held at the time of the barley harvest. The Feast of Pentecost, or of First Fruits, commemorated the giving of the Law on Mount Sinai and was held at the time of the wheat harvest. Both barley and wheat were harvested in the spring or in the early summer. The third feast, the Feast of Tabernacles, or of Ingatherings, was held at the time of the final harvest of olives and fruits in the fall, in commemoration of the beginning of Israel's wilderness wanderings. There were other feasts or festivals, but these three were established before the Babylonian Exile, and thus were integral to the established forms of worship, and attendance was obligatory within certain reasonable limitations. John tells of Jesus attending all of the great feasts. Two are mentioned by name: Passover (2:15; 6:4) and Tabernacles (7:2, 10). The unknown feast (5:1) may have been the Feast of Pentecost. He also attended the Feast of Dedication (10:22), which had been established at the rededication of the Temple by Judas Maccabaeus in 165 B.C. Jesus was a faithful worshiper in the religion of Judaism.

It was at this time that the public ministry of Jesus began. His mother and brothers were no longer with Him and He seemed to have left home to pursue His mission in life. While at the Feast of the Passover He cleansed the Temple. The Synoptic Gospels place this event at

---

[12] R. V. G. Tasker, *The Old Testament in the New Testament,* p. 69.

the close of Jesus' ministry and see it as one reason for the rise of opposition which led to His crucifixion. John's Gospel places it at the beginning of the ministry and uses it as a sign to show that Jesus came to offer Himself as a sacrifice for the sins of man, of which the Temple sacrifices were but a shadow and soon to pass away. Because of differences of detail in the two accounts, Westcott assumes that there were two distinct cleansings,[13] though not all scholars agree with this position.

The immediate reason for this act is plain to see. Jesus was a good Israelite, brought up in the tradition of His ancestors and zealous for the religion of His race. He was accustomed to seeing the sale of sheep and oxen and pigeons for sacrifice in the outer court of the Temple, the purchase of animals for sacrifice being the only way that many people had of obtaining them. He was aroused to action because not just the Temple but also the Temple worship was being defiled. The Temple rulers had cornered the market for sacrificial animals, were charging exorbitant prices, and demanding payment in temple currency for which the people had to pay a high rate of exchange. Worship had become big business. Priests had become merchants, "fleecing" the people on the one hand while on the other they served as mediators before God on behalf of the sins of the worshippers. Jesus knew that their own sins were standing between God and those to whom they ministered, making their religion of no effect. Hypocrisy such as this drew forth some of Christ's severest denunciations.

We are not told about the immediate reaction to the driving out of the animals, the removing of the bird cages, the upsetting of the exchange tables, and the spilling out of the money. One can almost see the frenzied chasing after sheep and oxen and the mad scramble to retrieve the money. Some of those who had been cheated may have rationalized that, under the circumstances, the money was public property and they proceeded to get back what had been taken from them — with a good rate of interest thrown in. The priests made no immediate response, probably being in the

Temple proper officiating at sacrifice while attendants carried on their business outside. We are told only that some Jews asked Jesus by what authority He had done as He did. This provided the opportunity for Jesus to give the real reason and thereby to announce that He was now launching upon His life's work in earnest. **Destroy this temple,** He said, **and in three days I will raise it up** (v. 19). By the temple He meant **the temple of his body** (v. 21) and, in a sense, the whole Levitical system of worship, which was destined in the plan of God to pass away and be replaced with the Gospel. It never was meant to be permanent, for its true value was prophetic of a reality for which it stood as a symbol. The sacrifices never had served to speak peace to the troubled conscience. They were intended by God to be acts of faith — faith for restoration of fellowship with God and faith that the promised One would come who would be at one and the same time the Messiah King and the Lamb of God.

Christ was demonstrating that by His coming crucifixion the Old would pass away, having accomplished its purpose, and, at His resurrection three days hence, the New would be instituted. In this one dramatic act of our Lord the whole scope of God's plan of salvation for the world is laid before us. What fearful majesty there must have been on Christ's countenance that day! What authority in every word and action! But what is more, the issue now involved the Jewish ecclesiastical authorities. Under the existing circumstances, no one could be expected to understand fully what Jesus was doing. But they could have listened. Following the Resurrection, the disciples who had been with Jesus in the Temple that day remembered what He had said, and their faith was strengthened.

To the account of the cleansing of the Temple John added a brief account of Christ's contact with people in general. Many of them believed on Him, but with reservations, placing their own interpretation on what He said and did. Jesus could see that their faith was not genuine. More than that, He knew men — He understood sinful human nature and how it performed under given circumstances. He would not be carried away

[13] Op. cit., p. 44.

by their show of acceptance and loyalty. The incident reminds one of the Parable of the Sower and the Seed. Some seed fell into shallow soil, sprouted quickly, and as quickly withered under the heat of the sun (Matt. 13:1-9).

B. THE NEW BIRTH (3:1-15)

1 Now there was a man of the Pharisees, named Nicodemus, a ruler of the Jews; 2 the same came unto him by night, and said to him, Rabbi, we know that thou art a teacher come from God; for no one can do these signs that thou doest, except God be with him. 3 Jesus answered and said unto him, Verily, verily, I say unto thee, Except one be born anew, he cannot see the kingdom of God. 4 Nicodemus saith unto him, How can a man be born when he is old? can he enter a second time into his mother's womb, and be born? 5 Jesus answered, Verily, verily, I say unto thee, Except one be born of water and the Spirit, he cannot enter into the kingdom of God. 6 That which is born of the flesh is flesh; and that which is born of the Spirit is spirit. 7 Marvel not that I said unto thee, Ye must be born anew. 8 The wind bloweth where it will, and thou hearest the voice thereof, but knowest not whence it cometh, and whither it goeth: so is every one that is born of the Spirit. 9 Nicodemus answered and said unto him, How can these things be? 10 Jesus answered and said unto him, Art thou the teacher of Israel, and understandest not these things? 11 Verily, verily, I say unto thee, We speak that which we know, and bear witness of that which we have seen; and ye receive not our witness. 12 If I told you earthly things and ye believe not, how shall ye believe if I tell you heavenly things? 13 And no one hath ascended into heaven, but he that descended out of heaven, *even* the Son of man, who is in heaven. 14 And as Moses lifted up the serpent in the wilderness, even so must the Son of man be lifted up; 15 that whosoever believeth may in him have eternal life.

In Jesus' encounter with Nicodemus, He sought to enforce the same central truth that we found in the cleansing of the Temple — that the Old was being replaced by the New in God's design for salvation. In this instance, however, the reference was to the Kingdom of God, a well-known Jewish concept, as it pertained to the individual rather than to the race. Nicodemus was a Pharisee, a member of the Sanhedrin, the ruling body of the Jews at Jerusalem. Most of the seventy members were Sadducees, the wealthy liberals of the day. As a general rule the Sadducees were not on friendly terms with the Pharisees, the conservatives, who were of the common people. Whenever the Sadducees and Pharisees were found in association, it was usually when they had formed a temporary union in opposition to Jesus.

Nicodemus appears to have been a man who, at least at this time, found it difficult to express his real thoughts. Jesus got closer to them in His answer than Nicodemus had in his opening remarks. **Rabbi,** he began, **we know that thou art a teacher come from God; for no one can do these signs that thou doest, except God be with him** (v. 2). The rejoinder of Jesus was not fitted to the words of Nicodemus, but it did get down to the real purpose in his coming to Jesus. He had come as a concerned man; he was concerned about certain theological implications of the ministry of Jesus. In many ways this Preacher from Nazareth was a good faithful Jew; but He had also set Himself up as a critic of the established religion, as a reformer or even as an innovator. Already by the cleansing of the Temple He had done enough to make Himself suspect. But Nicodemus, a student of Hebrew history and theology, observed something in this man which stamped Him as a man chosen of God; He had the mark of the prophet upon Him. In addition, Nicodemus found his own heart troubled.[14] And it was to this trouble in his heart that Jesus spoke: **Verily, verily, I say unto thee, Except one be born anew, he cannot see the kingdom of God.** Which is to say that the need of Nicodemus' heart was of first concern to Jesus. The things of the Spirit cannot be comprehended as they should be by an unregenerate heart. Nicodemus tried to "catch on," and even responded in the language Jesus had used. But his reply was absurd, hardly worthy of his high office: **How can a man be born when he is old?** Yet he was willing to think along with Jesus. The idea of

---

[14] For this insight into the attitude of Nicodemus I am endebted to Helen Waddell, *Stories From Holy Writ*, pp. 203-207.

renewal should not have been strange to Jews of Jesus' day; ceremonial purification by baptism was familiar; and there were the prophecies of Jeremiah concerning the new covenant when God's law would be written on men's hearts (Jer. 31:34): also that of Ezekiel who promised a new spirit to be given and the stony heart replaced with a heart of flesh (Ezek. 11:19).

Nicodemus had come to Jesus as a Church official might go to his pastor-counselor in our day, seeking spiritual guidance. This helps us to understand why he came alone by night. Questions by his colleagues about such actions might have had an adverse effect, because he was a mature, if not old, man, who by Jewish custom should have no need of seeking new dimensions in his religion, having been steeped in Judaism from his youth. And "according to the rabbinical view, unlike the N.T. teaching, the moral renewing of men belongs only to the future, which alone can bring the new spirit of promise, or the new heart."[15]

Yet his heart was not satisfied. Nicodemus proved to be the exception to the rule among the religious leaders of his day, and he may well serve as an example to those in every day who scorn to humble themselves by the admission of personal needs — those who appear to think that ecclesiastical position is evidence enough of inner grace and assurance; who sometimes become too big to be humble. **Art thou the teacher of Israel, and understandest not these things?** said Jesus. The attitude of Nicodemus implied, "Yes Lord, but I must have an answer." He has become known as the "secret disciple," and we do know that he did not leave his religious post to become a traveling companion of the Master. Yet he was a disciple. His was one voice raised in protest against the tactics of the Pharisees (7:50), and he supplied the preservative spices with which the body of Jesus was treated following the crucifixion (19:39).[16]

But what did Jesus mean by being born anew (or "from above," which is the more literal translation of the Greek *anothen*)? The concept of the new birth was an analogy for the giving to man of a new life, which constitutes the ultimate theme of John's Gospel and of the ministry of Christ, birth standing for new life in the same way that Jesus is said to be bread and light. These terms suggest an order of things higher than the temporal. In referring to them one must avoid substituting the term for the experience. In particular this is a danger in respect to the new birth. It is a reality, a realizable spiritual experience, but all the properties of physical birth must not be attributed to it. To say that to be reborn a child of God means always to be one, because it is impossible to be unborn (as in the natural realm), is to miss completely the import of what Jesus is saying. While there doubtless are similarities in the experience of the new birth to physical birth (else Jesus would not have used the term), the differences between them are equally evident. **That which is born of the flesh is flesh; and that which is born of the Spirit is spirit** (v. 6). The differences must not be used to teach things about the Christian life which are not in keeping with its character.

Jesus described this experience as being **born of water and the Spirit.** The beautiful analogy of the new birth need not be encumbered with strained interpretations, such as seeing in the water a reference to a phenomenon of the physical process of birth. The water referred to the rite of baptism. Conversion was very closely associated with baptism in those early days, being synonymous in time. Baptism, which was a ritual cleansing, became associated with Christian conversion as the evidence of having accepted the Gospel. A modern counterpart may be seen in the work of foreign missions. Among some of the more primitive people it is customary to place converts on probation. The confession of sins and the acceptance of the Gospel must be followed by a period of testing, and not until the leaders are convinced of the sincerity and genuineness of the candidates are they accepted for Christian baptism. Conversion dates from the baptism, and they are then taken into church membership.

15 W. F. Howard, *Christianity According to St. John*, p. 201.
16 For further comment on Nicodemus, see commentary on the two references given immediately above.

It is strange that only primitive folk need to be made sure of their commitment and to produce "fruit worthy of repentance." Has our modern civilization become a hindrance to effective evangelism? Has respectability become a substitute for godly living? Has conversion as preached by even the strictest evangelicals been made too easy, until all one needs to do is make a verbal assent to the Gospel in order to be heralded as another convert? Dr. E. Stanley Jones spoke to this point when he said in a New England sermon: "People who are born in Boston are liable to think that they do not need to be born again."

The new birth is also by the Spirit — from above, spiritual in nature and procedure. The new birth is the impartation of the life of Christ — eternal life — through the agency of His Spirit. One comes into a life having new dimensions and qualities as different from natural, physical life as spirit is from flesh. Jesus said that this new life is like the wind (the Greek *pneuma* means both wind and spirit) which can be experienced but not fully explained, either in its origin or in its final end. If one cannot understand the mysteries of physical birth, or even the common phenomeon of the blowing wind, both of which he accepts on the basis of having experienced and observed their effects, is it too much to ask that a man receive the new birth on equal terms? This argument of Jesus is a good one. Yet He realized that not all had been explained — verbal testimony must have a foundation. And so He carried His claim for speaking the truth of God back to His incarnation. True, no man had gone to heaven to get this truth from God; but He, the Divine *Logos* become flesh, had come from God with this good news. The words He spoke would one day be substantiated by His being lifted up in death on the cross. His death would make the new birth a reality for all who believed. **As Moses lifted up the serpent in the wilderness, even so must the Son of man be lifted up; that whosoever believeth may in him have eternal life (vv. 14-15).** Jesus was seeking to awaken Nicodemus

to truth — truth which one day would become a living experience if he would only believe it now.

C. GOD'S REDEMPTIVE LOVE (3:16-21)

16 For God so loved the world, that he gave his only begotten Son, that whosoever believeth on him should not perish, but have eternal life. 17 For God sent not the Son into the world to judge the world; but that the world should be saved through him. 18 He that believeth on him is not judged: he that believeth not hath been judged already, because he hath not believed on the name of the only begotten Son of God. 19 And this is the judgment, that the light is come into the world, and men loved the darkness rather than the light; for their works were evil. 20 For every one that doeth evil hateth the light, and cometh not to the light, lest his works should be reproved. 21 But he that doeth the truth cometh to the light, that his works may be made manifest, that they have been wrought in God.

In the Prologue (1:1-18) John gave his philosophy of creation; in this paragraph we have his philosophy of salvation. At first glance it is difficult to know whether these words represent John's comments upon the conversation with Nicodemus or whether Jesus is continuing to speak. Very probably these are the words of John. He said quite simply that the plan of salvation is rooted in the love of God for the world of His creation, especially man. The Incarnation arose out of the love of God rather than out of the fall of man, the latter providing only the occasion for the Incarnation and the circumstances under which it occurred. The parent strives to save the wayward son, not alone because he is wayward, but because he loves him as a son. The Incarnation, including Christ's atoning sacrifice, demonstrated God's love for man; man's sin necessitated Christ's death on the Cross. John's affirmation is positive and strong; going back to the beginning of man's need of salvation he finds the love of God already operative. He might have written, "In the beginning was love — the Love of God."

Christ the Incarnate Son came not to condemn the world of men, because man's sin had already condemned him. This can be observed in all those who do not believe on Christ. Unbelief is sin. Christ came to save man. His coming brought light, and because men choose to continue in the darkness of sin rather than walking in the light of righteousness, their condemnation is increased to the point of judgment. Their own sinful hearts condemn them; the light as it is in Christ judges them. They remain in darkness because they hate the light which reveals their sin, which they love. But those who will to be honest with themselves and with God come to the light. John could have said that coming to the light reveals sin which is taken away by the light. He does say that the light banishes the darkness, for the darkness could not put it out. The very turning to Christ in faith brings one into the light and thus to a new life.[17]

God so loved . . . that he gave his only begotten Son is closely related to **Ye must be born anew,** spoken to Nicodemus. All manifestations of life result from birth, the perpetuation of life already in existence. John does not speak of the Virgin Birth as such, but, in the present context, it is reasonable to affirm that he had it in mind. To him the Incarnation was a blessed reality. By giving His Son, God gave Himself to save man, and John finds agreement with this truth in Paul's statement that "God was in Christ reconciling the world unto Himself" (II Cor. 5:19). The marvellous truth is that God has taken the initiative, made all necessary provisions, paid the debt, and waits, as the father of the prodigal son, for sinful man to return to Him in faith. There are places and times for speaking of the need of repentance and other conditional prerequisites to the experience of salvation, but John gathered up everything into faith; believe what God has said, assent to what He has done, give Him a chance, come out into the light. "There is life for a look."

John believed that the love of God in Christ was a magnetic force, especially as it is seen in the Crucifixion. To inquiring Greeks Jesus said, "And I, if I be lifted up from the earth, will draw all men unto myself" (12:32). An analogy to this may be found in great music and art. Men are drawn to them

and pursue them with great passion and dedication. Not all men, however, respond in this way because not all have been "awakened to art." No form of art can be created to appeal to the inner sensitivities of all men, and so not all can be awakened to it. There is a story about a farmer who spent his enforced time at the symphony speculating how many tons of hay the hall would hold. But the Gospel has an appeal which corresponds to an inner, unsatisfied longing native to every man. All men are natively capable of accepting the Gospel and loving Christ. The man who rejects Him is like a man with musical tastes perverted by prejudice or willful ignorance, or because he has never nourished his artistic tastes, rather than like a man who has had no capacity for musical appreciation. Moreover, the will of man is involved. He can decide to allow himself to be exposed to the magnetic power of Christ, even though he may do so with doubting. To the Jews who doubted Christ's claims on the basis of His lack of formal training He said, "If any man willeth to do his will, he shall know of the teaching, whether it is of God, or whether I speak of myself" (7: 17). A man can allow himself to be drawn by and to Christ. There are no barriers that cannot be overcome by faith. The Gospel of Christ has both drawing and awakening powers.

D. FURTHER TESTIMONY OF JOHN THE BAPTIST (3:22-30)

22 After these things came Jesus and his disciples into the land of Judaea; and there he tarried with them, and baptized. 23 And John also was baptizing in Aenon near to Salim, because there was much water there: and they came, and were baptized. 24 For John was not yet cast into prison. 25 There arose therefore a questioning on the part of John's disciples with a Jew about purifying. 26 And they came unto John, and said to him, Rabbi, he that was with thee beyond the Jordan, to whom thou hast borne witness, behold, the same baptizeth, and all men come to him. 27 John answered and said, A man can receive nothing, except it have been given him from heaven. 28 Ye yourselves bear me witness, that I

---

[17] See comments on Christ's talk with the Samaritan woman for additional discussion of the relationship between love and light.

said, I am not the Christ, but, that I am sent before him. 29 He that hath the bride is the bridegroom: but the friend of the bridegroom, that standeth and heareth him, rejoiceth greatly because of the bridegroom's voice: this my joy therefore is made full. 30 He must increase, but I must decrease.

Jesus and John the Baptist came together for apparently the last time at Salim (of uncertain location), where there were many springs. Jesus and His disciples came for the purpose of baptizing. John was already there baptizing new followers, and immediately a contrast arose in the minds of some of the people concerning the comparative virtues of the two baptisms. From this we learn that the ministries of John and John overlapped. Jesus was gaining a larger number of followers than John, although the rite of baptism does not loom large in the ministry of Jesus. Actually we are told that "Jesus himself baptized not, but His disciples" (4:2).

A discussion soon arose between a certain Jew and some of John's disciples, and John was brought in to give an opinion. Evincing the same humble spirit as previously, he replied that the success of Jesus was evidence of God's approval, and that he was content to take second place and rejoice at His success. He then made a prophecy that Jesus would increase while he would decrease.

In recording this incident John did not attempt a comparative study of the two water baptisms; he left the issue unanswered. It was enough to say that John the Baptist and his movement would decrease to the vanishing point, while that of Jesus would continue to grow. Neither did John tell that Jesus received baptism at the hands of the Baptist, perhaps for the purpose of emphasizing the baptism of the Spirit (see 1:32; 14:16, 17, 26; 16:7:15). As in the case of the cleansing of the Temple and the Nicodemus incident, the Old is shown to be passing away and the New taking its place. The need of John, the forerunner or preparer of Christ's kingdom, would soon come to an end. It is significant that his last recorded words should be, **I must decrease.** One more reference is made to John (6:33-35) where he is spoken of in the past tense. Apparently

he was beheaded by Herod shortly after the beginning of Jesus' ministry.

E. A COMMENTARY ON JOHN'S WITNESS (3:31-36)

31 He that cometh from above is above all: he that is of the earth is of the earth, and of the earth he speaketh: he that cometh from heaven is above all. 32 What he hath seen and heard, of that he beareth witness; and no man receiveth his witness. 33 He that hath received his witness hath set his seal to *this*, that God is true. 34 For he whom God hath sent speaketh the words of God: for he given not the Spirit by measure. 35 The Father loveth the Son, and hath given all things into his hand. 36 He that believeth on the Son hath eternal life; but he that obeyeth not the Son shall not see life, but the wrath of God abideth on him.

This brief section is made up of a series of thoughts of John the Apostle on the final words of John the Baptist, and these serve as a commentary on the witness of the Baptist. Christ is from above where the new birth originates. He is sovereign over all of His created universe. Man, in contrast (including John the Baptist) is of the earth and speaks the language of earth. Man is earthbound; he is flesh. Christ came down and took on the flesh of man in order to reveal God's plan of salvation. When man is willing to accept the witness of Christ, he can be assured of the truth of God. The testimony of Christ to what God was doing is to be perpetuated by His disciples, the Church. As Christ was endued with the Holy Spirit at the beginning of His ministry, so God gives the Spirit to those who become Christ's witnesses. God is not sparing in the gift of the Spirit. It is by the Spirit that men are able to witness. Perhaps there is an oblique reference here to John the Baptist's being filled with the Spirit (cf. Luke 1:15).

Just as Christ was supreme in creation He is supreme in redemption. All things have been put into His hands by the Father. Reminiscent of Christ's conversation with Nicodemus, John closed these reflections with the promise of eternal Life to all who believe on Christ — in fact, to believe is to have it. Eternal life is withheld from the unbeliever, and the wrath of God becomes his portion.

F. JESUS AND THE SAMARITAN WOMAN (4:1-26)

1 When therefore the Lord knew that the Pharisees had heard that Jesus was making and baptizing more disciples than John 2 (although Jesus himself baptized not, but his disciples), 3 he left Judaea, and departed again into Galilee. 4 And he must needs pass through Samaria. 5 So he cometh to a city of Samaria, called Sychar, near to the parcel of ground that Jacob gave to his son Joseph: 6 and Jacob's well was there. Jesus therefore, being wearied with his journey, sat thus by the well. It was about the sixth hour. 7 There cometh a woman of Samaria to draw water: Jesus saith unto her, Give me to drink. 8 For his disciples were gone away into the city to buy food. 9 The Samaritan woman therefore saith unto him, How is it that thou, being a Jew, askest drink of me, who am a Samaritan woman? (For Jews have no dealings with Samaritans.) 10 Jesus answered and said unto her, If thou knewest the gift of God, and who it is that saith to thee, Give me to drink; thou wouldest have asked of him, and he would have given thee living water. 11 The woman saith unto him, Sir, thou hast nothing to draw with, and the well is deep: whence then hast thou that living water? 12 Art thou greater than our father Jacob, who gave us the well, and drank thereof himself, and his sons, and his cattle? 13 Jesus answered and said unto her, Every one that drinketh of this water shall thirst again: 14 but whosoever drinketh of the water that I shall give him shall never thirst; but the water that I shall give him shall become in him a well of water springing up unto eternal life. 15 The woman saith unto him, Sir, give me this water, that I thirst not, neither come all the way hither to draw. 16 Jesus saith unto her, Go, call thy husband, and come hither. 17 The woman answered and said unto him, I have no husband. Jesus saith unto her, Thou saidst well, I have no husband: 18 for thou hast had five husbands; and he whom thou now hast is not thy husband: this hast thou said truly. 19 The woman saith unto him, Sir, I perceive that thou art a prophet. 20 Our fathers worshipped in this mountain; and ye say, that in Jerusalem is the place where men ought to worship. 21 Jesus saith unto her, Woman, believe me, the hour cometh, when neither in this mountain, nor in Jerusalem, shall ye worship the Father. 22 Ye worship that which ye know not: we worship that which we know; for salvation is from the Jews. 23 But the hour cometh, and now is, when the true worshippers shall worship the Father in spirit and truth: for such doth the Father seek to be his worshippers. 24 God is a Spirit: and they that worship him must worship in spirit and truth. 25 The woman saith unto him, I know that Messiah cometh (he that is called Christ): when he is come, he will declare unto us all things. 26 Jesus saith unto her, I that speak unto thee am *he*.

The City of Samaria was founded by Omri, the sixth king of the Kingdom of Israel and the head of a dynasty of four kings. It was located on a 400-foot hill in the central Palestinian highlands and gave its name to the surrounding territory. It has also given its name to people who inhabited the territory. It has suffered all the vicissitudes of the land of the Jews, but has continued to survive. In the time of Jesus the land of Samaria was annexed to Judea as a single territory under Tetrarchs of the Roman Empire. As a result of the shift of populations brought about by the Assyrians at the fall of the Northern Kingdom in 721 B.C., the Samaritans became of mixed blood. At some time after the restoration in 536 B.C. and the refusal of the Jews to share with them the rebuilding of the Jerusalem Temple, a rival temple was constructed on Mount Gerazim, a short distance southeast of the City of Samaria. The Pentateuch served as their Scriptures. Apparently worship was carried on there in the time of Christ.

The woman of Samaria probably came from the countryside of Samaria rather than from the city by that name. The city of Sychar, near which was Jacob's well, where the woman's conversation with Jesus took place, probably is to be identified with Shechem. Sychar is not mentioned in the Old Testament. The field given to Joseph by Jacob is doubtless the extra portion or "mountain slope" which Jacob gave Joseph above that which he gave the other sons (Gen. 48:22).

It is said that the usual route taken by Jews from Judea to Galilee was east of the Jordan River, a detour around

Samaria. Because the Samaritans were of mixed race and worshiped at a rival temple, they were worse than heathens in the minds of the Jews and not to be associated with. "Dog" was a common name for them.

Jesus left Judea at this time apparently to avoid further comparisons between Him and John the Baptist in the minds of the people. John had set the record straight by announcing Jesus as the Messiah and himself no more than a fading voice, even though the Jews would have prolonged the discussion over the two baptisms. The encounter had been profitable, but there was no point in Jesus' keeping the issue alive by remaining on the scene. He left and started for Galilee.

Jesus took the route through Samaria because He wanted to minister to the people of that province. Whether by accident or by design, He met a woman who had come to the community well to get the family water supply. She proved to be a good listener and a ready propagandist or witness. This meeting of Jesus with the woman was one of the most successful missions recorded by John, both in terms of the ready reception of Christ's message and in the appreciation with which it was received.

Jesus chose an opportune time to arrive at the well, when women would be there rather than men with the flocks. The day was warm, and He was noticeably hot and weary. He took advantage of the situation to open a conversation, asking the woman for a drink of water. The disciples had gone to the city (Sychar-Shechem) for food; Jesus may have sent them. He and the woman were left alone. His speech, and perhaps even His dress, betrayed Him as a Jew, and the surprise of the woman was immediately evident. **How is it that thou, being a Jew, askest drink of me, who am a Samaritan woman?** John added the comment that Jews had no dealings with Samaritans. Besides the racial and religious barriers, and in part because of them, Samaritan women were said to be unclean, and a man who as much as spoke to one of them was defiled thereby. In speaking to her Jesus ran the risk of being thought unclean by those who knew Him; but He also showed that He regarded ceremonial religion ineffective in dealing with one's actual moral and spiritual condition. Little wonder that He was able to get the woman's attention at once. She was too amazed to get the water he had asked for.

Jesus soon revealed that water was not what He wanted. He was seeking an opening for His message — and He began to discourse on the water of life. He offered to give her living water, the water of eternal life. And like Nicodemus, she was unable to grasp more than the first meaning of His words. Yet she seemed to be groping for hidden meaning. Did this Man have some special means of drawing water from so deep a well? Or would He prove to be a greater man than Jacob (who had provided the well) and supply water in some other way? (v. 11-12). Ignoring the possible note of sarcasm in her remarks, Jesus told her that the water which He would give her would bring to her eternal life. Jacob's well water could quench only physical thirst and help to sustain physical life. The water which Jesus offered would quench the thirst of the soul and produce life that would be everlasting. The well water represented the Old ceremonialism; Jesus was bringing in the New era of grace. He offered her life from above — the life of the Spirit — even as He had to Nicodemus, to whom He spoke in terms of the new birth.

Eternal life has moral qualities as well as qualities of extension beyond time. Jesus sought to enforce this truth upon the woman, for He had seen her heart beginning to open, faith beginning to take hold of His words. In the only language she knew she asked for the water, not only for herself but for others, for to her water was to be shared — the well served all the people of the community and even wayfarers like Jesus. **Sir, give me this water, that I thirst not, neither come all the way hither to draw.** Jesus did not say, as might be expected, "I am the water of life." On other occasions He claimed to be the bread of life and the light of the world. But in this instance He was addressing one who had begun to probe beyond the analogy already made between the well water and the water promised her. She had begun to see the religious, even spiritual, significance in what Jesus was saying. And the language need not have been unfamiliar to her, She may have been reminded of Moses bringing water from the rock, or of Isaiah crying out, "with joy shall ye draw water out of the wells of salvation." Her true attitude became apparent when she made no attempt to justify her loose love life when Jesus revealed that He knew about it (doubtless by divine insight, which is more evident in John's Gospel than in the Synoptics). By this she knew that He was a prophet and immediately turned the conversation to religion. **Our fathers worshipped in this mountain; and ye say, that in Jerusalem is the place where men ought to worship.** In a few well-chosen sentences Jesus exposed the inadequacies of both Samaritan and Jerusalem worship, which differed very little from each other, both belonging to the old ceremonialism. Not that this worship had no place either in God's revelation to man or in man's reach after God. But Judaism had the advantage of being the special medium of God's revelation of salvation to the world, for through that revelation the Messiah had been promised. When the Messiah came, both Samaritanism and Judaism would have to give way, because true worship would then become spiritual rather than remain ceremonial.

The woman was apparently well versed in the Old Testament, even beyond the Pentateuch, which was the limit of the Samaritan canon. The promise of a Messiah was familiar to her. **I know that Messiah cometh,** she said. A hushed reverence comes into the narrative at this point. Jesus was about to make the plainest possible declaration of His divine origin — and that to a woman who was not of the Chosen People. This declaration Jesus had not been disposed to make to Nicodemus, a member of the Sanhedrin, the Jewish Council. The difference lay in the receptivity of the ones addressed. Often it happens that those who have had the greatest opportunity to gain the truth are duller of comprehension than others who come to it for the first time. The difference here is between a Jewish religious official and a common housekeeper. The woman was unhindered by the presuppositions and prejudices which blinded the Jews, and so Jesus said to her, **I that speak unto you am he** (v. 26)

Which is more important, the new birth or spiritual worship? Nicodemus needed the lesson on worship as much as did the Samaritan woman; and she, no less than he, stood in need of being born from above. One was no more, nor less, a disciple of Christ to begin with than the other. Evidently Jesus is saying that true worship is an approach to the kingdom of God and a way into a spiritual experience of conversion. His teachings on the new birth and on spiritual worship make a powerful treatise on Christian citizenship.

God is a Spirit: and they that worship him must worship in spirit and truth. This should read, "God is Spirit," for He is not one among many spirits, even the greatest, but His essential nature is spiritual and not material. The expression **Spirit and truth** refers to worship that is in keeping with the nature of God. John commented on this in the First Johannine Epistle where God is said to be love (4:8) and light (1:5). "God is love." Love is healing. Not only does He love; He *is* love. God was known to Israel by His deeds of love and mercy — He was the God who brought them out of the Land of Egypt. "He saved them for his name's sake, that he might make his mighty power to be known" (Ps. 106:8). Men are most like God when they love and perform loving deeds. Love is a Christian virtue, but it is also a spirit which permeates and spreads and grows. St. Paul said "the fruit of the Spirit is love" with its attendant qualities (Gal. 5:22).

God is also light, which speaks of revealed truth or of God revealing Himself. Christ came as the light of the world. James says that there is no variation in God, "neither shadow cast by turning" (1:17). No darkness, no falsehood, no imperfections are found in Him. He is truth — truth revealed. Walking in the light is walking in the truth of God in Christ.

It is proper to think of worship in **spirit and truth** as worship carried on in the spirit of love and on the basis of revealed truth. Worship, especially public worship, is a gathering together for mutual fellowship and edification and to give praise and honor to God. Its true intent and purpose are lost when the spirit of love is absent. Ceremonial worship, such as Nicodemus and the Samaritan woman knew — worship under the Old Covenant, worship which had served its purpose and could no longer bring men into the presence of God — could be conducted whether the participants practiced love for one another and for God or not. But worship under the New Covenant must be in the spirit of love, both for God and for man. Jesus taught that differences between brethren are to be cleared up before worship is acceptable (Matt. 5:23-24).

In similar fashion Christian worship must be conducted according to the truth of God as it has been revealed in Christ. Also, worship should constitute the quest for truth. The blessings from worship are a sense of acceptance and assurance which comes from the presence of God, but worship should mean more than this. Worshiping **in truth** will bring new light in which the worshiper will walk. The truth may come "close and searching" and be more sobering than joyous as one sees within himself attitudes and relationships which are unChristlike. It may "rock one back on his heels" or "drive him to his knees," "For the word of God is living and active, and sharper than any two-edged sword" (Heb. 4:12). Worship in **spirit and truth** is love-prompted and love-saturated worship which brings the light of God's truth upon one's heart and life.

G. CONSEQUENCES OF THE INTERVIEW (4:27-42)

27 And upon this came his disciples; and they marvelled that he was speaking with a woman; yet no man said, What seekest thou? or, Why speakest thou with her? 28 So the woman left the waterpot, and went away into the city, and saith to the people, 29 Come, see a man, who told me all things that *ever* I did: can this be the Christ? 30 They went out of the city, and were coming to him. 31 In the mean while the disciples prayed him, saying, Rabbi, eat. 32 But he said unto them, I have meat to eat that ye know not. 33 The disciples therefore said one to another, Hath any man brought him *aught* to eat? 34 Jesus saith unto them, My meat is to do the will of him that sent me, and to accomplish his work.

35 Say not ye, There are yet four months, and *then* cometh the harvest? behold, I say unto you, Lift up your eyes, and look on the fields, that they are white already unto harvest. 36 He that reapeth receiveth wages, and gathereth fruit unto life eternal; that he that soweth and he that reapeth may rejoice together. 37 For herein is the saying true, One soweth, and another reapeth. 38 I sent you to reap that whereon ye have not labored: others have labored, and ye are entered into their labor.

39 And from that city many of the Samaritans believed on him because of the word of the woman, who testified, He told me all things that *ever* I did. 40 So when the Samaritans came unto him, they besought him to abide with them: and he abode there two days. 41 And many more believed because of his word; 42 and they said to the woman, Now we believe, not because of thy speaking: for we have heard for ourselves, and know that this is indeed the Saviour of the world.

As soon as the disciples returned with food the woman left for the city. Conversation such as she and Jesus engaged in is spoiled when others are present. It was private — heart-to-heart. Some truths do not fit public discourse. Some people's problems are best cared for in private interviews. Reliance upon public services at the expense of personal counseling on the part of pastor and church cannot fail to leave untouched many of the deeper problems of people. Jesus was Master of the personal interview.

Leaving her water pot (for she planned to return), the woman hurried into Sychar to tell her friends of the prophet whom she half believed was the Jewish Messiah. Many believed what she told them; but it is doubtful whether their faith went any farther than hers regarding Christ's Messiahship. Others came out to the well and were persuaded to believe what Jesus Himself said to them. What they heard from Him confirmed what the woman had said. Perhaps prejudice against the Jews kept them from speaking of Christ as the Messiah — they called Him the Savior of the world (v. 42). But of greater significance is the fact that they believed more readily and heartily than the Jews.

The second result of this interview

with the woman is seen as Jesus talked with His disciples upon their return. It may not be proper to say that they were unappreciative of the greatness of the occasion. They had not heard the conversation, and for the moment they were fully absorbed with preparations for the evening meal. They failed to catch any of the atmosphere of what had transpired; the very air must have been charged as with electricity. The record implies that the disciples had started to eat before the woman left. When Jesus refrained from eating they urged food upon Him, unconscious of His pre-occupation. **I have meat to eat that ye know not.** They did not know what He meant. The Samaritans had come to accept Christ in a way not matched by this first band of disciples. The disciples had accepted Him as Rabbi (teacher — 1:38), and had asked to follow Him as interested novitiates. They had not been present to hear either the teaching on the New Birth or on the water of life. Their response to Jesus' refusal to eat — **Hath any man brought him ought to eat** — compares well with that of Nicodemus, "How can a man be born when he is old?" The woman had demonstrated keener insight and spiritual perception than anyone in John's record up to this time. Perhaps it was because she was a woman; or because she was not a Jewess. She would have had some comprehension of Jesus' next words to the disciples: **My meat is to do the will of him that sent me, and to accomplish his work** (v. 34). To the disciples this was something to be remembered and understood at a later date.

It must be observed, however, that readiness of comprehension seemed not to be of as great importance to Jesus as to us in this day of priorities, I.Q.'s, and Quiz Kids. The Samaritan woman is not heard of again in the Gospels. It was of greater importance that the disciples come to a full comprehension of Jesus and His mission with regard to their part in it and their dedication to it. And so Jesus pointed to the fields of unripened grain and drew forth a lesson. Unlike the grain, the spiritual harvest was already ripe for gathering, as evidenced by the people flocking out from the city. They, the disciples, were

to be reapers in God's harvest field, their reward would be sure, and they would rejoice with those who had gone before them in God's program of salvation. Jesus thought of both sowing and reaping going on simultaneously. Each man reaps where another has sown and in turn sows for another to reap. One man plants, another waters, and still another reaps, but it is "God that giveth the increase" (I Cor. 3:7).

H. HEALING THE OFFICIAL'S SON (4: 43-54)

43 And after the two days he went forth from thence into Galilee. 44 For Jesus himself testified that a prophet hath no honor in his own country. 45 So when he came into Galilee, the Galilaeans received him, having seen all the things that he did in Jerusalem at the feast: for they also went unto the feast.
46 He came therefore again unto Cana of Galilee, where he made the water wine. And there was a certain nobleman, whose son was sick at Capernaum. 47 When he heard that Jesus was come out of Judaea into Galilee, he went unto him, and besought *him* that he would come down, and heal his son; for he was at the point of death. 48 Jesus therefore said unto him, Except ye see signs and wonders, ye will in no wise believe. 49 The nobleman saith unto him, Sir, come down ere my child die. 50 Jesus saith unto him, Go thy way; thy son liveth. The man believed the word that Jesus spake unto him, and he went his way. 51 And as he was now going down, his servants met him, saying, that his son lived. 52 So he inquired of them the hour when he began to amend. They said therefore unto him, Yesterday at the seventh hour the fever left him. 53 So the father knew that *it was* at that hour in which Jesus said unto him, Thy son liveth: and himself believed, and his whole house. 54 This is again the second sign that Jesus did, having come out of Judaea into Galilee.

After two days in Samaria, at the urging of the people of Sychar, Jesus continued on His way to Galilee. The words of Jesus at this time — **a prophet hath no honor in his own country** — were probably spoken in reference to Judea and as part of His reason for having left there a few days before. They also indicate the attitude of resistance which Jesus was encountering and which would continue. They are also somewhat reminiscent of John's statement, "He came unto his own [things or home] and they that were his own received him not" (1:11). When He arrived in Galilee, the Galileans welcomed Him, probably those who had observed Him when He cleansed the Temple at the Passover Feast. It was said that they believed on Him then. Jesus, however, did not go among them as among friends and disciples for He knew the shallowness of their faith (2:24). This was more of a casual visit than a planned tour. He had accomplished His mission in Samaria and was spending a few days in familiar territory before returning to Jerusalem to an "unnamed" feast.

During this visit Jesus healed the son of a nobleman or Roman official at Cana, thereby completing His initial witness to the three chief representative groups in Palestine: Jews, Samaritans, and Gentiles (all non-Jews were Gentiles). The second miracle in the little town of Cana gives evidence of the degree of faith which He found there as against Nazareth, His boyhood home (Matt. 13:53-58). Each confrontation of Jesus with an individual person had its distinctive features, even though the end purpose in each case was the same — the development of faith in Him. Jesus never approached two people in exactly the same way. This man of Cana wanted Jesus to heal his son; Jesus wanted the man to believe in Him. The man pleaded, **Heal my son.** In substance Jesus replied, "Faith is necessary and you will not believe until you first see a miracle." The father's response showed that he was an exception to the common run of people — he accepted Christ's promise that his son would live and he returned to his home. The result was that the child was restored to health, the father's faith was vindicated, and the entire family became believers. The contrast between this officer of the Roman Court and the Galileans who had seen Jesus in Jerusalem shows that faith based only upon the occurrences (miracles) is not always strong nor genuine. John here revealed progress in Christ's presentation of redemptive truth. Miracles have their place as a means of faith, but ultimately faith must come through insight into the person and work of Christ, for Christians cannot live by miracles alone. In fact, faith is not really faith until it has gone beyond the ability to see. At the close of Christ's ministry, after the Resurrection, He spoke this truth to Thomas who wanted tangible support for his faith: "Because thou hast seen me, thou hast believed: blessed are they that have not seen, yet have believed" (John 20:29).

I. JESUS AND THE SABBATH (5:1-18)

1 After these things there was a feast of the Jews; and Jesus went up to Jerusalem. 2 Now there is in Jerusalem by the sheep gate a pool, which is called in Hebrew Bethesda, having five porches. 3 In these lay a multitude of them that were sick, blind, halt, withered. 5 And a certain man was there, who had been thirty and eight years in his infirmity. 6 When Jesus saw him lying, and knew that he had been now a long time in that case, he saith unto him, Wouldest thou be made whole? 7 The sick man answered him, Sir, I have no man, when the water is troubled, to put me into the pool: but while I am coming, another steppeth down before me. 8 Jesus saith unto him, Arise, take up thy bed, and walk. 9 And straightway the man was made whole, and took up his bed and walked.

Now it was the sabbath on that day. 10 So the Jews said unto him that was cured, It is the sabbath, and it is not lawful for thee to take up thy bed. 11 But he answered them, He that made me whole, the same said unto me, Take up thy bed, and walk. 12 They asked him, Who is the man that said unto thee, Take up thy bed, and walk? 13 But he that was healed knew not who it was; for Jesus had conveyed himself away, a multitude being in the place. 14 Afterward Jesus findeth him in the temple, and said unto him, Behold, thou art made whole: sin no more, lest a worse thing befall thee. 15 The man went away, and told the Jews that it was Jesus who had made him whole. 16 And for this cause the Jews persecuted Jesus, because he did these things on the sabbath. 17 But Jesus answered them, My Father worketh even until now, and I work. 18 For this cause therefore the Jews sought the more to kill him, because he not only brake the sabbath, but also called God his own Father, making himself equal with God.

The feast which was the occasion for the return of Jesus to Jerusalem is not named. John simply wanted to establish a setting for the first major conflict between Jesus and the Jews. In fact, the narration of the healing at the pool of Bethesda seems to have had a similar purpose, because much uncertainty gathers around it. The identity — not only of the feast, but also of the pool, its location, its healing properties and the account of the angel — has been a problem for scholars.

The matter is simplified by recognizing that the latter half of verse 3 and all of verse 4 are not found in the best Greek manuscripts from which our English New Testament is translated. In the King James Version this portion reads: "For an angel went down at a certain season into the pool, and troubled the water; whosoever then first after the troubling of the water stepped in was made whole of whatsoever disease he had." When this portion is omitted we have the simple, meaningful story of a group of sick folk gathered at what we would call a mineral spring, the water of which was known to have beneficial effects upon certain illnesses. The people who visited the pool waited for the moving of the water, which was probably the bubbling of the spring which fed the pool. The miracle which John relates is not a kind of magic, with angels giving healing power to water, but a miracle of healing by the Master Physician as evidence of His claim to being the Son of God. The pool, its borders lined with sick folk, became the setting for a remarkable case of healing by Jesus. There is little reason to think that He ignored the others, healing only one man. This would have been contrary to the nature of Jesus and the pictures given of Him elsewhere, especially in the Synoptics. This one case of healing, with its aftermath, was sufficient for John as a background for the ensuing conflict over the keeping of the Sabbath — for the healing had taken place on the Sabbath.

Jesus was necessarily critical of the Judaism of His day, and for this reason He was accused of trying to destroy the faith of the fathers. He stood in the true line of Hebrew prophets in this regard. Amos, for instance, cried out, "I hate, I despise your feasts, and I will take no delight in your solemn assemblies" (Amos 5:21). The rituals of which Amos spoke had been ordained of God, but he was opposed to them as practiced because both priest and people had perverted them to their own ends. The moral and religious values had been lost, and form was being substituted for reality. The prophets were looked upon as traitors to their country and to the Temple worship. Jesus demonstrated essentially this same attitude toward the religion of both Temple and synagogue and suffered a similar, and finally a worse, rejection than did the prophets.

In Jesus' day a Sabbath Day's journey was two thousand cubits (about three-fifths of a mile), and traveling farther constituted a breach of the Sabbath law. Many other forms were rigidly observed, such as ceremonial washing before meals and the wearing of prayer phylacteries. Such things could be observed as marks of piety, and the saying of lengthy prayers in public and the placing of large sums of money in the Temple treasury gave assurance that one was earning favor from God. There were at least four objections which Jesus had to the ceremonialism of that time. First, it placed the people in bondage — bondage to form and to public opinion. Second, it detracted from, or made unnecessary, faith in God as essential to religion. Originally the ceremonial law, the keeping of the Sabbath, the offering of sacrifices, circumcision, and the rest, were provided as evidence of the people's faith in God and as a means of expressing their allegiance to Him. But when these things ceased to be witnesses to faith and became only forms of approach to God, they lost their value. Third, there was the loss of personal moral values. Worship had ceased to make moral demands upon the worshipers. There was little in it to stir the conscience, nothing to move a man to the confession of sin. Fourth, formal ceremonialism was the perversion of what had formerly been the tools of pure worship. That which had been alive had died; that which had been sweet had gone sour; that which drew men to God now separated them from Him. And fifth, the saddest plight of all was that the participants themselves had taken on the deadness of their forms.

This is not the place to go into a full-scale dicussion of formalism versus freedom as it pertains to the keeping of the

Sabbath. John has not given us enough material to work with. The classic answer is given in Mark's Gospel: "The sabbath was made for man, and not man for the sabbath: so that the Son of man is lord even of the sabbath" (2:27). Religious observances are of value only as they minister to the needs of people, both individual and collective, and come under the wise counsel of the church and the leadings of the Spirit.

The healed man was accused by the Jews of breaking the Sabbath when they found him carrying his sleeping-mat. Either because he had not been a religious man, or because his joy at being healed caused him to be oblivious to formalistic religious demands, he attributed his breach of the Sabbath to the fact of his healing: **He that made me whole, the same said unto me, Take up thy bed and walk** (v. 11). As yet he did not know who Jesus was. To him, and to Jesus, the carrying of his cot was evidence of his healing; to the Jews it was a breach of the ceremonial law. The issue at stake was whether man or the law was of prime importance. Jesus was interested in the man, and He sought and found him in the Temple, and said to him, **Behold, thou art made whole: sin no more, lest a worse thing befall thee** (v. 14). For him to be influenced by his religious critics from then on would amount to sin, and this could lead to a recurrence of his illness. Jesus was suggesting that his sickness had been brought on by evil practices, the direct result of a sinful life. More than this, there are consequences of sin more dire than physical disease — these too the man must avoid. As Jesus said in another context, "Be not afraid of them that kill the body, but are not able to kill the soul: but rather fear him who is able to destroy both soul and body in hell" (Matt. 10:28).

The man who was healed told the Jews that his benefactor was Jesus. In his naive enthusiasm he did not realize that this was one of the worst things he could do — publicity was not what Jesus needed among the Jews. He was too well known by them already; and immediately a new wave of persecution arose, even attempts to kill Jesus. His only answer to them was, **My Father worketh still, and I am working** (v. 17).

In other words, He was working on the Sabbath because His Father was working: and the healing which He had performed was the work of God the Father. They thus had two charges against Him; He had broken the Sabbath by healing a man (causing him also to break it), and He claimed God as His father, which was an acknowledgement of equality with God. The power which He thus commanded was authority over both the physical and the moral worlds. He could heal a lame man when He chose; He could also break the Sabbath as they understood it, because He was greater in authority than both Moses (1:17) and the law which he had given.

J. JESUS AND THE FATHER (5:19-47)

19 Jesus therefore answered and said unto them, Verily, verily, I say unto you, the Son can do nothing of himself, but what he seeth the Father doing: for what things soever he doeth, these the Son also doeth in like manner. 20 For the Father loveth the Son, and showeth him all things that himself doeth: and greater works than these will he show him, that ye may marvel. 21 For as the Father raiseth the dead and giveth them life, even so the Son also giveth life to whom he will. 22 For neither doth the Father judge any man, but he hath given all judgment unto the Son; 23 that all may honor the Son, even as they honor the Father. He that honoreth not the Son honoreth not the Father that sent him. 24 Verily, verily, I say unto you, He that heareth my word, and believeth him that sent me, hath eternal life, and cometh not into judgment, but hath passed out of death into life. 25 Verily, verily, I say unto you, The hour cometh, and now is, when the dead shall hear the voice of the Son of God; and they that hear shall live. 26 For as the Father hath life in himself, even so gave he to the Son also to have life in himself; 27 and he gave him authority to execute judgment, because he is a son of man. 28 Marvel not at this: for the hour cometh, in which all that are in the tombs shall hear his voice, 29 and shall come forth; they that have done good, unto the resurrection of life; and they that have done evil, unto the resurrection of judgment.

30 I can of myself do nothing: as I hear, I judge: and my judgment is righteous; because I seek not mine own will, but the will of him that sent me. 31

If I bear witness of myself, my witness is not true. 32 It is another that beareth witness of me; and I know that the witness which he witnesseth of me is true. 33 Ye have sent unto John, and he hath borne witness unto the truth. 34 But the witness which I receive is not from man: howbeit I say these things, that ye may be saved. 35 He was the lamp that burneth and shineth; and ye were willing to rejoice for a season in his light. 36 But the witness which I have is greater than *that of* John; for the works which the Father hath given me to accomplish, the very works that I do, bear witness of me, that the Father hath sent me. 37 And the Father that sent me, he hath borne witness of me. Ye have neither heard his voice at any time, nor seen his form. 38 And ye have not his word abiding in you: for whom he sent, him ye believe not. 39 Ye search the scriptures, because ye think that in them ye have eternal life; and these are they which bear witness of me; 40 and ye will not come to me, that ye may have life. 41 I receive not glory from men. 42 But I know you, that ye have not the love of God in yourselves. 43 I am come in my Father's name, and ye receive me not: if another shall come in his own name, him ye will receive. 44 How can ye believe, who receive glory one of another, and the glory that *cometh* from the only God ye seek not? 45 Think not that I will accuse you to the Father: there is one that accuseth you, *even* Moses, on whom ye have set your hope. 46 For if ye believed Moses, ye would believe me; for he wrote of me. 47 But if ye believe not his writings, how shall ye believe my words?

Jesus was constrained to defend himself against the incriminations of the Jews concerning His authority and His relationship to God. He stated His claim to union with God, claiming no independent authority or power; He did only that which He observed the Father doing (v. 19). Jesus used the human analogy of the father-son relationship, not to establish a separateness between God and Him, but as a familiar background to His claim of an essential unity with God. **The Father loves the Son** (v. 20), in later Johannine thought becomes "God is love" (I John 4:8). By this analogy He also pointed out that His motivation was not the seeking of honor for Himself but rather doing the will of God and in love bringing life to man. The Hebrew concept of the father-son relationship, and even the concept found in our own Anglo-Saxon culture before the Industrial Revolution — when perforce the son followed his father in trade or business as a near duplicate of his parent — provides a clearer understanding of Christ's analogy than the concept of the father-son relationship today.

What the Jews had observed Jesus doing was actually the working of the Father — and greater works were still in store for them, to their increasing amazement. By this Jesus may have been referring to the raising of Lazarus from the dead, which occurred some time later. The Jews believed that God was able to raise the dead (Deut. 32:39; Isa. 6:19). Jesus was to show that He too could raise the dead. Yet not He alone, but as the Father worked through Him. At the same time, He did labor autonomously, for the power to do mighty works and the authority to judge when and where to act had been given Him as the Son of God. He was as truly God as was the Father, and no man could give honor to God the Father and at the same time dishonor God the Son. The source of all life rests in the Father and the Son (1:4) — not physical life only, even though the witness to life-giving reached a climax in the raising of Lazarus (ch. 11). In the Father and the Son resides also eternal life, or life from above, as Jesus told Nicodemus. However, it is the Son, not the Father, who became the focus of the life-giving process. The world of men is judged by the Son because of the unique relationship which He sustains to both God and man by the Incarnation. Men must deal, not with God as such, neither with God the Father, but with the Son who is the eternal Word made flesh (1:14). They who believe Him have eternal life (v. 24). He who would honor the Father can do so only by honoring the Son; and this he does by believing. To believe in the Son is to believe in the Father, both being equally God. By believing, one shares eternal life with Him, and the wonder of it all will be made plain in a coming day of resurrection.

These statements are abundant in paradox, but it is the paradox of grace, a paradox which is easy to live with when one has "passed from death unto life," when he gives himself to the truth in order to understand it, when he shares with John the secrets of the beloved.

Two more things must be said in order to make the witness of Jesus to Himself complete, and these are found in the reference to a final general resurrection, a greater experience than the raising of Lazarus from the dead. Lazarus must die another physical death because he rose on the earthly side of the grave. Those who experience the final resurrection will never again know physical death. Both the raising of Lazarus and the anticipated resurrection are evidences of that eternal life which Christ came to give. But more than this, the validity of this life in the believer will be tested by the resurrection, which will separate men to life or to judgment. They will be judged on the basis of their deeds, whether good or evil. In this life men are judged in respect to their believing on Christ; in the last day they will be judged in respect to their having done the will of God. Christ's claim to being the Son of God was evidenced by His works which testified to Him (5:36). Men's claim to new life in Him must finally rest upon similar evidence.

The witness of Jesus to Himself brought forth the claim that He was able to give life — physical and eternal — because He possessed it inherently, shared with and given by the Father (v. 26); and He had the authority to bestow life upon those who believed in Him. Life holds within it the power of judgment, because life is also light (1:4). "This is the judgment, that the light is come into the world, and men loved the darkness rather than the light; for their works were evil" (3:19). Judgment does not await the resurrection in the last day, but it adheres to the whole fabric of the Incarnation. The God-man brought about a relationship between man and His Creator whereby his every act is judged in the light of it. Man cannot stand, as it were, on the sidelines and ignore the Incarnation as if it never had happened; he is already involved through God's having taken on Himself human flesh, and he must decide to accept the life that is offered thereby or decide to reject it and suffer the consequences of tearing himself away from God. The decision is more than a Yes or No answer; it is either the acceptance or repudiation of the Incarnation: the union of God and man in Jesus Christ.

The debate between Jesus and the Jews continued over the authority by which He did as He was doing. He realized that His own testimony was not sufficient, because to the Jews two or more witnesses were required in every case. And so He presented the Father as a witness (v. 32), also John the Baptist whom the people would have remembered. Both the life and words of The Baptist testified brilliantly to Jesus, because he had burned himself out for Him. **He was the lamp that burneth and shineth; and ye were willing to rejoice for a season in his light** (v. 35). John's witness was bright and clear and the Jews had accepted it for a time. But the testimony of Jesus, given by both word and deed, was greater than that of John. Logic would demand that they give Jesus at least an equal hearing with John. They would not, even could not, believe Jesus because of two other witnesses which they had rejected: the Scriptures and Moses. Both had spoken — were still speaking — of Him, but the Jews had not received the message. The purpose of the Scriptures (the Old Testament) was to reveal Christ, and unless men were able to find Christ in them they gave no hope of salvation. Moses, too, testified of Christ, without whose life and work all that Moses did was fruitless. Both Scripture and Moses sat in judgment on those Jews who would not believe in Jesus. Those to whom Jesus was speaking were doubtless Scribes and Pharisees, also Sadducees to whom He may have addressed His words on the Resurrection, but in all their study of their Scriptures they had failed to see the promise of a Savior. Their false conception of the promised Messiah blinded them to Him when He was in their midst. They had become so perverse that they would sooner accept a leader who came in his own name than the One who had come in the name of God the Father. They had no real love for God, because they had neglected the admonition of the law of Moses: "Thou shalt love Jehovah thy God with all thy heart, and with all thy soul, and with all thy might" (Deut. 6:5). Consequently they could not recognize Him who was the embodiment of divine love.

We must recognize that Jesus never was unfair in what He expected of people, neither did He condemn them on insufficient grounds. Judaism had no power of salvation, and Jesus tried to show this to the Jews. At the same time, it had shown the path the Savior was to take and contained sufficient light by which to recognize Him. The law could not save, but it could and did condemn, when people accepted it as an end in itself, or when they used it to their own ends.

Still another emphasis of Jesus in this conflict of ideas is the unity of Scripture. If this be true of the Old Testament — that its central emphasis must be seen as Christ — how much more must the New Testament be seen as testifying primarily to Him. Jesus said of the Old Testament Scriptures, **These are they which bear witness of me** (v. 39). The unity of the whole Bible as we have it today cannot be found in its theology, or in its literary and historical consistency, but rather in its witness to the redeeming power of God in Jesus Christ the Son.

K. FEEDING THE MULTITUDE (6:1-15)

1 After these things Jesus went away to the other side of the sea of Galilee, which is *the sea* of Tiberias. 2 And a great multitude followed him, because they beheld the signs which he did on them that were sick. 3 And Jesus went up into the mountain, and there he sat with his disciples. 4 Now the passover, the feast of the Jews, was at hand. 5 Jesus therefore lifting up his eyes, and seeing that a great multitude cometh unto him, saith unto Philip, Whence are we to buy bread, that these may eat? 6 And this he said to prove him: for he himself knew what he would do. 7 Philip answered him, Two hundred shillings' worth of bread is not sufficient for them, that every one may take a little. 8 One of his disciples, Andrew, Simon Peter's brother, saith unto him, 9 There is a lad here, who hath five barley loaves, and two fishes: but what are these among so many? 10 Jesus said, Make the people sit down. Now there was much grass in the place. So the men sat down, in number about five thousand. 11 Jesus therefore took the loaves; and having

given thanks, he distributed to them that were set down; likewise also of the fishes as much as they would. 12 And when they were filled, he saith unto his disciples, Gather up the broken pieces which remain over, that nothing be lost. 13 So they gathered them up, and filled twelve baskets with broken pieces from the five barley loaves, which remained over unto them that had eaten. 14 When therefore the people saw the sign which he did, they said, This is of a truth the prophet that cometh into the world.

15 Jesus therefore perceiving that they were about to come and take him by force, to make him king, withdrew again into the mountain himself alone.

The feeding of the five thousand is recorded in all four Gospels, with some variations in the circumstances surrounding the incident. Matthew and Mark also record the feeding of the four thousand. John places the miracle after the account of the healing of the man at the pool of Bethesda. Some length of time must have elapsed between the two incidents in order for Jesus to go from Judea to Galilee and to heal a number of sick folk on the way (v. 2). The setting of this miracle is similar to that given by Matthew for the Sermon on the Mount — Jesus and His disciples on a mountain with a multitude of people nearby. The occasion was near the time of the Passover. This was one Passover during His ministry which Jesus did not attend, unless we transpose chapters five and six, so that the feast of 5:1 becomes the Passover of 6:4.[18] The multitude which He fed may have been on their way to the Passover. Jesus used the occasion for the discourse on the bread of life.

In the Synoptic Gospels, the disciples suggested to Jesus that something be done to care for the hungry crowd. In John, Jesus took the initiative, speaking to Philip and putting him to the test by asking him how they could purchase something for the people to eat. Why He asked Philip rather than Judas can only be guessed. Philip knew how much money was on hand — 200 denarii, worth about forty dollars — and it may be that he was treasurer of the disciple band in the early days, with Judas taking over the office at a later date. Philip failed

---

[18] G. H. C. Macgregor, "The Gospel of John," *The Moffatt New Testament Commentary*, p. 124.

utterly to think that Jesus might be going to perform another of His miraculous acts; he was not sensitive to the mood of Jesus and took His words literally, even as Nicodemus and the Samaritan woman had earlier. Philip responded that there was not enough money in the treasury to buy all the food that would be needed. Andrew seemed equally dull by suggesting that he had made an investigation and found only five loaves of bread and two fish in the crowd. On the other hand, Andrew may have caught a hint of what Jesus had in His mind, for John says that Jesus knew all the while what He would do. Perhaps like Mary at the wedding in Cana, Andrew did not think it amiss to give some suggestion to Jesus concerning what He should do.

Considerable detail is evident in the story, which seems to argue for its being an eye-witness report on the part of John. It may, however, signify no more than that the author saw the need of explaining details to his readers. He is the only writer who remembered that it was a lad who supplied the loaves and fish. He was careful to say that the Sea of Galilee was also called Tiberias, and that there was grass in the place where the people were gathered.

Nothing is said by John about the actual performing of the miracle, nothing which Jesus said or did as a signal for the multiplication of the food. He merely broke it up and passed it around until everyone had had enough. There is no indication that the miracle took place when Jesus returned thanks for the food. The evidence that a miracle had taken place was seen both in the amount of food which the crowd ate and in the amount which was left over. The twelve baskets which were required for the leftovers were doubtless the Jewish wallets or bags in which food for journeys was carried so that it would not be necessary to eat Gentile food. The facts that the people were hungry and that there were many empty baskets indicate that they had been away from home for some length of time. Their response to the miracle was typical of crowds of that day: **This is of a truth the prophet that cometh into the world** (v. 14. See also note on 4:19). They were ready to acclaim Him their king in fulfillment of

their messianic hope. They needed only a leader to incite them, or some encouraging word from Jesus. But He knew the weakness of their show of faith and purposefully avoided them by returning into the hills. Either He had come down onto the plain to meet the crowd, or He now withdrew deeper into the hill country to get away, apparently alone.

L. JESUS WALKING ON THE WATER (6:16-21)

16 And when evening came, his disciples went down unto the sea; 17 and they entered into a boat, and were going over the sea unto Capernaum. And it was now dark, and Jesus had not yet come to them. 18 And the sea was rising by reason of a great wind that blew. 19 When therefore they had rowed about five and twenty or thirty furlongs, they behold Jesus walking on the sea, and drawing nigh unto the boat: and they were afraid. 20 But he saith unto them, It is I; be not afraid. 21 They were willing therefore to receive him into the boat: and straightway the boat was at the land whither they were going.

John records another brief miracle — that of Jesus walking on the water. The disciples were on their way from Tiberias across the Lake to Capernaum when Jesus appeared to them on the water. His presence calmed the storm — "the winds ran away to their hiding, and the waves lay down at His feet like lambs." The Christian Church has found in this story a source of great comfort for those whose troubles distort the true image of things — the disciples were so afraid they did not recognize Jesus. But His **It is I, be not afraid** was enough to reassure them. And Matthew's version, telling of Peter's attempt to duplicate Jesus' act of water-walking and his fearful plunge into the lake, has become the classic illustration of bold action based upon weak faith; but at the same time it tells of Christ's nearness and His willingness and ability to save. It should not be forgotten, however, that Peter was the only one of the disciples who had enough courage to try to go to Jesus on the water.

The multiplication of the loaves and fish and the walking on the water are miracles which demonstrated the power of Jesus over nature in the realm of the preservation of life. He not only gives life, He also sustains it.

M. JESUS THE BREAD OF LIFE (6:22-71)

22 On the morrow the multitude that stood on the other side of the sea saw that there was no other boat there, save one, and that Jesus entered not with his disciples into the boat, but *that* his disciples went away alone 23 (howbeit there came boats from Tiberias nigh unto the place where they ate the bread after the Lord had given thanks) : 24 when the multitude therefore saw that Jesus was not there, neither his disciples, they themselves got into the boats, and came to Capernaum, seeking Jesus. 25 And when they found him on the other side of the sea, they said unto him, Rabbi, when camest thou hither? 26 Jesus answered them and said, Verily, verily, I say unto you, Ye seek me, not because ye saw signs, but because ye ate of the loaves, and were filled. 27 Work not for the food which perisheth, but for the food which abideth unto eternal life, which the Son of man shall give unto you: for him the Father, *even* God, hath sealed. 28 They said therefore unto him, What must we do, that we may work the works of God? 29 Jesus answered and said unto them, This is the work of God, that ye believe on him whom he hath sent. 30 They said therefore unto him, What then doest thou for a sign, that we may see, and believe thee? what workest thou? 31 Our fathers ate the manna in the wilderness; as it is written, He gave them bread out of heaven to eat. 32 Jesus therefore said unto them, Verily, verily, I say unto you, It was not Moses that gave you the bread out of heaven; but my Father giveth you the true bread out of heaven. 33 For the bread of God is that which cometh down out of heaven, and giveth life unto the world. 34 They said therefore unto him, Lord, evermore give us this bread. 35 Jesus said unto them, I am the bread of life: he that cometh to me shall not hunger, and he that believeth on me shall never thirst. 36 But I said unto you, that ye have seen me, and yet believe not. 37 All that which the Father giveth me shall come unto me; and him that cometh to me I will in no wise cast out. 38 For I am come down from heaven, not to do mine own will, but the will of him that sent me. 39 And this is the will of him that sent me, that of all that which he hath given me I should lose nothing, but should raise it up at the last day. 40 For this is the will of my Father, that every one that beholdeth the Son, and believeth on him, should have eternal life; and I will raise him up at the last day.

41 The Jews therefore murmured concerning him, because he said, I am the bread which came down out of heaven. 42 And they said, Is not this Jesus, the son of Joseph, whose father and mother we know? how doth he now say, I am come down out of heaven? 43 Jesus answered and said unto them, Murmur not among yourselves. 44 No man can come to me, except the Father that sent me draw him: and I will raise him up in the last day. 45 It is written in the prophets, And they shall all be taught of God. Every one that hath heard from the Father, and hath learned, cometh unto me. 46 Not that any man hath seen the Father, save he that is from God, he hath seen the Father. 47 Verily, verily, I say unto you, He that believeth hath eternal life. 48 I am the bread of life. 49 Your fathers ate the manna in the wilderness, and they died. 50 This is the bread which cometh down out of heaven, that a man may eat thereof, and not die. 51 I am the living bread which came down out of heaven: if any man eat of this bread, he shall live for ever: yea and the bread which I will give is my flesh, for the life of the world.

52 The Jews therefore strove one with another, saying, How can this man give us his flesh to eat? 53 Jesus therefore said unto them, Verily, verily, I say unto you, Except ye eat the flesh of the Son of man and drink his blood, ye have not life in yourselves. 54 He that eateth my flesh and drinketh my blood hath eternal life; and I will raise him up at the last day. 55 For my flesh is meat indeed, and my blood is drink indeed. 56 He that eateth my flesh and drinketh my blood abideth in me, and I in him. 57 As the living Father sent me, and I live because of the Father; so he that eateth me, he also shall live because of me. 58 This is the bread which came down out of heaven: not as the fathers ate, and died; he that eateth this bread shall live for ever. 59 These things said he in the synagogue, as he taught in Capernaum.

60 Many therefore of his disciples, when they heard *this*, said, This is a hard saying; who can hear it? 61 But Jesus knowing in himself that his disciples murmured at this, said unto them, Doth this cause you to stumble? 64 *What* then if you should behold the Son of man ascending where he was before? 63 It is the spirit that giveth life; the flesh profiteth noth-

ing: the words that I have spoken unto you are spirit, and are life. 64 But there are some of you that believe not. For Jesus knew from the beginning who they were that believed not, and who it was that should betray him. 65 And he said, For this cause have I said unto you, that no man can come unto me, except it be given unto him of the Father.

66 Upon this many of his disciples went back, and walked no more with him. 67 Jesus said therefore unto the twelve, Would ye also go away? 68 Simon Peter answered him, Lord, to whom shall we go? thou hast the words of eternal life. 69 And we have believed and know that thou art the Holy One of God. 70 Jesus answered them, Did not I choose you the twelve, and one of you is a devil? 71 Now he spake of Judas *the son* of Simon Iscariot, for he it was that should betray him, *being* one of the twelve.

The miracle of the feeding of the multitude took place on the eastern side of the Sea of Galilee. In the early morning, after the storm at sea, Jesus and His disciples anchored their boat at Capernaum. Meanwhile, some boats from Tiberias had stopped near the place of the feeding and some of the people took passage on the boats to Capernaum to find Jesus. There is no reason to think that there were enough boats to transport the entire crowd. As many went as the boats would hold. This explanation of the manner in which the people got across the lake is in keeping with John's custom of establishing proper settings for the discourses of Jesus.

The crowd to whom Jesus gave the discourse on the bread of life was probably made up largely of Jews. Jesus referred to the giving of manna by Moses (v. 32); The Jews murmured at Him (v. 41); they disputed among themselves (v. 52); and the meeting took place in the synagogue at Capernaum (v. 59). The Greek text suggests that in their disputings the Jews came to blows among themselves.[19] Seeing a number of people from the multitude of the day before, Jesus accused them of following Him for the food they had received gratis. At the same time He proceeded to tell them of the **true bread out of heaven** (v. 32). He knew there were hungers in the human heart that are deeper than the hunger for food, hungers

which must be awakened before they can be satisfied. Jesus looked beyond the dense materialism of the people and saw the inner needs of their lives. And there followed one of the greatest discourses of the entire ministry of our Lord. The great truth He taught has lingered through the centuries in the sacrament of the Lord's Supper. Opinion is divided over the eucharistic significance of this discourse. Most certainly verse 51 is eucharistic in content, but that the entire sermon was so intended is not certain.

There is a noticeable parallel between this occasion and that at Jacob's well (ch. 4). Bread takes the place of water. In the analogies water becomes the water of life — eternal or spiritual water — and bread becomes the bread of life — eternal or spiritual bread. In the present case the analogy is strengthened, and Jesus is the Bread of Life. As the result of the words of Jesus, the woman is brought to ask for the living water, and the crowd is brought to ask for bread. As would be expected, Jesus did not receive the believing response from the synagogue crowd that he had received from the Samaritan woman.

The crowd at Capernaum was a typical, curiosity-seeking group of people, interested primarily in what gain they might make of this miracle-worker whom they hoped would prove to be their messiah, their political deliverer from the lordship of Rome. They may have interpreted the feeding of the multitude as a political hand-out. At the same time, the claim of Jesus to the power and favor of God caught their imagination. **What can we do, that we may work the works of God?** they asked. What could they do to forward this movement which seemed to be taking root? The miracle of the loaves and fish the day before had not seemed to impress them very strongly. At least they wanted confirmation that what they had witnessed was the rule and not the exception, and so they asked Him for another sign or miracle. Moses had given Israel manna in the wilderness; could He prove His claim to national leadership as conclusively as Moses had proved his?

This was the lead which prefaced Jesus' bread-of-life discussion. It was not Moses

19 A. T. Robertson, *The Divinity of Christ,* p. 74.

but God who had provided the manna for Israel. Moreover, that "bread from heaven" typified the true Bread which God even then was offering them. Both the manna in the wilderness and yesterday's food on the mountain were meant to help them to recognize Him who was the Bread of Life. Their reply — **Lord, evermore give us this bread** — placed them with a growing number of listeners who asked naive questions or made inappropriate remarks because they could not comprehend divine truth. But they were still listening, and Jesus uttered one of His most direct statements of truth: **I am the bread of life: he that cometh to me shall not hunger, and he that believeth on me shall never thirst** (v. 36). Even then God was at work, offering them the bread of eternal life. If they could see and believe, bread for the soul and not just for the body was before them. **This is the will of my Father, that everyone that beholdeth the Son, and believeth on him, should have eternal life** (v. 40). No greater or more open appeal had been given by Jesus up to that time. At first He was annoyed by the callous materialism of the crowd; but soon He was the searching Savior who sought to win them. "Jesus almost cast pearls before swine in His patient endeavor to help these people see what sort of a Messiah He really was, in contrast to the political hopes expressed the afternoon before."[20] But they could only murmur among themselves over His claim to having come from heaven; He could not be of heavenly origin because His parents were well known in that area. It is worthy of note that John, who places greatest stress upon the deity of Jesus, in this instance records the fact that He is called the son of Joseph. He does not tell of the Virgin Birth, believing that the claim to Christ's deity must be substantiated by His life and works rather than only by the manner of His birth. Would the claim of Jesus to a virgin birth have been any more readily received than His declaration that He was the **living bread that came down out of heaven?** Doubtless not, because faith in both His person and His message must be based upon what God was doing through Him. Miracles were being wrought and a great

appeal for faith was going out. By all that Jesus did and said, He was trying to make God known. It is the appeal which has always been made by the Gospel. God draws, but men must respond in faith. "Accept Him who is the Bread of Life" was the message, but because people were dead to spiritual things, they turned away and continued to argue among themselves.

And so Jesus carried His analogy to its ultimate conclusion: **My flesh is meat indeed and my blood is drink indeed** (v. 55). **He who eats my flesh and drinks my blood has eternal life** (v. 54). It is impossible for Christians today to understand these sayings without a high degree of spiritual insight. The early Christians were accused of eating human sacrifices in their eucharistic feasts. And missionaries today in some parts of Africa must take great care to explain what is meant by "This is Christ's body, this is Christ's blood" in the observance of the Lord's Supper. And so it is not strange that Jesus met with only misunderstanding and criticism. John does not say what came of this discourse; the account closes with the people murmuring. The final response may have been more favorable than depicted, as in the case of Nicodemus. John tells only enough to get across the analogy of Jesus as the Bread of Life.

There was a definite reaction on the part of some of the disciples of Christ (not the twelve). "We cannot stomach this," they said (Weymouth). Jesus proceeded to explain to them the difference between flesh and spirit. Only a spiritual interpretation placed upon the words could possibly make sense. **The words that I have spoken unto you are spirit, and are life** (v. 63). Why had He not said this to the crowd of Jews? Because He had already gone further than they were able to follow. And even some disciples — those who previously had believed on Him — turned back and no longer followed Him. Thus were men tested — thus did Jesus become their judge — thus were their lives determined by their response to Him. Some had been drawn to Him, perhaps out of curiosity or because of the attractiveness which must have radiated from His personality, but faith had not become operative within them. They were like the hard soil upon which the seed fell, only to be stolen away before it had rooted. Others, the twelve included, heard and believed. **Would ye also go away?** Jesus asked. "The form of the question expects a negative answer, but the mere asking of it shows how much Jesus took to heart this rejection by the populace when He longed to save."[21] It was as though Jesus was giving the twelve an opportunity to follow the crowd. But Peter spoke for the group, **Lord, to whom shall we go? thou hast the words of eternal life. And we have believed and know that thou art the Holy One of God** (vv. 68-69). How this must have cheered the heart of our Lord! Yet there was sadness mingled with the joy. For He knew that Peter would one day deny Him — disown Him in public; and that Judas would betray Him to be crucified.

N. MISUNDERSTANDING AND DELAY (7:1-13)

1 And after these things Jesus walked in Galilee: for he would not walk in Judaea, because the Jews sought to kill him. 2 Now the feast of the Jews, the feast of tabernacles, was at hand. 3 His brethren therefore said unto him, Depart hence, and go into Judaea, that thy disciples also may behold thy works which thou doest. 4 For no man doeth anything in secret, and himself seeketh to be known openly. If thou doest these things, manifest thyself to the world. 5 For even his brethren did not believe on him. 6 Jesus therefore saith unto them, My time is not yet come; but your time is always ready. 7 The world cannot hate you; but me it hateth, because I testify of it, that its works are evil. 8 Go ye up unto the feast: I go not up unto this feast; because my time is not yet fulfilled. 9 And having said these things unto them, he abode *still* in Galilee.

10 But when his brethren were gone up unto the feast, then went he also up, not publicly, but as it were in secret. 11 The Jews therefore sought him at the feast, and said, Where is he? 12 And there was much murmuring among the multitudes concerning him: some said, He is a good man; others said, Not so, but he leadeth the multitude astray. 13 Yet no man spake openly of him for fear of the Jews.

The results of the rejection of Jesus by the Jews at Capernaum were not long in coming. As was suggested earlier, the multitude which Jesus fed may have been on their way to the Feast of Tabernacles in Jerusalem. And so those to whom He had spoken of the Bread of Life spread the word of His claim to equality with God and stirred up the Temple authorities against Him. Jesus stayed in Galilee because He knew that plans were afoot to do away with Him if He were caught in Jerusalem. The authority of the Sanhedrin, at that time, apparently did not extend beyond the borders of Judea. Later, however, its authority covered an expanded territory, because Saul of Tarsus received permission from the chief priests to persecute Christians as far away as Damascus, in Syria.

Jesus was now in home territory. He may even have taken a short trip to His old home in Nazareth because His brothers knew what was going on. They did not believe in Him and began to taunt Him, insinuating that He was a coward and did not dare to face the Jews again. Their slurs suggested that perhaps He realized that He had overextended Himself, having made claims that were too extravagant — that He would be ashamed to face again those who had heard Him. **Depart hence, and go into Judea, that thy disciples also may behold thy works which thou doest,** they said (v. 3). This is sarcasm pure and simple. The twelve were with Jesus, and so the brothers must have been referring to those who had recently ceased to follow Him. The brothers said, in effect: "They would still be your disciples and you would be on your way to success if you had not bungled things so badly." This must have been one of the low spots in the career of Jesus. The multitude, some of the disciples, and now His brothers, had all turned against Him. This whole episode made Him conscious of the fact that He was treading the winepress alone, and alone one day would go to the cross.

At the same time, Jesus did not take these insults without answering. To paraphrase His reply: "The people in Jerusalem seek to kill me, for I have revealed to them the evil of their ways. They do not hate you because you are a part of their following. Go on up to Jerusalem and celebrate the Feast with them. Worship with them while they plot to kill me." Whether or not His brothers felt the bite in His words, they left for Jerusalem and the Feast of Tabernacles, secure in the belief that they had a fanatic for a brother. In response to their urging that He go to Jerusalem, Jesus had given them the same answer He gave to Mary at the Cana wedding: **My time is not yet come** (v. 6). (This is not to say that Mary had spoken in the same spirit in which her sons talked with Jesus. Presumably she was at home at this time but took no part in their outburst.) Jesus did not say that He was not going to the feast, but that He was not going with them. The kind of publicity which He would have received by traveling in a public caravan would have been detrimental; therefore He chose to go privately. In this He proved to be right, because the Jews in Jerusalem were expecting Him to come, and they continued to search for Him when He did not arrive with the crowd. Their spirit of opposition to Him was so strong that the people of the city were afraid to express any opinion in public, either for or against Him. The Jews in this instance were probably the Jewish leaders who had been inflamed by those Jews from Galilee who had rejected Jesus at the meeting in the Capernaum synagogue.

It is proper to let a consecrated imagination take up the story at this point. By the time the Galileans had journeyed to Jerusalem on foot, all the while continuing among themselves the debate over the Bread of Life issue, they had probably developed a strong case against Him in their minds, regardless of the facts. It then became their religious duty to expose this man, and so they sought to set a trap for Him. There is no doubt that Jesus suffered much from the misrepresentation of events and circumstances by those who opposed Him.

O. CONTROVERSY WITH THE JEWS (7:14-52)

14 But when it was now the midst of the feast Jesus went up into the temple, and taught. 15 The Jews therefore marvelled, saying, How knoweth this man letters, having never learned? 16 Jesus therefore answered them, and said, My teaching is not mine, but his that sent me. 17 If any man willeth to do his will, he shall know of the teaching, whether it is of God, or *whether* I speak from myself. 18 He that speaketh from himself seeketh his own glory: but he that seeketh the glory of him that sent him, the same is true, and no unrighteousness is in him. 19 Did not Moses give you the law, and *yet* none of you doeth the law? Why seek ye to kill me? 20 The multitude answered, Thou hast a demon: who seeketh to kill thee? 21 Jesus answered and said unto them, I did one work, and ye all marvel because thereof. 22 Moses hath given you circumcision (not that it is of Moses, but of the fathers); and on the sabbath ye circumcise a man. 23 If a man receiveth circumcision on the sabbath, that the law of Moses may not be broken; are ye wroth with me, because I made a man every whit whole on the sabbath? 24 Judge not according to appearance, but judge righteous judgment.

25 Some therefore of them of Jerusalem said, Is not this he whom they seek to kill? 26 And lo, he speaketh openly, and they say nothing unto him. Can it be that the rulers indeed know that this is the Christ? 27 Howbeit we know this man whence he is: but when the Christ cometh, no one knoweth whence he is. 28 Jesus therefore cried in the temple, teaching and saying, Ye both know me, and know whence I am; and I am not come of myself, but he that sent me is true, whom ye know not. 29 I know him; because I am from him, and he sent me. 30 They sought therefore to take him: and no man laid his hand on him, because his hour was not yet come. 31 But of the multitude many believed on him; and they said, When the Christ shall come, will he do more signs than those which this man hath done? 32 The Pharisees heard the multitude murmuring these things concerning him; and the chief priests and the Pharisees sent officers to take him. 33 Jesus therefore said, Yet a little while am I with you, and I go unto him that sent me. 34 Ye shall seek me, and shall not find me: and where I am, ye cannot come. 35 The Jews therefore said among themselves, Whither will this man go that we shall not find him? will he go unto the Dispersion among the Greeks, and teach the Greeks? 36 What is this word that he said, Ye shall seek me, and shall not find me; and where I am, ye cannot come?

37 Now on the last day, the great *day* of the feast, Jesus stood and cried, saying, If any man thirst, let him come unto me and drink. 38 He that believeth on me, as the scripture hath said, from within him shall flow rivers of living water. 39 But this spake he of the Spirit, which they that believed on him were to receive: for the Spirit was not yet *given*; because Jesus was not yet glorified. 40 *Some* of the multitude therefore, when they heard these words, said, This is of a truth the prophet. 41 Others said, This is the Christ. But some said, What, doth the Christ come out of Galilee? 42 Hath not the scripture said that the Christ cometh of the seed of David, and from Bethlehem, the village where David was? 43 So there arose a division in the multitude because of him. 44 And some of them would have taken him; but no man laid hands on him.

45 The officers therefore came to the chief priests and Pharisees; and they said unto them, Why did ye not bring him? 46 The officers answered, Never man so spake. 47 The Pharisees therefore answered them, Are ye also led astray? 48 Hath any of the rulers believed on him, or of the Pharisees? 49 But this multitude that knoweth not the law are accursed. 50 Nicodemus saith unto them (he that came to him before, being one of them), 51 Doth our law judge a man, except it first hear from himself and know what he doeth? 52 They answered and said unto him, Art thou also of Galilee? Search, and see that out of Galilee ariseth no prophet.

The strategy of Jesus at this time is both important and interesting. By going to the Feast alone and in quiet, He thwarted any attempt to arrest Him upon His arrival. Then He went to the Temple, mingled with the people, taught them and gained their favor. For a time He seemed to have been lost in the crowd. The Jews who heard Him and marvelled at His teaching (v. 15) were doubtless the general populace of Jerusalem or visiting Jews attending the Feast, rather than the Temple leaders, the Sanhedrin. They were astonished at the ability of Jesus to speak as He did when He had not been a student of the Law at Jerusalem, as well as at the doctrine He taught. What follows reads like a continuation of the discourse in chapter 5. It contains the same defense of His

teachings as He had previously given of His miracles — in both instances He was doing the bidding of His heavenly Father. Some scholars think that a dislocation of the text has separated these two chapters by the insertion of chapter 6 from its original place before chapter 5.[22] In addition, His reference (v. 23) to an act of healing on the Sabbath seems to point to the healing of the lame man at the pool of Bethesda, for no such incident is found in either chapter 6 or chapter 7.

However this may be, Jesus not only again claimed divine authority for His teaching, but He also suggested a method whereby the people could know if He spoke the truth: **If any man willeth to do his will, he shall know of the teaching, whether it is of God, or whether I speak of myself** (v. 17). In other words, by an exertion of the will, by choosing deliberately to conform his life to the teaching of Jesus, a man could be assured of its divine origin and authority. The proof of His teaching can only be found in the doing of it. The Jews had not kept the Law of Moses (the Ten Commandments), and this failure set the pattern for them to reject Jesus. The Law had been given as a "tutor to bring us unto Christ" (Gal. 3:24), but it had not done that for them because they had neglected, if not rejected, it. At the same time they were observing the ceremonies of the Law on the Sabbath by circumcising a man. If they allowed this practice, why did they criticize Jesus for healing on the Sabbath Day? "If then the Sabbath could give way to ceremonial ordinance, how much more to a work of mercy? The law of charity is higher than any ceremonial law."[23]

The moving of Jesus from Galilee to Jerusalem in a secret manner, followed by His teaching in the Temple, may have been intended to remind the Jerusalem Jews of the promised Messiah for the Jews had a tradition among them, perhaps stemming from Malachi 3:1 and developed in some of the books of the Apocrypha, that the Messiah would appear suddenly and shrouded in mystery. The crowd conjectured that the Temple authorities had come to recognize Jesus as Messiah, this being the reason that

22 Macgregor, *op. cit.*, pp. 124f.
23 Alfred Plummer, "The Gospel According to St. John," *Cambridge Greek Testament,* p. 173.

they did not arrest Him, but rather allowed Him to teach. Yet this could not be, because the authorities knew where Jesus had come from, and His background could have been no mystery to them. But the way was again opened for Jesus to declare His relationship with God — that God had sent Him into the world and that He had come from God. And because neither His person nor His teaching fitted the pattern which the Jews had fashioned for their Messiah, efforts were made to arrest Him.

At this point John seems to refute any previous idea that Jesus had delayed this visit to Jerusalem in order to throw the authorities off the trail. He says that they were unable to take Him **because his hour was not yet come** (v. 30). Two things need to be said concerning this. First, these two aspects of the situation — which may be seen as the human and the divine — may be paradoxical, but they are not contradictory. Christ's dependence upon the Father for the working out of His life's plan, and His own essential deity, did not eliminate His need of care and caution. The strongest or greatest reliance upon God always produces the greatest degree of carefulness and vigilance, along with a high sense of responsibility. Careless faith is presumptuous. Jesus demonstrated personal, responsible faith.

Second, the expression "my time is not yet come" has a wider connotation here than when it was used previously (2:4; 7:6). There it was used when Jesus was requested to do something as an indication that He was following the directions of God, not those of man. In the present instance the expression explicitly states that a timetable has been established for the *main* events of the life of Jesus. The time would come in the providence of God when Jesus would be arrested and put to death, but until that time came no man could successfully lay hands on Him for these purposes.

As a result of this episode in the Temple, **many believe on him.** As has been noted before, such belief was very limited, to say the least. Probably it means that they believed what Jesus said without understanding it well enough for it to make a difference in their

attitude toward Him when the issues were clearly drawn. It was belief rather than conviction, a syllogistic rather than a committed faith. They said, **When the Christ shall come, will he do more signs than those which this man hath done?** (v. 31). Many more people, however, completely rejected all that Jesus taught, and the turmoil which resulted from this division within the crowd brought about the attempt to kill Jesus. The chief priests and Pharisees united against Him. The chief priests were Sadducees who came from aristocratic stock, while the Pharisees were from the common people. The officers who had been sent for the arrest were powerless to do anything (v. 30), and the people were mystified at Jesus and all that He did. His words at any time might have given pause to any group of people, because He talked of going away — going to one who had sent Him — going where they could neither find nor follow Him. They conjectured that He was going to the Greek-speaking Jews of the Diaspora to teach them; and this may be part of the immediate reason for the failure to arrest Him. Jesus apparently continued to teach throughout the days of the Feast. On seven of the eight days of the Feast the priests poured water from the pool of Siloam on the altar. The last day was a day of holy convocation, the day when the worshipers ceased to live in tents and returned to their normal dwellings.[24] On this last day, apparently sensing that many of the people were returning home with a deep sense of inner dissatisfaction and of spiritual needs unmet, Jesus got the attention of the milling crowd and made one of His most winsome appeals. **If any man thirst, let him come unto me and drink. He that believeth on me, as the scripture hath said, from within him shall flow rivers of living water.** (vv. 37-38). They would have been reminded of Isaiah 44:3 and 55:1. Jesus promised them living water with the guaranteed result that believers would themselves become fountains from which this water of life would flow to others. The Psalmist claimed that his cup was full to running over, as he slaked his thirst at the quiet waters of God's goodness and mercy (Ps. 23). To the woman of Sa-

24 Marcus Dods, "The Gospel According to St. John," *The Expositer's Greek Testament,* Vol. 1, p. 767.

maria Jesus said that the water He would give would be within her a well of eternal, life-giving water (John 4:14). And now to the Temple multitude Jesus offered rivers of living water. Little wonder that the Christian church has perpetuated this beautiful analogy in sermon and song.

John interpreted this living water as the Holy Spirit which was later given to the disciples on the Day of Pentecost. He was careful to explain that **the Spirit was not yet given: because Jesus was not yet glorified** (v. 39). "The rabbinical teaching was that the Holy Spirit had departed from Israel when the last of the prophets, Zechariah and Malachi, died. They looked for a fresh outpouring in the Messianic age."[25] In his sermon on the Day of Pentecost, Peter quoted from the prophecy of Joel: "And it shall be in the last days, saith God, I will pour out of my Spirit upon all flesh" (Acts 2:17).

Jesus was trying to make the Jews see that He was the fulfillment of their highest national and personal aspirations. John believed that the redemptive work of Christ became effectual on the Day of Pentecost when the Spirit descended on the group of disciples. The giving of the Spirit was necessary for the ministry and atoning death of Jesus to have its destined effect. In fact, that great collective experience in the upper room was no afterthought; it was as much a part of the redemptive plan as the Virgin Birth, the Crucifixion, or the Resurrection. The very evident corollary of this truth is that the redemptive work of Christ in the life of the individual is made effective by the Spirit working within and through him like a flowing, cleansing stream.[26]

It is difficult to imagine that an informed religious Jew would be unable to catch the truth Jesus sought to emphasize in the analogy of water, in relation to their own religious heritage. They could not be expected to understand all that the author John knew as the result of his own later experience. But at least honest minds could have demonstrated a receptive attitude. Many of them did perceive that He was the prophet promised by Moses (v. 40), or even that He was the

Messiah (v. 41). But as always there were those who could not see the truth because they would not see it. Jesus had led them to the water, but He could not make them drink. Others of the Jews (probably members of the Sanhedrin) managed to divide the crowd over the technicality that Jesus was from Nazareth in Galilee and not from Bethlehem in Judea where the messianic son of David was supposed to be born (v. 42-44). Jesus made no attempt to set them straight on His place of birth, doubtless feeling that men who chose to base their arguments on such a weak premise could never be convinced of the truth. The perversity of the human heart seldom has been seen in greater evidence than on that day.

The officers whom the chief priests and Pharisees sent to arrest Jesus must have lingered in the Temple until the last day of the Feast, hoping to find their opportunity. But the delay did something to them, for they found barriers to their mission higher than circumstances and stronger than their constituted authority. **Never man so spake,** they reported to their superiors. Here was a man whom they could not touch: overpowering awe gripped them, and the iron of their military discipline melted before Him. They were as Moses before the burning bush, the Israelites before the mountain that thundered and shook, or as Saul of Tarsus on the Damascus road. Perhaps these officers should be counted among the believers; they did not deny the charge (v. 47). And again here we find the strangers, the outsiders, responding to Jesus with interest and understanding, with those on the inside, the chosen people, rejecting the truth and cursing those who did accept it.

The condemnation of Jesus by the Pharisees (probably those on the Council) drew a remonstrance from one of their number — Nicodemus, the one who had come to Jesus by night. **Doth our law judge a man,** he said, **except it first hear from himself and know what he doth?** But they dismissed the plea and found in their law, not justice, but what they wanted to find — a technicality on which to support their verdict. As they chose to put it, the Messianic hope

[25] R. H. Strachan, *The Fourth Gospel*, p. 203.

[26] See commentary on chapters 14 and 16.

arose in Judah and would see its fulfillment in Judea; but Jesus was from Galilee. No other evidence was needed to settle the controversy. And so Nicodemus was silenced and the verdict against Jesus stood. But as we proceed, it will be seen how really weak and irresolute the Pharisees were. In the conflict with Jesus He beat them at their own game, and they threw up their hands in hopeless despair of ever disposing of Him.

In spite of this brave attempt by Nicodemus, he is considered a disappointment to this day. Could he have carried his case further? Could he have spearheaded a reform movement among his colleagues? What might have been the result? Did Nicodemus stand at a pivotal point in history, with the key to the future in his hands — and fail? Who can say? He was outnumbered, to be sure, by the Pharisees on the Council, and he was outweighed by the Sadducees among whom was the high priest; but only one is needed at such a time if he is of the right caliber. The stakes were high and Nicodemus had much to gain or lose; but he did not go far enough to run any risk. He let the flow of circumstances decide the issue for him. He reminds one of Eutychus, who sat on the window ledge (Acts 20:7-12) and finally fell off on the wrong side — the outside, three stories up. And he becomes the type of all those who try to serve Christ while allowing sin and the world to exert their pressure and decide the big issues of life — those who try to serve both God and mammon. Nicodemus must have lost influence among both the Pharisees and the disciples of Jesus, for by this incident he revealed his lack of full allegiance to either group. If not as bad as Judas who sold his Lord, Nicodemus was no better than Peter who denied Him.

P. JESUS AND THE ADULTEROUS WOMAN (7:53-8:11)

53 [And they went every man unto his own house: 1 but Jesus went unto the mount of Olives. 2 And early in the morning he came again into the temple, and all the people came unto him; and he sat down, and taught them. 3 And the scribes and the Pharisees bring a woman taken in adultery; and having set her in the midst, 4 they say unto him, Teacher, this woman hath been taken in adultery, in the very act. 5 Now in the law Moses commanded us to stone such: what then sayest thou of her? 6 And this they said, trying him, that they might have *whereof* to accuse him. But Jesus stooped down, and with his finger wrote on the ground. 7 But when they continued asking him, he lifted up himself, and said unto them, He that is without sin among you, let him first cast a stone at her. 8 And again he stooped down, and with his finger wrote on the ground. 9 And they, when they heard it, went out one by one, beginning from the eldest, *even* unto the last: and Jesus was left alone, and the woman, where she was, in the midst. 10 And Jesus lifted up himself, and said unto her, Woman, where are they? did no man condemn thee? 11 And she said, No man, Lord. And Jesus said, Neither do I condemn thee: go thy way; from henceforth sin no more.]

It is generally agreed that this portion of the Gospel of John was not part of the original; it cannot be supported with sufficient textual evidence. However, the story is true to the spirit of the Gospel and it fits quite naturally into the narrative at this point. The scribes (not chief priests as in the last story) and the Pharisees set the stage to trick Jesus into committing Himself concerning an interpretation of the law of Moses. There were the adulterous woman, her accusers (and His), and the pointed question, **In the law Moses commanded us to stone such: what then sayest thou of her? (8:5).** The effect of the response made by Jesus was to put the scribes and Pharisees, rather than the woman, under judgment. His silent writing in the dust provoked them to greater insistency for an answer, but His single remark caught them in their own guilt: **He that is without sin among you, let him first cast a stone at her.** One by one they slipped away silently. To the woman He pronounced His judgment upon her case: **Go thy way; from henceforth sin no more. (v. 11).** This is her sentence — freedom from her old life, with much more than a hint of God's grace to live by. "Her judgment is not one of condemnation, but of liberation."[27]

27 Strachan, *op. cit.*, p. 205.

Q. JESUS THE LIGHT OF THE WORLD (8:12-20)

12 Again therefore Jesus spake unto them, saying, I am the light of the world: he that followeth me shall not walk in the darkness, but shall have the light of life. 13 The Pharisees therefore said unto him, Thou bearest witness of thyself; thy witness is not true. 14 Jesus answered and said unto them, Even if I bear witness of myself, my witness is true; for I know whence I came, and whither I go; but ye know not whence I come, or whither I go. 15 Ye judge after the flesh; I judge no man. 16 Yea and if I judge, my judgment is true; for I am not alone, but I and the Father that sent me. 17 Yea and in your law it is written, that the witness of two men is true. 18 I am he that beareth witness of myself, and the Father that sent me beareth witness of me. 19 They said therefore unto him, Where is thy Father? Jesus answered, Ye know neither me, nor my Father: if ye knew me, ye would know my Father also. 20 These words spake he in the treasury, as he taught in the temple: and no man took him; because his hour was not yet come.

The controversy between Jesus and the Jews, especially the Pharisees, continued. This phase of it was introduced by the claim of Christ that He was the light of the world, and that He could dispense that light to all who believed in Him. This is similar to the Prologue statement: "In him was life; and the life was the light of men" (1:4). Light and life are closely associated in John's Gospel, having moral and spiritual significance. This topic is not elaborated upon as were the concepts of living water and living bread. The Pharisees challenged Jesus on the basis of His own testimony which stood alone, because the law of Moses required two witnesses to any claim. His answer was that the Father was His co-witness, making His claim valid. But He did not expect them to believe Him or to accept the testimony of the Father, because they were not able to discern spiritual truth. They did not know either Jesus or the Father. This was His indictment against them: the law of Moses had ceased to be a revelation of God to them. Knowledge of Jesus and of God the Father were alike, if not identical. There were those who would have liked to arrest Him, but **his time [was] not yet come.**

R. YE CANNOT FOLLOW ME (8:21-30)

21 He said therefore again unto them, I go away, and ye shall seek me, and shall die in your sin: whither I go, ye cannot come. 22 The Jews therefore said, Will he kill himself, that he saith, Whither I go, ye cannot come? 23 And he said unto them, Ye are from beneath; I am from above: ye are of this world; I am not of this world. 24 I said therefore unto you, that ye shall die in your sins: for except ye believe that I am *he*, ye shall die in your sins. 25 They said therefore unto him, Who art thou? Jesus said unto them, Even that which I have also spoken unto you from the beginning. 26 I have many things to speak and to judge concerning you; howbeit he that sent me is true; and the things which I heard from him, these speak I unto the world. 27 They perceived not that he spake to them of the Father. 28 Jesus therefore said, When ye have lifted up the Son of man, then shall ye know that I am *he*, and *that* I do nothing of myself, but as the Father taught me, I speak these things. 29 And he that sent me is with me; he hath not left me alone; for I do always the things that are pleasing to him. 30 As he spake these things, many believed on him.

Jesus seemed determined to continue the controversy with the Jews. He set Himself against the entrenched moral and religious leaders of His day. They could not come to an understanding of spiritual truth through the law or by logical processes, because they could not understand Him. They had no standard by which to judge Him. He stood among them, God incarnate, trying to touch something in them that would respond — to kindle some spark, to tap some latent desire, or, perhaps, to create an attitude of respect and willingness to listen. Their utter unawareness of His real person, their blindness to light, and their insensibility to their own amoral state, were in miniature the world which "knew him not" and "received him not" (1:10-11). There was a certain timelessness about the struggle; it was a cosmic struggle being waged in the arena of this world. It was the redeeming God giving Himself in total dedication to those who chose to resist the gift. It was a contest of wills, but it was more than that. By the Incarnation, by this intrusion of God upon man's complacent sinfulness,

God has stamped something of His image upon man in a way not known in the original creation, and man can never be the same again. The mark is there because of Him who became man in order to make God known. It became the mark of man's destiny. Its analogy is light: light spurned is darkness and death; light embraced is life. Its analogy is water and bread — refusal brings starvation and death; acceptance brings life eternal. Because God became man in Jesus *homo sapiens* carries upon it the mark of the world's Redeemer, just as deity was marked by taking the human form. Instinctively man recognizes this mark upon him. That mark is the mark of love; where love is not the basis of relationships, personal and national, man destroys himself. That mark is righteousness; where righteousness is not made the norm for the activities of life, man victimizes himself. That mark is holiness; where holiness of character and purpose does not prevail, man degenerates by his own moral diseases. That mark is a voice — "this is the way, walk ye in it." That mark is the sign of the cross — the guiltless dying for the guilty, that his guilt might be taken away. That mark is the golden rule; it is every noble impulse; it is the sinner's fear of punishment; it is the spontaneous prayer in times of need or danger. If man would but heed the law of conscience, he would find it a schoolmaster which would lead him to Christ.

In simpler terms, Jesus Christ is the determining factor in man's ultimate destiny. By the Incarnation, God designated men to be His children; by the Incarnation, the alternatives of man's choices are written within and pronounced without. He continues to struggle against the choice which God has made (Eph. 1:5); and Christ, in the person of the Holy Spirit, continues the struggle for men's hearts and minds, the struggle in which He engaged with the Jews in Jerusalem, essentially a contest of wills.

To return to the case history, the minds of the Pharisees could not rise above the natural plane. To them Christ's going away (v. 21) could mean only physical death, perhaps by suicide. His claim to supernatural origin mystified

them. After the many times when they had heard Him speak and had seen the signs (miracles) which He performed, they still saw no connection between Jesus and God, as they knew Him from the Old Testament. The reason for this was that they wanted to know before they would believe — and that would not be faith. Faith must always pioneer the way to the assurance of acquired knowledge. Because they would not believe, would not take a step in faith, they would die in their sins. When Jesus told of His coming death, also saying very bluntly that their continued efforts to find cause against Him would bring about that death, many of them relented and gave assent to what He had been saying — **Many believed in Him** (v. 30). This expression does not denote what we know theologically as saving faith. It means that the faith of these people was placed in Jesus as one who told the truth, and that they were willing to lay aside their own opinions on the controversial matters while they learned better what was the truth. It is stronger than the belief which only signified the acceptance of what Jesus said.[28]

S. THE TRUTH SHALL MAKE YOU FREE (8:31-59)

31 Jesus therefore said to those Jews that had believed him, If ye abide in my word, *then* are ye truly my disciples; 32 and ye shall know the truth, and the truth shall make you free. 33 They answered unto him, We are Abraham's seed, and have never yet been in bondage to any man: how sayest thou, Ye shall be made free? 34 Jesus answered them, Verily, verily I say unto you, Every one that committeth sin is the bondservant of sin. 35 And the bondservant abideth not in the house for ever: the son abideth for ever. 36 If therefore the Son shall make you free, ye shall be free indeed. 37 I know that ye are Abraham's seed, yet ye seek to kill me, because my word hath not free course in you. 38 I speak the things which I have seen with *my* Father: and ye also do the things which ye heard from *your* father. 39 They answered and said unto him, Our father is Abraham. Jesus saith unto them, If ye were Abraham's children, ye would do the works of Abraham. 40 But now ye seek to kill me, a man that hath told you the truth, which I heard from God:

28 Westcott, *op. cit.*, p. 132.

this did not Abraham. 41 Ye do the works of your father. They said unto him, We were not born of fornication; we have one Father, *even* God. 42 Jesus said unto them, If God were your Father, ye would love me: for I came forth and am come from God; for neither have I come of myself, but he sent me. 43 Why do ye not understand my speech? *Even* because ye cannot hear my word. 44 Ye are of *your* father the devil, and the lusts of your father it is your will to do. He was a murderer from the beginning, and standeth not in the truth, because there is no truth in him. When he speaketh a lie, he speaketh of his own: for he is a liar, and the father thereof. 45 But because I say the truth, ye believe me not. 46 Which of you convicteth me of sin? If I say truth, why do ye not believe me? 47 He that is of God heareth the words of God: for this cause ye hear *them* not, because ye are not of God. 48 The Jews answered and said unto him, Say we not well that thou art a Samaritan, and hast a demon? 49 Jesus answered, I have not a demon; but I honor my Father, and ye dishonor me.

50 But I seek not mine own glory: there is one that seeketh and judgeth. 51 Verily, verily, I say unto you, If a man keep my word, he shall never see death. 52 The Jews said unto him, Now we know that thou hast a demon. Abraham died, and the prophets; and thou sayest, If a man keep my word, he shall never taste of death. 53 Art thou greater than our father Abraham, who died? and the prophets died: whom makest thou thyself? 54 Jesus answered, If I glorify myself, my glory is nothing: it is my Father that glorifieth me; of whom ye say, that he is your God; 55 and ye have not known him: but I know him; and if I should say, I know him not, I shall be like unto you, a liar: but I know him, and keep his word. 56 Your father Abraham rejoiced to see my day; and he saw it, and was glad. 57 The Jews therefore said unto him, Thou art not yet fifty years old, and hast thou seen Abraham? 58 Jesus said unto them, Verily, verily, I say unto you, before Abraham was born, I am. 59 They took up stones therefore to cast at him: but Jesus hid himself, and went out of the temple.

Encouraged by this response, Jesus began to address Himself particularly to those who believed. The final outcome of the discussion shows that this belief did not bring about any change of heart.

It was a beginning, and Jesus endeavored to lead them on and bring them into a personal, individual comprehension of Him and His work. He dropped the use of allegory and spoke to them plainly and directly. **If ye abide in my word, then are ye truly my disciples; and ye shall know the truth and the truth shall make you free (v. 31).** Initial acceptance was not enough. "Those who have believed Jesus, that is, accepted his word, must continue in it if they are to be true disciples and to know the truth."[29] Not everyone who gives initial assent to the Gospel is able at once to accept all of its implications. Paul found some members of the Church at Corinth who were perpetual babes because they were unable (and perhaps unwilling) to take the "meat" of the Gospel (I Cor. 3:1-2). The author of the Epistle to the Hebrews spoke of a similar group who, when they should have become teachers of others, were still in need of being taught the primary principles of the Christian faith (Heb. 5:12-13). On at least two different occasions Jesus said, "He that endureth to the end, the same shall be saved" (Matt. 10:22; 24:13; Mark 13:13).

The Jews to whom Jesus was speaking were typical of those Christians who always argue with new truth. They claimed to be free men and, at least by inference, already in possession of the truth, because they were descendants of Abraham and were of the chosen people of God (v. 33). Their claim never to have been in bondage to any man was belied by the history of the Jewish nation. If they were sincere, and not talking just for effect, they may have had in mind the native independence of the Jews which would not accept the fact of bondage as their lot. The "day of the Lord" always loomed on their darkest horizon, and it was to be their day of deliverance and victory. Of course, Jesus was speaking of freedom from the bondage of sin. The fact that they, descendants of Abraham, sought to kill Him was sufficient proof of this bondage. In fact, they were not really and truly sons of Abraham, but were slaves in his household. Jesus, too, was Abraham's son, but He was free because He was also the Son of God. On this

29 Barrett, *op. cit.*, p. 285.

basis He offered them freedom from bondage (vv. 34-36).

The retaliation of the Jews was pointed and severe, and a most interesting exchange ensued. They expressed their claim to being Abraham's seed, went further to say that they had only one father, God, and then accused Jesus of being the product of an illegitimate birth (v. 41). Jesus replied that, judging by their actions, the devil was their father; he was a murderer, the father of all lies, and because they were like him they could not believe Jesus (v. 44). To a liar all men are liars. If Jesus' enemies had been truly sons of God, they would have believed the words of Jesus. By this Jesus denied them the status of true believers. What faith they may have had in Him had turned to unbelief in the face of increased truth. Initial belief did not make them children of God in the Gospel's sense of the term, and they were rejecting the truth which alone could make them God's children. Jesus defined a child of God as one who had been made free from sin, knowing a freedom that was moral and spiritual in contrast to the false freedom which the Jews claimed on the basis of race.

By this time the Jews were arrayed for full combat. He whom they had shortly professed to believe, they now charged with being a Samaritan (not a pure Jew) and demon-possessed or mentally deranged. Earlier the people at the Passover Feast had made the same accusation, but not with the growing deliberation evidenced at this time. This is in direct reply to His charge that they were the children of the devil. The manner of their speaking, **Say we not well that thou art . . .,** or "Are not we at last right . . ." (Westcott), seems to indicate that the epithets *Samaritan* and *demon* had come into more or less common use. The worst possible slander of a Jew was to call him a demented Samaritan. Jesus passed over the remark with the simple statement, "I am not out of my mind, but all I do and say springs from my desire to honor my Father, while you for your part and on this very account dishonour me" (v. 49).[30] The accusation recorded in the Synoptics — that Jesus was in league with Beelze-

bub — gave rise to a lengthy, reasoned refutation on His part (Matt. 10; Mark 3; Luke 10).

Then Jesus introduced a new idea: those who keep His word (remain in continued faith) will not see death (v. 51). Since physical death would be in the minds of His hearers (they spoke later of Abraham's death), the expression should probably read: "shall certainly not behold death forever," meaning that "death shall not be eternal."[31] The Jews understood Him to say that true believers would never have to die — or perhaps they were deliberately misrepresenting Him (v. 52). By such a claim He was making Himself superior to Abraham as a religious leader, and this a Jew could not tolerate. Anyone making this claim was certainly mentally unbalanced, they thought. Moreover, Abraham and all the prophets had died. Who or what was Jesus trying to make of Himself?

The answer to this query had been given many times as Jesus spoke to various groups. It was found in His relationship to God the Father. To deny what He had been teaching all along would make Him as big a liar as they were (v. 55). (One winces a little at this expression of Jesus.) Because of this fact, because He was the eternal Son of God, He was both superior to Abraham and before him in time. Moreover, He and Abraham were contemporaries (v. 56). Of course this was incredible to His hearers, who had been unable to lift their thinking one whit above the temporal. **Thou are not yet fifty years old,** they said, **and hast thou seen Abraham** ("and has Abraham seen you," as some manuscripts allow)? This remark concerning the age of Jesus at this time has led some scholars to believe that He was much more than thirty or so years old at the time of His crucifixion. The Jews were speaking about an old man, for the life-expectancy in those days was probably less than fifty years. The situation had now reached an impasse. Jesus and the Jews were getting further and further apart. His crowning statement, in their minds, was the most demonic of all: **Before Abraham was born, I am** (v. 58). Actually it was one

---

[30] W. R. Nicoll (ed.), *The Expositor's Greek Testament.*   [31] Plummer, *op. cit.,* p. 200.

of the clearest statements of His deity — a claim of pre-existence. Beside themselves with religious zeal and anger, and forgetting to seek an arrest and trial, **they took up stones to cast at him.** But Jesus hid from them for a time and then left the Temple. Their rash action may have been indicative of their sudden understanding of what Jesus meant, and the sudden prod to their conscience drove them to drastic action. The story of Saul of Tarsus on the road to Damascus provides an illustration of this kind of jealous hysteria: light resisted results in greater darkness; truth spurned makes room for additional error; righteousness flouted opens the door to the expression of evil passions. If this be so, how much greater was the condemnation of the Jews than if they had rejected Jesus out of simple ignorance.

T. JESUS AND THE BLIND MAN (9: 1-41)

1 And as he passed by, he saw a man blind from his birth. 2 And his disciples asked him, saying, Rabbi, who sinned, this man, or his parents, that he should be born blind? 3 Jesus answered, Neither did this man sin, nor his parents: but that the works of God should be made manifest in him. 4 We must work the works of him that sent me, while it is day: the night cometh, when no man can work. 5 When I am in the world, I am the light of the world. 6 When he had thus spoken, he spat on the ground, and made clay of the spittle, and anointed his eyes with the clay, 7 and said unto him, Go, wash in the pool of Siloam (which is by interpretation, Sent). He went away therefore, and washed, and came seeing. 8 The neighbors therefore, and they that saw him aforetime, that he was a beggar, said, Is not this he that sat and begged? 9 Others said, It is he: others said, No, but he is like him. He said, I am *he.* 10 They said therefore unto him, How then were thine eyes opened? 11 He answered, The man that is called Jesus made clay, and anointed mine eyes, and said unto me, Go to Siloam, and wash: so I went away and washed, and I received sight. 12 And they said unto him, Where is he? He saith, I know not.

13 They bring to the Pharisees him that aforetime was blind. 14 Now it was the sabbath on the day when Jesus made the clay, and opened his eyes. 15 Again therefore the Pharisees also asked him how he received his sight. And he said

unto them, He put clay upon mine eyes, and I washed, and I see. 16 Some therefore of the Pharisees said, This man is not from God, because he keepeth not the sabbath. But others said, How can a man that is a sinner do such signs? And there was a division among them. 17 They say therefore unto the blind man again, What sayest thou of him, in that he opened thine eyes? And he said, He is a prophet. 18 The Jews therefore did not believe concerning him, that had been blind, and had received his sight, until they called the parents of him that had received his sight, 19 and asked them, saying, Is this your son, who ye say was born blind? how then doth he now see? 20 His parents answered and said, We know that this is our son, and that he was born blind: 21 but how he now seeth, we know not; or who opened his eyes, we know not: ask him; he is of age; he shall speak for himself. 22 These things said his parents, because they feared the Jews: for the Jews had agreed already, that if any man should confess him *to be* Christ, he should be put out of the synagogue. 23 Therefore said his parents, He is of age; ask him. 24 So they called a second time the man that was blind, and said unto him, Give glory to God: we know that this man is a sinner. 25 He therefore answered, Whether he is a sinner, I know not: one thing I know, that, whereas I was blind, now I see. 26 They said therefore unto him, What did he to thee? how opened he thine eyes? 27 He answered them, I told you even now, and ye did not hear; wherefore would ye hear it again? would ye also become his disciples? 28 And they reviled him, and said, Thou art his disciple; but we are disciples of Moses. 29 We know that God hath spoken unto Moses: but as for this man, we know not whence he is. 30 The man answered and said unto them, Why, herein is the marvel, that ye know not whence he is, and *yet* he opened mine eyes. 31 We know that God heareth not sinners: but if any man be a worshipper of God, and do his will, him he heareth. 32 Since the world began it was never heard that any one opened the eyes of a man born blind. 33 If this man were not from God, he could do nothing. 34 They answered and said unto him, Thou wast altogether born in sins, and dost thou teach us? And they cast him out.

35 Jesus heard that they had cast him out; and finding him, he said, Dost thou believe on the Son of God? 36 He answered and said, And who is he, Lord, that I may believe on him? 37 Jesus said

unto him, Thou hast both seen him, and he it is that speaketh with thee. 38 And he said, Lord, I believe. And he worshipped him. 39 And Jesus said, For judgment came I into this world, that they that see not may see; and that they that see may become blind. 40 Those of the Pharisees who were with him heard these things, and said unto him, Are we also blind? 41 Jesus said unto them, If ye were blind, ye would have no sin: but now ye say, We see: your sin remaineth.

Earlier, Jesus had spoken of Himself as the light of the world (8:12). This became the subject for the controversy with the Pharisees which followed, but John did not elaborate upon it. In the present chapter Jesus the Light becomes the central theme, and it is illustrated by the account of healing of a blind man. The story of the healing in turn becomes the preface to the incidents and discourse of chapter 10. Several themes run through this story of healing: the problem of suffering, inherited results of sin, the miracle of healing, the method employed by Jesus, the miracle as a sign of His identity, the continued conflict between Jesus and the Pharisees, the act of excommunication of the healed man, the faith of the man, and the judgment of the Pharisees.

The storm of the previous chapter spent itself in the frenzy of Jesus' enemies collecting stones for an attack, before which Jesus made a hurried exit from the Temple. How much time elapsed between that incident and the present episode is not known, but a quiet now prevails and the disciples (probably the Twelve) are back with the Master. They have not been mentioned in John's narrative since the discourse on the Bread of Life in Galilee (6:71). During this interval Jesus appeared to be alone in His conflict with the chief priests and Pharisees. This would naturally mean He was in Jerusalem; and this is where the healing of the blind man took place. The usual haunt of beggars was the Temple area where the chances of receiving donations were good. People in a religious mood are usually good givers. Jesus **passed by**, with no indication given of where He and His disciples were going; perhaps Jesus was looking for an opportunity to proclaim His message,

since He would hardly feel free to enter the Temple so soon after being driven out. More than that, the days when crowds followed Him to hear Him speak and to witness His miracles were over. His witness was now to individuals and small groups. The sight of the blind man gave Him another opportunity to witness to the Light of the world.

This man was probably known to some of the disciples since it was known that he was thirty-eight years of age and that his blindness was congenital. The disciples asked why he was born blind — the age-old problem of human suffering. The Second Commandment teaches that the sins of a father are visited upon his children; could this be the answer, or had the man been born blind because of his own sin? To the latter idea four solutions have been offered: 1) the man was being punished for the sins God knew he would commit; 2) the transmigration of the soul — he might have sinned in a previous existence; 3) the pre-existence of the soul — the man's soul had sinned before it entered the body; 4) it was possible for an unborn baby to have sinful emotions.[32] Jesus dismissed the reasons for the blindness suggested by the disciples, but He made no attempt to offer what we would call a solution. Instead, He said that there was a purpose in the blindness which was being worked out to the glory of God.

In this case of healing, no mention is made of faith, either on the part of the man or of others. In general, faith — to John — is assent to the person and message of Jesus, rather than an expectancy that certain things will happen, or a condition of receiving something from God. The latter comes nearer the view of the Synoptic writers and the Apostle Paul. In the performance of this healing Jesus conformed to practices with which the people were familiar — He anointed the man's eyes with a solution of saliva and clay. A man's spittle was supposed to contain the essence of his character, and in popular thought it often had healing properties which enabled it to transfer health from one person to another. The pool of Siloam, which means **sent**, was probably used in order to indicate that Jesus was

[32] *Ibid.*, p. 204.

sent into the world to be the light of the world, and the washing became the test of the man's faith. After the washing of his eyes he went home cured. Later he was found in the Temple.

The purpose of this procedure would seem to be clear. In the miracles described by John up to this point there is no indication of how they were performed. The water just became wine; the son of the officer was well when the father arrived home; the lame man at the pool arose and walked at the mere word of Jesus. And the loaves and fish were not used up; they seemed only to expand when divided among the multitude. But in the present instance Jesus made use of a common medicinal remedy — clay moistened with spittle. The washing in the pool may have been ceremonial, or it may have been meant for the purpose of removing the clay at once in order to reveal that the cure had come about in an unusual way.

Jesus had a purpose in proceeding as He did. He wished to show that this miracle of healing took place according to laws which are known, although not fully understood. Miracles of healing do not go contrary to the laws which God has established for the functioning of the human body. This is universally recognized by those who teach divine healing; no one prays, after an amputation, for the leg stump to grow into a leg, because that would be contrary to the laws governing the human body as it has become understood. Dr. E. Stanley Jones has remarked that the miracle of healing is essentially the speeding up of those bodily processes by which man lives. We are not told what sort of blindness the man suffered from — only that he was born blind. He probably had eyes, and his blindness was the result of some malfunction. If he had had no eyes, the miracle would have differed radically from others described in the New Testament.

Recently the severed arm of a boy was replaced by surgery at a Boston, Massachusetts hospital. The surgeons were able to do their part because they knew how to cooperate with the laws of the human body. The miraculous element has been widely acknowledged. Miracle and mystery are not synonymous terms. "It is easier to believe, when means can be perceived; it is still easier, when means seem to be appropriate."[33] The Christian believer sees the supernatural in the natural — and the Incarnation shows that the supernatural can be seen by man in this way.

Jesus performed the miracle of healing on the eyes of the blind man in order to enforce the truth that He was the Light of the world. By this added witness, perchance some would see the light and believe. By calling attention to the man's blindness, Jesus emphasized the spiritual blindness of those around Him. By healing his blindness, Jesus showed that He was able to cure spiritual blindness. By telling the man to go and wash, Jesus sought to engender faith in His hearers.

The immediate results of the healing were not at all encouraging, except in the case of the man who had been cured. He proved to be one of the strongest converts to Jesus and His teachings up to this time. Of none was it said that he worshiped Jesus, except of this man. But most of those who had witnessed the miracle acted differently. The friends and neighbors of the man at first doubted his identity when they found him able to see. Then they took him to the Pharisees, probably because the miracle had been performed on the Sabbath day. And so has it always been with well-meaning but spiritually ignorant people — by hasty and thoughtless action they bring the Gospel of Christ into unnecessary conflict with the world.

After this healing there followed the most complete investigation of such an incident found in the Gospels. The Pharisees questioned the man who had been blind. They disputed among themselves: because Jesus healed the man He must have been from God; because He did it on the Sabbath He could not possibly have been. They questioned the man's parents, but got no satisfaction beyond the identification of the healed man as their son. The parents were inclined to follow their son in his faith in Jesus but feared to, because the Pharisees had been doing some ground work for their persecution of Him. Any one who confessed His Messiahship would be excommunicated. The man himself was cowed by neither the ban nor the brainwashing through which he was put. He did not know much about the man who had healed him, but he believed Him to be from God, as Moses had been. Whether breaking the Sabbath made Him a sinner the man did not know; but, he said, **One thing I know, that, whereas I was blind, now I see** (v. 25). The only answer from the Pharisees was to put him out of the synagogue.

There are differences of opinion concerning whether this was actual excommunication. Plummer[34] does not think so, and neither does Westcott,[35] who suggests that the Pharisees were not authorized to make such a declaration. If the Pharisees were the tools of the Jerusalem priesthood in the program of persecution, as some scholars think, this could have been excommunication of the most severe sort. There were three kinds practiced among the Jews: a thirty-day period, an indefinite period of time, and permanent dismissal. Strachan thinks that in the present case it was of the "severest form," because the man "had committed the heinous sin of attempting to teach his teachers."[36]

When Jesus heard of the noble defense which the man had made of Him, and the attending consequence, He hunted until He found him. **Dost thou believe on the Son of God,** asked Jesus. And after a brief conversation, he responded with one of the strongest declarations of faith given Jesus up to this time: **Lord, I believe. And he worshipped him** (vv. 35-38). Listening to Jesus was a judgmental experience, whether the listener was a blind man or a Pharisee. In making response to Him, they were at the same time answering something within themselves. The physically blind man was either healed or he continued in his blindness — he had faced a choice. The spiritually blind had the same alternative. The Pharisees professed spiritual sight, but because they rejected Jesus they were thereby revealed to be blind — blind leaders of the blind. Their blindness brought guilt upon them, because of their unbelief; while the blindness of the man brought sight

because of his faith. Light rejected becomes darkness; darkness acknowledged becomes light under the touch of Christ.

U. JESUS THE DOOR AND THE SHEPHERD (10:1-21)

1 Verily, verily, I say unto you, He that entereth not by the door into the fold of the sheep, but climbeth up some other way, the same is a thief and a robber. 2 But he that entereth in by the door is the shepherd of the sheep. 3 To him the porter openeth; and the sheep hear his voice: and he calleth his own sheep by name, and leadeth them out. 4 When he hath put forth all his own, he goeth before them, and the sheep follow him: for they know his voice. 5 And a stranger will they not follow, but will flee from him: for they know not the voice of strangers. 6 This parable spake Jesus unto them: but they understood not what things they were which he spake unto them.

7 Jesus therefore said unto them again, Verily, verily, I say unto you. I am the door of the sheep. 8 All that came before me are thieves and robbers: but the sheep did not hear them. 9 I am the door; by me if any man enter in, he shall be saved, and shall go in and go out, and shall find pasture. 10 The thief cometh not, but that he may steal, and kill, and destroy: I came that they may have life, and may have *it* abundantly. 11 I am the good shepherd: the good shepherd layeth down his life for the sheep. 12 He that is a hireling, and not a shepherd, whose own the sheep are not, beholdeth the wolf coming, and leaveth the sheep, and fleeth, and the wolf snatcheth them, and scattereth *them*: 13 *he fleeth* because he is a hireling, and careth not for the sheep. 14 I am the good shepherd; and I know mine own, and mine own know me, 15 even as the Father knoweth me, and I know the Father; and I lay down my life for the sheep. 16 And other sheep I have, which are not of this fold: them also I must bring, and they shall hear my voice; and they shall become one flock, one shepherd. 17 Therefore doth the Father love me, because I lay down my life, that I may take it again. 18 No one taketh it away from me, but I lay it down of myself. I have power to lay it down, and I have power to take it again. This commandment received I from my Father.

19 There arose a division again among the Jews because of these words. 20 And

---

34 *Op. cit.,* p. 211.   35 *Op. cit.* p. 149.   36 Strachan, *op. cit.,* p. 220.

many of them said, He hath a demon, and is mad; why hear ye him? 21 Others said, These are not the sayings of one possessed with a demon. Can a demon open the eyes of the blind?

The healing of the blind man (ch. 9) took place in Jerusalem, probably near the Temple. In the present chapter Jesus is said to be in Solomon's Porch in the Temple at the Feast of Dedication. Because of the close connection between these two chapters it may be supposed that the conflict over the blind man took place there also.

The discourse on the Good Shepherd is termed a parable (KJV and ASV), an allegory (Weymouth), and a figure (RSV). The Greek noun is *paroimia* which may be translated "parable" or "proverb." The account has some of the marks of the parable of the sower (Mark 4) with its allegorical interpretation. No single term can describe adequately the comparative kind of teaching which Jesus used.

No more familiar scene could have been chosen by Jesus than that of a shepherd and his sheep. He described briefly the immediate situation. The sheepfold enclosed the sheep at night. At times thieves and robbers would try to climb over the wall to kill and steal the sheep, for that was the only way they could get them; thieves and robbers could not pose as shepherds because the sheep would not follow strangers. But the true shepherd came each morning and called his sheep from a distance, and as the foldkeeper opened the door the sheep would rush out to their several shepherds. Where flocks were broken up and scattered among folds, each sheep would find its own shepherd.

It is evident that the thieves and robbers represent the chief priests and the Pharisees who had been trying to take from Jesus those who had begun to believe on Him, such as the man born blind. Everything about them was the opposite of Jesus, the Good Shepherd, who had come to save and lead the sheep into good pastures. The field probably was meant to represent the church, or the realm of God's redemptive love; but this cannot be carried too far, for Jesus certainly did not lead His followers in and out of the kingdom of God. The

porter, or gatekeeper, has no significance in the lesson Jesus sought to teach.

Jesus broke down His analogy into two parts, depicting Himself *first* as **the door** and *then* as **the good shepherd.** These two should be kept separate in the analysis of the analogy. The shepherd cannot also be the door. Jesus is **the door,** or "the way" (14:6), into the saving presence of God. Through Him men may come into abundant life. The Pharisees were not doors into **anything** — not even into the Old Testament church. If they ever had been able to bring people to God, that day had passed. No one could find God by following them. From this we can draw the lesson that men who would lead others into the Kingdom must themselves have entered by Christ the Door.

Jesus also said **I am the good shepherd.** The Pharisees were not shepherds, but hirelings, who did not love the sheep but forsook them in times of danger or handled them maliciously, as in the case of the man born blind. The Good Shepherd would lay down His life for His sheep; He would soon be crucified through a joint agreement with the Father. The love of Jesus for the sheep was to be demonstrated by His sacrifice. His death would come as the result of His own choice, because He had power to prevent it if He so wished. His love and death would take in Gentiles as well as Jews: **Other sheep I have, which are not of this fold: them also I must bring, and they shall hear my voice.** Therein would be created a unity among men, as well as a unity between God and man: **They shall become one flock, one shepherd** (v. 16).

By this manner of teaching Jesus again divided His hearers. All of them were able to understand the analogy of the shepherd from Psalm 23. The opposition came because of His calling the Pharisees hirelings, at the same time offering salvation to Gentiles and Samaritans. Even heaven would be spoiled for the Jews if they could not enjoy it by themselves. Added to this, Jesus reaffirmed His relation to God the Father, by whose authority He would allow Himself to be crucified and resurrected. **I lay down my life, that I may take it again . . . . I have power to lay it down, and I have power** to take it again. **This commandment received I from my Father** (vv. 17-18). To the Jews this was the claim of a demented fanatic. And so the interview closed in a stalemate.

V. FURTHER CONTROVERSY WITH JEWS (10:22-39)

22 And it was the feast of the dedication at Jerusalem: 23 it was winter; and Jesus was walking in the temple in Solomon's porch. 24 The Jews therefore came round about him, and said unto him, How long dost thou hold us in suspense? If thou art the Christ, tell us plainly. 25 Jesus answered them, I told you, and ye believed not: the works that I do in my Father's name, these bear witness of me. 26 But ye believe not, because ye are not of my sheep. 27 My sheep hear my voice, and I know them, and they follow me: 28 and I give unto them eternal life; and they shall never perish, and no one shall snatch them out of my hand. 29 My Father, who hath given *them* unto me, is greater than all; and no one is able to snatch *them* out of the Father's hand. 30 I and the Father are one. 31 The Jews took up stones again to stone him. 32 Jesus answered them, Many good works have I showed you from the Father; for which of those works do ye stone me? 33 The Jews answered him, For a good work we stone thee not, but for blasphemy; and because that thou, being a man, makest thyself God. 34 Jesus answered them, Is it not written in your law, I said, Ye are gods? 35 If he called them gods, unto whom the word of God came (and the scripture cannot be broken), say ye of him, whom the Father sanctified and sent into the world, Thou blasphemest; because I said, I am *the* Son of God? 37 If I do not the works of my Father, believe me not. 38 But if I do them, though ye believe not me, believe the works: that ye may know and understand that the Father is in me, and I in the Father. 39 They sought again to take him: and he went forth out of their hand.

The narrative of this section has the same flavor as found in previous records of encounters between Jesus and the Jews. They gathered around Him as if to hem Him in and exert psychological pressure upon Him. Like animals holding their quarry at bay, they continued their tactics of thrusting and striking,

seeking to wear Jesus down or to find some weakness in Him. They urged Him to make an open confession of His messiahship: **How long dost thou hold us in suspense? If thou art the Christ, tell us plainly** (v. 24). But this was only bait with which they hoped to catch Him — they sought for a specific statement to use as a whip with which to beat Him. But Jesus never did make direct statements concerning His relationship to God, except to those who had already manifested some degree of faith in Him; and He did not respond to the Jews at this time. Without faith it was — and still is — impossible for anyone to know that Jesus is the Christ. Both the works and words of Jesus were sufficient evidence for men of faith, or for those who were willing to listen in order to get the evidence, and nothing more could convince men who did not wish to believe. The Jewish interpretation of their messianic hope had dulled the powers of discernment to recognize their Messiah when He did come. **Ye believe not,** said Jesus, because ye are not of my sheep (v. 26).

This last statement might sound like a hard and unfair conclusion — the Pharisees did not believe in Jesus because they were not His disciples, while being a disciple was necessary to having true faith in Him. This principle seems to be moving in a circle, but the difficulty arises only when we think of Jesus and the Pharisees holding opposite beliefs. This was not entirely the case. "The great difference between him and the Pharisees was not that they held one set of beliefs and he another, but rather that he was morally in earnest about these beliefs and started to live as though they were really so."[37] Jesus was different from the Pharisees in that "he put human needs before law, . . . he emphasized the inner spirit or motive of the act rather than the outward act itself, . . . he put first things first and so made the ceremonial subservient to the moral."[38] There is an incident which illustrates this agreement between Jesus and the Pharisees. A scribe or lawyer asked Jesus which He considered the greatest commandment (Matt. 22:34f.; Mark 12:28f.), and Jesus replied with the

[37] Harold C. Phillips, *In the Light of the Cross*, p. 28.   [38] *Ibid.*, p. 26.

great *Shema* of Israel (Lev. 19:18) in its briefest form: "Thou shalt love the Lord thy God with all thy heart, and with all thy soul, and with all thy mind." On another occasion a lawyer asked Jesus what he must do to inherit eternal life (Luke 10:25-27), and when Jesus referred him back to the law for an answer, the lawyer quoted the same Old Testament passage. Jesus and the Jews were agreed on what was fundamental in religion. In this respect the Jews were not far from the Kingdom. If they had been willing to acknowledge this basic agreement, if they could have recognized that this love for God and man was inherent in the message of Jesus, and if they had allowed themselves to **follow** on from there to know and understand Jesus better, they would have been numbered among His **sheep.** They would have been included when He said, **I give unto them eternal life; and they shall never perish, and no one shall snatch them out of my hand.** Jesus guaranteed this on the basis of the power of God the Father, out of whose hand **no one is able to snatch them.**

A doctrine of unconditional eternal security has been sustained in part upon the strength of this promise of God's keeping power — if God is the Christian's protector, and nothing can take him from God, he is forever both safe and saved. In this regard Westcott points out the need of distinguishing "between the certainty of God's promises and His infinite power on the one hand, and the weakness and variableness of man's will on the other."[39] No one, no thing, can rob Christ of His followers, for He and the Father **are one,** but the disciple can cease to follow if he chooses. In the same connection, Westcott adds, "We cannot be protected against ourselves in spite of ourselves."

The zeal of the Pharisees for the law — the legal, not the moral law nor the law of love — prompted them to try to enforce it on the spot. They set about gathering stones, for Jesus had blasphemed by claiming oneness with God and blasphemy with punishable by stoning (Lev. 24:16). There were ten additional offences which could be punished with stoning, according to Old Testament law.[40] If the Pharisees had been equally zealous for the moral law there would have been no conflict. When one remembers that the whole life of the Pharisees was lived by the minute keeping of the law, as it was formulated and interpreted in the tradition of the elders, it is not difficult to understand their opposition to this young man who claimed to have come from God, speaking the words and doing the deeds of God while He boldly flouted the traditions of the elders. But while it is understandable, it is not excusable. The unlovely history of religions, sometimes even of the Christian religion, reveals that religious persecution has been of the most severe kind, and that the persecutors often condemn those who are closest to them in their doctrines and practices, but who deviate slightly from them. Unbelievers often are not molested; most martyrs come from the ranks of believers who are labeled heretics.

To the Pharisees Jesus was a heretic, a radical who was trying to change things, and in changing, to destroy. The only way they knew to cope with disagreement was to destroy it. But this method has always been the resort of weaklings and cowards, not of the brave and the true. If Jesus had adopted this principle, He would have welcomed the suggestion of James and John that they call down fire from heaven to "consume" the Samaritans who had refused to receive Jesus into their village because He was intending to go to Jerusalem (Luke 9:54). It is passing strange that the Church has been more ready to follow the Pharisees in similar situations than to follow the example of our Lord.

Once before the Pharisees threatened to stone Jesus (8:59), but He hid from them and got away. This time they were more deliberate, taking pains to search for stones and gather them together for the attack. They were ready to take matters into their own hands without due process of law. But Jesus stood His ground and kept them talking: **Many good works have I showed you from the Father; for which of those works do ye stone me?** They replied, **For a good work we stone thee not, but for blasphemy; and because that thou, being a**

---

[39] Westcott, *op. cit.,* p. 158.   [40] *The Interpreter's Dictionary of the Bible,* Vol. 4, p. 447.

man, makest thyself God (vv. 32, 33). And while the Pharisees continued to collect stones, Jesus continued to argue with them. Referring to Psalm 82, He reminded them that their own unbreakable Scripture called certain men gods — in fact it was God Himself doing so; why then should they say of Him **whom the Father sanctified and sent into the world, Thou blasphemest,** when He claimed to be **the Son of God** (v. 36). On the positive side, if they would but acknowledge the validity of His mighty works, they would soon come to a proper understanding of His relationship with God the Father. This argument from His works was a favorite one of Jesus. It does not appear on the surface that He was saying that miracles prove His diety, but that miracles plus all of His activities were evidences of it, and they were means whereby observers could build a firm faith. In this He went back to the fundamental principle by which Israel had come to a knowledge of God — they knew Him through His acts. They knew God as the One who had brought them up out of the land of Egypt and out of Babylonian captivity (Jer. 16:14-15; 23:7-8). Jesus challenged the Jews to be as aware and as sensitive to the workings of God as were their fathers. It seems evident that they did understand His reasoning; if not, they would have asked Him questions, for they had done so before. But because they did understand, and did not like what they had heard, they were going about to destroy Him.

Had the Pharisees carried through on their avowed purpose, their action would have been little short of mob violence. As it was, the process of gathering stones and the argument of Jesus gave them time to think about their rash intentions. They could not deny the fact that the blind man had been healed, so they dropped that issue. In like manner they dropped the charge of Sabbath breaking, because this was involved in the healing; the man had become a strong supporter of Jesus (9:24-34). The realization that Jesus had likened them to hireling shepherds (10:12) who had cast an afflicted sheep from the fold (9:34) came so close to the truth that they were glad to drop anything having to do with the blind man. They stood condemned before the jury of both their law and their conscience. Earlier they had accused Jesus of being in a demented state of mind (8:48), but now they knew that they were not dealing with an irresponsible public menace, but with a sane, fully responsible adult who knew what He was talking about and was prepared to prove it. And so blasphemy was their only recourse for a charge against Him. The heat of their initial rage having somewhat subsided under the pressure of reason, they decided not to stone Jesus but to put Him under arrest. "But He escaped from their hands" (v. 39 RSV).

W. THE RAISING OF LAZARUS (10:40-11:44)

40 And he went away again beyond the Jordan into the place where John was at the first baptizing; and there he abode. 41 And many came unto him; and they said, John indeed did no sign: but all things whatsoever John spake of this man were true. 42 And many believed on him there.

1 Now a certain man was sick, Lazarus of Bethany, of the village of Mary and her sister Martha. 2 And it was that Mary who anointed the Lord with ointment, and wiped his feet with her hair, whose brother Lazarus was sick. 3 The sisters therefore sent unto him, saying, Lord, behold, he whom thou lovest is sick. 4 But when Jesus heard it, he said, This sickness is not unto death, but for the glory of God, that the Son of God may be glorified thereby. 5 Now Jesus loved Martha, and her sister, and Lazarus. 6 When therefore he heard that he was sick, he abode at that time two days in the place where he was. 7 Then after this he saith to the disciples, Let us go into Judaea again. 8 The disciples say unto him, Rabbi, the Jews were but now seeking to stone thee; and goest thou thither again? 9 Jesus answered, Are there not twelve hours in the day? If a man walk in the day, he stumbleth not, because he seeth the light of this world. 10 But if a man walk in the night, he stumbleth, because the light is not in him. 11 These things spake he: and after this he saith unto them, Our friend Lazarus is fallen asleep; but I go, that I may awake him out of sleep. 12 The disciples therefore said unto him, Lord, if he is fallen asleep, he will recover. 13 Now Jesus had spoken of his death: but they thought that he spake of taking rest in sleep. 14 Then Jesus therefore said unto them plainly,

Lazarus is dead. 15 And I am glad for your sakes that I was not there, to the intent ye may believe; nevertheless let us go unto him. 16 Thomas therefore, who is called Didymus, said unto his fellow disciples, Let us also go, that we may die with him.

17 So when Jesus came, he found that he had been in the tomb four days already. 18 Now Bethany was nigh unto Jerusalem, about fifteen furlongs off; 19 and many of the Jews had come to Martha and Mary, to console them concerning their brother. 20 Martha therefore, when she heard that Jesus was coming, went and met him: but Mary still sat in the house. 21 Martha therefore said unto Jesus, Lord, if thou hadst been here, my brother had not died. 22 And even now I know that, whatsoever thou shalt ask of God, God will give thee. 23 Jesus saith unto her, Thy brother shall rise again. 24 Martha saith unto him, I know that he shall rise again in the resurrection at the last day. 25 Jesus said unto her, I am the resurrection, and the life: he that believeth on me, though he die, yet shall he live; 26 and whosoever liveth and believeth on me shall never die. Believest thou this? 27 She saith unto him, Yea, Lord: I have believed that thou art the Christ, the Son of God, even he that cometh into the world. 28 And when she had said this, she went away, and called Mary her sister secretly, saying, The Teacher is here, and calleth thee. 29 And she, when she heard it, arose quickly, and went unto him. 30 (Now Jesus was not yet come into the village, but was still in the place where Martha met him.) 31 The Jews then who were with her in the house, and were consoling her, when they saw Mary, that she rose up quickly and went out, followed her, supposing that she was going unto the tomb to weep there. 32 Mary therefore, when she came where Jesus was, and saw him, fell down at his feet, saying unto him, Lord, if thou hadst been here, my brother had not died. 33 When Jesus therefore saw her weeping, and the Jews also weeping who came with her, he groaned in the spirit, and was troubled, 34 and said, Where have ye laid him? They say unto him, Lord, come and see. 35 Jesus wept. 36 The Jews therefore said, Behold how he loved him! 37 But some of them said, Could not this man, who opened the eyes of him that was blind, have caused that this man also should not die? 38 Jesus therefore again groaning within himself cometh to the tomb. Now it was a cave, and a stone lay against it. 39 Jesus saith, Take ye away the stone. Martha, the sister of him that was dead, saith unto him, Lord, by this time the body decayeth; for he hath been *dead* four days. 40 Jesus saith unto her, Said I not unto thee, that, if thou believedst, thou shouldest see the glory of God? 41 So they took away the stone. And Jesus lifted up his eyes, and said, Father, I thank thee that thou heardest me. 42 And I knew that thou hearest me always: but because of the multitude that standeth around I said it, that they may believe that thou didst send me. 43 And when he had thus spoken, he cried with a loud voice, Lazarus, come forth. 44 He that was dead came forth, bound hand and foot with grave-clothes; and his face was bound about with a napkin. Jesus saith unto them, Loose him, and let him go.

In order to get out of reach of those who were seeking to take Him, Jesus left Judea and went into the territory of Herod Antipas in Perea (Transjordan) where He would be beyond the jurisdiction of the Sanhedrin at Jerusalem. For it was evident that this ruling body of the Jews was behind the many attempts to thwart His work. It will be noticed as time goes on that the Pharisees were less and less in authority among the enemies of Jesus. Following the raising of Lazarus (11:50) — the next event recorded by John — Caiaphas the high priest treated the Pharisees (doubtless members of the Sanhedrin of which Caiaphas was president) like ignorant servants, tools to be used or ignored as he chose. Jesus went into the Jordan Valley to the place where He had been baptized by John the Baptist (Matt. 3:14), and where John had introduced Him as the "Lamb of God" (John 1:29). This was at Bethany (John 1:18), or perhaps Bethabara.[41] While according to John's Gospel Jesus did not go there for the purpose of teaching and gathering disciples, the people recognized Him and believed on Him because of the testimony of the Baptist. However, this seems to be a reference to a pre-Passion mission beyond the Jordan which is spoken of in the Synoptics (Matt. 19:1; Mark 10:1). It may have lasted for a

---

[41] See *Interpreter's Dictionary of the Bible*, Vol. I, p. 388, for a discussion of the problem of location.

period of two months.[42] This points out that Jesus closed His public ministry at the same place where He was initiated into it by the baptism of the Spirit (John 1:32). It may have been as He passed the Mount of Olives on His way out of Jerusalem that He uttered His sad lament over the Holy City: "O Jerusalem, Jerusalem, thou that killeth the prophets, and stoneth them that are sent unto her! how often would I have gathered thy children together, even as a hen gathereth her chickens under her wings, and ye would not! Behold, your house is left unto you desolate" (Matt. 23:37-38).

We have here our last glimpse of John the Baptist, and it is a beautiful picture. **John indeed did no sign** (miracle) — he was never in competition with Jesus. A contrast is indicated between them, however. Jesus performed miracles and was the Truth; John did no miracles and was but the herald of the Truth. **All things whatsoever John spake of this man were true** (10:41). What a wonderful epitaph for a man to be remembered by!

While in this region Jesus received word that Lazarus, a friend who lived in Bethany, near Jerusalem, was ill. This is the first mention in the Gospel of John of Lazarus and his sisters Mary and Martha. They are identified through Mary whom John says was the woman **who anointed the Lord with ointment, and wiped his feet with her hair** (11:2). The account of this event comes later in John's Gospel (12:1-8) with the added details that she anointed His feet, and that she did it with nard ointment.

After receiving the word of the death of Lazarus, Jesus remained where He was for two days — and let Lazarus die. This is difficult to understand unless some purpose can be found in it. Jesus had been proclaiming Himself to be both the possessor and the giver of life. Jerusalem had rejected Him, but here was a great climactic opportunity to demonstrate His claim as never before. **This sickness is not unto death,** He said, **but for the glory of God, that the Son may be glorified thereby** (11:4). He did not mean by this that Lazarus would not die, but that death was not God's

purpose in allowing the illness, and that the end of the entire episode would be life and not death. The disciples understood Jesus to say that Lazarus would recover, and they were surprised when He later announced His intention to go to Bethany. They could see no good reason for it; moreover, the Jewish authorities in Jerusalem were looking for Him, and Bethany was less than two miles from Jerusalem. To return would be suicide. Jesus replied to them in terms of the will of God and the plan of God for His life: **Are there not twelve hours in the day?** (v. 9). The twelfth hour of His life was about to expire, but He had walked all the way in the light of God's will and had not stumbled; it was unthinkable now to turn back because of fear. His time was fast drawing to a close — the Father's time schedule for Him was nearing completion. He still had work to do and He would go forward unafraid.

Then He told His disciples the immediate reason for His decision to go to Bethany — Lazarus was dead. He broke the news in very beautiful language — not in words which sought to cover up the grim realities of death, but in words which robbed it of some of its sting and emphasized its temporary quality: **Our friend Lazarus is fallen asleep; but I go that I may awake him out of sleep** (v. 11). Since ancient times sleep has been an analogy of death. The disciples apparently did not understand this, or they were too disturbed over the matter to think in other than concrete terms, and so Jesus had to explain. By this expression Jesus was also saying that the death of Lazarus was like a sleep from which he would soon awaken (cf. Acts 7:60). The idea of death, with all of its permanence, lingered in the minds of the disciples. Only Thomas (whether out of doubt concerning the outcome of events so critical, or out of a loyalty which overcame his growing doubts) could think of anything to say: **Let us also go, that we may die with him** (v. 16). Thus also he may have expressed his growing conviction that sooner or later the Jews would kill Jesus.

Lazarus had died about the time that Jesus received word of his illness. Friends had gathered to mourn with the grieving sisters as was customary with the Jews, and everyone was watching to see if Jesus would come. Before He entered the village He was sighted and word of His coming was carried to the home. Martha hurried out to meet Him, for Jesus seemed to be waiting, while Mary remained at home in her grief. Perhaps she was more sensitive than Martha. Martha hurried out to meet Him, for containing elements of a rebuke; more probably she was complaining to Jesus, as most people do at times, over the unfavorable confluence of circumstances: **Lord, if thou hadst been here, my brother had not died** (v. 21). Why did things have to happen in this way? Why could not Lazarus have taken sick when the Great Physician was readily available? Why had something occurred to prevent Jesus from coming immediately? (Of course, she did not know why He had delayed). The matter of a few days was the difference between life and death. If only Jesus had been able to come sooner! If their home remedies could have kept Lazarus alive a little longer!

Martha seems to have been the head of the home, perhaps the oldest of the three. She took her responsibilities seriously. She was not one to quarrel with the inevitable for very long; and so she hastened to add, **Even now I know that, whatsoever thou shalt ask of God, God will give thee** (v. 22). Is this faith, or grasping at a straw? Did she think that Jesus would raise Lazarus from the grave? This is not likely, because the reply of Jesus that Lazarus would rise again registered no new thought in her mind — nothing but a reminder of the final Resurrection. It is more to the point to say that she had faith in Christ, but not faith for the raising of her brother from the dead. It was not faith that believed that He would do what she so much wanted, but rather faith that trusted Him to do whatever He thought best. This is the kind of faith which Jesus had been seeking to arouse or instill in people all during His ministry — faith in Him, in His Person. There was much more that Martha was to learn about Jesus, but in so far as she understood Him she believed in Him. People of this kind of faith are in a position to receive deeper spiritual revelations, and so Jesus said to her, **I am the resurrection, and the life: he that believeth on me, though he die, yet shall he live** (v. 25). Unable to respond fully to this great truth, she answered in a formal declaration of faith in His messiahship: **I have believed that thou art the Christ, the Son of God.** This confession was one of the purest testimonies to Jesus recorded in this Gospel of witness. Yet what she had said lacked something of true perception; it was something less than a truth which captivated her, which challenged her, which made demands upon her. She spoke the words as though she had memorized them — and then she was gone to tell Mary that Jesus had arrived.

The contrast between these two sisters is carefully worked out in this dramatic episode. Martha was practical, aloof, precise, self-sufficient, unemotional. No one followed her from the house, thinking that she was going to the grave of Lazarus to weep, as was the case with Mary (v. 31). She was not the kind of person who often shared her intimate feelings with others. She gave herself to things rather than to people. Even when the Master asked that the stone be removed from the mouth of the cave where the body of Lazarus had been placed, she expressed neither sorrow that he was dead nor expectancy at the words of Jesus that he would rise from the dead. Rather, she thought of how unsanitary and unsightly a spectacle the body would present after four days in the tomb.

Mary, on the other hand, was dependent, loving, sensitive, and expressive of her feelings. She found it easy to share her concerns with others, and people found themselves drawn to her by her every mood. She was more gentle than Martha, with a self-giving tenderness about her. In her sorrow she was not aware that Jesus was coming or that Martha had left the house. Friends were with her, sharing her grief. When she finally came to where Jesus was, she fell at His feet still weeping. And while she greeted Him with the same chiding admonition as had Martha (vv. 21, 32), the words sound like Martha's and not Mary's. Her grief moved Jesus deeply and He wept. Mary could get to one's heart without saying very much. Perhaps in her weeping there was a mingling of sorrow and joy — sorrow because of the death of Lazarus, but joy in the presence of Jesus with whom she had shared so much of her inner self. The next time we see her, she is anointing the feet of Jesus with costly perfumed ointment, wiping them with her hair.

Central to this series of events was the testimony they bore to Jesus as the giver of life. It proved to be Jesus' last chance to demonstrate this truth to the Jews who were already scheming to kill Him. He had come out of semi-retirement because Lazarus had sickened and died, but the raising of the dead forged the weapon with which His enemies condemned Him. Even the details of the visit to Bethany highlighted the Person of the Christ. In the presence of Martha, Jesus did little more than speak truths plainly and objectively, hoping that they would register with her. In the presence of Mary, Jesus responded with emotion to what was happening. He was the great Teacher, but He was more; He was the sorrowing, suffering Savior. His teachings are too high for men to reach unless they find in Him salvation from sin and enablement for righteousness. And so He **groaned in the spirit** (v. 33). The idea of indignation is expressed here. It indicates "an inward emotion which is accompanied by some physical expression, both in the voice and in some movement of the body."[43] The reason for this may have been the shallowness of the type of weeping of the "professional mourners," after the oriental fashion. Or He may have reacted in this manner to the lack of real faith evidenced by those present. More than this, Jesus may have at that moment felt the great weight of what the death and resurrection of Lazarus typified. Men were dead in sin; He had come to save them, but they would not accept Him, and now judgment was beginning to settle down upon them. No wonder that **Jesus wept.** While Mary and the others shed tears, Jesus wept aloud, probably partially in shared sympathy. There is no doubt that Jesus could have healed Lazarus without coming to Bethany, as He had healed the nobleman's son (4:46-54). But the need of this climactic sign was so great that the suffering of His friend became a

[43] Strachan, *op. cit.*, p. 237.

service to God — a symbol of the death and resurrection that would provide salvation for the world. The death of Lazarus was a type of the death of Christ, and his resurrection a type of the eternal life of the believer. The weeping of Jesus was a sign of His humanity, but, more than that, it was one of the highest expressions of His deity, a cry of involvement in all the struggle between good and evil for the souls of men. His humanity may be seen in His asking where the body had been placed (v. 34).

Again groaning in himself (v. 38), Jesus ordered the stone removed, offered a short prayer of thanksgiving (not petition), and then cried out in a tone of voice not spoken of in the other Gospels, **Lazarus, come forth.** In this Jesus demonstrated what He had been telling the Jews who had been seeking to arrest Him — that God was His Father, that God had given both power and authority into His hands, that He had power within Himself to raise the dead and give new life, because He was both the giver and the sustainer of that life. His demonstration was so conclusive and so damaging to the position taken by the Jews, that it became the immediate cause for the arrest and trial, and crucifixion of Jesus.

X. THE PLOT AGAINST JESUS (11:45-54)

45 Many therefore of the Jews who came to Mary and beheld that which he did, believed on him. 46 But some of them went away to the Pharisees, and told them the things which Jesus had done. 47 The chief priests therefore and the Pharisees gathered a council, and said, What do we? for this man doeth many signs. 48 If we let him thus alone, all men will believe on him: and the Romans will come and take away both our place and our nation. 49 But a certain one of them, Caiaphas, being high priest that year, said unto them, Ye know nothing at all, 50 nor do ye take account that it is expedient for you that one man should die for the people, and that the whole nation perish not. 51 Now this he said not of himself: but being high priest that year, he prophesied that Jesus should die for the nation; 52 and not for the nation only, but that he might also gather together into one the children of God that

are scattered abroad. 53 So from that day forth they took counsel that they might put him to death.

54 Jesus therefore walked no more openly among the Jews, but departed thence into the country near to the wilderness, into a city called Ephraim; and there he tarried with the disciples.

As on previous occasions, the crowd was divided, this time over the raising of Lazarus; some believed in Jesus because of it and others did not. The latter group reported to the Pharisees (probably members of the Sanhedrin) what had taken place. Immediately the Sanedrin was called in special session. Consternation reigned within the entire council. Jesus must be stopped. **If we let him thus alone, all men will believe on him; and the Romans will come and take away both our place and our nation** (v. 48). The issue before them was twofold. Jesus had claimed to be equal with God and had backed His claim by outstanding demonstrations of supernatural power which had embarrassed and enraged the Pharisees. And He had infuriated the Sadducees by raising a man from the dead, a phenomenon impossible according to their theology. Both of these groups, from which the membership of the ruling body came, agreed that Jesus must be destroyed. In addition to this, the fear of a national revolt was becoming acute. Unquestionably other seeds of revolt were being sown which finally led to the rising in A.D. 66 and culminated in the destruction of Jerusalem in A.D. 70. These Jewish leaders knew that a revolution, however largely supported, could only result in the destruction of their nation — both their religious life and national life would go. They did not believe that any one, Jesus least of all, could lead a successful coup against the Romans. He had maneuvered them into the position where they were saying that He must be sacrificed for their nation. Unless He were put out of the way, things would get out of hand and Rome would step in. Better the existing heel of Rome than the full weight of its might upon them.

It is a remarkable thing that the Jewish hope of a messiah should climax in this manner. Perhaps here can be seen the influence of the Pharisees who were looking for a religious rather than a political deliverer. Part of the confusion expressed in the question by the Pharisees, "What are we to do?" (v. 47, RSV), was due to the difference of opinion between the Pharisees and the Sadducees. The first had compromised with the Mosaic Law and the second had compromised with the Roman authorities; consequently, Jesus could not be acceptable to either group. Both had been chagrined and condemned in the face of His repeated teachings and works, and now they were united in seeking a way to destroy Him.

The significance of the action of Caiaphas the high priest can be found in the fear of a revolt among the people. He exerted the authority of his office to settle the problem in the quickest possible way. He was contemptuous of the Pharisees — **Ye know nothing at all,** he said. He may have felt that their repeated arguments with Jesus had helped to bring on the crisis. He was impatient with their lack of decisive action. His policy was not one of temporizing but of expediency; and he knew the answer to the problem of Jesus — put Him to death. In contrast to Caiaphas, the Pharisees can be seen in a milder light than heretofore — their threatening to stone Jesus had been warnings after all (8:59; 10:31; 11:8).[44] It may be they had been hoping to settle the matter "out of court." The policy of Caiaphas was one of aggressive action: it is always wise to sacrifice the few for the many, one man for the nation, he reasoned. **It is expedient for you that one man should die for the people, and that the whole nation should perish not** (v. 50). When he said this, everyone present knew that the issue had been settled, and **from that day forth they took counsel that they might put him to death** (v. 53). Word soon got to Jesus and He slipped away to the wilderness country to a little-known town by the name of Ephraim, near Bethel (II Chron. 13:19). Here He remained in seclusion with His disciples until it was time to return to Jerusalem for the next Passover Feast, His last fateful Passover. Jesus knew that He was moving swiftly toward the midnight hour of His earthly pilgrimage. He was preparing for His last trip to Jerusalem.

[44] Note also the attitude of Nicodemus, a Pharisee, in 7:50-52.

Caiaphas was high priest from A.D. 18 to 37. The statement, **being high priest that year,** punctuates the fact that he was the one in office who condemned Christ to death, representing the Jewish people in so doing. John interprets the judgment of Caiaphas, **that one man should die for the people,** as a prophecy of the death of Christ. As was suggested earlier in this section, it did appear that nothing but His death could prevent a rebellion and the consequent destruction of the Jewish people by the Roman Empire. As things turned out, His death had no such results. While Caiaphas was thinking in political terms, John, in recording the affair, may have had in mind the Jewish tradition that a high priest had the power of predictive prophecy, even though he might not know its full significance. The high priest did not need to be a man of high moral character in order to do this. Certainly Caiaphas was not speaking of the atoning death of Christ for the sins of the world, but by a peculiar kind of prophetic inspiration, or perhaps by the irony of circumstances, he spoke more truly than he knew. Herein John suggests two principles which may be resident in predictive prophecy: First, God speaks through men truths of which they themselves may be unaware at the time. And second, the coincidence of circumstances puts new meanings and interpretations upon the pronouncements. True predictive prophecy includes the voice of man, the voice of God, and the circumstance or event which is the fulfillment. John has provided the best philosophy of prophecy found in the New Testament.

Y. THE ANOINTING AT BETHANY (11: 55-12:11)

55 Now the passover of the Jews was at hand: and many went up to Jerusalem out of the country before the passover, to purify themselves. 56 They sought therefore for Jesus, and spake one with another, as they stood in the temple, What think ye? That he will not come to the feast? 57 Now the chief priests and the Pharisees had given commandment, that, if any man knew where he was, he should show it, that they might take him.

1 Jesus therefore six days before the passover came to Bethany, where Lazarus was, whom Jesus raised from the dead. 2 So they made him a supper there: and Martha served; but Lazarus was one of them that sat at meat with him. 3 Mary therefore took a pound of ointment of pure nard, very precious, and anointed the feet of Jesus, and wiped his feet with her hair: and the house was filled with the odor of the ointment. 4 But Judas Iscariot, one of his disciples, that should betray him, saith, 5 Why was not this ointment sold for three hundred shillings, and given to the poor? 6 Now this he said, not because he cared for the poor; but because he was a thief, and having the bag took away what was put therein. 7 Jesus therefore said, Suffer her to keep it against the day of my burying. 8 For the poor ye have always with you; but me ye have not always.

9 The common people therefore of the Jews learned that he was there: and they came, not for Jesus' sake only, but that they might see Lazarus also, whom he had raised from the dead. 10 But the chief priests took counsel that they might put Lazarus also to death; 11 because that by reason of him many of the Jews went away, and believed on Jesus.

The episode just discussed revealed that the Pharisees had been little more than tools of the Sadducaean high priests all the time. Now it is seen that the two groups were working hand in glove. The period of discussions concerning the relationship of Jesus to God the Father, and of His claim to eternal life, had ended. Miracles which had so troubled the Pharisees and confused their evidence against Jesus formed no part of the issue from then on. At last the case was clear-cut; the high priest was in complete control, and the case had been boiled down to its simplest solution: Jesus must die.

A net was immediately thrown out to catch Him. The lowliest citizen was asked to be a volunteer of the secret police. As people began to gather for the Passover, the main topic of conversation was whether Jesus would come to the Feast as had been His custom. **What think ye? That he will not come to the feast?** (11:56). They were coming **to purify themselves,** in preparation for the Feast. John has not mentioned this requirement in previous references to the Passover. In this instance he was presumedly thinking of both the need of moral cleansing in face of the evil attitude toward Jesus and the provision for such purification through the blood of Christ.

No more graphic picture of history-in-the-making has ever been witnessed than that which began when Jesus left His little haven of seclusion in Ephraim and started back to Jerusalem six days before the Passover. How He had needed those days of quiet and prayer! How important they were in preparation for the ordeal of the succeeding week! Not as one walking to his death, neither as one who might be surprised by some unexpected turn of events, but with the certainty of one who has considered all of the possibilities and risks and who moves ahead in the knowledge of a task to be done and a destiny to be fulfilled — this is the picture given in John's Gospel. While the agony in Gethsemane recorded in the Synoptics is not denied, it is omitted, and the focus is on the Master's inner security and equilibrium as He deliberately turned His face toward Jerusalem and the forces arrayed against Him.

This return from brief obscurity marked a new beginning in the ministry of Jesus — the beginning of the end. And it was celebrated with a banquet in Bethany in commemoration of the great miracle which IIc had performed there; this was done in defiance of the edict which had gone out to report Him to the Temple authorities. Matthew and Mark say that the gathering was at the home of Simon the leper (Matt. 26:6; Mark 14:3). Scholars have disagreed as to whether Mary of Bethany and Mary Magdalene were the same person.[45] Lazarus was there as an honored guest, and Martha maintained her reputation for efficiency and practicality by assisting with the meal. The disciples also were present.

Mary had good reason for anointing the feet of Jesus: He had raised her brother from the dead. In an act of supreme devotion she anointed His feet with a pound of pure nard ointment, and wiped them with her hair ("a woman's glory," I Cor. 11:15). The ointment was worth the equivalent of sixty dollars in today's American currency. The Synoptics say that she brought it in an alabaster jar.[46]

In the midst of this harmonious gathering a sour note was suddenly struck: Judas issued a public complaint against Mary for her act, because the perfume was so expensive. Why should he complain? It was costing neither him nor the treasury of which he was the custodian anything. Mary had apparently saved the money and purchased the ointment for this specific purpose. Judas was suggesting that she should have sold it — or perhaps never bought it in the first place — and given the money to him for the common treasury. He was officious to say the least and probably had some decided opinions concerning where people should put their tithes and offerings. All of which might have been proper under different circumstances, but not on this occasion. In the first place, Jesus (perhaps also Lazarus) was the guest of honor, and Mary was expressing in her own way her deep appreciation for what Jesus had done for her home; no one present had more reason for thanksgiving than Mary. If her action was really more costly than it should have been or more than the family thought wise, Martha would have spoken up or at least made some attempt to curb Mary. In the second place, it was very crude of Judas to bring up the matter of finance at that time — it was too late to change what Mary had done — and he might better have waited until later to voice his disapproval (if he thought the matter really did concern the philanthropic work of the group). In the third place, Judas' complaint was inopportune because of the rising tide of opposition to Jesus. If ever the group of disciples needed to stand together with Jesus, it was at that time. Was Judas beginning to show his real character? Any word or gesture unfavorable to Jesus would be looked upon with suspicion by those present. They would sense something ominous in the air. And as it turned out, Judas was more than a mere dissenter at the banquet; his actions indicated that the man who would deliver Jesus to the high priest would not be a careless

---

[45] For a favorable discussion see David Smith, *op. cit.*, pp. 208f. For the opposite view see R. H. Strachan, *op. cit.*, pp. 246f.

[46] For a good description of nard, see James Hastings, *A Dictionary of Christ and the Gospels*, Vol. II, p. 227. On alabaster see Vol. I, p. 41.

adventurer from the crowd, but one of the Twelve who had become associated with Him throughout His entire ministry. Mark's Gospel says that Judas went immediately after this to the chief priests to negotiate the betrayal of Jesus, and they promised to pay him if he succeeded (Mark 14:10-11). John says that he did it because he was a thief. How did John know? Perhaps it was discovered when the treasurer's book was taken over by another after the death of Judas. (And who would have been a more likely candidate for the job than John himself?)

This explosive outburst on the part of Judas came as no surprise to Jesus. Why had He not probed the matter? Why had He not exposed Judas? Why did He not expose him then? The answer is found in the several attempts which Jesus made to save Judas from his disastrous course.[47] As it was, Jesus defended Mary, interpreting her action in a way that Mary herself had hardly anticipated. **Suffer her to keep it against the day of my burying** (12:7), or "Let her alone, let her keep it for the day of my burial" (RSV).[48] The probable meaning is best expressed by Mark: "She hath done what she could; she hath anointed my body beforehand for the burying" (Mark 14:8). This remark by Jesus was also an indication to Judas that He knew which way events were trending as well as the part Judas was to play in them. This can be seen as the first attempt of Jesus to show Judas the error of his ways.

Either through Judas or by the grapevine, the people soon learned that Jesus was in Bethany and they came in crowds in order to see Him, but more particularly to see Lazarus, a dead man come to life. This shows that the common people did not share the feelings of the chief priests toward Jesus, for they came with no intention of betraying Him. Lazarus was the big attraction to the crowd. But because he had achieved a degree of notoriety, and as a result of his resurrection, many Jews believed on Jesus, and the hierarchy of priests were scheming to take Lazarus and put him to death. It is noticeable that Lazarus is not mentioned again. It has been suggested that he may have fled upon hear-

ing of this scheme and that Martha accompanied him (she too is lost to the narrative at this point). No one could blame Lazarus for such a retreat. He had been through enough of this sort of thing for a while and he could not be sure that Jesus would be on hand to perform another resurrection. Martha was probably the older of the two, and her brother was dependent upon her. Mary remained behind, and later she was one of three women who mourned for Jesus at the foot of the cross.

Z. THE TRIUMPHAL ENTRY INTO JERUSALEM (12:12-19)

12 On the morrow a great multitude that had come to the feast, when they heard that Jesus was coming to Jerusalem, 13 took the branches of the palm trees, and went forth to meet him, and cried out, Hosanna: Blessed *is* he that cometh in the name of the Lord, even the King of Israel. 14 And Jesus, having found a young ass, sat thereon; as it is written, 15 Fear not, daughter of Zion: behold, thy King cometh, sitting on an ass's colt. 16 These things understood not his disciples at the first: but when Jesus was glorified, then remembered they that these things were written of him, and that they had done these things unto him. 17 The multitude therefore that was with him when he called Lazarus out of the tomb, and raised him from the dead, bare witness. 18 For this cause also the multitude went and met him, for that they heard that he had done this sign. 19 The Pharisees therefore said among themselves, Behold how ye prevail nothing; lo, the world is gone after him.

The following day Jesus left Bethany for Jerusalem. The crowd of people was electrified by His boldness and sought to find a reason for it. Jesus was coming back to challenge the Sanhedrin and set Himself up as the Messiah in spite of the dictum of its high priest. Or perhaps He had changed His mind and was on His way to arrange a compromise with the Jews. At any rate, He was assured of plenty of popular support in whatever He intended to do. And so the people gathered palm leaves, the sign of victory, and went out from Jerusalem to meet Him. The people who had seen Lazarus raised from the dead spread

---

[47] See commentary on chapter 13.
[48] On the meaning of this see Westcott, pp. 177-178, also Barrett, pp. 343-344.

abroad the news (v. 17), and this had drawn the crowd together. They had gathered like those who followed Jesus to Capernaum after the feeding of the multitude on the mountain (ch. 6). But they were not true followers of Jesus, their professed belief being more curiosity than faith. At the same time the raising of Lazarus had brought about the decision on the part of the Sanhedrin to kill Jesus. He was now the center of attraction among all classes of people in Jerusalem, and little could happen to Him in secret. The Jewish authorities had not planned it this way, and that is why the arrest and trial took place in the night.

Jesus rode on **a young ass** while the crowd **cried out, Hosanna: Blessed is he that cometh in the name of the Lord, even the King of Israel** (v. 13). He rode "not on a war horse, suggestive of destruction, but on a colt, the beast of peace."[49] In relating the account John quoted from the prophet Zechariah as an item of proof that Jesus was the true Messiah to whom the prophets had looked forward (Zech. 9:9). When the Pharisees who were members of the Sanhedrin heard that Jesus was coming with a host of people in His train, they cried out, **Behold how ye prevail nothing; lo, the whole world is gone after him** (v. 19). In united despair because their own efforts had failed and because the plan of Caiaphas did not seem so likely to succeed as had appeared a short time previous, they laid the blame for their failure and the apparent success of Jesus upon their leaders: "We told you that nothing could be done to stop this man; why, the whole world has gone after him" (RSV). Apparently they did not know of the visit of Judas to the chief priests, "the hierarchical Sadducaean party."[50] At this moment Judas remained the one hope that the murderous plot of Caiaphas would be carried out. This illustrates how great an influence one man can wield over the course of history. And that man does not need of necessity to hold a place of leadership or of great power. His aims may be wholly self-centered and his actions irresponsible. He only needs to be the chief actor in a single nefarious

drama — a man at a sixth-floor window looking down his rifle barrel at the President of the United States riding by; or a backslidden disciple betraying his Lord for money in the office of the high priest. The one incident took place in Texas in 1963; the other, in Jerusalem in about the year 30. But the principle is the same in both cases. Such is the power of sin against which Jesus struggled, and to bring about its defeat He died.

The triumphal procession probably ended at the Temple; John did not specify where it ended. Neither did he tell of other events which followed immediately as recorded in the Synoptics. As is characteristic of John, he related only enough of the incident to get across the purpose in his mind — in this instance, to picture the living drama as the Son of God drew gradually nearer to His atoning death on the cross.

Z¹. GREEKS INQUIRE FOR JESUS (12-20-43)

20 Now there were certain Greeks among those that went up to worship at the feast: 21 these therefore came to Philip, who was of Bethsaida of Galilee, and asked him, saying, Sir, we would see Jesus. 22 Philip cometh and telleth Andrew: Andrew cometh, and Philip, and they tell Jesus. 23 And Jesus answereth them, saying, The hour is come that the Son of man should be glorified. 24 Verily, verily, I say unto you, Except a grain of wheat fall into the earth and die, it abideth by itself alone; but if it die, it beareth much fruit. 25 He that loveth his life loseth it; and he that hateth his life in this world shall keep it unto life eternal. 26 If any man serve me, let him follow me; and where I am, there shall also my servant be: if any man serve me, him will the Father honor. 27 Now is my soul troubled; and what shall I say? Father, save me from this hour. But for this cause came I unto this hour. 28 Father, glorify thy name. There came therefore a voice out of heaven, *saying*, I have both glorified it, and will glorify it again. 29 The multitude therefore, that stood by, and heard it, said that it had thundered: others said, An angel hath spoken to him. 30 Jesus answered and said, This voice hath not come for my sake, but for your sakes. 31 Now is the judgment of this world: now shall

---

49 R. H. Lightfoot, St. John's Gospel, p. 238.　　50 Westcott, op. cit., p. 174.

the prince of this world be cast out. 32 And I, if I be lifted up from the earth, will draw all men unto myself. 33 But this he said, signifying by what manner of death he should die. 34 The multitude therefore answered him, We have heard out of the law that the Christ abideth for ever: and how sayest thou, The Son of man must be lifted up? who is this Son of man? 35 Jesus therefore said unto them, Yet a little while is the light among you. Walk while ye have the light, that darkness overtake you not: and he that walketh in the darkness knoweth not whither he goeth. 36 While ye have the light, believe on the light, that ye may become sons of light.

These things spake Jesus, and he departed and hid himself from them. 37 But though he had done so many signs before them, yet they believed not on him: 38 that the word of Isaiah the prophet might be fulfilled, which he spake,

Lord, who hath believed our report? And to whom hath the arm of the Lord been revealed?

39 For this cause they could not believe, for that Isaiah said again,

40 He hath blinded their eyes, and he hardened their heart; Lest they should see with their eyes, and perceive with their heart, And should turn, And I should heal them.

41 These things said Isaiah, because he saw his glory; and he spake of him. 42 Nevertheless even of the rulers many believed on him; but because of the Pharisees they did not confess it, lest they should be put out of the synagogue: 43 for they loved the glory *that is* of men more than the glory *that is* of God.

Immediately after the universal note struck by the words of the Pharisees — **the whole world is gone after him** — some Greeks were introduced into the narrative. The term Gentiles or non-Jews describes these men better than the term Greeks. The Syrophoenician woman (Mark 7:26) was introduced as a Greek. These people represent a class which had turned to the worship of Jehovah, like Cornelius (Acts 10:22). The Greeks in the present account had come to Jerusalem to the Passover Feast. They had heard of Jesus and went to Philip to inquire if they could see Him. Philip and Andrew, both of whose names are Greek, took the petition to Jesus. But

this is as far as the story of the Gentiles goes. John introduced them into the story and then dropped them. It has been suggested that it would not have been proper for Gentiles to see Jesus before the crucifixion, because it was the crucifixion which brought the Gospel to the Gentiles.[51] More probably the omission is due to John's manner of writing. One can hardly imagine that Jesus would ignore the request which Philip and Andrew brought and begin to preach to them and the other disciples as if He had not heard them. It is very likely that the teaching which follows constitutes a summary report of what Jesus said to the Greeks when they were introduced to Him.

Perhaps this discourse should be included in the public ministry of Jesus. Yet it is of a semi-private nature and stands between His ministry previous to the raising of Lazarus and the subsequent private discourse to the Twelve in the upper room. To those present Jesus introduced the idea that life can only be perpetuated through death, and He illustrated the principle using the metaphor of a common seed being buried in the soil and being lost or consumed in order to produce another fruit-bearing plant. This is an analogy of the resurrection. By dying and rising again, He, the Son of God and the Son of man, would conquer the destroyer of life — death — and thereby guarantee the life of man beyond the grave. Jesus did not establish the idea of a future life upon some concept of the immortality of the soul, but upon the power of His own Resurrection. "Marvel not at this: for the hour cometh, in which all that are in the tombs shall hear his voice, and shall come forth: they that have done good, unto the resurrection of life; and they that have done evil, until the resurrection of judgment" (John 5:28-29).

This to Jesus was not only a parable of the Resurrection, but also the principle by which the Christian life is to be lived. **He that loveth his life loseth it; and he that hateth his life in this world shall keep it unto eternal life** (v. 25). The true disciple of Jesus Christ, like Him, both uses and loses his life —

51 Barrett, *op. cit.*, p. 250.

which is temporal — in the service of God and of others, in order to gain life which is eternal.

As if His own words had brought to Jesus a new realization that His **hour** had come, He cried out, **Now is my soul troubled; and what shall I say?** The agony of Gethsemane was upon Him. **Father, save me from this hour. But for this cause came I unto this hour. Father, glorify thy name** (vv. 27, 28). The hour which He had known was ahead of Him was now close at hand. But His agony of soul was not the result of fear or self-pity. It was the same as that expressed at the grave of Lazarus (11:33) when He reacted so strongly to the unbelief around Him and to the necessity of allowing Lazarus to die and be raised again as evidence of His life-giving powers. In this instance He was troubled as He faced the opposition and misunderstanding and moral blindness of the Jews at a time when Gentiles were making earnest inquiry about Him. He groaned within Himself at the awful necessity which lay ahead. He knew that that which would provide salvation for all men would also bring condemnation to those who refused to believe and accept. It was not a pleasant prospect for the one who loved even His enemies enough to die for them. And so He prayed with a troubled soul. He prayed for strength to endure, and He prayed that the Father's will would be done as it had been done throughout His life. Then there came a voice from heaven confirming Jesus in His resolution to fulfill the Father's will. The fact that all those present heard the voice, that some regarded it as thunder while still others thought it was the voice of an angel, would seem to indicate that it was a sound which not all could interpret. In this respect it was the counterpart of the teachings of Jesus which required spiritual insight on the part of the hearers in order to be understood. There is no indication that those who thought it thundered received any message from the sound. Those who thought an angel had spoken regarded the message as directed to Jesus. In answer to the questions which arose Jesus told them, **This voice hath not come for my sake, but**

for your sakes (v. 30). What had the voice meant when it said that Jesus would continue to be glorified even as He had been in the past (v. 28)? Not all had understood, and He told the group assembled the meaning of what they had heard. First, they were in a time of judgment for the whole world. His coming death and the attitude of men toward it judge men more accurately than any court of law.[52] Second, Satan would become a defeated foe and **be cast out.** This does not speak of the final end of the Devil, but of the curtailment of his authority as **the prince of this world.** Third, the death of Jesus on the cross would become the only force able to draw men from sin to salvation.

The response of the crowd lacked much of the argumentative spirit of the Pharisees. Reference was made to the law, but the question seemed sincere: **We have heard out of the law that the Christ abideth forever: and how sayest thou, The Son of man must be lifted up? who is this Son of man?** (v. 34). The answer of Jesus was brief: following Him and believing on Him was walking in light which would soon give them the answer to their question. Following only the law was walking in darkness and could give them no answer. He would soon be leaving them and so they should believe on Him while there was time. With those few words He went away and hid from them. In the telling of this incident John was reminded of the words of the prophet Isaiah (53:1; 6:10), which he interpreted as being spoken to the immediate situation. He seemed to say on the basis of Old Testament Scripture that the rejection of the Jews was as much pre-determined as the death of Christ — **that the word of the prophet Isaiah might be fulfilled.** Such fatalism differs from the spirit of Jesus in His many attempts to instill faith into His audiences. The foreknowledge of God could alone account for this judgment on the rejection of Jesus by the Jews.

Nevertheless, many of the Jewish rulers did believe on Him at this time, following the example of Nicodemus. They kept their change of mind to themselves lest they, like the blind man, be excommunicated. John's observation that

---

[52] See commentary on 5:22:30.

they loved the glory that is of men more than the glory that is of God shows that their faith fell far short of saving faith. Faith in Christ must be more than a mental assent in order to be effective. It is equally true today that multitudes of people believe in Christ who have never made any decision to be His followers. This is true for the greater part of those who are said to have believed in Jesus in the Gospel of John. There must be the faith of obedience as well as the faith of belief.

Z². CONCLUSION OF THE PUBLIC MINISTRY (12:44-50)

44 And Jesus cried and said, He that believeth on me, believeth not on me, but on him that sent me. 45 And he that beholdeth me beholdeth him that sent me. 46 I am come a light into the world, that whosoever believeth on me may not abide in the darkness. 47 And if any man hear my sayings, and keep them not, I judge him not: for I came not to judge the world, but to save the world. 48 He that rejecteth me, and receiveth not my sayings, hath one that judgeth him: the word that I spake, the same shall judge him in the last day. 49 For I spake not from myself; but the Father that sent me, he hath given me a commandment, what I should say, and what I should speak. 50 And I know that his commandment is life eternal; the things therefore which I speak, even as the Father hath said unto me, so I speak.

These few verses read like an echo from the teachings of Jesus to the Jews. They are the climax of His ministry to the mixed groupings of people. All of the ideas are familiar and constitute little more than a summary under three topics: hearing, believing and judgment. They serve as an outline to the response to His teachings, and the summary concludes with the very appropriate statement, **the things therefore which I speak, even as the Father hath said unto me, so I speak** (v. 50).

III. THE PRIVATE MINISTRY (13: 1-17:26)

A. THE LAST SUPPER (13:1-38)

1 Now before the feast of the passover, Jesus knowing that his hour was come that he should depart out of this world unto the Father, having loved his own that were in the world, he loved them unto the end. 2 And during supper, the devil having already put into the heart of Judas Iscariot, Simon's *son*, to betray him, 3 *Jesus* knowing that the Father had given all things into his hands, and that he came forth from God, and goeth unto God, 4 riseth from supper, and layeth aside his garments; and he took a towel, and girded himself. 5 Then he poureth water into the basin, and began to wash the disciples' feet, and to wipe them with the towel wherewith he was girded. 6 So he cometh to Simon Peter. He saith unto him, Lord, dost thou wash my feet? 7 Jesus answered and said unto him, What I do thou knowest not now; but thou shalt understand hereafter. 8 Peter saith unto him, Thou shalt never wash my feet. Jesus answered him, If I wash thee not, thou hast no part with me. 9 Simon Peter saith unto him, Lord, not my feet only, but also my hands and my head. 10 Jesus saith to him, He that is bathed needeth not save to wash his feet, but is clean every whit: and ye are clean, but not all. 11 For he knew him that should betray him; therefore said he, Ye are not all clean.

12 So when he had washed their feet, and taken his garments, and sat down again, he said unto them, Know ye what I have done to you? 13 Ye call me, Teacher, and, Lord: and ye say well; for so I am. 14 If I then, the Lord and the Teacher, have washed your feet, ye also ought to wash one another's feet. 15 For I have given you an example, that ye also should do as I have done to you. 16 Verily, verily, I say unto you, A servant is not greater than his lord; neither one that is sent greater than he that sent him. 17 If ye know these things, blessed are ye if ye do them. 18 I speak not of you all: I know whom I have chosen: but that the scripture may be fulfilled, He that eateth my bread lifted up his heel against me. 19 From henceforth I tell you before it come to pass, that, when it is come to pass, ye may believe that I am *he*. 20 Verily, verily, I say unto you, He that receiveth whomsoever I send receiveth me; and he that receiveth me receiveth him that sent me.

21 When Jesus had thus said, he was troubled in the spirit, and testified, and said, Verily, verily, I say unto you, that one of you shall betray me. 22 The disciples looked one on another, doubting of whom he spake. 23 There was at the table reclining in Jesus' bosom one of his disciples whom Jesus loved. 24 Simon Peter therefore beckoneth to him, and saith unto him, Tell *us* who it is of whom he speaketh. 25 He leaning back,

as he was, on Jesus' breast saith unto him, Lord, who is it? 26 Jesus therefore answereth, He it is, for whom I shall dip the sop, and give it him. So when he had dipped the sop, he taketh and giveth it to Judas, *the son* of Simon Iscariot. 27 And after the sop, then entered Satan into him. Jesus therefore saith unto him, What thou doest, do quickly. 28 Now no man at the table knew for what intent he spake this unto him. 29 For some thought, because Judas had the bag, that Jesus said unto him, Buy what things we have need of for the feast; or, that he should give something to the poor. 30 He then having received the sop went out straightway: and it was night.

31 When therefore he was gone out, Jesus saith, Now is the Son of man glorified, and God is glorified in him; 32 and God shall glorify him in himself, and straightway shall he glorify him. 33 Little children, yet a little while I am with you. Ye shall seek me: and as I said unto the Jews, Whither I go, ye cannot come; so now I say unto you. 34 A new commandment I give unto you, that ye love one another; even as I have loved you, that ye also love one another. 35 By this shall all men know that ye are my disciples, if ye have love one to another.

36 Simon Peter saith unto him, Lord, whither goest thou? Jesus answered, Whither I go, thou canst not follow me now; but thou shalt follow afterwards. 37 Peter saith unto him, Lord, why cannot I follow thee even now? I will lay down my life for thee. 38 Jesus answereth, Wilt thou lay down thy life for me? Verily, verily, I say unto thee, The cock shall not crow, till thou hast denied me thrice.

According to the Synoptic Gospels the Last Supper was a Passover Feast. John's Gospel places it on the evening preceding the Passover.[53] John alone records Jesus' washing of the disciples' feet. John records certain events which took place at the time of the supper rather than the details of the supper itself. Such details would not have been in keeping with John's mood or thought pattern, and least of all the purpose for which he wrote. To him Jesus was the Bread of Life, the giver and sustainer of life. He could not be consistent and say that household bread represented the body of Jesus. It is one thing to say that Jesus is Bread, but it is quite an-

other thing to say, no matter what meaning is intended, that bread is the body of Jesus. John's emphasis was not on the broken body of the Christ of the cross, but on the ever-living, incarnate, now glorified, Christ of God. And the picture of Jesus given by John on the occasion of the Last Supper is wonderful indeed.

Jesus had just come through the traumatic experience of being rejected by the Jewish authorities and by most of His friends and followers. A price was on His head; He had been condemned to die, untried and unconvicted, by the Sanhedrin. He was experiencing the full consciousness of impending death, at the same time keenly aware of His incarnate state. Being man, although also God, He could not escape death. He faced its inevitable approach with great concern, not for Himself but for His disciples.

First of all Jesus robed Himself like a household slave, using only the towel of His toil to cover Himself. He also did the work of a slave washing the feet of the disciples. He sought thereby to enforce a lesson: **If I then, the Lord and the Teacher, have washed your feet, ye also ought to wash one another's feet** (v. 14). It was a lesson on Christian humility and love. In the days following, the disciples would need to remember this great weapon against dissention, this powerful adhesive for Christian fellowship. Soon He came to Peter, the problem disciple, who could make an issue out of less material than any of the others — Peter, who always wanted to be ahead of other people and because of this was too often alone in what he did. It is not customary for commentators to be sympathetic toward Peter's impetuosity, but it must be remembered that it was part of what made him a leader among the disciples. Most leaders, civil or ecclesiastical, are strong individualists, if not egotists. There seemed to be little reason for Peter's refusing Jesus the right to wash his feet. Perhaps he felt that Jesus was humbling Himself unnecessarily. More probably he was embarrassed because he had failed to make preparation for this necessary courtesy — for he and John had comprised the committee which prepared for the supper. Because of the dusty roads in Palestine, and the open sandals commonly worn at that time, it was customary for the host to supply water, towel, and even a slave if he were able, to cleanse the dust from the feet of family and guests.

Jesus explained that back of the physical act which He was performing, there was a spiritual lesson to be learned. **If I wash thee not, thou hast no part with me** (v. 8). Peter, who had just said, **Thou shalt never wash my feet,** quickly reversed his demand: **Not my feet only, but also my hands and my head.** Patiently Jesus explained to Peter what He meant. An extended paraphrase of the few words recorded (v. 10) will bring out the meaning. "Peter, you probably had a full bath just before leaving home for this supper. On the way your feet became dusty; so you need only to wash your feet now. In similar fashion you, my disciples, may be said to have been cleansed from your old life; you have believed in Me, you have been my followers — these are your credentials for being here. But on the way to this hour, across the three years we have been together, in the midst of tension and stress, the bickering and the misunderstanding, the plotting and the scheming, you have accumulated some road dust. Doubt has become mixed with your faith, distrust with your love. Your purest thoughts of Me have become adulterated with questions. I understand — how could it have been otherwise under the circumstances? But, Peter, beware!"

Peter apparently was unable to grasp the full impact of this lesson. He was not fully aware of his own weaknesses. He was hesitant to admit that he had accumulated any road dust. Later that same evening he boasted to Jesus, **I will lay down my life for thee** (v. 37); to which Jesus replied, **The cock shall not crow, till thou shalt deny me thrice.** Before many hours had passed, Peter had denied his Lord in public.

Jesus also said that one in particular needed cleansing. He remembered the attitude of Judas Iscariot at the banquet in Bethany when Mary had anointed her Lord's feet. He also knew that Judas had already visited the chief priests in an effort to learn the terms laid down for turning Jesus over to them. Jesus, by the symbolic act of foot-washing, may have been making an even stronger appeal than he had made to Peter. It was all the more significant because Judas had allowed Jesus to wash his feet. Think of it! Jesus on His knees like a slave washing the feet of Judas who even then was scheming to betray Him to the authorities. "Judas," Jesus was saying, "let me wash this evil from your mind and heart. You have been one of my disciples, and I love you in spite of your plans. I know about them, and I understand — for I too know what it is like to be tempted. Our fellowship has been good. This need not be the end. Will you not begin to resist the thought of betrayal before it becomes too strong for you?"

Of course the other disciples did not know what was transpiring in either the mind of Jesus or that of Judas. Perhaps they had been tempted with thoughts similar to those of Judas. They had been shaken by the recent tide of events. Questions had arisen. Alternatives for action had come to their minds. Perhaps it was foolish to stand against the rising opposition. Thus they all may have shared in thoughts of desertion or denial. When Jesus spoke of one whom He knew would betray Him, all eyes probably turned toward Peter — he would have been the prime suspect because of his rebuke to Jesus during the foot-washing. By this time they were all seated or reclining at supper, and Peter, to cover his embarrassment, turned to the disciple who was probably least under suspicion — John the Beloved — and said, **Tell us who it is of whom he speaketh** (v. 24). Peter was not recovered sufficiently from his former chagrin to ask Jesus himself, and perhaps he was not sure but that Jesus meant him. Jesus was very frank when John asked Him who was meant: **He it is, for whom I shall dip the sop, and give it to him.** Then He deliberately gave it to Judas. On the surface this act appears cruel. But it was done in love, even as a surgeon's scalpel must be used at times in order to save a life. A struggle was going on within Judas. The Devil had his foot in the door of his mind. How long a time elapsed while Jesus and

Judas contended silently against each other — Jesus for love and Judas for money — we are not told. But the longer Judas debated the issue, the weaker became his will to resist and the weaker became whatever love he may have had for his Master. He gradually let down the inner barriers of his soul; he unbarred the door of his heart, and Satan came in.

Many have sought to understand how and why Judas could have betrayed Jesus. How could any man, however evil, live with the Son of God in intimate association for three or more years without having his life changed drastically and permanently? Reason would say that betrayal under such conditions would be impossible. But sin does not work by reasonable principles. Sin is irrational, the most unreasonable thing in the world. Judas betrayed Jesus with his eyes wide open. Men steal and murder and add sins to the catalogue of crime, knowing full well the probable consequences. But sin makes every man think himself an exception to the law of cause and effect. It takes reason captive while it batters down moral defenses. At the same time, however, some reasons can be deduced from the record for the behavior of Judas. He was the only Judean among the Twelve, and he may have felt, after the edict of Caiaphas that Jesus must die, that he would be a traitor to both his nation and his religion if he continued to support Jesus. What if he should be caught in a revolt for which he had no heart! We saw earlier that both the Pharisees and the Sadducees were opposed to Jesus, and to a Judean of strong nationalistic feelings, this fact would carry great weight. Judas may have entertained strong messianic hopes and, when Jesus failed to bear out his expectations, he may have become disillusioned. Perhaps the retreat of Jesus to the wilderness just prior to the banquet at Bethany convinced him that Jesus and he were not pursuing the same end. While the band of disciples was on the road and Judas heard Jesus repeat His exhortations over and over, everything sounded very plausible. But when he was on home territory, at Jerusalem and the Temple, observing the glory that was Israel, things took on a different cast. The bread and the water of a new spiritual kingdom, and even the promise of life eternal, faded quite easily before the tangible realities of the Mosaic law and ritual. No doubt other things, such as the money received, played their part. But before long, and under the shocked gaze of his fellow disciples, Judas had made up his mind. This must be the end. He arose and went out — **and it was night** (v. 30). He experienced not only the darkness of guilt and the blackness of sin — it was the darkness that only those know who have separated themselves from Him who is **the light of the world** — the only light by which man can be lighted.

Jesus had taken the initiative in revealing Judas as the traitor. It is evident that Jesus meant to precipitate the resignation and withdrawal of Judas from the group because he was no longer a disciple at heart. We are told that after he had gone out Jesus said, **Now is the Son of man glorified, and God is glorified in him** (v. 31). It was not to the glory of either God or Jesus that Judas should betray Him, but the entire situation in the company of the disciples changed when Judas departed. Peace and harmony was restored to the group. Judas would have been a detriment to anything Jesus sought to do if he had remained, so long as he continued to harbor thoughts of sedition. Better to be a silent disciple like Nicodemus, or a forgotten believer like the woman of Samaria, then to be a traitor in the camp like Judas. His departure was a blessing. It was necessary that he leave the group because Jesus had much to say to those of the inner circle, much that only loyal ears should hear and faithful hearts understand.

Peter soon became more like his old talkative self after Judas had gone. Jesus began to speak of His having to leave them soon and of the new commandment of love by which the disciples must learn to govern all of their relationships. Then Peter broke in: **Why cannot I follow thee even now? I will lay down my life for thee.** But how little Peter knew his own heart! For the second time that evening Jesus rebuked him for his impetuosity and lack of stability. **I say unto thee,** said Jesus, **The cock shall not crow, till thou hast denied me thrice** (v. 38).

B. I GO AWAY; I WILL COME AGAIN (14:1-31)

1 Let not your heart be troubled: believe in God, believe also in me. 2 In my Father's house are many mansions; if it were not so, I would have told you; for I go to prepare a place for you. 3 And if I go and prepare a place for you, I come again, and will receive you unto myself; that where I am, *there* ye may be also. 4 And whither I go, ye know the way. 5 Thomas saith unto him, Lord, we know not whither thou goest; how know we the way? 6 Jesus saith unto him, I am the way, and the truth, and the life: no one cometh unto the Father, but by me. 7 If ye had known me, ye would have known my Father also: from henceforth ye know him, and have seen him. 8 Philip saith unto him, Lord, show us the Father, and it sufficeth us. 9 Jesus saith unto him, Have I been so long time with you, and dost thou not know me, Philip? he that hath seen me hath seen the Father; how sayest thou, Show us the Father? 10 Believest thou not that I am in the Father, and the Father is in me? the words that I say unto you I speak not from myself: but the Father abiding in me doest his works. 11 Believe me that I am in the Father, and the Father in me: or else believe me for the very works' sake. 12 Verily, verily, I say unto you, He that believeth on me, the works that I do shall he do also; and greater *works* than these shall he do; because I go unto the Father. 13 And whatsoever ye shall ask in my name, that will I do, that the Father may be glorified in the Son. 14 If ye shall ask anything in my name, that will I do. 15 If ye love me, ye will keep my commandments. 16 And I will pray the Father, and he shall give you another Comforter, that he may be with you for ever, 17 *even* the Spirit of truth: whom the world cannot receive; for it beholdeth him not, neither knoweth him: ye know him; for he abideth with you, and shall be in you. 18 I will not leave you desolate: I come unto you. 19 Yet a little while, and the world beholdeth me no more; but ye behold me: because I live, ye shall live also. 20 In that day ye shall know that I am in my Father, and ye in me, and I in you. 21 He that hath my commandments, and keepeth them, he it is that loveth me: and he that loveth me shall be loved of my Father, and I will love him, and will manifest myself unto him. 22 Judas (not Iscariot) saith unto him, Lord, what is come to pass that thou wilt manifest thyself unto us, and not un-

to the world? 23 Jesus answered and said unto him, If a man love me, he will keep my word: and my Father will love him, and we will come unto him, and make our abode with him. 24 He that loveth me not keepeth not my words: and the word which ye hear is not mine, but the Father's who sent me.

25 These things have I spoken unto you, while *yet* abiding with you. 26 But the Comforter, *even* the Holy Spirit, whom the Father will send in my name, he shall teach you all things, and bring to your remembrance all that I said unto you. 27 Peace I leave with you; my peace I give unto you: not as the world giveth, give I unto you. Let not your heart be troubled, neither let it be fearful. 28 Ye heard how I said to you, I go away, and I come unto you. If ye loved me, ye would have rejoiced, because I go unto the Father: for the Father is greater than I. 29 And now I have told you before it come to pass, that, when it is come to pass, ye may believe. 30 I will no more speak much with you, for the prince of the world cometh: and he hath nothing in me; 31 but that the world may know that I love the Father, and as the Father gave me commandment, even so I do. Arise, let us go hence.

Resuming His topic after Peter's interruption, Jesus gave a lengthy discourse on His necessary departure from the world and His subsequent return. The style is not unlike that in Matthew's version of the Sermon on the Mount, an observation which does not confirm the commonly-alleged great diversity between John and the Synoptic Gospels concerning the manner of Christ's teaching.

There are some things about which the disciples had good reason to be troubled. The Jewish authorities had sworn to kill Jesus. Jesus had intimated on several occasions that He would soon die. Judas had deserted the band of disciples, and Peter had been charged with unfaithfulness. Their own safety, as well as their future, was uncertain. But most serious of all, there was the possibility that their faith in Jesus would prove to have been futile after all. Perhaps Judas had taken the best way out. How could Jesus be and do all He had promised if He were going to be betrayed and die at the hands of His enemies? They had good reason for being troubled — and Jesus knew and understood. Yet He could not minimize the facts nor mollify the situation with generalities. Neither did He prepare them for the ordeal by describing the possible course of events, nor by drawing sympathy to Himself in a series of invectives against the Sanhedrin. In every respect the calm objectivity of Jesus is outstandingly apparent as He kept the conversation on the plane of the personal relationship between Him and His disciples, assuring them that things were working out as planned. Not only was the will of God being achieved, but also all those who believed on Him would enjoy a richer and more lasting fellowship with Him through the Spirit than ever they had known. On this basis Jesus said, **Let not your heart be troubled.**

And He continued: **Believe in God, believe also in me.** This exhortation may be taken in several different ways. It may be that Jesus was simply encouraging the disciples to continue to believe in God and in Him. This uncomplicated interpretation is favored by many writers, but it is more probable, in view of the circumstances, that Jesus was affirming their faith in God as the basis of their faith in Him. As Jews they believed in God, and nothing had transpired to destroy that faith. Faith in God had never been a problem with them; faith in Jesus, on the other hand, had been a problem and at that time was undergoing its most severe test. His many attempts to bring the people to the point of belief had also been directed toward the disciples. Remembering the many people who had started to follow Him and had turned back, it is not plausible to suppose that while others wavered the Twelve believed with an unfaltering faith. The response to the Bread of Life discourse (ch. 6) and the events at the last Supper (ch. 13) show that their faith in Jesus was not unshakeable. And so He sought to tell them that faith in Him should flow naturally from their faith in God. This was another way of saying that He and the Father are one, the main thrust of His prolonged discussions with the Jews. The one thing that Jesus was depending on for the continuation of the Gospel was the faith and the faithfulness of His disciples. Could they stand the test? Was their faith strong enough to hold? That was

the great concern of Jesus, and the present discourse was given for the purpose of assuring their continued faith in Him.

Jesus made several major emphases at this time: first, His own oneness with God the Father; second, His necessary return to the Father whence He had come into the world; third, the provision that His followers would also leave this world to go to the Father at a later date; fourth, the prophecy that they would carry on a growing work after His departure; fifth, the promise that He would send to them the Holy Spirit; and sixth, the assurance that He Himself would one day return for them. These topics intertwine in the discussion of Jesus and will be treated here in like fashion.

The eleven disciples who were left had not fully comprehended the idea that Jesus and God the Father were a unity. They had heard most of the discussions between Jesus and the Jewish leaders, but still they were unable fully to take in this great truth, as well as some other truths. They had been willing to follow and listen and learn while others had closed their minds to anything that was different from what they already believed. The uncertainty in the minds of the disciples was expressed by Philip: **Lord, show us the Father, and it sufficeth us** (v. 8). Why Philip? Why not Peter? Peter could speak for himself, but at that time he was a poor spokesman for the group. Doubtless at that moment he was feeling quite humble and uncommunicative after having just been checked twice by Jesus for speaking without thinking. Philip was a highly trusted and respected disciple. John took notice of him on three separate occasions. He was among the first group of disciples chosen and the record says that Jesus **found him.** At the feeding of the five thousand Jesus discussed the matter of obtaining food with Philip as with a trusted lieutenant. And when some Greeks wanted to meet Jesus they first contacted Philip. It is perhaps not surprising that when a serious, thoughtful question was to be asked, Philip would ask it. What he expected Jesus to do can only be guessed. Perhaps he thought that if Jesus could give them some special bona fide revelation of the Father apart from Jesus Himself, he would no longer need to be concerned with the vexing question about the relationship between God the Father and God the Son — between Jesus and the Father. But that was not possible.

He that hath seen me hath seen the Father (v. 9), said Jesus. He Himself was the revelation of God the Father. This was absolutely basic. Philip must start there; he must believe that Jesus was such a revelation from God, or it would be impossible for him to know God at all. God can only be known as He has revealed Himself and the supreme revelation is Jesus Christ. By this time Jesus was addressing not just Philip but the whole band of disciples. **Believe** (plural) **me,** "my Person, my life, my words, . . . [or] from the divinity of my works deduce the divinity of my nature."[54]

As a second emphasis Jesus said that He was going to leave His disciples. This they could understand, and from His previous teachings they should have known the manner in which it would take place: **And whither I go, ye know the way.** But Thomas spoke up for the group: **we know not whither thou goest; how know we the way?** Was Jesus expecting too much of His disciples? Were they slower of understanding than they should have been? Jesus was not sitting in judgment upon them, but He was drawing them out by means of a question: You know where I am going, do you not? And when the answer was *No,* Jesus gave them one of the greatest capsules of truth recorded in the New Testament: **I am the way, and the truth, and the life** (v. 6). Jesus is the way for going to God, the truth for knowing about God, and the life for living with God. He was going back to the Father, in whose place of abode was plenty of room for all. His going was for the purpose of preparing a place for His disciples so that they could follow Him. Moreover, He would return for them.

It is impossible to exhaust the meaning of the truths on this objective basis — that Jesus was to ascend to heaven after the Resurrection and that He would come again at the end of the age. This is included in the total meaning of the passage, but the context will not allow

the interpretation to be limited to this. The Resurrection as a separate event had not been a part of the teaching of Jesus in this Gospel, and the framework of the discourse thus introduced is not eschatological in this sense of the term. The deeper and primary meaning is spiritual, relating to those to whom Jesus was speaking. By His death they would experience liberation from the sin which held them and gain an entrance into the presence of God. In this He was speaking of the new birth from above, or a birth of the Spirit, of which He had spoken to Nicodemus. It would be like going into the presence of the **Father.** They would be *in* the world but not *of* the world (17:14). They would experience a brand new dimension of living — life that was eternal.

Jesus enlarged on the truth of a life of personal fellowship with God in still another, yet not an entirely different, way. When I go away, He said, **I will pray the Father, and he shall give you another Comforter, that he may be with you forever, even the Spirit of truth** (v. 16). This is another way of saying, **I will not leave you desolate: I come unto you** (v. 18). For while the Spirit — the Paraclete — is ascribed both personality and deity, at the same time the Spirit is the Spirit of Jesus Himself. In the coming of the Spirit Jesus would return in a very real sense. Jesus had said, **I am the truth,** and the Spirit is the **Spirit of Truth** (v. 17). **He shall teach you all things, and bring to your remembrance all that I said unto you** (v. 26). The things which had been difficult to understand would be made plain, and new truths about Christ would be revealed to them. Many things He could not tell them then because they were not able to believe them without the aid of the Spirit.

This is the way the disciples understood the meaning of the gift of the Spirit, because the question was asked, **Lord, what is come to pass that thou wilt manifest thyself unto us, and not unto the world?** (v. 22). They seemed better able to comprehend an identity between Jesus and the Spirit sent from the Father than the identity between Jesus and the Father. Jesus was making progress with His students, and so He

---

[54] Westcott, *op. cit.,* p. 203.

showed them the next significant step of understanding and faith. **If a man love me, he will keep my word: and my Father will love him, and we will come unto him, and make our abode with him** (v. 23). The part that the disciple must play is obedience through love; start by loving Jesus — this is not difficult to do — and then obey what is known must be done. "If any man willeth to do his will, he shall know of the teaching" (7:17). He can then be assured of love in return — the love of the Father. And then — and this is the master stroke — **we will come unto him.** Father, Son, and Spirit, the great Three in One who make up the Godhead as He had revealed Himself to man, will be a part of the experience of those who believe and follow on to know Christ more perfectly. The going and the coming, the coming and the sending, the preparing and the abiding, are paradoxical phases of the one great transaction. God and man are brought together through the whole dramatic episode of the Incarnation. The believer finds a dwelling place for his soul in one of the many **mansions** in the kingdom of God, while the Triune God designs to make His dwelling place with man.

There is significance in the Greek word *monoi,* translated **mansions** or "rooms" (v. 2). The singular form means a way station or stopping place, such as one might use for lodging while on a trip away from home. While the concept of heaven as the final dwelling place of the Christian is inherent here, the contextual reference is to the present life of the Christian in fellowship with God. This is to say that living the new life (eternal life) on earth in the presence and by the power of the Spirit of God is like finding shelter and safety and sustenance at a hotel or camping site on one's way to his final heavenly home.

Jesus knew that, regardless of how well the disciples understood this great truth, there would be dark days ahead. He was thinking especially of the interim between the time He was speaking and the day when the coming of the Spirit would become an actuality. **He** told them of His coming death at the hands of **the prince of the world** (v. 30), who, however, had no lasting power

over Him. And He trusted that their love and obedience (v. 28), supported by His peace which He promised them on the very eve of His death, would sustain them and keep them unafraid. Moreover, if they continued to believe, they would be able to accomplish greater things than He had been able to do on earth. We should not think of **greater works** as being only miracles or signs of a more spectacular nature than those done by Jesus. What they would accomplish would still be done through Him, and because of this fact He would be able to do greater things through them by the power of the Spirit than He had been able to do in the flesh. His earthly ministry had been introductory and of short duration; the work which they would do would be progressive and would last as long as men believe in Christ and are endued with the Holy Spirit.

The **greater works** refer to the product of the Christian's fellowship with God. The promise, **if ye shall ask anything in my name, that will I do** (v. 14), must be seen within the scope of this relationship in which the Triune God makes His abode with the Christian (v. 23) and in which the Christian occupies his spiritual dwelling place in the kingdom of God on his way to his final heavenly home. Here is one of the most meaningful lessons on prayer found in the New Testament. It carries with it all of the spiritual force and insight for which the Gospel of John is noted. We frequently think of prayer as the petition of one who asks God for something, believing that God will give it to him and at the same time invoking the name of Christ who died for man and who thereby has peculiar influence over God the Father to obtain what man wants or needs. No doubt there is truth in this concept of prayer. But let us come a little closer to what John has tried to say. Think of a family in which the parent knows the needs of his children and is both able and willing to supply all they need. In that case, the supply of most of life's needs is there for the taking — the need, in the eyes of the Father, is petition enough. And so prayer in the name of Jesus is receiving with thanksgiving what belongs to one as a child of God. Permission to take becomes necessary only for the special or the doubtful things, those which may or may not be good for one under existing circumstances. Prayer then becomes communion, and communication, and fellowhip. It is abiding, dwelling; it is asking as a child asks and receiving from a parent who provides and gives willingly. In view of this Johannine concept, it seems strange that a Christian should need to keep asking for everything he needs from God with the feeling that if he does not ask he will not receive. John saw a gracious blending of asking on man's part and giving on the part of God. The asking heart of the child goes naturally to the father, even as a babe seeks the breast of its mother; and the giving heart of the Father goes naturally to the child, even as He has given him the very life he enjoys. The asker and the giver are locked in mutual embrace.

Let us move a little closer to this concept of prayer. The presence of God in the Christian is the abiding presence of His Holy Spirit. Spirit (*Pneuma*) is like wind (*pneuma*); it permeates and fills and creates its own power. The Holy Spirit is within the one who has received Him as a dynamic force, a living potential, a kind of incarnation, the life of Christ Himself within. This is a bold concept, yet it is perfectly in keeping with those concepts involved in the Bread of Life and Water of Life teachings of Jesus, and especially with His statement, **He that eateth my flesh and drinketh my blood abideth in me, and I in him** (6:56). Prayer, then, becomes asking of a very special kind; it is the body depending upon the bread and water for nourishment; it is the branch calling upon the vine for sustenance (ch. 15); it is the child receiving life and the wherewithal to sustain that life. "Whatsoever ye shall ask in my name, that will I do" (4:13) becomes **If ye abide in me, and my words abide in you, ask whatsoever you will, and it shall be done unto you** (15:7). "In the name of Jesus" becomes abiding in Him. Praying in His name is more than a formula, more than a policy, more than the best way to get things from God. Praying in His name is praying by one who has experienced the new life from above and in whom dwells the Holy Spirit, the Paraclete, whom Jesus promised to His followers.

There is no intention here to say that all that we receive from God comes automatically and that there is no need for prayer as petition or intercession. But when it is remembered that Jesus was here speaking to the inner group of His chosen disciples, and that John always thought and wrote in the highest of spiritual terms, it will be seen that prayer for the believer is essentially communion; a shared relationship, a relationship of love and obedience with God through the Spirit. There are other phases of prayer, but for John, and for every Christian, a life of prayer must be a life of fellowship; "yea, and our fellowship is with the Father, and with his Son Jesus Christ" (I John 1:3).

C. THE TRUE VINE AND THE BRANCHES (15:1-17)

1 I am the true vine, and my Father is the husbandman. 2 Every branch in me that beareth not fruit, he taketh it away: and *every* branch that beareth fruit, he cleanseth it, that it may bear more fruit. 3 Already ye are clean because of the word which I have spoken unto you. 4 Abide in me, and I in you. As the branch cannot bear fruit of itself, except it abide in the vine; so neither can ye, except ye abide in me. 5 I am the vine, ye are the branches: He that abideth in me, and I in him, the same beareth much fruit: for apart from me ye can do nothing. 6 If a man abide not in me, he is cast forth as a branch, and is withered; and they gather them, and cast them into the fire, and they are burned. 7 If ye abide in me, and my words abide in you, ask whatsoever ye will, and it shall be done unto you. 8 Herein is my Father glorified, that ye bear much fruit; and *so* shall ye be my disciples. 9 Even as the Father hath loved me, I also have loved you: abide ye in my love. 10 If ye keep my commandments, ye shall abide in my love; even as I have kept my Father's commandments, and abide in his love. 11 These things have I spoken unto you, that my joy may be in you, and *that* your joy may be made full. 12 This is my commandment, that ye love one another, even as I have loved you. 13 Greater love hath no man than this, that a man lay down his life for his friends. 14 Ye are my friends, if ye do the things which I command you. 15 No longer do I call you servants; for

the servant knoweth not what his lord doeth: but I have called you friends; for all things that I heard from my Father I have made known unto you. 16 Ye did not choose me, but I chose you, and appointed you, that ye should go and bear fruit, and *that* your fruit should abide: that whatsoever ye shall ask of the Father in my name, he may give it you. 17 These things I command you, that ye may love one another.

This chapter has a twofold connection with what has gone before — with prayer in the previous chapter and with analogies of bread and water in earlier chapters. The purpose here is an advance over what has gone before, because Jesus was interested in the permanent product and outreach of the new life experienced by the disciples. He would be leaving them soon. What would then happen to them and to the message which He had entrusted to them? It was inevitable that He should proceed to use the present analogy of the vine and branches, or one of like nature. For bread and water can only sustain — they cannot reproduce themselves. The vine with its branches is living and has the power to produce fruit, and so this becomes a more complete illustration of the relationship between Christ and the Christian and the consequences of the relationship. Praying and fruitbearing are closely related here — the one who abides in Christ asks and receives, and the one who abides in Him bears much fruit.

Jesus is the *vine,* the Christian is the *branch,* and the Father is the *husbandman* or vinedresser. The whole process of pruning and discarding of worthless branches is depicted here and hardly needs to be explicated because its meaning is so obvious. The main stress is upon the fact that men are not inanimate objects but are living, willing, choosing, fallible creatures. Jesus knew this better than anyone else. He had observed people coming and going, now believing, now deceiving, changing like the wind and moving with the crowd. One of His chosen Twelve had just decided to renounce his allegiance. What now of the remaining eleven? The lesson taught in this chapter is strong and pointed.

Ye did not choose me, but I chose you

(v. 16). Jesus here declared His sovereign authority over His followers. They were with Him because He had chosen them. Neither their own choice nor the confluence of circumstances could have brought about their relationship with Him. Yet, He was not thereby denying that they themselves had had a part in that which in reality was an agreement between them and Jesus. **Ye did not choose me** must be taken in a relative, not an absolute, sense. For actually they had responded to His **follow me,** had decided to stay when Judas had decided to leave; and the appeal of Jesus was to their wills and powers of choice — **abide in me; abide in my love; keep my commandments; love one another.** This same conclusion is understood in evangelistic campaigns today where the stress is laid upon accepting Christ, upon making a decision for Christ, giving oneself to Christ, or consecrating oneself to Him. The invitation goes out, "Jesus invites you to come to Him," and the response is, "O Lamb of God, I come." This kind of appeal has marked the advance of Evangelical Christianity throughout the centuries. John placed a strong theological content in his way of expressing this twofold character of the divine choice: man's response is based upon God's choice. Before we chose Him, He had already chosen us. The sovereignty of God does not destroy or nullify the God-given sovereignty of man, nor does the sovereignty of man exist apart from the sovereignty of God. God is sovereign in His sphere of action; man is sovereign in his sphere, by the will of God. Man's choices are real and not imaginary, else when Judas went out from the upper room and hanged himself, it was because God either chose him to that awful fate or failed to choose him for salvation.

This Johannine theology is strongly supported by Paul: God "chose us in him [Christ] before the foundation of the world, that we should be holy and without blemish before him in love" (Eph. 1:4). In Christ, God has chosen man to a life of holiness. The Incarnation with all of its implications was for this primary purpose. Nowhere in Scripture, interpreted in light of the Cross of Christ, can it be found that God chooses man to any other fate than salvation.

He has made but one choice for man — salvation. Any other fate for man comes contrary to the will of God. If this sounds like limiting the sovereign power of God, it need only be recognized that God does not have His way in much that goes on in the world. Paul refers to "world-rulers of this darkness" (Eph. 6:12) against which the Christian must wrestle. New Testament election is to salvation, never to damnation. Divine election is to salvation. St. Paul strengthens this concept by referring to it as the "good pleasure of God's will (Eph. 1:5), the "counsel" of his will (Eph. 1:11), the "eternal purpose" of His will (Eph. 3:11), all of which are involved in the "mystery" of His will (Eph. 1:9). True, it is a revealed mystery (*mysterion*), but not a fully understood mystery. It is possible for one to become overwise in claiming knowledge of the ways of God, whereas Paul stood in humble awe before the mystery of revealed truth. The sovereignty of God and the delegated sovereignty of man can best be understood when seen, each in relation to the other.

Jesus further said that the way of discipleship was not an easy way. The purpose of the disciple to follow must be strong if it is going to stand the stress of life; in fact, it must be renewed or perpetuated continually if it is to last. The disciples were chosen for the purpose of bearing fruit. And this purpose can be accomplished only by holding on, or abiding in Christ, while God prunes and labors to make better fruit-bearing vines. There is a certain amount of suffering associated with discipline — for that is what pruning in the Christian life is. If an apple tree, for instance, is not trimmed it will grow into a proliferation of branches and a profusion of blossoms, and it will bear fruit that is sure to be a disappointment. The fruit is of the same quality as the tree. A good tree produces good fruit (Matt. 7:17-18). Good fruit is glorifying to the husbandman.

The fruit of which Jesus spoke is love. What He had done for them — and also His soon-coming death on the cross — was done in love. The fruit of the Christian life is love for God and love for

mankind. **This is my commandment, that ye love one another, even as I have loved you** (v. 12). The Greek word is *agape*, self-giving, self-realizing love. The fruit is one, not many. Love has its many by-products and reaches its object or destination in many forms, just as fruit or grain reaches the customer in varied forms.[55] But love it must be, and love it will be, if God is allowed to prune and discipline.

Jesus said that the success of the Gospel depends on the fruit borne by His disciples. Twice in these few verses He commanded His disciples to love one another (vv. 12, 17). One cannot be commanded to love as one might be commanded to row a boat or sing a song. Yet, love begets love, love received responds in love, and love commands in the strongest possible way. Christ was not commanding as sovereign Lord but as Incarnate Savior. He commands that we love by His own demonstrations of love. **We love, because he first loved us** (I John 4:19). The wife of a brother minister died recently after a lingering illness covering a span of twelve years. He had nursed and cared for her when she could neither speak nor care for her own simplest needs. Medical advice might have said to place her in a rest home, and friends might have counseled other ways to meet the problem; but love commanded and he obeyed. The man was love-compelled. The commandments of Christ are the commandments of love (cf. II Cor. 5:14). When our lives and actions are love-impelled, then is the **Father glorified,** because we are bearing **much fruit,** and we are His disciples indeed.

D. THE HATRED OF THE WORLD (15: 18-27)

18 If the world hateth you, ye know that it hath hated me before *it hated* you. 19 If ye were of the world, the world would love its own: but because ye are not of the world, but I chose you out of the world, therefore the world hateth you. 20 Remember the word that I said unto you, A servant is not greater than his lord. If they persecuted me, they will also persecute you; if they kept my word, they will keep yours also. 21 But all these

[55] See Paul's many-sided description of love in Gal. 5:22. Read it, "The fruit of the Spirit is love: love manifested as joy, peace, etc."

things will they do unto you for my name's sake, because they know not him that sent me. 22 If I had not come and spoken unto them, they had not had sin: but now they have no excuse for their sin. 23 He that hateth me hateth my Father also. 24 If I had not done among them the works which none other did, they had not had sin: but now have they both seen and hated both me and my Father. 25 But *this cometh to pass,* that the word may be fulfilled that is written in their law, They hated me without a cause. 26 But when the Comforter is come, whom I will send unto you from the Father, *even* the Spirit of truth, which proceedeth from the Father, he shall bear witness of me: 27 and ye also bear witness, because ye have been with me from the beginning.

The experiences of Jesus in His public ministry became the pattern for the life of the disciples in the world. The term **world,** as used by John, has several meanings. It can mean the material creation, the world of men, or that system or society which evil men have organized in ignorance of or in opposition to the laws of God, including the adherents of the system. Jesus had been met with the hatred of entrenched Judaism, which was doubly guilty of sin because it not only perpetuated evil against Jesus, but did it in the name of its holy religion. But we must not blame the Jews as being solely responsible for the death of Jesus; neither can we think that others would not have done the same if they had been required to make a choice in the matter. Men of all nationalities are betraying Him in our own day, for everyone who hates his brother, everyone who murders and slanders and robs, has a share in the responsibility for Christ's death. The impression may come from the study of John's Gospel that the high priests and the Pharisees were the greatest of criminals, because they were responsible for having Jesus condemned. And from such an impression the church has often been hotly anti-Semitic because the Jews crucified Christ. But it should be remembered that the Gospel writers do not compare the Jewish people with other peoples to show that they were more evil. The Gospels reveal the conflict between the Jews and Jesus, but they also reveal that non-Jews, given the same chance, would have done essentially the same, although perhaps for different reasons. We can say this from our knowledge of human nature. The attitude of Jesus Himself is the exemplary attitude: "Father, forgive them, for they know not what they do" (Luke 23:34).

Of course, the Jews were of the **world** which hated Jesus and which also would hate His followers. Hatred of Jesus was also hatred of the Father. It was hatred of goodness, and truth and love, hatred of everything Jesus stood for. Jesus showed that the response to hate should not be more hate, but love. "Be not overcome of evil, but overcome evil with good" (Rom. 12:21).

Sin against love is worse than sin against law. The unpardonable sin can be understood or identified as the sin against love — the love of God. The disciples were **not of the world** because Jesus had chosen them **out of the world.** It was their identity with Him which would bring about hatred of them in the days to come. They, as Christ's slaves, would not expect any treatment more favorable than that shown their Master: **A servant** [slave] **is not greater than his lord** (v. 20). Jesus traced this hatred back to the fact that He had exposed the sins of the Jews. At first they had been hating Him through ignorance, but after hearing Jesus they could no longer be guiltless. **If I had not come and spoken unto them, they had not had sin; but now they have no excuse for their sin** (v. 22). Rather than turning to Christ who had come to save them, they turned against Him and became doubly guilty before God. The coming of Jesus did not bring about their sin; rather, it exposed sin and brought it under judgment. While the hatred of the world against Jesus and the Gospel will continue, so will the witness to Christ continue. Jesus was depending upon His disciples to be witnesses. In addition, the Holy Spirit which would come from the Father would also testify to Jesus.

Nowhere did Jesus say that His disciples were to hate the world. John, in his First Epistle, exhorted Christians not to love the world (I John 2:15). But "love not" does not mean *hate.* The hostility of the world must not be met with the hostility of the church. Christians are in the peculiar position of trying to win to Christ not only the world which hates them, but also the world from which they have drawn apart. The isolation of the church from sinful worldliness may often be interpreted by the world as a kind of holy snobbery which creates a barrier between the two. When this occurs, efforts to evangelize the unsaved take on the appearance of self-interest rather than love. And how much evangelism has been carried on for the single purpose of advancing the visible church, rather than out of love for the sinner, is sad to contemplate. Separation from the sinful world must never be so complete that one does not love those men who are responsible for it. The Jews hated Christ *without a cause* for the simple reason that He gave them no reason for doing so. Would that the church had always been as blameless in its approach to the world it seeks to save.

E. PROMISE OF BOTH PERSECUTION AND THE COMFORTER (16:1-33)

1 These things have I spoken unto you, that ye should not be caused to stumble. 2 They shall put you out of the synagogues: yea, the hour cometh, that whosoever killeth you shall think that he offereth service unto God. 3 And these things will they do, because they have not known the Father, nor me. 4 But these things have I spoken unto you, that when their hour is come, ye may remember them, how that I told you. And these things I said not unto you from the beginning, because I was with you. 5 But now I go unto him that sent me; and none of you asketh me, Whither goest thou? 6 But because I have spoken these things unto you, sorrow hath filled your heart. 7 Nevertheless I tell you the truth: It is expedient for you that I go away; for if I go not away, the Comforter will not come unto you; but if I go, I will send him unto you. 8 And he, when he is come, will convict the world in respect of sin, and of righteousness, and of judgment: 9 of sin, because they believe not on me; 10 of righteousness, because I go to the Father, and ye behold me no more; 11 of judgment, because the prince of this world hath been judged. 12 I have yet many things to say unto you, but ye cannot bear them now. 13 Howbeit when he, the Spirit of truth, is come, he shall guide you into all the truth: for he shall not speak from himself; but what things soever he shall hear, *these* shall

he speak: and he shall declare unto you the things that are to come. 14 He shall glorify me: for he shall take of mine, and shall declare *it* unto you. 15 All things whatsoever the Father hath are mine: therefore said I, that he taketh of mine, and shall declare *it* unto you. 16 A little while, and ye behold me no more; and again a little while, and ye shall see me. 17 *Some* of his disciples therefore said one to another, What is this that he saith unto us, A little while, and ye behold me not; and again a little while, and ye shall see me: and, Because I go to the Father? 18 They said therefore, What is this that he saith, A little while? We know not what he saith. 19 Jesus perceived that they were desirous to ask him, and he said unto them, Do ye inquire among yourselves concerning this, that I said, A little while, and ye behold me not, and again a little while, and ye shall see me? 20 Verily, verily, I say unto you, that ye shall weep and lament, but the world shall rejoice: ye shall be sorrowful, but your sorrow shall be turned into joy. 21 A woman when she is in travail hath sorrow, because her hour is come: but when she is delivered of the child, she remembereth no more the anguish, for the joy that a man is born into the world. 22 And ye therefore now have sorrow: but I will see you again, and your heart shall rejoice, and your joy no one taketh away from you. 23 And in that day ye shall ask me no question. Verily, verily, I say unto you, If ye shall ask anything of the Father, he will give it you in my name. 24 Hitherto have ye asked nothing in my name: ask, and ye shall receive, that your joy may be made full.

25 These things have I spoken unto you in dark sayings: the hour cometh, when I shall no more speak unto you in dark sayings, but shall tell you plainly of the Father. 26 In that day ye shall ask in my name: and I say not unto you, that I will pray the Father for you; 27 for the Father himself loveth you, because ye have loved me, and have believed that I came forth from the Father. 28 I came out from the Father, and am come into the world: again, I leave the world, and go unto the Father. 29 His disciples say, Lo, now speakest thou plainly, and speakest no dark saying. 30 Now know we that thou knowest all things, and needest not that any man should ask thee: by this we believe that thou camest forth from God. 31 Jesus answered them, Do ye now believe? 32 Behold, the hour cometh, yea, is come, that ye shall be scattered, every man to his own, and shall leave me alone:

and *yet* I am not alone, because the Father is with me. 33 These things have I spoken unto you, that in me ye may have peace. In the world ye have tribulation: but be of good cheer; I have overcome the world.

The main emphases of this chapter are the same as those in ch. 14 — that Jesus was going to leave the world and that He would send the Holy Spirit. Many considerations attend these two great events, and Jesus rehearsed them before His disciples in order that they might be fortified against the trials of persecution which were sure to come upon them. They would be cast out of the religious fellowship of the Jews; some of them would be martyred; but worst of all, these things would be done to them in the name of God, as if it were a service to Him. The basis for this opposition would be the same as that which prompted the Jews to reject and finally crucify Jesus — hatred based upon failure to recognize that Jesus had come to reveal God the Father, the old controversy over the claim of Jesus to deity. These things could not have been told to the disciples at the beginning of their association with Jesus, and even at the time of His death they understood such truths only slightly. Still other things the disciples would come to know when they were ready to bear them (v. 12), revealed by the Holy Spirit who would continue in them the work which Jesus had begun. By explaining things in this way Jesus sought to prepare the disciples for the rigors of the Christian life and to make full provision that they might not fall.

Both history and tradition tell of the persecution suffered by the disciples, who were later called apostles. Peter is said to have been crucified head downward; John was exiled to the Island of Patmos, probably a prison colony; James was slain by the sword; and the others were also martyred. But death was not the only experience that the disciples underwent for their Lord. The true martyr is the man who witnesses for Christ under all circumstances, whether he dies violently for his faith or not. Primarily a martyr (Greek *martyrios*) is a witness. John was exiled but died a natural death in old age. James his brother died by the sword early in life. But "both of the brothers drank the cup of the Lord"[56] (see Matt. 20:22-23). All that may be known or written about the New Testament apostles, including the Apostle Paul, was but the beginning of persecutions which fill the annals of Church History. Thus there has arisen the proverb, "The blood of the martyrs is the seed of the church."

In this chapter the Holy Spirit is again, as in ch. 14, termed **the Spirit of truth.** His coming will be for the purpose of leading men into truth. In this He will not work autonomously, but will act as the representative of Christ, even as Christ was the representative of the Father. His revelation of truth will be truth which concerns Christ who will remain central to the whole system of truth even after His departure from the world (v. 14). God the Father has turned over the reins of redemption to the Son who will be represented in the world by the Holy Spirit. In the entire arrangement the Holy Spirit, although the masculine pronoun is used, remains anonymous, the servant of Christ.

Many wonderful truths arise out of this very brief statement on the Holy Spirit. He is the Paraclete, the One who stands by the side of the Christian, to strengthen, to plead his case, to intercede for him and to be his counsel. He is as truly God as either the Father or the Son. The Father is most clearly known through the Son, while the Spirit continually makes the Son known. Jesus the Son is the highest revelation of God, because in Him God became incarnate. What the Spirit reveals is always truth as it is in Jesus Christ. The leadings of the Spirit never contradict truth already revealed in Christ as He is depicted in the Scriptures. The neglect of the study and understanding of the life and the teachings of Jesus, and an overly independent reliance upon one's own interpretation of the *inner voice*, has led to much confusion on the part of good people and to gross fanaticism on the part of others. John in his First Epistle warns his readers to "prove the spirits, whether they are of God" (I John 4:1). Unless there be some standard of truth,

---

[56] William Barclay, *The Master's Men*, p. 104. This is a brief book of biographies of the Twelve, which utilizes both Gospel and tradition, fact and fiction.

the spirit that speaks may not be the Holy Spirit. It may be one's own desires cropping up, one's own mind hatching ideas, or some evil spirit whispering within. Truth is only truth when it can be found to correlate with truth as it can be seen in the Incarnate Son.

The coming of the Spirit, Jesus promised, would be a convicting and a convincing force. This idea has moral significance. The work of the Spirit is in the realm of man's conscience. The truth involved is essentially moral, **all the truth** (v. 13), meaning truth for right living rather than for every intellectual curiosity. **And he, when he is come, will convict the world in respect of sin, and of righteousness, and of judgment** (v. 8). He will convict the world — the world of men in their sinful pursuits — indirectly through the Christian; the world as such cannot receive the Spirit (14:17). This places great responsibility upon the Christian to be the channel, an active, dynamic channel between heaven and earth, between Christ and the world. The Spirit convicts **the world of sin, because they believe not on me; of righteousness, because I go to the Father, and ye behold me no more; of judgment, because the prince of this world hath been judged** (vv. 9-11). Various interpretations have been given these three reasons for the work of the Spirit.[57] The meaning can be understood best against the background of the conflict between Jesus and the Jews. They had not believed Him when He claimed God as His Father; rather they condemned Him for it. The work of the Holy Spirit is to show that they and all who follow their example are wrong; to convict them of the sin of unbelief and the rejection of Jesus; to convince them that Jesus was right in claiming to be the Son of God. And the climactic work of the Spirit is to pronounce upon them the judgment which they had pronounced on Jesus — because by Jesus are all men judged. Even Satan has been judged and sentence has been passed upon him. Jesus said, "the prince of this world is coming. He has no power over me" (14:30, RSV). By His death and resurrection Jesus gained eternal victory over Satan, and he remains a defeated foe for all who trust in Christ. The work of the Spirit is to make men morally aware of these truths and so prepare their hearts for the Gospel.

The present discourse contains excellent material for understanding the doctrine of the Trinity. Father, Son, and Spirit are specified, each playing a separate role, yet — at the same time — intermingled, each at times playing the role of the other in some respects. Concerning the departure of Jesus and the coming of the Spirit we find what appear on the surface to be conflicting concepts. In the words of Jesus, "The Father . . . shall give you another Comforter" (14:16); "I come unto you" (14:18); "my Father will love him, and we will come unto him, and make our abode with him" (14:23); "the Holy Spirit, whom the Father will send in my name" (14:26); "if I go, I will send him unto you" (16:7); "when he is come" (16:8). All of this sounds confusing. The Father will send the Spirit, Jesus will send the Spirit, the Spirit Himself will come, Jesus will come again, the Spirit will come, both Jesus and the Father will come. But this is not just the confusion of paradox; it is the mystery of Deity. It is the mystery of the Triune God, revealed to man in the work of redemption.

Just how shall we look at this three-in-one revelation? First of all, in the entire discourse there is no mention of the name God except where the disciples finally proclaimed their faith: **by this we believe that thou camest forth from God** (16:30).[58] This fact is the key to the understanding of the problem. God has been revealed as Father, as Son, and as Spirit. The Son, Jesus, made the Father concept familiar and introduced the Holy Spirit, while He wrestled with the religious leaders of His day to declare and sustain His own claim to being the Son of God. The validity of belief in both the Father and the Spirit as doctrines of the Christian faith rests upon the fact of Christ as Son of God. The whole trinitarian structure falls if Jesus be not divine; but it stands because He is the Son of God, or God the Son. We

---

[57] Barrett, *op. cit.*, pp. 406-407.
[58] In John 16:2 God is mentioned as one to whom erroneous service is rendered, but this is aside from the references to God in His dealings with man in the plan of salvation.

are dealing, therefore, with three ways of knowing God: the Father concept which makes the Son concept real and understandable; the reality of the Incarnate Son; and the power of the Holy Spirit. And so we say: God the Father, God the Son, and God the Holy Spirit. One is no more God than the other. God cannot be said to be merely the sum total of the three; it is better to say that this is how God has chosen to be known to man.

The popular expression of the Trinity tends to equate God with the Father and to make the Son and the Spirit revelations of the Father. This is not the true Trinity as it is expressed in the New Testament. Also, there is a tendency to speak of Father, Son, and Spirit as three Persons in such a way that the result is a Tritheism (three Gods), rather than a Trinity (three-in-one God). The problem has arisen from a misunderstanding or reinterpretation in more modern terms of the word *Person* as used in the ancient creeds. The Second Council of Constantinople (553) used the expression "A trinity of the same essence [reality], one deity in three . . . persons."[59] This is a clear representation of the use of *person* in its early ecclesiastical context. In commenting on this term in respect to the Athanasian Creed (373) Philip Schaff says, "The term *persona* is taken neither in the old sense of a mere . . . form of manifestation . . . nor in the modern sense of an independent . . . individual, but in a sense which lies between the two conceptions."[60] Concerning the Christology of the Chalcedonian Creed he says, "Christ is not a *double* being, with two persons."[61] The Standard Catechism of the Methodist Church asks: "*Is the Trinity an incomprehensible mystery?* As to the manner of existence it is, but as a revealed fact it is not."[62] Schaff quotes Augustine as saying, "God is greater and truer in our thoughts than in our words; he is greater and truer in reality than in our thoughts."[63]

The material just presented is not meant as full explanation, but it is offered in the interest of understanding and appreciation. We can know God only as He has made Himself known. We must start with the three — Father Son, and Spirit — and we find therein a marvelous unity which we know as God. This is John's theology of the Trinity.

The teaching of Jesus concerning His leaving the world had a dual reference: to His death and to His ascension. About the first He said, **A little while, and ye behold me no more; and again a little while, and ye shall see me** (v. 16). When the disciples questioned the meaning of this statement, Jesus began to describe His going and returning without using the terms "crucifixion" and "resurrection," which were what He meant. **Ye shall weep and lament, but the world shall rejoice: ye shall be sorrowful, but your sorrow shall be turned into joy** (v. 20). It is evident that Jesus was speaking of the sorrow of the disciples and the joy of the Jews at His death, followed by the joy of the disciples at the Resurrection. He further illustrated His meaning in relation to the disciples by the case of the sorrow and pain of childbirth which is always followed by the joy of a new life begun. Birth and resurrection are parallel in that life is given in both experiences. However, the joy of resurrection is greater than the joy of birth because it is permanent — **your heart shall rejoice, and your joy no man taketh away from you** (v. 22). And then Jesus made a rather strange, yet significant, statement: **In that day ye shall ask me no question. But if ye shall ask anything of the Father, he will give it you in my name** (v. 23). Very little conversation between Jesus and His disciples is recorded in the Gospel accounts of the post-Resurrection appearances of Jesus. Nothing at all is said concerning the person of Jesus, which had been a major question in the minds of many and an issue in His discussions with the Pharisees. No one asked Him that question after the Resurrection. This does not mean that the faith of the disciples was perfected by the Resurrection, but it does signify a change of attitude on their part. "When they saw him, they worshipped him; but some doubted" (Matt.

---

[59] John H. Leith, *Creeds of the Churches* (New York: Doubleday & Company, 1963), p. 46.
[60] Philip Schaff, *The Creeds of Christendom*, Vol. I, p. 38.   [61] *Ibid.*, p. 31.
[62] *The Standard Catechism* of the Methodist Episcopal Church and the Methodist Episcopal Church South, p. 31.   [63] Schaff, *op. cit.*, p. 38.

28:17). "They were terrified and affrighted, and supposed that they beheld a spirit" (Luke 24:37). "None of the disciples durst inquire of him, Who art thou? knowing that it was the Lord" (John 21:12). There were questions in their minds about many things, but Jesus answered none of them. He sought only to make them realize that He was alive again (Luke 24:38-43). The questions needed to be asked, however, and they would be asked over and over again for they needed to be answered; but they would be asked in a new way — inquiring of the Father in the name of Jesus rather than asking Jesus Himself (John 16:23-24). The end result would be the same, even though He would not be present in the flesh, because of His unity with the Father; only the procedure would be different.

Admitting that He had been speaking in parables or figurative language, while leaving the disciples to understand the meaning after His Death and Resurrection, Jesus took up the second reference to His departure from the world — His return to the Father. This time He spoke, not in parables but in very plain language, and this time, not of His going and returning, but of His coming and His going. **I came out from the Father, and am come into the world: again, I leave the world, and go unto the Father** (v. 28). At last there dawned upon the minds of the disciples the truth which He had been declaring all along: **By this we believe that thou camest forth from God,** they said. This response, ever so sincere and significant, reminds one of the occasion of the first Passover, when "many believed" but Jesus would not "trust himself" to them because He knew the limitations of their expressed faith. On this occasion also, Jesus knew that the faith of the disciples was limited and insecure. **Do ye now believe?** He said. And referring again to the Crucifixion, He told them that they would forsake Him and He would be left alone except for the presence of the Father. But the Father would never forsake Him (v. 32). Herein lie both a fact and a truth: the faith which John attributed to the disciples of Jesus during His lifetime was never more than could be generated by the signs which He wrought as revelations

of His true Person; and their faith did not go further until the Spirit had been given.

After reading that Jesus was confident that the Father would never leave Him alone, one does not find in this Gospel the ninth-hour cry from the cross, "My God, my God, why hast thou forsaken me" (Matt. 27:46). John's concept of the unity of Jesus with God the Father was too strong. This expression is probably more figurative than actual as Matthew used it and as Jesus uttered it, being indicative of the great sense of loneliness which Jesus experienced in the hour when life was slipping from His body.

In this great discourse to His disciples, Jesus brought them face to face with the fact that His ministry was at an end, that His death was near and would be violent, that they would be expected to carry on the work which He had begun, and that they would have the presence of the Holy Spirit to lead them and help them. He could not promise them an easy time, but He could and did encourage them to believe for success in the deepest and most spiritual sense of the word. **These things have I spoken unto you, that in me ye may have peace. In the world ye have tribulation: but be of good cheer** — "be encouraged" — **I have overcome the world** (v. 33).

F. THE PRAYER OF JESUS (17:1-26)

1 These things spake Jesus; and lifting up his eyes to heaven, he said, Father, the hour is come; glorify thy Son, that the Son may glorify thee: 2 even as thou gavest him authority over all flesh, that to all whom thou hast given him, he should give eternal life. 3 And this is life eternal, that they should know thee the only true God, and him whom thou didst send, *even* Jesus Christ. 4 I glorified thee on the earth, having accomplished the work which thou hast given me to do. 5 And now, Father, glorify thou me with thine own self with the glory which I had with thee before the world was. 6 I manifested thy name unto the men whom thou gavest me out of the world: thine they were, and thou gavest them to me; and they have kept thy word. 7 Now they know that all things whatsoever thou hast given me are from thee. 8 for the words which thou gavest me I

have given unto them; and they received *them,* and knew of a truth that I came forth from thee, and they believed that thou didst send me. 9 I pray for them: I pray not for the world, but for those whom thou hast given me; for they are thine: 10 and all things that are mine are thine, and thine are mine: and I am glorified in them. 11 And I am no more in the world, and these are in the world, and I come to thee. Holy Father, keep them in thy name which thou hast given me, that they may be one, even as we *are.* 12 While I was with them, I kept them in thy name which thou hast given me: and I guarded them, and not one of them perished, but the son of perdition; that the scripture might be fulfilled. 13 But now I come to thee; and these things I speak in the world, that they may have my joy made full in themselves. 14 I have given them thy word; and the world hated them, because they are not of the world. even as I am not of the world. 15 I pray not that thou shouldest take them from the world, but that thou shouldest keep them from the evil *one.* 16 They are not of the world, even as I am not of the world. 17 Sanctify them in the truth: thy word is truth. 18 As thou didst send me into the world, even so sent I them into the world. 19 And for their sakes I sanctify myself, that they themselves also may be sanctified in truth. 20 Neither for these only do I pray, but for them also that believe on me through their word; 21 that they may all be one; even as thou, Father, *art* in me, and I in thee, that they also may be in us: that the world may believe that thou didst send me. 22 And the glory which thou hast given me I have given unto them; that they may be one, even as we *are* one; 23 I in them, and thou in me, that they may be perfected into one; that the world may know that thou didst send me, and lovedst them, even as thou lovedst me. 24 Father, I desire that they also whom thou hast given me be with me where I am, that they may behold my glory, which thou hast given me: for thou lovedst me before the foundation of the world. 25 O righteous Father, the world knew thee not, but I knew thee; and these knew that thou didst send me; 26 and I made known unto them thy name, and will make it known; that the love wherewith thou lovedst me may be in them, and I in them.

This prayer is part of the final discourse of Jesus to His disciples and was probably spoken audibly for their benefit. It has all the characteristics of prayer found in other portions of the discourse. That it was spoken in the Upper Room is held in doubt by some scholars. Westcott believes that Jesus and the disciples left the Upper Room at the close of ch. 14 and that the rest of the discourse was given on the way to Gethsemane,[64] the prayer probably being given in the Temple.[65] If chapters 14 and 16 are exchanged, only 17 was spoken on the way to Gethsemane. Plummer thinks that it was "spoken in the upper room, after the company had risen from supper, in the pause before starting for the Mount of Olives,"[66] along with chapters 15 and 16. "Arise, let us go hence" (14:31) has reference to their going out to meet the evil forces which would crucify Jesus.[67] If there is any way of sensing the situation out of which the prayer arose, the Upper Room would seem the most appropriate location.

This prayer is more properly called The Lord's Prayer than the model prayer commonly so-called. It is most often called The High-priestly Prayer, although Westcott calls it "The Prayer of Consecration."[68] Macgregor calls it a "sacramental prayer . . . the eternal intercession of the Great High Priest."[69] The prayer may be divided quite naturally into three parts: the prayer of Jesus for Himself (vv. 1-5) ; His prayer for the disciples (vv. 6-19) ; and His prayer for the general Church (vv. 20-26). The main portions rehearse much of the material and emphasis of the discourse.

The physical attitude of Jesus at prayer is in keeping with John's emphasis on His oneness with God. Both at the tomb of Lazarus (11:41) and in this instance **Jesus lifted up his eyes** in order to address the Heavenly Father. In contrast, in the Gethsemane prayer (Matt. 36:39) He "fell on his face and prayed." Luke says that "He kneeled" (Luke 22: 41). At other times it is recorded that He prayed, but we are not told of His physical posture. From these observations one is reminded of some significant physical attitudes of prayer, especial-

[64] *Op. cit.,* p. 211. [65] *Ibid.,* p. 237. [66] *Cambridge Greek Testament,* p. 298.
[67] *Ibid.,* p. 282. [68] *Op. cit.,* p. 314. [69] *Op. cit.,* p. 236.

ly of public prayer. A kneeling position bespeaks humility and submission. Standing with uncovered head signifies awe and reverence. Reclining and sitting may be the mark of trust and relaxation and are more appropriate for private than for public prayer. Bowed head and closed eyes imply that the world with its distractions is being shut out. The raised head and open eyes of Jesus demonstrated an intimacy with the Father which few Christians could hope to realize. Regardless of whether the body follows the heart, or vice versa, the attitudes just expressed are indicative of vital prayer under different circumstances.

The form of the prayer of Jesus under discussion here is that of simple address, with no repetition, no crying as though to attract God's attention, no imploring of God who may be found in an unwilling mood. From this it would seem that the closer one walks with God in his daily life, the more natural it becomes to pray in calmness and assurance. The opposite to the publican who "smote his breast, saying, God, be merciful to me a sinner" (Luke 18:13) is the Master who said, **I glorified thee on the earth, having accomplished the work which thou hast given me to do** (v. 4). By the prayer of Jesus, one is inclined to say that he who prays most effectively is he who least needs to pray for himself. Many prayers consist of beating a trail into the presence of God through the jungle of unfaithfulness and disobedience, so that praying becomes a remedy which restores rather than a food which nourishes. Weep and cry and repent if your path has strayed from God. But for the faithful Christian prayer begins with communion at the place where he and his Heavenly Father meet on prearranged terms: at the place where he, like Jesus, can turn his face heavenward and say **Father.**

As one approaches an analysis of this prayer of Jesus, his own heart reaches for the skies, he feels that the prayer of Christ for His disciples has been, or must be, answered for him, and he is brought into the Holy of Holies with Christ in both consecration and intercession.

This portion of the prayer which was for Jesus Himself was very simple, and made request only for that which it was His right to claim. **Father, glorify thou me with thine own self with the glory which I had with thee before the world was** (v. 5). Jesus was asking that He be restored to the heavenly state which He had had before His life on earth began. The hour had come for this restoration because He had been faithful in completing His Father-appointed task. He had been given the authority to grant eternal life to those disciples whom God had given Him according to the plan of grace and faith — grace on the part of God and faith on the part of man. When faith becomes united with grace it brings forth eternal life in the believer, and this reveals the glory of Jesus. His work on earth had glorified God the Father, and He was now ready to return to His former glory. The simplest definition of glory is the manifestation or revelation of one's true state or status, usually used in reference to good rather than to evil. Jesus had revealed the true nature of God to men and thus glorified God the Father. His own supreme glory would come from being restored as the divine *logos*.

Then Jesus prayed for His disciples — **not for the world** (v. 9), but for those **whom thou gavest me out of the world** (v. 6), those who **have kept thy word** (v. 7). God **gave**, they **kept**. God, as redeeming Savior rather than as sovereign Lord, had given them to Jesus as disciples and followers. Jesus described His disciples as men who had received His teachings and had believed that He had come from God. This is the minimum standard of faith for the follower of Christ, and though it seems very meagre when observed in the disciples, nevertheless it was enough to start with. And Jesus prayed for their continuance in the faith: **Holy Father, keep them in thy name . . . that they may be one, even as we are** (v. 11). In praying this way Jesus did not mention the Holy Spirit even though earlier He had promised to send the Spirit to lead them into all truth (16:13). From John's understanding of the plan of salvation, in no other way would a Holy Father preserve His chosen disciples than through the work of His Holy Spirit. This first use, by John, of **Holy** in addressing God signifies that the faith of discipleship and the knowledge of God are moral and spiritual in character. There must be more than a faith which brings understanding and a knowledge which brings certainty; faith must also bring sin into judgment and put men into a right relationship with a Holy God.

The petition for the disciples is threefold: **that they may be one, even as we are one** (v. 11), that they should be kept **from the evil one** (v. 15), and that they should be sanctified **in the truth** (v. 17). The first petition is for unity, the second is for victory, and the third is for purity. The unity which Jesus envisioned for His followers has its analogy in the unity of the Godhead: unity of purpose, unity of activity, and unity of character. But it must be more than unity within the group; that would create its own fluctuating, and eventually deteriorating, standard. It must also be unity with God the Father and God the Son. Otherwise it would be a false unity, for of itself unity is not a virtue unless it centers in a worthy norm.

This prayer for unity has been used as a strong argument for the uniting of churches in the interest of ecumenicity. If this be the meaning, such union could come only on a high plane of faith in Christ — nothing lower than that which John set forth. Some church leaders have advocated organizational unity and not theological or experiential unity. But this could not have been the aim of Christ's prayer, nor is it the prayer's best application for today. Without denying that value may be found in the uniting of religious bodies in the interest of Christian unity, true Christian unity, whether organizational or not, must be based upon a minimal creed of the deity of Jesus Christ and the efficacy of His atonement, and fortified by the answers to the other petitions for victory and purity.

The second prayer of Jesus for His disciples was that they might be brought safely through the trials which were ahead of them and be spared the evil fate which had befallen Judas. **I pray not that thou shouldest take them from the world, but that thou shouldest keep them from the evil one** (v. 15). The Greek for evil reads *poneroo* (masculine) — thus the translation **evil one**. Jesus may have been referring to "the prince of the world" (14:30), Satan. The disciples belonged to Jesus by right of the Father. He had given them God's Word as a defence against evil, and it had protected them during their years together. Soon they would be bereft of His physical presence, left "as sheep in the midst of wolves" (Matt. 10:16). They could be protected in either of two ways: by being isolated from the world of people, or by being kept in the midst of conflict with the sinful world. Jesus prayed in terms of the second. Victory over evil can be achieved only by serious struggle against the powers opposed to the Church. The one who tries to live his Christian life in isolation, such as the monk in his monastary cell or the church member who boasts that his church "may be small, but it is pure," has not necessarily found therein victory over sin, because evil comes from within as well as from without. Piety of this hothouse variety is too easily mistaken for self-righteousness or sanctified snobbery. Often the Church has found itself in the position of trying to win the world which it has shunned and condemned and even hated. The problem arises at the point of opposing evil and at the same time loving the ones who perpetrate it. The world cannot understand a man who professes to love the souls of men, who at the same time shuns contact with them as persons. Let Christians recognize that there are problems which must be faced by the believer who makes himself a part of the work-a-day world in which he lives and makes a living. The risk of evil influences is real, and the fear of being overcome is understandable; but Christ expects His disciples to be saving factors in the midst of life and to be overcomers, not to be overcome. The presence of the Holy Spirit is their guarantee of victory over sin and victory in winning others to Christ.

The third prayer of Jesus for His disciples was that they might be **sanctified**. This is first of all a ceremonial term, meaning to be set apart or consecrated for holy purposes. Such setting apart guarantees that the object shall be kept pure, free from everything which would defile its hallowedness. In this sense a building can be sanctified. People may be said to sanctify themselves when they devote or consecrate themselves totally to God and His service. This may take place at a definite date and time, but it must be perpetuated in order to be valid.

God also sanctifies by setting the person apart and by keeping him from evil. Christ shared with His disciples in this experience of sanctification; it was a part of His being born, living and dying. He lived a sanctified life. God had set Him apart, had dedicated Him to the great purpose of redemption, and had kept Him uncontaminated from the sin of the world. In similar fashion sanctification is also a part of the life of disciples in the world; they too must live sanctified lives because God has set them apart to share with Christ in the great work of redemption.

But this is not all. Sanctification comes through **the truth** (v. 17), which is the Word of God. The saving truth revealed by Jesus is the sanctifying agent. Truth is purifying: only truth can dispel falsehood, counteract error, and set men free. The earlier portion of the teaching of this discourse has led directly to this prayer for the sanctification of the disciples. They were to be sanctified through the truth; the Word of God is truth; Jesus is both the Word and the Truth. Because Jesus had to leave the world, the Holy Spirit would take His place and lead the disciples into all truth. The conclusion is that the Holy Spirit is the final agent for sanctification. Additional emphases on this truth may be found in other portions of the New Testament, and sound theology of sanctification makes necessary fine distinctions in the experience. But all the essentials are here: sanctification sets the Christian apart and dedicates him to God and His service; it cleanses and keeps him from evil that is in the world, and it is accomplished and perpetuated by the Holy Spirit.

It has already been suggested that the sanctification of Jesus was not essentially different from that of the disciples in the terms laid down by the prayer. The difference — and the problem of Jesus' needing to be sanctified — arises when the experience is limited to mean the cleansing of the heart from the carnal nature. This, of course, is implied in the term as understood from its wider use in the Bible, but here it is used of both Jesus and the disciples in relation to their service to God the Father in the world. God sanctified Jesus for this purpose (10:13), and Jesus reiterated this fact

in the present prayer (v. 19). He had been kept from sin, a pure vessel for the service of the Father. He prayed that the disciples likewise would be kept from sin, pure instruments for the service of God. The fact of the sinlessness of Jesus and the initial sinfulness of the disciples is not a part of the present topic, although the fact is implied. The identity of Jesus with man is stressed rather than His identity with God. And in this light, sanctification applies both to Jesus and His followers, each in his separate sphere.

The last emphasis of this prayer pertains to the Church in general. In essence Jesus prayed the same prayer as He had prayed for the eleven who heard Him. When the prayer would become answered in the disciples, their influence would cause others to believe in Christ, and a kind of chain-reaction would be set in operation. The oneness of the disciples with each other and with their Lord through the Spirit would spread to make Christians in every time and clime. Starting with Jesus whom the Father had sent and reaching to the farthest disciple, the revelation of God's redemption would be carried throughout the world. **I made known unto them thy name** [*character*], **and will make it known; that the love wherewith thou lovedst me may be in them, and I in them** (v. 26). With this petition the prayer closes. The answer to the things for which Jesus prayed for the little band of eleven disciples may become the glorious experience of every believer, provided he is willing to accept also its responsibility.

IV. THE PASSION STORY (18:1 — 19: 42)

A. THE ARREST OF JESUS (18:1-11)

1 When Jesus had spoken these words, he went forth with his disciples over the brook Kidron, where was a garden, into which he entered, himself and his disciples. 2 Now Judas also, who betrayed him, knew the place: for Jesus ofttimes resorted thither with his disciples. 3 Judas then, having received the band of *soldiers*, and officers from the chief priests and the Pharisees, cometh thither with lanterns and torches and weapons. 4 Jesus therefore, knowing all the things that were coming upon him, went forth, and saith unto them, Whom seek ye? 5 They answered him, Jesus of Nazareth.

Jesus saith unto them, I am *he*. And Judas also, who betrayed him, was standing with them. 6 When therefore he said unto them, I am *he*, they went backward, and fell to the ground. 7 Again therefore he asked them, Whom seek ye? And they said, Jesus of Nazareth. 8 Jesus answered, I told you that I am *he;* if therefore ye seek me, let these go their way: 9 that the word might be fulfilled which he spake, Of those whom thou hast given me I lost not one. 10 Simon Peter therefore having a sword drew it, and struck the high priest's servant, and cut off his right ear. Now the servant's name was Malchus. 11 Jesus therefore said unto Peter, Put up the sword into the sheath: the cup which the Father hath given me, shall I not drink it?

The account which John has given of the Passion and Resurrection is complete within itself and in keeping with his method of using selected events in the life of Jesus as signs or witnesses to His Person. John's story of the Passion serves this same end. Following also his concept of a timetable in the life of Jesus, John depicted Him as quietly and deliberately leaving the scene of the last discourse and going with the disciples to the Garden of Gethsemane (although he does not name it nor relate the agony of Jesus which took place there). To the disciples it was another occasion to get away in the cool of the evening with their Lord, whom they were beginning to observe with new insight. To Jesus it was keeping an appointment with Judas, His betrayer, and with death, the last great enemy of man. Judas **knew the place,** and Jesus seemed to know that Judas would look for Him in the garden. How the scene had changed from those times when Judas had been one of the Twelve, in fellowship with Jesus in the garden rendezvous!

The deliberateness of Jesus was matched by the intensity of Judas, which shows that evil can be as compelling as righteousness to the man who surrenders himself to it. A headlong mania seized Judas, and one can imagine his rush of activity in preparation for the arrest, as if he were afraid to stop lest a better impulse lay hold of him. Since the time of the Last Supper — which could not have been more than a few hours according to John — Judas had conferred with the Sanhedrin, made an agreement with that ruling body of the Jews, and hurried to find Jesus. He came to the garden with a band of soldiers provided by the Sanhedrin, having a **captain** and **officers** (v. 12). They were armed for night combat — **with lanterns, and torches and weapons** (v. 3). Certainly there was no need of such a force if they expected only to arrest Jesus. The soldiers may have been sent along to protect Judas in case Jesus or the disciples gave resistance. More probably the force was assigned to Judas in case the feared uprising (11:48) should occur, even though it was night when few people would be around. The fear was partly justified, for at the appearance of the soldiers Peter led a one-man resistance movement long enough to cut off a man's ear. It is a little surprising to find Peter with a sword. John took care to say that he had one, as if it were not the customary thing. Certainly there was nothing in the program of Jesus to require His disciples to have weapons of any kind. Peter may have obtained the sword on the way to the garden, anticipating trouble, and determined to prove his expressed loyalty to Jesus which the Master had so recently challenged (13: 37-38). At any rate, as soon as he learned that the soldiers had come for Jesus he went into action, attacking the first man he could reach; there seems to be no other reason why he struck the servant of the high priest. Peter was probably a poor swordsman, being a fisherman and not a soldier. Aiming to cleave the man's head, he missed and took off his right ear. This was a bad miss indeed if Peter chanced to be right-handed. He might have struck again, but he was stopped — not by the soldiers but by Jesus, for which Peter must have been thankful as he thought back upon the event. Luke says that the disciples asked Jesus if they should fight, and that one of them rushed with his sword before Jesus could answer. Whereupon Jesus rebuked him and healed the ear (Luke 22:49-50).

The soldiers who came with Judas were probably not Roman soldiers, who "would have taken Jesus at once to Pilate, not to the high priest."[70] Judas

[70] Barrett, *op. cit.*, p. 433.

came as their guide. Jesus identified Himself to them, according to John, whereas the Synoptics say that Judas identified Him by kissing Him. When Jesus said a second time, **I am he,** the soldiers fell back in consternation and fear, repelled by the very majesty of His bearing. John told this to show that they could not have taken Jesus unless He had allowed Himself to be taken. It may have been to Judas that Jesus said, **If therefore ye seek me, let these go their way** (v. 8), meaning for him to leave the group and let the soldiers return to their barracks. If so, this was an attempt to win Judas back. No further mention of Judas is made in John's Gospel; Matthew says that Judas hanged himself (Matt. 27: 5). Jesus may have meant to make this appeal to him, but the context of the account seems to point to the interest of Jesus in the eleven disciples rather than in Judas. Out of His concern for them, He asked the soldiers to take Him and let them go free. This may help to explain why none of the disciples were arrested, even though they had been closely associated with Jesus in all of His activities. As the arrest and trial proceeded, it became more and more evident that the Jewish authorities were not trying primarily to forstall an insurrection — they were bent on destroying just one man.

Two short remarks serve to maintain John's keen sense of the deity of Jesus, even in the period of His greatest humiliation. The first is by John: Jesus knew **all the things that were coming upon him** (v. 4). The second is by Jesus Himself: **the cup which the Father hath given me, shall I not drink it?** (v. 11). These words of Jesus are suggestive of his garden agony as given in detail by the Synoptics.

B. THE JEWISH TRIAL (18:12-27)

12 So the band and the chief captain, and the officers of the Jews, seized Jesus and bound him, 13 and led him to Annas first; for he was father in law to Caiaphas, who was high priest that year. 14 Now Caiaphas was he that gave counsel to the Jews, that it was expedient that one man should die for the people. 15 And Simon Peter followed Jesus, and

so did another disciple. Now that disciple was known unto the high priest, and entered in with Jesus into the court of the high priest; 16 but Peter was standing at the door without. So the other disciple, who was known unto the high priest, went out and spake unto her that kept the door, and brought in Peter. 17 The maid therefore that kept the door saith unto Peter, Art thou also *one* of this man's disciples? He saith, I am not. 18 Now the servants and the officers were standing *there,* having made a fire of coals; for it was cold; and they were warming themselves: and Peter also was with them, standing and warming himself.

19 The high priest therefore asked Jesus of his disciples, and of his teaching. 20 Jesus answered him, I have spoken openly to the world; I ever taught in synagogues, and in the temple, where all the Jews come together; and in secret spake I nothing. 21 Why askest thou me? ask them that have heard *me,* what I spake unto them: behold, these know the things which I said. 22 And when he had said this, one of the officers standing by struck Jesus with his hand, saying, Answerest thou the high priest so? 23 Jesus answered him, If I have spoken evil, bear witness of the evil: but if well, why smitest thou me? 24 Annas therefore sent him bound unto Caiaphas the high priest.

25 Now Simon Peter was standing and warming himself. They said therefore unto him, Art thou also *one* of his disciples? He denied, and said, I am not. 26 One of the servants of the high priest, being a kinsman of him whose ear Peter cut off, said, Did not I see thee in the garden with him? 27 Peter therefore denied again: and straightway the cock crew.

The trial of Jesus was twofold — ecclesiastical and civil. Each had three phases, as seen from a survey of the four Gospels at this point. John omitted the session before the Sanhedrin in the early morning, as well as that before Herod of Galilee. He also abbreviated many details given by one or more of the Synoptics. They in turn omit the session before Annas.[71]

The soldiers seem to have been instructed to avoid any conflict and to arrest Jesus as quietly as possible, because they stood by until they were assured that there would be no open op-

---

[71] For an uncritical, harmonized account of the trial see James Stalker, *The Life of Jesus Christ,* pp. 126-141. For a criticial appraisal see Hoskyns, *op. cit.,* pp. 511-525.

position. Then they seized **Jesus and bound him** (v. 12), to lesson the chances that any friends might try to rescue Him. He was kept bound before the high priest (v. 24), but apparently was given sufficient freedom to walk when taken to Pilate (v. 28). **They led him to Annas first; for he was father in law to Caiaphas, who was high priest that year** (v. 13). Annas was high priest from 7 to 14 A.D. and was followed by five sons and a son-in-law, Caiaphas. Whether he held office in the Sanhedrin at the time of the trial of Jesus is uncertain, but he evidently continued to exercise considerable control over its affairs.[72] The questioning seems to have taken place before Annas, after which Jesus was turned over to Caiaphas for the disposition of His case. "Note that according to John there is no formal trial, no citation of witnesses as in the Synoptics, but rather an attempt to gather damning evidence to lay before Pilate."[73] Jesus was questioned concerning His **disciples** and His **teachings.** In His answers He made no reference to the disciples, testifying only of Himself: **1 have spoken openly . . . and in secret spake I nothing. Why askest thou me? ask them that have heard me** (vv. 21-22). The only response came from one of the arresting officers, who struck Jesus with the flat of his hand, accusing Him of being discourteous to the high priest. One can well imagine that the officer did this in response to a silent signal from Caiaphas. But Jesus ignored the reference to the high priest and again made His plea on the basis of His teachings. **If I have spoken evil** [*in my public ministry*], **bear witness of the evil: but if well, why smitest thou me?** (v. 23). With this He was led away to the palace of Pilate.

Peter and another disciple had followed Jesus to the house of the high priest. The other disciple is traditionally thought to have been John the Apostle and author of this Gospel. How he, a Galilean fisherman, **was known unto the high priest** (v. 15) has long been a problem for scholars. This observation is easier to reconcile with a theory of authorship which attributes the Gospel to a Jerusalem elder rather than to John the son of Zebedee. Perhaps John, by

withholding the disciple's name, was not referring to himself. There was one disciple whom we know had access to the presence of the high priest — he had been there not very many hours before. We are not told what Judas was doing during the arrest and questioning of Jesus, but Matthew's Gospel says that at the close of the trial (before Jesus was taken to Pilate) he was "condemned" for what he had done; he returned the money to the chief priests and hanged himself. He was not asked to testify against Jesus, but as he observed the purpose and the tactics of the Jewish authorities, and when he saw the Master led away to certain death, he "repented" of what he had done. He and Peter were present at the ecclesiastical trial. And so the disciple who gained admittance for Peter could have been Judas. If this be so, Judas could have been an influencing factor in Peter's denying his Lord. If John knew Matthew's account that Judas repented of his evil deed, he may have been constrained to hope that Judas had obtained mercy and died a disciple at heart — therefore, perhaps, John called him a disciple rather than using his name.

We are not told why Peter followed Jesus into the chambers of the high priest, but the reason is obvious. It was like Peter to rush in and take risks. But it was more than impetuosity which propelled him. It was a follow-up of the sword episode by which he had sought to demonstrate his loyalty to Jesus. He hoped to be able to compensate for his inept remarks and actions; but as is so often the case, the result was over-compensation. He tried too hard and with poor discernment. If he had hoped to have the chance to defend Jesus before the high priest he was disappointed. He was caught off-guard at every turn. The receptionist, seeing Peter with **another disciple** whom she recognized, asked him: **Art thou also one of this man's disciples?** (v.17). And he quickly answered, **I am not.** Taken by surprise, he answered out of fear. But a lie, however unpremeditated, is difficult to recall. Like the occasion when he tried to walk on the water to reach Jesus (his attempt to reach Him this time was even more pathetic) Peter

---

[72] See Westcott, *op. cit.*, p. 255.   [73] Macgregor, *op. cit.*, p. 331.

began to sink with nothing to support him. And so he denied knowledge of Jesus again — and again — and the cock crew. Luke's Gospel says that "the Lord turned, and looked upon Peter" (Luke 22:61), and that Peter "went out, and wept bitterly." That look was the hand reaching out to save Peter, and the weeping was his response. Did Judas also see that look from Jesus? Is that what condemned him? Is that why he "repented" saying, "I have sinned in that I betrayed innocent blood"? (Matt. 27:4). Perhaps more hope can be held out for Judas than has been customary.

The prediction which Jesus had made of Peter's denial **before the cock crow** meant that he would do it before sunrise, for the **cock crow** was the herald of the dawn. Darkness was all around them — not just the darkness of night, but of circumstance — and Peter's denial was involved in it. But the coming dawn was not so evident. In his lessons from history, Dr. Beard says, "When it is dark enough, you can see the stars." Jesus had a better prospect for Peter than that: the night would be followed by morning. It was a promise of the Resurrection.

C. THE TRIAL BEFORE PILATE (18: 28-19:16)

28 They lead Jesus therefore from Caiaphas into the Praetorium: and it was early; and they themselves entered not into the Praetorium, that they might not be defiled, but might eat the passover. 29 Pilate therefore went out unto them, and saith, What accusation bring ye against this man? 30 They answered and said unto him, If this man were not an evil-doer, we should not have delivered him up unto thee. 31 Pilate therefore said unto them, Take him yourselves, and judge him according to your law. The Jews said unto him, It is not lawful for us to put any man to death: 32 that the word of Jesus might be fulfilled, which he spake, signifying by what manner of death he should die.

33 Pilate therefore entered again into the Praetorium, and called Jesus, and said unto him, Art thou the King of the Jews? 34 Jesus answered, Sayest thou this of thyself, or did others tell it thee concerning me? 35 Pilate answered, Am I a Jew? Thine own nation and the chief priests delivered thee unto me: what hast thou done? 36 Jesus answered,

My kingdom is not of this world: if my kingdom were of this world, then would my servants fight, that I should not be delivered to the Jews: but now is my kingdom not from hence. 37 Pilate therefore said unto him, Art thou a king then? Jesus answered, Thou sayest that I am a king. To this end have I been born, and to this end am I come into the world, that I should bear witness unto the truth. Every one that is of the truth heareth my voice. 38 Pilate saith unto him, What is truth?

And when he had said this, he went out again unto the Jews, and saith unto them, I find no crime in him. 39 But ye have a custom, that I should release unto you one at the passover: will ye therefore that I release unto you the King of the Jews? 40 They cried out therefore again, saying, Not this man, but Barabbas. Now Barabbas was a robber.

1 Then Pilate therefore took Jesus, and scourged him. 2 And the soldiers platted a crown of thorns, and put it on his head, and arrayed him in a purple garment; 3 and they came unto him, and said, Hail, King of the Jews! and they struck him with their hands. 4 And Pilate went out again, and saith unto them, Behold, I bring him out to you, that ye may know that I find no crime in him. 5 Jesus therefore came out, wearing the crown of thorns and the purple garment. And *Pilate* saith unto them, Behold, the man! 6 When therefore the chief priests and the officers saw him, they cried out, saying, Crucify *him*, crucify *him*! Pilate saith unto them, Take him yourselves, and crucify him: for I find no crime in him. 7 The Jews answered him, We have a law, and by that law he ought to die, because he made himself the Son of God. 8 When Pilate therefore heard this saying, he was the more afraid; 9 and he entered into the Praetorium again, and saith unto Jesus, Whence art thou? But Jesus gave him no answer. 10 Pilate therefore saith unto him, Speakest thou not unto me? knowest thou not that I have power to release thee, and have power to crucify thee? 11 Jesus answered him, Thou wouldest have no power against me, except it were given thee from above: therefore he that delivered me unto thee hath greater sin. 12 Upon this Pilate sought to release him: but the Jews cried out, saying, If thou release this man, thou art not Caesar's friend: every one that maketh himself a king speaketh against Caesar. 13 When Pilate therefore heard these words, he brought Jesus out, and sat down

on the judgment-seat at a place called The Pavement, but in Hebrew, Gabbatha. 14 Now it was the Preparation of the Passover: it was about the sixth hour. And he saith unto the Jews, Behold, your King! 15 They therefore cried out, Away with *him*, away with *him*, crucify him! Pilate saith unto them, Shall I crucify your King? The chief priests answered, We have no king but Caesar. 16 Then therefore he delivered him unto them to be crucified.

The Sanhedrin escorted Jesus to Pilate's palace, or official residence, where they hoped that He would speedily be given the death sentence. They themselves did not go in, for the Passover Feast was near and they would not defile themselves by entering a Gentile building. They wanted to put Jesus to death with clean hands. There was no direct contact between Jesus and the Jews from this time when they turned Jesus over to Pilate. Pilate was the fifth of the Procurators who had ruled Judea following the recall of Archaelaus, the son of Herod the Great. Pilate held office from A.D. 26 to 35 and was little more than a tax collector and a keeper of the peace. On several occasions he had been forced to yield to Jewish pressure in order to prevent trouble. He knew the Sanhedrin as a powerful religious body, and the Jews knew Pilate as essentially a corrupt governor. He placed himself at a distinct disadvantage before them the moment he met them outside his palace so early in the morning in deference to their wishes. He tried desperately to make the case seem like a bona fide trial with himself the sole arbitrator. But he knew from the beginning that the Sanhedrin had made up its mind and would settle for no less than the death penalty for their prisoner. And the Jews knew what kind of pressure to exert in order to obtain their demands. They brought no accusations against Jesus, nor did they ask Pilate to investigate His case. They asked only for the sentence of death as soon as possible. The hearing before Pilate was staged not only outside the palace but also inside, where Pilate took Jesus for questioning. There were three brief sessions between pilate and the Jews and two sessions between him and Jesus. After

Pilate's initial reluctance to become involved in the case and the reply of the Jews, It is not lawful for us to put any man to death (v. 31), Pilate took Jesus inside where he could confer with Him in private. Evidence is not conclusive that the Jews could not at that time put a man to death under their law.[74] Apparently they could do so by stoning, unless the two attempts to stone Jesus had been either mob violence or only vain threats. John explained the matter as being a fulfillment of prophecy, saying that the Jews asked Pilate to enforce the death penalty on Jesus, because under Roman law it would be by crucifixion, which was what Jesus had spoken of concerning the manner of His death. It is also possible that the Jewish reluctance to carry out their own sentence of death was due to the nearness of the Passover Feast.

To Pilate, the bringing of Jesus before him was evidence that there were political implications in the case. He had heard of Jesus, and he must have learned about the Triumphal Entry; and so he asked Jesus, Art thou the King of the Jews? (v. 33). Then there followed a clever exchange of words, Jesus taking the initiative from Pilate (v. 34), at the same time testifying to the truth of a higher kingship, and Pilate replying with sneering cynicism. Am I a Jew? he said. art thou the king of the Jews? What is truth? He was contemptuous and not serious, and he did not wait for answers because he was not seeking answers. In this confrontation of an earthly ruler and a heavenly King, the worst — and the best — Pilate could say was, I find no crime in Him (v. 38). Plainly he was disturbed. The inconvenience of so early an hour, the annoying insistence of the Jews, and the enervating effect of Jesus upon his personal morale, conspired to upset whatever purpose he may have had in mind. In his next move — the offer to substitute Barabbas for Jesus — he certainly failed to consider the mood of the Jews. One might wish that Pilate had been honestly trying to free Jesus, but this could not have been his serious intent because his very next move was to turn Jesus over to the soldiers for scourging and mockery. "He was bound in a stoop-

---

[74] Hoskyns, *op. cit.*, p. 519.

ing position to a low column . . . and beaten with rods or scourged with whips, the thongs of which were weighted with lead, and studded with sharp-pointed pieces of bone, so that frightful lacerations followed each stroke."[75] Such "scourging was itself a part of a capital sentence"[76]; but both Luke and John saw its use in this instance as a compromise to the Jews. Luke wrote, "I will therefore chastise him and release him" (Luke 23:16). John depicted Pilate as ordering the punishment in hope that it would satisfy the passion of the Jews for blood. While the soldiers threw a purple robe (the mark of a conqueror) over the bleeding back of Jesus and placed a crown of thorns on His head, mocking both Him and the Jews by crying, **Hail, King of the Jews,** Pilate went outside to tell the waiting Sanhedrin again that he could find no reason for condemning Jesus to death. And then, in a dramatic move, Jesus was brought out in His pitiful condition, and Pilate cried out, **Behold the Man.**

But like animals which have a taste of blood and cry for more, the crowd roared, **Crucify him, crucify him!** Jesus stood silent and calm while His fate continued to be argued in the heat of ignoble passions. In great disgust Pilate replied, **Take him yourselves, and crucify him** (19:6). He was trying to rid himself of the responsibility of determining the fate of Jesus; and the Jews found the case back where it had started. But they were not easily discouraged — evil never is. They had pressured Pilate with little success; now they would frighten him into action. And so they said, **he ought to die, because he made himself the son of God** (v. 7). Pilate was becoming more and more disconcerted. What sort of prisoner did he have on his hands? Might this man be possessed with the spirit of the gods? With a marked change of attitude he went into a second private conference with Jesus. The marvel is that any man could converse with Jesus and observe Him under such circumstances and not sense something of the majesty and holiness of His Person. So veiled was Christ in human flesh, and so blinded were His opponents with bigotry and hatred, that He was to them

only a man to be disposed of in the most brutal fashion. Again it was evident that only men of faith can come to know Him. There is some indication, however, that Pilate was open to reason, for when Jesus reminded him of the miscarriage of justice which both he and the Jews were perpetrating, as well as the misuse of a governor's constituted authority, he sought again to have Jesus released. But again the Jews were equal to the occasion. They had pressured and frightened Pilate to no avail — now they threatened him. **If thou release this man,** "who claims to be a king," **thou are not Caesar's friend** (v. 12). This was the Jews' most tactful device. Pilate could afford to lose almost anything except favor at the Roman court. He was at that time in no position to survive any serious accusation against him before the Roman Emperor.[77] Nothing more needed to be said. The issue was settled. Quickly regaining his official composure, Pilate sat down on what was probably an improvised seat from which he was to give his judgment; he was forced into making a decision — the Jews had raised the "sword of Damocles" over him. With bold sarcasm he said, **Behold, your King!** Their reply was "the final apostasy" of Israel. The "priests, speaking for the chosen nation, became traitors to its noblest traditions."[78] **Away with him, away with him, crucify him! We have no king but Caesar.** And without further comment, Pilate **delivered him unto them to be crucified.**

D. THE CRUCIFIXION (19:17-42)

17 They took Jesus therefore: and he went out, bearing the cross for himself, unto the place called The place of a skull, which is called in Hebrew Golgotha: 18 where they crucified him, and with him two others, on either side one, and Jesus in the midst. 19 And Pilate wrote a title also, and put it on the cross. And there was written, JESUS OF NAZARETH, THE KING OF THE JEWS. 20 This title therefore read many of the Jews, for the place where Jesus was crucified was nigh to the city; and it was written in Hebrew, *and* in Latin, *and* in Greek. 21 The chief priests of the Jews therefore said to Pilate, Write not, The King of the Jews; but, that he said, I

[75] *Expositor's Greek Testament,* Vol. I, p. 853. [76] Westcott, *op. cit.,* p. 268.
[77] See Plummer, *op. cit.,* p. 325. [78] Strachan, *op. cit.,* pp. 318-319.

am King of the Jews. 22 Pilate answered, What I have written I have written.

23 The soldiers therefore, when they had crucified Jesus, took his garments and made four parts, to every soldier a part; and also the coat: now the coat was without seam, woven from the top throughout. 24 They said therefore one to another, Let us not rend it, but cast lots for it, whose it shall be: that the scripture might be fulfilled. which saith,

They parted my garments among them.

And upon my vesture did they cast lots.

25 These things therefore the soldiers did. But there were standing by the cross of Jesus his mother, and his mother's sister, Mary the *wife* of Clopas, and Mary Magdalene. 26 When Jesus therefore saw his mother, and the disciple standing by whom he loved, he saith unto his mother, Woman, behold thy son! 27 Then saith he to the disciple, Behold, thy mother! And from that hour the disciple took her unto his own *home*.

28 After this Jesus, knowing that all things are now finished, that the scripture might be accomplished, saith, I thirst. 29 There was set there a vessel full of vinegar: so they put a sponge full of the vinegar upon hyssop, and brought it to his mouth. 30 When Jesus therefore had received the vinegar, he said, It is finished: and he bowed his head, and gave up his spirit.

31 The Jews therefore, because it was the Preparation, that the bodies should not remain on the cross upon the sabbath (for the day of that sabbath was a high *day*), asked of Pilate that their legs might be broken, and *that* they might be taken away. 32 The soldiers therefore came, and brake the legs of the first, and of the other that was crucified with him: 33 but when they came to Jesus, and saw that he was dead already, they brake not his legs: 34 howbeit one of the soldiers with a spear pierced his side, and straightway there came out blood and water. 35 And he that hath seen hath borne witness, and his witness is true: and he knoweth that he saith true, that ye also may believe. 36 For these things came to pass, that the scripture might be fulfilled, A bone of him shall not be broken. 37 And again another scripture saith, They shall look on him whom they pierced.

38 And after these things Joseph of Arimathaea, being a disciple of Jesus, but secretly for fear of the Jews, asked

of Pilate that he might take away the body of Jesus: and Pilate gave *him* leave. He came therefore, and took away his body. 39 And there came also Nicodemus, he who at the first came to him by night, bringing a mixture of myrrh and aloes, about a hundred pounds. 40 So they took the body of Jesus, and bound it in linen cloths with the spices, as the custom of the Jews is to bury. 41 Now in the place where he was crucified there was a garden; and in the garden a new tomb wherein was never man yet laid. 42 There then because of the Jews' Preparation (for the tomb was nigh at hand) they laid Jesus.

Crucifixion was a form of capital punishment which the Romans reserved for condemned slaves and provincials. Roman citizens were never crucified. It was the custom to force the condemned man to carry his own cross, although at times he carried only the crossbeam, perhaps because of his weakened condition following abuse such as Jesus suffered. The Synoptics say that Simon of Cyrene carried the cross of Christ (Matt. 27:32; Mark 15:21; Luke 23:26), while John's Gospel says that **They took Jesus therefore: and he went out, bearing the cross for himself** (v. 17). It is usually understood that Jesus faltered under the load and Simon was enlisted to carry the cross the remaining distance, walking behind Jesus. John wished to emphasize that Jesus alone was sufficient to atone for the sins of mankind.[79] The cross, whether it be Christ's cross or ours, is formed by the conflict between good and evil, by the will of God intercepting the will of Satan and the world. The Christian way is the way of the cross.

The site of Golgotha (Hebrew) or Calvary (Latin) has not been conclusively identified, but it was outside (Heb. 13:12), or near the City of Jerusalem (v. 20). A very old legend says that Adam's skull had been buried there, hence the title, **the place of a skull** (v. 17). The promontory is also said to resemble a man's skull in shape. Jesus was crucified there between two unidentified criminals, the central position of His cross perhaps meant by His executioners as a grim parody of His acclaimed dignity and honor. This may also have been intended by the Roman

---

[79] For a literary comparison of the crucifixion story in the four Gospels, see Smith *op. cit.*, p. 338.

authorities as an insult to the Jews.[80] Clearly an insult was the title which Pilate had placed over the cross, **Jesus of Nazareth, the King of the Jews** (v. 19). That Jesus, who was from Nazareth in Galilee, should be called the King of the Jews was a double insult; and when the sign, which was written in Hebrew, Latin, and Greek, began to attract the attention of the people of the city, the Sanhedrin asked Pilate to change it to read, **he said, I am King of the Jews.** Pilate's reply has become a classic expression of the principle that the past can never be rescinded. A man's life is a continuous line from his past, through his present, and into his future. Words once spoken can never be recalled. The words of Pilate, **What I have written, I have written,** will always serve to identify him as the one who finally condemned Jesus to the cross. This fact could not be erased, even if Pilate had obtained divine forgiveness for his sin.

The Old Testament hope for a king of the House of David was fulfilled in Jesus, although Pilate did not know it when he ordered the inscription placed upon the cross, and although the Jews did not want to recognize the fact. John believed that the death of Christ fulfilled prophecy in several ways. When the soldiers had broken the legs of the two criminals in order to insure their early death, they found Jesus already dead and did not break His legs. This was in keeping with the ordinance that no bones of the Paschal Lamb should be broken (Exod. 12:46; Num. 9:12), and John saw it as the fulfillment of Psalm 34:20. As was the custom, the four soldiers took the clothes of Jesus as a reward for their labor, and divided them four ways, probably "head-dress, shoes, outer-garment and girdle."[81] They drew lots for His inner garment or tunic because it was **without seam, woven from the top throughout** (v. 23). This, to John, was another fulfillment of prophecy (Ps. 22:18). His mind may also have gone to the seamless robe of the Levitical high priest (Exod. 28:32). He saw everything working out according to the will of God, both as to time and to circumstance. The fulfillment of prophecy meant that the plan of God was being accomplished.

Earlier in this Gospel, John told of Caiaphas' speaking prophetically without being aware that he was doing it. Here John said that prophecy "was most literally fulfilled by men who were utterly ignorant of it."[82] Besides the four soldiers, there were four women near the cross of Jesus, also **the disciple . . . whom he loved,** who was presumably John. There were Mary the mother of Jesus and her unnamed sister, Mary the wife of Clopas, and Mary Magdalene. For some unknown reason John rather frequently made mention of people whom he did not name. Who was this sister of Mary? The answer may be involved in the dramatic words of Jesus telling John to become a son to His mother. This seems an unnatural thing for Jesus to say, because He had brothers. But in light of their attitude toward Jesus at Capernaum (7:1-5), they may have been sons of Joseph by a previous marriage and hence not the sons of Mary. And if Mary's unnamed sister were Salome, wife of Zebedee and mother of John,[83] it would be quite natural for Jesus to thus turn to His cousin John in the hour of His death. It seems plausible that Mary, the Virgin Mother, spent her declining years in the home of her sister and family.

It was not until Jesus knew **that all things are now accomplished** that He turned His attention to His own needs and asked for a drink to slake His thirst. Some vinegar was near at hand for such occasions, and the soldiers, out of kindness, wet a sponge and lifted it to His lips. Thereupon He said, **It is finished: and he bowed his head, and gave up his spirit** (v. 30). All of the Gospel writers agree in saying that Jesus willingly gave up His life — none say that He died. He laid down His life, and He would receive it again at the Resurrection.

It becomes increasingly clear as the account of the Passion continues that the Jewish Sanhedrin was not seeking justice, allowing a fair trial and honestly believing that Jesus was worthy of death. If so, they would have been content to let Pilate care for the case in his own way. Neither were they acting entirely by the dictates of their religion. They

---

[80] Plummer, *op. cit.*, p. 328.   [81] Macgregor, *op. cit.*, p. 345.   [82] Plummer, *op. cit.*, p. 330.
[83] Expositor's Greek Testament, Vol. I, p. 858.

were seeking expression for the diabolical impulses which had arisen within them because of their reaction to the teachings and claims of Jesus. Their rejection of those teachings unleashed passions which were self-condemning and self-revealing, and which clamored for expression. Their perversity was demonstrated by an insistent petulance which was never satisfied. They had been impatient with Pilate's handling of the trial; they had complained about the title placed on the cross; and now they were demanding that Pilate have the three condemned men's legs broken, and the bodies buried so as not to desecrate the Jewish Sabbath. It was not mandatory to break the legs of crucified persons, for the soldiers did not do so to Jesus when they found Him already dead. It was the Roman custom to leave bodies on their crosses to decompose and to serve as spectacles of Roman justice. It was necessary that Jesus be entombed; thus there would be tangible evidence of the Resurrection to follow. But to the Jews even the dead body of Jesus was a trouble to them, and probably a prick to bad consciences. They must have it removed and buried. John wrote as one who knew that everything had worked out as God had planned. His writing at this point substantiates his claim to being an eye-witness. He observed that the soldiers did not break the legs of Jesus, and that when they pierced His side with a spear both blood and water came out. John wrote about what he had seen. The blood may be thought to symbolize Redemption and the water cleansing.

John did not disparage the value of what is commonly called secret discipleship. When we observe such men as Nicodemus and Joseph of Arimathea, it would appear that their discipleship may have been as effective as that of some of the Twelve, the difference being not in the quality of their allegiance but in the situations in which they demonstrated it. It is seldom, if ever, fair to judge another's Christian experience by his calling or status in life. Actions speak louder than words. As an old saying puts it:

You never can tell the depth of the well
By the length of the handle on the pump.

Both of these men demonstrated considerable boldness in the face of ex-

plosive conditions — Joseph by asking for the body of Jesus and Nicodemus in his preparing the body for burial. Out of devotion to Jesus they rescued the body from the soldiers, and gave it an honorable burial according to Jewish customs as far as was possible. What part any of the immediate disciples had in this procedure is not known. They had been so close to Jesus that the crucifixion shocked them; they could not undertsand such a swift and tragic climax to the ministry of their leader. To the disciples, Jesus and crucifixion did not belong together. They needed to get away in order to gain perspective. On the other hand, Joseph and Nicodemus were drawn to Jesus by the tragedy of the crucifixion. They were not so highly emotionalized as the others were and therefore could think more clearly and act with greater rationality. It was the purpose of John to give the best possible interpretation of the attitudes of everyone involved in the death of Jesus, including even Pilate and Judas Iscariot. In the case of the Jews he gave credit where credit was due; for at the close of his account of the public ministry of Jesus John stated that **even of the rulers many believed on him** (12:42).

E. THE RESURRECTION (ch. 20)

1 Now on the first *day* of the week cometh Mary Magdalene early, while it was yet dark, unto the tomb, and seeth the stone taken away from the tomb. 2 She runneth therefore, and cometh to Simon Peter, and to the other disciple who Jesus loved, and saith unto them, They have taken away the Lord out of the tomb, and we know not where they have laid him. 3 Peter therefore went forth, and the other disciple, and they went toward the tomb. 4 And they ran both together: and the other disciple outran Peter, and came first to the tomb; 5 and stooping and looking in, he seeth the linen cloths lying; yet entered he not in. 6 Simon Peter therefore also cometh, following him, and entered into the tomb; and he beholdeth the linen cloths lying, 7 and the napkin, that was upon his head, not lying with the linen cloths, but rolled up in a place by itself. 8 Then entered in therefore the other disciple also, who came first to the tomb, and he saw, and believed. 9 For as yet they knew not the scripture, that he must rise again from the dead.

10 So the disciples went away again unto their own home.

11 But Mary was standing without at the tomb weeping: so, as she wept, she stooped and looked into the tomb; 12 and she beholdeth two angels in white sitting, one at the head, and one at the feet, where the body of Jesus had lain. 13 And they say unto her, Woman, why weepest thou? She saith unto them, Because they have taken away my Lord, and I know not where they have laid him. 14 When she had thus said, she turned herself back, and beholdeth Jesus standing, and knew not that it was Jesus. 15 Jesus saith unto her, Woman, why weepest thou? whom seekest thou? She, supposing him to be the gardener, saith unto him, Sir, if thou hast borne him hence, tell me where thou hast laid him, and I will take him away. 16 Jesus saith unto her, Mary. She turneth herself, and saith unto him in Hebrew, Rabboni; which is to say, Teacher. 17 Jesus saith to her, Touch me not; for I am not yet ascended unto the Father: but go unto my brethren, and say to them, I ascend unto my Father and your Father, and my God and your God. 18 Mary Magdalene cometh and telleth the disciples, I have seen the Lord; and *that* he had said these things unto her.

19 When therefore it was evening, on that day, the first *day* of the week, and when the doors were shut where the disciples were, for fear of the Jews, Jesus came and stood in the midst, and saith unto them, Peace *be* unto you. 20 And when he had said this, he showed unto them his hands and his side. The disciples therefore were glad, when they saw the Lord. 21 Jesus therefore said to them again, Peace *be* unto you: as the Father hath sent me, even so send I you. 22 And when he had said this, he breathed on them, and saith unto them, Receive ye the Holy Spirit: 23 whose soever sins ye forgive, they are forgiven unto them; whose soever *sins* ye retain, they are retained.

24 But Thomas, one of the twelve, called Didymus, was not with them when Jesus came. 25 The other disciples therefore said unto him, We have seen the Lord. But he said unto them, Except I shall see in his hands the print of the nails, and put my finger into the print of the nails, and put my hand into his side, I will not believe.

26 And after eight days again his disciples were within, and Thomas with them. Jesus cometh, the doors being shut, and stood in the midst, and said,

Peace *be* unto you. 27 Then saith he to Thomas, Reach hither thy finger, and see my hands; and reach *hither* thy hand, and put it into my side: and be not faithless, but believing. 28 Thomas answered and said unto him, My Lord and my God. 29 Jesus saith unto him, Because thou hast seen me, thou hast believed: blessed *are* they that have not seen, and *yet* have believed.

30 Many other signs therefore did Jesus in the presence of the disciples, which are not written in this book: 31 but these are written, that ye may believe that Jesus is the Christ, the Son of God; and that believing ye may have life in his name.

John's account of the Resurrection of Jesus has but one purpose: to give witness to the fact that both His Death and the Resurrection are demonstrable events. This limited purpose is responsible for many omissions in the narrative. For instance, no mention is made that other women accompanied Mary Magdalene to the tomb in the early morning of that first Easter. But this manner of writing is the strength of John, recognizable throughout his Gospel. Certain narrative details are forfeited to the main intent, but because of their nature they are not seriously missed.

On the first day of the week — the Christian Sabbath — Mary Magdalene went to the garden tomb, **early, while it was yet dark.** Why did she go on that morning? Had she remembered what Jesus had said at the cleansing of the Temple? **Destroy this temple, and in three days I will raise it up** (2:19). She could not have been present; and if she had heard of the statement, there is small possibility that she would have understood its implication; John said the disciples understood only after the Resurrection. It is more probable that Mary had visited the tomb each morning following the burial, and the experiences of this special morning took her by surprise. She knew that a stone had been placed at the entrance to the tomb and she was greatly disturbed to find it moved. Without waiting to investigate, she ran to find Peter and John and broke the news to them. Her judgment was that someone had stolen the body of Jesus. She must have known where to find the two disciples. They too may have visited the tomb — John because his love drew him and Peter because the tragedy of his denial compelled him. The impression given by this Gospel is that a few of those closest to Jesus lingered for a period of mourning before going back to their homes. Luke's account of the walk to Emmaus (Luke 24:13f) suggests that by the time of the Resurrection the disciples were beginning to leave Jerusalem.

John remembered the foot race with Peter to the tomb, which he had won. In telling of the incident John was able to reveal the temperaments of the two men. John himself, more cautious than Peter and perhaps more reverent, merely peered into the tomb, while Peter rushed in without hesitating or thinking. He who was slower in running was also slower in stopping. Fortunately for Peter on this occasion, he fared somewhat better than when he had rushed to Jesus on the water and when he had cast himself headlong into the defense of Jesus at the Garden of Gethsemane: this was only because the empty tomb was more kindly than either the waters of Galilee or the soldiers of Pilate. When Peter and John were both inside the tomb, they found the linen clothes and the head cloth or turban lying as if "Jesus' physical body had passed into a spiritual and 'glorified' Risen Body without disturbing the grave clothes, which had simply settled down on the ledge within the tomb in their original positions."[84]

John himself **believed** — probably no more than the fact that the body of Jesus had gone from the tomb in some miraculous way. They did not know that Jesus was risen from the dead, **For as yet they knew not the scripture, that he must rise again from the dead** (v. 9). Peter and John returned home — probably to some lodging in Jerusalem rather than to their homes in Galilee. Nothing more could be done, so they left.

But Mary lingered behind weeping. As she peered into the empty darkness of the tomb, she saw a vision of two angels who enquired of her why she was weeping. Her reply was similar to her initial announcement to Peter and John: **Because they have taken away my Lord, and I know not where they have laid him** (v. 13). Immediately another form appeared beside her, who she thought was the gardener, a complete stranger to her. In answer to his questions, she begged to be shown where he had taken the body of Jesus. And such was her womanly devotion that she offered to remove the body and care for it properly; and she would have found a woman's strength to do it. Then there followed what has been described as "the greatest recognition scene in all literature — and one told in two words."[85] **Mary! Teacher!** Mary, like the sheep (ch. 10) had heard the voice of the true shepherd and recognized it. She may have flung herself at His feet (Matt. 28:9), washing them, as it were, with her tears. Doubtless she pleaded with Him not to leave. His reply signified that His work of redemption would not be completely finished until He had ascended to God the Father; then the promise of His continuous presence with them would be fulfilled. This follows naturally the teaching of the great discourse to the disciples. The Ascension was a necessary sequel to the Resurrection and a necessary prelude to the coming of the Holy Spirit. Mary took the news of her discovery of the Master to the disciples, who, according to John, had not left Jerusalem. The same evening Jesus appeared to the group gathered together. In the sequence of events related by John, the women are so closely associated with some of the chosen disciples and to the scene of the Resurrection that it is not amiss to suppose that the gathering on that first Easter evening was composed of a small mixed group of loyal disciples. Not all of the chosen eleven were there, for we know that Thomas was absent. Luke says that the eleven were together when the two disciples returned from Emmaus to report the appearance of Jesus to them (Luke 24:33). The meeting on this occasion was held behind closed doors **for fear of the Jews** (v. 19). Not that the disciples feared to be seen in public individually, but they were fearful that the Jewish authorities would be suspicious of their meetings if found out. They had reason to fear, because the history of the early church reveals that the initial persecutions came from the Jewish, not the Roman, authorities. Wit-

---

[84] Macgregor, *op. cit.*, p. 356.   [85] *Ibid.*, p. 358.

ness the threats and murder" of Saul of Tarsus (Acts 9:1, RSV). Those were dreadful days for that little band of believers. The contrast is aptly drawn between the clandestine meetings following the Crucifixion and the boldness of the apostles after the Baptism of the Spirit on the Day of Pentecost. But this must not be construed to mean that they were totally ineffective during that earlier period, and that the post-Resurrection appearances of Jesus wrought no change in the group. Thomas is an example of one affected by those appearances. And it must be noted that by the Day of Pentecost the group which was so small on the evening of the Resurrection had swelled to a total of one hundred twenty. Fearful men took on new courage, disbelievers regained their faith and deserters renewed their covenant. There is no evidence, however, that new converts were made during this period. Some scholars have ignored the baptism of the Spirit in its dynamic effect upon the Church. But the rebuttal to this misreading of the total picture is not to belittle the inspirational and strengthening value of the appearances of the Risen Lord to the inner group. Both the Resurrection and the continued presence of Jesus in the Person of the Holy Spirit were promised in the upper room discourse. And both the Resurrection and the New Testament Pentecost are indispensable to the ongoing of the work of Christ.

The appearance of Jesus in the room where the fearful group had locked themselves was a miracle of the Resurrection. Any attempt to suppose that Jesus secretly unlocked the door is contrary to the impression given by John. The mystery is the mystery of the resurrected body, which, "however changed in its substance, retained its characteristic marks."[86] Paul describes the resurrected body as a "spiritual body" (I Cor. 15:44), and we can suppose that he would include the risen body of Jesus. Upon making His appearance, Jesus greeted those gathered with a customary salutation, **Peace be unto you** (v. 19), probably a wish for well-being for those addressed. But, as with everything He touched, Jesus put a new meaning into the phrase. Its

significance must be understood in relation to the Resurrection. **And when he had said this, he showed unto them his hands and his side** (v. 20), which had been pierced during the crucifixion. Contrary to Docetic Gnosticism, here was proof of the reality of His Person and evidence of His Resurrection. No wonder that the disciples **were glad, when they saw the Lord.** Under such circumstances the benediction of peace was full of meaning. A second time Jesus said **Peace be unto you** (v. 21), this time relating it to His sending them into the world as His representatives, followed by a further benediction, **Receive ye the Holy Spirit.** The Father had sent the Son and in obedience the Son had found peace. Now the Son was sending the disciples, and in obedience they too would find peace. But this kind of peace is not the peace of quietude or of inactivity. Rather, it is peace in the midst of intense activity and even conflict with the sinful world. It is the peace of a good conscience, of adjustment to the demands of life, of coordinated activity, and of reliance upon the leadings of the Holy Spirit. The task of the disciples would be to carry on the work which Jesus had started. Jesus was a Son while they were ambassadors — yet ambassadors with the authority of Jesus Himself. **Whosoever sins ye forgive, they are forgiven unto them; whosoever sins ye retain, they are retained** (v. 23). This is an authority which neither the apostles nor the New Testament Church could presume to claim. Yet it is an authority conferred upon the Church by the baptism of the Holy Spirit, and not given to the Church *per se*. The Church does not have this authority because it is the Church but because it is indwelt and empowered by the Holy Spirit. The possession of a Church charter does not guarantee the possession of the Holy Spirit. The Spirit must be *received* by the Church as a body of dedicated individuals who have chosen to accept Christ's challenge of discipleship and have met the conditions for their own Pentecost. The authority, then, is the authority of the Spirit and not of the Church.

Many commentaries take the position that Jesus bestowed the Spirit upon the disciples at this time, the occasion being "for John almost certainly the counterpart of Pentecost."[87] Jesus **breathed on them, and saith unto them, Receive ye the Holy Spirit.** This spoke of the giving of new life after the fashion of the original creation (Gen. 2:7).[88] It was "the power of the new life proceeding from the Person of the Risen Christ. . . . the necessary condition for the descent of the Holy Spirit on the day of Pentecost."[89] Westcott also distinguishes between a Paschal and a Pentecostal gift of the Spirit, the relation between them being that of "quickening to endowing." These opinions dovetail with the position already taken in this commentary that belief in Jesus during His ministry, so often expressed by John, was limited — now on, now off — something less than saving faith even on the part of the disciples. These opinions support the doctrine of two works of grace. This would indicate that the disciples were true believers on the first Easter evening and sanctified on the day of Pentecost.

To John this incident stood by itself as the fulfillment of Christ's promise of the Spirit (ch. 14, 16), the impartation of new life and the new birth spoken of to Nicodemus — an all-inclusive experience of possessing the eternal life of God through the Spirit. Nowhere else in the Gospel does John give place for the actual achieving of the purpose of Christ's work in His contemporary followers. Jesus came that they might have life (10:10), and John wrote his Gospel for the same purpose (20:31). If this came to pass in the experience of the little band who gathered that evening, it happened when Jesus said, **Receive ye the Holy Spirit.** Otherwise, the statement of Jesus was a promise. At least, according to John (and he was at Pentecost), the meeting on that first Easter was eventful in the lives of the few gathered there, even as the day of Pentecost was in the lives of the one hundred twenty people assembled in the upper room. The one does not destroy the necessity of the other.

For some reason Thomas was not at the meeting when Jesus made His first Resurrection appearance. When told later that the risen Lord had been there, he was not easily convinced. He must be able to see and feel the body of the Lord and be assured of the wounds which had killed Him. He was only asking for signs sufficient to satisfy himself, even as others had done all through the ministry of Jesus; and Jesus obliged him by appearing to the group at their next meeting, evidently for the sake of Thomas alone. Thomas' problem was not the Person of Christ and His relationship to God — that seems to have been taken care of in the Upper Room Discourse (14:4-11). It was the Resurrection which bothered him. Thomas has become so thoroughly labeled a doubter that it is difficult to think of him in any other light. But some of the greatest doubters are also the greatest believers, because their powers of perception are more penetrating than those of the average believer. The worst that one can say of Thomas is that he was an honest doubter — that he doubted only that he might secure more evidence for his understanding. If one allows that he had been satisfied that Jesus was **the way, and the truth, and the life,** and that the next words were spoken directly to Thomas — **If ye had known me, ye would have known my Father also; from henceforth ye know him, and have seen him** (14:7) — it is possible to believe that he achieved greater insight into the deity of Jesus, and a deeper comprehension of His teaching on the Holy Spirit than the average listener. If so, the appearance of Jesus in Resurrection form bothered him, for he was not prepared for it. John said that those who came first to the tomb **did not know the scripture, that he must rise from the dead** (20:9). While the others were gathered behind barred doors, Thomas was by himself, seeking a reconciliation in his own mind for conflicting concepts. The promise of Christ's return had been so fused in his mind with the promise of the Holy Spirit that the physical appearance of the Risen Christ added a dimension to his problem for which he was not prepared. He needed to know that the Resurrection was both inevitable and necessary. But for the moment he needed tangible evidence for what others said was true. Perhaps he

[87] Macgregor, *op. cit.*, p. 365.   [88] *Ibid.*   [89] Westcott, *op. cit.*, p. 295.

was slower than the rest of the group and needed to follow through logically on every point of his syllogism, but this should not be held against him. Would to God more Christians would follow the example of Thomas and strive for greater assurance for their beliefs. The other disciples had apparently learned to be patient with him, and Jesus invited him to observe (both see and feel) the evidence and believe. **Reach hither thy finger, and see my hands; and reach hither thy hand, and put it into my side: and be not faithless, but believing** (v. 27). Jesus was not suggesting that Thomas had been faithless prior to this time; He was urging him to respond with faith rather than with unbelief. The answer of Thomas is one of the great mountain crests of the Gospel of John: **My Lord and my God.** "The discipline of self-questioning, followed by the revelation of tender compassion, enabled Thomas to rise to the loftiest view of the Lord given in the Gospels."[90] Those five words encompassed the totality of his faith in Christ; they were not the words of a chronic doubter, but those of a believer with an ever-expanding faith; and they best expressed the faith which John himself came to know. In fact, John may be indirectly acknowledging his debt to Thomas for the faith which he himself held.

Knowing that few, if any, would be able to satisfy their doubts in the way that Thomas did, Jesus responded to him with a beatitude which is both a blessing and a promise: **Blessed are they who have not seen, and yet have believed** (v. 29). He might have said, Blessed are those who read the story of Thomas and thereby believe on Me.

This is the concluding episode of John's Gospel. The two verses which follow constitute his concluding statement. He had not sought to write a life of Jesus, but had chosen only certain items as signs for the purpose which he had in mind for writing the Gospel. He had written that men **may believe that Jesus is the Christ** — most certainly for his Jewish readers — and that He is the Son of God — perhaps wishing to appeal especially to Gentile readers. **And that believing ye may have life in his name:** eternal life, life from above, the New Birth, life in Christ, life through the indwelling of the Holy Spirit. All who read must agree that John did a convincing piece of work.

F. THE EPILOGUE (ch. 21)

1 After these things Jesus manifested himself again to the disciples at the sea of Tiberias; and he manifested *himself* on this wise. 2 There were together Simon Peter, and Thomas called Didymus, and Nathanael of Cana in Galilee, and the *sons* of Zebedee, and two other of his disciples. 3 Simon Peter saith unto them, I go a fishing. They say unto him, We also come with thee. They went forth, and entered into the boat; and that night they took nothing. 5 But when day was now breaking, Jesus stood on the beach: yet the disciples knew not that it was Jesus. 5 Jesus therefore saith unto them, Children, have ye aught to eat? They answered him, No. 6 And he said unto them, Cast the net on the right side of the boat, and ye shall find. They cast therefore, and now they were not able to draw it for the multitude of fishes. 7 That disciple therefore whom Jesus loved saith unto Peter, It is the Lord. So when Simon Peter heard that it was the Lord, he girt his coat about him (for he was naked), and cast himself into the sea. 8 But the other disciples came in the little boat (for they were not far from the land, but about two hundred cubits off), dragging the net *full* of fishes. 9 So when they got out upon the land, they see a fire of coals there, and fish laid thereon, and bread. 10 Jesus saith unto them, Bring of the fish which ye have now taken. 11 Simon Peter therefore went up, and drew the net to land, full of great fishes, a hundred and fifty and three: and for all there were so many, the net was not rent. 12 Jesus saith unto them, Come *and* break your fast. And none of the disciples durst inquire of him, Who art thou? knowing that it was the Lord. 13 Jesus cometh, and taketh the bread, and giveth them, and the fish likewise. 14 This is now the third time that Jesus was manifested to the disciples, after that he was risen from the dead.

15 So when they had broken their fast, Jesus saith to Simon Peter, Simon, *son* of John, lovest thou me more than these? He saith unto him, Yea, Lord; thou knowest that I love thee. He saith unto him, Feed my lambs. 16 He saith to

90 Westcott, *op. cit.*, p. 297.

him again a second time, Simon, *son* of John, lovest thou me? He saith unto him, Yea, Lord; thou knowest that I love thee. He saith unto him, Tend my sheep. 17 He saith unto him the third time, Simon, *son* of John, lovest thou me? Peter was grieved because he said unto him the third time, Lovest thou me? And he said unto him, Lord, thou knowest that I love thee. Jesus saith unto him, Feed my sheep. 18 Verily, verily, I say unto thee, When thou wast young, thou girdest thyself, and walkedst whither thou wouldest: but when thou shalt be old, thou shalt stretch forth thy hands, and another shall gird thee, and carry thee whither thou wouldest not. 19 Now this he spake, signifying by what manner of death he should glorify God. And when he had spoken this, he saith unto him, Follow me. 20 Peter, turning about, seeth the disciple whom Jesus loved following; who also leaned back on his breast at the supper, and said, Lord, who is he that betrayeth thee? 21 Peter therefore seeing him saith to Jesus, Lord, and what shall this man do? 22 Jesus saith unto him, If I will that he tarry till I come, what *is that* to thee? follow thou me. 23 This saying therefore went forth among the brethren, that that disciple should not die: yet Jesus said not unto him, that he should not die; but, If I will that he tarry till I come, what *is that* to thee?

24 This is the disciple that beareth witness of these things, and wrote these things: and we know that his witness is true.

25 And there are also many other things which Jesus did, the which if they should be written every one, I suppose, that even the world itself would not contain the books that should be written.

This chapter was probably added to the Gospel in its initial form by the author in order to present some post-Resurrection appearances of Jesus in Galilee, as well as in Jerusalem, where the greater portion of the material for John's Gospel originated. He may have felt this need in recognition of the Galilean emphasis in the Synoptics. The disciples — seven of them — went fishing on Lake Galilee at the invitation of Peter. Jesus appeared to them for the third time after the Resurrection (v. 14) (the other occasions being those in 20:19-23 and 20:26-29). It has been suggested that the fishing trip represented

"complete apostasy" on the part of the disciples as a fulfillment of the forecast of Jesus that they would leave Him and be scattered (16:32).[91] One finds it difficult to think that the disciples would apostatize after having received the benediction of Jesus with its possible effect on their lives (20:22). They had scattered at the time of the Crucifixion, but had been brought together again. It is more conceivable that the fishing trip was a holiday diversion on the part of the disciples rather than a return to their former vocation. Only **Simon Peter** and **the sons of Zebedee** are known to have been fishermen. They were waiting for the day of Pentecost (Luke 24:49) when the work of the Church would begin under the power of the Holy Spirit; and they were waiting also for others to assemble. Many others were witnessing appearances of Jesus (I Cor. 15:3-8); thus the one hundred twenty were being readied for that great day. Because of those first appearances, the atmosphere among the little group that went fishing had changed noticeably, and we find them in a more relaxed frame of mind.

In the list of seven disciples Peter was named first and Thomas second. With the exception of John himself, these were the two men most prominently involved in the Passion and Resurrection of Jesus. In addition, the author mentioned two unnamed disciples, neither of them being John. This reference to unnamed persons follows a familiar pattern found in John's Gospel. Their long absence from boat and net cost Peter and his companions much of their old-time skill; they toiled all night without success. The miraculous draught of fish, which they took after the appearance of Jesus served to reveal to them His identity; and, at the same time, it contains certain symbolical truths. No significance should be placed on the casting of the net **on the right side of the boat** rather than from any other spot. The fact that they followed instructions serves to show their obedience to Jesus; that is, if they had recognized Him immediately. Or it may only show that they were open for suggestions, which would be rather revealing, since Peter was the leader of the expedition. It was their great catch of

91 Hoskyns, *op. cit.*, p. 552.

fish which confirmed their recognition of the man on the shore as being Jesus. By this miracle Jesus sought to show them what it would mean for them to be "fishers of men." Their success would depend upon both God and man — neither could catch fish alone. The purpose of the Incarnation is seen in this necessity of God and man working together for the salvation of the world. The number of fish (153) may represent an actual count,[92] but the large number represents great success, and promises success to the Church. **The net was not rent** — and so the Church will be able to stand the greatest strain which can be placed upon it: "the gates of Hades shall not prevail against it" (Matt. 16:18). The number of fish may also represent the universal nature of the Gospel, for the ancient world believed that there were 153 species of fish.

Peter and John were again paired in this narrative. John immediately perceived that it was Jesus on the shore, and at the news Peter splashed his way a hundred yards to get to Him. As usual John was quick to see while Peter was quick to act. The primary purpose of Jesus in appearing to the seven disciples seems not to be the great catching of fish. After He told Peter to go back to the boat and help bring in the catch, the fish are forgotten in the narrative. Jesus already had fish frying on the coals, and they all were aware that it was Jesus by the time He invited them to share breakfast with Him. The serving of the bread and fish is suggestive of the Lord's Supper. The breakfast became the setting for a further commissioning of the disciples which Jesus did by 1) suggesting that they were to be fishers of men; 2) emphasizing to Peter that the basis of true discipleship is love-loyalty; and 3) by showing that each man must serve Him as an individual as well as a member of the group.

Peter became the center of the conversation. Three times he had denied His Lord (18:18-27). And now three times he was asked to acknowledge his loyalty to Him. **Simon, son of John** [*Joanes, mar*], **lovest thou me more than these?** (v. 15). It is conceivable that Jesus meant "more than the boats and nets," but not probable. The question refers to Peter's earlier boasting: "If all shall be offended in thee, I will never be offended" (Matt. 26:33), and Jesus was "asking him whether he now professes to have more loyalty and devotion than the rest."[93] The episode which followed was, in the first place, a full restoration of Peter to his former place of favor and discipleship in the presence of the other disciples. A public denial must be cancelled out by a public declaration of loyalty. In the second place, Jesus was saying that the Christian must be bound to his Lord by cords of love. And, third, that love and loyalty to Christ must find their expression in obeying the commission to win others to Him.

Much emphasis has been placed upon the fact that Jesus, in talking with Peter, used two different Greek words which are translated love — *agapao* and *phileo*. Greek scholars are not agreed on whether one is stronger than the other, and some think that there is no significance in the change from one to the other, because both terms were used by John for the love of God (14:23; 16:27); *agapao* is used for loving both God and man (14:23), and for loving the sinful world (I John 2:15): Also, the Beloved Disciple is both *hon agapa* and *hon ephile*. Barrett thinks that the use of the two Greek words in the Gospel of John shows that they are synonyms.[94] Those who lay stress upon the change of meaning in the use of the two words often fail to note that a change is also made in words from **lambs** to **sheep** and from **feed** to **tend** (or shepherd); also, that there are three words used for fish in this chapter. To be wholly consistent, one should find meaning in all of these changes of words. At the same time it must be recognized (and modern Americans should know this best) that distinctions must be made between love as a virtue, love as affection, and love as passion. There are words available for such distinctions, but they are little used in popular speech. It is not certain that New Testament writers always used words with fine distinctions of meaning. Westcott, along with others, has legitimate grounds for his interpretation of this passage. It goes like this:[95]

[92] Plummer, *op. cit.*, p. 351.   [93] Plummer, *op. cit.*, p. 353.   [94] Barrett, *op. cit.*, p. 486.
[95] Westcott, *op. cit.*, pp. 302-304.

Jesus used *agapao,* the stronger term, and twice Peter replied with *phileo,* the weaker term. Then Jesus accommodated his question to Peter, not demanding the highest love of Peter because he was not yet capable of giving it. Peter was in turn exhorted to **feed lambs, tend sheep,** and **feed sheep.** The chief need of small lambs is to be fed, while grown sheep need to be tended or cared for by the shepherd; but sheep also need to be fed. This, to me, is the most satisfactory interpretation which can be placed upon this passage. However, it is well to observe that such distinctions can easily be carried too far. Did Jesus find as much reason for changing from *agapao* to *phileo* as He had for changing from lambs to sheep and from feed to tend? Certainly it is not correct to say that *agapao* means divine love and *phileo* means human love.

This message of demonstrating one's love was for all those who heard and all those who would read; but in particular Jesus spoke to Peter, for immediately He told Peter what would be his final end as a man of such devotion to Christ and His cause — he would be crucified as Jesus had been. **Follow me** to the cross, Jesus was saying. The expression **gird thee** seems to refer to the manner of being bound to the cross by ropes rather than being fastened by spikes. This was more torturous than nailing because one was left longer to die in the sun and heat, in hunger and thirst.[96] The invitation to follow Christ had taken on an infinitely richer meaning than it had when first the disciples were called. Tradition says that Peter was crucified head downward because he did not feel worthy to be crucified upright as was Jesus.

Little wonder that Peter hesitated before answering. He wanted to know what might be required of the other disciples, and what they thought about it. He who had always rushed ahead now be-

came very deliberate. Life has a way of doing this to all of us in one way or another. Peter wanted to know if John would be required the same measure of devotion. There was almost a note of criticism in his voice, as much as to imply that John might be required less sacrifice because he was **the disciple Jesus loved.** "Lord, what about this man?" (v. 21, RSV), Peter asked. The answer of Jesus was hypothetical as John later explained. He answered in this vein: "Whether John lives until I return again while you have to die on a cross is not the real issue. Only one issue is involved — willingness to follow Me wherever I may lead." There are no ways of equalizing the demands which Christian devotion makes upon various Christians. In a very true sense, each man determines how much he is willing to sacrifice or give in order to be a witness to Christ. Neither is it possible to evaluate any one man's contribution over against that of another. Human computations and standards cannot analyze or weigh love. Faithfulness is the measure of love.

After claiming to be an eye-witness to what he had written — perhaps to the first twenty chapters, as well as to chapter 21 — John closed his writing on a high note of praise for Christ. He was thinking not only of His earthly life and ministry, but also of the effect of His life and death upon the world. What he — and the Synoptists — had written was but a drop in a bucket. "Men would always keep writing about Jesus because He will always be making history. The Jesus of history is the Jesus of all history since his coming. The 'gesta Christi,' the achievements of Christ, are not yet ended."[97] The world, and beyond — all time and space — are full of what Jesus did, and is doing, and will continue to do, world without end, Amen!

[96] James Hastings, *A Dictionary of Christ and the Gospels,* Vol. I, pp. 398.
[97] Strachan, *op. cit.,* p. 340.

Bibliography

Askwith, E. H. *The Historical Value of the Fourth Gospel.* London: Hodder and Stoughton, 1910.

Baillie, D. M. *God Was in Christ.* New York: Charles Scribner's Sons, 1948.

Barclay, William. *The Gospel of John,* 2 vols. Philadelphia: Westminster Press, 1955.

——— *The Master's Men.* New York: Abingdon Press, 1959.

Barrett, C. K. *The Gospel According to St. John.* London: S. P. C. K., 1962.

Bruce, F. F. *The New Testament Documents.* Grand Rapids: Wm. B. Eerdmans Publishing Co., 1943.

Buttrick, G. A. (ed.). *The Interpreter's Dictionary of the Bible.* 4 vols. New York: Abingdon Press, 1962.

Charnwood, Lord. *According to St. John.* Boston: Little, Brown, and Company, 1925.

Cross, Frank M. Jr. *The Ancient Library of Qumran.* New York: Anchor Books, Doubleday, 1961.

Daniel-Rops, Henri. *Daily Life in the Time of Jesus.* Translated by Patrick O'Brian. New York: Hawthorn Books, Inc., 1962.

Dodd, C. H. *The Interpretation of the Fourth Gospel.* London: Cambridge University Press, 1953.

Dods, Marcus. *The Gospel of St. John.* Vol. I. New York: A. C. Armstrong and Son, 1906.

Drummond, James. *An Inquiry into the Character and Authorship of the Fourth Gospel.* London: Williams and Norgate, 1903.

Edersheim, Alfred. *The Life and Times of Jesus the Messiah.* 2 vols. New York: Longmans, Green and Co., 1901.

Edwards, R. A. *The Gospel According to St. John.* London: Eyre and Spottiswoods, 1954.

Eisler, Roberts. *The Enigma of the Fourth Gospel.* London: Methuen & Co., Ltd., 1938.

Fuller, Reginald H. *The New Testament in Current Study.* New York: Scribners, 1962.

Gaebelein, A. C. *The Gospel of St. John.* New York: Publication Office "Our Hope," Arno C. Gaebelein, Inc., 1936.

Gardner-Smith, P. *St. John and the Synoptic Gospels.* Cambridge: The University Press, 1938.

Harrisville, Roy A. *The Concept of Newness in the New Testament.* Minneapolis: Augsburg Publishing House, 1960.

Hastings, James (ed.). *A Dictionary of Christ and the Gospels.* 2 vols. New York: Charles Scribner's Sons, 1911.

Hayes, D. A. *John and His Writings.* New York: The Methodist Book Concern, 1917.

Headlam, A. C. *The Fourth Gospel as History.* London: Basil Blackwell, 1948.

Holland, H. S. *The Fourth Gospel.* Edited by W. J. Richmond. London: John Murray, 1923.

Hoskyns, E. C. *The Fourth Gospel.* Edited by Francis N. Davey. London: Faber and Faber Limited, 1948.

Howard, W. F. *The Fourth Gospel in Recent Criticism and Interpretation.* London: The Epworth Press, 1935.

——— *Christianity According to St. John.* Philadelphia: The Westminster Press, 1946.

Hunt, B. P. W. S. *Some Johannine Problems.* London: Skeffington and Son, 1958.

Hunter, A. M. "Recent Trends in Johannine Studies," *Expository Times,* March, 1960.

——— *Interpreting the New Testament.* Philadelphia: The Westminster Press, 1951.

——— *Interpreting the Parables.* Philadelphia: The Westminster Press, 1960.

——— *A Pattern for Life.* Philadelphia: The Westminster Press, 1953.

Jeremias, Joachim. "The Qumran Texts and the New Testament." *The Expository Times,* December, 1948.

Klassen, Wm. and Snyder, G. F. (eds.). *Current Issues in New Testament Interpretation.* New York: Harper and Brothers, 1962.

Leith, John H. (ed.). *Creeds of the Churches.* New York: Doubleday & Company, Inc., 1963.

Lenski, R. C. H. *The Interpretation of St. John's Gospel.* Columbus, Ohio: Lutheran Book Concern, 1931.

Lüthi, Walter. *St. John's Gospel.* Translated by Kurt Schoenenberger. Edinburgh and London: Oliver and Boyd, 1960.

Manson, T. W. *Studies in the Gospels and Epistles.* Edited by Matthew Black. Philadelphia: The Westminster Press, 1962.

Macgregor, G. H. C. *The Gospel of John.* "The Moffatt New Testament Commentary." New York: Harper and Brothers, 1928.

Milligan, Wm. and Moulton, W. F. *Commentary on the Gospel of St. John.* Edinburgh: T. & T. Clark, 1898.

Moffatt, James. *An Introduction to the Literature of the New Testament.* Edinburgh: T. & T. Clark, 1911.

Nunn, H. P. V. *The Fourth Gospel.* London: The Tyndale Press, 1946.

Nicoll, W. Robertson (ed.). *The Expositor's Greek Testament.* Vol. I. London: Hodder and Stoughton, n.d.

Plummer, Alfred. *The Gospel According to St. John.* "The Cambridge Bible for Schools and Colleges." Cambridge: The University Press, 1923.

————. *The Gospel According to St. John.* "Cambridge Greek Testament for Schools and Colleges." Cambridge: The University Press, 1905.

Phillips, H. C. *In the Light of the Cross.* New York: Abingdon-Cokesbury Press, 1947.

Robinson, B. W. *The Gospel of John.* New York: Macmillan, 1925.

Robinson, J. A. T. *Twelve New Testament Studies.* Napierville, Ill.: Allenson, 1962.

Robertson, F. W. *Sermons.* New York: Harper and Brothers, New Edition, n.d.

Richardson, Alan. *The Gospel According to St. John.* London: S.C.M. Press, Ltd., 1960.

Salmon, George. *A Historical Introduction to the Study of the Books of the New Testament.* London: John Murray, 1892.

Sanday, Wm. *The Criticism of the Fourth Gospel.* Oxford: Clarendon Press, 1905.

Schaff, Philip. *The Creeds of Christendom,* Vol. I. New York: Harper and Brothers, 1877.

Schmiedel, Paul. *The Johannine Writings.*

Translated by M. A. Canney. London: Adam and Charles Black, 1908.

Scott, E. F. *The Crisis in the Life of Jesus.* New York: Charles Scribner's Sons, 1952.

————. *The Fourth Gospel, Its Purpose and Theology.* Edinburgh: T. & T. Clark, 1951 (reprint).

Smith, David. *John.* "Commentary on the Four Gospels," 3 vols. New York: Doubleday, Doran and Company, 1928.

Stalker, James. *The Life of Jesus Christ.* Rev. ed. New York: American Tract Society, 1891.

Standard Catechism of the Methodist Episcopal Church and the Methodist Episcopal Church South. New York: Eaton and Mains, 1905.

Stendahl, Krister (ed.). *The Scrolls and the New Testament.* New York: Harper and Brothers, 1957.

Strachan, R. H. *The Fourth Gospel.* Third Edition. London: SCM Press, Ltd., 1960 (reprint).

Streeter, B. H. *The Four Gospels.* New York: The Macmillan Co., 1825.

————. *Reality.* New York: The Macmillan Co., 1927.

Tasker, R. V. *The Old Testament in the New Testament.* Philadelphia: The Westminster Press, 1957.

Temple, Wm. *Readings in St. John's Gospel.* London: Macmillan, 1949.

Tenney, Merrill. *New Testament Survey.* Grand Rapids: Eerdmans, 1961.

Vincent, Marvin R. *Word Studies in the New Testament,* vol. II. New York: Charles Scribner's Sons, 1889.

Westcott, B. F. *The Gospel According to St. John.* London: James Clarke & Co., 1958.

Waddell, Helen. *Stories From Holy Writ.* New York: The Macmillan Co., 1950.

The Acts of the Apostles

by Charles W. Carter

Preface

Professor Charles W. Carter, the author of the *Wesleyan Bible Commentary*: "The Acts," is Chairman of the Division of Religion and Philosophy and Professor of Philosophy and Religion at Taylor University. He is Chairman of the Editorial Board and General Editor of the *Wesleyan Bible Commentary*.

Professor Carter holds the following degrees: Th.B. and A.B., Marion College; M.A., Winona Lake School of Theology; B.D., Asbury Theological Seminary; M.A., Butler University; and the Th.M. from Butler University Graduate School of Religion (now Christian Theological Seminary). He has studied at several other schools, including Ohio State University and Chicago Lutheran Theological Seminary. In 1949 he was elected to membership in the Phi Kappa Phi, national scholastic honor society, and in 1950 to membership in Theta Phi, international honor society (Butler University chapter). He has been recognized and listed in such works as *Who's Who in the Mid-West* (1949); *Who Knows and What* (1st ed., 1949); *Who's Who in American Education* (16th ed., 1953-'54); and *Directory of American Scholars, Pt. IV, Philosophy* (4th ed., 1964). He holds membership in the Metaphysical Society of America; the American Association of University Professors; the National Association of Professors of Missions; American Academy of Political Science; and the Evangelical Theological Society, in which he is a member of the Editorial Committee.

Professor Carter has authored eight books. These include *Transformed Africans* (Wesleyan Methodist Publishing Association, 1938); *A Half-Century of American Wesleyan Missions in West Africa* (Wesleyan Methodist Publishing Association, 1940); *Akafa Ka Malen Ma Themne.* "Christian Songs in Temne," co-authored, compiled and translated with George H. Hemminger (General Council — Assemblies of God, 1948); *The Bible Gift of Tongues* (The Wesley Press, 1952); *Road to Revival* (Higley Press, 1959); *The Evangelical Commentary,* "The Acts of the Apostles," co-authored with Ralph Earle (Zondervan Publishing House, 1959); *Higley's Sunday School Lesson Commentary* (Higley Press, 1960); *Higley Sunday School Lesson Commentary* (Higley Press, 1961). Professor Carter was Editor of the Higley Press and the Higley Sunday School Literature in 1958 and 1959. He has also been a frequent contributor to various religious periodicals and journals.

Professor Carter is an ordained minister in the Wesleyan Methodist Church of America, and a member of the North Michigan Conference of that denomination. For seventeen years he served with the missionary department of his church to Sierra Leone, West Africa, where he was for several years principal and professor in the Clark Memorial Biblical Seminary and General Superintendent of the American Wesleyan Mission of Sierra Leone. He has spent about nine years in the pastoral ministry of his church in America. His preaching and lecturing in churches, camps, conventions and colleges have taken him to almost every part of the United States, and into Canada,

Mexico, the Island world, Africa and parts of Europe. In 1952 he was chosen to deliver the Lienard Lectures at Nazarene Theological Seminary.

For eleven years the author was Professor of Philosophy and Missions at Marion College, where he was also Chairman of the Division of Religion and Philosophy. Since 1959 he has been at Taylor University. His years of teaching the Book of Acts in college, plus his many years of practical service in the ministry and on the mission field, will be reflected to the readers in this commentary. The *Wesleyan Bible Commentary*: "The Acts" represents many years of preparation and applied scholarship. The bibliography represents the scholarly and practical works consulted in the preparation of this work.

The American Standard Version is the basic text of the Scriptures used in the *Wesleyan Bible Commentary*: "The Acts," as in the *WBC* generally. However, many parallel versions have been consulted and on occasion cited for the additional light which they may throw on the text.

While the author has aimed at a high level of accuracy and scholarship, the purpose of the commentary is practical rather than technical. It is designed to serve the interest of students of the Book of Acts both on the lay and ministerial levels, as well as those more specialized students in formal preparation for Christian service.

The author has sought diligently to rediscover the spirit and purpose of the writer of Acts, and accurately to interpret and convey that spirit and purpose to the readers of this commentary. That Luke's prime purpose in writing Acts was to present Jesus Christ as the risen and victorious "Lord of All" is evident from the recurrence of the title "Lord" no less than 110 times in the Acts. This title, as applied to the risen Christ, occurs more than any other important word in Acts. The Holy Spirit working in and through Christ's first-century disciples is represented by Luke as witnessing to the universal Lordship of Jesus Christ. This is evident from Christ's words in the key verse of the Acts: **But ye shall receive power, when the Holy Spirit is come upon you: and ye shall be my witnesses** (Acts 1:8a), as also in His words to His disciples as recorded in the Great Commission in the Gospel According to Matthew: **All authority hath been given unto me in heaven and on earth; Go ye therefore, and make disciples of all the nations** (Matt. 28:18b, 19a). All else in the Acts record is incident to this prime purpose. Luke never loses sight of this divine objective in his Acts account from the opening to the closing words of the book.

The natural divisions of the Acts have been followed in the development of this commentary. Chapters 1-7 are devoted to the witness to Christ's Lordship in Jerusalem and Judaea. Chapters 8 through 12 are devoted to the witness to Christ's Lordship in transition from the Jewish to the Gentile world. Chapters 13 through 28 are concerned with the witness to Christ's Lordship to all the world of the first century, with implications of its significance for the entire world of every succeeding generation of mankind. The Analytical Outline, printed in its entirety in the Introduction and then incorporated into the expositions, has served to direct the expositor's efforts in attempting to present clearly and systematically the meaning and purpose of the author of the Acts. It is sincerely hoped that it will serve as an aid to the reader as well.

The author has sought to bring to life the spirit and meaning of first-century Christianity with their relevance to the twentieth century, as they are revealed in the Acts record.

The *Wesleyan Bible Commentary*: "The Acts" is presented to all who seek for the true meaning of Christianity at its source, with the earnest prayer that it may prove to be a safe and accurate guide to the readers' realization of that desired objective.

Special appreciation is here expressed to Dr. Ralph Earle of Nazarene Theological Seminary for his kind permission to use his Introduction to the Acts which formerly appeared in the *Evangelical Commentary*: "The Acts of the Apostles," Charles W. Carter and Ralph Earle (Grand Rapids, Michigan: Zondervan Publishing House, 1959).

The author wishes also to express his appreciation to the Editorial Board of the *Evangelical Commentary* for their permission to incorporate into the *Wesleyan Bible Commentary*: "The Acts" the expositional material which he contributed to that volume. Acknowledgment of indebtedness to all authors and publishers of works consulted or quoted in the *Wesleyan Bible Commentary*: "The Acts" is hereby made. Due credit is given to these sources in the footnotes and in the bibliography.

Outline

Introduction

I. AUTHORSHIP

A. EXTERNAL EVIDENCE

The earliest testimony to Luke as the author of Acts is found in the Anti-Marcionite Prologue to St. Luke's Gospel (ca. A.D. 150-180). There it is stated: "Moreover, the same Luke afterwards wrote the Acts of the Apostles."[1]

The Muratorian Fragment (ca. A.D. 170-200) says:

> But the Acts of all the Apostles [a strangely exaggerated title!] were written in one volume. Luke compiled for 'most excellent Theophilus' what things were done in detail in his presence, as he plainly shows by omitting both the death of Peter and also the departure of Paul from the city, when he departed for Spain.[2]

Likewise coming from the latter part of the second century is the witness of Irenaeus[3] and Clement of Alexandria[4] that Acts was written by Luke. Eusebius speaks of "the testimony of Luke in the book of Acts."[5] There appears not to have been raised in the early church any question about the Lukan authorship of Acts. Zahn says: "No other position concerning its authorship had been expressed in any quarter."[6]

B. INTERNAL EVIDENCE

One of the most certain results of modern New Testament study is that *the Third Gospel and Acts were written by the same author.* This is definitely implied by the reference in the first verse of Acts to "the former treatise" and the fact that both books are addressed to Theophilus. There is also a great similarity of style and vocabulary. Moffatt notes that there are no less than 57 words which in the New Testament are found only in both the Third Gospel and Acts.[7] Windisch admits: "Lexical, stylistic, and material points of contact between the two prove that both documents derive from the same author."[8] A. C. Clark has sought to deny this.[9] But his arguments have been answered in careful detail by W. L. Knox[10]

In the second place, *the one who wrote the "we" section*[11] *also wrote the rest of the book,* so that the author of Acts was a *companion of Paul.* Again Windisch, who is opposed to Lukan authorship, writes: "Attention must be called to the pervasive lexical, stylistic, and redactional *unity* of Acts as it has been demonstrated by the representatives of the most varied points of view, and, what is especially important, with the inclusion of the 'we' sections."[12] Harnack emphasizes in strongest terms the unity of the "we" sections with the rest of the book.[13]

In the third place, *the author was a physician.* Without doubt Hobart overstated the case in his book, *The Medical Language of St. Luke.*[14] But Harnack gave weighty support to the thesis. Not only did he examine the evidence offered by Hobart, but he made a fresh investigation of the subject.[15] His final conclusion was: "The evidence is of overwhelming force; so that it seems to me that no doubt can exist *that the third gospel and the Acts of the Apostles were composed by a physician.*"[16] Zahn accepted this view. He writes: "W. K. Hobart has proved to the satisfaction of anyone open to conviction, that the author of the Lucan work was familiar with the technical language of Greek medicine, and hence was a *Greek physician.*"[17] Moffatt asserts that Harnack's

---

[1] H. D. Major, T. W. Manson, and C. J. Wright, *The Mission and Message of Jesus,* p. 253.
[2] Kirsopp Lake and Silva Lake, *An Introduction to the New Testament,* p. 280.
[3] *Against Heresies, III.* 14, 1.   [4] *Stromata,* V, 12.
[5] Pamphilus Eusebius, *Ecclesiastical History,* III, 4.
[6] Theodor Zahn, *Introduction to the New Testament,* III, 3.
[7] James Moffatt, *An Introduction to the Literature of the New Testament,* p. 297.
[8] H. Windisch, "The Case Against the Tradition," *The Beginnings of Christianity,* II, 306.
[9] A. C. Clark, *The Acts of the Apostles,* pp. 393ff.
[10] Wilfrid L. Knox, *The Acts of the Apostles,* see especially pp. 2-15, 100-109.
[11] Acts 16:10-17; 20:5-21:18; 27:1-28:15.   [12] *Op. cit.,* p. 305.
[13] Adolf Harnack, *Luke the Physician,* pp. 52f.   [14] W. K. Hobart, *The Medical Language of St. Luke.*
[15] Harnack, *op. cit.,* pp. 175-198.   [16] *Ibid.,* p. 198.   [17] Zahn, *op. cit.,* III, 146.

study "has proved this pretty conclusively."[18]

More recently Cadbury claims to have demolished Hobart's theory. He says: It is doubtful whether his [Luke's] interest in disease and healing exceeds that of his fellow evangelists or other contemporaries who were not doctors, while the words that he shares with the medical writers are found too widely in other kinds of Greek literature for us to suppose that they point to any professional vocabulary."[19]

It would seem that Cadbury's claim is as far exaggerated one way as Hobart's case is the other. More reasonable is the statement of H. D. A. Major: "Nevertheless, there are passages in the Lucan writings, which although they cannot be said to prove, yet do support the hypothesis, that the author was a physician."[20] Bruce has stated the case very fairly: "We shall probably be right in concluding that while the presence of medical diction in Luke-Acts cannot by itself prove anything about authorship, the more striking instances may properly be used to illustrate, and perhaps even to support, the conclusion reached on other grounds, that the author of the twofold history was Luke the physician."[21]

In Colossians 4:14, Paul refers to "Luke, the beloved physician." The only other places in the New Testament where Luke is named are II Timothy 4:11 and Philemon 24.

One other argument for the Lukan authorship of Acts may be mentioned. That is the fact that such a relatively obscure person as Luke — as far as the New Testament record goes — should be named unanimously by the early church as author. Creed states the case well: "If the Gospel and Acts did not already pass under his name there is no obvious reason why tradition should have associated them with him."[22]

II. DATE

John Knox thinks that "Luke-Acts as a finished work belongs to the middle of the second century."[23] That is because he feels that it did not appear until after Marcion had appropriated an earlier, shorter version of Luke's Gospel. Overbeck would place the writing of Acts in "the second and third decades of the second century."[24] Moffatt prefers a date around A.D. 100.[25] Goodspeed[26] and Scott[27] suggest A.D. 90. It should be noted that the last three named hold that Luke wrote Acts. Dibelius a bit more generously chooses "the last ten to thirty years of the first century."[28] Zahn says, "It may be assumed with practical certainty that Luke wrote his work about the year 75."[29]

Harnack has been the outstanding exponent of a date before A.D. 70. He declared that Luke wrote "perhaps even so early as the beginning of the seventh decade of the first century."[30] A little later he expressed himself thus: "The concluding verses of the Acts of the Apostles, taken in conjunction with the result of the trial of St. Paul and to his martyrdom, make it in the highest degree probable that the work was written at a time when St. Paul's trial in Rome had not yet come to an end."[31] The above quotation indicates the main reason for holding to an early date for Acts.

C. C. Torrey thinks that "the Third Gospel was written before the year 61, probably in the year 60" and that Acts was written soon after.[32] This is the commonly accepted view of conservative scholars today: that Luke probably wrote his Gospel during Paul's two years' imprisonment at Caesarea and Acts during the Apostle's two years' imprisonment at Rome. Bruce gives a very clear and

[18] Moffatt, op. cit., p. 298.   [19] Henry J. Cadbury, The Making of Luke-Acts, p. 358.
[20] Major, loc. cit.
[21] F. F. Bruce, The Acts of the Apostles, p. 5.   Notice should also be taken of the Early Church tradition that the writer of Acts was a physican (Eusebius, Ecclesiastical History, III, 4).
[22] J. M. Creed, The Gospel According to St. Luke, p. xiii.
[23] John Knox, Marcion and the New Testament, p. 121.
[24] See Edward Zeller, The Contents and Origin of the Acts of the Apostles, to which is prefixed Dr. F. Overbeck's Introduction to the Acts, I, 71.   [25] Op. cit., p. 312.
[26] Edgar J. Goodspeed, An Introduction to the New Testament, p. 196.
[27] E. F. Scott, The Literature of the New Testament, p. 94.
[28] Martin Dibelius, A Fresh Approach to the New Testament and Early Christian Literature, p. 264.
[29] Op. cit., III, 159.   [30] Adolf Harnack, The Acts of the Apostles, p. 297.
[31] Adolf Harnack, The Date of the Acts and the Synoptic Gospels, p. 99.
[32] C. C. Torrey, The Composition and Date of Acts, p. 68.

III. PURPOSE

Probably the preface to Luke's Gospel (Luke 1:1-4) was intended to serve as a statement of the purpose for writing the two-volume work, Luke-Acts. Luke desired to give Theophilus an authoritative history of the beginnings of Christianity, in order that he might "know the certainty concerning the things wherein thou wast instructed."

More specifically, the purpose of Acts is suggested in its first verse, where it is stated that the "former treatise" gave what Jesus *began* to do. Here, then, we are to read what He *continued* to do through His apostles and prophets.

Kirsopp Lake and Silva Lake give a threefold purpose for the book as follows: "a. A desire to prove the supernatural inspiration and guidance given to the Church on the day of Pentecost. . . . b. A desire to show that the best Roman magistrates never decided against the Christians. . . . c. A more purely historical desire to show how the Church ceased to be Jewish and became Greek."[34]

The apologetic purpose of Acts seems unquestionable.[35] There is every evidence to indicate that Luke wanted Theophilus to know that Christianity was not officially persecuted by Roman rulers in the first generation of its history.

The Tübingen school of criticism in Germany, as is well known, subordinated this apologetic emphasis to an irenic purpose. Acts was written primarily as an effort to harmonize and reconcile the Petrine and Pauline parties in the church.[36] Consequently it was claimed that Acts is unreliable; it gives an intentionally distorted view of the primitive church. The epistles of Paul give the true picture: Paul rebuking Peter publicly (Gal. 2:11-14), Pauline and Petrine parties in Corinth in mutual opposition (I Cor. 1:12), etc., etc. But this Tübingen theory has been largely discredited in this century, so that it is no longer widely held. Henshaw says that "the Tübingen school launched an attack on the authenticity of the history presented in 'Acts,' by representing it as a second-century work, written to cover up a controversy between Jewish and Pauline Christianity, which, it was alleged, divided the whole of the early Church," and then adds: "Investigation has now completely refuted the theory."[37]

The highest purpose for Luke's writing is perhaps expressed in these words of Barnett: "To put Christianity in its true light, therefore, the author of Luke-Acts described the life and message of Jesus and showed how He remained the determining influence in the Christian movement through the person of the Spirit."[38] Clogg thinks that Acts 1:8 gives the twofold aim of the book; namely, the emphasis on the power of the Holy Spirit and on the rapid expansion, numerically and geographically, of the church.[39]

In seeking to sum up the theological purpose of the book, Cadbury notes that three important convictions of the early church are presented therein: (1) the resurrection of Jesus; (2) His return from heaven; (3) the coming of the Holy Spirit into the hearts of His disciples.[40]

IV. TRUSTWORTHINESS

The Tübingen school of German criticism in the nineteenth century dismissed the Book of Acts as historically unreliable.[41] But as early as 1896 Ramsay could assert that Acts "was written by a great historian, a writer who set himself to record the facts as they occurred."[42] In 1911 he stated even more emphatically: "The present writer takes the view that Luke's history is unsurpassed in respect of its trustworthiness."[43]

---

[33] *Op. cit.*, pp. 10-14. Some of the reasons are: (1) little evidence of acquaintance with Paul's letters; (2) abrupt close of book; (3) no hint of Paul's death; (4) no reflection of Neronian persecution; (5) no hint of Jewish War; (6) primitive theology.   [34] *Op. cit.*, p. 66.
[35] Streeter calls it "the first of the Apologies" (B. H. Streeter, *The Four Gospels*, p. 539).
[36] See Zeller, *op. cit.*, II, 111-160.   [37] T. Henshaw, *New Testament Literature*, p. 185.
[38] Albert E. Barnett, *The New Testament*, p. 174.
[39] F. B. Clogg, *An Introduction to the New Testament*, p. 247.
[40] Henry J. Cadbury, "Acts and Eschatology," *The Background of the New Testament and Its Eschatology*, p. 300.   [41] Cf. Zeller, *op. cit.*, II, 111ff.
[42] W. M. Ramsay, *St. Paul the Traveller and the Roman Citizen*, p. 14.
[43] W. M. Ramsay, *The Bearing of Recent Discovery on the Trustworthiness of the New Testament*, p. 81.

In the meantime F. H. Chase had taken up the gauntlet against the extreme radical criticism. In 1902 he wrote: "Thus the 'traditional' view of the Book, which we know to have been that of the Christian society since the time of Irenaeus, stands the test of careful and thorough investigation, and may claim to be accounted the 'critical' view."[44]

Since the epochal work of Ramsay and Harnack, the Book of Acts has been held in higher respect. The main point at which some scholars today would question its complete trustworthiness is in the matter of the speeches. For instance, one of the most recent writers of a text in New Testament introduction says: "The speeches of Acts . . . look like deliberate compositions of the writer himself, following the methods of Greek historians, in which he seeks to give the essential items in the earliest proclamation of the Gospel."[45] That is, the speeches do not give us what Paul or Peter or Stephen actually said but only a sample of the apostolic *kerygma*.[46]

The confirmation of the Acts record at so many points by archaeological discovery in modern times ought to make the honest student slow to doubt the reliability of Acts as a trustworthy account of what happened in the first generation of the Christian church.

by Ralph Earle

[44] Frederick H. Chase, *The Credibility of the Book of the Acts of the Apostles*, p. 296.
[45] Donald T. Rowlingson, *Introduction to New Testament Study*, pp. 108f.
[46] For a further discussion of the speeches in Acts see the Exegesis by Ralph Earle contained in *The Evangelical Commentary* by Charles W. Carter and Ralph Earle, "The Acts of The Apostles," pp. 34-38, where the writer accepts a middle view — that what is given is "a faithful reproduction of the thought, spirit, and main content of each of the speeches."

The Acts of the Apostles

I. THE CHURCH IN PREPARATION
(Acts 1:1-26)

A. THE AUTHOR'S PROLOGUE (1:1-5)

The prologue to the *Book of Acts* links .he authorship of this later work to that of the *Third Gospel*. It also links the acts and instructions of the Lord Jesus which were begun in Luke with their continuance by the Holy Spirit in His disciples in the Acts record. Further, it confirms these works and teachings by reference to Christ's appearances to His disciples subsequent to His death and resurrection. It records His command to His disciples to remain in Jerusalem until the Father's promise had been fulfilled to them, and it concludes with a promise of their not far distant baptism with the Holy Spirit.

1. The Author's Purpose (1:1)

1 The former treatise I made, O Theophilus, concerning all that Jesus began both to do and to teach,

The former treatise (a systematic presentation of facts and principles) unquestionably refers to the *Third Gospel* written by the same author as *Acts*. Says Cadbury:

> It is necessary once more to remind the reader that it was the custom in antiquity, on account of the purely physical conditions of writing, to divide works into volumes, to prefix to the first a preface for the whole, and to add secondary prefaces to the beginning of each later one. . . . The book of Acts is no afterthought. The word "treatise" implies a more complete work than does *logos* . . . . Luke 1:1-4 . . . is the real preface to Acts as well as to the Gospel, written by the author when he contemplated not merely one but both volumes. . . . It is as necessary to apply the phraseology of the preface [to Luke] to Acts as to the Gospel.[1]

The continuity of Acts with Luke is suggested in the identity of *authorship,*

Luke; the *reader,* Theophilus; and the *subject,* Jesus Christ, though He is now in the person of the Holy Spirit working in and through His disciples. What Jesus began to do in the days of His flesh He planned and prepared to continue in a larger measure by His Spirit indwelling His disciples. Said Jesus to His disciples, "Verily, verily, I say unto you, He that believeth on me, the works that I do shall he do also; and greater works than these shall he do; because I go unto the Father" (John 14:12). Thus Luke's purpose in writing Acts is clearly to supplement his Gospel narrative of Jesus' earthly life and works with an historical record of the works of the ascended Christ through the Holy Spirit with whose personality and power His followers were soon to be endued. Acts is Luke's history of the infant church. The word "began" suggests the continued activity of the church indefinitely.

Theophilus is an enigmatical character. History can help us but little in knowing who or what he was. Tradition is for the most part unreliable. The latter links Theophilus with Antioch of Syria, and thus some think him to have been a Greek or Roman official of governmental rank at that city. Dummelow[2] considers him more likely a distinguished Roman citizen residing at Rome, since the title "most excellent" was applied to high-ranking Romans, and especially was a technical title in the second century, designating equestrian (knight-hood) rank. This title was applied to both Felix and Festus in Acts 23:26; 24:3, and 26:25. However, it was sometimes used solely to designate friendship. The tradition contained in the *Clementine Recognitions* (X. 71), about the middle of the second century, holds that Theophilus was a superior-ranking governmental officer at Antioch, and that he consecrated the palace in which he resided (the great basilica), under the name of a church.

In any event, the name Theophilus ap-

[1] Henry J. Cadbury, "Commentary on the Preface of Luke," *The Beginnings of Christianity*, Part one, II, 491, 492.   [2] J. R. Dummelow, ed., *A Commentary on the Holy Bible*, p. 737.

plies to a Gentile of rank and honor who had likely been converted to Christianity by Luke or Paul. He may have been a Christian of wealth who financed the publication of Luke and Acts, which fact may account for Luke's having dedicated these works to him.

That Theophilus was a real person, and not a fictitious name for all the Christians or "friends of God" as some suppose, is attested by the fact that the singular number is used, and the title "most excellent" could not apply to all the Christians as with an individual. Cadbury holds that, when the form of this preface is considered in the light of contemporary Hellenistic literature,

> its adoption at once suggests a certain flavour of conventionality on the part of the author as consciously presenting his book to the public. The dedication to Theophilus means this, rather than that the book is intended for a limited circle.[3]

2. The Lord's Confirmation (1:2, 3)

> 2 until the day in which he was received up, after that he had given commandment through the Holy Spirit unto the apostles whom he had chosen: 3 to whom he also showed himself alive after his passion by many proofs, appearing unto them by the space of forty days, and speaking the things concerning the kingdom of God:

The incarnation, life and work, death, resurrection, appearances, commission of His disciples, ascension to the Father, and the descent of the Holy Spirit are all continuous and integrated factors in the divine plan of human redemption. No one factor may be intelligibly considered apart from the whole divine process. Thus the personal work of Christ continued on earth until His ascension; **the day he was received up.**

Christ's ascension did not occur until He had made provision for the continuance of His redemptive work by giving **commandment through the Holy Spirit unto the apostles whom he had chosen** for that purpose. This "Commandment," or "Great Commission," as it is popularly designated, has its fullest and most specific record in Matthew 28: 18-20. Here, following His death and resurrection and just prior to His ascension, on the occasion of His appearance

to the disciples on a mountain in Galilee, Jesus issued His kingdom command. "All authority hath been given unto me in heaven and on earth. Go ye therefore, and make disciples of all nations, baptizing them into the name of the Father and of the Son and of the Holy Spirit: teaching them to observe all things whatsoever I commanded you: and lo, I am with you always, even unto the end of the world." Corresponding but less detailed accounts of this commission occur in Mark 16:14-18; Luke 24:45-49; and John 20:23; and finally, in its epitomized form in Acts 1:8. Matthew's account sets forth: *First,* the "resource and authority" of the commission as vested in Christ's victory over death and His consequent universal Lordship; "All authority hath been given unto me in heaven and on earth." This is a claim which Christ nowhere makes for Himself until after His death and resurrection (see also Rev. 1:17b, 18). *Second,* the "objective" of the commission is defined as twofold: "make disciples," and "teaching them to observe all things whatsoever I commanded you." *Third,* the "extent" of the commission is suggested in the words, "Go ye therefore [unto] . . . all the nations." These words should be understood to imply all nations of every generation from that day until the close of the Gospel Age. Finally, Christ presents the divine "assurance" of the commission. "Lo, I am with you always, even unto the end of the world" (or the consummation of the age).

Let the universality of this commission be carefully noted as indicated by the word "all": "All authority . . . all the nations . . . all things . . . always" (all-ways).

Christ's issuance of the commandment **through the Holy Spirit** unto the apostles is clear testimony to the inseparableness of the third person of the Holy Trinity from any communication of divinity to humanity.

A. T. Robertson takes note of eleven appearances of Christ. They are as follows: *first,* Mary Magdalene (Mark 16:9 and John 20:11-18) ; *second,* other women (Matt. 28:9, 10) ; *third,* two disciples including Cleopas, en route to Emmaus (Mark 16:12, 13 and Luke 24:13-32) ;

³ Cadbury, *op. cit.,* p. 490.

fourth, Simon Peter (Luke 24:33, 34 and I Cor. 15:5); *fifth,* the disciples, Thomas being absent (Mark 16:14; Luke 24:36-43; and John 20:19-25); *sixth,* to the disciples including Thomas (John 20:26-31 and I Cor. 15:5); *seventh,* the seven disciples by the Sea of Galilee (John 21:1, 2); *eighth,* the eleven on a mountain in Galilee (Mark 16:14-18; Matt. 28:16-20) and above 500 (I Cor. 15:6); *ninth,* James the brother of Jesus (I Cor. 15:7); *tenth,* the disciples at Jerusalem with another commission (Luke 24:44-49 and Acts 1:3-8); *eleventh,* the last appearance to the disciples on Mount Olivet between Jerusalem and Bethany (Mark 16:19, 20; Luke 24:50-53; and Acts 1:9-12).[4] If included, the post-ascension appearance to Paul (I Cor. 15:8) on the Damascus road would make twelve. Christ's appearances to Stephen in his hour of martyrdom (Acts 7:55, 56) and to John the Revelator on the Isle of Patmos (Rev. 1:9-18) are also noteworthy. Except for the last three mentioned, these appearances of Christ occurred within the forty days between His resurrection in His glorified form and His ascension. Thus the appearance of Christ to Stephen, Paul, and the Revelator were not different from His appearances to His disciples before His ascension. This fact supports Paul's argument that his apostleship was validated by Christ's appearance to him on the Damascus road.

The **many** ["infallible"] **proofs** attesting Christ's resurrection from the dead included: (1) the carefully guarded but empty tomb (Luke 24:5, 6); (2) the declaration of the angels (Luke 24:4-7); (3) the testimony of the Roman guards (Matt. 28:11-15); (4) the post-resurrection appearances, above enumerated (see notes on previous verse); (5) the release of the saints from their graves following Christ's resurrection (Matt. 27:51-53); (6) the occurrence of Pentecost in fulfillment of the promise of the Holy Spirit to His disciples (Acts 1:8; 2:1-4); (7) the arrest of, and appearance to, the persecutor Saul on the Damascus road (Acts 9:1-18); (8) the appearance to Stephen in the hour of his death (Acts 7:55, 56); (9) the appearance to John on Patmos (Rev. 1:9-18); (10) His eating and drinking with the disciples (Luke 24:39-43); (11) His important instructions and commission to His disciples (Matt. 28:18-20); (12) the forty days of ministration during which time His claims could be adequately investigated and substantiated or denied by His friends or foes; (13) His fulfillment of Old Testament prophecy; and (14) His fulfillment of His own predictions. Finally, perhaps the greatest evidence of Christ's resurrection has been His influence upon the lives of men and nations throughout the subsequent ages. The "Good News" of Christ's atoning death and victorious resurrection has ever borne the evidence of **many** [infallible] **proofs** (see Romans 1:16, 17 and I Thess. 1:5).

The things concerning the kingdom of God, about which Jesus spoke to His disciples, pertained to the spiritual nature of that kingdom which He came to establish. This spiritual kingdom was to be wrought in, and outworked through, the lives of His disciples by the personal operation of the Holy Spirit: the doctrines that would mould it, the discipline that would direct and preserve it, and the spirit and methods that would propagate it.

3. The Lord's Command (1:4a)

4 and, being assembled together with them, he charged them not to depart from Jerusalem, but to wait for the promise of the Father,

The **being assembled together with them** on the occasion of this command may refer to the meeting with the more than 500 disciples on a mountain in Galilee (I Cor. 15:6), since the promise of the Holy Spirit to be fulfilled at Pentecost was for all believers and not just the apostles. Luke's gospel record of this event would rather appear to locate the place and time of Christ's command on the Mount of Ascension; however, the actual time of the command and the promise that follows may have preceded the ascension.

Luke's earlier recorded command, "But tarry ye in the city, until ye be clothed with power from on high" (Luke 24:49b), agrees with the later Acts account concerning **the promise of the Father** (Acts 1:4); and here, as always, is conditioned for its fulfillment upon the obedience of the disciples to the divine

---

[4] A. T. Robertson, *A Harmony of the Gospels,* pp. 242-252.

command to "tarry" or "wait" in Jerusalem. Christ's supreme authority qualified Him to issue the command. Obedience to that command assured the fulfillment of the promise. Had they in impatience failed to wait in obedience, there would have been no Christian Pentecost, and had there been no Pentecost, there would have been no church for the evangelization of the first-century world. There is no substitute for obedience, and there is no spiritual Pentecost without obedience. The church signs her own spiritual death warrant when she fails to obey the divine command to wait for her spiritual Pentecost. Dr. Edwin S. Johnson has quoted D. L. Moody as having said, "You might as well try to see without eyes, hear without ears, or breathe without lungs, as to live the Christian life without the Holy Spirit."

4. The Lord's Promise (1:4b, 5)

> which, *said he,* ye heard from me:
> 5 for John indeed baptized with water;
> but ye shall be baptized in the Holy
> Spirit not many days hence.

Just as the whole of the Jewish economy looked forward to and found its fulfillment and meaning in Christ the Messiah crucified, dead, buried, and victoriously resurrected, so the New Testament economy finds its fulfillment and significance in the Father's verification of His promise to every believer through the baptism with the Holy Spirit. He, the Holy Spirit, is the Father's promise to all believers by His holy prophets (Acts 2:16-21), by John the Baptist (Matt. 3:11, 12), by Christ Himself (John 16:7), and finally as directly given by the Father. Nor was this promise restricted to the apostles or immediate disciples of Jesus. Peter applies Joel's prophecy concerning Pentecost to the assembled multitudes at Jerusalem thus: "Ye shall receive the gift of the Holy Spirit. For to you is the promise, . . . and to all that are afar off, even as many as the Lord our God shall call unto him" (Acts 2:38b, 39).

John's baptism was with water unto repentance, but Christ's baptism was with the Holy Spirit unto purification, animation, and power. Says Clarke:

> Christ baptizes with the Holy Ghost, for the destruction of sin, the illumination of

the mind, and the consolation of the heart. . . . Christ's baptism *established* and *maintained* the kingdom.[5]

This promise most evidently refers to the communication of the Holy Spirit on the following Pentecost "to *illuminate, regenerate, refine,* and *purify* the heart. With this, sprinkling or immersion are equally efficient: without this both are worth nothing."[6]

In Luke 12:49 and 50, Christ declared that He "came to cast fire upon the earth. . . . But," said He, "I have a baptism to be baptized with; and how am I straitened till it be accomplished!" His casting of fire, in the Pentecostal effusion, could not be realized until the accomplishment of His baptism of suffering and death. His baptism is now past and He is about to cast Himself upon earth in the unrestrained and unlimited fiery baptism of His disciples by the Holy Spirit.

B. THE LORD'S PLAN (1:6-11)

In this paragraph is recorded the disciples' continued misapprehension of the divine plan for the kingdom, Christ's revelation of His plan to His disciples, and the Father's attestation of that plan.

1. The Disciples' Misapprehension of the Plan (1:6)

> 6 They therefore, when they were come together, asked him, saying, Lord, dost thou at this time restore the kingdom to Israel?

Lord, dost thou at this time restore the kingdom to Israel? How reminiscent are these words of the remark of one of the disciples on the road to Emmaus, after Christ's death: "But we hoped that it was he who should redeem Israel" (Luke 24:21a).

These Jewish disciples of Christ had been so thoroughly imbued with the age-old Jewish materialistic concept of the Messianic kingdom that, until the hour of Christ's ascension, they were unable to grasp the spiritual significance of the kingdom Christ came to establish. They, like the Pharisees, had not yet learned that "The kingdom of God cometh not with observation: . . . for lo, the kingdom of God is within you" (Luke 17:20b, 21b); or, as Paul later voiced it, "The

---

[5] Adam Clarke, *The New Testament of Our Lord and Saviour Jesus Christ,* I, 683.   [6] *Ibid.*

kingdom of God is not eating and drinking, but righteousness and peace and joy in the Holy Spirit" (Rom. 14:17; see also Matt. 20:21 and Heb. 12:16, 17).

The Romans, not the Israelites, wielded the scepter of government. The Jews hoped and prayed for deliverance from this galling foreign yoke. Even Christ's disciples shared, in a measure, this materialistic hope. Pentecost was necessary to disillusion Christ's disciples of the false notion of the kingdom. Pentecost is ever a necessity to clarify and establish spiritual realities. With Pentecost spiritual values will be clarified; without Pentecost they will become obscured and confused. No Spirit baptized and directed ministry will ever lose its way doctrinally or otherwise.

2. The Divine Revelation of the Plan (1:7, 8)

7 And he said unto them, It is not for you to know times or seasons, which the Father hath set within his own authority. 8 But ye shall receive power, when the Holy Spirit is come upon you: and ye shall be my witnesses both in Jerusalem, and in all Judaea and Samaria, and unto the uttermost part of the earth.

Christ mildly rebukes the disciples' query concerning the restoration of the kingdom. He does not deny that He has a kingdom to restore. In fact He admits that His plan provides for a universal kingdom over the souls of men (v. 8), though that plan is not for a narrow limited material kingdom such as His Jewish disciples had conceived.

In His rebuke, It is not for you to know times or seasons, which the Father hath set within his own authority (v. 7), Christ implies that God is never the agent of a fatalistic determinism. Says Clarke:

Infinite, eternal liberty to act or not to act, to create or not to create, to destroy or not to destroy, belongs to God alone, and we must take care how we imagine decrees, formed even by His own prescience, in reference to futurity, which power is from the moment of their conception laid under the *necessity* of performing. In every point of time and eternity, God must be free to act or not to act, as may seem best to His godly wisdom.[7]

It must ever be remembered that God's respect for the intelligent moral freedom with which He has endowed man influences His provision of, and decisions in, human events (see Jonah).

On the positive side it was *power*, or *divine energy,* not the divine *authority* of verse seven, that the disciples were to receive through their enduement with the Holy Spirit. Nor was the divine energy a gift to be received apart from the personal Lordship of Christ through the Holy Spirit in their lives. An interesting and helpful reading of verse eight is found in the margin of another version (KJV). "Ye shall receive the power of the Holy Spirit coming upon you." This rendering directly relates the "power" to the "person" of the Holy Spirit. His power is never disassociated from His personality. God does not parcel out His power. This promise became a reality on the day of Pentecost when "they were all filled with the Holy Spirit" (Acts 2:4a), which Holy Spirit Chadwick designates as the "Other Self of the Christ."[8]

The geographic, national, and temporal plan of the universal spiritual kingdom is then outlined by Christ for His disciples in this passage, as well as the whole plan of the Book of Acts. This passage which reveals the divine plan for the Christian witness to Christ's finished work to the world may be viewed thus:

I. *The enduement of the disciples with the Spirit for the world witness*: **But ye shall receive power, when the Holy Spirit is come upon you.**

II. *The divine commission of the disciples to the world witness*: **And ye shall be my witnesses.**

III. *The universal scope of the world witness*: **In Jerusalem, and in all Judaea and Samaria, and unto the uttermost part of the earth.**

Otherwise considered this key verse to the Book of Acts (Acts 1:8) may be analyzed as follows:

I. *The Pentecostal Promise*: ye "**shall receive.**"

II. *The Pentecostal power*: ye shall receive "**power.**"

III. *The Pentecostal person*: the "**Holy Spirit.**"

7 *Ibid.,* I, 684.   8 Samuel Chadwick, *The Way to Pentecost,* p. 21.

IV. *The Pentecostal purpose*: Ye shall be "my witnesses."

V. *The Pentecostal plan*: in "Jerusalem," and in all "Judaea" and "Samaria," and unto "the uttermost part of the earth."

The divine commission of the disciples was to witness to Christ. A witness is one who gives testimony to that which he has seen or experienced, and of which he consequently has personal firsthand knowledge; and the witness given is an attestation of a known fact or event. Now in the realm of personal subjective experience, religious or otherwise, the individual is the final authority. From his experience and testimony there is no further human appeal, since he only can know what transpires within his subjective self, or between that self and God. Such knowledge of personal experience is a matter of personal faith. In fact, all knowledge of whatever kind is finally based upon personal faith. This principle was grasped and expressed by the great apostle Paul: "For who among men knoweth the things of a man, save the spirit of the man, which is in him?" (I Cor. 2:11). Now, the knowledge of the person, work, teachings, death, and resurrection of Jesus Christ was a matter of personal experience with these disciples. Peter implies that one of the requirements for a first-century Christian apostle was that he must have known Christ in the flesh (Acts 1:21, 22; also I John 1:1-4). Having reiterated the accomplishments of His suffering, death, and resurrection, Jesus declared to His disciples: "Ye are witnesses of these things" (Luke 24:48). Nor was their witness to consist of the mere historical fact of Christ's death and resurrection, of which they had certain knowledge, but theirs was to be a living witness to the personal, ever living presence of Christ who was to indwell and abide with them forever through the Holy Spirit with whom they were to be endued on the day of Pentecost. This was the commission of the first-century Christian disciples, and this is the abiding commission to the disciples of Christ in every age and for all time. (For O.T. parallel see Isa. 6.)

The universal scope of the divine plan of witnessing arrests our attention: **In Jerusalem, and in all Judaea and Samaria,**

and unto the uttermost part of the earth. What a Herculean task Jesus assigns to this little flock of first-century Christians!

That the universal scope of the Christian world witness is geographic, racial, and temporal appears evident from the words of this commission, as well as those of Matthew 28:18-20. The apostles themselves were Jewish Christians, and the Holy Spirit first descended on them in Jerusalem. This effusion of the Spirit next influenced the Jews residing in, or assembled at, Jerusalem for the Jewish Pentecost, resulting in the conversion of 3,000 souls. The gospel was declared to be first for the Jews, and the early Christian disciples and apostles consistently practiced witnessing first to the Jews wherever they went. Jerusalem was the religious capital of the Jews. Christ and Christianity were the fruit of the faith of the Jews, the end product of the Jewish economy. Saint Augustine is reported as having said that "the Old Testament is the New Testament infolded; the New Testament is the Old Testament unfolded. The New is the Old concealed; the Old is in the New revealed. The Old Testament is the New Testament in bud; the New Testament is the Old Testament in full bloom."

The scope of the commission broadens both geographically and racially with the mention of Judaea and Samaria. While primarily a geographic province of southern Palestine throughout which Jews for the most part resided, the term Judaea also embraced the Gentile administrative capital of Caesarea. The country of Samaria to the north of geographic Judaea, on the other hand, consisted of a despised, mongrel people, half Jew, half Gentile, both racially and religiously. They, together with the Jews of the Dispersion, formed the bridge of transition for the Christian witness from the Jerusalem Jews to the Gentile nations and the uttermost part of the earth. (See ADDITIONAL NOTE VII, *Samaria and the Samaritans*.)

The last division of this scope of the Christian witness is all-inclusive of peoples, geography, and ages or generations, to the close of the Gospel Age.

The foregoing analysis of the scope of the Christian witness clearly underlies Luke's plan in setting forth the history of the Christian witness in the Book of Acts. In outline it would be as follows:

I. *The witness in Jerusalem,* Acts 1-7.

II. *The witness in transition,* Acts 8-12.

III. *The witness in all the world,* Acts 13-28.

The principal characters in the first division are Peter and Stephen; in the second, Peter, Philip, and Barnabas; and in the third, Paul. In Paul is found a combination of the characteristics of all the foregoing, and the task he began continues unfinished in our day. However, that the first-century disciples of Christ realized in large measure the fulfillment of the scope of this commission for their generation is the clear testimony of Paul in his epistles. To the church at Rome, Paul could write within 30 years of Pentecost: "First, I thank my God through Jesus Christ for you all, that your faith is proclaimed throughout the whole world" (Romans 1:8). And again in the Colossian letter, written during his first Roman imprisonment about A.D. 60, Paul made a like declaration: "The gospel . . . is come unto you; even as it is also in all the world bearing fruit and increasing, as it doth in you also, since the day ye heard and know the grace of God in truth" (Col. 1:5b, 6).

Nor does Paul stand alone in his testimony to the early wide spread of the Christian gospel. Justin Martyr (100?-165?), writing in the second Christian century, is reported by Harnack to have said:

> There is not a single race of human beings, barbarians, Greeks, or whatever name you please to call them, nomads or vagrants or herdsmen living in tents, where prayers in the name of Jesus the crucified are not offered up. . . .
> Through all the members of the body is the soul spread; so are Christians throughout the cities of the world.[9]

While Tertullian lived and wrote at a slightly later date (A.D. 160-230), yet his memorable tribute to the far-reaching influences of the Christian religion reflects, according to Harnack, the success of the first-century Christian evangel:

> We [the Christians] are but of yesterday. Yet we have filled all the places you frequent — cities, lodging houses, villages, townships, markets, the camp itself, the tribes, town councils, the palace, the senate, and the forum. All we have left you is your temples. . . . Behold, every corner of the universe has experienced the gospel, and the whole ends and bounds of the world are occupied with the gospel.[10]

Writing of the rapid spread of the gospel in the days of the cruel emperor Nero, a contemporary of the Apostle Paul, Lactantius, observes, according to Harnack, "Nero noticed that not only at Rome but everywhere a large multitude were daily falling away from idolatry and coming over to the new religion."[11]

Adolf Harnack takes note of these reports of the universal proclamation of the gospel within the Apostolic Age as follows:

> This belief, that the original apostles had already preached the gospel to the whole world, is therefore extremely old. . . . The belief would never have arisen unless some definite knowledge of the apostles' labours and whereabouts (i.e., in the majority of cases) had been current. Both Clemens Romanus and Ignatius assume that the gospel had already been diffused all over the world. . . . Finally, as the conception emerges in Hermas, it is exceptionally clear and definite; and this evidence of Hermas is all the more weighty, as he may invariably be assumed to voice opinions which were widely spread and commonly received. On earth, as he puts it, there are twelve great peoples, and the gospel has already been preached to them all by the apostles.[12]

Many more testimonies, of biblical and extra-biblical writers, could be added as evidence that these disciples of Jesus Christ at Pentecost caught a vision under the powerful illumination of God as revealed in the person of the Holy Spirit that irresistibly impelled them to proclaim the glorious gospel of Jesus Christ to the ends of the earth. Pentecost then, as ever, set on fire the hearts of these first-century Christians. They were inflamed with a passion that could not be satisfied as long as a creature remained who had not heard of Christ and His saving provisions.

---

[9] Adolf von Harnack, *The Mission and Expansion of Christianity in the First Three Centuries,* II, 4, 5. [10] *Ibid.,* pp. 7, 16. [11] *Ibid.,* p. 16. [12] *Ibid.,* p. 24.

3. The Divine Attestation of the Plan (1:9-11)

9 And when he had said these things, as they were looking, he was taken up; and a cloud received him out of their sight. 10 And while they were looking stedfastly into heaven as he went, behold two men stood by them in white apparel; 11 who also said, Ye men of Galilee, why stand ye looking into heaven? this Jesus, who was received up from you into heaven, shall so come in like manner as ye beheld him going into heaven.

The ascension of Jesus Christ to the Father in the sight of His disciples at the completion of His instructions to them was conclusive evidence of the Father's approval of His plans. Following the Resurrection, He had more than once appeared and vanished from their sight only to reappear again. This ninth verse, however, records His final departure in physical form. The heaven into which He disappeared was primarily the cloud-enshrouded physical atmosphere. These clouds swallowed His physical presence from their sight, but His spiritual presence was to remain with them forever, though the fuller revelation and realization of that presence must await the day of Pentecost.

Amazed and dazed by the final bodily disappearance of their Lord, these disciples were suddenly shocked to the realization of their responsibility to Christ's last command by the question of two messengers. These messengers are here designated "men," but they are, when correctly understood, angels in the physical form of men, who were fresh from the throne of God, to the right hand of which Christ had just ascended. These messengers seem to say: "Why further concern yourselves about your Lord's person? His work is completed; you have His blueprint for the construction of His universal spiritual kingdom in the hearts of men on earth. This same incarnate God-man, who by reason of the Father's acceptance of His person and work in the Ascension, is made Lord of the universe and will indeed **so come in like manner as ye beheld him going into heaven.** However, His return **in like manner** as He departed will depend upon your faithfulness in executing the command.

He will personally return to receive and rule over the spiritual kingdom which you, His disciples, prepare for Him through the power of His Spirit working through you in witnessing to all the world. To Pentecost, and from thence to the challenge of a world witness!" This is the message of the two heaven-sent messengers to the "heavenward gazing" disciples on the Mount of Ascension. How much like the disciples on the Mount of Transfiguration they were (see Matt. 17:4 and Mark 9:9, 17-29).

The kingdom of Christ has ever suffered from two fatal deficiencies on the part of its servants: a heavenward gaze, on the one hand, without a sense of manward responsibility; and, on the other hand, a disproportionate sense of manward responsibility without the heavenward gaze. The true religion of Jesus Christ places redeemed man in a position of ambassadorial mediatorship (II Cor. 5:20). Christ's promise, "and lo, I am with you alway, even unto the end of the world" [the consummation of the age], is forever conditioned upon the disciples' obedience to the Master's command, "Go ye" (Matt. 28:20b and 19a). Morgan's observation on this passage is pertinent.

> The realization of the promise of His abiding presence is entirely dependent upon the church's willingness to fulfill her responsibility. She has no right to apply this gracious word to herself save as she fulfills the conditions imposed. If we have no passion in our hearts for the discipling of the nations, we have no warrant for believing that He remains in fellowship with us.[13]

The religion of the Lord Jesus Christ is like a carpenter's square, one arm of which points Godward, and the other manward; the first is religious or spiritual and the second, social (see Matt. 22:37-40). "Adventism" has overemphasized the first, while the "social gospel" has overemphasized the second (cf. I Thess. 1:9, 10). These messengers' words, **this Jesus** — denoting His human nature, and **as ye beheld him going into heaven** — denoting His identity, distinguish Christ's second coming from the Holy Spirit's manifestation at Pentecost, as well as exposing the mistaken notion of some that it refers to Christ's coming

---

[13] G. Campbell Morgan, *The Missionary Manifesto*, p. 56.

for His saints at death. There is no more certain scriptural fact than the personal Second Coming of Jesus Christ at the end of the Gospel Age. While it was clearly the purpose of Luke in the Acts to portray the universal Lordship of Jesus Christ, the Second Coming of Christ is a dominant concern in the epistles.

C. THE DISCIPLES' PRAYER (1:12-14)

Following the account of Christ's ascension, Luke records the place, personnel, and nature of the disciples' prayer in preparation for Pentecost.

1. The Place of the Prayer (1:12, 13a)

12 Then returned they unto Jerusalem from the mount called Olivet, which is nigh unto Jerusalem, a sabbath day's journey off. 13 And when they were come in, they went up into the upper chamber, where they were abiding;

At last disillusioned of their mistaken materialistic concept of Christ's kingdom and fully committed to His spiritual program of world evangelization, the disciples returned to Jerusalem, which was a sabbath day's journey off. A sabbath day's journey is generally regarded as 2,000 cubits, and a cubit, according to Josephus, was approximately 1 1/2 feet; thus a distance of approximately 3,000 feet seems to be indicated. This distance was established by Mosaic law as the spacing between the ark and the people. When the ark halted in its course at sundown Friday, the people were allowed to traverse the intervening distance of 2,000 cubits for worship on the sabbath, hence the origin of this "sabbath day" measurement.[14]

The exact location of the disciples' ten-day prayer meeting, between Christ's Ascension and Pentecost, is a disputed question among scholars. Some hold that the upper chamber to which they resorted for prayer was the identical location of the "last supper." Some have thought that they were in a compartment of the temple, which view seems to find support in Luke 24:53. However, upper rooms of private houses were not uncommonly used for religious purposes. It would be a pleasant thought that they were guests in the evidently well-to-do and commodious home of the disciple Mary, the

mother of John Mark, where Christian disciples later assembled for prayer (see Acts 12:12-16). Certainly such a private dwelling is more fitting to the Acts statement, where they were abiding (or residing) for a period of ten days, then would be a room in the temple. Further, Luke's statement descriptive of the Pentecostal effusion, "it filled all the 'house' where they were sitting" (Acts 2:2), lends weight to this position.

2. The Personnel of the Prayer (1:13b, 14b)

both Peter and John and James and Andrew, Philip and Thomas, Bartholomew and Matthew, James *the son* of Alphaeus, and Simon the Zealot, and Judas *the son* of James. 14 with the women, and Mary the mother of Jesus, and with his brethren.

With two exceptions, consisting of a slight difference in the order of listing and the omission of Judas from the Acts record, Luke's record of the apostles in Acts 1:13 agrees with his earlier record in Luke 6:12-16. The priority given to Peter here and in the following early chapters of Acts indicates Luke's purpose in presenting Peter as the divinely chosen leader of the infant Judaeo-Christian church. Luke is careful to make special note of Mary the mother of Jesus, of whom this is the last mention in the Bible, and his brethren who had not believed in His Messiahship before His death and resurrection (Matt. 12:46-50). The women mentioned must have included those who remained with Him at the Cross and were present at the Resurrection, and certainly included Mary Magdalene from whom Christ had cast seven demons. Likely the wives of some of the apostles, including Peter's (Matt. 8:14) and those wives and other relatives of devout men, were present. Most probably Joanna the wife of Herod's steward, Susanna and other women who had been cured of illness or demon possession and who in grateful loyalty had followed and ministered to Him (Luke 8:2, 3), were there. Mary, the mother of James and Joses, Salome the wife of Zebedee (Mark 15:40), Mary and Martha of Bethany and certainly Mark's mother Mary, who was probably hostess

---

[14] James Hastings, ed., *Dictionary of the Bible*, p. 968.

to the company, were all most likely present. The total company consisted of approximately 120 persons (v. 15). A deep sense of sadness settles over the soul at the deathly silence concerning Judas.

3. The Persistence of the Prayer (1:14a)

14 These all with one accord continued stedfastly in prayer,

This appears in Williams' translation: "with one mind they were all continuing to devote themselves to prayer."[15]

What a diversity of persons constituted this praying assembly, and yet what unity of spirit and purpose those words, "with one mind," suggest to the serious reader! **Unity** is the keynote of the sacred occasion — "with one mind." They were characterized by: *first,* unity of plan to assemble *en masse* at a designated location in Jerusalem and pray and wait in faith for the fulfillment of the Father's promise (Luke 24:49); *second,* unity of place where physical proximity would lend strength and faith to their vigil (see Matt. 18:20); *third,* unity of purpose which gave direction and focus to their praying (see Mark 11:24); *fourth,* unity of persistence which afforded drive to their praying (see James 5:16b); and *fifth,* unity of prayer which integrated their desires with their objective and thus sealed to them by faith the fulfillment of the Father's promise to endue them with power from on high.

D. THE DISCIPLES' PURPOSE (1:15-26)

The purpose of the disciples in preparation for Pentecost appears to have been twofold: *first,* to realize the fulfillment of Jewish prophecy in relation to the betrayer Judas; and *second,* to supply the vacancy left in the apostolate by Judas' failure.

1. A Purpose to Realize the Fulfillment of Prophecy (1:15-20)

15 And in these days Peter stood up in the midst of the brethren, and said (and there was a multitude of persons gathered together, about a hundred and twenty), 16 Brethren, it was needful that the scripture should be fulfilled, which the Holy Spirit spake before by the mouth of David concerning Judas, who was guide to them that took Jesus. 17 For he was numbered among us, and received his portion in this ministry. 18 (Now this man obtained a field with the reward of his iniquity; and falling headlong, he burst asunder in the midst, and all his bowels gushed out. 19 And it became known to all the dwellers at Jerusalem; insomuch that in their language that field was called Akeldama, that is, The field of blood.) 20 For it is written in the book of Psalms,

Let his habitation be made desolate,
And let no man dwell therein: and,
His office let another take.

The inauguration or dedication (not the birthday as some suppose — see **Additional Note II,** *The Practical Significance of Pentecost*) of the Christian church was about to occur with the Pentecostal effusion. Peter having been restored to the grace of his Lord and his appointed office, which he had temporarily forfeited by his triple apostasy (Luke 22:54-62 and John 21:15-19), now resumed his former role as the apostolic chairman and called the assembly to order for the business of electing an apostolic successor to replace the fallen Judas.

The assumption of this initiative and office by Peter (**Peter stood up in the midst of the brethren,** v. 15; cf. 2:14) is clearly personal and not offcial as the church of Rome assumes. In support of this position are the following evidences: *First,* Peter's understanding and confession of Christ's divinity, not Peter's character, was to be the foundation of the church (Matt. 16:18). *Second,* Christ committed the apostolic authority to all the apostles and not to Peter exclusively, not even primarily (see John 20:19-23). *Third,* the whole New Testament regards the twelve apostles, and not Peter alone, as the church's foundation (see Matt. 19:28; Eph. 2:19-22; Rev. 21:14). *Fourth,* the church called Peter into question for having preached the gospel to the household of the Gentile Cornelius (Acts 11:1-3). *Fifth,* Peter assumed a role subordinate to James at the first general church council in Jerusalem (Acts 15). *Sixth,* Paul regarded his apostleship equal to, and independent of, that of Peter and the other apostles (II Cor.

---

[15] For a full treatment of "one accord" in the Book of Acts the reader is referred to *Golden Treasures from the Greek New Testament for English Readers,* by Jasper Abraham Huffman, pp. 155-160, as quoted in Additional Note I at end of this volume.

11:5; Gal. 2:6-9). *Seventh,* Paul rebuked and reprimanded Peter for his divisive conduct at Antioch (Gal. 2:11-18). *Eighth,* Peter himself assumed a position of equality with, and not superiority to, his fellows (I Peter 5:1). And, *ninth,* Luke made no further mention of Peter in the Acts record after his appearances at the Jerusalem conference (Acts 15).

Thus Peter's primacy on this occasion, as well as elsewhere, was the natural expression of his personal character and ability, rather than of divine appointment. His characteristic zeal, courage, readiness, even venturesomeness and audacious faith, naturally brought him into prominence as the leader of the apostles.

Peter recognizes and asserts that the church of Christ is to be built upon the divinity of Christ. The revelation of that divinity was given to and through the twelve apostles. The apostolate is now incomplete in Judas' absence, and thus an inadequate foundation for the church is afforded. It is therefore necessary to choose an apostolic successor to Judas.

The number of brethren assembled for this occasion, **about a hundred and twenty,** fulfilled the Jewish requirement for the number of a council in any city, and thus was the election of an apostle to be made both official and legal.

The meaning of Peter's statement, **Brethren, it was needful that the scripture should be fulfilled,** is best understood in the light of the last part of verse 20, **his office let another take.** There are no scriptural or logical grounds for a conclusion that Judas' betrayal and fall was made necessary to fulfill a divine decree. In consideration of the fact of Judas' apostasy, it was necessary to choose an apostolic successor in order to fulfill the divine prophecy, as well as the divine plan for the Christian church. Indeed Judas' fall and the related events recorded in verses 15 through 20 are the fulfillments of the divine prophecy, but as consequences of Judas' decisions and conduct, and not of necessity to the fulfillment of a divine prediction. Dummelow offers a pertinent observation on Peter's words, **it was needful that the scripture should be fulfilled.** Says this authority:

Just as the scandal and stumbling block of the death of Jesus was diminished by the discovery that it was foretold in the O.T., and was part of the determinate council of God (Luke 24:26, 46; Acts 2:23; 3:17, 18, etc.), so the scandal of the fall of an Apostle was relieved by the discovery that David had foretold it in the Psalms: cf. John 13:18; Matt. 26:24. Peter quotes Ps. 69:25 and 109:8. David really spoke of his own enemies, perhaps (in Ps. 109) of Ahithophel, but Peter regards the words as a typical prophecy of the treachery of Judas.[16]

That Judas had been a genuinely regenerated member of the body of Christ is suggested: *first,* by the words of Peter, **he was numbered among us** (v. 17; see also John 13:18); and *second,* by his divine election to the apostleship, having **received his portion in this ministry** (v. 17b). Certainly Judas could not be thought to have actually received his apostolic appointment by the authority of Christ had he not first become partaker of the divine nature. Such a sacred commission could not have been given to an enemy of the kingdom of grace by the omniscient king Himself. Further, that Judas fell from both his divine relationship and his apostolic office by a deliberate choice of material gain at the expense of his loyalty to Christ is made clear by Peter's continued address: **Now this man obtained a field with the reward of his iniquity; and falling headlong, he burst asunder in the midst, and all his bowels gushed out.**

This passage may be better understood in relation to the words in verse 25, which read: **this ministry and apostleship from which Judas fell away, that he might go to his own place.** On this latter passage Dummelow remarks: "St. Peter speaks with merciful reserve, but probably means Hell ('Gehenna'). The same euphemism is found in rabbinical writings."[17]

The most likely explanation of this whole matter concerning Judas Iscariot seems to be as follows: *First,* he was chosen a disciple and elected an apostle by Jesus Christ (John 14:12; 17:11, 12; and Acts 1:17). *Second,* he neglected or otherwise failed to grasp the spiritual significance of Christ's kingdom and his own personal discipleship and ministry and consequently became covetous of ma-

---

[16] Dummelow, *op. cit.,* p. 819.   [17] *Ibid.*

terial gain and betrayed his sacred trust as treasurer of the apostolic group (John 12:3-6). *Third,* he became deceptively hypocritical (Matt. 26:25, 48; Luke 22: 47, 48). *Fourth,* he spurned every overture of divine mercy designed to restore him to grace and save him from his ultimate tragedy, both when he was made the honored guest of the last supper by the Lord (John 13:26), and when Jesus tenderly addressed him as "friend" on the occasion of His arrest in the garden (Matt. 26:50). *Fifth,* he transferred his will, devotion, and obedience from Christ to Satan (John 13:27). *Sixth,* he deliberately took his leave of the Master to execute his evil purpose (John 13:30). *Seventh,* he purposely and calculatively bargained with the enemies of the Lord for Christ's betrayal into their hands (Matt. 26:14-16; Luke 22:3-6). *Eighth,* he deliberately and purposely executed his evil intention of Christ's betrayal by identifying himself with and directing the Sanhedrin's servants to the place of Christ's arrest (Mark 14:11; Matt. 26:16, 47-49). *Ninth,* upon his awakening to the shocking consequences of his deed, at the condemnation of Christ to death, Judas' repentance and confession (Matt. 27:3, 4) were the self-imposed result of the remorseful "sorrow of the world [which] worketh death," and not that "godly sorrow [which] worketh repentance which bringeth no regret" (II Cor. 7:10). *Tenth,* he consequently went out and committed suicide by hanging himself (Matt. 27:5), from which position he likely fell on a rocky cliff by reason of the rope having broken, and thus his abdomen was ruptured on the jagged rocks and his intestines were forcefully ejected from their body cavity (Acts 1:18b). *Eleventh* and finally, his career terminated in final and awful separation from God as the natural consequences of the willful choices which he made and the evil course that he deliberately followed; as Peter who knew Judas so well phrases his awful doom: **that he might go to his own place** (Acts 1:25b), or the place of his own choosing, the end and state for which he had conditioned himself by rejection of all that he knew to be right, and deliberate conformity to that which he knew to be wrong. Satan promises much but affords little. Somewhere Ethymius

is reported as having said, "Before we sin, he [Satan] suffers us not to see the end of it, lest we repent. But after the sin is committed he suffers us to see it to cause us remorse and to drive us to despair."

That Judas could have sincerely repented and experienced restoration to God at any moment prior to his fatal suicide there can be no reasonable doubt (cf. Luke 23:39-43); but that he did so there lacks scriptural evidence. Thus the eternal fate of his soul will best remain in the determinate council of an all-wise and just God.

The problem of the reconciliation of Luke's parenthetical statement concerning Judas' obtaining **a field with the reward of his iniquity** (Acts 1:18, 19), with Matthew's account (Matt. 27:3-10) is not without a likely resolution. It is possible that Judas was motivated by economic interest in his betrayal of Jesus for thirty pieces of silver, which money he intended to invest in a parcel of land containing soil especially valuable for pottery-making. Thus he may have bargained with the owners for this field, but may not as yet have paid the money for it before his remorseful awakening at the sight of Jesus' condemnation, and his consequent suicide. His return of this money to the chief priests may have eventuated in their use of it to consummate the deal begun by Judas, with a view to its use as a cemetery in which to bury poor strangers who came to Jerusalem and died there away from home and friends, since it was unlawful to put such money into the temple treasury. Thus in this sense it could be said that Judas **obtained a field with the reward of his iniquity.** On the other hand, it may be simply meant to imply that the purchase of this field by the priests was a consequence of Judas' monetary betrayal of Christ, though no part of his intelligent purpose. Either view leaves no particular problem in the reconciliation of Luke's account with that of Matthew.

That this parcel of land was called **The field of blood** by the inhabitants of Jerusalem (v. 19), may be accounted for by either one of two factors, or even a possible combination of both. *First,* it may have been so called by reason of the fact that it was purchased with "blood money," the thirty pieces of silver for which Christ was betrayed unto death. *Second,* it is possible that it was so called because Judas may have committed suicide in the field and was buried in this very field from which he had intended to enrich himself by material gain. In either event **this man obtained . . . The field of blood . . . with the reward of his iniquity.** Ill-gotten gain can never procure spiritual security. That is obtained solely by giving, and never by getting. Judas won a dismal burying ground as a reward. His fellow apostles won an eternal spiritual kingdom for their loyalty to Christ.

2. A Purpose to Fulfill the Apostolate (1:21-26)

21 Of the men therefore that have companied with us all the time that the Lord Jesus went in and went out among us, 22 beginning from the baptism of John, unto the day that he was received up from us, of these must one become a witness with us of his resurrection. 23 And they put forward two, Joseph called Barsabbas, who was surnamed Justus, and Matthias. 24 And they prayed, and said, Thou, Lord, who knowest the hearts of all men, show of these two the one whom thou hast chosen, 25 to take the place in this ministry and apostleship from which Judas fell away, that he might go to his own place. 26 And they gave lots for them; and the lot fell upon Matthias; and he was numbered with the eleven apostles.

Peter presents three specific requirements to be met by the apostolic successor of Judas. These conditions are, as implied in the address of Peter: *first,* a true discipleship to Jesus Christ: **beginning from the baptism of John,** the baptism of repentance and saving faith in Christ (v. 22a); *second,* faithful and loyal membership in the Christian disciple family (vv. 21, 22a); *third,* a personal witness to the personal resurrection of Jesus Christ from the dead (v. 22b). These requirements advanced by Peter as qualifications for Christian apostleship placed Paul under necessity of defending his apostleship before his enemies as being directly from God, and not of men, as witness the introductions of most of his epistles.

Though the eleven apostles might have selected a successor for Judas without reference to the lay disciples, they rather consulted the assembly and thus set a precedent by introducing a popular element into the policy of the infant church's government. This precedent is followed through the church in the Acts record (cf. Acts 5:3-6). The organizational weaknesses of the church at this juncture is evidenced by the following facts: *first,* that two candidates were advanced for the apostolic position clearly indicated the disciples' uncertainty of the divine will in the matter; *second,* that the disciples' choice was made from among the disciples and their candidates presented to God before prayer was offered for divine direction; *third,* that they employed the **lot** (Urim), a sacred device used under the law to ascertain the divine will, but here for the first and last time employed by the followers of Christ. Dummelow thinks it may have consisted in the writing of the names of the candidates on tablets and then shaking them up until one fell out. In any event, there is no evidence that it was ordered or approved of God on this occasion.

Joseph, called Barsabbas, not to be confused with Barnabas of later date, and **Matthias** were the disciples' choice. Their prayer for God's choice between the candidates is the first recorded "post-ascension" Christian prayer, and it was directed to the **Lord** Jesus Himself. Such became the accepted practice of the apostolic church (see Acts 9:14). It is natural that they should have petitioned Christ in the choice of this apostle, since He had chosen the original twelve.

That neither Joseph nor Matthias was Christ's choice of a successor for Judas seems evident from the fact that, though the lot fell on Matthias, he is not heard of again in the New Testament and evidently did not fill the office, though, of course, "silence" is not conclusive evidence. All subsequent evidence seems to point to Paul as the divine selection to complete the apostolate.

Morgan, while acknowledging that it is a debated question in Biblical interpretation, nevertheless unhesitatingly asserts that the disciples were mistaken in their choice of Matthias to succeed Judas.

. . . my own conviction is that we have a revelation of their inefficiency for olganization; that the election of Matthias was wrong. Their idea of what was necessary as a witness to the resurrection was wrong. They said that a witness must have been with them from the baptism of John. They thought a witness must be one who had seen Jesus prior to His ascension. As a matter of fact the most powerful incentive to witness was the seeing of Christ after resurrection, as when He arrested Saul of Tarsus on his way to Damascus. So their principle of election was wrong. Their method of selection was also wrong. The method of casting lots was no longer necessary. Thus we have the wrong appointment of Matthias. He was a good man, but the wrong man for this position, and he passed out of sight; and when presently we come to the final glory of the city of God, we see twelve foundation stones, and twelve apostles' names, and I am not prepared to omit Paul from the twelve, believing that he was God's man for the filling of the gap.

These men were perfectly sincere, proceeding on the lines of revealed truth, but they were ignorant of God's best method; unable to bear their witness; unable to organize themselves for the doing of the work; and consequently needing the coming of the Paraclete.[18]

II. THE CHURCH'S FIRST PENTECOST (Acts 2:1-47)

A. THE FACT OF PENTECOST (2:1-11)

The Pentecost of Acts 2 occurred at Jerusalem during the annual Jewish feast which, in the opinion of some scholars, commemorated the giving of the Law on Mount Sinai. At the Jewish Pentecost God wrote His Law on tables of stone for Israel's moral government. At the Christian Pentecost He wrote His moral laws on hearts of flesh for the moral government of mankind. The former was external; the latter was internal. The former was legal; the latter was spiritual.

1. The Preparation for Pentecost (2:1)

1 And when the day of Pentecost was now come, they were all together in one place.

The allusion to **the day of Pentecost** is primarily to the first day of the week when the Jewish Pentecost was held at Jerusalem (Lev. 23:15). However, in ref-

erence to the outpouring of the Holy Spirit, it bespeaks the culmination of the divine plan of redemption and the full preparation of the Christian disciples to receive the special effusion and dispensation of the Holy Spirit, and to begin the worldwide witness to which Christ had commissioned them (see Matt. 28:18-20 and Acts 1:8). It was that "fulness of time" to which Paul later referred (Gal. 4:4). The disciples' unity of spirit,[19] purpose, plan, and place made possible the divine effusion of the Holy Spirit. Whether Christ's disciples were in a compartment of the temple or in the upper room of a private home where they may have eaten the last supper with the Lord, when Pentecost occurred, is not known for certain. The latter seems likely (Acts 1:12-14). That they were in Jerusalem appears certain (Luke 24:49).

2. The Occurrence of Pentecost[20] (2:2-4)

2 And suddenly there came from heaven a sound as of the rushing of a mighty wind, and it filled all the house where they were sitting. 3 And there appeared unto them tongues parting asunder, like as of fire; and it sat upon each one of them. 4 And they were all filled with the Holy Spirit, and began to speak with other tongues, as the Spirit gave them utterance.

And suddenly. . . . The suddenness of the Pentecostal effusion was resultant from fourteen and a half centuries (Lightfoot) of preparation, from the giving of the Law on Mount Sinai. God may take long to prepare, but when His plans are completed and the time is propitious, He moves suddenly and significantly. Four words may summarize the significance of this first Christian Pentecost: namely, *power,* **the rushing of a mighty wind;** *purity,* **tongues parting asunder, like as of fire, . . . sat upon each one of them;** *possession,* **they were all filled with the Holy Spirit;** and *proclamation,* **they began to speak with other tongues, as the Spirit gave them utterance.** Christ had promised divine power as a concomitant of Pentecost (Acts 1:8; Luke 24:49). John the Baptist had likewise promised the divine purifying fire (Matt.

---

[18] G. Campbell Morgan, *The Acts of the Apostles,* p. 21.
[19] See Additional Note I, *Homothumadon — One Accord.*
[20] See Additional Note II, *The Practical Significance of Pentecost.*

3:11; see also Heb. 12:29). Christ's plan for the full and abiding possession of His disciples by the Holy Spirit at Pentecost was made explicit to them by Him while He was still with them (John 14: 16, 25, 26; 15:26; 16:7). That immediate effective proclamation of the Gospel was the purpose of the miracle of **other tongues** is evident from prophecy (Isa. 66:18), and the need arising out of the occasion and opportunity where **there were dwelling at Jerusalem Jews, devout men, from every nation under heaven** who, when they heard the Spirit-animated disciples proclaiming Christ, **were confounded, because that every man heard them speaking in his own language** (see also vv. 7-11).[21]

3. The Effects of Pentecost (2:5-8)

5 Now there were dwelling at Jerusalem Jews, devout men, from every nation under heaven. 6 And when this sound was heard, the multitude came together, and were confounded, because that every man heard them speaking in his own language. 7 And they were all amazed and marvelled, saying, Behold, are not all these that speak Galilaeans? 8 And how hear we, every man in our own language wherein we were born?

Pentecost was a threefold miracle of interpretation, clarification, and conviction. The assembled multitude heard these disciples proclaim **the mighty works of God** in their own languages and were deeply convicted in their hearts of the truthfulness of that message. Said Christ: "And when he [the Holy Spirit] is come, he will reprove [convict] the world of sin, and of righteousness, and of judgment" (John 16:8, KJV).

4. The Nations at Pentecost (2:9-11)

9 Parthians and Medes and Elamites, and the dwellers in Mesopotamia, in Judaea and Cappadocia, in Pontus and Asia, 10 in Phrygia and Pamphylia, in Egypt and the parts of Libya about Cyrene, and sojourners from Rome, both Jews and proselytes, 11 Cretans and Arabians, we hear them speaking in our tongues the mighty works of God.

Fifteen different nations are listed in this passage. They consisted of Gentile proselytes to the Jewish faith, *God-fearers*

(Gentiles who worshipped the God of the Jews but who did not subscribe to the Jewish ceremonials), Jews of the *Diaspora,* and the Judaean Jews. Here it may be noted that the first phase of the *Diaspora* occurred in 722 B.C. when the ten Northern Tribes were carried away into captivity at the hands of the cruel Assyrians, while the second phase occurred in 586 B.C. when the Southern Kingdom was taken to Babylonia under the conquest of Nebuchadnezzar. While there is no record of the restoration of the Northern Kingdom, the Southern Kingdom, after some 70 years, was in part returned to its native land under the benevolent Cyrus. However, the greater percentage of these later captives was widely distributed throughout the Persian Empire which followed in political succession the Babylonian. During the height of the Persian Empire, there occurred the incidents recorded in the Book of Esther. It is of particular interest that the author of this book notes that there were 127 provinces in the Persian Empire, ranging from India to Ethiopia, whatever the significance of these place-names may be to history, and further that there were Jews dwelling in all of these Persian provinces (see Esther 1:1; 3:8). In addition to the *Diaspora* there were, according to Benjamin Robinson,[22] three other major dispersions. The first of these latter occurred in the third century B.C. during the control of Palestine by Egypt, when the Jews migrated in large numbers to the city of Alexandria where they formed a sizable colony, adopted the Greek language, imbibed much of the Greco-Egyptian culture, and translated the Old Testament into the Greek, giving to the world the version known as the Septuagint.

In the second century B.C., when Palestine fell under the power of Syria, the Jews migrated in large numbers northward and settled in and about Antioch, from which place they further penetrated into Cilicia, and from thence scattered into the cities of Asia Minor and crossed over into Macedonia and Greece, establishing colonies and synagogues wherever they went.

This third stage of this latter migration occurred after the Roman conquest of

---

[21] See Additional Note III, *The Bible Gift of Tongues.*
[22] Benjamin Willard Robinson, *The Life of Paul,* pp. 9f.

Palestine under Pompey in the first century B.C. At this time there occurred a general dispersion of the Jews throughout the whole Roman Empire and even into lands beyond Rome's domain. Robinson holds that there were at least 150 Jewish colonies throughout the Empire of Rome by the time of Christ's appearance. In most of these Jewish communities there were synagogues which were in close relationship with the temple at Jerusalem and paid revenue to the Temple. Though these synagogues were much more simple and modest in their architecture and forms of worship than was the Temple, as well as more liberal in their attitude toward the Gentile world, they were at the same time an integral part of the Jewish religious system. It was from these Jewish settlements out in the Roman Empire, and even beyond, that the Jewish representation at Pentecost, as recorded in Acts 2, had come. The latter probably constituted by far the greater percentage of the foreign population present for the Jewish Pentecost.

B. THE EXPLANATION OF PENTECOST (2:12-21)

The new spiritual dispensation inaugurated by the Pentecostal descent of the Holy Spirit required a divinely inspired explanation. God's Word properly understood and expounded always clarifies His acts.

1. The Pentecostal Question (2:12, 13)

12 And they were all amazed, and were perplexed, saying one to another, What meaneth this? 13 But others mocking said, They are filled with new wine.

Those who heard the preaching of the **mighty works of God** in their own languages by the Spirit-filled disciples felt the mighty influence of that Spirit and found themselves in a state of spiritual ecstasy, for such is the meaning of the word **amazed,** beyond their ability to understand. That something supernatural had happened certain of the multitude were well aware, but what it signified they could not tell. The manifestations of God always arrest attention, awaken interest, and provoke inquiries concerning spiritual truth. Nothing produces moral sanity and spiritual inquiry like mighty divine manifestations. When

man begins to inquire, God stands ready to inform. One has said that it is only at the point of man's recognized need that God can help him.

But while some were moved to honest, reverent inquiry, under the Spirit's influence, others sceptically mocked and scoffed at the divine manifestation, giving the sacred a secular and profane interpretation, saying, **They are filled with new wine.** A lump of moist clay and a block of ice placed together in the sun react differently, with quite opposite results. The one is melted, the other hardened. So by the same divine manifestation, one person may be melted into submission to the divine will, while another may reject that manifestation and become spiritually calloused.

2. The Pentecostal Spokesman (2:14)

14 But Peter, standing up with the eleven, lifted up his voice, and spake forth unto them, *saying,* Ye men of Judaea, and all ye that dwell at Jerusalem, be this known unto you, and give ear unto my words.

But Peter . . . . Peter, ever the ready and gifted spokesman, once having ignominiously failed his Lord, but now fully restored, answers the charge of the scoffers by standing erect before the multitude to prove that he was not drunk, to which the other disciples add their support by standing also. Peter **lifted up his voice** in full confidence and conviction of the divine origin of the phenomenon, ready to courageously witness to the risen Christ in the face of violent opposition.

3. The Misapprehension of Pentecost (2:15)

15 For these are not drunken, as ye suppose; seeing it is *but* the third hour of the day;

Very evidently there was a sharp division of the people, as well as of opinions concerning the spiritual manifestations. While the Jews of the dispersion inclined to the influence of the Spirit, the Judaean Jews who had been responsible for the rejection and crucifixion of Jesus Christ and did not wish to hear that He was alive again, labelled the whole affair irrational intoxication. It is to this latter class of Judaean Jews that

Peter addresses his great Pentecostal sermon, and that in their common language, as witness his words, **Ye men of Judaea, and all ye that dwell at Jerusalem.** Doubtless the other disciples witnessed to Christ likewise in the various languages of those present and less prejudiced than the former. The third hour (nine o'clock in the morning) would in itself rule out the charge of drunkenness. "They that are drunken are drunken in the night" (I Thess. 5:7).

4. The Truth Concerning Pentecost (2:16-20)

16 but this is that which hath been spoken through the prophet Joel:
17 And it shall be in the last day, saith God,
I will pour forth of my Spirit upon all flesh:
And your sons and your daughters shall prophesy,
And your young men shall see visions,
And your old men shall dream dreams:
18 Yea and on my servants and on my handmaidens in those days
Will I pour forth of my Spirit; and they shall prophesy.
19 And I will show wonders in the heaven above,
And signs on the earth beneath;
Blood, and fire, and vapor of smoke:
20 The sun shall be turned into darkness,
And the moon into blood,
Before the day of the Lord come,
That great and notable *day:*

This is that which hath been spoken through the prophet Joel. Peter makes the Spirit's manifestation the fulfillment of the Jewish prophecy by Joel, with which they were familiar and which they readily accepted. Pentecost was the fulfillment of their own prophecies.

In verses 17 through 20, Peter quotes Joel's prediction of Pentecost and interprets it as an impartial and universal divine evangelical visitation. Joel's prophecy of Pentecost reflects four major constituents: namely, (1) *the Holy Spirit's universal effusion,* **I will pour forth of my Spirit upon all flesh;** (2) *the universal proclamation of the Gospel,* **your sons and your daughters shall prophesy . . . my servants and . . . my handmaidens . . . shall prophecy (preach);** (3) *spiritual illumination,* **your young men shall see visions** (the illuminating

and animating *forward look;* see Isa. 6:1-8), **and your old men shall dream dreams** (the clarified and rewarding *retrospect* of advanced age); and (4) *arresting and confirmatory miracles,* **I will show wonders in the heaven above, and signs on the earth beneath** (see I Thess. 1:5, 6).

5. The Purpose of Pentecost (2:21)

21 And it shall be that whosoever shall call on the name of the Lord shall be saved.

Purpose, or what the philosophers call teleology — that is, plan or design directed to a given end — characterizes all the acts of God from His creative work to the final restoration of all creation (sinfully rebellious man excepted) through the redemptive plan and provision. Pentecost was the culmination of a long process of divine planning for human redemption. Here Peter openly declares to the Jewish opponents of Christ, as well as those favorably inclined, that the threefold Pentecostal purpose is: (1) a *universal evangelical invitation,* **whosoever;** (2) a *universal evangelical condition,* **call on the name of the Lord;** and (3) a *universal evangelical provision,* **shall be saved** (see Matthew 11:28-30 and John 7:37-39).

C. THE DECLARATION OF PENTECOST: PETER'S PENTECOSTAL SERMON (2:22-40)

22 Ye men of Israel, hear these words: Jesus of Nazareth, a man approved of God unto you by mighty works and wonders and signs which God did by him in the midst of you, even as ye yourselves know; 23 him, being delivered up by the determinate counsel and foreknowledge of God, ye by the hand of lawless men did crucify and slay: 24 whom God raised up, having loosed the pangs of death: because it was not possible that he should be holden of it. 25 For David saith concerning him,
I beheld the Lord always before my face;
For he is on my right hand, that I should not be moved:
26 Therefore my heart was glad, and my tongue rejoiced;
Moreover my flesh also shall dwell in hope:
27 Because thou wilt not leave my soul unto Hades,

Neither wilt thou give thy Holy One
to see corruption.
28 Thou madest known unto me the ways
of life;
Thou shalt make me full of gladness
with thy countenance.
29 Brethren, I may say unto you freely
of the patriarch David, that he both died
and was buried, and his tomb is with
us unto this day. 30 Being therefore a
prophet, and knowing that God had
sworn with an oath to him, that of the
fruit of his loins he would set *one* upon
his throne; 31 he foreseeing *this* spake of
the resurrection of the Christ, that neither
was he left unto Hades, nor did his flesh
see corruption. 32 This Jesus did God
raise up, whereof we all are witnesses.
33 Being therefore by the right hand of
God exalted, and having received of the
Father the promise of the Holy Spirit,
he hath poured forth this, which ye see
and hear. 34 For David ascended not
into the heavens: but he saith himself,
The Lord said unto my Lord, Sit thou
on my right hand,
35 Till I make thine enemies the footstool of thy feet.
36 Let all the house of Israel therefore
know assuredly, that God hath made
him both Lord and Christ, this Jesus
whom ye crucified.
37 Now when they heard *this*, they
were pricked in their heart, and said
unto Peter and the rest of the apostles,
Brethren, what shall we do? 38 And
Peter *said* unto them, Repent ye, and be
baptized every one of you in the name
of Jesus Christ unto the remission of
your sins; and ye shall receive the gift
of the Holy Spirit. 39 For to you is the
promise, and to your children, and to all
that are afar off, *even* as many as the
Lord our God shall call unto him. 40
And with many other words he testified,
and exhorted them, saying, Save yourselves from this crooked generation.

Having prefaced his sermon by the confirmatory prophecy of Joel, Peter proceeds directly to an assertion of Jesus
Christ's divine approval and redemptive
mission, and then openly charges the
Judaean Jews with His rejection and
crucifixion (vv. 22, 23). The divine
irony, and the Jew's resultant burning
shame and consternation, is scathingly
depicted by Peter in God's miraculous
resurrection of His Son from the dead,
confirmed by their illustrious father
David's own testimony (vv. 24-32).
Christ's acceptance with the Father in His

ascension, supported likewise by David's
testimony, is presented next in order
(vv. 33a, 34). All of this, Peter reasons,
adds up to the incontrovertible deity
and universal Lordship of Jesus Christ
(vv. 34, 36; see also Matt. 28, esp. vv. 18-
20). It is noteworthy that the burden of
the message of Acts may be summed up
in six phrases: namely, (1) *Christ crucified;* (2) *Christ resurrected* (the word
with its cognates occurs at least 22 times
in Acts); (3) *Christ ascended;* (4) *the
Holy Spirit descended;* (5) *Christ Jesus
declared Lord of all* (*Lord* occurs at least
110 times in Acts); (6) *the door of salvation opened to all.*

In response to the inquiry, **What shall
we do?,** made by those of his audience
who were convicted by the Spirit, Peter
opens wide the door of salvation universally provided in Christ's redemptive
work on the Cross, and invites all to
enter by the way of repentance, remission
of sins, and the gift of the Holy Spirit
(vv. 37-40).

D. THE CHURCH OF PENTECOST (2: 41-47)

41 They then that received his word
were baptized: and there were added
unto them in that day about three thousand souls. 42 And they continued stedfastly in the apostles' teaching and fellowship, in the breaking of bread and the
prayers.
43 And fear came upon every soul: and
many wonders and signs were done
through the apostles. 44 And all that
believed were together, and had all
things common; 45 and they sold their
possessions and goods, and parted them
to all, according as any man had need.
46 And day by day, continuing stedfastly
with one accord in the temple, and
breaking bread at home, they took their
food with gladness and singleness of heart,
47 praising God, and having favor with
all the people. And the Lord added to
them day by day those that were saved.

The Pentecostal church has remained
a model for Christians of all subsequent
ages. Briefly characterized: (1) *its converts* joyfully received the gospel, were
baptized, and identified themselves with
the church (v. 41); (2) *its sacred communion* consisted in steadfastness of purpose, doctrinal instruction, Christian fellowship, observance of the Lord's Supper

(Lange), and prayers (v. 42); (3) *its moral and spiritual influence* profoundly affected the community, and frequent miracles confirmed its divine mission (v. 43); (4) *its liberality* abounded toward the needs of the entire body of Christ (vv. 44, 45); (5) *its service* reflected constancy, unity, fellowship, joy, and guileless sincerity (v. 46); and (6) *its spiritual prosperity* is reflected in its victorious praises, its confidence of and favor with the community, and its evangelical fervor and success (v. 47).

III. THE CHURCH'S FIRST RECORDED PHYSICAL MIRACLE (Acts 3:1-26)

A. A NOTABLE MIRACLE (3:1-11)

Luke evidently singled out this one notable miracle from among the "many wonders and signs . . . done through the apostles" (Acts 2:43b) for the purpose of depicting the mighty onmoving power of the Holy Spirit through the apostolic church. It is the first recorded miracle of divine healing, following Pentecost, and it is fully validated by its salutary moral and spiritual results. The Pentecostal power of the Holy Spirit indwelling and working through the apostles (Acts 1:8) here becomes effective in removing opposition and unbelief and in paving the way for the preaching of salvation through Christ to the Jews and the pagan world beyond.

1. The Power of Prayer (3:1)

1 Now Peter and John were going up into the temple at the hour of prayer, *being* the ninth *hour.*

As yet the disciples of Christ and the apostles constituted but a new spiritual life movement within the Jewish communion. It remained for Stephen to gain the larger vision of the mission of Christianity to the Gentile world, which vision cost him his life, but which also produced the great apostle to the Gentiles, Paul. The disciples were not even called Christians until later at Antioch (Acts 11:26). They worshipped Christ, but as yet after the Jewish pattern. They observed the three, daily, stated Jewish periods of prayer in the temple (Acts 2:42, 46): namely, "the third hour" (Acts

2:15), about nine o'clock in the morning; "the sixth hour" (Acts 10:9), about noon; and "the ninth hour" (Acts 3:1; 10:3), about three o'clock in the afternoon (cf. Ps. 55:17). Vitalized by the Holy Spirit, their communion with God became a prime source of sweet fellowship and spiritual power for life and service. Prayer was a prized privilege and a chief practice of the apostolic church (Acts 6:4), and accounted for many mighty miracles and victories (Acts 12:3-17). The habit and engagement of prayer is ever the secret of Christian victory (see Dan. 6:10 and Ps. 55:17). Lange[23] holds that Christian custom had firmly established the observance of these three hours of prayer by later apostolic times. A prayerless church is a powerless church. A praying church is an invincible church. The miracle of healing that followed was resultant from the united prayers of these Spirit-filled, Christian brother apostles.

2. The Opportunity for Service (3:2)

2 And a certain man that was lame from his mother's womb was carried, whom they laid daily at the door of the temple which is called Beautiful, to ask alms of them that entered into the temple;

God often selects the apparently hopeless cases for the demonstration of His power. It was no recent or temporary affliction which might be remedied by time or natural means, from which this man suffered. Rather, from birth he had been unable to walk and must be carried on a litter if he went about at all. He was a common spectacle **whom they laid daily at the door of the temple which is called Beautiful.** What a contradiction! A poor, ragged, wretched, helpless, and hopelessly deformed beggar lying dejectedly, with his beggar's cup feebly extended to passers-by. There he lay framed in the most ornate and expensive gate, **called Beautiful,** of the great Jewish temple, **to ask alms of them that entered into the temple** in selfish, hypocritical, ceremonial, religious masquerade.

Dummelow[24] holds that the gate referred to here was the *Gate of Nicanor* and that it was constructed of fine Corinthian brass. He regards it as having

---

23 John Peter Lange, *Commentary on the Holy Scriptures,* p. 62.   24 Dummelow, *op. cit.,* p. 882.

been far more expensive than the other gates of the temple which were overlaid with silver and gold. The *Gate of Nicanor* opened to the east by the "gate of the holy house" itself. Josephus says, concerning this gate: "its height was fifty cubits, and its doors were forty cubits, and it was adorned after a most costly manner, as having much richer and thicker plates of silver and gold upon them than the others."[25] It may be that Peter got his text from this gold-and-silver-plated brass gate when he said, **Silver and gold have I none.**

The cripple had got no nearer to God than the gate of the temple, and he got no more from the religionists that passed through the gate than their scornful glances and pitiful pittances. Nor will morally and spiritually injured and helpless society ever receive more from the church than this man received, until the latter experiences a new spiritual revival. So long as the church "fares sumptuously every day" (see Luke 12:16-21 and Rev. 3:14-22), the beggars, "full of sores," will lie at her gate. So long as priests and Levites "pass by on the other side," the robbed, beaten, and bleeding world will lie "half dead" at the side of the road (Luke 10:25-37).

3. The Appeal of Helplessness (3:3)

3 who seeing Peter and John about to go into the temple, asked to receive an alms.

Long exposed to the spiritual deadness and compassionlessness of formal religion, the crippled beggar could conceive of religion only in the terms of materiality. No more than a pittance could he hope for from the temple. He was there for what he could get, and he got little indeed. Meager will be the benefits to society from the church when she loses her spiritual power and mission.

4. The Stimulus to Faith (3:4, 5)

4 And Peter, fastening his eyes upon him, with John, said, Look on us. 5 And he gave heed unto them, expecting to receive something from them.

Peter, fastening his eyes upon him, with John, said, Look on us. The apostles, moved by his sad condition and

25 Flavius Josephus, *War*, V, v, 3.

pitiful plea for alms, conceived, under divine inspiration, a better and a permanent way of alleviating the wretched man's plight. Physical healing would not only restore him to normality, independence, and self-respect, but it would also demonstrate to the world God's compassion for the suffering and His miraculous power to restore the afflicted. There radiated from the Spirit-filled apostles' countenances a confidence and faith born of communion with the living God which, as he looked expectantly on them, inspired renewed hope and challenged him to believe. Faith is contagious. Faith in the Christian begets faith in the unbelieving world. Faith, like love, comes to birth under the influence of another in whom it is manifested. Thus John could say, "We love [him], because he first loved us" (I John 4:19). The world will believe little and the church's influence will remain sadly limited until Christians renew their faith in the goodness and power of God. Faith flourishes in the soil of spiritual manifestations. Prayer produces such manifestations. Likewise Christ's faith in man begets man's faith in Christ (see Gal. 2:20).

5. The Healing Virtue in the Name (3:6-8a)

6 But Peter said, Silver and gold have I none; but what I have, that give I thee. In the name of Jesus Christ of Nazareth, walk. 7 And he took him by the right hand, and raised him up: and immediately his feet and his ankle-bones received strength. 8 And leaping up, he stood, and began to walk;

Obedience to the Apostle's command was a human impossibility, but inspired by the sheer confidence and authority of that command, **in the name of Jesus Christ of Nazareth,** and supported by Peter's extended hand, the cripple forthwith sprang up, **stood, and began to walk.** He suddenly realized himself to have been made every whit whole. A divine healing current surged through his twisted and deformed body, straightening, restoring, healing, and animating it throughout, **and immediately his feet and his ankle-bones received strength.** The suddenness with which his feet and ankle-bones received strength was proof of a miraculous cure, and that cure was evidenced by his standing, **walking, and leaping, and praising God.**[26] The miracle was more than a physical healing. Here a man immediately stands, walks, and leaps who, crippled from birth, had never learned to stand, not to mention walking or leaping. Divine animation often restores unavoidably lost opportunities and facilitates progress in the life of the restored one.

While Peter and John possessed and exercised the authority to command the cure of the cripple in the name of Jesus, his responsive cooperation was required to effect the cure. Though devoid of money, either for the church treasury or alms for the crippled beggar, these apostles had access to a far richer treasure with which none else could compare (Phil. 4:19), and which they stood ready to dispense where worthy needs existed. **Silver and gold have I none,** said Peter, **but what I have that give I thee.** Thomas Aquinas is reported by Clarke[27] to have once appeared in the chamber of Pope Innocent IV, where vast sums of church money were being counted. The Pope remarked to Thomas: "You see that the church is no longer in an age in which she can say, *Silver and gold have I none?*" "It is true, holy father," replied the angelic doctor, "nor can she now say to the lame man, '*Rise up and walk!*'" (cf. Rev. 3:14-22).

6. The Spiritual Transformation (3:8b)

8b and he entered with them into the temple, walking, and leaping, and praising God.

A purported divine cure that produces no spiritual or moral change in the patient is subject to legitimate suspicion. With the affliction at last removed, that had all his lifetime barred him from the temple worship and service, the well and normal man now enters the temple with the apostles to worship God. A faith healing that does not lead to the worship and service of God is worse than useless. A cure had been effected in this man that made him a joyful worshipper of God and brought new life and interest into the temple service. When divine healing leads the soul to God in Christ

and spiritually animates the church it is creditable indeed.

7. The Salutary Results (3:9-11)

9 And all the people saw him walking and praising God: 10 and they took knowledge of him, that it was he that sat for alms at the Beautiful Gate of the temple; and they were filled with wonder and amazement at that which had happened unto him.
11 And as he held Peter and John, all the people ran together unto them in the porch that is called Solomon's greatly wondering.

The lifelong impotency of the cripple and his normally dejected spirits, as he lay at the *Gate Beautiful* begging, were well known by the citizens, and especially the temple patrons. Thus their attention was arrested, and **wonder** and **amazement** gripped them at his sudden restoration to normal physique and activity. His animated spirit and action, as was evidenced by his **walking, leaping, and praising God** in the temple, were sufficient evidence of his cure. This miraculous cure not only afforded Peter a text from which to preach, but also an interested and expectant audience to hear his powerful sermon which followed. Pews will not long remain empty when hearts are Spirit-filled and God's wonder-working power is in evidence. God revealed insures transforming results (see Luke 7:19-23 and Acts 16:18).

B. A POWERFUL SERMON (3:12-18)

12 And when Peter saw it, he answered unto the people, Ye men of Israel, why marvel ye at this man? or why fasten ye your eyes on us, as though by our own power or godliness we had made him to walk? 13 The God of Abraham, and of Isaac, and Jacob, the God of our fathers, hath glorified his Servant Jesus; whom ye delivered up, and denied before the face of Pilate, when he had determined to release him. 14 But ye denied the Holy and Righteous One, and asked for a murderer to be granted unto you, 15 and killed the Prince of life; whom God raised from the dead; whereof we are witnesses. 16 And by faith in his name hath his name made this man strong, whom ye behold and know: yea, the faith which is through him hath given him this perfect sound-

---

[26] Clarke, *op. cit.*, I, 705.   [27] *Ibid.*

ness in the presence of you all. 17 And now, brethren, I know that in ignorance ye did it, as did also your rulers. 18 But the things which God foreshowed by the mouth of all the prophets, that his Christ should suffer, he thus fulfilled.

There is much in this second recorded sermon of Peter that is reminiscent of his Pentecostal Day sermon (Acts 2:22-40). The occasion, like the first, was produced by a divine miracle; there the gift of languages, here the healing of a cripple. Both arrested the attention and heightened the interest and expectations of the multitudes, and Peter was thus given audience. Here Peter and John, like Paul and Barnabas later at Lystra under very similar circumstances (Acts 14:8-18), disclaimed any human, miracle-working power (v. 12). Rightfully, Peter ascribes the power and the glory to God in the vindication of His Son Jesus Christ (v. 13a). How unlike so many modern professed faith healers and miracle workers was Peter's response to this miracle. Taking advantage of the occasion, Peter delivered a direct, penetrating indictment of the Jews, in which he made them responsible for the rejection, condemnation, and cruel execution of God's Son and their Messiah. They had counted Him less than the murderer Barabbas (vv. 13b-15a). This charge was immediately followed by a declaration of God's victory, through Christ's resurrection, over their wicked designs, to which victory the apostles joyfully gave witness (v. 15b). The validity of Christ's resurrection from the dead was attested by the miracle of healing through faith in His Name, which they had just witnessed (v. 16). The irony of the situation, Peter pointed out, was that the Jews ignorantly served the end against which they fought (vv. 17, 18).

C. A FERVENT EXHORTATION (3:19-26)

19 Repent ye therefore, and turn again, that your sins may be blotted out, that so there may come seasons of refreshing from the presence of the Lord; 20 and that he may send the Christ who hath been appointed for you, *even* Jesus: 21 whom the heaven must receive until the times of restoration of all things, whereof God spake by the mouth of his holy prophets that have been from of old. 22 Moses indeed said, A prophet shall the Lord God raise up unto you from among your brethren, like unto me; to him shall ye hearken in all things whatsoever he shall speak unto you. 23 And it shall be, that every soul that shall not hearken to that prophet, shall be utterly destroyed from among the people. 24 Yea and all the prophets from Samuel and them that followed after, as many as have spoken, they also told of these days. 25 Ye are the sons of the prophets, and of the covenant which God made with your fathers, saying unto Abraham, And in thy seed shall all the families of the earth be blessed. 26 Unto you first God, having raised up his Servant, sent him to bless you, in turning away every one of you from your iniquities.

Having convincingly presented his argument and having made his charge against the Jews, Peter observed the convicting effect of the truth on his hearers and proceeded directly to exhort them to repent and turn from the wickedness of their thoughts and deeds, that they might receive forgiveness of sins and the favor of God (v. 19). But the preacher warns that they must now be willing to receive Christ as their Savior and the personal Lord of their lives, though formerly having rejected Him, if they are to be saved (vv. 20-22). Personal divine judgment is inescapable if they again reject Christ in the light of this convincing truth and the miracle of healing which they have witnessed (v. 23). His hearers are the heirs of the promises, given through the prophets, of free universal salvation and blessing in this Holy Spirit dispensation (2:23, 25). Peter's exhortation closes with the solemn reminder that Christ was first raised for, and that salvation is first offered to, the Jews. There is evidence that this sermon and exhortation bore immediate fruit unto salvation in Peter's hearers and precipitated the first apostolic persecution.

IV. THE CHURCH'S FIRST PERSECUTION (Acts 4:1-37)

A. THE APOSTLES' ARREST (4:1-4)

1 And as they spake unto the people, the priests and the captain of the temple and the Sadducees came upon them, 2 being sore troubled because they taught

the people, and proclaimed in Jesus the resurrection from the dead. 3 And they laid hands on them, and put them in ward unto the morrow: for it was now eventide. 4 But many of them that heard the word believed; and the number of the men came to be about five thousand.

Those most adversely affected by the healing of the crippled man and the apostles' preaching in the name of the risen Christ were: *first, the priests.* They were the prime and most bitter enemies of Christ from the beginning. The *second* was **the captain of the temple,** a superior priest next in rank to the high priest, who supervised a body of temple order-lies, consisting of lesser priests and Levites. And the *third* consisted of the **Sadducees,** who rejected the oral tra-ditions, the existence of spirits and angels, predestination and fatalism, im-mortality and the bodily resurrection (see Acts 5:17; 23:6; and Matt. 3:7; 16:1). The Pharisees evidently took no part in the arrest, for reasons that will ap-pear later.

The cause of the arrest appears to have been fourfold: *first,* jealousy of the apostles' influence over the multitude (v. 2); *second,* the apostles' assumption of teaching authority without formal education or rabbinical ordination (v. 13a); *third,* possibly a fear that the en-thusiasm of the multitude would pre-cipitate trouble with the Roman author-ities.[28] But chiefly, Sadducean objection to the doctrine of the resurrection seems to have motivated their arrest. The Pharisees believed in the resurrection; many were favorably disposed to Chris-tianity (Acts 5:34; 23:6); and some be-lieved on Christ (Acts 15:5).

Since the arrest of the apostles was at evening and Jewish trials at night were illegal, the apostles were incarcerated in the public prison until the next day (v. 3). The utter failure of the opposition's purpose is evidenced by the fact that **many of them that heard the word be-lieved,** and the church thus increased until **the number of the men came to be about five thousand,** probably mean-ing the total male Christian communion to that date (exclusive of women and

children; cf. Matt. 14:21; Luke 9:14; Acts 5:14).[29]

B. THE APOSTLES' TRIAL (4:5-12)

This is the Christians' first appearance before an ecclesiastical or civil court after Pentecost. Here begins the Christian heritage of persecution, promised by Christ (Mark 10:28-30; John 15:20, 21), and which was to play such an important part in the church's subsequent history. The church began by giving a good ac-count of herself before the ruling author-ities.

1. The Personnel of the Court (4:5, 6)

5 And it came to pass on the morrow, that their rulers and elders and scribes were gathered together in Jerusalem; 6 and Annas the high priest *was there,* and Caiaphas, and John, and Alexander, and as many as were of the kindred of the high priest.

Seldom has anyone been honored by trial before such an imposing tribunal. The importance of the case is evidenced by the assemblage of the full Sanhedrin, or Grand Council of the Jews, the na-tional Jewish council of seventy members (possibly seventy-one including the high priest), which consisted of **their rulers,** or the chief priests; the **scribes,** or rabbis, professional teachers; and the **elders,** or those members who were neither scribes nor rabbis, but who with the **rulers** came to judge the apostles. Present with the council was **Annas,** not actually the high priest, but who had been for nine years, and still retained the office in his family and exercised the supreme authority as president of the Sanhedrin (see John 18:13); **Caiaphas,** the nominal high priest and son-in-law to Annas, who had con-demned Christ to death; **John,** possibly the son of Annas;[30] **Alexander,** a brother to the famous Greco-Jewish philosopher Philo Judaeus and one of the richest men of his day, according to Josephus;[31] **and the kindred of the high priest,** who prob-ably came to add the weight of their votes to his decision. What a formidable foe the infant church faced!

The forerunner of the Jewish Sanhe-drin was the Gerousia or Senate of Jeru-

28 Dummelow, *op. cit.,* p. 823.   29 Lange, *op. cit.,* p. 72.
30 Matthew Henry, *Commentary on the Whole Bible,* VI, comment on Acts 4:5, 6.
31 Flavius Josephus, *Ant.,* XIX, v. 1.

salem, the exact origin of which is in doubt, though it may have emerged from the assembly of 150 chief citizens under Nehemiah (Neh. 5:17). The Gerousia was designed to provide limitations upon the high priest who was supreme in politics and religion in Judea during the Egyptian subjugation in the third century B.C. Its effectiveness was doubtful, however.

In the first Christian century there were local Sanhedrins in eleven troparchies of Judaea which were responsible, under the Roman procurator, for the collection of taxes. Further, it appears that those local Sanhedrins were empowered to handle such civil and criminal cases as involved Jews only, or they might refer them to the Jerusalem national Sanhedrin. The appointment and removal of the Jewish high priests were in the power of the Roman procurator or governor, except by concession to the Herods.

Concerning the national Sanhedrin in the first Christian century, Mould remarks:

> The Jerusalem Sanhedrin administered Jewish law covering civil, criminal, moral, and religious questions. Its civil authority was limited to Judea. It could make arrests and its authority over Jews, provided they did not possess Roman citizenship, was practically unlimited except in the matter of capital punishment, which required the procurator's approval. However, the Jews did have the right to kill on the spot any gentile who entered the sacred courts of the temple beyond the Court of the Gentiles. The Jerusalem Sanhedrin consisted of seventy members. The high priest was its head. Apparently it was a self-perpetuating body, filling its own vacancies by members chosen from the ranks of the high-priestly families, the scribes, and the elders. The religious prestige of this body extended wherever there were Jews.[32]

With the destruction of Jerusalem in A.D. 70 the Sanhedrin disappeared, though the synagogue survived.

2. The Question of the Court (4:7)

7 And when they had set them in the midst, they inquired, By what power, or in what name, have ye done this?

Note the similarity of this question to the one asked Christ by the chief priests and elders (Matt. 21:23b). The question itself is twofold. *First,* it implies illegality and was intended to incriminate the apostles: "Where are your credentials for the performance of miracles and teaching the people?" The Sanhedrin claimed the exclusive right to authorize religious healers and teachers, and they had given no such rights to the apostles. *Second,* the question hints at magical practices for which, if convicted, the apostles could be condemned to death by the Sanhedrin, if the sentence were approved by the Roman procurator. Such practices were not uncommon, and even the name of Jesus was later used by magicians (see Acts 19:13-20).

3. The Answer to the Court (4:8-12)

8 Then Peter, filled with the Holy Spirit, said unto them, Ye rulers of the people, and elders, 9 if we this day are examined concerning a good deed done to an impotent man, by what means this man is made whole; 10 be it known unto you all, and to all the people of Israel, that in the name of Jesus Christ of Nazareth, whom ye crucified, whom God raised from the dead, *even* in him doth this man stand here before you whole. 11 He is the stone which was set at nought of you the builders, which was made the head of the corner. 12 And in none other is there salvation: for neither is there any other name under heaven, that is given among men, wherein we must be saved.

Peter, who cringed before a maid's question and denied Christ in Pilate's judgment hall, now, **filled with the Holy Spirit,** boldly makes answer to the Sanhedrin (see Luke 12:11, 12). Pentecost makes courageous men out of cowards and witnesses out of moral weaklings. Peter's defense before the court is fourfold. *First,* the miracle of healing was beneficial to the cripple and injurious to no one; **a good deed done** (v. 9). *Second,* **in the name of Jesus Christ of Nazareth** the impotent man had been made **whole,** and his presence bore undeniable testimony (v. 10). *Third,* God had outwitted the rulers of the Jews through victory over death: **He is the stone [Christ] which was set at nought [rejected] of you the builders [rulers of the Jews], which was made the head of the corner [raised up**

[32] Elmer W. K. Mould, *Essentials of Bible History,* pp. 467, 468.

in power] (v. 11). *Fourth,* Christ is unique in that **neither is there any other name under heaven, that is given among men, wherein we must be saved** (v. 12). Peter leaves no place for the modern liberal view of "other ways of salvation."

C. THE APOSTLES' VICTORY (4:13-22)

There were three insurmountable obstacles to the designs of the Jewish court on the lives of the apostles: namely, (1) the boldness of the apostles (v. 13); (2) the evidence of the man made whole (v. 16); and (3) their fear of the people already convicted of the validity of the risen Christ (v. 21b).

1. The Apostles' Secret (4:13)

13 Now when they beheld the boldness of Peter and John, and had perceived that they were unlearned and ignorant men, they marvelled; and they took knowledge of them, that they had been with Jesus.

Courage born of confidence is the most disarming weapon known to man. Here there was no anticipation of objections met by subtle arguments of logic. Rather, the apostles believed so certainly and witnessed so definitely that their faith became contagious, even in testimony to the unbelieving Sanhedrin. The rulers discerned that they were but unschooled laymen, as far as literary education went. Then, however, they learned, from the apostles or elsewhere, that they had been disciples of Jesus Christ, and they seemed to grasp the reason for their superhuman wisdom. That the secret of their power was in Christ at last dawned upon the Sanhedrin.

2. The Apostles' Evidence (4:14)

14 And seeing the man that was healed standing with them, they could say nothing against it.

There is an inescapable logic in the situation before the Sanhedrin. If the apostles' doctrine of the resurrected Christ were false, then the man could not have been healed in Christ's Name. If the man, whom they all knew to have been a cripple for more than forty years (v. 22), is healed through the Name of

Christ, then the doctrine must necessarily be true. The man stands in their midst perfectly whole, through the Name of Christ. Therefore the doctrine of the apostles is true, and consequently, they could say nothing against it. One demonstration of divine power is worth ten thousand theological or philosophical arguments. Christ commissioned His disciples to witness (Acts 1:8), and here is a convincing testimony.

3. The Court's Consternation (4:15, 16)

15 But when they had commanded them to go aside out of the council, they conferred among themselves, 16 saying, What shall we do to these men? for that indeed a notable miracle hath been wrought through them, is manifest to all that dwell in Jerusalem; and we cannot deny it.

What shall we do to these men? Having put the apostles out of the courtroom, the Sanhedrin went into a huddle. They were convinced by the miracle of healing, by the witness of the apostles, by the capitulation of the multitudes to Christ, and by their own consciences, that the doctrine of Christ's resurrection was true. They should have asked: "What shall we do about our relation to Christ's claims upon our lives?" But they hardened their hearts and refused to believe, even though the evidence was undeniable. They only sought to know how they might keep the fame of the miracle, and consequently the name of the risen Christ, from spreading further. It was already **manifest to all that dwell in Jerusalem.** How could they keep it from spreading beyond Jerusalem?[33]

4. The Court's Decision (4:17, 18)

17 But that it spread no further among the people, let us threaten them, that they speak henceforth to no man in this name. 18 And they called them, and charged them not to speak at all nor teach in the name of Jesus.

The court's decision involved three serious considerations: *first,* it was based on no previous apostolic offense: they **let them go, finding nothing how they might punish them** (v. 21); *second,* it included an official and authoritative

---

[33] See notes concerning Sanhedrin on Acts 4:5, 6, relative to the limitations of Jewish authority.

command to cease all witnessing, preaching, or teaching in Christ's name, whether to individual, congregation, or multitude, in private or in public (vv. 17b and 18b); and *third,* the command was enforced by an illegal threat of the severest punishment, perhaps even death, should they resume their testimony for Christ, though that testimony had brought only good (v. 9). Thus the court's decision was groundless, unreasonable, and unjust.

5. The Apostles' Reply (4:19, 20)

19 But Peter and John answered and said unto them, Whether it is right in the sight of God to hearken unto you rather than unto God, judge ye: 20 for we cannot but speak the things which we saw and heard.

The apostles' answer was resolute, appealing to the consciences and the judgment of the judges (Lange). They clearly placed the responsibility for the continuance of their testimony on the Sanhedrin. You, our judges, profess to serve the same God whom we serve, and since He has commanded us to witness, and has honored our witness as you behold by the evidence before you, should we place your prohibitive command above His positive command? **Judge ye.** The assumed reply is negative. They are silenced. We must and will continue to witness to Christ's resurrection, was the audacious apostolic reply to the court. They would obey the higher authority.

6. The Apostles' Release (4:21, 22)

21 And they, when they had further threatened them, let them go, finding nothing how they might punish them, because of the people; for all men glorified God for that which was done. 22 For the man was more than forty years old, on whom this miracle of healing was wrought.

They . . . let them go. The court had no alternative. They simply added empty threats of punishment to save face for the court, which they were restrained from inflicting through fear of the popular support of the apostles' teaching, and then released them. Nor does man ever have an alternative when he is forced to face the verities of divine reality.

D. THE CHURCH'S PRAYER (4:23-31)

23 And being let go, they came to their own company, and reported all that the chief priests and the elders had said unto them. 24 And they, when they heard it, lifted up their voice to God with one accord, and said, O Lord, thou that didst make the heaven and the earth and the sea, and all that in them is: 25 who by the Holy Spirit, *by* the mouth of our father David thy servant, didst say,

Why did the Gentiles rage,
And the peoples imagine vain things?
26 The kings of the earth set themselves
     in array,
And the rulers were gathered together,
Against the Lord, and against his
     Anointed:

27 for of a truth in this city against thy holy Servant Jesus, whom thou didst anoint, both Herod and Pontius Pilate, with the Gentiles and the peoples of Israel, were gathered together, 28 to do whatsoever thy hand and thy counsel foreordained to come to pass. 29 And now, Lord, look upon their threatenings: and grant unto thy servants to speak thy word with all boldness, 30 while thou stretchest forth thy hand to heal; and that signs and wonders may be done through the name of thy holy Servant Jesus. 31 And when they had prayed, the place was shaken wherein they were gathered together; and they were all filled with the Holy Spirit, and they spake the word of God with boldness.

They . . . lifted up their voice to God with one accord. This prayer embodies three considerations. *First,* there were the release and the report of the apostles to the church (v. 23). How natural that **being let go, they came to their own company.** So does man ever do. They required the understanding and prayer support of the whole church of which they were but the advance representatives. There they shared their burdens and their victories in Christ. *Second,* the church took seriously the situation and prayed in faith unitedly,[34] intelligently, and effectively that God would **grant unto [His] servants to speak . . . [the] word with all boldness.** *Third,* God heard their prayer and granted their request with a renewed spiritual manifestation, **and they spake the word of God with boldness.** God's answers are certain

---

[34] See Additional Note I, "*Homothumadon*" — *One Accord.*

when His people pray in faith in accordance with His will.

E. THE CHURCH'S PROSPERITY (4:32-37)

32 And the multitude of them that believed were of one heart and soul: and not one *of them* said that aught of the things which he possessed was his own; but they had all things common. 33 And with great power gave the apostles their witness of the resurrection of the Lord Jesus: and great grace was upon them all. 34 For neither was there among them any that lacked: for as many as were possessors of lands or houses sold them, and brought the prices of the things that were sold, 35 and laid them at the apostles' feet: and distribution was made unto each, according as any one had need.

36 And Joseph, who by the apostles was surnamed Barnabas (which is, being interpreted, Son of exhortation), a Levite, a man of Cyprus by race, 37 having a field, sold it, and brought the money and laid it at the apostles' feet.

The prosperity of the church consisted in (1) its spiritual unity (v. 32a), (2) its boundless generosity (vv. 32b, 34-37),[35] (3) its undaunted witness to Christ (v. 33a), and (4) the measureless grace of God's manifest presence and approval (v. 33b).

V. THE CHURCH'S FIRST DIVINE JUDGMENT (Acts 5:1-16)

A. DIVINE JUDGMENT AND HYPOCRISY (5:1-11)

This incident of hypocrisy and consequent divine judgment is the first recorded "fly in the precious ointment" (cf. Eccl. 10:1) of the apostolic church. The offense is glaring and the punishment severe. Both are intended as a warning to the church, for all time, of God's displeasure with insincerity and its deadening threat to the spiritual life of the church. When insincerity moves into the church, God moves out.

1. The Occasion of the Judgment (5:1-2)

1 But a certain man named Ananias, with Sapphira his wife, sold a possession, 2 and kept back *part* of the price, his wife also being privy to it, and brought a certain part, and laid it at the apostles' feet.

No one was under compulsion to sell his property and pool the proceeds in the church. Such was purely voluntary (v. 4). However, the practice appears to have become popular with the Christian community. It gave good standing to the Christian, and herein lay the danger. Who Ananias and Sapphira were, why they sold all their property, or whether they had been sincere believers, we are left to conjecture. We are only told, as Weymouth graphically translates the passage, that "Ananias with his wife, Sapphira, sold some property, but, with her full knowledge and consent, dishonestly kept back part of the price received for it, though he brought the rest and gave it to the apostles."

Plumptre[36] thinks that the account of Ananias' experience here must be understood against the background of the act of Barnabas in selling his property and giving the proceeds to the church (cf. Acts 4:36, 37). Ananias thought he could get the same results of praise and power, acquired by Barnabas at the cost of genuine sacrifice, by a cheaper means. Plumptre sees in Ananias,

. . . a strange mingling of discordant elements. Zeal and faith of some sort had led him to profess himself a believer. Ambition was strong enough to win a partial victory over avarice; avarice was strong enough to triumph over truth. The impulse to sell came from the Spirit of God; it was counteracted by the spirit of evil, and the resulting sin was therefore worse than that of one who lived altogether in the lower, commoner forms of covetousness. It was an attempt to serve God and mammon; to gain the reputation of a saint, without the reality of holiness.[37]

There are certain respects in which the sin of Ananias resembles that of Achan (Josh. 7:1), as also that of Gehazi (II Kings 5:20-27). However, Ananias' sin was greater than that of either Achan or Gehazi in that he had greater light and consequently his hypocrisy was more glaring. Ananias appears to have been afflicted with the sin of "double-mindedness" against which James warns (James

---

1:8; 4:8). Possibly it was from this incident that James was impressed with the peril of such a state. It was not the fact that he offered only a part that constituted his sin, but rather because he offered the part as though it were the whole. He was guilty of purloining (cf. Titus 2:10), or "stealthy and dishonest appropriation."

Plumptre understands Peter's rebuke (v. 3) to imply,

> . . . the perversion of conscience and will, just at the moment when they seemed to be, and, it may be, actually were, on the point of attaining a higher perfection than before. The question 'Why' implies that resistance to the temptation had been possible (James 4:7).[38]

Insincerity and incomplete obedience are the lessons clearly taught, and the penalty is spiritual death. While on earth, Christ's most severe condemnations were of hypocrisy in the lives of the religionists. The church begins with this same divine disapprobation on insincerity.

2. The Detection of the Hypocrisy (5:3)

3 But Peter said, Ananias, why hath Satan filled thy heart to lie to the Holy Spirit, and to keep back *part* of the price of the land?

Ananias' sin was no unpremeditated accident. He had deliberately agreed with his wife to deceive the church by professing to give all the proceeds from the sale, while he was giving only a part. The motive appears to have been twofold: *first*, selfishness in retaining part of the price; and *second*, glory in the recognition for generosity which he hoped to receive from the church. He tarried and toyed with temptation and Satan deceived and ensnared him. Nothing can be clearer than the apostolic belief in the personality of Satan, from this word of Peter. The Holy Spirit of God to whom he lied revealed to Peter Ananias' sin. Sin is ever revealed where the Spirit of God is present.

3. The Necessity of the Judgment (5:4)

4 While it remained, did it not remain thine own? and after it was sold, was it not in thy power? How is it that

38 *Ibid.*

thou hast conceived this thing in thy heart? thou hast not lied unto men, but unto God.

All sin is finally against God, and though it may never be detected by man, it is never hidden from God. David realized this fact when he exclaimed: "Against thee, thee only, have I sinned, and done that which is evil in thy sight" (Ps. 51:4a). Weymouth reads: "How is it that you have cherished this design in your heart?" Thus it was an act for which Ananias was fully responsible, and in which he attempted to deceive God so as to realize his unworthy purposes. The judgment that followed was necessary to label hypocrisy in the church as forever condemned of God.

4. The Administration of the Judgment (5:5, 6)

5 And Ananias hearing these words fell down and gave up the ghost: and great fear came upon all that heard it. 6 And the young men arose and wrapped him round, and they carried him out and buried him.

Sin will not only be exposed, but it must die in the presence of God's revealed holiness. It was not Peter's words, but God's revealed wrath against the sin of hypocrisy that occasioned the death of Ananias. It was when Isaiah saw God in His exaltation and holiness that he cried out: "Woe is me! for I am undone" (Isa. 6:5a). Sin withers and dies in the presence of God's holiness as surely as snow melts when the sun shines on it. Unless the sinner detaches himself from sin, through repentance and renunciation, he must die with it. God destroys sin, and it remains only for the church to dispose of its remains. **The young men . . . carried him out and buried him** (v. 6). The immediate effect on the church was most salutary and is graphically portrayed in Weymouth's translation: "all who heard the words were awe-struck."

5. The Accomplice in Hypocrisy (5:7-10)

7 And it was about the space of three hours after, when his wife, not knowing what was done, came in. 8 And Peter answered unto her, Tell me whether ye

sold the land for so much. And she said, Yea, for so much. 9 But Peter *said* unto her, How is it that ye have agreed together to try the Spirit of the Lord? behold, the feet of them that have buried thy husband are at the door, and they shall carry thee out. 10 And she fell down immediately at his feet, and gave up the ghost: and the young men came in and found her dead, and they carried her out and buried her by her husband.

It was either at a subsequent service of the church three hours after her husband's death, and probably at a later stated "hour of prayer," or three hours later in the same service in which her husband died, that Sapphira appeared. She had become an accomplice with her husband in his sin, and she intended to carry through with the deception. Peter repeated the question to her, to which she replied as had her husband. She was rebuked by the apostle and the judgment of death swiftly followed. The evident lesson is that as "none . . . liveth to himself" (Rom. 14:7a), so no man sins unto himself, but he must ever draw another into his evil company and partnership. God desired the infant church to learn that sin is contagious and that the one influenced to evil shares the guilt and judgment of the one who influences. Sin is a lonely creature and must soon die in solitude.

6. The Effects of the Judgment (5:11)

11 And great fear came upon the whole church, and upon all that heard these things.

Weymouth reads: "all who heard of this incident." The incident incited three kinds of fear: *first,* a reverential fear of God's holiness and majesty which was revealed; *second,* a disciplinary fear, by reason of the divine judgment against hypocrisy which fell upon and purified the church; and *third,* an arresting fear that fell upon the unbelieving who saw or heard of the incident. God is one, but His manifestations and administrations are as varied as the needs of men.

B. DIVINE JUDGMENT AND SPIRITUAL RENEWAL (5:12-16)

12 And by the hands of the apostles were many signs and wonders wrought

among the people: and they were all with one accord in Solomon's porch. 13 But of the rest durst no man join himself to them: howbeit the people magnified them; 14 and believers were the more added to the Lord, multitudes both of men and women: 15 insomuch that they even carried out the sick into the streets, and laid them on beds and couches, that, as Peter came by, at the least his shadow might overshadow some one of them. 16 And there also came together the multitude from the cities round about Jerusalem, bringing sick folk, and them that were vexed with unclean spirits: and they were healed every one.

It will be noted that the miraculous events of verses 12-16 are in answer to the prayer of the church following the release of the apostle from prison (see Acts 4:30). Indeed, the tragedy of divine judgment on hypocrisy within the church had intervened (vv. 1-10) and served to inspire reverence and respect for God and His apostles (v. 11). God then, as now, worked in mysterious ways His wonders to perform, and indeed "his ways [are] past tracing out!" (Rom. 11:33b). These happenings are the unbroken continuance of the miraculous character of the church from Pentecost onward (Acts 2:43). It was due to the prayer of the church, however, that the revival continued.

The unity of the disciples in the Lord (v. 12b) bespoke their invincibility and afforded the necessary channel for divine manifestation and operation (v. 12a). Their location was most advantageous. *Solomon's porch* was a spacious court on the east side of the temple, bearing Solomon's name, and was supposed to have been a remnant of the original temple built by him (see II Chron. 4:9; 6:13). The particular location appears to have been advantageous both to Christ and to the Christians (see John 10:23; Acts 3:11; Acts 5:12). So far the Christians had not broken with the temple worship.

The popular support accorded the Christians, and the apostles in particular, is indicated by Luke's words, **howbeit the people magnified them** (v. 13b), or as Weymouth reads: "the people held them in high honour." God's presence always magnifies human instruments. "Little is much, when God is in it." The resultant revival was more than excitement and mere sensationalism. It was characterized by genuine spiritual fruit. Says Luke: **And believers were the more added to the Lord, multitudes both of men and women** (v. 14). Two special notes are striking in this passage: *first,* the believers **were added** [joined] **to the Lord;** and *second,* **women** are mentioned as of importance in the church for the first time since Pentecost. Finally, the healings and demon expulsions (vv. 15, 16) represent the beneficent implications of the gospel extended to suffering humanity. Such was the example that Jesus personally set for the church (Matt. 9:32-35), and such was the commission which He gave His disciples (see Matt. 9:36-38; 10:8 and Mark 3:14, 15). While the so-called modern "social gospel" is scripturally invalid, the social implications of the personal gospel of Christ are unlimited. Little wonder, or matter, that the pagan thinkers confused magical concepts with the divine miracles of healing (v. 15b). It is not said, nor is it to be supposed, that the shadow of Peter actually healed anyone. A sharp distinction is made here by Luke between **sick folk** and **them that were vexed with unclean spirits** (v. 16). The recognition of demon possession and demon expulsion is evident in the apostolic church. The modern church may be overlooking an important matter here. It became common practice in the primitive church to appoint a special officer to each church whose ecclesiastical duty consisted in expelling demons from the possessed through the use of Jesus' name.[39]

VI. THE CHURCH'S SECOND PERSECUTION (Acts 5:17-42)

A. IMPRISONMENT AND DELIVERANCE OF THE APOSTLES (5:17-21a)

The occasion for this second arrest of Peter and John is found in Acts 5:12-16, which incident has been dealt with previously. At their first trial they had been strictly warned by the court not to speak nor teach in the name of Jesus (Acts 4:18b). This prohibition they boldly disregarded, and the great revival continued.

1. The Arrest and Imprisonment (5:17, 18)

17 But the high priest rose up, and all they that were with him (which is the sect of the Sadducees), and they were filled with jealousy, 18 and laid hands on the apostles, and put them in public ward.

Whether by the high priest is meant Annas, the president of the Sanhedrin, or Caiaphas, the actual high priest, it is difficult to know. The former is likely indicated. The high priest, probably Annas the president of the Sanhedrin, was supported by the Sadducean party in his indignation or "angry jealousy" (Weymouth) and intentions against the apostles, at the sight of the influence of the apostles over the multitude. Generally, the arrest was based on the apostles' disregard of the court's command, their continued preaching in Christ's Name, their miracles of healing, and their influence over the people. However, more really and specifically, it was based on the Sadducean opposition to their doctrine of the resurrection and the operations of the Holy Spirit, both of which the Sadducees denied. It would appear that these court officials so undignified themselves as to have personally laid hands on the apostles and put them in the common prison (v. 18). As at their first arrest, it was evening, and therefore they could not be legally tried by the Sanhedrin before the next day. Thus they were compelled to spend the night in the common prison among vile criminals. It was not fear of their escape, but desire to stop their work, that accounted for their imprisonment.

2. The Divine Deliverance (5:19)

19 But an angel of the Lord by night opened the prison doors, and brought them out, and said,

God has a master key that will unlock all the prison doors where His servants may be incarcerated by the enemy. "The Lord knoweth how to deliver the godly out of temptation" (II Pet. 2:9). The irony of the situation rests in the fact that the Lord sent an angel to deliver the apostles, while the Sadducees, who dominated the Sanhedrin, did not believe in

---

[39] See Additional Note V, *Demon Possession and Expulsion.*

angels. Man's unbelief does not alter divine reality. The existence and ministry of angels is a clear testimony of the Scriptures (see Additional Note VIII, Angelology. The apostles' deliverance from prison was perfectly right, since it was accomplished by God; and its purpose was to encourage the apostles in their dark hour (**by night** [the angel] **opened the prison doors)**, and the church that doubtless prayed for their release, and to confound and convince the rulers who fought against Christ.

3. The Divine Commission (5:20)

20 Go ye, and stand and speak in the temple to the people all the words of this Life.

The apostles were divinely delivered that they might resume their ministry, not that they might retire into solitude and safety. If it is for personal safety or profit that man seeks deliverance of God he may have little hope of divine intervention. God saves man that he may serve Him (see I Thess. 1:9b).

The commission was, **Go ye, and stand and speak in the temple.** Here was where the people would gather for worship, according to the Law. They were to enter into the very temple itself and boldly stand and proclaim **all the words of this Life,** the whole gospel of Jesus Christ, to a people condemned to death by the Law. God's true church is ever a "going concern," even in the face of opposition and danger.

4. The Apostles' Obedience (5:21a)

21 And when they heard *this,* they entered into the temple about daybreak, and taught.

Without hesitation the apostles, encouraged and fortified by their deliverance and the renewed commission, appear to have entered directly into the temple where they resumed their teaching. Weymouth says, "they went into the temple just before daybreak," or as soon as the doors were opened. The divine commission is ever the divine enabling.

B. THE CHARGES AND REPLY OF THE APOSTLES (5:21b-33)

In this account we have very much of a repetition of the first trial of the apostles as recorded in Acts 4:1-22, with, however, certain important differences which will appear. The rulers' indignation, or "angry jealousy," as Weymouth translates it, was greatly heightened at the apparent defiance of the apostles and their increased influence over the people. The Sanhedrin was now wrathfully resolved to stop this whole business forever.

1. The Court's Design (5:21b)

21 But the high priest came, and they that were with him, and called the council together, and all the senate of the children of Israel, and sent to the prison-house to have them brought.

The president of the Sanhedrin planned and purposed to make this second trial of the apostles more auspicious and effective than the first. At the first trial the regular court and certain other important persons were present. For this second trial an extraordinary session of the Sanhedrin was evidently called for the occasion. This contained, it would appear, the Sanhedrin, with its seventy elders, and two other judicatories, one of which was stationed in the outer-court temple gate, and the other in the inner Gate Beautiful, each of which was comprised of twenty-three judges. The full Sanhedrin thus assembled would have consisted of 116 judges. While the high priest sought to overawe and intimidate the apostles and Christians in general by assembling this extraordinary court and thus finally to stop their activities, God on the other hand turned it into a larger opportunity for the Christian witness.

2. The Court's Consternation (5:22-25)

22 But the officers that came found them not in the prison; and they returned, and told, 23 saying, The prison-house we found shut in all safety, and the keepers standing at the doors: but when we had opened, we found no man within. 24 Now when the captain of the temple and the chief priests heard these words, they were much perplexed concerning them whereunto this would grow. 25 And there came one and told them, Behold, the men whom ye put in the prison are in the temple standing and teaching the people.

What an embarrassment it must have occasioned the president to have summoned this extraordinary court and called it to order, only to find that the prisoners docketed for trial, whose arrest and incarceration he had personally conducted the evening before, were missing from the jail. **The officers that came found them not in the prison** (v. 22a). Man purposes, but God disposes. No prison is sufficiently secure to hold God's true servants. Even Paul was "an ambassador in bonds" (Eph. 6:20), and considered himself not the prisoner of man, but of the Lord Jesus Christ (see Eph. 3:1; 4:1; Philemon 1, 9).

No blame could be placed on the prison guards, for they had done their duty well. Upon learning of the prisoners' escape, the high priest, the temple captain, and the chief priests seem to have recognized that it was by supernatural means that the apostles escaped. Their real concern is expressed by the narrator in his words: **they were much perplexed concerning them whereunto this would grow** (v. 24b); or in Weymouth's translation, "they were utterly at a loss with regard to it, wondering what would happen next." They had not long to wonder. As if to add to their consternation, a messenger appeared and made his announcement.

3. The Apostles' Rearrest (5:26, 27a)

26 Then went the captain with the officers, and brought them, *but* without violence; for they feared the people, lest they should be stoned. 27 And when they had brought them, they set them before the council.

The apostles' influence seems to have reached an all-time high, which was doubtless due to a knowledge of their divine deliverance from prison, the many benefits received from God at the hands of the people, and the special manifestations of divine power and favor on their lives and ministry. Fear of stoning by the multitude only restrained the officers from violently beating and dragging the apostles from the temple. Evidently the apostles accompanied them readily and willingly, possibly having been entreated of the officers, knowing that He who had delivered them from prison would deliver them in court.

4. The Court's Charge (5:27b, 28)

27 And the high priest asked them, 28 saying, We strictly charged you not to teach in this name: and behold, ye have filled Jerusalem with your teaching, and intend to bring this man's blood upon us.

Having placed the apostles in the midst of this august assembly, arranged as it was in a semicircle, the high priest brought a threefold charge against them. *First*, they had violated the previous command of the court not to teach in Christ's name; *second*, they had filled Jerusalem with the Christian doctrine; and *third*, they had made the rulers of Israel responsible for the death of Christ (v. 28). Matthew Henry[40] sees in the *second*, disorderly conduct in the disturbance of the exciting doctrine; and in teaching of an exciting doctrine; and in the *third*, sedition and faction, with a view to setting the people against the rulers. The latter charge doubtless reflects the guilt of their own consciences. It is noteworthy that they were not charged with breaking jail.

5. The Apostles' Reply (5:29-32)

29 But Peter and the apostles answered and said, We must obey God rather than men. 30 The God of our fathers raised up Jesus, whom ye slew, hanging him on a tree. 31 Him did God exalt with his right hand *to be* a Prince and a Saviour, to give repentance to Israel, and remission of sins. 32 And we are witnesses of these things; and *so is* the Holy Spirit, whom God hath given to them that obey him.

Without denial or hesitation, the apostles replied to the charges, indicating in each instance that the rulers were fighting a losing battle against God. *First*, they replied that God's authority was greater than man's, and since they served Him, they said, **We must obey God rather than men** (v. 29b). They reasoned, *second*, that Jesus was the especially appointed messenger of God whose crucifixion at their hands was a direct and vicious affront to God Himself. And *third*, they gave the answer to the second charge of the court, to the effect that the popularity of the Christian doctrine was due to

---

[40] Matthew Henry, *op. cit.*, VI. Comment on Acts 5:27b, 28.

the work of God through His risen Christ, who was now supplanting the Jewish ecclesiastical rulers and teachers (v. 31). *Finally*, they frankly identified themselves as propagators (witnesses) of the whole and claimed the cooperation and approbation of God. Thus they placed full responsibility upon the court.

6. The Court's Indignation (5:33)

33 But they, when they heard this, were cut to the heart, and were minded to slay them.

Like maddened beasts, wounded and inescapably cornered, they now saw as their only alternative the destruction of their pursuers. They literally "were sawn asunder"[41] or became violently enraged and **were minded to slay them.** Justice was forgotten and judges' benches were forsaken as personal passion dethroned reason, bared wicked fangs, and viciously panted for blood. "They were disposed to kill the Apostles" (Weymouth).

C. THE DEFENSE AND RELEASE OF THE APOSTLES (5:34-42)

34 But there stood up one in the council, a Pharisee, named Gamaliel, a doctor of the law, had in honor of all the people, and commanded to put the men forth a little while. 35 And he said unto them, Ye men of Israel, take heed to yourselves as touching these men, what ye are about to do. 36 For before these days rose up Theudas, giving himself out to be somebody; to whom a number of men, about four hundred, joined themselves, who was slain; and all, as many as obeyed him, were dispersed, and came to nought. 37 After this man rose up Judas of Galilee in the days of the enrolment, and drew away *some of the* people after him: he also perished; and all, as many as obeyed him, were scattered abroad. 38 And now I say unto you, Refrain from these men, and let them alone: for if this counsel or this work be of men, it will be overthrown: 39 but if it is of God, ye will not be able to overthrow them; lest haply ye be found even to be fighting against God. 40 And to him they agreed: and when they had called the apostles unto them, they beat them and charged them not to speak in the name of Jesus, and let them go. 41 They therefore departed from the presence of the council, rejoicing that they were counted worthy to suffer dishonor for the Name. 42 And every day, in the temple and at home, they ceased not to teach and preach Jesus *as* the Christ.

Had not the court been restrained by the collected and wise advice of Gamaliel, the rulers probably would have stoned the apostles, as they later did Stephen. However, their work was not done. Three important things are said about Gamaliel; namely, he was **a Pharisee, a doctor of the law, and** he was **had in honor of all the people** (v. 34). Thus he was best qualified for this defense. Gamaliel was the teacher of Saul who became Paul the Apostle (Acts 22:3), and he was the grandson of the great Hillel and the most influential rabbi of his time.[42] His reason for defense of the apostles seems to have sprung from his party affiliation (a Pharisee), and thus his regard for the doctrine of the resurrection, his favorable impression of the lives and ministry of the apostles, his sense of justice, and his faith in providence. He cites two examples of Jewish leaders whose work came to naught, and then advised the court to leave these men and their work in God's hands, lest they should fight against God.

Gamaliel's advice was accepted by the court, and though they gave partial vent to their indignation by flogging the apostles for their disobedience to the court's previous command, probably with thirty-nine stripes each, the rulers accordingly released them with a renewal of the futile command, as they must have realized, charging **them not to speak in the name of Jesus** (v. 40b). The apostles returned forthwith and resumed their ministry to the waiting multitude in the temple and extended their services to private homes as well, where **they ceased not to teach and to preach Jesus as the Christ** (v. 42b). How futile the efforts of man to stay the work of God!

VII. THE CHURCH'S FIRST ORGANIZATIONAL PROBLEMS (Acts 6:1-7)

A. THE CHURCH'S NEW PROBLEMS (6:1, 2)

The apostolic church, like the church of every subsequent generation, had its problems. Those problems were met

---

[41] Dummelow, *op. cit.*, p. 825.   [42] *Ibid.*

under divine guidance as they arose. The first was insincerity and was punished by divine judgment (Acts 5:1-11). The second had its origin in the enlargement of the church and consisted in discriminatory accusations, if not practices, and the division of church responsibilities. These problems were settled by divinely aided human wisdom.

1. The Problem of Enlargement (6:1a)

1 Now in these days, when the number of the disciples was multiplying,

The narrator here uses a new arithmetic for the first time in regard to the church's growth. Previously believers have been "added to the church" (see Acts 2:41, 47; 5:14); but now the growth, resultant from the apostolic victories under God's blessings, has become so rapid that it can be referred to as "multiplication." Nor was this rapidly growing church without its growing pains. Growth is normal and healthy, but it always produces its problems of new adaptations, as expansion and maturity continue. An unwillingness to meet and solve those problems will ever stifle the growth and destroy the organism. The apostles accepted it as a challenge.

2. The Problem of Discrimination (6: 1b)

1 there arose a murmuring of the Grecian Jews against the Hebrews, because their widows were neglected in the daily ministration.

There arose a murmuring . . . . A muffled undertone of complaint finally broke through and began to evidence itself on the surface. **The Grecians** were Hellenists, or Jews who had imbibed the Greek culture, including language, of the countries in which they were born in the dispersion. They were considered inferior by the Hebrews, or Palestinian Jews, who were in the majority in the church.[43] The order of widows, supported by the church from the common treasury and devoted to prayer and works of mercy (Acts 9:41; I Tim. 5:3, 9-11, 16), was one of the earliest Christian institutions.[44] This neglect of the Grecian widows by the Hebrew-Christian administrators of

temporal goods probably was unintentional, but it revealed an essential weakness of early Christian communalism.

3. The Problem of Responsibilities (6: 2)

2 And the twelve called the multitude of the disciples unto them, and said, It is not fit that we should forsake the word of God, and serve tables.

Originally, in the Christian communal system, the apostles were the administrators of the common treasury (Acts 2:45; 5:2). Increased ministerial responsibilities in the growing church made it inevitable that this could not continue. The apostles' first duty was to minister the Word of God (Matt. 28:18-20; Acts 1:8). They assembled the multitude and declared their first duty to be a direct spiritual ministry. The *apostolate* appeared first in the church, then the *diaconate,* and later the *presbyterate,* as the need for each arose.[45] Whenever the ministry neglects its spiritual service to man for temporal concerns, it has failed the divine calling. Janitorial duties or secular employment by the minister may be justifiable in the beginning of a church, but it can seldom be long continued without injury to both the minister and the church.

B. THE PROPOSED SOLUTION (6:3-5a)

The apostolic church here sets forth a workable example for the solution of church problems. The entire church was represented (v. 2a), and though the apostles suggested the solution, responsibility for the choosing of the officers was left with the church. While these officers are simply designated **seven men** in this early Acts record, it would appear that the office to which they were appointed was that known as the *diaconate* in later times,[46] though this is questioned if not denied by some scholars. The fuller qualifications of deacons are given by Paul (Phil. 1:1; I Tim. 3:8, 12) .

1. The Necessary Consideration (6:3a)

3 Look ye out therefore, brethren, from among you seven men of good report,

43 Dummelow, *op. cit.,* p. 825.   44 H. D. M. Spence, ed., *Pulpit Commentary,* XVIII, 192.
45 *Ibid.,* p. 193.   46 Dummelow, *loc. cit.*

Here is a perfect model of lay representation in official church matters. Weymouth reads: "Pick out from among yourselves." The church best knew who among its number were efficient, reliable, and impartial. Its careful consideration and choice is reflected in the care of the church under those chosen. No particular significance need be attached to the number seven, unless for the sacredness of the number with the Jews, or that each might supervise the temporal affairs one day a week.

2. The Required Qualifications (6:3b, 4)

3 full of the Spirit and of wisdom, whom we may appoint over this business. 4 But we will continue stedfastly in prayer, and in the ministry of the word.

The apostles specify the qualifications of the seven officers to be chosen; namely, (1) *good reputation,* of **good report;** (2) *spirituality,* **full of the Spirit;** and (3) *practicality,* **full . . . of wisdom.** These qualifications are few, but they cover much territory. Such church officers will ever do credit to Christianity, and under them the cause of Christ will prosper; and thus the ministry will be freed from temporal time-consuming interests that it may **continue** [itself] **stedfastly in prayer, and in the ministry of the word.**

3. The Amicable Solution (6:5a)

5 And the saying pleased the whole multitude:

Any solution of such an acute problem that will please the whole church must indeed be of divine origin. How insignificant do personal or group differences become when Christian people are disposed to settle their problems in God's way.

C. THE PLAN OF PROCEDURE (6:5b, 6)

Divine wisdom is clearly reflected in the apostolic plan for the selection, presentation, and dedication of these church officers to their duties. As is revealed by their later ministerial activities, especially in the case of Stephen and Philip, they were more than temporal officials.

1. The Church's Choice (6:5b)

5 and they chose Stephen, a man full of faith and of the Holy Spirit, and Philip, and Prochorus, and Nicanor, and Timon, and Parmenas, and Nicolaus a proselyte of Antioch;

While it was the duty of the church to choose the officials, it was the responsibility of the apostles to dedicate (v. 6b) and appoint them (v. 3b). All seven of those chosen bore Greek names. However, as it was not uncommon for Jews, especially Hellenist Jews, to have Greek names, this does not argue that all of them were pure Greeks. Three of the seven are of special interest. Stephen turned evangelist and became the first Christian martyr, of whom we learn more later. Philip likewise became an effective evangelist, whose record we have in Acts 8:5; 8:26; and 21:8. Nicolaus is called a proselyte of Antioch, indicating that he was a Gentile converted to the Jewish faith, and from that to Christianity. This mention of his nationality may seem to indicate that the rest were Jews by nationality.

2. The Church's Recommendation (6: 6a)

6 whom they set before the apostles:

Here is a beautiful example of respect for rights within the church. The church has used its best judgment in selecting the officers in accordance with the specifications given, and now they present their choice to the apostles for their approval. It may be seriously questioned whether anyone is divinely called into Christian service who does not have the recognition and recommendation of at least some responsible party or parties within the church.

3. The Officers' Dedication (6:6b)

6 and when they had prayed, they laid their hands upon them.

How like the selection and dedication of Barnabas and Paul for their missionary work by the church at Antioch (Acts 13:2, 3). The essential elements in their ordination were prayer and the laying on of hands by the apostles. This custom was very ancient and was borrowed from the Jews by the Christians (see Num. 27:18-23; Deut. 34:9). It simply betokened the Christians' acceptance of God's selection (John 15:16).

D. THE BENEFICENT RESULTS (6:7)

When the mind and will of God is sought and followed in the solution of problems and the conduct of church business, spiritual prosperity will always follow.

1. The Word of God Increased (6:7a)

7 And the word of God increased;

With the apostles wholly devoted to prayer, study, and the preaching of the Word of God (v. 4), and the church's temporal offices wisely and satisfactorily administered by the newly elected officers, there is little wonder that the revival went on. **The word of God increased** in arresting, illuminating, convicting, converting, delivering, and cleansing power. Under the Spirit's quickening power, produced by earnest prayer, God's Word becomes "quick and powerful" (Heb. 4:12, 13). The Spirit-animated Word is ever productive of revivals.

2. The Church Multiplied (6:7b)

7 and the number of the disciples multiplied in Jerusalem exceedingly;

It is possible that this reference gives a hint of the division of the disciples into separate congregations in Jerusalem, for more efficient administrative purposes. Some scholars think that each of the seven officers was appointed to a different congregation. However, there is no evidence of this. It is enough to know that the spiritual movement continued, and that the word **multiplied** best expressed the narrator's concept of the rapid growth.

3. The Priests Converted (6:7c)

7 and a great company of the priests were obedient to the faith.

While some scholars doubt the genuineness of this reading, Clarke[47] observes that it represents the greatest of all apostolic miracles, since the priests were the most bitter foes of Christian and Christianity (see John 12:42). Since there were 24 courses in Jerusalem, literally multi-

tudes, there is no problem about the conversion of **a great company of the priests.**

VIII. THE CHURCH'S FIRST MARTYR (Acts 6:8-7:60)

A. STEPHEN'S ARREST AND ARRAIGNMENT (6:8-15)

Stephen was the first of the seven lay church officers chosen to administer the temporal affairs of the disciples (Acts 6:5a). He well met the qualifications of *good reputation, spirituality,* and *practicality,* as laid down by the apostles (Acts 6:3). While Peter has been considered the greatest of the apostolic preachers, and Paul the greatest missionary, it is hardly too much to say that Stephen was the greatest first-century Christian. He evidently was a Hellenistic Jew and was possessed with a passion for the conversion of his fellow Hellenists. He evidences a remarkable knowledge of the Jewish Scriptures and history; and he reflects a wider and more liberal view of the gospel of Jesus Christ as the fulfillment of the Law, and God's provision of salvation for all nations and peoples, than even the apostles themselves. He was willing to seal his testimony to this conviction in martyrdom with his own blood.

1. The Activities of Stephen (6:8)

8 And Stephen, full of grace and power, wrought great wonders and signs among the people.

And Stephen . . .

Though Stephen had been chosen by the church as an official lay leader, it soon became evident that God had higher designs for his life. He came up through the ranks, as have so many great preachers and church leaders since. As a lay leader he was **a man full of faith and of the Holy Spirit** (Acts 6:5a), and now impelled by the quickening power of the Spirit and a passion for the evangelization of his fellows, he is seen doing **great wonders and signs** (v. 8b). Stephen's temporal office in the church brought him into contact with the poor, the sick, and the suffering, whether from demon possession or otherwise, of the congregation, and thus afforded ample opportunity for the supplying by miraculous means such needs of many of the

47 Clarke, *op. cit.,* I, 725.

people as could not be met by the temporal treasury. Filled with faith (some read "grace"), and thus giving unlimited credence to the promises of God for the people, and of the energizing power of God's Spirit (Acts 1:8), Stephen was enabled to witness mighty miracles of healing, demon expulsion, and spiritual and moral transformations among the peoples he served. The possibilities for Spirit-filled and faithful lay leadership in the church are quite unlimited. However, this spiritual service was not without its price.

2. The Synagogue's Opposition (6:9-12)

9 But there arose certain of them that were of the synagogue called *the synagogue* of the Libertines, and of the Cyrenians, and of the Alexandrians, and of them of Cilicia and Asia, disputing with Stephen. 10 And they were not able to withstand the wisdom and the Spirit by which he spake. 11 Then they suborned men, who said, We have heard him speak blasphemous words against Moses, and *against* God. 12 And they stirred up the people, and the elders, and the scribes, and came upon him, and seized him, and brought him into the council,

But there arose certain of them that were of the synagogue (v. 9a). Satan will never see his territory invaded and his subjects lost without a battle. This new activity of a Hellenist Christian especially directed toward the more liberal Hellenistic Jews of the synagogues was particularly dangerous to the cause of the enemy. It is striking that this opposition arose from among the Hellenists. Possibly they were incited by the rulers of the Sanhedrin.

Concerning the synagogue it should be noted that at least 10 adults were required by law for the organization of a synagogue, and there were at this time about 150 Jewish communities throughout the Roman Empire and beyond, though they may not all have had synagogues.[48] There were 480 synagogues in Jerusalem, according to Josephus (some say 250). They were simpler in form of worship and more liberal than the temple, in that they allowed Gentile proselytes and God-fearing non-proselytes to worship in them.

Mould says concerning the Jewish Synagogue of the first century:

> The synagogue controlled by scribes and Pharisees, was the vital center of Jewish religious thought and life. In the time of Jesus it was required that there be a synagogue in every place where ten would agree to be regular attendants. The larger cities had several synagogues. The synagogue building was so constructed that the worshippers faced toward Jerusalem. At the end of the room which the worshippers faced was the *ark*, a chest or closet in which were kept the rolls of Holy Scripture in linen cases. In front of the ark was a curtain and before that a lamp which was always kept burning. The elders and the Pharisees occupied *chief seats* facing the congregation. There was a reading desk upon a raised platform. Control of the synagogue was vested in the council of elders. Officers of the synagogue consisted of (1) *the ruler of the synagogue,* who had the immediate management of the building and its services, and who sat in the "seat of Moses" during service; (2) the *chazzan* or attendant, who had charge of the sacred rolls, kept the building in condition, and administered the scourgings which were meted out to criminals by the local synagogue courts. The chazzan may also have served as village school teacher in the synagogue schools. (3) A third group of synagogue officials was the *almoners* who collected and disbursed the alms.
>
> Synagogue services were held on all Sabbath mornings and feast days. Less formal services occurred on Sabbath afternoons, on Mondays, and on Thursdays. The order of worship included (1) the Shema (Deut. 6:4-9; 11:13-21; Num. 15:37-41), recited in unison with certain benedictions; (2) prayers, with responses by the congregation, standing; (3) a reading of passages selected by the ruler from the Torah and the Prophets, with an accompanying translation from Hebrew into Aramaic; (4) an address by any person selected by the ruler; and (5) a benediction, provided a priest were present to give it; otherwise a prayer was substituted.[49]

Those mentioned here, the members of which attacked Stephen, are **the synagogue of the Libertines,** consisting of freedmen of the Roman descendants of prisoners taken by Pompey (Chrysostom);

[48] Robinson, *op. cit.,* p. 10.
[49] Mould, *op. cit.,* pp. 479, 480. For further information on the Jewish synagogue, see Edersheim, *Life and Times of Jesus the Messiah,* I, 430-49.

Cyrenians, consisting of members from Cyrene, capital of Upper Libya in Africa, one-fourth part of which city was Jewish; **Alexandrians,** consisting of peoples from Alexandria in Egypt, two-fifths of which city was Jewish, or about 100,000 people, and the place of the translation of the Old Testament into Greek (the Septuagint); **Cilicia,** consisting of people from the province of Cilicia in Asia Minor, which was the home of Paul and the residence of many Jews (see Acts 15: 23, 41); and **Asia,** with members from the province of Asia in Asia Minor where many bigoted Jews resided (v. 9).

Unable to match the wisdom and the Spirit with which Stephen preached and reasoned with these Hellenist Jews in their Jewish synagogue or synagogues, they resorted to the foul means of employing certain lewd fellows to do their dirty work of bringing false witness against him before the Sanhedrin (v. 12; cf. Acts 17:5); and thus by these means they had him dragged into the court and falsely accused by testimonies designed to inflame the wrath and prejudice the judgments of the rulers (v. 13).

3. The Charges Against Stephen (6:13, 14)

13 and set up false witnesses, who said, This man ceaseth not to speak words against this holy place, and the law: 14 for we have heard him say, that this Jesus of Nazareth shall destroy this place, and shall change the customs which Moses delivered unto us.

The accusations brought against Stephen by these hired **false witnesses** remind one very much of the like proceedings against Christ at His trial. Indeed there is very much in the trial and death of Stephen to remind one of the trial and death of Christ. Nor is this surprising when it is remembered that his attacks on Judaism were but the continuation of the attacks which Christ had made, and that he proclaimed the gospel of Jesus Christ. Specifically, the accusations brought against Stephen were four. *First,* he was accused of blasphemy (a very serious religious crime) against Moses, the Jewish Law-Giver, and against God (v. 11); *second,* they accused him of blaspheming against, and even predicting, the

destruction of the Jewish temple (13b); *third,* he was accused of blasphemy against the Law itself (13b); and *finally,* they accused him of saying that Jesus would destroy the temple and change or destroy the customs handed down from Moses. The accusations are all doubtless a perversion of what Stephen had actually said, but the overall charge is blasphemy. Both the contemptuous scorning of sacred places and the persistent willful transgression of the commands of God and disregard for the word of God (Num. 15: 30f.), were regarded as blasphemy of the highest order by the Jews. It was the most frequent charge brought against Jesus by His enemies, the Jews, both on the grounds of His claims to divinity and His interpretation of the Law (Matt. 9:3; 26:65; Mark 2:7; John 10:33, 36). The legal punishment for blasphemy was death (Lev. 24:16), and thus Jesus' death was regarded as just by the Jews (John 8:58, 59; 10:33; 19:7). Likewise Stephen is placed under accusation for the crime of blasphemy, for which, if convicted, he might be executed, though such execution could only be carried out legally by official approval of the Roman procurator of Judaea.

The rulers had their last warning from God in His vindication of Stephen before the council, as he stood to make his defense with his face in a halo of divine glory resembling **the face of an angel** (v. 15).

B. STEPHEN'S DEFENSE AND INDICTMENT OF THE COUNCIL (7:1-53)

A semblance of justice appears in the high priest's permission granted Stephen to answer before the Sanhedrin the charges made against him. Bruce correctly observes that Stephen's speech "is obviously not a speech for the defense in the forensic sense of the term." Bruce continues:

Such a speech as this was by no means calculated to secure an acquittal before the Sanhedrin. It is rather a defense of pure Christianity as God's appointed way of worship; Stephen here shows himself to be the precursor of the later Christian apologists, especially those who defended Christianity against Judaism.[50]

The very crux of Stephen's address re-

[50] F. F. Bruce, *Commentary on the Book of the Acts,* p. 141.

veals that he had grasped the true significance of the universality of Christianity as expressed by Christ to the Samaritan woman at the well of Jacob:

> Woman, believe me, the hour cometh, when neither in this mountain, nor in Jerusalem [the temple], shall ye worship the Father. . . . But the hour cometh, and now is, when the true worshippers shall worship the Father in spirit and truth: for such doth the Father seek to be his worshippers. God is a Spirit: and they that worship him must worship him in spirit and truth (John 4:21b-24).

1. Stephen's Address to the Council (7:1, 2a)

1 And the high priest said, Are these things so? 2 And he said, Brethren and fathers, hearken:

Addressing the council as **brethren and fathers,** or fellow Jews and official rulers, thus respectfully identifying himself with the nationality and the religion of his accusers, Stephen proceeds to reply to the charges. This same mark of sympathetic identification with the audience addressed is in evidence in each of Peter's and Paul's recorded public addresses. It will characterize the successful gospel minister's message today, or in any day.

2. Stephen's Answer to the First Charge (7:2b-37)

2 The God of glory appeared unto our father Abraham, when he was in Mesopotamia, before he dwelt in Haran, 3 and said unto him, Get thee out of thy land, and from thy kindred, and come into the land which I shall show thee. 4 Then came he out of the land of the Chaldaeans, and dwelt in Haran: and from thence, when his father was dead, *God* removed him into this land, wherein ye now dwell: 5 and he gave him none inheritance in it, no, not so much as to set his foot on: and he promised that he would give it to him in possession, and to his seed after him, when *as yet* he had no child. 6 And God spake on this wise, that his seed should sojourn in a strange land, and that they should bring them into bondage, and treat them ill, four hundred years. 7 And the nation to which they shall be in bondage will I judge, said God: and after that shall they come forth, and serve me in this place. 8 And he gave him the covenant of circumcision: and so *Abraham* begat Isaac,

and circumcised him the eighth day; and Isaac *begat* Jacob, and Jacob the twelve patriarchs. 9 And the patriarchs, moved with jealousy against Joseph, sold him into Egypt: and God was with him, 10 and delivered him out of all his afflictions, and gave him favor and wisdom before Pharaoh king of Egypt; and he made him governor over Egypt and all his house. 11 Now there came a famine over all Egypt and Canaan, and great affliction: and our fathers found no sustenance. 12 But when Jacob heard that there was grain in Egypt, he sent forth our fathers the first time. 13 And at the second time Joseph was made known to his brethren; and Joseph's race became manifest unto Pharaoh. 14 And Joseph sent, and called to him Jacob his father, and all his kindred, three score and fifteen souls. 15 And Jacob went down into Egypt; and he died, himself and our fathers; 16 and they were carried over unto Shechem, and laid in the tomb that Abraham bought for a price in silver of the sons of Hamor in Shechem. 17 But as the time of the promise drew nigh which God vouchsafed unto Abraham, the people grew and multiplied in Egypt, 18 till there arose another king over Egypt, who knew not Joseph. 19 The same dealt craftily with our race, and ill-treated our fathers, that they should cast out their babes to the end they might not live. 20 At which season Moses was born, and was exceeding fair; and he was nourished three months in his father's house: 21 and when he was cast out Pharaoh's daughter took him up, and nourished him for her own son. 22 And Moses was instructed in all the wisdom of the Egyptians; and he was mighty in his words and works. 23 But when he was well-nigh forty years old, it came into his heart to visit his brethren the children of Israel. 24 And seeing one *of them* suffer wrong, he defended him, and avenged him that was oppressed, smiting the Egyptian: 25 and he supposed that his brethren understood that God by his hand was giving them deliverance; but they understood not. 26 And the day following he appeared unto them as they strove, and would have set them at one again, saying, Sirs, ye are brethren; why do ye wrong one to another? 27 But he that did his neighbor wrong thrust him away, saying, Who made thee a ruler and a judge over us? 28 Wouldest thou kill me, as thou killedst the Egyptian yesterday? 29 And Moses fled at this saying, and became a sojourner in the land of Midian, where he begat two sons. 30 And when forty years were fulfilled, an angel appeared to him in the wilderness of Mount Sinai, in a flame of fire in a bush. 31 And when Moses saw it, he wondered at the sight: and as he drew near to behold, there came a voice of the Lord, 32 I am the God of thy fathers, the God of Abraham, and of Isaac, and of Jacob. And Moses trembled, and durst not behold. 33 And the Lord said unto him, Loose the shoes from thy feet: for the place whereon thou standest is holy ground. 34 I have surely seen the affliction of my people that is in Egypt, and have heard their groaning, and I am come down to deliver them: and now come, I will send thee into Egypt. 35 This Moses whom they refused, saying, Who made thee a ruler and a judge? him hath God sent *to be* both a ruler and a deliverer with the hand of the angel that appeared to him in the bush. 36 This man led them forth, having wrought wonders and signs in Egypt, and in the Red sea, and in the wilderness forty years. 37 This is that Moses, who said unto the children of Israel, A prophet shall God raise up unto you from among your brethren, like unto me.

The God of glory appeared. . . . This is that Moses, who said unto the children of Israel, A prophet shall God raise up unto you from among your brethren, like unto me (vv. 2b, 37). By a studied and extended recounting of Jewish history, with which his hearers are familiar, Stephen reflects his extreme reverence for, and faith in, both God and His servant Moses and thus refutes their charge that he blasphemed God and Moses.

The facility with which Stephen relates the history of God's chosen people, from the call of Abraham in Ur to the giving of the Law on Sinai, reveals both his thorough knowledge of those historical facts and his grasp of their spiritual significance, culminating in the promise of the Messiah (v. 37b; cf. Deut. 18:15 and Acts 3:22). Thus Stephen shows, not only that he believes in and reverences God and Moses, but that God through Moses prepared the way for the coming of the Christ whom he preached. Instead of blaspheming God and Moses, as they charged, Stephen shows that faith in God and Moses is established through faith in Christ, who is the Son of the first and the fulfillment of the type of the second.

3. Stephen's Answer to the Third Charge (7:38-43)

38 This is he that was in the church in the wilderness with the angel that spake to him in the mount Sinai, and with our fathers: who received living oracles to give unto us: 39 to whom our fathers would not be obedient, but thrust him from them, and turned back in their hearts unto Egypt, 40 saying unto Aaron, Make us gods that shall go before us: for as for this Moses, who led us forth out of the land of Egypt, we know not what is become of him. 41 And they made a calf in those days, and brought a sacrifice unto the idol, and rejoiced in the works of their hands. 42 But God turned, and gave them up to serve the host of heaven; as it is written in the book of the prophets,

Did ye offer unto me slain beasts and sacrifices
Forty years in the wilderness, O house of Israel?
43 And ye took up the tabernacle of Moloch,
And the star of the god Rephan,
The figures which ye made to worship them:
And I will carry you away beyond Babylon.

Stephen continues his defense by indicating that Moses was part and parcel of the true **church** [of God] **in the wilderness** (v. 38a), which culminated in Christ the Messiah, and that it was by the hand of this Moses that God, through an angel, gave Israel the Law, the living oracles. Further, he shows from their own history that their fathers had rejected Moses and the Law which God gave them through him; while he, Stephen, rather than blaspheming the Law, reverenced it for what it was intended of God: **living oracles** designed as a "tutor to bring us unto Christ" (Gal. 3:24b).

4. Stephen's Answer to the Second Charge (7:44-50)

44 Our fathers had the tabernacle of the testimony in the wilderness, even as he appointed who spake unto Moses, that he should make it according to the figure that he had seen. 45 Which also our fathers, in their turn, brought in with Joshua when they entered on the possession of the nations, that God thrust out before the face of our fathers, unto the days of David; 46 who found favor in the sight of God, and asked to find a

habitation for the God of Jacob. 47 But Solomon built him a house. 48 Howbeit the Most High dwelleth not in *houses* made with hands; as saith the prophet, 49 The heaven is my throne,
And the earth the footstool of my feet: What manner of house will ye build me? saith the Lord:
Or what is the place of my rest?
50 Did not my hand make all these things?

Our fathers had the tabernacle of the testimony in the wilderness (v. 44a). Stephen replies to the charge of blasphemy against the temple by showing that God was worshipped by the Israelites in the wilderness in the tabernacle which was God's pattern for the temple which was later to be constructed by Solomon. However, he clearly implies that the true spiritual worship of God is not confined to material buildings, and that as God was worshipped in the wilderness before there was a temple, so He may now be worshipped without the temple: **Howbeit the Most High[51] dwelleth not in houses made with hands. . . . The heaven is my throne, And the earth the footstool of my feet** (vv. 48, 49a). To this very fact their own prophet has borne testimony: **as saith the prophet,** (v. 48b; cf. I Kings 8:27; II Chron. 2:6; 6:18).

5. Stephen's Indictment of the Council (7:51-53)

51 Ye stiffnecked and uncircumcised in heart and ears, ye do always resist the Holy Spirit: as your fathers did, so do ye. 52 Which of the prophets did not your fathers persecute? and they killed them that showed before of the coming of the Righteous One; of whom ye have now become betrayers and murderers; 53 ye who received the law as it was ordained by angels, and kept it not.

Ye stiffnecked and uncircumcised in heart and ears, ye do always resist the Holy Spirit; as your fathers did, so do ye (v. 51). Finally, having incontestably cleared himself of the charge of blasphemy, Stephen turns the whole argument on the rulers of the Jews and directly indicts them with the height of the crime of blasphemy, through their willful and persistent disobedience to, and rejection of, God's Law and its realized fulfillment in Jesus Christ their Messiah (see

[51] See Additional Note VI, *The High-God Theory.*

Num. 15:30, 31). Thus he has established two great facts: *first,* that, as Paul later stated (Gal. 3:23-26), the Law only served to bring man to Christ, and that its instrumental value is now past, since Christ the Messiah has already come; and *second,* that they, his accusers, themselves stand inescapably condemned for the very crime of which they have accused him, blasphemy, which carries the penalty of death.

C. STEPHEN'S GLORIOUS MARTYRDOM (7:54-60)

Stephen became the first Christian martyr, and he gave his life that the gospel might be unshackled from Jewish legalism to find its way to the hearts of all men throughout the world.

1. The Council's Indignation (7:54)

54 Now when they heard these things, they were cut to the heart, and they gnashed on him with their teeth.

Weymouth says, "They became infuriated and gnashed their teeth at him." The realization of their humiliating situation, after Stephen's speech, should have brought them to repentance and submission to Christ, as on the day of Pentecost. However, it only inflamed their wrath and dethroned their reason, and thus an orderly and dignified court suddenly became a scene of mob-mad chaotic violence. The volcano had long smouldered, but now it suddenly burst forth in all of its destructive fury, inundating its innocent victim with its scalding wrath.

2. The Consolation of Stephen (7:55, 56)

55 But he, being full of the Holy Spirit, looked up stedfastly into heaven, and saw the glory of God, and Jesus standing on the right hand of God, 56 and said, Behold, I see the heavens opened, and the Son of man standing on the right hand of God.

But he . . . saw the glory of God. Through the hail of death-stones, Stephen caught a vision of God's revealed glory that was laid up in store for him and saw Jesus standing on the right hand of God, in identification with His martyred saint, waiting to receive him into everlasting glory. It is said that this is the only scriptural record of Christ standing, after His ascension. With David, Stephen could say: "Yea, though I walk through the valley of the shadow of death, I will fear no evil; for thou art with me" (Ps. 23:4a).

3. The Council's Illegal Procedure (7: 57, 58)

57 But they cried out with a loud voice, and stopped their ears, and rushed upon him with one accord; 58 and they cast him out of the city, and stoned him: and the witnesses laid down their garments at the feet of a young man named Saul.

Justice and legality were thrown to the wind as the rulers, **with one accord,** rushed upon the defendant and, without verdict or sentence, dragged him out of the city and violently stoned him to death. Nor had the Jewish Sanhedrin the right of execution without Roman authority, with one exception (see note on Acts 4:5, 6). This was reserved for the Roman government. Thus Stephen's death was a violent, unjust, and illegal murder at the hands of the Jewish rulers, though the people of Acts 6:12 may have been employed as their unwitting instruments.

4. The Prayer of Stephen (7:59, 60a)

59 And they stoned Stephen, calling upon *the Lord,* and saying, Lord Jesus, receive my spirit. 60 And he kneeled down, and cried with a loud voice, Lord, lay not this sin to their charge.

Amidst the confusion and fury of violent death, Stephen makes two requests. *First,* he prays for the privilege of continued identification with his Master: **Lord Jesus, receive my spirit.** *Second,* he prays for his enemies: **Lord, lay not this sin to their charge.** St. Augustine is reported to have said, "If Stephen had not prayed, Saul would not have been converted." Saul heard Stephen's prayer. How like the Master's dying prayer was that of Stephen (Luke 23:34a)! Some of Christ's own murderers may have heard both the dying prayer of the Master and that of His martyred saint, Stephen.

5. The Death of Stephen (7:60b)

60 And when he had said this he fell asleep.

Luke had caught the spirit of hope that animated the first Christians when he recorded, concerning Stephen's death, **he fell asleep.** Taylor remarks: "Such a mode of speech suggests a future awakening."[52] Thereafter the Christians appear to have largely substituted the word "sleep" for "death," in the event of the decease of a Christian (cf. John 11:23-26; I Cor. 15; I Thess. 4:13-18). The word bespeaks the continuance of the new life which they already enjoyed. It suggests that they had grasped the significance of immortality through Christ.

Vincent significantly observes concerning Stephen's death, as expressed in the words, **he fell asleep,** that this expression marks

> . . . his calm and peaceful death. Though the pagan authors sometimes used *sleep* to signify *death,* it was only as a poetic figure. When Christ, on the other hand, said, 'Our friend Lazarus *sleepeth* . . .,' he used the word, not as a figure, but as the expression of a *fact.* In the mystery of death, in which the pagan saw only nothingness, Jesus saw continued life, rest, waking — the elements which enter into sleep. And thus, in Christian speech and thought, as the doctrine of the resurrection struck its roots deeper, the word *dead,* with its hopeless finality, gave place to the more gracious and hopeful word *sleep.* The pagan burying-place carried in its name no suggestion of hope or comfort. It was a *burying-place,* a *hiding-place,* a *monumentum,* a mere *memorial* of something gone; a *columbarium* or dove-cot, with its little pigeonholes for cinerary urns; but the Christian thought of death as sleep, brought with it into Christian speech the kindred thought of a chamber of rest, and embodied it in the word *cemetery* . . . the place to lie down to sleep.[53]

IX. THE CHURCH'S FIRST DISPERSION (Acts 8:1-25)

A. THE ORIGIN OF THE DISPERSION (8:1-4)

1 And Saul was consenting unto his death.

52 William M. Taylor, *Paul the Missionary*, p. 23.
53 Marvin R. Vincent, *Word Studies in the New Testament*, I, 486.

And there arose on that day a great persecution against the church which was in Jerusalem; and they were all scattered abroad throughout the regions of Judaea and Samaria, except the apostles. 2 And devout men buried Stephen, and made great lamentation over him. 3 But Saul laid waste the church, entering into every house, and dragging men and women committed them to prison.

4 They therefore that were scattered abroad went about preaching the word.

Prior to the incident of this record, Christian evangelization, since Pentecost, had been confined to Jerusalem, as far as we know. Nor does there appear to be any scriptural evidence that the "apostles" as yet envisioned their responsibility for world-wide evangelization. Indeed Christ had so commissioned them (Matt. 28:18-20; Acts 1:8), but the larger significance of that commission had not as yet dawned upon them. As stated previously, it was Stephen, a Hellenist Jew, who first caught this larger vision of the gospel for the whole world, and who paid for its declaration with his life.

Devout men buried Stephen, and made great lamentation over him (v. 2). Jewish law forbade public mourning at the death of a condemned criminal. Thus the **great lamentation** over Stephen testified to his innocence and the illegality of his martyrdom. Nor was the body of a criminal buried by official Judaism (see Christ's burial, Matt. 27:57-60; John 19:28-42).

It was Stephen's heroic and glorious death that shattered the iron bars of Jewish legalism and emancipated the gospel of Christ for world-wide dissemination. The corn of wheat fell into the ground and died, and it brought forth much fruit (John 12:24). Stephen means "crown," and thus he was the first to wear the "Christian martyr's crown" (see Rev. 2:10). He had "fallen asleep" that a great spiritual awakening might occur. God buries His workmen, but His work goes on.

Stephen's death was followed by the first organized, systematic, concerted persecution of the disciples, which appears to have been directed primarily against the Hellenist Christians who had caught the larger vision of the gospel from Stephen. Under the impact of persecu-

tion, the disciples were **scattered abroad** (thus far they had been concentrated in Jerusalem) **throughout the regions of Judaea and Samaria, except the apostles.** This dissemination was in accord with Christ's command (Matt. 10:23), not for the security of the disciples, but for the spread of the Gospel. It is noteworthy that the apostles are excepted in the scattering: **except the apostles** (v. 1b), which probably indicates that the persecution fell mainly on the Hellenist disciples, but not on the Jewish Christian apostles.

Saul, who probably was a member of the Cilician synagogue and had been worsted in debate with Stephen (Acts 6:9), who guarded the garments of Stephen's murderers (Acts 7:58b), and who had given his full consent to Stephen's martyrdom (Acts 8:1a), now becomes the ringleader of the Jewish official persecution of the Christians. **Saul laid waste the church.** Disregarding the rights of domestic privacy and sex differences, he hunted down Christians wherever they might be found and **committed them to prison** (v. 3b). What a dark day for the church, but what unforeseen blessed results. The concentrated blaze of divine glory in Jerusalem was thereby scattered to become a devouring fire throughout the regions beyond (see Rom. 1:8; Col. 1:6). **They therefore that were scattered abroad** [because of the persecution] **went about** [everywhere] **preaching the word** (v. 4). "Surely the wrath of man shall praise thee: The residue of wrath shalt thou gird upon thee [restrain]" (Ps. 76: 10).

B. PHILIP AND THE SAMARITAN MISSION (8:5-13)[54]

The author of Acts seems to single out, from among the many witnessing activities of the disciples scattered abroad under the terrible persecution of Saul, the case of Philip as an example of the tenor of those disciples.

1. The Ministry of Philip (8:5)

5 And Philip went down to the city of Samaria, and proclaimed unto them the Christ.

Philip, like Stephen, was one of the seven lay officers chosen to supervise the

---

[54] See Additional Note VII, *Samaria and the Samaritans.*

temporal affairs of the church (Acts 6:5). Also, like Stephen, he was doubtless a Hellenist Christian, who with a heart aflame for Christ and a mind illumined by the larger vision of the gospel for the whole world, derived from the teachings and example of Stephen, found himself among the scattered Hellenist disciples who had gone about [everywhere] preaching the word. This Philip is not to be confused with the Apostle Philip. In evidence of this fact, the apostles did not leave Jerusalem under the persecution of Saul (v. 1b), nor until they were apprised of the revival in Samaria. A later note on Philip the deacon, who from a lay church officer became an effective evangelist, is found in Acts 21:8, 9. Exactly what city of Samaria Philip went to, whether Sebaste the capital or possibly Sychar, is not certain, nor important. It may have been the latter, where Christ saw the Samaritan woman and many others converted (John 4:3-42). It evidently was a populous center, and it represented the transition of the gospel from the Jews to the Gentiles. The Samaritans were a racially mixed Jewish-Gentile people, and quite as mongrel in religion. Consequently, they were more despised by the Jews than were the Gentiles. Philip's going down to the city of Samaria only indicates the greater importance of Jerusalem, and not geographic elevation. There he preached to these Samaritans Christ as the Messiah, whom they expected, both from the Jewish Scriptures which they possessed and from Christ's earlier ministry among them.

2. The Response of the Samaritans (8: 6)

6 And the multitudes gave heed with one accord unto the things that were spoken by Philip, when they heard, and saw the signs which he did.

The height of this expectancy of the coming Messiah quickened these semipagan Samaritans to perceive in Philip's preaching of Christ, from the Jewish Scriptures (Acts 8:35), the fulfillment of those Scriptures and of their personal hopes, which faith was confirmed by the accompanying demonstrations of divine power and approval in the miracles wrought among them through Philip (cf.

Thess. 1:5). Thus the multitudes gave heed with one accord, or with one mind, to Philip's message. That they tended to credulity appears evident from verse 10, but that they had solid ground for their faith in Christ through Philip's ministry is certain from verse 12. The expression, gave heed, is meant to suggest an obedience of faith unto salvation on the part of the people, and not merely a mental assent or mere interest.

3. The Success of the Mission (8:7, 8)

7 For from many of those that had unclean spirits, they came out, crying with a loud voice: and many that were palsied, and that were lame, were healed. 8 And there was much joy in that city.

The validity of demon possession and expulsion among the Samaritans, as opposed to the view that they were merely insane persons whose delusions took the form of a belief that they were possessed, appears evident from two considerations. *First,* Luke clearly states that they were unclean spirits and indicates that their personalities are evident from the fact of their crying with a loud voice as they came out. Indeed Matthew refers to lunatics who were healed by Christ, but in the same passage he also mentions the demon possessed as a different class (Matt. 4:24, 25). Luke, who was a physician and thus well qualified to judge the nature of maladies of his day, both here and in the case of the Gadarene (see Luke 8:26-36), refers clearly to demon possession. *Second,* the author clearly differentiates, in this passage, between demon possession and the disease of palsy and afflictions of lameness, both of which later are healed, while the former is expelled. Little wonder that there should have been much joy in the hearts and homes of emancipated and healed individuals restored to normality. The gospel wrought social and economic benefits, as well as physical and spiritual.

4. The Case of Simon the Sorcerer (8: 9-13)

9 But there was a certain man, Simon by name, who beforetime in the city used sorcery, and amazed the people of Samaria giving out that himself was some great one: 10 to whom they all gave heed, from the least to the greatest, saying,

This man is that power of God which is called Great. 11 And they gave heed to him, because that of long time he had amazed them with his sorceries. 12 But when they believed Philip preaching good tidings concerning the 'kingdom of God and the name of Jesus Christ, they were baptized, both men and women. 13 And Simon also himself believed: and being baptized, he continued with Philip; and beholding signs and great miracles wrought, he was amazed.

It is sufficient to note that this Simon was one of the many opportunist wizards of the land in his day who took advantage of the prevalent expectation of a Messiah popularized by the Jews of the *Diaspora* and played upon the credulity of the people with the practices of conjuring, juggling, and soothsaying. Probably a superpsychic, as well as a trickster and a demon-trafficker, this man had for long amazed the Samaritans and held them bound under his spells of sorcery. These spells were validated, in the minds of the people, by his claim to be **some great one.** Actually he professed deity, and many unsubstantiated legends about him grew up even in the church. Simon himself was put to consternation by the genuine miracles and wonders wrought through Philip, and then, motivated by selfish evil desires, he professed faith in Christ, was baptized and for a time followed Philip and studied most diligently *the signs and great miracles wrought* by Philip (v. 13b). There appears to be little grounds for a belief in his genuine conversion under Philip.

C. THE APOSTLES AND THE SAMARITAN MISSION (8:14-25)

It is noteworthy that the apostles were excepted in the scattering of the disciples under persecution at the martyrdom of Stephen (v. 1b). This likely indicates that the persecution fell mainly on the Hellenist disciples because of their larger vision of the gospel for the Gentile world, as Stephen clearly indicated in his defense. Too, it likely indicates that the apostles as yet had thought of the gospel of Christ for the Jews only.

1. The Apostles' Commission (8:14)

14 Now when the apostles that were at Jerusalem heard that Samaria had received the word of God, they sent unto them Peter and John:

News of the reception of the gospel of Christ by the Samaritans was indeed epochal. The word indicates something of a national turning to Christ and not just a revival in a given city. A meeting of the apostolate in Jerusalem was immediately called, and official decision was made to dispatch Peter and John to Samaria with full powers to act in whatever capacity they deemed wise in the interest of the church. This is the first action of its kind recorded of the Jerusalem apostles.

2. The Apostles' Confirmation (8:15-17)

15 who, when they were come down, prayed for them, that they might receive the Holy Spirit: 16 for as yet it was fallen upon none of them: only they had been baptized into the name of the Lord Jesus. 17 Then laid they their hands on them, and they received the Holy Spirit.

Most authorities seem to agree that the mission of Peter and John to Samaria was to consecrate or ordain, through the imposition of hands and prayer on the human side, and through the special gifts of the Holy Spirit on the divine side, certain of the Samaritans for special Christian service to their own people. While this may be true, it cannot be denied that with the manifestation of the Holy Spirit, in whatever capacity, there is always the sanctifying efficacy of the holiness of His personal presence. Whether the Samaritans were sanctified on this occasion or another, they were sanctified by the Holy Spirit (Acts 15:8, 9). Thus the apostles recognized, approved, and confirmed that God had visited with salvation the Samaritans also.

3. The Apostles' Rebuke of Simon (8:18-24)

18 Now when Simon saw that through the laying on of the apostles' hands the Holy Spirit was given, he offered them money, 19 saying, Give me also this power, that on whomsoever I lay my hands, he may receive the Holy Spirit. 20 But Peter said unto him, Thy silver perish with thee, because thou hast thought to obtain the gift of God with money. 21 Thou hast neither part nor

lot in this matter: for thy heart is not right before God. 22 Repent therefore of this thy wickedness, and pray the Lord, if perhaps the thought of thy heart shall be forgiven thee. 23 For I see that thou art in the gall of bitterness and in the bond of iniquity. 24 And Simon answered and said, Pray ye for me to the Lord, that none of the things which ye have spoken come upon me.

Verses 18-24 present the true character of another impostor who, like Ananias, desired Christian connections and divine powers for selfish reasons. He had previously amazed the people with his magic and sorcery before professing Christianity. If he could but obtain these special gifts of the Holy Spirit by the imposition of the apostles' hands, he would be able to supersede his former practices and powers and thus his fame and fortune would grow greatly. He makes his request, and Peter, perceiving the wickedness of his heart, delivers to him the withering rebuke contained in verses 20, 21, and 23, and then exhorts him to true repentance and earnest prayer to God for forgiveness. Simon, still thinking magically, asks the prayers of Peter, not for salvation, but that he might escape the consequent judgment of his evil (v. 24). Luke does not relate the sequel, and we are left to conjecture the outcome.

4. The Apostles' Evangelization (8:25)

25 They therefore, when they had testified and spoken the word of the Lord, returned to Jerusalem, and preached the gospel to many villages of the Samaritans.

So enlightened and inspired by God's visitation of the Samaritans with salvation were Peter and John, that as they returned to Jerusalem, they engaged in the evangelization of the villages of the very people upon whom James and John once besought the Master for permission to "bid fire to come down from heaven, and consume them."

X. THE CHURCH'S FIRST AFRICAN CONVERT (Acts 8:26-40)

A. THE MESSENGER OF GOD (8:26-30, 40)

When God has a special mission to perform, He does not appoint someone who is sitting idly by waiting for something to do, but rather chooses one who is actively engaged in the task at hand. Philip was such, and he became God's messenger for the special missionary undertaking in relation to the Ethiopian nobleman. We have already observed Philip engaged in the successful evangelization of the Samaritans. Mighty miracles and powerful conversions were occurring under his ministry among the people, until it could be said that **Samaria had received the word of God** (v. 14). Likewise, after this mission was completed, **Philip . . . passing through . . . preached the gospel to all the cities, till he came to Caesarea** (v. 40).

1. The Messenger's Commission (8:26)

26 But an angel of the Lord spake unto Philip, saying, Arise, and go toward the south unto the way that goeth down from Jerusalem unto Gaza: the the same is desert.

It appears most unusual that God should have commissioned Philip, who was being so successfully used in the evangelization of the Samaritans, to leave his labors there among the hungry hearted multitudes and depart to an uninhabited wilderness in southern Palestine. Since there were several roads leading to Gaza, and God knew well the road over which the nobleman would return to his native land from Jerusalem, he specifies to Philip the exact route to follow, **the way that goeth down from Jerusalem unto Gaza.** It is always safe to follow His directions.

2. The Messenger's Obedience (8:27a)

27 And he arose and went:

Philip was not only living near enough to God to receive His instructions, but his unbounded faith prompted him to immediate obedience to God's will. Had he been a day late, or perhaps even an hour, he would have missed the opportunity of his lifetime to witness the conversion of a great foreign nobleman. Indeed there are times when "the king's business [requires] haste" (I Sam. 21:8b).

3. The Messenger's Opportunity (8:27b, 28)

27 and behold, a man of Ethiopia, a eunuch of great authority under

Candace, queen of the Ethiopians, who was over all her treasure, who had come to Jerusalem to worship; 28 and he was returning and sitting in his chariot, and was reading the prophet Isaiah.

The Ethiopian was most likely a negro from the country south of Egypt in Africa which included the modern Nubia, Cordofan, and northern Abyssinia, of which great kingdom he was treasurer under the queen who bore the dynastic title of Candace. He may not have been a eunuch, in the literal sense of the word, but bore the title as was common with ancient oriental high court officials (see Gen. 37:36 with marginal notes). This important officer was evidently a Jew by religion who had been to Jerusalem to worship at the temple. He most likely was only a *proselyte of the gate*. He was returning and reading en route the prophecy of Isaiah. He clearly expected the Messiah, as all Jews did. This was Philip's opportunity!

4. The Messenger's Approach (8:29, 30)

29 And the Spirit said unto Philip, Go near, and join thyself to this chariot. 30 And Philip ran to him, and heard him reading Isaiah the prophet, and said, Understandest thou what thou readest?

Philip, whose faith in God had been rewarded in the finding of the hungry-hearted Ethiopian, was quick to respond to the Spirit's prompting to **Go near, and join thyself to this chariot** (v. 29b). **And Philip ran** [thither] **to him** (v. 30a). The nobleman may have appeared to be out of the class of the humble, dust-covered Christian disciple by the way, but God's servants must be ready to reach up for spiritual fruit as well as down. There is a suggestion of sympathetic identification in those words **join thyself,** of urgency in the words **Philip ran to him,** and of wise and understanding tactfulness in Philip's question, **Understandest thou what thou readest?** This is the nobleman's interest which the evangelist wisely seeks.

B. THE SEEKER AFTER GOD (8:31-34)

The nobleman had worshipped at Jerusalem and possibly was present at Pentecost. He had reading knowledge of the Jewish Scriptures, most likely in the Alexandrian Greek version (Septuagint), and was in earnest quest of the Messiah.

1. The Seeker's Bewilderment (8:31a)

31 And he said, How can I, except some one shall guide me?

In answer to Philip's question, **Understandest thou?** he replied, **How can I?** unless I have a teacher, a guide. His bewilderment immediately opened the way for Philip's exceptional opportunity. Man's sincere quest for God will always be met by God if He can but find a human instrument through whom He can work.

2. The Seeker's Request (8:31b)

31 And he besought Philip to come up and sit with him.

The nobleman's request was both an expression of confidence in the evangelist and a gesture of courtesy and desired companionship. Clearly Philip had won both the confidence and respect of the treasurer. His invitation became the evangelist's enlarged opportunity. It is seriously doubtful if anyone is ever won to Christ until his confidence has been secured by some Christian. Herein lies the weakness of much professional evangelism.

3. The Seeker's Interest (8:32, 33)

32 Now the passage of the scripture which he was reading was this,
He was led as a sheep to the slaughter;
And as a lamb before his shearer is dumb,
So he openeth not his mouth:
33 In his humiliation his judgment was taken away:
His generation, who shall declare?
For his life is taken from the earth.

The point of his scriptural interest was most opportune. It spoke to his heart of Christ's shameful trial before Pilate: **He was led as a sheep to the slaughter;** of His non-retaliatory sufferings: **so he openeth not his mouth;** of the ignominy and injustice of the treatment accorded Him: **in his humiliation** [sufferings] **his judgment was taken away** [or, He was denied justice]; of the immeasurable wickedness of His opposers and murderers: **His generation who shall declare** [or declare their wickedness]; and of His death: **his** life is taken from the earth. Such a record is sufficient to awaken the moral and spiritual interest of any sincere soul.

4. The Seeker's Question (8:34)

34 And the eunuch answered Philip, and said, I pray thee, of whom speaketh the prophet this? of himself, or of some other?

The height of interest had become so great in the nobleman's mind that he broke forth with a demand for an explanation. This is always the crucial point in dealing with the sincere seeker after God. It is only the man who knows God himself that can lead another to Christ at this juncture. Philip had patiently and painstakingly awaited this moment. The clock had struck, and now it was Philip's time and turn to speak, and he spoke in season.

C. THE READY INSTRUCTOR (8:35-37)

There are many who can talk about religion, but there are few indeed who can instruct men into a saving relationship with the Lord Jesus Christ, as did Philip in dealing with the Ethiopian.

1. The Evangelist's Wisdom (8:35a)

35 And Philip opened his mouth,

There is a time to listen to the sorrows, griefs, and longings of others, and there is a time to speak forth in instruction and consolation. Philip had listened until he knew well the thoughts and secret desires of his spiritual patient and then he **opened his mouth** and spoke forth with assurance and certainty. Starting at the point of the seeker's greatest interest and question, concerning the Scripture under consideration, Philip **preached** unto him Jesus. It is always at man's point of extremity that God's greatest opportunity presents itself. Happy and wise is the soul winner who can detect that point. "He that is wise winneth souls" (Prov. 11:30).

2. The Evangelist's Message (8:35b)

35 and beginning from this scripture, preached unto him Jesus.

The nobleman earnestly sought, in the Jewish Scriptures, for the Messiah promised by the prophets. Christ the Messiah is the ultimate object of the earnest and sincere religious quest of every man. Many indeed are not following, in their religious quests, the road that leads to God in Christ. This man had found in the Old Testament Scriptures an intimation of the fulfillment of his hopes. Philip began with Isaiah's prophecy of the Christ, the Messiah, and showed the nobleman that this Jesus, of whom he may have heard, was the fulfillment of that Messianic prophecy, and thus the Savior of all men. Evangelism that does not lead to Christ misses the mark.

3. The Seeker's Conversion (8:36)

36 And as they went on the way, they came unto a certain water; and the eunuch saith, Behold, *here is* water; what doth hinder me to be baptized?

Though omitted by the American Standard Version, the King James Version includes verse 37, which reads in part: "I believe that Jesus Christ is the Son of God." The Ethiopian's request for baptism expressed in his words, **Behold, here is water; what doth hinder me to be baptized?** indicates that Philip's instruction in salvation, even to the outward sign of water baptism, had been thorough, even perhaps well beyond the conversation recorded in Acts. It also indicates the genuineness and sincerity of the man's conversion. But Philip, anxious for a thorough commitment and open confession of Christ, replied: "If thou believest with all thy heart, thou mayest." Philip wanted no halfway conversion of a man who would return to his pagan countrymen with an opportunity for a wide and vital witness to Christ. His open confession, "I believe that Jesus Christ is the Son of God," fully satisfied the evangelist of his thorough conversion to Christ. "For with the heart man believeth unto righteousness; and with the mouth confession is made unto salvation" (Rom. 10:10).

D. THE JOYFUL CONVERT (8:38-40)

Philip's personal evangelistic efforts led the Ethiopian to wholehearted faith in Christ, an open confession of Christ, and a joyous experience with Christ.

1. The Convert's Baptism (8:38)

38 And he commanded the chariot to stand still: and they both went down into the water, both Philip and the eunuch; and he baptized him.

The Ethiopian's baptism reveals four things: *first,* that personal salvation precedes water baptism (see v. 37) ; *second,* that water baptism was a recognized practice of the apostolic church (Matt. 28:19) ; *third,* that performance of the rite of baptism was not restricted to the apostles, since Philip was but a lay evangelist; and *fourth,* that water baptism, whether by immersion or otherwise, was but an outward sign or testimony to the inner-soul work of grace.

2. The Evangelist's Disappearance (8:39a)

39 And when they came up out of the water, the Spirit of the Lord caught away Philip; and the eunuch saw him no more,

Without questioning the miraculous disappearance of Philip, let us note the practical effects of that disappearance on the convert. *First,* he was thus early weaned from dependence on the human instrument of his new faith; and *second,* he was left wholly dependent on God and the Scriptures for the sustenance and development of his new Christian life. Little wonder that tradition has assigned to this man the early evangelization of Ethiopia.

3. The Convert's Joy (8:39b)

39 for he went on his way rejoicing.

The Ethiopian continued in the course of his former life, but now with a new life in Christ. His joy consisted in the soul rest and satisfaction found in Christ, and in the glorious prospect of carrying his new faith to his native countrymen where his influential position gave him a great advantage for Christ and righteousness.

4. The Evangelist's Continued Ministry (8:40)

40 But Philip was found at Azotus: and passing through he preached the gospel to all the cities, till he came to Caesarea.

The expression, **But Philip was found at Azotus,** is meant to convey the idea, Wesley thinks, that "Probably none saw him from his leaving the eunuch till he was there."[55] The distance from Gaza, near which place Philip likely met the eunuch, was about twenty miles to Azotus. From here he carried out an evangelizing mission until he reached **Caesarea,** the Roman capital of Judaea and an important seaport, where Philip eventually settled and reared his family, including four unmarried daughters who were prophetesses. **All the cities** which Philip evangelized must have included Ashdod, Ekron, Joppa, Jamnia, Ascalon, and Apollonia of the Philistine country, as these all lay in his course between Gaza and Caesarea. The extent of the spiritual fruitage of this evangelism we do not know, but the activities of the evangelist suggest his impelling zeal for Christ and his passion to see men brought under His Lordship. The earlier spiritual fruitage in Samaria and the conversion of the Ethiopian added their impetus to the evangelist's activities. Good fuel always causes the flames to leap higher and the fire to burn brighter. *The evangelistic ministry* of Philip may be summarized as threefold: *first,* mass evangelism at Samaria (Acts 8:5-8) ; *second,* personal evangelism, as represented in the conversion of the Ethiopian nobleman (Acts 8:26-39a) ; and *third,* itinerant evangelism, as represented by his preaching to the coastal cities (Acts 8:40) .

XI. THE CHURCH'S FIRST CONVERTED PERSECUTOR (Acts 9:1-43)

A. THE PERSECUTOR ARRESTED (9:1-9)

Whatever may have been the extent of the persecution that fell upon the church following the martyrdom of Stephen, it is evident that Saul was the ringleader of these vicious activities.

1. The Persecutor's Activities (9:1, 2)

1 But Saul, yet breathing threatening and slaughter against the disciples of the Lord, went unto the high priest, 2 and asked of him letters to Damascus unto the synagogues, that if he found

---

[55] John Wesley, *Explanatory Notes Upon the New Testament,* p. 427, n. 40.

any that were of the Way, whether men or women, he might bring them bound to Jerusalem.

At the stoning of Stephen he was present and guarded the garments of the murderers (Acts 7:58b), and Luke takes pains to say that Saul gave his full approval of the martyrdom of Stephen (Acts 8:1a). Although the author of Acts has deviated from Saul to relate the conversion of the Samaritans and the Ethiopian nobleman, he resumes the subject in chapter nine. Nor has the persecution abated in the meantime, for we read, "But Saul laid waste [made havoc] the church, entering into every house, and dragging men and women committed them to prison" (Acts 8:3). The intensity of his wrathfully destructive activities is graphically depicted in Luke's words: **But Saul, yet breathing threatening and slaughter against the disciples of the Lord.** Lange observes that "menace and slaughter constituted the vital air which he inhaled (and exhaled)."[56] Time and the growth of the church under the labors of the apostles, Philip, and the scattered disciples, only served to intensify his wrath and activities against the Christians. As a servant of the Sanhedrin, if indeed not a member, he secured warrants from the high priest for the arrest of any disciples who might be associated with the synagogue at faraway Damascus. This was a civil and religious right permitted the Jews by the Roman government concerning members of their own race. His utter disregard for Christian women is evidenced by the fact that their persecution by Saul is specifically mentioned three times in Acts (Acts 8:3; 9:2; 22:4).

The disciples, not yet called Christians, are here for the first time referred to as the people of **the Way.** The word thus used and capitalized in the ASV occurs six times in the Acts (Acts 9:2; 19:9, 23; 22:4; 24:14, 22).

2. The Persecutor's Encounter (9:3-7)

3 And as he journeyed, it came to pass that he drew nigh unto Damascus: and suddenly there shone round about him a light out of heaven: 4 and he fell upon the earth, and heard a voice saying unto him, Saul, Saul, why persecutest thou

me? 5 And he said, Who art thou, Lord? And he *said,* I am Jesus whom thou persecutest: 6 but rise, and enter into the city, and it shall be told thee what thou must do. 7 And the men that journeyed with him stood speechless, hearing the voice, but beholding no man.

Who art thou, Lord? . . . I am Jesus whom thou persecutest (v. 5). Saul's visit to Damascus in quest of Christians indicates something of the widespread of Christianity by this time, as well as his blind and cruel determination to arrest its progress, or to stamp it out completely. The light of God's ineffable glory suddenly flashed forth, probably in answer to the prayer of the Christians in Damascus who may have heard of his coming (Acts 9:13, 14), and smote the persecutor down in the road near the city. The voice of God spoke to the arrested and startled enemy of Christ, clearly reflecting that Saul's battle was not against men, but against God and His Son, who is Lord of all. The Lord, in response to Saul's question, **Who art thou, Lord?** immediately identified Himself as the Jesus whom Saul and the Jews rejected. Christ's identification of Himself with His suffering disciples is likewise very clearly intimated. Saul's inevitable capitulation is suggested by Christ's words, as recorded in the King James Version, though omitted from the American Standard Version, "it is hard for thee to kick against the pricks" (v. 5b; cf. 26:14b). Saul the persecutor, who had made many tremble under his wrath, was suddenly arrested by God and stood trembling and astonished before his conqueror, humbly inquiring for His will.

3. The Persecutor's Apprehension (9: 8, 9)

8 And Saul arose from the earth; and when his eyes were opened, he saw nothing; and they led him by the hand, and brought him into Damascus. 9 And he was three days without sight, and did neither eat nor drink.

And he was three days without sight (v. 9a). When man will not heed the overtures of God's mercy, he will have to suffer the judgments of the Lord. He who had dragged innocent men and wom-

---

[56] Lange, *op. cit.,* p. 161.

en away from their homes to prison in chains was now so helpless that he required to be led about by the hand. Startled, shocked, humbled, and blinded by the stroke of God, for three days Saul groped helplessly about, eating nothing. He was led, a harmless captive of God, into the very city from which he had purposed to ruthlessly take captive the disciples of God's Son. He had gone to Damascus to imprison Christ's disciples, but he had been arrested by their Master, and for a time was imprisoned in the dismal dungeon of sightlessness that he might become the disciple and loving servant of Christ ever after. Paul later reflects this experience in his words, as Weymouth translates them: "I press on, striving to lay hold of that for which I was also laid hold of by Christ Jesus" (Phil. 3:12b; cf. Williams' translation).

B. THE PERSECUTOR CONVERTED (9:10-18)

The conversion of Saul was so momentous that Luke thrice records the event in the Acts (9:1-19; 22:5-21; 26:12-20). Contributing to the conversion of Saul was his likely unsuccessful dispute with Stephen, as a member of the Cilician synagogue (Acts 6:9, 10); the profound impression made on his mind by Stephen's defense, as evidenced by the similarities in all his later recorded messages and arguments to Stephen's address; the practical demonstrations of Christianity which he must have witnessed in the lives of the disciples he so doggedly persecuted; and his growing personal sense of dissatisfaction with the inability of the Law to give peace with God, as he later records (see Rom. 7). The sudden revelation of Christ to him on the Damascus road removed the last objection, and forever convinced him that the Christian way was right. It was this personal appearance of Christ to him upon which he ever after relied to validate his apostleship (Acts 22:7-11, 21; I Cor. 9:1; 15:8; II Cor. 11:5; 12:12; Gal. 2:8). Dummelow significantly remarks:

> Saul's conversion at once gave Christianity a higher social status. He was an educated man, of good family, a rabbi, and (probably) a member of the San-

hedrin. It could no longer be objected to the teachers of the new faith that they were all ignorant and unlettered men.[57]

1. The Human Agent (9:10)

10 Now there was a certain disciple at Damascus, named Ananias; and the Lord said unto him in a vision, Ananias. And he said, Behold, I *am here*, Lord.

Ananias may have been the leader of the Christian disciples at Damascus. Tradition holds that he was one of the Seven, later consecrated a bishop of Damascus by Andrew and Peter, and that he finally became a martyr. He is later described by Luke as "a devout man according to the law, well reported of by all the Jews that dwelt there" (Acts 22:12). That these Damascus disciples were still worshipping in the Jewish synagogue appears evident (v. 2).

2. The Divine Commission (9:11, 12)

11 And the Lord *said* unto him, Arise, and go to the street which is called Straight, and inquire in the house of Judas for one named Saul, a man of Tarsus: for behold, he prayeth; 12 and he hath seen a man named Ananias coming in, and laying his hands on him, that he might receive his sight.

The task assigned Ananias was indeed a hazardous one, as humanly viewed, but it was definite and specific. Judas' house was likely the regular lodging place of Saul when in Damascus. Here Luke records perhaps the most hopeful news that the disciples had received since the death of Stephen. **Behold,** said the Lord to Ananias concerning the former persecutor, **he prayeth.** As God prepared Ananias for his mission to Saul by a vision, He at the same time prepared Saul for Ananias' visit.

3. The Human Objection (9:13, 14)

13 But Ananias answered, Lord, I have heard from many of this man, how much evil he did to thy saints at Jerusalem: 14 and here he hath authority from the chief priests to bind all that call upon thy name.

Ananias' objection rested, *first,* on the cruelties of Saul against the disciples at Jerusalem, which were well known at

Damascus; and *second,* on the fact that Saul was authorized by the high priest to arrest all who called upon the name of Christ in connection with the synagogue at Damascus. Only a fool would walk into such a dangerous trap, Ananias objected.

4. The Divine Purpose (9:15, 16)

15 But the Lord said unto him, Go thy way: for he is a chosen vessel unto me, to bear my name before the Gentiles and kings, and the children of Israel: 16 for I will show him how many things he must suffer for my name's sake.

Ananias' objection is met by God's renewal of the commission to fulfill his mission to Saul: **Go thy way: for he is a chosen vessel unto me,** or an instrument of choice, to carry the gospel to the Gentiles, God informed Ananias.

Saul's birth and upbringing in the Gentile city of Tarsus in Asia Minor, his theological training in the more liberal school of Gamaliel at Jerusalem, his likely graduate training in the Greek university at Tarsus,[58] and his membership in the Cilician synagogue, combined to qualify him for this great mission to the Gentiles, a mission which must entail great suffering.

5. The Divine Transformation (9:17, 18)

17 And Ananias departed, and entered into the house; and laying his hands on him said, Brother Saul, the Lord, *even* Jesus, who appeared unto thee in the way which thou camest, hath sent me, that thou mayest receive thy sight, and be filled with the Holy Spirit. 18 And straightway there fell from his eyes as it were scales, and he received his sight; and he arose and was baptized;

That this experience under the human instrumentality of Ananias culminated in the genuine conversion of Saul, which had begun with his spiritual arrest on the Damascus road, is evident from the following facts: *first,* Ananias' tender prayer and announcement of his divinely appointed mission to Saul (v. 17b); *second,* the falling away of the scales of blinding pride, prejudice, hatred, and vain imaginations that had darkened his spiritual vision; and *third,* his baptism and experience of the regenerating Holy Spirit and forgiveness of sins through prayer to God in Christ. The last is particularly evident in the account in Acts 22:16, where we read: "arise, and be baptized, and wash away thy sins, calling on his name." This spiritual transformation of Saul marks the turning point in the history of early Christianity.

C. THE PERSECUTOR PREACHES (9: 19-30)

19 and he took food and was strengthened.

And he was certain days with the disciples that were at Damascus. 20 And straightway in the synagogues he proclaimed Jesus, that he is the Son of God. 21 And all that heard him were amazed, and said, Is not this he that in Jerusalem made havoc of them that called on this name? and he had come hither for this intent, that he might bring them bound before the chief priests. 22 But Saul increased the more in strength, and confounded the Jews that dwelt at Damascus, proving that this is the Christ. 23 And when many days were fulfilled, the Jews took counsel together to kill him: 24 but their plot became known to Saul. And they watched the gates also day and night that they might kill him: 25 but his disciples took him by night, and let him down through the wall, lowering him in a basket.

26 And when he was come to Jerusalem, he assayed to join himself to the disciples: and they were all afraid of him, not believing that he was a disciple. 27 But Barnabas took him, and brought him to the apostles, and declared unto them how he had seen the Lord in the way, and that he had spoken to him, and how at Damascus he had preached boldly in the name of Jesus. 28 And he was with them going in and going out at Jerusalem, 29 preaching boldly in the name of the Lord: and he spake and disputed against the Grecian Jews; but they were seeking to kill him. 30 And when the brethren knew it, they brought him down to Caesarea, and sent him forth to Tarsus.

Immediately following his conversion, Saul identified himself with the Damascus disciples, began to preach Christ as the living Son of God now risen from the dead, amazed the people with his radical

---

[58] Jewish boys desiring a liberal education had to study at Alexandria, Tarsus, or Athens. E. W. K. Mould, *op. cit.,* p. 473.

change of spirit and purpose from the persecutor of Christ's disciples to the preacher of Christ's gospel, and began to grow in favor with God and in influence with the people.

Concerning Saul's Damascus road conversion experience, Robinson[59] observes that there was a threefold significance. *First,* in that vision he received the profound personal conviction that Jesus Christ was alive from the dead; *second,* there came to him a clear conception that the fact and saving significance of Christ's resurrection was to be made known to all nations (Acts 9:15; 22:15; 26:17; Rom. 1:5; I Cor. 9:1; 15:8ff.; Gal. 1:16); and *third,* he was deeply convinced that he was the divinely chosen messenger to bear this gospel message to all nations (Acts 26:16-18; Rom. 1:5; Gal. 1:16).

Soon after his conversion, Saul departed to Arabia, possibly to the ancient Petra, where he prepared himself for his lifework by study, meditation, and prayer. Returning to Damascus, he began to preach Christ in the synagogues openly. The Jews were moved with envy and laid a plot to kill him, from which plot Saul escaped, with the aid of the disciples, over the city wall in a basket. He proceeded to Jerusalem where he met Barnabas who commended him to the apostles. His preaching incited the Hellenist Jews to murderous intent against him, which occasioned his departure to his home country in Cilicia, where he lived and labored for about seven years, until summoned to Antioch to assist Barnabas in the ministry of the church there.

D. THE CHURCH PROSPERS (9:31-43)

31 So the church throughout all Judaea and Galilee and Samaria had peace, being edified; and, walking in the fear of the Lord and in the comfort of the Holy Spirit, was multiplied. 32 And it came to pass, as Peter went throughout all parts, he came down also to the saints that dwelt at Lydda. 33 And there he found a certain man named Æneas, who had kept his bed eight years; for he was palsied. 34 And Peter said unto him, Æneas, Jesus Christ healeth thee: arise, and make thy bed. And straightway he arose. 35 And all that dwelt at Lydda and in Sharon saw him, and they turned to the Lord.

59 Robinson, *op. cit.,* pp. 54, 55.

36 Now there was at Joppa a certain disciple named Tabitha, which by interpretation is called Dorcas: this woman was full of good works and almsdeeds which she did. 37 And it came to pass in those days, that she fell sick, and died: and when they had washed her, they laid her in an upper chamber. 38 And as Lydda was nigh unto Joppa, the disciples, hearing that Peter was there, sent two men unto him, entreating him, Delay not to come on unto us. 39 And Peter arose and went with them. And when he was come, they brought him into the upper chamber: and all the widows stood by him weeping, and showing the coats and garments which Dorcas made, while she was with them. 40 But Peter put them all forth, and kneeled down, and prayed; and turning to the body, he said, Tabitha, arise. And she opened her eyes; and when she saw Peter, she sat up. 41 And he gave her his hand, and raised her up; and calling the saints and widows, he presented her alive. 42 And it became known throughout all Joppa: and many believed on the Lord. 43 And it came to pass, that he abode many days in Joppa with one Simon a tanner.

Saul's conversion resulted in a cessation of persecution long suffered by the church at his hands and allowed for the edification and rapid increase of its ministry (v. 31). Luke follows this account with a notation concerning the disciples at Lydda (v. 32b), where Peter healed Aeneas of palsy, which healing precipitated a great turning to God (v. 35). Finally, he relates the restoration to life of Dorcas at Joppa through Peter's prayers (v. 40) with the resultant spiritual awakening at Joppa (v. 42).

It is noteworthy that Luke's expression in verse 31, **So the church throughout all Judaea and Galilee and Samaria had peace, being edified,** contains the only reference to Christianity in "Galilee" in the entire Book of Acts.

XII. THE CHURCH'S FIRST GENTILE EVANGELISM (Acts 10:1-11:18)

A. THE HEAVENLY VISIONS (10:1-16)

The first Gentile mission had a most opportune entrance at Caesarea, the Roman colony and Roman capital of Judaea and the most important commercial and political cosmopolitan port of Palestine during that time. Caesarea was built by Herod the Great and named Caesarea Augustus in honor of the emperor, Augustus Caesar. The inhabitants were mostly Greeks and other Gentiles, but the Jews were accorded equal privileges. Besides the governor's royal palace, the city had a theater, amphitheater, and a temple housing the image of the emperor of Rome. The chief characters in the gospel drama were Peter and Cornelius. Peter, the Apostle, was at Joppa lodging with Simon the tanner whose house, for ceremonial reasons incident to his tanner's trade, was removed from the city and located near the seaside.

1 The Man Cornelius (10:1, 2)

1 Now *there was* a certain man in Caesarea, Cornelius by name, a centurion of the band called the Italian *band*, 2 a devout man, and one that feared God with all his house, who gave much alms to the people, and prayed to God always.

Cornelius was by occupation and position a centurion, or captain, of an Italian century (band) or a cohort. If it were the latter, which appears more likely than the former, then he was in command of 600 soldiers, men recruited in Italy and thus likely Roman citizens. The duties of a Roman centurion were similar to a present-day army captain. Like all the centurions appearing in the New Testament, Cornelius is favorably represented (cf. Matt. 8:5 and Luke 7:1-10). By religion he was an uncircumcised Gentile worshipper of the one true God, "a proselyte of the gate," or a "God-fearer"; a devout, generous, prayerful, and religiously influential man. Luke is specific in designating Cornelius a devout man, or a sincere worshipper of the Jewish Jehovah, as opposed to Gentile idolatry. Luke's statement that he was one that feared God is to be understood in reference to reverential fear that inspired worship, rather than a servile fear. His sound character and religious influence are evidenced by the fact that his family followed his faith, as Weymouth renders Luke's words, "and so was every member of his household." His Jewish faith is attested by his observance of the stated Jewish hours of prayer (vv. 3, 30), fastings, and almsdeeds (v. 31).

Although Philip had earlier visited Caesarea and doubtless preached the Christian gospel there (see Acts 8:40), there appears no evidence that Cornelius had ever heard that message before the appearance of Peter. Thus this "God-fearing" Gentile, one of the first to hear and believe the gospel of Jesus Christ (see exception Acts 8:27-40), was prophetic of the entrance of the gospel would have into the cities of the empire, where Paul later traveled, through the nucleus of "God-fearers" who formed the gateway to the various communities. Such an individual was Lydia at Philippi (see Acts 16:14).

2. The Vision of Cornelius (10:3-8)

3 He saw in a vision openly, as it were about the ninth hour of the day, an angel of God coming in unto him, and saying to him, Cornelius. 4 And he, fastening his eyes upon him, and being affrighted, said, What is it, Lord? And he said unto him, Thy prayers and thine alms are gone up for a memorial before God. 5 And now send men to Joppa, and fetch one Simon, who is surnamed Peter: 6 he lodgeth with one Simon a tanner, whose house is by the sea side. 7 And when the angel that spake unto him was departed, he called two of his household-servants, and a devout soldier of them that waited on him continually; 8 and having rehearsed all things unto them, he sent them to Joppa.

He saw in a vision openly (v. 3a). While praying at about three o'clock in the afternoon, the ninth hour, Cornelius was suddenly confronted with a supernatural vision in which an angel appeared to him from God with a special message. Luke is careful to indicate that Cornelius' vision was genuine, since it was at the stated hour of prayer when he would not have been asleep. The word openly implies "plainly" or "evidently," thus delivering the worshipper of any suspicion of imposition. Supernatural visions were to be a valid characteristic of the Pentecostal dispensation (Acts 2: 17).

In the Old Testament "visions and dreams" are commonly mentioned together, and even Peter's quotation of Joel's prophecy at Pentecost associates the two.

Concerning the earlier Old Testament concept, one has observed:

The two words are repeatedly used of the same experience, the dream being rather the *form*, the vision the *substance* (e.g., Dan. 1:17; 2:28; 4:5; cf. Jer. 23:28). . . . The earlier prophets had already attained to the idea of vision as inspired insight.[60]

Among the important visions recorded by Luke in Acts are those of Ananias on the occasion of Saul's conversion (Acts 9:10); Saul in the house of Judas at Damascus (Acts 9:12); Cornelius at Caesarea (Acts 10:3); Peter at Joppa (Acts 10:17, 19; 11:5); Paul at Troas (Acts 16:9, 10); Paul at Corinth (Acts 18:9); and Paul's vision on the occasion of the shipwreck en route to Rome (Acts 27:23, 25).

The special messenger of Cornelius' vision was a divinely commissioned angel. The whole subject of angelology in the Bible, though difficult, is exceedingly interesting.[61]

Cornelius' fear at the sight of the angel in his vision is assuaged by the angel's citation of God's remembrance of his prayers and alms. The devotion and service of a godly man are a standing memorial before God. The angel's directions are specific, including the name of the city, **Joppa** (Joppa was about thirty miles south of Caesarea and thirty-five miles northwest of Jerusalem, now a flourishing city known as Jafa or Jaffa — one of the most ancient cities of the world, and once the chief seaport of Palestine).

God's directions were specific: **Simon, whose surname is Peter, . . . Simon a tanner.**

Note the name and occupation of Peter's host, and the location of Simon's house, **whose house is by the sea side** (cf. Acts 9:10, 11). When we are near enough to hear God's voice, His directions are always clear.

Forthwith Cornelius dispatched two **household-servants,** under the command of **a devout,** or "God-fearing," **soldier** to Joppa to summon Peter, having revealed God's message to them.

3. The Trance of Peter (10:9-16)

9 Now on the morrow, as they were on their journey, and drew nigh unto the city, Peter went up upon the housetop to pray, about the sixth hour: 10 and he became hungry, and desired to eat: but while they made ready, he fell into a trance; 11 and he beholdeth the heaven opened, and a certain vessel descending, as it were a great sheet, let down by four corners upon the earth: 12 wherein were all manner of fourfooted beasts and creeping things of the earth and birds of the heaven. 13 And there came a voice to him, Rise, Peter; kill and eat. 14 But Peter said, Not so, Lord; for I have never eaten anything that is common and unclean. 15 And a voice *came* unto him again the second time, What God hath cleansed, make not thou common. 16 and this was done thrice: and straightway the vessel was received up into heaven.

Peter went up upon the housetop to pray . . . he fell into a trance (vv. 9, 10). As God prepared Cornelius to receive His message through Peter, so He also prepared Peter to deliver that message to Cornelius. Such was the case with Philip and the Ethiopian treasurer (Acts 8: 26-39), with Saul and Ananias (Acts 9: 10-19), and with Jacob and Esau (Gen. 32:9-12, 24, 29; 33:4); and such is ever true where God can get the audience and obedience of those through whom He would work.

At about twelve o'clock noon, **the sixth hour,** Peter ascended to the flat roof of his host's house (likely by an outside stairway), for prayer and meditation while he awaited the preparation of the midday meal. These housetops of oriental houses commonly served as places of prayer, meditation, recreation, and even for sleeping purposes (cf. I Sam. 9:25, 26; II Sam. 11:2; II Kings 23:12; Neh. 8:5, 6). Overcome with hunger and drowsiness, he fell into a trance. Nor is Peter's trance to be identified with the vision as such. The trance, of far less importance than the vision in Bible experiences, was a sort of waking vision. Webster defines the trance as: "1. A state of partly suspended animation or of inability to function; a daze; a stupor. 2. A state of profound abstraction of mind or spirit, as in religious contemplation; ecstasy. 3. A sleeplike state such as that of deep hypnosis."

And Willett defines the trance as:

A condition in which the mental powers

60 S. W. Green, "Vision," *Dictionary of the Bible*, ed. James Hastings, p. 959.
61 See Additional Note VIII, *Angelology*.

are partly or wholly unresponsive to external impressions while dominated by subjective excitement, or left free to contemplate mysteries incapable of apprehension by the usual rational processes.[62]

In the entire Bible there are but two occurrences of the trance recorded: namely, that of Peter at Joppa, and of Paul's early Christian experience at Jerusalem when he was warned of impending danger (Acts 22:17). Other implied trances may be found in Isa. 6; Dan. 7:1, 2; 9:21; II Cor. 12:2; and Rev. 1:10.

During this trance experience, God gave Peter an object lesson in the form of a **great sheet** filled with all manner of animals, both clean and unclean. The **great sheet**-like **vessel** which was **let down by four corners upon the earth** may be best understood as a "sail canvas," perhaps suggested in part by Peter's fishing trade and in part by the appearance of sail ships at sea near Simon's house (see Acts 10:6). Likewise Peter's hunger may account for the revelation having centered about food.

Weymouth's translation of the passage is illuminating:

> He had got very hungry and wished for some food; but, while they were preparing it, he fell into a trance. The sky had opened to his view, and what seemed to be an enormous sheet was descending, being let down to the earth by ropes at the four corners. In it were all kinds of quadrupeds, reptiles, and birds, and a voice came to him which said, "Rise, Peter, kill and eat."

Clarke significantly observes concerning Peter's revelation, that it was

> Perhaps intended to be an emblem of the *universe*, and its *various nations*, to the four corners of which the Gospel was to extend, and to offer its blessings to all the inhabitants, without distinction of nation (cf. Matt. 28:18-20; Acts 1:8; 2:21, 39).[39]

It appears that God's command to Peter to **kill and eat** carried the idea of sacrificial slaughter, rather than simply slaughter for food, suggesting Peter's appointed mission to offer up Jews and Gentiles alike as a spiritual sacrifice to God through a universal gospel ministry (cf. Rom. 12:1, 2).

The expression, **What God hath**

cleansed, make not thou common (v. 15b), is intended to shatter Jewish conservatism and prejudice. Indeed God had earlier, under the Levitical system, distinguished between the clean and the unclean beasts and had forbidden the Jews to eat or sacrifice the latter, as He had also distinguished between Jew and Gentile, all for a purpose in that preparatory period. But now that Christ has come "and brake down the middle wall of partition" (Eph. 2:14b) by His sacrificial death, these distinctions have been forever abolished (see Eph. 2:11-22). Happy are the people who are discerning of divine progress and are adaptable to the on-moving program of God in human history. Prejudice and undue conservatism lock the gates of the Kingdom of God against the world for whose salvation Christ died (cf. Matt. 23:13).

Three times this array descended before the gaze of Peter, thus fulfilling the requirements of the Mosaic law, "that at the mouth of two witnesses or three every word may be established" (Matt. 18:16b; cf: Deut. 19:15).

Clearly the admixture of clean and unclean animals, which Peter was commanded of God to kill and eat, an act repugnant to Peter's Jewish training and taste (cf. Lev. 11), was designed to convey to the apostle that the gospel of Christ was for Gentiles, who were considered by the Jews unclean, as well as for the Jews. Finally convinced that the revelation was from God, Peter's Jewish prejudices against the admission of the Gentiles into the church were shattered, and he was thus prepared for the reception of the Gentile messengers from Cornelius (v. 28).

However, the distinction between clean and unclean meats had to be abolished before the barriers to social intercourse between the Jews and Gentiles in the church could be removed, and thus Christian equality be established. Jesus clearly taught this in principle (Mark 7:19).

God's supernatural acts toward men are always validated by their moral worth.

B. THE DIVINE MISSION (10:17-33)

As Peter meditated on the significance of the housetop sheet or canvas sail ob-

---

[62] H. L. Willett, "Trance," *Dictionary of the Bible*, ed. James Hastings, p. 946.
[63] Clarke, *op. cit.*, I, 761.

ject lesson, Cornelius' servants arrived at Simon's house and inquired for him.

1. The Mission Summons (10:17-23a)

17 Now while Peter was much perplexed in himself what the vision which he had seen might mean, behold, the men that were sent by Cornelius, having made inquiry for Simon's house, stood before the gate, 18 and called and asked whether Simon, who was surnamed Peter, were lodging there. 19 And while Peter thought on the vision, the Spirit said unto him, Behold, three men seek thee. 20 But arise, and get thee down, and go with them, nothing doubting: for I have sent them. 21 And Peter went down to the men, and said, Behold, I am he whom ye seek: what is the cause wherefore ye are come? 22 And they said, Cornelius a centurion, a righteous man and one that feareth God, and well reported of by all the nation of the Jews, was warned of God by a holy angel to send for thee into his house, and to hear words from thee. 23 So he called them in and lodged them.

Arise, and get thee down, and go with them, nothing doubting: for I have sent them (v. 20). While the messengers were inquiring for Peter at the gate of the house, the Spirit was prompting Peter to descend to meet them. In ready obedience Peter descended and inquired of their quest. Accordingly, the messengers related their mission and Peter recognizing the hand of God in it all, received and entertained the messengers until the following day.

2. The Mission Accepted (10:23b-33)

23 And on the morrow he arose and went forth with them, and certain of the brethren from Joppa accompanied him. 24 And on the morrow they entered into Caesarea. And Cornelius was waiting for them, having called together his kinsmen and his near friends. 25 And when it came to pass that Peter entered, Cornelius met him, and fell down at his feet, and worshipped him. 26 But Peter raised him up, saying, Stand up; I myself also am a man. 27 And as he talked with him, he went in, and findeth many come together: 28 and he said unto them, Ye yourselves know how it is an unlawful thing for a man that is a Jew to join himself or come unto one of another nation; and *yet* unto me hath God showed that I should not call any man

common or unclean: 29 wherefore also I came without gainsaying, when I was sent for. I ask therefore with what intent ye sent for me. 30 And Cornelius said, Four days ago, until this hour, I was keeping the ninth hour of prayer in my house; and behold, a man stood before me in bright apparel, 31 and saith, Cornelius, thy prayer is heard, and thine alms are had in remembrance in the sight of God. 32 Send therefore to Joppa, and call unto thee Simon, who is surnamed Peter; he lodgeth in the house of Simon a tanner, by the sea side. 33 Forthwith therefore I sent to thee; and thou hast well done that thou art come. Now therefore we are all here present in the sight of God, to hear all things that have been commanded thee of the Lord.

Accompanied by six Jewish brethren (Acts 11:12) as witnesses to what was about to occur, Peter set out with Cornelius' messengers the following day. Upon arrival at Caesarea, evidently a day later, Cornelius awaited them, together with his **kinsmen and his near friends.** These latter probably included his domestic servants, as well as such "devout soldiers" from the barracks as the one sent in charge of the party that summoned Peter (v. 7). That the company assembled was sizable is evident from verse 27.

Cornelius' conduct toward Peter upon his arrival at Caesarea, as he **fell down at his feet, and worshipped him** (v. 25), seems to indicate that he mistook Peter for an angel who had come to fulfill the implied promise of the angel in his vision (v. 3). However, it is evident that that former announcement concerned a man **Simon, who is surnamed Peter.** In any event Cornelius' act is one of reverential obeisance commonly accorded superiors in the Orient (see Gen. 33:3), and not an act of worship directed to God (cf. Gen. 18:3; 19:3). Peter's humility and sense of divine mission are reflected in his courteous refusal of superior recognition, even when offered by a Gentile: **But Peter raised him up, saying, Stand up; I myself also am a man** (v. 26), or as he seems to imply, I am but your equal, and not your superior. The true Christian spirit is ever the world's greatest social equalizer.

Possibly for the sake of the Gentile proselytes and God-fearers, as well as Jews present in Caesarea who had knowledge of his mission, Peter reiterates his "housetop trance experience," recounting the manner in which God had shattered his anti-Gentile prejudice. Indeed Peter goes beyond the verbal message of God regarding the animals and reveals that he had grasped the significance of the revelation as it concerned the relation of Jews and Gentiles in the plan of Christian redemption: **unto me hath God showed that I should not call any man common or unclean** (v. 28b).

As a preparatory factor to the message he was about to deliver, Peter requested a fuller statement of Cornelius' purpose in sending for him (v. 29). Cornelius proceeded to relate a full account of his vision before the entire company, which account corroborates Peter's trance experience and confirms the faith of all, in preparation for Peter's message. This is most remarkable in the light of the strict Jewish prohibitions against Jewish social intercourse with Gentiles (see John 4:9; 18:28; Acts 11:3; Gal. 2:12, 14).

C. THE APOSTLE'S MESSAGE (10:34-43)

The message of Peter to the household of Cornelius consists of three essential considerations; namely, the impartiality of God, the universal lordship of Jesus Christ, and the way of salvation for all men.

1. The Divine Impartiality (10:34, 35)

34 And Peter opened his mouth, and said,
Of a truth I perceive that God is no respecter of persons: 35 but in every nation he that feareth him, and worketh righteousness, is acceptable to him.

Peter began his message to the Gentile household of Cornelius, probably including many Italian soldiers from the barracks, by frankly acknowledging his shattered Jewish prejudices and his new understanding of the impartiality of God in His great plan of human redemption. While with us today the universality of divine redemption is taken for granted, to both Jew and Gentile in Peter's day the whole matter was an entirely new concept. Indeed, it was implicit in the teachings of the prophets and in Christ's works

and words, but it required a special divine revelation for it to become explicit in the ministry of the Christian apostles. Thus, in a single sentence, Peter's utterance is effective, as Bruce[64] phrases it, in "sweeping away the racial prejudices of centuries." Peter had "perceived" the divine impartiality, and he was prompt to declare it.

Race prejudice has been one of the persistent problems of society from early ages. Nor has man as yet been successful in his attempts to eradicate this loathsome disease from the social organism. Notwithstanding the high ideals and clear teachings of the equality of man and the unity of the body of Christ, the church has not infrequently stood self-condemned as a result of her racial attitudes that have closed the doors of the Kingdom of God to the souls of men. An early indication of this racial problem is reflected by one of the Pharaohs, as recorded by Groves:

> Egypt varied with political and military fortunes, but may be taken as passing just below the First Cataract, and including the island of Philae, the most famous centre in all Egypt in Roman times for the worship of Isis, and one of the last pagan strongholds to yield to Christianity. The First Cataract was the ethnological as well as the geographical boundary. As early as 2000 B.C. the Pharaoh set this as the frontier no Negro should pass save in special circumstances. There is good evidence, however, of active commercial intercourse, and of Egyptian influence on Nubian culture. The people were of mixed Hamitic and Negro descent.[65]

The foregoing citation clearly indicates that while the racial barrier stood opposed to both social and religious intercourse between the Nubian Negro and the Egyptian, it did not prevent an "active commercial intercourse," nor the influence of Egyptian culture on the Nubian Negro.

Indeed, Stephen and Philip, both Jewish Hellenist Christian laymen, had earlier grasped the broader significance of the gospel for the Gentiles as well as the Jews, but Peter was the first Jewish Christian "apostle" to enter into that universal concept.

---

[64] F. F. Bruce, *op. cit.*, p. 224.
[65] C. P. Groves, *The Planting of Christianity in Africa*, I, 47; see also Serigman, *Races of Africa*, p. 111.

Nothing new or great is ever undertaken or accomplished until someone has "perceived," or seen through, and grasped the pattern and possibilities of things yet unrealized. Divine revelations, when properly understood, ever have a transforming moral and spiritual effect on man and human history. "Where there is no vision, the people perish" (Prov. 29:18a, KJV). Let it be noted that Peter refers to **nations**, a political designation, and not "races," a physical designation. The latter term is not found in the Bible in reference to divisions of mankind.

2. The Universal Divine Lordship (10:36-41)

36 The word which he sent unto the children of Israel, preaching good tidings of peace by Jesus Christ (he is Lord of all) — 37 that saying ye yourselves know, which was published throughout all Judaea, beginning from Galilee, after the baptism which John preached; 38 *even* Jesus of Nazareth, how God anointed him with the Holy Spirit and with power: who went about doing good, and healing all that were oppressed of the devil; for God was with him. 39 And we are witnesses of all things which he did both in the country of the Jews, and in Jerusalem; whom also they slew, hanging him on a tree. 40 Him God raised up the third day, and gave him to be made manifest, 41 not to all the people, but unto witnesses that were chosen before of God, *even* to us, who ate and drank with him after he rose from the dead.

He is Lord of all (v. 36). Peter's first gospel message to this eager Gentile congregation is a succinct, but dynamic, summation of the entire person and work of Jesus Christ in relation to the redemptive scheme. In rapid succession he presents Jesus Christ in the clear aspects of His peace, His universal lordship, His requirement of repentance, His humanity, His deity, His sacrificial death, His victorious resurrection, His post-resurrection appearances, His universal judgeship, and remission of sins through faith in His Name.

Analytically outlined, Peter's message to Cornelius' household might look something like the following:

1. *The Gospel of Peace by Jesus Christ:* **preaching good tidings of peace by Jesus Christ** (v. 36).

2. *The Universal Lordship of Jesus Christ:* **he is Lord of all** (v. 36b).

3. *The Repentance of Sins through Jesus Christ:* **the baptism which John preached** (v. 37b).

4. *The Humanity of Jesus Christ:* **Jesus of Nazareth** (v. 38a).

5. *The Deity of Jesus Christ:* **God anointed him with the Holy Spirit and with power** (v. 38).

6. *The Crucifixion of Jesus Christ:* **whom also they slew, hanging him on a tree** (v. 39b).

7. *The Resurrection of Jesus Christ:* **Him God raised up the third day** (v. 40a).

8. *The Appearances of Jesus Christ:* **and gave him to be made manifest** (v. 40b).

9. *The Universal Judgeship of Jesus Christ:* **this is he who is ordained of God to be the Judge of the living and the dead** (v. 42b).

10. *The Impartial Remission of Sins through Jesus Christ:* **through his name every one that believeth on him shall have remission of sins** (v. 43b).

3. The Way of Salvation (10:42, 43)

42 And he charged us to preach unto the people, and to testify that this is he who is ordained of God *to be* the Judge of the living and the dead. 43 To him bear all the prophets witness, that through his name every one that believeth on him shall receive remission of sins.

It is significant that Peter concludes his message with the clear implication that the way of salvation for these Gentiles, as also for the Jews, is open through faith in the name, and submission to the lordship of Jesus Christ.

Thus Peter sets an example of expository evangelistic preaching in the first Christian century, which was both eagerly received by his Gentile hearers and signally approved and blessed of God. Nor has this type of preaching ever lost its usefulness throughout the subsequent centuries.

D. THE SPIRIT'S EFFUSION (10:44-48)

That Peter's hearers believed on Christ unto the salvation of their souls is evidenced by two facts: *first, that* God poured forth upon them the gift of the Holy Spirit; and *second,* that they were judged by Peter as worthy candidates for water baptism.

1. The Spirit Outpoured (10:44-46)

44 While Peter yet spake these words, the Holy Spirit fell on all them that heard the word. 45 And they of the circumcision that believed were amazed, as many as came with Peter, because that on the Gentiles also was poured out the gift of the Holy Spirit. 46 For they heard them speak with tongues, and magnify God. Then answered Peter,

While Peter yet spake these words, the Holy Spirit fell on all them that heard the word (v. 44). Usually the outpouring of the Holy Spirit followed water baptism and the laying on of hands by the apostles (cf. Acts 2:38; 8:17; 19:6); but in this instance the order was reversed. While God may honor and use human symbols, He is never confined to them for His spiritual operations. The reversal of the order here is probably the miraculous evidence that the Gentiles were to be included in the gift of the Holy Spirit, and thus were to be baptized.

That the spiritual significance of the outpouring of the Holy Spirit on these Gentiles is identical with that of the Pentecostal effusion of Acts 2 is attested by Peter's declaration, on the occasion of his defense of the Gentile cause at the Jerusalem Council. In this rehearsal he states: "And God, who knoweth the heart, bare them witness, giving them the Holy Spirit, even as he did unto us; and he made no distinction between us and them, cleansing their hearts by faith" (Acts 15:8, 9).

Thus as the baptism of the Holy Spirit wrought purity of heart in the disciples on the day of Pentecost, so the hearts of these Gentile believers were cleansed by His gracious personal manifestations at the close of Peter's message to them. One is reminded of Christ's words to His disciples: "Already ye are clean because of the word which I have spoken unto you" (John 15:3). **While Peter yet spake these words, the Holy Spirit fell on all them that heard the Word** (v. 44), "cleansing their hearts by faith" (Acts 15:9b).

A purported Pentecost that does not purify the Christian's inner nature of the carnal principle and pollution is spurious indeed, notwithstanding the external manifestations or significations of such a purported experience. The manifestation of the personality of the Holy God, to the inner nature of the unholy heart, inevitably consumes the sin nature of that heart and recreates it in His likeness (cf. Ps. 51:10).

This spiritual effusion on the Gentiles amazed Peter's Jewish-Christian companions, for they **heard them speak with tongues, and magnify God** (v. 46). This miraculous phenomenon of **tongues,** or "languages," recurred at Caesarea as an aid to the evangelization of the polyglot Gentile inhabitants of this great seaport city.[66] But as Clarke observes:

> They had got *new hearts* as well as *new tongues;* and, having believed with the heart unto righteousness, their tongues made confession unto salvation; and God was magnified for the mercy which he had imparted.[67]

Through faith they had believed unto righteousness of heart, and by the miraculous divine gift of languages these Spirit-baptized Gentile believers began to proclaim that righteousness to their polyglot neighbors, and thus they "magnified God."

The amazement of the Jewish-Christian believers present with Peter at this Gentile Pentecost is due to the fact that the Jews held that the Divine Spirit could not be communicated to any Gentile, or be bestowed upon anyone who dwelt beyond the promised land.[68]

2. The Disciples' Baptism (10:47, 48)

47 Can any man forbid the water, that these should not be baptized, who have received the Holy Spirit as well as we? 48 And he commanded them to be baptized in the name of Jesus Christ. Then prayed they him to tarry certain days.

The incontestable right of these uncircumcised Gentile Christians to be baptized, as a token of their acceptance into the body of Christ, is made evident by the miraculous divine approval, and the Apostle's declaratory question of verse 47. Peter then commands their baptism

---

[66] See Additional Note III, *The Bible Gift of Tongues.*   [67] Clarke, *op. cit.,* I, 767.   [68] *Ibid.*

and thus shows a vital, saving relationship through faith in Jesus Christ, the Son of God and the Savior of men. God had witnessed to His acceptance of the Gentiles by giving them the Holy Spirit, and Peter witnesses to their acceptance into the church by baptizing them in the Name of Jesus without the requirement of circumcision. On the question of the baptismal formula employed by Peter on this occasion, Wesley remarks:

> In the Name of the Lord — Which implies the Father who anointed Him, and the Spirit with which He was anointed, to His office. But as these Gentiles had before believed in God the Father, and could not but now believe in the Holy Ghost, under whose powerful influence they were at this very time, there was the less need of taking notice that they were baptized into the belief and profession of the sacred Three; though doubtless the apostle administered the ordinance in that very form which Christ Himself had prescribed.[69]

Certainly, in the light of Wesley's explanation, no ground remains for a Unitarian interpretation of this passage.

E. THE DEFENSE OF PETER (11:1-18)

The news of the success of Peter's mission to the Gentiles at Caesarea spread rapidly throughout Judaea as the apostles and disciples heard of the mighty workings of God in the household of Cornelius and passed that good news along to their fellows. In addition to their moral and spiritual transforming power in the lives, homes, and communities of people, spiritual awakenings always have a restraining influence against wickedness among non-Christian people. However, they are no less likely to arouse opposition from unsympathetic sources. Such was the case with the Gentile awakening at Caesarea.

1. The Occasion of the Defense (11:1-4)

1 Now the apostles and the brethren that were in Judaea heard that the Gentiles also had received the word of God. 2 And when Peter was come up to Jerusalem, they that were of the circumcision contended with him, 3 saying, Thou wentest in to men uncircumcised, and didst eat with them. 4 But Peter began, and expounded *the matter* unto them in order, saying,

69 Wesley, *op. cit.*, pp. 436, 437, n. 48.

Upon his return to Jerusalem, Peter was met by a delegation of the anti-Gentile Jewish Christians. This was likely the Judaizing party (Acts 15:1-5), which soon charged him with illegal association with Gentiles (v. 3). These Jewish-Christian legalists did not attack the baptism of the Gentiles, perhaps because of the Lord's command and God's evident visitation of these Gentiles, but they made an acute issue of Peter's breach of Jewish ceremonial law and custom: **Thou wentest in to men uncircumcised, and didst eat with them** (v. 3). Legalism always places externalities above spirituality and seeks to stifle the latter by enforcement of the former. Paul declared, "the letter killeth, but the spirit giveth life" (II Cor. 3:6). The legalists wished at best to regard the Gentiles as an inferior class and require of them subscription to the Jewish ceremonial law (Gal. 2:12-21). Legalism invariably tends toward "classism" in the church, the "holier-than-thou" attitude.

2. The Explanation of Peter (11:5-10)

5 I was in the city of Joppa praying: and in a trance I saw a vision, a certain vessel descending, as it were a great sheet let down from heaven by four corners; and it came even unto me: 6 upon which when I had fastened mine eyes, I considered, and saw the fourfooted beasts of the earth and wild beasts and creeping things and birds of the heaven. 7 And I heard also a voice saying unto me, Rise, Peter; kill and eat. 8 But I said, Not so, Lord: for nothing common or unclean hath ever entered into my mouth. 9 But a voice answered the second time out of heaven, What God hath cleansed, make not thou common. 10 And this was done thrice: and all were drawn up again into heaven.

What God hath cleansed, make not thou common (v. 9b). Peter by-passed the general principles embodied in their accusation and built his defense on the grounds of the special divine revelation that commanded, and thus authorized, his act in the special case in question. He proceeded to expound in order unto his opponents the details of the Caesarean incident (v. 4). It originated in answer to prayer to God at Joppa, was revealed to the Apostle in a vision from God, in which God clearly (by a thrice-repeated revelation) showed him that the Gentiles were not to be considered ceremonially unclean by the Jews. The genuineness of the sheet-vision is accentuated, Peter indicates, by the fact that it was not only thrice lowered but finally retracted into heaven from whence it had been let down. Peter intimates that he had been quite as reluctant to break ceremonial rules and eat meat considered unclean by the Jews, as the Jewish Christians were to see that the ceremonial law had been fulfilled and abrogated by Christ, and thus that the Gentiles were to be admitted to fellowship in the body of Christ without imposition of the Jewish law. In short, it was God's doing, and who were the Jewish Christians to object?

3. The Obedience of Peter (11:11-14)

11 And behold, forthwith three men stood before the house in which we were, having been sent from Caesarea unto me. 12 And the Spirit bade me go with them, making no distinction. And these six brethren also accompanied me; and we entered into the man's house: 13 and he told us how he had seen the angel standing in his house, and saying, Send to Joppa, and fetch Simon, whose surname is Peter; 14 who shall speak unto thee words, whereby thou shalt be saved, thou and all thy house.

As Peter continued his defense of the gospel for the Gentiles before the Jewish-Christian opposition, he clearly implied the divine origin and authorization of the mission, and then adduced a number of evidences in support of his obedience in ministering to, and associating with, the Gentiles. *First,* no sooner had the trance of divine origin been withdrawn than three men appeared from Caesarea inquiring for him in behalf of Cornelius, who had been instructed of God in a vision to send for him (v. 11). *Second,* the Holy Spirit spoke directly to him, prompting him to accompany the messengers to Caesarea, and that without misgivings (v. 12). *Third,* six Jewish Christian men accompanied Peter to Caesarea to testify to the divine leadings and approval in all the events (v. 12). *Fourth,* by comparing notes with Cornelius, after arriving at Caesarea, Peter found that all the circumstances of the divine directions, both on his part and with Cornelius, perfectly corresponded. And *fifth,* he stated

the object of the mission as being the salvation of Cornelius and his household (vs. 14), a most worthy mission indeed.

4. The Reward of Peter (11:15-18)

15 And as I began to speak, the Holy Spirit fell on them, even as on us at the beginning. 16 And I remembered the word of the Lord, how he said, John indeed baptized with water; but ye shall be baptized in the Holy Spirit. 17 If then God gave unto them the like gift as *he did* also unto us, when we believed on the Lord Jesus Christ, who was I, that I could withstand God? 18 And when they heard these things, they held their peace, and glorified God, saying, Then to the Gentiles also hath God granted repentance unto life.

Peter clearly saw the divine approval and reward of his obedience (in transcending the ceremonial bounds of Judaism to take the gospel to the Gentiles) was the outpouring of the Holy Spirit upon them, even as on the day of Pentecost (v. 15). We have previously observed that the significance of the divine spiritual effusion at Pentecost was fourfold (see Acts 2:1-4). So likewise, Peter relates, the Holy Spirit was outpoured on the Gentiles in His *personal power, sanctifying purity, spiritual enduement* and *possession,* and in a *miraculous proclamation* through the gift of *tongues* (or languages) for the purpose of evangelization. This spiritual effusion Peter then recognized to be the fulfillment of Christ's promise (v. 16).

Verses 17 and 18 clearly reveal that Peter's vivid and convincing presentation of the events at Caesarea won, for the time being, the complete approval of the Jewish Christians at Jerusalem upon the mission to the Gentiles.

XIII. THE CHURCH'S FIRST GENTILE MISSIONARY CENTER (Acts 11:19-30)

A. THE CHURCH AT ANTIOCH (11:19-21)

We have previously noted the approval of the Gentile evangelization at Caesarea, by the Jewish Christians at the close of Peter's defense (Acts 11:17, 18). It becomes clear, however, from verse 19 that the evangelization of Antioch was carried out by the disciples scattered abroad under the persecution that followed Stephen's death (Acts 8:1), rather than by Gentile disciples from Caesarea, as some have supposed. The dispersed disciples followed the great trade routes by land and sea northward to Phoenicia, Cyprus, and Antioch. Antioch in northern Syria ranked the third greatest city (about 800,000 inhabitants, including suburbs[70]) of the Roman Empire and was called "The Queen of the East," "Antioch the Beautiful," and "Antioch the Great." It was beautifully situated on the Orontes River about 15 or 20 miles from its seaport city of Seleucia. It was the capital of Syria and seat of the Roman governor. The population was mainly Syrian, but Greek in language and culture, with a considerable Jewish representation who had equal rights with the Greeks. Here Christianity first contacted and came to grips with Roman and Greek civilization. The moral corruption of Antioch is reflected in Juvenal's statement, when he wished to say the worst about Rome: "The Orontes has flowed into the Tiber."[71] Antioch soon superseded Jerusalem as the center of Christianity and remained so for long, producing such honorable Christian names as Ignatius and John Chrysostom, and a famous school of theology.

1. The Jewish Evangelization (11:19)

19 They therefore that were scattered abroad upon the tribulation that arose about Stephen travelled as far as Phoenicia, and Cyprus, and Antioch, speaking the word to none save only to Jews.

The dispersion that took place after the martyrdom of Stephen seems at first to have extended only into Judaea and Samaria. However, Jewish Christians, many of whom may have been present for Pentecost and were converted there, soon moved on northward, visiting and witnessing in the Jewish synagogues throughout the coastland of Phoenicia (Phenice), on the western Mediterranean island of Cyprus (home of Barnabas), and in Antioch of Syria. That they preached **the word to none save only to Jews** seems evidence that these evangelists were themselves Jewish Christians,

and not proselytes. While accepting Christ as the Messiah, they thought of Christianity only as a new spiritual life movement within the Jewish religion. They knew nothing of Peter's vision and did not understand that God had opened the door of faith to the Gentiles also.

2. The Grecian Evangelization (11:20)

20 But there were some of them, men of Cyprus and Cyrene, who, when they were come to Antioch, spake unto the Greeks also, preaching the Lord Jesus.

These particular Christian disciples were Hellenists (Greek-speaking Jews), or perhaps some were even converted proselytes, and consequently were more liberal in their views than were the Jewish Christians. Representatives of Cyrenian Africa and Cyprus are named. The mention of Cyrenians at Antioch, who naturally would have returned to their homes in Africa, may indicate a purposeful evangelization mission to the Greeks of Antioch, on their part. In any event, to Hellenist Africans and Cyprian Christians belongs credit for the first-known Grecian evangelization after Pentecost. Groves remarks:

That there were Christians quite early in Cyrenaica seems clear. The existence of a Jewish community in contact with Jerusalem is attested in Acts (2:10; 6:9); these more enlightened Jews of the Dispersion, when converted, were not unnaturally among the first missionaries to the Gentiles (11:20; 13:1). That their own home settlements received the Gospel early is to be safely presumed. We know nothing, however, about Christian beginnings in Cyrenaica (alternatively known as Pentapolis). Catacombs are said to have been discovered in Cyrene belonging to the period before Constantine.[72]

Further, the foregoing authority[73] observes that Simon of Cyrene, who bore Christ's cross, came from northern Africa (Luke 23:26). He is regarded as a Jewish settler in a Greek settlement of Barca, a district of modern Tripoli (cf. Acts 2:10; 6:9; 11:20; 13:1). Apollos (Acts 18:24-19:1) is declared to have been an Alexandrian Christian (cf. Acts 6:9). Luke's account of the conversion of the

[70] Madeline S. and J. Lane Miller, *Harper's Bible Dictionary*, p. 21.
[71] James Hastings, *Dictionary of the Bible*, p. 37.   [72] Groves, *op. cit.*, p. 46.   [73] *Ibid.*, p. 34.

Ethiopian nobleman (Acts 8:26-40) further testifies to the early impact of Christianity upon Africa.

Tradition in the apostolic age gives no account of any of the original apostles evangelizing in Africa. Indeed, tradition depicts Thomas as the apostle to India, whose route likely took him via the Nile and across the Red Sea, and possibly through Alexandria. J. N. Farquhar regarded this tradition very favorably and actually considered Thomas as one of the evangelists who proclaimed Christ in Egypt, Cyrene, and westward in Africa. Eusebius is the authority for a tradition that John Mark was a missionary to Egypt, but especially the establisher of churches in Alexandria. Demetrius, Pantanus, Clement, and Origen were all associated with the famous Catechetical School of Alexandria, which became a center of Christian learning which stood unrivaled in the Christian world of its day.

Returning to the dispersed disciples, we note that some of them preached **only to Jews** (v. 19b), while others **spake unto the Greeks also, preaching the Lord Jesus.** As previously noted, the population of Antioch was mainly Gentiles of Greek culture and with many pure Greek residents, and the church that subsequently developed in Antioch was largely Gentile in membership.

3. The Extent of the Evangelization (11:21)

21 And the hand of the Lord was with them: and a great number that believed turned unto the Lord.

These disciples had preached **the Lord Jesus** (v. 20b), or Jesus as the Messiah and Lord, to the Greeks, and a great number of them were saved, or **believed** and were converted, **turned,** to the Lordship of Christ in their lives. How many were converted we are not told, but that the demands of the church soon required Saul to assist Barnabas in the pastoral care of the flock indicates an extensive movement. Further, Antioch was very soon to become the missionary center from which the gospel would be sent to the Gentile world afar.

Something of the extent of this early evangelization movement among the Grecian Antiochians is indicated by the fact that by the time of the Nicean Council in A.D. 325, there are reported to have been more than 200,000 Christians in Antioch alone. Between A.D. 253 and 380, Antioch was the seat of no less than ten church councils,[74] and its patriarchs took precedence over those at Rome, Constantinople, Jerusalem, and Alexandria.[75]

B. THE MINISTRY OF BARNABAS (11: 22-24)

The fame of the Antiochian mission among the Greeks soon reached the Jerusalem church. The Jewish Christians there, restrained by God's acknowledged visitation of the Caesarean Gentiles, wisely did not condemn the movement at Antioch, but rather selected and authorized a most honorable and trustworthy man of their number, Barnabas (v. 24), to proceed to that city.

1. The Commission of Barnabas (11:22)

22 And the report concerning them came to the ears of the church which was in Jerusalem: and they sent forth Barnabas as far as Antioch:

Barnabas' commission was evidently principally to investigate the situation and report to the Jerusalem church. The extent of his commission may be inferred from the duration of his service there and his acquisition of Saul to assist him in the ministry of the church. His more liberal Cypriote background well qualified him for work among the Gentiles. If Barnabas may not have had the honor of founding the church at Antioch, he at least holds the credit for being the first known pastor. That he was not one of the original (Acts 14:14) apostles, but a Jewish Levite who owned land in Cyprus, which land he sold and gave the proceeds to the church, we learn from Acts 4:36. This passage likewise informs us of his special gifts for Christian service, as the very name Barnabas signifies, "the son of consolation" (ASV).

2. The Consolation of Barnabas (11:23)

23 who, when he was come, and had seen the grace of God, was glad; and he

---

[74] For an account of Christianity at Antioch, see Additional Note IX, *Christianity at Antioch.*
[75] Hastings, *op. cit.,* p. 37.

exhorted them all, that with purpose of heart they would cleave unto the Lord:

Upon his arrival in Antioch, Barnabas evidently wisely played the part of an unbiased auditor and observer of the Gentile revival. The evidences of transforming divine grace at work in the lives of these Gentile people were soon sufficient to convince him that it was indeed a genuine and great work of God. Concerning Barnabas, Luke says: **who, when he was come, and had seen the grace of God, was glad.** Though he was neither the originator nor director of this work, he was sufficiently magnanimous to appreciate and rejoice in it. Barnabas at once adjusted himself to the new situation, stepped into the movement and lent the full weight of his support by exhortations (encouragements: Weymouth) to them all; that is, Jews as well as Gentiles. The import of his exhortations was unity in the body of Christ and fixedness of purpose and steadfastness in the Lord Jesus Christ. His very name, Barnabas, means "son of prophecy" (see Acts 13:1), and this name may have been gained from an especially comforting or consoling prophecy which he delivered to the disciples at Jerusalem after his conversion.[76] Thus he consoled or encouraged the Antioch church.

3. The Character of Barnabas (11:24)

24 for he was a good man, and full of the Holy Spirit and of faith: and much people was added unto the Lord.

Something of the esteem in which Barnabas was held by the author of the Book of Acts is indicated by the fact that he is mentioned in Acts no less than twenty-five different times, besides five references to him by Paul outside Acts. Luke here characterizes Barnabas as a man of sterling "character": **a good man;** a man of "spirituality": **full of the Holy Spirit;** and a man of "faith": **full of . . . faith.** His character stems from two sources: *first,* his strict Levitical training in the moral law; and *second,* his sound Christian conversion (Acts 4:36, 37). His spirituality was attributable to the sanctifying work and abiding presence of the Holy Spirit in his life. His faith was the natural fruit of the first two, plus an un-

wavering devotion to Christ and an unquestioned obedience to His will. His fullness of faith may imply: *first,* that "natural or intellectual faith" that is the property of every normal man, without which life would be impossible; *second,* "evangelical faith" by which he experienced a saving and sanctifying relationship with Christ; *third,* "fiduciary faith" ·by which he maintained the constancy of his relationship with Christ; and *fourth,* "achieving faith" by which he saw the mighty works of God performed.

Little wonder that Luke states, after this characterization of Barnabas: **and much people was added unto the Lord** (v. 24b). The fruit of increased spiritual conversions was consequent upon the divine commission, consolation, and unimpeachable character of Barnabas as a prophet of God to Antioch. Nor did Barnabas win men to himself, only for them to be lost to the cause of Christ after his departure, but rather to the Lord Christ, for they were **added** [joined] **unto the Lord.** This building up of the Antioch church under the ministry of Barnabas probably extended over a considerable period of time.

C. THE ENGAGEMENT OF SAUL (11: 25, 26)

Following the attack made on Saul's life by the Hellenist Jews at Jerusalem he had gone to Tarsus, his home city in Cilicia, where he had most likely engaged in evangelistic labors until called to Antioch to assist Barnabas. It is possible, and some scholars think likely, that Barnabas and Saul had attended the Greek university together at Tarsus, and that Barnabas had known for long the character and worth of Saul. In any event, his thorough acquaintance with, and confidence in, Saul are evident (see Acts 9:27).

1. The Summons of Saul (11:25, 26a)

25 And he went forth to Tarsus to seek for Saul; 26 and when he had found him, he brought him unto Antioch.

When the Antioch church had grown beyond Barnabas' ability to shepherd it alone, it was Saul that he desired to aid

[76] Dummelow, *op. cit.,* p. 824.

him. Saul's more liberal education, long residence among Gentiles,[77] thorough spiritual transformation, and his subsequent evangelistic activities at Damascus, possibly in Arabia for some time, at Jerusalem, and then in Cilicia for approximately seven years, combined to recommend him to Barnabas as a man fitted to assist him in the work at Antioch. Thus Barnabas departed to Tarsus, not far distant from Antioch, where he sought Saul. The fact that he probably did not have definite knowledge of Saul's exact whereabouts may suggest that Saul was already traveling somewhere in Asia Minor evangelizing. When found, Saul readily accompanied Barnabas to Antioch.

2. The Service of Saul (11:26)

26 and when he had found him, he brought him unto Antioch. And it came to pass, that even for a whole year they were gathered together with the church, and taught much people; and that the disciples were called Christians first in Antioch.

Saul's service at Antioch was primarily a teaching ministry. In consideration of his thorough Jewish theological training, his radical conversion to Christianity, and his sympathetic understanding of the Gentiles (see Acts 15), Saul was in a strategic position to indoctrinate and edify in the Christian faith these Gentiles recently converted to that faith, many of them at least from gross paganism, and to effect a workable plan of church membership and fellowship between them and the Jewish-Christian element of the church.

3. The Disciples' New Name (11:26b)

26b And it came to pass, that even for a whole year they were gathered together with the church, and taught much people; and that the disciples were called Christians first in Antioch.

Until now the followers of Christ were known by such designations as **disciples, believers, brethren, saints,** the people of the Way (or **this Way, the church of God, Galileans,** or **Nazarenes** (Acts 24:5). This last name was likely given in derision, as nothing good was supposed to come out of Nazareth (John 1:46). The

term **Christian** occurs only three times in the New Testament (Acts 11:26; 26:28; I Peter 4:16), and only in the last instance is it used by a Christian of Christians. It is quite clear that they did not assume the name themselves, as they were so **called,** and the Jews could not have given them this name without admitting the Messiahship of Christ. Therefore, it probably was given to them by the Antiochians, not in derision as some suppose, but in recognition of their avowed devotion to Christ as their Lord and leader. It was here at Antioch that the disciples of Christ more nearly earned the right to the name Christian than at any previous place or time, and they were rewarded with it. Harnack gives an interesting and illuminating treatment of the various names accorded the early Christians.[78]

D. THE JERUSALEM FAMINE RELIEF (11:27-30)

27 Now in these days there came down prophets from Jerusalem unto Antioch. 28 And there stood up one of them named Agabus, and signified by the Spirit that there should be a great famine over all the world: which came to pass in the days of Claudius. 29 And the disciples, every man according to his ability, determined to send relief unto the brethren that dwelt in Judaea: 30 which also they did, sending it to the elders by the hand of Barnabas and Saul.

This incident reflects the important part played by prophets, as distinguished from apostles or deacons in the apostolic church, and the spirit of genuine charity that characterized the Antioch Christians in their relief of the needy at Jerusalem. It further indicates the good will of these young Gentile Christians toward the mother Judaeo-Christian church at Jerusalem (see note on Acts 2:41-47).

XIV. THE CHURCH'S FIRST SECULAR PERSECUTION (Acts 12:1-25)

A. THE DESIGNS OF HEROD (12:1-4)

1 Now about that time Herod the king put forth his hands to afflict certain of the church. 2 And he killed James the brother of John with the sword. 3 And when he saw that it pleased the Jews, he proceeded to seize Peter also. And *those* were the days of unleavened bread. 4

---

[77] Mould, *op. cit.*, pp. 570ff.   [78] See Additional Note X, *Early Names of Christ's Followers.*

And when he had taken him, he put him in prison, and delivered him to four quaternions of soldiers to guard him; intending after the Passover to bring him forth to the people.

From the prosperity of the Gentile work at Antioch (Acts 11:19-30), Luke returns in chapter 12 to the Jerusalem church, where for the third time the cruel hand of organized persecution had fallen upon the disciples. The *first* persecution was by the Sadducees and the chief priests (Acts 4:1; 5:17); the *second* was incited by the Hellenists (Acts 6:9-15), though executed by the Jewish council (Acts 7:1-60), and followed up by the Pharisees and Hellenists with Saul as their chief representative, until his conversion (Acts 8:1; 9:1, 2, 29). This *third* persecution came by the hand of **Herod the king,** though doubtless it was incited by the anti-Christian Jews. The next great Christian persecution was to come from the official Roman government. That this persecution occurred at about the time of the Jerusalem famine relief (Acts 11:29, 30; 12:1) is evident from the known date of Herod's death, A.D. 44.

This **Herod the king** was Herod Agrippa I,[79] grandson of Herod the Great and nephew to Herod Antipas, who beheaded John the Baptist. It may be noted that upon the death of Herod the Great, king of the Jews, in about 4 B.C., his kingdom was divided between his three sons as follows: Philip was made tetrarch of Iturea, the country north and east of the Sea of Galilee, where he reigned until A.D. 34; Herod Antipas became tetrarch of Galilee and Perea until his recall by Rome for maladministration and a suspected plot against the emperor's life in A.D. 39. Archelaus was made ethnarch of Judaea, which also included Samaria to the north and Idumaea in the south, with his capital at Caesarea, until his deposition and banishment to Gaul by Rome in A.D. 6, also for maladministration. Though some of the Jews, especially the political party of the Herodians, wished another descendant of Herod the Great to succeed Archelaus, many of the Judaean Jews preferred a direct Roman rule. Thus Rome added Judaea to the province of Syria and established in Judaea the procurator-

ship which lasted from A.D. 6 until A.D. 41. There were seven of these procurators, between Archelaus and Herod Agrippa I, of which Pilate was the fifth in order. Caponius ruled from A.D. 7-9; M. Ambibulus A.D. 9-12; Annius Rufus A.D. 12-15; Valerius Gratus A.D. 15-26; Pontus Pilatus A.D. 25-36; Marcellus A.D. 36; and Marullus A.D. 37-41.

These procurators were chiefly fiscal agents for Rome. Judaea was divided into eleven toparchies, or major towns with their adjacent country and villages, with Jerusalem as the Jewish capital. Each toparchy had a synagogue with a minor Sanhedrin responsible to the Temple and Sanhedrin at Jerusalem.

While the Sanhedrin was permitted to administer Jewish law relating to civil, criminal, moral, and religious questions involving Jews within Judaea, except where such Jews possessed Roman citizenship, the execution of all capital punishment and the charge of all Gentiles, fell under Roman authority. There was the one exception that the Jews had the right to kill on the spot any Gentile who ventured beyond the court of the Gentiles at the Jerusalem Temple. The procurator was the final court of appeal, except that Roman citizens had the right of direct appeal to Caesar. The procurator had the power to appoint and remove the Jewish high priest of the Sanhedrin. In fact, the robes of the Jewish high priest were kept in the tower of Antonia. Otherwise the Jews were allowed complete religious freedom. Taxes were collected by the procurators mainly through the local Sanhedrins of the eleven toparchies.[80]

For a brief period of three years (A.D. 41-44) the whole of Palestine was ruled by Herod Agrippa I. This Herod Agrippa I had a checkered career. He grew up in Rome where from luxury and extravagance he descended to poverty and want. To evade his debts he fled to southern Judaea where he contemplated suicide in despondency over his bankruptcy, but from which he was saved by his wife Kypros, who gained favor for her husband with Herod Antipas through his wife Herodias, who was the sister of Agrippa I. Agrippa I was given a minor appointment in Tiberias, but he soon fell

[79] Mould, *op. cit.,* pp. 550, 551.   [80] *Ibid.,* pp. 391, 467, 468.

out with Antipas and resigned. He then found brief favor with Flaccus the legate of Syria at Damascus until his own brother Aristobulus charged him with bribery. He eluded his Palestinean creditors and fled back to Rome via Alexandria, where he borrowed a vast sum of money from Alexander, the brother of the Jewish philosopher Philo.

Back in Rome he developed a friendship with Caius Caligula, who succeeded his foster father to the throne upon the death of the latter in A.D. 37. Caligula released Agrippa I from prison where Tiberius had incarcerated him for wishing his death, and appointed him king over the former tetrarchy of Philip. Two years later (A.D. 39), Caligula extended Agrippa's domain to include the tetrarchy of Herod Antipas, who was banished through the instigation of Agrippa.

When Caligula was murdered and succeeded by Claudius in A.D. 41, Claudius, out of a sense of obligation to Agrippa, added Judaea and Samaria to his kingdom. Thus Agrippa became the king of all the territory which had belonged to his grandfather Herod the Great.

With the Jews Agrippa I was successful as a ruler. He deferred to their scruples, observed their regulations, and was careful to avoid offense in every respect. It was this disposition toward, and deference to, his Jewish subjects at Jerusalem that elicited his persecution of the Christians, his beheading of the apostle James, and his intention to execute Peter after the Jewish feast of the Passover at Jerusalem. These acts were all designed to curry favor with the Jews: **And when he saw that it pleased the Jews, he proceeded to seize Peter also** (v. 3a).

In A.D. 44, at the conclusion of an oration at Caesarea to the peoples of Tyre who had sued for his favor, Herod Agrippa I suddenly died by a stroke of God for receiving the ascriptions of divinity from his favor-seeking subjects (Acts 12:21-24).

Following Herod's death Rome returned the government of Judaea to a succession of seven procurators, until the destruction of Jerusalem and the end of Jewish national life in A.D. 70. These later procurators were Fadus, A.D. 44-48; Alexander, A.D. 48; Cumanus, A.D. 48-52;

Felix, A.D. 52-60; Festus, A.D. 60-62; Albinus, A.D. 62-64; and Florus, A.D. 64-66. After declining to appoint him king of Judaea in A.D. 44, Claudius did, in A.D. 48, give Herod's twenty-one-year-old son, Agrippa, the small kingdom of Chalcis in Lebanon. In A.D. 50 he exchanged this for Philip's former kingdom, and later Nero gave him parts of Galilee and Julias in Perea. His capital was Caesarea Philippi and, though he maintained a residence in Jerusalem, he had no authority in Judaea. It was this Agrippa II that heard Paul's defense at Caesarea (Acts 25:13 — 26:32). He reigned from A.D. 48 until about A.D. 100.[81]

Whatever the immediate incitement of this persecution of the Christians, with the resultant martyrdom of James and the intended martyrdom of Peter, may have been, it is evident that it arose with the Jews. Herod, out of respect for his Jewish subjects, had proceeded to Jerusalem to be present for the great annual Jewish feast of the Passover. Here he observed the cumulative opposition of the non-Christian Jews to the progress of the new Christian movement, and considering it good policy to please these troublesome Jewish subjects (v. 3a), "laid hands on certain members of the church, to do them violence" (Weymouth). James the Great, son of Zebedee and brother of John (see Matt. 20:20) — not James the less, son of Alphaeus — was the first victim to fall. The Jews, Clarke[82] observes, had four methods of execution: namely, *stoning, burning, beheading* with the sword, and *strangling*. Crucifixion was later adopted, probably from the Romans. Beheading with the sword was the punishment (according to the Talmud) for one who drew the people away to a strange worship. This probably accounts for the verdict against James and thus indicates something of his influence. He had the honor of being the *first apostle* to be martyred for Christ. No more is known of the incident. Herod evidently sought to stamp out the new movement by eliminating James and Peter, whom he thought to be the ringleaders. Therefore, after beheading James and observing that it improved his position with the Jews, as a foreign ruler, he proceeded to arrest and securely im-

[81] *Ibid.*, pp. 466-470; 550-554.   [82] Clarke, *op. cit.*, I, 774.

prison Peter by placing him under a special guard of sixteen soldiers, intending to execute him publicly after the Jewish passover.

B. THE DELIVERANCE OF PETER (12: 5-11)

Why God allowed James to be executed while He miraculously delivered Peter from the same fate is not known for certain. That an apostle's heroic martyrdom should have strengthened the faith of the church, as well as convinced the unbelieving of the real value of the Christian Way, seems most likely. Possibly James was Christ's best example of devotion, even unto death. The Hebrew children did not claim immunity from the fiery furnace, but they did declare their undivided devotion to God, even unto death, if necessary (Dan. 3:16-18). David likewise did not claim immunity from "the valley of the shadow of death," but he did claim Jehovah's comforting presence in that valley (Ps. 23:4). Perhaps James, like certain other ancient worthies, was "tortured, not accepting their deliverance; that they might obtain a better resurrection" (Heb. 11:35). In any event, for reasons best known to God, He allowed James to be martyred and spared Peter for further service.

1. The Prayer of the Church (12:5)

5 Peter therefore was kept in the prison: but prayer was made earnestly of the church unto God for him.

Is it possible that the martyrdom of James may have been due to the Jerusalem disciples having slacked their prayer vigil when rest from persecution came to the church with the conversion of the persecutor Saul (Acts 9:31)? Possibly it required this advantage of the enemy to drive them back to earnest and incessant prayer for Peter's deliverance from prison and impending execution. That these disciples knew the power of prayer is evident from Peter's earlier deliverances from the murderous designs of the Sanhedrin (Acts 4). Weymouth's translation of the passage is instructive: "but long and fervent prayer was offered to God by the church on his behalf." With Peter locked in prison and secured by a sixteen-man guard, the only hope of his deliverance lay in a miracle. Man's extremity again becomes God's opportunity, and the church learned the power of prayer in a crisis. Never was it truer than then that prayer alters apparently impossible situations.

2. The Plight of Peter (12:6)

6 And when Herod was about to bring him forth, the same night Peter was sleeping between two soldiers, bound with two chains: and guards before the door kept the prison.

Just how a condemned man may feel the night before his scheduled execution probably only that individual can know. Peter had likely watched the recent trial and bloody execution of his brother-apostle James. The memory of that gory spectacle was fresh in his mind. How would he stand up to the ordeal on the morrow? Many a man has lost his reason under similar circumstances. But we read concerning Peter: **the same night Peter was sleeping.** Indeed he slept between two soldiers to whom he was bound with two chains, **and guards before the door kept the prison,** or "were keeping" the prison. The language of the text seems to be intended to emphasize the security and apparent inescapableness of the prison, and at the same time the "rest of faith" that characterized the Apostle. Peter had learned the secret that "he giveth unto his beloved sleep" (Ps. 127:2b). Perhaps it was from this experience that Peter later wrote: "The Lord knoweth how to deliver [rescue: Weymouth] the godly out of temptation" (II Pet. 2:9a).

3. The Intervention of God (12:7-10)

7 And behold, an angel of the Lord stood by him, and a light shined in the cell: and he smote Peter on the side, and awoke him, saying, Rise up quickly. And his chains fell off from his hands. 8 And the angel said unto him, Gird thyself, and bind on thy sandals. And he did so. And he saith unto him, Cast thy garment about thee, and follow me. 9 And he went out, and followed; and he knew not that it was true which was done by the angel, but thought he saw a vision. 10 And when they were past the first and the second guard, they came unto the iron gate that leadeth into the city; which opened to them of its own accord: and they went out, and passed on through

one street; and straightway the angel departed from him.

And behold, an angel of the Lord stood by him. As the hour for execution drew near and the victory looked certain for the Jews who had instigated Peter's arrest and intended execution, and the disciples saw no hope of Peter's escape outside of God, it was then that the angel of the Lord appeared and things began to happen. The glory of God's presence illumined the inky black cell in which Peter was incarcerated. The angel gently smote Peter, awakening him without so much as disturbing the guards, took him by the hand and raised him to his feet, as the chains that had bound him to the soldiers fell as noiselessly to the floor as a feather to a cushion (v. 7). The angel then bade Peter, in a soundless language, to gird himself and follow him (v. 8). The whole procedure seemed to Peter to be too good to be real, and he thought it to be only an illusion or dream (v. 9). They passed the first and second guards without even arousing their suspicions that a major jail-break was in progress and then came to the great outer iron gate of the prison which, like an electric-eye door, automatically opened as they approached it. From here they passed into the open street where the angel left Peter a free man. What a miraculous and glorious deliverance! Who but God could have executed it? How utterly futile are man's efforts to outwit God!

4. The Considerations of Peter (12:11, 12a)

11 And when Peter was come to himself, he said, Now I know of a truth, that the Lord hath sent forth his angel and delivered me out of the hand of Herod, and from all the expectation of the people of the Jews. 12 And when he had considered *the thing,* he came to the house of Mary the mother of John whose surname was Mark;

The events of his deliverance had been so rapid that it took Peter a while to get his bearings as he stood there alone in the dark street as a free man.

The circumstances of Peter's deliverance from prison may be summed up as follows: he was conscious that he had his freedom; he stood alone in the street; he

realized that he must go somewhere; and he thought of the prospect of the friendly shelter of Mary's home where the comforts of life and kindly friends would welcome him. Perhaps he took in much more than the foregoing as he **considered the thing.** How much more we often see after some great deliverance than we were able to see before the deliverance came. God's emergency movements are too rapid for men either to follow or fully comprehend by reflection.

C. THE DILIGENCE OF THE CHURCH (12:12b-17)

Mention of the house of Mary greatly humanizes the church at Jerusalem. This Mary, mother of John Mark and thus an aunt to Barnabas, was evidently a Christian widow of considerable wealth and influence, as her home would indicate. She evidently played an important part in the lay life of the early church at Jerusalem. It should be observed that her house was approached by an imposing gate at which the portress Rhoda (Rose) attended (v. 3). Her spacious home provided for the assemblage of the church for worship (v. 12b), though this occasion could not have been an official meeting of the church since James and the other apostles were absent (v. 17b). It has been previously suggested (see note on Acts 1:12, 13) that her house was the scene of the Last Supper and the location of the Pentecostal effusion.

1. The Church's Concern (12:12b)

12 where many were gathered together and were praying.

This was no ordinary perfunctory mid-week prayer meeting. The life of the leading apostle, Peter, and perhaps the very existence of the church was at stake, and at this special, though unofficial, prayer meeting **many were gathered together and were praying.** Perhaps from this experience James learned that: "The effectual fervent prayer of a righteous man availeth much" (James 5:16—KJV).

2. The Church's Surprise (12:13-15)

13 And when he knocked at the door of the gate, a maid came to answer, named Rhoda. 14 And when she knew Peter's voice, she opened not the gate for joy, but ran in, and told that Peter

stood before the gate. 15 And they said unto her, Thou art mad. But she confidently affirmed that it was even so. And they said, It is his angel.

And they said, It is his angel. Common Jewish opinion held that guardian angels were generally provided for God's servants. However, only twice in the New Testament are special personal guardian angels mentioned: namely, in this instance and in Matthew 4:11. Popular belief allowed that on occasion one's guardian angel might assume his physical appearance and represent him. Such seems to have been the first thought of the disciples on the appearance of Peter at the home of Mary. Indeed, the damsel was convinced that Peter was present, but the disciples first judged her mad and then concluded that what she saw was Peter's angel. How human were these early disciples to fear to believe that God had answered their prayers!

3. The Church's Reward (12:16, 17)

16 But Peter continued knocking: and when they had opened, they saw him, and were amazed. 17 But he, beckoning unto them with the hand to hold their peace, declared unto them how the Lord had brought him forth out of the prison. And he said, Tell these things unto James, and to the brethren. And he departed, and went to another place.

In amazement they beheld Peter (v. 16b). Here was the answer to their prayers knocking for recognition while they prayed on for what they already had. Nowhere is the reality of answered prayer more clearly taught than in this instance. For their edification Peter rehearsed the details of the deliverance, authorized them to relay the report to James and the brethren, and then departed for regions unknown.

D. THE DEFEAT OF HEROD (12:18-25)

18 Now as soon as it was day, there was no small stir among the soldiers, what was become of Peter. 19 And when Herod had sought for him, and found him not, he examined the guards, and commanded that they should be put to death. And he went down from Judaea to Caesarea, and tarried there.

20 Now he was highly displeased with them of Tyre and Sidon: and they came with one accord to him, and having made Blastus the king's chamberlain their friend, they asked for peace, because their country was fed from the king's country. 21 And upon a set day Herod arrayed himself in royal apparel, and sat on the throne, and made an oration unto them. 22 And the people shouted, *saying*, The voice of a god, and not of a man. 23 And immediately an angel of the Lord smote him, because he gave not God the glory: and he was eaten of worms, and gave up the ghost.

24 But the word of God grew and multiplied.

25 And Barnabas and Saul returned from Jerusalem, when they had fulfilled their ministration, taking with them John whose surname was Mark.

Once again God outwitted Satan and removed the carefully designed plot to defeat and destroy the church. Peter made good his escape. Only once again is he mentioned in Acts, that in chapter 15, where some six years later he was present at the general church council held in Jerusalem, in A.D. 49 or 50.

The guards were unable to give a satisfactory account of the escape of the special prisoner, and consequently suffered execution. Herod suffered a horrible death, as divine judgment, at Caesarea consequent upon his assumption of a divine prerogative.

Consequent upon these events **the word of God grew and multiplied** (v. 24). The prosperity and progress of the church are assured when she finds her victories through faith in her glorified head, Christ. (For the meaning of v. 25, see exegetical note by Ralph Earle in Carter and Earle, *The Evangelical Commentary*, "The Acts of the Apostles," pp. 171, 172.)

XV. THE CHURCH'S FIRST GENTILE MISSIONARY CAMPAIGN (Acts 13:1-14:28)

A. THE MISSION INITIATED (13:1-3)

The missions of Philip to Samaria (Acts 8:5-13) and to the Ethiopian nobleman (Acts 8:26-40), of Peter to Caesarea (Acts 10:23-48), and the general preaching of the scattered disciples after the martyrdom of Stephen (Acts 8:1, 4), were all expressions of the infant church's missionary spirit and outlook. However, the record of Acts 13 gives us the first account of an organized missionary campaign to the great Gentile world outside of Judaism. Further, with the launching of the first missionary campaign, we observe the transfer of the base of missionary operation from the Jewish church at Jerusalem where she experienced her spiritual enduement, to the predominantly Gentile Christian church at Antioch, from which all three of the great missionary campaigns of Paul were launched.

1. The Source of the Mission (13:1, 2a)

1 Now there were at Antioch, in the church that was *there*, prophets and teachers, Barnabas, and Symeon that was called Niger, and Lucius of Cyrene, and Manaen the foster-brother of Herod the tetrarch, and Saul. 2 And as they ministered to the Lord, and fasted,

The first great Gentile missionary campaign found its origin among a spiritually vital and active corps of preachers (**prophets**), and **teachers,** who were carrying forth the work of the church at Antioch. Nor were their services merely perfunctory, but rather vital, as is evidenced by the fact that **they ministered to the Lord, and fasted** (v. 2a). A praying, supplicating, fasting, and praiseful church will ever be an active and fruitful church. One of the first laws of life in the spiritual organism, as in nature, is vital insurgency, or a disposition for life to break out of bounds and express itself. A second law of life is self-reproduction. The noted soul winner and church builder, Dr. John Timothy Stone, once presented the following telling illustration, bearing on the question of soul-winning. Hypothetically he produced two objects, the one a beautiful, ornate, symmetrical, and attractive agate, which any boy would desire. Beside it was placed an object that was rough and coarse in exterior appearance, unsymmetrical and unattractive, just a worthless acorn admired and desired by no one. "Should these two objects," stated Dr. Stone, "be buried together in fertile soil where the rain would moisten and the sun warm the earth, producing conditions favorable to germination, the acorn would soon sprout, grow, and eventually develop into a great spreading oak of beauty and value. The agate, on the other hand, would remain forever unresponsive to the atmospheric challenges. The difference in these two objects is the fact that the acorn is possessed of the germ of life, and life is insurgent and must ever reproduce itself, while the agate is inanimate and can never reproduce itself; it can never be other than what it is — just a beautiful, glossy, cold agate. It may deteriorate, but it will never reproduce itself. Likewise the church, regardless of culture, beauty of form, perfection of ritual, architectural impressiveness or material prosperity, that does not have in it the germ of spiritual life will die with the generation that produced it. The church possessed of the Spirit of God, though lacking any or all of these other admirable graces and characteristics, will reproduce itself spiritually, and there will be another generation of Christians."

When the ministers and teachers of a church sustain the vital relationship of the branch to the vine (John 15:5), there will be spiritual fruition.

There were no apostles in the Antioch church at this time. Prophets were of secondary rank to apostles. Both apostles and prophets characterized first-century Christianity and distinguished it from subsequent ages. Upon the foundation of the divine revelation given through these two offices, the church of Christ is built (Eph. 2:20). While the predictive element was not absent, New Testament prophets were for the most part "forth tellers" or preachers of the gospel. Paul defines their function as "edification," "exhortation," and "consolation" (I Cor. 14:3). The gift of prophecy was widely diffused (I Cor. 14:1), and even women not uncommonly exercised it (Acts 2:17). Philip is said to have had "four virgin daughters who prophesied" (Acts 21:9). Five prophets, or prophets and teachers, are here named in the Antioch church. Judas and Silas are later referred to as prophets at Antioch (Acts 15:32). Paul lists the divine order of the officers as "apostles, prophets, teachers, miracle workers, gifts of healing, helps, governments, and gifts of languages" (I Cor. 12:28). Those named at Antioch are Barnabas (see Acts 11:22-24), later the missionary companion of Paul; Symeon, otherwise known as Niger or Black, the latter a Roman surname, possibly a freedman from Africa; Lucius of Cyrene, an ancient African city state (see Acts 11: 20); Manaen, here designated the foster brother of Herod the tetrarch, but designated by the RSV, "a member of the court of Herod the tetrarch." Herod Antipas became ruler of Galilee and Perea after his father (Herod the Great) died, but was exiled to Gaul where he died in A.D. 39. Finally, Saul, who was to become the Great Apostle, is named.

The vital relationship of these Christians with Christ made them sensitive to the will of God and the directions of His Spirit (see Acts 8:29, 39; 10:19; 11:12; 13:4; 16:6). The Spirit, possibly through one of the several prophets, instructed the church to separate Barnabas and Saul for special missionary service. Thus the first great missionary campaign of the church was initiated by the Holy Spirit in and through a vitally spiritual ministering, fasting, and praying church at Antioch. Such situations always give birth to missionary endeavor. It was in a "haystack prayer meeting" that the modern American foreign missionary movement had its inception.

2. The Personnel of the Mission (13:2b)

2b the Holy Spirit said, Separate me Barnabas and Saul for the work whereunto I have called them.

The voice of God by the Holy Spirit (**the Holy Spirit said**) here indicates both His personality and office work in directing the affairs of the church.

Selection unto divine service is always conditioned upon spiritual relationship to God, moral worth, special gifts and graces, and holy zeal for Christ. A call to special divine service is characterized by: *first,* a period of unconscious preparation; *second,* a secret inner consciousness of God's will; *third,* the church's recognition and confirmation of the call; *fourth,* a period of specific preparation for the special service; *fifth,* human dedication to the field of service; *sixth,* an open door of service; and *seventh,* a fruitful ministry (see John 15:16). Careful examination will reveal how well Barnabas and Saul met these qualifications.

While it is Luke's primary purpose to narrate the history of Paul, rather than of Barnabas or another, throughout the remaining chapters of Acts, the evidence is conclusive that the divine wisdom was fully justified in selecting these men to become the first, great, Christian missionaries.

3. The Consecration of the Mission (13:3)

3 Then, when they had fasted and prayed and laid their hands on them, they sent them away.

The church's separation of Barnabas and Saul, at the Spirit's command, may well be regarded as their ordination unto apostleship by the church, as well as a sacred consecration to missionary service. Hereafter, from Acts 14:4, 14, they are both designated "apostles" by Luke. Whether Barnabas had met the requirements laid down by Peter for apostleship is a matter of doubt. That Paul had not, his enemies persistently contended (see Acts 1:21, 22). However, Paul's right of claim to the apostleship is well established: *first,* by his training (Acts 22:3); *second,* by his Christian experience on the Damascus road when the Lord appeared to him in a vision (I Cor. 15:8); *third,* by Christ's direct revelation of His Gospel unto him (Gal. 1:11, 12 and Eph. 3:1-4); *fourth,* by the Jerusalem apostles' recognition of him (Gal. 2:6-10); *fifth,* by the Antioch church's ordination and consecration of him to missionary service (Acts 13:2, 3); *sixth,* by the fruit of his service (Acts 13:49; 14:1, 21); *seventh,* by the divine miracles that accompanied his ministry (Acts 13:11; 14: 3, 10); and *eighth,* by his success in founding Christian churches in Asia Minor during his first missionary journey (Acts 14:23), and subsequently throughout much of the Roman world.

The moral and spiritual security afforded these heroic Christian apostles by the imposition of hands, backed up by fastings and earnest prayers on the part of the church at Antioch, doubtless accounted in large measure for the success of their enterprise. There is no substitute for the prayers of the home church in the missionary enterprise.

B. THE MISSION INAUGURATED (13:4-12)

The missionary campaign which was initiated by God through the Antioch church was now launched by the apostles under the evident direction of the Holy Spirit.

1. A Divinely Approved Campaign (13: 4a)

4 So they, being sent forth by the Holy Spirit, went down to Seleucia;

They [the church] **sent them away,** but the higher commission and personal direction of the campaign is expressed in Luke's statement here. Thus the divine commission and the human consecration collaborated in the inauguration of the first missionary enterprise of the church. On these words, **being sent forth by the Holy Spirit,** Clarke significantly observes: "By his *influence, authority,* and his *continual direction.* Without the *first,* they were not *qualified* to go; without the *second,* they had no *authority* to go; and without the *third,* they would not know *where to go.*"[83]

2. A Thoroughly Executed Campaign (13:4b-6a)

4 and from thence they sailed to Cyprus. 5 And when they were at Salamis, they proclaimed the word of God in the synagogues of the Jews: and they had also John as their attendant. 6 And when they had gone through the whole island unto Paphos,

That Barnabas and Paul had a very definite strategy in their missionary campaign becomes increasingly evident, both from the first and subsequent campaigns. Robinson[84] sees four elements in Paul's plan of advance. *First,* there was the selection of the strategic points of the empire as bases of operation; *second,* the establishment of self-sustained churches in each of these centers; *third,* the charging of these churches with the responsibility of evangelizing the surrounding area; *fourth,* the projection of Paul's personal evangelistic efforts through Asia Minor, Greece, Italy, and possibly Spain, thus planting Christianity clear across the Roman Empire.

Seleucia, from where the apostles set sail, was the seaport city of Antioch located near the mouth of the Orontes River, and about sixteen miles from Antioch. From thence they sailed in a southwesterly direction across the eastern Mediterranean Sea to the island of Cyprus. Cyprus, an island in the eastern Mediterranean Sea, sixty miles west of Syria, the chief cities of which were Salamis in the east and Paphos located at the west end, was the first target of the missionary campaign. The island had many Jewish communities.

At Salamis two important factors came to light. The first was Paul's lifelong strategy of evangelizing the Gentile world via the Jewish synagogue. Robinson[85] reckons that there were some 150 Jewish communities (and most, if not all, likely had synagogues in them) throughout the empire by the time of Paul. He further observes that they were relatively simple in structure and form of worship; that they maintained a close tie with the Jerusalem temple; and that they exercised a liberalizing influence upon Judaism by reason of their adaptation of the Jewish religion to their environment. Robinson also notes their reduction of the ceremonial law and greater emphasis upon the ethical and spiritual elements of religion, plus wide use of the Greek Septuagint in the services, and their intensive proselyting activities among the Gentiles, with special concessions to these converts. Paul, brought up in the synagogue of Tarsus, could best use the synagogue as a springboard for his evangelizing activities. The second factor was the appearance of John Mark at Salamis. Luke notes (Acts 12:25) that Barnabas and Saul took Mark with them from Jerusalem. Whether he accompanied them via Antioch or met them at Salamis is not known definitely. That Barnabas was from Cyprus (Acts 4:36) and that Mark was his cousin, may account for the expedition having been directed first to Cyprus where they had friends and acquaintances, and where already the gospel had been introduced (11:19, 20); and that John Mark was a sort of apprentice missionary appears likely; **they had also John** [Mark] **as their attendant** (v. 5b).

For a distance of 140 miles they traversed the island, visiting the towns and proclaiming the gospel until they came to Paphos. The incidents and fruits of their ministry en route from Salamis to Paphos are passed over by Luke, since

[83] Clarke, *op. cit.,* I, 780. [84] Robinson, *op. cit.,* pp. 74, 75. [85] *Ibid.,* pp. 9-12.

his primary concern is with certain important events at Paphos.

Paphos ranked second in importance to Salamis, but while Salamis was the capital of eastern Cyprus, Paphos, in the west, was the seat of the Roman government. Cyprus was a Roman senatorial province over which a proconsul (Sergius Paulus) presided, rather than a Caesarean or imperial province presided over by propraetors. The island was annexed by Rome in 57 B.C. and had formerly enjoyed the latter status but was given to the people by Augustus. Paphos was, further, the seat of the island's chief deity, Aphrodite or Venus, the worship of whom rendered Paphos one of the most immoral and dissolute centers of the world. The superb temple of Venus here with all its elaborate, but immoral, rites won for her the title "Queen of Paphos." To this stronghold of Satan, the Holy Spirit with purpose led the Christian apostles.

3. A Strongly Opposed Campaign (13: 6b-11)

6b they found a certain sorcerer, a false prophet, a Jew, whose name was Bar-Jesus; 7 who was with the proconsul, Sergius Paulus, a man of understanding. The same called unto him Barnabas and Saul, and sought to hear the word of God. 8 But Elymas the sorcerer (for so is his name by interpretation) withstood them, seeking to turn aside the proconsul from the faith. 9 But Saul, who is also *called* Paul, filled with the Holy Spirit, fastened his eyes on him, 10 and said, O full of all guile and all villany, thou son of the devil, thou enemy of all righteousness, wilt thou not cease to pervert the right ways of the Lord? 11 And now, behold, the hand of the Lord is upon thee, and thou shalt be blind, not seeing the sun for a season. And immediately there fell on him a mist and a darkness; and he went about seeking some to lead him by the hand.

Several things concerning Elymas or Bar-Jesus are noteworthy. *First,* he was an apostate Jewish prophet (v. 6), a man who had known the light of the divine revelation and had turned from the light to darkness (cf. Matt. 6:23; Luke 11:35; John 3:19-21). *Second,* he was **a false prophet** who subtly used his knowledge of the secret mysteries of the divine revelation, into which he had been

initiated as a Jewish prophet, to pervert the truth of God (v. 10b). *Third,* he was a **sorcerer,** or one who trafficked in "black magic," the most wicked and demoniacal of all known practices (v. 6). *Fourth,* he was a learned, wise, shrewd, cunning man, as his name Elymas (wise, skilled, learned) signifies. Since Bar-Jesus was his Jewish name, ironically signifying his purposes, in its Anglicized form, Elymas was probably the title given him ·by the inhabitants of Paphos in recognition of his skillful, though wicked, practices. Thus he was known at Paphos as Elymas, Bar-Jesus, or a doctor. *Fifth,* he seems to have been totally devoid of any remnants of such moral principles as sincerity, honesty, or good intentions, and so far depraved as to be capable of the most vicious or heinous crimes, as suggested by Paul's rebuke: **O full of all guile and villany.** *Sixth,* he appears to have so yielded himself to Satanic influence as to become partaker of the demoniacal nature to the extent that Paul could address him as **thou son of the devil.** *Seventh,* though strategically situated in a position of tremendous influence as the proconsul's moral and religious adviser or court chaplain (v. 7a), his evil influence was cast against every moral, religious, social, economic, and political good of humanity and the community. This appears evident from Paul's charge: **thou enemy of all righteousness.** What a formidable foe these "first term" missionaries confronted! Men of lesser conviction, courage, and faith might well have forsaken the field at this first serious engagement as they attempted to invade these fortified realms of Satan's dark domain.

Paul's assumption of the initiative in handling the case of Elymas may indicate a recognition of his superior wisdom and training to that of Barnabas, required to match the skill and cunning of this servant of Satan. That God wisely selects His servants with a view to their fitness for the occasion or situation is evidenced by successful experience and history alike. Nor are we to overlook the influence of the **Holy Spirit,** with whom Paul was **filled,** for this encounter with Satan. The wisest are helplessly weak in the presence of satanic forces without the wisdom and power of God's Spirit, and the unlearned and weak often become spiritual giants under the Spirit's influence (see I Cor. 1:26-29). Further, at this juncture Luke introduces the Apostle's Gentile name "Paul," by which he is consistently designated throughout the remainder of Acts and the New Testament, except in the reiteration of his conversion experience (see Acts 14:14; 15:12, 25; 22: 13; 26:14). While "Saul" was his Jewish name, now that his ministry has carried him into contact with the official Roman world, in which empire he has legal citizenship, it is both to his personal advantage and that of the Kingdom of Christ which he represents to be officially known as "Paul." Again, hereafter the order of names presented by Luke is usually Paul and Barnabas, instead of Barnabas and Saul as before, thus indicating the prominence of leadership into which Paul had entered.

Sergius Paulus gave every evidence of intelligent sincerity as he **called unto him Barnabas and Saul, and sought to hear the word of God** (v. 7b). The very presence of Elymas at his court may indicate a spiritual concern on the ruler's part. The Christian messenger is as obligated to reach up to those in high positions as to reach down to the social outcast. According to Finegan, "An inscription of the year A.D. 55 has been found at Paphos with the words 'in the time of the proconsul Paulus.' "[86] This evidence adds validity to Luke's account.

Paul's withering rebuke administered to Elymas produced results vividly reminiscent of the apostle's own Damascus road encounter with Christ (see Acts 9:3-9, 18). Origen and Chrysostom mention a tradition to the effect that Elymas became a Christian, and indeed the words of Paul, **thou shalt be blind . . . for a season,** seem to offer a ray of hope.

4. A Definitely Victorious Campaign (13:12)

12 Then the proconsul, when he saw what was done, believed, being astonished at the teaching of the Lord.

A practical-minded Roman officer could not be other than profoundly impressed by such demonstration of divine power.

The miracle of judgment inspired his faith in Christ's power to save and conditioned his mind for the reception and understanding of the teaching of the Lord. Thus Paul's first recorded convert is both a Gentile and a distinguished government official; "a member of the ancient patrician gens of the Sergii."[87]

The larger success of this mission of planting Christianity in Cyprus is indicated by Harnack's[88] citation of three bishops, Gelasues of Salamis, Cyrl of Paphos, and Spryidon of Trimithus, who attended the council of Nicaea in A.D. 325. Again, Harnack relates that the register of the synod of Sardica (A.D. 343) reveals the signatures of twelve bishops from Cyprus; both of which evidences are a testimony to the rapid growth of Christianity in Cyprus.

C. THE MISSION EXTENDED (13:13-43)

Having rapidly covered the homeland of Barnabas on Cyprus, the missionary party set sail across 170 miles of the Mediterranean toward the native country of Paul, for whose salvation his impassioned soul yearned.

1. The Geographical Exension (13:13, 14a)

13 Now Paul and his company set sail from Paphos, and came to Perga in Pamphylia: and John departed from them and returned to Jerusalem. 14 But they, passing through from Perga, came to Antioch of Pisidia;

Perga was the capital of the province of Pamphylia. Here Mark, for reasons unknown, forsook the party and evidently returned to Jerusalem. Whether he resented the ascension of Paul to leadership of the party over his cousin Barnabas, or became homesick, or was unable to stand the rigors of pioneer missionary travel, or was fearful of the wild mountain country before them, or whether Paul's more liberal views irked his Jewish prejudices, is left to conjecture. That Paul was displeased with Mark's conduct and made an issue of this incident at the outset of the second missionary journey, Luke frankly records (see Acts 15:36-39). However, Paul later testifies to the worth of Mark and thus indirectly credits the

86 Jack Finegan, *Light from the Ancient Past*, p. 260.
87 Dummelow, *op. cit.*, p. 835.   88 Harnack, *op. cit.*, II, 141.

judgment of Barnabas as superior in having given Mark another chance (see II Tim. 4:11).

Though some hold that a possible case of malaria or other illness contracted by Paul in the lowlands of Pamphylia accounted for his having moved on to the higher country northward (see Gal. 4:13-15), it would seem that the more likely explanation lies in Paul's passion to evangelize the regions beyond throughout Galatia. The Galatian letter's reference to Paul's infirmity appears more likely to indicate an eye affliction (see Gal. 4:15). The cities falling within the scope of his immediate objective were Pisidian Antioch, Iconium, Lystra, and Derbe, all of which were located in the southern section of the Roman province of Galatia.

Certain scholars of note, including Bishop Lightfoot, support the "Northern Galatian Theory," to the effect that the churches to which Paul wrote the Galatian letter were located in north Galatia proper, and included Tavium, Ancyra, and Pessimus. However, this position seems to lack sufficient support, especially in the light of the fact that there is no specifically recorded missionary journey nor account of the establishment of churches in those parts. On the other hand, Luke records the missionary journey to the cities of southern Galatia and gives an account of the establishment of the several churches there. This latter view holds that the Galatian epistle was written to churches of Pisidia, Antioch, Iconium, Lystra, and Derbe, established on Paul's first missionary journey.

In support of the southern view are the following evidences: *first,* we have a clear record of the Apostle's visit to, and establishment of churches in, the cities of the Roman province of southern Galatia, whereas we have no definite record of either a visit to, or establishment of, churches in northern Galatia proper; nor is there any reference to the existence of any churches in northern Galatia until about a century and a half later. *Second,* the Roman province of Galatia included the southern states mentioned in Acts 13 and 14, as well as northern ethnic Galatia (see I Pet. 1:1). *Third,* Paul repeatedly alludes to Barnabas in the Galatian letter as though he were

well known to the Galatians, and we know that he accompanied Paul on this first journey to southern Galatia, whereas he was not with Paul on his second or any subsequent journey as far as is known. *Fourth,* Paul refers to his readers as Galatians (Gal. 3:1), the customary Roman designation and the only term by which· he could correctly address both Lycaonians and Phrygians. The principal exponents of this southern Galatian theory are Ramsay and Findlay. If this more likely position is adopted, then Paul's letter to the Galatians will serve as an illuminating commentary on the Acts account of this missionary journey to Asia Minor. It is noteworthy that, outside of the Galatian letter, there are but five New Testament references to Galatia (Acts 16:6; 18:23; I Cor. 16:1; II Tim. 4:10; I Pet. 1:1).

Antioch of Pisidia, the next objective of the apostles, was the Roman capital of Antioch of Pisidia or "Pisidian Antioch," and is so called because of its unusual location. It was situated at an altitude of approximately 3,600 feet and was traversed by the great overland highway passing from Syria and the East to Ephesus, and thence by sea route to the West. It had been made a free city about 189 B.C., and a Roman colony with citizenship rights by Augustus Caesar sometime before 11 B.C. Its extensive ruins indicate its prominence in Paul's day. It was located near the modern Turkish city of Yalovath. It was a thoroughly Hellenized and Romanized city, though the Phrygians and Pisidians were a less highly civilized people. It was the seat of Roman civil and military administration for southern Galatia. Being a Roman citizen (Acts 22:29) as well as a citizen of the kingdom of heaven, Paul's wisdom and the Holy Spirit's leadings are clearly evidenced in the selection of this advantageous location for the Apostle's ambassadorial entry into Galatia. Main overland routes, governmental capitals, centers of population, and Jewish synagogues were a part of Paul's strategy for the spread of the gospel.

2. The Evangelical Extension (13:14b-43)

14b and they went into the synagogue on the sabbath day, and sat down. 15 And after the reading of the law and the prophets the rulers of the synagogue sent unto them, saying, Brethren, if ye have any word of exhortation for the people, say on. 16 And Paul stood up, and beckoning with the hand said,

Men of Israel, and ye that fear God, hearken: 17 The God of this people Israel chose our fathers, and exalted the people when they sojourned in the land of Egypt, and with a high arm led he them forth out of it. 18 And for about the time of forty years as a nursing-father bare he them in the wilderness. 19 And when he had destroyed seven nations in the land of Canaan, he gave *them* their land for an inheritance, for about four hundred and fifty years: 20 and after these things he gave *them* judges until Samuel the prophet. 21 And afterward they asked for a king: and God gave unto them Saul the son of Kish, a man of the tribe of Benjamin, for the space of forty years. 22 And when he had removed him, he raised up David to be their king; to whom also he bare witness and said, I have found David, the son of Jesse, a man after my heart, who shall do all my will. 23 Of this man's seed hath God according to promise brought unto Israel a Saviour, Jesus; 24 when John had first preached before his coming the baptism of repentance to all the people of Israel. 25 And as John was fulfilling his course, he said, What suppose ye that I am? I am not *he*. But behold, there cometh one after me the shoes of whose feet I am not worthy to unloose. 26 Brethren, children of the stock of Abraham, and those among you that fear God, to us is the word of this salvation sent forth. 27 For they that dwell in Jerusalem, and their rulers, because they knew him not, nor the voices of the prophets which are read every sabbath, fulfilled *them* by condemning *him*. 28 And though they found no cause of death *in him*, yet asked they of Pilate that he should be slain. 29 And when they had fulfilled all things that were written of him, they took him down from the tree, and laid him in a tomb. 30 But God raised him from the dead: 31 and he was seen for many days of them that came up with him from Galilee to Jerusalem, who are now his witnesses unto the people. 32 And we bring you good tidings of the promise made unto the fathers, 33 that God hath fulfilled the same unto our children, in that he raised up Jesus; as also it is written in the second psalm, Thou art my Son, this day have I begotten thee. 34 And as concerning that he raised him up from the dead, now no more to return to corruption, he hath spoken on this wise, I will give you the holy and sure *blessings* of David. 35 Because he saith also in another *psalm*, Thou wilt not give thy Holy One to see corruption. 36 For David, after he had in his own generation served the counsel of God, fell asleep, and was laid unto his fathers, and saw corruption: 37 but he whom God raised up saw no corruption. 38 Be it known unto you therefore, brethren, that through this man is proclaimed unto you remission of sins: 39 and by him every one that believeth is justified from all things, from which ye could not be justified by the law of Moses. 40 Beware therefore, lest that come upon *you* which is spoken in the prophets:

41 Behold, ye despisers, and wonder, and perish;

For I work a work in your days,

A work which ye shall in no wise believe, if one declare it unto you.

42 And as they went out, they besought that these words might be spoken to them the next sabbath. 43 Now when the synagogue broke up, many of the Jews and of the devout proselytes followed Paul and Barnabas; who, speaking to them, urged them to continue in the grace of God.

And they went into the synagogue on the sabbath day, . . . And Paul stood up (vv. 14b, 16a). No inconsiderable number of Jews dwelt in the cities of Asia Minor, and it was natural that they should have possessed a synagogue at this important location. As was his strategy, Paul with Barnabas resorted to the synagogue at Antioch on their first sabbath in the city, both for worship and with a view to an opportunity to present the gospel of Christ. Here they sat down until after the customary reading of the Law and the Prophets. Dummelow's Commentary outlines the order of the synagogue services as follows:

(1) the recitation of the Shema (i.e., of Deut. 6:4-9; 11:13-21; Num. 15:37-41); (2) fixed prayers and benedictions; (3) a lesson from the Law; (4) a lesson from the Prophets, intended to illustrate the law; (5) a sermon or instruction. The ruler of the synagogue (at Antioch there appears to have been more than one) decided who was to read or preach.[89]

Recognized by the rulers of the synagogue as Jewish brethren, though

89 Dummelow, *op. cit.*, p. 835.

strangers, Paul and Barnabas were bidden to bring the congregation an exhortation, or better a "consolation," or encouragement to their hopes. Scattered throughout the ancient world with no independent national life, these people, like Simeon at the birth of Christ, were "looking for the consolation of Israel," their coming Messiah (Luke 2:25). Any message by a credentialed Jew that could direct their hopes to the soon-coming of their long-awaited Messiah would be welcome indeed; and so especially welcome were messengers from Jerusalem, as was the case with Paul and Barnabas. Such an invitation afforded a coveted opportunity for Paul to deliver to his brethren in Israel at Antioch the glorious gospel that this Messiah of their fond hopes was at hand. The sermon that follows is Paul's first recorded address and here, as in all of his subsequent recorded sermons, is clearly revealed the influence of the underlying principles of Stephen's valedictorian address of Acts 7. Indeed the influence of Peter's Pentecostal Day sermon on Paul may not be entirely lacking, but even this may more likely have come to the Apostle indirectly through Stephen's address to which Paul, as Saul the youthful persecutor, listened and from the influence of which he was never quite able to free himself (cf. Acts 7:58; 8:1; 26:10b; and 26:14).

An analysis of Paul's sermon, which follows in verses 16 through 47, might appear as follows:

1. *An address of recognition and courtesy* (v. 16).
2. *A Jewish historical frame of reference,* with the facts of which his audience was familiar (vv. 17-25).
3. *Certain scriptural, historical, and logical deductions from the foregoing,* concerning Christ as the Messiah of the Jews and the Savior of all mankind (vv. 26-37).
4. *A practical application of these truths to his audience* (vv. 38, 39).
5. *A solemn warning and impassioned appeal to his hearers,* lest they suffer the fate of their ancient forefathers in the wilderness (vv. 40, 41).

First, concerning the address, it need be noted that when **Paul stood up, and** [beckoned] **with the hand,** he was employing a familiar gesture designed to arrest attention and establish rapport with his audience. Further, the address, **Men of Israel, and ye that fear God,** clearly indicates that Paul recognized two general classes of hearers before him: *first,* the "Jews of the dispersion"; and, *second,* "God-fearers," or those Gentiles who were privileged to worship the true God, Jehovah, in the non-liturgical services of the synagogue, but who did not subscribe to the Jewish ceremonials of circumcision or strict observance of the Law. They were "God-fearers," but not full proselytes. That there were many such Gentiles out in the empire and beyond who benefited from the spiritual worship of Jehovah through the synagogue is clearly evident. When a minister fails to recognize properly his audience and its components, he will usually fail to gain its attention and interest for his message. When a minister duly recognizes and respects his audience, he will usually gain the respect of the audience for himself and his message.

Whether Paul meant to include the **devout proselytes** of verse 43 in the class of **Men of Israel,** or **ye that fear God,** in verse 16, is not clear. However, from the foregoing facts it would seem that they were among the former, and that the special mention made of these **devout proselytes** in verse 43 is intended to indicate that they, like the Jews, had a more profound understanding of the relationship of the Law of Moses to the promised Messiah and consequently grasped more easily and clearly the implications of Paul's message. Further, to have recognized them as **Men of Israel** in his address would have been a distinct compliment to them and no offense to the Jews, if indeed not a compliment to the Jews also.

Second, Paul launches abruptly into his message: (1) he sympathetically relates his congregation to the God of Israelitish history, then identifies himself with them: **The God of this people Israel chose our fathers** (v. 17); (2) he makes a patriotic allusion to the Israelitish nation's deliverance from Egyptian bondage under the direct intervention of God; **exalted the people** [delivered and vindicated them] **when they sojourned in the land of Egypt, and with a high arm** [a demonstration of divine power over their enemies] **led them forth out of it** (v. 17b); (3) in a sweeping statement he covers forty years of wilderness wanderings followed with a reminder of God's patience with, and care over, them: **as a nursing-father bare he them in the wilderness** (v. 18b); (4) next he summarily reviews God's power and the fulfillment of His promise in destroying the Canaanites, after which He fulfilled His promise and **gave them their land for an inheritance, for about four hundred and fifty years** (v. 19); (5) the period of the Judges is briefly cited with the notation of its termination with their illustrious prophet Samuel (v. 20); (6) God's compliance with their request for a king follows with the coronation of Saul of the tribe of Benjamin whose reign lasted forty years (v. 21); (7) a delicate reference to Saul's removal follows (v. 22a), after which Paul arrives at the crux of his message in the introduction of King David of whom God testified: **a man after my heart, who shall do all my will** (v. 22b); (8) through the posterity of David, Paul declares that God has fulfilled His age-old promise to Israel, of a Messiah (**a Saviour**) in the person of **Jesus** (v. 23); (9) this conclusion is then collaborated by John the Baptist's prediction of Christ's coming, his mission of repentance to Israel, and the personal testimony of John to Christ as the Messiah (vv. 23, 24), all facts with which his hearers were familiar. Thus the historical foundation of this sermon is complete.

Third, the Apostle proceeds to make his deductions, from these known and acknowledged facts, concerning Christ as the Jews' Messiah and the Savior of all men.

Paul (1) tightens his psychological grasp upon his audience by a renewed direct address: **Brethren, children of the stock of Abraham, and those among you that fear God** (v. 26a); (2) he then boldly asserts that Israel has already given birth to the child of her age-old expectations, and that his mission is to announce to them that glorious consummation: **to us is the word of this salvation sent forth** (v. 26); (3) then, anticipating their likely objections to his identification of Jesus Christ with the Messiah, because of the Jews' rejection of Christ at Jerusalem, of which fact they would have had knowl-

edge, Paul proceeds to disqualify the adverse judgment of the Sanhedrin on the grounds (a) that they really did not know Jesus Christ, (b) that they did not understand the real significance of the prophetic writing which they regularly read, (c) that they actually fulfilled those prophecies concerning Christ by their official condemnation of him, (d) that they had dishonestly and unjustly rendered their judgment in demanding the death sentence for Christ when **they found no cause of death in him** (vv. 28, 29).

Next (4) Paul proceeds to declare the culminating fact of Christianity that **God raised him from the dead** (v. 30a), and (5) he supports this claim by the fact of His post-resurrection appearances to His disciples who, including the speaker, **are now his witnesses unto the people** (v. 31b). How well Paul has grasped the significance of Christ's words in Acts 1:8! (6) Paul personally applies the benefits of Christ's resurrection from the dead to his hearers (v. 33), and then supports the resurrection of Christ by reference to the Psalms of David wherein His eternal victory over death is clearly predicted (vv. 34-37).

Fourth, Paul offers the practical benefits of Christ's atoning death and resurrection to his hearers as (1) remission of sins (v. 38b); (2) justification by faith (v. 39a); and (3) superiority of Christian grace to the Mosaic Law in doing for man what the Law could never do (v. 39b).

Fifth, while Paul's sermon differs from Peter's and Stephen's in his appeal to David as against their appeal to Moses for support, it does nevertheless correspond with their addresses in its conclusion. This conclusion consists of (1) a solemn warning against his hearers suffering the fate of their forefathers who rejected the voice of God in the wilderness (vv. 40, 41a); (2) a reference to the exhibition of divine power designed to produce their salvation (v. 41b).

In this, Paul's first recorded sermon, is distinctly advanced his great doctrine of "justification by faith," as opposed to justification by the works of the Law (v. 39), a doctrine the discovery of which spiritually awakened the slumbering soul of a German monk nearly fifteen centuries later and produced the history-changing Protestant Reformation of A.D. 1517. Further, this sermon reveals that the people, to whom he later wrote the Galatian Epistle on this subject of justification, had already been enlightened (see Gal. 2:16; 3:16; 3:1-15). Some doctrines that emerge from this sermon are divine providence, divine omnipotence, divine judgment, repentance, divine revelation, the death of Christ, the resurrection of Christ, the appearances of Christ, the divine sonship of Christ, and forgiveness of sins. Interestingly, the doctrine of baptism is totally absent, even though there were converts (vv. 48, 52).

The spiritual interest and desire awakened in the minds of Jew and Gentile alike by Paul's sermon is evident; and **as they went out, they** [both Jews and Gentile proselytes] **besought that these words might be spoken to them the next sabbath** (v. 42). The apostles, taking advantage of their awakened souls, further instructed and encouraged these new believers **to continue in the grace of God** (v. 43).

D. THE MISSION INTERRUPTED (13: 44-52)

As at Paphos, so at Antioch, the enemy would not allow his domain to be invaded and his subjects taken captive by the gospel of Christ without violent opposition. At Antioch, as usual in the ministry of Paul, the Jews were the greatest opponents of the gospel of Christ.

1. The Cause of the Interruption (13: 44, 45)

44 And the next sabbath almost the whole city was gathered together to hear the word of God. 45 But when the Jews saw the multitudes, they were filled with jealousy, and contradicted the things which were spoken by Paul and blasphemed.

The broadcasting of Paul's sermon throughout the week by those who had heard him, especially the God-fearers, and those who were spiritually awakened, resulted in an assemblage of **almost the whole city** on the following sabbath **to hear the word of God** (v. 44).

The resultant jealousy and opposition of the Jews likely arose from two causes: *first,* out of their envy at seeing the God-fearing Gentiles, whom they had hoped to convert to Judaism, drawn away to Chris-

tianity; and *second,* from their fear that the teachings of the apostles would undermine and destroy the whole structure of Judaism, and thus the new faith would supersede that system, as indeed Paul had already intimated in his first sermon (vv. 27-31). The form of their opposition is said to be "contradiction" and "blasphemy." The former probably consisted of historical and theological arguments, and the latter of insinuations and charges against the person and character of Christ, based on reports they had acquired from Jerusalem.

2. The Nature of the Interruption (13: 46-51)

46 And Paul and Barnabas spake out boldly, and said, It was necessary that the word of God should first be spoken to you. Seeing ye thrust it from you, and judge yourselves unworthy of eternal life, lo, we turn to the Gentiles. 47 For so hath the Lord commanded us, *saying,*
I have set thee for a light of the Gentiles,
That thou shouldest be for salvation unto the uttermost part of the earth.
48 And as the Gentiles heard this, they were glad, and glorified the word of God: and as many as were ordained to eternal life believed. 49 And the word of the Lord was spread abroad throughout all the region. 50 But the Jews urged on the devout women of honorable estate, and the chief men of the city, and stirred up a persecution against Paul and Barnabas, and cast them out of their borders. 51 But they shook off the dust of their feet against them, and came unto Iconium.

In verse 46 Paul clearly indicates that it is a part of his missionary strategy to preach the gospel first to the Jews, using the synagogue as a door of entrance to the Gentile world (see Rom. 1:14-16). Herein Paul reveals what so many Bible scholars until today have failed to see: namely, that the Jews were not a people chosen especially of God unto salvation, to the exclusion of the Gentiles, but rather they were chosen and prepared to become a missionary nation to proclaim the gospel of God to all people of the earth. This is the thesis of Paul in his letter to the Romans where in chapter 9 he presents God's election of Israel as a missionary people, in chapter 10 His rejection of Israel from this office and function because of their rejection of Christ and His gospel (thus leaving them without a message), and in chapter 11 His partial restoration of Israel based on their acceptance of Christ. Nowhere in His word has God revealed an election of the Jews, as a nation, to salvation, to the exclusion of the Gentiles, nor their rejection, as a nation, from salvation. Salvation is always and everywhere a matter of the "personal" acceptance of God's offered mercy in Christ.

Paul's declaration, **lo, we turn to the Gentiles** (v. 46b), does not close the door of hope to the Jews, nor does it indicate that he will not hereafter preach to the Jews. It is to be understood that since the Jews at Antioch have rejected the gospel and thus "judged themselves" (not "are judged") **unworthy of eternal life,** the apostles will henceforth address themselves to the Gentiles at Antioch. This decision the apostles justify by reference to their own prophet who foresaw the universal implications of the great plan of redemption (cf. Isa. 49:6 and Acts 2:39; see also Acts 18:6 and 28:28).

The Gentiles having grasped the universal implications of Paul's words greatly rejoiced and **glorified the word of God** (v. 48a).

Luke's statement, **and as many as were ordained to eternal life believed,** receives a most illuminating treatment by Dummelow:

> This expresses the Pauline and Apostolic doctrine of predestination, according to which God desires the salvation of all men (I Tim. 2:4; 4:10, etc.), but insomuch as He foresees that some (in the exercise of their free will) will actually repent and believe, while others will refuse to do so, He ordains the former to eternal life, and the latter to eternal death (Rom. 8:28-30, etc.).[90]

What is clear from this passage and its setting, and is consistent with the whole plan of divine redemption, is that while God ordains unto eternal life all that will believe, and to eternal death all that do not believe, it must be observed that God neither ordains the "act of believing" nor the "act of unbelief." These are acts of man's intelligent moral volition, for the exercise of which he bears

[90] *Ibid.,* p. 836.

full moral responsibility (see John 3:16-21 and 3:36).

When it is understood that the words of verse 44, **almost the whole city was gathered together,** would imply not just the town residents but those of the country as well, or the regions of Pisidia (Clarke), then Luke's statement of verse 49 takes on meaning: **And the word of the Lord was spread abroad throughout all the region.** Thus the apostles' wisdom is justified in their selection of Antioch as their first strategic Galatian center from which to evangelize.

The **devout women of honorable estate** affected by the Jewish propaganda against the apostles were likely the wives of prominent Gentile citizens, if not government officers, who had become proselytes to the Jewish faith. These women were now used by these Jews to influence their husbands, the chief men of the city, to take action against Paul and Barnabas by arresting, roughly treating, and expelling them from Antioch and Pisidia. How like the tactics of the Sanhedrin in handling the case of Jesus, and later those against Paul at Jerusalem upon his arrest.

The action of Paul and Barnabas, upon leaving Antioch, when **they shook off the dust of their feet against them** (v. 51), was well understood by the Jews who regarded it as a curse pronounced upon their enemies. When traveling in heathen lands outside of Canaan, the Jews paused at the borders and shook the contaminated dust from their feet and garments before re-entering their sacred land, lest they defile it. Thus, this act of the apostles signified that the Jews of Antioch had taken a curse upon themselves in rejecting the gospel and its messengers (see Matt. 10:14; Mark 6:11; Luke 9:5; and Acts 18:6).

3. The Results of the Interruption (13:52)

52 And the disciples were filled with joy and with the Holy Spirit.

Again the irony of the situation turns out to the glory of God and the benefit of His disciples. These disciples, like those at Thessalonica, "received the word in much affliction," but "with joy of the Holy Spirit" (I Thess. 1:6b). Such discipleship bids fair for the success of the church in any situation.

The ultimate success of this initial invasion of Antioch with the gospel is in evidence at a later date. Says Finegan:

> Also there was a Christian basilica at Antioch which was more than 200 feet long, and which dates, according to an inscription, in the time of Optimus, who was bishop of Antioch in the last quarter of the fourth century.[91]

E. THE MISSION RESUMED (14:1-7)

Feeling that their work in Antioch was completed and nothing daunted by their persecution, Paul and Barnabas followed the injunctions of the Lord (Matt. 10: 23) and moved on to the next important city of Iconium. This distance of sixty miles southeastward they traversed by the Roman highway that followed the ancient Alexandrian route eastward to a verdant and fruitful plateau watered by Pisidian mountain streams. Here Iconium, a flourishing city of strategic importance located at a crossroads in Pisidia, and honored with the title Caludiconium but later named a Roman colony by Hadrian, met the vision and challenged the spirits of these Christian ambassadors. A modern Turkish city of 47,000 people, bearing the name of Konia, is located at the site of ancient Iconium.

1. The Methods Employed (14:1-3a)

1 And it came to pass in Iconium that they entered together into the synagogue of the Jews, and so spake that a great multitude both of Jews and of Greeks believed. 2 But the Jews that were disobedient stirred up the souls of the Gentiles, and made them evil affected against the brethren. 3 Long time therefore they tarried *there* speaking boldly in the Lord,

Luke employs three phrases that subtly suggest the successful methods of the apostles at Iconium: namely, **entered together into the synagogue . . . so spake. . . . Long time therefore they tarried there speaking boldly in the Lord** (vv. 1, 3a). Here, as always, the missionaries chose the little synagogue for the initiation of the gospel among the Iconians. Experience gained and success attained at Antioch afforded them definite advantages here.

The words **so spake** characterize the ministry of Paul and Barnabas as probably tactful in approach, understanding of the constituency and mental attitudes of their audiences, but with such faith and holy boldness as enabled the Spirit of God to be demonstrated in mighty power (cf. I Thess. 1:5). Their recent success at Antioch revealed its influence on the beginning of their ministry at Iconium. Experience may serve either to strengthen or weaken the ministry of God's servants, depending on the manner in which it is used.

Luke's expression, **Long time therefore they tarried there speaking boldly in the Lord** (v. 3a), can only be properly understood in the light of the persecution directed against Paul and Barnabas at Iconium. The first persecution likely consisted in a legal attempt of the Jews to have the apostles officially expelled. This would appear to be the sense of the words, **But the Jews . . . stirred up the souls of the Gentiles** [likely the Roman officials as they are not called Greeks], **and made them evil affected against the brethren** (v. 2). Whether considered as disturbers of the peace, or slanderously charged, the attempt apparently failed. However, it evidently required time among this strange people for the apostles to "live down" the false accusations and prejudices and prove to the people the truth of the gospel. As when God sought to deliver Israel from Egypt by the hand of Moses, He demonstrated His power as superior to that of the Egyptian magicians and deities, so God here manifested Himself through Paul and Barnabas in **signs and wonders . . . done by their hands** (v. 3b). Thus their ministry of the Word, their perseverance, and God's manifest power combined to accomplish success in Iconium.

2. The Results Achieved (14:3b-7)

.3b who bare witness unto the word of his grace, granting signs and wonders to be done by their hands. 4 But the multitude of the city was divided; and part held with the Jews, and part with the apostles. 5 And when there was made an onset both of the Gentiles and of the

91 Finegan, *op. cit.*, p. 262.

Jews with their rulers, to treat them shamefully and to stone them, 6 they became aware of it, and fled unto the cities of Lycaonia, Lystra and Derbe, and the region round about: 7 and there they preached the gospel.

Luke's statement in verse 1, that a **great multitude both of Jews and of Greeks believed** (Jews and Greek God-fearers or proselytes to the Jewish faith), indicates the initial success of the gospel ministry in Iconium.

However, the great success of their ministry had the further effect of precipitating a second persecution in which **the city was divided; and part held with the Jews, and part with the apostles** (v. 4). Doubtless it was the sword of truth that sharply divided the believing from the unbelieving (Matt. 10:34-36), but it was the Jews who instigated the actual attack against the apostles, of which Luke says: **there was made an onset both of the Gentiles and of the Jews with their rulers, to treat them shamefully and to stone them** (v. 5). Legal procedure having evidently failed in the first attempt (v. 2), the Jews finally resorted to mob violence, as at Thessalonica (see Acts 17:5), to rid themselves of these emissaries of the gospel of Christ. Seeing that every principle of justice was cast to the wind by their enemies, so that they could accomplish nothing further under the circumstances and that the new believers would be safer for their absence, the apostles decided, as in like circumstances at Thessalonica (Acts 17:9, 10), to evade further trouble by departing **to the cities of Lycaonia, Lystra and Derbe, and the region round about:** [where] they preached the gospel (vv. 6b, 7).

Three items of interest accompany the introduction of the gospel at Iconium. In the *first* place, it is here that Paul and Barnabas are first called "apostles" by Luke, though they were evidently ordained or consecrated to that office at Antioch of Syria (Acts 13:1-3). The *second* item concerns a legend recorded by Dummelow:

The curious second-century romance, 'The Acts of Paul and Thecla,' gives many additional particulars of St. Paul's proceedings at Iconium, some of which, perhaps are authentic. Thecla, who belonged to one of the chief families of

Iconium, overheard from a window the preaching of the apostle. She was at that time engaged to a young man named Thamyris, but on hearing St. Paul's words she became so enamoured of virginity that she broke off her engagement. For this interference with family life, and for impiety, St. Paul was scourged and expelled from the city, and Thecla was condemned to be burnt alive. A fall of rain extinguished the fire, and she escaped and followed Paul to Antioch. Here again she was persecuted, but was rescued by Tryphaena, a lady of great influence. The presbyter who composed this romance (though it was probably founded on a fact) was deposed from his office.[92]

The *third* item of interest associated with Iconium is a famous description of Paul, as contained in the apocryphal *Acts of Paul* and recorded by Finegan. The account reads as follows:

A man of little stature, thin-haired upon the head, crooked in the legs, of good state of body, with eyebrows joining, and nose somewhat hooked, full of grace; for some times he appeared like a man, and sometimes he had the face of an angel.[93]

F. THE APOSTLES IDOLIZED (14:8-20)

To understand the attempted worship of the apostles at Lystra it is necessary to understand, at least in a measure, these Lycaonian peoples of **Lystra and Derbe, and the region round about** (v. 6b).

The distance from Iconium to Lystra was eighteen miles in a south-southwestward direction, and the elevation of this city was approximately 3,800 feet. The modern city of this site is likely Zolders. Both Lystra and Derbe were in the Lycaonian region, and at the time of the apostles' visit, the peoples spoke the Lycaonian vernacular (Acts 14:11), though Latin was the official language. Lystra, like Antioch, was a Roman colony. Derbe was located some twenty miles southeast of Lystra and is supposed to be represented by the modern village of Zosta or Losta.

No mention is made of a synagogue here, and it is apparent that the inhabitants were largely without Judaistic influence. They were a grossly superstitious heathen people who had de-

92 Dummelow, *op. cit.*, p. 836.   93 Finegan, *op. cit.*, p. 263.

scended from the Gauls, who in turn had settled there in the third century B.C. They were characterized (if we are to judge from Paul's letter to the Galatians) by mental alertness, generosity, impressibility, impulsiveness, inconstancy, vehemence, treacherousness, quarrelsomeness, discouragement, extreme and gross superstition (see Gal. 1:6; 4:8; 5:15; Acts 14:11, 12). It is noteworthy that of the fifteen works of the flesh listed in Galatians 5: 20, 21, five are sins of strife. Such were the people to whom the apostles preached the gospel at Lystra and Derbe (cf. Acts 5:42; 13:32; 14:15).

1. The Occasion of the Idolization (14:8-10)

8 And at Lystra sat a certain man impotent in his feet, a cripple from his mother's womb, who never had walked. 9 The same heard Paul speaking: who, fastening his eyes upon him, and seeing that he had faith to be made whole, 10 said with a loud voice, Stand upright on thy feet. And he leaped up and walked.

How similar is this incident to the healing of the cripple at the Gate Beautiful in Acts 3:1-10! Here sat, or probably better — sprawled, a pitiable wretch of humanity who had likely been born with clubfeet that were totally useless for locomotion, a familiar daily spectacle to the citizens of the city, an object of charity to whom they occasionally tossed alms. As is common among such primitive pagans, his deformity was likely regarded as a curse of the gods or fate, for some sin committed by his ancestry, a fatalistic view (Karma) imbibed also by some of the Jews (see John 9:1-3) and refuted by the experiences and faith of Job. How utterly helpless is paganism to alleviate the sufferings and elevate the status of unfortunate humanity! But what an opportunity and challenge was afforded the Christian apostles to demonstrate to this pagan community the power of the God of Christianity!

What this cripple **heard Paul speaking** we are not told. Possibly he related an incident of healing from the ministry of Christ, or possibly the very incident of the healing of the cripple at the Gate Beautiful. In any event what he heard awakened faith within him (see Rom. 10:14-17), a fact Paul was quick to detect:

seeing that he had faith to be made whole (v. 9b). A twofold human assistance was afforded his faith. The first was the electrifying eye contact through which the Apostle radiated the faith of his own living soul to the dormant soul of the cripple, thereby awakening and inspiring him to life and hope. The second consisted in the Apostle's authoritative command, most probably given in the name of the Lord Jesus, when he **said with a loud voice, Stand upright on thy feet** (v. 10a). In the first, "faith begets faith," while in the second, "authority begets action." God's living messengers are always animating, and his authoritative commands are always action-producing. The full evidence of his miraculous healing is seen in the fact that **he leaped up and walked** (v. 10b). His was not a psychological superimposed benefit by a super-psychic healer giving him temporary relief, only to slump back into a deeper despair after the excitement subsided and the human inspiration had been removed; but now, restored, he proceeded on a normal course of life, as suggested by the word **walked.**

The word **leaped** may suggest a natural and joyful emotional reaction to the sudden realization of his having been made whole, as well as prompt obedience to Paul's command, but the word **walked** suggests the permanence of his cure. Thus God selected for the demonstration of His power before these pagans a hopeless, organically disordered victim which no power or trick of magic or super-psychic influence could change, but which His power could make every whit whole.

2. The Attempt at Idolization (14:11-13)

11 And when the multitude saw what Paul had done, they lifted up their voice, saying in the speech of Lycaonia, The gods are come down to us in the likeness of men. 12 And they called Barnabas, Jupiter; and Paul, Mercury, because he was the chief speaker. 13 And the priest of Jupiter whose *temple* was before the city, brought oxen and garlands unto the gates, and would have done sacrifice with the multitudes.

So profoundly overcome by the evident miracle of divine healing were these impressionable peoples that with one voice they gave expression in their Lycaonian vernacular to their natural, pagan, religious concepts: **The gods are come down to us in the likeness of men** (v. 11b). Nor was this anthropomorphic idea of the pagan divinities new to the Lycaonians. It was commonly believed that the gods visited men in human form. In part, the idea may have been a corrupt borrowing by the pagans from Jewish history and theology, taken from such accounts as the visit of the angels to Abraham. In the main, it probably reflected the disposition of the pagan mind to conceive of the gods as being human, with a view to attaining a sense of kinship with them. One legend has it that Jupiter and Mercury visited Baucis and Philemon, virtuous peasants in the neighboring province of Phrygia.

It appears from Luke's account that the Roman Jupiter or Greek Zeus, their chief deity, was best represented by Barnabas who was likely older, larger, heavily bearded, and more impressive in physical appearance, than was Paul. On the other hand, the smaller stature, more youthful appearance, quick movements, and eloquent speech of Paul best represented their concept of the Roman Mercury or Greek Hermes. Luke phrases it thus: **because he was the chief speaker** (v. 12b).

It appears that Jupiter was the patron deity of Lystra, and it is likely that there was an image of Jupiter in the temple dedicated to him and situated before the city gates, where also the priest of Jupiter officiated.

Believing the apostles to be the gods, it was quite natural that the officiating priest should have sought to honor these deities with a special sacrifice. Thus oxen for sacrifice and garlands for festive decoration were brought, and the animals were about to be slain in their honor before the apostles realized what this priest and the populace were about. Likely their use of the Lycaonian language, a tongue unknown to the apostles, accounted for their ignorance of the procedures.

3. The Renunciation of Idolization (14:14-20)

14 But when the apostles, Barnabas and Paul, heard of it, they rent their garments, and sprang forth among the multitude, crying out 15 and saying, Sirs, why do ye these things? We also are men of like passions with you, and bring you good tidings, that ye should turn from these vain things unto a living God who made the heaven and the earth and the sea, and all that in them is: 16 who in the generations gone by suffered all the nations to walk in their own ways. 17 And yet he left not himself without witness, in that he did good and gave you from heaven rains and fruitful seasons, filling your hearts with food and gladness. 18 And with these sayings scarce restrained they the multitudes from doing sacrifice unto them.

19 But there came Jews thither from Antioch and Iconium: and having persuaded the multitudes, they stoned Paul, and dragged him out of the city, supposing that he was dead. 20 But as the disciples stood round about him, he rose up, and entered into the city: and on the morrow he went forth with Barnabas to Derbe.

The apostles rent their garments in a familiar token of horror at the thought of so blasphemous a consideration as their deification (see Matt. 26:65).

The apostles appear to have run in among the peoples, possibly waving their arms in violent protest, in an attempt to prevent the sacrificial slaughter of the oxen. While the language barrier would have prevented the apostles from understanding the Lycaonian speech, the Lycaonians evidently understood and spoke the Greek used by the apostles.

The speech that follows, likely an address by Paul, differs radically from Paul's synagogue sermons, in that it is an address on "natural religion" such as these pagan Lycaonians could understand, rather than on "revealed religion" designed for the Jewish mind. There are close similarities between this address and Paul's Mars' Hill sermon, likewise delivered to pagan hearers (cf. Acts 17:22-31).

Even under the extremity of the circumstances, the apostles retained their equilibrium and maintained a courteous manner toward the people, as witnessed their address: **Sirs, why do ye these things?** (v. 15a); not a condemnation of their conduct, but an arresting question. Nor did the apostles make a tirade of attacks upon their pagan deities, but rather positively and sympathetically identified themselves with the humanity of the Lycaonians and thus denied any suspicion of their personal divinity: **we also** are men of like passions with you (v. 15). Here it should be remarked that the words, **of like passions,** are to be understood as identifying their human nature, and not an allusion to the base or perverted nature of sinful man, as some have mistakenly supposed.

In the apostles' words, [we] **bring you good tidings** (v. 15), the Christian evangel appears as natural and as fresh as the water that flows from the nearby mountain source to irrigate the arid plateau on which Lystra stood. This is the evangel of the **living God** who vitalizes all that He touches. How different from the **vain things,** valueless and meaningless objects of their pagan worship, from which they are exhorted to turn in true repentance.

The brief address on "natural religion," contained in verses 15 through 17, likely delivered by Paul, while not primarily a Christian sermon is nevertheless foundational to Christianity for the thought of the Lycaonians. This address may be analyzed as follows:

1. *The Vitality of God;* a **living God** (v. 15).
2. *The Creatorship of God:* **who made the heaven and the earth and the sea, and all that in them is** (v. 15b).
3. *The Mercy of God:* **who in the generations gone by suffered all the nations [Gentiles] to walk in their own ways** (v. 16).
4. *The Revelation of God:* **and yet he left not himself without witness** (v. 17a).
5. *The Providence of God:* **he did good and gave you from heaven** (v. 17).

First, Paul's letter to the Thessalonians affords an illuminating commentary on the striking contrast between pagan idolatry and Christian theism: "and how ye turned unto God from idols to serve a living and true God" (I Thess. 1:9). Their conversion was: (1) "voluntary," in that it represented an intelligent moral choice on their part — "ye turned." Thus Paul exhorts the Lycaonians to turn from vanity to reality. Their conversion was (2) "vital," in that they established relationship with "a living God," as opposed to the non-living character of their former idols, called **vain things** among the Lycaonians. And their conversion was (3) "victorious," as it involved deliverance from slavish servitude to vain

idolatry, and liberty "to serve a living and true God" (cf. Acts 26:18). How many of the Lycaonians entered into this gracious experience we do not know, but that some did we know from the subsequent life of Timothy (see Acts 16:1-3).

Second, faith in the existence and creatorship of God is absolutely essential to evangelical or saving faith (see Heb. 11:1-6). Naturalistic Evolution strikes at the very foundation of man's hope of salvation, "the creatorship of God." This humanistic scheme seeks to rob God of His rightful ownership of all things and thus render impossible their redemption by, and to, God.

Third, the thought of God's mercy in allowing the unenlightened pagan Gentiles **to walk in their own ways** (v. 16b) [religiously] until light should be afforded them, when He might have destroyed them in their ignorance and vanity, should influence them to comprehend His goodness and repent and turn to Him for saving grace (cf. Acts 17:29, 30).

Fourth, God's revelation of Himself to the Lycaonians through nature makes them responsible for faith in His unitary nature, divine creatorship, and providential goodness. In the Roman letter Paul argues the fourfold revelation of God to man, in chapters one and two, and then makes him morally responsible to each of these revelations. In the *first* place, he presents the revelation of God in the very moral constitution of man who is created in the personal spiritual image of God (Rom. 1:19 and 2:14, 15); *second,* he represents God as revealed in nature, His handiwork (Rom. 1:20); *third,* God is revealed in the Mosaic Law (Rom. 2:12); and *finally,* God is revealed in Christ and His gospel (Rom. 2:16). To these first two revelations of God the Lycaonians had been responsible. To what extent they had been enlightened by the law of Moses through the Jewish religion we cannot say, but that they now had a far greater responsibility because the gospel of Christ had been delivered to them by the apostles is evident.

Fifth, God's revelation of Himself through His providential goodness in so directing the seasons and elements as to afford the earth's fruit for the supply of their temporal necessities is presented in verse 17. This last citation is especially designed to impress upon the hearers the goodness and love of God with a view to producing repentance and acceptance of His spiritual goodness through Jesus Christ.

How much more was contained in the Apostle's message Luke does not tell us, but how little they were impressed with what was said is suggested by the author's words: **And with these sayings scarce restrained they the multitudes from doing sacrifice unto them** (v. 18).

Like persistent bloodhounds on the trail of a criminal, the Antioch and Iconian Jewish enemies of the gospel of Christ trailed Paul and Barnabas to Lystra where they took advantage of the half-civilized, fickle Lycaonians (see Gal. 1:6; 3:1; 4:15), whose minds they poisoned and perverted and whose emotions they inflamed to violent action against the apostles of the Lord. Thus under their influence these very people who had but so recently sought to worship the apostles as gods, now sought to destroy them as devils: **they stoned Paul, and dragged him out of the city, supposing that he was dead** (v. 19b).

How changeable is popular acclaim! One day the crowds acclaimed Christ king (Matt. 21:9, 15), but another day not far distant they cried for His blood (Luke 23:21). First Paul is Mercury from heaven; now he is an impostor worthy of death by stoning.

The violence enacted against Paul, but from which Barnabas and the new disciples were evidently exempt, is possibly due to the fact that Paul was regarded by the Jews, some of whom may have been present to incite the pagans to mob violence, as the most damaging to their cause, by reason of his courage, wisdom, logic, and convincing eloquence in preaching the gospel of Christ. It was these qualities in Stephen that so enraged his enemies and precipitated his martyrdom by stoning at the hands of the Sanhedrin (see Acts 6:10).

Whether the Jews took part in the actual stoning, or whether Paul was actually dead, Luke does not say. Since stoning was the Jewish method of punishment, while flogging and crucifixion were mainly Roman methods, this is evidently a Jewish-incited mob, and they likely participated in the violence. The fact that he was dragged outside the city may indicate their utter disdain for him and their purpose that his blood should not pollute their town. How like the rejection and execution of the Christ whom Paul preached (Heb. 13:12)! How reminiscent of the occasion on which Paul had cast his lot with the persecutors of Stephen! (Acts 7:58 and 8:1). One may wonder if Paul, like Stephen, had any vision of heaven during his ordeal (see Acts 7:55, 50).

Whether Paul was actually dead, or whether the life was still in his body and his persecutors just "supposed that he was dead," it was their full intent to have killed him, and in either case his recovery is miraculous (cf. Acts 20:9-12 and Rom. 8:11). Luke's notation that **the disciples stood round about him** (v. 20a) is likely intended to mean that their sympathies were deeply stirred and their hearts were lifted in passionate and faithful prayer for his recovery. What part those prayers played in his restoration to life and service only heaven will reveal. Paul's return to the city after his restoration probably was due to the fact that his enemies thought him dead and supposed that his friends had disposed of his body. On the other hand, what an encouragement to the faith of these young Christians to see Paul so miraculously restored by the power of the **living God** he preached, and what an example of Christian courage that he should return to the very city from which he had been dragged to his supposed death! Likely the home of Timothy, a new Christian disciple (II Timothy 1:3-6), was the abode of Paul and Barnabas while in Lystra.

The extent of Paul's early recovery from this ordeal is suggested by Luke's words: **And on the morrow he went forth with Barnabas to Derbe** (v. 20b), though the mention of his having accompanied Barnabas may indicate the temporary safeguard of the protection afforded him by this fellow apostle.

The success of their ministry at Derbe is indicated by Luke's statement that they **made many disciples** (v. 21). Among those **many disciples** made at Derbe was one Gaius, who later became one of Paul's trusted assistants in the gospel ministry (Acts 20:4).

The importance of Derbe, a small Lycaonian city on the extreme borders of Galatia, is indicated by the Roman title accorded it, Claudio-Derbe.

G. THE CHRISTIANS REVISITED (14: 21-25)

21 And when they had preached the gospel to that city and had made many disciples, they returned to Lystra, and to Iconium, and to Antioch, 22 confirming the souls of the disciples, exhorting them to continue in the faith, and that through many tribulations we must enter into the kingdom of God. 23 And when they had appointed for them elders in every church, and had prayed with fasting, they commended them to the Lord, on whom they had believed. 24 And they passed through Pisidia, and came to Pamphylia. 25 And when they had spoken the word in Perga, they went down to Attalia;

Luke's record states that the apostles **returned to Lystra, and to Iconium, and to Antioch** (v. 21b), in the face of their former opposition and persecution, and in full consideration of the fact that they could easily have crossed the Taurus Mountains through the Cilician Gates and returned via Tarsus, Paul's home. This indicates the extent of their devotion to the Christian cause. The work of the apostles on the return trip may be summed up as consisting in *confirmation, exhortation, organization,* and *commendation* of the new Asia Minor disciples.

First, as they revisited these cities where the gospel had been introduced, they did so for the purpose of **confirming the souls of the disciples** (v. 22a). A disciple is a follower of a master, a learner, or a scholar. These new believers are so designated, and as such Luke's choice of words here is apt. The apostles confirmed their souls by instruction in the Christian doctrines and principles which Luke designates as **the faith** (v. 22). To convert but not to confirm the souls of men is to leave them a likely prey to vicious error. Probably in small classes by day and by flickering lights at night, in homes, in the markets, or by the wayside, these apostles confirmed the young disciples in the Christian truth.

Second, they set themselves to the task of **exhorting them to continue in the faith, and that through many tribula-**

tions we must enter into the kingdom of God (v. 22). While confirmation was primarily instructional and its principal appeal was to the intelligence, exhortation, on the other hand, was primarily hortatory, and its appeal was mainly to the emotions and will. Citation of the Lord's teaching concerning the Christian heritage of suffering (Mark 10:29, 30), examples from Old Testament history, and the recent vivid personal experiences of the apostles themselves, doubtless served as data for these exhortations delivered with a view to encouraging and fortifying these new believers in the midst of immoral pagan environment and violent Jewish opposition. To have left them unwarned would have been to leave them unarmed against powerful godless foes (see Acts 20:31).

Third, for the conservation of their evangelistic work, the apostles effected a simple form of organization for each church by appointing **for them elders in every church** (v. 23a). The question of church officers has been dealt with elsewhere (see Acts 6). These men were selected for their faith, character, wisdom, conduct, and perseverance. This selection was delayed until the apostles' return journey in order to give those with leadership qualities and moral worth time and opportunity to be revealed to their fellow Christians, as well as to the apostles (see Acts 16:1-3a). In this Paul was practicing what he later enjoined upon Timothy (I Tim. 5:18-22). It would appear to be a valid inference from this incident that wherever Paul established churches, he provided a ministry for them. The method of selecting and electing these under-shepherds (elders) for their office is aptly treated by Clarke thus:

> I believe the simple truth to be this, that in ancient times the people chose by the *cheirotonia* (lifting up of hands) their spiritual pastor; and the *rulers* of the Church, whether *apostles* or others, appointed that person to his office by the *cheirothesia,* or *imposition of hands;* and perhaps each of these was thought to be equally necessary: the *Church agreeing* in the *election* of the person; and the *rulers* of the Church appointing, by *imposition of hands,* the person thus elected.[94]

94 Clarke, *op. cit.*, I, 797.

The accompanying fasting and prayer were customary to ascertain God's will and insure God's approval and blessings upon the church's ministry (Acts 13:2, 3). Here is a first-century apostolic precedent and model of democratic congregational church government.

The *final act* of the apostles in relation to these young churches was performed when **they commended them to the Lord, on whom they had believed** (v. 23b). Here, as always, there is no safer refuge for the young Christian believers than in the hands of the Lord.

H. THE RESULTS REPORTED (14:26-28)

26 and thence they sailed to Antioch, from whence they had been committed to the grace of God for the work which they had fulfilled. 27 And when they were come, and had gathered the church together, they rehearsed all things that God had done with them, and that he had opened a door of faith unto the Gentiles. 28 And they tarried no little time with the disciples.

In rapid succession Luke carries the apostles homeward through Pisidia and Pamphylia to Perga, where they are said to have **spoken the word** (v. 25), from there they went to Attalia, the seaport of Perga, and sailed to Antioch of Syria. Luke is careful to note that upon their return the apostles could report that the work to which they had been committed by the church **they had fulfilled** (v. 26b). Their conference report was completed.

The last two verses of this chapter record the first church missionary service ever conducted by returned missionaries sent forth by the church body. Several items of interest appear in conjunction with this event. *First*, **they . . . gathered the church together** (v. 27a). Thus they assembled the whole church which had been responsible for sending them on the mission, that they might benefit from the report. The missionary task and concern is one belonging to the entire church, and not a small group of "special interest" enthusiasts. *Second*, they made a complete positive report of their tour in which they **rehearsed all things that God had done with them** (v. 27). Whatever apparent adversities had befallen them, they seem to have regarded as in the permissive will of God, and thus were

counted to His glory. They gave these "investors" in the cause of world evangelism what they expected, a report of the returns on their investment in the cause. One might like to know if they related the departure of Mark from the work at Lystra, but Luke does not say. Even that may have been regarded as one of the **all things that God had done with them** (v. 27). *Third*, they threw out a new and greater challenge to the churches in their report, that God **had opened a door of faith unto the Gentiles** (v. 27b).

It was the last item of their report that challenged the Antioch church to launch a second and third missionary enterprise with Paul as the principal organizer and leader. Successful endeavor for God always inspires and challenges to further and more heroic undertakings.

The entire journey covered about 1,400 miles, and the total time may have occupied about eighteen months or more. The furlough time spent at Antioch, between one and two years, was for rest, recuperation, replenishment, recruitment, and reorganization for a second mission.

XVI. THE CHURCH'S FIRST GENERAL COUNCIL (Acts 15:1-35)

A. THE OCCASION OF THE COUNCIL (15:1-5)

In this chapter Luke records the greatest crisis with which the young church had yet been confronted, if indeed not the greatest crisis the church has yet faced in her history. It was the first serious internal conflict of the body ecclesiastic, and it threatened to precipitate a cleavage in the body that might never have been healed. The apostles' handling of the situation set a model for all time.

Two different views of the circumcision controversy in relation to the Jerusalem Council have characterized the thinking of scholars. Both are summarily presented here.

The position which is probably the most widely accepted places the Jerusalem Council between the first and second missionary journeys. *First*, word of the conversion of the Gentiles on Paul's first missionary journey, and that he had not required their circumcision, had reached

Jerusalem and there greatly disturbed the strict Judaeo-Christian legalist party. *Second,* this party sent representatives to Antioch, who falsely professed to have authority from the Jerusalem apostles, to teach that all Gentile converts had to be circumcised before they could be saved (Acts 15:1). *Third,* Paul challenged the validity of their doctrines and ecclesiastical authority and questioned the sincerity of their motives (Gal. 2:4). *Fourth,* Paul, possibly challenged by the Judaizers, decided to go to Jerusalem and present the question to the Jerusalem church for solution. This he finally decided to do only after he had received a special divine revelation that it was God's will and that the results would accord with God's former revelation to him (Gal. 2:4). *Fifth,* the Antioch church accorded with this plan and endorsed a delegation to the Jerusalem Council, consisting of Paul, Barnabas, and Titus (Gal. 2:1-5), and possibly unnamed others. Galatians 2:1-10 is an account of this third visit of Paul to Jerusalem after his conversion. *Sixth,* Paul and his party met with the apostles and elders of the Jerusalem church in a private pre-council session in which they presented the cause of Gentile freedom and apparently secured their concurrence. *Seventh,* the legalist party made a test case of Titus in which they demanded his circumcision, since he was a Gentile, to which Paul steadfastly refused to give consent. The apostles evidently favored the legalists' contention at first, since Titus was to be Paul's companion; but, judging from James's decision, as expressed in the decrees of the Council (Acts 15:19, 20), and Paul's argument in the Galatian letter (Gal. 2:6-10), they eventually concurred with Paul. *Eighth,* the Council unanimously rendered its decision in favor of the exemption of the Gentile Christians from circumcision (see Acts 15:19-21) and approved the ministry of Paul and Barnabas to the Gentiles (cf. Acts 15:25-27 and Gal. 2:9). *Ninth,* Paul and Barnabas, in company with Judas and Silas, returned to Antioch where they delivered the decrees, to the great joy and edification of the church (Acts 15:30, 31). *Tenth,* subsequently Peter, under pressure from the disgruntled Judaizers, whose cause had been lost at the Council, went to Antioch, where his devisive conduct in the church was openly condemned by Paul (Gal. 2:11-14). *Eleventh,* the Galatian letter was written after the Jerusalem Council and before the second missionary journey. *Twelfth,* the second missionary journey was launched from Antioch, with its attendant incidents (Acts 15:36-41).

Certain other scholars take quite a different view of the incidents outlined in the foregoing view. In brief they contend: *first,* the Jerusalem visit of Galatians 2:1-10 is not the same as that of Acts 15, but rather of that described in Acts 11:29, 30; *second,* that the Galatian letter was written sometime before the Jerusalem Council during the heat of the circumcision controversy; and *third,* that Peter's visit to Antioch, related in Gal. 2:11-21, occurred before the Jerusalem Council.

Ramsay is possibly the ablest supporter of the latter view in general. However, the first view is the most generally accepted, and all factors considered, it appears to fit most satisfactorily the recorded events. This view is held by Clarke, Wesley, Lightfoot, and many other eminent scholars. It will afford the frame of reference for the exposition of this chapter, except for the time of Peter's visit to Antioch and the possible date of the Galatian letter, both of which are in dispute among scholars.

1. The Activities of the Judaizers (15:1)

1 And certain men came down from Judaea and taught the brethren, saying, Except ye be circumcised after the custom of Moses, ye cannot be saved.

That these **certain men** of verse 1 were the representatives of the "believing" **sect of the Pharisees** in the Jerusalem Christian church, mentioned in verse 5, appears evident. Further, that they were sent by this Judaeo-Christian legalist party to Antioch to propagate their doctrines, though they falsely claimed to have been sent by the Jerusalem apostles (see Gal. 2:4), is equally evident. Again, that they were the same as those mentioned in Galatians 2:12 is likely. This sect of Pharisees consisted of Jews whom Christ frequently rebuked (see Matt. 23:4, 15, 23 and Luke 11:42,

46), and from which party there had been converts to Christianity (v. 5).

To understand properly these Judaizers, as they are called, it is necessary to know something of the strict Jewish Pharisaic party from which they were converted to Christianity. It appears from history that the sect of the Pharisees came into existence for the preservation and propagation of the essence of Judaism following the exile and during the Inter-Testament period, when they developed a "Theocracy" in lieu of their former "Monarchy." Thus they became the rulers of a religious state in which Mosaic monotheism was preserved, the Mosaic Law was strictly imposed, and the Messianic hope was widely diffused.

This was all to their credit, and to them both Judaism and the Christian world are deeply indebted. However, by the dawn of the Christian era, their religious beliefs and practices had crystallized into a fanatical advocacy of binding and blinding legalism that stifled the last breath of life from religion. They had become blind leaders of the blind (Matt. 15:14), and bound burdens upon their followers which none could bear (Matt. 23:4; Luke 11:46; Acts 15:10b). They had made the fatal mistake of confusing means with ends and had mistaken the former for the latter. Whereas the Mosaic law was designed as a tutor to lead men to Christ and liberty, they thought it to be the savior in itself (see Gal. 3:24, 25). They failed to recognize in Christ the fulfillment of the law, never attained to the spiritual idea of "the church," and placed their interpretations of the law above the law itself (see Matt.23:2). Rabbi Eleazer is reported to have said: "He who expounds the Scriptures in contradiction to tradition has no inheritance in the world to come." They degraded Judaism into a narrow nationalistic religion with an elaborate ritual and extreme Sabbatarianism, from which all but the strictest were excluded. Of this persuasion they became fanatical advocates (Matt. 23:15), and from this sect Paul had sprung (Acts 26:5).

The Jewish-Christian legalists consisted of those from this Judaeo-Pharisaic party who had embraced Christianity but had attempted to incarcerate it behind the iron bars of Jewish legalism, both for themselves and for the Gentiles. The epistles to the Galatians, to the Romans, and to the Hebrews at a later period, were all written to refute this error, and the segment of the the church at Jerusalem that held it never outlived the first Christian generation. In fact, its influence seems to have extended widely over the Jerusalem church in time, and to have robbed that church of her vital spirituality and mission to the world. There is evidence that there developed in the Jerusalem church an increasing disposition to restrict the privileges of membership to those who had conformed strictly to the Jewish law. That the "pillar apostles" did not fully share this position is equally evident from the decisions of the Jerusalem Conference (Acts 15:19-21). Harnack observes that this Jewish-Christian church fled to Pella, a small pagan town to the north and across the river in Decapolis, in A.D. 68 upon the first Roman attack on Jerusalem, where it remained for the most part, and evidently never enjoyed prosperity nor wielded any noticeable influence on its hosts.

Of the disappearance of this legalistic Jewish-Christian church, Lietzmann remarks:

> The original church disappeared with the migration to Pella and the destruction of Jerusalem. At the same time it sank below the horizon of Gentile Christianity which was in process of conquering the world and which had thereby become dominant in Christendom after the judgment of God over the Holy City had made plain to all eyes His punishment for the crucifixion of the Lord, i.e., by the destruction of the temple and its worship and the abolition of the Law. Jewish Christianity had lacked not only a racial, but also a religious basis for its former claims and thus was forgotten in the church Catholic. It sank to oblivion in the lonely deserts of East Jordan.[95]

Had these legalists won their contention at the Jerusalem Conference, either the church would have been divided into Judaeo-Christian and Gentile-Christian sections, or the whole body would have likely suffered the fate described above.

This legalistic teaching was extremely disturbing to the faith of the young Gen-

---

[95] Hans Lietzmann, *The Beginnings of the Christian Church*, I, 78-80.

tile disciples at Antioch, since they already believed on Christ for salvation, and were now told that **Except ye be circumcised after the custom of Moses, ye cannot be saved** (v. 1b). It further threatened to effect a cleavage between the Jewish and Gentile Christians of the Antioch church (see Gal. 2:11-13).

2. The Appointment of the Antioch Delegation (15:2, 3)

2 And when Paul and Barnabas had no small dissension and questioning with them, *the brethren* appointed that Paul and Barnabas, and certain other of them, should go up to Jerusalem unto the apostles and elders about this question. 3 They therefore, being brought on their way by the church, passed through both Phoenicia and Samaria, declaring the conversion of the Gentiles: and they caused great joy unto all the brethren.

When it is remembered that no Gentile, in the first generation, could become a true proselyte to the Jewish religion without circumcision, if indeed at all, it is understandable that these representatives of Judaeo-Christian legalism should have contended for the circumcision of the Gentile disciples at Antioch before they could regard themselves as being truly saved and worthy of membership in the Christian church. Since the principle of salvation with them was "law," while it was "grace" with the apostles, there naturally arose strong differences of opinions and points of view, as well as pointed and sharp questionings. Contentiousness is no stranger to legalism, and *dissensions* are her favored devices. She looks on externals and judges spiritual values by appearances, while God looks on the heart and judges spiritual values by true moral worth and purity of motives (cf. I Sam. 16:7).

Because of the dangers involved to the Antioch church, as well as the issues involved for the whole Christian movement, the Antioch church decided to send a delegation to the apostles at Jerusalem for a decision on the matter. This decision may have been due in part to the fact that these Judaizers claimed to have been sent on their mission by the Jerusalem apostles, a claim likely suspected by Paul and Barnabas (Acts 15:24).

While Paul and Barnabas were the elected delegates of the church at Antioch, Paul claims the support of direct revelation in the venture (see Gal. 2:2). Among the **certain other of them** sent to Jerusalem was Titus, who became a test case in this matter of Gentile circumcision (see Gal. 2:3-5), and who later became one of Paul's most trusted companions and emissaries for delicate and difficult tasks (see II Cor. 7:6; 8:6, 16-18), but who strangely is not mentioned in the Acts account. Paul's justification in not allowing the circumcision of Titus at the Jerusalem Council, while requiring it in the case of Timothy at a later date (see Acts 16:3), is found: first, in the fact that Titus was evidently a pure Gentile, while Timothy was of mixed parentage, his mother a Jewess and his father a Greek; second, since "they all knew that his father was a Greek" (Acts 16:3b) and he was to be Paul's traveling companion, the apostle realized that, uncircumcised, Timothy would be a barrier to the gospel with the prejudiced Jews wherever they traveled throughout the empire. This reason is given by Luke: "because of the Jews that were in those parts; for they all knew that his father was a Greek" (Acts 16:3b). However, since his mother was a Jewess and Timothy had followed her religion (II Tim. 1:5), it seemed logical that he should bear the outward signs of his nationality. Thus, for expediency's sake, Paul had him circumcised (cf. I Cor. 8:9-13; Acts 18:18; 20:16; 21: 23). Again, Titus was a test case at Jerusalem involving the question of the observance of the Jewish law as necessary to salvation, which for Paul to have yielded would have been against his cause of freedom for the Gentiles, in that he would have sacrificed a religious principle, while such was not true in the case of Timothy.

Since the question concerning circumcision is purported to have arisen with the apostles at the mother church in Jerusalem, it is only logical that it should be referred to them.

The expression, **They therefore, being brought on their way by the church** (v. 3a), is probably meant to suggest that the church which delegated them to attend the conference provided the necessary means, financial and otherwise, to meet their travel expenses, rather than that members of the church accompanied them for a distance, as some suppose (cf. Rom. 15:24).

This was to be Paul's third visit to Jerusalem since his conversion. The first occurred about A.D. 37 or 38 and followed his escape from Damascus (Acts 9:26); the second took place about A.D. 45 on the occasion of the famine offering taken to Jerusalem by Paul and Barnabas (Acts 11:29, 30).

The Apostle's reports, concerning Gentile conversions, to the disciples in Phoenicia and Samaria as they were en route to Jerusalem, were received with joyful gratitude on their part. Though there were evidently Jewish Christians in Phoenicia (Acts 11:19), they seem not to have been prejudiced against the Apostle's ministry to the Gentiles.

3. The Report of the Delegation (15:4)

4 And when they were come to Jerusalem, they were received of the church and the apostles and the elders, and they rehearsed all things that God had done with them.

Upon arrival in Jerusalem, the delegation was cordially and warmly received by the church body, its elders, and the apostles. Whether the latter included all the apostles, or just the "pillar apostles," James, Cephas, and John, who are named in this connection (Gal. 2:9), we are not informed. From Luke's statement that **they were received of the church** (v. 4a), we may safely infer that the Judaizers were greatly in the minority.

Here, as at Antioch, Paul and Barnabas gave a full and detailed report of their missionary activities and experiences. This initial report appears to have been made to a private session of the apostles (Gal. 2:2) before the opening of the full church conference on the matter. This report included a detailed statement of the doctrinal content of Paul's Gentile message: "I laid before them the gospel which I preach among the Gentiles" (Gal. 2:2). Paul's strategy in this pre-conference session with the apostles is evident from his words, "but privately before them who were of repute, lest by any means I should be running, or had run, in vain" (Gal. 2:2b), a strategy which appears to have been ef-

fective, judging from the support given him by the apostles in the subsequent church conference.

4. The Opposition of the Pharisees (15:5)

5 But there rose up certain of the sect of the Pharisees who believed, saying, It is needful to circumcise them, and to charge them to keep the law of Moses.

This is the sole mention by name of believing Pharisees, though it is likely that the Judaizers in general were of this sect. It is possible that the words of verse 5 are a part of the report of Paul and Barnabas to the apostles concerning the activities of these Pharisees at Antioch. However, it seems more likely that they are a record of the concerted opposition of this party at Jerusalem, possibly in the pre-conference session. (Concerning these Pharisees, see the note on verse 1.) The Pharisaic requirements of the Gentile ·disciples for church membership, **It is needful to circumcise them, and to charge them to keep the law of Moses** (v. 5b), are even more demanding here than as stated at Antioch, according to verse 1. As the crisis approaches, the emotional temperature of these legalists rises. They foresee the issues involved, in which Christianity may become an extra-Jewish movement embracing the Gentile world and resulting in the disintegration of the whole Mosaic economy.

B. THE DEFENSE OF THE GENTILES (15:6-12)

This is the occasion of the first general Christian council ever held, and certainly the greatest of the first century. It dealt with some of the weightiest problems ever considered by the church.

1. The Defense of Peter (15:6-11)

6 And the apostles and the elders were gathered together to consider of this matter. 7 And when there had been much questioning, Peter rose up, and said unto them,

Brethren, ye know that a good while ago God made choice among you, that by my mouth the Gentiles should hear the word of the gospel, and believe. 8 And God, who knoweth the heart, bare them witness, giving them the Holy Spirit, even as he did unto us; 9 and he made no distinction between us and them, cleansing their hearts by faith. 10 Now therefore why make ye trial of God, that ye should put a yoke upon the neck of the disciples which neither our fathers nor we were able to bear? 11 But we believe that we shall be saved through the grace of the Lord Jesus, in like manner as they.

The speech of Peter here delivered in defense of the Gentiles clearly reveals the principles involved. They are: *first,* the direct will of God for the salvation of the Gentiles by faith, as attested by Peter's experience at Caesarea (v. 7b); *second,* the divine impartation of the Holy Spirit in the regeneration of the souls of the believing Gentiles (v. 8); *third,* the divine impartiality in sanctifying the souls of the Gentile believers in response to their faith (v. 9); *fourth,* the insulting affront to God in substituting an unbearable and ineffective human device for the grace of God (v. 10; cf. Gal. 5:1); *fifth,* the grace of God received through faith is the only means of salvation for Jews as well as Gentiles (v. 11; cf. Rom. 3:24; Gal. 2:16; 3:6).

Clarke succinctly summarizes Peter's address as follows:

> 1. Circumcision is a sign of the purification of heart. 2. That purification can only be effected by the Holy Ghost. 3. This Holy Spirit was hitherto supposed to be the portion of those only who had received circumcision. 4. But the Gentiles, who were never circumcised, nor kept any part of the law of Moses, have had their hearts purified by faith in Christ Jesus. 5. As God, therefore, has given them the thing signified, He evidently does not intend that the sign should be administered. 6. Should we impose this burdensome rite, we should most evidently be provoking God, who plainly shows us that He intends no more to save in this way. 7 Therefore it is evident that both Jews and Gentiles are to be saved through the grace of the Lord Jesus Christ.[96]

Peter's entire speech is in full accord doctrinally with the theology of the apostle Paul, though Paul claims independence of all the apostles in the origin of his theology (Gal. 2:6). That James and the other apostles were in accord with Peter's defense of the Gentiles is clear from James's address recorded in verses 13-21.

There is an apparent divergence in point of view between Paul and Peter in their concept of God's choice of an apostle to the Gentiles. In the Acts account (15:7), Peter appears to claim the priority on the divine election to Gentile apostleship, whereas in Paul's account (Gal. 2:7, 8), he claims for himself the divine right to Gentile apostleship and ascribes to Peter the divine right of apostleship to the Jews. However, this apparent difference may find its reconciliation in the chronological fact that Peter was divinely called to preach to the Gentile household of Cornelius at Caesarea before Paul had begun his larger Gentile ministry, but that Peter's larger ministry was to the Jews.

2. The Declaration of Barnabas and Paul (15:12)

12 And all the multitude kept silence; and they hearkened unto Barnabas and Paul rehearsing what signs and wonders God had wrought among the Gentiles through them.

The arguments presented by Peter based upon experience, Scripture, and logic evidently left his opponents totally defeated and disarmed for the time being, and the assembled multitude awesomely convinced.

Paul and Barnabas corroborated the conclusions of Peter by a vivid recital of instances of divine manifestations and the gracious salvation of the Gentiles through their ministry on the first missionary journey. Doubtless the blinding of Elymas, the conversion of Sergius Paulus, the effect of the gospel on the Gentiles at Antioch of Pisidia, the healing of the lame man, the conversion of Timothy, and Paul's deliverance from death at Lystra were among the **signs and wonders God had wrought among the Gentiles through them** (v. 12b). And all of this was accomplished by, and approved of, God quite independent of the Jewish ceremonial law. What a fitting conclusion to, and what a convincing demonstration of, the truth of Peter's apologia for Gentile salvation by grace and freedom from the burden of ceremonial law.

---

[96] Clarke, *op. cit.,* I, 801.

C. THE DECISION OF THE CHAIRMAN (15:13-21)

Naturally Peter would be expected to have taken charge of the assembly and rendered the decision concerning the status of the Gentiles in the Christian church, as well as the requirements to be met by them for membership. Certainly, if the contention of the Roman church, that Peter was the pope, were correct, he should have presided at this first general church council. However, the office is assumed by another while Peter quite gracefully gives place.

1. The Position of the Chairman (15:13)

13 And after they had held their peace, James answered, saying, Brethren, hearken unto me:

James, the Lord's brother, who was pastor of the Jewish-Christian church at Jerusalem, evidently assumed the role of president or moderator of the Council, by calling the assembly to attention. A note of recognized authority seems to characterize his manner and ring in his introductory words, **Brethren, hearken unto me** (v. 13b). While humbly and sympathetically identifying himself with the Council, he had a decision to render, and he demanded a hearing. Since the Judaizers centered in the mother church of which he was pastor, and since it was from this church that their activities had been launched, it was quite logical that James should have assumed command, as chairman of the assembly, as also in a certain sense, the judge who rendered the final decision.

2. The Summary of the Chairman (15:14-18)

14 Symeon hath rehearsed how first God visited the Gentiles, to take out of them a people for his name. 15 And to this agree the words of the prophets; as it is written,
16 After these things I will return,
And I will build again the tabernacle of David, which is fallen;
And I will build again the ruins thereof,
And I will set it up:
17 That the residue of men may seek after the Lord,
And all the Gentiles, upon whom my name is called,

18 Saith the Lord, who maketh these things known from of old.

Though a Jewish Christian himself and primarily concerned with the affairs of the Jewish-Christian church, James nevertheless had caught the significance of Christ's commission and the universal implications of His gospel. He threw the full weight of his authority behind the address of Peter delivered in favor of the Gentiles' salvation by grace and freedom from the ceremonial law. He fully approved Peter's conduct in preaching the gospel to Cornelius' household, and he credited their conversion as a genuine work of God. Further, James quoted to this Jewish-Christian assembly a Jewish prophecy from Amos 9:11, 12, which he declared to be in full agreement with the contention of Peter. Thus the Jewish prophets knew better than the Judaizers God's place for the Gentiles in His spiritual Kingdom.

Amos prophesied before the exile and foretold the partial historical restoration of Israel, but thereby implied the spiritual inclusion of this Jewish remnant who should **seek after the Lord** (v. 17) together with **all the Gentiles, upon whom my name is called** [better, who call upon my name] — (see Acts 2:21), in His great spiritual Kingdom, the church of Jesus Christ. This divine purpose was made known by God **from of old** or "from the beginning" (v. 18b), and was revealed to Amos and the other Messianic prophets, but only now is it discovered that the prophecy is being fulfilled. God is giving the Gentiles a spiritual visitation for the purpose of completing His spiritual Kingdom, the *ecclesia,* the body of Christ of which He is the rightful head (cf. 1:22, 23; 2:11-22; 3:6).

It is interesting that James here called Peter by his common Hebrew name **Symeon,** and not Peter, a fact that would not honor him with any special significance on this important occasion.

3. The Sentence of the Chairman (15:19-21)

19 Wherefore my judgment is, that we trouble not them that from among the Gentiles turn to God; 20 but that we write unto them, that they abstain from the pollutions of idols, and from fornication, and from what is strangled, and

from blood. 21 For Moses from generations of old hath in every city them that preach him, being read in the synagogues every sabbath.

James speaks with the authority vested in him as chairman of the Council. This is evident in the decision which he renders, and it is recognized by the Council in its adoption of his recommendations.

It is noteworthy that James recommends that the decisions he is about to make be sent to the churches by letter from the Council. This is probably intended not only to make the decision official but also to prevent its denial or distortion by the Judaizers.

Negatively considered, James cast his decision in favor of the position of Peter, Barnabas, and Paul; that we trouble not . . . the Gentiles (v. 19b) with the burden of the Mosaic ceremonial law. Positively, James advanced four prohibitions to be observed by Gentile Christians, designed, in part at least, to facilitate Jewish-Gentile social and religious relationships, but all of which pertained to approved Christian deportment and were not requisites to salvation. When analyzed, these prohibitions appear to fall into four categories as follows:

1. A Religious Prohibition: that they abstain from the pollutions of idols (v. 20).
2. A Moral Prohibition: that they abstain from . . . fornication (v. 20b).
3. A Hygienic Prohibition: that they abstain from . . . what is strangled (v. 20b).
4. A Civil Prohibition: that they abstain from . . . blood (v. 20b).

The first, or religious prohibition, did not pertain primarily to the worship of idols, a practice renounced by Gentiles at their conversion (see I Thess. 1:9b), but rather to meat which had been sacrificed to the heathen idols, as indicated in verse 29. This prohibition would be observed by refusing to buy such meat in the markets as was known to have been sacrificed to idols; by declining to receive or to eat, in heathen homes, meat known to have been offered to idols; by avoiding heathen religious feasts which were both an incentive to idolatry and moral impurities.

Second, the moral prohibition, was directed, not only against fornication as such, but as the word seems to allow, against adultery (I Thess. 4:3-7), prostitution, homosexuality (Rom. 1:26, 27), incest, and bestiality (cf. Lev. 15 and I Cor. 5:1). These vices, frequently practiced in connection with heathen worship, were an especial danger to the young Gentile converts environed by evil influences as they were. Wesley remarks: "Which even the philosophers among the heathens did not account any fault. It was particularly frequent in the worship of their idols; on which account they [pollutions of idols and fornication] are here named, together."[97] Lightfoot holds that this prohibition was especially directed against the Gentile practice of marriage within the forbidden degrees, especially such as is described in Leviticus, chapter 18, against which the Jews had a strong antipathy but which was common among the Gentiles (I Cor. 5:1).

Third, the hygienic prohibition pertained to the heathen practice of strangling, rather than butchering an animal killed for meat. Such meat was considered a delicacy by some of the pagans, but the practice was forbidden by God (see Lev. 17:10-14 and Deut. 12:16, 23, 25), and it was highly obnoxious to the Jews, a fact which would have caused the Gentile Christians no limit of difficulty in their religious and social intercourse with the Jewish Christians.

On the fourth prohibition scholars have differed, some holding that blood here refers to the use of animal blood as food, a position apparently rendering the fourth prohibition quite unnecessary because of its close similarity, if not identity, with the third prohibition. Another and more likely view is that it is a prohibition against cruelty, murder, manslaughter, or other acts of violence (Clarke). God's prohibitions contained in Genesis 9:4-6 appear to have a bearing on this question. Weymouth remarks on this problem:

There is some evidence, both in verses 20 and 29, for the omission of 'things strangled,' as well as for the addition of a negative form of the Golden Rule, 'Do not to others what you would not

97 Wesley, op. cit., p. 454, n. 20.

have done to yourselves.' Some inter-preters, accepting the shortened text, regard the Decree as a threefold *moral* prohibition, of idolatry, bloodshed (mur-der), and fornication.98

One view of verse 21 is that James considered these prohibitions unnecessary for the Jewish Christian, since they were all contained in the Scriptures which they regularly heard read in the synagogues and with which they would be familiar (Clarke). Another view holds that these prohibitions are rendered necessary for the amicable relations of the Gentile Christians with the Jews, who were so widely diffused over the empire. Yet another view holds that James is simply recommending that the Jewish Christians are still to attend the synagogues and ob-serve the ceremonial law (Dummelow).

D. THE DECREES OF THE COUNCIL (15:22-29)

With no dissenting voice, and an ap-parent satisfaction on the part of all with the conclusions reached, the Coun-cil proceeded to formulate the decrees.

1. The Support of the Decrees (15:22)

22 Then it seemed good to the apostles and the elders, with the whole church, to choose men out of their company, and send them to Antioch with Paul and Barnabas; *namely,* Judas called Barsabbas, and Silas, chief men among the brethren:

Concurring in the decision to formu-late and publish the decrees stated by James were the body of original apostles at Jerusalem, who were responsible for the general oversight and direction of the church, the ruling elders of the local churches as represented at the Council, and the entire lay membership of the Jerusalem church and the Council. No voice of dissent is heard from the Juda-izers, and had they been content to leave the matter as settled by the Council, how much trouble the young church would have been saved (see Gal. 1:6-10)!

Had the decrees been left with Paul and Barnabas to deliver, they might have been suspected by the Judaizers, since they were involved in the controversy. Therefore, in accordance with the Mosaic legal requirement for the establishment

of evidence, and recommended by Christ (Matt. 18:16), they, the whole Council in democratic concurrence, chose two honored and representative men from the Council to accompany Paul and Barnabas and deliver the decrees, primarily to the church at Antioch where the controversy had arisen. **Judas, called Barsabbas,** a Hebrew Christian, and possibly the brother of Joseph Barsabbas who was a candidate for apostleship to replace Judas (Acts 1:23), was the first elected, likely to represent the Christian-Jewish point of view. **Silas,** or Silvanus, whose Latin name identifies him as a Hellenist, is next chosen to represent the Gentile interest and point of view. How provi-dential that Silas, one of the **chief men among the brethren** (v. 22b) at the Council, should have been chosen for this mission. The appointment opened the door to him for a larger ministry as the companion of Paul on his second missionary journey (see Acts 15:40; 16:19; 17:4, 10, 14; 18:5 and II Cor. 1:19). His Roman citizenship, like that of Paul, was a valuable credential for travel and mis-sionary service out in the empire (see Acts 16:37-39). At a later date he ap-pears to have been associated with Peter (I Peter 5:12).

2. The Script of the Decrees (15:23-29)

23 and they wrote *thus* by them, The apostles and the elders, brethren, unto the brethren who are of the Gentiles, in Antioch and Syria and Cilicia, greeting: 24 Forasmuch as we have heard that certain who went out from us have troubled you with words, subverting your souls; to whom we gave no commandment; 25 it seemed good to us, having come to one accord, to choose out men and send them unto you with our beloved Barnabas and Paul, 26 men that have hazarded their lives for the name of our Lord Jesus Christ. 27 We have sent therefore Judas and Silas, who themselves also shall tell you the same things by word of mouth. 28 For it seemed good to the Holy Spirit, and to us, to lay upon you no greater burden than these necessary things: 29 that ye abstain from things sacrificed to idols, and from blood, and from things strangled, and from fornication; from which if ye keep yourselves, it shall be well with you. Fare ye well.

98 Richard Francis Weymouth, *The New Testament in Modern Speech,* p. 320, n. 20.

In writing the decrees to the churches, they supplied a threefold witness to the decisions of the Council; *first,* that of Paul and Barnabas; *second,* that of Judas Barsabbas and Silas; and *third,* that of the written statement (Matt. 18:16). Further, a written record of the decrees would prevent distortion of the Council's decision, support the oral report of the apostles, and preserve a record of the historic Council's agreement on the issue.

The Address of the epistle reflects, not only the unanimity of the participating personnel (**The apostles and the elders, brethren,** v. 23a), but also a tender and endearing fraternalism and Christian affection, as suggested by the words of specific greeting which may be read: from the brethren of the Jerusalem Council **unto the brethren who are of the Gentiles, in Antioch and Syria and Cilicia, greeting** (v. 23b). Further, here is designated both the places and persons for which the epistle was intended. It had been designed for the Gentile disciples in whose interest the decrees had been made. It was directed to those disciples in Antioch where the controversy had arisen, and throughout Syria and Cilicia where Gentile Christians were located among the Jews and would require the decrees both for their protection and instruction. There was no need to address the Jewish Christians, as the epistle concerned only the Gentile Christians.

The epistle takes passing note of the Judaizing adversaries who had given rise to the necessity of this epistle. The Council assumes a proportionate share of responsibility for the activities of these disturbing legalists, who, they write, **went out from us** [and] **have troubled you with words subverting your souls** (v. 24). So must the church ever assume responsibility for her whole constituency, the defective or injurious as well as the saintly and benevolent (cf. Isa. 6:5 and Gal. 6:1-3). Indeed the church owns them: **they went out from us;** but the church does not approve their subversive activities nor take responsibility for their unauthorized teachings: **to whom we gave no commandment** (v. 24b).

Briefly the epistle reviews the account of the Council proceedings, by relating the unanimity of spirit (see Additional

Note I, *One Accord*) and judgment in the decisions reached and the plans formulated. A special word of confidence is accorded the apostles: **our beloved Barnabas and Paul, men that have hazarded their lives for the name of our Lord Jesus Christ** (vv. 25b, 26). This is especially significant in view of the fact that they have been, and will again be, under attack by the Judaizers.

Special divine inspiration is claimed for the decrees about to be written: **For it seemed good to the Holy Spirit** (v. 28a). Paul claimed divine revelation in attending the Council (Gal. 2:2), Peter claimed divine direction in his ministry to the Gentiles as reported at the Council (Acts 15:7), and there was every evidence of divine approval in the decisions reached by the Council. Therefore it is in order that these decrees be sent forth as the voice of God.

Reference to **these necessary things** (v. 28b) indicates the disposition of the church to keep external regulations of the church over its members at a minimum (cf. Matt. 11:28-30).

Finally, the admonitions contained in the decrees set forth in the letter are reiterated with some change in their order from James's original statement (see comment on v. 20). The observance of these regulations will be in the interest of their spiritual welfare and prosperity, the letter informs them, and then closes with an expression of Christian good will (v. 29b).

E. THE DELIVERY OF THE DECREES (15:30-35)

30 So they, when they were dismissed, came down to Antioch; and having gathered the multitude together, they delivered the epistle. 31 And when they had read it, they rejoiced for the consolation. 32 And Judas and Silas, being themselves also prophets, exhorted the brethren with many words, and confirmed them. 33 And after they had spent some time *there,* they were dismissed in peace from the brethren unto those that had sent them forth. 35 But Paul and Barnabas tarried in Antioch, teaching and preaching the word of the Lord, with many others also.

Officially released from and authorized by the Council, the delegation proceeded to Antioch, where before the assembled church they read the epistle, with the result that the disciples **rejoiced for the consolation** (v. 31b), which its message afforded them. They were now officially free from the threatened yoke of legalism and could devote themselves to spiritual edification and vital evangelism. Judas and Silas, both of whom were prophets (preachers), took advantage of the Antiochians' jubilant spirits and delivered a series of exhortations, probably on brotherly love, spiritual unity, loyalty, steadfastness in the Christian faith, and devotion to the continued evangelization of their non-Christian fellows. They concluded by confirming them in the truths they had previously been taught. How long they remained we are not told, but that they were farewelled under the blessings of God is suggested by Luke's words, **they were dismissed in peace from the brethren unto those that had sent them forth** (v. 33b).

How long Paul and Barnabas remained at Antioch, **teaching and preaching the word of the Lord** (v. 35), we are not told, but the entire time elapsing between the first and second missionary journeys certainly did not exceed two years.

The problem of fitting the conduct of Peter, as recorded in Galatians 2:11-21, into the pattern of events at Antioch has plagued the minds of many scholars. Certainly the view that Peter went to Antioch soon after the Jerusalem Council and became guilty of the divisive conduct attributed to him in the Galatian account hardly seems logical, if possible. On the other hand, to relate the second chapter of Galatians to the eleventh chapter of Acts is highly unsatisfactory. Where then does the conduct of Peter, described in Galatians 2, best fit?

First, let it be observed that in the Galatian letter Paul is arguing the case for Gentile freedom, and not recording history, as is the case with Luke in Acts. Indeed, Paul is drawing on historical events to enforce his argument, but that without necessary regard to the sequence of events.

Second, therefore, we shall assume that Peter's conduct as recorded in Galatians 2:11-21 actually occurred at some time before the Jerusalem Council events recorded in Galatians 2:1-10. Thus Peter's conduct and Paul's rebuke of that conduct may have taken the form of an afterthought with the Apostle. This he relates to the Galatians to show what issues were finally settled at the Council and that even Peter and Barnabas, who had been influenced by Peter at Antioch, were both so far convinced as to champion the cause of Gentile freedom at the Council.

Third, granted the foregoing conclusions, then the conduct of Peter in Galatians 2:11-21 would appear to fit best into an earlier visit of this apostle to Antioch, possibly in a supervisory capacity during the ministry of Paul and Barnabas, prior to the First Missionary Journey. It might best fit into the period described in Acts 11:25, 26.

The foregoing conclusion has the following support: (1) there were both Jew and Gentile Christians in the Antioch church (Acts 11:19-21); (2) that Barnabas faced difficulty in reconciling the Jew and Gentile elements at Antioch likely accounted for his seeking Saul, who possessed special qualification by nature and training for such a delicate task (Acts 11:25-26); (3) Paul, who labored at this task with Barnabas for a year (Acts 11:26), would naturally have been greatly disturbed at such a time by the official conduct of Peter on a social occasion among the Christians at Antioch, which even influenced Barnabas, just when the reconciliation of the Jews and Gentiles seemed imminent; (4) the conduct of Peter did not involve the question of circumcision, which was dealt with at the Jerusalem Council, but rather the matter of the social relations of the two nationalities. Peter had been severely censured by the Pharisaic party at Jerusalem for this same breach of Jewish religious and social etiquette while at Caesarea (Acts 11:1-3), and their presence at Antioch could easily account for his deflection there; (5) both Peter and Barnabas seemed to have fully recovered themselves, without resentment, after Paul's rebuke, and thus after a lapse of between two to three years, it is not surprising that they defended the Gentiles' liberty so vigorously at the Council.

XVII. THE CHURCH'S FIRST EURO-PEAN MISSION (Acts 15:36-18:22)

A. THE APOSTLES' PLANS FOR THE MISSION (15:36-41)

Certainly the Second Missionary Journey was more opportune at this juncture than had it occurred before the Jerusalem Council, as now the Christian Gentiles' relation to the church had been officially determined. That the apostles had long contemplated this second evangelistic enterprise is likely.

1. The Proposal of Paul (15:36)

36 And after some days Paul said unto Barnabas, Let us return now and visit the brethren in every city wherein we proclaimed the word of the Lord, *and see* how they fare.

Three things become evident in the plans for the second missionary campaign. *First,* it is Paul who takes the initiative and suggests the plans and purposes of this campaign. *Second,* it seems clear that in his original plan, Paul purposed to follow the course of the first missionary journey, judging from his reference to **every city wherein we proclaimed the word of the Lord** (v. 36). *Third,* the objective of the campaign is specifically stated to be a review of the progress of the Christian faith where they planted it during the first campaign, as the words, **and see how they fare** (v. 36b) would imply.

That Paul did not have a European mission in mind at this time seems further evident from the fact that his plans to evangelize in the province of Asia (Acts 16:6) were thwarted by the Holy Spirit, as were his subsequent plans to evangelize in Bithynia (Acts 16:7).

Thus it would appear that the whole procedure of the divine scheme for the second missionary journey was revealed step by step as the apostles followed the divine leadings. While Paul proposed a worthy missionary plan, God purposed a much more extensive and fruitful campaign that was to penetrate to the very heart of first-century European-Hellenist civilization. Paul's plans were always subject to revision by the divine wisdom. Only a careful review of the fruits of this second journey will reveal the spiritual

losses, had Paul missed God's plan for the campaign. How much more is seen by Him who looks down from above the circle of heavens (Isa. 40:22), than by man who looks up from the valley hemmed in by mountain walls.

2. The Problem of John Mark (15:37, 38)

37 And Barnabas was minded to take with them John also, who was called Mark. 38 But Paul thought not good to take with them him who withdrew from them from Pamphylia, and went not with them to the work.

The first serious recorded apostolic church leadership problem arose over the question of John Mark's accompanying Paul and Barnabas on the second missionary journey. The departure of Mark from the missionary party at Perga, on the first journey, was treated in relation to Acts 13:13. At the outset of the second missionary journey, John Mark is at Antioch with plans to accompany the apostles. Barnabas, his cousin, has a deep interest in him and his welfare, as well as a devotion to the missionary cause. Paul, a non-relative of Mark and possessed of a supreme devotion to the cause of Christ, is unable to see in Mark the values discernible by Barnabas. Paul remembers the departure of Mark from the work at Perga and thinks of the words of Christ (Luke 9:62). Robinson[99] thinks, further, that there may have been other problems involved in the contention, including too ambitious a program for Barnabas; Barnabas' act of siding with Peter (Gal. 2:11); difference of opinion as to the route to be followed; and Paul's desire to visit his own Cilician country first.

3. The Parting of the Apostles (15:39-41)

39 And there arose a sharp contention, so that they parted asunder one from the other, and Barnabas took Mark with him, and sailed away unto Cyprus: 40 but Paul chose Silas, and went forth, being commended by the brethren to the grace of the Lord. 41 And he went through Syria and Cilicia, confirming the churches.

Leaving the foregoing speculations, we are on certain ground when we center the

99 Robinson, *op. cit.,* pp. 111, 112.

problem in John Mark and observe that the sharp contention over the problem resulted in their parting asunder, Barnabas taking Mark and Paul taking Silas. Barnabas followed the former route to Cyprus where we lose sight of him. Paul took a northwesterly route through Syria and into Cilicia confirming the churches en route. Paul and Silas are said to have been **commended by the brethren to the grace of the Lord** (v. 40b). Nothing is said of the church's approval of the program of Barnabas and Mark. However, this may be due to Luke's purpose to record the history of Paul henceforth and thus may have no bearing on Barnabas.

Notwithstanding the nearly, if not quite, facetious remark of D. A. Hayes that he is quite sure one of the two brethren lost his perfect love over the contention, Clarke argues with learning and force that there is nothing in the expression, **sharp contention** (v. 39a), to justify the conclusion that ill will characterized either of them. That they were both perfectly sincere in their positions may well be granted. That they were both right from their respective points of view is possible. Let us sum up the resultant facts: *first,* there appears to have been no breach of fellowship between Paul and Barnabas (I Cor. 9:6); *second,* Barnabas was evidently right in giving Mark another chance, as his history reveals and as Paul later recognizes (see Col. 4:10; Philemon 24; II Tim. 4: 11); *third,* two missionary parties went forth, each of which had special qualifications for its respective field of service; *fourth,* the division appears to have had no ill effects on the church at Antioch, nor to have created any problems on the fields visited; *fifth* and finally, the incident apparently opened the door of opportunity for Silas to accompany Paul on his second missionary journey, and thus to gain experience that developed him into one of Paul's closest companions and most useful co-workers in the gospel ministry.

Thus we are taught the lesson from first-century Christianity that even great men may forcefully disagree on what they regard as principles and still maintain Christian grace and charity while proceeding on their respective courses, and that out of such vigorous disagreements of energetic men may come greater good than from apathetic acquiescence (Rom. 8:28).

B. THE NEW MISSIONARY PERSONNEL (16:1-5)

Reference to Acts 15:41, which logically belongs to the sixteenth chapter, indicates that Paul's course at the commencement of the second missionary journey led overland through northern Syria, likely touching at Issus and Alexandria, and then passed through the Syrian Gates (now the Belian or Beilan Pass) in Mount Amanus and thence into the Cilician province of Asia Minor. In Cilicia he most probably visited Tarsus, the metropolis of Cilicia and Paul's home, from whence he ascended toward Mount Taurus and on to the Lycaonian plateau via the Cilician Gates and thence to Derbe and Lystra. Luke's statement, "confirming the churches" (Acts 15:41b), expresses the primary purpose and nature of Paul's visit to the churches of Syria and Asia Minor. Whether or not the reading of some versions of Acts 15:41 is valid (namely, "They delivered unto them the decrees of the apostles and elders to keep"), certainly Acts 16:4 expresses an essential part of their ministry to all the churches revisited on this journey. That their faith had been disturbed by Judaizing activities appears evident from Paul's Galatian letter (cf. Gal. 1:6-9 and 3:1), if we regard this letter as having been written after the Jerusalem Council and before the second missionary journey, even to the extent of undermining confidence in the validity of his apostleship. Their reception of the Jerusalem Council decrees (Acts 15:23-29) afforded an official statement of their Christian freedom from the Mosaic Law (Gal. 5:1-13), and that their faith should rest in divine grace producing hope and brotherly love (Gal. 5:5-14), and not in the ceremonial law that could but lead to bondage and the forfeiture of their relationship with Christ (Gal. 5:2-4), with inevitable resultant confusion, strife, and destruction (Gal. 5:15).

1. The Heritage of Timothy (16:1, 2)

1 And he came also to Derbe and to Lystra: and behold, a certain disciple was there, named Timothy, the son of a

Jewess that believed; but his father was a Greek. 2 The same was well reported of by the brethren that were at Lystra and Iconium.

Timothy's home was at Lystra. An element of surprise and amazement are suggested by the manner in which Luke introduces him into the narrative, **And behold a certain disciple was there, named Timothy** (v. 1). At Lystra a cripple had been healed, the apostles had been beaten, and then Paul was stoned by the Jewish-incited mob and left for dead (see Acts 14:8-20). Could any good possibly have emerged from these misfortunes? In just one phrase of verse 20, Luke gives us the key to the almost hidden success of the apostles' first mission to Lystra: "But as the disciples stood round about him." Among those new converts who were present and witnessed the miraculous restoration of Paul was a lad in his late teens whose name was Timothy, and likely his newly converted Jewish mother, Eunice, and grandmother, Lois, in whose home the apostles may have resided. Possibly the souls of the great Apostle and this bright, lovable young lad had been "knit together" in love and mutual admiration, like Jonathan and David of old, as they lived and associated together in the home of his mother. Or is it too fanciful to suppose that, since as some hold, Timothy's mother was a widow, Paul came to fill the place of an absent father's love in the boy's life? Such seems to have been the subsequent relationship of the two (cf. I Tim. 1:2, 18; II Tim. 1:2; 2:1). There was indeed great cause for amazement as this young man, physically mature and spiritually developed, stands before the Apostle upon his re-entry into Lystra. His name Timothy, or Timotheus, simply means "dear to God," likely suggesting his pious Jewish mother's hopes at his birth. Or did Paul rechristen him "Timothy" at his conversion?

No mention is made of Timothy's father, except that he was a Greek; thus he was the son of one of those forbidden, but not uncommonly practiced, mixed marriages of that day. That he had the advantages of upbringing by a pious Jewish mother and grandmother, both of whom became Christians, we know (cf. II Tim. 1:5; 3:14, 15; and Acts 16:1).

Further, such had been the exemplary faith and conduct of this young man that Luke can observe that he was held in high esteem by the Christians at Lystra and Iconium, 18 miles away. A vital faith always manifests itself in an energetic service for Christ (cf. I Thess. 1:8).

2. The Circumcision of Timothy (16:3)

3 Him would Paul have to go forth with him; and he took and circumcised him because of the Jews that were in those parts: for they all knew that his father was a Greek.

Paul's judicious decision to take Timothy with him on this journey finds its justification both in Timothy's reputation in the church (v. 2) and his subsequent usefulness to the Apostle in the cause of Christ. (For a record of their later relationship, compare the following Scriptures: Acts 17:14; I Thess. 3:2; Acts 18:5; I Thess. 1:1; II Thess. 1:1; Acts 19:22; I Cor. 4:17; 16:10; II Cor. 1:1; Rom. 16:21; Acts 20:4; Col. 1:1; Phil. 1:1; Philemon 1.)

The circumcision of Timothy finds its justification in the fact that while his father was a Greek, his mother was a Jewess, and Timothy had been brought up in her faith. Thus he would be regarded as a Jew in religion, and consequently, uncircumcised, he would have been regarded by the Jews as unclean. Therefore, both Paul's association with him and any attempt on his part to minister in the synagogue would have been resented and resisted by the Jews everywhere they traveled. His circumcision was voluntary and for the sake of expediency, and not necessary for his salvation. For a reconciliation of this incident with Paul's refusal to circumcise Titus at Jerusalem, see the comment on Acts 15:2, 3. While Paul's policy was never to compromise where principle was involved, he was always ready to compromise, even sacrifice, when expediency not involving principle required it for the sake of the cause of Christ (cf. Gal. 2:3-5 and I Cor. 8:8-13; 9:22, 23).

3. The Help of the Decrees (16:4, 5)

4 And as they went on their way through the cities, they delivered them the decrees to keep which had been or-

dained of the apostles and elders that were at Jerusalem. 5 So the churches were strengthened in the faith, and increased in number daily.

The subsequent cities visited in Asia Minor are not specified by Luke, but they most certainly included Iconium and Antioch of Pisidia, where churches were planted on the first missionary journey, if not others, that these disciples might have the benefit of the decisions of the Jerusalem Council and the confirmation of Paul's ministry, since such was Paul's original purpose for this second journey (see Acts 15:36). Concerning the decrees of verse 4, see the comment on the introduction to chapter 16.

Two benefits accrued from Paul's second ministry to these churches. The first was "edification," they **were strengthened in the faith,** and the second was "evangelization." The first was a passive benefit received by them from the missionaries, the second an active benefit communicated by them to the world. This is an abiding divine principle exemplified by Christ in the training and commission of His disciples, and everywhere found in His teachings (cf. John 7:37-39; Gal. 5:6). Here is a recurrence of the normal spiritual life of the church of Pentecost (see Acts 2:42, 47b). When disturbing and divisive factors are eliminated from the body of Christ, confidence and faith will be restored, and the church will return to her supreme mission of world evangelization. Such is the spiritual norm of the body ecclesiastic. The "spiritually animate" will always seek to reproduce itself as normally as does the "naturally animate" world.

The early and widespread growth of the church in these regions, as suggested by Luke's words, **the churches . . . increased in number daily** (cf. Acts 13:44, 48, 49; 14:1, 21) is amply attested by extra-biblical sources. Harnack indicates two factors that especially prepared the soil of Asia Minor for Christianity. *First,* he declares,

> Here there were no powerful and unifying national religions to offer . . . fanatical resistance to Christianity . . . although there were strong local sanc-

100 Harnack, *op. cit.,* II, 181-184.

tuaries and several attractive cults throughout the country.
Second, he continues,
> The older national memories had almost died out everywhere. There was a total lack of any independent political life. Here, the imperial cultus established itself, therefore, with success. But while the imperial cultus was an anticipation of universalism in religion, it was a totally unworthy expression of that universalism, nor could it permanently satisfy the religious natures of the age . . . . Here Hellenism had assumed a form which rendered it peculiarly susceptible to Christianity.[100]

C. THE ENLARGED PROSPECT (16: 6-10)

That Paul had plans for the further evangelization of Asia Minor which were not immediately in accord with the divine will is clearly evident from Luke's account.

1. The Divine Prohibition (16:6-8)

6 And they went through the region of Phrygia and Galatia, having been forbidden of the Holy Spirit to speak the word in Asia; 7 and when they were come over against Mysia, they assayed to go into Bithynia; and the Spirit of Jesus suffered them not; 8 and passing by Mysia, they came down to Troas.

While at Lystra, Paul and his party received a divine intimation that they should not attempt the evangelization of Proconsular Asia in western Asia Minor, for reasons left to conjecture. Possibly a further seasoning of the Galatian Christians with a view to a gradual penetrating impact of their new faith on the western peoples, through travel and commercial intercourse, was needed to prepare the soil of Asia for Christianity. Possibly an encircling of Asia by Christian influences, through the planting of churches in Macedonia and Achaia, was necessary as a preparatory factor. Possibly the "occupational missionary service" of Priscilla and Aquila, whom Paul was to meet and engage at Corinth, was a requisite to the establishment of Christianity in Ephesus, from which location Asia was eventually evangelized. Possibly the ripeness of Europe for the gospel message accounted for the divine prohibition to preach in Asia; or a combination of two or more of these factors, if not others, may have occasioned the divine directive. The Holy Spirit's directives are always right, when properly understood and obeyed. Man can always afford to lay his plans aside in deference to the divine will. It is wise that he should plan, but his plans must always be subject to alteration by the will of God.

Phrygia and Galatia, through which Paul passed, doubtless visiting Iconium and Antioch, may be best understood, Goodwin thinks, by considering Phrygia and Galatia as adjectives rather than nouns, and thus reading, "the country which is Phrygian and Galatic."[101]

Arriving at the borders of Mysia, Paul's party made plans to enter **Bithynia,** evidently with the purpose of the evangelization of that territory, since the Spirit had forbade them to preach in Asia; **the Spirit of Jesus suffered them not** (v. 7b). Of these words, **Spirit of Jesus,** Dummelow remarks: This remarkable expression, which makes the Holy Spirit the Spirit not only of the Father, but also of the Son, is an evidence that the true divinity of Jesus was firmly held when St. Luke wrote.[102]

That these divine prohibitions had a purpose, as they always have in man's life, becomes evident in the next verse.

The divine method of forbidding Paul to preach in Asia (v. 6b), or enter Bithynia (v. 7b), needs to be considered circumstantial, as God often manifests His will directly to His servants, as also sometimes circumstantially. Says Wesley: "Sometimes a strong impression, for which we are not able to give any account, is not altogether to be despised."[103]

2. The Macedonian Invitation (16:9, 10)

9 And a vision appeared to Paul in the night: There was a man of Macedonia standing, beseeching him, and saying, Come over into Macedonia, and help us. 10 And when he had seen the vision, straightway we sought to go forth into Macedonia, concluding that God had called us to preach the gospel unto them.

The missionary party arrived at Troas, the chief port of Mysia on the Aegean

Sea, which was located near the site of the legendary Troy, the scene of Homer's *Iliad.* Troas had been made a Roman colony by Augustus, and was afforded special privileges by the Romans because of their traditional origin in this region.

While at Troas Paul most certainly preached and founded a church, as he met disciples there on a subsequent visit (Acts 20:7). Here the apostle experienced one of the several significant visions of his life (cf. Acts 9:3-6, 12; 18:9; 27:23-25; II Cor. 12:1-7). While Paul stands alone in the significance of his visions, there are many historic parallels of the fact of his vision, including Socrates, Mohammed, St. Bernard, Saint Francis, Ansgar, George Fox, Jacob Boehme, David Joris, and Swedenborg. That this or any other vision of Paul was indicative of epilepsy, as some hold, is too fanciful for serious consideration. If epileptic seizures produced such results as to influence human history as did the visions of Paul, then it would be to the interest of God and humanity that world religious and political leaders have "epileptic fits."

Says Wesley:

A vision appeared to Paul by night — It was not a dream, though it was by night. No other dream is mentioned in the New Testament, than that of Joseph and of Pilate's wife. *A man of Macedonia* — Probably an angel clothed in the Macedonian habit, or using the language of the country, and respresenting the inhabitants of it. *Help us* — Against Satan, ignorance, and sin.[104]

It is entirely possible that Paul became ill at Troas and was attended by a young Gentile Christian physician from Philippi whose name was Luke, on business or conducting a clinic at Troas, and who may have told the Apostle of the great needs and opportunities for the gospel in his home city. Others have thought the man to have been the guardian angel of Macedonia (Dan. 10:10-14). His Macedonian speech or dress may have identified him (Dummelow). Be this as it may, we have scriptural evidence that it was at Troas that Luke joined the party, for here the author of Acts identifies himself for the first time with the missionaries by the use of

---

[101] Frank J. Goodwin, *A Harmony and Commentary of the Life of St. Paul,* p. 65.
[102] Dummelow, *op. cit.,* p. 840.   [103] Wesley, *op. cit.,* p. 458, n. 7.   [104] *Ibid.,* n. 9.

the pronoun "we" in verse 10. Paul's vision produced the European mission, and this is sufficient to validate its divine origin. Such was to characterize the Spirit-baptized church (see Acts 2:17). In any enterprise, sacred or secular, the vision is essential to afford the form, ideal, or pattern, as a guide for actualization.

How fitting that Christianity should have been introduced into Europe by a special divine revelation to Paul! God forever stands at the threshold and opens the doors for His servants into great new spiritual enterprises.

D. THE MINISTRY AT PHILIPPI (16: 11-15)

Though not revealed to Paul in the divine prognostication at Troas, nevertheless God foresaw the open door for the gospel at Philippi and unerringly directed the missionary party to the **place of prayer**, which was not only to afford access to God but also to the great country of Macedonia, by way of the heart of a prominent merchant woman.

1. The Mission's Advance (16:11, 12)

11 Setting sail therefore from Troas, we made a straight course to Samothrace, and the day following to Neapolis; 12 and from thence to Philippi, which is a city of Macedonia, the first of the district, a *Roman* colony: and we were in this city tarrying certain days.

Luke makes clear that there was now a sense of certainty and urgency characterizing the missionaries. **And when he had seen the vision, straightway we sought to go forth into Macedonia, concluding that God had called us to preach the gospel unto them** (v. 10). Zeal, good intentions, and earnest or feverish efforts for God will all end in failure and frustration until the divine will is ascertained (see vv. 6 and 7). When God's will is clearly understood by His obedient servants, there comes to their hearts a rest of conviction and purposefulness that clears the moral and spiritual atmosphere and gives drive and direction to life and service. There is no stabilizing and securing force in the life of man equal to a clear knowledge of God's

will, when the mind of man accords with that divine will.

Since Philippi was the party's goal, Luke hurried on with only a passing notice of **Samothrace,** an island midway of the northern Aegean Sea, to their port of disembarkation on the following day at **Neapolis**, the seaport of **Philippi**. Luke's special notes on **Philippi** indicate its importance as the **first** city of the district, and a **Roman colony**. Whether **first** in importance, or in the course of travel from the sea, is in doubt; probably the former is meant.

Finegan gives an interesting account of this once proud city. Philippi was founded in the middle of the fourth century B.C. by Philip of Macedonia, father of Alexander the Great; but a small settlement named Crenides had preceded it, according to Strabo. It was made a Roman colony to celebrate the victory of Antony and Octavian over Brutus and Cassius in the battle of Philippi 42 B.C. and given the name Colonia Julia Philippenis, in honor of Julius Ceasar, with the first citizenship rights accorded the veterans of this battle. Neapolis, located nine miles from Philippi, was included in the Philippian territory. The famous overland route from Asia to Rome (the Via Egnatia) passed from Neapolis over Mount Symbolum into Philippi, traversing the full length of the city's forum, a structure 300 by 150 feet. The fame of this once proud city is further indicated by the acropolis, Roman baths, the theater, and the "colonial archway," the latter located at the west entrance of the city, which forbade foreign deities to enter the city. About a mile west of Philippi, the Via Egnatia crossed the river Ganga or Gangites. Thus the gate of Acts 16:13 is likely the "colonial archway" through which the apostles passed to the riverside where Paul ministered to the women assembled for prayer, in the absence of a Jewish synagogue.[105]

2. The Mission's Success (16:13-15)

13 And on the sabbath day we went forth without the gate by a river side, where we supposed there was a place of prayer; and we sat down, and spake unto the women that were come together.

105 Finegan, *op. cit.*, pp. 269-271.

14 And a certain woman named Lydia, a seller of purple, of the city of Thyatira, one that worshipped God, heard us: whose heart the Lord opened to give heed unto the things which were spoken by Paul. 15 And when she was baptized, and her household, she besought us, saying, If ye have judged me to be faithful to the Lord, come into my house, and abide *there*. And she constrained us.

Luke's words in verse 13 suggest five things. *First,* either that there were insufficient Jews in Philippi to afford a synagogue, or that their religion was forbidden by the Romans to be practiced within the city. The latter may be intimated by the author's words, **And on the sabbath day we went forth without the gate** (v. 13a). *Second,* they indicate that the Jews maintained a place of prayer (Gr. *proseuche*), "a *place* used for *worship,* where there was no synagogue. It was a large building uncovered, with seats, as in an amphitheatre. Buildings of this sort the Jews had by the seaside, and by the sides of rivers."[106] *Third,* this passage suggests that such Jews or proselytes as may have resided at Philippi were women, since no men are mentioned. Clarke's suggestion that this may have been a pre-service assembly of women to whom Paul spoke appears quite unlikely. *Fourth,* the riverside location of the *proseuche* was likely due to the convenience of water for ceremonial or purification purposes. And, *fifth,* it is clear that Paul's manner of approach was one of informal religious conversation with these women, rather than a direct formal proclamation of the gospel, as indicated by the record: **we sat down, and spake unto the women that were come together** (v. 13b). Paul usually stood to preach. How like Christ's informal approach to the Samaritan woman at Jacob's well (John 4:6-26), or that of Philip with the Ethiopian nobleman (Acts 8:29-39). The most effective preaching has not always been done from the high pulpits, nor to great audiences. The Christian message is a witness, and to be effective it must ever be on the personal level.

Lydia was likely an influential leader of these women of Jewish faith, possibly even the director of this simple act of worship. That she was a Gentile proselyte to the Jewish faith, as were the other women, is most likely. That she was a native of Thyatira, the city of Thyatira in Lydia of Asia Minor (the country that probably gave her her name), and a merchandiser of a very beautiful and expensive cloth of purple dye, Luke suggests. Her circumstances indicate that she was a woman of considerable means (v. 15). It was such a person as this that God sought out to become the human door of entrance for the gospel in Macedonia.

Luke's statement that she was **one that worshipped God** implies a sincerity and devotion out of the usual course. Wesley suggests that she was "Probably acquainted with the prophetic writings,"[107] in which case she would have been one of those Grecian-Jews who earnestly expected the Messiah and gladly heard the message of the Apostle. She was near to the Kingdom of God, and Paul's message of truth was used of God to turn the key that unlocked her heart to the entrance of Christ. The same Spirit that directed and inspired the Apostle's message conditioned her spiritual understanding to receive that message. Wesley remarks concerning Luke's expression, **whose heart the Lord opened** (v. 14), "The Greek word properly refers to the opening of the eyes. And the heart has its eyes (Eph. 1:18). These are closed by nature; and to open them is the peculiar work of God."[108] This very thing Paul declares to be the purpose and function of the gospel: "to open their eyes, that they may turn from darkness to light and from the power of Satan unto God, that they may receive remission of sins and an inheritance among them that are sanctified by faith in me" (Acts 26:18). On the contrary, he asserts that Satan, "the god of this world hath blinded the minds of the unbelieving, that the light of the gospel of the glory of Christ, who is the image of God, should not dawn upon them" (II Cor. 4:4).

Satan darkens, God illumines; Satan closes the spiritual eyes, Christ opens the eyes of the spiritually blind. No amount of oratory, elocution, logical argumentation, exposition, or persuasion can effect this spiritual illumination. It is a work that belongs exclusively to God. Until

---

[106] Clarke, *op. cit.,* I, 815.   [107] Wesley, *op. cit.,* p. 459, n. 14.   [108] *Ibid.*

the Lord opens the hearts of the unsaved, they will remain entombed in the dark dungeon of this world of spiritual death.

Awakened and illumined, Lydia gave **heed unto the things which were spoken by Paul** (v. 14b). In his Ephesian letter Paul implies that the soul may be truly awakened without responding and realizing the benefits of salvation: "Awake thou that sleepest, and arise from the dead, and Christ shall shine upon thee" (Eph. 5:14). Thus the Apostle suggests that initial salvation consists of a threefold process: (1) spiritual awakening, (2) spiritual resurrection, and (3) spiritual illumination. Such appears to have been the experience of this first European convert.

And when she was baptized (v. 15a). Like the Ethiopian nobleman converted and baptized under the personal ministry of Philip (Acts 8:36-39), this European noblewoman, converted under Paul's ministry, sealed her faith and offered her testimony to the pagan citizens of Philippi by that outward material symbol of a gracious inner work of grace already wrought by God in her inner spiritual nature. So genuinely converted and so influential was her life that her entire household followed her in baptism. Her household would have included her domestic servants and slaves, as well as her children and relatives, if any resided with her (cf. 16:33; 18:8; I Cor. 1:16; Matt. 19:13-15). Since no mention is made of her husband, it is as logical to believe that she was a widow, if indeed she was married and had children, as it is to so conclude concerning Eunice, the mother of Timothy (Acts 16:1). Renan is reported to have entertained the unsupported notion that Lydia became Paul's wife.

Lydia's conversion served the further practical benefit of providing lodging and entertainment for Paul's missionary party while they remained in Philippi and this by constraint of Lydia and not of choice by the missionaries. God's doings are always practical, when properly understood. Though she was God's chosen instrument in the gospel's European initiation, she appears either to have left Philippi or died, as Paul does not mention her name in the Philippian letter.

E. THE EXPULSION OF A DEMON (16:16-18)

Though the gospel had a peaceful European entrance through the conversion of Lydia, this state of affairs was not to last for long.

1. The Occasion of the Demon Expulsion (16:16-18a).

16 And it came to pass, as we were going to the place of prayer, that a certain maid having a spirit of divination met us, who brought her masters much gain by soothsaying. 17 The same following after Paul and us cried out, saying, These men are servants of the Most High God, who proclaim unto you the way of salvation. 18 And this she did for many days.

The evangelistic activities of the missionaries by the riverside were disturbing to Satan's interests. Interference began through the annoying conduct of a "clairvoyant" slave girl whose "mediumship" had been exceedingly gainful to her masters. That she was both possessed of a demon and mentally unsound is a reasonable inference from Luke's account. Her supposed, if not real, ability to divine, or clairvoyantly explore and discern the transomatic world, and then to display this occult knowledge in soothsaying or fortune-telling, was unquestionably due to the intelligence of the unclean demon by whom she was possessed. Such individuals and practices were not uncommon in the ancient Orient, nor are they uncommon in the dark regions of paganism today. Though in a more refined fashion and with greater cultural pretenses, occultism is experiencing a shocking recrudescence in the modern western world through practices of clairvoyance, telepathy, spiritualistic mediumship and materialization, palmistry, and crystal-gazing. Especially has this become increasingly true in the wake of three great wars when so many devoid of a knowledge of Bible truth or faith in God have attempted to make contact with their deceased loved ones. There are always those who are ready to sell their souls and service to forbidden occultism.

Jan Karel Van Baalen has analyzed this occult practice as consisting in either trickery, such as sleight of hand performance, superpsychic powers of occult personalities, and demon possession, or possibly a combination of any two or all three of these factors. Again the same authority has outlined the results of occultism under the heading of three "Black I's," namely, "infidelity," "immorality," and "insanity."[109]

That ventriloquism has been associated with divination and soothsaying is not strange when it is remembered that not infrequently these practitioners are characterized by dual personalities, one of whom may be a possessing demon. Many sober-minded thinkers are becoming increasingly aware of the reality of demon possession as accounting for much personality abnormality even in modern civilized society, as witnesses the appearance of a recent significant publication by J. Stafford Wright, Principal of Tyndale Hall, Bristol, England.[110] A chapter in this book entitled, "Man and His Unseen Neighbors" treats and gives full credence to "Demons," "Fallen Angels," "Demon Possession," and "The Method and Manner of Possession." A widely read work of the late C. S. Lewis likewise accepts the credibility of demon personality.[111]

That Luke, a physician capable of distinguishing between symptoms of a natural physical or mental disorder and those superimposed by a demon personality, should diagnose this and other cases as demon possession cannot be without significance.

This unfortunate girl's discernment reflected in her often repeated exclamation, **These men are servants of the Most High God** (v. 17), is not surprising in the light of Christ's experiences when the demons recognized Him (cf. Matt. 8:28, 29 and Acts 19:15). Possessed of a knowledge of Christ's person, the demon would also know His redemptive work; and thus the exclamation, **who proclaim unto you the way of salvation** (v. 17b). Paul neither required nor desired this demoniacal counterfeit publicity, as it threatened to weaken the missionaries' position with the people by reason of the demon's profession of a knowledge of God and His salvation and a proclamation of this through the possessed girl. Paul, like Jesus (Mark 1:25), while recognizing that what the demon said was true, rejected

the testimony, because of its source. The demon-possessed girl's reference to the **Most High God** antedates the "Highgod" discoveries of modern anthropologists by nearly two thousand years. (See Additional Note VI, *The High-God Theory.*

2. The Accomplishment of the Demon Expulsion (16:18b)

18 But Paul, being sore troubled, turned, and said to the spirit, I charge thee in the name of Jesus Christ to come out of her. And it came out that very hour.

The girl recognized in Paul a servant and minister of the **Most High God,** or the supreme God, and therefore supreme over the demon that possessed her. Consequently, Paul's authoritative command in the Name of Jesus Christ, that the spirit leave the girl, automatically expelled the demon, who by reason of his inferiority to Christ was compelled to obey. Note that it was Paul's command **in the name of Jesus Christ** that expelled the demon (cf. Mark 5:8).

F. THE VICTORY OVER PERSECUTION (16:19-34)

Though the gospel had a peaceful entrance into Philippi, the enemy was soon to raise a storm of violent opposition against the invasion of his territory.

1. The Cause of the Persecution (16: 19-21)

19 But when her masters saw that the hope of their gain was gone, they laid hold on Paul and Silas, and dragged them into the market place before the rulers, 20 and when they had brought them unto the magistrates, they said, These men, being Jews, do exceedingly trouble our city, 21 and set forth customs which it is not lawful for us to receive, or to observe, being Romans.

This slave girl was the chattel of unprincipled mercenary pagan men who had no respect for her personal worth nor concern about the teachings of the missionaries, until their monetary gain was affected. She was to them but an instrument, and when her instrumental worth to them was destroyed, they were en-

---

[109] J. K. Van Baalen, *The Chaos of Cults,* pp. 33-38.
[110] Wright, *op. cit.*   [111] C. S. Lewis, *The Screwtape Letters.*

raged. Paul's expulsion of the evil spirit from the girl had left her quite incapable of divining for stolen goods or telling fortunes to their material profit. Clarke sees no evidence that the girl was converted, and therefore the protests of her masters were from mercenary and not religious or patriotic motives, as they represent their cause before the magistrates. How helpless are the evil devices of unprincipled men apart from the support of Satanic intelligence! How much evil would be eliminated from society were the profit motive absent! (See I Tim. 5:10.) Truth always suffers opposition when it touches the purse of the greedy.

Doubtless the missionaries were ruthlessly dragged to the market place with a view to exciting and inflaming the passions of the rabble gathered there and thus gaining support for their accusers.

Note that when Paul and Silas were arraigned before the magistrates (or Praetors),[112] whose offices were likely near the central market, they do not present their real reasons for attacking them, the loss of gain (v. 19a), but from pretense of patriotism they make a threefold charge against them. *First,* they prejudice the minds of the magistrates at the outset by representing Paul and Silas as Jews, **These men, being Jews** (v. 20b), (only a half-truth as Silas was likely a Gentile proselyte), a people despised by the Romans as troublemakers throughout the empire. Roman hostility to the Jews may account for the absence of many Jews, or even a synagogue at Philippi. *Second,* they charge them with disturbance of the peace, **These men, being Jews, do exceedingly trouble our city** (v. 20b), a charge totally devoid of factual evidence. On the contrary, Paul had silenced a disturbance of the peace by casting the demon out of the noisy damsel. *Third,* they were charged with introducing religious customs forbidden to Romans, though not to non-Roman citizens. Nor is there any validity to this charge since there is no evidence that the missionaries had preached to other than Jews. As a slave the soothsaying damsel would not have been a citizen, nor is there evidence that she was converted. Thus there is not a valid charge against them.

2. The Nature of the Persecution (16: 22-24)

22 And the multitude rose up together against them: and the magistrates rent their garments off them, and commanded to beat them with rods. 23 And when they had laid many stripes upon them, they cast them into prison, charging the jailor to keep them safely: 24 who, having received such a charge, cast them into the inner prison, and made their feet fast in the stocks.

The likely protest of Paul and Silas that they were Roman citizens and should be treated as such was probably drowned by the clamor of the excited and inflamed mob. Six steps are clearly discernible in the persecution proceedings against Paul and Silas. *First,* every semblance of rationality or justice was removed from their makeshift trial by the influence of the mob spirit that motivated the proceedings (v. 22a). *Second,* official shame and regard for justice and legal procedure were cast aside as the magistrates stripped the missionaries of their clothing and commanded them to be beaten (v. 22b). *Third,* they were mercilessly beaten with rods by the police (lictors). Though the Jews had borrowed this form of punishment from the Romans, they limited it to thirty-nine stripes, whereas the Romans applied it without limit. Paul possibly alludes to this very incident at Philippi in his later words, "stripes above measure" (II Cor. 11: 23). *Fourth,* they were thrown or cast, like vicious criminals, into the dark, damp, unsanitary, prison dungeon and secured there (v. 23b). *Fifth,* for self-protection the jailer cast them into the solitary confinement of the inner prison cells. *Sixth,* their feet were securely and painfully locked in the heavy wooden stocks of the prison. This cruel form of punishment the writer has often witnessed among the West Africans. A heavy hardwood log, twelve to eighteen inches in diameter and ten to fifteen feet long, is hewn square and then sawed in half lengthwise. Round holes the size of a man's ankles are then cut at the division of the log at intervals of about two feet. The halves are hinged together at one end and then tapered off to a flat point

---

[112] Weymouth, *op. cit.,* observes, "Their proper title was 'duumviri,' but they often assumed the higher rank of praetors, to which they had no right, although Luke concedes it to them five times in this chapter."

at the opposite end and provided with a hasp and staple for locking. The prisoner secured in such a set of stocks is required to place his feet in the grooves of the lower half of the log while attendants raise the upper half from the unhinged end. When the feet are in place, the upper section is lowered over the victim's feet and securely padlocked. Here prisoners are sometimes left for days in a dark, unventilated room without food, water, or sanitation. This device is aptly named an "alligator" (*uquie*) in the Temne language of Sierra Leone. In a similar device Paul and Silas were secured in the inner prison. The likelihood of Luke's residence in Philippi and Timothy's youthfulness, if not his Greek father's resemblance, may have exempted these men from the punishment accorded their companions.

3. The Consequences of the Persecution (16:25-30)

25 But about midnight Paul and Silas were praying and singing hymns unto God, and the prisoners were listening to them; 26 and suddenly there was a great earthquake, so that the foundations of the prison-house were shaken: and immediately all the doors were opened; and everyone's bands were loosed. 27 And the jailor, being roused out of sleep and seeing the prison doors open, drew his sword and was about to kill himself, supposing that the prisoners had escaped. 28 But Paul cried with a loud voice, saying, Do thyself no harm: for we are all here. 29 And he called for lights and sprang in, and, trembling for fear, fell down before Paul and Silas, 30 and brought them out and said, Sirs, what must I do to be saved?

The sequence, as well as significance, of transpiring events recorded by Luke is striking.

Wearied, beaten, maltreated and bloody, these two missionaries uncomfortably sat in their inner dungeon cell with feet secured in the torturous stocks. Then *first*, in these circumstances and at the darkest hour of the night, **about midnight** (v. 25a), Paul and Silas were praying and singing hymns **unto God** (v. 25a). What Paul and Silas prayed about we are not told; we may suppose that they prayed for their persecutors, for the salvation of their fellow prisoners and for grace to sustain them in this situation. Nor do we know the hymns that they sang, except that they were **unto God**. All self-pity was absent. What better occupation could they have engaged in at such a time and place. They had learned with afflicted Job that God "giveth songs in the night" (Job 35:10). Their physical sufferings had been spiritually sublimated, and they were transported into "heavenly places, in Christ Jesus" (Eph. 2:6). Nor have they been the last to experience mental and spiritual transcendence in the hour of most intense affliction. *Second,* though cut off from the normal channels of missionary activity, they were not without an audience, and such an audience without their presence could not have heard the gospel. Their prayers and songs of praise ascended to the ears of God and extended to the ears of the prisoners: **the prisoners were listening to them** (v. 25b). Who can say that some of these very prisoners were not among Paul's beloved disciples to whom he later wrote the endearing Epistle to the Philippians? Possibly it was from this experience that Paul learned the great philosophy which he phrased in Romans 8:28. *Third,* the earth began to rise and fall, like a panting monster, under a seismic shudder that vibrated the stones out of their positions and sent iron doors clattering to the prison floor. Freed from their cells, the prisoners quickly assisted one another in gaining freedom from their bonds. Clarke regards this incident as symbolical of the shattering dynamic of the gospel with its consequent liberation of the spiritually bound, and consternation of the impenitent and wicked (see Luke 4:18). There need be no question about the miraculous character of an incident so productive of moral and spiritual benefit as was this earthquake. *Fourth,* the same jailer, who had so heartlessly and ruthlessly thrust them into the prison, now frightfully awakened, first thought to commit suicide and then sought and found peace with God. Roman law demanded that in the event prisoners escaped, the prison keeper or guard should suffer the same punishment intended for the escaped prisoner (cf. Acts 12:19). Pagan philosophy of the day, especially Stoicism, commended suicide to escape execution, and the jailer, thinking death inevitable, supposing that the prisoners were escaped, in desperation intended suicide. Little did he realize that though so near the gates of death and hell, the doors of mercy and eternal life were about to open to him. The alertness of Paul became the means of his salvation. From fear and despair his mind turned to hope and inquiry: Sirs, what must I do to be saved? (v. 30b). If man could but see that the calamities of life are often God's methods of leading him to hope and salvation, how different would be the issues of life!

4. The Fruits of the Persecution (16: 31-34)

31 And they said, Believe on the Lord Jesus, and thou shalt be saved, thou and thy house. 32 And they spake the word of the Lord unto him, with all that were in his house. 33 And he took them the same hour of the night, and washed their stripes; and was baptized, he and all his, immediately. 34 And he brought them up into his house, and set food before them, and rejoiced greatly, with all his house, having believed in God.

How different the attitude and address of the jailer toward Paul and Silas now than yesterday! Then he ruthlessly cast them into prison as malefactors; now he falls down before them in reverence and addresses them as Sirs. The arrester has been arrested by God.

Certainly, as Clarke observes, it is absurd to think that the jailer was concerned about his personal safety when he asked this question, What must I do to be saved? (v. 30b). It was now certain that none of the prisoners had escaped. Rather let us soberly and realistically conclude with Wesley that his question, What must I do to be saved? (v. 30b), implied: "From the guilt I feel, and the vengeance I fear. Undoubtedly God then set his sins in array before him, and convinced him in the clearest and strongest manner that the wrath of God abode upon him."[113]

Their answer was confident and unequivocal: Believe on the Lord Jesus [or believe that Jesus is Lord supreme even to your need] and thou shalt be saved (v. 31). To supply the needed further instruction for the salvation of the

113 Wesley, op. cit., p. 461, n. 30.

jailer and his family, Paul and Silas spoke the word of the Lord unto him, with all that were in his house, and this may have included the prisoners by now. This was no vague or shallow personal instruction which Paul and Silas gave these spiritually awakened souls. The genuineness of the jailer's repentance and faith in God is further evidenced by his restitutional service to Paul and Silas in the washing of their wounds and the likely application of soothing and healing ointment. A profession of religion that does not right the wrongs of the past, where possible and practical, is of little value to either the professor or society.

Like the Ethiopian nobleman, this jailer seals the inner work of divine grace wrought in his heart by the outward symbol of water baptism. By what mode he was baptized we are not told, nor is that of primary importance; but Clarke's argument against the employment of immersion under the circumstances will hardly stand in the light of the modern archeological discovery of elaborate baths in ancient Philippi.

Though the profound influence of the jailer's conversion on his household in bringing them to repentance and salvation is not to be discredited, it should also be observed that it was not unusual for whole households to be proselytized to Judaism, and it not infrequently occurred in the Christian church. That they were individually saved on the grounds of their own faith appears evident from verse 34. His new-found faith in Christ was productive of generosity and joy, as the saving grace of Christ must ever be (v. 34b).

G. THE APOSTLES' PEACEFUL DEPARTURE (16:35-40)

35 But when it was day, the magistrates sent the serjeants, saying, Let those men go. 36 And the jailor reported the words to Paul, saying, The magistrates have sent to let you go: now therefore come forth, and go in peace. 37 But Paul said unto them, They have beaten us publicly, uncondemned, men that are Romans, and have cast us into prison; and do they now cast us out privily? nay verily; but let them come themselves and bring us out. 38 And the serjeants reported these words unto the magis-

trates: and they feared when they heard that they were Romans; 39 and they came and besought them; and when they had brought them out, they asked them to go away from the city. 40 And they went out of the prison and entered into *the house of* Lydia: and when they had seen the brethren, they comforted them, and departed.

It is quite possible that when the fervor of the frenzied mob had subsided, the magistrates had learned the truth concerning the supposed offense of the men who had been beaten and imprisoned, and sought to wash their hands of this miscarriage of justice. Wesley thinks, and that not without reason, the earthquake may have influenced their decision to release the missionaries. In any event they ordered the prisoners' release the following day (v. 35).

Paul asserted their Roman citizenship rights and demanded a respectable release by the very magistrates who had unjustly treated them. The reply to the sergeants brought to light the citizenship of Paul and Silas, which fact struck terror to the hearts of the magistrates. Such official conduct might, if known at Rome, cost them their positions or even severe punishment. In compliance with Paul's request, the magistrates came personally and besought them, probably apologized for the treatment accorded them, and then asked them to leave the city.

For how long we are not told, but they returned to the home of Lydia where they ministered to the disciples, and then feeling that their work in Philippi was done, they went on their way.

No New Testament church became dearer to the heart of the Apostle Paul than that at Philippi. His epistle addressed to the Philippians exceeds all the others in its spirit of personal affection, abounding gratitude, and exuberant joy, notwithstanding the fact that it was written from Paul's Roman jail cell. The care of these Christians for the Apostle of their salvation finds its fullest expression in his words: "And ye yourselves also know, ye Philippians, that in the beginning of the gospel, when I departed from Macedonia, no church had fellowship with me in the matter of giving and receiving but ye only; for even in Thessalonica ye sent once and again unto my need" (Phil. 4:15, 16). This epistle is so joyful and grateful in its spirit and tone that one has said that it may be summed up in a single sentence, "I rejoice, do you rejoice?"

H. THE EVANGELIZATION OF THE THESSALONIANS (17:1-9)

And some of them were persuaded (v. 4a). Perhaps nowhere is the immediate record of Paul's evangelistic success more pronounced than at Thessalonica. The fuller account of this initial ministry at Thessalonica is revealed in Paul's first and second letters written to the Thessalonian Christians from Corinth on his second missionary journey.

1. The Proclamation of the Gospel (17:1-3)

1 Now when they had passed through Amphipolis and Apollonia, they came to Thessalonica, where was a synagogue of the Jews: 2 and Paul, as his custom was, went in unto them, and for three sabbath days reasoned with them from the scriptures, 3 opening and alleging that it behooved the Christ to suffer and to rise again from the dead; and that this Jesus, whom, *said he,* I proclaim unto you, is the Christ.

Since Luke drops the "we" of personal identification with the missionary party from his historical record as they leave Philippi, it is generally assumed that he remained there, which likely signifies that either Philippi was his home or that he remained as pastor of the new church, or possibly both. Nor is Luke identified with Paul again until Paul arrives at Philippi the second time on his third missionary journey (see Acts 20:5, 6), after which Luke is with him to the close of the Acts record. Leaving Philippi, the party followed a southwesterly course for thirty-three miles over the *via Egnatia* to **Amphipolis,** originally the Roman capital of one of the four districts of Macedonia, but now having taken second place to Philippi and being devoid of a synagogue or Jewish population and generally decadent, it is avoided by Paul as a field of missionary activity. Thirty miles farther southwest they passed through the important city of **Apollonia,** without stopping to evangelize, and from thence on westward upward of forty miles to **Thessalonica.** This was the important capital of the entire province of Macedonia, and it had a large Jewish population and a synagogue. Thessalonica was founded by Cassander about 315 B.C. and named after his wife, Thessalonica, who was the sister of Alexander the Great. It was made a free city in reward for "its support of Antony and Octavian in the Battle of Philippi."[114] Thessalonica was the modern Salonika, an important Allied military base during the First World War, having a present population of about one-quarter million. It is located on the favored Thurmic Bay.

Here Paul, in keeping with his strategy to evangelize the capitals and commercial centers on the main trade routes that the gospel might spread from these centers throughout the empire, addressed himself to the Jewish synagogue as was his custom, where the way had been prepared for the gospel by the Old Testament revelation and the Gentile proselytes, mediums which Paul always sought to use for the evangelization of the Gentile world. Clarke thinks that the use of the definite article in reference to the Thessalonian synagogue indicates that this was the only synagogue in Macedonia, all other places of Jewish worship being only *proseuchas,* as at Philippi (see comment on Acts 16.13).

Paul's method of ministry in the synagogue is made evident in verses 2 and 3. *First,* he, like Philip with the Ethiopian nobleman (Acts 8:30-35), began at the point of Jewish interest in their own Scriptures concerning the promised Messiah, from which he reasoned with them (v. 2b). *Second,* he expounded the prophecies to the effect that this Messiah was to redeem humanity, not by the route of a materialistic earthly kingdom as they supposed, but through His suffering and atoning death and His glorious universal Lordship through the conquest of death in His resurrection, and this he did positively and with strong conviction as Luke suggests in his use of the word **alleging,** which means to declare as under oath (v. 3a). How great was the Apostle's passion for their salvation! *Third,* he identified the Jesus of his message with the Messiah of the Jewish Scriptures. Thus did Paul tactfully, logically, and passionately lead his hearers from the Scriptures to the Christ that he knew as Savior and Lord. He proceeded from promise in the Scriptures to fulfillment in his Christ.

That Paul remained at Thessalonica much longer, evangelizing the Gentiles with greater success, appears to be suggested by Luke's references to his three weeks' initial ministry in the synagogue.

2. The Acquisition of Converts (17:4)

4 And some of them were persuaded and consorted with Paul and Silas; and of the devout Greeks a great multitude, and of the chief women not a few.

That those who were persuaded went beyond mental assent to the logically inescapable conclusions of Paul is evidenced by the fact they **consorted with Paul and Silas.** Wesley renders these words, "And some of them believed and were joined to Paul and Silas"; while Weymouth's version states: "Some of the people were won over, and attached themselves to Paul and Silas." Thus they joined the company of the Christians. That these conversions were deep and genuine, effecting a saving relationship with Christ, there can remain no reasonable doubt. The great multitude of **devout Greeks** (v. 4b) who became Christians indicates, *first,* the extensive influence of the Jewish synagogue in winning Gentiles to the Jewish faith at Thessalonica; *second,* that these were not full proselytes, but "God-fearers" or those Greeks who worshipped Jehovah in the synagogue but did not subscribe to the Jewish ceremonials; and *third,* that the Greeks at Thessalonica much more readily became Christians than did the Jews. In fact, there is evidence from the Thessalonian letter that the church here was largely comprised of Gentile believers, as indeed it could not have been said of Jews, "ye turned unto God from idols, to serve a living and true God" (I Thess. 1:9b), since Jews were not idol worshipers at this time, and they already professed to be servants of the "living and true God," in contrast with the inanimate false idols. **The chief women not a few** (v. 4b) likewise were most probably the wives of prominent Gentile citizens and governmental officials, as was the case at Antioch of Pisidia (see note on Acts 13:50) . Here, as in so many other places, women figured largely in the church of the first century.[115]

3. The Jews' Attack on the Missionaries (17:5-9)

5 But the Jews, being moved with jealousy, took unto them certain vile fellows of the rabble, and gathering a crowd, set the city on an uproar; and assaulting the house of Jason, they sought to bring them forth to the people. 6 And when they found them not, they dragged Jason and certain brethren before the rulers of the city, crying, These that have turned the world upside down are come hither also; 7 whom Jason hath received: and these all act contrary to the decrees of Caesar, saying that there is another king, *one* Jesus. 8 And they troubled the multitude and the rulers of the city, when they heard these things. 9 And when they had taken security from Jason and the rest, they let them go.

At Thessalonica, as at Antioch (Acts 13:45, 50) , the deflection of so many Gentiles from the synagogue to Christianity, whom the Jews had hoped to win as proselytes to Judaism, aroused within them a jealous hatred that expressed itself in a most incredible manner. Unleashed jealousy knows no principles. Nor are religious people immune to its impassioned, blinding, perverting, cruel venom, if they are not cleansed and sustained by the Holy Spirit of God. Motivated by the cruel monster, the subjects throw to the wind every principle of right and justice and pant for the blood of their innocent victims. Jealousy was one of the viperous brood of the "sins of the spirit" characterizing the elder son in Christ's parable (Luke 15: 25-32) . That this elder son represented the Pharisees and scribes in their jealous resentment of Christ's receiving and eating with the Gentiles (publicans and sinners) is made clear in Luke 15:1. And though the lost sheep, coin and prodigal son were all recovered and restored, the curtain falls on the elder son, leaving him out of the Kingdom of God. When jealousy motivates the pursuer, the victim's only hope is in the "divine city of refuge," as witnesses the relation of Saul and David.

There are two views concerning the **vile fellows of the rabble** (v. 5a) whom these Jews used as instruments against the missionaries. One holds that they were idle, unprincipled, underworlding scavengers of the city who loafed about the central market and eked out a living by stealing, cheating, or begging, spending as much of their time in jail as outside, fellows everywhere alert to engage in any disorder that would afford them either excitement or personal gain. The other view holds that these **vile fellows of the rabble** were, rather, cheap, incompetent, unprincipled, and largely unemployed shyster lawyers with a degree of judicial authority, comparable perhaps to the so-called American "justice of the peace," of whom there were many in the country in Paul's day. Clarke calls them "wicked men of the forensic tribe." They were likely the descendants of the Greek Sophists and were ever ready to be employed for a pittance. Strange bedfellows for these proud Jewish religionists in their attack upon the missionaries.

Whichever view is taken, these **vile fellows** were employed by the Jews to the great discredit of the religion of Jehovah in Thessalonica. Either they were employed to shout slogans or taunts, and thus inflame the passions of the ignorant masses and set them like packs of dogs on Paul and Silas, or, if lawyers, then their approach probably was to charge them with religious heresy and, or, political sedition. In either event, they gathered **a crowd, [and] set the city on an uproar (v. 5).**

Learning that the missionaries were housed in the home of Jason, these Jews attempted, either directly or through their representatives, to secure custody of them, not legally to try them for any supposed misdemeanor, but to turn them over to the mob violence of the waiting, frenzied populace. How like the incident in Sodom when the sin-intoxicated Sodomites attacked the house of Lot, demanding custody of the heaven-sent investigating angels (cf. Gen. 19:1-11) !

Jason was evidently a Jew who had believed on Christ and, like Lydia at Philippi, had become the host of the mis-

---

[115] See Additional Note XI, *The Place of Women in the Primitive Church.*

sionaries. He may be the same Jason from whom Paul sends greetings to the Romans from Corinth (Rom. 16:21), having gone to that city from Thessalonica to be with Paul on the occasion of the Apostle's second visit there. Unable to find the missionaries, for reasons untold — possibly Jason hid them — they apprehended Jason and certain of the new believers and hauled them into the court before the magistrates with one of the most complimentary charges, ironically made against the missionaries *in absentia,* that they ever received, **These that have turned the world** [the inhabited earth] **upside down are come hither also** (v. 6b). These accusers appear to have had an inverted perspective of the world. Actually, it was already upside down, and the missionaries were simply turning it right side up. Men may become so accustomed to inverted circumstances and ways of life that wrong appears right, and right appears to be wrong. Widespread knowledge of the power and effectiveness of the gospel at this early stage of Christian progress is suggested in these words of accusation.

Their accusation of sedition (v. 7) was totally without foundation. Indeed, the missionaries declared Jesus to be Lord of the universe by His resurrection from the dead, but always and everywhere they made clear that His was a spiritual Kingdom and never after Pentecost did they confuse it with the material. Nor is there any evidence that the missionaries' conduct contravened Roman law, as is implied in their words, **these all act contrary to the decrees of Caesar** (v. 7). By these devices the accusers poisoned the minds of the populace and strongly prejudiced them against the Christians.

The **security** (v. 9), which the rulers took from Jason and the other Christians arraigned before the rulers for harboring and consorting with the missionaries, appears to have been a guarantee that the missionaries would leave the city (see I Thess. 2:17, 18). Paul was never cowardly when the gospel or its interests were at stake, but always considerate of the interests and welfare of others; having completed his service at Thessalonica, he peacefully went on his way, but not

until a powerful church had been planted there.

Paul's first and second letters to the Thessalonians, written from Corinth, are illuminating commentaries on his first visit to this city. At the very outset of the first letter, he remarks that he has only thanks to God for them, and that always (1:2); after which he commends them for the three greatest and abiding Christian virtues (1:3) with which Paul closes his dissertation on the *Summum Bonum* in First Corinthians, the thirteenth chapter. Note, however, that the Thessalonian Christians possessed *a working faith, a laboring love,* and *a patient hope.* In verse 5 he reviews the effectiveness with which he preached the gospel at Thessalonica — "in power, and in the Holy Spirit, and in much assurance." Further, he relates of them that they "became imitators of us, and of the Lord, having received the word in much affliction, with joy of the Holy Spirit" (I Thess. 1:6). The Apostle continued to the effect that they lived exemplary lives before all (1:7), and that from these Christians "sounded forth the word of the Lord" (1:8a) to the extent that they had largely, if not completely, covered Macedonia and Achaia with their witness. Salvation, suffering, and the Second Coming of Jesus Christ are the three golden strands that run throughout the whole of First Thessalonians and form the essential structure of the epistle.

A word need be said concerning the **rulers** at Thessalonica, since they are unique in the New Testament record. Finegan observes concerning these rulers, who are called *politarchai,* that an inscription found on an arch (the Vardar Gate), spanning the *Via Egnatia* at the western entrance to the city but now in the British Museum, begins with these words: "In the time of the Politarchs...." He further states that this inscription should probably be dated between 30 B.C. and A.D. 143. Other Thessalonian inscriptions, he states, one mentioning *Politarchs,* are definitely dated in Augustus' reign. Then says Finegan, "The term is otherwise unknown [outside of Acts 17:6] in extant Greek literature, but Luke's accuracy in the matter is entirely vindicated by the inscriptions."[116]

[116] Finegan, *op. cit.,* p. 271. See also Ernest De Witt Burton, *The American Journal of Theology,* II (1898), pp. 598-632.

I. THE SPIRITUAL QUEST OF THE BEROEANS (17:10-15)

Under the protective cover of darkness, the Christian disciples at Thessalonica sent Paul and Silas away. While Timothy is not mentioned by name, he certainly accompanied Paul and Silas in the escape, since he is later mentioned with Silas at Beroea in verse 14.

Paul and his company proceeded overland southwest from Thessalonica for a distance of about fifty miles to the small city of Beroea, now known as Verria or Veroia and presently having a population of about 6,000. The city lay on the eastern side of Mount Olympus near Pella, the birthplace of Alexander the Great. It had a community of Jews and a synagogue. It is thought that Paul resorted to Beroea for rest and comparative seclusion for a time, but if so, he had not long to enjoy it. Cicero designates the city as "an out of the way place."

1. The Beroeans' Pursuit of Eternal Life (17:10-12)

10 And the brethren immediately sent away Paul and Silas by night unto Beroea: who when they were come thither went into the synagogue of the Jews. 11 Now these were more noble than those in Thessalonica, in that they received the word with all readiness of mind, examining the scriptures daily, whether these things were so. 12 Many of them therefore believed; also of the Greek women of honorable estate, and of men, not a few.

As usual Paul resorted to the Jewish synagogue at Beroea. Here he found not only sincere, earnest-hearted Jews but many prominent Greek women and men. The nobility of these Beroean Jews is evidenced *first*, by their likely higher culture and learning than those of Thessalonica; *second*, by their sincerity and eager-mindedness, **they received the word with all readiness of mind** (v. 11) ; *third*, by their unbiased, earnest quest for truth, **examining the scriptures daily, whether these things were so** (v. 11b). That is, they heard the word of the gospel readily, and then they earnestly examined the Old Testament prophecies with which they were conversant to ascertain whether the allegations of Paul concerning Christ and His redeeming work were in truth the fulfillment of these prophecies concerning the Messiah. They were following the injunction of Christ to the Jews of His day to "search the scriptures" which testified of Him (John 5:39).

There appear to have been three classes among the many who came to believe on Christ unto salvation at Beroea. *First,* there were many believers from the class of noble Scripture-searching Jews; *second,* there were prominent Greek women, probably wives of governmental officials and merchantmen; *third,* there were not a few Greek men who also came into the faith. Luke has taken special pains to note this latter class who have not been prominent, when present at all elsewhere.

Thus if Paul thought to rest at Beroea, the results of these evangelistic activities appear to indicate otherwise.

2. The Jews' Pursuit of the Missionaries at Beroea (17:13-15)

13 But when the Jews of Thessalonica had knowledge that the word of God was proclaimed of Paul at Beroea also, they came thither likewise, stirring up and troubling the multitudes. 14 And then immediately the brethren sent forth Paul to go as far as to the sea: and Silas and Timothy abode there still. 15 But they that conducted Paul brought him as far as Athens: and receiving a commandment unto Silas and Timothy that they should come to him with all speed, they departed.

How long Paul remained at Beroea we do not know, but as soon as word reached Thessalonica concerning Paul's preaching at Beroea, the Jewish enemies there hotly pursued him to Beroea, thirsting for his blood and employing the same tactics of inciting the multitudes to violence against the Apostle.

Since it was evident that Paul was the object of their jealous wrath and they could not rest until they were done with him, the disciples held council and decided that in the interest of the work and Paul's safety, it would be best for him to depart. However, Silas and Timothy were left at Beroea to confirm the faith of the disciples.

An apparent camouflage move was made by Paul's Beroean escorts, who pretended to take him to the sea as though to take shipping out of the country. However, it appears likely that they escorted him overland to Athens. Others hold that they actually took shipping at Driem and sailed to Athens. However that may be, he gave his escort a command to deliver to Silas and Timothy that they should come to him at Athens immediately.

There appears to be evidence in First Thessalonians (3:1-3) that Silas and Timothy joined Paul at Athens in accordance with his instructions, but that Paul's anxiety over the welfare of the Christians at Philippi and Thessalonica was such that he soon dispatched Silas to Philippi and Timothy to Thessalonica to ascertain their welfare, confirm them in the faith, and report to him, which they did. They then returned with their favorable reports to find Paul at Corinth (Acts 18:1, 5).

J. THE MINISTRY AT ATHENS (17:16-34)

Arriving at Athens, Paul found himself in one of the most famous centers of philosophy, religion, art, and architecture the ancient world had ever known. It was in "the city of the violet-crown" that the greatest pinnacle of ancient world culture was attained. Its golden age was realized during the administration of Pericles, about 443-429 B.C. While not the political capital of Achaia or Greece, a position held by Corinth, it was the cultural capital of the whole ancient world. It was located five miles northeast of the Saronic Gulf between two streams, Caphessus and Ilissus. Long walls connected the city with its two seaports, and the Piraeus and Phaleric Gulfs. It was surrounded by mountains and within its walls were four famous hills; (1) A precipitous rocky eminence of 512 feet altitude, known as the Acropolis, was surmounted by the crown of Greek architecture, the Parthenon. (2) The Areopagus, or Hill of Ares, lay northwest of the Acropolis and was perhaps the location of Paul's famous Mars' Hill sermon. This Areopagus was provided with rock benches constituting three sides of a square, the meeting place of the Areopagus court, which exercised both religious and political authority, but with special interest in religion and education. However, some hold that the Areopagus

sometimes met in the Stoa Basileios or Royal Stoa and that Paul's sermon may have been delivered there. (3) The Pynx was farther west. (4) The Museum was located to the south. Says Finegan:

> Of the Parthenon-crowned Acropolis J. P. Mahaffy wrote, 'There is no ruin all the world over which combines so much striking beauty, so distinct a type, so vast a volume of history, so great a pageant of immortal memories. . . . All the Old World's culture culminated in Greece — all Greece in Athens — all Athens in its Acropolis — all the Acropolis in the Parthenon.[117]

The next most important structure was the Agora or marketplace, which constituted the center of the commercial and civic life of the city. The Agora covered a large area to the north of the west end of the Acropolis. Eastward from the Agora stood the Stoa of Attalos, a colonnaded portico, and nearby the Stoa of the Giants. On the south were two large parallel stoas, and on the west several other important buildings including the Stoa of Zeus Eleütherios, the Temple of Apollo Patroos, the Sanctuary of the Mother of the Gods, the Bouleuterion, the assembling place of the famous Athenian Council of Five Hundred, and the Tholos, where the executive divisions of the Council were held. Other buildings were the Temple of Ares, the Odeum or Music Hall, and the Library, which was dedicated to Trajan, south of the Stoa of Attalos.

The Temple of Hephaistos, the god of fire and metallurgy, overlooked the Agora from the hill of Kolonos Agoraios westward. A variety of shops and arcades and the Horologium or Tower of the Winds were located to the east of the Roman Agora.

Achaia was a Roman senatorial province governed by a proconsul such as Cyprus (see comment on Acts 13:4-6), though the city of Athens was governed by the aristocratic court of the Areopagus (v. 19).

The modern city has a population of approximately one-half million.

It was to this awe-inspiring city of ancient culture, filled with altars and temples to the uncounted gods, that Paul

[117] *Ibid.*, p. 273.

made his way alone from Beroea to await the arrival of Silas and Timothy.

1. The Ministry in the Synagogue (17: 16, 17)

16 Now while Paul waited for them at Athens, his spirit was provoked within him as he beheld the city full of idols. 17 So he reasoned in the synagogue with the Jews and the devout persons, and in the marketplace every day with them that met him.

To the sensitive Jewish soul of Paul, cultured in opposition to all forms of idolatry, the ornate imagery and idols of Athens were naturally exceedingly repugnant. Little wonder that Luke records, **his spirit was provoked within him as he beheld the city full of idols** (16b). Paul must have felt as Quartilla is made to say of Athens in Petronius' Satyr (Cap. XVIII): "Our region is so *full of deities* that you may more frequently meet with a *god* than a *man*."[118]

Little wonder that Paul resorted to the Jewish synagogue where from the Old Testament Scriptures he could reason with the **Jews** and **devout persons**, or God-fearing Gentiles, concerning Christ as the fulfillment of their Messianic prophecies. It would appear that his daily meetings in the marketplace were at first with the peoples of these classes. The synagogue itself at Athens appears to have been near the marketplace.

2. The Message on Mars's Hill (17:18-31)

18 And certain also of the Epicurean and Stoic philosophers encountered him. And some said, What would this babbler say? others, He seemeth to be a setter forth of strange gods: because he preached Jesus and the resurrection. 19 And they took hold of him, and brought him unto the Areopagus, saying, May we know what this new teaching is, which is spoken by thee? 20 For thou bringest certain strange things to our ears: we would know therefore what these things mean. 21 (Now all the Athenians and the strangers sojourning there spent their time in nothing else, but either to tell or to hear some new thing.) 22 And Paul stood in the midst of the Areopagus, and said,
Ye men of Athens, in all things I perceive that ye are very religious. 23 For as I passed along, and observed the objects of your worship, I found also an altar with this inscription, TO AN UNKNOWN GOD. What therefore ye worship in ignorance, this I set forth unto you. 24 The God that made the world and all things therein, he, being Lord of heaven and earth, dwelleth not in temples made with hands; 25 neither is he served by men's hands, as though he needed anything, seeing he himself giveth to all life, and breath, and all things; 26 and he made of one every nation of men to dwell on all the face of the earth, having determined *their* appointed seasons, and the bounds of their habitation; 27 that they should seek God, if haply they might feel after him and find him, though he is not far from each one of us: 28 for in him we live, and move, and have our being; as certain even of your own poets have said,
For we are also his offspring.
29 Being then the offspring of God, we ought not to think that the Godhead is like unto gold, or silver, or stone, graven by art and device of man. 30 The times of ignorance therefore God overlooked; but now he commandeth men that they should all everywhere repent: 31 inasmuch as he hath appointed a day in which he will judge the world in righteousness by the man whom he hath ordained; whereof he hath given assurance unto all men, in that he hath raised him from the dead.

Eventually Paul was encountered by the Epicurean and Stoic philosophers, who misjudged him to be another of the wandering teachers who gathered bits of information here and there and dispensed it at will.

Athens was the famed city and center of philosophy. The four famous historic schools had been founded and had flourished here. They were the Academy of Plato, the Lyceum of Aristotle, the Porch of Zeno, and the Garden of Epicurus. However, only the Stoics and the Epicureans remained in Athens until Paul's day. The former were the predominant philosophers of the religious and sober-minded thinkers, while the latter characterized the irreligious and loose-living element. One may doubt whether the Epicureans, who regarded pleasure in one way or another as the *Summum Bonum,* had many points of

[118] Clarke, *op. cit.,* p. 824.

contact with Pharisaic Judaism, or much in common with Christianity. Josephus sees the similarities of the Stoics and Pharisees: (1) their common narrowness and austerity; (2) their willingness to suffer for piety and virtue's sake rather than compromise; (3) their devotion to law, the Pharisees to the law of Moses and its commentaries and the Stoics to the law of nature; (4) the Stoics were naturalistic fatalists and the Pharisees, predestinarian fatalists; (5) the Pharisees held to a theistic providence; the Stoics, to a pantheistic providence; (6) the Pharisees were monotheists; the Stoics, though pantheists, approximated this position in their concept of the *Nous* or Divine Reason or *Logos,* that pervaded and ordered all things; (7) they both held a view of a future life, though the Stoics' pantheistic concept necessarily precluded personal immortality; (8) and both were severe ethicists, though neither was highly consistent in this respect.

The Epicureans, on the other hand, were irreligious materialists whose atheistic outlook ascribed all good to pleasures of the senses and of necessity limited them to the present life. Theirs was a world of chance without God or meaning.

Cushman presents an interesting table of comparisons and contrasts between these two schools of philosophy. In agreement: both subordinated theory to practice, and both had the same practical purpose in their philosophy; namely, to gain peace of mind for the individual and to gain independence of the world for the individual. In disagreement: with the Stoics universal law was supreme, with the Epicureans the individual was supreme; to the Stoics man was a rational being, to the Epicureans he was a feeling being; with the Stoics independence was attained by idealizing the feelings through serenity; the Stoics were religious, the Epicureans anti-religious, though both subscribed to the popular gods; to the Stoics the world was a moral order, to the Epicureans it was a mechanical order; with the Stoics the universal determined the individual, with the Epicureans the universal was the result of the individual; to the Stoics the world was the expression of an imminent

reason, but with the Epicureans it was but a combination of atoms.[119]

Thus it is not difficult to understand that, while finding many points of sympathy and agreement with the Stoics, Paul would have had little, if any, kinship with the Epicureans.

That neither the Stoics nor Epicureans initially understood the nature of Paul's message appears evident from their remarks. **What would this babbler say? . . . He seemeth to be a setter forth of strange gods** (v. 18). This first remark is highly uncomplimentary in that it accuses Paul of being one who picked up knowledge indiscriminately. There were many itinerate philosophers of such a nature in the country in Paul's day, heirs of the Sophist rhetoricians of an earlier day in Athens. In the second remark they fell far short of comprehending Paul, in that they appear to have understood him to refer to a new female deity, possibly the wife of Jesus, when he spoke of **the resurrection,** a conclusion likely drawn from the feminine gender of the noun. The Stoics conceived only of an impersonal continuance of life after death, while the Epicurean materialism terminated all with death; and thus to both schools of thought, the doctrine of the resurrection was entirely new and strange indeed. Clarke contends, as noted in the comment on Acts 16:21, that both among the Athenians and Romans it was unlawful to teach or worship legally unauthorized gods. If this contention is valid, then Paul was in grave danger of arrest at Athens, as at Philippi. This would seem to be the reason he was taken to the Areopagus, or court, that they might assure themselves of the true nature of his teachings (vv. 19, 22). If Paul was actually arrested at this time and made to appear before the Areopagus, as Luke's words, **and they took hold of him, and brought him unto the Areopagus** (v. 19a), would seem to warrant, their treatment of the Apostle is eloquent testimony to Athenian justice in allowing Paul to defend himself and prohibiting such mob violence as had occurred at Philippi and Thessalonica. And indeed the Areopagus was famous for its justice, where the court of twelve superior judges so impartially and fairly conducted the trials of the

[119] Hubert Ernest Cushman, *A Beginner's History of Philosophy,* I, 225, 226.

accused that it became proverbial that "both the plaintiff and defendant departed satisfied with the decision" (Clarke). This was indeed a high standard of justice and approximated the ideal set forth by the founder of the Academy, Plato, who said, "Justice is having and doing what is one's own." However, Luke remarks that it was the custom of the Athenians to pass their time in idle speaking and hearing new speculations. Such was the degeneracy of philosophy at Athens by this time. The profounder meaning of the old schools had been lost, and this generation dabbled in the foamy surf of a departed tide of learning.

As Paul stood in the midst of the Areopagus, he delivered a sermon to the proud Athenians on natural religion, which sermon bears many similarities to his address to the Lycaonians at Lystra (see notes on Acts 14:15-18).

Paul had clearly discerned the Athenian mind and presented a divinely inspired message suited to meet their greatest needs, something "newer" to them indeed than they had ever heard. Certainly if our thesis is correct that Paul's address before the Areopagus was his defense against charges of advocating a new, unauthorized, and in Athens illegal, religion, then his choice of the inscription from the altar, **TO AN UNKNOWN GOD** (v. 23), was indeed a master stroke. Their **UNKNOWN GOD** whose worship was fully authorized and thus made legal in Athens, Paul declared to be the subject of his preaching in Athens. Thus the Athenian charge, **He seemeth to be a setter forth of strange** [*foreign divinities*] **gods** [*demons*] (v. 18), was abrogated by Paul's declaration concerning their authorized **UNKNOWN GOD, What therefore ye worship in ignorance, this I set forth unto you** (v. 23b). If Paul could but prove that his preaching concerning **Jesus and the resurrection** (v. 18b) was an exposition of their **UNKNOWN GOD,** then his indictment by the Areopagus of preaching an illegal religion in Athens could not stand. How well Paul succeeded in establishing this claim his address and its effect on the court revealed. Of course, this defense afforded Paul a coveted opportunity to proclaim the gospel of Jesus Christ to a people who had never learned of the Messiah.

Paul presents his address in three clearly discernible steps. The choice of the Apostle's words of address, **Ye men of Athens** (v. 22), is apt. If it was the Areopagus that he was addressing, then they were honored as the "first men of Athens"; if otherwise, he still was speaking respectfully. He recognized their all-pervasive religious interest and implied that for this reason he was especially happy to address them, since his chief interest also was religion.

The genuineness of the text of Paul's address, purportedly taken from an altar **TO AN UNKNOWN GOD** (v. 23), has been called into question by some scholars. However, Finegan points out that near the time of Paul, Apollonius of Tyana, a noted Neo-Pythagorean philosopher, visited Athens and is reported by his biographer to have remarked that it is a proof of wisdom "to speak well of all the gods, especially at Athens, where altars are set up in honour even of unknown gods."[120] Further, Finegan cites the geographer Pausanias, who visited Athens between A.D. 143 and 159 and produced extensive and accurate topographical accounts of the city. Pausanias says that "on the road from the Phaleron Bay harbor to the city he had noticed 'altars of the gods named Unknown, and of heroes,' and also mentions 'an altar of Unknown Gods' at Olympia."[121]

Other instances are cited by Finegan, such as the inscription on the altar found at Pergamum in 1909 in the temple of Demeter, which is thought to read, "To unknown gods, Capito, torch-bearer." Thus the absence at present of such an altar in Athens is no disproof of its existence in Paul's day. Whether the Athenians identified this "unknown God" with the Supreme Being, or the "High-God" of the modern science of religion, is an unanswered question. That Paul made this application of the "altar text," there can be no reasonable doubt.[122]

Paul recognizes the philosophical cast of mind of his audience and presents his message understandingly to them in answer to the three great questions of philosophy: "Whence," "What," "Whither";

[120] Finegan, *op. cit.,* p. 276. [121] *Ibid.* [122] See Additional Note VI, *The High-God Theory.*

or otherwise stated, "the origin," "the nature," and "the end of all things." Analyzed, his message would appear somewhat as follows:

1. *The Origin of All Things,* vv. 24-26.
2. *The Nature of All Things,* vv. 27-30.
3. *The End of All Things,* v. 31.

Neither the Epicureans nor Stoics believed in, or understood, the doctrine of creation by a divine fiat. The materialistic Epicureans regarded matter as eternal and thus uncreated, while the Stoics, being pantheistic, did not distinguish the Divine Reason from Matter. Neither naturalistic materialism nor pantheistic naturalism can ever answer the question of origins, since neither recognizes an originator. Paul's presentation of a personal, supreme, and transcendent God (v. 24b), who created all things by a divine fiat (v. 24a) was an answer to the question of origin, for which pagan philosophers had long sought in vain. God then is not only, as the Stoics suppose, the directive, spiritual principle living and working within nature, but a personal, divine Providence. Further, Paul declared that this "unknown God" is the providential dispenser of life and breath to all things and therefore is quite independent of man, thus abrogating the necessity of sacrificial worship (v. 25). Paul then proceeded to show that man himself is the creature of this "unknown God" and thus dependent upon Him. Nor are men to be categorized, as do the proud Greeks, into Greek and barbarian, with a decided discount on the latter; a proposition with which the Stoics, who believed in the spiritual equality of man through pantheism, would have readily agreed.

Though Paul declared the providential supervision and location of the various nationalities, as to the places and times of their respective locations in the various parts of the earth, for which in the divine wisdom they were best fitted (v. 26b), at the same time he declared the essential unity of the human race. And indeed the Apostle is supported in his view of "homo sapiens" (v. 26a) by the testimony of modern science. The science of religion testifies that men are homogenous in their disposition to worship a supernatural being, and indeed anthropology points to a universal concept of a High or Supreme God, though he is not the direct object of worship by all. Psychology testifies to the psychological unity of the human race. Biology witnesses to the fact that mankind is one specie. Physiology predicates a common anatomical structure and blood content, as witnesses the modern blood bank. Sociology finds all people with common social characteristics. Indeed three and a half centuries before Paul in Athens, Socrates had discovered a common universal ethical principle in mankind which neither the ancient Sophists' relativism nor its modern social relativistic counterpart has been able to deny successfully. The Apostle used the term **nation** and not "race" to distinguish the varied peoples, for he recognized that there is but one race. The word "race" is not used in the Bible, except in regard to contest of speed. **Nation** is a political designation, whereas "race" is a physical designation. God recognizes no essential physical or psychological difference of peoples, nor does modern science. Again Paul refuted the hoary doctrine of Evolution, which was born in the unenlightened minds of the ancient Greeks and has reappeared in a but slightly altered garb in modern pagan thought. Creation, and not Evolution or emanation, is the answer to origins, Paul told his Greek auditors.

Next Paul proceeded to the nature and meaning of all things. First, he declared that since man is the creation of the supreme personal God, he should search after God, even though it may be the groping of a blind man in unfamiliar and uncertain circumstances, not through the pride of intellect, for "the [Greeks] through . . . wisdom knew not God" (I Cor. 1:21a). But even in the absence of the Jewish divine revelation, man has the revelation of God in nature about him and in his ethical values, which could aid him in finding peace with God, for **he is not far from each one of us** (v. 27b. See also Rom. 1:18-20 and 2:11-16). Paul quoted, in support of the eminence of God, from the Greek poet Aratus, who was from Paul's home country of Cilicia, though some 300 years earlier, and also a Stoic (cf. I Cor. 15:33 and Titus 1:12). Since the same lines are found in Cleanthus' Hymn to Jupiter, Paul may have referred to both poets. Nor does this mean that Paul was going beyond certain bounds in his agreement with the Stoics. Indeed Christian Theism has many more points of agreement with Stoicism than with Epicureanism, but neither are Christian philosophies, and both have serious divergences from, and irreconcilable conflicts with, Christianity. Concerning this dependence of man on God, Clarke quotes from Synopsis Sohar, p. 104: "The holy blessed God never does evil to any man. He only withdraws his gracious presence from him, and then he necessarily perisheth"; and then Clarke adds, "This is philosophical and correct."[123]

Paul drove to an inescapable conclusion in verse 29, concerning the nature of God and man. Since man is the creature, offspring, of God and thus bears the nature of God in His creation, then God must be superior to man, else He could not be his Creator Father. But these gold, silver, and stone, graven images of Athens are inferior to man, as his proud Greek Areopagus auditors would readily agree. Therefore, how can they be likenesses of God who is superior to man? Thus Paul had shown the nature of God to be a personal, transcendent, and yet eminently spiritual being; and man, whose nature is by creation Godlike, is therefore an essentially personal, spiritual being. From the answer to the second great philosophical question concerning the nature of things, Paul proceeded to the third and last great question concerning the ends or purposes of all things.

In verse 30 Paul argues that, though God has in His providential goodness overlooked this insulting idolatry, **now he commandeth men that they should all everywhere repent;** or, like the Thessalonians, turn to "God from idols, to serve a living and true God" (I Thess. 1:9b). In the light of this new truth, they cannot continue in the wickedness of idolatry without condemnation now and judgment to come. Such a day of universal righteous judgment for the inhabited world of unrepentant mankind is assured by reason of the resurrection of Jesus Christ, who is to be the judge, since the salvation He provided by His death will have been spurned. The end of man is fellowship with God through

repentance and saving faith in the resurrection of Christ. To reject God is certain self-destruction. What a profound impression such an argument must have made upon the august Areopagus that prided itself in pure justice!

3. The Product of the Ministry (17: 32-34)

32 Now when they heard of the resurrection of the dead, some mocked; but others said, We will hear thee concerning this yet again. 33 Thus Paul went out from among them. 34 But certain men clave unto him, and believed: among whom also was Dionysius the Areopagite, and a woman named Damaris, and others with them.

Whether Paul had finished his sermon when the assembly broke up, on the occasion of his mention of the resurrection, is not clear. It was likely the Epicurean element that mockingly laughed and scorned at Paul's doctrine of the resurrection of Jesus Christ, and not the Stoics, who expressed a desire to hear him further. Wesley says concerning Luke's words **some mocked,** "They took offense at that which is the principal motive of faith, from the pride of reason. And having once stumbled at this, they rejected all the rest."[124] In any event, the court found no cause for punishment in his teachings and thus Paul, seeing no possibility of further discourse, left the Areopagus.

How many were won over to faith in Christ by Paul's message we are not told; but among the believers was Dionysius the Areopagite, who was a member of the august court of Areopagus and had of necessity passed through the office of Archon or chief governor of the city. This meant that he was a man of the highest intelligence, of good reputation in the city, and of high social position. Thus in Athens, as at Paphos on Cyprus, the Christian message first bore fruit in a governmental person of high rank. **Damaris, and others** — how many we are not told — with Dionysius constituted the first fruits of the gospel in Athens. Paul's reference to the household of Stephanas as being the first fruits of the gospel in Achaia may be due to his having considered Athens as a free and

---

[123] Clarke, op. cit., p. 827.   [124] Wesley, op. cit. p. 467, n. 32.

independent city. There is a tradition that made Dionysius a bishop of Athens and a martyr of the Christian faith.

Whether a church immediately developed out of Paul's ministry in Athens is a matter of difference of opinion among scholars. That the high court of Athens and many of the populace had the opportunity of hearing the glorious message of redeeming grace from the lips of Paul is evident.

K. THE CORINTHIAN MISSION (18:1-4)

1 After these things he departed from Athens, and came to Corinth. 2 And he found a certain Jew named Aquila, a man of Pontus by race, lately come from Italy, with his wife Priscilla, because Claudius had commanded all the Jews to depart from Rome: and he came unto them; 3 and because he was of the same trade, he abode with them, and they wrought; for by their trade they were tentmakers. 4 And he reasoned in the synagogue every sabbath, and persuaded Jews and Greeks.

Following his Mars' Hill address at Athens, Paul traversed the forty miles westward to Corinth, the political capital of Achaia, which was situated on the isthmus between Hellas and Peloponnesus. Corinth was in Paul's day both the political and commercial metropolis of Greece and was the residence of the Roman Proconsul.[125]

The wickedness of Corinth made it a byword for corruption and licentiousness throughout the Roman world. Allusions to its sensuality and moral corruption are found in Paul's Corinthian letters and were such in fact as to outrage even pagan sentiment. Without question Paul got his inspiration and much of his information for his description of the revolting degeneracy and immorality of the Gentiles, as recorded in the first chapter of Romans (see Rom. 1:21-32), from observation of the Corinthian situation, especially as he wrote Romans from Corinth while there on his third missionary journey.

The worship of Aphrodite, the goddess of love and beauty, identified by the Romans with Venus, the worship of whom was cleverly designed to excite lust, was the distinctive cult of Corinth from ages past. The temple of Aphrodite was situated on the summit of Acro Corinth, a mountain 1,500 feet in elevation above the city and 1,886 feet above the sea. North of the market place on a low hill stood the temple of Apollo.

Finegan's description of the topography of Corinth is helpful. He locates the large agora or market place in the center of the city, surrounded by colonnades and monuments. Northwest of the market was the theater of Corinth. In 1898 a heavy stone was found which had formed the lintel over a doorway and which bore the Greek inscription, "Synagogue of the Hebrews." The inscription has been dated between 100 B.C. and A.D. 200. Since it was found near the market place, it appears likely that the synagogue was located near the agora. The lettering is poorly carved which, Finegan thinks, suggests that the Jews of Corinth were poor, and thus it accords with Paul's characterization of the Corinthian Christians (see I Cor. 1:26-31). If the synagogue was on the east side of the street opposite the shops and colonnades of the west side, then, as Finegan supposes, it was located in the residential section as indicated by the remaining house walls, and thus Titus Justus' house could have **joined hard to the synagogue** (Acts 18:7).

The **judgment-seat** where Paul appeared before Gallio is thought to have been the Latin *rostrum,* or elevated platform, located in the agora and constituting one of its most prominent features (see Acts 18:12-17).

At Corinth Paul associated himself with two Jews who were evidently Christian believers, since it is not recorded that they were converted under Paul, and who were to assist him greatly in his evangelization of Corinth and elsewhere later. The home of this man Aquila and his wife Priscilla was in Pontus, one of the two easternmost provinces of Asia Minor. Whether for commercial or other reasons, they had settled in Rome. But due to a disturbance there among the Jews which appears to have centered around a contention over Christ, the Emperor Claudius, not able to distinguish between Jews and Christians, nor understanding the

---

[125] See Additional Note XII, *Corinth.*

nature of the controversy, expelled the Jews from Rome, including Christian believers, in about A.D. 49. These disturbances likely arose as a result of the Christian witness and preaching by concerted Jews who returned to Rome after Pentecost (see Acts 2:10), or possibly they were some of Paul's converts from Asia Minor who had traveled to Rome. The real source of the trouble was always the Christ-rejecting Jews of Paul's day. Suetonius wrote, "He [Claudius] expelled the Jews from Rome, because they were in a state of continual tumult at the instigation of one Chrestus." By Chrestus is likely meant "Christus" or Christ.

At Corinth Aquila and Priscilla became the hosts of Paul, even as Eunice and Lois at Lystra, Lydia at Philippi, and Jason at Thessalonica. Apart from their common faith in Christ, Paul had an occupational affinity with this couple, since they were all tent-makers. In fact, it was required of every Jewish boy, regardless of the wealth, education, or social standing of the parents, that he learn a manual trade by which he would be capable of supporting himself in case of necessity. It appears from Luke's words, **they wrought** (v. 3), that they may have earned a livelihood while preaching the gospel in Corinth. We hear more of this Jewish-Christian couple who accompanied Paul to Ephesus (v. 18), and later returned to Rome where they likely prepared for the coming of Paul and also established a Christian church in their house, as at Ephesus (cf. I Cor. 16:19 and Rom. 16:3-5). They are last seen in the Biblical record at Ephesus, where they returned following Paul's trial at Rome (II Tim. 4:19). Only eternity will reveal the credit due such faithful, sacrificing, occupational missionaries who have contributed so much to the spread of the gospel and the establishment of Christianity, both in Paul's day and throughout subsequent centuries. Often have evangelistic reapers been credited with the fruit of their labors. The self-support of Paul and his companions in the gospel at Corinth, as well as with Paul at Thessalonica and elsewhere, enabled them to introduce the gospel among a new people without laying themselves liable to the charge that they were preaching for material gain, as was the custom with the wandering philosopher-teachers of that day and formerly.

On the one hand, Paul did thus labor and support himself when he first arrived at Corinth (v. 3), in Thessalonica (II Thess. 3:8-12), and later at Ephesus (Acts 20:33-35; I Cor. 4:9-13). However, on the other hand, he saw the advantage to his disciples of their giving of their material means for the support of the gospel and its ministers, and he both commended them for so doing and recommended their continuance in giving. This is especially evident in the Philippian letter (Phil. 4:10-20), but it also appears in the Corinthian letter (II Cor. 9), and possibly Paul alludes to a gift from the Thessalonians in his first Thessalonian letter (I Thess. 3:6-10).

If, as evidence would seem to indicate, the synagogue was near the market place, it is understandable that Paul would likely have had an interested hearing, as **he reasoned in the synagogue every sabbath** (v. 4a), from the Gentiles who heard him in the market preaching and teaching daily throughout the week. Thus Luke informs us that in these sabbath synagogue services Paul persuaded Jews and Greeks alike. While the initial fruit of his sabbath-to-sabbath synagogue labors is not evident in Luke's record, such fruit is suggested by Luke's statement that he **persuaded Jews and Greeks** (v. 4b). From Paul's epistles we glean information concerning the identity of these "first-fruit converts" in Corinth. Indeed, Epenetus is given in some versions as the first fruit of the gospel in Achaia, but in other versions he is recorded as the first fruit of proconsular Asia. Wesley takes the latter view while Clarke as confidently takes the former view. We are on surer ground however when we note the family of Stephanas (I Cor. 1:16), and Crispus and Gaius (cf. I Cor. 1:14 and Acts 18:8). That there were many more we learn from verse 8.

L. THE CORINTHIAN PEOPLE (18:5-11)

5 But when Silas and Timothy came down from Macedonia, Paul was constrained by the word, testifying to the

Jews that Jesus was the Christ. 6 And when they opposed themselves and blasphemed, he shook out his raiment and said unto them, Your blood *be* upon your own heads; I am clean: from henceforth I will go unto the Gentiles. 7 And he departed thence, and went into the house of a certain man named Titus Justus, one that worshipped God, whose house joined hard to the synagogue. 8 And Crispus, the ruler of the synagogue believed in the Lord with all his house; and many of the Corinthians hearing believed, and were baptized. 9 And the Lord said unto Paul in the night by a vision, Be not afraid, but speak and hold not thy peace: 10 for I am with thee, and no man shall set on thee to harm thee: for I have much people in this city. 11 And he dwelt *there* a year and six months, teaching the word of God among them.

In Acts 17:15 it was noted that Paul had instructed his Beroean escorts to dispatch Silas and Timothy to him at Athens immediately. Upon their final arrival at Corinth, they evidently delivered to him an offering from the Philippian church (cf. II Cor. 11:8, 9 and Phil. 4:15, 16). Doubtless Luke means to imply in the words, **Paul was constrained by the word** [the gospel, Acts 4:4; 16:6, 32; 17:11], **testifying to the Jews that Jesus was the Christ** (v. 5b), that Paul had found great encouragement in their reports of the progress of the work in Macedonia, as well as the relief of his stringencies by the offering which they brought and the support of their presence. And thus his faith was rewarded, and he took courage to renew and intensify his evangelistic efforts toward the Jews. He was now released from the necessity of manual employment and could, together with Silas and Timothy, give himself wholly to the preaching of the gospel. Vincent gives the meaning to the effect that "Paul was engrossed by the word." This appears to be the true meaning of this rather difficult passage. It should be noted at this juncture that this is the last biblical mention of Silas. Clarke thinks he may have died in Macedonia. Since Luke's primary concern is with Paul, Silas is henceforth dropped from the record.

The Jews' reaction to Paul's intensified evangelistic efforts at Corinth was an *organized* or *concerted* resistance

against Paul and his preaching. It is noteworthy that in railing and blaspheming against the gospel of Christ these Corinthian Jews actually **opposed themselves** (v. 6a). And so does man always work against his own best interest when he opposes truth. Paul's act of shaking his garments was typical and signified the transfer of responsibility for truth preached and witness given to these blasphemous Jews. It may further indicate that they were soon to be delivered to their enemies by God.[126] Paul's testimony had been so given that he bore no further responsibility to these Jews. **I am clean** (v. 6b), or as Weymouth renders it, "I am not responsible" any longer for you. The Apostle's expressed purpose to turn to the Gentiles was here limited to his ministry at Corinth. He subsequently goes first to the Jews at Ephesus and elsewhere.

Paul's entry into the house of Titus Justus, likely a Roman colonist who was a "God-fearer" or "proselyte of the gate" and whose house was next door to the synagogue, was for the purpose of finding a new preaching place after leaving the synagogue. He doubtless continued to lodge with Aquila and Priscilla.

The conversion of the chief ruler of the synagogue, Crispus, was a signal victory for Christianity at Corinth. By his office he presided at all meetings in the synagogue, interpreted and rendered technical decisions in law, solemnized marriages, granted divorces, declared excommunications, and performed other important functions.

It appears likely that Sosthenes was chosen to fill the office of Crispus after the latter's conversion to Christianity. The conversion of this prominent Jewish leader, even after the Apostle had been closed out of the synagogue, was the signal for many to follow him in the faith; first those of his own household, as with the Philippian jailer, and then **many of the Corinthians hearing believed, and were baptized** (v. 8b), most likely Gentiles. How effective for Christ's Kingdom is such a key individual when brought to the Lord! In I Corinthians 1:14 Paul indicates that Crispus was one of the few of his converts who was baptized by his own hands.

---

[126] Wesley, *op. cit.*, p. 468, n. 6.

It would appear from verse 9 that Paul may have been near discouragement or even departure from Corinth. The odds were against him, humanly speaking (cf. I Cor. 2:3). However, "the Lord knoweth how to deliver the godly out of temptation" (II Pet. 2:9a). God had further work for Paul in Corinth, and thus He appeared to him in a vision of the night with instructions to continue his ministry (cf. Acts 27:23-26), and assurance that he will not be prevented in his work nor personally harmed: **For I am with thee, and no man shall set on thee to harm thee** (v. 10a; cf. Matt. 28:18-20). However, Paul's greater encouragement comes with the Lord's prophetic declaration concerning the spiritual fruit of the Apostle's ministry: **for I have much people in this city** (v. 10b). How often are souls who are not yet saved cut off from a future saving faith in Christ because of the fear or failure of God's messengers to stand by and declare the offered mercies of God in Christ!

Reassured of God, Paul remained at Corinth for about eighteen months, during which time he established the Corinthian church and wrote the first and second letters to the Thessalonians. Some scholars hold that he wrote the Galatian letter at this time, though this is not the conviction of the present writer.

M. THE CORINTHIAN PROCONSUL (18:12-17)

12 But when Gallio was proconsul of Achaia, the Jews with one accord rose up against Paul and brought him before the judgment-seat, 13 saying, This man persuadeth men to worship God contrary to the law. 14 But when Paul was about to open his mouth, Gallio said unto the Jews, If indeed it were a matter of wrong or of wicked villany, O ye Jews, reason would that I should bear with you: 15 but if they are questions about words and names and your own law, look to it yourselves; I am not minded to be a judge of these matters. 16 And he drove them from the judgment-seat. 17 And they all laid hold on Sosthenes, the ruler of the synagogue, and beat him before the judgment-seat. And Gallio cared for none of these things.

Gallio, brother of the Roman philosopher Seneca (tutor of the emperor Nero) and uncle of the poet Lucan, was a well-educated, accomplished, and amiable Roman who had been advanced from the office of consul to the proconsulship of Achaia, with its capital at Corinth, in about A.D. 52. He was noted for his sense of justice and administrative ability.

Exasperated with Paul's success in winning believers to the Lord, **the Jews with one accord**[127] **rose up against Paul and brought him before the judgment seat** (v. 12). Though divided among themselves on many issues, **the Jews** were of **one accord** in their purpose to destroy Paul and stop the preaching of the gospel of Christ. They had no legal right under Roman law to punish Paul, as they had not to crucify Christ, so they charged him before Gallio in hopes of his execution by the Romans. Roman law permitted the Jewish religion, as well as the authorized Gentile religions, to be present in the colonies. However, the introduction of any new and unauthorized religion was forbidden and even punishable by death. Thus in the Jews' charge, **This man persuadeth men to worship God contrary to the law** (v. 13), is implied a criminal act on Paul's part in introducing and propagating a new religion that was neither of an authorized Gentile brand nor Jewish, and consequently he was guilty of a grave civil offense and liable to execution.

Before Paul could open his mouth in explanation or self-defense, the astute Gallio discerned the wicked devices of the Jews and completely abrogated their designs. Indeed, Gallio asserted, "were Paul allegedly a villainous person, possibly suspect of sedition, then it would be a matter for my court and it would be for me to hear your charges against him." However, coolly and disdainfully Gallio continues, "O ye Jews, since your complaints concern doctrines, practices, and names (as perhaps whether Jesus was their Messiah) within your own religion, then that is something for you to settle without violence, but it is not a matter for the civil court." With this he dismissed the case and expelled the Jews from the court.

---

[127] See Additional Note I, *Homothumadon − One Accord.*

The Jews'[128] violent treatment of Sosthenes, the ruler of the synagogue who had succeeded Crispus on the occasion of the latter's conversion to Christianity, was likely due to the fact that he had already embraced Christianity and defended Paul, or that he was known to have been influenced by Paul and was inclining toward Christianity. That he eventually became a Christian and one of Paul's closest companions we infer from I Corinthians 1:1. Possibly his treatment at the hands of the Jews sealed his decision to become a Christian. How many other converts Paul made in Corinth we do not know. Of the following we have record: Stephanas and his household (I Cor. 16:15), Fortunatus (I Cor. 16:17), Achaicus (I Cor. 16:17), Erastus (Rom. 16:23), Gaius (I Cor. 1:14), Tertius (Rom. 16:22), Quartus (Rom. 16:23), Chloe (I Cor. 1:11), and Phoebe of Cenchrea (Rom. 16:1).

Gallio's attitude as expressed in the words, [he] cared for none of these things (v. 17b), is not to be taken as an indifference toward religion, but rather toward the internal disputations and religious wranglings of the Jews. He was doubtless well informed of their disorderly conduct that eventuated in their expulsion from Rome under the rule of Claudius in ça A.D. 49. How faithfully is God's promise to Paul, as recorded in verses 9 and 10, fulfilled in these threatening circumstances! His promises are always worthy of man's implicit faith.

N. THE EPHESIAN PROSPECT (18:18-21)

18 And Paul, having tarried after this yet many days, took his leave of the brethren, and sailed thence for Syria, and with him Priscilla and Aquila: having shorn his head in Cenchreae; for he had a vow. 19 And they came to Ephesus, and he left them there: but he himself entered into the synagogue, and reasoned with the Jews. 20 And when they asked him to abide a longer time, he consented not; 21 but taking his leave of them, and saying, I will return again unto you if God will, he set sail from Ephesus.

Paul's continued stay, expressed as yet many days (v. 18), was at the close of his eighteen months' ministry at Corinth and after his arraignment before Gallio; and it was doubtless employed in the edification of the Christian converts.

While Paul left Corinth with a view to returning to Antioch of Syria, he nevertheless had in his plans a brief visit to Ephesus where he intended leaving Priscilla and Aquila to prepare the way for the founding of a church in this great center of western Asia Minor.

It is of interest that the names of this couple here appear in the order of Priscilla and Aquila, thus placing the woman first. They occur likewise in Romans 16:3 and II Timothy 4:19. This is probably due to the greater ability, prominence, and personality of Priscilla over her husband Aquila.

Luke's statement, having shorn his head at Cenchreae: for he had a vow (v. 18b), most likely is spoken in reference to Paul, though Weymouth remarks: "[He] Probably Paul, possibly Aquila." In any event, this was a Jewish custom in the keeping of vows (cf. Acts 21:24; Num. 6:18). What this particular vow was we are not told. It was likely a private vow voluntarily assumed in appreciation of some great mercy or deliverance wrought by God. Vincent thinks that this was not the Nazarite vow, though similar in its obligations, since that vow could only be concluded by the cutting of the hair in Jerusalem, whereas this one was marked by the shearing of the head at the small seaport village of Cenchrea, en route to Ephesus. However, this may have been a modification of the Nazarite vow which began and ended with the shaving of the head. For the duration of the vow, intercourse with the Gentiles was forbidden. Thus Paul may have postponed the initiation of the vow until he had left Corinth and then concluded it at Jerusalem where the hair, grown during this period, was offered on the altar at the temple together with certain specified sacrifices. This was not a conciliatory vow for the benefit of the Jews or Jewish Christians, but just the usual Jewish way of rendering thanks to God for blessings received. Nor is there any reason to suppose that Paul violated his

[128] While Bruce, op. cit., p. 375, regards Sosthenes' assaulters as bystanding Greeks, Wesley, op. cit., p. 469, with apparent better reasons, regards them as the Jews who were disappointed with Sosthenes' efforts to obtain a conviction against Paul.

Christian principles in deferring to a Jewish custom, any more than in the circumcision of Timothy at Lystra. An imposing array of scholars are found on either side of the question, some assigning the vow to Aquila and others with equal force to Paul. The weight of evidence seems to point to Paul. This appears the more likely when it is noted that Paul evidently was planning to keep the feast of Pentecost (or possibly the Passover) at Jerusalem, though reference to this feast is omitted from the RV.

Upon arrival at Ephesus (see comments on Ephesus in Acts 19:1), Paul apparently left Priscilla and Aquila there to do occupational missionary work in preparation for his return and his three-year evangelistic ministry on his third missionary journey. Paul himself seems to have spent but a single Sabbath in Ephesus (Clarke) reasoning with the Jews concerning Christ as the Messiah. This initial contact appears favorable, as the record states that **they asked him to abide a longer time** (vs. 20), which invitation he declined, taking his leave with the promise of a future return if such were God's will.

It is interesting to note that the former divine prohibition to preach in Asia (see Acts 16:6) has now been lifted, and Paul apparently plans the Ephesian campaign under the direction of God. As one has said, "God's clock keeps perfect time." He closes doors that no man can open and opens doors that no man can close (Rev. 3:7). The omniscient mind knows best when to prohibit and when to permit. To run before God is as hazardous as to refuse to follow. Here, indeed, "a great door and effectual is opened" (I Cor. 16:9a) for the gospel ministry.

O. THE APOSTLE'S RETURN (Acts 18:22)

22 And when he had landed at Caesarea, he went up and saluted the church, and went down to Antioch.

Having disembarked at Caesarea in Palestine, Paul **went up** to Jerusalem where he greeted the mother church. The prominence of Jerusalem in Jewish and Christian thought was sufficient to justify

the omission of the name of Jerusalem — thus the expression **went up** (cf. John 7:8, 10; John 12:20; Acts 24:11).

Luke's statement that Paul **saluted the church,** indicates the prominence of the Jerusalem church in the first century. Of this expression Wesley says, "Eminently so called, being the mother church of Christian believers."[129] And on this expression Clarke remarks:

That is, the Church at Jerusalem, called emphatically The Church, because it was the first church — the Mother, or Apostolic *Church*; and from it all other Christian Churches proceeded: those in *Galatia, Philippi, Thessalonica, Corinth, Ephesus, Rome,* &c. Therefore, even this last [Rome] was only a *daughter* Church, when in its *purest* state.[130]

Paul evidently kept the feast of the Passover at Jerusalem before he proceeded down to Antioch of Syria where he most likely gave a full account of the activities of his second missionary journey (cf. Acts 14:26-28) to the church which had commissioned him to both the first and second journeys (see Acts 13:2, 3 and 15:40).

XVIII. THE APOSTLE'S THIRD MISSIONARY JOURNEY (Acts 18:23-21:14)

(Time: A.D. 53-57? Personnel: Timothy, Titus, Priscilla, Aquila, Tychicus, Trophimus, Luke, Sopater, Aristarchus, Secundus, Gaius, Erastus, and Silas? Area: Asia Minor, Macedonia, and Achaia).

A. THE DEPARTURE FROM ANTIOCH (18:23)

23 And having spent some time *there*, he departed, and went through the region of Galatia, and Phrygia, in order, establishing all the disciples.

It does not appear that Paul remained long at Antioch, as the language employed seems to indicate that he moved eagerly back toward Ephesus, where a great challenge awaited him. En route he **went through the region of Galatia, and Phrygia, in order, establishing all the disciples** (v. 23). Weymouth remarks: "In the South Galatian view the phrase may mean the shorter hill route from

---

[129] Wesley, *op. cit.,* p. 470, n. 22.   [130] Clarke, *op. cit.,* I, 838.

Antioch to Ephesus, a little north of the main road down the Lycus Valley."[131] Wesley thinks that Paul spent about four years in Asia Minor, including the time spent in Ephesus on this third journey. Though not recorded in detail, to judge from the words, **in order,** Paul likely revisited the churches at Derbe, Lystra, Iconium, and Antioch in Pisidia, where he confirmed and established these converts of his first missionary journey.

B. THE EMERGENCE OF APOLLOS (18:24-28)

24 Now a certain Jew named Apollos, an Alexandrian by race, an eloquent man, came to Ephesus; and he was mighty in the scriptures. 25 This man had been instructed in the way of the Lord; and being fervent in spirit, he spake and taught accurately the things concerning Jesus, knowing only the baptism of John: 26 and he began to speak boldly in the synagogue. But when Priscilla and Aquila heard him, they took him unto them, and expounded unto him the way of God more accurately. 27 And when he was minded to pass over into Achaia, the brethren encouraged him, and wrote to the disciples to receive him: and when he was come, he helped them much that had believed through grace; 28 for he powerfully confuted the Jews, *and that* publicly, showing by the scriptures that Jesus was the Christ.

During the time intervening between Paul's first and second visits to Ephesus, Apollos made his appearance at that city.

It is strange indeed that this man, designated a Jew, should bear the Roman name of a heathen deity "Apollo," in view of the Jewish aversion to idolatry. Possibly, as Clarke suggests, his parents were Gentiles who were converted to Judaism as proselytes after his birth and christening, and thus Apollos was a Jew by religion but not by nationality. Dummelow's Commentary regards his name as a contraction of Apollonius. Other references to Apollos are found in I Corinthians 1:12; 3:4, 5; 4:6; 16:12 and Titus 3:13.

In any event, he was by religion a Jew who was designated **an Alexandrian by race** (v. 24). For more than three centuries before Christ, Alexandria of Egypt had been one of the most cosmopolitan centers of the ancient world. Here Egyptians, Hindus, Greeks, Latins, Jews, and other nationalities met and pooled their wisdom to produce the greatest university of the day. Of this school Philo Judaeus (20 B.C.—A.D. 54), the Jewish Hellenistic philosopher, is probably the greatest representative. His purpose was to reconcile Greek philosophy with Jewish theology. Out of Jewish scholarship influenced by this Alexandrian school of thought, the famous Septuagint version of the Old Testament was produced.

While there is no other reference to Alexandrian or Egyptian Christianity in the New Testament, extra-biblical records reveal that by the opening of the second century A.D. there were approximately a million Christians in Egypt. It has been previously noted that in the third century B.C. a great migration of Jews to the region of Alexandria occurred. Exactly when, how, and by whom Christianity was first carried to Egypt we do not know. Luke's mention of Christ's African cross-bearer, Simon a Cyrenian (Luke 23:26), the presence of those from "Egypt, and the parts of Libya about Cyrene" at Pentecost (Acts 2:10), those of "the synagogue of the Cyrenians, and of the Alexandrians" who were "disputing with Stephen" (Acts 6:9) just before his martyrdom, "men . . . of Cyrene" (Acts 11:20) who preached to the Greeks at Antioch, "and Symeon that was called Niger, and Lucius of Cyrene" (Acts 13:1), who were included among the prophets and teachers at Antioch, are all tantalizingly interesting, but what, if any, part they played in carrying the gospel to Egypt we do not know for certain. Whether Apollos became a disciple of John the Baptist and learned of the promised Messiah on the occasion of a visit to Judaea during an annual feast, or whether he was converted to John's gospel by another in Egypt, we are not certain. In coming to Ephesus he likely had in mind the enlightenment and instruction of the Jews in the Christian way, so far as he understood it. How far his knowledge of Christ went seems not very clear. He certainly regarded Christ Jesus as the Messiah (Mark 1:1-11), and he likely knew Him as the divine "Son of God" and "the world's sin bearer" (John 1:29-34). It

---

[131] Weymouth, *op. cit.,* p. 321, n. 24.

appears that his knowledge was factually accurate so far as it extended. That he was genuinely sincere is without question, even to the point of **being fervent in spirit** (v. 25). Of this expression Vincent remarks: "Fervent . . . *to boil* or *ferment*, is an exact translation of this word, which means to *seethe* or *bubble*, and is therefore used figuratively of mental states and emotions."[132] (Cf. Matt. 13:33.) Nor was this a religious zeal without knowledge, for Luke remarks concerning him that he was both **an eloquent man** and **mighty in the Scriptures** (v. 24).

Of Apollos' eloquence (*logios*) Vincent observes that this is the only New Testament usage of the term. The term *logios* has several usages in Greek literature, however. Thus Vincent remarks, "As *logos* means either *reason* or *speech*, so this derivation [*logios*] may signify either one who has thought much and has much to say, or one who can say it well."[133] Vincent continues to observe that Herodotus uses it in the sense of "one *skilled in history*"; or as "an *eloquent* person," especially the "epithet of Hermes or Mercury, as the god of speech and eloquence," or "a *learned* person generally."[134]

From the foregoing it may be deduced that the intellectual acumen, thorough training in the general history and philosophy of the ancients, a reasoned knowledge of Jewish history and religion, plus an acquaintance with the teachings of John the Baptist to the effect that Jesus was the Messiah, wrought a burning conviction of these truths in the soul of Apollos that expressed itself in a zealous, logical flow of brilliant eloquence which his opponents found it difficult to match and under which his hearers found themselves swept into his persuasions.

Whether Apollos had experienced true Christian conversion before coming to Ephesus is not quite certain. However, Luke's characterization of him would seem to indicate that he had. In any event, he knew John's baptism of repentance and believed Jesus to be the promised Messiah. If he was not "in" he certainly was "near" the Kingdom of God. He seems to have received Christian baptism at the hands of Priscilla and Aquila. Even that he entered into a deeper sanctifying relationship with Christ under the ministry of this Christian couple appears likely from Luke's account (see Acts 18:26b). What a great ministry, though indirectly rendered, some of God's humble lay-servants have performed! The earnest prayers of two saintly, fervent ladies that D. L. Moody might receive the baptism of the Holy Spirit resulted in the mighty ministry of that man. Natural or acquired abilities without God are utterly meaningless to the Kingdom, but when filled, possessed, and employed of God, they become mighty to the destruction of Satan's kingdom and the construction of Christ's Kingdom.

The vision and zeal of Apollos impelled him to move on to Achaia where at Corinth he was to render a great service to the young church. In this enterprise he was encouraged by the brethren at Ephesus, likely including Priscilla and Acquila, even to the extent of their writing a letter of introduction to the Corinthian church in which letter he was earnestly commended to their confidence (cf. II Cor. 3:1).

The success of the ministry of Apollos at Corinth is attested by the fact that he soon became so popular that his admirers formed a faction or party of Apollos within the Corinthian church (see I Cor. 1:12-3:6).

Luke informs us that the ministry of Apollos at Corinth was twofold: first, **he helped them much that had believed through grace** (v. 27b), and second, **he powerfully confuted the Jews** (v. 28a). Thus, in the first instance, his newly acquired grace at Ephesus became the means of edifying the Corinthian converts, and that grace plus his learning and eloquence became an effective instrument for confuting the Jews publicly, both to the encouragement of the Christians and the discouragement of Jewish opposition to Christianity.

Of the word **confuted,** used here by Luke, Vincent observes that it is not elsewhere used in the New Testament and that it implies that "he confuted them *thoroughly* (*diá*), *against* (*katá*) all their arguments."[135]

---

[132] Vincent, *op. cit.,* I, 549.   [133] *Ibid.*   [134] *Ibid.*   [135] *Ibid.,* p. 550.

On the work of Apollos at Corinth Wesley remarks:

Who greatly helped through grace — It is through grace only that any gift of any one is profitable to another. Them that had believed — Apollos did not plant, but water [I Cor. 3:6]. This was the peculiar gift which he had received. And he was better able to convince the Jews than to convert the heathens.136

The burden of Apollos' ministry at Corinth was **that Jesus was the Christ** (v. 28b). Any ministry that falls short of this objective is short of Christianity, and the ministry that attains this objective is the true Christian ministry.

C. THE APOSTLE'S MISSION TO EPHE-SUS (19:1-22)

On his first missionary journey Paul did not go farther west than Antioch of Pisidia in Asia Minor. On his second missionary journey he by-passed Ephesus on the north, because he was "forbidden of the Holy Spirit to speak the word in Asia (Acts 16:6b). However, when returning from Corinth to Jerusalem at the close of his second missionary journey, he briefly visited Ephesus where he "entered into the synagogue, and reasoned with the Jews," after which he departed leaving them Priscilla and Aquila and his personal promise to return again in God's will (Acts 18:19, 21). Thus it would appear that Ephesus must have been an objective of the Apostle from the beginning of his missionary career. But until now the time for its invasion by the gospel had not been propitious. An earlier attempt might easily have proved abortive. The discernment of God's will for God's work in God's time is indeed a work of divine wisdom.

1. Paul Returns to Ephesus (19:1a)

1 And it came to pass, that, while Apollos was at Corinth,

Luke's description of Paul's return to Ephesus is probably designed to indicate that he revisited and confirmed the churches of Asia Minor established on his first missionary journey, en route to Ephesus. This would have constituted

his third pastoral visit to these churches since their establishment. Thus Antioch of Pisidia would have been the last and westernmost church from which Paul departed for Ephesus. From this point he evidently proceeded, not by the usual level trade route that passed through the Lycus and Maeander valleys and the cities of Colossae and Laodicea, but rather by the more direct mountainous northern route that passed down through the Cayster valley. Paul's words to the Colossians (Col. 2:1) seem clearly to indicate that he had never been to that city.

In certain respects (especially religiously) Ephesus was the most important city which Paul had so far visited in his missionary travels. Indeed there is a noticeable ascending order in the successive cities attacked by the Apostle in his missionary strategy. His next and probably last great objective was to be the city of Rome itself.

Ephesus was a city of Lydia located on the west coast of Asia Minor, at the mouth and on the left bank of the Cayster River, about midway between Miletus on the south and Smyrna on the north and just opposite the island of Samos, about three miles from the open sea. The city was situated at a transportation junction of the main sea and land trade routes between Rome and the Orient (Acts 19: 21; 20:1, 17; I Tim. 1:3; II Tim. 4:12). It possessed an elaborately constructed harbor.

Ephesus came under Rome's control about A.D. 133. While it evidently became the capital of the province of Asia in western Asia Minor, it is uncertain whether it was such in Paul's day. It "ranked along with Antioch in Syria and Alexandria in Egypt as one of the three great cities of the eastern Mediterranean."137 Eventually the mouth of the river silted up, the harbor became a marsh, and the city disappeared, except for its extensive ruins. Only the small village of Ayasoluk, or Seljuk (Turkish), constructed mainly of stone from the ruins of Ephesus, located a mile or so to the northeast, remains to memorialize the once illustrious city.

At the harbor's head stood the famed temple of Diana (Roman) or Artemis (Greek), which goddess was represented

136 Wesley, *op. cit.*, pp. 470, 471, n. 27.   137 Finegan, *op. cit.*, p. 265.

in statue as a multi-breasted mother goddess.

Croesus and Cyrus (sixth century B.C.) and Alexander the Great (fourth century B.C.) had all left their mark on the Asiatic people in general and the Ionian Greeks, who originally populated the province of Asia, in particular. From Croesus' time (ca. 560 B.C.) a fertility goddess of Lydia, who resembled Ashtoreth of the Phoenicians, had been the chief deity of the city. Her worship was characterized by a magnificent temple, commercialized subsidiaries, and legalized prostitution. Ephesus was "a worshiper" (KJV), "a temple-keeper" (ASV), and "a warden" (Moffatt) of the goddess (Acts 19:35). Magic was commercialized and widely practiced at Ephesus. Charlatans exacted fees for consultation (Acts 19: 13-16, 19), and the general prevalence of superstition was evidenced by inscriptions on buildings and walls throughout the city. The Millers aptly remark: "Under liberal Roman rule, . . . Ephesus became a racial melting pot, a cosmopolitan commercial center of the Empire, and a battlefield of religion."[138]

The temple of Diana was discovered by the English architect and anthropologist, J. T. Wood, on May 2, 1869. It was 120 years in building and the original temple, according to tradition, burned in 356 B.C. However, it was replaced by the "Hellenistic Temple" which was completed in the latter part of the fourth century B.C. The temple rested on a platform about 240 feet wide and over 400 feet long. The temple proper was over 160 feet wide and 340 feet long with 100 columns over 55 feet high. Gold and silver images, weighing from three to seven pounds each, were made of the goddess by the smiths (Acts 19:23-26). Little wonder that this temple was regarded as "one of the seven wonders" of the ancient world.

The great Ephesian theater, which was the scene of the tumult raised against Paul (Acts 19:29), was a semi-circular auditorium 495 feet in diameter, excavated in the hollow of a hill that commanded a clear view of the city and accommodated an audience of nearly 25,000 people.

The further magnificence of this city is suggested by Finegan's description:

> Another important feature of ancient Ephesus was the agora or marketplace. This was a great rectangular, colonnaded area entered by magnificent gateways and surrounded by halls and chambers. Nearby was the library, built with fine columns and with its walls recessed with niches for bookcases [cf. Acts 19:9b]. Other buildings which have been excavated include gymnasia, baths, and burial monuments. One of the city's finest streets ran directly from the theater to the river harbor, being nearly one-half mile long and about 35 feet wide, and lined with halls on either side. Also at the harbor there were monumental gateways.[139]

At this famous, ancient city Paul evangelized for upward of three years between the autumn of A.D. 52 and the spring of A.D. 55, and out from Ephesus the whole of western Asia Minor was evangelized. Here a great Christian church was founded by Paul, over which Timothy was later made pastor. And if tradition is reliable, at Ephesus both the apostle John and Mary the mother of Christ spent their last days. The churches' third general council, which defined the doctrine of Christ's person as "two natures, but one person," was held at Ephesus in A.D. 430. To this church Paul later wrote the Ephesian epistle, though likely intended for other churches as well, and to this church Christ directed the message recorded in Revelation 2:1-7.

There appear to be indications that Paul may have regarded Ephesus as the third great missionary base from which the gospel was to radiate forth to the central eastern section of the Roman Empire, Jerusalem and Antioch of Syria having been the first two and the city of Rome designed to become the fourth.

2. Paul Finds Certain Disciples at Ephesus (19:1b-7)

1b Paul having passed through the upper country came to Ephesus, and found certain disciples: 2 and he said unto them, Did ye receive the Holy Spirit when ye believed? And they *said* unto him, Nay, we did not so much as hear whether the Holy Spirit was *given*. 3 And he

---

[138] Miller and Miller, *op. cit.*, p. 167.   [139] Finegan, *op. cit.*, pp. 268, 269.

said, Into what then were ye baptized? And they said, Into John's baptism. 4 And Paul said, John baptized with the baptism of repentance, saying unto the people that they should believe on him that should come after him, that is, on Jesus. 5 And when they heard this, they were baptized into the name of the Lord Jesus. 6 And when Paul had laid his hands upon them, the Holy Spirit came on them; and they spake with tongues, and prophesied. 7 And they were in all about twelve men.

[He] **found certain disciples** (v. 1b). Paul's discovery of these disciples at Ephesus is one of the most momentous and, in certain respects at least, vexing accounts of the Book of Acts. If they were at Ephesus when he briefly visited that city near the close of his second missionary journey (Acts 18:19-21), he evidently did not meet them then. Dummelow holds that they had arrived at Ephesus, between the departure of Apollos for Corinth (v. 1a) and the return of Paul to Ephesus; else Apollos would have instructed them in the Christian doctrine after "Priscilla and Aquila . . . took him unto them and expounded unto him the way of God more accurately" (Acts 18: 26). However, this need not be supposed, as Apollos appears to have left Ephesus for Corinth almost immediately after having met Priscilla and Aquila (Acts 18:26, 27).

Clarke thinks that these men were Asiatic Jews who, a quarter-century earlier, had heard John preach at Jerusalem (perhaps at an annual feast) and were there baptized by him, in anticipation of Christ's coming. Bruce allows that

> They may have received their knowledge of Christianity from a source similar to that from which Apollos received his, or they may have received it from Apollos and been baptized by him during his earlier days in Ephesus, when he knew only the baptism of John.[140]

Of greater importance, however, is the state of grace that characterized these disciples. There seems to be no warrant for the common assumption that these **certain disciples** were the disciples of John the Baptist. Indeed they had received **John's baptism** (v. 3b), which

Paul defines as **the baptism of repentance** (v. 4b), a factor common to all baptisms that were administered to proselytes by the Jews; but faith in Him that was to come was peculiar to John's baptism (Clarke: v. 4b). Thus they were the disciples of Christ, though imperfectly instructed, and not John's disciples, as many mistakenly suppose. Bruce is specific and significant in his statement:

> But that these men were Christians is certainly to be inferred from the way in which Luke describes them as 'disciples'; this is a term which he commonly uses for Christians, and had he meant to indicate that they were disciples, not of Christ but of John the Baptist (as has sometimes been deduced from v. 3), he would have said so explicitly.[141]

Paul's question, **Did ye receive the Holy Spirit when ye believed?** (v. 2a), was answered by these disciples in the negative: **Nay, we did not so much as hear whether the Holy Spirit was given** (v. 2b). This reply probably does not warrant the inference that these disciples had no knowledge of the person, dispensation, or office work of the Holy Spirit in the life of the believer. No more can be deduced from their reply than that they were uninformed concerning the fulfillment of His dispensation and effusion which occurred at the Jerusalem Pentecost. Dummelow remarks:

> Of course they had heard of the Holy Ghost, but St. Paul means, had they experienced that new power of holiness, that peace and love and joy which the ascended Messiah had first given at Pentecost, and was still ready to bestow on all believers.[142]

On this problem Bruce remarks:

> Paul's question . . . suggests strongly that he regarded them as true believers in Christ . . . the addition of the word "given," as in A.R.V., may give the real intention of their words. Even if they had only been baptized with John's baptism, they conceivably knew that John had spoken of a coming baptism with the Holy Spirit [see Matt. 3:11]; they did not know, however, that this expected baptism was now an accomplished fact.[143]

Thus it may be safely concluded that these disciples had been instructed in the teaching of John concerning the saving

[140] Bruce, op. cit., p. 385. See also F. Davidson (ed.), The New Bible Commentary, Acts 18: 24-28. [141] Ibid. [142] Dummelow, op. cit., p. 845. [143] Bruce, op. cit., pp. 385, 386.

efficacy of the coming Christ, had believed on Him (cf. Eph. 1:13), had received water baptism as a token of their repentance, "A baptism of expectation rather than one of fulfillment as Christian baptism now was."[144] They had become recipients of a measure of Christian grace through the ministry of the Holy Spirit (Rom. 8:5) and had lived in anticipation of a spiritual Pentecost, the historical occurrence of which they had not been informed.

The re-baptism of these Ephesian disciples is the only New Testament account of such an occurrence. Whoever of the apostles had been baptized with John's baptism, it appears that "their Pentecostal enduement with the Spirit transformed the preparatory significance of the baptism which they had already received into the consummative significance of Christian baptism."[145]

However, these Ephesian Christian disciples had neither experienced nor learned of the Pentecostal baptism. Therefore, it was evidently their desire and Paul's judgment that they should be re-baptized into the name of the Lord Jesus (v. 5b). It appears most likely that if these disciples had already received Christian baptism they would have heard of the Holy Spirit, and it further appears probable that the Trinitarian formula (Matt. 28:19) was used at this time.

More important, however, is the fact that this second baptism was not likely administered by Paul personally but by some other, such as Priscilla or Aquila, if we are to take Paul's own words to the Corinthians seriously (see I Cor. 1:14-16). Thus whatever measure of Christian grace accompanied their second water baptism, by whatever mode they were baptized, that experience of grace is not to be confused with what they experienced **when Paul had laid his hands upon them, [and] the Holy Spirit came upon them; and they spake with tongues, and prophesied** (v. 6). Under John's teachings they had experienced the baptism of repentance and faith in the coming Messiah. Under their second baptism at Ephesus their Christian experience had been confirmed, animated and enriched by the accompanying power and grace of the Holy Spirit (cf. John 20:22, 23). But under the imposition of hands by Paul, they received the baptism of the Holy Spirit and fire in the purification of their natures, as promised by John (Matt. 3:11; Luke 3:16) and provided by the very nature of God (Heb. 12:29). Thus the complete possession and empowerment of their lives, as experienced by the Christian disciples on the day of Pentecost (cf. Acts 1:8; 2:1-4; and 15:8, 9), as well as by the Samaritans under the ministry of Peter and John (Acts 8:14-17) and the Gentile household of Cornelius at Caesarea under Peter's ministry (Acts 10:44-48; 11:15-17; 15:8, 9), became a reality with these believers.

Luke's remark, that **they spake with tongues, and prophesied** (v. 6b), seems clearly to indicate that these twelve disciples were divinely earmarked for special witnessing to the Gentiles of Ephesus and western Asia Minor. There is no reason for believing that their prophesying was other than "forthtelling" or witnessing for Christ to their fellow countrymen, from their personal experiences and possibly also from the Jewish Scriptures with which they may have had an acquaintance. As previously noted, it is not known for certain whether they were Jews, Gentiles, proselytes, or God-fearers. But if they were not Jews, they were most likely either Gentile proselytes to Judaism or God-fearers. In any event, there is every evidence of the fact that when **they spake with tongues** (v. 6) they had received a divine gift of languages designed to enable them to minister the gospel of Christ to the exceedingly polyglot cosmopolitan city of Ephesus, as well as the entire western section of Asia Minor. Who can say that from among these very disciples there may not have come some of Paul's most efficient and effective helpers in the evangelization of western Asia Minor from his Ephesian base during the nearly three years that followed? It is entirely possible that some of his helpers named in his epistles were from this original company of disciples who **spake with tongues, and prophesied**. In support of this interpretation, Bruce says:

---

[144] *Ibid.,* p. 386.   [145] *Ibid.*

Ephesus was to be a new centre of the Gentile mission — the next in importance after the Syrian Antioch — and these twelve disciples were to be the nucleus of the Ephesian church. By this exceptional procedure, then, they were associated in the apostolic and missionary task of the Christian Church.146

Clarke adds the further weight of his testimony to this position thus:

> They [the Ephesian twelve] received the miraculous gift of different languages; and in those languages they *taught* to the people the great doctrines of the Christian religion; for this appears to be the meaning of the word *Proefateuon*, prophesied, as it is used above.147

And Matthew Henry significantly remarks,

> This was indeed to introduce the gospel at Ephesus, and to awaken in the minds of men an expectation of some great things from it; and some think that it was further designed to qualify these twelve men for the work of the ministry, and that these twelve men were the elders of Ephesus, to whom Paul committed the care and government of the church. They had the spirit of prophecy, that they might understand the mysteries of the kingdom of God themselves, and the gift of tongues, that they might preach them to every nation and language.148

Certainly, while there is found no basis in this incident for the interpretation of an "unknown tongue," there is strong evidence for a valid conclusion that what occurred was a miraculous divine gift of *bona fide* languages designed for the enablement of these Spirit-baptized Christian disciples to preach (*prophesy*) Christ to the polyglot peoples of one of the greatest centers of the ancient world.

Luke records two specific localities of Paul's ministry at Ephesus: namely, the Jewish synagogue and the school of Tyrannus. However, it is not to be supposed that Paul confined his ministry to these places while he remained in Ephesus. Paul's associates here were Timothy, Titus, Erastus, and Sosthenes (Acts 19:22; I Cor. 1:1; II Cor. 1:1; and 12:17f.).

3. Paul Ministers in the Jewish Synagogue (19:8, 9a)

8 And he entered into the synagogue, and spake boldly for the space of three months reasoning and persuading *as to* the things concerning the kingdom of God. 9 But when some were hardened and disobedient, speaking evil of the Way before the multitude,

Paul followed his usual custom, as at Antioch of Pisidia (Acts 13:14), at Thessalonica (Acts 17:2), at Beroea (Acts 17:10), at Athens (Acts 17:17), and at Corinth (Acts 18:4), by beginning at Ephesus in the Jewish synagogue. On his earlier visit to Ephesus (Acts 18:19-21), Paul had established contact with the Jews here by ministering in their synagogue. It appears from Luke's words, "they asked him to abide a longer time" (Acts 18:20), that their impression of his person and ministry had been favorable. This is further borne out by the fact that he continued to minister in **the synagogue . . . for the space of three months** (v. 8), an unusually long time, before opposition forced him out. However, here as always, when the light of Christ's Messiahship had sufficiently illumined their darkness, **some were hardened and** [became] **disobedient** (v. 9), with the consequence that they spoke **evil of the Way before the multitude** (v. 9), thus poisoning their minds against the Christian missionaries and the Christian gospel. Consequently Paul was forced to leave the synagogue, as he had had to do in so many other instances.

Thus having offered the gospel first to the Jews at Ephesus, who had been providentially placed there as God's emissaries to the Gentiles, Paul then turns to the Gentiles, seeing that certain Jews were determined to reject and oppose the light of God's truth (cf. Acts 18:6).

Luke's expression, **reasoning and persuading** (v. 8), or conversing with them, with a view to persuading them of the truth of the Christian doctrine, may suggest that there were those of the synagogue who believed unto eternal life. However, apparently the majority closed their minds, hardened their hearts, and

146 *Ibid.*, p. 387.   147 Clarke, *op. cit.*, I, 842.
148 Matthew Henry, *op. cit.*, VI. Comment on Acts 19:6, 7.

set themselves in active opposition against Christianity. Thus prejudiced they became active propagandists against the Christian mission. Here at Ephesus, as always, the Word of God was "to the one a savor from death unto death; to the other a savor from life unto life" (II Cor. 2:16). The twelve initial subjects of Paul's Ephesian ministry (vv. 1b-7) affectionately received his message and became partakers of the Holy Spirit, but these latter propagandists were hardened by their unbelief and rejection of the same truth. Thus they not only brought condemnation upon themselves but became the active agents of Satan among the multitude, perhaps both those within and outside the synagogue, prejudicing their minds against the Christian Way (cf. Acts 17:5).

4. Paul Ministers in the School of Tyrannus (19:9b-20)

9b he departed from them, and separated the disciples, reasoning daily in the school of Tyrannus. 10 And this continued for the space of two years; so that all they that dwelt in Asia heard the word of the Lord, both Jews and Greeks. 11 And God wrought special miracles by the hands of Paul: 12 insomuch that unto the sick were carried away from his body handkerchiefs or aprons, and the diseases departed from them, and the evil spirits went out. 13 But certain also of the strolling Jews, exorcists, took upon them to name over them that had the evil spirits the name of the Lord Jesus, saying, I adjure you by Jesus whom Paul preacheth. 14 And there were seven sons of one Sceva, a Jew, a chief priest, who did this. 15 And the evil spirit answered and said unto them, Jesus I know, and Paul I know; but who are ye? 16 And the man in whom the evil spirit was leaped on them, and mastered both of them, and prevailed against them, so that they fled out of that house naked and wounded. 17 And this became known to all, both Jews and Greeks, that dwelt at Ephesus; and fear fell upon them all, and the name of the Lord Jesus was magnified. 18 Many also of them that had believed came, confessing, and declaring their deeds. 19 And not a few of them that practised magical arts brought their books together and burned them in the sight of all; and they counted the price of them, and

found it fifty thousand pieces of silver. 20 So mightily grew the word of the Lord and prevailed.

In the face of Jewish opposition in the synagogue, there was nothing left for Paul to do, in fairness to the believers, but to separate them from the unbelieving Jews and launch his Christian mission quite independent of the synagogue. When existing sources of spiritual truth and life are deliberately and determinately clogged, new fountains of spiritual life will break forth elsewhere. Paul said, "But the word of God is not bound" (II Tim. 2:9b). The many branches of Christianity have arisen largely as a result of the failure of the existing nominal churches to express, or allow expression of, spiritual life. Jan Karel Van Baalen, in his book, *The Chaos of Cults,* goes so far as to suggest that the recrudescence of "Sects and cults [has represented] 'the unpaid bills of the [Christian] church.' "[149]

The school of Tyrannus to which Paul resorted for the continuance of his gospel ministry in Ephesus, was either rented or borrowed for his purposes at such hours as this philosopher did not require it for his lectures. It was a secular lecture hall with no other consecration than that given it by Paul's ministry there. Who Tyrannus was, what school of philosophy he represented, or how Paul happened to acquire the building we are not told. That this new and likely central location for Paul's ministry was a decided advantage over the synagogue appears evident from the fact that he no longer was identified with the Jews. Consequently, the Gentiles would experience a freedom to listen to his discussions, which they could not have had in the Jewish synagogue. This appears evident from Luke's words, **reasoning daily in the school of Tyrannus** (v. 9b), and again, **this continued for the space of two years; so that all they that dwelt in Asia heard the word of the Lord, both Jews and Greeks** (v. 10). Thus Paul's long entertained desire, hitherto prevented (Acts 16:6), to evangelize the peoples of Proconsular Asia in western Asia Minor, was now fulfilled.

Concerning Paul's hours of discussion in Tyrannus' lecture hall, it may be

[149] Van Baalen, *op. cit.,* p. 17.

observed that believers and others favorably impressed by his previous ministry in the synagogue accompanied him, as well as new people attracted to the truth. His messages and discussions were conducted in the hall at such time as Tyrannus did not require the building for his lectures. Indeed, the Western Text indicates that Paul used the building from 11 A.M. to 4 P.M. Tyrannus likely held his classes in the early morning. General public activities in the Ionian cities terminated at 11 A.M. Thus Paul probably spent the early morning hours in tent-making (cf. Acts 20: 34), and then devoted the succeeding hours to his evangelistic ministry in the hall of Tyrannus.

Bruce[150] thinks Paul's unusual display of energy and personal sacrifice in preaching while the populace customarily slept may have so impressed the Ephesians as to have induced them to sacrifice their siesta to hear him preach.

Paul's **two years'** ministry in **the school of Tyrannus** is likely meant as an approximate period and may have been longer, which taken together with the **three months** (v. 8) spent in the synagogue, made up the approximate three-year period spent at Ephesus (Acts 20: 31). Luke's statement, **all they that dwelt in Asia heard the word of the Lord, both Jews and Greeks** (v. 10), indicates the extent of Paul's evangelizing ministry during this period and accounts for the establishment of the several churches of Asia, namely, Ephesus, Smyrna, Pergamum, Thyatira, Sardis, Philadelphia, Laodicea, Colossae, Hierapolis, and Troas, the first seven of which are mentioned in Revelation 1:11. Nor is it to be supposed that Paul visited and evangelized all these locations personally, but rather that he directed the campaign from his Ephesian headquarters, which campaign was carried out in large part by his faithful helpers. Possibly these included the twelve earlier recipients of the Holy Spirit (vv. 5-7), who were likely the elders of the Ephesian church to whom Paul later gave his final charge at Miletus (Acts 20: 17ff.).

The special miracles attributed to Paul in verses 11 and 12 are reminiscent of the people's faith in Peter's shadow at an earlier period (Acts 5:15), and they bear a definite resemblance to the healings attributed to the touching of Jesus' garments (Mark 5:25-34; 6:53-56).

It should be noted that there is a distinction between the **special miracles which God wrought by the hands of Paul** (v. 11) and the statement **that unto the sick were carried away from his body handkerchief or aprons, and the diseases departed from them, and the evil spirits went out** (v. 12).

In the first instance it would seem that the miracles were wrought by the power of God working directly in Paul through the imposition of his hands on the sick, afflicted, and demon-possessed. Such was the usual divine method in the early church. However, in the second instance, the faith of his Ephesian followers seems not unmixed with the magical concepts rife in Ephesus (vv. 18, 19). They conceived of the divine power transmitted from his person to his personal effects, especially his handkerchiefs and aprons, or "sweatrags being used for tying round his head and the aprons for tying around his waist"[151] as he applied himself to his arduous task of tent-making. Magic has always associated personal effects of those regarded as possessed of such powers, especially soiled or perspiration-soaked clothing. That even some of Paul's Ephesian disciples were not completely free from these magical concepts appears evident from verse 18. To recognize these magical concepts on the part of some of Paul's Ephesian followers at this early stage of their faith is neither to attribute such concepts to Paul or the Christian religion which he preached, nor is it to say that the healings or demon expulsions were occasioned by any power resident in the hankerchiefs or aprons. However, that these objects, coming as they did from the person of so spiritually animated and popularly acclaimed a person as Paul, should have served as an aid to the faith of both those who bore them and those to whom they were borne appears entirely likely. Nor does Luke state that Paul either ordered or approved the practice. That God may have wrought miracles of healing and demon expulsion in response to the faith of these

150 Bruce, op. cit., pp. 388, 389.   151 Ibid., p. 389.

believers, though not because of, nor through, the **handkerchiefs or aprons** borne by them, is indeed credible, and such Luke doubtless means.

The incident of the attempted exorcism of the demons from the possessed man by the sons of Sceva, in verses 13 through 17, is the most remarkable of its kind in the Bible. **And there were seven sons of one Sceva, a Jew, a chief priest, who did this (v. 14).** It appears from verse 13 that the practice of demon exorcism by a certain class of vagabond Jews who may have capitalized on this art for monetary gain was not uncommon nor limited to the sons of Sceva. Such an individual was Bar-Jesus or Elymas (Acts 13:6, 8) whom Paul earlier rebuked; and, while his nationality is not given, such may Simon the sorcerer (Acts 8:9-13) have been. His Hebrew name, Simon, would indicate that he belonged to this class. Such conditions are indeed an illuminating though sad commentary on the degenerate state of Judaism in the first Christian century. Magic was the means employed in this art of demon exorcism. Correct formulae employing the sacred name of Jehovah were recited over the possessed, in the effort to deliver him of his demon.

Whether a **chief priest** (v. 14), as Luke suggests, or an impostor as may be allowed, this man had seven sons who were all vagabond magicians, who practiced, or pretended to practice, demon exorcism. Beholding the miracles wrought by God through Paul (vv. 11, 12) in the use of Christ's name, these lewd fellows conceived the prospect of material gain through the use of this divine name and so attempted its employment on a demoniac (v. 15).

Immediately the accosted demon recognized and acknowledged the name of Christ (Mark 1:23, 24), as demons must ever do, and admitted acquaintance with Paul, whose activities were well known in Ephesus, but disclaimed the authority of Sceva's sons over him: **Jesus I know, and Paul I know; but who are ye? (v. 15b)**. Whatever other magical formulae they may have known and successfully used, they certainly fouled on this one; for they were overcome by the enraged demon, stripped of their garments, and severely beaten.

Luke suggests in verse 17 that this incident served to reveal the superior power of Paul's use of the Name of Christ to that of the Jewish exorcists, and thus Christ's name was magnified in the minds of the populace. Again God made the wrath of man to praise Him. Wesley remarks:

> Several of the Jews about this time pretended to a power of casting out devils, particularly by certain arts or charms, supposed to be derived from Solomon. *Undertook to name* — Vain undertaking! Satan laughs at all those who attempt to expel him either out of the bodies or the souls of men but by divine faith. All the light of reason is nothing to the craft and strength of that subtle spirit. His craft cannot be known but by the Spirit of God; nor can his strength be conquered but by the power of faith.[152]

Evidence seems to indicate that this class of vagabond Jewish exorcists commonly employed or professed to employ the Ineffable Name of the Jehovah of the Jews in magical practices, and this the more effectively with the Gentiles because of the Jews' supposed secret knowledge of this name.

That it was the man possessed by this evil spirit, enraged and animated by the demon, and not the disembodied demon himself, **who leaped upon them and mastered both of them, and prevailed against them, so that they fled out of the house naked and wounded (v. 16),** is made clear by Luke. Further, it is in question whether Sceva's seven sons who were engaged in this nefarious business all participated in this incident, or whether only two of them were involved.

The resultant effects of the foregoing incident upon the Ephesians is suggested by Luke's statement: **Many also of them that had believed came, confessing, and declaring their deeds (v. 18 . . . . So mightily grew the word of the Lord and prevailed (v. 20).**

The evident contrast, between the effectiveness of Paul's use of the name of Jesus in benevolent miraculous deeds and the utter failure and humiliating defeat of these Jewish extortionists in their attempt to practice demon exorcism by the same divine name, was so rapidly and widely heralded throughout the city that **this**

---

[152] Wesley, *op. cit.*, p. 472, n. 13.

became known to all, both Jews and Greeks, that dwelt at Ephesus (v. 17a). The result was a reverential fear of God and a heightened respect for His servant Paul, in the mind of the populace. Thus it appears from Luke's words, and the name of the Lord Jesus was magnified (v. 17b), that this whole incident became "the talk of the town" and consequently focused general interest on Paul and his preaching in the hall of Tyrannus, with the result that a powerful spiritual awakening occurred in Ephesus. Wesley remarks: *"And the name of the Lord Jesus was magnified — So that even the malice of the devil wrought for the furtherance of the gospel."*[153]

Luke's statement, Many also of them that believed came, confessing, and declaring their deeds (v. 18), seems clearly to indicate that, to this juncture, many in Ephesus had come under the influence of the gospel and had partially yielded to its claims, who had not fully grasped the spiritual significance of the Christian gospel nor purified themselves from their pagan practices. Dummelow supports this conclusion as follows:

> The incident led to a reformation within the church. Many converts had continued their magical practices after their baptism. They now came forward and publicly renounced them, proving their sincerity by burning their books of spells.[154]

Wesley's remarks on this passage are pertinent:

> *Many came, confessing* — Of their own accord. *And openly declaring their deeds* — The efficacy of God's word, penetrating the inmost recesses of their soul, wrought that free and open confession to which perhaps even torments would not have compelled them.[155]

So will the genuinely revealed presence of God ever produce conviction for sin and wrongdoing and elicit frank and open confession, with the resultant forsaking of that which is unlike and opposed to God (cf. John 16:7-11; Acts 26:18; I Thess. 1:9, 10; Ps. 51:1-3). Spiritual manifestation always awakens, illumines, and inspires moral ideals. Without divine illumination, man will always grope in moral darkness and error. Their confessing, and declaring their deeds (v. 18), or divulging the secrets and forces of their magical spells had the effect of rendering them valueless, both to the users and to the people, as confidence in them would now be destroyed. So must the works of Satan ever be treated if genuine righteousness is to be established. Whenever the secrets of Satan are known, his power is broken.

Luke takes pains to specify the nature of the pagan practices at Ephesus. Topping the list was the practice of magical arts (v. 19). It appears that the cult of magic throve in the city of Ephesus among the Jews as well as Gentiles (Acts 19:19f.). The books of magic which were sold about the country were formulas in the form of amulets or inscriptions for doorposts, garden gates, and such like. Many of the magical papyri still survive. Mould states that "The emperor cult was there,"[156] and there is scriptural reference to the Ephesian high priests of this cult, which priests are known as Asiarchs (Acts 19:31). However, Artemis or Diana was the most important cult at Ephesus.

How like the half-Mohammedan, half-pagan practices of so many peoples influenced by Mohammedanism in Africa today! Sebbies (portions of Koranic writings encased in leather), worn as charms about the neck, around the forehead and forearms or the ankles, or suspended by cords under the clothing about the waist, are common in these lands.

Luke's account indicates that these magical practices were of such great reputation as to enhance the value of the "books." Wesley[157] sees in the bringing together of these books an evidence of common consent on the part of those who became Christians. Certainly when they brought their books together and burned them in the sight of all (v. 19), they were thoroughly convinced of the truth of Christianity and of the unlawfulness of their former practices. By thus publicly (in the sight of all) burning these things, they witnessed to their valuelessness, cleared themselves of any possible temptation to return to their former use, and declared to the

---

[153] *Ibid.*, p. 472, n. 17.   [154] Dummelow, *op. cit.*, p. 845.
[155] Wesley, *op. cit.*, p. 472, n. 18.   [156] Mould, *op. cit.*, p. 575.   [157] Wesley, *op. cit.*, p. 473, n. 19.

Ephesian populace their change of religious loyalties from Satan to Christ. He who does not burn his bridges behind him when he crosses the great gulf between "the kingdom of Satan" and "the Kingdom of God" may find future occasion to return over those bridges to his former loyalties.

The value of these works, stated by Luke to be **fifty thousand pieces of silver** (v. 19b), is somewhat in dispute among scholars.

Here again, Luke's observation indicates the beneficent effects of a great spiritual victory: **So mightily grew the word of the Lord and prevailed** (v. 20). This statement appears to suggest both the geographic expansion of Christianity in western Asia Minor and the intensification of its power and efficacy, both in Ephesus and wherever it spread.

Paul's ministry at Ephesus was now nearly completed. Though accompanied by many personal hazards and even possible sufferings, the fruits of his enterprise for Christ at Ephesus were rewarding. Whether Paul was actually imprisoned at Ephesus is uncertain. Luke is silent concerning the matter. In the second Corinthian letter, probably written from Philippi shortly after Paul left Ephesus, he alludes to imprisonments and sufferings, some of which may have occurred at Ephesus (II Cor. 11:23-27). Bruce[158] notes that Deissmann supports this position, as also do H. Lisco, W. Michaelis, G. S. Duncan, and M. Dibelius, while it is opposed by T. W. Manson.

During his three (about two and a half) years at Ephesus, Paul had thoroughly evangelized that city and western Asia Minor. Having securely planted an indigenous church in those parts, he now felt confident in leaving these young converts to carry on their Christian witness under the superintendency of the Holy Spirit. The Apostle's soul was restless with a passion for the evangelization of regions yet unreached. Says Wesley:

> Paul sought not to rest, but pressed on as if he had yet done nothing. He is already possessed of Ephesus and Asia. He purposes for Macedonia and Achaia. He has his eye upon Jerusalem; then upon Rome; afterward on Spain (Rom. XV, 24). No Caesar, no Alexander the Great, no other hero, comes up to the magnanimity of this little Benjamite. Faith, and love to God and man, had enlarged his heart, even as the sand of the sea.[159]

5. Paul Purposes to Visit Jerusalem (19: 21a)

21a Now after these things were ended, Paul purposed in the spirit,

While Spain became what Bruce calls Paul's "new Macedonia,"[160] yet the Apostle had other more immediate objectives en route. Among these were a revisitation of Macedonia and Achaia, a final visit to Jerusalem, and afterward a voyage to Rome where he prayed and hoped to realize spiritual fruit (cf. Rom. 1:8-15; 15:20, 24, 28). Though Luke but once hints at Paul's purpose in visiting Jerusalem (Acts 24:17), it becomes clear that his final visit to Macedonia and Achaia has as its objective the taking of a collection from the European churches, which he purposed to deliver to the Jerusalem church in person (cf. I Cor. 16:1-5; II Cor. 8:1-15; Rom. 15:25-28).

Paul's expressed intention of personally conveying the collection from the younger Gentile churches to the mother Jewish-Christian church at Jerusalem had a threefold significance. *First,* it indicated the continued poverty of the Jerusalem church, which was evidenced soon after Pentecost and to which the Gentile Christians had ministered from the beginning (Acts 11:29, 30). It appears quite likely that, in addition to the disposal of their property and the pooling of the proceeds in the first communal venture at Jerusalem following Pentecost, many of these Judaean Christian Jews had suffered heavy economic losses at the hands of their Jewish countrymen (cf. Heb. 10:32-34). (For further comment on the causes of Jewish-Christian poverty at Jerusalem, see note on Acts 2:44, 45). *Second,* it reflected the Christian gratitude and generosity of these Gentile Christians for their Jewish-Christian brethren from whom they had received the gospel. *Third,* it evidenced Paul's purpose to maintain the spirit of unity and good will between the Jewish and Gentile elements of the Christian church. Such was the purpose of the General

---

[158] Bruce, *op. cit.,* p. 393, n. 29.   [159] Wesley, *op. cit.,* p. 473, n. 21.   [160] Bruce, *op. cit.,* p. 394.

Church Council of Acts 15, and such continued to be Paul's purpose. He, who had so frequently been accused of abrogating the Jewish Law in his Gentile ministry, was careful to allay Jewish-Christian suspicion by demonstrating the charity of the Gentiles toward the Jews.

6. Paul Plans to Visit Rome (19:21b, 22)

21b when he had passed through Macedonia and Achaia, to go to Jerusalem, saying, After I have been there, I must also see Rome. 22 And having sent into Macedonia two of them that ministered unto him, Timothy and Erastus, he himself stayed in Asia for a while.

Ramsay speaks of Paul's "clear conception of a far-reaching plan"[161] as revealed in this twenty-first verse. Paul's association with Aquila and Priscilla at Corinth, and later at Ephesus, afforded ample opportunity for them to inspire the mind and soul of the Apostle with the challenges to Christianity which that great capital and metropolis, Rome, presently afforded. Only recently had Aquila and Priscilla come from Rome (Acts 18:2), and erelong they evidently returned there (Rom. 16:3). As "all roads led to Rome," so Paul regarded this great capital city as the hub of the ancient world, out from which the gospel would radiate to all parts of the empire (Rom. 1:8). Indeed, from Rome he purposed to convey personally the gospel to Spain in the west. Says Ramsay:

> Such an intention implies in the plainest way an idea already existent in Paul's mind of Christianity as the religion of the Roman Empire. Spain was by far the most thoroughly romanized district of the Empire, as was marked soon after by the act of Vespasian in 75, when he made the Latin status universal in Spain. From the centre of the Roman world Paul would go on to the chief seat of Roman civilization in the West, and would thus complete a first survey, the intervals of which should be filled up by assistants, such as Timothy, Titus, etc.[162]

Whether Paul ever reached Spain we cannot be certain. However, Luke's chief interest was with Rome as the terminus of his history, and from henceforth his narrative points to that great capital.

D. THE APOSTLE'S MALTREATMENT AT EPHESUS (19:23-41)

Whether Paul personally made a journey to Corinth during his stay at Ephesus, or whether that journey (II Cor. 12:14; 13:1) was made from Troas after his departure from Ephesus, is not clear. In any event before he finally departed from Ephesus, he met with an attack of violent opposition led by one Demetrius, a silversmith.

1. The Cause of the Opposition (19: 23-27)

23 And about that time there arose no small stir concerning the Way. 24 For a certain man named Demetrius, a silversmith, who made silver shrines of Diana, brought no little business unto the craftsmen; 25 whom he gathered together, with the workmen of like occupation, and said, Sirs, ye know that by this business we have our wealth. 26 And ye see and hear, that not alone at Ephesus, but almost throughout all Asia, this Paul hath persuaded and turned away much people, saying that they are no gods, that are made with hands: 27 and not only is there danger that this our trade come into disrepute; but also that the temple of the great goddess Diana be made of no account, and that she should even be deposed from her magnificence whom all Asia and the world worshippeth.

Evidently the fierce opposition which arose against Paul at Ephesus had a two-fold basis. First, the Christian Way had undermined confidence in the pagan nature worship of Artemis, the great goddess of the Ephesians. (For a description of this influential pagan goddess and her cult, see the note on Acts 19:1a.)

Luke's designation of Christianity as a Way occurs six times in the Acts record (cf. 9:2; 19:9; 19:23; 22:4; 24:14; 24:22). The word is clearly designed to indicate the progressive force of the new religion. The author of the Hebrew letter caught the significance of this Way and designated it "a new and living Way" (Heb. 10:20a). Thus Christian grace became a spiritual and moral escalator, in contrast with the laborious ladder of Jewish legalism (cf. Rom. 1:16; 8:11; Col. 1:27). Here at Ephesus, as at Thessalonica, these people of the Way were turning the world upside down (cf. Acts 17:6). Pa-

---

[161] W. M. Ramsay, St. Paul the Traveller and the Roman Citizen, p. 274.   [162] Ibid., p. 255.

ganism, however entrenched and influential, must ever crumble and fall before the irresistible impact of the "new and living Way." How significant are Christ's words in this relation: "upon this rock I will build my church; and the gates of Hades shall not prevail against it" (Matt. 16:18b). Weymouth's translation reads: "and the might of Hades shall not triumph over it." Indeed the Apostle had the "keys of the kingdom of heaven" (Matt. 16:19a), and many were they whom he had loosed from their bondage to the pagan cult of Artemis.

In the second place, the Ephesian opposition to Paul arose from an economic motive, caused by the loss of business to the guild of silversmiths who appear to have been led by Demetrius. Bruce holds that they regarded their very craft as falling under the patronage of their goddess, Diana or Artemis, in whose honor many of their wares were made. Ramsay observes that

> "a certain Demetrius was a leading man in the associated trades, which made in various materials, terracotta, marble, and silver, small shrines (*naoi*) . . . representing the Goddess Artemis sitting in a niche or *naiskos*, with her lions beside her."163

Bruce remarks:

> Among these wares were miniature silver niches, containing an image of the goddess, which her votaries bought to dedicate in her temple. The sale of these small shrines was a source of considerable profit to the silversmiths, and they were alarmed at the fall in the demand for them which the spread of Christianity was causing.164

How like the resentment of the owners of the demon-possessed slave girl at Philippi, when Paul cast the soothsaying demon out of her, with the resultant loss of their nefarious gain (Acts 16:19)! And how like the unrestrained opposition of slave-holding Christian clergy and laymen to the activities of the ardent abolitionists of the first half of the nineteenth century in the United States!

Thus the offense of the gospel to the combined religious devotion and economic gain of these Ephesian silversmiths produced a mob violence from which the Apostle narrowly escaped with his life. Religious fanaticism and greed for

monetary gain are two of the greatest enemies to Christ and Christianity. Bruce165 thinks that the special festival to Artemis which fell at the time of the spring equinox, at the beginning of the month of Artemision, may have coincided with the mob violence against Paul and the gospel in A.D. 55. Religious patriotism and fanaticism frequently flourish at festivals, as witnesses the uncurbed fervor at the breaking of the Mohammedan fast of Ramadan.

2. The Nature of the Attack (19:28-34)

28 And when they heard this they were filled with wrath, and cried out, saying, Great *is* Diana of the Ephesians. 29 And the city was filled with the confusion: and they rushed with one accord into the theatre, having seized Gaius and Aristarchus, men of Macedonia, Paul's companions in travel. 30 And when Paul was minded to enter in unto the people, the disciples suffered him not. 31 And certain also of the Asiarchs, being his friends, sent unto him and besought him not to adventure himself into the theatre. 32 Some therefore cried one thing, and some another: for the assembly was in confusion; and the more part knew not wherefore they were come together. 33 And they brought Alexander out of the multitude, the Jews putting him forward. And Alexander beckoned with the hand, and would have made a defence unto the people. 34 But when they perceived that he was a Jew, all with one voice about the space of two hours cried out, Great *is* Diana of the Ephesians.

Paul was no stranger to mob violence and plots laid against his life by enemies of the gospel which he preached. Luke records ten such attacks in Acts. The *first* was waged by the Jews at Damascus following Paul's conversion (Acts 9:23-25) ; the *second* by the Grecian Jews at Jerusalem (Acts 9:29-30) ; the *third* was instigated by the Jews at Antioch of Pisidia (Acts 13:50) ; the *fourth* was motivated by the Jews from Antioch and Iconium at Lystra, but executed by the pagan Lycaonians (Acts 14:19); the *fifth* occurred at Philippi at the hands of the Philippian officials, who were influenced by the owners of the slave girl from whom Paul expelled the evil spirit (Acts 16:19-24) ; the *sixth* occurred at Thessalonica

---

163 *Ibid.*, pp. 277, 278.   164 Bruce, *op. cit.*, p. 398.   165 *Ibid.*

at the hands of the jealous Jews and the Gentile rabble (Acts 17:5-9); the *seventh*, at Corinth by the Jews before Gallio (Acts 18:12-17); the *eighth*, at Ephesus by the pagan craftsmen of Diana or Artemis (Acts 19:23-41); the *ninth*, in Greece after Paul left Ephesus (Acts 20:2, 3); and the *tenth* occurred at Jerusalem at the hands of the Jews, on the occasion of Paul's last visit to that city (Acts 21:27-32; 23:9, 10, 12-14).

Demetrius, who as Ramsay phrases it, "must have had a good deal of capital sunk in his business"[166] summoned his fellow tradesmen to a meeting in the union hall where he inflamed their minds with propaganda against the Apostle. The Christian propaganda, he charged, devaluated the images and diverted the populace from the purchase of their crafts, as also from the worship of Artemis. Upon this, says Ramsay,

> The tradesmen were roused; they rushed forth into the street; a general scene of confusion arose, and a common impulse carried the excited crowd into the great theatre. The majority of the crowd were ignorant [of] what was the matter; they only knew from the shouts of the first rioters that the worship of Artemis was concerned.[167]

During the two-hour riot that followed they screamed their frenzied loyalty to the goddess, in the repetitious phrase, **Great is Diana of the Ephesians.** Ramsay significantly remarks:

> In this scene we cannot mistake the tone of sarcasm and contempt, as Luke tells of this howling mob; they themselves thought they were performing their devotions, as they repeated the sacred name; but to Luke they were merely howling, not praying.[168]

Quite naturally the concourse rushed to the great theater (v. 29). (For a description of the Ephesian theater, see note on Acts 19:1.) The rioters seized as hostages Gaius and Aristarchus of Macedonia (see Acts 20:4), Paul's fellow travelers. Bruce thinks, without sufficient reason it would seem, that Luke received his story of the Ephesian riot from one of these men.

Apparently Paul was absent when the riot began but appeared when he learned of the peril of his fellow Christians. His self-forgetfulness appears in his endeavor to enter the theater at the risk of his life (vv. 30, 31). Perhaps he sought to protect Gaius and Aristarchus, who had been seized by the mob (v. 29), by assuming personal responsibility for the movement that had provoked the riot. In any event, the Christian disciples' regard and love for Paul was evidenced by their refusal to allow him to hazard his life in entering the theater (v. 30).

Luke's reference to **certain . . . Asiarchs** (v. 31) who were Paul's friends and who sought to restrain him from entering the theater, is both interesting and instructive. On this question Ramsay remarks:

> The Asiarchs, or High Priests of Asia, were the heads of the imperial, political-religious organization of the province in the worship of "Rome and the Emperors"; and their friendly attitude is a proof both that the spirit of the imperial policy was not as yet hostile to the new teaching, and that the educated classes did not share the hostility of the superstitious vulgar to Paul.[169]

Ramsay thinks further that some of these **Asiarchs** may have been priests of Artemis, or other deities of the cities, and that evidently the Ephesian priests were not hostile to Paul. It is even possible that they may have regarded the Christian religion with favor as a cultural contribution to the religious eclecticism of the day, of which Artemis was the center in Asia. Viewed thus, it would appear that the monetary motive dominated the riot, rather than any sincere religious consideration.

Typical of mob violence, the greater part of those participating were totally ignorant of the real purpose of the riot (v. 32). When emotion dethrones reason, purpose is lost in the fog of confusion.

That the riotous resentment was as strongly anti-Jewish as it was anti-Christian is clear from the fact that when they put forth Alexander to address the mob, he was forthwith rejected and the hysteria was intensified (vv. 33, 34).

Who this Alexander was and who put him forth to speak to the mob, we are not told. Wesley thinks he was a well-known Christian who was forcefully projected into the situation by the artificers and workmen and pushed on by the Jews

[166] Ramsay, *op. cit.*, p. 278.   [167] *Ibid.*   [168] *Ibid.*, p. 279.   [169] *Ibid.*, p. 281.

as a religious scapegoat.[170] However, Bruce[171] holds that Alexander was put forth by the Jews to make clear to the rioters that they were no part of the Christian community responsible for the resentment created. Bruce and Dummelow[172] take the same position. Whether this Alexander is identical with "Alexander the coppersmith" (II Tim. 4:14), or whether he is the same as Alexander the apostate (I Tim. 1:20), is not known for certain. However, both of the latter characterizations appear to fit a Jew such as the Ephesian Alexander, who may have professed faith in Christ and subsequently apostatized to become a bitter enemy of the Christian cause.

3. The Arrest of the Attack (19:35-41)

35 And when the town-clerk had quieted the multitude, he saith, Ye men of Ephesus, what man is there who knoweth not that the city of the Ephesians is temple-keeper of the great Diana, and of the *image* which fell down from Jupiter? 36 Seeing then that these things cannot be gainsaid, ye ought to be quiet, and to do nothing rash. 37 For ye have brought *hither* these men, who are neither robbers of temples nor blasphemers of our goddess. 38 If therefore Demetrius, and the craftsmen that are with him, have a matter against any man, the courts are open, and there are proconsuls: let them accuse one another. 39 But if ye seek anything about other matters, it shall be settled in the regular assembly. 40 For indeed we are in danger to be accused concerning this day's riot, there being no cause *for it*: and as touching it we shall not be able to give account of this concourse. 41 And when he had thus spoken, he dismissed the assembly.

The **town clerk** or secretary of the city, who published the civic assembly decrees, was greatly disturbed by the disorderly conduct of the Ephesians. Bruce designates him "'the most important Ephesian official . . . [who] acted as liaison officer between the civil administration and the Roman provincial administration, whose headquarters were also in Ephesus."[173] As such he was responsible to the provincial administration for the conduct of civic affairs and thus was liable for the disorders of the day.

The town-clerk's address to the people was both shrewd and effective. He first appealed to their common sense by citing the universal recognition of Ephesus as the **temple-keeper of the great Diana, and of the image which fell down from Jupiter** (v. 35b). In the light of such recognition it was folly, he reasoned, for them to madly acclaim that which was taken for granted. Further, this officer seems to imply, Diana will stand or fall on her own merit (v. 36). He then proceeded to exonerate the accused Christians by citing their unimpeachable character and conduct at Ephesus. Next he indited Demetrius and the craftsmen for their illegal procedures against the Christians. They should have presented their case to the regular court of the proconsul.

If their complaints were such as not to require the decisions of the proconsul, then the town-clerk advised them that the regular meetings of the civic assemblies were open to them. According to Chrysostom these assemblies met three times each month. By their riot and irregular assembly they had acted illegally and made both themselves and the city liable to punishment by Rome.

Withal, Luke reflects in his record of this incident the liberal attitude of Rome toward all religions and the consequent legal freedom and protection which Christianity enjoyed under the Roman Empire at that time. Says Ramsay concerning the town-clerk's address:

His speech is a direct negation of the charges commonly brought against Christianity as flagrantly disrespectful in actions and in language to the established institutions of the State. . . .

This address is . . . entirely an *apologia* of the Christians . . . it is included by Luke in his work, not for its mere Ephesian connection, but as bearing on the universal question of the relation in which the church stood to the Empire . . . the basis for the Church's claim to freedom and toleration.[174]

E. THE APOSTLE'S FINAL MISSION TO MACEDONIA AND ACHAIA (20:1-5)

It appears likely that the Ephesian riot of Acts 19 shortened Paul's stay there and accounted for an earlier visit to Europe than had been previously planned. In

---

[170] Wesley, *op. cit.*, p. 474, n. 33. [171] Bruce, *op. cit.*, pp. 400, 401. [172] Dummelow, *op. cit.*, p. 845.
[173] Bruce, *op. cit.*, p. 401. [174] Ramsay, *op. cit.*, pp. 281, 282.

the first Corinthian letter (16:8), which he wrote from Ephesus near the close of his stay there, Paul expressed his intention of remaining in Ephesus until after Pentecost, which he did not do. Correspondence with the Corinthians previous to our first Corinthian letter seems to be indicated in I Corinthians 5:9 and 7: 1. Among Paul's verbal informants concerning the Corinthians are mentioned Chloe (I Cor. 1:11) and Stephanas (I Cor. 16:15). The latter was accompanied by Fortunatus and Achaicus, the bearers of a special gift to Paul from the Corinthian church (I Cor. 16:17).

Benjamin Robinson[175] gives an interesting analysis of Paul's correspondence with the Corinthians, as that correspondence is found in our two Corinthian letters, though his analysis may not be acceptable to many conservative readers.

Apparently Paul had personally visited Corinth once during his stay at Ephesus (see II Cor. 12:14; 13:1). He had likely sent Timothy to Corinth from Ephesus twice in the interest of the church there (cf. Acts 19:22; I Cor. 4:17; and 16:10, 11). A crisis had arisen in the Corinthian church, while Paul was at Ephesus, which called forth a lively correspondence and communication between Paul and the Corinthians. Finally he discharged Titus to Corinth on a conciliatory mission (II Cor. 8:6, 16-18). Paul expected to meet him at Troas upon his return. However, likely because of the hazards of winter sailing, Titus was delayed. Thus Paul, because of his restless anxiety over the Corinthian crisis and his desire to complete the European mission and get on to Jerusalem, and from thence to Rome (Acts 19:21) without further delay, sailed from Troas to Philippi (II Cor. 2:12, 13). There appears to be some evidence that Paul may have suffered a severe illness at about this time, possibly while at Troas waiting for Titus or in Macedonia after having crossed over to Europe. This illness may have been the result of maltreatment at Ephesus (see II Cor. 4:7-5: 10).

1. Paul's Mission to Macedonia (20:1, 2a, 3b)

1 And after the uproar ceased, Paul having sent for the disciples and exhorted them, took leave of them, and departed to go into Macedonia. 2a And when he had gone through those parts, and had given them much exhortation, . . . 3b and a plot was laid against him by the Jews as he was about to set sail for Syria, he determined to return through Macedonia.

Paul had formerly planned to sail directly from Ephesus to Corinth (II Cor. 1:16), but the acuteness of the Corinthian situation disposed him rather to send Titus with a letter (II Cor. 7:6-8). Titus had previously visited Corinth in the interest of the collection (II Cor. 12:18). Failing to find his messenger Titus at Troas, Paul feared lest the Corinthians had rejected his appeal for the Jerusalem collection (II Cor. 2:13). Probably at Philippi (in February or early March, A.D. 56)[176] he met Titus, who brought the good news from Corinth of their restored loyalty, which news revived the spirits of Paul (II Cor. 7:5, 6). Paul then proceeded to revisit the cities of Macedonia where he had established churches on his second missionary journey, giving them **much exhortation.**

Chapters 8 and 9 of II Corinthians indicate that a chief reason for this European visit was the Jerusalem collection. These two chapters, which concern the collection, may have been written while Paul was in Macedonia and following the letter of reconciliation in II Corinthians 1:1-6:13. Paul's purpose to deliver this collection from the younger Gentile churches to the Jerusalem mother church may well reflect the Apostle's sacred regard for the decisions of the General Council of Acts 15 (cf. Gal. 2: 10 and see note on Jerusalem Council, Acts 15).

En route from Macedonia to Achaia, Paul may have reached Illyricum (Rom. 15:19-23), as indeed there seems to be no other place in his travels into which this reference fits.[177]

2. Paul's Mission to Achaia (20:2b, 3a)

2b he came into Greece. 3a And when he had spent three months *there,*

Paul's purpose in visiting Greece, or Achaia, was twofold. *First,* he wished to revisit and edify the Corinthian church which had been so severely tried. *Second,*

[175] Robinson, *op. cit.,* p. 174.   [176] Ramsay, *op. cit.,* p. 390.   [177] *The Interpreter's Bible,* IX, 264.

he desired to receive a collection for the Jerusalem church.

During his three-month stay at Corinth in the winter of A.D. 55-56 (cf. I Cor. 16:6), Paul may have resided in the home of his old friend and convert, Gaius (I Cor. 1:14), where he penned the letter to the Romans, which he evidently sent to Rome by Phoebe (Rom. 16:1, 2). Indeed, Gaius joined Paul in sending words of greetings to the Christians at Rome in that letter (Rom. 16:23; cf. I Cor. 1:14). The Roman letter is the maturest and fullest expression of Paul's religious philosophy that remains. But even here his missionary soul-passion for the unreached regions finds expression (Rom. 15:20-28).

At the close of his Corinthian ministry, Paul thought to sail to Syria and from thence travel to Jerusalem with the collection. However, upon discovery of a Jewish plot to kill him, perhaps aboard a pilgrim ship sailing with Jews to the Jerusalem Passover, he altered those plans and returned through Macedonia (v. 3), from whence he sailed to Troas (v. 6). The five days required for the return voyage, as against the earlier two-day voyage, was doubtless occasioned by the inclement weather of the season.

3. Paul's Companions in Travel (20:4, 5)

4 And there accompanied him as far as Asia, Sopater of Beroea, *the son* of Pyrrhus; and of the Thessalonians, Aristarchus and Secundus; and Gaius of Derbe, and Timothy; and of Asia, Tychicus and Trophimus. 5 But these had gone before, and were waiting for us at Troas.

Luke reveals evident purpose in mentioning Paul's companions at this juncture. The collection was both Paul's principal mission to Europe and the occasion of his intended visit to Jerusalem. Slanderous insinuations of ulterior and even selfish personal motives in the taking of the collection were made by Paul's enemies. This disposed him to exercise scrupulous care in handling the money (II Cor. 8:18-21). His letter to the Corinthians indicates that he wished them to receive and handle the collection quite independent of himself, even to its conveyance to the Jerusalem church by a specially authorized representative of the

Corinthian church (I Cor. 16:1-4). Paul intended only to head a delegation of representatives from the various Gentile churches bearing their respective offerings, with a view to closing breaches between the Jerusalem church and the Gentile Christians by this token of Christian charity, loyalty, and unity (cf. Acts 24:17 and Rom. 15:25-27).

Paul's companions representing Macedonia were: *first,* **Sopater of Beroea,** *the son of Pyrrhus.* Macgregor remarks:

> One Sosipater is mentioned in Rom. 16:21 along with Timothy and Lucius. If the two are identified and Lucius is assumed to be Luke, then . . . Romans and Acts agree that Timothy, Luke, and Sopater were all three with Paul at this point.[178]

Bruce likewise favors identification of Sopater with Sosipater of Rom. 16:21,[179] as does also Clarke.[180] Thus the earlier "nobility" of these, many of whom became Christians (Acts 17:10-12), is reflected in their church loyalty and financial support. *Second,* **Aristarchus and Secundus,** with the doubtful inclusion of Gaius, represented the church of Thessalonica.[181] The liberality of the Macedonian and Achaian churches in this instance is highly commended by Paul (cf. 15:26 and II Cor. 8:1-5). Aristarchus is of special interest as Paul's companion in travel at Ephesus (Acts 19:29); his fellow traveller to Rome (Acts 27:2); his fellow laborer in Rome (Philemon 24); and his fellow prisoner at Rome (Col. 4:10, 11). There appears to be no other New Testament reference to Secundus. *Third,* the Achaian, and especially Corinthian, collection which was likely under the charge of Titus, received Paul's special consideration (cf. Rom 15:26; I Cor. 16:1, 2; II Cor. 8:6; 9:2).

Fourth, if the **Gaius** here mentioned is identical with the Gaius of Acts 19:29, where he is designated a *Macedonian,* then he also represented those churches along with Aristarchus and Secundus. Clarke remarks: "Some suppose he was a *native* [of Macedonia], but descended from a family that came from Derbe; but as *Gaius,* or *Caius,* was a very common name, these might have been two distinct persons."[182] It would be a pleasing thought

[178] *Ibid.,* p. 265.   [179] Bruce, *op. cit.,* p. 405.   [180] Clarke, *op. cit.,* I, 850.
[181] Bruce, *op. cit.,* p. 403, n. 5.   [182] Clarke, *loc. cit.*

that this Gaius was Paul's Corinthian convert (I Cor. 1:14) and the gracious host of the Apostle while he abode in Corinth (Rom. 16:23), as well as the beloved elder to whom John addressed his third epistle (III John 1:1). If such were true, then Gaius together with Titus may have represented the Corinthian church with its offering, although Luke lists him with the Macedonian delegates. Such would solve the problem of Luke's apparent silence concerning a Corinthian representative. Otherwise, either Titus (II Cor. 8:6, 19) or Paul himself must have been authorized to bear the Corinthian collection. However, in the absence of sufficient evidence we cannot press the point. Ramsay suggests that Luke's apparent silence concerning Titus may be due to the fact that Titus was a close relative of Luke. Ramsay states:

> Thus it may very well have happened that Luke was a relative of one of the early Antiochian Christians; . . . Further, it is possible that this relationship gives the explanation of the omission of Titus from *Acts,* an omission which everyone finds it so difficult to understand. Perhaps Titus was the relative of Luke; and Eusebius found this statement in an old tradition, attached to II Cor. VIII, 18; XII, 18, where Titus and Luke (the latter not named by Paul, but identified by an early tradition) are associated as envoys to Corinth. Luke, as we may suppose, thought it right to omit his relative's name, as he did his own name from his history.[183]

In the *fifth* place, however the foregoing concerning Gaius may fall, we appear to be on safe ground in ascribing to Timothy representation of the Lycaonian churches. Timothy was Paul's convert at Lystra on his first missionary journey (I Tim. 1:1, 2) and became his travelling companion on his second missionary journey (Acts 16:1-3). To this Timothy Paul later wrote the two epistles that bear his name.

Sixth, other representatives of Asia were **Tychicus and Trophimus.** Tychicus is later found with Paul in Rome and is sent by the Apostle with the letter to Ephesus (Eph. 6:21, 22; II Tim. 4:12). He subsequently bore the Colossian letter from Paul's Roman imprisonment to Colossae (Col. 4:7, 8). It appears that

Paul later appointed him to supervise the church at Crete, in Titus' absence from the island (Titus 3:12). He was one of Paul's most intimate and beloved friends.

While Luke does not specifically mention an Ephesian representative as such, it appears reasonable from the presence of Trophimus, "an Ephesian," with Paul at Jerusalem (Acts 21:29) that he was there to represent the church. Paul later left Trophimus ill at Miletus. Probably he travelled with the Apostle and may have been en route to his home in Ephesus (II Tim. 4:20).

Seventh, it appears most likely that Luke represented the Philippian church, as he rejoined Paul there and sailed with him from Macedonia to Troas. This is inferred from the author's use of the first person plural pronoun (v. 6), indicating his identification with the Apostle. In fact, judging from the so-called *"We"* sections of Acts, Luke first joined Paul at Troas on his first missionary journey (Acts 16:10) and then dropped out of the picture upon Paul's departure from Philippi (Acts 16:40). Nor does he again appear until he joins Paul on his voyage from Philippi to Jerusalem (Acts 20:6). Hereafter Luke continued with Paul for the most part until the end of his first Roman imprisonment, unless an exception be allowed for the Apostle's two-year imprisonment at Caesarea. The *"We"* sections are hereafter found in the Acts narrative as follows: 20:5-15; 21:1-18; 27:1-37; 28:16.

F. THE APOSTLE'S MINISTRY AT TROAS (20:6-12)

After a seven-day stay at Troas, the activities of which time can only be conjectured, Paul and his party assembled in an upper chamber of a private dwelling for worship. Such places were the common assembly rooms of the early Christians (Luke 22:12; Acts 1:13). That this meeting occurred on Sunday evening, rather than our Saturday or the Jewish Sabbath, is indicated by Paul's plans to resume his journey on the following morning. It is likely that he planned Sunday as a day of worship rather than a day of travel. Macgregor remarks: "Almost certainly the latter [Sunday evening], as **the morrow,** when Paul intended

183 Ramsay, *loc. cit.*

to depart, most naturally means the day after the first mentioned, and therefore is presumably Monday."[184] On this problem Bruce observes:

> On Sunday evening, not Saturday evening; Luke is not using the Jewish reckoning from sunset to sunset but the Roman reckoning from midnight to midnight; although it was apparently after sunset that they met, 'break of day' (v. 11) was 'on the morrow' (v. 7).[185]

Two important facts emerge from this meeting at Troas. *First,* it reflects the earliest clear record of Sunday as the Christian day of worship, as opposed to the Jewish Sabbath or our Saturday. Indeed Paul appears to allude to this fact in his Corinthian letter (I Cor. 16:2), but he is not explicit. Likewise there appears to be a strong implication favorable to Sunday as the Christian day of worship in John 20:19, 26. It is worthy of note that the expression, "Lord's day," is first used in Rev. 1:10. *Second,* it depicts the order of a first-century Christian worship service. This likely began with a fellowship meal which was followed by the Eucharist or Lord's Supper. Next was a prolonged discourse by Paul, during which time there was probably opportunity for questions and discussions. Finally, there was a later fellowship meal, and then the service came to a close.

1. The Message at Troas (20:6, 7, 11)

6 And we sailed away from Philippi after the days of unleavened bread, and came unto them to Troas in five days; where we tarried seven days.
7 And upon the first day of the week, when we were gathered together to break bread, Paul discoursed with them, intending to depart on the morrow; and prolonged his speech until midnight.
11 And when he was gone up, and had broken the bread, and eaten, and had talked with them a long while, even till break of day, so he departed.

Luke does not inform us of the nature or content of Paul's message at Troas, though he does indicate its length. That it contained both instruction and exhortation for the Christians may be safely inferred from Paul's recorded addresses, as well as the content of his epistles.

Probably slaves and other working people had no free time for religious congregational worship except at night. Since this is likely Paul's third visit to Troas, many would wish to hear the great Apostle.

The length of Paul's address here is most interesting in that it reflects the intensity of interest on the part of his audience. Bruce remarks:

> Church meetings were not regulated by the clock in those days, and the opportunity of listening to Paul was not one to be cut short; what did it matter if he went on conversing with them until midnight.[186]

Clarke reckons that the sun set at Troas at about 7 P.M. and rose at 5 A.M., thus affording a night of eight hours. Then allowing two hours for interruption, he concludes that Paul must have preached a sermon not less than six hours long.[187] Certainly time is a negligible factor when spiritual truth is ministering to recognized spiritual need. Someone has remarked, with a note of sarcasm, that "the modern sermonette is delivered by a preacherette to Christianettes." The briefest religious discourse may be too long in the absence of spiritual content or spiritual interest by the audience, while the longest may seem too brief in the presence of recognized spiritual need. Some justification for the length of Paul's sermon here may be found in the fact that it was his last message to these people. That there was purpose in its length appears from Luke's words, [he] prolonged his speech (v.b).

2. The Miracle at Troas (20:8-10, 12)

8 And there were many lights in the upper chamber where we were gathered together. 9 And there sat in the window a certain young man named Eutychus, borne down with deep sleep; and as Paul discoursed yet longer, being borne down by his sleep he fell down from the third story, and was taken up dead. 10 And Paul went down, and fell on him, and embracing him said, Make ye no ado; for his life is in him. 12 And they brought the lad alive, and were not a little comforted.

Wesley thinks the many lights in the upper chamber (v. 8) were designed "to

---

[184] *The Interpreter's Bible,* IX, 267.   [185] Bruce, *op. cit.,* p. 408, n. 25.   [186] *Ibid.*
[187] Clarke, *op. cit.,* I, 851.

prevent any possible scandal"[188] against the Christian meeting at night. However, Macgregor[189] depreciates such a suggestion. Indeed it appears likely that the torches consumed so much of the oxygen in the room as to produce a drowsiness on some of the congregation already weary from the day's toil. Such may have been the plight of the young man Eutychus, who sank into a deep sleep while he perched in an open window of the room and tumbled three stories to the ground outside.

Much controversy has raged over the question whether Eutychus was really dead. However, Luke the physician was present and has given us his medical verdict to the effect that he **was taken up dead** (v. 9b). No such verdict is given by Luke in the case of Paul's "supposed" death at Lystra (Acts 14:19). Nor do Paul's words of comfort to the relatives and friends, **his life is in him** (v. 10b), abrogate Luke's decisions. These words may be regarded as the prophecy of faith. Ramsay[190] credits Luke's verdict, as do Bruce,[191] Robinson,[192] and Dummelow[193] while the death of Eutychus is discredited by Macgregor.[194]

Paul interrupted his address to mix works with faith and descended to embrace the young man and reassure the Christians that he was restored to life. Parallels are found in Elijah's action in I Kings 17:21 and Elisha's in II Kings 4:34. This miracle finds its moral validation in part in the comfort which it brought to the Christian friends and relatives (v. 12). True divine miracles are always a source of strength to the faith of Christian believers.

G. THE APOSTLE'S MEETING AT MILETUS (20:13-38)

1. The Journey to Miletus (20:13-16)

13 But we, going before to the ship, set sail for Assos, there intending to take in Paul: for so had he appointed, intending himself to go by land. 14 And when he met us at Assos, we took him in, and came to Mitylene. 15 And sailing from thence, we came the following day over against Chios; and the next day we touched at Samos; and the

day after we came to Miletus. 16 For Paul had determined to sail past Ephesus, that he might not have to spend time in Asia; for he was hastening, if it were possible for him, to be at Jerusalem the day of Pentecost.

Why Paul did not sail with his companions on Monday morning but went overland to meet them at Assos, is not certain. Bruce suggests that he wished to remain at Troas until "assured of Eutychus' complete restoration to consciousness and health."[195] Dummelow[196] thinks rather that Paul wished to avoid the tedious voyage around Cape Lectum en route to Assos. Ramsay offers a more plausible explanation. He observes that at this season the wind in the Aegean Sea generally blows from the north from early morning until sundown, at which time it reaches a dead calm. This is followed by a gentle south wind during the night. The ship would harbor from evening until the change of wind sometime before sunrise. Thus it was necessary for all passengers to be aboard very early in the morning that the ship might "be ready to sail with the first breath of north wind."[197] Since Paul had not completed his service at Troas, he permitted his party to precede him by ship, while he travelled nineteen miles south overland by a road that paralleled the coast, though some miles inland. Thus he crossed the river valley and ascended to the gates of Assos at a half-mile altitude. This city was famed as the home of Cleanthes, the Stoic philosopher, and possessed one of the most imposing and beautiful locations among the Greek cities. It was famous for its excellent wheat which it exported, and here Aristotle taught 348-345 B.C. It is presently marked by an archaeological site and the Turkish village of Behram or Behramkoy. Here Paul boarded the ship and rejoined his Jerusalem-bound party.

The following is a curious though humanly interesting observation on Paul's departure from Troas.

From II Tim. 4:13 we learn that Paul lost some of his baggage, which presumably his friends omitted to put on

[188] Wesley, op. cit., p. 476, n. 8. [189] The Interpreter's Bible, loc. cit. [190] Ramsay, op. cit., p. 291.
[191] Bruce, op. cit., p. 408. [192] Robinson, op. cit., p. 182. [193] Dummelow, op. cit., p. 846.
[194] The Intrepreter's Bible. IX, 268. [195] Bruce, op. cit., p. 409; cf. Ramsay, loc. cit.
[196] Dummelow, loc. cit. [197] Ramsay, op. cit., p. 293.

the ship; for he asks Timothy to bring on from Troas a cloak — or possibly a case for books — some papyrus volumes, and some parchment rolls.[198]

If the foregoing is intended to refer to a planned visit of Timothy to the Apostle during a later period in his life, then no particular problem is posed.

Probably following a night's anchorage at Assos, they sailed the next day to the port of Mitylene on the mountainous island of Lesbos. The next day found them en route toward the island of Chios and from thence the following day to the island of Samos. The fifth day was spent en route to Miletus, where they likely anchored Friday evening. Miletus was second only to Ephesus among the cities of Asia. It was founded by Ionians in the eleventh century B.C., and here Greek philosophy had its origin with Thales, who was born in 625 B.C. Alexander destroyed the city in 334 B.C., but it was soon rebuilt.

Paul's reason for avoiding Ephesus appears to have been a problem of time, as he planned to reach Jerusalem on schedule for Pentecost. It is further possible that he considered his reappearance at Ephesus so soon after his stormy departure (Acts 20:1) might make unnecessary trouble for himself and the Christians there.

He could much more effectively represent and vindicate the Gentile Christians by delivering their offering to the Jerusalem church in the presence of the vast representation of Jews and Jewish Christians attending the feast. Robinson observes: "This day was not only a Jewish celebration, but an anniversary of the outpouring of the Spirit described in Acts, chapter 2. It would be a particularly opportune and appropriate occasion for presenting the contribution of the Gentile churches to the Jewish Christians."[199] Luke does not say that he arrived on time at Jerusalem, but the fact that he spent "some days" (Acts 21:10) at Caesarea in the house of Philip appears to indicate that he was running ahead of schedule. In fact, Ramsay holds that Paul had fully fifteen days to spare when he reached Caesarea.[200]

2. The Charge to the Ephesian Elders (20:17-35)

17 And from Miletus he sent to Ephesus, and called to him the elders of the church. 18 And when they were come to him, he said unto them,

Ye yourselves know, from the first day that I set foot in Asia, after what manner I was with you all the time, 19 serving the Lord with all lowliness of mind, and with tears, and with trials which befell me by the plots of the Jews; 20 how I shrank not from declaring unto you anything that was profitable, and teaching you publicly, and from house to house, 21 testifying both to Jews and to Greeks repentance toward God, and faith toward our Lord Jesus Christ. 22 And now, behold, I go bound in the spirit unto Jerusalem, not knowing the things that shall befall me there: 23 save that the Holy Spirit testifieth unto me in every city, saying that bonds and afflictions abide me. 24 But I hold not my life of any account as dear unto myself, so that I may accomplish my course, and the ministry which I received from the Lord Jesus, to testify the gospel of the grace of God. 25 And now, behold, I know that ye all, among whom I went about preaching the kingdom, shall see my face no more. 26 Wherefore I testify unto you this day, that I am pure from the blood of all men. 27 For I shrank not from declaring unto you the whole counsel of God. 28 Take heed unto yourselves, and to all the flock, in which the Holy Spirit hath made you bishops, to feed the church of the Lord which he purchased with his own blood. 29 I know that after my departing grievous wolves shall enter in among you, not sparing the flock; 30 and from among your own selves shall men arise, speaking perverse things, to draw away the disciples after them. 31 Wherefore watch ye, remembering that by the space of three years I ceased not to admonish every one night and day with tears. 32 And now I commend you to God, and to the word of his grace, which is able to build you up, and to give you the inheritance among all them that are sanctified. 33 I coveted no man's silver, or gold, or apparel. 34 Ye yourselves know that these hands ministered unto my necessities, and to them that were with me. 35 In all things I gave you an example, that so laboring ye ought to help the weak, and to remember the words of the Lord Jesus, that he himself

---

[198] The Interpreter's Bible, IX, 269.   [199] Robinson, op. cit., p. 183.   [200] Ramsay, op. cit., p. 297.

said, It is more blessed to give than to receive.

Kraeling[201] reckons that it required three days for messengers to reach Ephesus (Ephesus lay about thirty miles from Miletus) and return with the Ephesian elders to meet Paul. That such a delay argues strongly that Paul's party must have sailed in a chartered ship, which was subject to the Apostle's orders, has been discredited by Ramsay.[202]

The suggestion that these "Ephesian elders" were the twelve disciples whom Paul met upon his arrival in that city has been dealt with earlier (see note on Acts 19:1-7).

Thus far in Acts, Luke has recorded three of Paul's public addresses, *first,* his message to the Jews in the synagogue at Antioch of Pisidia (Acts 13:16-41); *second,* an address, based upon natural religion, to the pagan Lycaonians at Lystra (Acts 14:14-17) and *third,* an address, based upon natural religion, to the intelligent Athenians (Acts 17:22-31). This account of Paul's final charge to the Ephesian elders is Luke's first and only record of a message by Paul delivered specifically and exclusively to Christian believers. It contains many striking parallels to his epistles. This address is by nature mainly hortatory, though it contains an element of the apologetic.[203] It falls naturally into four principal divisions:

I. *The Apostle's Personal Example and Ministry* (vv. 18a-21).
II. *The Apostle's Devotion to Duty* (vv. 22-27).
III. *The Apostle's Charge to the Ephesian Elders* (vv. 28-32).
IV. *The Apostle's Personal Vindication* (vv. 33-35).

Paul's appeal to his personal example while he was at Ephesus closely parallels a similar appeal to the Thessalonians (cf. I Thess. 1:9; 2:1-11). Nothing hidden or secretive characterized Paul's conduct at Ephesus or elsewhere. The Jews possessed the Old Testament Scriptures and the instruction and examples they afforded for their directives. Before Paul wrote them, the Gentiles at Ephesus were devoid of any written instruction in Chris-

tian righteousness, as were the Thessalonians. Hence the importance of Paul's godly example before them, if they were to attain unto correct Christian deportment. Such examples of righteousness in the midst of wickedness either become a blessing unto salvation, or a curse unto damnation, depending on the reaction to the example. Clarke observes, on verse 19:

> This relates not only to his zealous and faithful performance of his *apostolic function,* but also to his *private walk* as a Christian; and shows with what carefulness this apostle himself was obliged to walk, in order to have his calling and election, as a Christian, ratified and made firm.[204]

It is noteworthy that Paul gives priority to his service to Christ — serving the Lord (v. 19). Paul is ever and foremost "a servant of Jesus Christ," after which he is "called to be an apostle" (Rom. 1:1. Cf. Phil. 1:1; Titus 1:1). This same humility Paul could later recommend to the Ephesian Christians (Eph. 4:2). Twice he alludes to his tears in this address (vv. 19 and 31. Cf. II Cor. 2:4; Phil. 3:18).

Wesley remarks:

> Holy tears from those who seldom weep on account of natural occurrences, are no mean specimen of the efficacy, and proof of the truth, of Christianity. Yet joy is well consistent therewith (verse 24). The same person may be sorrowful, yet always rejoicing.[205]

Nor does the Apostle omit trials by the Jews from the tool kit of his effective service for Christ at Ephesus. Even the plots of the Jews (a possible allusion to Alexander's attempt to incriminate Paul and the Christians at the Ephesian riot) Paul employed to further the cause of Christ. From his Roman prison, Paul could write of himself as "the prisoner of the Lord" (Eph. 4:1) and not of Nero, as the Jews and Rome thought.

How well did Paul demonstrate at Ephesus his confidence in the gospel, later expressed in Rom. 1:16! With boldness he executed his ministry both in public and in private (v. 20). House to house dissemination of the gospel charac-

[201] Emil G. Kraeling, *Rand McNally Bible Atlas,* pp. 451, 452.   [202] Ramsay, *op. cit.,* p. 295.   [203] Bruce, *op. cit.,* p. 413.   [204] Clarke, *op. cit.,* p. 853.   [205] Wesley, *op. cit.,* p. 477, n. 19.

terized the first-century Christians from the beginning (cf. Acts 2:46; 5:42).

Paul seems to summarize his Ephesian ministry in three words, *First,* his personal witness, **testifying;** *second,* **repentance;** and *third,* encouragement unto **faith.** In the first he is exemplifying the true spirit of early Christianity, the personal witness to Christ. Such Christ commanded (Acts 1:8). Whenever Christians lose their witness they lose Christ. No amount of eloquent preaching or profound teaching or convincing argumentation will ever substitute for the humble witness to Jesus Christ. Men are saved only by Christ, and they can know Him only as witness is borne to Him by those who know Him.

Jesus' own words concerning repentance are final: "Except ye repent, ye shall all in like manner perish" (Luke 13:3). Repentance bespeaks a genuine renunciation of one's loyalty to the former way of life with a consequent turning therefrom. Faith, on the other hand, is a new relationship with a new master. **Repentance is toward God,** against whom all, both Jew and Gentile, have sinned, whereas **faith is toward our Lord Jesus Christ.** There can be no true saving faith in Christ until there has been a genuine repentance toward God. Repentance is heartbreak for sin; saving faith is heartbreak with sin.

The loyal devotion of Paul to the cause of Christ impelled him to move on to Jerusalem for the accomplishment of his mission. Not even the Spirit's warnings of forthcoming **bonds and afflictions** (v. 23; Acts 21:10-14; Rom. 15:30, 31) could deter Paul from his sense of duty. How like his Master, on a similar occasion, who "stedfastly set his face to go to Jerusalem" (Luke 9:51)!

The Apostle regarded his life as expendable for the cause of Christ to **testify the gospel of the grace of God** (v. 24. Cf. II Tim. 4:7; Col. 4:17).

Paul's prediction, **ye . . . shall see my face no more** (v. 25b), is to be understood in the light of his devotion to Christ as he faced Jerusalem and the future (vv. 22, 23). In reality, there is strong evidence that he did later visit these parts and probably again saw some of the Ephesian Christians whom he

knew (cf. Phil. 1:25-27; 2:24; Philemon 22; I Tim. 1:3). He had thoroughly discharged his responsibility both to Jews and Gentiles at Ephesus, and they were left without excuse if they perished in their sins (cf. Ezek. 33:1-6). In verse 27 Paul returns to the emphasis of verse 20. Concerning **the whole counsel of God,** Clarke observes: "All that God has *determined* and *revealed* concerning the salvation of man — the doctrine of Christ crucified, with repentance towards God, and faith in Jesus as the Messiah and great atoning priest."[206]

Paul's charge to the Ephesian elders was twofold. *First,* they were exhorted to give diligence to their own lives: **Take heed unto yourselves** (v. 28a). *Second,* they were admonished to give diligent care to the church: **to all the flock** (v. 28). This was their divine appointment made by the Holy Spirit.

Christ has purchased the church at the expense of His lifeblood (cf. I Pet. 1:18, 19; Eph. 5:25-27; Rev. 5:9). It is the responsibility of the ministry to sustain, edify, and **feed** Christ's treasured possession, **the church** (cf. John 10:12, 13; 21:15-17).

Verses 29 and 30 clearly indicate Paul's fear of the activities of the ubiquitous Judaizers, whose subtle and damaging work is so clearly and forcefully depicted in the Galatian letter. That this prophecy came true in a measure appears evident from Paul's letter to Timothy while the latter pastored the Ephesian church (see I Tim. 4:1-6; II Tim. 3:1-13); but that the Ephesian elders maintained doctrinal correctness in the church, though having left their "first love," is equally evident from Rev. 2:2.

Paul's benediction in verse 32 accords with the purpose of his ministry as set forth in Acts 26:18. Indeed Paul uses a very similar expression in II Thess. 2:13. Salvation is an inheritance which comes only to those who appropriate the sanctifying blood of the redeeming Christ.

In his personal vindication, Paul *first* declared himself innocent of covetousness (a charge so often brought against him by his enemies). *Second,* he reminded them that he not only was self-supporting by his craft while he labored at Ephesus, but that he also supported

206 Clarke, *op. cit.,* p. 854.

the members of his party (v. 34). *Third,* he reminded them of his personal example, which they should follow, in sympathetic service and Christian generosity (v. 35).

3. The Farewell at Miletus (20:36-38)

36 And when he had thus spoken, he kneeled down and prayed with them all. 37 And they all wept sore, and fell on Paul's neck and kissed him, 38 sorrowing most of all for the word which he had spoken, that they should behold his face no more. And they brought him on his way unto the ship.

Three factors characterize Paul's leave-taking of the Ephesian elders: namely, *first,* his departing prayer **with them all** (v. 36); *second,* their sorrowful reaction, especially at the prospect of not seeing Paul again (vv. 37, 38a); and *third,* their conveyance of the Apostle to his ship (v. 38b). The first manifests Paul's concern and care over the church of Christ (cf. Eph. 3:14-21); the second reveals the Ephesian elders' personal love and regard for the Apostle; and the third reflects their solicitude for Paul.

H. THE APOSTLE'S RETURN TO JUDAEA (21:1-14)

Paul's parting from the Ephesian elders reminds the reader of the tender relationship between Jonathan and David, of whom it is said, "the soul of Jonathan was 'knit' with the soul of David" (cf. I Sam. 18:1 and Col. 2:2, 19).

At the ship to which these elders escorted Paul (in the rendering of Bruce) "we tore ourselves away from them."[207] Wesley remarks concerning the parting: "Not without doing violence to both ourselves and them."[208] Paul's farewell parting from his friends at the various locations, as he closes his third missionary journey, is tender and touching in the extreme. Nowhere is the humanity of the great Apostle more evident than on these occasions (cf. Phil. 4:1).

Certainly Paul must have faced the last lap of his third missionary journey with mixed emotions — sorrow in leaving behind his many converts and friends, eager anticipation of the accomplishment of Christian love and unity between the Gentile-Jewish Christian elements, and

thrusts of sharp, apprehensive fear at the threat of Jewish hostility to his plan and person at Jerusalem. But a sense of Christian duty impelled him to accomplish his mission.

1. The Voyage from Miletus to Tyre (21:1-6)

1 And when it came to pass that we were parted from them and had set sail, we came with a straight course unto Cos, and the next day unto Rhodes, and from thence unto Patara: 2 and having found a ship crossing over unto Phoenicia, we went aboard, and set sail. 3 And when we had come in sight of Cyprus, leaving it on the left hand, we sailed unto Syria, and landed at Tyre; for there the ship was to unlade her burden. 4 And having found the disciples, we tarried there seven days: and these said to Paul through the Spirit, that he should not set foot in Jerusalem. 5 And when it came to pass that we had accomplished the days, we departed and went on our journey; and they all, with wives and children, brought us on our way till we were out of the city: and kneeling down on the beach, we prayed, and bade each other farewell; 6 and we went on board the ship, but they returned home again.

A day's voyage brought Paul's party to the island of Cos, one of the Dodecanese, which lay at the entrance to the Ceramian Gulf, where they may have anchored at the city of Cos on the east end of the island. Luke's expression, **we came with a straight course** (v. 1), probably suggests that they had both the wind and the tide in their favor. Kraeling[209] observes that this island was famous for its production of silk, ointments, wine, and wheat, as well as for its luxurious country life. It was further noted as the home of Hippocrates, the father of medical science, whose "oath" every medical graduate in the western world is required to take. Aesculapius, the god of healing, was the chief deity of Cos. Juno was also an important goddess here. Apelles, the celebrated painter, is reported to have been born at Cos.

From Cos they sailed a day's voyage to the city of Rhodes (v. 1b) on the island of the same name. This island was about 20 by 43 miles in size. The city, which was founded in 408 B.C., was situated on

---

[207] Bruce, *op. cit.,* p. 420.   [208] Wesley, *op. cit.,* p. 480, n. 1.   [209] Kraeling, *op. cit.,* p. 452.

the northern tip of the island. The Colossus of Rhodes was one of the "seven wonders of the ancient world." It was a bronze statue of the sun god Apollo which towered 150 feet above the harbor at the entrance to which it stood. It had been erected in 280 B.C. in commemoration of the successful repulsion of an enemy siege, and it stood for 56 years. Clarke remarks that "ships in full sail could pass between its legs. It was the work of Chares, a pupil of Lysippus, who spent 12 years in making it."[210] It was finally destroyed by an earthquake in 224 B.C. Its fragments remained undisturbed until A.D. 656. Kraeling observes that "Strabo, the Greek geographer, calls Rhodes the most splendid city known to him with respect to harbors, streets, walls, and other equipment."[211] This ancient geographer makes further note of its "excellent government" and the "social-mindedness" of its inhabitants toward the unemployed and poor. Rhodes was formerly mistress of Caria and Lycia on the mainland but eventually came under the power of Rome, whose favor it enjoyed as a free city in Paul's day where it remained an important trade city.

From Rhodes Paul's party sailed to Patara on the southwest coast of Lycia and possibly to Myra further east on the coast of Lycia (cf. Acts 27:5). Patara was located on the mouth of the Xanthus River and constituted the chief port of several nearby islands, being itself an important coastal trade center. However, Myra appears to have been more important in this respect, and it may have been here, rather than at Patara, that Paul's party transshipped to Phoenicia.

The ship boarded by Paul's party was likely a large merchant vessel, as it took to open sea rather than following the coast line, as a coastal vessel would have done. This voyage to Tyre covered about 350 miles and likely occupied about five days. En route to Syria their vessel left Cyprus on the left, or "port side," as they struck a direct course from Lycia to Tyre, where its cargo was destined (v. 3b). Doubtless Paul had revived memories of early missionary experiences at Paphos as their ship sailed within sight of Cyprus (v. 3).

This was unlikely Paul's first visit to Tyre, as he had doubtless called here during his earlier travels between Palestine and Syria or Cilicia. Tyre had formerly been an island city but was joined to the mainland by Alexander the Great, while it was under siege by this monarch. By ocean accretion, it eventually became an isthmus. Kraeling remarks:

> Here thirty thousand women, children, and slaves were taken and sold into slavery by Alexander; nearly one-third as many men were killed in the defense of the city or executed. The woe of an Ezekiel over Tyre (Ezek. 27-28) was thus completely fulfilled, though later than the prophet expected.[212]

Tyre was annexed by Rome in 65 B.C. and made a free city. The Lord's prediction (Matt. 11:21, 22) suggests something of both the importance and wickedness of this city. It was the accommodative applause of the inhabitants of Tyre to Herod's oration that occasioned that ruler's untimely and horrible death (Acts 12:21-23). Dummelow states that Tyre was,

> the greatest maritime city of the ancient world, claiming to have been founded as early as 2750 B.C. It produced glass and purple dye, but its chief wealth came from the fact that it almost monopolized the carrying-trade of the world. The Tyrian mariners were so skilled in astronomy and constructed such accurate charts, that they sailed by night as well as by day, and made long voyages out of sight of land. They are known to have circumnavigated Africa — an extraordinary feat for the small ships of the ancients.[213]

The present city is known as Tyr or Sour (Fr.), Es Sur (Arab), or Zor (Heb.). It has some 7,500 people and is located in southern Lebanon.

At Tyre Paul found a Christian church which had been begun by disciples of the Hellenist dispersion, following the martyrdom of Stephen (Acts 11:19). With these disciples Paul and his party spent a week, probably while they waited for the ship to unload and reload cargo (v. 3b). Among these disciples were those who appear to have had the spirit of prophecy, in the sense of "foretelling" events. It is, however, quite possible that

[210] Clarke, op. cit., I, 857.   [211] Kraeling, loc. cit.   [212] Ibid.   [213] Dummelow, op. cit., p. 847.

they spoke in part from actual knowledge of Jewish hostility to Paul and of a plot to kill him, made earlier at Corinth (Acts 20:3), which plot may have been relayed by Jews who had passed through Tyre en route to the Passover in Jerusalem (cf. Acts 23:12-16). In any event, they warned Paul against going on to Jerusalem at this time (v. 4; cf. Acts 20:23). We are not to suppose that Paul openly disobeyed God in the continuance of his journey to Rome following these warnings. Rather we would agree with Clarke's conclusion:

> Through the Spirit, must either refer to their own great earnestness to dissuade him from taking a journey which they plainly saw would be injurious to him . . . ; or, if it refers to the Holy Spirit, it must mean that if he regarded his personal safety he must not, at this time, go up to Jerusalem.214

Indeed the Spirit foretold that Paul would meet persecutions, but it would not appear that he was forbidden of God to go to Jerusalem. Paul was willing to take whatever personal risk was necessary to glorify God in the extension of His cause. The purport of the warning seems to be that if Paul went to Jerusalem, the Jews would persecute and imprison him, and possibly he would be killed. Thus he could go and face the personal consequence for God's glory, or he might desist without losing God's favor. Thus Paul was left to the free exercise of his own personal judgment and conscience, as he was neither commanded of God to go nor to stay. God is always fair in aiding His servants to foresee the consequences of their decisions and actions. Bruce views this incident likewise.

> We should not conclude that his determination to go on was disobedience to the guidance of the Spirit of God; this determination of his was the fruit of an inward spiritual constraint which would not be gainsaid.215

In his purpose to fulfill his Jerusalem mission, Paul here again parallels his Master (cf. Luke 9:51).

As at Miletus, the Christian disciples at Tyre, including the women and children, showed their love and respect for Paul by accompanying him to the sandy seashore outside the city where he was to embark for Caesarea. There, unashamed, they knelt together, most likely in the presence of the mariners and other passengers, and offered their prayers to God, possibly concluding with a Christian hymn of praise. The God who fills heaven and earth with His presence can as well be worshipped under the canopy of the open heavens as in the great stone temples (cf. John 4:21-24; Acts 16:13). Open-air services are not without a New Testament precedent. After tender Christian farewells the party boarded the ship, while the Tyrian disciples returned home, thankful to God for the encouragement and enrichment of their lives by the visit and ministry of the missionary party.

2. The Voyage from Tyre to Caesarea (21:7-14)

7 And when we had finished the voyage from Tyre, we arrived at Ptolemais; and we saluted the brethren, and abode with them one day. 8 And on the morrow we departed, and came unto Caesarea: and entering into the house of Philip the evangelist, who was one of the seven, we abode with him. 9 Now this man had four virgin daughters, who prophesied. 10 And as we tarried there some days, there came down from Judaea a certain prophet, named Agabus. 11 And coming to us, and taking Paul's girdle, he bound his own feet and hands, and said, Thus saith the Holy Spirit, So shall the Jews at Jerusalem bind the man that owneth this girdle, and shall deliver him into the hands of the Gentiles. 12 And when we heard these things, both we and they of that place besought him not to go up to Jerusalem. 13 Then Paul answered, What do ye, weeping and breaking my heart? for I am ready not to be bound only, but also to die at Jerusalem for the name of the Lord Jesus. 14 And when he would not be persuaded, we ceased, saying, The will of the Lord be done.

The first day's sailing from Tyre brought the ship to Ptolemais, a distance of some twenty miles, which was the most southerly of the Phoenician ports. This city was successor to the Old Testament Acco or Accho (Judg. 1:31) and was of considerable importance. In modern times it is known as Acre or Akka (Fr. Saint'-Jean'-d'Acre) and has a popu-

---

214 Clarke, op. cit., I, 857, 858 (cf. I Sam. 23:9-13).
215 Bruce, op. cit., p. 421 (cf. Acts 19:21; 20:22).

lation of 10,695 (1944 est.). It is now largely superseded by Haifa, just across the bay into which the river Belus empties. Here, as at Tyre, they found Christian believers with whom the party spent a day (v. 7b), doubtless ministering to their spiritual welfare while the Christians ministered to the material comfort of the party.

It is interesting, if not important, that while Luke designates the Christian believers at Tyre "disciples" (v. 4a), here at Ptolemais he calls them "brethren" (see **Additional Note X,** "Early Names of Christ's Followers").

The following day they departed for Caesarea, a distance of some forty miles, which probably occupied about two days' travel time. Thus the long voyage "that may have begun about April 15 . . . finally terminated about May 14, two weeks before the Pentecost festival that Paul wanted to spend at Jerusalem."[216]

The fact of this extra time, **some days** (v. 10), before Pentecost may account for Paul's lack of haste to reach Jerusalem. (For a description of the city of Caesarea, see opening explanatory paragraph under Acts 10.)

Quite naturally Paul's missionary party lodged, during their stay in Caesarea, in the home of Philip the Evangelist (not Philip the Apostle), **who was one of the seven** (v. 8). Later tradition seems to have tended to confuse **Philip the Evangelist** and "Philip the Apostle," as also "John the Apostle" and "John the Elder."

> Evangelists were itinerant officers, whose duty it was to break new ground and establish new churches. They ranked below the prophets and above the presbyters or pastors. . . . The N. T. never uses 'evangelist' in the same sense of the writer of a Gospel.[217]

Philip has not been mentioned by Luke since his arrival in Caesarea following the conversion of the Ethiopian nobleman (Acts 8:40). From a member of the "seven lay deacons" chosen by the church to look after the temporal affairs of the Grecian widows (Acts 6:1-6), Philip had risen to the position of an effective evangelist, witnessed the conversion of the Samaritans *en masse* (Acts 8:5-8), be-

came God's instrument for the conversion of the Ethiopian treasurer (Acts 8:26-39), and evangelized all the coastal cities between Gaza and Caesarea (Acts 8:40). Doubtless Philip had witnessed Paul's (then Saul) part in the martyrdom of his fellow Christian deacon, Stephen (Acts 7:58; 8:1) and had followed with enthusiastic interest and joy Paul's conversion and subsequent Gentile ministry.

Conybeare and Howson observe that Paul's conversion on the Damascus road likely occurred at about the same time that Philip witnessed the Ethiopian nobleman's conversion on the Gaza road. Further, these authorities remark concerning Caesarea,

> Thenceforth it became his [Philip's] residence if his life was stationary, or it was the centre from which he made other missionary circuits through Judaea. . . . The term "evangelist" seems to have been almost synonymous with our word "Missionary." It is applied to Philip and to Timothy.[218]

The introduction of Philip's **four virgin daughters, who prophesied** (v. 9) is most interesting. This notation indicates: *first,* Philip's godly parental influence in turning their lives into the service of the Lord; and *second,* the place of importance to which women were already attaining within the ministry of the church (cf. Acts 18:26; Phil. 4:3). It might also be questioned whether Paul's advice concerning celibacy and marriage (see I Cor. 7) may not have reached their ears and influenced their lives in this respect. As prophetesses, Philip's daughters were not without precedent. Miriam (Ex. 15:20), Deborah (Judg. 4:4), Noadiah (Neh. 6:14), Huldah (II Kings 22:14), and the wife of Isaiah (Isa. 8:3) are designated prophetesses in the Old Testament. Indeed Joel's prophecy clearly states that one characteristic of the Pentecostal influence was to be that "your daughters shall prophesy" (Acts 2:17, 18). On the other hand, Clarke simply remarks:

> Probably these were no more than *teachers* in the church: for we have already seen that this is a frequent meaning of the word *prophesy;* and thus is undoubtedly one thing intended by the word prophecy by Joel. . . . If Philip's

---

216 Kraeling, *op. cit.,* p. 453.   217 Dummelow, *loc. cit.*
218 W. J. Conybeare and J. S. Howson, *The Life and Epistles of St. Paul,* p. 615, n. 2.

daughters might be *prophetesses* why not teachers?[219]

It appears that Philip and his daughters (his wife is not mentioned) with other Judaean Christians later settled in the province of Asia. Some or all of the daughters lived to a good old age and became esteemed as historical informants on early Judaean Christianity. In fact, several scholars of note think that much of Luke's information for Acts may have been supplied by this family during these few days and later during Paul's two-year imprisonment at Caesarea (Acts 24-27). Is it too fanciful to conjecture that Luke may have resided in Philip's home for two years while Paul was a prisoner at Caesarea? One authority suggests: "It is not improbable that these inspired women gave St. Paul some intimation of the sorrows which were hanging over him." And this authority continues, "Perhaps the force of 'who did prophesy' (v. 9) is to be found in the fact that they did foretell what was to come."[220]

The prophet Agabus (v. 10), who came down to Caesarea from Judaea, was likely the prophet of the same name earlier met at Antioch of Syria (Acts 11:28), whose first prophecy is declared to have been fulfilled in the days of Claudius, A.D. 46. Agabus was evidently a true prophet in the sense of "foretelling," rather than a preacher or "forthteller" of God's message. The object lesson which he employed to make more vivid and impressive his prophetic warning to Paul was no uncommon practice among the Jews of the Old Testament (cf. I Kings 11:29f.; 22:11; Isa. 20:2; Jer. 13:4; 27: 2, 3; Ezek. 4:1-12). This prophecy was literally fulfilled (Acts 21:27f.).

Agabus indeed claims divine inspiration for his prophetic warning to Paul, **Thus saith the Holy Spirit** (v. 11), but unlike the Tyrian Christians (v. 4), he does not interpret this warning as a divine prohibition against Paul's intended visit to Jerusalem. A parallel with Christ's own prediction of Himself is found in Mark 10:33. The statement, **shall deliver him into the hands of Gentiles** (v. 11b), indicates the restrictions placed upon the Jews by the Romans in the handling of criminal cases in Judaea (see notes on Acts 7:57, 58). However, this statement also indicates that Agabus placed full responsibility upon the Jews for Paul's arrest (cf. Acts 2:23).

Out of personal love and solicitation, both Paul's party and the Christians at Caesarea earnestly besought Paul to give up his purpose to visit Jerusalem (v. 12). However, Paul rebuked them for the demoralizing influence which their entreaties were having upon him (v. 13a) and reasserted his purpose to complete his mission, even at the expense of his life **for the name of the Lord Jesus** (v. 13b), if need required. Thus Paul reflects the "early Christian martyr spirit," for Christ's sake. Indeed, from Christ's first message to him through Ananias at his conversion experience in Damascus (Acts 9:16), Paul had accepted suffering for Jesus' sake as a part of his heritage. As previously noted, Paul's resolution to visit Jerusalem at this time involved "the collection," with its hoped-for benefits (see comment on Acts 20:4, 5). Finally Paul's friends acquiesced, yielding human sentiments to the wisdom and will of God (v. 14). How often has human sentiment and solicitation, growing out of personal friendships or relationships, served to deter God's servants from His higher will. Bruce regards the Christians' words, **The will of the Lord be done** (v. 14b), as a prayer which may contain an "echo of the Lord's own prayer in Gethsemane [Luke 22:42]."[221]

XIX. THE APOSTLE'S LAST VISIT TO JUDAEA (Acts 21:15-23:35)

A. PAUL CONFERS WITH THE JERUSALEM ELDERS (21:15-25)

1. The Journey from Caesarea to Jerusalem (21:15-17a)

15 And after these days we took up our baggage and went up to Jerusalem. 16 And there went with us also *certain* of the disciples from Caesarea, bringing *with them* one Mnason of Cyprus, an early disciple, with whom we should lodge. 17 And when we were come to Jerusalem,

In due time the party packed their baggage (v. 15)[222] and proceeded to Jeru-

[219] Clarke, *op. cit.*, I, 858.　[220] Conybeare and Howson, *loc. cit.*　[221] Bruce, *op. cit.*, p. 426.
[222] Ramsay takes this expression to mean that they "equipped horses for the journey." If this is correct then it is the first of two instances in Acts where beasts are mentioned in conjunction with Paul's travels. The second was when the Roman cavalry placed Paul on a beast and spirited him away to Caesarea (Acts 23:24). W. M. Ramsay, *The Cities of St. Paul*, p. 301.

salem. They were accompanied by certain Caesarean disciples. It would be of interest to know whether Philip was in the party. In any event, it appears that **Mnason of Cyprus**, here designated an early disciple (v. 16), was to be their host. Mnason may have been a convert at Pentecost, or even of the Lord Himself. He "may have been one of those Cyprian Jews who first made the gospel known to the Greeks at Antioch."[223] He was likely a Hellenist, thus accounting for his more liberal outlook in entertaining Paul's missionary party. Mnason either may have been at Caesarea on business when contacted by Paul's party, or he may have been sent for from Jerusalem by Philip to meet Paul at Caesarea. However, Dummelow[224] holds that Mnason's house was probably nearly halfway between Caesarea and Jerusalem and that they lodged with him the first night of the sixty-mile journey. With this position Kraeling agrees (as also Ramsay),[225] supposing that Mnason's town may have been Antipatris, from which they proceeded "to Jerusalem via the Beth-horon Road"[226] (cf. Acts 23:31-33). However, Bruce[227] sees little merit in this latter view but adds that Luke likely gathered valuable data concerning the early days of Christianity from this early disciple, Mnason.

Luke records five definite visits of Paul to Jerusalem following his conversion at Damascus, of which this is the last. The *first* was on the occasion of Paul's introduction to the elders by Barnabas (Acts 9:26); the *second,* on the occasion of the delivery of the relief fund from Antioch during the famine (Acts 11:29, 30; 12:25); the *third* was on the occasion of the General Church Council (Acts 15:1, 2); the *fourth* was a brief visit at the close of his second missionary journey (Acts 18:22); while the *fifth* and last visit was at the close of his third missionary journey (Acts 21:15, 17). On all but the fourth he encountered stormy opposition from either the Jews or the Judaizers. On the occasion of his fifth visit the Jews, probably incited by the

Judaizers, bent every effort to destroy him and put an end to his work. Conybeare and Howson remark:

> we do find in *the Epistle written to the Romans* . . . a remarkable indication of discouragement, and almost despondency, when he asked the Christians at Rome to pray that, on his arrival in Jerusalem, he might be delivered from the Jews who hated him, and be well received by those Christians who disregarded his authority . . . Rom. XV, 31. We should remember that he had two causes of apprehension, — one arising from the Jews, who persecuted him everywhere; the other from the Judaizing Christians, who sought to depreciate his apostolic authority.[228]

The foregoing authorities further state:

> Now he had much new experience of the insidious progress of error and of the sinfulness even of the converted. Yet his trust in God did not depend on the faithfulness of man; and he went to Jerusalem calmly and resolutely, though doubtful of his reception among the Christian brethren, and not knowing what would happen on the morrow.[229]

2. The Reception by the Christian Elders (21:17b-20a).

17b the brethren received us gladly. 18 And the day following Paul went in with us unto James; and all the elders were present. 19 And when he had saluted them, he rehearsed one by one the things which God had wrought among the Gentiles through his ministry. 20 And they, when they heard it, glorified God;

In verse 18 is Luke's last identification with Paul, by the use of the plural pronoun, until Acts 27:1 (cf. Acts 16:17). Upon their arrival at Jerusalem, Paul's party was joyously received by the brethren (cf. Acts 28:15). This enthusiastic reception was probably accentuated by the presentation of the gift for the church from the Gentile Christians, though Luke does not mention this matter. Bruce[230] suggests that the Jerusalem church may have regarded these Gentile offerings as a parallel "to the annual

---

[223] Conybeare and Howson, *op. cit.*, p. 617.   [224] Dummelow, *loc. cit.*
[225] Ramsay, *loc. cit.*   [226] Kraeling, *loc. cit.*   [227] Bruce, *op. cit.*, pp. 426-427.
[228] Conybeare and Howson, *op. cit.*, p. 618.   [229] *Ibid.*, p. 619.
[230] Mould holds that "Every Jew, upon reaching the age of twenty, paid an annual tax of one-half shekel into the temple treasury," and he further states that the "gold shekel" was worth about $10.00 at this time, while the "silver shekel" was worth about $.62. Probably the former is to be understood as the temple tax. Mould, *op. cit.*, p. 276.

half shekel which proselytes to Judaism (like other Jews) paid into the temple treasury at Jerusalem.[231]

Whether Paul accompanied the party on its first meeting with the brethren at Jerusalem (v. 17), or whether James was absent from the first meeting seems uncertain. Possibly the latter was the case. In any event, a meeting of the entire party with **James; and all the elders** (v. 18) was arranged the next day. James was the brother of our Lord and the acknowledged head of the Jerusalem church. He was commonly known as James the Just." The importance of his role in the Jerusalem church was evident from the beginning (Acts 12:17; 15:13). It appears that all the other "pillar apostles" were gone from Jerusalem by this time. Perhaps they were either dead or engaged in mission work elsewhere, since none are mentioned by name. Bruce remarks:

> But James remained in Jerusalem, exercising wise and judicious leadership over the Nazarene community there, greatly respected not only by the members of that community but by the ordinary Jews of Jerusalem as well.[232]

It appears likely that the Jerusalem church was organizationally patterned after the Jewish temple. James may have had a body of seventy elders, corresponding to the Sanhedrin, to assist him in the administration of the Judaean church. Since "the collection" was for this church, it was fitting that this body of elders should have been present with James to receive it officially. Such an organization appears justified in the light of James's statement that there were **many thousands** (v. 20) of believers among the Jews, probably meaning Judaean believers, but possibly including believers from other parts also who were present for Pentecost.

As on the occasion of Paul's return from his first missionary journey (Acts 14:27) and his address before the Jerusalem Council (Acts 15:4), so now before the Jerusalem elders, he presented his cause in the form of a vivid rehearsal of the mighty works of God among the Gentiles through his ministry (v. 19b). From the assembly there arose a unanimous chorus, "Glory to God" (v.

20b). Thus by the presentation of the offering and the recounting of God's visitation to the Gentiles, Paul won the coveted approval and loyalty of the Jerusalem church. However, there is no record of expressed appreciation for the gift, unless verse 20 is to be so understood.

It is of interest to note here that this is the last mention of James in Acts. In fact, Josephus says that he was illegally tried and condemned to death by stoning at the hands of the Sanhedrin under the high priest Ananus, between the Judaean governorships of Festus, who died in A.D. 62, and Albinus, who succeeded Festus in the same year. This Ananus was of the Sadducean party, which was noted for its harshness and rigidity in judgment even above the Pharisees. James, with some other Christians, was arraigned before the Sanhedrin and accused of having broken the law, for which they were condemned and stoned to death (for permissions and prohibitions of the Jewish Sanhedrin under the Romans, see notes on Acts 4:5, 6; 7:57, 58; 12:1-4). That the whole affair was considered unjust and repellent to the Jewish populace, as well as to the Christians, is evinced by the fact that the Jews protested the action to Albinus, who deposed Ananus.[233]

3. The Advice of the Elders (21:20b-25)

20b and they said unto him, Thou seest, brother, how many thousands there are among the Jews of them that have believed; and they are all zealous for the law: 21 and they have been informed concerning thee, that thou teachest all the Jews who are among the Gentiles to forsake Moses, telling them not to circumcise their children, neither to walk after the customs. 22 What is it therefore? they will certainly hear that thou art come. 23 Do therefore this that we say to thee: We have four men that have a vow on them; 24 these take, and purify thyself with them, and be at charges for them, that they may shave their heads: and all shall know that there is no truth in the things whereof they have been informed concerning thee; but that thou thyself also walkest orderly, keeping the law. 25 But as touching the Gentiles that have believed, we wrote, giving judgment that they should

---

[231] Bruce, *op. cit.*, p. 429.   [232] *Ibid.*   [233] Josephus, *Antiquities*, XX, ix, 1.

keep themselves from things sacrificed to idols, and from blood, and from what is strangled, and from fornication.

The final victory of the legalistic Judaizing party in the Judaean church over the liberals appears evident from Acts 21:20. Though the Jerusalem Council had won liberty from the Jewish law for the Gentile Christians out in the empire (cf. Acts 15; 21:25), such Christian liberty was never accorded Gentile Christians in Judaea. The **many thousands** (v. 20) of Jewish believers in Judaea were all extremely **zealous for the law** of Moses (cf. Acts 15:5; Gal. 1:14). It appears very likely that the Hebrew letter was written to this very people to show them the superiority of Christ and His grace to Moses and the Law, with a view to saving them from the death-dealing influence of legalism to the Christian spirit and liberty. The final effect of this legalism in the church is evidenced by the fact that Palestinian Jewish Christianity never outlived the first century. Little wonder that Paul wrote to the Corinthian church, which had come under the influence of these Judaizers, "the letter killeth, but the spirit giveth life" (II Cor. 3:6b).

That the slanderous accusations brought against Paul contained in Acts 21:21 were clearly false is seen from Acts 16:1-4. But Dummelow remarks, "it had this amount of truth in it that St. Paul's principle that a man is saved by faith in Christ and not by the works of the law would naturally lead to the abandonment of the ceremonial law even by the Jews."[234] However, for expediency's sake, the elders advised Paul to reassure both the Jews and Jewish Christians by joining **four men that have a vow on them** (v. 23) in their purification rites. These men were evidently Nazarites (cf. Num. 6:1-21). Paul was advised to associate himself with them in the vow during the week that remained (v. 27) and to pay for their sacrifices. Thus by taking the Nazarite vow and defraying the sacrificial expenses of these men, Paul could reassure both Jews and Christians of his loyalty to Moses, as well as to Christ (cf. Acts 18:18 with notes). Further, such

an act on Paul's part would reflect an acceptable mark of charity toward those of his own race who were unable to pay the expenses of their sacrificial vows. Such appears to have been the intent of Herod Agrippa I, according to Josephus.[235] C. W. Emmet raises the question: "Was Paul's action, as Harnack suggests, a way of expending part of the contribution he had brought?"[236]

In verse 21 James appears only to reassure Paul of the position of the Jerusalem church concerning conditions for the admission of Gentile Christians to the church, as decided by the Jerusalem Council.[237] That these conditions had not changed for the Gentile Christians, James here makes clear.

Of verse 26 Dummelow offers the following free translation:

He entered into the Temple, informing the priests that within seven days (see v. 27) the days of their purification would be accomplished and he purposed to remain with them in the Temple for a whole week until the legal sacrifice had been offered for each of them.[238]

Windisch offers, with considerable reservation and misgiving but by concession, the following considerations of Paul's conduct at this juncture:

(1) It is not impossible that Paul, following the principle enunciated in I Cor. IX, 20 (cf. also X, 23, VIII, 1 ff.; Rom. XIV.), made a point of observing the ceremonial Law when he lived among the Jews and especially, when he was at a festival in Jerusalem. (2) Paul may have felt that circumstances, of which we are unaware, justified his concession to Jewish legal scruples on this occasion. (3) Luke may even have related the incident with the special purpose of showing how grievously the Jews had sinned against one so scrupulous to obey the Law as Paul.[239]

Withal it appears most satisfactory to view this incident in the light of the principles which Paul lays down for himself in the Corinthian letter: "I am become all things to all men, that I may by all means save some" (I Cor. 9:22b; see also vv. 19-23). Jackson and Lake remark:

[234] Dummelow, op. cit., pp. 847, 848.   [235] Josephus, Ant., XIX, vl, 1.
[236] F. J. Foakes-Jackson and Kirsopp Lake, The Beginnings of Christianity, Pt. 1, II, 294, n. 2.
[237] For a full discussion of this whole matter, see notes on Acts 15.1-34, but especially vv. 13-21.
[238] Dummelow, op. cit., p. 848.   [239] Jackson and Lake, op. cit., II, 231.

Hence Luke's object was not so much to show that Paul was a strict Jew, but that he was still so far in sympathy with Judaism as to be able to take his part in a religious rite which did not compromise his principles . . . . Paul's action does not necessarily imply that he himself had taken a vow, still less that he recognized the ceremonial law as a means of securing salvation.240

B. PAUL CONFRONTS JEWISH HOSTILITY (21:26-36)

It is impossible to state whether Paul was mistaken in accepting the advice of the elders. However, four facts emerge from his compliance with this advice. *First,* Paul's well-intentioned conduct did not accomplish the desired end (v. 27); *second,* there is no spiritual evidence that either the elders or other Jerusalem Christians supported Paul in his trials here, though a final conclusion cannot be based upon the absence of evidence (see exception in Acts 23:16-22); *third,* the motives of both the elders and Paul remain unquestioned in the light of all available evidence; and *fourth,* the eventuation of the whole affair brought Paul on his way to his desired goal, Rome. Thus if there were well-intended human mistakes, nevertheless God overruled them to the accomplishment of His purpose in the life and ministry of Paul, and thus Paul's philosophy of Romans 8:28 was vindicated. Further, who can say that God was not at this time affording the Judaean Jews their last opportunity for repentance and the acceptance of the Messiah before the sharp ax of Roman destruction should fall in A.D. 70.

Rackham has suggested the following parallels between Paul's and Christ's last days in Jerusalem:

The history of the Lord's passion seems to be repeating itself. Like the Lord Jesus, Paul is carried before the Sanhedrin and smitten on the mouth; the multitude of the people cry out, *Away with him;* his fellow countrymen deliver him into the hands of the Gentiles; he is accused before the Roman governor and stands before a Herod; his accusers are the same, the Sadducean highpriesthood, as also the counts of the indictment which culminate in the charge of treason against Caesar; three times he is

pronounced to have done nothing worthy of death, yet he narrowly escapes a scourging, and the governor leaves him bound in order to please the Jews [Lk. xxiii, 25]: incidentally the trial of Jesus resulted in the renewal of friendly relations between Pilate and Herod Antipas, so likewise Paul's case enables Festus to pay a compliment to Herod Agrippa II. Finally, the close of the book leaves the apostle in a state of comparative freedom and activity: like S. Peter in ch. xii, he has experienced a deliverance — almost, we might say, a resurrection from the dead. This resemblance is not due to arbitrary invention. It is the natural working out of a law which had been enunciated by the Lord himself: 'as the master so shall the servant be.' In the Revelation, in a symbolical picture (xi, 1-12), S. John has shown that the experience of the Lord's witnesses must be the same as that of the Lord, the Faithful Witness, himself. How much more certain this will become, when the servant is standing in the same position and on the same spot as the master. Granted the same situation, then the greater the inward likeness of the servant to his master, the greater will be the outward likeness of their experience.241

1. Paul Attacked by the Jewish Mob (21:26-31a)

26 Then Paul took the men, and the next day purifying himself with them went into the temple, declaring the fulfillment of the days of purification, until the offering was offered for every one of them.

27 And when the seven days were almost completed, the Jews from Asia, when they saw him in the temple, stirred up all the multitude and laid hands on him, 28 crying out, Men of Israel, help: This is the man that teacheth all men everywhere against the people, and the law, and this place; and moreover he brought Greeks also into the temple, and hath defiled this holy place. 29 For they had before seen with him in the city Trophimus the Ephesian, whom they supposed that Paul had brought into the temple. 30 And all the city was moved, and the people ran together; and they laid hold on Paul, and dragged him out of the temple: and straightway the doors were shut. 31 And as they were seeking to kill him,

Mention of the **Jews from Asia** (v. 27),

240 *Ibid.,* II, 294.
241 Richard B. Rackham, *The Acts of the Apostles,* "Westminster Commentary," p. 404.

who were responsible for the incitement of mob violence against Paul at Jerusalem, appears to give validity to the suggestion that Alexander had been used by these very Jews in an attempt to aggravate the similar riotous situation at Ephesus (see Acts 19:33). In fact, there are certain similarities between the Ephesian and Jerusalem riots; to wit, the multitudinous uproar (vv. 27, 28, 30), the attempted violence (vv. 30, 31), the rescue by the Roman officials (vv. 31-33), and the confused issue of the occasion (v. 34).[242]

The occasion of the Jerusalem riot against Paul appears to have been due to the presence of Trophimus in Jerusalem. When the Asian orthodox Jews saw Paul in the Temple (v. 27), they assumed that Trophimus, an Ephesian Gentile Christian whom they knew and who had before been seen with Paul in Jerusalem, was with him in the Temple (vv. 28b, 29). Had their assumption been correct, they would have had legal right to kill Trophimus, who was a Gentile,[243] though not Paul, who was both a Jew and a Roman citizen (see notes on Acts 7:57, 58).

The outer court of the Temple was designated the "Court of the Gentiles." Within this was the "Court of the Women." Between the two was a high wall with doors. An inscription on a stone found in Jerusalem in 1871 and now in the Museum of the Ancient Orient at Istanbul reads: "No foreigner may enter within the balustrade and enclosure around the sanctuary. Whoever is caught will render himself liable to the death penalty which will inevitably follow."[244] Speaking of this wall, Josephus quotes Titus the Roman general as saying to the Jews at the siege of Jerusalem, A.D. 70, "Have not you been allowed . . . to engrave in Greek, and in your own letters [Hebrew or Aramaic], this prohibition, that no foreigner should go beyond the wall? Have not we given you leave to kill such as go beyond it, though he were a Roman?"[245] However, there is not a shred of evidence that their assumption was correct. They were guilty of the logical fallacy of "false association." Paul most likely had in mind this temple barrier between Jewish and Gentile Christians

when he later wrote of Christ's removal of "the middle wall of partition" (Eph. 2:13-19).

The accusations shouted against Paul by the mob are reminiscent of similar accusations hurled against Stephen, who under like circumstances became the church's first illegal martyr. The charges consisted of teaching, *first*, **against the people,** or perhaps better, the customs of the Jewish people (cf. Acts 6:14); *second,* against **the law** (cf. Acts 6:13b); *third,* against the Temple, **this place** (cf. Acts 6:13b); and *fourth,* they charged that he **defiled this holy place,** which was equivalent to blasphemy (cf. Acts 6:11). This last accusation was later modified by Paul's enemies before the governor Felix, to the effect that "he assayed to profane the temple" (Acts 24:6; cf. Acts 21:29b). This marks the disposition to greater accuracy in legal procedure where the accuser is held responsible for his statements than when he is under the emotional excitement of irresponsible and unrestrained mob psychology.

Upon the violent eviction of Paul (cf. v. 32b) from the Temple, the guards hurriedly closed the doors between the "Court of the Jews" and the "Court of the Gentiles" (v. 30). This measure was likely in part to insure against any other Gentiles entering the inner court, and possibly also to prevent profanation of the Temple by the violence of the mob. Wesley thinks that this action was designed in part "to prevent Paul's taking sanctuary at the horns of the altar."[246] That the Jews' intention was to commit an illegal act of murder on Paul is clear (Acts 21:31a; cf. Acts 7:57-8:1a).

2. Paul Rescued by the Roman Army (21:31b-36)

31b tidings came up to the chief captain of the band, that all Jerusalem was in confusion. 32 And forthwith he took soldiers and centurions, and ran down upon them: and they, when they saw the chief captain and the soldiers, left off beating Paul. 33 Then the chief captain came near, and laid hold on him, and commanded him to be bound with two chains; and inquired who he was, and what he had done. 34 And some shouted one thing, some another, among the

---

[242] For comparison, see Acts 19:23-41. [243] So states Josephus, *War*, VI, ii, 4.
[244] Finegan, *op. cit.,* p. 246. [245] Josephus, *loc. cit.* [246] Wesley, *op. cit.,* p. 484, n. 30.

crowd: and when he could not know the certainty for the uproar, he commanded him to be brought into the castle. 35 And when he came upon the stairs, so it was that he was borne of the soldiers for the violence of the crowd; 36 for the multitude of the people followed after, crying out, Away with him.

News of the riot quickly reached Claudius Lysias, the chief captain or tribune of the "Italian Band" or "Cohort," which was quartered in the tower of Antonia. The location of this tower where troops were stationed, especially during Jewish feast occasions as a protection against riots, commanded a clear view of the "Court of the Gentiles."[247]

The statement that the captain **took soldiers and centurions** (v. 32) indicates that at least 200 militia were called out, since a centurion commanded 100 soldiers. Immediately upon the arrival of the soldiers, Paul's assailants ceased beating him (v. 32b). Both as a measure against the escape of a possible criminal and as a protection against further violence by the Jews, the captain arrested **Paul and bound** [him] **with two chains** (v. 33a). This likely means that Paul was handcuffed to a soldier on either side (cf. Acts 12:6, 7b). The captain neither knew who Paul was, nor what his offense had been (v. 33b). Nor was the mob of any help in clarifying the issue, since in their emotional confusion **some shouted one thing, some another** (v. 34). Duty demanded that he know the truth of the matter, as well as afford protection and justice to the accused. Therefore Lysias took Paul to the castle barracks (v. 34).

Under the violent impulse of a recurrent surge of uncontrolled emotion and hatred the mob bore in on the soldiers as they led Paul to the tower, like a great wave of the turbulent ocean that drives the vessel against the rocky cliff. Here, as on the occasion of Christ's last experience in Jerusalem, the frenzied mob of religious fanatics cried, **Away with him** or "slay him" (v. 36; cf. Luke 23:18; John 19:15).

C. PAUL PREPARES TO ADDRESS THE JEWS (21:37-40)

Paul had planned and labored long to bring the collection to the Jerusalem church. He did not propose to lose any opportunity to vindicate his cause, which apparently had so seriously aborted. Thus he requested permission to speak to the captain, evidently with the future purpose of gaining permission to address the Jews.

1. Paul's Mistaken Identity (21:37, 38)

37 And as Paul was about to be brought into the castle, he saith unto the chief captain, May I say something unto thee? And he said, Dost thou know Greek? 38 Art thou not then the Egyptian, who before these days stirred up to sedition and led out into the wilderness the four thousand men of the Assassins?

The captain's question, **Dost thou know Greek?** (v. 37b) appears to indicate that he was not familiar with the Latin and hoped to converse with Paul in Greek, with which he evidently was familiar. That Lysias was not a Roman appears further evident from Acts 22:28. It may be observed here that, as a Jew, Paul had a perfect right to be in the Temple worshiping, and that, as a citizen of Tarsus (a free Roman city), he might naturally claim to speak the Greek language.

Immediately upon learning that Paul spoke Greek, the captain jumped to the conclusion that he was the long-sought Egyptian leader of a band of Assassins that had harassed the Romans in Judaea (v. 38). Such bands of Assassins were common in Judaea at this time. They were known as "Sicarii" because they hid a knife, "sica," in their clothing, and then during religious festivals engaged in "patriotic assassinations."[248] They seem to have been members of the extremely patriotic party of the Zealots. They assassinated influential Jews who were friendly to the Roman rule, as well as Roman officials. They arose during the governorship of Felix (A.D. 52-60), or possibly earlier, and their activities were finally responsible for misleading Judaea into revolt and consequent destruction by the Romans in A.D. 70.[249]

According to Josephus,[250] an Egyptian had come to Jerusalem about three years earlier and set himself forth as a prophet,

---

[247] For a description of this Roman fortress see Josephus, *War*, V, v, 8.
[248] *Ibid.*, II, xiii, 3.   [249] Mould, *op. cit.*, p. 471.
[250] Josephus, *Ant.*, XX, viii, 6.

and likely as a purported patriotic deliverer of the Jews from the Romans. He acquired a sizable following,[251] as such "Messiahs" usually do, from among the disgruntled Jewish populace. He led his band to the Mount of Olives with the promise that the Jerusalem walls would fall at his command (cf. Josh. 6), and they would then easily defeat the Roman garrison and fall into command of the country. However, the governor Felix sent a contingent of soldiers against them with the result that many were killed, while others were taken prisoners. The leader himself escaped. Thus Lysias reasoned that the sullen resentment of the Jews had at last found expression in their manhandling of this insurrectionist by whom they had been misled and who had now appeared to attempt a second insurrection.

2. Paul's True Identity (21:39, 40)

39 But Paul said, I am a Jew, of Tarsus in Cilicia, a citizen of no mean city: and I beseech thee, give me leave to speak unto the people. 40 And when he had given him leave, Paul, standing on the stairs, beckoned with the hand unto the people; and when there was made a great silence, he spake unto them in the Hebrew language, saying,

Though Lysias seems not to have been unduly impressed with Paul's statement that he was **a Jew, of Tarsus in Cilicia, a citizen of no mean city** (v. 39), he nevertheless granted him permission to address the Jews who waited below in the outer court of the Temple. Ramsay states:

The view which we take is that the Jews of Tarsus were, as a body, citizens with full burgess rights. That does not, of course, exclude the possibility that there were some or even many resident stranger Jews in the city. The right of citizenship could only be got by inheritance from a citizen father, apart from exceptional cases in which it was bestowed by a formal law on an individual as a reward for services rendered to the city; but such cases were comparatively few in any one city, for the right was jealously guarded.[252]

According to his custom, Paul **beckoned with the hand unto the people** (v. 40) as a gesture for attention (cf. Acts 13:16) and then proceeded to address the Jews in the Hebrew, or possibly Aramaic, language which "was not only the vernacular of Palestinian Jews but was the common speech of all non-Greek speakers in western Asia, as far east as (and including) the Parthian empire beyond the Euphrates."[253] It is noteworthy that Paul's speech here reiterates the exact opening words of Stephen's defense, **Brethren and fathers**, before the Sanhedrin (cf. Acts 7:2). Nor is this the only instance in which Paul's speeches reflect the influence of Stephen's earlier address on his thought, manner, and life.

D. PAUL'S DEFENSE BEFORE THE JEWS (22:1-21)

From the steps of the castle Paul stretched forth his hand for attention and spoke forth in the Hebrew (Aramaic) dialect of Judaea, though he might have employed the Greek, addressing his assailants as **Brethren and fathers** (v. 1). Plumptre thinks this was the "received formula"[254] in addressing any assembly of which the scribes and elders were a part. Both the gesture for attention and the employment of his nation's language were designed to identify the speaker with his audience and secure respect and good will. That this purpose was in a measure achieved is evident from their increased interest and attention: **they were the more quiet** (v. 2b). Their surprise at hearing "the sound of their holy mother-tongue awed them into deeper silence,"[255] occurring as it did at the moment when they expected the renegade to address them in Greek. Lechler[256] observes that Paul's employment of the address **brethren** expressed his love for his own race, while his use of **fathers** conveyed his respect for the eminent rulers of the Jews, some of whom may have been in his audience. Bruce remarks that Paul's speech which follows is both "autobiographical and apologetic."[257]

---

[251] Josephus, *War*, II, xlll, 5.   [252] W. M. Ramsay, *The Cities of St. Paul*, p. 174.
[253] Bruce, *op. cit.*, p. 437.   [254] Ellicott, *op. cit.*, VII, 150.
[255] Jamieson, Faussett, and Brown, *Commentary, Critical and Explanatory on the Old and New Testaments*, II, 211.   [256] Lange, *op. cit.*, p. 398.   [257] Bruce, *op. cit.*, p. 440.

1. Paul's Jewish Heritage (22:1-5)

1 Brethren and fathers, hear ye the defence which I now make unto you.

2 And when they heard that he spake unto them in the Hebrew language, they were the more quiet: and he saith,

3 I am a Jew, born in Tarsus of Cilicia, but brought up in this city, at the feet of Gamaliel, instructed according to the strict manner of the law of our fathers, being zealous for God, even as ye all are this day: 4 and I persecuted this Way unto the death, binding and delivering into prisons both men and women. 5 As also the high priest doth bear me witness, and all the estate of the elders: from whom also I received letters unto the brethren, and journeyed to Damascus to bring them also that were there unto Jerusalem in bonds to be punished.

Paul's declaratory statement, **I am a Jew**, seems designed to answer two questions and allay suspicion accordingly. First, by this assertion Paul re-emphasized his answer to the captain's question, "Art thou not then the Egyptian?" (Acts 21: 38a); and second, he refuted the Jews' accusation that he was a renegade Jew. This fundamental statement is supported by the evidence that follows.

First, Paul reminded his hearers that his education had been in the cultural environment of their sacred, religious capital, Jerusalem (v. 3). This likely began soon after he became "a son of the Law" at twelve years of age (cf. Luke 2:42). Further, he implies that he had benefited from the personal instruction of the single greatest teacher Judaism had ever produced, Gamaliel (v. 3). Paul's expression, **at the feet of Gamaliel**, reflects the custom of the Jewish rabbinical school where the scholars sat on the floor with the rabbi on a high chair above them. Thus the expression "sitting at the feet" of a superior instructor persists. Like his Master, Paul had sat "in the midst of the teachers [doctors], both hearing them, and asking them questions" (Luke 2:46).

Paul makes clear that his education under this revered Gamaliel had been thorough and accurate, in accordance with the Jewish educational system (v. 3). In fact, there appears a subtle suggestion in his defense, to the effect that he had more nearly adhered to Gamaliel's teaching than had his countrymen. One authority points out that "Paul's version of what the rabbis commonly taught concerning the law shows little sign of the influence of Gamaliel, who laid much stress on the importance of repentance rather than on 'works.' "[258] The foregoing writer continues: "Indeed one feels that at times Paul's Christian doctrine is nearer to the mind of the great rabbi than is the type of rabbinical doctrine which he attacks."[259]

Second, in consequence of the foregoing exact and rigorous instruction, Paul compares his religious **zeal** to that of his hearers (v. 3b). Plumptre significantly remarks:

> The Apostle . . . claims their sympathy as having at one time shared all their dearest convictions. There is, perhaps, a touch of higher enthusiasm in the Apostle's language. He was a zealot for God: they were zealots for the law.[260]

As Lechler phrases it, "The Apostle . . . remarks: '*I* was once what *ye* are; ye are still today, indeed, at this very moment, what I too was at a former period.' "[261] In support of the assertion of his former role as a zealot, Paul describes his persecutions of the Christians by a tactfully guarded allusion: **this Way** (cf. Acts 9:2; 19:9, 23; 24:14, 22) **unto the death** (cf. Gal. 1:14; Phil. 3:5, 6). In this last statement Paul may well have been assuming responsibility for his part in the martyrdom of Stephen. In a subtle manner Paul appears to set in contrast **the Way** (cf. John 14:6) of eternal life which belongs to the Christian believer, with *the death* which can never extinguish that life in Christ (cf. John 11:25, 26). This fact he discovered for himself as the chief persecutor of the Christians. Paul's testimony here accords with Luke's earlier account (Acts 8:3; 9:2), that he completely disregarded the sanctity of the home, as well as sex differences, in his vicious onslaughts against the Christians.

Paul's statement, **binding and delivering into prisons** (v. 4), is more specific than Luke's earlier account of these activities (cf. Acts 9:2). The Millers state that the "prisons of the Near East were sordid"[262] in Bible times. Offenders were incarcerated in *natural* pits or cave-

[258] *The Interpreter's Bible*, IX, 290.　　[259] *Ibid*.　　[260] Ellicott, *op. cit.*, p. 151.
[261] Lange, *op. cit.*, p. 399.　　[262] Miller, *op. cit.*, p. 580.

like dungeons where life was eked out by the bread and water "of affliction" (cf. I Kings 22:27). Prisoners were sometimes cast into these pits where their feet were caught in snares (see Jer. 18:22; 48:43). Some were bound with chains (Isa. 61:1), and yet others had their feet fast in stocks (Acts 16:24). Even the dead bodies of the slain were sometimes concealed in these prison pits (Jer. 41:7; cf. 38:11-13, 28; 39:15-18). The punishments alluded to (v. 5b) would have included scourgings and brutal violence (cf. Acts 9:2; 26: 10, 11). The Acts' record gives numerous accounts of the imprisonment of Christians (Acts 4:3; 5:19; 12:1, 4ff.). Paul himself had various occasions to reflect on his treatment of the Christians before his conversion, as he subsequently suffered like fate (see II Cor. 11:23; Eph. 4:1; Acts 16:23ff.; Acts 21:33, 37; 23: 35; II Tim. 4:16). Characteristics of jailers and prisoners are depicted in various Bible accounts (see Acts 12:6ff.; 16:25, 27-34; Gen. 40). Something of Christ's tender compassion for prisoners (Matt. 25:36, 39, 43f.) seems to be indicated in Paul's reflection on his former maltreatment of Christ's followers (v. 4b).

In support of the truth of his zeal for the law and deadly hatred of Christians, Paul appeals to the testimony of the high priest Ananias, son of Nebaeus, who may have been present and who would have been apprised of the official acts of his predecessors. His further appeal for support to **all the estates of the elders** is doubtless an allusion to the Sanhedrin and Senate, if indeed the latter is to be distinguished from the former. The permanent records of this body would have revealed the official documents issued to Paul for the arrest, return, and punishment of Christians who had likely taken refuge in Damascus following the martyrdom of Stephen (vv. 4b, 5). All of this Paul did as a zealous Jew. **The brethren** (v. 5) were Jews with whom Paul subtly identified himself in his defense.

2. Paul's Encounter with Christ (22: 6-14)

6 And it came to pass, that, as I made my journey, and drew nigh unto Damascus, about noon, suddenly there shone from heaven a great light round about me. 7 And I fell unto the ground, and heard a voice saying unto me, Saul, Saul, why persecutest thou me? 8 And I answered, Who art thou, Lord? And he said unto me, I am Jesus of Nazareth, whom thou persecutest. 9 And they that were with me beheld indeed the light, but they heard not the voice of him that spoke to me. 10 And I said, What shall I do, Lord? And the Lord said unto me, Arise, and go into Damascus; and there it shall be told thee of all things which are appointed for thee to do. 11 And when I could not see for the glory of that light, being led by the hand of them that were with me I came into Damascus. 12 And one Ananias, a devout man according to the law, well reported of by all the Jews that dwelt there, 13 came unto me, and standing by me said unto me, Brother Saul, receive thy sight. And in that very hour I looked up on him. 14 And he said, The God of our fathers hath appointed thee to know his will, and to see the Righteous One, and to hear a voice from his mouth.

The three accounts of Paul's encounter with Christ on the Damascus road, as recorded by Luke, vary but little in their essential elements. The first, in Acts 9: 1-19, is recorded in the third person, while the other two accounts in Acts 22:5-21 and Acts 26:12-20, respectively, are recorded in the first person. (For a full treatment of this experience, see notes on Acts 9:1-19. Only such items of the experience as are recorded in Acts 22, but not in Acts 9, will be discussed here).

Paul's special note of the hour, **about noon** (v. 6), when his encounter with Christ occurred is not recorded in Acts 9, though a similar expression, **at midday** (26:13a) is employed in Acts 26. Plumptre says that this expression "may fairly be taken as characteristic of a personal recollection of the circumstances of the great event."[263] Nor is it to be supposed that so unusual an experience as Paul had with Christ at this time, with its transforming effects on his whole future, could ever be forgotten, either as to the place or time of its occurrence.

Concerning Paul's introduction of the appellation **Jesus of Nazareth** (v. 8), not found in Acts 9:5 or 26:15, Lechler observes that "it is very appropriately employed when Paul addresses an assemblage

[263] Ellicott, *op. cit.*, p. 151.

of unconverted Jews, to whom he mentions Jesus for the first time."[264]

Verse 9 is found only in this chapter. It seems to signify that while his companions in travel saw the light that blinded Paul they did not understand the meaning of the voice that spoke to him from heaven (cf. John 12:28, 29).

Verse 10 is found in neither of the other accounts of Paul's conversion. It appears clearly to imply that Paul recognized himself to be no longer master of his own fate, but now subject to the will of the divine. The Galilean had conquered, and Paul was ever after "a servant of Jesus Christ" (cf. Rom. 1:1).

Paul takes pains to mention that **Ananias** [was] **a devout man according to the law, well reported of by all the Jews that dwelt there** (v. 12). Thus he indicates that this man who is called a **disciple** (a Christian) in Acts 9:10 was also a pious and law-abiding Jew who was highly esteemed by all the Jews at Damascus. Yet it was he who visited Paul and prayed for his recovery (v. 13). This description was intended as a reconciliatory gesture toward the Jews whom Paul addressed. Such a person as Ananias would not have associated himself with Paul, had he been a renegade blasphemer. Further, this pious Ananias would have required evidence that Paul's conversion was of divine origin.

Three things are recorded of Ananias' message to Paul in this chapter, which are not in chapter 9. *First,* Paul is **to know his will.** It was Paul's final submission to Christ that brought to him a knowledge of God's will (cf. John 7:17). *Second,* Paul was appointed **to see the Righteous One** (cf. Isa. 6:1). *Third,* he was appointed to receive God's message from heaven for communication to **all men** (cf. vv. 14 and 15).

Paul's use of the name **Righteous One** (v. 14b) for Christ is both striking and instructive. Plumptre remarks:

The name does not appear to have been one of the received titles of the expected Messiah, but may have been suggested by Isa. XI, 4, 5. It seems to have been accepted by the Church of Jerusalem, and in I John ii, 1, and, perhaps, in Jas. V, 6 [also Acts 3:14] we find examples of

its application. The recent use of it by Pilate's wife (Matt. XXVII, 19) may have helped to give prominence to it. He who had been condemned as a malefactor was emphatically, above all the sons of men, the "righteous," the "Just One."[265]

It is plain at this juncture that Paul is vindicating his "apostleship" above question, against the persistent attacks of the Judaizing party. He claims to have been appointed by **the God of our Fathers**, the God of the Jews, to see Christ, **the Righteous One**, thus fulfilling the requirement of a Christian apostle (cf. I Cor. 15:8) and then to have been appointed a **witness for him unto all men** (v. 15).

Indeed Bruce holds,

That Paul actually saw the risen Lord outside Damascus in addition to hearing His voice is emphasized more implicitly in the Pauline letters than in Acts . . . . Paul himself makes it plain that to him the vision of Christ was the central and all-important feature of his conversion-experience.[266] (cf. I Cor. 9:1; 15:8).

3. Paul's Commission from Christ (22: 15, 16)

15 For thou shalt be a witness for him unto all men of what thou hast seen and heard. 16 And now why tarriest thou? arise, and be baptized, and wash away thy sins, calling on his name.

Luke is careful to record in all three accounts (9:15; 22:15; 26:16) Paul's commission to apostleship by Jesus Christ. The object of his commission in the first account is declared to be "the Gentiles and kings, and the children of Israel" (9:15). In the third account before Agrippa, it is simply stated, "to appoint thee a minister and a witness both of the things wherein thou hast seen me, and of the things wherein I will appear unto thee" (26:16b). However, in the present account Paul tactfully states before this mob-mad Jewish audience that Christ commissioned him to **be a witness for him unto "all men"** of **what thou hast seen and heard** (v. 15). Thus Paul avoids further irritation of his Jewish audience by not accentuating his mission to the Gentiles while at the same time he validates his universal mission to bear the good news of salvation to "all men." Bruce remarks:

> henceforth he was to tell forth with confidence what he had seen and heard, with all that implied — that Jesus of Nazareth, crucified by men, exalted by God, was Israel's Messiah, glorified Son of God, and the Saviour of mankind.[267]

The words **arise, and be baptized, and wash away thy sins, calling on his name** (v. 16), while not found in either Acts 9 or Acts 26, are of very special significance. They reflect the fact of compliance with Jesus' command (Matt. 28: 19), and that for Paul baptism was more than a formal or ceremonial act. Repentance and saving faith are clearly presupposed by the Apostle, which in turn produced the witness of certain forgiveness (cf. Eph. 5:14). Paul's clear concept of the relationship of "the washing of regeneration" to the "renewing of the Holy Spirit" (Titus 3:5) stemmed from his own vital experience in Christ. That this experience was in answer to his prayer to the **Righteous One** (v. 14) who had appeared to him on the way is evident from Ananias' instruction to call on His name (v. 16b). Thus Paul's experience in Christ as here recorded involved, *first,* the revelation of Christ to him (v. 8); *second,* Paul's response to that revelation, **arise;** *third,* baptism, **be baptized;** *fourth,* forgiveness, **wash away thy sins;** and *fifth,* prayer to Christ, **calling on his name.** Without pressing the order, it may be safely assumed that all genuine experience in Christ will embody these elements. (For a fuller treatment of Paul's experience in Christ, see notes on Acts 9:3-19.)

4. Paul's Premonition of Jewish Hostility (22:17-21)

17 And it came to pass, that, when I had returned to Jerusalem, and while I prayed in the temple, I fell into a trance, 18 and saw him saying unto me, Make haste, and get thee quickly out of Jerusalem; because they will not receive of thee testimony concerning me. 19 And I said, Lord, they themselves know that I imprisoned and beat in every synagogue them that believed on thee: 20 and when the blood of Stephen thy

witness was shed, I also was standing by, and consenting, and keeping the garments of them that slew him. 21 And he said unto me, Depart: for I will send thee forth far hence unto the Gentiles.

In an effort to reassure the Jews that his Damascus experience in Christ had not divorced him from his national and religious loyalty, Paul relates his subsequent return to Jerusalem and worship in the temple (v. 17b. Cf. Acts 9:26; Gal. 1:17-19). That this was Paul's first visit to Jerusalem following his conversion appears evident from the fact that he here received his commission to the Gentiles, which would seem quite out of place had he already engaged in that mission in Cilicia and Syria as he did between the first and second visits to Jerusalem.[268]

Paul's **trance** experienced **while** [he] **prayed in the temple** (v. 17) at Jerusalem may be identified with the one mentioned in II Cor. 12:1-4.[269] (For a fuller treatment of trances and visions, see notes on Peter's "trance" at Joppa, Acts 10:9-16.)

Paul's statement that he **saw him saying unto me** appears unusual. It may be intended to suggest the soundless communication of Christ's message to him. Christ's command to Paul to leave Jerusalem immediately implies that the Jews would reject Paul then for the same reasons that they were rejecting him now, namely because of his witness for Christ. Plumptre remarks concerning Paul's reply (v. 19):

> It was partly an extenuation of the unbelief of the people [Jews]. They were, as he had once been, sinning in ignorance, which was not invincible. Partly it expressed the hope that they too might listen when they saw him whom they had known as a vehement persecutor preaching the faith which he had once destroyed.[270]

Paul implies (v. 20) that in his ignorance and religious zeal, he had participated in Stephen's martyrdom even as they, in their fanatical but ignorant zeal, sought now to take his life. As Paul had sought then to stamp out Christianity by destroying the witness to it, so they sought to do likewise now.

---

[267] *Ibid.*   [268] With this position Lechler, Bruce, Maogregor, Plumptre, and others agree.
[269] Dummelow, *op. cit.,* p. 848. Dummelow thinks this identification unlikely for chronological reasons.
[270] Ellicott, *op. cit.,* p. 152.

Again, Paul reaffirms the divine origin of his apostleship to the Gentiles: **Depart: for I will send thee forth far hence unto the Gentiles** (v. 21). Plumptre sees in these words "the promise of a mission rather than the actual mission itself."[271] Thus understood the experience fits better into Paul's first visit to Jerusalem than his second. Nor do these words necessarily imply immediate entry upon that mission. Eventually there was to be a human acceptance and confirmation by the church of the inner divine conviction that impelled him to go **far hence unto the Gentiles** (see Acts 13:2, 3).

E. PAUL'S APPEAL TO HIS ROMAN CITIZENSHIP (22:22-30)

The multitude of Jews appears to have given Paul uninterrupted, though perhaps impatient, audience until **this word . . . I will send thee forth far hence unto the Gentiles** (vv. 22a, 21b). That God should turn from the Jews to the Gentiles with the offered hope of redemption was more than the fanatical mob could bear. As when Stephen reached a like juncture in his defense before the Sanhedrin (Acts 7:51-54), so now mob violence was unleashed in all its mad fury against Paul. Only the protective presence of the Roman garrison prevented Paul from suffering a like fate with Stephen at their hands.

1. The Jews Reject Paul (22:22, 23)

22 And they gave him audience unto this word; and they lifted up their voice, and said, Away with such a fellow from the earth: for it is not fit that he should live. 23 And as they cried out, and threw off their garments, and cast dust into the air,

That the Jews' intention was murder is clear from their own words (v. 22b). Without trial or legality, they would have slaked their mad thirst with the blood of this blasphemer. These words, **Away with such a fellow from the earth: for it is not fit that he should live,** are but the wild echo of similar demands of the same people against the Christ whom Paul now preached (cf. Luke 23:18; John 19:15).

The casting off of their garments (v.

23) is vividly reminiscent of the conduct of the Jews who illegally executed Stephen by stoning him to death (cf. Acts 7:58). Even their casting of **dust into the air** (v. 23b) may have represented ominous threats of stoning; though Plumptre[272] allows that the reference to the garments and casting of dust may only signify the custom of shaking the dust from the garments against one whom they rejected (cf. Matt. 10:14; Acts 18:6).

2. The Captain Examines Paul (22: 24, 25a)

24 the chief captain commanded him to be brought into the castle, bidding that he should be examined by scourging, that he might know for what cause they so shouted against him. 25 And when they had tied him up with the thongs, Paul said unto the centurion that stood by,

It would appear that Paul's defense in the Aramaic tongue had been imperfectly understood by the Roman captain. Consequently the resurgent uproar against Paul by the Jews confirmed his suspicion that they had a valid complaint against the accused. In order to elicit the truth of the offense from Paul's own lips, the captain planned to follow the customary Roman method of scourging (cf. Acts 16:20-23). Thus Paul was stripped to the waist and bound with leather thongs to the whipping post or column in the fortress in preparation for the torture at the hands of the Roman soldiers — all at the command of the captain and not the Jews. Bruce takes a slightly divergent view of the method of Paul's intended punishment. Instead of the "whipping post" he remarks "it is more likely that he was suspended some little distance above the ground."[273] Bruce depicts this mode of Roman punishment most vividly:

The scourge (Latin *flagellum*) was a fearful instrument of torture, consisting of leather thongs, weighted with rough pieces of metal or bone, and attached to a stout wooden handle. If a man did not actually die under the scourge (which frequently happened), he would certainly be crippled for life. Paul had been beaten with rods on three occasions (presumably at the hand of Roman lictors), and five times he had been sentenced to the disciplinary lash inflicted by Jewish

---

[271] *Ibid.*   [272] *Ibid.*, p. 153.   [273] Bruce, *op. cit.*, p. 445, n. 35.

authority, but neither of these penalties had the murderous quality of the *flagellum*.[274]

3. The Roman Law Protects Paul (22:25b-30)

25b Is it lawful for you to scourge a man that is a Roman, and uncondemned? 26 And when the centurion heard it, he went to the chief captain and told him, saying, What art thou about to do? for this man is a Roman. 27 And the chief captain came and said unto him, Tell me, art thou a Roman? And he said, Yea. 28 And the chief captain answered, With a great sum obtained I this citizenship. And Paul said, But I am *a Roman* born. 29 They then that were about to examine him straightway departed from him: and the chief captain also was afraid when he knew that he was a Roman, and because he had bound him. 30 But on the morrow, desiring to know the certainty wherefore he was accused of the Jews, he loosed him, and commanded the chief priests and all the council to come together, and brought Paul down and set him before them.

Paul's appeal to his rights as a Roman citizen through the centurion saved him the cruel ordeal of flogging, as also the captain a likely severe penalty for having commanded his punishment.

Bruce[275] holds that Roman citizens were exempt from this penalty, and that under the Empire it could be inflicted on a citizen after he had been legally convicted by the court. In any event it was not permissible against a citizen as a "third degree" measure, as the captain was about to employ it in the case of Paul.

Plumptre observes concerning the scourging of a Roman citizen:

> It was the heaviest of all the charges brought by Cicero against Verres, the Governor of Sicily, that he had broken this law: "*Facinus est vinciri civem Romanum seclus verberari.*" (Cic. in Verr. v. 57). The words *civis Romanus sum* acted almost like a charm in stopping the violence of provincial magistrates.[276]

Actually Paul had been in an almost identical position once before at Philippi, but there for reasons untold he did not avail himself of his citizenship rights and consequently was beaten and im-

prisoned, though due apologies were later made by the Roman officials (see Acts 16:36-39).

The captain's question concerning Paul's citizenship (v. 27) seems to imply that Paul did not present a figure that bespoke such a status. Well may this have been true after the violent treatment given him by the mob.

The captain's citizenship had been purchased at a great price (v. 28a), possibly during the reign of Claudius (A.D. 41-54) as he bore the name of Claudius Lysias. His last name Lysias, being Greek, indicates that he was of that race, though possessing Roman citizenship and holding a high Roman office.

Paul's reply indicates that his citizenship was by birth (v. 28b), and thus his father or grandfather may have gained the citizenship as a reward for some superior service to the Roman government in Asia Minor or by other means unknown to us. Citizenship carried with it certain commercial as well as personal advantages.

The discovery of Paul's citizenship status struck fear to the hearts of all who had placed hands on him, but especially so to the captain who had ordered him bound (v. 29).

The captain's decision to submit the prisoner to a "grand jury" investigation by the Jewish Sanhedrin the next day was made with a view to discovering, through the Jewish court, the information concerning Paul which he had intended to force from him by scourging the day before.

F. PAUL'S EXAMINATION BEFORE THE SANHEDRIN (23:1-11)

According to Acts 22:30, Lysias' failure to ascertain the real cause for the Jewish hostility against Paul prompted him to arrange a hearing before the Sanhedrin the following day. Whether this assembly was presided over by the high priest or the chief captain is not certain. In either event it was a special, rather than a regular, session of the council.

1. Paul Rebukes the High Priest (23:1-5)

1 And Paul, looking stedfastly on the council, said, Brethren, I have lived be-

---

[274] *Ibid.*   [275] *Ibid.*   [276] Ellicott, *op. cit.*, p. 109.

fore God in all good conscience until this day. 2 And the high priest Ananias commanded them that stood by him to smite him on the mouth. 3 Then said Paul unto him, God shall smite thee, thou whited wall: and sittest thou to judge me according to the law, and commandest me to be smitten contrary to the law? 4 And they that stood by said, Revilest thou God's high priest? 5 And Paul said, I knew not, brethren, that he was high priest: for it is written, Thou shalt not speak evil of a ruler of thy people.

Luke's statement, **And Paul, looking stedfastly on the council** (v. 1a), seems clearly designed to indicate that Paul closely scrutinized the personnel and attitude of this sullenly hostile body and then drew his conclusions accordingly. In Acts 6:15 the same expression is used of Stephen before this council. In Acts 7:55 it is used of Stephen as he gazed heavenward when the council unleashed its wrath against him. Again in Acts 14:9 it is used of the cripple at Lystra who was healed by Paul (cf. Acts 3:4; 13:9).

Paul's declaration that he had **lived before God in all good conscience until this day** (v. 1b) at once posed a problem for scholars and elicited a violent protest from the high priest (cf. Acts 24:16; Rom. 8:5; I Cor. 4:4; I Tim. 1:5; II Tim. 1:3). The very mention of a **good conscience** appears to make Paul self-contradictory. In his letter to Timothy he declared himself to be the chiefest of all sinners saved by the grace of God (I Tim. 1:15). However, here and elsewhere (cf. Acts 24:16; Rom. 2:15; 9:1; 13:5), Paul avows that he lived a perfectly conscientious life. Two things are essential to an understanding of Paul's utterance: namely, what he meant by conscience, and how he applied the term to his life in this instance.

Conscience may be best understood as the moral judging function of the mind or intelligence. It is not something added or separate from the unitary spiritual nature of personality, but it is rather the constitutional intelligence functioning in relation to moral matters. Indeed, conscience may be neglected, educated, perverted, or suppressed. But so may other constitutional functions of

human personality. Before any of these things may happen to conscience, its existence is essential. Rackham has well said,

> The conscience is a consciousness which bears testimony with, or to, our personality within; and the subject matter of the testimony is the moral value of actions, the testimony itself being a pronouncement whether they are right or wrong. A good conscience gives a good verdict, and this it can only do if the faculty of judgment is itself clear.[277]

Thus Paul's moral judgment, conditioned as it was by his Pharisaic training, had informed him that his treatment of the Christians was commensurate with the strict requirements of the law as he then understood it (cf. Acts 26:9-11). But Paul had not yet understood, at that time, that "the law is become our tutor to bring us to Christ, that we might be justified by faith" (Gal. 3:24). Williams' translation is graphic: "So the law has been our attendant to lead us to Christ, so that we might through faith obtain right standing with God."[278] The attendant was "usually a slave who cared for the Greek child on the way to and from the teacher."[279]

Paul's great fallacy before his conversion was the common fallacy of confused values. He ascribed intrinsic value to the law, whereas it possessed only extrinsic or instrumental value. He made the law "an end" rather than "a means" to the end, which was Christ. Thus to Paul the law was final, and consequently it was inevitable that it would destroy Christ and His teachings since He purported to supersede the law (Matt. 5:17, 18). Thus as a strict adherent to the law, Paul could rightfully say that he had **lived before God in all good conscience until this day.** He had been conscientious as a Jew, and after his spiritual enlightment he had been conscientious as a Christian. This Jewish conscientiousness was, however, attained by the conformity of his conduct with the requirements of the law. The unsuccessfully attempted reconciliation of his inner motives, desires, and aspirations with the higher ideals and requirements of the law was quite another matter. In this area Paul

[277] Rackham, *op. cit.*, pp. 432f.
[278] Williams, *op. cit.*, p. 418.   [279] *Ibid.*

made no such claims to conscientiousness before God, prior to his Christian conversion (see Rom. 7). His conscientiousness here referred to was in persecuting the Christians and not in attaining to the divine moral ideal.

Paul's argument in verse 1 implied that as he had been wrong before God in persecuting the Christians, so were the Jews now; but now enlightened he saw Christ as the end of the law, which they if enlightened would likewise see.

The high priest's reaction was immediate and violent in spirit and intent as he ordered Paul to be smitten on the mouth. How similar his reactions, when worsted in reason, to those of the synagogue who "were not able to withstand the wisdom and the Spirit by which [Stephen] spake" (Acts 6:10)! There is no better evidence of a defenseless cause than the loss of temper and the employment of violence against the victor.

This high priest, Ananias, was the son of Nedebaios. He had succeeded Joseph, son of Camithos, and he was the twentieth high priest in order from the accession of Herod the Great in 40 B.C. He had received his appointment in A.D. 47 or 48 from Herod of Chalcis (A.D. 41-48), a brother to Herod Agrippa I, and held it about a dozen years. Perhaps a more infamous individual never occupied the office. Ananias was a bold, insolent, violent-tempered member of the Sadducean party, noted for its stern and exacting judgment on others. Josephus[280] depicts his infamy. He made himself exceedingly wealthy on the ill-gotten gain of his office, forcibly took the tithes that belonged to the priests, thus leaving some to starve, sheltered a wicked brood of henchmen, and collaborated with the Sicarii, or Assassins of the country. He convened the Sanhedrin in the interim between the governorship of Festus and Albinus and condemned to death by stoning James, the brother of Jesus and pastor of the Jerusalem church, with other Christians, besides innumerable other wicked deeds, according to Josephus.[281] As a member of the Sadducean party he was hated by the extreme nationalistic parties of Judaea because of his pro-Roman sympathies and policy. Once, five years earlier, he had been ordered to

Rome to answer for his conduct on suspicion of involvement in a Judaeo-Samaritan incident of violence. However, he was vindicated and restored by the emperor. Eventually, during the war against Rome in A.D. 66, Ananias, with his brother Hezekiah, was slain by the insurrectionists in an aqueduct where they were hiding.[282]

It was to this Ananias that Paul administered his withering rebuke (v. 3). Paul's analogy, **thou whited wall**, was not without precedent (cf. Matt. 23:27; Luke 11:44). Some have thought they have seen an allusion to Ezekiel's "wall . . . daubed with untempered mortar" (Ezek. 13:10-16) in the words of Paul's rebuke.[283] Plumptre aptly remarks:

> The whole utterance must be regarded by St. Paul's own confession as the expression of a hasty indignation, recalled after a moment's reflection; but the words so spoken were actually a prophecy, fulfilled some years after, by the death of Ananias by the hands of the Sicarii.[284]

Paul knew his rights of defense both by Jewish and Roman law, and until proven guilty he should be considered innocent (cf. Deut. 19:15; John 7:51). Thus the command of Ananias — whether executed or not we are not told — made him a violator of Paul's rights. For this breach of law (cf. Rom. 2:1) and for flagrant hypocrisy, Paul rebuked the high priest. There was no more excuse for the first offense than for the second. In fact, the first may have issued from the second. Not infrequently insincerity and hypocrisy are products of censoriousness, unreasonable demands, and severe reprehensions of the legalists. It is a subtle psychological device in which the guilty party, consciously or unconsciously, projects his own perverted spirit or misdemeanor to some other person of his disfavor, with a view to diverting attention from himself to another. It has been suggested that Paul's allusion to the **whited wall** may have signified the precariousness of Ananias' position, like a tottering wall, as well as the veneer of whitewash over corruption and injustice in his life. Of how little worth are priestly garb and office to the production of moral character or its preservation from moral

[280] Josephus, *Ant.*, XX, ix, 1, 2.   [281] *Ibid.*   [282] Josephus, *War*, II, xvii, 9.
[283] *The Interpreter's Bible*, IX, 298.   [284] Ellicott, *op. cit.*, VII, 154.

corruption (cf. Matt. 7:15; John 10:12; Acts 20:29).

The rebuke of Paul by the bystanders (v. 4) closely parallels a similar incident in the experience of Jesus as He stood trial before Caiaphas (John 18: 19-22).

Paul's apology (v. 5) has been variously viewed by Bible interpreters. Possible reasons suggested for his reply, **I knew not, . . . that he was high priest** (v. 5), include the fact that Ananias had taken the office since Paul had last been associated with the Sanhedrin and thus he was unknown to Paul; that possibly another than Ananias (perchance Lysias) was presiding at this special session; that Paul did not know who had given the order to smite him; that Paul was ironically suggesting that such an order could not have been expected from the high priest; that Paul was afflicted with poor eyesight (cf. Acts 9:18); that he was looking in the opposite direction when the words were spoken and thus did not know who gave the order; and finally, that Paul made an honest mistake. Plumptre[285] favors the view that either Paul's defective eyesight or that Ananias was not presiding, accounts for his mistake. Rackham[286] takes the view that Paul had not sufficiently reflected that the words came from the high priest and that he should have been more deliberate and less vigorous in his reply. Whether Paul should or should not have spoken these words, they were in any event both penetratingly true and prophetically suggestive. Paul's respect for the ceremonial and ethical requirements of the law is reflected in his quotation of Exodus 22:28 (cf. Rom. 13:1-7). Even an apostle's apology should serve as an apt model for the Christian's spirit and deportment in similar circumstances. It has been suggested that Paul apologized to the office, if he did not to the man! As with Elijah, who "was a man of like passions with us" (James 5:17a), so Paul the Apostle was a fellow human being (cf. Acts 15:37-40).

2. Paul Divides the Council (23:6-9)

6 But when Paul perceived that the one part were Sadducees and the other

Pharisees, he cried out in the council, Brethren, I am a Pharisee, a son of Pharisees: touching the hope and resurrection of the dead I am called in question. 7 And when he had so said, there arose a dissension between the Pharisees and Sadducees; and the assembly was divided. 8 For the Sadducees say that there is no resurrection, neither angel, nor spirit; but the Pharisees confess both. 9 And there arose a great clamor: and some of the scribes of the Pharisees' part stood up, and strove, saying, We find no evil in this man: and what if a spirit hath spoken to him, or an angel?

Paul's strategy in dividing the council has been assailed by some as being unworthy of Christian ethics.[287] However, it seems that Christ's words in the parable of the unrighteous steward, "the sons of this world are for their own generation wiser than the sons of the light" (Luke 16:8b), have a bearing on Paul's conduct at this juncture. Having failed in his attempt at a straightforward, courteous defense before the council, the Apostle counters with a new surprise strategy. He took stock and concluded that the Sanhedrin consisted of a Sadducean majority with a strong, Pharisaic minority party. The situation seems to have changed from Christ's day, if Mould is correct when he states, "But a few members of the Sanhedrin were Sadducees in the time of Jesus."[288] This Sadducean majority in the Sanhedrin in Paul's time may have been due to the influence of Ananias, a Sadducee, as president. Again Mould states:

> The Sadducees, as descendants of the high priestly family, were originally a religious group, but they had long been mixed up in politics by virtue of their civil powers. Since they got and held their wealth and power by virtue of Roman support, their policy was to keep on good terms with Rome. Thus they were diametrically opposed to the Pharisees politically.[289]

Again Mould observes:

> The Pharisees, while not primarily a political party, became such virtually by force of necessity. As Jews loyal to their religious past, they were patriots. They disliked the rule of Rome but considered it a just punishment for the sins of the

---

[285] *Ibid.*   [286] Rackham, *op. cit.*, p. 433.
[287] F. W. Farrar, *The Life and Work of St. Paul*, pp. 327f.   [288] Mould, *op. cit.*, p. 468.
[289] *Ibid.*, p. 471.

nation. They believed that when the law should be perfectly kept the Messiah would come and Rome's sway would be miraculously brought to an end.[290]

The Pharisees were the largest and most influential group in Judaism at this time. They were anti-Hellenizing and neutralized the liberalizing influence of Greek and Roman culture on the Jewish religion. They held the model ideal of a life in full accord with God's will, which ideal accounted for their tendency to legalism. They were separatistic and held strictly to orthodox Judaism but became formalistic, narrow, censorious, self-righteous, and conceited. They stifled the spirit while rigorously demanding the letter of the law. Indeed, the party had its exceptions in such noble souls as Gamaliel (Acts 5:33-40) and Nicodemus (John 3:1-15). The Pharisees believed in a coming Messiah, the existence of spirits and angels, and they accepted the doctrine of the resurrection from the dead.

The Sadducees, on the other hand, though the smaller party, were in the main aristocratic and very influential. They favored Hellenization and courted Roman favor. They were worldly in their outlook, accepted only the Torah, rejected the oral law, and hated the doctrine of the resurrection and belief in angels and spirits. Plumptre states: "They were, in fact, carried along by one of the great waves of thought which were then passing over the ancient world and were Epicureans and Materialists without knowing it, just as the Pharisees were . . . the counterpart of the Stoics."[291]

Thus Paul's identification of himself with the Pharisaic party not only placed him in alignment with all that was best in the Judaism of his day, but it also sharply divided the council. Nor was Paul either amiss or dishonest in thus identifying himself, as the following evidence indicates. *First*, before his conversion he had been a conscientious member of the party (Acts 26:4, 5; cf. Phil. 3:4, 5). *Second*, there appears to have been no inconsistency between membership in the Pharisaic party as such and saving faith in, and loyalty to, Jesus Christ (Acts 15:5). *Third*, Paul regarded the Christian faith as the fulfillment

and fruition of all that was best in Judaism as conserved by the Pharisaic party (Phil. 3:3).

Thus Paul's citation of three things effectively achieved his purpose to divide the council. *First*, as previously indicated, he identified himself with the Pharisaic party, as against the Sadducees. *Second*, he implied that his preaching had accorded with the hope (v. 6b) of the nation, or the promise of the Messiah, which hope Paul held had been fulfilled in Christ (cf. Gal. 4:4). Such a hope the Pharisees held, and those among the party who had believed (Acts 15:5) recognized Christ as the Messiah. Bruce states that "it was not until A.D. 70 or thereby that steps were taken to exclude Jewish Christians from participation in the synagogue worship by the addition of a prayer — the *birkath ha-minim* — that 'the Nazarenes and the heretics might perish as in a moment and be blotted out of the book of life.' "[292] *Third*, Paul held with the Pharisees the doctrine of the resurrection, and for him Christ's resurrection was necessary to the fulfillment of this hope, as also for personal salvation (cf. I Cor. 15:12-26).

The resurgence of Jewish orthodoxy in the council greatly agitated the liberal materialistic party of the Sadducees, with the result that there arose a dissension so severe that the assembly was divided (v. 7). Josephus[293] once employed this ruse, though of questionable honesty, to escape the violence of a mob. Consequently certain Pharisaic scribes rose to Paul's defense, declaring, We find no evil in this man (v. 9. Cf. Matt. 27: 23, 24). Most of the scribes were Pharisees (cf. Mark 2:16; Luke 5:30), and their allowance that a spirit or angel might have spoken to Paul is reminiscent of Gamaliel's defense of the apostles when they were on trial before the Sanhedrin some twenty-five years earlier (Acts 5:34-39). It has been thought that the scribes' remark was an allusion either to Paul's conversion experience which he had related the previous day (Acts 22: 6-11), or to his vision in the Temple upon his first return to Jerusalem (Acts 22: 17-21).[294] In any event, in their position, as Plumptre remarks, "After twenty-five

---

[290] *Ibid.*   [291] Ellicott, *op. cit.*, p. 155.   [292] Bruce, *op. cit.*, p. 453, n. 14.
[293] Josephus, *Life*, p. 8.   [294] *The Interpreter's Bible*, IX, 300.

years they have not got further than the cautious policy of those who halt between two opinions."[295] How sad that they were unable to come clear over and repose their trust in Him whom they allowed had appeared unto Paul, for such may have been the import of their words, **what if a spirit hath spoken to him, or an angel?** (v. 9b).

3. Paul Rescued and Reassured (23:10, 11)

10 And when there arose a great dissension, the chief captain, fearing lest Paul should be torn in pieces by them, commanded the soldiers to go down and take him by force from among them, and bring him into the castle.
11 And the night following the Lord stood by him, and said, Be of good cheer: for as thou hast testified concerning me at Jerusalem, so must thou bear witness also at Rome.

The Sadducees, incited by an angry, wounded, and vindictive Ananias, threw the full weight of their strength against the Pharisaic defenders of orthodoxy, whose champion Paul had become. Between the contending parties, Paul was in grave danger of being physically dismembered (v. 10a). Sensing the gravity of the situation with a Roman citizen's life at stake for whom he was personally responsible, the captain forthwith ordered Paul's rescue by the soldiers. Thus Paul was forcibly extricated and returned to the safety of the fortress barracks. Plumptre thinks his prison may have been "the selfsame guard-room as that which had witnessed our Lord's sufferings at the hands of Pilate's soldiers."[296] Luke's words, **And the night following the Lord stood by him** (v. 11a), seem to imply four things. *First,* Paul felt the keen edge of discouragement in the apparent failure of his whole mission to Jerusalem on this last visit. There is no evidence that his long-planned and carefully executed mission with the offering to his nation had either been appreciated, or that it had accomplished its purpose. *Second,* his attempted personal witness for Christ had apparently miscarried. *Third,* Paul's own personal future stood in uncertainty and jeopardy. *Fourth,* in the darkest hour of Paul's apparent defeat and discour-

agement, **the Lord stood by him** to comfort and sustain. **Be of good cheer,** says the Lord to Paul, your testimony at Jerusalem has not been in vain as you have supposed. I have yet a greater witness for you to bear for me at Rome (cf. Rom. 1:13; 15:23). Paul must here have learned the lesson concerning temptation about which he wrote to the Corinthians (I Cor. 10:13). On more than one occasion when Paul stood "at wits' end," a special visitation from the Lord succored him, renewing his courage and strength. Such was his case under trial at Corinth (Acts 18:9, 10); such was to be his experience during the storm en route to Rome (Acts 27:23-25); or again when on trial for his life at Rome (II Tim. 4:16-18); and such was this Jerusalem experience. How faithful Christ ever is to His promise, "I am with you always, even unto the end of the world" (Matt. 28:20b), when His servants obey His command to "Go . . . , and make disciples of all the nations" (Matt. 28:19a)!

G. PAUL'S DELIVERANCE FROM THE JEWS' PLOT (23:12-35)

Again foiled and frustrated by the escape of the coveted victim from their net, some forty Jews in desperation committed themselves to a rash oath (v. 12).

1. The Plot to Kill Paul Designed (23:12-15)

12 And when it was day, the Jews banded together, and bound themselves under a curse, saying that they would neither eat nor drink till they had killed Paul. 13 And they were more than forty that made this conspiracy. 14 And they came to the chief priests and the elders, and said, We have bound ourselves under a great curse, to taste nothing until we have killed Paul. 15 Now therefore do ye with the council signify to the chief captain that he bring him down unto you, as though ye would judge of his case more exactly: and we, before he comes near, are ready to slay him.

The band of some forty Jews who took the oath neither to **eat nor drink till they had killed Paul** were most likely of the *Sicarii* or Assassins (cf. Acts 21:38), of which there were many in Judaea by this

[295] Ellicott, *loc. cit.*　　[296] *Ibid.*

time. They were likely of the extreme Zealot party (see Acts 1:13b), and it is more than likely that they were instigated to this plot by Ananias the high priest. Josephus[297] informs us that he (Ananias) regularly employed the *Sicarii* to execute his foul and murderous purposes during his high priesthood. Thus we may well imagine that Ananias was the "master mind" behind the plot. Nor was such a scheme without precedent in Palestine. Plumptre remarks:

> The casuistry of the more fanatical Jews led them to the conclusion that a blasphemer or apostate was an outlaw, and that, in the absence of any judicial condemnation, private persons might take on themselves the execution of the divine sentence.[298]

The technique of their plot seems to imply an intended ambush against Paul. It is an illuminating commentary on the fanatical and frenzied state of their minds that they did not consider the near impossibility of their undertaking and the almost certain heavy loss of life to themselves in an attempt to extricate Paul from the custody of the Roman soldiers en route to the council. In their oath they literally placed themselves under a curse or an *anathema* (cf. Rom. 9:3; I Cor. 16:22; Gal. 1:8, 9). Bruce suggests that it may have taken such a form as, "So may God do to us, and the more also, if we eat or drink until we have killed Paul."[299] Another authority remarks: "Fortunately the rabbis were able to devise means of release from such oaths; so the plot having failed, we need not assume that the plotters starved to death!"[300] When these Assassins presented their scheme to **the chief priests and the elders** of the Sadducean party, it is noteworthy that **the scribes,** who were mostly Pharisees and who championed Paul's cause in the council the day before, are not mentioned as having been consulted. It appears further that they were proposing to ask of Lysias an opportunity for a verdict against Paul and not simply an inquiry. Thus it would appear that they intended to do by subtle and ruthless violence what they could not hope to do by legal procedure because of their inability to secure a majority in the council.

2. The Plot to Kill Paul Foiled (23: 16-22)

16 But Paul's sister's son heard of their lying in wait, and he came and entered into the castle and told Paul. 17 And Paul called unto him one of the centurions, and said, Bring this young man unto the chief captain; for he hath something to tell him. 18 So he took him, and brought him to the chief captain, and saith, Paul the prisoner called me unto him, and asked me to bring this young man unto thee, who hath something to say to thee. 19 And the chief captain took him by the hand, and going aside asked him privately, What is it that thou hast to tell me? 20 And he said, The Jews have agreed to ask thee to bring down Paul tomorrow unto the council, as though thou wouldest inquire somewhat more exactly concerning him. 21 Do not thou therefore yield unto them: for there lie in wait for him of them more than forty men, who have bound themselves under a curse, neither to eat nor to drink till they have slain him: and now are they ready, looking for the promise from thee. 22 So the chief captain let the young man go, charging him, Tell no man that thou hast signified these things to me.

The appearance of Paul's nephew affords the only reference to Paul's family in the Acts (cf. Rom. 16:7, 11). It has been suggested that possibly Paul's sister had married into a high-priestly family and that Paul's nephew thus inadvertently stumbled onto the plot by having overheard it discussed by the *Sicarii,* after which he secretly reported it to Paul and thence to the chief captain. However, it is not known for certain whether his sister resided in Judaea or was there for the Pentecost feast, or possibly for the education of her son in the rabbinical school. Of course, if she were married into a priestly family, the hostility of that caste toward Paul might well account for his not lodging at her home. Nor is it known whether she and her family were Christians. We are on safe ground, however, when we note that this lad had a love and loyalty to his uncle that enabled him to handle

---

[297] Josephus, *Ant.,* XX, ix, 2.   [298] Ellicott, *op. cit.,* p. 156.   [299] Bruce, *op. cit.,* p. 457.
[300] *The Interpreter's Bible,* IX, 302.

privately and judiciously a secret that involved a matter of life and death for Paul. Further, we learn from the incident that Paul was accessible to his friends and acquaintances, even while in custody. This fact may account for Luke's rather full information on the happenings of these days, since he would have been at Jerusalem. Nor is it necessary to suppose that Paul was bound in fetters, even though he is designated **Paul the prisoner** (cf. Eph. 3:1; 4:1; Philemon 1).

Bruce[301] thinks that Paul was likely disinherited from a wealthy father and family in Silicia (cf. Phil. 3:8) upon his having become a Christian.

It appears that the centurions were available to him and complied with his wishes. That the chief captain welcomed the information from Paul's nephew appears evident, and the manner in which he treated the whole affair indicates that he favored Paul's position against the Jews, though of course his responsibility to a Roman citizen might well color his treatment of Paul.

3. The Transfer of Paul Planned (23: 23, 24)

23 And he called unto him two of the centurions, and said, Make ready two hundred soldiers to go as far as Caesarea, and horsemen threescore and ten, and spearmen two hundred, at the third hour of the night: 24 and *he bade them* provide beasts, that they might set Paul thereupon, and bring him safe unto Felix the governor.

The skirmishes of the two previous days in the Sanhedrin, plus information of the plot to kill Paul, sufficiently convinced the chief captain of the gravity and hazards of the situation. From the garrison of about a thousand soldiers he ordered, through two centurions, that two hundred soldiers, seventy cavalrymen and two hundred spearmen, with special beasts for Paul to ride, be prepared to leave Jerusalem for Caesarea at about nine o'clock at night. It is noteworthy that this affords the only definite instance in Acts, or elsewhere in the New Testament, where Paul ever mounted a beast of transport. Otherwise he walked or sailed, for all we know. Thus safely escorted, both the interests

of the chief captain and those of Paul the prisoner would be safeguarded. Lysias could not rest easy with such a plot pending until he knew that Paul was safely in the hands of the chief administrative and executive officer of the colony, Felix. If the *Sicarii* knew of Lysias' plan to spirit Paul out of Jerusalem, there is no evidence that they offered resistance or interference.

4. The Letter Concerning Paul Written (23:25-30)

25 And he wrote a letter after this form:

26 Claudius Lysias unto the most excellent governor Felix, greeting. 27 This man was seized by the Jews, and was about to be slain of them, when I came upon them with the soldiers and rescued him, having learned that he was a Roman. 28 And desiring to know the cause wherefore they accused him, I brought him down unto their council: 29 whom I found to be accused about questions of their law, but to have nothing laid to his charge worthy of death or of bonds. 30 And when it was shown to me that there would be a plot against the man, I sent him to thee forthwith, charging his accusers also to speak against him before thee.

How Luke knew the content of Lysias' letter to Felix we are not told. Paul may have had a copy of it, but it appears more likely that Luke heard it read in court at Caesarea before Felix. Such was the custom, to read openly the charge against the accused.

The practice of letter-writing in the first Christian century afforded the chief means of communication. It was an epistolary age. Much is revealed in the few sentences of this letter preserved for us. Plumptre[302] observes that the epithet, **most excellent,** is the same as that used by Luke of Theophilus (Luke 1:3; cf. Acts 24:3; 26:25), and that the formal salutation, **greeting,** is the same as that used in the Jerusalem Council letter by James (Acts 15:23), as well as the Epistle of James (James 1:1). Further, the captain herein reveals his own name, Claudius Lysias, the first being Roman and the last Greek.

Mention of Felix, the governor (more properly *procurator* of an imperial province), throws a painting of varied and conflicting hues on the canvas of Judaean administration. Certainly Lysias' address, **most excellent governor Felix** (v. 26), can be taken as nothing more than a gesture of diplomatic respect, for Felix might be regarded as anything short of **most excellent**. Bruce holds that "The 'most excellent' . . . belongs properly to the equestrian order in Roman history (of which Felix was not a member) and was also given to the governors of subordinate provinces such as Judaea who were normally drawn from the equestrian order."[303] He ruled Judaea for seven or eight years (A.D. 52-59 or 60), having been preceded by the unhappy Cumanus and succeeded by Festus. The country had been left in a sad and disordered state upon the banishment of the inefficient and corrupt Cumanus by the emperor in A.D. 52. There had been a gruesome massacre of Jews at the Jerusalem Passover because of their riotous activities when a Roman soldier insulted the Temple. There had been a small scale war between the Galileans and the Samaritans when certain Galileans en route to a Jerusalem festival had been attacked, in the unsuccessful settlement of which Cumanus had been accused of accepting bribes to favor the cause of the Samaritans, which accusation effected his downfall. Felix inherited too grave a political situation for his ability. The country was a seething mass of disorder with the "dagger-carrying" *Sicarii* terrorizing the land and pressing the people to revolt against Rome. Assassin and "Messianic" outbreaks were frequent (cf. Acts 21:38). The patronizing high priest, Jonathan, who had helped Felix get his office had been assassinated, either at the instigation of Felix or otherwise.

The Emperor Claudius' mother, Antonia, retained two slave brothers, Antonius Felix and Pallas, who were later made freedmen. Felix became the companion and favored minister of Claudius, and thus he obtained the procuratorship of Judaea by the grace of Claudius and the help of Pallas and the high priest Jonathan. Bruce thinks that he may previously "have occupied a subordinate post in Samaria under Cumanus from

A.D. 48."[304] It thus appears that he considered the favor of the emperor, his foster brother, immunized him against imperial responsibility for any crime that he might commit. He wielded, in the words of Tacitus, "the power of a tyrant in the temper of a slave."[305] Lust and cruelty characterized his entire rule. He is reported to have married thrice. Plumptre[306] relates that his first wife was Drusilla, the daughter of Selena, who was the wife of Juba king of Mauritania and the daughter of Antonius and Cleopatra. Drusilla, the daughter of Agrippa I and sister of Agrippa II, who had left her husband Azizus, king of Emesa, was his second wife (cf. Acts 24:24).[307] The name of his third wife is unknown. Before such a ruler and judge, Paul the Apostle was to stand trial for his faith in Christ. Though the orator Tertullus, in an effort to curry favor with the Jews, complimented Felix with the words, "Seeing that by thee we enjoy much peace, and that by thy providence evils are corrected for this nation" (Acts 24:2b), it may be doubted if he was either sincere or realistic. Paul's address (Acts 24: 10) seems better to suggest Felix's knowledge of Jewish administrative difficulties.

It is noteworthy that Lysias avoids all reference to his binding of Paul and the intended scourging. Nor does he intimate that he had been ignorant of Paul's Roman citizenship at the outset. He ingeniously colors the whole affair to give the impression that he had dutifully rescued, from Jewish mob violence, a victim, whom he knew to be a Roman citizen (v. 27). He gives a fair and honest account of Paul's examination before the Sanhedrin (vv. 28, 29). This was clearly intended as "a preliminary investigation with a view to preparing a charge to lay before the Roman Court."[308] He states also the Jews' plot to kill Paul and his purpose to place Paul in the safe custody of Felix the governor for fair trial (v. 30). He gives his judgment that the whole affair is a Jewish doctrinal disputation, not a Roman legal question. Withal, Lysias was a typical office holder who arranged the stage to present himself in the most favorable light before those to whom he owed his

---

303 Bruce, *op. cit.*, pp. 459, 460.   304 *Ibid.*, p. 402.
306 Ellicott, *loc. cit.*   307 Josephus, *Ant.*, XX, vii, 1.
308 *The Interpreter's Bible*, IX, 305.

305 Tacitus, *Annals*, XIII, 54; History, V, 9.

position, by taking credit for what did not rightfully belong to him and by taking diligent care to veneer his official mistakes with an appearance of excellence in judgment and service.

5. The Transfer of Paul Accomplished (23:31-35)

31 So the soldiers, as it was commanded them, took Paul and brought him by night to Antipatris. 32 But on the morrow they left the horsemen to go with him, and returned to the castle: 33 and they, when they came to Caesarea and delivered the letter to the governor, presented Paul also before him. 34 And when he had read it, he asked of what province he was; and when he understood that he was of Cilicia, 35 I will hear thee fully, said he, when thine accusers also are come: and he commanded him to be kept in Herod's palace.

It appears that the first half, or possibly two-thirds, of the approximately sixty-mile journey from Jerusalem to Caesarea was reached at Antipatris before daybreak (v. 31). Bruce holds that Antipatris was 35 miles from Jerusalem. And it was, he continues, "at the foot of the Judaean hills, on the site of the modern Ral el-'Ain, built by Herod the Great in the well-watered and well-wooded plain of Kaphar-Saba and called after his father Antipater."[309] Such was quite possible, allowing a distance of some thirty-five miles to Antipatris and remembering that they had left at about nine o'clock in the evening. From Antipatris the foot soldiers returned to Jerusalem leaving the cavalry to escort Paul the remaining 27 miles to Caesarea. This was considered safe as the Jews loathed the use of horses as unclean animals, and thus the *Sicarii* could not have overtaken the party, even if they had learned of Paul's transfer to Caesarea. Also, the remaining journey was through territory that was principally Gentile.

Felix's inquiry concerning Paul's province (v. 34) was a requirement of Roman jurisprudence. An accused citizen could be tried in either his home province or in the one where the crime was alleged to have been committed (cf. Luke 23:6, 7).

Felix's expressed decision, **I will hear thee fully . . . when thine accusers also**

are come (v. 35a), indicates that upon learning that Paul's home province was Cilicia, he at once knew that he had "jurisdiction over Paul, either as procurator over Judea, in which the 'crime' had been committed, or as the deputy of the legate of Syria and Cilicia, Paul's native province, who would rank as his administrative superior."[310] Possibly his immediate decision to try Paul rather than defer to his superior officer (as Pilate had done with Christ, Luke 23:6-12), the Syrian legate, was but a reflection of his characteristic impetuosity and pride of position.

It is apparently at this juncture that Paul assumed an active role in the proceedings. Thenceforth he seems to have asserted his Roman citizenship rights in a fourfold relation. *First,* he did so to escape scourging (Acts 22:25). *Second,* he evidently appealed his right of jurisdiction from the Jewish Sanhedrin to the Roman procurator, in which case his transfer to Caesarea was in compliance with his own expressed rights as a citizen, a demand Lysias would have gladly acceded to, in any event, to relieve his own responsibility. *Third,* he asserted his right of fair trial before the Roman provincial court (Acts 25:10). And *fourth,* Paul asserted his citizenship rights by appeal to the supreme court of Caesarea at Rome (Acts 25:11b, 12b).

With promise of a full and just trial upon the appearance of his accusers, Felix ordered Paul detained under guard in Herod's palace. This was likely the palace built by Herod the Great and later converted into an official residence for the Roman Judaean procurator, though it may have served as a fortress and have had a guard room (cf. Mark 15:16; Phil. 1:13). It is not to be supposed that Paul was incarcerated in a common prison such as that into which he and Silas were thrown at Philippi (Acts 16:23, 24).

XX. THE APOSTLE ON TRIAL BEFORE FELIX AT CAESAREA (Acts 24:1-26)

A. PAUL'S INDICTMENT BEFORE FELIX (24:1-9)

Once more, as at Corinth before the Roman governor, the proconsul Gallio

---

[309] Bruce, *op. cit.*, p. 461.   [310] *The Interpreter's Bible,* IX, 306.

(Acts 18:12-17), Paul was arraigned before an official Roman court presided over by Felix, the eleventh procurator of Judaea (A.D. 52-59 or 60). Before Felix, as before Gallio, his accusers were the Jews who were enraged because he preached Christ as their Messiah and the Savior of all men. Before Gallio in Corinth, the capital of a Gentile province where the Jews were a hated minority, he was acquitted, and Christianity was thus given legal status as a form of Judaism. But at Caesarea Paul was being tried by the Roman procurator of Judaea, which was predominantly Jewish and where the laws and customs of the Jews were carefully respected by the Roman rulers. Paul was more anxious for the status of Christianity in Judaea than he was for his own personal welfare. However, Christianity had ceased to be regarded as a form of Judaism in Judaea. A growing hostility of the Jews against the Christians was developing. Erelong James, pastor of the Jerusalem church, with others, was to suffer martyrdom at the hands of the Sanhedrin at the instigation of Ananias (see comment on Acts 23:1-5). Rome did not yet have a hostile attitude toward the Christians, but Jewish pressure on the Roman procurator of Judaea was very strong. There was no assurance that Felix would not yield to their demands, even as Pilate had when Christ was on trial before him (cf. Matt. 27:23-26). The cause of Christianity throughout the Roman empire hinged on the outcome of Paul's trial at Caesarea. We may only imagine with what earnestness Paul must have prayed before he went on trial for the defense of Christianity in this most strategically situated Roman provincial court of justice. Nor was the issue to be finally settled until it was carried to the supreme court of Caesar in Rome itself.

1. The Witnesses Against Paul (24:1)

1 And after five days the high priest Ananias came down with certain elders, and *with* an orator, one Tertullus; and they informed the governor against Paul.

Plumptre[311] thinks that the **five days'** intervention may have afforded time for the messenger from Felix to go to Jeru-

salem, summon Paul's accusers, and return. However, he allows that the **five days** may have begun with Paul's departure from Jerusalem, which seems to accord better with verse 11.

The bloodthirsty persistence of Ananias is eloquently evidenced by his appearance before Felix's court to secure, if possible, either the conviction or custody of Paul. (For the office and character of Ananias, see notes on Acts 23:1-5.) The **certain elders** were his supporting delegation from the Sanhedrin and most certainly such as had participated in the council's attack on Paul at Jerusalem (Acts 23:1-10). Tertullus was evidently a cheap, though "professional, Roman pleader and probably [?] a heathen."[312] Macgregor likewise considers Tertullus as "a Roman professional counsel for the prosecution, a *causidicus* or advocate."[313] However, Bruce regards him as "probably a Hellenistic Jew."[314] From Tertullus' identification of himself with the activities of the Sanhedrin against Paul (**on whom "we" laid hold,** v. 6), it would appear that he was a Jew or at best a Hellenist. Tertullus is one of two lawyers named in the New Testament, the other Zenos, a Christian convert and worker for whom Paul sent (Titus 3:13). These lawyers are not to be confused with the "scribes and doctors of the law" found in the Gospels. The latter were ecclesiastics and theologians. The lawyers of Tertullus' tribe were many in the first century (see notes on Acts 17:5). If not actually Greeks, they were likely influenced by the Sophist school of philosophy. In any event, Paul had great respect for the law of the nation of which he was a citizen (cf. I Tim. 2:2), as well as for the law of Moses.

Bruce aptly states: "They enlisted the services of an advocate named Tertullus to state it [their case against Paul] in the conventional terms of forensic rhetoric."[315] It sounds very modern when Plumptre remarks:

Men of this class were to be found in most of the provincial towns of the Roman empire, ready to hold a brief for plaintiff or defendant, and bringing to bear the power of their glib eloquence,

[311] Ellicott, *op. cit.,* VII, 158.
[312] A. T. Robertson, *Luke the Historian in the Light of Research,* p. 190.
[313] *The Interpreter's Bible,* IX, 307.   [314] Bruce, *op. cit.,* p. 463.   [315] *Ibid.*

as well as their knowledge of Roman laws, on the mind of the judge.[316]

Here is a case where two, yea even three, cultures met in conflict. The Jews were accusing a Christian apostle before a Roman court.

2. The Address to the Judge (24:2-4)

2 And when he was called, Tertullus began to accuse him, saying, Seeing that by thee we enjoy much peace, and that by thy providence evils are corrected for this nation, 3 we accept it in all ways and in all places, most excellent Felix, with all thankfulness. 4 But, that I be not further tedious unto thee, I entreat thee to hear us of thy clemency a few words.

With flattering eloquence and personal compliments, Tertullus paved the way for his indictment of Paul. Concerning Tertullus' words, of thy clemency (v. 4b), Plumptre remarks: "The epithets of the hired orator stand in striking contrast with the 'righteousness, temperance, and judgment to come,' of which the Apostle afterwards spoke to the same rulers."[317] Clarke analyzes Tertullus' oration thus: "1. The exordium.   2. The proposition. 3. The conclusion."[318]   In the first is contained his praise for Felix and his administration of Judaea. Clearly his purpose was to curry favor and win the esteem of Felix for his cause.

Obviously Felix had certain accounts to his credit in his Judaean administration. In addition to the dispersing of the Egyptian *Sicarii's* insurrection (Acts 21: 38), he had quelled uprisings and banditry under the leadership of one Eliezer[319] and a serious disturbance between the Syrians and the Caesarean Jews.   But the other side of the ledger was seriously overbalanced with discredits.   He was reprehensible for both bad character and maladministration.   His lustful, mercenary, oppressive, unjust, and cruel conduct was all too well known by his Jewish subjects.   (For a description of Felix's character and conduct, see notes on Acts 23:25-30.)

Tertullus' claim that the Jews graciously and universally accepted Felix's administration (v. 3) was flagrant hypocrisy. Indeed many of the Sadducees favored

him, but there were far more of the loyalists who thirsted for his blood.

Tertullus' reference to Felix's providence (v. 2) led Plumptre to observe:

Men spoke then as now of the "providence of God," and the tendency to clothe the emperors with quasi-divine attributes led to the appearance of this word — "the providence of Caesar" — on their coins and on medals struck in their honor. Tertullus, after this manner, goes one step further, and extends the term to the procurator of Judea.[320]

This tendency to deify Roman rulers was evidenced by the ascription of divinity to Herod Agrippa I by the peoples of Tyre with his resultant divine judgment in death in A.D. 44 (Acts 12:21-23). Robertson sees evidence of Roman emperor worship in Paul's experience at Thessalonica:

Evidently, Paul, while in Thessalonica, had been stirred up by the worship of the Roman emperor and may have employed language that gave some color to the specious charge of his enemies. Here in Thessalonica Paul began to face the inevitable conflict between Christ and Caesar. The shadow of Rome was cast upon the Cross.[321] (Cf. II Thess. 2:3.)

Treason seems to have been the charge that threw both the Thessalonian politarchs and the crowd into pandemonium, and thus Jason was required to give security to insure their good behavior against treason (Acts 17:9).

Concerning Tertullus' words, **that I be not further tedious unto thee,** Bruce remarks:

It was . . . customary to promise brevity, as Tertullus does here (v. 4); the promise was sometimes kept, sometimes not, but it was calculated to secure good will for the speaker at the outset of his speech.[322]

3. The Charges Against Paul (24:5-9)

5 For we have found this man a pestilent fellow, and a mover of insurrections among all the Jews throughout the world, and a ringleader of the sect of the Nazarenes: 6 who moreover assayed to profane the temple: on whom also we laid hold: 8 from whom thou wilt be able, by examining him thyself, to take knowl-

[316] Ellicott, *loc. cit.,*   [317] *Ibid.,* p. 159.   [318] Clarke, *op. cit.,* I, 873.
[319] Josephus, *Ant.,* XX, viii, 5, and *War,* XI, xiii, 2.
[320] Ellicott, *op. cit.,* p. 159.   [321] Robertson, *op. cit.,* p. 197.   [322] Bruce, *op. cit.,* p. 464.

edge of all these things whereof we accuse him. 9 And the Jews also joined in the charge, affirming that these things were so.

Though Tertullus advances four general things against Paul, they seem to resolve themselves logically into three specific charges: *First,* he is charged with being a confirmed agitator and promoter of subversive activities: **a pestilent fellow . . . a mover of insurrections.** *Second,* he is charged with being the self-appointed chief of a revolutionary movement: **a ringleader of the sect of the Nazarenes.** And *third,* he is charged with intent to profane the Jewish Temple: **who moreover assayed to profane the temple.**

First, Tertullus shrewdly leveled his charge against Paul before Felix when he alleged that he had been found to be **a pestilent fellow,** or perhaps by implication a deadly, poisonous, pernicious, demoralizing, peace-disturbing, infectious Sicarius at large in the empire who had come to Judaea with the purpose of directing a revolt against Rome. It was, as we have seen, in the suppression of these *Sicarii* of Judaea that Felix most prided himself. "Messianic" movements were many; and though they began as a religion, they sometimes became political. The charge of Tertullus against Paul seems to imply that he was head of such a movement. Tertullus well knew that if the Jews could secure a verdict against Paul on this first charge, his execution by Felix in the interest of Roman government in Palestine would be assured.

The *second* charge was designed to be cumulative in its import. Herein Paul is depicted as the organizer and director of a subversive, political movement which, under the false guise of the legalized Jewish religion in the empire, had bored its way into every part of the Roman Empire. Tertullus is subtly drawing the lines of demarcation between Judaism and Christianity with the purpose of pushing the latter out into the unfavorable recognition of Rome. Had he succeeded, not only would Paul have suffered execution but the Roman ax would have fallen on the Christians of Judaea and perhaps throughout the em-

pire. If he failed, Christianity would come into favorable notice and recognition of Rome and would attain legal status, as indeed it did in A.D. 313 under the emperor Constantine. Tertullus employed no new device in his attempt to set Caesar against Christ. The Jews employed this device against Christ Himself (John 19:12); it was employed against the Christian apostles at Philippi (Acts 16:19-21); and again at Thessalonica (Acts 17:6-8); and at Corinth (Acts 18:12, 13).

Bruce[323] observes that this is the single New Testament employment of the name *Nazarene* in application to the followers of Christ. As such they are designated a party or organization (cf. Acts 5:17). The *third* charge of the attempted profanation of the Temple lacks the detail of the earlier charge against Paul where the Jews actually accused him of doing so by taking the Gentile Trophimus into the Temple. There they accused him of the act, but here Tertullus, perhaps either because of the difficulty of proof or because of the discovery of their mistake, resorts to an accusation against Paul's motives: he **assayed to profane the temple.** Of course if this charge could have been sustained, the Jews would have had the legal right to execute Paul themselves. Perhaps it is this that they most hoped to accomplish in the trial. A verdict here would have been a final victory for them over Paul, if not over Christianity.

Tertullus closed his prosecution by committing the case to the judge with the complimentary assurance that Felix would, by examination, find the charges true as he had presented them (v. 8). The Jewish delegation gave assent to the charges as presented by Tertullus.

B. PAUL'S DEFENSE BEFORE FELIX (24:10-21)

That both the prosecution and the defense began their addresses at the beckoning of Felix (cf. vv. 2 and 10) makes clear that this was a formal trial.

1. Paul's Address to the Judge (24:10)

10 And when the governor had beckoned unto him to speak, Paul answered, Forasmuch as I know that thou hast

been of many years a judge unto this nation, I cheerfully make my defence:

There is a marked difference between the address of the defense (v. 10) and that of the prosecution (vv. 2-4). Paul is briefer, less ornate, and more direct in his approach. Both are complimentary of the judge, but instead of an enumeration of doubtful achievements ascribed to Felix by Tertullus, Paul, in a straightforward manner, recognizes Felix's knowledge of Jewish affairs, possibly gained in large measure through Drusilla and his experience as administrator and judge of Judaea, as favorable criteria for judging the case in question. Plumptre says, "We note at once the difference between St. Paul's frank manliness and the servile flattery of the advocate."[324]

2. Paul's Reply to the First Charge (24:11-13)

11 seeing that thou canst take knowledge that it is not more than twelve days since I went up to worship at Jerusalem: 12 and neither in the temple did they find me disputing with any man or stirring up a crowd, nor in the synagogues, nor in the city. 13 Neither can they prove to thee the things whereof they now accuse me.

Paul replies to the three charges of Tertullus in order (see notes on vv. 5-9). *First,* he denies that he had any seditious intent at Jerusalem. This denial he supports by numerous evidences. Concerning the problem raised by the twelve days (v. 11), Bruce remarks:

The notes of time from Paul's arrival in Jerusalem (Ch. 21:17f.) are given in great detail. But the seven days of Ch. 21:27 and the five days of Ch. 24:1 would in themselves make up twelve days, without taking into consideration the time-notes of Chs. 21:18, 26; 22:30; 28:11f., 23, 30. We have therefore to suppose (with Rackham . . .) that the five days of Ch. 24:1 are reckoned from Paul's arrest in the temple (which strikes one as most improbable), or that the week prescribed for the four Nazarites' purification was nearly completed when Paul joined them, or that he was arrested early in the week. The last alternative seems to accord with the wording of Ch. 21:27 less well than the second one does.[325]

Concerning the chronological problem, Macgregor simply states: "The truth probably is that Paul is simply speaking in round numbers — as we might say, 'about a fortnight.' "[326]

Paul's purpose in going to Jerusalem had not been for political agitation as Tertullus alleged, but rather for religious worship: **I went up to worship** (v. 11b; cf. v. 18). Paul's nationality and training supported this claim. As a provincial Jew it was perfectly natural and right that he should have come to Jerusalem to worship at the Pentecostal feast. The brevity of time spent there (12 days) would have been against seditious activities, especially as he accounted for his conduct during that time.

He makes a flat denial that the Jews had found him disputing with any man or gathering and agitating a following, either in the Temple, in a Jerusalem synagogue, or in any other part of the city (v. 12). Tertullus had generalized in his charges. Paul categorically denied these generalities with their subtle implications. When one has been honest in speech and upright in conduct, it will not be difficult to give a straightforward and satisfactory account of his words and deeds. This categorical denial of seditious activities Paul clinches with a straightforward challenge to his accusers to offer satisfactory evidence of their accusations (v. 13).

3. Paul's Reply to the Second Charge (24:14-16)

14 But this I confess unto thee, that after the Way which they call a sect, so serve I the God of our fathers, believing all things which are according to the law, and which are written in the prophets; 15 having hope toward God, which these also themselves look for, that there shall be a resurrection both of the just and unjust. 16 Herein I also exercise myself to have a conscience void of offence toward God and men always.

While ignoring his alleged position as ringleader of the sect of the Nazarenes (v. 5b), Paul denied Tertullus' allegation that the Christian movement was politically subversive under the cloak of Judaism throughout the empire (v. 5). Positively, he proudly identified himself with

[324] Ellicott, *loc. cit.*   [325] Bruce, *op. cit.,* p. 468, n. 13.   [326] *The Interpreter's Bible,* IX, 310.

the Way which they call a sect (v. 14). But immediately he defended this sect as a perfectly lawful and orthodox movement within Judaism. In systematic order Paul asserts that he (and these people) of the Way **worship** (v. 11b) [and] **serve . . . the God of our Fathers** (v. 14), or the Jehovah of the Jews. Further, he asserts that they believe **all things which are according to the law and which are written in the prophets** (v. 14). While not so stated, Paul subtly implies that the Christian faith accepts the essence of Judaism while rejecting the oral additions and accretions of the Jews (cf. Matt. 23:4). Thus Paul places Christianity in direct descent from the law of Moses and implies that it is the fulfillment of the prophets. Christianity is founded upon the teachings of Moses — it rests upon the moral content of the law, and it is the realized fulfillment of what the prophets promised. Further, Paul boldly asserts that his "saving faith" (**hope toward God,** v. 15a) rests upon the very one (the Messiah) to whom the Jews still look forward. Paul seems to say, I repose my faith for salvation in the Messiah who has already come, and in whom the Jews hope to repose their faith when He shall have come. For Paul and the Christians the Messiah was a present savior; for the Jews He was still a future anticipation. Clearly Paul implies that the object of his hope toward God (Christ) was identical with the Messiah for whom they had long looked and for whom they still looked (cf. John 1:11, 12). Again he asserts his faith, and that of the Christians, in the resurrection, **both of the just and the unjust** (v. 15b). This latter statement need not be regarded as in conflict with Paul's doctrine of the two resurrections in the Thessalonian letter (cf. I Thess. 4:13-18; I Cor. 15; Rev. 20:13-15).

Macgregor[327] would deny that reference to the resurrection in verse 15 is Pauline, on the ground that Paul taught two separate resurrections, for the righteous and for the unjust, and that Paul's faith centered in Christ's resurrection which the Jews denied. It seems appropriate to reply, first, that there is no apparent good reason to deny that Paul may have allowed for separate resurrections — **both of the just and the unjust** — in this utterance. It did not fit his purpose to deal with them separately at this time. He is countering Sadducean denial of any resurrection by identifying his belief with that of orthodox Judaism. In the second place, Paul assumed the resurrection of Christ as the condition and the guarantee of the resurrection of the dead (cf. I Cor. 15:12-22). Nor did it serve Paul's purpose to assert or argue the resurrection of Christ at this juncture. Continuity of orthodox and Christian theology was Paul's purpose here, with a view to vindicating the Christian cause.

Mention of the resurrection here, as before the Sanhedrin at Jerusalem (Acts 23:6), immediately identified Paul and Christianity with the Pharisees and orthodox Judaism as opposed to the Sadducees, who rejected the doctrine and thus forfeited their right of claim to orthodox Judaism. Most likely the certain elders who accompanied Ananias (v. 1), who was known to be a Sadducee, were "hand-picked" Sadducees for the occasion, as probably was Tertullus, if indeed he was a Jew. Thus Paul's assertion of faith in the resurrection placed the Christians in the position of orthodoxy, while leaving his accusers in the position of heterodoxy, a subtle move of defense indeed on Paul's part. Could it have been that Paul knew that Felix's wife Drusilla, who was a Jewess and evidently listened to Paul with great interest, was of the orthodox party and that Felix's religious sympathies would have been with her, rather than with the Sadducees (cf. v. 24)?

Paul returned (v. 16) to the reassertion of his strict conscientiousness, a proposition which he had stated before the Sanhedrin at Jerusalem and for which the Jews had attempted to mob him. (See Acts 23:1-5 with notes on "conscience.")

4. Paul's Reply to the Third Charge 24:17-21)

17 Now after some years I came to bring alms to my nation, and offerings: 18 amidst which they found me purified in the temple, with no crowd, nor yet with tumult: but *there were* certain

327 *Ibid.,* p. 311.

Jews from Asia — 19 who ought to have been here before thee, and to make accusation, if they had aught against me. 20 Or else let these men themselves say what wrong-doing they found when I stood before the council, 21 except it be for this one voice, that I cried standing among them, Touching the resurrection of the dead I am called in question before you this day.

As further evidence of his loyalty to orthodox Judaism, Paul advances the prime purpose of his last visit to Jerusalem: namely, "the collection" (v. 17). Here however, Paul judiciously refers to it as **alms to my nation, and offerings.** Nor does Paul here differentiate between the Christian and non-Christian Jews in his use of the word "nation." But it must be remembered that in his defense he is attempting to establish that Christianity is the very spiritual essence of orthodox Judaism. Thus there is no shading of truth in his statement here. Concerning the **alms** Plumptre remarks:

> The "alms" were, of course, the large sums of money which St. Paul had been collecting, since his last visit, for the disciples (possibly in part, also, for those who were not disciples) at Jerusalem. It is noticeable that this is the only mention in the Acts of that which occupies so prominent a place in the epistles of this period (see Rom. 15:25; I Cor. 16:1-4; II Cor. 8:1-4).[328]

Plumptre sees a "refined courtesy" in Paul's use of the term **nation** instead of the usual term, "people," for the Jews. "Nation" was commonly used of the heathen, but to have referred to the Jews here as "people" would have "implied a certain assumption of superiority to the magistrate before whom he stood."[329] Such would have weakened his cause with Felix.

Rather than profaning the Temple, Paul declares that he was found **purified in the temple, with no crowd, nor yet with tumult** (v. 18). The relation between Paul's purification in the Temple (see notes on Acts 21:23, 24) and "the offering" of verse 17 appears to be inseparable. In fact, it would appear that the Jews discovered him in the Temple presenting his offering during the completion of his Nazarite vow. Plumptre remarks that "he was, as it

were, occupied with them [the offerings] when the Jews from Asia found him, not profaning the Temple, but purified with all the completeness which the Nazarite vow required."[330] Macgregor[331] agrees with this position.

The **certain Jews from Asia** (v. 18b) were evidently those who had seen and recognized Trophimus in the city and then, upon seeing Paul in the Temple, assumed that he had taken Trophimus into the "court of the Jews," and thus started the riot (Acts 21:28, 29). However, these very Asian Jews who were responsible for initiating the whole affair appear to have completely forsaken their cause by evading the consequences of their charges and probably returning to Asia after Pentecost. Thus the Sadducees, forsaken by both their Asian Jewish witnesses and the supporting Pharisaic party of the Sanhedrin, were left to carry on the prosecution of an alleged capital offense without witnesses and with a Sanhedrin divided on the issue involved. Paul assumes the absence of the witnesses as evidence of the untenableness of their cause (v. 19). He then cleverly turns the burden of proof on the prosecution, which is without witnesses or evidence (v. 20). Then with a withering blow of irony, Paul concludes his defense by an allusion to the doctrine of the resurrection which had so sharply divided the council and defeated its cause against him. It was as though he said, "The real issue at stake is the doctrine of the resurrection, on which doctrine the Jews are divided and I stand with the orthodox party." And in this conclusion Paul was not amiss, for the difference between the true Jew as expressed in the Christian faith, and the non-Christian Jew, was the resurrection of the dead — first of Christ and then of His followers (I Cor. 15:20-23).

C. PAUL'S TRIAL DEFERRED BY FELIX (24:22-27)

Felix was shrewd enough to see that the Jews had no real case against Paul. To have rendered a verdict against the Apostle in the light of the evidence would have been a violation of his sense of Roman justice and might have involved him in serious trouble with Rome. To

[328] Ellicott, op. cit., p. 160.   [329] Ibid.   [330] Ibid.   [331] The Interpreter's Bible, loc. cit.

have acquitted Paul would have incurred for Felix the violent disfavor of the Sadducean majority in the Sanhedrin. Thus his position was almost identical to that of Pilate at the trial of Jesus (Matt. 27: 20-24), but Felix appears to have been shrewder than Pilate in that he escaped between the horns of the dilemma by deferring the trial rather than accepting either of the alternatives of acquittal or condemnation of Paul.

1. Felix's Reason for Deferring the Trial (24:22)

22 But Felix, having more exact knowledge concerning the Way, deferred them, saying, When Lysias the chief captain shall come down, I will determine your matter.

Felix's deference of Paul's trial seems to have been the result of his **more exact knowledge concerning the Way**, or concerning Christianity. "The comparative, [**more exact**] implies a reference to an average standard,"[332] Plumptre thinks. From whence did he obtain his knowledge of Christianity? There are several possible answers. *First,* he had ruled Judaea for some years and had had opportunity to observe Christianity there. *Second,* he may have contacted the Christians in Rome before coming to Judaea as procurator. *Third,* he may well have observed Christianity at Jerusalem, especially during the annual feasts which he quite naturally had visited, at least in the interests of his wife who was a Jewess. *Fourth,* he doubtless contacted and observed the Christians in Caesarea where Christianity had invaded the Roman army itself through the conversion of Cornelius and his household under Peter some twenty-five years earlier (Acts 10). Likewise Philip had lived here for a quarter of a century evangelizing and had doubtless founded and developed a Christian community. *Fifth,* he may have acquired considerable knowledge of Christianity from his present wife Drusilla, who was a Jewess and may have been informed of Christianity. In any event, Felix's knowledge of Christianity appears to have been favorable.

The conflicting accounts of Tertullus and Paul made it imperative that Felix

gain further information on the whole matter from Lysias, who had arrested Paul and sent him to Felix for trial (v. 22b).

2. Felix's Solicitude for Paul (24:23)

23 And he gave order to the centurion that he should be kept in charge, and should have indulgence; and not to forbid any of his friends to minister unto him.

Felix's charge concerning Paul following the trial was threefold. *First,* he ordered a centurion to keep Paul **in charge.** In other words, Paul was to be kept in custody. Macgregor says of Paul's detention: "The **custody** would be military confinement which would safeguard the accused pending trial without subjecting him to the discomfort of a public jail."[333] *Second,* Paul was to **have indulgence.** This seems to imply such consideration as would be fitting a Roman citizen who had not been proven guilty of any crime. *Third,* he was to have free intercourse with his friends or relatives who might wish to visit him and minister to his comfort and needs (cf. Acts 23:16).

3. Felix's Conferences with Paul (24:24-26)

24 But after certain days, Felix came with Drusilla, his wife, who was a Jewess, and sent for Paul, and heard him concerning the faith in Christ Jesus. 25 And as he reasoned of righteousness, and self-control, and the judgment to come, Felix was terrified, and answered, Go thy way for this time; and when I have a convenient season, I will call thee unto me. 26 He hoped withal that money would be given him of Paul: wherefore also he sent for him the oftener, and communed with him.

That Paul's defense before Felix had definitely awakened an interest in his mind in the Christian religion is evident from the fact that Felix and Drusilla subsequently **sent for Paul and heard him concerning the faith in Christ Jesus** (v. 24b). Felix's second wife, Drusilla, was the daughter of Herod Agrippa I and sister of Herod Agrippa II. (For Drusilla's life, see notes on Acts 24:24-26.) Drusilla was but six years old when her father died in A.D. 44 (Acts 12:21-23). Thus Drusilla must have had some, possibly much, acquaint-

---

[332] Ellicott, *op. cit.,* p. 161.   [333] *The Interpreter's Bible,* IX, 312.

ance with the history and development of Christianity in Judaea. She would have known of her father's execution of James the brother of John and of his imprisonment and planned execution of Peter (Acts 12:1-4). Plumptre thinks that "She may have connected her father's tragic end at Caesarea with the part he had taken in persecuting the faith, of which one of the chief preachers was now brought before her."[334] Thus her evident renewed interest in Christianity appears to have influenced her husband, and together they sought opportunity to learn more of his **Way** by private interviews with Paul. Here, as later at Rome, Paul's prison became his parish. Little wonder that Paul came to consider himself the "prisoner of Christ" (Eph. 3:1; 4:1; II Tim. 1:8; Philemon 1, 9). We would concur with Plumptre that "The procurator and his wife were apparently in the first stage of an earnest inquiry which might have led to a conversion."[335]

Paul took advantage of the awakened interest in Christianity in Felix and Drusilla and proceeded to deliver a carefully reasoned evangelistic *message* to their minds and consciences. Three elements constitute that *message*: namely, **righteousness** or justice, **self-control** or moderation, and **judgment to come** or man's final and personal accountability to God for his life and conduct on earth. A more fitting approach and application to the pair before him could not have been made. Paul's address may be analyzed thus:

1. **Righteousness**, *God's ideal for man.*

2. **Self-control**, *God's requirement for man.*

3. **Judgment to come**, *God's assessment of man.*

First, righteousness, as Paul used the term, may be fairly equated with justice. Paul is reasoning with a Gentile ruler who had been influenced by Greek and Roman philosophical thought more than Jewish. To the Greek philosophers' ideal of justice, neither Paul nor Felix, himself of Greek nationality, would have been strangers. Plato had defined *justice as having and doing what is one's own*. This was understood at once as a *responsibility*,

a *privilege*, and a *prohibition*. As a responsibility it meant that man was obligated to acquire and to do those things that were expected of him as a member of society, whether possessions, position, or performance. As a privilege, it granted to man permissions of possession and performance that made life rich and meaningful. But as a prohibition, it forbade man to infringe upon the rights of his fellows, either as to the acquisition of their property or position. Such became the Greek concept of justice or righteousness. This ideal will accord with the Jewish and Christian ethical requirements. Thus Paul used the known to lead his hearers to the unknown. But Felix, like Herod (Mark 6:17, 18), had taken another man's wife (see notes on Acts 24:24-26) and thus he stood condemned by the Greek ethical ideal, as also by the Christian. *Second*, the Greek ethical ideal of **self-control** had received its highest treatment in Aristotle's *summum bonum* or the *via media* – *the golden mean*. This noble concept of moderation in the use of all things struck directly at the sensuous and emotional nature of Felix. Thus it established the principle that "things" can only have instrumental or utilitarian value and must be used only as means to worthy ends, unless they are to destroy their own users. Noble manliness is thus the end, while things are but means (cf. Matt. 6:19-34 and Phil. 4:5). With the Christian ideal and requirement this again fully accorded, and thus Paul brought to bear on the conscience of Felix and Drusilla both the requirements of the Greek philosophy and the Christian religious ideal. *Third*, Paul did not end as a philosopher by simply presenting the ideal, but he proceeded to bring to bear upon their moral judgment and their emotional sense the fact that as these noble ideals were inherent in the very nature of a righteous God, so God would ultimately bring man to account for his use of the ideals. **Judgment to come** was to be the final measurement of man's earthly life and conduct (cf. Psa. 51:4). Felix and Drusilla had been weighed in the balances and were found wanting. Little wonder that **Felix was terrified** (v. 25). Sinful man will always be terrified when thus arraigned be-

[334] Ellicott, *loc. cit.*   [335] *Ibid.*

fore the bar of divine justice by such faithful preaching.

Felix, unable to bear more of Paul's message, bade him retire until such future time as would be conveniently suited to hear more of this **Way**. His conscience was rudely awakened, but in Plumptre's words, "Its voice was silenced by the will which would not listen."[336] Felix with Paul, and Herod Antipas with John the Baptist, are striking parallels at this juncture (cf. Mark 6:20). There is no evidence that for Felix the **convenient season** ever bore fruit in repentance and saving faith. Like so many since, Felix played for time to rationalize himself out of the severe conviction which had gripped his soul. Procrastination became the enemy that robbed his soul of its prize of salvation.

But Felix was plainly a man of mixed motives in relation to his interest in Paul. **He hoped withal that money would be given him of Paul** (v. 26). Ramsay makes much of Paul's supposed wealth.[337]

A worthy counter suggestion to Ramsay's hypothesis might be that Paul was not a wealthy man, but that Luke was likely a man of means and that, as the missionary companion and friend of the Apostle, he generously expended his resources on Paul's imprisonments and trials.

After discrediting the theory that Paul may have used any of the "collection" for his personal expense, Ramsay states: "There seems no alternative except that Paul's hereditary property was used . . . we must regard Paul as a man of some wealth during these years.[338] Whether or not Ramsay's hypothesis concerning Paul's wealth merits respect (it does appear quite strained), Paul was nevertheless, for some reason which Luke does not tell us, regarded by Felix as a favorable prospect for a substantial bribe. Possibly Paul's allusion to **alms** . . . and **offerings** (v. 17), which he had brought to his nation, led Felix to the mistaken notion that these were Paul's personal contributions and thus that he was a man of financial means.

Felix's hopes for a bribe from Paul were but the natural outflow of his perverted character and conduct. Plumptre

remarks: "This greed of gain in the very act of administering justice was the root-evil of the weak and wicked character."[339]

Felix's subsequent interviews with Paul are aptly suggested by Plumptre as follows:

> It is not difficult to represent to ourselves the character of these interviews, the suggestive hints — half promises and half threats of the procurator, the steadfast refusal of the prisoner to purchase the freedom which he claimed as a right, his fruitless attempt to bring about a change for the better in his judge's character.[340]

Again there is a striking parallel between Paul and the philosopher Socrates at this juncture. Socrates refused to allow his disciples to bribe the judge or guards for his release when he was condemned to die by the hemlock cup for the principles which he taught in Athens.

We should like to know the effect of Paul's life and ministry on Drusilla, but Luke passes this over.

4. Felix's Disposal of Paul (24:27)

27 But when two years were fulfilled, Felix was succeeded by Porcius Festus; and desiring to gain favor with the Jews, Felix left Paul in bonds.

What Paul did during his two years of Caesarean imprisonment is left untold by Luke, and we can do no more than conjecture. That he was afforded comfortable circumstances and possibly a considerable degree of liberty appears likely from the circumstances of the case. Some have conjectured that he wrote the Epistle to the Hebrews during this period (if indeed it was written by Paul); others that the Ephesian, Colossian and Philippian epistles, with perhaps Philemon, were written here. However, evidence is lacking for any of these hypotheses. It seems most probable that he had contact and encouraging fellowship with Luke, Philip, and other Christians at Caesarea. Doubtless they ministered to his material, as also to his spiritual, comfort. It seems possible that Luke may have utilized the time and opportunity in association with Paul for further collection of materials for his histories. It would have been here,

---

[336] *Ibid.*, p. 162. [337] See Additional Note XIII, *Paul's Supposed Wealth.*
[338] W. M. Ramsay, *St. Paul the Traveller and the Roman Citizen,* p. 312.
[339] Ellicott, *loc. cit.* [340] *Ibid.*

at least in part, that Paul learned the secret of patient resignation to God's will (Phil. 4:11) .

The Jews multiplied complaints against the abuses of Felix's government, and finally he was recalled by Nero. His brother Pallas' influence with the emperor saved him from more serious punishment. Porcius Festus succeeded Felix as procurator of Judaea and died in the second year of his administration. Josephus[341] gives Festus credit with suppressing the ravaging *Sicarii* activities of the country and maintaining peace while he lived.

Characteristically patronizing, Felix, on the occasion of his recall, left Paul in prison at Caesarea as a favor to the Jews who might have added this to their charges against him before Caesar had he released Paul. Too cowardly to condemn Paul to death or release him to the Sanhedrin, which would have done so, and too deferent to Jewish pressure groups to acquit and release him, Felix committed the logical fallacy of "decision by indecision" and left Paul to be disposed of by his successor. Plumptre remarks of Luke's words **desiring to gain favor with the Jews, Felix left Paul in bonds** (v. 27b) , "It was, so to speak, an investment in iniquity."[342] How often do people leave their personal and official responsibilities for others to execute while they thus attempt to evade the consequences of their own acts!

XXI. THE APOSTLE'S DEFENSE BEFORE FESTUS AND AGRIPPA II (Acts 25:1-26:32)

In the year of Felix's recall by Nero (or possibly a little later) , Porcius Festus came into the office of procurator of Judaea where he lived but two years and then died in office. Little is known concerning the life or character of this man, apart from a brief account by Josephus. He appears to have been an honorable and prudent man, for the most part. Had the circumstances of his reign been more favorable, his success might have been greater. However, the impossibility of his situation was brought about by the corruption and maladministration of his predecessor, Felix. Violence, intrigue,

sedition, and extreme loyalist bigotry made of the Jews an impossible people for this Roman procurator. Josephus describes the beginning of his rule thus: "Festus succeeded Felix as procurator, and made it his business to correct those that made disturbances in the country. So he caught the greatest part of the robbers, and destroyed a great many of them."[343] Josephus[344] describes somewhat in detail the nature of these disorders and the measures employed by Festus to correct them. Withal his task proved impossible and the situation grew worse, a condition which may have contributed to his early death.

A. PAUL'S CASE REVIEWED BY FESTUS (25:1-12)

1 Festus therefore, having come into the province, after three days went up to Jerusalem from Caesarea. 2 And the chief priests and the principal men of the Jews informed him against Paul; and they besought him, 3 asking a favor against him, that he would send for him to Jerusalem; laying a plot to kill him on the way. 4 Howbeit Festus answered, that Paul was kept in charge at Caesarea, and that he himself was about to depart *thither shortly.* 5 Let them therefore, saith he, that are of power among you go down with me, and if there is anything amiss in the man, let them accuse him.

6 And when he had tarried among them not more than eight or ten days, he went down unto Caesarea; and on the morrow he sat on the judgment-seat, and commanded Paul to be brought. 7 And when he was come, the Jews that had come down from Jerusalem stood round about him, bringing against him many and grievous charges which they could not prove; 8 while Paul said in his defence, Neither against the law of the Jews, nor against the temple, nor against Caesar, have I sinned at all. 9 But Festus, desiring to gain favor with the Jews, answered Paul and said, Wilt thou go up to Jerusalem, and there be judged of these things before me? 10 But Paul said, I am standing before Caesar's judgment-seat, where I ought to be judged: to the Jews have I done no wrong, as thou also very well knowest. 11 If then I am a wrong-doer, and have committed anything worthy of death, I refuse not to die; but if none of those things is

[341] Josephus, *War,* II, xiv, 1.   [342] Ellicott, *loc. cit.*   [343] Josephus, *loc. cit.*
[344] Josephus, *Ant.,* XX, viii, 9, 10.

true whereof these accuse me, no man can give me up unto them. I appeal unto Caesar. 12 Then Festus, when he had conferred with the council, answered, Thou hast appealed unto Caesar: unto Caesar shalt thou go.

Three days after taking his office Festus went up from Caesarea, the Roman seat of government, to Jerusalem (v. 1), the religious capital of the Jews whom he was to rule. It was a conciliatory visit to the capital and court of this troublesome people, as well as an informative visit for Festus. Early acquaintance with the ruling Jews of Judaea was both desirable and wise on Festus' part.

Though Ananias had been replaced by a new high priest, Ishmael ben Phabi, there had been no change in the policy of the Sanhedrin.[345]

The chief priests and the principal men of the Jews (v. 2a), the same Sadducean element that had not ceased to thirst for Paul's blood, made a quick move to prejudice the mind of the new ruler (cf. v. 24) against the prisoner left by Felix, by renewing their indictment of Paul. Bruce states, "They lost no time in exploiting the favor which Felix had done them in leaving Paul in prison in Caesarea."[346] Rackham identifies **the principal men of the Jews** (v. 2), or "leaders of the Sanhedrin" with "the First Ten [who] were a board of magistrates in the Greek cities of the East. In Roman colonies in Italy the name had been given to the ten who ranked first on the roll of the senate."[347] It appears that they sought to take advantage of Festus' recent arrival and lack of experience in Judaea by requesting as an official favor that he would grant the Sanhedrin custody of the prisoner whose offense concerned Jewish law and jurisdiction. Macgregor states, "The point would be that the Jews asked Festus to issue an official 'order' handing over Paul to their own jurisdiction at Jerusalem."[348] It is further probable that they sought to intimidate Festus by impressing him with their influence in having effected the recall of Felix.

Luke's statement concerning the Jews' **plot to kill him** [Paul] **on the way** (v. 3b) may indicate that this was either a revival of the foiled plot that the "more than

forty men" (Acts 23:12ff.) had earlier made, or it was a new plot laid by others quite as zealous for revenge who hoped for greater success in waylaying Paul en route to Jerusalem from Caesarea. These assassination plots reveal how intricately related the Jewish religious leaders of this time were with the *Sicarii* or Assassins of the land. Festus' refusal to allow Paul to fall into their trap may have been due to knowledge which he had of their previous plot.

Festus informed the Sanhedrin that Paul was legally a charge of the Roman government at Caesarea and could not be transferred to their court (v. 4a). He himself was soon to return to Caesarea (v. 4b) in anticipation of an official visit from Agrippa II and other official provincial dignitaries who appear to have customarily staged an official welcome for a new procurator of Judaea (cf. vv. 13, 23). Therefore, if they thought they had a case against Paul they should select a delegation of responsible and influential men (cf. I Cor. 1:26) to proffer the charges and produce substantial evidence (v. 5), and not send some hired "rhetorician" and "pleader" such as Tertullus had been before Felix (cf. Acts 17:5; 24:1).

Within eight or ten days Festus returned to Caesarea where the following day he opened a formal trial of Paul (v. 6). Bruce remarks: "The whole case against Paul was now opened afresh, thanks to Felix's neglect to pronounce his acquittal and discharge him.[349]

The many and grievous charges (v. 7) which were brought against Paul by the Jews before Festus were likely a reiteration of the earlier charges brought against him by Tertullus before Felix, with certain variations and additions (see Acts 24:5, 6 with notes). However, they were all totally without support (v. 7b). Rackham significantly remarks: "The prosecutors **from Jerusalem surrounded him** and made up for their want of evidence by the violence of their *outcries,* declaring that *he was unfit to live*"[350] (cf. Luke 23:10). Plumptre observes:

> The line of St. Paul's defense indicates the three counts of the indictment. He had broken, it was alleged, the law of Israel, which Rome recognized as the

[345] Rackham, *op. cit.,* p. 454.   [346] Bruce, *op. cit.,* p. 475.   [347] Rackham, *op. cit.,* p. 222, n. 5.
[348] *The Interpreter's Bible,* IX, 317.   [349] Bruce, *op. cit.,* p. 476.   [350] Rackham, *op. cit.,* p. 454.

religion of the province, and was therefore subject to the spiritual jurisdiction of the Sanhedrin; he had profaned the Temple; he was a disturber of the peace of the empire, and taught that there was another king than Nero.351

The last charge was quite clearly a revival of the second charge brought against Paul by Tertullus (cf. Acts 21: 27, 28; 24:5, 6).

Paul proceeded to deny categorically all three of the charges in order: **Neither against the law of the Jews, nor against the temple, nor against Caesar, have I sinned at all** (v. 8). As there was no supporting evidence for the charges (v. 7b), there could be no verdict of guilt.

Festus, eager to improve his position and influence with his Jewish subjects, as Felix had been (Acts 24:27), offered a counter proposition to Paul's outright acquittal. **"Wilt thou [Paul] go up to Jerusalem and there be judged of these things before me?"** (v. 9b). The whole proposition appeared perfectly reasonable. Festus, not having Felix's "more exact knowledge concerning the Way" (Acts 24:22), was at a loss to understand the case between the allegations of the Jews and the denials of Paul. The principal charge that concerned the Sanhedrin was the profanation of the Temple. Any violation of Caesar's rights was no concern of the Jews and should be dealt with by the Roman court. Therefore an investigation before the Sanhedrin at Jerusalem with Festus presiding seemed the logical method of resolving the whole problem. And thus Festus would favor the Jews and gain their favor in return, so he hoped. Festus certainly was unaware of the similar abortive attempt made by Lysias (Acts 22:30 — 23:10).

Although Festus seemed to assure Paul that the Jerusalem investigation would still be under the control of the Roman court, Paul had a wholesome distrust of the Jews and thus replied: **"I am standing before Caesar's judgment-seat, where I ought to be judged** (v. 10a). Macgregor states: "The provincial tribunal, before which he is already standing, derives its power by delegation from Caesar himself, and as a Roman citizen he *ought to be*

tried by Caesar's representative and none other."352 Rackham states: "But Paul was a Roman citizen, and his case could not be submitted to a provincial tribunal without his own consent. This he refused to give."353

Paul made a final appeal to Festus' sense of justice when he stated, **to the Jews have I done no wrong, as thou very well knowest** (v. 10b). This being the case, why submit the case to the Sanhedrin, with the personal perils involved?

Paul was quite willing to pay the supreme penalty if he could be proven guilty of anything worthy of death (v. 11). However, in the absence of such proof and faced with a choice between two alternatives, trial before the treacherous unfair Sanhedrin or the supreme secular court of Caesar at Rome, he accepted the latter and declared, **I appeal unto Caesar** (v. 11b). Bruce thinks that Paul "may even have hoped to secure recognition for Christianity as a *religio licita* distinct from Judaism"354 in his appeal to Caesar.

Rackham remarks:

> He [Paul] refused as a confessedly innocent man, *to be made a present* of to the Jews [as had been the case with the Lord — Acts 3:13-15]. This he once for all made *impossible* by uttering the two words, *Caesarem appello, I appeal unto Caesar.*355

Rackham further states:

> . . . it was with great reluctance that St. Paul made his appeal. It was the final and complete assertion of his Roman citizenship and acceptance of Caesar as his king: to the Jews it meant repudiation of the theocracy and apostasy from Moses. But the apostle in the past two years must have thoroughly weighed the question. The Lord himself in the vision at Jerusalem (XIII, 11) might almost be said to have suggested it; for it seemed at the time the only possible method of reaching Rome.356

Concerning Paul's appeal to Caesar, Bruce remarks:

> The right of appeal to the emperor (*prouocatio ad Caesarem*) took the place of the earlier right of appeal to the sovereign people of Rome (*prouocatio ad populum*), which Roman citizens had en-

---

351 Charles J. Ellicott, ed., *Ellicott's Commentary on the Whole Bible*, VII, 163.
352 *The Interpreter's Bible*, IX, 318.   353 Rackham, *op. cit.*, p. 455.
354 Bruce, *op. cit.*, p. 478, n. 7.   355 Rackham, *loc. cit.*   356 *Ibid.*, p. 452.

joyed from time immemorial. It was usually exercised by appealing against the verdict of a lower court, but might be exercised at any stage in the proceedings, the defendant claiming that the case be tried at Rome and the verdict pronounced by the emperor. Ordinary provincial subjects of the Roman Empire had no such privilege.[357]

Paul's appeal to Caesar must have elicited from Festus mixed emotional reactions. *First,* his personal and official pride would likely have been wounded in having had the first (known) court trial of his new administration appealed from his court to that of Caesar. Rackham sees an indication of this displeasure in Festus' reply, **Thou hast appealed unto Caesar: unto Caesar shalt thou go** (v. 12b) and remarks: "The interrogative translation . . . gives it a ring of annoyance, as if Festus was not pleased with being appealed against in his first trial"[358] (cf. I Cor. 1:13; 7:18, 21, 27).

Second, upon reflection Paul's appeal to Caesar must have come as something of a relief to Festus as it delivered him from the unwelcome and vexing responsibility of deciding Paul's case at either the expense of the Jews' favor or Roman justice. Consequently, after a brief conference with his council he acceded Paul's appeal. This appeal forever took the case out of the Sanhedrin's reach. Rackham graphically puts it: "By these solemn and decisive words the Jews, who had been thronging Paul like hungry wolves, were balked of their prey."[359] Thenceforth Paul was bound for Rome.[360]

According to Macgregor[361] the right of a Roman citizen to appeal against a magistrate's verdict dated from an early time and was ratified by the *Lex Valeria* of 509 B.C. The appeal had originally been to the people and then to the "tribunes of the people" and from thence to the emperor himself who by reason of his tribunitial power constituted the highest and final court of appeal. Thus from the instant of appeal, all lower court proceedings were arrested. Though such right of appeal had at first been limited to the city and immediate environs (within a mile of the walls), by

Paul's day it appears to have extended to all citizens throughout the empire.

The foregoing authority holds that Paul's motive in appealing to Caesar was primarily to escape the unjust jurisdiction of the Sanhedrin to which Festus seemed disposed to deliver him. Indeed, it is allowed, Paul likely considered it providential that he should have this opportunity of reaching his coveted destination, Rome (cf. Acts 19:21; 23:11; Rom. 1:7-16). However, in this view, Paul is motivated by the evidence that Festus is inclining toward an unfavorable view of his case, possibly influenced in part by derogatory reports left by Felix in deference to the Jews, whose accusations he sought to mitigate in view of his recall and trial in Rome. Should Paul be condemned on the religious charges by the Sanhedrin, which was inevitable, then his chances of acquittal before Festus on the political charges, reserved for judgment by Rome, would be slim indeed, since to acquit Paul on the second charge would be tantamount to vetoing the Sanhedrin's guilty verdict on the first charge. Thus Festus would lose favor with the Jews. Paul's only alternative was appeal to Caesar.

B. PAUL'S CASE REFERRED TO AGRIPPA II (25:13-21)

13 Now when certain days were passed, Agrippa the king and Bernice arrived at Caesarea, and saluted Festus. 14 And as they tarried there many days, Festus laid Paul's case before the king, saying, There is a certain man left a prisoner by Felix; 15 about whom, when I was at Jerusalem, the chief priests and elders of the Jews informed *me,* asking for sentence against him. 16 To whom I answered, that it is not the custom of the Romans to give up any man, before that the accused have the accusers face to face, and have had opportunity to make his defence concerning the matter laid against him. 17 When therefore they were come together here, I made no delay, but on the next day sat on the judgment-seat, and commanded the man to be brought. 18 Concerning whom, when the accusers stood up, they brought no charge of such evil things as I supposed; 19 but had certain questions against him of their own religion, and of one Jesus, who was

357 Bruce, *loc. cit.*   358 Rackham, *op. cit.,* p. 455.   359 *Ibid.*
360 Rackham, *ibid.,* pp. 408, 409, significantly treats Paul's appeal.
361 *The Interpreter's Bible,* IX, 314, 315.

dead, whom Paul affirmed to be alive.
20 And I, being perplexed how to inquire
concerning these things, asked whether he
would go to Jerusalem and there he
judged of these matters. 21 But when
Paul had appealed to be kept for the
decision of the emperor, I commanded
him to be kept till I should send him to
Caesar.

Festus laid Paul's case before the king,
(v.14). This is not the first, though it is
the last, known appearance of a Christian
before a member of the Herodian dynasty.
Rackham significantly remarks of this occasion:

And now Paul the apostle is brought
into contact with this worldly and philo-
Roman family of the Herods. It is
striking how the fortunes of that family
were bound up with the origins of the
church, but it was an ill-starred connection for the Herods. Their founder,
Herod the Great, had tried to destroy
the infant Jesus. His son Antipas, the
tetrarch of Galilee, beheaded John the
Baptist, and won from the Lord the title
of 'fox.' His grandson Agrippa I slew
James the son of Zebedee with the sword.
Now we see Paul brought before Agrippa's
son. As the Lord before Herod Antipas,
so Paul stands before Herod Agrippa
II; and on each occasion the trial served
to cement the friendship between the
Herodian prince and the Roman governor. S. Peter also had the honour of
being arrested by a Herod: and the
pomp of this scene is an evident counter-
picture to the ostentatious display made
at Caesarea by the first Agrippa [Matt.
2; 14:1-12; Luke 3:19, 20; 9:9; 13:32; 23:
7-12; Acts 4:27; 12:21-23]. Of all these
Herods, Agrippa II comes out the best.
The Lord would not open his lips before
Antipas; nor would Paul give an exposition of his faith before Drusilla. But
before Agrippa II the apostle makes his
most elaborate 'apologia pro vitâ suâ'; he
bears witness to the king's Jewish faith;
he had even hopes of winning him to
Christianity. It is true that Agrippa
somewhat cynically warded off S. Paul's
advances, but had he been as morally
worthless as the other Herods, we feel sure
that the apostle would have adopted a
different tone.[362]

Herod Agrippa II was the son of Herod
Agrippa I, who died under divine judg-

ment at Caesarea in A.D. 44 (Acts 12:23).
At that time Agrippa II was at Rome in
the court of Claudius Caesar in training
for future Palestinian governmental service. Agrippa II was but seventeen years
old at his father's death; and because of
his youth and the governmental problems
inherent in Judaea he was some years
later given the former tetrarchies of
Philip and Lysanias, which later included
certain towns in Galilee and Perea,[363]
rather than his father's kingdom. He was
given the responsibility for the temple
treasury and the appointment of the
Jewish high priest, as well as the custody
of the high priestly ceremonial vestments
which were worn on the Great Day of
Atonement. Thus he was something of
a co-ruler of the Jews, with Festus as
procurator of Judaea. His greater knowledge and experience in Jewish affairs
(himself being part Jew) disposed Festus
to refer Paul's exasperating case to
Agrippa II upon his arrival in Caesarea.
Rackham[364] holds that Agrippa II was
first given the small kingdom of Chalcis
upon the death of his father's brother,
Herod King of Chalcis (A.D. 48) four
years after his father's death, and then in
A.D. 53 Claudius exchanged Chalcis for the
larger realms before referred to, at which
time Agrippa II was given the *title of
King*. For these favors Agrippa II re-
named Caesarea Philippi, the capital of
Philip's tetrarchy from 4 B.C. to A.D.
34, Neronias in honor of Nero. This
Agrippa remained loyal to Rome to the
last, lived to see the destruction of Jerusalem in A.D. 70, but died childless in
A.D. 100 at 73 years of age in the reign
of Trajan. Thus ended the Herod
dynasty.[365]

Agrippa I also had three daughters:
namely, Berenice or Bernice, a year
younger than Agrippa II, Mariamne,
and Drusilla. The last named was the
wife of Felix, whose sordid story has already been related (see notes on Acts
24:24). Bernice had married her father's
brother, Herod of Chalcis, and was left
a widow upon his death. She then went
to live with her brother, Herod Agrippa
II. Macgregor says of her:

[362] Rackham, *op. cit.*, pp. 457, 458.   [363] Josephus, *Ant.*, XIX, ix, 1; X, i, 3; viii,5.
[364] Rackham, *op. cit.*, pp. 455, 456.
[365] For further accounts of Agrippa II see Josephus, *War*, II, xii, 1, 7; xv, 1; xvi, 4; VII, v, 1; *Ant.*, XIX,
ix, 2; vi, 3; vii, 1; viii, 4; ix, 6.

She was a fascinating but utterly profligate woman, and eventually became the mistress of the Emperor Titus. Yet once she displayed real magnanimity by appearing as a suppliant with bare feet to intercede for the Jews, and narrowly escaped with her life from the brutal procurator Gessius Florus.[366]

Scandalous reports of criminal incestuous relations between Bernice and Herod II spread, and she left Herod to marry a Cilician potentate by the name of Polemo who professed the name of the Jewish religion and was circumcised for her sake. But she soon forsook him (and he forthwith forsook the Jewish religion) and she returned to her brother with whom she appeared on the occasion of Paul's trial.[367]

Agrippa's arrival at Caesarea was exceedingly fortunate for Festus since Agrippa was a Jew, an authoritative administrator, and thoroughly conversant with Jewish custom and administration, as well as religion. However, in culture and loyalty he was thoroughly Roman. He seems to have been out of favor with the Jewish rulers at this time, due perhaps to the fact that he had deposed Ananias. (Incidentally it was Agrippa II who later deposed the high priest Ananus after he had illegally put to death James, the pastor of the Jerusalem church.) He had also built a tower in his Jerusalem palace which overlooked the temple courts, but which view was obstructed by a counter wall constructed by the high priest. The quarrel which ensued was settled at Rome. All of this may have accounted for Agrippa's interest in, and likely sympathies with, Paul's case (cf. v. 22). Festus' relating of Paul's case to Agrippa II adds little to our knowledge of the whole affair. Festus appears especially concerned to obtain Agrippa's aid in composing intelligible charges against Paul to send with him to Rome (cf. vv. 14, 20, 26).

Festus relates his inheritance of Paul's case from Felix (v. 14b); the demand of the Sanhedrin at Jerusalem for custody of Paul that they might pass sentence on him (v. 15); his refusal to accede to their demand, with the explanation that the Roman policy is fair trial for everyone (v. 16); his subsequent arraignment of

trial for Paul at Caesarea (v. 17); the Jews' failure to produce any charges of concern to the Roman government (v. 18); and their introduction of certain religious questions which focused on **one Jesus who was dead, whom Paul affirmed to be alive** (v. 19). Festus then admits his personal and official perplexity as to how to obtain clear and correct evidence in the case that he might justly judge the man. Thinking, as Lysias had earlier done, that such evidence might be obtained through a grand jury investigation of the whole matter before the Jerusalem Sanhedrin, Festus had proposed to Paul that the matter be referred to that court (v. 20). He concluded his narration to Agrippa II with the information that Paul had appealed to Caesar rather than return to Jerusalem, and that he had ordered him held in custody until he could be sent to Rome (v. 21). Thus the case is summarized for Agrippa II. Agrippa with his greater knowledge of Judaism, and probably Christianity as well, read much between the lines in the case which was not evident to Festus. His curiosity was aroused and his appetite whetted to know more of this unusual case and the unusual man involved in it.

C. PAUL'S CASE REVIEWED BY AGRIPPA II (25:22-27)

22 And Agrippa *said* unto Festus, I also could wish to hear the man myself. Tomorrow, saith he, thou shalt hear him.

23 So on the morrow, when Agrippa was come, and Bernice, with great pomp, and they were entered into the place of hearing with the chief captains and the principal men of the city, at the command of Festus Paul was brought in. 25 And Festus saith, King Agrippa, and all men who are here present with us, ye behold this man, about whom all the multitude of the Jews made suit to me, both at Jerusalem and here, crying that he ought not to live any longer. 25 But I found that he had committed nothing worthy of death: and as he himself appealed to the emperor I determined to send him. 26 Of whom I have no certain thing to write unto my lord. Wherefore I have brought him forth before you, and specially before thee, King Agrippa, that after examination had, I may have somewhat to write. 27 For it seemeth to me

---

[366] *The Interpreter's Bible*, IX, 319.
[367] For further accounts of Bernice see Josephus, *War*, II, xi, 6; xvii, 6; *Ant.*, XIX, v, 1; ix, 1; XX vii, 3.

unreasonable, in sending a prisoner, not withal to signify the charges against him.

And Agrippa said unto Festus, I also could wish to hear the man myself (v. 22a). Plumptre remarks that this expressed desire of Agrippa implies "that the wish was not now formed for the first time."[368] Macgregor observes concerning Agrippa's words: "If, more literally, we translate 'I had a desire,' we shall have an interesting parallel with another Herod who 'had long desired to see [Jesus]' "[369] (Luke 23:8). Agrippa, like his sister Drusilla, the wife of Felix, doubtless had vivid memories of his father's execution of James, the Lord's brother (Acts 12:1, 2), and the general persecution of the Christians some fifteen years earlier. Too, he had likely known something of the disturbance between the Jews and Christians in Rome while resident there under Claudius (cf. Acts 18:2). There were, of course, many Christians in his realm to the north. He had likely heard much of Paul and his missionary activities, but such knowledge as he possessed was flamed into anxious desire at the opportunity that presented itself for him to see and hear Paul in person.

Luke's description of the pompous court procession and array in preparation for Paul's hearing on the following day (v. 23) strongly suggests that he was an eyewitness. Bruce remarks of the **chief captains** who attended the hearings: "The 'chief captains' . . . would be five in number, as there were five auxiliary cohorts stationed at Caesarea."[370] Macgregor states of the chief captains and the principal men of the city: "These play much the same part as the 'council' or 'assessors' in v. 12. They are called in 26:30 'Those who were sitting with them.' "[371]

The contrast between the humble, shackled, missionary prisoner before the bar and the richly robed formal procession of Roman royalty that assembled to hear his defense was most striking. Comparisons were then impossible, but native greatness will eventually assert itself, while the sham and show will disappear before the ravages of time as the proverbial mist before the rising sun. The tables have turned, and Paul marches on down the way of time touching and animating the lives of men wherever his life and works are read or heard. He has become the moral and spiritual giant of the ages, while **Felix** and **Drusilla** and **Festus** and **Agrippa** and **Bernice** and **the chief captains** and **the principal men** before whom he once made his defense are but the forgotten ghosts of a pretentious past. And so must it ever be when true greatness meets superficial show and sham.

Rackham remarks: "The solemnity of the occasion is marked by its elaborate setting and the repetitions which it involves. Three times over we read the account of Festus' dealings with the Jews; and thereby three times is the apostle's innocence insinuated"[372] (vv. 10, 18, 25).

With due official dignity, Festus introduced Paul to the court and briefly summarized the previous proceedings against him, both by the Sanhedrin and by his own Roman court, and then announced the fact of Paul's appeal to Caesar (vv. 24, 25).

Festus concluded his remarks in opening the case with a frank acknowledgment of his complete bewilderment concerning charges to accompany Paul before Caesar (v. 26a) and humbly deferred to the superior knowledge and experience of Agrippa for this needed information which he hoped Agrippa would obtain by his review of the case (vv. 26, 27).

Dummelow summarizes Festus' purpose in Agrippa's review of the case thus: "As Agrippa was expert in all matters of the Jewish law, Festus hoped that he would help him to compose a letter to the Emperor, which would make it clear what the charges against Paul really were."[373] "According to the Digest (XLIX. b) such written reports, called *litterae dimissoriae,* had to be sent when cases were remanded to the supreme court."[374]

The recurrence of emperor deification is in evidence in Festus' reference to Nero as **my lord** (v. 26). Bruce remarks:

> The title "lord" (*kyrios*) with a divine connotation was given to Roman emperors in the eastern provinces as it had been given to the Ptolemies and other

[368] Ellicott, *op. cit.,* VII, 165.   [369] *The Interpreter's Bible,* IX, 320.
[370] Bruce, *op. cit.,* p. 484, n. 23   See also Josephus, *Ant.,* XIX, ix, 2.
[371] *The Interpreter's Bible,* IX, 321.   [372] Rackham, *op. cit.,* p. 456.   [373] Dummelow, *op. cit.,* p. 850.
[374] *The Interpreter's Bible, loc. cit.*

dynasts; Deissmann notes that there is a remarkable rise in the frequency of such inscriptions in the time of Nero and his successors (*Light From the Ancient East* [Eng. tr., London, 1927], pp. 353ff.) .[375]

Macgregor remarks:

Caligula was the first to style himself *Dominus,* and Domitian improved on this with the title *Dominus deus.* The papyri show that in Egypt from the middle of the first century B.C. *kyrios* is more and more frequently used of the emperor.[376]

Whether Paul knew the words of the Master as recorded by Mark (Mark 13:9-11) we cannot say; but that he felt the assurance of the divine wisdom and strength for this occasion, as promised in those words, appears evident from his confident manner. This was not only to be his last opportunity to declare his innocence of the charges which the Jews had brought against him, but it was also a challenging opportunity to witness for Christ before Roman royalty and officialdom (cf. Acts 25:23 and 26:30) .

D. PAUL'S FORMAL DEFENSE (26:1-3)

1 And Agrippa said unto Paul, Thou art permitted to speak for thyself. Then Paul stretched forth his hand, and made his defence:
2 I think myself happy, king Agrippa, that I am to make my defence before thee this day touching all the things whereof I am accused by the Jews: 3 especially because thou art expert in all customs and questions which are among the Jews: wherefore I beseech thee to hear me patiently.

Paul's introduction consisted of two phases. *First,* Festus introduced the prisoner to the august assembly with official permission to deliver an address in his self-defense. There is no evidence of Jewish enemies or accusers at this hearing, and therefore we are left free to assume that Paul was addressing a private assembly of Roman officials (see Acts 25: 23; 26:1). *Second,* Paul made his formal introduction to the assembly. Luke's statement that he **stretched forth his hand** (v. 1) is evidently a gesture of greeting to the king, as perhaps also to his company. Bruce holds that "the expression

is different from that in Acts 13:16 and 21:40 . . . [where it is intended] to denote a gesture inviting silence and attention."[377] Plumptre remarks: "Here it acquires a fresh pictorial vividness from the fact that St. Paul now stood before the court as a prisoner, with one arm, probably the left, chained to the soldier who kept guard over him. (Comp. verse 29.) "[378]

It would appear that Paul intended something more than a formal compliment in his address to Agrippa (v. 2). In faithfulness to the Herodian dynasty, Agrippa II remained loyal to Rome to the end, even during the subsequent Jewish War with Rome. However, he bore his national Jewish interest at heart and strove earnestly to avert the catastrophe. As a Jew he knew well their customs and was sympathetic with their interests. Thus Paul's knowledge of Agrippa's Judaeo-Roman character and sympathies made him the more ready to answer before him. Bruce remarks: "He, at least, might appreciate the strength of Paul's argument that the message which he proclaimed was the proper consummation of Israel's ancestral faith."[379] However, Paul's address was both frank and courteous. He would not flatter a ruler whose character he knew to be corrupt (cf. Acts 24:2-4), but he recognized his advantages in making his defense before a ruler who knew well the doctrinal distinctions between Pharisees and Sadducees, especially on the question of the "resurrection" and their common anticipation of the Messiah, plus the fact that the hopes of some, at least of the Pharisees if not also of the Sadducees, had found fulfillment in Christ (Acts 6:7; 15:5; 21:20).

Paul expresses no such intent of brevity as was promised Felix by Tertullus (cf. Acts 24:4), but rather recognizing the necessity of time to present adequately his case and the cause of Christ he simply and courteously requested patience of his audience while he made a fair presentment. Perhaps the difference between Tertullus' brevity and Paul's more extended address was due to the fact that Tertullus had little of import to say while Paul was about to narrate the most important story ever told.

---

[375] Bruce, *op. cit.,* p. 485, n. 24. [376] *The Interpreter's Bible, loc. cit.*
[377] Bruce, *op. cit.,* p. 488, n. 9. [378] Ellicott, *loc. cit.* [379] Bruce, *loc. cit.*

Macgregor observes concerning the word **especially** (v. 3a) that it might possibly be placed in the sentence in three different ways: " (a) **Because you are especially familiar;** (b) Especially because you are familiar. (c) That is, especially before you, which would be in line with the use of the word in 25:26."[380]

E. PAUL'S FORMER LIFE (26:4-5)

4 My manner of life then from my youth up, which was from the beginning among mine own nation and at Jerusalem, know all the Jews; 5 having knowledge of me from the first, if they be willing to testify, that after the straitest sect of our religion I lived a Pharisee.

It appears evident that Luke records only a brief summary outline of Paul's address before Agrippa II. Dummelow remarks: "This speech, though in form of a defense to the Jews, is really intended by St. Luke to be Paul's defense to the world — an apology for his whole life and work."[381] Bruce notes that Paul's address largely covers the ground of the speech delivered before the Jews from the steps of the fortress of Antonia (Acts 21:40-22:22):

but the general tone and atmosphere of the two speeches are different, each being adapted to its very distinctive audience. Here, in the calm and dignified setting of the governor's audience-chamber at Caesarea, he delivered the speech which, above all his other speeches recorded in Acts, may worthily claim to be his *Apologia Pro Vita Sua.*[382]

The dignity and literary style of this address is somewhat reminiscent of Paul's earlier address before the Areopagus at Athens (Acts 17:22-31), though the content is quite different.

Paul's words, **mine own nation and at Jerusalem** (v. 4), seem to imply that his former life was common knowledge to the Jews, both in his youth among the Jews at Tarsus in Cilicia and during his subsequent education and activities at Jerusalem. Here, as before Felix (Acts 24:10), Paul's employment of the term "nation," instead of the usual term "people" used of the Jews, seems designed to soften the common harsh distinction between Jews and heathen, likely in courtesy to Festus and the chief captains present (see note on Acts 24:10). Macgregor states: "Alternatively it is just possible that *ethnos* was technically used to mean a "province" — here Judea, in 26:4, Cilicia."[383] In any event he is making his accusers, the Judaean Jews, responsible for knowledge of his Jewish upbringing at Tarsus and his Pharisaic training and activities at Jerusalem (cf. Gal. 1:13ff.; Phil. 3:5, 6). It is clear that Paul intended to establish before Agrippa the fact of his strict orthodox education and life, to which his accusers, if honest, would be forced to admit (v. 5). Macgregor[384] observes that Paul here places greater emphasis on his practice and form of worship than on the Jewish creed or system of beliefs, as was commensurate with the custom of the better Jewish teachers (cf. James 1:26, 27).

F. PAUL'S VERSION OF THE ISSUE (26:6-8)

6 And now I stand *here* to be judged for the hope of the promise made of God unto our fathers; 7 unto which *promise* our twelve tribes, earnestly serving God night and day, hope to attain. And concerning this hope I am accused by the Jews, O king! 8 Why is it judged incredible with you, if God doth raise the dead.

Having historically and logically established his claim to Jewish orthodoxy in belief and practice, Paul next proceeded to set before Agrippa **the hope of** [in] **the promise** (v. 6) in relation to the "resurrection of the dead" (v. 8), which is the real issue at stake between Paul and his accusers. Weymouth aptly renders the passage thus: "And now I stand here impeached because of my hope in the promise made by God to our fathers,"[385] while the RSV reads: "And now I stand here on trial for hope in the promise made by God to our fathers." Wesley remarks that Paul's claim shows "that what the Pharisees rightly taught concerning the resurrection Paul likewise asserted at this day."[386]

Paul proceeded to indicate that it was but a matter of fact that a good Pharisee

---

[380] *The Interpreter's Bible,* IX, 323. [381] Dummelow, *loc. cit.* [382] Bruce, *op. cit.,* p. 488.
[383] *The Interpreter's Bible,* IX, 308. [384] *Ibid.,* p. 323. [385] Weymouth, *op. cit.,* p. 339.
[386] Wesley, *op. cit.,* pp. 499-500.

believed in the resurrection from the dead, and that he rested his faith on the resurrection for the fulfillment of Israel's ancient hope, **the hope in the promise.** This may appear to allude to the "Messianic hope," but when considered in relation to Acts 23:6; 24:15, and 26:8, it becomes quite clear that it was the resurrection which Paul had ultimately in mind. On the other hand, Paul implicitly reasoned that the hope of the resurrection rested upon God's fulfillment of His promise of the Messiah, and that without the Messiah the hope in the resurrection was in vain. But again Christ's claim to be God's fulfillment of the Messianic hope rested for its validation on Christ's own resurrection from the dead. However, both the fulfillment of the Messianic hope and Christ's resurrection from the dead which validated that hope, were requisite to the forgiveness of our sins and the ultimate hope of our resurrection from the dead (cf. I Cor. 15:12-23). Bruce remarks: "It was the hope which gave life and meaning and purpose to the ordinances of divine worship, faithfully maintained by all twelve tribes of Israel."[387]

It has been suggested that Paul's words, **our twelve tribes** (v. 7), imply "that in their hope the twelve tribes are one single community."[388] Bruce significantly observes: "Neither Paul nor any other NT writer knows anything of the fiction of the ten 'lost' tribes. (Cf. Matt. 19: 28; Luke 22:30; Jas. 1:1; Rev. 7:4ff.; 21:12.)"[389] And again the same authority remarks on the Jews gathered from the Diaspora for the Jerusalem Pentecost of Acts 2:

> "Parthians and Medes and Elamites, and the dwellers in Mesopotamia," lived to the east of Judea. . . . These were the lands of the earliest dispersion, to which exiles from the ten northern tribes of Israel had been carried by the Assyrians. They did not lose their identity so completely as is commonly supposed.[390]

Thus Paul agrees with James (James 1:1), and perhaps also with Peter in part (I Pet. 1:1), in his view that the **twelve tribes** (v. 7) were sharers alike in the common hope of Israel. How devastating

Paul's utterance is to the ancient and oft revived legend, that following Shalmaneser's conquest of the ten Northern Tribes they lost themselves in remote regions of the earth. This legend seems to have made its first appearance in the apocryphal literature[391] where they are represented as having gone to an uninhabited country where they might keep the laws of Jehovah which they had failed to keep in their native land. This unfounded legend played a large role in the origin and development of the American Mormon movement. The American aboriginal Indians have likewise been identified with the supposed "ten lost tribes," and some have tried to identify them with the gypsies.

Paul returned to his thesis with the words: **And concerning this hope I am accused by the Jews, O king** (v. 7b). Having sufficiently demonstrated that his position was identical with that of the orthodox Jews on the question of the resurrection, Paul then proceeded to assert that it was for his faith in, and advocacy of, this very blessed hope of orthodox Judaism that he was indicted by the Jews. It is implicit in this argument that Paul is still driving the sharp edge of doctrinal division through the center of the Sanhedrin, thus separating the orthodox Pharisees from the liberal, materialistic Sadducees, and then identifying himself with the former and placing the blame for his indictment on the latter. In fact, it would appear that Paul was implying that the real controversy was one of the liberal Sadducean Jewish party against the orthodox Pharisaic party, rather than the Jews against him personally. Having clearly defined the issue and drawn the line of demarcation, Paul then directly appealed to Agrippa by a direct question for a personal verdict (v. 8; cf. I Kings 17:17-23; II Kings 4:18-37). One could almost suspect that Paul regarded Agrippa's religious sympathies and beliefs to be Pharisaic rather than Sadducean, though according to Plumptre, "the rest of his kindred had been [allied] with the Sadducean high priest, not a few of whom he had himself nominated."[392] It has been observed that Paul's question to Agrippa (v. 8) was

[387] Bruce, op. cit., p. 489.   [388] The Interpreter's Bible, IX, 324.   [389] Bruce, op. cit., p. 489, n. 13.
[390] Ibid., p. 61.   [391] II Esdras 13:40-46.   [392] Ellicott, op. cit., VII, 166.

general, but that he had in mind specifically the resurrection of Jesus Christ, since for Paul the resurrection of the dead in general was dependent upon Christ's resurrection (cf. I Cor. 15:12-23) .[393]

The import of Paul's argument, Bruce thinks, was

> that this belief had now been validated in that God had already raised up one man from the dead, and had by that very fact demonstrated that man to be Israel's long-expected Messiah and Deliverer, the one in whom the age-old hope was realized. Why should those who believed in the resurrection of the dead refuse to believe that God had in fact raised up Jesus, and so declared Him to be the Son of God? If God did not raise up Jesus, why believe that He raised up the dead at all?[394]

G. PAUL'S PERSECUTION OF THE CHRISTIANS (26:9-11)

9 I verily thought with myself that I ought to do many things contrary to the name of Jesus of Nazareth. 10 And this I also did in Jerusalem: and I both shut up many of the saints in prisons, having received authority from the chief priests, and when they were put to death I gave my vote against them. 11 And punishing them oftentimes in all the synagogues, I strove to make them blaspheme; and being exceedingly mad against them, I persecuted them even unto foreign cities.

Paul's words in these verses are an illuminating commentary on the persecution that followed the martyrdom of Stephen (cf. Acts 8:1-4; 9:1, 2). In fact, they seem to suggest even a much more extensive and ferocious persecution of the church than do the earlier records. Paul's part in that persecution receives special emphasis here, likely as an indication of his fanatical devotion to Judaism. Thus Paul shows his sympathetic understanding of the present Jewish opposition to the doctrine of Christ's Messiahship and resurrection. This sympathetic understanding appears to give birth to a degree of hope for Israel's salvation, in the heart of the Apostle. He had passed from unbelief in Christ and persecution of the Christians to saving faith in Christ as the resurrected Messiah. He could not despair of hope for Israel, and even for Agrippa himself (cf. Rom. 9:1-8; I Tim. 1:12-17) .

Paul again called the Jews to witness his pre-Christian conduct in Jerusalem (v. 10a). In contrast he now made bold, even before Agrippa, whose father had beheaded James and sought to execute Peter (Acts 12:1-6), to call the Christians **saints,** or the "holy ones" of Israel.[395]

While the Scriptures record Paul's direct implication in the death of but one Christian, Stephen, it appears from the Apostle's words here that he may have participated in many other martyrdoms also (cf. Acts 9:1, 2; I Thess. 2:14-16; Heb. 10:32).

Paul's assertion, **I gave my vote against them** (v. 10b), has been the subject of much controversy among scholars, some holding that it identifies him as a member of the Sanhedrin, but others denying this meaning of the expression. Macgregor states: "This does not necessarily prove that Paul had been an official member of the Sanhedrin, for the expression is often used metaphorically. It may mean little more than 22:20. 'I also was standing by and approving' " (cf. 8:1) .[396] Plumptre remarks: "The words show that St. Paul, though a 'young man' . . . must have been a member either of the Sanhedrin itself or of some tribunal with delegated authority."[397] Bruce remarks: "The expression 'was consenting' (ch. 8:1; it recurs in ch. 22:20) need not be taken to mean that Saul was actually a member of the Sanhedrin."[398]

However, Conybeare and Howson state:

> There are strong grounds for believing that if he was not a member of the Sanhedrin at the time of St. Stephen's death, he was elected into that powerful senate soon after; possibly as a reward for the zeal he had shown against the heretics. He himself says that in Jerusalem he not only exercised the power of imprisonment by commission from the High Priests, but also, when the Christians were put to death, gave his vote against them. From this expression it is natural to infer that he was a member of the supreme court of judicature.[399]

---

[393] *The Interpreter's Bible, loc. cit.*   [394] Bruce, *op. cit.*, pp. 489, 490.
[395] See I Maccabees 7:13 and II Maccabees 14:6.   [396] *The Interpreter's Bible*, IX, 325.
[397] Ellicott, *loc. cit.*   [398] Bruce, *op. cit.*, pp. 172, 173.   [399] Conybeare and Howson, *op. cit.*, p. 12.

The foregoing authority notes that membership in the Sanhedrin was restricted to fathers with children, since such would dispose them to mercy. Since it was customary for Jews to marry young, Paul may well have qualified, though it is not known what became of his wife and family.[400] Dummelow is specific when he says, "The Gk. means 'the vote of a judge' and establishes the fact that at the time of the death of Stephen, Paul, though so young a man, was a member of the Sanhedrin."[401] Thus we must be content to conclude that Paul was either a member of the Sanhedrin, or if he was not, then he was invested with very special authority by that body, before his conversion.

Paul's allusion to his punishment of the Christians, **oftentimes in all the synagogues** (v. 11a), indicates the widespread activities of his persecutions. There are reported to have been several hundred Jewish synagogues in Jerusalem at this time. Paul's trip to faraway Damascus suggests the wide range of his activities. Bruce notes that "the ruling body of each synagogue constituted a minor lawcourt or *beth din*."[402]

Paul does not claim to have succeeded in forcing any of the Christians to blaspheme, but that such was his purpose is evident: **I strove to make them blaspheme** (v. 11). He evidently considered it more profitable to his cause to secure apostates from the Christian faith than to have killed the Christians. Pliny observes that renegade Christians could be made to curse Christ (*maledicere Christo*), but that the true Christians could not be compelled to do so.[403] Empty profession under persecution has no sustaining power, but the true Christian is fortified against external pressures by an inward power that is greater than the outer (I John 4:4).

Paul's statement that he was **exceedingly mad against them** (v. 11) expresses "with a wonderful vividness, . . . [his] retrospective analysis of his former state. It was not only that he acted in ignorance (I Tim. 1:13); he might plead also the temporary insanity of fanaticism."[404]

Nor was Paul the last instance of this "religious insanity of fanaticism" which made of him the mad murderer of the saints. The "Spanish Inquisition," the "New England Witch-burning Craze," and many other more modern instances of the merciless persecution of non-conformist Christians by the established church have effectively testified to a violent insanity produced by religious fanaticism. It would appear that Paul had in mind the distinction between this "insanity of fanaticism" and the "sobriety" that grace works in the heart when he wrote, "For the spirit which God has given us is not a spirit of cowardice, but one of power and of love and of sound judgment" (II Tim. 1:7; Weymouth).

Paul's words, **I persecuted them even unto foreign cities** (v. 11b), indicate that Damascus was not the only instance of such activities, but that Samaria, Phoenicia, Galilee, Perea, Decapolis, and other regions likely felt the fury of his mad rage.

H. PAUL'S ENCOUNTER WITH CHRIST (26:12-15)

12 Whereupon as I journeyed to Damascus with the authority and commission of the chief priests, 13 at midday, O king, I saw on the way a light from heaven, above the brightness of the sun, shining round about me and them that journeyed with me. 14 And when we were all fallen to the earth, I heard a voice saying unto me in the Hebrew language, Saul, Saul, why persecutest thou me? it is hard for thee to kick against the goad. 15 And I said, Who art thou, Lord? And the Lord said, I am Jesus whom thou persecutest.

We are again confronted, for the third time in Acts, with Luke's account of Paul's Damascus road experience.[405] Here, however, it is characterized by certain variants evidently designed for the special occasion. With those variants we are especially concerned in this section.

Concerning Paul's **authority and commission** (v. 12), Plumptre observes: "The former word [authority] implies the general power delegated to him, the latter [commission] the specific work assigned

---

[400] *Ibid.*, p. 67, n. 2 and p. 72, n. 3.   [401] Dummelow, *op. cit.*, p. 851.   [402] Bruce, *op. cit.*, p. 490, n. 15.
[403] Pliny, *Letters*, X, 96.   [404] Ellicott, *op. cit.*, VII, 167.
[405] For the most part Paul's experience as here related has been treated in Acts 9:1-0 and 22:5-10, to which the reader is referred for the exposition.

to him, and for the execution of which he was responsible."406

In this account only, of the three, Luke records Christ's words to Paul, **it is hard for thee to kick against the goad** (v. 14b). It is doubtless designed especially for his Gentile hearers, as also for the Hellenistic Agrippa on this occasion. Macgregor observes that the expression was

> a proverbial saying, found both in Greek and Latin, usually with reference to fighting against the will of the gods, but not yet paralleled from any Semitic source. The word . . . means, in this context, not "difficult" but "painful," hence RSV, It hurts you to kick . . . ."407

Another remarks of the expression: "It supplies an apt figure for resistance to God; and here it conveys an important intimation that Saul's zeal for Judaism had not been according to knowledge, but rather against the driving of the divine will."408 Withal it is apparent from the figure employed that Paul was already subconsciously convinced of the truth of Christianity. This conviction probably arose in part from the unanswerable "wisdom and . . . spirit" (Acts 6:10) with which Stephen worsted his Jewish contestants of the synagogues (Acts 6:9), and likely in part from the noble example of Stephen in his life and death (Acts 6:8, 15; 7:54-8:1a), as well as that of other Christians whom he unsuccessfully attempted to force to blaspheme the name of Christ (v. 11). It would be revealing to discover how many Communists have been convinced of the truth of Christianity behind the "Iron and Bamboo Curtains" by the faithful witness of Christians who under persecutions and "brainwashings" have refused to recant their faith in Christ or become "turncoats." The deeper the conviction of the truth of Christianity in the mind of Paul before his conversion, the more ferociously did he fight against that conviction. Bruce states:

> It was probably in large measure to stifle this conviction and impression that Paul threw himself so furiously into the campaign of repression. But the goad kept on picking his conscience, until at last the truth that Jesus was risen indeed burst forth into full realization and

acknowledgment as He appeared to Paul in person and spoke to him by name outside the walls of Damascus.409

Many of Christianity's greatest victories and accomplishments have occurred under the most severe circumstances, and Christian faithfulness under extreme opposition and suffering has always been productive of spiritual prosperity and progress in the church.

I. PAUL'S COMMISSION FROM CHRIST (26:16-18)

> 16 But arise, and stand upon thy feet: for to this end have I appeared unto thee, to appoint thee a minister and a witness both of the things wherein thou hast seen me, and of the things wherein I will appear unto thee; 17 delivering thee from the people, and from the Gentiles, unto whom I send thee, 18 to open their eyes, that they may turn from darkness to light and from the power of Satan unto God, that they may receive remission of sins and an inheritance among them that are sanctified by faith in me.

In blunt language, Paul the determined opponent and persecutor of Christianity had to be "knocked down" by God before he could qualify to **arise, and stand upon** . . . [his] **feet** (v. 6) for Christ.

Like certain prophets of old, Paul is commanded of Christ to stand upon his feet and receive the divine commission (see Ezek. 2:1, 3; cf. Acts 22:14, 18; Isa. 6:6-13; 42:1-4; Jer. 1:7-10). No mention is made of the mission of Ananias in relation to Paul's commission, perhaps for the obvious reason that it would not have been important to his purpose before his largely Gentile audience, and the fact that he was compressing the whole experience into such brief compass. Plumptre410 thinks that Paul's summary of his commission as given here was designed to embody the substance of the "visions and revelations of the Lord" (II Cor. 12:1-7), in which his future had been charted for him and he had received the revelation of the gospel which he was to preach to the world. In any event, Paul's commission to the Gentiles was evidently first delivered to him through Ananias (Acts 22:12-15) and then was subsequently directly and defi-

---

406 Ellicott, *loc. cit.*   407 *The Interpreter's Bible,* IX, 326.   408 Rackham, *op. cit.,* p. 468.
409 Bruce, *op. cit.,* p. 491.   410 Ellicott, *op. cit.,* VII, 167.

nitely revealed to him in the temple at Jerusalem in a vision by the Lord Himself (Acts 22:17-21). Thus Paul apparently summarized the contents of more than one vision.

Christ's purpose to appoint . . . [Paul] **a minister and a witness** (v. 16) makes evident the fact that his divine commission was twofold. He was to be a herald of the gospel to the nations, of which gospel he was, through encounter with Christ, a personal witness. No man can be an effective minister (John 15:16; Eph. 6:19-20; cf. I Cor. 4:1) until he has had a saving encounter with Christ (cf. Isa. 6:5-8; II Cor. 5:17-20; II Tim. 2:6). Thus the true gospel ministry is inseparable from the personal witness to the saving efficacy of Christ.

While on the one hand, **the things wherein thou hast seen me** (v. 16) may relate both to the revelation of Christ to Paul on the Damascus road and to the revelation of Christ in the lives of the Christians Paul had formerly persecuted, on the other hand, **the things wherein I will appear unto thee** (v. 16) related to Christ's subsequent revelations to Paul (Acts 18:9, 10; 22:17-21; 23:11).

Christ's promise to Paul in relation to the execution of his commission was twofold: **delivering thee from the people, and from the Gentiles, unto whom I send thee** (v. 17). Indeed the protective power of Christ over His servant Paul while he was under attack both from **the people** (the Jews) and **the Gentiles** has been in evidence frequently in the Acts record, and without doubt this interpretation of Christ's promise has validity. However, Macgregor offers a challenging variant to the foregoing interpretation.[411]

It was doubtless this last qualification that especially recommended Paul to Barnabas for the ministry of the mixed Greco-Jewish Christian congregation at Antioch (see Acts 11:25, 26).

Paul's Gentile ministry is specifically delineated in verse 18. In outline form it might appear as follows:

1. *A Ministry of Spiritual Illumination:* **to open their eyes.**

2. *A Ministry of Spiritual Conversion:* **that they may turn from darkness to light.**

3. *A Ministry of Spiritual Deliverance:* **from the power of Satan unto God.**

4. *A Ministry of Spiritual Remission:* that **they may receive remission of sins.**

5. *A Ministry of Spiritual Inheritance:* that **they may receive . . . an inheritance among them that are sanctified by faith in me.**

First, the Apostle likely thought of his own recovery from physical (and spiritual) blindness when he had met Christ (cf. 9:8, 9, 17, 18; 22:11-15), as he uttered these words of his commission. Indeed light became one of Paul's prime symbols for Christian conversion and life (cf. Rom. 13:12; II Cor. 4:6; Eph. 5:8-14; Col. 1:12-14; I Thess. 5:4-8; see also Isa. 2:5; 9:2; 35:5; 42:6; 49:6; 60:1, 19, 20).

Second, Paul is equally clear in his emphasis on man's moral freedom and responsibility in responding to the initiative of God and His offered mercies in Christ. Nowhere does the Apostle represent God as imposing Christ and His salvation upon man (cf. Eph. 5:14; I Thess. 1:9b, 10). While the KJV reads "to turn them from darkness to light," the ASV conveys the better sense of the passage: **that they may turn from darkness to light;** thus representing the non-Christian as responding to the divine appeal.

Third, it is evident that Paul clearly recognized the personality and dominance of Satan over the lives of unconverted men. Here it is not simply a decision on man's part to accept and follow Christ, but it involves a demonstration of divine power by which man is extricated from Satan's authority over his life and placed under the Lordship of Jesus Christ (cf. Rom. 1:16; 12:1, 2). The universal Lordship of Jesus Christ, as opposed to the dominance of Satan over the lives of men, is the burden of the first-century Christian message (cf. Matt. 28:18-20; Acts 1:8).

Fourth, the remission of sins is the gateway to the Kingdom of God, through which all who would enter must pass. That repentance, as a condition of remission of sins is implied, becomes evident both from Paul's previous statement (v. 20), and from Christ's own words: "I tell you, Nay: but, except ye

411 *The Interpreter's Bible,* IX, 327.

repent, ye shall all in like manner perish" (Luke 13:3, 5). It was an orthodox Jewish doctrine that the power to forgive sins rested exclusively with God (Luke 5:21). However, Christ offered a miracle of healing before the skeptical scribes and Pharisees as evidence of His divine authority to forgive sins (Luke 5:24-26). Divine forgiveness is likewise assured by the Apostle John (I John 1:9).

Fifth and finally, Paul declares that the ultimate aim of Christ's gospel is to offer converted man an assured holy heritage through faith in Christ (cf. I Cor. 1:30; Eph. 5:25-27; I Thess. 4:3, 4; 5:23; II Thess. 2:13; Heb. 13:12; I Peter 1:2). Phillips' translation of the passage is graphic: ". . . that they may . . . take their place with all those who are made holy by their faith in Me."[412] This great divine provision was the principal import of Christ's high priestly prayer (John 17:15, 17, 19).

In summary it may be noted that Paul's commission implies a series of spiritual transferences for the converted man: (1) *from blindness to sight;* (2) *from darkness to light;* (3) *from the kingdom and dominion of Satan to the kingdom and dominion of Christ* (cf. Rom. 1:18-32); (4) *from condemnation unto death to remission of sins unto eternal life;* and (5) *from spiritual poverty and moral pollution to a heavenly inheritance and moral purity.*

J. PAUL'S FAITHFULNESS TO CHRIST (26:19-23)

19 Wherefore, O king Agrippa, I was not disobedient unto the heavenly vision: 20 but declared both to them of Damascus first, and at Jerusalem, and throughout all the country of Judaea, and also to the Gentiles, that they should repent and turn to God, doing works worthy of repentance. 21 For this cause the Jews seized me in the temple, and assayed to kill me. 22 Having therefore obtained the help that is from God, I stand unto this day testifying both to small and great, saying nothing but what the prophets and Moses did say should come; 23 how that the Christ must suffer, *and* how that he first by the resurrection of the dead should proclaim light both to the people and to the Gentiles.

I was not disobedient unto the heavenly vision (v. 19b). Plumptre remarks:

The language of the Apostle is significant in its bearing on the relations of God's grace and man's freedom. Even here, with the "vessel of election" (chap. IX, 15) "constrained" by the love of Christ (2 Cor. V, 14), there was the possibility of disobedience. There was an act of will in passing from the previous state of rebellion to that of obedience.[413]

Paul's experience had been definitely a vision, as contrasted with a dream or trance (cf. Luke 1:22; II Cor. 12:1; see also notes on Peter's trance, Acts 10:10-17).

From the day of his conversion Paul had but one supreme object of affection, Christ, and but one ultimate purpose, the fulfillment of Christ's purpose for his life (cf. Phil. 3:13, 14).

In verse 20 the Apostle reviews his witness to Christ at **Damascus, Jerusalem, Judaea, and to** the **Gentiles** (possibly his Cilician ministry before going to Antioch) following his conversion. However, this may be a general summary of Paul's entire ministry from his conversion until his arrest at Jerusalem, as verse 20 seems to suggest. Paul's ministry was designed to produce a threefold effect in the lives of his hearers: *first,* repentance: **that they should repent;** *second,* conversion: **that they should . . . turn to God;** and *third,* good works: **that they should . . . [do] works worthy of repentance** (cf. Matt. 3:8). Nowhere does Paul ever recognize works as the grounds of man's justification, either before conversion or after, but everywhere, as here, Paul requires good works as the criterion of salvation. The order set forth here is logical and scriptural. Nor should anyone, not even the Jews or Agrippa himself, object to the preaching of a doctrine that made good men out of bad ones by way of repentance and by the forsaking of wicked ways to follow the righteousness of God in Christ. However, Paul concluded that it was for this very reason that the Jews had seized him in the Temple and had attempted to kill him (v. 21). Thus Paul indicts his accusers for attempting to destroy the very righteousness which they professed to stand for and teach. But it is clear

---

[412] J. B. Phillips, *The Young Church in Action,* p. 68. (Cf. Rom. 1:7; 6:22; II Cor. 7:1; Eph. 4:24; I Thess. 3:13; 4:7.)   [413] Ellicott, *loc. cit.*

(here Paul appeals to Agrippa's sympathies with Rome, as well as to the Gentile members of his audience) that Paul's unpardonable sin in the sight of the Jews was that he taught the Gentiles that they were fellow heirs of the promise made to the Jews. For this same cause Stephen had become the first Christian martyr, and Paul had consented unto his death (cf. Acts 13:46; Eph. 3:6, 7).

His deliverance from the murderous intent of the Jews Paul attributed to the very God they profess to serve (v. 22a). He then declared that his message was but the message of orthodox Judaism based upon a correct interpretation of the Messianic predictions of the Jewish prophets and the law which God gave to Moses (v. 22b). Plumptre states: "The name of Moses was added by an instantaneous afterthought to meet the case of those among the hearers who, like the Sadducees, placed the Pentateuch on a higher level of authority than the prophets."[414] That message, more specifically, concerned the sufferings and death of Christ (cf. Isa. 35), His resurrection from the dead, and the proclamation of the good news of salvation for all men thus procured, first to the Jews and then to the Gentiles (v. 23).

But the concept of a suffering Messiah had always been a stumbling block to the Jews, as also foolishness to the Greeks (I Cor. 1:23). Though the Jews had conceived of, and emphasized only, the glories of the coming Messiah's kingdom, thus missing the import of the Cross, Paul's principal emphasis was ever on Christ crucified and resurrected (cf. Acts 13:27-35). Even Christ's Jewish disciples were exceedingly dull of understanding in this respect (cf. Matt. 16:22). It was not until after His death and resurrection that the truth of His sufferings began to dawn upon them (see Luke 24:25, 26, 44). In fact, not until Pentecost were they completely disillusioned of their materialistic concepts of His Kingdom (see Acts 1:6-8).

It is noteworthy that it was by the preaching of the resurrection of Christ that **light** (v. 23b) should come to Jew and Gentile alike. Christ's resurrection then, as now, was the hope of the world.

K. PAUL'S IMPACT ON FESTUS AND AGRIPPA (26:24-29)

24 And as he thus made his defence, Festus saith with a loud voice, Paul, thou art mad; thy much learning is turning thee mad. 25 But Paul saith, I am not mad, most excellent Festus; but speak forth words of truth and soberness. 26 For the king knoweth of these things, unto whom also I speak freely: for I am persuaded that none of these things is hidden from him; for this hath not been done in a corner. 27 King Agrippa, believest thou the prophets? I know that thou believest. 28 And Agrippa *said* unto Paul, With but little persuasion thou wouldest fain make me a Christian. 29 And Paul *said*, I would to God, that whether with little or with much, not thou only, but also all that hear me this day, might become such as I am, except these bonds.

Under the impact of Paul's inescapable logic and undeniable evidence for the truth of Christianity, Festus momentarily forgot the dignity of his position and unrestrainedly exclaimed, **Paul, thou art mad; thy much learning is turning thee mad** (v. 24b). Macgregor remarks, "Paul had deliberately been using language which while intelligible to Agrippa the Jew, to whom the defense is chiefly directed, might well appear to the sophisticated Roman as the ravings of a demented apocalyptist!"[415] Whether Festus spoke in scorn, unrestrained sincerity, or utter amazement, it is equally evident that Paul's defense had made a tremendous impact upon him.

Paul's protest (v. 25) reflects his self-control and the courtesy due Festus' position (cf. Acts 24:3). In contrast to Festus' accusation of "madness," Paul asserts that he has spoken **words of truth and soberness** (v. 25b). Excesses, of which Festus accused Paul, are denied by the Apostle in his claim to **soberness,** or a harmony of the reason and impulses. Aristotle[416] made much of the· virtue of this state of mind to which Paul laid claim, a fact of Greek philosophy with which Paul may have been well acquainted. In support of his claim to **truth and soberness,** which to Festus' Greek mind appeared to be madness, Paul appealed to the Greco-Jewish judg-

[414] *Ibid.,* p. 168.   [415] *The Interpreter's Bible,* IX, 329.
[416] Aristotle, "Nicomachean Ethics," *On Man in the Universe,* III, 10.

ment of Agrippa (v. 26). That appeal appears to have been, *first,* to Agrippa's knowledge that the Law and the Prophets had predicted a coming Messiah who was known to the Jews as the Christ. *Second,* Agrippa knew that from the days of Jesus of Nazareth there had been communities of Jews throughout Palestine, Syria, Asia Minor, Europe, and even in Rome (cf. Acts 9:31), who believed that the Christ had come, suffered, died, and had risen again. These congregations of Nazarenes, as they were commonly known to the Jews, were not by now an obscure people, nor were their doctrines unknown to Agrippa (v. 26b).

Paul evidently sought to establish a more satisfactory point of contact with Agrippa and thus afford a basis for discussion in his question directed to the king (v. 27). As a Jew, Agrippa could not deny faith in the prophets, but he was not to be forced into an admission of unwelcome truth. Whether Agrippa's reply (v. 28) is to be understood as an evasive cynical sneer, as many scholars hold, or whether Agrippa spoke in sincerity, it is equally evident that he had been forced by Paul's logic into a position where he could offer no counter argument to Paul's conclusions concerning Christianity. Conybeare and Howson remark concerning Agrippa's reply:

> The words were doubtless spoken ironically and in contempt: but Paul took them as though they had been spoken in earnest, and made that noble answer, which expresses, as no other words ever expressed them, that union of enthusiastic zeal with genuine courtesy, which is the true characteristic of a Christian.[417]

Paul made one last appeal (v. 29) to Agrippa, and perhaps Bernice as well as the Gentile members of his audience, for a realistic facing of truth. Bruce paraphrases Paul's reply thus: " 'In short or at length,' said Paul, 'I could pray that not only Your Majesty, but all who are here today listening to me were Christian like myself — except for these chains' (holding up his shackled wrists)."[418] Thus Paul stood before this august assembly of Roman rulers, himself a prisoner in chains,

wishing that they might be as he was:

> . . . pardoned and at peace with God and man with a hope stretching beyond the grave, and an actual present participation in the powers of the eternal world — this was what he was desiring for them. If that could be effected, he would be content to remain in bonds, and to leave them upon their thrones.[419]

The lingering effect of Paul's defense on the minds of Paul's audience we cannot know. That he had been a faithful witness for Christ before a court of Roman officials is evident and sufficient.

L. PAUL'S INNOCENCE AFFIRMED (26:30-32)

30 And the king rose up, and the governor, and Bernice, and they that sat with them: 31 and when they had withdrawn, they spake one to another, saying, This man doeth nothing worthy of death or of bonds. 32 And Agrippa said unto Festus, This man might have been set at liberty, if he had not appealed unto Caesar.

Paul's defense before Agrippa was at an end. It had not been a trial but simply a review of the case by Agrippa that he might aid Festus in the formulation of charges to accompany Paul to Rome. The company withdrew and conferred. Whatever their personal opinion of Paul, the unanimous verdict was, **this man doeth nothing worthy of death or of bonds** (v. 31b). Not guilty, they said, but there is nothing that can be done for him short of Caesar's court. Agrippa said to Festus, **this man might have been set at liberty, if he had not appealed unto Caesar** (v. 32). The case had passed to the highest court of appeal, and thus it was forever removed from provincial jurisdiction.

XXII. THE APOSTLE'S VOYAGE TO ROME (Acts 27:1-28:31)

The presence of Luke with Paul at this juncture is evidenced by the author's resumption of the plural pronoun **"we"** (v. 1). The last **"We"** section had dropped off upon the party's arrival at Jerusalem (cf. Acts 21:18; Acts 16:10-17; 20:6-21:18 for other **"We"** sections). From that point to the present we have been

---

[417] Coneybeare and Howson, *op. cit.,* p. 675. [418] Bruce, *op. cit.,* p. 496.
[419] Ellicott, *op. cit.,* VII, 169.

left to conjecture the whereabouts of Luke and the other members of Paul's party, except for a single note concerning Trophimus (Acts 21:29).

A. THE VOYAGE FROM CAESAREA TO CRETE (27:1-8)

Here begins the most dramatic section of the entire Acts record. The account that follows is of special interest and importance for the light that it sheds upon ancient nautical terms and methods. The impression is received that the account of the entire voyage was written by an eyewitness, which impression is supported by the author's identification of himself with the party and the events by his use of the personal plural pronoun "we" almost throughout.

Bruce's comment is both interesting and instructive:

> Luke . . . viewed the sea through Greek eyes and tells us what he saw in unforgettable word-pictures. He could also draw upon a well-established literary tradition for the description of a storm and wreck at sea — not that this in any way depreciates the factual worth of his narrative. From Homer's *Odyssey* onwards, the account of a Mediterranean voyage in antiquity almost invariably included a storm or shipwreck. Homer, in fact, set the fashion in which such accounts continued to be related for many centuries. Luke himself has in this chapter one or two unmistakable Homeric reminiscences.[420]

Bruce[421] further suggests that Luke appears to have been influenced by the OT narrative of Jonah's "storm experience" on the Mediterranean. He notes that this voyage has afforded a rich source for the allegorical interpretation of the experiences, all the way from a comparison of life to a storm-wrought sea voyage to the figurative prediction of the course of church history through the ages. While there are dangerous pitfalls in such allegorical interpretation of the Scriptures, at the same time there are valid moral and spiritual lessons of great worth to be found in the account. Perhaps the example of Paul under the stress of adverse circumstances affords the greatest single

source of instruction and encouragement to the Christian. Bruce states:

> . . . we have seen Paul in many roles but here he stands erect as the practical man in a critical emergency. Not once or twice the world has had to thank the great saints and mystics for providing timely help in moments of crisis when realistic, practical men of affairs were unable to supply it.[422]

It has been noted that:

> The important features in the account are: first, the light it throws on the dominating personality of Paul who, prisoner though he is, exerts his influence at every crisis; and second, the sobriety of the narrative in spite of all its vividness.[423]

1. The Ship's Personnel (27:1, 2)

1 And when it was determined that we should sail for Italy, they delivered Paul and certain other prisoners to a centurion named Julius, of the Augustan band. 2 And embarking in a ship of Adramyttium, which was about to sail unto the places on the coast of Asia, we put to sea, Aristarchus, a Macedonian of Thessalonica, being with us.

Both Ramsay[424] and Bruce[425] acknowledge heavy indebtedness to the work of James Smith[426] for "seafaring technicalities" in their treatment of Paul's voyage to Rome.

Presumably the Roman officials took the first opportunity to place Paul aboard a ship en route to Italy, along with **certain other prisoners** (v. 1) who evidently were of a different class than Paul. Though they too may have appealed to Caesar, as Paul had,[427] Rackham regards them "not as appellants but criminals, condemned it may be to suffer their penalty in the games of the amphitheater. . . . The word for *prisoner* is peculiar to this passage in the N.T.S. Paul was in bonds but not a (convicted) prisoner"[428] (cf. Luke 23:32 where "two 'other malefactors' [were] led with him to be put to death"). Ramsay agrees with Rackham on the position of these **certain other prisoners.**

> He [Paul], of course, occupied a very different position from the other prison-

420 Bruce, *op. cit.*, p. 498.   421 *Ibid.*, pp. 498, 499.   422 *Ibid.*, p. 499.
423 *The Interpreter's Bible*, IX, 331, 332.   424 Ramsay, *op. cit.*, p. 314.   425 Bruce, *loc. cit.*
426 James Smith, *The Voyage and Shipwreck of St. Paul.*   427 Ellicott, *op. cit.*, VII, 170.
428 Rackham, *op. cit.*, 480.

ers. He was a man of distinction, a Roman citizen who had appealed for trial to the supreme court in Rome. The others had been, in all probability, already condemned to death and were going to supply the perpetual demand which Rome made on the provinces for human victims to amuse the populace by their death in the arena.[429]

Reference to **the centurion named Julius, of the Augustan band** (v. 1b), to whom Paul and the other prisoners were delivered, has long puzzled Bible scholars. Ramsay's conclusion appears to be the most satisfactory:

It would naturally be a legionary centurion on detached service for communication between the Emperor and his armies in the provinces. . . . That the centurion [Julius] to whom Luke alludes was one of this body is confirmed by the fact that, when he reached Rome, he handed Paul over to his chief. We conclude, then, that the "troops of the Emperor" was a popular colloquial way of describing the corps of officer couriers; and we thus gather from Acts an interesting fact, elsewhere unattested but in perfect conformity with the known facts.[430]

Macgregor cautiously concludes:

Possibly the name was given to a body of imperial couriers, elsewhere called *frumentarii*, who were detailed for such duties as keeping open communications between the emperor and his provincial armies, controlling the commissariat, and conducting prisoners to Rome. It seems likely that one entrusted with such responsible duties as was Julius would belong rather to such a select corps than to a Syrian auxiliary cohort.[431]

Plumptre[432] interestingly suggests that possibly Julius and his band may have escorted Festus to his Judaean province and that this was their return voyage to Rome. Could this have been a detachment of the 3,000-man bodyguard of the equestrian order recently formed by Nero and named Augustiani, which was assigned to accompany the emperor to the games and to applaud his public performances in the theater?

The port of embarkation is assumed to have been Caesarea. The ship which they boarded belonged to, and was bound for, Adramyttium, an important seaport of Mysia across the bay northeast of the island of Lebos and southeast of Troas. Adramyttium was situated on the old Roman road that passed from Assos and Troas to Pergamus, Ephesus, and Miletus. The gulf (Adramytti) still bears its ancient name. En route the ship was booked to call at certain **places on the coast of Asia** (v. 2). Due to the difficulty of securing direct passage to Rome at that season, it may have been the original intention of Julius to sail to Adramyttium and from thence to Greece or more likely Macedonia, after which they would have proceeded overland, probably via the *Egnatian Way* to the Adriatic Sea.

The presence of Aristarchus of Macedonia (v. 2; cf. Acts 19:29; 20:4; Col. 4:10; Philemon 24) as also of Luke, with Paul en route to Rome poses a problem which Ramsay holds can only be solved by allowing that they were permitted to accompany Paul as his personal slaves, "not merely performing the duties of slaves . . . , but actually passing as slaves."[433] Ramsay regards this as having greatly enhanced Paul's position with the Roman officer Julius. Bruce remarks that "Ramsay's argument merits the respect due to his great knowledge of social history in the Roman Empire of the first century A.D."[434] However, it might be suspected that Ramsay unconsciously read into the narrative more of the aristocratic cultural influence of the British society of his day than the known facts of the case would warrant. Aristarchus, who had accompanied Paul to Jerusalem from Macedonia (Acts 20:4), may have remained with Paul during the two years of his imprisonment at Caesarea and was now intending to return home, but due to changed plans in the sailing (v. 6), went to Rome with Paul where he is later found sharing Paul's imprisonment, possibly still serving his comforts (Col. 4:10). Kraeling regards Aristarchus as "the diarist whose journal [was] used by Luke."[435] The total passenger complement of the ship is given later by Luke as 276 persons (v. 37).

[429] Ramsay, *loc. cit.*
[430] *Ibid.*, p. 315. With this position, Rackham, *op. cit.*, p. 408; Bruce, *op. cit.*, p. 500; Ellicott, *loc. cit.*, and others agree.   [431] *The Interpreter's Bible*, IX, 332.
[432] Ellicott *loc. cit.* [433] Ramsay, *op. cit.*, p. 316. [434] Bruce, *op. cit.*, p. 501. [435] Kraeling, *op. cit.*, p. 454.

2. The Officer's Treatment of Paul at Sidon (27:3)

3 And the next day we touched at Sidon: and Julius treated Paul kindly, and gave him leave to go unto his friends and refresh himself.

The day following their embarkation the ship came to Sidon, some 20 miles north of Tyre. Here 40,000 people had perished in the flames of the city when it was destroyed by the Persian monarch Artaxerxes III in 351 B.C.

In the third century B.C. a new Hellenistic city had arisen under the Seleucids. By Paul's time it was a free city with its own municipal government and magistrates. It had become noted for its artists and scholars, especially in mathematics and astronomy. It was a chief center of wealth and trade, as well as of skilled workmen in glass and purple dyes. Thus it afforded a challenging opportunity for Christian evangelism and the development of a church. That the Christians had taken advantage of this opportunity is evidenced by the Christian friends whom Paul visited in the city, and who were likely the fruit of the gospel planted there more than a quarter of a century earlier (Acts 11:19). Sidon has a present population of about 10,000 people and is known by the French as Saidan but to Arabs as Saida. Its ancient spacious harbor has been largely silted up.

Paul appears to have favorably impressed Julius (cf. Acts 18:14-16; 19:31, 37), who treated him philanthropically, though he was in custody.

The friends to whom Paul went at Sidon were, according to Harnack,[436] Christian believers. Harnack thinks friends may have been one of the current names by which Christians greeted one another in Paul's day (cf. John 15: 14, 15; III John 14). The church at Sidon likely originated with the witness of the scattered disciples following the martyrdom of Stephen (Acts 11:19). In addition to the mutual spiritual edification and encouragement shared by Paul and the Sidon Christians, they likely contributed to his personal comfort in food and clothing for the voyage, which would have been welcomed by Paul after a two-year imprisonment. He was most likely in the custody of a soldier while ashore.

3. The Ship's Course from Sidon to Myra (27:4, 5)

4 And putting to sea from thence, we sailed under the lee of Cyprus, because the winds were contrary. 5 And when we had sailed across the sea which is off Cilicia and Pamphylia, we came to Myra, *a city* of Lycia.

En route from Patara to Tyre two years earlier, the vessel on which Paul and his companions sailed passed by a direct course across the eastern Mediterranean (Acts 21:1-3). Ramsay[437] holds that while it was common for vessels to follow this course eastward it was hardly possible for them to return thus, for there was seldom a steady easterly wind that could be trusted for such a voyage. The westerly breezes were constant throughout the summer months, and consequently the westward-bound vessels sailed northward east of Cyprus and from thence westward along the coast of Asia Minor leaving Cyprus on the south. Since Luke explains the reason for the course followed (v. 4b), Ramsay[438] considers it evident that he was a stranger to the sea and had expected that the vessel should have followed the direct course taken from Myra to Sidon two years earlier. However, it may be legitimately questioned whether Luke may not have made his explanation, **because the winds were contrary** (v. 4b), in the interest of his uninformed readers, rather than as an expression of his personal surprise. The ship moved along the coasts of Cilicia and Pamphylia, aided by the local offshore breezes and a steady westward coastal current. "The Adramyttian ship," says Ramsay, "crept on from point to point up the coast, taking advantage of every opportunity to make a few miles, and lying at anchor in the shelter of the winding coasts, when the westerly wind made progress impossible."[439]

One authority notes that Luke's expression, **sailed across** (v. 5), "seems to imply that after a time they ceased to hug the coast and cut across from point to point presumably from the southwest point of **Cilicia** to the promontory of

436 Adolf Harnack, *op. cit.*, I, 419f.   437 Ramsay, *op. cit.*, pp. 316, 317.
438 *Ibid.*   439 *Ibid.*, p. 317.

Lycia just east of **Myra,** across the great bay made by the coast of **Pamphylia.**"440

After fifteen days441 of sailing they reached the harbor of Myra, which was the great port for Syrian and Egyptian commerce. The city of Myra, a port of Lycia, on the most southerly point of Asia, was located some two miles inland from the harbor. Ramsay states that Myra was "the seat of the sailors' god."442

The site of the ancient city is marked by ruins of the theater, an aqueduct, rock tombs and other buildings.

Conybeare and Howson relate concerning Myra: "In the seclusion of the deep gorge of Dembra is a magnificent Byzantine church, — probably the cathedral of the diocese, when Myra was the ecclesiastical and political metropolis of Lycia."443 Thus it would appear that eventually Christianity made its impact upon the city whose honor had been stolen from Paul and the gospel by St. Nicholas, the patron saint of the Greek sailors, who had been born at Patara and was buried at Myra.

4. The Ship's Course from Myra to Fair Havens (27:6-8)

6 And there the centurion found a ship of Alexandria sailing for Italy; and he put us therein. 7 And when we had sailed slowly many days, and were come with difficulty over against Cnidus, the wind not further suffering us, we sailed under the lee of Crete, over against Salmone; 8 and with difficulty coasting along it we came unto a certain place called Fair Havens; nigh whereunto was the city of Lasea.

If Julius' plan had originally been to sail to Macedonia and from there to take the overland route to the Adriatic, then his plans were changed at Myra in favor of a continued sea voyage direct to Italy. What may have changed his plans can only be conjectured. Plumptre thinks it may have been the presence of an Alexandrian grain ship bound for Rome, in the harbor of Myra upon their arrival, that offered:

An easier and more expeditious route to go straight to Rome, instead of landing at Myra, and then taking another ship to Macedonia in order to journey by land to the coast of the Adriatic. A local inscription described Myra as a "horrea," or store-house of corn . . . and the Alexandrian ship may therefore have gone thither to discharge part of its cargo.444

Plumptre thinks that this ship had been driven out of its course by a strong westerly wind (an argument that does not seem consistent with his account otherwise) en route from Alexandria to Rome. Ramsay considers such a conclusion both "unnecessary and incorrect."445 He holds rather that it was on its "regular and ordinary course" and had likely experienced favorable sailing. The colossal city of Rome had by this time become largely dependent upon foreign markets, of which Egypt was chief, for her corn (wheat) supply, and consequently such government grain vessels were common on the sea and in the ports between Alexandria and Rome by this time. If this was a government-owned grainship, then it is quite understandable that Julius should have requisitioned passage to Rome for himself, his troops, and the prisoners. These vessels which carried grain "were of a specially large build,"446 and consequently such a ship could have accommodated so large a passenger complement as 276 people (v. 38).447

Troubles began when the Alexandrian ship set sail from Myra for Cnidus. The difficulties encountered were occasioned by the strong northwesterly Etesian gales which prevail in those regions during late July and throughout August. The **many days** (v. 7) of slow sailing consumed about 25 days, for the distance of about 130 miles,448 which with favorable weather could have been done in a day. The lateness of the season likely accounted for their not having put in port at Cnidus to wait for better weather. Though Cnidus appears to have been too far north for their course, it is evident that the coast afforded them pro-

---

440 *The Interpreter's Bible,* IX, 333.　　441 Rackham, *op. cit.,* p. 481.
442 Ramsay, *op. cit.,* p. 298. For further description of eastern Mediterranean sailing in relation to Myra, see *ibid.,* pp. 298, 316-319, 399.　　443 Conybeare and Howson, *op. cit.,* p. 691.
444 Ellicott, *op. cit.,* VII, 171.
445 Ramsay, *op. cit.,* p. 319 — For an interesting description of a wind-driven ship by Lucian in his dialogue *The Ship,* see *Ibid.,* pp. 319, 320.　　446 Rackham, *op. cit.,* p. 482.
447 One of these ships, that of Lucian, has been described as 180 feet by 45 feet with a calculated tonnage of about 1200. James Hastings, ed., *Dictionary of the Bible,* p. 851.
448 Kraeling, *op. cit.,* p. 455.

tection from the northerly wind and enabled the ship to sail more southerly toward Crete than otherwise possible, while at the same time keeping clear of the treacherous northern coast of Rhodes.

Cnidus was located on a peninsula on the southwest coast of Asia Minor with a harbor on either side. Since the coast of Asia Minor bends away northward here, they were exposed to the full force of the Etesian (periodical or annual Mediterranean) winds. Thus the impossibility of "heading" these winds disposed the ship's captain to take the only course open and sail southward with a view to coming under the lee of the coast of Crete, which is modernly known as Candia. From Cape Salmone at the eastern tip of the island they sailed with difficulty, but with some protection, westward under the lee of the coast until they came to the harbor known as Fair Havens, near the city of Lasia, where they remained for some time. Fair Havens was a small bay lying east of Cape Matalda. It is still known by this name.

Concerning the island of Crete, Souther remarks:

> Crete, the modern Candia, is an island 60 miles S. of Greece proper, about 150 miles long, and varying in breadth from 30 to 7 miles, with mountains as high as 8000 feet. It is about equidistant from Europe, Asia, and Africa, and was inhabited from the earliest times of which we have any knowledge.
> . . . The epithets which a native of the island, the poet Epimenides (flourished B.C. 600), flung at the Cretans, are quoted in a somewhat unapostolic manner in the Epistle to Titus (1:12). Epimenides styled them 'always liars, evil beasts of prey, lazy gluttons.'[449]

The record of Christianity in Crete is somewhat obscure. We know that there were Cretan Jews present at Pentecost (Acts 2:11), and it is likely that some of them were converted (Acts 2:37-42) and carried the Christian faith back to their island with them. In any event, Christianity seems to have been well established in the island in the first century. That Titus was placed here by Paul to superintend the churches of the island, we learn from Paul's letter to Titus (Titus 1:4-9). Further, the con-

siderable extent of Christianity by the time of this epistle (ca. A.D. 65) is indicated by Paul's instructions, "ordain elders in every city, as I had appointed thee" (Titus 1:5b). How many cities there were we are not told, but Hurlbut[450] lists eighteen towns in all on the island, three of which are on the west end, eight on the north side, five on the south side, and two in the interior. So if Paul's words to Titus (1:5) are to be taken literally, the Christian community on Crete must have been considerable. Both the influence of Judaizing Christianity on the native Cretans and the influence of pagan Cretan culture on the Christians become apparent from Paul's letter to Titus. That there were Christians here when Paul was en route to Rome seems evident, but there is no indication that Paul made contact with them at Fair Havens, as he did at Tyre (Acts 21:4) and Sidon (v. 3).

There is no evidence that Paul founded the church on Crete, although he may have reorganized it. At all events, it is evident that he visited the island at a time other than on his voyage to Rome, that he was acquainted with the Christian community there (Titus 1:5), and that Titus was with him, whom he left in charge of the churches of Crete, not as a bishop but as a superintendent (Titus 1:5). From A.D. 54 or 55 (see II Cor. 7:5-16; 8:16-24), nothing is known of Titus until following Paul's release from his first Roman imprisonment, or perhaps until after Paul had written I Timothy in about A.D. 64 or 65. It appears to have been at this time that he accompanied Paul to visit the Christians of Crete. Paul subsequently promised to send Artemas or Tychicus to Crete to relieve Titus, at which time Titus was instructed to join Paul to winter at Nicopolis (Titus 3:12). Further, it seems evident that Titus was with Paul in his second Roman imprisonment and that Paul sent him to Dalmatia on an errand (II Tim. 4:10).

Regarding the Epistle to Titus as a commentary on the church in Crete, three things become evident. *First*, false teachers, especially a branch of Judaizers, were doing a damaging work. They stressed Jewish ceremonials such as circumcision, taught Jewish fables, laid down the commandments of men, raised and discussed foolish questions, contended about genealogies, and strove about technical points of the Jewish law. *Second,* Paul wrote to instruct Titus concerning the organization and direction of the church and to offer his personal encouragement for his difficult task. *Third,* Paul sent his letter to Titus by the hands of Zenas and Apollos who had evidently planned a missionary journey to Crete, possibly as Apollos had gone from Ephesus to Corinth to edify the church there (Acts 18:24-28).

There appears a slight indication that Paul may have joined Apollos at Corinth on his third missionary journey and there have sent the Epistle to Titus by Apollos and Zenas (cf. I Cor. 16:12), in which event Paul would have visited Crete with Titus, at an earlier date, possibly from Corinth on his second missionary journey. In that case Paul might have had one of his three previous shipwrecks en route to, or returning from, Crete (cf. II Cor. 11:25). Such an hypothesis could account for Paul's apparent knowledge of the hazards of sailing in the region of Crete (see Acts 27:9, 10). However, scholars have generally noted the similarity of the style of Titus to I Timothy and have dated the epistle at about A.D. 65. Thiessen summarizes Paul's purpose and plan in the writing of Titus.[451]

B. THE VOYAGE FROM CRETE TO MALTA (27:9-26)

Luke's notation that the **Fast was now already gone by** (v. 9) is a chronological landmark for Paul's voyage to Rome. Kraeling[452] and Bruce[453] agree with Ramsay (as also many other scholars) that this **Fast** of "The Great Day of Atonement," fell on October 5 in A.D. 59 and that as Paul and Aristarchus observed this occasion, Luke used it as a mark of time. Ramsay[454] further notes that September 14 to November 11 was a dangerous season for navigation, and from November 11 to March 15 it appears that all open-sea sailing was discontinued. Ramsay thinks the ship reached Fair Havens in late September and did not leave until after October 5.

Bruce succinctly treats this chronological problem thus:

> By the 'Fast' he [Luke] means, of course, the Great Day of Atonement, which falls on Tishri 10. Luke's remark has point only if that date fell rather late in the solar calendar that year. In A.D. 59 it fell on October 5, but in all the neighboring years from A.D. 57 to 63 it fell earlier. A late date for the Day of Atonement is required also by the subsequent time notes of the journey to Italy. When they set sail from Fair Havens, fifty or sixty miles brought them under the lee of Candia (v. 16): on the fourteenth night from Candia (V. 27) they drew near land, and the following day (V. 39) they landed on Malta, where they spent three months (Ch. 28:11). The seas were closed to sailing until the beginning of February at the earliest; the three months spent in Malta must therefore have corresponded roughly to November, December and January; they must have left Fair Havens not much earlier than mid-October. The solar date of the Day of Atonement in A.D. 59 thus accords well with Luke's implication that the Fast took place while they were at Fair Havens.[455]

1. The Decision to Sail from Crete (27: 9-12)

9 And when much time was spent, and the voyage was now dangerous, because the Fast was now already gone by, Paul admonished them, 10 and said unto them, Sirs, I perceive that the voyage will be with injury and much loss, not only of the lading and the ship, but also of our lives. 11 But the centurion gave more heed to the master and to the owner of the ship, than to those things which were spoken by Paul. 12 And because the haven was not commodious to winter in, the more part advised to put to sea from thence, if by any means they could reach Phoenix, and winter *there; which is* a haven of Crete, looking north-east and south-east.

Paul's experience in ocean travel was more extensive than may appear on the surface of the Acts record. (cf. II Cor. 11: 25, 26). Thus he felt confident and made bold to offer advice against sailing from Fair Havens (v. 9b). However, Julius, who appears to have made the decision (v. 11), took the advice of the ship's master who wished to proceed to the more

451 Henry Clarence Thiessen, *Introduction to the New Testament,* pp. 266, 267.
452 Kraeling, *loc. cit.*   453 Bruce, *op. cit.,* p. 506.   454 Ramsay, *op. cit.,* p. 322.
455 Bruce, *loc. cit.*

commodious harbor of Phoenix near the western end of Crete for wintering quarters (v. 12). Ramsay[456] suggests that a council was held to consider the advisability of sailing and that Paul was consulted as a man of rank and travel experience. Ramsay[457] goes on to argue that the evidence is conclusive that there was an "official council" at which Julius presided and that this fact, plus his final and official decision to sail, indicates that they were sailing on a government ship on which a high-ranking military officer such as Julius, rather than the master of the ship, would have had the final decision to make. Rome's absolute dependence upon grain from the foreign ports to feed and pacify the urban masses made it imperative that the government own and control these merchant vessels. Further, Ramsay thinks, this naturally placed matters of decisions for movement and directions of such grain ships under military or naval officers (which were not at that time distinct) rather than the sea captains, though such authority did not extend to navigation as such. This vessel, Ramsay believes, belonged to the "Alexandrian fleet in the Imperial service." The problem of **the owner of the ship** (v. 11) Ramsay[458] resolves by rejecting the rendering as incorrect, both in the KJV and the RV. Indeed Williams' translation would allow Ramsay's position where it reads, "But the colonel was influenced by the pilot and the captain of the ship rather than by what Paul said"[459] (v. 11). Similarly Phillips' version reads: "But Julius paid more attention to the helmsman and the captain than to Paul's words of warning."[460]

"The harbor of Phoenix or Phenice," says Kraeling, "was forty geographical miles farther up the Cretan coast. It was better protected and in every way more attractive, and there was reasonable hope of being able to make it in a few hours under favorable circumstances."[461] A southerly breeze bade fair for their voyage, and so they set sail, with difficulty rounding Cape Matala, which cape projects south six miles, and then entered the Gulf of Messara.

Concerning Julius' acceptance of the master's advice rather than Paul's, Wesley remarks: "And indeed it is a general rule, Believe an artificer in his own art. Yet when there is the greatest need, a real Christian will often advise even better than him."[462] How well advised would governmental administrators often be if they consulted the judgment of experienced God-fearing missionaries, though their training might not have been in the technicalities of administration. Here is a case in which "the wish became the father of the deed." Though the decision of **the more part** (v. 12) or the majority carried, subsequent events proved the minority judgment and advice to have been right. There is hardly sufficient historical evidence that majority decisions have always been right and minorities wrong. Especially are majority decisions dangerous when they have been motivated by selfish desires, as is so often the case. Plumptre sees in Paul's admonition (v. 9), "The tone . . . of a man who speaks more from the foresight gained by observation than from a direct, supernatural prediction."[463] In fact, Bruce quotes James Smith as saying, "the prudence of the advice given by the masters and owners was extremely questionable and that the advice given by St. Paul may probably be supported even on nautical grounds."[464] Besides his previous sea and shipwreck experiences, Paul evidenced an acquaintance with Crete itself in his Epistle to Titus, though it is not known for certain when he acquired that knowledge, as the epistle was written at a later date. Paul speaks in warning of the loss of the precious cargo of grain, as also of the more precious lives of the passengers. The former prediction was fulfilled, but by divine intervention the latter was averted (see v. 20).

On the problem of **a haven of Crete looking northeast and southeast** (v. 12), Bruce remarks:

> But it is not necessary to suppose that any mistake was made. A short distance west of Lutro, on the other side of the peninsula of Muros, lies Phineka, which evidently preserves the ancient name Phoenix. Phineka lies open to the wester-

---

[456] Ramsay, op. cit., 323.   [457] Ibid., pp. 323-326.   [458] Ibid., p. 324.
[459] Williams, op. cit., p. 323.   [460] Phillips, op. cit., p. 70.   [461] Kraeling, loc cit.
[462] Wesley, op. cit., p. 405, n. 11.   [463] Ellicott, op. cit., VII, 172.
[464] James Smith, op. cit., p. 85 n., as quoted by Bruce, op. cit., p. 507.

ly wind and may have had quite a good harbour in the first century; the two streams shown as entering the bay in its vicinity may have silted up in the course of the centuries.[465]

Dummelow's explanation is both clear and simple: "The bay or harbour formed a semicircle, of which one half looked SW. and the other half NW."[466]

2. The Storm at Sea (27:13-20)

13 And when the south wind blew softly, supposing that they had obtained their purpose, they weighed anchor and sailed along Crete, close in shore. 14 But after no long time there beat down from it a tempestuous wind, which is called Euraquilo: 15 and when the ship was caught, and could not face the wind, we gave way *to it,* and were driven. 16 And running under the lee of a small island called Cauda, we were able, with difficulty, to secure the boat: 17 and when they had hoisted it up, they used helps, undergirding the ship; and, fearing lest they should be cast upon the Syrtis, they lowered the gear, and so were driven. 18 And as we labored exceedingly with the storm, the next day they began to throw *the freight* overboard; 19 and the third day they cast out with their own hands the tackling of the ship. 20 And when neither sun nor stars shone upon *us* for many days, and no small tempest lay on *us,* all hope that we should be saved was now taken away.

Luke makes a sharp distinction between the opinionated decision of Julius and the seamen to sail from Fair Havens, and the studied sober judgment of Paul that safety required them to remain in port. Such is suggested by his placement of responsibility for sailing upon "them": **supposing that "they" had obtained "their" purpose, "they" weighed anchor and sailed** (v. 13). Previously, as later, Luke identifies Paul and his party with the movements of the ship by the use of the pronouns **we** and **us** (see vv. 1-5, 7, 8). Here however, the picture has changed and **"they"** ventured forth against the sober advice and warnings of the man of God and the lessons that nature itself should have taught them. Such presumptiveness is always dangerous and is certain to carry its own re-

ward. Nor would Paul bear responsibility for conduct which was against his own best judgment and advice. The necessity of circumstances demanded that he accompany the ship on its ill-fated course, but he could not commit himself to a course of action which he foresaw would be disastrous.

They found slight circumstantial confirmation for their decision in a gentle south wind which arose and promised to bring them safely on to their desired haven at Phoenix. However, this temporary breeze proved only to be as the miraged lake on the burning desert sands that lures the thirst-mad traveller on, only to vanish, leaving him in disillusionment and deeper despair of hopelessness. Luke's statement that they **sailed along Crete, close in shore** (v. 13b) suggests how little they trusted the out-of-season **south wind** which promised to take them to their destination. The rounding of Cape Matala threatened to be their greatest danger. However, this was accomplished without incident, and from thence they hopefully charted a course across the gulf of Messara to Phoenix. Erelong their rising hopes of reaching Phoenix some seventeen miles across the bay were **dashed to pieces** by the sudden conversion of the promising south wind into the **tempestuous Euraquilo** or "Levanter," (v. 14) which **beat down** upon them from the 7000-foot Mount Ida of legendary fame. Ramsay calls it "a sudden eddying squall,"[467] but Luke describes it as a "typhonic wind" suggesting "the whirling motion of the clouds and sea caused by the meeting of contrary currents of air. From this derives our English typhoon."[468]

"The sailors recognized this wind as an old enemy and had a name for it — Euraquilo."[469] Having passed Cape Matala, they lost the further protection of the coast line which they had thus far closely followed (v. 13b). Consequently as **the ship was caught, and could not face the wind, we gave way to it and were driven** (v. 15b). Kraeling vividly describes the incident that followed thus:

The ship, with a single large sail which could not be slackened quickly, was in great peril. They drifted with starboard

[465] Bruce, *op. cit.,* p. 508.   [466] Dummelow, *op. cit.,* p. 852.   [467] Ramsay, *op. cit.,* p. 327.
[468] Pliny the Elder describes this as the chief plague of sailors, "not only breaking up the spars but the hull itself." Pliny, *Natural History,* II, 132.   [469] Bruce, *op. cit.,* p. 509.

toward the wind until they got into calmer water under the shelter of an island named Gauda or Clauda (Gozzo), [or the modern Gavdho] some twenty-three miles to the south. Here they were able to take refuge. The water-logged lifeboat [or the "dinghy"] which they had been towing, was got aboard — a hard job ['with difficulty,'] says Luke, probably remembering his blisters] in which the diarist seems to have helped. [There were certain jobs which only trained members of the crew could carry out, but any landlubber could haul on a rope and some of the passengers were pressed into service]. The ship was then undergirded with ropes to reinforce her, lest she break apart from the strain caused by shifting cargo. This could be done by lowering a cable under the hull in U-shaped manner, drawing it along both sides to the center and fastening it there.470

Vivid as is Kraeling's description, there remains some doubt as to the exact nature of the operation suggested by Luke in verse 17. Macgregor offers the following possible explanations. This authority questions the afore-described operation and then asks:

> Or (b), [were they] undergirders of ropes or chains stretched across the ship's hold under the deck and made fast to one of the stout ribs on each side? Or (c), as shown in ancient pictures of Egyptian ship rope trusses, 'stretched above decks from stern to stem intended to prevent the boat from breaking its back amid-ship by binding the stern and stem together'? . . . The last suggestion is attractive because such trusses were kept taut by being raised from the deck by props — which might well be the function of the helps.471

Kraeling's view appears the more likely as his description of **the helps** accords with Bruce's472 identification of **the helps** with the "undergirders," or "frapping cables," nautical terms attested by Aristotle, Philo, and Josephus. The practice is sometimes followed by modern seamen and is called "frapping."473 Plumptre sees an allusion to this practice in the lines of Horace (Od. 1:14), which he translates thus "['And scarcely can our keels keep sound, e'en with the ropes

that gird them around and against the imperious wave']."474

Why the ship did not attempt to find refuge at Cauda Luke does not say, but it is assumed that there may have been no harbor available there.

A new fear arose with the seamen lest the **Euraquilo** should drive them on the Syrtis (v. 17b). The Syrtis was a great stretch of sand-banks along the coast of Cyrene and Carthage, Africa, the major one to the southwest of Cauda, and directly· toward which the wind was blowing. Kraeling remarks: "The Syrtes were two areas on the coast of Africa — the westerly one being the Syrtis Minor and the easterly one the Syrtis Major; both were greatly feared by ancient navigators."475 And Dummelow cites Farrar as authority that "The 'Greater Syrtis,' 'the Goodwin Sands of the Mediterranean' . . . lay to the SW of Cauda."476

Luke's expression, **they lowered the gear, and so were driven** (v. 17b), may be best understood in Dummelow's words, "They probably lowered the main sail more than halfway, but left the sail 'artemon' or storm sail extended."477 Phillips renders the passage, "so they shortened sail and lay to drifting,"478 and Williams says, "they lowered the sail and let her drift."479 According to Ramsay, the ship drifted with her bow to the north, held on course by a low sail "making leeway proportionate to the power of the wind and waves on her broadside."480 Kraeling describes the operations at this point in vivid, nautical terminology:

> Precautions were taken to reduce the hazards by 'straking sail,' or 'lowering the gear.' This meaning getting flat on the deck every bit of fair-weather sailing equipment such as spars, rigging, sails, etc. But this precaution was not enough to keep Paul's ship from being blown southward. A ship in this situation had either to scud or heave to. The former was out of the question, since that would have taken them to the Syrtis. They had to heave to with some storm-sail set. This was necessary to keep her on the starboard track in order to hold a course west of north.481

470 Kraeling, op. cit., p. 456.
471 The Interpreter's Bible, IX, 336. See also Cadbury, The Beginnings of Christianity, pt. II, vol. V, 351.
472 Bruce, op. cit., p. 509, n, 38.   473 Dummelow, loc. cit.   474Ellicott, op. cit., VII, 173.
475 Kraeling, loc cit.   476 Dummelow, loc. cit.   477 Ibid.   478 Phillips, op. cit., p. 71.
479 Williams, op. cit., p.323.   480 Ramsay, op. cit., pp. 330, 331.   481 Kraeling, loc. cit.

Ramsay cites James Smith as authority that the resultant speed would vary, depending upon the size of the vessel and the velocity of the wind, from three-fourths to two miles per hour, with a likely mean rate of about one and one-half miles per hour. The direction, he thinks, would have been eight degrees north of west. Thus he calculates that by leaving Cauda at evening, the ship would have neared Malta by the fourteenth night, having covered roughly five hundred miles of ocean. It appears that their greatest danger was foundering the ship because of leakage due to the sail and heavy winds at the starboard side, for which excessive strain ancient vessels were not constructed. This fact seems to account for the conduct of the fearful seamen in lightening the ship by throwing the cargo overboard the following day (v. 18; cf. Jonah 1:5).

On the third day desperation demanded that even the equipment be cast into the sea to save the ship. This they began to do, which seems to have been progressively carried out (cf. v. 38). Thus they made the supreme sacrifice which, says Ramsay, "makes a striking picture of growing panic."[482] The tackling of the ship (v. 19), which may have included spars, ("including the mainyard . . . , an immense spar, probably as long as the ship, which would require the united efforts of passengers and crew to launch overboard"),[483] the ropes, the ship's furniture, such as tables, benches, chests, boxes, beds, and such like were heaved overboard. It is amazing how easily expendable material possessions become when life itself is at stake. Satan's words to God concerning Job are near the truth when taken from their setting and applied to material possessions: "all that a man hath will he give for his life" (Job 2:4b).

Luke does not fail to depict the progressiveness of their dawning despair. Caught in the storm, driven out of course, personal possessions and the ship's equipment plus most of the cargo overboard, and now for eleven more weary days and nights they were driven blindly on with the raging tempest hiding the sun by day and the stars by night. Thus they were robbed of direction or distance as no astronomical bearings could be taken. They were doubtless hard pressed to bail a leaking ship and stay it from foundering. All hope of driving the vessel ashore to elude a watery interment seemed to be lost. For fourteen days they had been too sick or distraught to eat. The bad had come to the worst. There remained no alternative. They were helpless victims trapped in the death grasp of a mad and raging sea! How utterly helpless! Luke, perhaps expressing the pagan mariner's perspective, seems almost to personalize their fate in his words, **all hope that we should be saved was now taken away** (v. 20b). Perhaps Paul had looked upon his pagan travelling companions in this extreme hour and learned from them what he later wrote from his Roman prison: "having no hope, and without God in the world" (Eph. 2:12b). It would seem that God allowed them to be utterly robbed of every human or material source of dependence or hope that He might "show himself strong in the behalf of them whose heart is perfect toward him" (II Chron. 16:9). Or in the words of the author of Hebrews, "He taketh away the first, that he may establish the second" (Heb. 10:9).

3. The Reassurance of Paul (27:21-26)

21 And when they had been long without food, then Paul stood forth in the midst of them, and said, Sirs, ye should have hearkened unto me, and not have set sail from Crete, and have gotten this injury and loss. 22 And now I exhort you to be of good cheer; for there shall be no loss of life among you, but *only* of the ship. 23 For there stood by me this night an angel of the God whose I am, whom also I serve, 24 saying, Fear not, Paul; thou must stand before Caesar: and lo, God hath granted thee all them that sail with thee. 25 Wherefore, sirs, be of good cheer: for I believe God, that it shall be even so as it hath been spoken unto me. 26 But we must be cast upon a certain island.

We may well imagine that while panic and frustration reigned in the pagan minds of these men, Paul, perhaps with his Christian companions, was hidden away somewhere in the dark hold of the ship keeping his prayer vigil with God. The hymn writer so aptly expressed what

---

[482] Ramsay, *op. cit.,* p. 332.   [483] James Smith, *op. cit.,* p. 116, as quoted by Bruce *op. cit.,* p. 511.

we may well imagine characterized the content of Paul's prayer on this occasion, when she wrote,

> Master, the tempest is raging!
> The billows are tossing high!
> The sky is o'er-shadowed with blackness,
> No shelter or help is nigh:
> Carest Thou not that we perish?
> How canst Thou lie asleep,
> When each moment so madly is threatening
> A grave in the angry deep?

Then out of the darkness of despair came the answer of God through an angel who **stood by** (v. 23) Paul this night and said, **Fear not, Paul** (v. 24).

> The winds and the waves shall obey
> My will,
> Peace, be still!
> Whether the wrath of the storm-tossed sea,
> Or demons, or men, or whatever it be,
> No water can swallow the ship where lies
> The Master of ocean and earth and skies;
> They all shall sweetly obey My will;
> Peace, be still! Peace, be still!
> They all shall sweetly obey My will;
> Peace, peace, be still![484]

Then suddenly out of the midnight darkness there shone a light, not the light of the sun that had broken through the storm clouds, but the light of God's glory that had illumined with new rays of hope, out of the midst of despair, the countenance of the "man of God" aboard.

Their abstinence from food (v. 21) does not imply that their provisions were exhausted, (vv. 35, 38), but probably suggests that extreme seasickness had largely deprived them of appetite (v. 33), and the uncertainties ahead may have placed them on slim rations. Added to this was the likely fact that the violent storm had prevented them from preparing food.

Julius, the captain, and the seamen had rejected Paul's counsel in their self-sufficiency at Fair Havens (v. 11), but now, however, with all hope gone (v. 20), they were glad to listen to his advice (v. 21). Bruce remarks: "It warms our hearts to see . . . that in some human respects he

was so like ourselves; he would not resist the temptation to say, 'I told you so,' to those who had despised his good advice at Fair Havens."[485]

It appears that Luke's narrative implies that the pagan mariners and passengers had turned in vain to wailing to their gods (cf. Jonah 1:5), while Paul prayed faithfully on in confidence until he had God's answer (v. 22-25).

Paul had received from God, and was now prepared to deliver to his fellows what the situation most needed, a message of good cheer and hope. His very manner and message reflected the confidence born of divine assurance (cf. Acts 3:6, 7). At Fair Havens Paul had spoken out of experience and human judgment and his prediction had been fulfilled, except for the loss of life (vv. 9, 10). However, now as Bruce phrases it:

> No amount of experience or shrewd calculation could have given him this assurance; he ascribes his new confidence to a supernatural revelation made to him during the past night by an angel of God. Not only would he himself survive to stand before the emperor; the lives of his shipmates were also to be spared for his sake. The world has no idea how much it owes, in the mercy of God, to the presence in it of righteous men.[486]

It would be interesting to know if the **angel of God that stood by** Paul (v. 23) on this dark night and reassured him that he should **stand before Caesar** (v. 23) was the same messenger that appeared to him earlier with assurance that he should **bear witness also at Rome** (Acts 23:11; cf. Gen. 18:26ff.).

The angel of the Lord had dispelled Paul's doubts and fears, **Fear not, Paul** (v. 24a), and now Paul was prepared to encourage his fellows: **Wherefore, sirs, be of good cheer** (v. 25a). Before he could offer encouragement to others, Paul had to experience their depression and be divinely lifted from it (cf. Heb. 2:18).

Of Paul's statement **whose I am, whom also I serve** (v. 23), Plumptre remarks: "The service implied is that of worship rather than labour. The word and thought were eminently characteristic of St. Paul"[487] (cf. Rom. 1:9; II Tim. 1:3).

Paul assumed the role of a prophet and shared the divine revelation which

---

[484] Written by Mary A. Baker, quoted from *Power and Praise*, p. 105.
[485] Bruce, *op. cit.*, pp. 511, 512.   [486] *Ibid.*, p. 512.   [487] Ellicott, *op. cit.*, VII, 174.

had been made to him: **But we must be cast upon a certain island** (v. 26). Nor is it necessary to suppose that Luke added these words after the occurrence.

C. THE SHIPWRECK AT MALTA (27: 27-44)

The detailed accuracy with which God's revelation to Paul was fulfilled in the events that follow is most amazing.

1. The Surmise of Land (27:27, 28)

27 But when the fourteenth night was come, as we were driven to and fro in the *sea of* Adria, about midnight the sailors surmised that they were drawing near to some country: 28 and they sounded, and found twenty fathoms; and after a little space, they sounded again, and found fifteen fathoms.

The fourteenth night (v. 27) seems to have been calculated from the time of their departure from Fair Havens (cf. vv. 18, 19, 33), as based upon James Smith's calculations referred to earlier in this chapter. Bruce states that "The soundings recorded in vs. 28 indicate that the ship was passing the Point of Koura located on the east coast of Malta, at the east extremity of St. Paul's Bay."[488] It is quite possible that the sound of breakers against the rocky shore and a dim line of sea foam alerted the seamen to approaching land. When they sounded (measured the depth of the sea), they first found it to be 20 fathoms or about 120 feet, but a second sounding indicated only 15 fathoms or about 90 feet. Thus their suspicions that they were approaching land were confirmed. These soundings have been found to agree with modern measurements taken among the breakers of Cape Koura.

Reference to the **sea of Adria** (v. 27) may be best understood as a name which was commonly applied to the whole of the eastern Mediterranean, though in a more technical sense it belonged to the waters lying to the northeast between Sicily and Achaia.

2. The Sailors' Plan of Escape (27: 29-32).

29 And fearing lest haply we should be cast ashore on rocky ground, they let go

four anchors from the stern, and wished for the day. 30 And as the sailors were seeking to flee out of the ship, and had lowered the boat into the sea, under color as though they would lay out anchors from the foreship, 31 Paul said to the centurion and to the soldiers, Except these abide in the ship, ye cannot be saved. 32 Then the soldiers cut away the ropes of the boat, and let her fall off.

Cognizance was taken of approaching dangerous rocks. The sailors cast out four anchors from the stern of the ship and wished for the day (v. 29). Ancient ships were equipped for stern anchors as well as bow anchors. This appears to indicate that they were anchored off the north shore of Malta, and thus, with a heavy northeasterly wind blowing, the bow of the ship would be aimed at the shore in readiness to run aground at such time as the anchors should be lifted or severed from the ship.

Once the ship was thus anchored the sailors sought to insure their own safety at the expense of the other passengers by escaping to land (v. 30). Thus they lowered the lifeboat under pretense of laying out anchors from the bow of the ship. Paul immediately detected their scheme and divulged to Julius and his soldiers the plot, with the warning that their escape would preclude the salvation of the remainder of the ship's passenger complement. Obviously the sailors were necessary for the management and maneuvering of the ship as occasion should arise. At Julius' command the soldiers cut away the ropes and let the dinghy drop into the sea. This appears to have been a rash move as the dinghy might have been used in getting passengers to shore after daybreak, and thus it is possible that the ship itself might have been saved from wreckage by beaching. However, it may have been considered by Julius as a necessary precautionary move against the sailors' further attempt to escape.

3. The Seamen's Fast Broken (27:33-38).

33 And while the day was coming on, Paul besought them all to take some food, saying, This day is the fourteenth day that ye wait and continue fasting, having taken nothing. 34 Wherefore I

---

[488] Bruce, *op. cit.,* p. 514.

beseech you to take some food: for this is for your safety: for there shall not a hair perish from the head of any of you. 35 And when he had said this, and had taken bread, he gave thanks to God in the presence of all; and he brake it, and began to eat. 36 Then were they all of good cheer, and themselves also took food. 37 And we were in all in the ship two hundred threescore and sixteen souls. 38 And when they had eaten enough, they lightened the ship, throwing out the wheat into the sea.

Paul's advice, as day dawned, that they **take some food: for this is for your safety** (v. 34), reflects its own merit. For fourteen days they had taken little if any food. They would naturally have become very weak and unfit for the difficult task that lay ahead in beaching the ship and getting ashore. The food, though simple and quickly prepared, would afford renewed physical strength and moral courage. Though Paul **gave thanks to God in the presence of all** (an act of piety; cf. I Tim. 4:4-6), **and broke the bread and began to eat,** (v. 35), this is not to be confused with the Eucharist (cf. Luke 24:30).

The number of passengers aboard need not surprise us as Josephus[489] relates a voyage to Rome in A.D. 63 where there were 600 passengers aboard, which ship went down in the Adriatic Sea. It has been suggested that the enumeration may have been with a view to the distribution of the food supplies.

The operation of lightening the ship by jettisoning the wheat cargo, begun at verse 18, was completed here perhaps in order that the ship might better run aground well up the beach.

4. The Ship's Wreckage (27:39-41)

39 And when it was day, they knew not the land: but they perceived a certain bay with a beach, and they took counsel whether they could drive the ship upon it. 40 And casting off the anchors, they left them in the sea, at the same time loosing the bands of the rudders; and hoisting up the foresail to the wind, they made for the beach. 41 But lighting upon a place where two seas met, they ran the vessel aground; and the foreship struck and remained unmoveable, but the stern began to break up by the violence *of the waves.*

When day dawned they saw land, but they were unable to identify it. Bruce[490] thinks they may have been familiar with the main harbor of Valletta where the other Alexandrian ships anchored (Acts 28:11) some eight miles distance from St. Paul's Bay, which itself lay some five miles from Melita the capital, located in the heart of the island. However, from St. Paul's Bay where they were shipwrecked, and with which location they were not familiar, they were unable to identify the island. When they saw a certain bay with a beach they (probably the ship's officers, Julius, and Paul) held consultations and decided in favor of beaching the ship at this spot (v. 39). Kraeling states:

> Tradition has localized the shipwreck on the eastern side of the bay and here was built a church of St. Paul *ad Mare;* that church was rebuilt in 1610, at which time the Tower of St. Paul was also erected near by.[491]

In the operation that followed (v. 40), **casting off the anchors,** for which they had no further use, **loosing the bands of the rudders,** or steering paddles, that they might drop into position and guide the ship, and **hoisting up the foresail** used only to direct the ship, they let her drive for the beach. Bruce vividly describes the bay and what happened to the ship thus:

> But there was something which they had not noticed, because it could not be seen until they had entered into the bay. "From the entrance of the bay, where the ship must have been anchored, they could not possibly have suspected that at the bottom of it there should be a communication with the sea outside" (Smith, *Voyage,* p. 143). St. Paul's Bay is sheltered on the northwest by the island of Salmonetta, which is separated from the Maltese mainland by a narrow channel about a hundred yards wide. This channel is the "place where two seas met."[492]

Ramsay[493] suggests that the ship probably drew about eighteen feet of water. When it struck the muddy bottom, it plowed on into tenacious clay which held the forepart of the ship fast and exposed the stern to the violence of the waves. Though the ship's stern began

---

[489] Josephus, *Life,* p. 3.
[490] Bruce, *op cit.* p. 518.   [491] Kraeling, *op cit.,* p. 457.   [492] Bruce, *loc. cit.*   [493] Ramsay, *op. cit.,* p. 341.

to break up under the impact, the bow was held together until every passenger safely escaped to shore.

5. The Passengers' Escape (27:42-44)

42 And the soldiers' counsel was to kill the prisoners, lest any *of them* should swim out, and escape. 43 But the centurion, desiring to save Paul, stayed them from their purpose; and commanded that they who could swim should cast themselves overboard, and get first to the land; 44 and the rest, some on planks, and some on *other* things from the ship. And so it came to pass, that they all escaped safe to the land.

The soldiers' counsel . . . to kill the prisoners (v. 42) may be best understood by the fact that Rome's rigid laws demanded that capital punishment be inflicted upon those in charge of prisoners if they allowed them to escape — especially in the case of capital crimes (cf. Acts 12:19; 16:27). The suggestion to slaughter the prisoners seems to have come from the soldiers, possibly some under-officer, and not from Julius himself.

Julius' admiration for, and confidence in, Paul by this time was such (v. 1) that he at once countermanded the order or intention of the soldiers (v. 43a). Thus we again see "the man of God" as the instrument of the salvation of those who otherwise would have perished.

Julius evidenced his disciplinary command of the situation and followed a plan, which Paul may have suggested, in which those able were to swim ashore and then give assistance to the non-swimmers as they attempted to get ashore on pieces of wreckage (v. 43). Paul may have been among the former, judging from his previous shipwreck experiences (cf. II Cor. 11:25).

The non-swimmers made for shore on planks and such other pieces of wreckage as were available from the disintegrating ship (v. 44). They all made it safely to shore with no loss of life, though the ship and its cargo were a total loss (v. 22).

6. Some Lessons from Paul's Voyage and Shipwreck

a. The beneficent influence of a godly life among the ungodly.

b. The spiritual and moral transcendence of physical handicap and limitation. Paul sets sail a prisoner bound for Caesar's court under a Roman centurion but ends in command of the army and the ship.

c. The advice of one sober experienced man of God may be safer than that of many motivated by selfish desires.

d. Prayer and divine aid may avail when all other hope is lost.

e. Man's extremity often becomes God's special opportunity.

f. The darkest hour of human despair is often just before the breaking of spiritual dawn and new hope.

g. All things temporal and material can profitably be sacrificed for life itself.

h. Things often turn out much better than a threatening situation promises.

i. The example of moral courage under extreme stress and strain when others have fallen into confusion and despair.

D. THE WINTER ON MALTA (28:1-10)

There seems to be no reasonable doubt that the island of Malta (or Melita) was the place of Paul's shipwreck and three months' stay en route to Rome. The name Melita, later Malta, means "refuge," and it was given to the island by the Phoenicians. The island is 17½ miles long and has 95 square miles of land surface. It is located about 60 miles south of Sicily. It has a present population of approximately 235,000. The present capital is its chief city Valletta. Its harbors are excellent, the finest of which is Valletta, which is reported to be one of the strongest naval bases of Great Britain. It was the most bombed spot of the world during World War II, having undergone over 1,200 air raids. Originally a Phoenician and Carthaginian colony, it was captured by Rome in 218 B.C. It was taken by the British from Napoleon in 1800 and given dominion status in 1921, but it reverted to a crown colony in 1933 following a church-state controversy in 1930-32. Though treeless, it has a thin layer of fertile soil over a limestone formation which is agriculturally productive. It originally had a wealthy temple dedicated to Juno.

The Christian faith planted by Paul on Malta continues to the present. Traditional landmarks associated with Paul

and Publius live on to the present.
Publius' home is said to have become a
Christian church. A Christian bishop
represented Malta at the Council of
Chalcedon in A.D. 451.

1. The Incident of the Viper (28:1-6)

1 And when we were escaped, then
we knew that the island was called
Melita. 2 And the barbarians showed
us no common kindness: for they kindled
a fire and received us all, because of the
present rain, and because of the cold.
3 But when Paul had gathered a bundle
of sticks and laid them on the fire, a
viper came out by reason of the heat, and
fastened on his hand. 4 And when the
barbarians saw the *venomous* creature
hanging from his hand, they said one
to another, No doubt this man is a
murderer, whom, though he hath escaped
from the sea, yet Justice hath not suffered to live. 5 Howbeit he shook off the
creature into the fire and took no harm.
6 But they expected that he would have
swollen, or fallen down dead suddenly:
but when they were long in expectation
and beheld nothing amiss come to him,
they changed their minds, and said that
he was a god.

The Maltese were regarded as barbarians both by the Romans and the
Greeks. The word does not signify that
they were an uncivilized people, but
rather that they were neither Greeks nor
Romans, perhaps the equivalent of the
modern word "native," or those who
speak a foreign language, a somewhat
patronizing term. Plumptre remarks that
"The language of Malta at the time, if
not absolutely Punic, was probably a
very bastard Greek."[494]

Luke must have understood their dialect, for upon landing he learned that the
island was called Malta (v. 1).

The hospitality of the Maltese was most
heartening to the shipwrecked men. They
quickly built a large bonfire and warmly
brought the drenched and cold victims
of the merciless sea to the inviting heat,
or as one authority says, "gave us first
aid."[495] In fact Plumptre[496] sees an implication of both hospitality and shelter
in Luke's words. They made no difference between soldiers, sailors, and prisoners, but received and treated them all
alike (v. 2) as brothers in need (cf. Rom.

14:1, 3). It is amazing how considerate
and compassionate the heart of even pagan peoples may be in the presence of
human suffering or calamity. Even a
mongrel Samaritan had compassion on a
helpless, suffering, wayside victim of heart-
less robbers, while Jewish religionists
"passed by on the other side" (Luke 10:
30-35). The cold of the late autumn intensified by the heavy rain that followed
the windstorm greatly added to the discomfort of the wretched sea victims.

The unbounded energy of Paul was,
as usual, in evidence as he gathered wood
to feed the flames. Perhaps by the chain
on his wrist, the Maltese recognized him
as one of the prisoners. Thus, when under
duress of the heat, a viper slithered out
of the burning wood and fastened itself
upon Paul's hand (v. 3b), the natives at
once judged him to be a murderer (cf.
Luke 13:1-5; John 9:1, 2) pursued by the
inescapable law of fate or Justice, or what
the Hindus call Karma (v. 4).

Two objections to Luke's account of
the events immediately following the
landing have been offered. First, it is
held that no trees grow on Malta and
therefore there could have been no wood
to gather. There are two possible answers to this objection. The Maltese required fire for comfort and cooking.
They did not have coal on the island.
There may have been trees on the island in Paul's day, though there are not
now, or wood may have been one of
the items of trade by sea with other
peoples to supply their need. Or, more
likely, the reply of Plumptre may be adequate: "The Greek word, however, is
applied to the dry stalks of herbaceous
plants rather than to the branches of
trees, and, as such exactly describes the
stout, thorny heather that still grows near
the bay."[497]

The second objection is that there are
no poisonous serpents on the island of
Malta. Here again, however, this is
hardly sufficient evidence that there were
not such creatures there in Paul's day.
They may well have become extinct
under the heavy population of so small
an island in subsequent centuries. It
has been observed[498] that wolves were
still existent in England for many centuries after Paul visited Malta, though

494 Ellicott, *op. cit.*, p. 178. 495 *The Interpreter's Bible*, IX, 342.
496 Ellicott, *loc. cit.* 497 *Ibid.* 498 Rackham, *op. cit.*, p. 492, n. 7.

they are now extinct, as also with poisonous snakes in Ireland.

Whether the serpent was actually poisonous or just thought by Luke to be so, and whether it actually bit Paul's hand or just fastened itself on his hand by some manner, is in considerable dispute. Macgregor suggests that the serpent may have been "the *Coronella Austriaka,* which bites though it has no poison fangs. In any case Luke, and certainly the onlookers, thought that the snake was poisonous and that it had struck Paul, and not merely coiled around his hand."[499] Certainly a trained medical man in ancient times would have been well informed about serpents, to which great respect was paid in ancient medicine and custom.[500]

Luke likely saw a relationship between this incident and Mark 16:18, if indeed he was acquainted with this work (cf. Luke 10:19).

The pagan concept of **Justice,** while it may have been derived from the Greeks, clearly carried the connotation of retribution rather than the Platonic concept of equity. Plato had defined justice as having and doing what is one's own. The would-be comforters of Job reflected the idea of the inescapable mechanical law of justice. In the absence of any clear concepts of divine providence, primitive people have usually been disposed to consider nature as divine in something of the Greek hylozoistic, or cruder pagan, animistic sense. Though there may be a disposition to semi-personalize natural objects or manifestations and think of them as quasi-gods, this view usually involves a fatalistic concept of the universe. Thus there arises the idea that all beneficent conduct procures its own good reward while all malevolent conduct likewise procures its own evil rewards. The philosophy is the result of reasoning from effect to cause. Macgregor states, concerning *Justice* (v. 4), that "Probably the word should be understood in a personal sense as the name of *Dike,* the goddess of justice and vengeance."[501] This authority further states: "There is extant an interesting epitaph (quoted by Wettstein from *Anthol. Pal.* VII. 290) to a man [a murderer] who, though he came safely through a shipwreck on the sandy shores of Libya, was immediately afterward killed in his sleep by the bite of a viper."[502]

As the natives watched in wonderment, they beheld Paul dispatch the serpent into the flames with no personal harm. They supposed that either **he would have swollen** rapidly or that he would have **fallen down dead suddenly** (v. 6). Lucan is reported to have written the following lines concerning the effect of the bite of a venomous African serpent known as the Prestes (or inflamer): "The Prestes bit him, and a fiery flush lit up his face, and set the skin a-stretch, and all its comely grace had passed away" (Lucan, IX. 790).[503]

How like the pagans at Lystra (cf. Acts 14:11-19), however, set in reverse, as the former first acclaimed Paul and Barnabas gods and then stoned Paul and left him for dead, perhaps as a devil, while the Maltese first judged Paul to be a murderer and then changed their minds and said that he was a god (v. 6b). How easily swayed are the minds of primitive peoples controlled by superstitions! Plumptre thinks that "their thoughts may have travelled quickly to the attributes of the deities who, like Apollo or Aesculapius, were depicted as subduing serpents."[504] Bruce states, "It is not difficult to detect Luke's quiet humor in his account of this remarkable change of mind."[505]

2. The Healing of Publius' Father (28: 7-10)

7 Now in the neighborhood of that place were lands belonging to the chief man of the island, named Publius; who received us, and entertained us three days courteously. 8 And it was so, that the father of Publius lay sick of fever and dysentery: unto whom Paul entered in, and prayed, and laying his hands on him healed him. 9 And when this was done, the rest also that had diseases in the island came, and were cured: 10 who also honored us with many honors; and when we sailed, they put on board such things as we needed.

It appears that Publius owned an estate near the location of the shipwreck. Such is not surprising when it is considered

499 *The Interpreter's Bible,* loc. cit.   500 See Dummelow, *op. cit.,* p. 852.
501 *The Interpreter's Bible,* IX, 343.   502 *Ibid.*   503 Quoted in Ellicott, *loc. cit.*
504 *Ibid.,* p. 178.   505 Bruce, *op. cit.* p. 523.

that the Maltese of this time were reported to be a wealthy and even somewhat luxurious people in their manner of life. Publius is correctly designated **the chief man of the island** (v. 7). Macgregor remarks: "The exact word (*protos*) has been found in two inscriptions as a title of an official in Malta, so that we may list this with the use of the title 'politarch' of the Thessalonian officials (17:6) as an illustration of Luke's accuracy in small details of local color."[506]

It does not appear to be quite clear whether Publius was a representative of the Roman government or a native official on Malta. The island was evidently attached to the province of Sicily in Paul's day, in which case Publius may have been the legate of the proconsul of Sicily, with which his Latin name would agree. Kraeling remarks:

> One would expect the official [Publius] to have resided at the capital (Citta Vecchia). And indeed tradition, which would make him the first bishop of Malta, seeks his residence where the cathedral of that town now stands; but he may have had a country estate near the seashore. A prominent villa, found near the church of St. Paul at Mare, but covered up again for protection, is a candidate for indentification with the country house of Publius, if one favors the traditional landing place. . . . Whether a Christian group was created through his efforts is, however, unknown. . . . There are believed to be traces of Christian influence in second-century art on the island, but the first reference to a churchman from Malta dates from the fifth century.[507]

It is interesting that there seems to be neither Biblical nor historical evidence of any Jews on Malta.

It seems unlikely that Publius' three days of courteous hospitality was extended to the entire group of 276 persons. Luke's omission of the word **all** (v. 7b) seems to imply that only a select number of the party, possibly including Paul, Julius, the ship's captain, and Luke, were entertained in Publius' home, though he may have contributed toward the comforts of the other members.

Publius' courtesy and kindness to the shipwrecked men was richly rewarded in the healing of his seriously ill father

for whom Paul prayed the prayer of faith (v. 8).

The cause of Publius' father's illness is given by Luke as **fever and dysentery** (v. 8). Luke's medical knowledge supports his diagnosis of this particular case (cf. Luke 4:38-40). Bruce designates his condition as "intermittent attacks of gastric fever and dysentery."[508] The same authority states that "Malta has long had a peculiar unpleasant fever of its own 'Malta fever,' due to a microbe in goat's milk."[509] From the character of the disease it may be suspected that Publius' father was afflicted with amoebic dysentery in combination with the fever, a disease not uncommon in such countries. Hyppocrates (Hyppocrates, Aph. VI. 3) lends support to Luke's diagnosis.

Luke's statement that Paul **prayed, and laying his hands on him healed him** (v. 8b), suggests the combination of the two acts recommended by James (James 5:14, 15). Again the relation of the viper's bite to this healing suggests the juxtaposition of Christ's promises in Mark 16:18, though this passage is of doubtful authority. It should be observed that in Luke we have a firsthand medical witness to the miraculous character of the healing of Publius' father.

The many healings that followed may well have received "medical treatment" at Luke's hands, as there appears to have been a distinction between the healing of Publius' father in answer to Paul's prayers and the others who were cured (v. 9b). Indeed, Luke's statement that the Maltese **honored us with many honors** (v. 10) is taken by some to mean that they paid him liberal fees or gave him an honorarium for his services (cf. Acts 3:7, 16; 4:34; 5:2, 19:19; I Tim. 5:17, and especially Ecclus. 38:1, which says, "Honor a physician according to thy need of him with the honor due unto him").

As the party departed the island the Maltese, out of their appreciation, lavished on them such things as they would need for their journey to Rome. Luke does not name the articles donated, but we may well imagine that they included provisions and clothing of which they had been deprived in the storm and shipwreck.

[506] *The Interpreter's Bible, loc. cit.*   [507] Kraeling, *op. cit.,* p. 458.
[508] Bruce, *loc. cit.*   [509] *Ibid.,* n. 17.

E. THE ARRIVAL AT ROME (28:11-16)

Beyond the aforementioned incidents of the serpent and the healings, Luke does not tell us of the activities of Paul's party or of the other shipwrecked men during their three winter months' stay on Malta. We may well imagine, however, that Paul busied himself evangelizing among the natives while Luke ministered to the physical welfare of the people.

1. The Voyage from Malta to Puteoli (28:11-13)

11 And after three months we set sail in a ship of Alexandria which had wintered in the island, whose sign was The Twin Brothers. 12 And touching at Syracuse, we tarried there three days. 13 And from thence we made a circuit, and arrived at Rhegium: and after one day a south wind sprang up, and on the second day we came to Puteoli;

The three-months' stay on Malta were made necessary because of the winter weather which forbade sailing on the open sea. They left Crete sometime after October (see note on Acts 27:9) and two weeks later arrived at Malta. Thus a three-months' stay on Malta would have placed their departure in late January or early February. This departure would have been before the safe sailing season opened about March 5, according to Vegetius (Vegetius *De Re Militari* IV. 39). Pliny the Elder (Pliny *Natural History* II. 47, 122) placed the reopening date nearly a month earlier, February 8. Vegetius may refer to longer voyages on the open sea than Pliny. It is evidently nearer the latter date that they sailed, and that probably because of unseasonably favorable weather. They boarded another grain ship from Alexandria which had wintered at Malta, probably in the harbor of Valletta. This ship, as was customary, took its name from its figurehead, The Twin Brothers, or "Castor and Pollux" (KJV), or the "Dioscuri," the two sons of Zeus and Lida. They were regarded as patron deities of the sailors. Bruce remarks: "Their constellation, Gemini, was considered a sign of good fortune in a storm."[510] Ramsay[511] suggests that Luke's reason for giving the

name of this vessel, but no others, lies in the fact that he heard the name of this ship before he saw it, and thus it was fixed in his mind. To Luke, a non-sailor, ships were only means of conveyance. Ramsay thinks that Paul's party may have learned that The Twin Brothers of the Alexandrian Imperial fleet was lying in the great harbor of Valletta while they were entertained by Publius shortly after the shipwreck (v. 7).

After about a day's sailing, they arrived at the great port of Syracuse on the east coast of the island of Sicily some eighty miles from Malta. Sicily was divided into two parts and the whole was under a *praetor,* with a *quaestor* over each half. Syracuse was the capital and principal city of the eastern half. It had been a very prosperous Greek state but had suffered decline under the Rome rule in the second century B.C. It had only begun to recover from the days of Augustus Caesar.

Perhaps due to either a lull or adverse winds, their vessel harbored at Syracuse for three days. With the appearance of favorable weather, the ship made a circuit (the KJV reads "we fetched a compass") or followed a circuitous route (cf. II Sam. 5:23; II Kings 3:9) and arrived at Rhegium (v. 13) on the southwest coast of Italy, where they evidently remained in harbor for one day, again because of adverse weather.

Rhegium (now Reggio) was situated close by the narrow straits of Messina, where the famed Scylla and Charybdis were situated. Scylla was a great rock to the north of the cape and Charybdis was a dangerous whirlpool near the Strait of Messina. Thus The Twin Brothers, like many other ships that called at Rhegium, had to lie in harbor awaiting a favorable wind to avoid the dangerous currents and the whirlpool. The Twin Brothers appear on the coins of Rhegium, indicating perhaps both that they were invoked here for the safety of the ship as it passed through the straits and that the ship was a frequent caller at this port. Josephus[512] records that Caligula undertook the construction of a harbor for Egyptian corn-ships at Rhegium, "a great and kindly undertaking," but he never completed the enterprise.

With the appearance of a south wind,

---

[510] Bruce, *op. cit.*, pp. 525, 526.　　[511] Ramsay, *St. Paul the Traveller*, p. 346.
[512] Josephus, *Ant.*, XIX, ii, 5.

they set sail and a day later entered the port of Puteoli (now Pozzuoli) on the coast of Italy to the north (v. 13). Since the distance from Rhegium to Puteoli was approximately 180 miles, the wind evidently favored their voyage. Puteoli, which lay at the northern part of the bay of Naples was the chief port of Rome in Paul's day. Here the ocean voyage for the passengers ended. En route they had sailed past Pompeii framed against Vesuvius and on past Neapolis (now Naples). Puteoli was probably the principal cargo depot for Rome. The ruins of the mole where Paul landed are said to be still visible at Puteoli. Only the ruins of the amphitheater, where Nero once performed, and the Serapeum remain to mark the site of the ancient city.

2. The Journey from Puteoli to Rome (28:14-16)

14 where we found brethren, and were entreated to tarry with them seven days: and so we came to Rome. 15 And from thence the brethren, when they heard of us, came to meet us as far as The Market of Appius and The Three Taverns; whom when Paul saw, he thanked God, and took courage.
16 And when we entered into Rome, Paul was suffered to abide by himself with the soldier that guarded him.

At Puteoli Paul's heart was gladdened by the presence of Christians, with whom he and his party were permitted to tarry and fellowship for a full week. Paul's last known contact with any Christians, apart from the members of his party and converts he may have made en route, had been at Sidon some six months earlier. It is possible that Julius awaited further orders here from his superior officer before proceeding to Rome with his troops and the prisoners.

The presence of Christians at Puteoli is significant in that it indicates the wide spread of Christian faith in the absence of any distinct record of these parts (cf. Rom. 1:8; Col. 1:6). It is possible that here, even as likely at Rome, the Christian faith was carried back from Pentecost by Jews and proselytes converted there (Acts 2:10). Then, as Plumptre remarks, "a city which was *en rapport*, like Puteoli,

with both Alexandria and Rome, may have received it from either."[513] Plumptre[514] further advances the hypothesis that the Epistle to the Hebrews was written from Puteoli by Apollos (Acts 18: 24) to Hebrew Christians of the ascetic class in the Nile Delta. He argues that the salutation, "They of [or from] Italy salute you" (Heb. 13:24), was not a natural way of speaking of Christians at Rome, and since there was no other known Christian church in Italy, it must have reference to these Christian disciples at Puteoli. Thus, according to this hypothesis, Apollos would have been at some later date associated with these Christians at Puteoli, possibly as their pastor, and from here wrote the Hebrew letter to Egyptian Hebrew-Christians. While the hypothesis seems to have certain merits, it lacks sufficient evidence for unqualified acceptance. That there were Jews at Puteoli is attested by Josephus.[515]

It appears that Paul's **seven days** (v. 14) with the Christians at Puteoli, as also at Troas (Acts 20:6) and at Tyre (Acts 21:4), were designed to enable him to fellowship with and minister to them on the Lord's day. Julius' courtesy in granting Paul this privilege would have been but the repetition of an earlier like incident at Sidon (v. 3).

Luke's statement, **and so we came to Rome** (v. 14), simply indicates that the city of Rome was the next stage of their journey. En route Christian disciples from Rome who had heard of his arrival, perhaps by messengers during the week Paul was at Puteoli, came out to officially greet and welcome the Great Apostle of their faith to the city. In fact, they appear to have constituted an official delegation from the church at Rome. It seems that some came as far as the **Market of Appius** (about 40 miles from Rome), while others met him at **The Three Taverns** (about 40 miles from Rome). Possibly Luke intends to indicate that there were two different delegations that came to welcome him, one having received the word of his arrival earlier than the other. From his letter written to Christians of Rome from Corinth nearly three years earlier, they knew

513 Ellicott, *op. cit.*, VII, 180.   514 *Ibid.*
515 Josephus, *Ant.*, XVII, xii, 1, and *War*, II, vii, 1.

of his plans to visit Rome, though they probably had little idea of when he might arrive. Over the Appian Way Paul travelled with the company of soldiers and his fellow prisoners. Plumptre[516] thinks that the reason Paul's Christian friends had not come farther than **Appii Forum** was because they did not know whether he would come thence by road or canal. As quoted by Plumptre, "Horace (Sat. i, 5, 1. 4) had condemned the town to a perpetual infamy, as . . . [with sailors filled, and scoundrel publicans!]".[517] However, as Paul met here with the Christians from Rome, it may well be imagined that they conducted together a service of prayer and thanksgiving to God that would have given a moral complexion to the place not before experienced.

The next mentioned place on their Rome-ward journey was **The Three Taverns** (v. 15) where the second contingent of Christians met them. Little wonder that **Paul . . . thanked God and took courage** (v. 15) as he met these Christians. He had long desired to visit Rome (cf. Acts 19:21; Rom. 1:9ff.; 15:23f.), and at last he had realized his desire. If he had been apprehensive about his reception by the Christians at Rome (as his words in v. 15 seem to imply), this warm welcome more than allayed any fears he may have had. Many questions may have plagued his mind since his departure from Caesarea such as: Would there be friends to welcome him or would he enter Rome unescorted as a common criminal? Were the Christians, to whom he wrote his Roman letter nearly three years earlier and who were so much in his mind (Rom. 1:10-12), still safe, or had they been killed or driven from Rome by persecution? Had they been deflected from the faith or poisoned against him by the deadly work of the Judaizers? All of these fears were dispelled in an instant by the welcome accorded him by his Christian friends from Rome. Thus reassured and re-animated, Paul entered Rome, perhaps by the "Porta Capena," like a victor returning from the defeat of a powerful enemy. His goal, Rome, was at last realized, and Luke triumphantly announces: **and . . . we entered into Rome** (v. 16a).

Luke's notation that **Paul was suffered to abide by himself with the soldiers that guarded him** (v. 16) indicates the special privilege accorded him by the Romans. This was unquestionably due to the favorable recommendation of Julius and may also have possibly been augmented by a favorable report on his case by Festus. Concerning the officer to whom Paul was delivered, Macgregor states:

> This official was either the *princips peregrinorum*, an officer of the praetorian guard in command of the courier troops or *frumentarii* . . . or, perhaps more probably, the *praefectus praetorii*, commander of the praetorian guard, who took prisoners into custody on their arrival at Rome. Paul himself was granted the privilege of *custodia libera* and would be permitted to *stay by himself* in his own quarters under the supervision of *the soldier that guarded him*.[518]

F. THE CONFERENCES WITH THE JEWS OF ROME (28:17-29)

As was Paul's policy throughout his ministry, he desired at the earliest possible opportunity to meet with the Jews at Rome. However, his confinement prevented him from going to their synagogue for a meeting where he might preach Christ. There appear to have been a number of synagogues in Rome at this time, and the Jews were a well-known community to the Romans, though sometimes a very troublesome one (cf. Acts 18:2).

1. The First Conference (28:17-22)

17 And it came to pass, that after three days he called together those that were the chief of the Jews: and when they were come together, he said unto them, I, brethren, though I had done nothing against the people, or the customs of our fathers, yet was delivered prisoner from Jerusalem into the hands of the Romans: 18 who, when they had examined me, desired to set me at liberty, because there was no cause of death in me. 19 But when the Jews spake against it, I was constrained to appeal unto Caesar; not that I had aught whereof to accuse my nation. 20 For this cause therefore did I entreat you to see and to speak with *me*: for because of the hope of Israel I am bound with this chain. 21 And they said unto him, We neither received let-

[516] Ellicott, *op. cit.*, VII, 181. [517] *Ibid.* [518] *The Interpreter's Bible*, IX, 346.

ters from Judaea concerning thee, nor did any of the brethren come hither and report or speak any harm of thee. 22 But we desire to hear of thee what thou thinkest: for as concerning this sect, it is known to us that everywhere it is spoken against.

Paul invited the Jewish leaders at Rome to a conference at his residence. After brief introductions he summarized the events that had brought him to Rome, from his arrest at Jerusalem to the present. He declared his innocence of any adverse activities against the Jewish people or their customs, thus implying his loyalty to Judaism (v. 17b). Nevertheless, he related, his own people had brought accusations against him and delivered him to the Roman officials for trial (v. 17c). He asserted that the Romans had carefully examined the accusations brought against him by the Jews at Jerusalem and found them groundless and had desired to set him free (v. 18). However, when the Jews insisted upon his punishment, he had found that his only recourse was appeal to Caesar. He assures them that he has no accusations to bring against his own nation before Caesar (v. 19). Since Rome had been so greatly plagued by the troublesome Jews in the city, as elsewhere, and had at one time expelled them from Rome (Acts 18:2), it must have been a relief to these leaders to learn that Paul was not there to make further trouble for them.

Having carefully avoided placing undue responsibility upon the Jewish authorities at Jerusalem for his arrest and appeal, Paul then proceeded to bear his ever faithful witness to Christ: **Because of the hope of Israel I am bound with this chain** (v. 20b). "He is a prisoner because as a Christian he believes that in Jesus Christ **the hope of Israel** had been fulfilled."[519] Bruce states, "In Rome as in Jerusalem he emphasized that the Christian message which he proclaimed far from undermining the religion of Israel, was its divinely appointed fulfillment"[520] (cf. Acts 23:6; 24:14-15; 26:6ff.).

The reply of the Jewish leaders was to the effect that they had no adverse reports on Paul, either by letter from the Jerusalem Jews or by personal communication from travelling Jews (v. 21). Bruce[521] thinks that the failure of the Jerusalem Jews to succeed in prosecuting Paul before the provincial magistrates may have discouraged them from attempting further prosecution before Caesar. It should be noted, however, that Paul's appeal to Caesar was made very soon before his actual sailing and that due to the lateness of the season, with the soon closing of the seas to sailing, they may not have had opportunity to send complaints to Rome against him. If, as Bruce[522] thinks, it had been a bit later when Nero married Poppaia Sabina in A.D. 62, who was friendly to the Jews and as Josephus[523] asserts was a God-fearing proselyte to the faith, their chances to influence the emperor against Paul might have been better.

Whether the Jews knew more about Paul than they admitted, we cannot be certain. However, they planned to keep themselves clear of any involvement with the Roman authorities against a Roman citizen. They cautiously reflected their suspicions of Paul by admitting their knowledge of Christianity as a sect which was, they said, in ill repute everywhere (v. 22). Just when and how the Christian church came into being at Rome is not certain, but it is clear that when Paul wrote his letter to Rome from Corinth in about A.D. 57, it was then a well-established Christian community widely and favorably renowned (cf. Rom. 1:8). The unfavorable attitude of the Jews toward Christianity may even have been influenced by the Roman suppression of riots by dispersing the Jews from Rome under Claudius (Acts 18:2), which riots may have been characterized by Jewish attacks upon the Christians. In any event the Jews, while noncommittal, were willing to hear Paul further on the subject of Christianity. Their professed ignorance of firsthand knowledge of Christianity may be due to the fact that the synagogue and the church here were already separated, the church having started mainly as a non-Jewish body. Indeed, the number of Latin names found in the sixteenth chapter of Romans would seem to lend weight to this theory.

519 *Ibid.*   520 Bruce, *op. cit.,* p. 530.   521 *Ibid.*   522 *Ibid.*   523 Josephus, *Life,* p. 3.

2. The Second Conference (28:23-28)

23 And when they had appointed him a day, they came to him into his lodging in great number; to whom he expounded *the matter*, testifying the kingdom of God, and persuading them concerning Jesus, both from the law of Moses and from the prophets, from morning till evening. 24 And some believed the things which were spoken, and some disbelieved. 25 And when they agreed not among themselves, they departed after that Paul had spoken one word, Well spake the Holy Spirit through Isaiah the prophet unto your fathers, 26 saying,

Go thou unto this people, and say,
By hearing ye shall hear, and hall in no wise understand;
And seeing ye shall see, and shall in no wise perceive:
27 For this people's heart is waxed gross,
And their ears are dull of hearing,
And their eyes they have closed;
Lest haply they should perceive with their eyes,
And hear with their ears,
And understand with their heart,
And should turn again,
And I should heal them.
28 Be it known therefore unto you, that this salvation of God is sent unto the Gentiles: they will also hear.

Paul's method of approach on this occasion was as always when preaching to the Jews: namely, exposition and witness (v. 23). From both the law of Moses and the prophets, Paul reasoned throughout the entire day that Jesus was the Messiah and that His Kingdom was the church. Bruce states that "His text was the whole volume of Hebrew scripture, interpreted by the events of the advent, passion, and triumph of Jesus of Nazareth, 'declared to be the Son of God with power, according to the spirit of holiness, by the resurrection from the dead' (Rom. 1:4)."[524] Without question there was much debate and possibly no little contention over the meaning and application of certain Messianic prophecies throughout the day, as Paul earnestly labored to convince these leading Jews of Rome that Jesus Christ was the fulfillment of Israel's age-old hope.

That the Apostle's efforts were not in vain is clear from the fact that **some believed** (v. 24). However, others disbelieved, with whom Paul renounced fellowship, with the inevitable result that, as usual, strife arose among them (v. 25). Paul, as so often before, rebuked the unbelieving Jews with the words of their own prophets (Isa. 6:9, 10). Then he declared to them the universal import of the **salvation of God** in Christ, with his personal confidence that the Gentiles in Rome as elsewhere would hear and believe the message concerning Christ (v. 28).

G. THE AMBASSADOR IN BONDS (28:30-31)

30 And he abode two whole years in his own hired dwelling, and received all that went in unto him, 31 preaching the kingdom of God, and teaching the things concerning the Lord Jesus Christ with all boldness, none forbidding him.

Paul was evidently accorded the utmost leniency while a prisoner at Rome. He was permitted to dwell in his own rented house or apartment in the city at his personal convenience (and evidently at his personal expense) [525] under the surveillance of a soldier-guard who was responsible to give account of his charge. A light chain, presumably fastened by the wrist, evidently secured Paul to his guard, which guard would naturally have been changed regularly. He was at liberty to invite his friends to his quarters and to preach or minister to all who came to him, though he was not permitted to go out at liberty. He doubtless found ample opportunity to rest and recuperate after the rigorous and trying experiences of the sea. His spirits would have been revived from the ordeals of the past two years and more, as he enjoyed the fellowship and encouragement of his visiting friends at Rome, and especially as he engaged in a profitable and victorious ministry for Christ to those who came to him for help (cf. Philemon 9-12). He carried on correspondence with his friends and former converts at such places as Philippi, Colossae, and Ephesus.

At Rome Paul did not regard himself as a prisoner of Caesar, but rather as "the prisoner of Jesus Christ in behalf of . . . [the] Gentiles" (Eph. 3:1; also cf. Eph. 4:1; Philemon 1, 9). In fact, he was

---

[524] Bruce, *op. cit.*, p. 532.   [525] See Additional Note XIII, *Paul's Supposed Wealth*.

a prisoner of Christ by divine appointment that he might be God's special ambassador to the Gentiles at Rome (Eph. 6:20). To the end that he might execute well this divine appointment at Rome, Paul earnestly requested the prayers of his Christian friends in other parts (see Eph. 6:18-20). Withal, Paul was not without his severe spiritual conflicts and temptations to discouragement during his Roman imprisonment, which he likens to a warfare against a subtle and powerful enemy, the victories over which he uses to encourage his Christian friends (see Eph. 6:10-20). Well did Paul set the example of Christian courage and fortitude, while in prison, for such subsequent saints as Madame Guyon and John Bunyan.

That Paul wrote Ephesians, Colossians, Philippians, and Philemon from his Roman imprisonment has been held by most scholars. The exact order and dates of the writing have less agreement among scholars. These letters likely dated from the middle of the two-year imprisonment at about A.D. 61. That Philippians was written last, and at a time when it seems that Paul's trial was in progress and he felt confident of acquittal, appears fairly evident from the tone of the Philippian letter.

The character of Paul's ministry in Rome, **with all boldness** (v. 31), and the liberty and favor that he enjoyed at the hands of the Roman officials as he carried on his preaching ministry, is suggested by Luke's statement: **none forbidding him** (v. 31b). Though delays of justice were not uncommon at Rome, the two-year delay in Paul's trial (v. 30), Dummelow thinks, was caused " (1) by the loss of the official papers in the wreck, (2) by the non-appearance of the accusers, (3) by the difficulty of getting together the witnesses."[526]

Luke drops out of the picture at verse 16, though we learn from Paul's epistles that he was with him there during his imprisonment (cf. Col. 4:14; II Tim. 4:11). He closes his record with Paul actively engaged in the ministry he loved so well. What better conclusion could he have given to this great record than to present the great Apostle as an ambassador of Jesus Christ, the Lord and

King of the universe, to the court of the most ungodly of all earthly rulers, Nero? (Eph. 6:19, 20).

That he was not unsuccessful in his ambassadorship, even within the household of Nero Caesar, we seem to have evidence for in his epistle to the Philippians, where he says, "All the saints salute you, especially they that are of Caesar's household" (Phil. 4:22).

Only a few times in the Acts does Luke use the full title for Christ, as here, **the Lord Jesus Christ** (v. 31; cf. Acts 11:17; 15:11; 16:31; 20:21). As earlier noted, the title **Lord** is the most often repeated important word in Acts (110 times) and constitutes the burden of the apostolic message.

That Christ was redemptively the Lord of the universe gave validity to Paul's universal concept and proclamation of the gospel of Jesus Christ. Thus Luke closes this great record of the life and ministry of the greatest of all Christian apostles in a triumphant display of (1) the transcendence of the Christian faith over all obstacles: Paul the ambassador of Christ in wicked Nero's prison (Eph. 6:19, 20); (2) the freedom and independence of Paul, even as Nero's prisoner: **in his own hired dwelling** (cf. II Tim. 2:9); (3) the universal reach of the gospel: **"all" that went in unto him** (cf. Acts 1:8; 2:38, 39); (4) the universal spiritual Kingdom of Christ over men: **preaching the kingdom of God** (cf. Acts 1:3; 8:12; 19:8; 20:25; 28:23); (5) the exposition of Christ's teachings and work for man's salvation and edification: **teaching the things concerning the Lord Jesus Christ** (cf. Matt. 9:35; 28:18-20); (6) the Christian confidence and boldness commensurate with the proclamation of Christ's salvation for man: **with all boldness** (cf. Acts 4:13, 29, 31; Eph. 6:18, 19); and (7) the favor accorded the gospel proclamation by the ruling authorities: **none forbidding him.**

Luke brought his Acts account to a conclusion, having accomplished his historical purpose. That his purpose was severalfold became evident in the course and culmination of the record. *First,* in accordance with his thesis implied at the outset of the book (Acts 1:1-5), Luke traced the continuance of Christ's work,

526 Dummelow, *op. cit.,* p. 853.

begun while He was in the flesh, from Pentecost throughout the Roman empire. *Second,* he traced the spread of the gospel and the development of the church according to the plan which he laid down in the first chapter of the book (Acts 1:8). *Third,* he demonstrated the power of the Christian faith to invade the non-Christian world and establish itself wherever it went. *Fourth,* he revealed the inherent and relentless animosity and opposition of the Jewish church to Jesus Christ and His gospel of salvation, while at the same time demonstrating the victory of the new faith over the old religion. *Fifth,* he portrayed in succession the leading characters in the gospel drama of the first Christian century: Peter, Stephen, Philip, Barnabas, and the greatest of all, Paul. *Sixth,* he traced the break of the new Christian faith with the old Jewish system, beginning at Jerusalem at Pentecost with the Christian disciples worshipping in the Temple and ending with Christianity established in the capital of the empire as a religion distinct from Judaism (Acts 28:22). *Seventh,* Luke demonstrated the ability of the Christian faith to win the favor of, and legal status in, the pagan Roman Empire (Acts 28:30, 31), though it required to await the Emperor Constantine's Edict of Toleration (A.D. 313) for final governmental confirmation.

Whether Paul was acquitted or convicted in the court of Nero at the end of his two-year imprisonment seems not to have been in the purpose of Luke to relate. Evidence from Paul's *Pastoral Epistles,* plus the testimony of tradition, seems to point favorably toward his acquittal, a fourth missionary journey in which he may have gone to Spain, Crete, Nicopolis, and other regions, then to have been again arrested, tried at Rome, condemned, and executed by beheading in about A.D. 67. Whether Paul suffered martyrdom at the close of his first or a second imprisonment at Rome, he left his clear testimony to a finished life work, his readiness to meet God by way of Nero's beheading-block, and a clear assurance of a heavenly coronation in righteousness by the Lord of the universe whom he served and whose lordship he proclaimed across the ancient world, and who is the "righteous judge," in distinction from the unrighteous Nero (II Tim. 4:6-8).

Additional Note I

HOMOTHUMADON = ONE ACCORD

Through the Book of Acts with Homothumadon

This . . . word [*homothumadon*] . . . occurs only eleven times in the Westcott and Hort Greek New Testament and all these instances, with one exception only, in the Books of Acts. . . . The one exception is found in Rom. 15:6.

Homothumadon is compounded of the Greek words, *homos,* which means *together* or in *unison,* and *thumos,* which primarily means to *rush along,* or to *breathe violently.* The best English phrase with which *homothumadon* can be translated is, *with one accord.* In the pronunciation of the word *homothumadon,* the letter u of the third syllable is pronounced like the English e with a macron over it.

The Greek word itself cannot be said to be a musical term, but the best English word with which to translate it, *accord,* is decidedly musical. It means, among other things, to *agree in pitch and tone.* The other uses of this word in the Book of Acts are varied, even including the united opposition of the people to the preaching of the gospel in 18:12; but it is in relation to the church that we wish to examine the use of *homothumadon.*

Here is a picture: As chairman of the Music-Lecture Course Committee of the college with which he has been connected, this writer, two or three times, secured the services of one of America's best-known and greatly loved harpists. Before beginning her program, and always as she began a new series of selections, this harpist would run her nimble fingers across the strings of the harp, and then, with her delicately trained ear, would listen intently for some discordant sound. Sometimes she must have heard some sound not in perfect accord, though the audience would not have been able to detect it; for she would take the large key which lay beside her, put it on the particular post of the instrument to which the string of the harp was attached, and adjust it. This she continued to do until there was no longer heard the least sound of disharmony. The music which then came from that great golden harp was well-nigh heavenly. There was no discord, but accord. This is *homothumadon*.

I. Homothumadon as the Pentecostal Prerequisite

The first use of *homothumadon* in the Book of Acts is in 1:14, where the setting is that of the upper room, during the ten days intervening between the ascension of Jesus and the day of Pentecost. "These all *with one accord* continued stedfastly in prayer, with the women, and Mary the mother of Jesus, and with his brethren."

"These all" refers to the twelve apostles (now eleven, Judas counted out) and the other persons mentioned. Keeping the apostles particularly in mind, there had not always been *homothumadon*. There had been wrangling, jealousy, and strife. But these existed no longer. Confessions had been made, apologies offered, old scores, whatever they were, settled; and now pre-Pentecostally, they were *with one accord*: there was *homothumadon*. The exact details of the procedure we are not told, but we are apprised of the fact of the absence of all discord.

Why ten days? God who knows the end from the beginning, and all the contingencies of the way, knew how to schedule this period between the Ascension and Pentecost. It was not how long it would take God, but how much time His people needed to meet the Pentecostal prerequisite — *homothumadon*.

II. Homothumadon as a Pentecostal Requisite

The American Standard Version reads: "And when the day of Pentecost was now come, they were all together in one place." The King James reads: "And when the day of Pentecost was fully come, they were all with one accord in one place." The difference is that the phrase "with one accord," is omitted in the American Standard Version. The reason that this phrase is not found in the American Standard Version is that this version is an accurate translation here of the Westcott and Hort Greek New Testament, and the word *homothumadon* is

not in this verse of that Greek Manuscript where variations are found. Westcott and Hort spent 27 years in the examination of the Greek Manuscripts and found the preponderance of evidence in favor of the text which they produced.

Since however *homothumadon* is found pre-Pentecostally, and also post-Pentecostally, even if the word itself were not found in Acts 2:1 in the Greek Manuscripts, the King James translators were justified in inferring that the Pentecostal prerequisite and the post-Pentecostal requisite must have obtained Pentecostally. The logic of this is sound, and the conclusion inescapable.

That the Pentecostal participants should be in one place is easy to comprehend. That it is possible for a group of people to be in *one place* without being with *one accord* is as readily understood, as most people have seen such situations. But that the Pentecostal participants should be both in one place and with one accord as an absolute necessity cannot be disputed. What obtained in Acts 1:14 must have equally obtained in Acts 2:1.

III. Homothumadon in Post-Pentecostal Fellowship

The next appearance of this interesting word in the Book of Acts is in 2:46, where the verse reads as follows: "And they, continuing daily with one accord [*homothumadon*] in the temple, and breaking bread from house to house, did eat their meat with gladness and singleness of heart."

Here is one of the references which shows that even post-Pentecostally the Christian religion was a movement within Judaism, and the temple continued to be generally recognized as their regular place of service. The break which caused the Christians to abandon the temple for private houses for worshipping places, and later chapels, came more or less gradually.

Here, however, the Christians are depicted as living with one accord, even in the midst of the temporary Christian communion of goods which was made necessary by the unusual circumstances under which they found themselves. The acid test of Christianity is not in the temple or church services, but in the daily grind of the commonplace. These early Christians stood the test of *homothumadon,* even under the irregularities of that day and situation.

IV. Homothumadon in Post-Pentecostal Prayer and Worship

Perhaps the secret of *homothumadon* in Acts 2:46 is found in Acts 4:24, where the word is used in relation to prayer and worship of the early church. It reads as follows: "And when they heard that, they lifted up their voice to God with one accord. . . ."

This is the reaction of the early Christians to the arrest of Peter and John when they had healed the lame man at the temple gate. They had preached, had been arrested, had been imprisoned, preached some more, had been threatened, and commanded to preach no more in the name of Jesus. They had placed God first, and refused to become subject to the decrees of the magistrates. Being let go, they returned to their own company of believers and reported. Immediately the above statement is made by the writer of the sacred narrative, in which *homothumadon* is employed in relation to their praying.

Here the baptism with the Holy Spirit and *homothumadon* are linked together in a post-Pentecostal way, as it was in chapters one and two, pre-Pentecostally and Pentecostally. Those persons who had been previously filled with the Spirit on this prayer meeting occasion were *homothumadon.*

V. Homothumadon in Relation to Christianity's Difficult Problem

No general body of the Christian church ever met a more difficult problem than that first gathering of the Christians held in Jerusalem about A.D. 50. James the brother of our Lord was chairman and, besides others representing the two extreme oppositions, Paul and Peter were present as expert witnesses.

The extremely difficult problem before this conference was the relation of Jew and Gentile in the Christian body: Must Gentile become Jew to become Christian?

The detailed minutes of this gathering would have made a volume of interesting and exciting reading. God has seen fit, however, to hand down this report in the small compass of verses 1-35 in chapter 15 of the Acts.

There was testimony, disputation, a recourse to prophecy, and evidently much prayer and patience, and finally the "Great Magna Charta of Christian Liberty" was agreed upon, emerged, and was written down.

It was a magnificent technique which was employed, resulting in a document with fundamental applications to all problems for all times.

The whole account of this conference merits very close and prayerful study by all charged with the solution of the doctrinal and practical problems of the Christian church. But couched among the things written down is found again our interesting Greek word, *homothumadon.* Here it is: "It seemed good unto us, being assembled with one accord (*homothumadon*) . . .," (v. 25, KJV). No, it is not strange, but significant that in the same document are also found these words: "It seemed good to the Holy Ghost, and to us," (verse 28, KJV).

Where there is *homothumadon* among Christians, there the Holy Spirit is present. What men think in the *homothumadon* way, the Holy Spirit can think with them and inspire their difficult problem solutions.

In our first *homothumadon* reference, Acts 1:14, the Twelve were involved. In the second reference, Acts 2:1, the one hundred and twenty were involved. In the subsequent references, and particularly the last one, the interests of the whole church are at stake. Why not give *homothumadon* a chance in our churches and conferences today?[527]

Additional Note II

THE PRACTICAL SIGNIFICANCE OF PENTECOST

I. Pentecost Signifies Divine Power

And suddenly there came from heaven a sound as of the rushing of a mighty wind, and it filled all the house where they were sitting (Acts 2:2).

[527] Jasper Abraham Huffman, *Golden Treasures from the Greek New Testament for English Readers,* pp. 155-160.

There appears to have been a two-fold purpose in this divine phenomenon described by Luke as, **a sound as of the rushing of a mighty wind.** *First,* it was intended to stimulate the faith of the disciples for all that was to follow. *Second,* its purpose was to arrest the attention of the masses of people assembled in Jerusalem for the Jewish Pentecost and thus provide audience for that inspired apostolic preaching which was to result in the initial conversion of 3,000 people.

Power has ever been the passion of man. Nor does the acquisition and exercise of power appear to have been absent from God's plan and purpose for man. Immediately following creation we read the divine commission to man: "Be fruitful, and multiply, and replenish the earth, and subdue it; and have dominion over the fish of the sea, and over the birds of the heavens, and over every living thing that moveth upon the earth" (Gen. 1:28b). A review of man's material and intellectual achievements through the centuries would bear near conclusive testimony to the fulfillment of that commission. But there are two important realms in which man, devoid of the grace of God, has ever failed to fulfill the commission to "subdue . . . and have dominion," namely, the realms of the spiritual and the moral. Solomon grasped this truth when he said, "He that ruleth his spirit [is greater] than he that taketh a city" (Prov. 16:32). Man has, through the exercise of his native abilities, become a giant, but in the absence of divine grace he is a morally insane giant, a giant who will inevitably destroy himself by his own powers, unless he places himself under the control of God. It is an inner divine power that man requires if he is to fulfill God's purpose in his existence.

The application of the divine power to the personal indwelling presence of the Holy Spirit in the life of the Spirit-baptized Christian believer is multifold. A few examples of these practical applications will be helpful.

First, Pentecostal power is the assurance of the sanctified Christian's victory over temptation and sin. It was this provisional assurance that the Apostle John had in mind when he wrote, "Ye are of God, *my* little children, and have overcome them: because greater is he that is in you than he that is in the world" (I John 4:4). And again, the Apostle Paul set forth the assurance of this spiritual victory through the indwelling presence of the Holy Spirit most forcibly and beautifully in the eighth chapter of the letter to the Romans, especially verses 11, 31-39.

Second, the Pentecostal power is an effective enablement to the execution of the Christian witness. Said Jesus, "But ye shall receive power, when the Holy Spirit is come upon you: and ye shall be my witnesses both in Jerusalem, and in all Judaea and Samaria, and unto the uttermost part of the earth" (Acts 1:8). Again, of the early disciples subsequent to Pentecost, Luke wrote, "with great power gave the apostles their witness of the resurrection of the Lord Jesus" (Acts 4:33a). The indwelling presence of the Holy Spirit is quite as much an enabling to witness by a consistent, righteous, exemplary life as by oral testimony. Each validates the other.

Third, the efficacy of Pentecostal power for the endurance of persecution is well exemplified by the first Christian martyr, Stephen. Repeatedly in the early chapters of the Acts of the Apostles, we read of the spiritual victories of the apostles through the energizing presence of the Holy Spirit in the experiences of most extreme and severe persecution.

Fourth, the practice of demon expulsion by the Spirit-filled apostles dots the pages of the first-century Christian history. A notable failure of such an attempt in the name of Jesus, but in the absence of the indwelling presence of the Holy Spirit, is that of the sons of Sceva at Ephesus (Acts 19:14-17).

Fifth, Pentecostal power for Christian healing in the first-century church is quite at much in evidence as is demon expulsion. The Acts of the Apostles is replete with such divine healings at the hands of the Spirit-filled apostles.

Sixth and finally, death itself was made to give up its victim at the command of these Spirit-filled servants of God. The restoration of Dorcas to life at the hands of Peter is a familiar example. Paul would seem to be thinking of both the healing of the body and of the final resurrection of the body when he uttered those words: "But if the Spirit of him that raised up Jesus from the dead dwelleth in you, he that raised up Christ Jesus from the dead shall give life also to your mortal bodies through his Spirit that dwelleth in you" (Rom. 8:11).

II. Pentecost Signifies Divine Purification

And there appeared unto them tongues parting asunder [parting among them or, distributing themselves], **like as of fire; and it sat upon each of them** (Acts 2:3). John the Baptist's prophetic words concerning Christ are here fulfilled:

> I indeed baptize you with water unto repentance: but he that cometh after me is mightier than I, whose shoes I am not worthy to bear: he shall baptize you in [or with] the Holy Spirit and *in* fire: whose fan is in his hand, and he will thoroughly cleanse his threshing-floor; and he will gather his wheat into the garner, but the chaff he will burn up with unquenchable fire (Matt. 3:11).

The meaning of the phenomenon of fire on the day of Pentecost is not far to seek. It must be borne in mind that in the Pentecostal effusion God was manifesting or revealing Himself primarily to the believing disciples of Jesus Christ, who on the day of Pentecost **were all together in one place.** They had given up the world and had dedicated themselves in faith to the pursuit and execution of the will of God in Christ. At last their hopes of an earthly kingdom were forever gone (see Acts 1:6, 7). They were now in earnest and desperate pursuit of the inner spiritual Kingdom which Christ had promised to them. Before the inner reign of Christ could be fully realized in their lives, there must be an inner purification, a consuming of the inner nature of self and sin, a renovation of every secret chamber of the soul, that nothing foreign or opposed to the nature of God might remain within. It was God's purpose that His disciples should be so inwardly pure that they might declare their independence of the domain of sin and the devil, as did Christ when He said, "The prince of the world [Satan] cometh: and he hath nothing in me" (John 14:30). There was to be no claim foreign to the claim of Christ

upon, or within, the lives of these disciples of Jesus.

For the purpose of this inner purification, God revealed Himself to the waiting disciples under the symbol of **tongues parting asunder like as of fire.** Consistently throughout the Scriptures, "fire" is employed as a symbol of divine purification. Fire has ever been a symbol of the holiness and justice of God. Thus God revealed Himself to His servants in ancient times (Deut. 4:24; Exod. 3:2; 19:18; Isa. 6:4; Ezek. 1:4; Dan. 7:10).

Malachi predicted the coming and the work of Christ under the symbol of fire.

> The Lord, whom ye seek, will suddenly come to his temple; and the messenger of the covenant, whom ye desire, behold, he cometh, saith Jehovah of hosts. But who can abide the day of his coming? and who shall stand when he appeareth? for he is like a refiner's fire, and like fullers' soap: and he will sit as a refiner and purifier of silver, and he will purify the sons of Levi, and refine them as gold and silver; and they shall offer unto Jehovah offerings in righteousness (Mal. 3:1-3).

Likewise in His post-ascension and second-coming appearances, Jesus is represented under the symbol of fire (Rev. 1:12-18). Even the Word of God is likened unto fire: "Is not my word like fire? saith Jehovah" (Jer. 23:29a).

Finally, God Himself is represented by the author of the letter to the Hebrews under the symbol of fire: "Our God is a consuming fire" (Heb. 12:29). Thus it was God the Holy Spirit in consuming fire who manifested Himself in **tongues like as of fire** to the disciples on the day of Pentecost, purifying, sanctifying their inner natures (cf. Acts 15:8, 9).

At the first great general Christian council held at Jerusalem Peter, speaking in defence of the gospel for the Gentiles, declared that their purification was on the same basis as that of the disciples at Pentecost. Said Peter: "And God, who knoweth the heart, bare them witness, giving them the Holy Spirit, even as he did unto us; and he made no distinction between us and them, cleansing their hearts by faith" (Acts 15:8, 9). At this juncture the testimony of Adam Clarke is significant: "Christ baptizes with the Holy Ghost, for the destruction of sin, the illumination of the mind, and the consolation of the heart."[528]

Finally, the tongues of fire were the manifestation of God's personal purifying presence to the inner impure natures of the disciples, making them inwardly clean in preparation for complete and uncontested possession and dominion by His Spirit. In the midst of the general manifestation of God's presence there was an individualization, or "personal" manifestation, providing for the personal conditions and needs of each disciple. Thus, while this purification or sanctification of the disciples' inner natures was primarily negative, it was a necessary and adequate provision of God for the positive work which was immediately to follow; namely, the complete possession of their inner beings by the personal presence of the Holy Spirit, giving them power over sin, the world, and the devil, and energizing them with a dynamic spiritual fervor for the proclamation of the gospel of Christ to all men throughout the world of their day.

III. Pentecost Signifies Divine Possession

And they were all filled with the Holy Spirit (Acts 2:4a).

It was God's evident purpose in the creation of man personally to indwell him by His Spirit. The "Fall" evicted the Spirit of God from the heart of man. Redemption through Christ provided a means of reconciliation between an offended God and offending man. However, reconciliation, important and essential as it is, is not enough to satisfy the heart of God. He longs to indwell the soul of man. Before such an unrivaled establishment of God in the soul of man could be realized, the inner nature of pollution and enmity against God must be cleansed away. For this purpose "Jesus also, that he might sanctify the people through his own blood, suffered without the gate" (Heb. 13:12). God's purpose in this great cleansing work, provided for the soul of converted man by Christ, is set forth by Paul in his first letter to the Thessalonian Christian converts thus: "This is the will of God, *even* your sanctification" (I Thess. 4:3).

But, the question may be fairly asked,

was not the Spirit of God in these disciples from the time of their conversion before Pentecost? That such was the case no careful student of the Word of God would attempt to deny. The regenerative work of God in the lives of penitent sinners is the work of the Holy Spirit in the inner nature of man. Indeed, Jesus declared to Nicodemus on this subject: "Verily, verily, I say unto thee, Except one be born of water and the Spirit, he cannot enter into the kingdom of God. That which is born of the flesh is flesh; and that which is born of the Spirit is spirit" (John 3:5, 6). And Paul declared, "But ye are not in the flesh but in the Spirit, if so be that the Spirit of God dwelleth in you. But if any man have not the Spirit of Christ, he is none of his" (Rom. 8:9). There is, in fact, no stage or part of the redemptive work that can be divorced from the direct operation of the Spirit of God. Jesus declared that even the work of conviction for sin on the world was to be the work of the Holy Spirit (see John 16:7-11). According to Jesus there can be no true worship apart from the Holy Spirit: "God is a Spirit, and they that worship him must worship him in spirit and truth" (John 4:24).

It will be noted that it was after His death and resurrection, and in conjunction with the Great Commission, which was not to be carried out until after Pentecost, that Jesus "breathed on them [His disciples], and saith unto them, Receive ye the Holy Spirit" (John 20:22). That this was a prophetic act and word of the Master to be fulfilled on the day of Pentecost is evident from the prophetic commission of the preceding and following verses. In fact, the divine outpouring of the Holy Spirit on the day of Pentecost cannot be separated from the Great Commission. "But ye shall receive power, when the Holy Spirit is come upon you: and ye shall be my witnesses" (Acts 1:8). If the witnessing could not begin until Pentecost was a reality in the lives of the disciples, Pentecost could not become a reality in their lives until the outpouring of the Holy Spirit on the day of Pentecost. So likewise it is in the prophetic sense of this Pentecostal fullness that Christ's words in John 4:17

---

[528] Adam Clarke, *op. cit.,* I, 683.

must be understood. There is no indication in Christ's words, "for he abideth with you, and shall be in you," that the Holy Spirit had not become the vital principle of their new lives in Christ. Rather the utterance is a prediction of that fulness of the Spirit which they were to experience on the day of Pentecost. Says Samuel Chadwick: "the change from *with* to *in* marks the transition from one dispensation to another." It is indeed the difference between the personal, physical presence of Christ with His disciples, and what His spiritual inner abiding presence through the Holy Spirit would be as a result of Pentecost.

Again Chadwick remarks:

> There is often some confusion in the interchange of terms, and the elimination of the middle factor. The Son comes in the coming of the Spirit, and abides in the soul in the presence of the Spirit; and in the coming of the Son through the Spirit the Father comes and abides also. "He will come . . . I will come . . . We will come" all refer to the coming of the Spirit as promised in our Lord's farewell talk with His disciples (John 14: 16-23). "In their relation to the human soul the Father and the Son act through and are represented by the Holy Spirit. And yet the Spirit is not merged in either the Father or in the Son." This is absolute unity with perfect distinction of persons in the Trinity. They are never confused in the unity nor divided in the distinction. Each is Divine and all are one.529

IV. Pentecost Signifies Universal Proclamation

And [they] began to speak with other tongues, as the Spirit gave them utterance (Acts 2:4b).

Pentecost was a miracle of **other tongues**. Someone has said that any purported miracle must possess a moral value to validate itself. If the moral value validates a miracle, the miracle of **other tongues** on the day of Pentecost was well established.

Peter, taking advantage of the arrested attention and interest of the assembled multitude, consequent upon this miracle of proclamation in their diverse languages, arose and interpreted the meaning of the Pentecostal phenomena with

such effectiveness as to result in the conversion of 3,000 souls (Acts 2:41).

Thus the miracle of **other tongues, as the Spirit gave them utterance,** was not only the direct means in the hands of God for the confounding and conversion of this multitude on the day of Pentecost, but there was also precipitated that great world-wide missionary movement that was to follow the inauguration of the church on the day of Pentecost. As there were present there at Jerusalem representatives **from every nation under heaven,** so this gospel of Jesus Christ was to be carried to "every nation under heaven" by fire-baptized and Holy Spirit-possessed men and women. The **other tongues** were necessary vehicles for the expression of **the mighty works of God,** and the result was the conversion of the multitude. This phenomenon was an intelligent and intelligible proclamation of the **wonderful works of God** (the gospel of Christ) to a people who otherwise could not have understood it. It was the work of the Holy Spirit in the lives of the sanctified disciples. It marked the beginning and made possible the great missionary evangelistic program to which Christ commissioned His disciples when He said, "Go ye therefore, and make disciples of all nations" (Matt. 28:19); and again, "Ye shall receive power, when the Holy Spirit is come upon you; and ye shall be my witnesses . . . unto the uttermost part of the earth" (Acts 1:8).

Additional Note III

THE BIBLE GIFT OF TONGUES

I. The First Occurrence of the Bible Gift of Tongues

And they . . . began to speak with other tongues, as the Spirit gave them utterance (Acts 2:4b).

Among the accompanying miracles of Pentecost was the gift of languages. It is logical that any purported miracle must demonstrate a moral value to validate its claims. On the basis of this principle, the miracle of **other tongues** given on the day of Pentecost was amply validated. The gospel was thus proclaimed, and

529 Chadwick, *op. cit.,* p. 44.

they witnessed the conversion of about 3,000 souls (Acts 2:41).

It should be noted from the very outset that the word *unknown,* in relation to "the Bible gift of tongues," does not occur in the original Greek of the New Testament. Nor is it found in the *American Revised Version.* The word *unknown* occurs only in italics in the KJV of the New Testament (and that misleadingly) in an attempt to clarify the meaning of the word **tongues.** Thus, properly speaking, there is no *unknown tongue* in the language of the New Testament. The Greek word *glossa,* meaning a tongue, or a language (Acts 2:11), or a nation of people distinguished by their language (Rev. 5:9; 7:9), is consistently used in its various forms throughout the New Testament, except where the word *dialektos,* meaning speech, dialect, or language, is used (Acts 1:19; 2:6, 8; 21:40; 22:2; 26:14).

Webster defines the word "tongue" as "The power of communication through speech . . . Act of speaking; esp., a spoken language." Hence a tongue, in this sense, is an articulate, intelligible speech or language used for the purpose of communicating ideas from one person to another. *That the foregoing definition of "tongues" accords with the Biblical use of the word throughout the New Testament it is the purpose of this study to show.*

Let it be noted that, with the occurrence of the divine miracle of languages at Pentecost, the disciples **began to speak with other tongues, as the Spirit gave them utterance** (Acts 2:4b), and the multitude exclaimed, **How hear we, every man in our own language wherein we were born? . . . we hear them speaking in our tongues the mighty works of God** (Acts 2:8, 11). Again, in the case of Cornelius' household, it is said that the Jews who accompanied Peter **heard them speak with tongues, and magnify God** (Acts 10:46). Matthew Henry remarks on this passage:

> They spoke with tongues which they never learned . . . that they might communicate the doctrine of Christ to the hearers. . . . Or being enabled to speak with tongues intimated that they were all designated for ministers, and by this first descent of the Spirit upon them were

qualified to preach the gospel to others, which they did but now receive themselves . . . when they spoke with tongues, they *magnified* God, they spoke of Christ and the benefits of redemption, which Peter had been preaching to the glory of God.[530]

Likewise when this phenomenon occurred at Ephesus, it is stated that **they spake with tongues, and prophesied** (Acts 19:6). Both Clarke and Matthew Henry take the position that this **prophesying** was preaching in the miraculously given tongues (languages), to people who could not otherwise have heard the gospel message.

As to the significance of "tongues," as Paul deals with that problem in the church at Corinth, due consideration will be given in the commentary on First Corinthians, chapters 12-14 of the WBC.

II. The Necessity of the Bible Gift of Tongues

The Acts record informs us that,

There were dwelling at Jerusalem Jews, devout men, from every nation under heaven. And when this sound [the sound as of the rushing of a mighty wind] **was heard, the multitude came together, and were confounded, because that every man heard them speaking in his own language. And they were all amazed and marvelled, saying, Behold, are not all these that speak Galileans? And how hear we, every man in our own language wherein we were born?** (Acts 2:5-8).

There then follows a list of fifteen different nations which were represented at the Jerusalem Pentecost, into the countries of which Jews of the *Diaspora* had been born whose language these representative Jewish people spoke and understood.

In order to comprehend the fuller significance of this necessity for the miracle of other tongues on the day of Pentecost, it is necessary to examine briefly the character of the hearers of the message at Pentecost. The record states that **there were dwelling at Jerusalem Jews, devout men, from every nation under heaven** (Acts 2:5). Whether these devout men were proselytes (Gentile converts to the Jewish faith and practice), or Gentile

---

[530] *Matthew Henry's Commentary on the Whole Bible,* VI, Comment on Acts 10:46.

worshippers of Jehovah but not full prose-lytes, or whether the expression is meant to characterize the Jewish dwellers at Jerusalem, seems uncertain. In any event, they represented the dwellers at Jerusalem, who for the most part had been attracted there by the temple worship, from the lands of the *Diaspora*. However, there is also another class of people concerned in the Pentecostal effusion. They are represented by Luke thus: **And when this sound was heard, "the multitude" came together, and were confounded, because that every man heard them speaking in his own language** (Acts 2:6). Very evidently this multitude comprised not only the dwellers at Jerusalem, but also those who had gathered from the various lands to keep the feast of Pentecost, which was one of the principal annual Jewish feasts to which Jewish worshipers were expected, if at all possible, to come.

The linguistic problem at Pentecost, presented by this multitude, is suggested by the presence of **Parthians, Medes,** and **Elamites,** nations beyond the Roman Empire, and the influence of Rome where the Ten Tribes of the Northern Kingdom were supposed to have settled after their captivity in 722 B.C. (see II Kings 17:6). **Mesopotamia,** the chief Jewish center of which Babylon, famed for its rabbinical schools and formerly the point of the "confusion of tongues" at the construction of the Tower of Babel, had its representatives present at Pentecost. **Judaea,** probably as distinguished from Galilee, the home of Christ's disciples, was naturally represented. **Cappadocia, Pontus, Asia, Phrygia** and **Pamphylia** represented the countries of Asia Minor from which foreign-born Jews and proselytes had come to Pentecost. **Egypt,** where according to Philo, the famed Greco-Jewish philosopher of Alexandria, a million Jews resided and formed a large part of the population of Alexandria and imbibed much of the Hellenic[531] culture, including language, had sent its representatives to Jerusalem. North African **Libya** and the North African Greek city of **Cyrene,** a quarter of the great population of which consisted of Jews with full citizenship rights, also sent representatives

to the Jerusalem feast of Pentecost. It is of special interest that it was Simon of *Cyrene* who bore the cross of Christ en route to Calvary (Matt. 27:32). There were those of the synagogue of the Cyrenians who disputed with Stephen on the occasion of his martyrdom (Acts 6:9). There were Christian representatives of Cyrene who first bore the gospel to the Greek population of Antioch of Syria (Acts 11:20); and there was a Christian prophet, Lucius of Cyrene, in the Antioch church who played an important part in instigating the first Christian missionary journey of Paul and Barnabas (Acts 13: 1). **Sojourners from Rome, both Jews and Proselytes** (v. 10b), were present. And finally, inhabitants of the large Mediterranean island of Crete and of the Arabian peninsula are named as present at Pentecost.

These dwellers at Jerusalem, sojourners, Hellenistic Jews, Gentile proselytes, and "God-fearers" exclaimed, **we hear them speaking in our tongues the mighty works of God** (Acts 2:11b).

A. J. Maclean[532] observes that the languages enumerated in Acts 2, in which the disciples spoke on the day of Pentecost, may have been in large part but varied dialects of the Greek and the Aramaic,[533] especially the latter, since the Jews of the *Diaspora* may have spoken principally Greek or Aramaic. However, thus allowing, it is nevertheless necessary to consider that dialects may and often do vary so greatly that they practically amount to different languages as far as speaking communication is concerned. Also, there were many parts of the ancient world in which Jews had settled, and where proselytes to Judaism had been made, that had been but superficially Hellenized, if at all, and where the native pagan dialects only were spoken at this time. Therefore, a miracle of speaking would be necessary to cover these varied dialects at Pentecost, to say nothing of the distinct languages that may have been represented. It is also necessary to note that, beside the Jerusalem and Hellenic Jews present at Pentecost, there were many "proselytes" and "God-fearers" present. The latter were a people who were

---

[531] Hellenic — A term characterizing the classical Greek culture. Thus, a Hellenist is "one who affiliates with Greeks or imitates Greek manners; esp., a Jew who used the Greek language as his mother tongue" (Webster).
[532] A. J. Maclean, "Gift of Tongues," *Dictionary of the Bible*, ed. James Hastings, pp. 943, 944.
[533] Aramaic: the Semitic-Hebrew vernacular in use in Palestine at this time.

not of the Jewish nationality, but were nevertheless worshippers of Jehovah in the more liberal fashion of the Jewish synagogues out in the countries of the Roman Empire and beyond. These Jewish communities, Benjamin Robinson thinks, may have reached 150 by the time of Paul.[534] In addition, there were those synagogues that were established in Jerusalem, which are supposed to have numbered about 250. Some put the number much higher. It is hardly logical to assume that all of these latter people understood and spoke either Greek or Aramaic, but they did hear the disciples preaching Jesus and His resurrection: **the mighty works of God , . . . every man in . . . his own language wherein . . . [he was] born** (Acts 2:8b).

From the foregoing considerations it becomes evident that this initial occurrence of the miraculous gift of languages is to be understood as the use of the *bona fide* languages of people present who otherwise would have been incapable of hearing the gospel of Jesus Christ, and that by men who themselves were unfamiliar with the languages which they were using.

Adam Clarke's comment is interesting at this juncture.

> At the beginning of Babel the *language* of the people was *confounded*; and, in consequence of this, they became scattered over the face of the earth; at this *foundation* of the *Christian Church*, the gift of various languages was given to the apostles, that the scattered nations might be *gathered;* and united under one shepherd and superintendent (*episkopos*) of all souls.[535]

That this Pentecostal miracle may have been in part a miracle of the interpretation of the speech of the disciples into the language of the hearers by the Holy Spirit was suggested by Gregory of Nyssa and others, but from Acts 2:6 this appears extremely unlikely. Thus it is impossible to deny that the **other tongues,** with which these Spirit-filled disciples spoke, were divine miraculous gifts of speech to the disciples for the purpose of evangelizing the representative multitude present at Pentecost.

The miracle of the proclamation of the gospel in the different languages of those present for the Jewish Pentecost, and which resulted in the great spiritual awakening, seems to anticipate the fulfillment of the "Great Commission" of Christ (Matt. 28:18-20 and Acts 1:8). This is further suggested by the universal representation of redeemed humanity as depicted in Revelation (see Rev. 5:9, 10; 7:9, 10).

III. The Purpose of the Bible Gift of Tongues

Maclean holds that "Tertullian apparently judged the gift [of tongues] to be an ecstatic utterance of praise."[536] This position seems impossible to defend when all of the scriptural facts are considered. Nevertheless, he admits that most of the Church Fathers, including Origen (A.D. 185?-A.D. 254?), Chrysostom (A.D. 347-A.D. 407), Theodoret (A.D. 396-A.D. 457), Gregory of Nyssa (A.D. 331--A.D. 394), and Gregory of Nazianzus (A.D. 329-A.D. 390), understood the miraculous gift of tongues, as recorded in Acts, to be for the purpose of evangelizing the nations. The preaching of **the mighty works of God** (the resurrection of Jesus Christ from the dead) was made intelligible to the people of the nations enumerated in the second chapter of Acts by reason of the miracle of tongues, with the result that some 3,000 were initially converted to Christ and added to the church. This event in itself is sufficient to establish the fact that the divine gift of tongues was for evangelization purposes.

In perfect accord with the evangelistic purpose of the gift of tongues on the day of Pentecost is the prediction of Isaiah, which prediction looks ultimately to the Gospel Age, and possibly embodies Pentecost itself. Says the prophet: "The time cometh, that I will gather all nations and tongues; and they shall come, and shall see my glory. And I will set a sign among them, . . . and they shall declare my glory among the nations" (Isa. 66:18, 19). And it is in conjunction with the Great Commission that Mark records Christ's prediction of the phenomenon of "new tongues" (Mark 16:15-17).

But the evangelistic purpose of the divine gift of tongues does not rest exclusively upon the Pentecostal incident.

---

[534] Robinson, *op. cit.*, pp. 9-12. [535] Clarke, *op. cit.*, p. 693. [536] A. J. Maclean, *op. cit.*, p. 943.

There are three other distinct occurrences of this phenomenon recorded in the New Testament; indeed some think they see even a fourth, in the incident of the outpouring of the Holy Spirit on the Samaritan Christians when they were visited by Peter and John from Jerusalem, as recorded in Acts 8:14-24. However, there is no mention made, in this account concerning Samaria, of the gift of tongues accompanying the bestowment of the Holy Spirit, and there appears to have been no need for it in the presence of a common language spoken by these people.

IV. The Bible Gift of Tongues at Caesarea

The first record of the miracle of "tongues," following the Jerusalem Pentecost, is found in Acts 10, when the household of Cornelius received the Holy Spirit and spake with tongues, under the ministry of Peter. The record is specific and very significant. It reads in part as follows:

> While Peter yet spake these words, the Holy Spirit fell on all them that heard the word. And they of the circumcision that believed were amazed, as many as came with Peter, because that on the Gentiles also was poured out the gift of the Holy Spirit. For they heard them speak with tongues, and magnify God (Acts 10:44-46).

In his defense of the gospel for the Gentiles at Jerusalem, following his return from Caesarea, Peter identifies this divine phenomenon that occurred at Caesarea with that of the Pentecost at Jerusalem. Says Peter:

> And as I began to speak, the Holy Spirit fell on them, even as on us at the beginning [or on the day of Pentecost]. . . . If then God gave unto them the like gift as he did also unto us, when we believed on the Lord Jesus Christ, who was I, that I could withstand God? (Acts 11:15, 17).

Now, there are two circumstances that validate the evangelistic significance of the gift of tongues at Caesarea. The first

lies in the location of Caesarea and the second in the person and the position of Cornelius. As to the first, it must be noted that Caesarea was the most important seacoast and port city of Palestine at that time. It was a Roman colony and the Roman capital of Palestine. Caesarea was a large and important commercial and political cosmopolitan city, to which came, and through which passed, peoples of all parts of the Roman empire, representing the many linguistic divisions of that empire. Caesarea was the main port for the East-West overland route through southern Palestine, and it was the principal Palestinian port of call for the marine intercourse of the Mediterranean world with Egypt. Here, where Christianity first invaded the polyglot Gentile world, it was fitting that the gift of tongues should have occurred as an intrument for Gentile evangelization.

As to Cornelius and his position, it remains to be noted that he was a Gentile "proselyte of the gate"[537] or "devout man," in relation to the Jewish religion, and a Roman centurion of the Italian cohort[538] in relation to the Roman government. As such he had in his garrison of a hundred or more men (some hold a cohort of 600 men rather than a century of a 100),[539] a considerable linguistic representation of soldiers recruited from the various parts of the Roman Empire. It is easily possible that "the household of Cornelius" included the soldiers' barracks, as well as his servants and the members of his family. When these factors are considered, then the gift of tongues, both in getting the message to the soldiers of the barracks and perhaps his servants as well, and in turn aiding these Gentile Christian soldiers to witness for Christ to others who were of a different language, begins to take on meaning at Caesarea. Nor is it necessary to assume that there was no time element between their reception of the Holy Spirit and their speaking with tongues, any more than is such an assumption warranted concerning the day of Pentecost, or in subsequent occurrences of this miraculous phenomenon. It is

---

[537] 'Proselytes of the gate,' Gentiles "who dwelt in the land of Israel, or even out of that country, and who, without obliging themselves to circumcision, or to any other ceremony of the law, feared and worshipped the true God, observing the [seven] rules that were imposed upon the children of Noah." Alexander Cruden, A Complete Concordance.

[538] Italian cohort: one of the 10 divisions, consisting of 600 soldiers, of a Roman military legion.

[539] Lange, op. cit., p. 191.

entirely likely that between the records of verses 45 and 46 in Acts 10, these Spirit-baptized Christians scattered throughout the city witnessing for Christ to the peoples of various languages. Such was likewise most probable in Jerusalem, on the day of Pentecost, and elsewhere when the disciples of Christ received this gift. The two remaining occurrences of this phenomenon — the gift of tongues — will be dealt with in the expositions of Acts 19 and I Corinthians 12-14, in the WBC, Vols. IV and V.

Additional Note IV

CHRISTIAN COMMUNISM IN THE BOOK OF ACTS[540]

There are two passages in the Acts of the Apostles which are especially used by some people as proof-texts for the argument that real communism was practiced in the Christian church after Pentecost. These passages as they appear in the King James Version are as follows: "And all that believed were together, and had all things common; And sold their possessions and goods, and parted them to all men, as every man had need" (Acts 2:44-45).

"Neither was there any among them that lacked: for as many as were possessors of lands or houses sold them, and brought the prices of the things that were sold, And laid them down at the apostles' feet: and distribution was made unto every man according as he had need" (Acts 4:34-35).

These passages supposedly describe a genuine "Christian communism" — a society in which private property was abolished and where the ruling principle could be stated in the words, "From each according to his ability, to each according to his need" — or at least, in which there was a redistribution of wealth, in which all shared equally.

It is evident that this communism, if it was practiced, did not survive for long. Why did it not survive? Two answers fairly well include those which have been offered. The first answer is that the communistic practices were God's will for the Christian community, but that selfishness and other non-Christian attitudes made

God's ideal impossible and forced a return to "capitalism," where each person had his own personal property. This answer assumes that if we could establish a truly Christian city or country today, it would then be God's will to have such communism again. Indeed, this assumption helped lead to the establishment of the Shaker settlements, the experiment at Zion, Illinois, and other such ill-fated attempts during the past century.

The second answer, which is probably the more common one in our day, is that these early Christians were generous to a fault, becoming starry-eyed idealists who were either so overcome by the joy of their Christian fellowship that they gave their money away unwisely, or else were convinced that Jesus would return to set up His Kingdom so soon that money and possessions were worthless. At least one Sunday School lesson commentator, who seems quite sound in many respects, implies that the collections for the Christians in Jerusalem which Paul mentions in his epistles (I Cor. 16:1-4; II Cor. 8-9; etc.) were necessary because this mistaken experiment in communism had so impoverished the Jerusalem Christians that they were thrown on the mercies of other Christians who had not been involved.

Neither of these two answers is satisfactory. In reply to the first, there seems to be abundant evidence that God has ordained the principle of private ownership. The right of private ownership, which is capitalism, and the legitimate rewards of one's own initiative and work, are far more consistent than is communism with the high evaluation which God has placed upon us as individuals, made in His own image. The commandments "Thou shalt not steal" and "Thou shalt not covet" are based upon the right of private property. Sharing with others, based upon love and issuing in love, would be impossible if nothing were our own to share.

The second answer suggested is equally unacceptable. The New Testament nowhere warns us that what these early Christians did in these matters was mistaken. If they were mistaken, then the New Testament is not a completely safe guide for our lives. This conclusion we do not accept.

[540] J. Harold Greenlee, The Asbury Seminarian, Vol. V (Fall, Winter, 1950), pp. 92-94. Used by permission.

It seems that the whole assumption of communism in Acts, even a so-called "Christian communism," is due to a misunderstanding of the author of Acts. This misunderstanding is of two kinds. One is a misunderstanding of the author's point of view. He is trying to emphasize very strongly the attitude of generosity which prevailed among the Christians. He was describing an attitude of heart which would be found in any truly Christian home. He meant that the Christian love was so sincere that, if someone was in need, others would share with him as though their possessions were his. A pagan writer about A.D. 100 described the Christians as Acts intends to describe them, with these words: "He who has gives to him who has not without grudging. And if there is a man among them who is poor and needy and they have not an abundance of necessaries, they fast for three days that they may help the needy with the necessary food." Here is not communism, but Christian love. Moreover, the author of Acts shows that he is not describing complete communism by the story of Ananias and Sapphira (Acts 5:2, 4); for he writes that Peter rebuked Ananias with the words, "While it remained, was it not thine own? And after it was sold, was it not in thine own power?" How could Peter have said this if all the Christians were expected to surrender their possessions?

The second misunderstanding of Acts in these passages is a misunderstanding of what the author actually said. The description given in Acts 2:45 and 4:34, 35 is a picture of progressive selling of possessions and distribution of the money. Every verb — five of them — in these descriptions is a Greek imperfect tense, describing not a single act, as implied in the KJV and RSV, but a continuing, repeated, or customary action. We might read them in this way: ". . . they were selling . . . and were distributing . . ."; and ". . . they were bringing the prices . . . and they were placing them . . . and it was being distributed. . . ." In other words the disciples were prompted by Christian love to aid those of their company who were in need, *whenever anyone was in need*, even if it meant selling possessions to provide the assistance. This assistance was evidently carried out by the apostles for the church,

rather than being a purely individual matter, as Acts 4:35 points out. It may, therefore, have involved some sort of systematic contributions by those who were able. But it is clearly not a case of everyone's selling all his possessions and giving it all to the church.

The misunderstanding is not lessened, moreover, by the translations, ". . . and parted them to all men, as every man had need" (2:45), and ". . . unto every man according as he had need" (4:35). The meaning of each of these passages is more nearly, ". . . and distributed them so often as anyone had need." Indeed, in both passages in the original the words "had need" are preceded by the Greek particle *an* which makes the idea more indefinite — that is, the distribution was made to people *when and if* they were in need.

The translation in 2:44, "*had* all things common," can also easily be misunderstood to mean that the disciples owned everything in common. The verb *echō* usually does mean "to have," in the sense of "to possess."

However, this verb is also used (1) to refer to the people's opinion of John the Baptist — "they *counted* him as a prophet" (Matt. 14:5), "for all *hold* John as a prophet" (Matt. 21:26), "for all men *counted* John, that he was a prophet indeed" (Mark 11:32); (2) to refer to the people's opinion of Jesus — "they *took* him for a prophet" (Matt. 21:46); and (3) in St. Paul's words in Phil. 2:29, "*hold* such in reputation" — that is, consider such people precious. The meaning of the verb in these passages, in other words, is to have or to hold an opinion about someone or something, or to consider someone or something in a certain light. It is this meaning which should be used in Acts 2:45, which gives the meaning that "they considered all things common" — that is, they had the truly Christian spirit of the motto, "What is mine is yours to share, if you need it."

Perhaps a paraphrase or free translation may summarize what we believe to be the proper meaning of these two passages we have been discussing:

And all who believed were accustomed to consider their possessions as common property; and they would sell their properties and possessions and distribute them to anyone who was in need (Acts 2:44-45).

For neither was anyone in need among them; for as many as were owners of fields or houses would sell them and bring the price of the things which were sold and would place it at the feet of the apostles, and it would be distributed to anyone who was in need (Acts 4:34-45).

The idea that the Christians were attempting to set up a "communistic utopia" rests upon a view which misreads the author's glowing description of vital Christian stewardship and love among what was doubtless a large percentage of poor people, and mistakenly forces into his words a description of a legalistic system which was forced upon the entire Christian community. A fair interpretation of relevant passage does not seem to bear out such a Utopian thesis.

Additional Note V

DEMON POSSESSION AND EXPULSION

A significant statement has been made by J. Stafford Wright concerning the problem of demon possession and expulsion. Says this author:

Demon possession demands serious consideration. It has been accepted as a fact by most nations from early times, and is still recognized today: It was apparently accepted by Jesus Christ, and many of the cures that He and His disciples practised were based on the real existence of demons which had to be cast out. Jesus and His disciples distinguished clearly between normal physical illnesses, that were cured generally by the laying on of hands or anointing with oil, and those cases of possession which were cured by the word of command (e.g., Matt. 10:8; Mark 6:13; Luke 13:32), even though these latter cases often showed the symptoms of ordinary diseases such as dumbness and blindness (Matt. 9:32, 33; 12:22).

The chief characteristic of demon possession appears to have been the control of the body of the possessed in an abnormal way, against what was believed to be the will of the person. Where the possessing spirit was prepared to speak, it spoke of itself as an entity different from the man it was possessing. Thus the spirits in Mark 5 recognized Jesus for what He was, and gave their name as Legion.

Similar characteristics have been noted in recent times from various parts of the world, and they have attracted particular notice in China. The stories may lack the amount of corroboration in detail that we should desire, but their similarity in general outline, as they come from different parts, makes them inherently likely. A person suddenly exhibits another personality, and speaks in a different voice, which Miss Mildred Cable describes as "the weird minor chant of the possessed, the voice, as in every case I have seen, clearly distinguishing it from insanity" (*The Fulfilment of a Dream*, p. 118). The person often becomes violent, and may exhibit supernatural knowledge. Usually his words are evil, and often blasphemous.

A very full study of cases in China was made by a missionary, Dr. J. L. Nevius, in 1892, in *Demon Possession and Allied Themes* (Fleming H. Revell). . . . Dr. Nevius began his studies with a detailed questionnaire, which he sent to many missionaries and Chinese Christians, so as to discover as much firsthand information as possible. His conclusion in the light of all the evidence is that demon possession is what the name suggests, and it cannot be equated with any ordinary physical or psychological derangement. . . .

Certainly the casting out of demons is no light thing. . . . He [Christ] spoke of the danger of the spirit returning to his former victim, accompanied by other spirits also, unless the victim has in the meantime filled the house of his life with another Owner (Luke 11:24-26) .[541]

Additional Note VI

THE HIGH-GOD THEORY

Stephen's allusion to the Most High (Acts 7:48), here clearly identified with the Jehovah of the Hebrews, is both interesting and provoking. Twice in the Acts the expression occurs (Acts 7:48 and 16:17), once in Hebrews (Heb. 7:1), and once in Mark (Mark 5:7). Paul's allusion to "The Unknown God" of the Athenians (Acts 17:23) appears to bear the same significance as the other references. At Philippi the demon-pos-

[541] J. Stafford Wright, *Man in the Process of Time*, pp. 131-134. For further discussion of this subject, see Richard Chenevix Trench, *Notes on the Parables of Our Lord*, pp. 117-138.

sessed damsel referred to the Christian apostles as servants of "the Most High God, who proclaim . . . the way of salvation" (Acts 16:17). Likewise the demon-possessed Gadarene addressed Jesus as the "Son of the Most High God" (Mk. 5:7). In the Epistle to the Hebrews Melchizedek is referred to as the "priest of the God Most High" (Heb. 7:1).

All of the foregoing adds up to a strong suspicion that, even apart from the special divine revelation as given of God to the Hebrews through the law, but later and fuller to the world through Christ, there is in man's moral consciousness the inescapable conviction of a Supreme God. In the science of religion this concept has become known as the "High-God Theory."

In general the "High-God Theory" maintains that all people, including the most primitive, have a concept of a Supreme Being, above and beyond their polytheistic concepts. This "High-God" is seldom an object of worship for primitives, though he may be recognized as the Supreme God. Zwemer[542] treats the subject at considerable length.

Andrew Lang, nearly half a century ago, was one of the earliest modern scholars to advance and champion this "High-God" theory. Lang spoke of his "anachronistic views regarding the prevalence of the idea of a Sky-god or Highest god among primitive tribes."[543] Though Lang was largely ignored at first, in due time Wilhelm Schmidt, the well-known German anthropologist, revived the theory and brought it to scholarly recognition and wide acceptance. Thus Zwemer writes:

> Through endless transformations, myths, and legends, the Sky-god or High-god is found at the base of all the ethnic religions in the Mediterranean area and in the Far East. We find him also among primitive tribes in most widely scattered areas and the belief in such a Supreme Spirit is characterized by spontaneity, universality, and persistency which can only point to a veritable primitive revelation or an innate perception.[544]

Lang stated:

> Of the existence of a belief in a Supreme Being, among primitive tribes there is as good evidence as we possess for any fact in the ethnographic region . . . certain low savages are as monotheistic as some Christians. They have a Supreme Being and the distinctive attributes of Deity are not by them assigned to other beings.[545]

J. K. Archer,[546] following Wilhelm Schmidt, classifies primitives on the "lower" and "higher" cultural levels. The former include the Negritos, certain Micronesian and Polynesian tribes, Papuans, Aruntas, Andamanese, the Kols and Pariaks, the Pygmies and Bushmen, the Caribs and the Yohgans. The latter include the Samoans, Hawaiians, Kalmuks, Veddas, Todas, Bantus, Eskimos, and the American Indians.

In his Oxford Lectures ("High Gods in North America" — 1932), Schmidt asserted:

> It is precisely among the three oldest primitive peoples of North America that we find a clear and firmly established belief in a High-god. . . . It is only now that we can produce the final proof that these High-gods, in their oldest form, come before all other elements, be they naturalism, fetishism, Ghost-worship, animism, totemism, or magism, from one or other of which of the earlier evolutionistic theories had derived the origin of religion.[547]

Schmidt[548] further observes that among a large number of these tribes the High-god concept includes the creatorship of the universe *ex nihilo*.

Grace H. Turnbull cites ample evidence from the ritual of the Omaha Indians to the effect that "Wakonda" was their High-god and as such was the creator of all things: "At the beginning all things were in the mind of Wakonda . . . Wakonda [was] the Maker of all things."[549]

Schmidt observes that primitives generally represent the Supreme Being as absolutely good, ascribe to him fatherhood, creative power, and sky residence.

[542] Samuel Marinus Zwemer, *The Origin of Religion, Evolution or Revelation,* pp. 75-99.
[543] *Ibid.,* p. 75.
[544] *Ibid.,* cf. "Sky-Gods" by Foucart in *Encyclopedia of Religion and Ethics,* James Hastings,, ed. pp. 580-585.   [545] Andrew Lang, *The Making of Religion,* pp. 181, 183.
[546] J. K. Archer, *Faiths Men Live By,* pp. 18, 19.
[547] Wilhelm Schmidt, *High Gods in North America,* p. 19.   [548] *Ibid.*
[549] Grace H. Turnbull, *Tongues of Fire: A Bible of Sacred Scriptures of the Pagan World,* p. 10.

African pygmies and bushmen, Philippine Negritos, and Southeast Australians use the name "father" for their High-god. Creator is a common designation for him among the American Indians. The Ainu of Hokkadio have three unusual names for their High-god: "Upholder, Cradle (of children), and Protector."[550]

Among the High-god attributes on which there is rather general agreement among primitives, Schmidt[551] observes, are eternity, omniscience, beneficence, omnipotence, and the authority to administer rewards and punishments.

Likewise missionaries and anthropologists have found this High-god concept in the ethnic religions of China (Shang-ti=supreme ruler), Japan (Ama no Mi Naka Nusho no Mikoto), and India (Varuna, perhaps the original Ouranos).[552]

Ancient Egypt, Assyria (Ashur), and the Arabs (Orotal, a corruption of Alah Taal) have all had their High-god concepts as expressed in their respective deities.[553]

Zwemer observes that Calvin held that

. . . in every man there is still a seed of religious truth and an ineradicable consciousness of God. Light is still shining in the darkness and all men still retain a degree of love for truth, for justice, and a social order. This knowledge of God, said Calvin, is innate but quickened by the manifestation of God in nature. It fails in its proper effect because of sin, and could only be restored by special grace in a special objective revelation.[554]

Zwemer concludes that "although Calvin's doctrine of the knowledge of God and of Common Grace was wholly based on the Scriptures, this very doctrine is now largely confirmed by anthropology and the history of religion."[555]

We conclude therefore that the origin of the idea of God is not due to magic, fetishism, manism, animism, or any process of evolution on man's part, but to God himself, the Creator of man and his Redeemer. "For ever since the world was created, his invisible nature, his everlasting power and divine being, have been quite perceptible in what he had made. So they have no excuse. Though they knew God, they have not glorified him as God nor given thanks to him; they have turned to futile speculations till their ignorant minds grew dark. . . . Since they have exchanged the truth of God for an untruth, worshipping and serving the creature rather than the Creator who is blessed for ever. Amen. (Rom. 1:20, 21, 25).[556]

Therefore, it appears most probable that the Philippian demoniac's "Most High God" (Acts 16:17), the Athenians' "Unknown God" (Acts 17:23), and Melchizedek's "God Most High" (Heb. 7:1), with their varying concepts, were one and the same with the "Most High God" (Acts 7:48) of Stephen's address and the "Most High God" (Mark 5:7), recognized by the demon-possessed Gadarene.[557]

Additional Note VII

SAMARIA AND THE SAMARITANS[558]

The district of Samaria lay to the north of Judaea and was bounded on the west by the Mediterranean, and on the east by the Jordan River, and on the north and northwest by Phoenicia and Galilee. Caesarea, the capital of Judaea, of which Samaria was a political part in Paul's

[550] Wilhelm Schmidt, The Origin and Growth of Religion: Facts and Theories, pp. 263-269.
[551] Ibid., pp. 270-275. [552] Zwemer, op. cit., pp. 84-88. [553] Ibid., pp. 89-93.
[554] Ibid., p. 98. [555] Ibid. [556] Ibid., pp. 98, 99.
[557] For further evidence on the "High-God" theory, the reader is referred to the following works:
P. S. Deshmukh, Religion in Vedic Literature (Oxford: 1933).
Alexander LeRoy, The Religion of the Primitives. Tr. Newton Thompson (New York: 1922).
R. H. Lowie, Primitives. Tr. Newton Thompson (New York: 1922).
John Murphy, Primitive Man: His Essential Quest (Oxford: 1927).
Paul Radin, The Method and Theory of Ethnology (London: 1933).
Paul Radin, Primitive Man As Philosopher (New York: 1927).
Paul Radin, The Racial Myth (New York: 1933).
Benjamin B. Warfield, "Antiquity and Unity of the Human Race," in Studies In Theology (New York: 1932), pp. 235-258.
William L. Thomas, Source Book for Social Origins (Chicago: 1909).
H. J. D. Ashtey, Biblical Anthropology (Oxford U. Press, 1929).
Robert Henry Lowie, The History of Ethnological Theory (New York: Rhinehart, 1937).
[558] The following treatment is largely based upon R. A. S. Macalister, "Samaria and the Samaritans," in Dictionary of the Bible, ed. James Hastings, p. 821; Madalene S. and J. Lane Miller, "Samaria, District of" and "Samaritans," in Harper's Bible Dictionary, pp. 638, 639; and Elmer W. K. Mould, op. cit., pp. 637-640.

day, was located on the seacoast of Samaria. In Solomon's time Samaria was
peopled by Israelites (mainly Ephraim
and the half-tribe of Manasseh).

Upon the death of Herod the Great
(4 B.C.?), his will provided for Samaria
and northern Idumaea to be given to his
son, King Archelaus, who ruled the country until he was deposed by Rome in A.D.
6. Thereafter the country came under
the Roman procurators.

When Israel, the Northern Kingdom,
fell under the Assyrians in 722 B.C., most
of the ruling and artisan classes were
taken into captivity. Many of the peasant
class were left in the country. Foreigners
were introduced to replace the captive
Israelites, resulting in a mixed population (Ezra 4:2, 9ff.). They had neither
the Hebrew standards of racial nor religious purity. The resultant condition
greatly offended the Judaean Jews, in
consequence of which an imaginary line
was drawn between the two nations which
was never to be erased.

After the restoration of the Southern
Kingdom, the Jerusalem Jews rejected the
proffered assistance of the Samaritans
under their governor Sanballat, in rebuilding the temple (Neh. 6). The
Samaritans thereafter tried to prevent the
rebuilding of Jerusalem (Ezra 4:4-7; Neh.
4:7), and in general opposed the Jewish
restoration.[559]

In consequence of their rebuff, the
Samaritans built their own temple on
Mt. Gerizim and organized themselves
into a distinct sect. This was probably accomplished in the fourth century
B.C. under permission of Alexander the
Great, though it may have been at an
earlier date. Thereafter the Jews considered the Samaritans a mongrel people, both racially and religiously, and
had no more dealings with them than
absolutely necessary. In fact, because of
their racial and religious corruption, the
orthodox Jews regarded the Samaritans
with greater disdain than they did the
heathen nations. They denied them the
privilege of offerings at the Jerusalem
temple, restricted their commerce, and
forbade them to intermarry with the
Jews. In short the "Jews . . . [had] no
dealings with the Samaritans" (John
4:9b).

The Samaritans had much in common
with the Jews. They observed the Sabbath, kept the sacred feasts, practiced
circumcision, anticipated the Messiah
(however He was to be a Samaritan
Messiah who would convert all to their
religion and nation). On the other hand,
they had certain marked differences with
the Jews. They held only the Pentateuch to be divinely authoritative, while
they rejected the rest of the Old Testament. They believed in a god who was
unique and without associate, in Moses,
the Torah, the sacredness of Mt. Gerizim,
and in future rewards and punishments.
Their belief that Mt. Gerizim was the
true earthly abode of God was the main
theological contention with the Jews who
held Jerusalem to be His earthly abode
(see John 4:19-25). Thus the Samaritans
assigned many Old Testament events to
Mt. Gerizim which the Jews attributed to
Moriah. Among these were the home of
Abraham (Gen. 22), the place of Isaac's
intended sacrifice, the vision of Jacob
(Gen. 31:13), Joseph's tomb (Josh. 24:
32), Jacob's Bethel, and others. They
gave many honorific titles to Mt. Gerizim,
such as " 'the Ancient Mountain,' 'Bethel,'
'the House of Angels,' 'the Gate of
Heaven,' 'Luzah,' ('to God in This
Place'), 'Sanctuary,' 'Mt. Gerizim,' 'Beth-
yhwh, the very name of the Highest,' 'the
Beautiful Mountain,' 'the Chosen Place,'
'the Highest in the World,' 'the First of
Mountains,' 'God is Seen,' and 'the Mountain of the Inheritance of the Shekinah.' "[560]

The Gerizim temple was destroyed by
the Maccabeans under John Hyrcanus
and was never rebuilt, though they continued to venerate Mt. Gerizim. The
Jewish-Samaritan animosity was finally
taken to Rome for settlement.[561]

Throughout the first century the Jewish-Samaritan animosity continued. Samaritans were considered strangers (Luke
17:18), and their mixed Jewish-heathen
worship (John 4:22) was an abomination
to the Jews. Only a handful of Samaritans remained, sacrificing, and celebrating
the Passover and waiting for the Messiah
at Mt. Gerizim.

While in His earlier ministry, Jesus'
disciples appear to have shared the Jewish hostility to the Samaritans (Luke 9:

---

[559] Josephus, Ant., XII, v, 5.   [560] Madelene S. and J. Lane Miller, op. cit., p. 640.
[561] Josephus, War, II, xii, 3-7.

51-56), it is quite evident that Jesus Himself was not infected with this spirit. It is recorded that He cleansed ten Samaritan lepers (Luke 17:11-19) and that an ill-famed Samaritan woman and many of her acquaintances came to believe on Him (John 4:21-42). In conversation with this woman, He set the Kingdom of God in correct perspective as consisting in a spiritual relationship with God and not dependent on earthly sacred places or ritual. Christ paid His highest respects to the Samaritans in His famous parable of "The Good Samaritan" delivered to a Jewish lawyer (Luke 10:25-37).

Persecuted Christians, following Stephen's martyrdom, fled to Samaria among other places, and in Samaria Philip preached and witnessed a great spiritual awakening accompanied by many miracles and conversions (Acts 8:1-25).

Additional Note VIII

ANGELOLOGY

The following discussion of angelology is based in part upon Oesterley's[562] treatment of the subject. In general angels are recognized in the Bible as divinely created beings (Col. 1:16), who possess superhuman powers (II Kings 6:17; Zech. 12:8). They assume human forms and converse (I Kings 19:5); eat (Gen. 18:8) and fight in defense of men on earth (Gen. 32:1, 2; II Sam. 5:24; Joel 3:11). Though they are regarded as wise (II Sam. 14:17, 20), they do not possess divine perfection (Job 4:18). If angels and seraphim are identical, they move by flight (Isa. 6:2, 6).

The mission of angels in relation to men appears to be that of guidance (Gen. 24:7, 40; Exod. 23:20ff.; Job 33:23); instructors of the Old Testament prophets (I Kings 13:18; 19:5ff.; II Kings 1:3, 15; Zech. 1:9); the destroyers of the evil and destructive (II Sam. 24:16, 17; II Kings 19:25; Job 33:23; Ps. 35:6; 78:49; Acts 12:23); the guardians of men (Gen. 19:15ff.; Ps. 34:7; 91:11); carriers of the answers to men's prayers on earth (Dan. 10:10-21); and messengers for God to men (Matt. 1:20; 2:13; 28:5; Luke 1:28; 24:23).

In their relation to God the function of angels consists principally in reporting the affairs of men on earth (Job 1:6; 2:1; cf. Zech. 1:8-10; Ps. 18:11; Isa. 19:1), and of participating in praise to God (Gen. 28:12; Ps. 103:20; Isa. 6:2).

Christ indicates in the gospels that heaven is the dwelling place of angels (Matt. 18:10; Luke 12:8, 9; John 1:51); that they are above men (Luke 20:36); that they escort the souls of the righteous dead to their heavenly abode (Luke 16:22); that they are without sex (Matt. 22:30); and that they are very great in number (Matt. 26:53). They are represented as accompanying Christ at his second coming (Matt. 13:39; 16:27; 24:31; 25:31; Mark 8:38; Luke 9:26; John 1:51). The Bible indicates that there are evil as well as good angels (Matt. 25:41); but that they are limited in knowledge (Matt. 24:36). Children have their guardian angels (Matt. 18:10). Angels are represented as rejoicing at the repentance of sinners and their return to the heavenly Father (Luke 15:10).

The ministry of angels seems to play a larger part in the Acts account than in the gospel stories. Luke gives us the account of the release of Peter and John from their imprisonment at the hands of an angel (Acts 5:19). An angel carried the Law to Moses on Mount Sinai (Acts 7:30, 35, 38). It was an angel that spoke to Philip during his work in Samaria (Acts 8:26). An angel appeared to Cornelius in his home at Caesarea (Acts 10:3, 7, 22; 11:13). Peter was released from his prison by an angel (Acts 12:7-11, 15). The judgment of death was inflicted upon Herod by an angel (Acts 12:23). Just before his shipwreck experience at Malta, an angel visited Paul with a message of assurance (Acts 27:23).

That angels and spirits are not one and the same is clearly attested (Acts 23:8, 9). Paul's treatment of angels accords in general with the Acts account (see Rom. 8:38; I Cor. 4:9; 11:10; I Tim. 5:21), except that he seems to give greater place to the direct communication of God to man (Gal. 1:12; cf. Acts 9:5). Paul forbids the worship of angels (Col. 2:18), and goes so far as to equate this practice with the worship of demons (I Cor. 10:20).

If the traditional view be true that one third of the angels fell with Lucifer, and if Lucifer is to be identified with Satan, then it would be a logical conclusion that two thirds of the angels remain righteous and unfallen. Thus it is a logical conclusion that to every evil angel attacking righteous man upon earth, there may be assigned two unfallen protecting angels to preserve him against their attacks. Thus indeed, "They that be for us are more than they that be against us."

Additional Note IX

CHRISTIANITY AT ANTIOCH

Harnack furnishes the following most enlightening information on the status of Christianity in Antioch:

In accordance with its tendency towards universal dominion, Christianity streamed from Jerusalem as far as Antioch (Acts xi), the greatest city of the East and the third city in the Roman empire, ere a few years had passed over its head. It was in Antioch that it got its name, which in all probability was originally a nickname; for Antioch was a city of nicknames and of low-class literature. Here the first Gentile Christian community grew up; for it was adherents of Jesus drawn from paganism who were called "Christians" (cf. vol. i, pp. 411f.). Here Barnabas labored. Here the great apostle Paul found his sphere of action for some years, and ere long the Christian community became so important, endowed with such a vigorous self-consciousness and such independent activity, that its repute rivalled that of the Jerusalem church itself. Between the churches of Jerusalem and Antioch the cardinal question of the Gentile Christians was debated; it was the church of Antioch — mentioned along with Syria and Cilicia in Acts xv, 23, and the only city noted in this connection — which took the most decided step forward in the history of the gospel; and as early as the second century it gave further expression to its church-consciousness by designating the apostle Peter as its first bishop — although, to judge from Gal. ii, 11 f., it was no glorious role that he had played in Antioch. One of its churches was traced back to the apostolic age.

Its fame is established by Ignatius, after Paul. Several features (though they are not many) in the contemporary situation of the church at Antioch can be made out from the epistles of Ignatius who proudly terms it "the church of Syria." In Smyrn, xi, 2, he says that after the persecution it had regained its proper size. The claim which he advances, under cover of an exaggerated modesty, to instruct foreign churches probably sprang, not simply from his personal attainments as a confessor, but also from the ecclesiastical and commanding position of the city of which he was bishop. The central position of the church is indicated by the fact that all the Asiatic churches sent envoys to congratulate the church of Antioch upon its recovery. It now occupied the place once held by Jerusalem.

Once more, it was in this church that the dynamic Christology received its most powerful statement; here Arianism arose; and here the ablest school of exegesis flourished. Thanks to the biblical scholarship of Lucian, the teacher of Arius, Antioch acquired a widespread importance for the development of exegesis and theology in the East (Arianism, the Antiochene school of exegesis, Nestorianism).

The central position of the church is reflected in the great synods held at Antioch from the middle of the third century onwards.

It is impossible to draw up any statistical calculations with regard to the church about A.D. 320, but at any rate there were several churches in the city (Theod., H.E., i, 2), and if the local Christians really were in the majority in Julian's reign, their number must have been very large as early as the year 320. Diodorus and Chrysostom [347-407] preached in what was substantially a Christian city, as the latter explicitly attests in several passages. He gives the number of the inhabitants (excluding slaves and children) at 200,000 (Hom. in Ignat. 4), the total of members belonging to the chief church being 100,000 (Hom. 85, 86, c. 4). Antioch in early days was always the stronghold of Eastern Christianity, and the local church was perfectly conscious of its vocation as the church of the metropolis. The horizon and effective power of the Antiochene bishop extended as far as Mesopotamia and Persia, Armenia and Georgia. He felt himself in duty bound to superintend the missions and the consolidation of the church throughout these countries. The execution of this task led to the steady growth of certain rights, which were never formally defined, but which were exercised by the Antiochene bishop throughout the East. Similarly, he recognized his duties with regard to the defence of the church against heretics, who were fond of resorting to the East. It was from Antioch that the missionary impulse of Chrysostom proceeded, as well as the vigorous campaign against the heretics waged by the great exegetes, by Diodorus and Theodoret, and by Chrysostom and Nestorius.563

Additional Note X

EARLY NAMES OF CHRIST'S FOLLOWERS564

The term "disciples" fell into disuse, because it no longer expressed the relationship in which Christians now found themselves placed. It meant at once too little and too much. Consequently other terms arose, although these did not in every instance become technical.

The Jews, in the first instance, gave their renegade compatriots special names of their own, in particular "Nazarenes," "Galileans," and perhaps also "Poor" (though it is probably quite correct to take this as a self-designation of Jewish Christians, since "Ebionim" in the Old Testament is a term of respect). But these titles really did not prevail, except in small circles. "Nazarene" alone enjoyed, and for long retained, a somewhat extensive circulation.

The Christians called themselves "God's people," "Israel in spirit" . . . "the seed of Abraham," "the chosen people," "the twelve tribes," "the servants of God," "believers," "saints," "brethren," and "the church of God."

The three characteristic titles, however, are those of "saints," "brethren," and "the church of God," all of which hang together.

Closely bound up with the name of "saints" was that of "brethren" (and "sisters"), the former denoting the Christians' relationship to God and to the future life . . . the Kingdom of God, the latter the new relationship in which they felt themselves placed towards their fellow men, and, above all, towards their fellow believers (cf. also the not infrequent title of "brethren in the Lord"). After Paul, this title became so common that the pagans soon grew familiar with it, ridiculing and besmirching it, but unable, for all that, to evade the impression which it made. For the term did correspond to the conduct of Christians.

Yet even the name of "the brethren,"

though it outlived that of "the saints," lapsed after the close of the third century; or rather, it was only ecclesiastics who really continued to call each other "brethren."

We now come to the name "Christians," which became the cardinal title of the faith. The Roman authorities certainly employed it from the days of Trajan downwards (cf. Pliny and the rescripts, the "cognitiones de Christians"), and probably even 40 or 50 years earlier (I Pet. iv, 16; Tacitus), whilst it was by this name that the adherents of the new religion were known among the common people (Tacitus; cf. also the well-known passage in Suetonius).

One name still falls to be considered, a name which of course never became really technical, but was (so to speak) semi-technical; I mean that of . . . (miles Christi, a soldier of Christ). With Paul this metaphor had already become so common that it was employed in the most diverse ways.

It is indeed strange that Harnack appears to overlook one name by which the early Christians were well known and often called, that is, the designation "friends."

Additional Note XI

THE PLACE OF WOMEN IN THE PRIMITIVE CHURCH

It is most interesting and instructive to note Harnack's observation on the recognition given to, and the prominence of, women in the church of the first century.

No one who reads the New Testament attentively, as well as those writings which immediately succeeded it, can fail to notice that in the apostolic and subapostolic age women played an important role in the propaganda of Christianity and throughout the Christian communities. The equalizing of man and woman before God (Gal. iii, 28) produced a religious independence among women, which aided the Christian mission. Jesus himself had a circle of women among his adherents, in addition to the disciples. . . .

Concerning the Roman and Philippian letters, as also Priscilla in Acts, Harnack states:

---

563 Adolf Harnack, The Mission and Expansion of Christianity, II, 125, 127, 128, 133.
564 Harnack, op. cit., I, 401-406, 410, 414.

Thus no fewer than fifteen women are saluted, alongside of eighteen men, and all these must have rendered important services to the church or to the apostle, or to both, in the shape of the work with which they are credited. . . .

In Philippians, which contains a few personal items, we read (iv, 2) : "I exhort Euodia and I exhort Syntyche to be of the same mind in the Lord. Yea, I pray thee also, true yokefellow, to help these women, for they have wrought with me in the service of the gospel, together with Clement and the rest of my fellow-workers, whose names are in the book of life." These two women, then, had helped to found the church at Philippi, and consequently occupied a position of high honour still (perhaps as presidents of two churches in their houses, like Nymphe at Colosse) . . . .

Yet in Acts also (xviii, 18, 26) the woman is first and it was the woman who — as Chrysostom rightly infers from xviii, 26 — converted Apollos, the disciple of John the Baptist. As the latter was a cultured Greek, the woman who was capable of instructing him, must have been herself a person of some culture. She was not merely the mother of a church in her house. As we find from Paul as well, she was a missionary and a teacher. The epistle to the Hebrews probably came from her or from her husband."565

Additional Note XII

CORINTH

Finegan aptly describes the Corinth of Paul's day as follows:

In going from Athens to Corinth (Acts 18:1), Paul was moving from the intellectual center of Greece to its most splendid commercial city. . . . Corinth was just across the isthmus which connected central Greece with the Peloponnesus. This isthmus was a natural meeting place for trade from East and West. Ships from Asia Minor, Syria, and Egypt put in to the port of Cenchreae (cf. Romans 16:1) on the east side of the isthmus, those of Italy, Sicily, and Spain docked at Lechaeum the harbor on the west side. The distance between these two ports was less than ten miles. . . . Situated but one and one-half miles south of this isthmus and commanding the ports on either side of it, the city of Corinth obviously was destined for com-

mercial greatness. Pindar called the Isthmus of Corinth 'the bridge of the sea' and Strabo summed up the situation accurately when he said, "Corinth is called 'wealthy' because of its commerce, since it is situated on the Isthmus and is master of two harbors, of which the one leads straight to Asia, and the other to Italy; and it makes easy the exchange of merchandise from both countries that are so far distant from each other.

. . . She dominated extensive trade routes, and Corinthian bronze and pottery were exported widely over the Mediterranean. About 146 B.C., Corinth warred with Rome and upon defeat was completely destroyed, probably because of commercial jealousy. The inhabitants were sold into slavery and for one hundred years the site of the city lay desolate. Then in 46 B.C. Julius Caesar refounded the city as the colonial Laus Julia Corinthiensis, and peopled it with Italian freedmen and dispossessed Greeks. Its commercial prosperity was recovered rapidly, and Augustus made Corinth the capital of Achaia and seat of its proconsul (Acts 18:12) .566

Additional Note XIII

PAUL'S SUPPOSED WEALTH

Ramsay argues most persuasively that Paul was a man of considerable material means.

Several other factors show clearly that, during the following four years, Paul had considerable command of money. Imprisonments and a long lawsuit are expensive. Now, it is clear that Paul during the following four years did not appear before the world as a penniless wanderer, living by the work of his hands. A person in that position will not, either at the present day or in the first century, be treated with such marked respect as was certainly paid to Paul, at Caesarea, on the voyage, and in Rome. The governor Felix and his wife, the Princess Drusilla, accorded him an interview and private conversation. King Agrippa and his Queen Bernice also desired to see him. A poor man never receives such attentions or rouses such interest. Moreover, Felix hoped for a bribe from him; and a rich Roman official did not look for a small gift. Paul, therefore, wore the outward appearance of a man of means, like one in a position to bribe a Roman procurator. The minimum in the way of personal attendants

565 Harnack, *op. cit.*, II, 64, 67, 68.   566 Finegan, *op. cit.*, pp. 278-279.

that was allowable for a man of respectable position was two slaves; and, as we shall see, Paul was believed to be attended by two slaves to serve him. At Caesarea he was confined in the palace of Herod; but he had to live, to maintain two attendants, and to keep up a respectable appearance. Many comforts, which are almost necessities, would be given by the guards, so long as they were kept in good humor, and it is expensive to keep guards in good humor. In Rome he was able to hire a lodging for himself and to live there, maintaining, of course, the soldier who guarded him.

An appeal to the supreme court could not be made by everybody that chose. Such an appeal had to be permitted and sent forward by the provincial governor; and only a serious case would be entertained. But the case of a very poor man is never esteemed as serious; and there

is little doubt that the citizen's right of appeal to the Emperor was hedged in by fees and pledges. There is also one law for the rich man and another for the poor: at least, to this extent, that many claims can be successfully pushed by a rich man in which a poor man would have no chance of success. In appealing to the Emperor, Paul was choosing undoubtedly an expensive line of trial. All this had certainly been estimated before the decisive step was taken. Paul had weighed the cost; he had reckoned the gain which would accrue to the Church if the supreme court pronounced in his favor; and his past experience gave him every reason to hope for a favorable issue before a purely Roman tribunal, where Jewish influence would have little or no power. The importance of the case, as described in the preceding section, makes the appeal more intelligible.[567]

---

[567] Ramsay, *op. cit.*, pp. 310-312.

Bibliography

I. Archaeology

Caiger, Stephen L. *Archaeology and the New Testament.* London: Cassell and Co., 1939.

Cobern, Camden M. *The New Archaeological Discoveries* (6th ed.). New York: Funk & Wagnalls, 1922.

Deissmann, Adolph. *Bible Studies.* Translated by Alexander Grieve. Edinburgh: T. & T. Clarke, 1901.

————. *Light from the Ancient East* (new rev. ed.). Translated by Lionel R. M. Strachan. New York: George H. Doran Co., 1927.

Finegan, Jack. *Light from the Ancient Past.* Princeton: University Press, 1946.

Free, Joseph, P. *Archaeology and Bible History.* Wheaton: Van Kampen Press, 1950.

Wright, G. Ernest. *Biblical Archaeology.* Philadelphia: Westminster Press, 1957.

II. Bible Atlases

Hurlbut, Jesse L. *Bible Atlas* (rev. ed.). Chicago: Rand McNally & Co., 1910.

Kraeling, Emil G. *Rand McNally Bible Atlas.* Chicago: Rand McNally & Co., 1956.

Stirling, John. *An Atlas of the Acts of the Apostles and the Epistles.* London: George Philip and Son, Ltd., 1939.

Wright, G. E. and Filson, F. V. (eds.). *The Westminster Historical Atlas* (rev. ed.). Philadelphia: Westminster Press, 1945, 1956.

III. Bible Dictionaries

Davis, John D. *The Westminster Dictionary of the Bible.* Revised and rewritten by Henry S. Gehman. Philadelphia: Westminster Press, 1944.

Douglas, J. (ed.). *The New Bible Dictionary.* Grand Rapids: Wm. B. Eerdmans Publishing Co., 1962.

Hastings, James (ed.). *Dictionary of the Apostolic Church.* 2 vols. New York: Charles Scribner's Sons, 1916 (rep. 1921).

————. *A Dictionary of the Bible.* 5 vols. New York: Charles Scribner's Sons, 1898.

Miller, M. S. and Miller, J. L. *Harper's Bible Dictionary.* New York: Harper & Brothers, 1952.

Orr, James (ed.). *The International Standard Bible Encyclopedia.* Revised by Melvin Grove Kyle. Chicago: Howard-Severance Co., 1929.

IV. Commentaries

Aberly, John. "The Acts," *New Testament Commentary* (rev. ed.). Edited by H. C. Alleman. Philadelphia: Muhlenberg Press, 1936.

Alexander, Joseph Addison. *Commentary on the Acts of the Apostles.* 2 vols in 1. Grand Rapids: Zondervan Publishing House, 1956 (reprint).

Alford, Henry. *The Greek Testament,* 6th ed. Vol. II. London: Rivingtons, 1871 (Moody Press, 1958, reprint).

————. *The New Testament for English Readers* (3rd ed.). 2 vols. (each bound in two parts). Boston: Lee and Shepard, 1872 (Moody Press, 1955, reprint).

Barclay, William. *The Acts of the Apostles.* Philadelphia: Westminster Press, 1955.

Barnes, Albert. *Notes on the New Testament: Acts of the Apostles.* Edited by Robert Frew. Grand Rapids: Baker Book House, 1949 (reprint).

Bartlet, J. V. *The Acts.* "The Century Bible." Edinburgh: T. C. & E. C. Jack, n.d.

Benson, Joseph. *The New Testament of Our Lord and Saviour Jesus Christ.* Vol. I. New York: Carlton & Phillips, 1856.

Blunt, A. W. F. *The Acts of the Apostles.* "The Clarendon Bible." Oxford: Clarendon Press, 1923.

Bloomfield, S.T. *The Greek Testament, with English Notes, Critical, Theological, and Exegetical* (5th Am. ed.). Vol. I. Philadelphia: H. C. Peck and Theo. Bliss, 1836.

Bruce, F. F. *The Acts of the Apostles.* The Greek text with Introduction and Commentary. Grand Rapids: Wm. B. Eerdmans Publishing Co., 1952.

————. *The Acts of the Apostles.* "The New Bible Commentary." Edited by F. Davidson. Grand Rapids: Wm. B. Eerdmans Publishing Co., 1953.

————. *Commentary on the Book of the Acts.* "The New International Commentary on the New Testament." Grand Rapids: Wm. B. Eerdmans Publishing Co., 1954.

Burch, Ernest W. *Acts of the Apostles.* "The Abingdon Bible Commentary." Edited by F. C. Eiselen *et al.* New York: Abingdon-Cokesbury Press, 1929.

Calvin, John. *Commentary Upon the Acts of the Apostles*. Edited by Henry Beveridge. 2 vols. Grand Rapids: Wm. B. Eerdmans Publishing Co., 1949 (reprint).

Carroll, B. H. *The Acts, "An Interpretation of the English Bible."* Edited by J. B. Cranfill. Nashville: Broadman Press, 1942 (1st ed., 1916).

Carter, C. W., and Earle, Ralph. *The Acts of the Apostles*. "The Evangelical Commentary." Grand Rapids: Zondervan Publishing House, 1959.

Carver, William Owen. *The Acts of the Apostles*. Nashville: Broadman Press, 1916.

Clarke, Adam. *The New Testament of Our Lord and Savior Jesus Christ*. 2 vols. New York: Methodist Book Concern, n.d. Also Nashville: Abingdon-Cokesbury Press, n.d.

Clarke, W. K. L. *Concise Bible Commentary*. New York: Macmillan Co., 1953.

Cook, F. C. (ed.). *The Holy Bible*. Commentary . . . by Bishops and Other Clergy of the Anglican Church. New Testament, Vol. II. New York: Charles Scribner's Sons, 1907.

Cowles, Henry. *Acts of the Apostles*. New York: D. Appleton and Co., 1883.

Cox, Lilian E. *The Acts of the Apostles*. "The Twentieth Century Bible Commentary" (rev.). Edited by G. H. Davies *et al.* New York: Harper & Brothers, 1955 (1st ed., 1932).

Davidson, F. (ed.). *The New Bible Commentary*. Grand Rapids: Wm. B. Eerdmans Publishing Company, 1954.

Dummelow, J. R. (ed.). *A Commentary on the Holy Bible*. London: Macmillan Co., 1909. Also New York: Macmillan Co., 1936 (rep. 1951).

Ellicott, Charles John (ed.). *Ellicott's Commentary on the Whole Bible*. Grand Rapids: Zondervan Publishing House. n.d. "Acts," E. H. Plumptre, Vol. VII.

Erdman, Charles R. *The Acts: An Exposition*. Philadelphia: Westminster Press, 1919.

Exell, Joseph S. *The Biblical Illustrator: The Acts*. 3 vols. Grand Rapids: Baker Book House, 1954 (reprint).

Furneaux, William M. *The Acts of the Apostles*. Oxford: Clarendon Press, 1912.

Gaebelein, A. C. *The Acts of the Apostles: An Exposition*. New York: "Our Hope," 1912.

Gloag, Paton J. *A Critical and Exegetical Commentary on the Acts of the Apostles*. 2 vols. Edinburgh: T. & T. Clark, 1870.

Godbey, W. B. *Commentary on the New Testament*. Vol. V. Cincinnati: Revivalist Press, 1899.

Gore, Charles, Goudge, H. L., and Guillaume, Alfred. *A New Commentary on Holy Scripture*. New York: Macmillan Co., 1928.

Gould, Ezra P. *A Critical and Exegetical Commentary*. New York: Charles Scribner's Sons, 1896.

Hackett, H. B. *A Commentary on the Acts of the Apostles* (rev. ed.). Edited by Alvah Hovey. Philadelphia: American Baptist Publication Society, 1882.

Hastings, Edward (ed.). *The Speaker's Bible: The Acts of the Apostles*. 2 vols. Aberdeen: "The Speaker's Bible" Office, 1927.

Henry, Matthew. *Commentary on the Whole Bible*. Vol. VI. New York: Fleming H. Revell Co., n.d.

Hervey, A. C. and others. *The Acts of the Apostles*. "The Pulpit Commentary." Edited by H. D. Spence and J. S. Exell. Grand Rapids: Wm. B. Eerdmans Publishing Co., 1950 (reprint).

Jackson, F. J. Foakes. *The Acts of the Apostles*. "The Moffatt New Testament Commentary." New York: Harper and Brothers, 1931.

Jackson, F. J. Foakes, and Lake, Kirsopp (eds.). *The Beginnings of Christianity*. Part I. "The Acts of the Apostles." 5 vols. London: Macmillan & Co., Ltd., 1920-33. Also 1942 (reprint).

Jamieson, Robert, Fausset, A. R., and Brown, David. *A Commentary Critical Experimental and Practical on the Old and New Testaments*. 6 Vols. (Am. ed.) Grand Rapids: Wm. B. Eerdmans Publishing Co., 1948. Also Grand Rapids: Zondervan Publishing House, n.d. (1 vol.).

Knowling, R. J. "The Acts of the Apostles," *The Expositor's Greek Testament*. Edited by W. R. Nicoll. Grand Rapids: Wm. B. Eerdmans Publishing Co., n.d.

Knox, Ronald A. *A New Testament Commentary*. Vol. II. New York: Sheed & Ward, 1954.

Lange, John Peter. *Commentary on the Holy Scriptures* (Critical, Doctrinal, and Homiletical. Trans. from Ger. and ed. by Philip Schaff). "Acts." Grand Rapids: Zondervan Publishing House (reprint).

Lechler, G. V., and Gerok, Charles. *The Acts of the Apostles*. "A Commentary on The Holy Scriptures." Edited by John Peter Lange. Translated and edited by Philip Schaff. Grand Rapids: Zondervan Publishing House, n.d.

Lenski, R. C. H. *The Interpretation of the Acts of the Apostles*. Columbus, O.: Wartburg Press, 1944.

Lumby, J. R. *The Acts of the Apostles*. "The Cambridge Bible." Edited by J. J. S. Perowne. Cambridge: University Press, 1890.

――――. *The Acts of the Apostles.* "Cambridge Greek Testament." Cambridge: University Press, 1885.

Macaulay, J. C. *A Devotional Commentary on the Acts of the Apostles.* Grand Rapids: Wm. B. Eerdmans Publishing Co., 1946.

McGarvey, J. W. *New Commentary on the Acts of the Apostles.* 2 vols. in 1. Cincinnati: Standard Publishing Co., 1892.

Macgregor, G. H. C. *The Acts of the Apostles* (Exegesis). "Interpreter's Bible." Edited by G. A. Buttrick *et al.* Vol. IX. New York: Abingdon-Cokesbury Press, 1954.

Maclaren, Alexander. *Exposition of Holy Scripture: The Acts.* Grand Rapids: Wm. B. Eerdmans Publishing Co., 1932 (rep. 1944).

Menzies, Allan. *The Acts of the Apostles.* "A Commentary on the Bible." Edited by A. S. Peake. London: Thomas Nelson and Sons, 1919.

Meyer, H. A. W. *Critical and Exegetical Handbook to the Acts of the Apostles.* Translated from the 4th German ed. by Paton Gloag. Revised and edited by W. P. Dickson. Am. ed. by William Ormiston. New York: Funk & Wagnalls, 1883.

Moorehead, William G. *Outline Studies* (Acts, Romans, I & II Corinthians, Galatians). London & Edinburgh: Fleming H. Revell, 1902.

Morgan, G. Campbell. *The Acts of the Apostles.* New York: Fleming H. Revell Co., 1924.

Nicoll, W. Robertson (ed.). *The Expositor's Greek Testament.* Vol. II. Grand Rapids: Wm. B. Eerdmans Publishing Company, n.d.

Olshausen, Hermann. *Biblical Commentary on the New Testament.* 1st Am. ed. by A. C. Kendrick. Vol. III. New York: Sheldon, Blakeman & Co., 1857.

Page, T. E. *Acts of the Apostles.* London: Macmillan and Co., 1886.

Parker, Joseph. *Apostolic Life.* 3 vols. New York: Funk & Wagnalls, 1883-85.

――――. *The People's Bible* (Discourses upon the Holy Scriptures), Vols. XXIII-XXV. New York: Funk and Wagnalls Company, 1883.

Plumptre, E. H. *The Acts of the Apostles.* "Commentary on the Whole Bible." Edited by C. J. Ellicott. Vol. VII. Grand Rapids: Zondervan Publishing House, n.d.

Rackham, R. B. *The Acts of the Apostles.* "Westminster Commentaries" (8th ed.). London: Methuen & Co., Ltd., 1919 (1st ed., 1901).

Robertson, A. T. *Word Pictures in the New Testament.* Vol. III. New York: Richard R. Smith, 1930.

Sadler, M. F. *The Acts of the Apostles.* London: G. Bell and Sons, 1887.

Scott, Thomas. *The Holy Bible* (5th ed.). Boston: Crocker and Brewster, 1849.

Simpson, A. B. *The Acts of the Apostles.* "Christ in the Bible Series." Harrisburg, Pa.: Christian Publications, n.d.

Spence, H. D. M. (ed.). *Pulpit Commentary, Acts and Romans.* Grand Rapids: Wm. B. Eerdmans Publishing Company, 1950 (rep.).

Stillhorn, F. W. *Annotations on the Acts of the Apostles.* "The Lutheran Commentary." Edited by H. E. Jacobs. Vol. VI. New York: Christian Literature Co., 1896.

Stokes, G. T. *The Acts of the Apostles.* 2 vols. "The Expositor's Bible." New York: A. C. Armstrong and Son, 1892.

Thomas, David. *Acts of the Apostles: A Homiletic Commentary.* Grand Rapids: Baker Book House, 1955 (reprint of 1870 edition).

Vincent, Marvin R. *Word Studies in the New Testament.* Vol. I. Grand Rapids: Wm. B. Eerdmans Publishing Co., 1946 (1st ed., 1887).

Weiss, Bernhard. *A Commentary on the New Testament.* Translated by G. H. Schodde and E. Wilson. Vol. II. New York: Funk & Wagnalls, 1906.

Wesley, John. *Explanatory Notes Upon the New Testament.* London: Epworth Press, 1954.

Whedon, D. D. *Commentary on the New Testament.* Vol. III. New York: Hunt & Eaton, 1871.

Whitby, Daniel. *A Commentary on the Gospels and Epistles of the New Testament.* "A Critical Commentary and Paraphrase on the Old and New Testament and the Apocrypha." Edited by Patrick *et al.* Vol. IV. Philadelphia: Carey and Hart, 1848.

Whitelaw, Thomas. *A Homiletical Commentary on the Acts of the Apostles.* "The Preacher's Complete Homiletical Commentary on the New Testament." New York: Funk & Wagnalls, 1896.

Williams, George. *The Student's Commentary on the Holy Scriptures* (4th ed.). Grand Rapids: Kregel Publications, 1949 (reprint).

Williams, R. R. *The Acts of the Apostles.* "Torch Bible Commentaries." Edited by John Marsh *et al.* London: SCM Press, 1953.

V. CONCORDANCES

Cruden, Alexander. *Cruden's Unabridged Concordance.* Grand Rapids: Baker Book House, 1953.

Ellison, J. W. (ed.). *Nelson's Complete Concordance of the Revised Standard*

Version. New York: Thomas Nelson & Sons, 1957.

Hazard, M. C. *A Complete Concordance to the American Standard Version of the Holy Bible.* New York: Thomas Nelson & Sons, 1922.

Moffatt Bible Concordance. New York: Harper & Brothers, 1950.

Moulton, W. F., and Geden, A. S. *A Concordance to the Greek Testament* (3rd ed.). Edinburgh: T. & T. Clark, 1950.

Smith, J. B. *Greek-English Concordance to the New Testament.* Scottdale, Pa.: Herald Press, 1955.

Strong, James. *The Exhaustive Concordance of the Bible.* New York: Abingdon-Cokesbury Press, 1890.

Walker, J. B. R. *The Comprehensive Concordance to the Holy Scriptures.* New York: Macmillan Co., [1929], 1936.

Young, Robert. *Analytical Concordance to the Bible* (22nd Am. ed., revised by W. B. Stevenson). New York: Funk & Wagnalls Co., n.d.

VI. LEXICONS

Abbott-Smith, G. *A Manual Greek Lexicon of the New Testament* (2nd ed.). Edinburgh: T. & T. Clark, 1923.

Arndt, W. F., and Gingrich, F. W. *A Greek-English Lexicon of the New Testament and Other Early Christian Literature.* Chicago: University of Chicago Press, 1957.

Cremer, Hermann. *Biblico-Theological Lexicon of New Testament Greek.* Translated from the German of the 2nd edition by William Urwick. Edinburgh: T. & T. Clark, 1878.

Liddell, H. G., and Scott, Robert. *A Greek-English Lexicon.* New edition revised and augmented throughout by Henry S. Jones. Oxford: Clarendon Press, 1940.

Moulton, J. H., and Milligan, George. *The Vocabulary of the Greek Testament Illustrated from the Papyri and Other Non-literary Sources.* Grand Rapids: Wm. B. Eerdmans Publishing Co., 1949.

Thayer, J. H. *A Greek-English Lexicon of the New Testament.* Grimm's Wilke's *Clavis Novi Testamenti,* translated, revised, and enlarged. New York: American Book Co., n.d. (Copyright, 1886, by Harper & Brothers; corrected edition, 1889).

VII. NEW TESTAMENT VERSIONS

Confraternity Edition of the New Testament. New York: P. J. Kenedy & Sons, 1950.

English Revised Version of *The New Testament.* Oxford: University Press, 1881.

Goodspeed, Edgar J. *The New Testament: An American Translation.* Chicago: University of Chicago Press, 1923.

Holy Bible-Old and New Testaments (ASV). New York: Thomas Nelson and Sons, 1901.

King James Version of *The Holy Bible.* 1611 (1st ed.).

Knox, Ronald. *The New Testament of Our Lord and Saviour Jesus Christ: A New Translation.* New York: Sheed & Ward, 1944.

Moffatt, James. *The New Testament: A New Translation* (rev. ed.). New York: George H. Doran, 1922.

Phillips, J. B. *The Young Church in Action: A Translation of the Acts of the Apostles.* New York: Macmillan Co., 1955.

Revised Standard Version of the New Testament. New York: Thomas Nelson & Sons, 1946.

Spencer, F. A. *The New Testament of Our Lord and Saviour Jesus Christ.* New York: Macmillan Co., 1937.

Verkuyl, Gerrit. *Berkeley Version of The New Testament.* Grand Rapids: Zondervan Publishing Co., n.d.

Wesley, John. *The New Testament.* Introduction by George C. Cell. Philadelphia: John C. Winston Co., 1938 (1st ed., 1755).

Weymouth, R. F. *The New Testament in Modern Speech* (5th ed.). Newly revised by J. A. Robertson. Boston: Pilgrim Press, 1929 (1st ed., 1902).

Williams, Charles B. *The New Testament: A Translation in the Language of the People.* Chicago: Moody Press, 1950 (original edition, 1937).

VIII. OTHER WORKS CITED

Aberly, John. *An Outline of Missions.* Philadelphia: Muhlenburg Press, 1945.

Andrews, Samuel. *The Life of Our Lord Upon the Earth.* Grand Rapids: Zondervan Publishing House, 1954 (reprint).

Angus, S. *The Environment of Early Christianity.* New York: Charles Scribner's Sons, 1915.

Archer, J. K. *Faiths Men Live By.* New York: Thomas Nelson & Sons, 1934.

Aristotle. *On Man in the Universe.* New York: D. van Nostrand Co., Inc., 1943.

Barnett, Albert E. *The New Testament.* New York: Abingdon-Cokesbury Press, 1946.

Blass, Frederick. *Philology of the Gospels.* London: Macmillan Co., 1898.

Bowen, C. R. *Studies in the New Testament.*

Edited by R. J. Hutcheon. Chicago: University of Chicago Press, 1936.

Brightman, Edgar Sheffield. *A Philosophy of Religion*. New York: Prentice-Hall, Inc., rep. 1947.

Bringle, F. J., and Grubb, Kenneth G. *World Christian Handbook*. London: World Dominion Press (rev. ed.).

Bruce, F. F. *The Acts of the Apostles*. Chicago: Inter-Varsity Christian Fellowship, 1952.

————. *Second Thoughts on the Dead Sea Scrolls*. Grand Rapids: Wm. B. Eerdmans Publishing Co., 1956.

Burrell, David James and Joseph Dunn. *The Early Church* (Studies in the Acts of the Apostles). New York: American Tract Society, 1897.

Burrows, Millar. *The Dead Sea Scrolls*. New York: Viking Press, 1955.

Cadbury, Henry J. *The Book of Acts in History*. New York: Harper & Brothers, 1955.

————. *The Making of Luke-Acts*. New York: Macmillan Co., 1927.

Carver, William Owen. *The Bible a Missionary Message*. New York: Fleming H. Revell and Company, 1921.

————. *Missions in the Plan of the Ages*. Nashville: Broadman Press, 1951.

Chadwick, Samuel. *The Way to Pentecost*. Berne, Ind.: Light and Hope Publications, 1937 (reprint).

Chase, Frederick H. *The Credibility of the Book of the Acts of the Apostles*. London: Macmillan Co., 1902.

Clarke, A. C. *The Acts of the Apostles*. Oxford: University Press, 1933.

Clogg, F. B. *An Introduction to the New Testament*. New York: Charles Scribner's Sons, 1937.

Coates, J. R. (ed. and trans.). *Bible Key Words*. New York: Harper & Brothers, 1951.

Conybeare, W. J., and Howson, J. S. *The Life and Epistles of St. Paul*. Hartford, Conn.: S. S. Scranton and Co., 1899.

Cowles, Henry. *The Date of the Acts and the Synoptic Gospels*. New York: Williams and Norgate, J. P. Putnam's Sons, 1911.

Creed, J. M. *The Gospel according to St. Luke*. New York: Macmillan and Co., 1930.

Cushman, Herbert Ernest. *A Beginner's History of Philosophy*. New York: Houghton Mifflin Company, 1946.

Dalman, G. H. *Jesus-Jeshua*. New York: Macmillan Co., 1929.

————. *The Words of Jesus*. Edinburgh: T. & T. Clark, 1909.

Davies, J. G. *Daily Life of Early Christians*. New York: Duell, Sloan and Pearce, 1953.

Davies, W. D., and Daube, D. (eds.). *The Background of the New Testament and Its Eschatology*. Cambridge: University Press, 1956.

Dibelius, Martin. *A Fresh Approach to the New Testament and Early Christian Literature*. New York: Charles Scribner's Sons, 1936.

————. *Studies in the Acts of the Apostles*. Edited by H. Greenen. New York: Charles Scribner's Sons, 1956.

Dodd, C. H. *According to the Scriptures*. New York: Charles Scribner's Sons, 1953.

Dods, Marcus. *An Introduction to the New Testament*. New York: Thomas Whittaker, 1902.

Earle, Ralph. *The Gospel According to Mark*. Grand Rapids: Zondervan Publishing House, 1957.

Edersheim, Alfred. *The Life and Times of Jesus the Messiah* (8th ed.). 2 vols. New York: Longmans, Green, & Co., 1903.

————. *Sketches of Jewish Social Life in the Days of Christ*. London: Religious Tract Society, 1876.

Eusebius, Pamphilus. *Ecclesiastical History*. Translated by Frederick Cruse. Grand Rapids: Baker Book House, 1955 (reprint).

Exell, Joseph S. *The Biblical Illustrator*. Acts Vol. I. New York: Fleming H. Revell Company, n.d.

Farmer, William R. *Maccabees, Zealots, and Josephus*. New York: Columbia University Press, 1956.

Farrar, F. W. *The Life and Work of St. Paul*. New York: E. P. Dutton & Co., 1896 (Exegesis). London: Cassell, Petter, Galpin and Co., 1879 (Exposition).

————. *Messages of the Books*. New York: Macmillan Co., 1927.

Ferm, Vergilius (ed.). *An Encyclopedia of Religion*. New York: The Philosophical Library, 1943.

Field, F. *Notes on the Translation of the New Testament*. Cambridge: University Press, 1899.

Glover, Robert Hall. *The Bible Basis of Missions*. Los Angeles: Bible House of Los Angeles, 1946.

Glover, Robert Hall, and Kain, J. Herbert *The Progress of World Wide Missions* (rev. ed.). New York: Harper and Brothers, Publishers, 1960.

Goodspeed, Edgar, J. *An Introduction to the New Testament*. Chicago: University of Chicago Press, 1937.

Goodwin, Frank J. *A Harmony and Commentary on the Life of St. Paul*. Grand Rapids: Baker Book House, 1951.

Green, Bryan. *The Practice of Evangelism*. New York: Charles Scribner's Sons, 1955.

Groves, C. P. *The Planting of Christianity in Africa*. Vol. I London: Lutterworth Press, 1948 (1st ed. 1840).

Harnack, Adolf von. *The Acts of the Apostles.* Translated by J. R. Wilkinson. New York: G. P. Putnam's Sons, 1909.

————. *The Date of the Acts and of the Synoptic Gospels.* Translated by J. R. Wilkinson. New York: G. P. Putnam's Sons, 1911.

————. *Luke the Physician.* Translated by J. R. Wilkinson. Edited by W. D. Morrison. London: Williams & Norgate. New York: G. P. Putnam's Sons, 1907.

————. *The Mission and Expansion of Christianity.* Vol. I, II. New York: G. P. Putnam's Sons, 1908.

Hayes, D. A. *Paul and His Epistles.* New York: Methodist Book Concern, 1915.

Henshaw, T. *New Testament Literature.* London: George Allen and Unwin, 1952.

Higdon, E. K. *New Missionaries for New Days.* St. Louis: The Bethany Press, 1956.

Hobart, W. K. *The Medical Language of St. Luke.* Grand Rapids: Baker Book House, 1954 (original ed., 1882).

Hocking, William Earnest. *Living Religions and a World Faith.* New York: MacMillan Company. 1940.

Huffman, Jasper A. *Golden Treasures from the Greek New Testament for English Readers.* Winona Lake: Standard Press, 1951.

Josephus, Flavius. *Works.* Translated by William Whiston. Philadelphia: Henry T. Coates & Co., n.d. (also Exposition, Philadelphia: David McKay, n.d.)

Kent, Charles F. *The Work and Teachings of the Apostles.* New York: Charles Scribner's Sons, 1916.

Kilgour, R. *The Bible Throughout the World.* London: World Dominion Press, 1939.

Klausner, Joseph. *From Jesus to Paul.* Translated from the Hebrew by W. F. Stinespring. New York: Macmillan Co., 1943.

Knox, John. *Marcion and the New Testament.* Chicago: University of Chicago Press, 1942.

Knox, Wilfred L. *The Acts of the Apostles.* Cambridge: University Press, 1948.

Kraemer, Hendrick. *The Christian Message in a Non-Christian World.* London: The Edinburgh House Press, 1938.

Lake, Kirsopp. *The Earlier Epistles of St. Paul.* London: Rivingtons, 1911.

Lake, Kirsopp, and Lake, Silva. *An Introduction to the New Testament.* New York: Harper & Brothers, 1937.

Latourette, Kenneth Scott. *A History of the Expansion of Christianity,* Vol. I. New York: Harper and Brothers, 1937.

Lewis, C. S. *The Screwtape Letters.* New York: Macmillan Co., 1948.

Lewis, Edwin. *The Creator and the Adversary.* New York: Abingdon-Cokesbury Press, 1948.

Lietzmann, Hans. *The Beginning of the Christian Church,* Vol. I. New York: Charles Scribner's Sons, 1949.

Lightfoot, J. B. *St. Paul's Epistle to the Galatians.* Grand Rapids: Zondervan Publishing House, n.d.

————. *St. Paul's Epistle to the Philippians.* London: Macmillan Co., 1894.

Love, Julian Price. *The Missionary Message of the Bible.* New York: Macmillan Company, 1941.

Luckock, H. M. *Footprints of the Apostles as Traced by St. Luke in the Acts.* London, 1897.

Mackie, G. M. *Bible Manners and Customs.* London: A. and C. Black, Ltd., 1936.

Major, H. D. A., Manson, T. W., and Wright, C. J. *The Mission and Message of Jesus.* New York: E. P. Dutton and Co., 1938.

Mathews, Basil. *Forward through the Ages.* New York: Friendship Press, 1951.

Mayor, J. B. *The Epistle of St. James.* Grand Rapids: Zondervan Publishing House, 1954 (reprint).

Moe, Olaf. *The Apostle Paul.* Translated by L. A. Vigness. Minneapolis: Augsburg Publishing House, 1950.

Moffatt, James. *An Introduction to the Literature of the New Testament* (3rd ed.). New York: Charles Scribner's Sons, 1918.

Morgan, G. Campbell. *The Missionary Manifesto.* New York: Fleming H. Revell Co., 1909.

Morton, H. V. *In the Steps of St. Paul.* New York: Dodd, Mead & Co., 1936.

Mould, Elmer W. K. *Essentials of Bible History* (rev. ed.). New York: T. Nelson & Sons, 1951.

Mowinckel, S. *He That Cometh.* Translated by G. W. Anderson. New York: Abingdon-Cokesbury Press, 1954.

Peake, Arthur S. *A Critical Introduction to the New Testament.* New York: Charles Scribner's Sons, 1911.

————. *The People and the Book.* Oxford: Clarendon Press, 1925.

Pierson, Arthur T. *The Acts of the Holy Spirit.* New York: Fleming H. Revell Company, 1898.

Plummer, Alfred. *A Critical and Exegetical Commentary on the Gospel According to St. Luke.* "International Critical Commentary." New York: Charles Scribner's Sons, 1896.

Ramsay, W. M. *The Bearing of Recent Discovery on the Trustworthiness of the New Testament.* Grand Rapids: Baker Book House, 1953 (reprint).

————. *The Church in the Roman Empire, before* A.D. 170. Grand Rapids: Baker Book House, 1954 (1st ed., 1897).

————. *The Cities of St. Paul.* Grand Rapids: Baker Book House, 1949 (reprint).

————. *St. Paul the Traveller and the Roman Citizen.* Grand Rapids: Baker Book House, 1949 (1st. ed., 1895).

————. *Was Christ Born at Bethlehem?* New York: G. P. Putnam's Sons, 1898.

Robertson, A. T. *A Harmony of the Gospels.* New York: George Doran Co., 1922.

————. *Luke the Historian in the Light of Research.* New York: Charles Scribner's Sons, 1920.

Robinson, Benjamin Willard. *The Life of Paul.* Chicago: University of Chicago Press, 1928 (rep. 1946).

Rowlingson, Donald. *Introduction to New Testament Study.* New York: Macmillan Co., 1956.

Sabatier, A. *The Apostle Paul.* London: Hodder and Stoughton, Ltd., 1903.

Saltau, T. Stanley. *Missions at the Crossroads.* Grand Rapids: Baker Book House, 1954.

Schaff, Philip. *The Nicene and Post-Nicene Fathers of the Christian Church.* Grand Rapids: Wm. B. Eerdmans Publishing Company, (rep. 1956).

Schmidt, Wilhelm. *High God's in North America.* Oxford: University Press, 1933.

————. *The Origin and Growth of Religion: Facts and Theories.* Trans. H. J. Rose, New York: Dial, 1935.

Schürer, Emil. *A History of the Jewish People in the Time of Jesus Christ.* 2 vols. Edinburgh: T. & T. Clark, 1885.

Schweitzer, Albert. *The Mysticism of Paul the Apostle.* Translated by W. Montgomery. New York: Henry Holt and Co., 1931.

Scott, E. F. *The Literature of the New Testament.* New York: Columbia Univeristy Press, 1936.

Scroggie, W. Graham. *Know Your Bible.* Vol. II. London: Pickering and Inglis, Ltd., 1940, and New York: Loizeaux Bros., n.d.

Selwyn, E. G. *The First Epistle of Peter* (2nd ed.). London: Macmillan & Co., Ltd., 1947.

Smith, George Adam. *The Historical Geography of the Holy Land* (16th ed.). New York: George H. Doran, 1919.

Smith, James. *The Voyage and Shipwreck of St. Paul* (4th ed.). London: Longmans, Green, and Co., 1880.

Soper, Edmund Davison. *The Philosophy of the Christian World Mission.* New York: Abingdon-Cokesbury Press, 1943.

Stendahl, Krister (ed.). *The Scrolls and the New Testament.* New York: Harper & Brothers, 1957.

Stonehouse, N. B. *Paul Before the Areopagus.* Grand Rapids: Wm. B. Eerdmans Publishing Co., 1957.

Taylor, William M. *Paul the Missionary.* New York: Richard R. Smith Inc., 1930.

Thiessen, Henry C. *Introduction to the New Testament.* Grand Rapids: Wm. B. Eerdmans Publishing Co., 1943.

Torrey, C. C. *The Composition and Date of Acts.* Cambridge: Harvard University Press, 1916.

Trench, Richard Chenevix. *Notes on the Parables of Our Lord.* Philadelphia: William Sychelmoore, n.d.

————. *Synonyms of the New Testament.* Grand Rapids: Wm. B. Eerdmans Publishing Co., 1947.

Turnbull, Grace H. *Tongues of Fire: A Bible of Sacred Scriptures of the Pagan World.* New York: Macmillan Co., 1929.

Van Baalen, J. K. *The Chaos of Cults.* Grand Rapids: Wm. B. Eerdmans Publishing Co., 1949.

Walker, James. *Philosophy of the Plan of Salvation.* New York: Chautauqua Press, 1887. (Edited by Chas. W. Carter and retitled *God's Wisdom in the Plan of Salvation.* Butler, Indiana: The Higley Press, rep. 1958).

Wright, J. Stafford. *Man in the Process of Time.* Grand Rapids: Wm. B. Eerdmans Publishing Co., 1956.

Zahn, Theodor. *Introduction to the New Testament.* Translated by John Trout *et al.* Grand Rapids: Kregel Publications, 1953 (reprint).

Zeller, Eduard. *The Contents and Origin of the Acts of the Apostles.* Translated by Joseph Dare. London: Williams & Norgate, 1875.

Zwemer, Samuel. *Into All the World.* Grand Rapids: Zondervan Publishing House, 1943.

————. *The Origin of Religion.* New York: Loizeaux Brothers, 1945.

ACKNOWLEDGMENTS

Grateful acknowledgement is made to the following authors and publishers for permission granted to quote from their publications:

Bruce, F. F. *A Commentary on the Book of the Acts.* "The New International Commentary on the New Testament." Grand Rapids: Wm. B. Eerdmans Publishing Co., 1954.

Cushman, Herbert Ernest. *A Beginner's History of Philosophy.* New York: Houghton Mifflin Company, 1946.

Dummelow, J. R. *A Commentary on the Holy Bible*. New York: Macmillan Co., 1936 (rep. 1951).

Finegan, Jack. *Light From the Ancient Past*. Princeton: University Press, 1946.

Greenlee, Harold. "Christian Communism in the Book of Acts." *The Asbury Seminarian*. Wilmore, Ky.: Fall & Winter, 1950.

Groves, C. P. *The Planting of Christianity in Africa*. London: Luttherworth Press, n.d. (U.S. distributor, Allenson, Naperville, Illinois.)

Hastings, James (ed.). *A Dictionary of the Bible*. New York: Charles Scribner's Sons, 1898.

Huffman, Jasper A. *Golden Treasures From the Greek New Testament for English Readers*. Winona Lake: Standard Press, 1951.

Jackson, F. J. Foakes, and Lake, Kirsopp (eds.). *The Beginnings of Christianity*. Part I, "The Acts of the Apostles." New York: Macmillan Company.

Kraeling, Emil G. *Rand McNally Bible Atlas*. Chicago: Rand McNally & Co., 1956.

Lietzmann, Hans. *The Beginnings of the Christian Church*, Vol. I. New York: Charles Scribner's Sons, 1949.

Macgregor, G. H. C. "The Acts of the Apostles" (Exegesis) in *The Interpreter's Bible*, Vol. IX. New York: Abingdon-Cokesbury Press, 1954.

Miller, Madeline S. and J. Lane. *Harper's Bible Dictionary*. New York: Harper & Brothers, 1952. Used by permisison.

Morgan, G. Campbell. *The Missionary Manifesto*. New York: Fleming H. Revell Co., 1909.

————. *The Acts of the Apostles*. New York: Fleming H. Revell Co., 1924.

Mould, Elmer W. K. *Essentials of Bible History* (rev. ed.). New York: Ronald Press, 1951.

Phillips, J. B. *The Young Church in Action*: *The Translation of The Acts of the Apostles*. New York: Macmillan Co., 1955.

Rackham, R. B. *The Acts of the Apostles*. "Westminster Commentaries" (8th ed.). London: Methuen & Co., Ltd., 1919.

Robertson, A. T. *Luke the Historian in the Light of Research*. New York: Charles Scribner's Sons, 1920.

Robinson, Benjamin Willard. *The Life of Paul*. Chicago: University of Chicago Press, 1928 (rep. 1946).

Schmidt, Wilhelm. *High Gods in North America*. Oxford: University Press, 1933.

Weymouth, R. F. *Weymouth's New Testament in Modern Speech*. New York: Harper & Brothers. Used by permission.

Williams, Charles B. *The New Testament: A Translation in the Language of the People*. Chicago: Moody Press, 1950.

Wright, J. Stafford. *Man in the Process of Time*. Grand Rapids: Wm. B. Eerdmans Publishing Co., 1956.

Zwemer, Samuel. *The Origin of Religion*. New York: Loizeaux Brothers, 1945.